•BLOOMSBURY THEMATIC
DICTIONARY OF QUOTATIONS

•BLOOMSBURY THEMATIC DICTIONARY OF QUOTATIONS

BLOOMSBURY

First published 1988

This edition published 1990

Copyright ©1990 by Bloomsbury Publishing Limited
Bloomsbury Publishing Limited, 2 Soho Square,
London W1V 5DE

A CIP catalogue record for this book is available from the
British Library

ISBN 0 7475 0735 X

Compiled and typeset by
Market House Books, Ltd., Aylesbury
Printed in Great Britain by
Butler & Tanner Limited, Frome and London

• Contents

• Acknowledgments

Editors

John Daintith
Rosalind Fergusson
Anne Stibbs
Edmund Wright

Contributors

Elizabeth Bonham
Deborah Chapman
Sue Cope
Eve Daintith
Hazel Egerton
Joan Gallagher
Joanna Gosling
Jock Graham
Lawrence Holden
Alan Isaacs
Amanda Isaacs
Valerie Illingworth
Stephen Jones
Elizabeth Martin
Jennifer Monk
David Pickering
Kathy Rooney
Ruth Salomon
Jessica Scholes
Gwynneth Shaw
Mary Shields
Kate Smith
Tracey Smith

• Introduction

This book is a companion volume to the *Bloomsbury Dictionary of Quotations* (first published in 1987), which is arranged alphabetically by author. The present volume contains quotations listed in that work but many other quotations have been added.

Here we have classified over 10,000 quotations under about 800 thematic headings. These are arranged alphabetically. Many of them are subjects that one might expect — 'big issues' such as *love, marriage, youth, age, death,* etc. But we have also included current topics such as *pollution, feminism,* and *healthy living.* At the beginning of each entry there is a list of cross references to related themes. For example, those interested in *adultery* are also advised to read about *sex, unfaithfulness,* and *marriage.*

In general, the quotations under a theme are things said **about** the subject, but we have also used quotations that are **examples** of a theme. For instance, under the heading *epitaphs* will be found quotations that are epitaphs as well as things said about epitaphs.

The entry on *last words* contains examples of last words, *Goldwynisms* gives a selection of Goldwyn's supposed sayings, *insults* provides the reader with a number of possibilities, and so on. Some of the themes have been sub-classified, for example sayings in favour of *feminism* and sayings against. This has not always been possible — thus, it proved too difficult to find much to be said in favour of *critics.* And in most cases sub-classifying is not desirable. One of the interesting features of this method of organization is the juxtaposition of different viewpoints on the same subject.

Within a thematic entry itself, the quotations are arranged alphabetically by author; for the first appearance of an author within an entry, the author's dates and brief biographical note are given. This is followed by any explanatory note that may be required and the source, if it is known. Anonymous quotations come at the beginning of a thematic entry and biblical quotations will be found alphabetized under **Bible** within the entry.

The thematic arrangement is ideal for seeking an apt quotation on a particular theme. But it is also an interesting and amusing book through which to browse. For example, under the entry *politicians* a wide variety of quotations appear, from Shakespeare, through Curzon and Churchill, to Kinnock and Thatcher.

In addition, an author index provides the user with the opportunity of seeking *bon mots* from their favourite personalities. This index lists the themes under which each author is represented, thus providing an entirely different way of making use of the thematic arrangement.

The other index provided, is based on the *keyword* or *-words* in a quotation, directing the user to the theme under which a particular quotation is listed. So users who remember only one or two words of a quotation can complete it correctly and find the source. As Dorothy Parker once said

'I might repeat to myself . . . a list of quotations beautiful from minds profound — If I can remember any of the damn things.'

We hope that this book will help jog the memory as well as providing an informative and enjoyable selection.

The Editors

LIST OF SUBJECTS

ABSENCE
ABSTINENCE
ACADEMICS
ACCUSATION
ACHIEVEMENT
ACCIDENTS
ACTING
ACTION
ACTORS
ADDICTION
ADDRESSES
ADMIRATION
ADAPTABILITY
ADULTERY
ADVICE
ADVERTISING
AFFECTATION
AFTERLIFE
AGE
AGRICULTURE
AGGRAVATION
AGREEMENT
AIDS
ALCOHOL
AMBITION
AMERICA
AMERICANS
ANALOGY
ANCESTRY
ANGER
ANIMALS
ANIMALISM
ANTICIPATION
APOLOGIES
APPEARANCE
APPEARANCES
ARCHITECTURE
ARGUMENTS
ARISTOCRACY
ARROGANCE
ARMY
ART
ARTHURIAN LEGEND
ARTISTS
ARTS
ASTRONOMY
ATHEISM
ASSASSINATION
AUTHORITARIANISM
AUDIENCES
AUTUMN
BABIES
BEAUTY
BED
BELIEF
BEGINNING
BEQUESTS
BIBLE
BETRAYAL
BIRDS

BIOGRAPHY
BIRTH
BITTERNESS
BLESSING
BOASTS
BLINDNESS
BOATS
BOLDNESS
BOOKS
BOOK, SONG, AND PLAY
    TITLES
BOREDOM
BORROWING
BORES
BRIBERY
BREVITY
BRITAIN
BRITISH
BRITISH EMPIRE
BUSINESS
BUREAUCRACY
CAMBRIDGE
CANNIBALISM
CAPITALISM
CATHOLICISM
CAUTION
CATS
CENSORSHIP
CHANGE
CERTAINTY
CHANCE
CHARACTER
CHARITY
CHARM
CHAUCER
CHILDREN
CHOICE
CHIVALRY
CHRISTIANITY
CHRISTMAS
CHURCHILL
CHURCH
CINEMA
CIVILIZATION
CLARITY
CLASS
CLASSIFICATION
CLASSICS
CLEANNESS
CLERGY
CLOCKS
CLOTHES
COLD WAR
COMFORT
COMMITMENT
COMMUNICATION
COMMUNISM
COMPLAINTS
COMPLIMENTS
COMPOSERS

COMPROMISE
CONCEIT
CONFLICT
CONFORMITY
CONFUSION
CONSCIENCE
CONSERVATION
CONSERVATISM
CONSTANCY
CONTEMPT
CONTENTMENT
CONTRACEPTION
CONVERSATION
CORRUPTION
COSMETICS
COUNTRYSIDE
COURAGE
COURTESY
COWARDICE
CREATION
CRICKET
CRIME
CRITICISM
CRITICS
CRUELTY
CULTURE
CURIOSITY
CURSES
CYNICISM
CUSTOM
DAMNATION
DANCING
DAY
DANGER
DEATH
DECEPTION
DEBAUCHERY
DECISION
DECLINE
DEFEAT
DEMOCRACY
DELUSION
DENIAL
DEPARTURE
DESIRE
DESIGN
DESTINY
DESPAIR
DETERMINATION
DEVIL
DIARIES
DIFFERENCE
DIPLOMACY
DICKENS
DISABILITY
DISAPPOINTMENT
DISCONTENT
DISASTER
DISEASE
DISCOVERY

DISILLUSION
DISMISSAL
DOGS
DOCTORS
DOUBT
DOOMSDAY
DREAMS
DRINKS
DROWNING
DRUGS
DRUNKENNESS
DUTY
ECOLOGY
ECONOMICS
EDITORS
EDUCATION
EFFORT
EGOTISM
EMBARRASSMENT
EMOTION
ENDING
ENDURANCE
ENGLAND
ENEMIES
ENGLISH
ENVIRONMENT
ENTHUSIASM
ENVY
EPITAPHS
EQUALITY
ESCAPE
ETERNITY
EUROPE
ETIQUETTE
EVIL
EVOLUTION
EXAMINATIONS
EXCELLENCE
EXAMPLE
EXCESS
EXECUTION
EXISTENCE
EXPEDIENCY
EXPECTATION
EXPERIENCE
EXPERTS
EXPLANATIONS
EXPLOITATION
EXPLORATION
EXTRAVAGANCE
EYES
FACTS
FAITH
FAILURE
FAIRIES
FAITHFULNESS
FAME
FAMILIARITY
FAMILY
FASCISM

PERSPECTIVE
PERSISTENCE
PERSUASION
PERVERSITY
PETULANCE
PESSIMISM
PHILISTINISM
PHILOSOPHY
PHILOSOPHERS
PHOTOGRAPHY
PLACES
PLAYS
PLEASURE
POETRY
POETRY AND PROSE
POETS
POLITICIANS
POLICE
POLITICS
POLLUTION
POP MUSIC
PORNOGRAPHY
POPULARITY
POSSIBILITY
POVERTY
POSTERITY
POVERTY AND WEALTH
POWER
POWER POLITICS
PRAISE
PRACTICALITY
PRAYER
PRECOCITY
PRESENT
PREJUDICE
PRIDE
PRINCIPLES
PRIVACY
PROCRASTINATION
PROGRESS
PROMISCUITY
PROMOTION
PROMPTNESS
PROMISES
PRONUNCIATION
PROOF
PROPAGANDA
PROPHECY
PRUDENCE
PROSE
PROTESTANTISM
PRUDERY
PROVOCATION
PSYCHIATRY
PSYCHOLOGY
PUBLIC
PURPOSE
QUOTATIONS
RABBITS
RACISM
READING
REALISM
REALITY
REASON
REGRET

REBELLION
RELIGION
REMEDIES
RENUNCIATION
REPARTEE
REPRESENTATION
REPUBLIC
RESEARCH
REPUTATION
RESPONSIBILITY
RESPECT
RESPECTABILITY
RETRIBUTION
REST
RESULTS
RETURN
REVENGE
REVOLUTION
RIDICULE
RIGHT
RIGHTEOUSNESS
ROYALTY
RIVERS
RUSSIA
RUSSIAN REVOLUTION
RUDENESS
RULES
RUTHLESSNESS
SARCASM
SATISFACTION
SATIRE
SAYINGS
SCIENCE
SCEPTICISM
SCIENCE FICTION
SCIENTISTS
SCOTLAND
SCOTS
SCULPTURE
SEA
SEASIDE
SEASONS
SELF
SECRECY
SELF-CONFIDENCE
SELF-CONTROL
SELFISHNESS
SELF-DENIAL
SELF-KNOWLEDGE
SELF-INTEREST
SELFLESSNESS
SELF-MADE MEN
SELF-PRESERVATION
SELF-RELIANCE
SENSATION
SENTIMENTALITY
SELF-RESPECT
SEPARATION
SERVICE
SERIOUSNESS
SERMONS
SERVILITY
SEX
SEXES
SHAKESPEARE

SHYNESS
SIGNATURES
SILENCE
SIMILARITY
SIMPLICITY
SIN
SINCERITY
SLAVERY
SINGERS
SLEEP
SINGING
SMALLNESS
SMOKING
SNOBBERY
SOCIALISM
SOCIETY
SOLDIERS
SOLITUDE
SORROW
SOUL
SPACE
SPEECH
SPECULATION
SPELLING
SPONTANEITY
SPEECHES
SPOONERISMS
SPORT AND GAMES
SPRING
STATE
STARING
STARS
STATELY HOMES
STRIKES
STATISTICS
STUBBORNNESS
STUPIDITY
STYLE
SUBJECTIVITY
SUBURBIA
SUCCESS
SUFFERING
SUICIDE
SUMMER
SUMMONS
SUN
SUITABILITY
SUNDAY
SUPERIORITY
SUPERNATURAL
SUPERSTITION
SUPPORT
SUSPICION
SWITZERLAND
SURVIVAL
SYMPATHY
TACT
TALENT AND GENIUS
TALENT
TASTE
TAXATION
TECHNOLOGY
TEETH
TELEGRAMS

TELEVISION
TEMPTATION
THEATRE
THEFT
THINKING
THEORY
THIRST
THREATS
TIME
THRIFT
TITLES
TRANSIENCE
TOLERANCE
TRANSLATION
TRAVEL
TREES
TREASON
TRIVIALITY
TRUST
TRUTH
TYRANNY
UNCERTAINTY
UNDERSTANDING
UNEMPLOYMENT
UNFAITHFULNESS
UNIVERSE
UNITY
VENICE
VERBOSITY
VICE
VICTORY
VIRTUE
VIOLENCE
VIRTUE AND VICE
VULGARITY
WALES
WAR
WAR AND PEACE
WATER
WASTE
WEAKNESS
WEALTH
WEAPONS
WEATHER
WINTER
WISDOM
WELSH
WHISTLING
WISDOM AND
   FOOLISHNESS
WOMAN'S ROLE
WOMEN
WORDS
WONDER
WORK
WORLD
WORLD WAR I
WORLD WAR II
WORLD-WEARINESS
WORRY
WRITERS
WRITING
YIELDING
YOUTH

A

ABSENCE

See also separation

1 Long absent, soon forgotten.
Proverb

2 Out of sight, out of mind.
Proverb

3 When the cat's away, the mice will play.
Proverb

4 Absence makes the heart grow fonder,
Isle of Beauty, Fare thee well!
Thomas Haynes Bayly (1797–1839) British writer.
Isle of Beauty

5 What's become of Waring
Since he gave us all the slip?
Robert Browning (1812–89) British poet.
Waring

6 Absence is to love what wind is to fire; it
extinguishes the small, it inflames the great.
Bussy-Rabutin (Roger de Rabutin, Comte de Bussy;
1618–93) French soldier and writer.
Histoire amoureuse des Gaules

7 What's the good of a home, if you are never
in it?
George Grossmith (1847–1912) British singer and
comedian.
The Diary of a Nobody, Ch. 1

8 Has anybody here seen Kelly?
Kelly from the Isle of Man?
C. W. Murphy (19th century) British songwriter.
Has Anybody Here Seen Kelly?

9 We seek him here, we seek him there,
Those Frenchies seek him everywhere.
Is he in heaven? – Is he in hell?
That damned elusive Pimpernel?
Baroness Orczy (1865–1947) British novelist.
The Scarlet Pimpernel, Ch. 12

10 Why art thou silent! Is thy love a plant
Of such weak fibre that the treacherous air
Of absence withers what was once so fair?
William Wordsworth (1770–1850) British poet.
Miscellaneous Sonnets, III

ABSTINENCE

See also alcohol, self-denial, sex, smoking

1 He neither drank, smoked, nor rode a
bicycle. Living frugally, saving his money, he
died early, surrounded by greedy relatives. It
was a great lesson to me.
John Barrymore (1882–1942) US actor.
The Stage, Jan 1941 (J. P. McEvoy)

2 If someone asks for a soft drink at a party,
we no longer think he is a wimp.
Edwina Currie (1946–) British politician.
Speech, Dec 1988

3 Teetotallers lack the sympathy and
generosity of men that drink.
W. H. Davies (1871–1940) British poet.
Shorter Lyrics of the 20th Century, Introduction

4 It was a brilliant affair; water flowed like
champagne.
William M. Evarts (1818–1901) US lawyer and
statesman.
Describing a dinner given by US President Rutherford B.
Hayes (1877–81), an advocate of temperance
Attrib.

5 If you resolve to give up smoking, drinking
and loving, you don't actually live longer; it
just seems longer.
Clement Freud (1924–) British Liberal politician and
broadcaster.
The Observer, 27 Dec 1964

6 Mr Mercaptan went on to preach a brilliant
sermon on that melancholy sexual perversion
known as continence.
Aldous Huxley (1894–1964) British novelist.
Antic Hay, Ch. 18

7 My experience through life has convinced me
that, while moderation and temperance in all
things are commendable and beneficial,
abstinence from spirituous liquors is the best
safeguard of morals and health.
Robert E. Lee (1807–70) US general.
Letter, 9 Dec 1869

8 The few bad poems which occasionally are
created during abstinence are of no great
interest.
Wilhelm Reich (1897–1957) Austrian-born US
psychiatrist.
The Sexual Revolution

9 The people who are regarded as moral
luminaries are those who forego ordinary
pleasures themselves and find compensation
in interfering with the pleasures of others.
Bertrand Russell (1872–1970) British philosopher.
Sceptical Essays

10 Lastly (and this is, perhaps, the golden rule),
no woman should marry a teetotaller, or a
man who does not smoke.
Robert Louis Stevenson (1850–94) Scottish writer.
Virginibus Puerisque

11 She belongs to a Temperance Society and
wears one of those badges in the shape of a
bow of ribbon to show that she would never
take a drink, not even brandy if she were

dying. Of course by temperance they all mean the opposite – total abstinence.
Elizabeth Taylor (1912–75) British writer.
Angel

12 Though in silence, with blighted affection, I pine,
Yet the lips that touch liquor must never touch mine!
G. W. Young (19th century) British writer.
The Lips That Touch Liquor

ACADEMICS

See also education, intellectuals

1 A professor is one who talks in someone else's sleep.
W. H. Auden (1907–73) British poet.
Attrib.

2 First come I; my name is Jowett.
There's no knowledge but I know it.
I am Master of this college:
What I don't know isn't knowledge.
H. C. Beeching (1859–1919) British academic.
Referring to Benjamin Jowett, master of Balliol College, Oxford
The Masque of Balliol

3 It's no use trying to be *clever* – we are all clever here; just try to be *kind* – a little kind.
F. J. Foakes Jackson (1855–1941) British academic.
Advice given to a new don at Jesus College, Cambridge
Noted in A. C. Benson's Commonplace Book

4 Like so many ageing college people, Pnin had long ceased to notice the existence of students on the campus.
Vladimir Nabokov (1899–1977) Russian-born US novelist.
Pnin, Ch. 3

5 I am the Dean of Christ Church, Sir:
There's my wife; look well at her.
She's the Broad and I'm the High;
We are the University.
Cecil Arthur Spring-Rice (1859–1918) British diplomat.
The Masque of Balliol

ACCIDENTS

See also chance, disaster, misfortune

1 The Act of God designation on all insurance policies; which means, roughly, that you cannot be insured for the accidents that are most likely to happen to you.
Alan Coren (1938–) British humorist and writer.
The Lady from Stalingrad Mansions, 'A Short History of Insurance'

2 Accidents will occur in the best-regulated families.
Charles Dickens (1812–70) British novelist.
David Copperfield, Ch. 28

3 My good man, I'm not a strawberry.
Edward VII (1841–1910) King of the United Kingdom.
Rebuking a footman who had spilt cream on him
The Last Country Houses (C. Aslat)

4 Heard there was a party. Came.
Beatrice Lillie (Constance Sylvia Munston, Lady Peel; 1898–1989) Canadian-born British actress.
On arriving breathlessly at a friend's house seeking help after a car crash
Attrib.

5 O Diamond! Diamond! thou little knowest the mischief done!
Isaac Newton (1642–1727) British scientist.
Said to a dog that set fire to some papers, representing several years' work, by knocking over a candle
Wensley-Dale . . . a Poem (Thomas Maude)

6 Knocked down a doctor? With an ambulance? How could she? It's a contradiction in terms.
N. F. Simpson (1919–) British dramatist.
One-Way Pendulum, I

7 The chapter of accidents is the longest chapter in the book.
John Wilkes (1725–97) British politician.
Attrib. in *The Doctor* (Southey), Vol. IV

ACCUSATION

See also responsibility

1 I do not know the method of drawing up an indictment against an whole people.
Edmund Burke (1729–97) British politician.
Speech on Conciliation with America (House of Commons, 22 Mar 1775)

2 Never make a defence or apology before you be accused.
Charles I (1600–49) King of England.
Letter to Lord Wentworth, 3 Sept 1636

3 *J'accuse.*
I accuse.
Émile Zola (1840–1902) French novelist.
Title of an open letter to the French President, denouncing the French army's conduct in the Dreyfus affair
L'Aurore, 13 Jan 1898

ACHIEVEMENT

See also effort, success

1 Ye shall know them by their fruits. Do men gather grapes of thorns, or figs of thistles? Even so every good tree bringeth forth good fruit; but a corrupt tree bringeth forth evil fruit.
A good tree cannot bring forth evil fruit, neither can a corrupt tree bring forth good fruit.
Every tree that bringeth not forth good fruit is hewn down, and cast into the fire.
Wherefore by their fruits ye shall know them.
Bible: Matthew
7:16–20

2 Be not afraid of growing slowly, be afraid only of standing still.
Chinese Proverb

3 Our greatest glory is not in never falling, but in rising every time we fall.
Confucius (K'ung Fu-tzu; 551–479 BC) Chinese philosopher.
Analects

4 One never notices what has been done; one can only see what remains to be done. . . .
Marie Curie (1867–1934) Polish chemist.
Letter to her brother, 18 Mar 1894

5 We never do anything well till we cease to think about the manner of doing it.
William Hazlitt (1778–1830) British essayist.
On Prejudice

6 I do not want to die . . . until I have faithfully made the most of my talent and cultivated the seed that was placed in me until the last small twig has grown.
Käthe Kollwitz (1867–1945) German sculptor and graphic artist.
Diaries and Letters, 15 Feb 1915

7 For, as I suppose, no man in this world hath lived better than I have done, to achieve that I have done.
Thomas Malory (1400–71) English writer.
Morte d'Arthur, Bk. XVII, Ch. 16

8 Log-cabin to White House.
W. M. Thayer (1820–98) US writer.
The title of his biography of James Garfield, US president

9 To achieve great things we must live as though we were never going to die.
Marquis de Vauvenargues (1715–47) French soldier and writer.
Réflexions et maximes

ACTING

See also action, actors, cinema, criticism, plays, theatre

1 Theatre director: a person engaged by the management to conceal the fact that the players cannot act.
James Agate (1877–1947) British theatre critic.
Attrib.

2 It's not whether you really cry. It's whether the audience thinks you are crying.
Ingrid Bergman (1915–1982) Swedish film and stage actress.
Halliwell's Filmgoer's and Video Viewer's Companion

3 Acting is the expression of a neurotic impulse. It's a bum's life. Quitting acting, that's the sign of maturity.
Marlon Brando (1924–) US film star.
Halliwell's Filmgoer's and Video Viewer's Companion

4 For the theatre one needs long arms; it is better to have them too long than too short.

An *artiste* with short arms can never, never make a fine gesture.
Sarah Bernhardt (Sarah Henriette Rosine Bernard; 1844–1923) French actress.
Memories of My Life, Ch. 6

5 Pray to God and say the lines.
Bette Davis (Ruth Elizabeth Davis; 1908–89) US film star.
Advice to the actress Celeste Holm
Attrib.

6 It is easier to get an actor to be a cowboy than to get a cowboy to be an actor.
John Ford (Sean O'Feeney; 1895–1973) US film director.
Attrib.

7 It is. But not as hard as farce.
Edmund Gwenn (1875–1959) British actor.
On his deathbed, in reply to the comment 'It must be very hard'
Time, 30 Jan 1984

8 Acting is therefore the lowest of the arts, if it is an art at all.
George Moore (1852–1933) Irish writer and art critic.
Mummer-Worship

9 The art of acting consists in keeping people from coughing.
Ralph Richardson (1902–83) British actor.
The Observer

10 In music, the punctuation is absolutely strict, the bars and the rests are absolutely defined. But our punctuation cannot be quite strict, because we have to relate it to the audience. In other words, we are continually changing the score.
Ralph Richardson
The Observer Magazine, 'Tynan on Richardson', 18 Dec 1977

11 Imagination! imagination! I put it first years ago, when I was asked what qualities I thought necessary for success upon the stage.
Ellen Terry (1847–1928) British actress.
The Story of My Life, Ch. 2

12 Ladies, just a little more virginity, if you don't mind.
Herbert Beerbohm Tree (1853–1917) British actor and theatre manager.
Directing a group of sophisticated actresses
Smart Aleck (H. Teichmann)

ACTION

See also acting

1 Barking dogs seldom bite.
Proverb

2 Doing is better than saying.
Proverb

3 Easier said than done.
Proverb

4 Footprints on the sands of time are not made by sitting down.
Proverb

5 Saying is one thing, and doing another.
Proverb

6 Let's meet, and either do, or die.
Francis Beaumont (1584–1616) English dramatist.
The Island Princess, II:2

7 He who desires but acts not, breeds pestilence.
William Blake (1757–1827) British poet.
The Marriage of Heaven and Hell, 'Proverbs of Hell'

8 Liberty's in every blow!
Let us do or die!
Robert Burns (1759–96) Scottish poet.
Scots, Wha Hae

9 Deliberation is the work of many men. Action, of one alone.
Charles De Gaulle (1890–1970) French general and statesman.
War Memoirs, Vol. 2

10 Suit the action to the word, the word to the action; with this special observance, that you o'erstep not the modesty of nature.
William Shakespeare (1564–1616) English dramatist.
Hamlet, III:2

11 If to do were as easy as to know what were good to do, chapels had been churches, and poor men's cottages princes' palaces.
William Shakespeare
The Merchant of Venice, I:2

12 So many worlds, so much to do,
So little done, such things to be.
Alfred, Lord Tennyson (1809–92) British poet.
In Memoriam A.H.H., LXXIII

13 It's dogged as does it. It ain't thinking about it.
Anthony Trollope (1815–82) British novelist.
Last Chronicle of Barset, Ch. 61

ACTORS

General quotes

See also acting, cinema, criticism, plays, theatre

1 An actor's a guy who, if you ain't talking about him, ain't listening.
Marlon Brando (1924–) US film star.
The Observer, 'Sayings of the Year', Jan 1956

2 An actor is something less than a man, while an actress is something more than a woman.
Richard Burton (Richard Jenkins; 1925–84) British actor.
Halliwell's Filmgoer's and Video Viewer's Companion

3 Never meddle with play-actors, for they're a favoured race.
Miguel de Cervantes (1547–1616) Spanish novelist.
Don Quixote, Pt. II, Ch. 11

4 Remember you are a star. Never go across the alley even to dump garbage unless you are dressed to the teeth.
Cecil B. de Mille (1881–1959) US film producer and director.
Halliwell's Filmgoer's and Video Viewer's Companion

5 Actors should be treated like cattle.
Alfred Hitchcock (1889–1980) British film director.
Said in clarification of a remark attributed to him, 'Actors are like cattle'
Quote, Unquote (N. Rees)

6 At one time I thought he wanted to be an actor. He had certain qualifications, including no money and a total lack of responsibility.
Hedda Hopper (1890–1966) US writer.
From Under My Hat

7 They didn't act like people and they didn't act like actors. It's hard to explain. They acted more like they knew they were celebrities and all. I mean they were good, but they were *too* good.
J. D. Salinger (1919–) US novelist.
The Catcher in the Rye, Ch. 17

Specific quotes

8 Can't act. Can't sing. Can dance a little.
Anonymous
Studio report after Fred Astaire's first screen test

9 John Wayne is dead.
The hell I am
Anonymous
Inscription on a wall in Bermondsey Antique Market, together with a ghostly denial
Evening Standard, 1980

10 If she was a victim of any kind, she was a victim of her friends.
George Cukor (1899–1983) US film director.
Referring to Marilyn Monroe
On Cukor (Gavin Lambert)

11 Garrick was pure gold beat out into thin leaf.
James Boswell (1740–95) Scottish lawyer and writer.
Referring to David Garrick

12 I remember Sarah Bernhardt's funeral perfectly. I have never had to wait so long to cross the street.
Eric Dunstan
Ego 9, 14 Oct 1946

13 I'm just a lucky slob from Ohio who happened to be in the right place at the right time.
Clark Gable (1901–60) US film actor.
Attrib.

14 Olivier's was, to my mind, the definitive Macbeth. Olivier had murder in his heart from the moment he came on the stage.
John Gielgud (1904–) British actor.
An Actor and His Time

15 Chaplin is no business man – all he knows is that he can't take anything less.
Samuel Goldwyn (Samuel Goldfish; 1882–1974) Polish-born US film producer.
Attrib.

16 You can't direct a Laughton picture. The best you can hope for is to referee.
Alfred Hitchcock (1889–1980) British film director.

17 She looked as though butter wouldn't melt in her mouth – or anywhere else.
Elsa Lanchester (1902–86) British-born US actress.
Referring to Maureen O'Hara
Attrib.

18 Goodbye Norma Jean
Though I never knew you at all
You had the grace to hold yourself
While those around you crawled.
They crawled out of the woodwork
And they whispered into your brain
Set you on the treadmill
And made you change your name.
Bernie Taupin (1950–) British songwriter.
Lyrics for a song by Elton John
Candle in the Wind (song)

19 I don't pretend to be an ordinary housewife.
Elizabeth Taylor (1932–) British-born US actress.
Interview

20 As Romeo Irving reminded me of a pig who has been taught to play the fiddle. He did it cleverly, but would be better employed in squealing.
Ellen Terry (1847–1928) British actress.
Notes on Irving

21 Ah, every day dear Herbert becomes *de plus en plus Oscarié*. It is a wonderful case of nature imitating art.
Oscar Wilde (1854–1900) Irish-born British dramatist.
Referring to Beerbohm Tree's unconscious adoption of some of the mannerisms of a character he was playing in one of Wilde's plays
Great Theatrical Disasters (G. Brandreth)

ADAPTABILITY

See also change

1 Remember that to change your mind and follow him who sets you right is to be none the less free than you were before.
Marcus Aurelius (121–180 AD) Roman emperor.
Meditations, Bk. VIII, Ch. 16

2 Mahomet made the people believe that he would call a hill to him . . . when the hill stood still, he was never a whit abashed, but said, 'If the hill will not come to Mahomet, Mahomet will go to the hill.'
Francis Bacon (1561–1626) English philosopher.
Often misquoted as 'If the mountain will not come to Mohammed'
Essays, 'Of Boldness'

3 President Robbins was so well adjusted to his environment that sometimes you could not tell which was the environment and which was President Robbins.
Randall Jarrell (1914–65) US author.
Pictures from an Institution, Pt. I, Ch. 4

4 As time requireth, a man of marvellous mirth and pastimes, and sometimes of as sad gravity, as who say: a man for all seasons.
Robert Whittington (16th century) English writer.
Referring to Sir Thomas More; after Erasmus
Vulgaria, Pt. II, 'De constructione nominum'

ADDICTION

1 Cocaine isn't habit-forming. I should know – I've been using it for years.
Tallulah Bankhead (1903–68) US actress.
Pentimento (Lillian Hellman), 'Theatre'

2 Every form of addiction is bad, no matter whether the narcotic be alcohol or morphine or idealism.
Carl Gustav Jung (1875–1961) Swiss psychoanalyst.
Memories, Dreams, Reflections, Ch. 12

ADDRESSES

1 Addresses are given to us to conceal our whereabouts.
Saki (Hector Hugh Munro; 1870–1916) British writer.
Cross Currents

2 Three addresses always inspire confidence, even in tradesmen.
Oscar Wilde (1854–1900) Irish-born British dramatist.
The Importance of Being Earnest, III

ADMIRATION

See also compliments, love, praise, respect, wonder

1 Miss J. Hunter Dunn, Miss J. Hunter Dunn, Furnish'd and burnish'd by Aldershot sun.
John Betjeman (1906–84) British poet.
A Subaltern's Love Song

2 Here's looking at you, kid.
Humphrey Bogart (1899–1957) US film star.
Casablanca

3 A fool always finds a greater fool to admire him.
Nicolas Boileau (1636–1711) French writer.
L'Art poétique, I

4 There is a garden in her face,
Where roses and white lilies grow;
A heav'nly paradise is that place,
Wherein all pleasant fruits do flow.
There cherries grow, which none may buy
Till 'Cherry ripe' themselves do cry.
Thomas Campion (1567–1620) English poet.
Fourth Book of Airs

5 I do think better of womankind than to

suppose they care whether Mister John
Keats five feet high likes them or not.
John Keats (1795–1821) British poet.
Letter to Benjamin Bailey, 18 July 1818

6 'There is a report that Piso is dead; it is a
great loss; he was an honest man, who
deserved to live longer; he was intelligent
and agreeable, resolute and courageous, to
be depended upon, generous and faithful.'
Add: 'provided he is really dead'.
Jean de La Bruyère (1645–96) French satirist.
Les Caractères

7 On Richmond Hill there lives a lass,
More sweet than May day morn,
Whose charms all other maids surpass,
A rose without a thorn.
Leonard MacNally (1752–1820) Irish dramatist and poet.
The Lass of Richmond Hill

8 Many a man has been a wonder to the
world, whose wife and valet have seen
nothing in him that was even remarkable.
Few men have been admired by their
servants.
Michel de Montaigne (1533–92) French essayist.
Essais, III

9 Charlie is my darling, my darling, my darling,
Charlie is my darling, the young Chevalier.
Carolina Nairne (1766–1845) Scottish songwriter.
Referring to Bonnie Prince Charlie
Charlie is my Darling

10 Not to admire, is all the art I know
To make men happy, and to keep them so.
Alexander Pope (1688–1744) British poet.
Imitations of Horace, 'To Mr. Murray'

11 Where'er you walk, cool gales shall fan the
glade,
Trees, where you sit, shall crowd into a shade:
Where'er you tread, the blushing flow'rs shall
rise,
And all things flourish where you turn your
eyes.
Alexander Pope
Pastorals, 'Summer'

12 But search the land of living men,
Where wilt thou find their like agen?
Walter Scott (1771–1832) Scottish novelist.
Marmion, I

13 The barge she sat in, like a burnish'd throne,
Burn'd on the water. The poop was beaten
gold;
Purple the sails, and so perfumed that
The winds were love-sick with them; the oars
were silver,
Which to the tune of flutes kept stroke and
made
The water which they beat to follow faster,
As amorous of their strokes. For her own
person,

It beggar'd all description.
William Shakespeare (1564–1616) English dramatist.
Antony and Cleopatra, II:2

14 Age cannot wither her, nor custom stale
Her infinite variety. Other women cloy
The appetites they feed, but she makes hungry
Where most she satisfies.
William Shakespeare
Antony and Cleopatra, II:2

15 'A was a man, take him for all in all,
I shall not look upon his like again.
William Shakespeare
Hamlet, I:2

16 Who is Silvia? What is she,
That all our swains commend her?
Holy, fair, and wise is she.
William Shakespeare
The Two Gentlemen of Verona, IV:2

17 He was a great patriot, a humanitarian, a
loyal friend – provided, of course, that he
really is dead.
Voltaire (François-Marie Arouet; 1694–1778) French
writer.
Giving a funeral oration
Attrib.

18 The sweetest thing that ever grew
Beside a human door!
William Wordsworth (1770–1850) British poet.
Lucy Gray

ADULTERY

See also marriage, sex, unfaithfulness

1 What men call gallantry, and gods adultery,
Is much more common where the climate's
sultry.
Lord Byron (1788–1824) British poet.
Don Juan, I

2 I have looked on a lot of women with lust.
I've committed adultery in my heart many
times. God recognises I will do this and
forgives me.
Jimmy Carter (1924–) US statesman and president.
Remark

3 Sara could commit adultery at one end and
weep for her sins at the other, and enjoy
both operations at once.
Joyce Cary (1888–1957) British novelist.
The Horse's Mouth, Ch. 8

4 I say I don't sleep with married men, but
what I mean is that I don't sleep with happily
married men.
Britt Ekland (1942–) Swedish film actress.
Attrib.

5 You know, of course, that the Tasmanians,
who never committed adultery, are now
extinct.
W. Somerset Maugham (1874–1965) British novelist.
The Bread-Winner

6 Madame, you must really be more careful. Suppose it had been someone else who found you like this.

Duc de Richelieu (1766–1822) French statesman.
Discovering his wife with her lover
The Book of Lists (D. Wallechinsky)

7 With all my heart. Whose wife shall it be?

John Horne Tooke (1736–1812) British clergyman, politician, and etymologist.
Replying to the suggestion that he take a wife
Attrib.

ADVERTISING

1 Any publicity is good publicity.

Proverb

2 It pays to advertise.

Anonymous
Already current by c. 1912 when Cole Porter used it as the title of an early song

3 Advertising is the most fun you can have with your clothes on.

Jerry Della Femina (1936–) Advertising executive.
From those wonderful folks who gave you Pearl Harbor

4 Half the money I spend on advertising is wasted, and the trouble is I don't know which half.

Viscount Leverhulme (1851–1925) British industrialist.
Confessions of an Advertising Man (D. Ogilvy)

5 Freedom of the press in Britain is freedom to print such of the proprietor's prejudices as the advertisers don't object to.

Hannen Swaffer (1879–1962) British journalist.
Attrib.

Advertising Slogans

6 A diamond is forever.

7 A Mars a day helps you work rest and play.

8 Drinka pinta milka day.

9 Go to work on an egg.

10 Guinness is good for you.

11 Heineken refreshes the parts other beers cannot reach.

12 I'd like to teach the world to sing.

Coca Cola

13 I'll bet he drinks Carling Black Label.

14 It beats as it sweeps as it cleans.

Hoover

15 It's fingerlickin' good.

Kentucky Fried Chicken

16 It's the real thing.

Coca Cola

17 Sch . . . you know who.

Schweppes

18 The bank that likes to say yes.

Trustee Savings Bank

19 Vorsprung durch Technik.

Audi

ADVICE

1 A good scare is worth more than good advice.

Proverb

2 Don't teach your grandmother to suck eggs.

Proverb

3 He that has no children brings them up well.

Proverb

4 He that has no wife, beats her oft.

Proverb

5 Advice would be more acceptable if it didn't always conflict with our plans.

Anonymous

6 Advice is seldom welcome; and those who want it the most always like it the least.

Earl of Chesterfield (1694–1773) English statesman.
Letter to his son, 29 Jan 1748

7 Your business is to put me out of business.

Dwight D. Eisenhower (1890–1969) US general and statesman.
Addressing a graduating class at a university
Procession (J. Gunther)

8 I intended to give you some advice but now I remember how much is left over from last year unused.

George Harris (1844–1922) US congressman.
Said when addressing students at the start of a new academic year
Braude's Second Encyclopedia (J. Braude)

9 It is a good thing to follow the first law of holes; if you are in one, stop digging.

Denis Healey (1917–) British Labour politician.
Speech, May 1988

10 On my twenty-first birthday my father said, 'Son, here's a million dollars. Don't lose it.'

Larry Niven (1938–) US science-fiction writer.
When asked 'What is the best advice you have ever been given?'
Attrib.

11 One gives nothing so freely as advice.

Duc de la Rochefoucauld (1613–80) French writer.
Maximes, 110

12 Don't tell your friends their social faults, they will cure the fault and never forgive you.

Logan Pearsall Smith (1865–1946) US writer.
Afterthoughts

13 No one wants advice – only corroboration.

John Steinbeck (1902–68) US novelist.

14 It's queer how ready people always are with advice in any real or imaginary emergency, and no matter how many times experience has shown them to be wrong, they continue to set forth their opinions, as if they had received them from the Almighty!

Annie Sullivan (1866–1936) US teacher of the handicapped.
Letter, 12 June 1887

15 I have lived some thirty years on this planet, and I have yet to hear the first syllable of valuable or even earnest advice from my seniors.

Henry David Thoreau (1817–62) US writer.
Walden, 'Economy'

16 Are you in trouble? Do you need advice? Write to Miss Lonelyhearts and she will help.

Nathaniel West (Nathan Weinstein; 1903–40) US novelist.
Miss Lonelyhearts

AFFECTATION

See also ostentation

1 We have become a grandmother.

Margaret Thatcher (1925–) British politician and prime minister.
Remark, Mar 1989

2 Don't you sit there and sigh gal like you was Lady Nevershit.

Arnold Wesker (1932–) British dramatist.
Roots, III

3 She keeps on being Queenly in her own room with the door shut.

Edith Wharton (1862–1937) US novelist.
The House of Mirth, Bk. II, Ch. 1

AFTERLIFE

See also death, heaven

1 CLOV. Do you believe in the life to come?
HAMM. Mine was always that.

Samuel Beckett (1906–89) Irish novelist and dramatist.
Endgame

2 That which is the foundation of all our hopes and of all our fears; all our hopes and fears which are of any consideration: I mean a Future Life.

Joseph Butler (1692–1752) British churchman.
The Analogy of Religion, Introduction

3 We have no reliable guarantee that the afterlife will be any less exasperating than this one, have we?

Noël Coward (1899–1973) British dramatist.
Blithe Spirit, I

4 We sometimes congratulate ourselves at the moment of waking from a troubled dream; it may be so the moment after death.

Nathaniel Hawthorne (1804–64) US novelist and writer.
American Notebooks

5 Death is nothing at all. I have only slipped away into the next room. I am I and you are you. Whatever we were to each other, that we are still . . . . What is death but negligible accident? Why should I be out of mind because I am out of sight? I am waiting for you, for an interval, somewhere very near just around the corner. All is well.

Henry Scott Holland (1847–1918) British Anglican clergyman.
Attrib.

6 Is there another life? Shall I awake and find all this a dream? There must be, we cannot be created for this sort of suffering.

John Keats (1795–1821) British poet.
Letter, 1820

7 My doctrine is: Live that thou mayest desire to live again – that is thy duty – for in any case thou wilt live again!

Friedrich Wilhelm Nietzsche (1844–1900) German philosopher.
Eternal Recurrence

8 After your death you will be what you were before your birth.

Arthur Schopenhauer (1788–1860) German philosopher.
Parerga and Paralipomena

9 The dread of something after death –
The undiscover'd country, from whose bourn
No traveller returns.

William Shakespeare (1564–1616) English dramatist.
Hamlet, III:1

10 I am going a long way
With these thou seest – if indeed I go
(For all my mind is clouded with a doubt) –
To the island-valley of Avilion;
Where falls not hail, or rain, or any snow,
Nor ever wind blows loudly; but it lies
Deep-meadow'd, happy, fair with orchard lawns
And bowery hollows crown'd with summer sea,
Where I will heal me of my grievous wound.

Alfred, Lord Tennyson (1809–92) British poet.
Idylls of the King, 'The Passing of Arthur'

11 One world at a time.

Henry David Thoreau (1817–62) US writer.
On being asked his opinion of the hereafter
Attrib.

AGE

See also longevity, old age, youth

1 Never too late to learn.
Proverb

2 There's many a good tune played on an old fiddle.
Proverb

3 All evil comes from the old. They grow fat on ideas and young men die of them.

Jean Anouilh (1910–87) French dramatist.
Catch as Catch Can

4 I am past thirty, and three parts iced over.
Matthew Arnold (1822–88) British poet and critic.
Letter to A. H. Clough, 12 Feb 1853

5 I refuse to admit that I am more than fifty-two, even if that does make my sons illegitimate.
Nancy Astor (1879–1964) US-born British politician.
Attrib.

6 I think your whole life shows in your face and you should be proud of that.
Lauren Bacall (1924–) US actress.
Remark, Mar 1988

7 Age will not be defied.
Francis Bacon (1561–1626) English philosopher.
Essays, 'Of Regiment of Health'

8 A man that is young in years may be old in hours, if he have lost no time.
Francis Bacon
Essays, 'Of Youth and Age'

9 The only thing I regret about my past life is the length of it. If I had my past life over again I'd make all the same mistakes – only sooner.
Tallulah Bankhead (1903–68) US actress.
The Times, 28 July 1981

10 What is an adult? A child blown up by age.
Simone de Beauvoir (1908–86) French writer.
La Femme rompue

11 If thou hast gathered nothing in thy youth, how canst thou find any thing in thine age?
Bible: Ecclesiasticus
25:3

12 No man also having drunk old wine straightway desireth new: for he saith, The old is better.
Bible: Luke
5:39

13 Old age is . . . a lot of crossed off names in an address book.
Ronald Blythe (1922–) British author.
The View in Winter

14 Being now come to the years of discretion.
The Book of Common Prayer
Order of Confirmation

15 Therefore I summon age
To grant youth's heritage.
Robert Browning (1812–89) British poet.
Rabbi ben Ezra, XIII

16 Ah well, perhaps one has to be very old before one learns how to be amused rather than shocked.
Pearl Buck (1892–1973) US novelist.
China, Past and Present, Ch. 6

17 A lady of a 'certain age', which means
Certainly aged.
Lord Byron (1788–1824) British poet.
Don Juan, VI

18 A man is as old as he's feeling,
A woman as old as she looks.
Mortimer Collins (1827–76) British writer.
The Unknown Quantity

19 Youth is a blunder; manhood a struggle; old age a regret.
Benjamin Disraeli (1804–81) British statesman.
Coningsby, Bk. III, Ch. 1

20 I am resolved to grow fat and look young till forty, and then slip out of the world with the first wrinkle and the reputation of five-and-twenty.
John Dryden (1631–1700) British poet and dramatist.
The Maiden Queen, III

21 Men are but children of a larger growth;
Our appetites as apt to change as theirs,
And full as craving too, and full as vain.
John Dryden
All for Love, IV

22 The years between fifty and seventy are the hardest. You are always being asked to do things, and you are not yet decrepit enough to turn them down.
T. S. Eliot (1888–1965) US-born British poet and dramatist.
Time, 23 Oct 1950

23 Here I am, an old man in a dry month,
Being read to by a boy, waiting for rain.
T. S. Eliot
Gerontion

24 Si jeunesse savait; si vieillesse pouvait.
If only youth knew, if only age could.
Henri Estienne (1528–98) French scholar.
Les Prémices

25 At sixteen I was stupid, confused, insecure and indecisive. At twenty-five I was wise, self-confident, prepossessing and assertive. At forty-five I am stupid, confused, insecure and indecisive. Who would have supposed that maturity is only a short break in adolescence?
Jules Feiffer (1929–) US writer, cartoonist, and humorist.
The Observer, 3 Feb 1974

26 Though the Jazz Age continued, it became less and less an affair of youth. The sequel was like a children's party taken over by the elders.
F. Scott Fitzgerald (1896–1940) US novelist.
The Crack-Up

27 At twenty years of age, the will reigns; at thirty, the wit; and at forty, the judgement.
Benjamin Franklin (1706–90) US scientist and statesman.
Poor Richard's Almanack

28 A diplomat is a man who always remembers a woman's birthday but never remembers her age.
Robert Frost (1875–1963) US poet.
Attrib.

29 She may very well pass for forty-three
In the dusk, with a light behind her!
W. S. Gilbert (1836–1911) British dramatist.
Trial by Jury

30 'Old Cary Grant fine. How you?'
Cary Grant (Archibald Leach; 1904–86) British-born US film star.
Replying to a telegram sent to his agent inquiring: 'How old Cary Grant?'
The Filmgoer's Book of Quotes (Leslie Halliwell)

31 You will recognize, my boy, the first sign of old age: it is when you go out into the streets of London and realize for the first time how young the policemen look.
Seymour Hicks (1871–1949) British actor-manager.
They Were Singing (C. Pulling)

32 What do the ravages of time not injure? Our parents' age (worse than our grandparents') has produced us, more worthless still, who will soon give rise to a yet more vicious generation.
Horace (Quintus Horatius Flaccus; 65–8 BC) Roman poet.
Odes, III

33 Whenever a man's friends begin to compliment him about looking young, he may be sure that they think he is growing old.
Washington Irving (1783–1859) US writer.
Bracebridge Hall, 'Bachelors'

34 It is sobering to consider that when Mozart was my age he had already been dead for a year.
Tom Lehrer (1928–) US university teacher and songwriter.
An Encyclopedia of Quotations about Music (N. Shapiro)

35 I am just turning forty and taking my time about it.
Harold Lloyd (1893–1971) US silent-film comedian.
Reply when, aged 77, he was asked his age
The Times, 23 Sept 1970

36 Growth is a greater mystery than death. All of us can understand failure, we all contain failure and death within us, but not even the successful man can begin to describe the impalpable elations and apprehensions of growth.
Norman Mailer (1923–) US writer.
Advertisements for Myself

37 But at my back I always hear
Time's winged chariot hurrying near;
And yonder all before us lie
Deserts of vast eternity.
Andrew Marvell (1621–78) English poet.
To His Coy Mistress

38 A man is only as old as the woman he feels.
Groucho Marx (Julius Marx; 1895–1977) US comedian.
Attrib.

39 I am old enough to be – in fact am – your mother.
A. A. Milne (1882–1956) British writer.
Belinda

40 How soon hath Time, the subtle thief of youth,
Stolen on his wing my three-and-twentieth year!
John Milton (1608–74) English poet.
Sonnet: 'On Being Arrived at the Age of Twenty-three'

41 Do you think my mind is maturing late,
Or simply rotted early?
Ogden Nash (1902–71) US poet.
Lines on Facing Forty

42 At 50, everyone has the face he deserves.
George Orwell (Eric Blair; 1903–50) British novelist.
Last words in his manuscript notebook, 17 Apr 1949

43 Each generation imagines itself to be more intelligent than the one that went before it, and wiser than the one that comes after it.
George Orwell
Book Review

44 From forty to fifty a man is at heart either a stoic or a satyr.
Arthur Pinero (1855–1934) British dramatist.
The Second Mrs Tanqueray, I

45 One of the pleasures of middle age is to *find out* that one WAS right, and that one was much righter than one knew at say 17 or 23.
Ezra Pound (1885–1972) US poet.
ABC of Reading, Ch. 1

46 You know, by the time you reach my age, you've made plenty of mistakes if you've lived your life properly
Ronald Reagan (1911–) US politician and president.
The Observer, 'Sayings of the Week', 8 Mar 1987

47 It is fun to be in the same decade with you.
Franklin D. Roosevelt (1882–1945) US Democratic president.
After Churchill had congratulated him on his 60th birthday
The Hinge of Fate (Winston S. Churchill), Ch. 4

48 I have always felt that a woman has the right to treat the subject of her age with ambiguity until, perhaps, she passes into the realm of over ninety. Then it is better she be candid with herself and with the world.
Helena Rubinstein (1882–1965) Polish-born US cosmetics manufacturer.
My Life for Beauty, Pt. I, Ch. 1

49 The young have aspirations that never come to pass, the old have reminiscences of what never happened.
Saki (Hector Hugh Munro; 1870–1916) British writer.
Reginald at the Carlton

50 The young man who has not wept is a savage, and the old man who will not laugh is a fool.
George Santayana (1863–1952) US philosopher.
Dialogues in Limbo, Ch. 3

51 When I was young, I was told: 'You'll see,

when you're fifty. I am fifty and I haven't seen a thing.

Erik Satie (1866–1925) French composer.
From a letter to his brother
Erik Satie (Pierre-Daniel Templier), Ch. 1

52 Thou hast nor youth nor age;
But, as it were, an after-dinner's sleep,
Dreaming on both.

William Shakespeare (1564–1616) English dramatist.
Measure for Measure, III:1

53 Doth not the appetite alter? A man loves the meat in his youth that he cannot endure in his age.

William Shakespeare
Much Ado About Nothing, II:3

54 Crabbed age and youth cannot live together:
Youth is full of pleasure, age is full of care;
Youth like summer morn, age like winter weather;
Youth like summer brave, age like winter bare.

William Shakespeare
The Passionate Pilgrim, XII

55 All that the young can do for the old is to shock them and keep them up to date.

George Bernard Shaw (1856–1950) Irish dramatist and critic.
Fanny's First Play

56 It's a funny thing about that bust. As time goes on it seems to get younger and younger.

George Bernard Shaw
Referring to a portrait bust sculpted for him by Rodin
More Things I Wish I'd Said (K. Edwards)

57 One's prime is elusive. You little girls, when you grow up, must be on the alert to recognize your prime at whatever time of your life it may occur. You must then live it to the full.

Muriel Spark (1918–) British novelist.
The Prime of Miss Jean Brodie, Ch. 1

58 The mark of the immature man is that he wants to die nobly for a cause, while the mark of the mature man is that he wants to live humbly for one.

Wilhelm Stekel (1868–1940) Viennese psychiatrist.
The Catcher in the Rye (J. D. Salinger), Ch. 24

59 Men come of age at sixty, women at fifteen.

James Stephens (1882–1950) Irish novelist.
The Observer, 'Sayings of the Week', 1 Oct 1944

60 I was born old and get younger every day. At present I am sixty years young.

Herbert Beerbohm Tree (1853–1917) British actor and theatre manager.
Beerbohm Tree (Hesketh Pearson)

61 Life begins at forty.

Sophie Tucker (Sophia Abuza; 1884–1966) Russian-born US singer.
Attrib.

62 From birth to age eighteen, a girl needs good parents. From eighteen to thirty-five, she needs good looks. From thirty-five to fifty-five, she needs a good personality. From fifty-five on, she needs good cash.

Sophie Tucker
Attrib.

63 There are no old men any more. *Playboy* and *Penthouse* have between them made an ideal of eternal adolescence, sunburnt and saunaed, with the grey dorianed out of it.

Peter Ustinov (1921–) British actor.
Dear Me, Ch. 18

64 It is charming to totter into vogue.

Horace Walpole (1717–97) British writer.
Letter to G. A. Selwyn, 1765

65 No woman should ever be quite accurate about her age. It looks so calculating.

Oscar Wilde (1854–1900) Irish-born British dramatist.
The Importance of Being Earnest, III

66 One should never trust a woman who tells one her real age. A woman who would tell one that, would tell one anything.

Oscar Wilde
A Woman of No Importance, I

67 The older one grows the more one likes indecency.

Virginia Woolf (1882–1941) British novelist.
Monday or Tuesday

68 My heart leaps up when I behold
A rainbow in the sky:
So was it when my life began;
So is it now I am a man;
So be it when I shall grow old,
Or let me die!
The Child is Father of the Man;
And I could wish my days to be
Bound each to each by natural piety.

William Wordsworth (1770–1850) British poet.
My Heart Leaps Up

69 One that is ever kind said yesterday:
'Your well-belovèd's hair has threads of grey,
And little shadows come about her eyes.'

W. B. Yeats (1865–1939) Irish poet.
The Folly of Being Comforted

70 Where, where but here have Pride and Truth,
That long to give themselves for wage,
To shake their wicked sides at youth
Restraining reckless middle age?

W. B. Yeats
On hearing that the Students of our New University have joined the Agitation against Immoral Literature

71 Though leaves are many, the root is one;
Through all the lying days of my youth
I swayed my leaves and flowers in the sun;
Now I may wither into the truth.

W. B. Yeats
The Coming of Wisdom with Time

72 Wine comes in at the mouth

And love comes in at the eye;
That's all we shall know for truth
Before we grow old and die.
W. B. Yeats
A Drinking Song

73 Be wise with speed,
A fool at forty is a fool indeed.
Edward Young (1683–1765) British poet.
Love of Fame, II

AGGRAVATION

1 This is adding insult to injuries.
Edward Moore (1712–57) British dramatist.
The Foundling, V

2 The point is that nobody likes having salt
rubbed into their wounds, even if it is the
salt of the earth.
Rebecca West (Cicely Isabel Fairfield; 1892–1983) British
novelist and journalist.
The Salt of the Earth, Ch. 2

AGREEMENT

1 My cousin Francis and I are in perfect accord
– he wants Milan, and so do I.
Charles V (1500–58) Holy Roman Emperor.
Referring to his dispute with Francis I of France over Italian
territory
The Story of Civilization (W. Durant), Vol. 5

2 I am always of the opinion with the learned,
if they speak first.
William Congreve (1670–1729) British Restoration
dramatist.
Incognita

3 'My idea of an agreeable person,' said Hugo
Bohun, 'is a person who agrees with me.'
Benjamin Disraeli (1804–81) British statesman.
Lothair, Ch. 35

4 We seldom attribute common sense except to
those who agree with us.
Duc de la Rochefoucauld (1613–80) French writer.
Maximes, 347

5 Very like a whale.
William Shakespeare (1564–1616) English dramatist.
Hamlet, III:2

6 Our agenda is now exhausted. The secretary
general is exhausted. All of you are
exhausted. I find it comforting that, beginning
with our very first day, we find ourselves in
such complete unanimity.
Paul Henri Spaak (1899–1972) Belgian statesman.
Concluding the first General Assembly meeting of the United
Nations

7 Ah! don't say you agree with me. When
people agree with me I always feel that I
must be wrong.
Oscar Wilde (1854–1900) Irish-born British dramatist.
The Critic as Artist, Pt. 2

8 If two men on the same job agree all the
time, then one is useless. If they disagree all
the time, then both are useless.
Darryl F. Zanuck (1902–79) US film producer.
The Observer, 'Sayings of the Week', 23 Oct 1949

AGRICULTURE

See also countryside

1 We plough the fields, and scatter
The good seed on the land,
But it is fed and watered
By God's Almighty Hand.
He sends the snow in winter,
The warmth to swell the grain,
The breezes and the sunshine,
And soft refreshing rain.
Jane Montgomery Campbell (1817–78) British hymn
writer.
Hymn

2 Three acres and a cow.
Jesse Collings (1831–1920) British politician.
Slogan used in his land-reform propaganda

3 Is my team ploughing,
That I was used to drive?
A. E. Housman (1859–1936) British scholar and poet.
A Shropshire Lad, 'Bredon Hill'

4 'O Mary, go and call the cattle home,
And call the cattle home,
And call the cattle home,
Across the sands of Dee.'
The western wind was wild and dank with
foam,
And all alone went she.
Charles Kingsley (1819–75) British writer.
The Sands of Dee

5 This bread I break was once the oat,
This wine upon a foreign tree
Plunged in its fruit;
Man in the day or wind at night
Laid the crops low, broke the grape's joy.
Dylan Thomas (1914–53) Welsh poet.
This bread I break

AIDS

1 Everywhere I go I see increasing evidence of
people swirling about in a human cesspit of
their own making.
James Anderton (1932–) British Chief Constable of
Greater Manchester.
Referring to AIDS

2 It could be said that the Aids pandemic is a
classic own-goal scored by the human race
against itself.
Princess Anne (1950–) The Princess Royal, only
daughter of Elizabeth II.
Remark, Jan 1988

3 We hope people will learn to love condoms.

In the past people like Casanova had lots of fun with their condoms.

David Cox TV producer.
Remark, Mar 1987

4 My message to the businessman of this country when they go abroad on business is that there is one thing above all they can take with them to stop them catching AIDS, and that is the wife.

Edwina Currie (1946–) British politician.
The Observer, 15 Feb 1987

5 Every time you sleep with a boy you sleep with all his old girlfriends.

Government-sponsored AIDS advertisement, 1987

6 We're all going to go crazy, living this epidemic every minute, while the rest of the world goes on out there, all around us, as if nothing is happening, going on with their own lives and not knowing what it's like, what we're going through. We're living through war, but where they're living it's peacetime, and we're all in the same country.

Larry Kramer (1935–) US dramatist and novelist.
The Normal Heart

ALCOHOL

See also abstinence, drinks, drunkenness, public houses

1 A cask of wine works more miracles than a church full of saints.

Proverb

2 Adam's ale is the best brew.

Proverb

3 A good drink makes the old young.

Proverb

4 He who drinks a little too much drinks much too much.

Proverb

5 Take a hair of the dog that bit you.

Proverb

6 There's many a slip 'twixt the cup and the lip.

Proverb

7 When the wine is in, the wit is out.

Proverb

8 If all be true that I do think,
There are five reasons we should drink;
Good wine – a friend – or being dry –
Or lest we should be by and by –
Or any other reason why.

Dean Aldrich (1647–1710) English poet.
Reasons for Drinking

9 I feel no pain, dear mother, now
But oh, I am so dry!
O take me to a brewery

And leave me there to die.

Anonymous
Shanty

10 So who's in a hurry?

Robert Benchley (1889–1945) US humorist.
When asked whether he knew that drinking was a slow death
Attrib.

11 He is believed to have liked port, but to have said of claret that 'it would be port if it could'.

Richard Bentley (1662–1742) English academic.
Bentley (R. C. Jebb)

12 Woe unto them that rise up early in the morning, that they may follow strong drink; that continue until night, till wine inflame them!

Bible: Isaiah
5:11

13 Drink no longer water, but use a little wine for thy stomach's sake and thine often infirmities.

Bible: I Timothy
5:23

14 When the ruler of the feast had tasted the water that was made wine, and knew not whence it was: (but the servants which drew the water knew;) the governor of the feast called the bridegroom,
And saith unto him, Every man at the beginning doth set forth good wine; and when men have well drunk, then that which is worse: but thou hast kept the good wine until now.

Bible: John
2:9–10

15 No man also having drunk old wine straightway desireth new: for he saith, The old is better.

Bible: Luke
5:39

16 Look not thou upon the wine when it is red, when it giveth his colour in the cup, when it moveth itself aright.
At the last it biteth like a serpent, and stingeth like an adder.

Bible: Proverbs
23:31–32

17 If we heard it said of Orientals that they habitually drank a liquor which went to their heads, deprived them of reason and made them vomit, we should say: 'How very barbarous!'

Jean de La Bruyère (1645–96) French satirist.
Les Caractères

18 The heart which grief hath cankered
Hath one unfailing remedy – the Tankard.

C. S. Calverley (1831–84) British poet.
Beer

19 Alcohol is like love: the first kiss is magic,

the second is intimate, the third is routine. After that you just take the girl's clothes off.
Raymond Chandler (1888–1959) US novelist.
The Long Good-bye

20 So was hir joly whistle wel y-wet.
Geoffrey Chaucer (c. 1342–1400) English poet.
The Canterbury Tales, 'The Reve's Tale'

21 I must point out that my rule of life prescribed as an absolutely sacred rite smoking cigars and also the drinking of alcohol before, after, and if need be during all meals and in the intervals between them.
Winston Churchill (1874–1965) British statesman.
Said during a lunch with the Arab leader Ibn Saud, when he heard that the king's religion forbade smoking and alcohol
The Second World War

22 Apart from cheese and tulips, the main product of the country is advocaat, a drink made from lawyers.
Alan Coren (1938–) British humorist and writer.
Referring to Holland
The Sanity Inspector, 'All You Need to Know about Europe'

23 Then trust me, there's nothing like drinking So pleasant on this side the grave;
It keeps the unhappy from thinking,
And makes e'en the valiant more brave.
Charles Dibdin (1745–1814) British actor and dramatist.
Nothing like Grog

24 'Did you ever taste beer?' 'I had a sip of it once,' said the small servant. 'Here's a state of things!' cried Mr Swiveller . . . . 'She *never* tasted it – it can't be tasted in a sip!'
Charles Dickens (1812–70) British novelist.
The Old Curiosity Shop, Ch. 57

25 First you take a drink, then the drink takes a drink, then the drink takes you.
F. Scott Fitzgerald (1896–1940) US novelist.
Ackroyd (Jules Feiffer), '1964, May 7'

26 Best while you have it use your breath, There is no drinking after death.
John Fletcher (1579–1625) English dramatist.
With Jonson and others
The Bloody Brother, II:2

27 And he that will go to bed sober,
Falls with the leaf still in October.
John Fletcher
The Bloody Brother, II:2

28 A taste for drink, combined with gout, Had doubled him up for ever.
W. S. Gilbert (1836–1911) British dramatist.
The Gondoliers, I

29 Let schoolmasters puzzle their brain, With grammar, and nonsense, and learning, Good liquor, I stoutly maintain,
Gives genius a better discerning.
Oliver Goldsmith (1728–74) Irish-born British writer.
She Stoops to Conquer, I

30 He that goes to bed thirsty rises healthy.
George Herbert (1593–1633) English poet.
Jacula Prudentum

31 Malt does more than Milton can
To justify God's ways to man.
A. E. Housman (1859–1936) British scholar and poet.
A Shropshire Lad, 'The Welsh Marches'

32 Claret is the liquor for boys; port for men; but he who aspires to be a hero must drink brandy.
Samuel Johnson (1709–84) British lexicographer.
Life of Johnson (J. Boswell), Vol. III

33 No, Sir; there were people who died of dropsies, which they contracted in trying to get drunk.
Samuel Johnson
Scornfully criticizing the strength of the wine in Scotland before the Act of Union in response to Boswell's claim that there had been a lot of drunkenness
Tour to the Hebrides (J. Boswell)

34 Come, let me know what it is that makes a Scotchman happy!
Samuel Johnson
Ordering for himself a glass of whisky
Tour to the Hebrides (J. Boswell)

35 My friends should drink a dozen of Claret on my Tomb.
John Keats (1795–1821) British poet.
Letter to Benjamin Bailey, 14 Aug 1819

36 O, for a draught of vintage! that hath been Cool'd a long age in the deep-delved earth.
John Keats
Ode to a Nightingale

37 O for a beaker full of the warm South, Full of the true, the blushful Hippocrene, With beaded bubbles winking at the brim, And purple-stained mouth.
John Keats
Ode to a Nightingale

38 Even though a number of people have tried, no one has yet found a way to drink for a living.
Jean Kerr (1923–) US dramatist.
Poor Richard

39 Frenchmen drink wine just like we used to drink water before Prohibition.
Ring Lardner Jnr (1885–1933) American humorist.
Wit's End (R. E. Drennan)

40 It takes a good deal of physical courage to ride a horse. This, however, I have. I get it at about forty cents a flask, and take it as required.
Stephen Leacock (1869–1944) English-born Canadian economist and humorist.
Literary Lapses, 'Reflections on Riding'

41 If die I must, let me die drinking in an inn.
Walter Map (c. 1140–c. 1209) Welsh clergyman and writer.
De Nugis Curialium

42 The tranquilizer of greatest value since the early history of man, and which may never become outdated, is alcohol, when administered in moderation. It possesses the distinct advantage of being especially pleasant to the taste buds.
Nathan Masor (1913–)
Attrib.

43 I've made it a rule never to drink by daylight and never to refuse a drink after dark.
H. L. Mencken (1880–1956) US journalist.
New York Post, 18 Sept 1945

44 No man is genuinely happy, married, who has to drink worse gin than he used to drink when he was single.
H. L. Mencken
Prejudices, 'Reflections on Monogamy'

45 Then to the spicy nut-brown ale.
John Milton (1608–74) English poet.
L'Allegro

46 A torchlight procession marching down your throat.
John L. O'Sullivan (1813–95) US writer.
Referring to whisky
Collections and Recollections (G. W. E. Russell), Ch. 19

47 *In vino veritas.*
Truth comes out in wine.
Pliny the Elder (Gaius Plinius Secundus; 23–79 AD)
Roman scholar.
Natural History, XIV

48 It is WRONG to do what everyone else does – namely, to hold the wine list just out of sight, look for the second cheapest claret on the list, and say, 'Number 22, please'.
Stephen Potter (1900–69) British writer.
One-Upmanship, Ch. 14

49 A good general rule is to state that the bouquet is better than the taste, and vice versa.
Stephen Potter
One-Upmanship, Ch. 14

50 It is the unbroken testimony of all history that alcoholic liquors have been used by the strongest, wisest, handsomest, and in every way best races of all times.
George Edward Bateman Saintsbury (1845–1933)
British writer and critic.
Notes on a Cellar-Book

51 People may say what they like about the decay of Christianity; the religious system that produced green Chartreuse can never really die.
Saki (Hector Hugh Munro; 1870–1916) British writer.
Reginald on Christmas Presents

52 By insisting on having your bottle pointing to the north when the cork is being drawn, and calling the waiter Max, you may induce an impression on your guests which hours of laboured boasting might be powerless to achieve. For this purpose, however, the guests must be chosen as carefully as the wine.
Saki
The Chaplet

53 It provokes the desire, but it takes away the performance. Therefore much drink may be said to be an equivocator with lechery.
William Shakespeare (1564–1616) English dramatist.
Macbeth, II:3

54 I am only a beer teetotaller, not a champagne teetotaller.
George Bernard Shaw (1856–1950) Irish dramatist and critic.
Candida

55 Alcohol is a very necessary article . . . It enables Parliament to do things at eleven at night that no sane person would do at eleven in the morning.
George Bernard Shaw
Major Barbara, II

56 Gin was mother's milk to her.
George Bernard Shaw
Pygmalion, III

57 Well, then, my stomach must just digest in its waistcoat.
Richard Brinsley Sheridan (1751–1816) British dramatist.
On being warned that his drinking would destroy the coat of his stomach
The Fine Art of Political Wit (L. Harris)

58 Another little drink wouldn't do us any harm.
Edith Sitwell (1887–1964) British poet and writer.
Façade, 'Scotch Rhapsody'

59 Selwyn Macgregor, the nicest boy who ever committed the sin of whisky.
Muriel Spark (1918–) British novelist.
The Go-Away Bird, 'A Sad Tale's Best for Winter'

60 Fifteen men on the dead man's chest
Yo-ho-ho, and a bottle of rum!
Drink and the devil had done for the rest –
Yo-ho-ho, and a bottle of rum!
Robert Louis Stevenson (1850–94) Scottish writer.
Treasure Island, Ch. 1

61 There are two things that will be believed of any man whatsoever, and one of them is that he has taken to drink.
Booth Tarkington (1869–1946) US novelist.
Penrod, Ch. 10

62 It's a Naive Domestic Burgundy, Without Any Breeding. But I think you'll be Amused by its Presumption.
James Thurber (1894–1961) US humorist.
Men, Women and Dogs

63 'Joe,' I said, 'was perhaps the first great nonstop literary drinker of the American nineteenth century. He made the indulgences of Coleridge and De Quincey seem like a bit

of mischief in the kitchen with the cooking sherry.'
James Thurber
Alarms and Diversions, 'The Moribundant Life . . . '

64 I prefer temperance hotels – although they sell worse kinds of liquor than any other kind of hotels.
Artemus Ward (Charles Farrar Browne; 1834–67) US humorous writer.
Artemus Ward's Lecture

65 I hadn't the heart to touch my breakfast. I told Jeeves to drink it himself.
P. G. Wodehouse (1881–1975) British humorous novelist.
My Man Jeeves

66 It was my Uncle George who discovered that alcohol was a food well in advance of modern medical thought.
P. G. Wodehouse
The Inimitable Jeeves, Ch. 16

67 I must get out of these wet clothes and into a dry Martini.
Alexander Woollcott (1887–1943) US journalist.
Reader's Digest

68 Father, dear father, come home with me now,
The clock in the steeple strikes one.
Henry Clay Work (1832–84) US songwriter.
A temperance song
Come Home, Father

AMBITION

See also desire

1 He who rides a tiger is afraid to dismount.
Proverb

2 *Per ardua ad astra.*
Hard and high to the stars!
Anonymous
Motto of the Royal Air Force

3 Ah, but a man's reach should exceed his grasp,
Or what's a heaven for?
Robert Browning (1812–89) British poet.
Andrea del Sarto

4 Man partly is and wholly hopes to be.
Robert Browning
A Death in the Desert

5 You seem to have no real purpose in life and won't realize at the age of twenty-two that for a man life means work, and hard work if you mean to succeed. . .
Jennie Jerome Churchill (1854–1921) US-born British hostess and writer.
Letter to Winston Churchill, 26 Feb 1897
Jennie (Ralph G. Martin), Vol. II

6 I have found some of the best reasons I ever

had for remaining at the bottom simply by looking at the men at the top.
Frank More Colby (1865–1925) US editor.
Essays, II

7 If thy heart fails thee, climb not at all.
Elizabeth I (1533–1603) Queen of England.
Written on a window in reply to Walter RALEIGH's line
Worthies of England (Fuller), Vol. I

8 Hitch your wagon to a star.
Ralph Waldo Emerson (1803–82) US poet and essayist.
Society and Solitude, 'Civilization'

9 I would like to throw an egg into an electric fan.
Oliver Herford (1863–1935) British-born US humorist.
When asked if he really had no ambition beyond making people laugh
Attrib.

10 I am going to build the kind of nation that President Roosevelt hoped for, President Truman worked for and President Kennedy died for.
Lyndon B. Johnson (1908–73) US statesman.
The Sunday Times, 27 Dec 1964

11 A slave has but one master; an ambitious man has as many masters as there are people who may be useful in bettering his position.
Jean de La Bruyère (1645–96) French satirist.
Les Caractères

12 The shades of night were falling fast,
As through an Alpine village passed
A youth, who bore, 'mid snow and ice,
A banner with the strange device,
Excelsior!
Henry Wadsworth Longfellow (1807–82) US poet.
Opening of a poem best known as a Victorian drawing-room ballad, and the butt of many music-hall jokes. Excelsior means 'higher' (Latin)
Excelsior

13 If you would hit the mark, you must aim a little above it;
Every arrow that flies feels the attraction of earth.
Henry Wadsworth Longfellow
Elegiac Verse

14 Fain would I climb, yet fear I to fall.
Walter Raleigh (1554–1618) English explorer.
Written on a window pane. For the reply *see* ELIZABETH I
Attrib.

15 Ambition should be made of sterner stuff.
William Shakespeare (1564–1616) English dramatist.
Julius Caesar, III:2

16 I have no spur
To prick the sides of my intent, but only
Vaulting ambition, which o'er-leaps itself,
And falls on th' other.
William Shakespeare
Macbeth, I:7

17 And he that strives to touch the stars,

Oft stumbles at a straw.
Edmund Spenser (1552–99) English poet.
The Shepherd's Calendar, 'July'

18 There is always room at the top.
Daniel Webster (1782–1852) US statesman.
When advised not to become a lawyer because the profession
was overcrowded
Attrib.

19 Well, good luck to you, kid! I'm going to
write the Great Australian Novel.
Patrick White (1912–) British-born Australian novelist.
The Vivisector, 112

AMERICA

See also Americans

1 Our society distributes itself into Barbarians,
Philistines, and Populace; and America is just
ourselves, with the Barbarians quite left out,
and the Populace nearly.
Matthew Arnold (1822–88) British poet and critic.
Culture and Anarchy, Preface

2 God bless the USA, so large,
So friendly, and so rich.
W. H. Auden (1907–73) British poet.
On the Circuit

3 Yankee Doodle came to town
Riding on a pony;
Stuck a feather in his cap
And called it Macaroni.
Edward Bangs (fl. 1775) US songwriter.
Yankee Doodle; or Father's Return to Camp

4 O beautiful for spacious skies,
For amber waves of grain,
For purple mountain majesties
Above the fruited plain!
America! America!
God shed His grace on thee
And crown thy good with brotherhood
From sea to shining sea!
Katharine Lee Bates (1859–1929) US writer and poet.
America the Beautiful

5 I called the New World into existence to
redress the balance of the Old.
George Canning (1770–1827) British statesman.
Speech, 12 Dec 1826

6 This is virgin territory for whorehouses.
Al Capone (1899–1947) Italian-born US gangster.
Talking about suburban Chicago
The Bootleggers (Kenneth Allsop), Ch. 16

7 How beautiful it would be for someone who
could not read.
G. K. Chesterton (1874–1936) British writer.
Referring to the lights on Broadway
Attrib.

8 America is the only nation in history which
miraculously has gone directly from barbarism
to degeneration without the usual interval of
civilization.
Georges Clemenceau (1841–1929) French statesman.
Attrib.

9 Patriotism is easy to understand in America;
it means looking out for yourself while
looking out for your country.
Calvin Coolidge (1872–1933) US president.
Attrib.

10 The business of America is business.
Calvin Coolidge
Speech, Washington, 17 Jan 1925

11 Poor Mexico, so far from God and so near to
the United States!
Porfirio Díaz (1830–1915) Mexican general and
statesman.
Attrib.

12 Whatever America hopes to bring to pass in
this world must first come to pass in the
heart of America.
Dwight D. Eisenhower (1890–1969) US general and
statesman.
Inaugural address, 1953

13 America is a country of young men.
Ralph Waldo Emerson (1803–82) US poet and essayist.
Society and Solitude, 'Old Age'

14 Our country is the world – our countrymen
are all mankind.
William Lloyd Garrison (1805–79) US abolitionist.
The Liberator, 15 Dec 1837

15 New York . . . that unnatural city where
every one is an exile, none more so than the
American.
Charlotte Perkins Gilman (1860–1935) US writer.
The Living of Charlotte Perkins Gilman

16 The United States is like a gigantic boiler.
Once the fire is lighted under it there is no
limit to the power it can generate.
Lord Grey (1862–1933) British statesman.
Their Finest Hour (Winston S. Churchill), Ch. 32

17 The United States, I believe, are under the
impression that they are twenty years in
advance of this country; whilst, as a matter
of actual verifiable fact, of course, they are
just about six hours behind it.
Harold Hobson (1904–) British theatre critic and
writer.
The Devil in Woodford Wells, Ch. 8

18 The American system of rugged
individualism.
Herbert Clark Hoover (1874–1964) US statesman.
Speech, New York, 22 Oct 1928

19 The United States has to move ·very fast to
even stand still.
John Fitzgerald Kennedy (1917–63) US statesman.
The Observer, 'Sayings of the Week', 21 July 1963

20 'Tis the star-spangled banner; O long may it
wave

O'er the land of the free, and the home of the brave!

Francis Scott Key (1779–1843) US lawyer.
The Star-Spangled Banner

21 Give me your tired, your poor,
Your huddled masses yearning to breathe free,
The wretched refuse of your teeming shore,
Send these, the homeless, tempest-tossed to me,
I lift my lamp beside the golden door!

Emma Lazarus (1849–87) US poet and philanthropist.
Used as an inscription on the Statue of Liberty
The New Colossus

22 In other countries, art and literature are left to a lot of shabby bums living in attics and feeding on booze and spaghetti, but in America the successful writer or picture-painter is indistinguishable from any other decent business man.

Sinclair Lewis (1885–1951) US novelist.
Babbitt, Ch. 14

23 In an English ship, they say, it is poor grub, poor pay, and easy work; in an American ship, good grub, good pay, and hard work. And this is applicable to the working populations of both countries.

Jack London (1876–1916) US novelist.
The People of the Abyss, Ch. 20

24 First the sweetheart of the nation, then the aunt, woman governs America because America is a land of boys who refuse to grow up.

Salvador de Madariaga y Rogo (1886–1978) Spanish diplomat and writer.
The Perpetual Pessimist (Sagitarius and George)

25 If there is any country on earth where the course of true love may be expected to run smooth, it is America.

Harriet Martineau (1802–76) British writer.
Society in America, Vol. III, 'Marriage'

26 The immense popularity of American movies abroad demonstrates that Europe is the unfinished negative of which America is the proof.

Mary McCarthy (1912–89) US novelist.
On the Contrary

27 The national dish of America is menus.

Robert Robinson (1927–) British writer and broadcaster.
BBC TV programme, *Robinson's Travels*, Aug 1977

28 I pledge you, I pledge myself, to a new deal for the American people.

Franklin D. Roosevelt (1882–1945) US Democratic president.
Speech accepting nomination for presidency, Chicago, 2 July 1932

29 America . . . where law and customs alike are based on the dreams of spinsters.

Bertrand Russell (1872–1970) British philosopher.
Marriage and Morals

30 In the United States there is more space where nobody is than where anybody is. That is what makes America what it is.

Gertrude Stein (1874–1946) US writer.
The Geographical History of America

31 I like to walk around Manhattan, catching glimpses of its wild life, the pigeons and cats and girls.

Rex Todhunter Stout (1886–1975) US writer.
Three Witnesses, 'When a Man Murders'

32 I found there a country with thirty-two religions and only one sauce.

Talleyrand (Charles Maurice de Talleyrand-Périgord; 1754–1838) French politician.
Autant en apportent les mots (Pedrazzini)

33 America is a large, friendly dog in a very small room. Every time it wags its tail it knocks over a chair.

Arnold Toynbee (1889–1975) British historian.
Broadcast news summary, 14 July 1954

34 By the waters of Babylon we sit down and weep, when we think of thee, O America!

Horace Walpole (1717–97) British writer.
On the eve of the American Revolution
Letter to Mason, 12 June 1775

35 Up from the meadows rich with corn,
Clear in the cool September morn,

The clustered spires of Frederick stand
Green-walled by the hills of Maryland.

John Greenleaf Whittier (1807–92) US poet.
Barbara Frietchie

36 There exists in the world today a gigantic reservoir of good will toward us, the American people.

Wendell Lewis Willkie (1892–1944) US lawyer and businessman.
One World, Ch. 10

37 Sometimes people call me an idealist. Well, that is the way I know I am an American. America is the only idealistic nation in the world.

Woodrow Wilson (1856–1925) US statesman.
Speech, Sioux Falls, 8 Sept 1919

38 America . . . is the prize amateur nation of the world. Germany is the prize professional nation.

Woodrow Wilson
Speech, Aug 1917
Mr Wilson's War (John Dos Passos), Pt. III, Ch. 13

39 New York is a small place when it comes to the part of it that wakes up just as the rest is going to bed.

P. G. Wodehouse (1881–1975) British humorous novelist.
My Man Jeeves, 'The Aunt and the Sluggard'

40 America is God's Crucible, the great Melting-

Pot where all the races of Europe are melting and re-forming!
Israel Zangwill (1864–1926) British writer.
The Melting Pot, I

AMERICANS

1 Good Americans, when they die, go to Paris.
Thomas Gold Appleton (1812–84) US writer.
Autocrat of the Breakfast Table (O. W. Holmes), Ch. 6

2 A Boston man is the east wind made flesh.
Thomas Gold Appleton
Attrib.

3 There is nothing the matter with Americans except their ideals. The real American is all right; it is the ideal American who is all wrong.
G. K. Chesterton (1874–1936) British writer.
New York Times, 1 Feb 1931

4 Scratch an American and you get a Seventh Day Adventist every time.
Lord Hailsham (1907–) British Conservative politician.
The Observer, 'Sayings of the Week', 1 June 1969

5 I am willing to love all mankind, *except an American.*
Samuel Johnson (1709–84) British lexicographer.
Life of Johnson (J. Boswell), Vol. III

6 Does that mean that because Americans won't listen to sense, you intend to talk nonsense to them?
John Maynard Keynes (1883–1946) British economist.
Said before a monetary conference, 1944 or 1945

7 There won't be any revolution in America . . . The people are too clean. They spend all their time changing their shirts and washing themselves. You can't feel fierce and revolutionary in a bathroom.
Eric Linklater (1899–1974) Scottish novelist.
Juan in America, Pt. V, Ch. 3

8 No one can kill Americans and brag about it. No one.
Ronald Reagan (1911–) US politician and president.
The Observer, 'Sayings of the Week', 27 Apr 1986

9 An American is either a Jew, or an anti-Semite, unless he is both at the same time.
Jean-Paul Sartre (1905–80) French writer.
Altona

10 That strange blend of the commercial traveller, the missionary, and the barbarian conqueror, which was the American abroad.
Olaf Stapledon (1886–1950) British philosopher and science-fiction writer.
Last and First Men, Ch. 3

11 Americans have been conditioned to respect newness, whatever it costs them.
John Updike (1932–) US novelist.
A Month of Sundays, Ch. 18

12 American writers want to be not good but great; and so are neither.
Gore Vidal (1925–) US novelist.
Two Sisters

13 MRS ALLONBY. They say, Lady Hunstanton, that when good Americans die they go to Paris.
LADY HUNSTANTON. Indeed? And when bad Americans die, where do they go to?
LORD ILLINGWORTH. Oh, they go to America.
Oscar Wilde (1854–1900) Irish-born British dramatist.
See Thomas Gold APPLETON
A Woman of No Importance, I

14 Like so many substantial Americans, he had married young and kept on marrying, springing from blonde to blonde like the chamois of the Alps leaping from crag to crag.
P. G. Wodehouse (1881–1975) British humorous novelist.
Wodehouse at Work to the End (Richard Usborne), Ch. 2

ANALOGY

See also similarity

1 Though analogy is often misleading, it is the least misleading thing we have.
Samuel Butler (1835–1902) British writer.
Notebooks

2 She, and comparisons are odious.
John Donne (1573–1631) English poet.
Elegies, 8, 'The Comparison'

3 My mistress' eyes are nothing like the sun; Coral is far more red than her lips' red.
William Shakespeare (1564–1616) English dramatist.
Sonnet 130

4 And yet, by heaven, I think my love as rare As any she belied with false compare.
William Shakespeare
Sonnet 130

5 Jeeves coughed one soft, low, gentle cough like a sheep with a blade of grass stuck in its throat.
P. G. Wodehouse (1881–1975) British humorous novelist.
The Inimitable Jeeves, Ch. 13

ANCESTRY

See also aristocracy, family

1 I am my own ancestor.
Duc d'Abrantes (1771–1813) French general.
Said on being made a duke
Attrib.

2 I can trace my ancestry back to a protoplasmal primordial atomic globule. Consequently, my family pride is something in-conceivable. I can't help it. I was born sneering.
W. S. Gilbert (1836–1911) British dramatist.
The Mikado, I

3 The difference between us is that my family begins with me, whereas yours ends with you.

Iphicrates (d. 353 BC) Athenian general.
Reply to a descendant of Harmodius (an Athenian hero), who had derided Iphicrates for being the son of a cobbler
Attrib.

4 Being Southerners, it was a source of shame to some members of the family that we had no recorded ancestors on either side of the Battle of Hastings.

Harper Lee (1926–) US writer.
To Kill a Mockingbird, Pt. I, Ch. 1

5 I don't know who my grandfather was; I am much more concerned to know what his grandson will be.

Abraham Lincoln (1809–65) US statesman.
Taking part in a discussion on ancestry
Attrib.

ANGER

1 The man who gets angry at the right things and with the right people, and in the right way and at the right time and for the right length of time, is commended.

Aristotle (384–322 BC) Greek philosopher.
Nicomachean Ethics, Bk. IV

2 When they heard these things, they were cut to the heart, and they gnashed on him with their teeth.

Bible: Acts
7:54

3 Never go to bed mad. Stay up and fight.

Phyllis Diller (1917–) US writer and comedienne.
Phyllis Diller's Housekeeping Hints

4 Anger is one of the sinews of the soul.

Thomas Fuller (1608–61) English historian.
The Holy State and the Profane State

5 Spleen can subsist on any kind of food.

William Hazlitt (1778–1830) British essayist.
On Wit and Humour

6 Anger has overpowered him, and driven him to a revenge which was rather a stupid one, I must acknowledge, but anger makes us all stupid.

Johanna Spyri (1827–1901) Swiss writer.
Heidi, Ch. 23

7 Anger supplies the arms.

Virgil (Publius Vergilius Maro; 70–19 BC) Roman poet.
Aeneid, Bk. I

ANIMALISM

See also evolution, lust, mankind, sex

1 My brain: it's my second favourite organ.

Woody Allen (Allen Stewart Konigsberg; 1935–) US film actor.
Sleeper

2 But oh, the farmyard world of sex!

Harley Granville-Barker (1877–1946) British actor and dramatist.
The Madras House, IV

3 Be a good animal, true to your animal instincts.

D. H. Lawrence (1885–1930) British novelist.
The White Peacock, Pt. II, Ch. 2

4 It's all this cold-hearted fucking that is death and idiocy.

D. H. Lawrence
Lady Chatterley's Lover, Ch. 14

5 The soul started at the knee-cap and ended at the navel.

Wyndham Lewis (1882–1957) British novelist.
The Apes of God, Pt. XII

6 – 'Do you come here often?'
'Only in the mating season.'

Spike Milligan (1918–) British comic actor and author.
The Goon Show

7 The wren goes to't, and the small gilded fly
Does lecher in my sight.

William Shakespeare (1564–1616) English dramatist.
King Lear, IV:6

ANIMALS

See also cats, dogs, horses, rabbits

1 There was a young lady of Riga,
Who went for a ride on a tiger;
They returned from the ride
With the lady inside,
And a smile on the face of the tiger.

Anonymous

2 The fox knows many things – the hedgehog one *big* one.

Archilochus (c. 680–c. 640 BC) Greek poet.
Attrib.

3 And God said, Let the earth bring forth the living creature after his kind, cattle, and creeping thing, and beast of the earth after his kind: and it was so.

Bible: Genesis
1:24

4 Tiger! Tiger! burning bright
In the forests of the night,
What immortal hand or eye
Could frame thy fearful symmetry?

William Blake (1757–1827) British poet.
Songs of Experience, 'The Tiger'

5 Rats!
They fought the dogs and killed the cats,
And bit the babies in the cradles.

Robert Browning (1812–89) British poet.
The Pied Piper of Hamelin

6 And the muttering grew to a grumbling;
And the grumbling grew to a mighty rumbling;

And out of the houses the rats came tumbling.
Robert Browning
The Pied Piper of Hamelin

7 Wee, sleekit, cow'rin', tim'rous beastie,
O what a panic's in thy breastie!
Robert Burns (1759–96) Scottish poet.
To a Mouse

8 Whenever you observe an animal closely, you feel as if a human being sitting inside were making fun of you.
Elias Canetti (1905–) Bulgarian-born novelist.
The Human Province

9 The devil's walking parody
On all four-footed things.
G. K. Chesterton (1874–1936) British writer.
The Donkey

10 Animals are such agreeable friends – they ask no questions, they pass no criticisms.
George Eliot (Mary Ann Evans; 1819–80) British novelist.
Scenes of Clerical Life, 'Mr Gilfil's Love Story', Ch. 7

11 Mary had a little lamb,
Its fleece was white as snow,
And everywhere that Mary went
The lamb was sure to go.
Sarah Josepha Hale (1788–1879) US writer.
Poems for Our Children, 'Mary's Little Lamb'

12 'Twould ring the bells of Heaven
The wildest peal for years,
If Parson lost his senses
And people came to theirs,
And he and they together
Knelt down with angry prayers
For tamed and shabby tigers
And dancing dogs and bears,
And wretched, blind, pit ponies,
And little hunted hares.
Ralph Hodgson (1871–1962) British poet.
The Bells of Heaven

13 The stars grew bright in the winter sky,
The wind came keen with a tang of frost,
The brook was troubled for new things lost,
The copse was happy for old things found,
The fox came home and he went to ground.
John Masefield (1878–1967) British poet.
Reynard the Fox

14 I never nurs'd a dear gazelle,
To glad me with its soft black eye
But when it came to know me well,
And love me, it was sure to die!
Thomas Moore (1779–1852) Irish poet.
Lalla Rookh

15 Dogs, like horses, are quadrupeds. That is to say, they have four rupeds, one at each corner, on which they walk.
Frank Muir (1920–) British writer and broadcaster.
You Can't Have Your Kayak and Heat It (Frank Muir and Denis Norden), 'Ta-ra-ra-boom-de-ay!'

16 The cow is of the bovine ilk;

One end is moo, the other, milk.
Ogden Nash (1902–71) US poet.
The Cow

17 Nothing can be more obvious than that all animals were created solely and exclusively for the use of man.
Thomas Love Peacock (1785–1866) British novelist.
Headlong Hall, Ch. 2

18 *Exit, pursued by a bear.*
William Shakespeare (1564–1616) English dramatist.
Stage direction
The Winter's Tale, III:3

19 There are two things for which animals are to be envied: they know nothing of future evils, or of what people say about them.
Voltaire (François-Marie Arouet; 1694–1778) French writer.
Letter, 1739

20 Let dogs delight to bark and bite,
For God hath made them so;
Let bears and lions growl and fight,
For 'tis their nature too.
Isaac Watts (1674–1748) English theologian and hymn writer.
Divine Songs for Children, 'Against Quarrelling'

21 Feather-footed through the plashy fen passes the questing vole.
Evelyn Waugh (1903–66) British novelist.
Scoop, Bk. I, Ch. 1

22 I think I could turn and live with animals, they're so placid and self-contained,
I stand and look at them long and long.
Walt Whitman (1819–92) US poet.
Song of Myself, 32

ANTICIPATION

See also expectation

1 A stitch in time saves nine.
Proverb

2 Don't cross the bridge till you get to it.
Proverb

3 The early bird catches the worm.
Proverb

4 Don't count your chickens before they are hatched.
Aesop (6th century BC) Reputed Greek writer of fables.
Fables, 'The Milkmaid and her Pail'

5 To swallow gudgeons ere they're catched,
And count their chickens ere they're hatched.
Samuel Butler (1612–80) English satirist.
Hudibras, Pt. II

6 He told me never to sell the bear's skin before one has killed the beast.
Jean de La Fontaine (1621–95) French poet.
Fables, V, 'L'Ours et les deux Compagnons'

7 To travel hopefully is a better thing than to arrive, and the true success is to labour.
Robert Louis Stevenson (1850–94) Scottish writer.
Virginibus Puerisque

APOLOGIES

See also regret

1 Very sorry can't come. Lie follows by post.
Charles Beresford (1846–1919) British naval officer.
Reply, by telegram, to a dinner invitation at short notice from Edward, Prince of Wales
The World of Fashion 1837–1922 (R. Nevill), Ch. 5

2 Miss Otis regrets she's unable to lunch today.
Cole Porter (1893–1964) US songwriter.
Hi Diddle Diddle, Miss Otis Regrets

3 Love means never having to say you're sorry.
Erich Segal (1937–) US writer.
Love Story

4 Mr. Speaker, I said the honorable member was a liar it is true and I am sorry for it. The honourable member may place the punctuation where he pleases.
Richard Brinsley Sheridan (1751–1816) British dramatist.
On being asked to apologize for calling a fellow MP a liar
Attrib.

5 It is a good rule in life never to apologize. The right sort of people do not want apologies, and the wrong sort take a mean advantage of them.
P. G. Wodehouse (1881–1975) British humorous novelist.
The Man Upstairs and Other Stories

APPEARANCE

See also appearances, beauty, clothes, cosmetics, eyes

1 Fine feathers make fine birds.
Proverb

2 Handsome is as handsome does.
Proverb

3 A homely face and no figure have aided many women heavenward.
Minna Antrim (1861–?) US writer.
Naked Truth and Veiled Allusions

4 Take a close-up of a woman past sixty! You might as well use a picture of a relief map of Ireland!
Nancy Astor (1879–1964) American-born British politician.
When asked for a close-up photograph
Attrib.

5 But if a woman have long hair, it is a glory to her: for her hair is given her for a covering.
Bible: I Corinthians
11:15

6 Alas, after a certain age every man is responsible for his face.
Albert Camus (1913–60) French existentialist writer.
The Fall

7 Ears like bombs and teeth like splinters: A blitz of a boy is Timothy Winters.
Charles Causley (1917–) British poet and broadcaster.
Timothy Winters

8 It was a blonde. A blonde to make a bishop kick a hole in a stained-glass window.
Raymond Chandler (1888–1959) US novelist.
Farewell, My Lovely, Ch. 13

9 Sunburn is very becoming – but only when it is even – one must be careful not to look like a mixed grill.
Noël Coward (1899–1973) British dramatist.
The Lido Beach

10 The ring so worn, as you behold, So thin, so pale, is yet of gold.
George Crabbe (1754–1832) British poet.
His Mother's Wedding Ring

11 The most delightful advantage of being bald – one can hear snowflakes.
R. G. Daniels (1916–) British magistrate.
The Observer, 'Sayings of the Week', 11 July 1976

12 He had but one eye, and the popular prejudice runs in favour of two.
Charles Dickens (1812–70) British novelist.
Said by Mr Squeers
Nicholas Nickleby, Ch. 4

13 It was not a bosom to repose upon, but it was a capital bosom to hang jewels upon.
Charles Dickens
Describing Mrs Merdle
Little Dorrit, Bk. I, Ch. 21

14 I am so changed that my oldest creditors would hardly know me.
Henry Stephen Fox (1791–1846) British diplomat.
Remark after an illness
Letter from Byron to John Murray, 8 May 1817

15 There is a great difference between painting a face and not washing it.
Thomas Fuller (1608–61) English historian.
Church History, Bk. VII

16 The flowers that bloom in the spring,
Tra la,
Have nothing to do with the case.
I've got to take under my wing,
Tra la,
A most unattractive old thing,
Tra la,
With a caricature of a face.
W. S. Gilbert (1836–1911) British dramatist.
The Mikado, II

17 Where's the cheek that doth not fade, Too much gaz'd at? Where's the maid Whose lip mature is ever new?
John Keats (1795–1821) British poet.
Fancy, I

18 It always seemed to me that men wore their beards, like they wear their neckties, for show. I shall always remember Lewis for saying his beard was part of him.
D. H. Lawrence (1885–1930) British novelist.
St Mawr

19 There was an Old Man with a beard,
Who said, 'It is just as I feared! –
Two Owls and a Hen,
Four Larks and a Wren,
Have all built their nests in my beard!'
Edward Lear (1812–88) British artist and writer.
Book of Nonsense

20 A smile that snapped back after using, like a stretched rubber band.
Sinclair Lewis (1885–1951) US novelist.
Attrib.

21 The Lord prefers common-looking people. That is why he makes so many of them.
Abraham Lincoln (1809–65) US statesman.
Our President (James Morgan), Ch. 6

22 He looks as if he had been weaned on a pickle.
Alice Roosevelt Longworth (1884–1980) US hostess.
Referring to John Calvin Coolidge, US president 1923–29
Crowded Hours

23 Gentlemen always seem to remember blondes.
Anita Loos (1891–1981) US novelist.
Gentlemen Prefer Blondes, Ch. 1

24 In high school and college my sister Mary was very popular with the boys, but I had braces on my teeth and got high marks.
Betty MacDonald (1908–58) US writer.
The Egg and I, Ch. 2

25 There's a man outside with a big black moustache.
 – Tell him I've got one.
Groucho Marx (Julius Marx; 1895–1977) US comedian.
Horse Feathers

26 To Crystal, hair was the most important thing on earth. She would never get married because you couldn't wear curlers in bed.
Edna O'Brien (1936–) Irish novelist.
Winter's Tales, 8, 'Come into the Drawing Room, Doris'

27 Men seldom make passes
At girls who wear glasses.
Dorothy Parker (1893–1967) US writer.
Attrib.

28 All I say is, nobody has any business to go around looking like a horse and behaving as if it were all right. You don't catch horses going around looking like people, do you?
Dorothy Parker
Horsie

29 Had Cleopatra's nose been shorter, the whole face of the world would have changed.
Blaise Pascal (1623–62) French philosopher and mathematician.
Pensées, II

30 To church; and with my mourning, very handsome, and new periwig, make a great show.
Samuel Pepys (1633–1703) English diarist.
Diary, 31 Mar 1667

31 My nose is huge! Vile snub-nose, flat-nosed ass, flat-head, let me inform you that I am proud of such an appendage, since a big nose is the proper sign of a friendly, good, courteous, witty, liberal, and brave man, such as I am.
Edmond Rostand (1868–1918) French poet and dramatist.
Cyrano de Bergerac, I:1

32 In the spring . . . your lovely Chloë lightly turns to one mass of spots.
Ronald Searle (1920–) British cartoonist.
The Terror of St Trinian's, Ch. 7

33 LORD NORTHCLIFFE. The trouble with you, Shaw, is that you look as if there were famine in the land.
G.B.S. The trouble with you, Northcliffe, is that you look as if you were the cause of it.
George Bernard Shaw (1856–1950) Irish dramatist and critic.
Attrib.

34 Why not be oneself? That is the whole secret of a successful appearance. If one is a greyhound why try to look like a Pekinese?
Edith Sitwell (1887–1964) British poet and writer.
Why I Look As I Do

35 A short neck denotes a good mind . . . You see, the messages go quicker to the brain because they've shorter to go.
Muriel Spark (1918–) British novelist.
The Ballad of Peckham Rye, Ch. 7

36 But Shelley had a hyper-thyroid face.
John Collings Squire (1884–1958) British journalist.
Ballade of the Glandular Hypothesis

37 . . . his nicotine eggyellow weeping walrus Victorian moustache worn thick and long in memory of Doctor Crippen.
Dylan Thomas (1914–53) Welsh poet.
Under Milk Wood

38 Very hard for a man with a wig to keep order.
Evelyn Waugh (1903–66) British novelist.
Decline and Fall, Pt. I, Ch. 3

39 Enclosing every thin man, there's a fat man demanding elbow-room.
Evelyn Waugh
Officers and Gentlemen, Interlude

40 But there are other things than dissipation that thicken the features. Tears, for example.
Rebecca West (Cicely Isabel Fairfield; 1892–1983) British novelist and journalist.
Black Lamb and Grey Falcon, 'Serbia'

41 Grief has turned her fair.
Oscar Wilde (1854–1900) Irish-born British dramatist.
Referring to the fact that a recently-bereaved lady friend had dyed her hair blonde
Attrib.

42 Big chap with a small moustache and the sort of eye that can open an oyster at sixty paces.
P. G. Wodehouse (1881–1975) British humorous novelist.
The Code of the Woosters

43 The stationmaster's whiskers are of a Victorian bushiness and give the impression of having been grown under glass.
P. G. Wodehouse
Wodehouse at Work to the End (Richard Usborne), Ch. 2

APPEARANCES

See also appearance, deception, hypocrisy

1 All that glitters is not gold.
Proverb

2 Appearances are deceptive.
Proverb

3 Never judge from appearances.
Proverb

4 Still waters run deep.
Proverb

5 Things are not always what they seem.
Proverb

6 Vice is often clothed in virtue's habit.
Proverb

7 You can't tell a book by its cover.
Proverb

8 The lamb that belonged to the sheep whose skin the wolf was wearing began to follow the wolf in the sheep's clothing.
Aesop (6th century BC) Reputed Greek writer of fables.
Fables, 'The Wolf in Sheep's Clothing'

9 The French are wiser than they seem, and the Spaniards seem wiser than they are.
Francis Bacon (1561–1626) English philosopher.
Essays, 'Of Seeming Wise'

10 No-wher so bisy a man as he ther nas,
And yet he semed bisier than he was.
Geoffrey Chaucer (c. 1342–1400) English poet.
Referring to the man of law
The Canterbury Tales, Prologue

11 Keep up appearances; there lies the test
The world will give thee credit for the rest.
Charles Churchill (1731–64) British poet.
Night

12 I may not hope from outward forms to win
The passion and the life, whose fountains are within.
Samuel Taylor Coleridge (1772–1834) British poet.
Dejection: An Ode

13 Appearances are not held to be a clue to the truth. But we seem to have no other.
Ivy Compton-Burnett (1892–1969) British novelist.
Manservant and Maidservant

14 No man could be so wise as Thurlow looked.
Charles James Fox (1749–1806) British Whig politician.
Lives of the Lord Chancellors (Campbell), Vol. V

15 Ah, pray make no mistake,
We are not shy;
We're very wide awake,
The moon and I.
W. S. Gilbert (1836–1911) British dramatist.
The Mikado, II

16 An' for all 'is dirty 'ide
'E was white, clear white, inside
When 'e went to tend the wounded under fire!
Rudyard Kipling (1865–1936) Indian-born British writer.
Gunga Din

17 Strip the phoney tinsel off Hollywood and you'll find the real tinsel underneath.
Oscar Levant (1906–72) US pianist and actor.
Attrib.

18 And you cannot tell by the way a party looks or how he lives in this town, if he has any scratch, because many a party who is around in automobiles, and wearing good clothes, and chucking quite a swell is nothing but a phonus bolonus and does not have any real scratch whatever.
Damon Runyon (1884–1946) US writer.
More than Somewhat, 'The Snatching of Bookie Bob'

19 Things are entirely what they appear to be and *behind them* . . . there is nothing.
Jean-Paul Sartre (1905–80) French writer.
Nausea

20 Care I for the limb, the thews, the stature, bulk, and big assemblance of a man! Give me the spirit.
William Shakespeare (1564–1616) English dramatist.
Henry IV, Part Two, III:2

21 Through tatter'd clothes small vices do appear;
Robes and furr'd gowns hide all.
William Shakespeare
King Lear, IV:6

22 Our purses shall be proud, our garments poor;
For 'tis the mind that makes the body rich;
And as the sun breaks through the darkest clouds,
So honour peereth in the meanest habit.
William Shakespeare
The Taming of the Shrew, IV:3

23 It is only shallow people who do not judge by appearances.
Oscar Wilde (1854–1900) Irish-born British dramatist.
The Picture of Dorian Gray, Ch. 2

ARCHITECTURE

See also houses, stately homes

1 Sir Christopher Wren
Said, 'I am going to dine with some men.
If anybody calls
Say I am designing St Paul's.'
Edmund Clerihew Bentley (1875–1956) British writer.
Biography for Beginners

2 A very stately palace before him, the name of which was Beautiful.
John Bunyan (1628–88) English writer.
The Pilgrim's Progress, Pt. I

3 You have to give this much to the Luftwaffe – when it knocked down our buildings it did not replace them with anything more offensive than rubble. We did that.
Charles, Prince of Wales (1948–) Eldest son of Elizabeth II.
See also SITWELL
The Observer, 'Sayings of the Week', 6 Dec 1987

4 Like a carbuncle on the face of an old and valued friend.
Charles, Prince of Wales
Referring to a proposed modern extension to the National Gallery
Speech, 1986

5 'Fan vaulting' . . . an architectural device which arouses enormous enthusiasm on account of the difficulties it has all too obviously involved but which from an aesthetic standpoint frequently belongs to the 'Last-supper-carved-on-a-peach-stone' class of masterpiece.
Osbert Lancaster (1908–86) British cartoonist.
Pillar to Post, 'Perpendicular'

6 What has happened to architecture since the second world war that the only passers-by who can contemplate it without pain are those equipped with a white stick and a dog?
Bernard Levin (1928–) British journalist.
The Times, 1983

7 I declare this thing open – whatever it is.
Prince Philip (1921–) The consort of Queen Elizabeth II.
Opening a new annex at Vancouver City Hall
Attrib.

8 No person who is not a great sculptor or painter can be an architect. If he is not a sculptor or painter, he can only be a *builder*.
John Ruskin (1819–1900) British art critic and writer.
Lectures on Architecture and Painting

9 When we build let us think that we build for ever.
John Ruskin
The Seven Lamps of Architecture, Ch. 6, 'The Lamp of Memory'

10 Architecture in general is frozen music.
Friedrich Wilhelm Joseph von Schelling (1775–1854) German philosopher.
Philosophie der Kunst

11 Many of my buildings are condemned now in advance.
Richard Seifert (1910–) British architect.
He designed Centre Point, London and other office block schemes
The Observer, 'Sayings of the Week', 6 Aug 1972

12 How simple-minded of the Germans to imagine that we British could be cowed by the destruction of our ancient monuments! As though any havoc of the German bombs could possibly equal the things we have done ourselves!
Osbert Sitwell (1892–1969) British writer.
See also CHARLES, PRINCE OF WALES
The Collected Essays, Journalism and Letters of George Orwell, Vol. III

13 It's beige! My color!
Elsie De Wolfe (1865–1950) US designer.
On first sighting the Acropolis
Elsie de Wolfe (J. Smith)

14 In *Architecture* as in all other *Operative* Arts, the *end* must direct the *Operation*. The *end* is to build well. Well building hath three Conditions. *Commodity, Firmness*, and *Delight*.
Henry Wotton (1568–1639) English poet and diplomat.
Elements of Architecture, Pt. I

ARGUMENTS

1 It takes two to make a quarrel.
Proverb

2 Least said soonest mended.
Proverb

3 For every why he had a wherefore.
Samuel Butler (1612–80) English satirist.
Hudibras, Pt. I

4 There is only one way under high heaven to get the best of an argument – and that is to avoid it.
Dale Carnegie (1888–1955) US lecturer and writer.
Dale Carnegie's Scrapbook

5 Many a long dispute among divines may be thus abridged: It is so. It is not so. It is so. It is not so.
Benjamin Franklin (1706–90) US scientist and statesman.
Poor Richard's Almanack

6 In every age and clime we see,
Two of a trade can ne'er agree.
John Gay (1685–1732) English poet and dramatist.
Fables

7 Scholars dispute, and the case is still before the courts.
Horace (Quintus Horatius Flaccus; 65–8 BC) Roman poet.
Ars Poetica c. 8 BC

8 'It's like the question of the authorship of the *Iliad*,' said Mr Cardan. 'The author of that poem is either Homer or, if not Homer, somebody else of the same name.'
Aldous Huxley (1894–1964) British novelist.
Those Barren Leaves, Pt. V, Ch. 4

9 It takes in reality only one to make a quarrel. It is useless for the sheep to pass resolutions in favour of vegetarianism while the wolf remains of a different opinion.
Dean Inge (1860–1954) British churchman.
Outspoken Essays

10 Sir, I have found you an argument; but I am not obliged to find you an understanding.
Samuel Johnson (1709–84) British lexicographer.
Life of Johnson (J. Boswell), Vol. IV

11 Though a quarrel in the streets is a thing to be hated, the energies displayed in it are fine; the commonest man shows a grace in his quarrel.
John Keats (1795–1821) British poet.
Letter

12 When men understand what each other mean, they see, for the most part, that controversy is either superfluous or hopeless.
Cardinal Newman (1801–90) British theologian.
Sermon, Oxford, Epiphany 1839

13 Quarrels would not last so long if the fault were on only one side.
Duc de la Rochefoucauld (1613–80) French writer.
Maximes, 496

14 The most savage controversies are those about matters as to which there is no good evidence either way.
Bertrand Russell (1872–1970) British philosopher.
Unpopular Essays

15 I love argument, I love debate. I don't expect anyone just to sit there and agree with me, that's not their job.
Margaret Thatcher (1925–) British politician and prime minister.
The Times, 1980

16 I did not know that we had ever quarrelled.
Henry David Thoreau (1817–62) US writer.
On being urged to make his peace with God
Attrib.

17 I am, sir for the last time in my life, Your Humble Servant Horace Walpole.
Horace Walpole (1717–97) British writer.
Ending a letter written to an uncle with whom he had recently quarrelled
Horace Walpole (R. Ketton-Cremes)

18 I am not arguing with you – I am telling you.
James Whistler (1834–1903) US painter.
The Gentle Art of Making Enemies

19 No question is ever settled
Until it is settled right.
Ella Wheeler Wilcox (1850–1919) US poet.
Settle the Question Right

ARISTOCRACY

See also ancestry, class, Houses of Parliament, nobility, stately homes, titles

1 One has often wondered whether upon the whole earth there is anything so unintelligent, so unapt to perceive how the world is really going, as an ordinary young Englishman of our upper class.
Matthew Arnold (1822–88) British poet and critic.
Culture and Anarchy, Ch. 2

2 Like many of the upper class
He liked the sound of broken glass.
Hilaire Belloc (1870–1953) French-born British poet.
See also Evelyn WAUGH
New Cautionary Tales, 'About John'

3 The nobility of England, my lord, would have snored through the Sermon on the Mount.
Robert Bolt (1924–) British playwright.
A Man for All Seasons

4 We, my lords, may thank heaven that we have something better than our brains to depend upon.
Earl of Chesterfield (1694–1773) English statesman.
Speech, House of Lords
The Story of Civilization (W. Durant), Vol. 9

5 Democracy means government by the uneducated, while aristocracy means government by the badly educated.
G. K. Chesterton (1874–1936) British writer.
New York Times, 1 Feb 1931

6 The Stately Homes of England
How beautiful they stand,
To prove the upper classes
Have still the upper hand.
Noël Coward (1899–1973) British dramatist.
Operette, 'The Stately Homes of England'

7 If human beings could be propagated by cutting, like apple trees, aristocracy would be biologically sound.
J. B. S. Haldane (1892–1964) British geneticist.
The Inequality of Man, title essay

8 There are no credentials They do not even need a medical certificate. They need not be sound either in body or mind. They only require a certificate of birth – just to prove that they are first of the litter. You would not choose a spaniel on these principles.
David Lloyd George (1863–1945) British Liberal statesman.
Budget Speech, 1909

9 A fully equipped Duke costs as much to keep up as two Dreadnoughts, and Dukes are just as great a terror, and they last longer.
David Lloyd George
Speech, Limehouse, 30 July 1909

10 An aristocracy in a republic is like a chicken whose head has been cut off: it may run about in a lively way, but in fact it is dead.
Nancy Mitford (1904–73) British writer.
Noblesse Oblige

11 He is without strict doubt a Hoorah Henry, and he is generally figured as nothing but a lob as far as doing anything useful in this world is concerned.
Damon Runyon (1884–1946) US writer.
Short Takes, 'Tight Shoes'

12 Kind hearts are more than coronets,
And simple faith than Norman blood.
Alfred, Lord Tennyson (1809–92) British poet.
Lady Clara Vere de Vere, VI

13 If the French noblesse had been capable of playing cricket with their peasants, their chateaux would never have been burnt.
George Macaulay Trevelyan (1876–1962) British historian.
English Social History, Ch. XIII

14 My Lord Bath, you and I are now two as insignificant men as any in England.
Robert Walpole (1676–1745) British statesman.
Said to William Pulteney, Earl of Bath, when they were promoted to the peerage (1742)
Political & Literary Anecdotes (W. King)

15 The sound of the English county families baying for broken glass.
Evelyn Waugh (1903–66) British novelist.
See also Hilaire BELLOC
Decline and Fall, Prelude

16 Unlike the male codfish which, suddenly finding itself the parent of three million five hundred thousand little codfish, cheerfully resolves to love them all, the British aristocracy is apt to look with a somewhat jaundiced eye on its younger sons.
P. G. Wodehouse (1881–1975) British humorous novelist.
Wodehouse at Work to the End (Richard Usborne), Ch. 5

ARMY

See also officers, soldiers, war, weapons

1 Oh! the grand old Duke of York
He had ten thousand men;
He marched them up to the top of the hill,
And he marched them down again.
And when they were up they were up,
And when they were down they were down,
And when they were only half way up,
They were neither up nor down.
Anonymous
Traditional

2 Conduct . . . to the prejudice of good order and military discipline.
Anonymous
Army Act, 40

3 The chief attraction of military service has consisted and will consist in this compulsory and irreproachable idleness.
Leo Tolstoy (1828–1910) Russian writer.
War and Peace, Bk. VII, Ch. 1

4 An army is a nation within a nation; it is one of the vices of our age.
Alfred de Vigny (1797–1863) French writer.
Servitude et grandeur militaire, 1

5 Ours is composed of the scum of the earth.
Duke of Wellington (1769–1852) British general and statesman.
Of the British army
Remark, 4 Nov 1831

6 The army ages men sooner than the law and philosophy; it exposes them more freely to germs, which undermine and destroy, and it shelters them more completely from thought, which stimulates and preserves.
H. G. Wells (1866–1946) British writer.
Bealby, Pt. VIII, Ch. 1

ARROGANCE

See also conceit, egotism, pride

1 The need to be right – the sign of a vulgar mind.
Albert Camus (1913–60) French existentialist writer.
Notebooks, 1935–42

2 I am sure no man in England will take away my life to make you King.
Charles II (1630–85) King of England.
To his brother James following revelation of Popish Plot fabricated by Titus Oates
Attrib.

3 He was like a cock who thought the sun had risen to hear him crow.
George Eliot (Mary Ann Evans; 1819–80) British novelist.
Adam Bede

4 If this young man expresses himself in terms too deep for *me*,
Why, what a very singularly deep young man this deep young man must be!
W. S. Gilbert (1836–1911) British dramatist.
Patience, I

5 There, but for the Grace of God, goes God.
Herman J. Mankiewicz (1897–1953) US journalist and screenwriter.
Said of Orson Welles in the making of *Citizen Kane*. Also attributed to others
The Citizen Kane Book

6 The bullet that is to kill me has not yet been moulded.

Napoleon I (Napoleon Bonaparte; 1769–1821) French emperor.
In reply to his brother Joseph, King of Spain, who had asked whether he had ever been hit by a cannonball
Attrib.

7 What His Royal Highness most particularly prides himself upon, is the excellent harvest.

Richard Brinsley Sheridan (1751–1816) British dramatist.
Lampooning George IV's habit of taking credit for everything good in England
The Fine Art of Political Wit (L. Harris)

8 A LADY. This landscape reminds me of your work.

WHISTLER. Yes madam, Nature is creeping up.
James Whistler (1834–1903) US painter.
Whistler Stories (D. Seitz)

9 Well, not bad, but there are decidedly too many of them, and they are not very well arranged. I would have done it differently.

James Whistler
His reply when asked if he agreed that the stars were especially beautiful one night
Attrib.

10 The Admiral of the Atlantic salutes the Admiral of the Pacific.

Wilhelm II (1859–1941) King of Prussia and Emperor of Germany.
Telegram sent to Czar Nicholas II during a naval exercise
The Shadow of the Winter Palace (E. Crankshaw)

11 All men think all men mortal, but themselves.

Edward Young (1683–1765) British poet.
Night Thoughts

ART

See also artists, arts, design, painting

1 The works of art, by being publicly exhibited and offered for sale, are becoming articles of trade, following as such the unreasoning laws of markets and fashion; and public and even private patronage is swayed by their tyrannical influence.

Prince Albert (1819–61) The consort of Queen Victoria.
Referring to the Great Exhibition
Speech, Royal Academy Dinner, 3 May 1851

2 The object of art is to give life a shape.

Jean Anouilh (1910–87) French dramatist.
The Rehearsal

3 The lower one's vitality, the more sensitive one is to great art.

Max Beerbohm (1872–1956) British writer.
Seven Men, 'Enoch Soames'

4 It would follow that 'significant form' was form behind which we catch a sense of ultimate reality.

Clive Bell (1881–1964) British art critic.
Art, Pt. I, Ch. 3

5 Art is the only thing that can go on mattering once it has stopped hurting.

Elizabeth Bowen (1899–1973) Irish novelist.
The Heat of the Day, Ch. 16

6 Art for art's sake.

Victor Cousin (1792–1867) French philosopher.
Lecture, Sorbonne, 1818

7 Art is a jealous mistress.

Ralph Waldo Emerson (1803–82) US poet and essayist.
Conduct of Life, 'Wealth'

8 Works of art, in my opinion, are the only objects in the material universe to possess internal order, and that is why, though I don't believe that only art matters, I do believe in Art for Art's sake.

E. M. Forster (1879–1970) British novelist.
Art for Art's Sake

9 . . . I rarely draw what I see. I draw what I feel in my body.

Barbara Hepworth (1903–75) British sculptor.
World of Art Series (A. M. Hammersmith)

10 Art has to move you and design does not, unless it's a good design for a bus.

David Hockney (1937–   ) British painter, draughtsman and printmaker.
Remark, Oct 1988

11 In free society art is not a weapon . . . Artists are not engineers of the soul.

John Fitzgerald Kennedy (1917–63) US statesman.
Address at Dedication of the Robert Frost Library, 26 Oct 1963

12 But the Devil whoops, as he whooped of old: 'It's clever, but is it art?'

Rudyard Kipling (1865–1936) Indian-born British writer.
The Conundrum of the Workshops

13 Art is not a special sauce applied to ordinary cooking; it is the cooking itself if it is good.

W. R. Lethaby (1857–1931) British architect.
Form in Civilization, 'Art and Workmanship'

14 I do not know whether he draws a line himself. But I assume that his is the direction . . . It makes Disney the most significant figure in graphic art since Leonardo.

David Low (1871–1963) New-Zealand-born newspaper cartoonist.
Walt Disney (R. Schickel), Ch. 20

15 In England, pop art and fine art stand resolutely back to back.

Colin MacInnes (1914–76) British novelist.
England, Half English, 'Pop Songs and Teenagers'

16 Art is not a mirror to reflect the world, but a hammer with which to shape it.

Vladimir Mayakovsky (1893–1930) Soviet poet.
The Guardian, 11 Dec 1974

17 Nothing unites the English like war. Nothing divides them like Picasso.

Hugh Mills (1913–71) British screenwriter.
Prudence and the Pill

18 To be aristocratic in Art one must avoid polite society.
George Moore (1852–1933) Irish writer and art critic.
Enemies of Promise (Cyril Connolly), Ch. 15

19 All art deals with the absurd and aims at the simple. Good art speaks truth, indeed *is* truth, perhaps the only truth.
Iris Murdoch (1919–) Irish-born British novelist.
The Black Prince, 'Bradley Pearson's Foreword'

20 All art constantly aspires towards the condition of music.
Walter Pater (1839–94) British critic.
The Renaissance, 'The School of Giorgione'

21 When I was their age, I could draw like Raphael, but it took me a lifetime to learn to draw like them.
Pablo Picasso (1881–1973) Spanish painter.
Visiting an exhibition of drawings by children
Picasso: His Life and Work (Ronald Penrose)

22 Burnings of people and (what was more valuable) works of art.
A. L. Rowse (1903–) British historian and critic.
Historical Essays (H. R. Trevor-Roper)

23 Life without industry is guilt, and industry without art is brutality.
John Ruskin (1819–1900) British art critic and writer.
Lectures on Art, 3, 'The Relation of Art to Morals', 23 Feb 1870

24 Fine art is that in which the hand, the head, and the heart of man go together.
John Ruskin
The Two Paths, Lecture II

25 The trouble, Mr Goldwyn is that you are only interested in art and I am only interested in money.
George Bernard Shaw (1856–1950) Irish dramatist and critic.
Turning down Goldwyn's offer to buy the screen rights of his plays
The Movie Moguls (Philip French), Ch. 4

26 Skill without imagination is craftsmanship and gives us many useful objects such as wickerwork picnic baskets. Imagination without skill gives us modern art.
Tom Stoppard (1937–) Czech-born British dramatist.
Artist Descending a Staircase

27 Art is not a handicraft, it is the transmission of feeling the artist has experienced.
Leo Tolstoy (1828–1910) Russian writer.
What is Art?, Ch. 19

28 What a delightful thing this perspective is!
Paolo Uccello (1397–1475) Italian painter.
Men of Art (T. Craven)

29 . . . any authentic work of art must start an argument between the artist and his audience.
Rebecca West (Cicely Isabel Fairfield; 1892–1983) British novelist and journalist.
The Court and the Castle, Pt. I, Ch. 1

30 Art is the imposing of a pattern on experience, and our aesthetic enjoyment is recognition of the pattern.
A. N. Whitehead (1861–1947) British philosopher.
Dialogues, 228

31 Art never expresses anything but itself.
Oscar Wilde (1854–1900) Irish-born British dramatist.
The Decay of Lying

32 All Art is quite useless.
Oscar Wilde
The Picture of Dorian Gray, Preface

33 Art is the most intense mode of individualism that the world has known.
Oscar Wilde
The Soul of Man Under Socialism

ARTHURIAN LEGEND

1 What were they going to do with the Grail when they found it, Mr Rossetti?
Max Beerbohm (1872–1956) British writer.
Caption to a cartoon

2 On either side the river lie
Long fields of barley and of rye,
That clothe the wold and meet the sky;
And thro' the field the road runs by
To many-tower'd Camelot.
Alfred, Lord Tennyson (1809–92) British poet.
The Lady of Shalott, Pt. I

3 An arm
Rose up from out the bosom of the lake,
Clothed in white samite, mystic, wonderful.
Alfred, Lord Tennyson
Idylls of the King, 'The Passing of Arthur'

ARTISTS

General quotes

See also art, painting

1 Poets and painters are outside the class system, or rather they constitute a special class of their own, like the circus people and the gipsies.
Gerald Brenan (Edward Fitzgerald Brenan; 1894–1987) British writer.
Thoughts in a Dry Season, 'Writing'

2 Remember I'm an artist. And you know what that means in a court of law. Next worst to an actress.
Joyce Cary (1888–1957) British novelist.
The Horse's Mouth, Ch. 14

3 Beware of the artist who's an intellectual also. The artist who doesn't fit.
F. Scott Fitzgerald (1896–1940) US novelist.
This Side of Paradise, Bk. II, Ch. 5

4 I don't advise any one to take it up as a business proposition, unless they really have talent, and are crippled so as to deprive them of physical labor.

Grandma Moses (Anna Mary Robertson Moses; 1860–1961) US primitive painter.
Referring to painting
The New York Times, 'How Do I Paint?', 11 May 1947

5 An amateur is an artist who supports himself with outside jobs which enable him to paint. A professional is someone whose wife works to enable him to paint.

Ben Shahn (1898–1969) US artist.
Attrib.

6 What is an artist? For every thousand people there's nine hundred doing the work, ninety doing well, nine doing good, and one lucky bastard who's the artist.

Tom Stoppard (1937–) Czech-born British dramatist.
Travesties, I

7 A painter should not paint what he sees, but what will be seen.

Paul Valéry (1871–1945) French poet and writer.
Mauvaises Pensées et Autres

8 An artist is someone who produces things that people don't need to have but that he – for *some* reason – thinks it would be a good idea to give them.

Andy Warhol (Andrew Warhola; 1926–87) US pop artist.
From A to B and Back Again, 'Atmosphere'

9 A living is made, Mr Kemper, by selling something that everybody needs at least once a year. Yes, sir! And a million is made by producing something that everybody needs every day. You artists produce something that nobody needs at any time.

Thornton Wilder (1897–1975) US novelist and dramatist.
The Matchmaker, II

Specific quotes

10 It is comparatively easy to achieve a certain unity in a picture by allowing one colour to dominate, or by muting all the colours. Matisse did neither. He clashed his colours together like cymbals and the effect was like a lullaby.

John Berger (1926–) British author and art critic.
Toward Reality

11 When Sir Joshua Reynolds died
All Nature was degraded;
The King dropped a tear in the Queen's ear,
And all his pictures faded.

William Blake (1757–1827) British poet.
On Art and Artists

12 One of the reasons why medieval and renaissance architecture is so much better than our own is that the architects were artists. Bernini, one of the great artists of seventeenth-century Rome, was a sculptor.

Kenneth Clark (1903–83) British art historian.
Civilisation

13 I do not paint a portrait to look like the subject, rather does the person grow to look like his portrait.

Salvador Dali (1904–89) Spanish painter.
Diary of a Genius

14 The Epstein makes me feel physically sick. The wretched woman has two sets of breasts and a hip joint like a merry thought.

John Galsworthy (1867–1933) British novelist.
Letter to Edward Garnett, 14 June 1925

15 His subjects are softened and sentimentalised too much. It is not simple unaffected nature that we see, but nature sitting for her picture.

William Hazlitt (1778–1830) British essayist.
Referring to Thomas Gainsborough's pictures

16 If people dug up the remains of this civilization a thousand years hence, and found Epstein's statues and that man Ellis, they would think we were just savages.

Doris Lessing (1919–) British novelist.
Martha Quest, Pt. I, Ch. 1

17 I paint objects as I think them, not as I see them.

Pablo Picasso (1881–1973) Spanish painter.
Cubism (John Golding)

18 I should desire that the last words which I should pronounce in this Academy, and from this place, might be the name of – Michael Angelo.

Joshua Reynolds (1723–92) British portrait painter.
Discourse to Students of the Royal Academy, 10 Dec 1790

19 See what will happen to you if you don't stop biting your fingernails.

Will Rogers (1879–1935) US actor and humorist.
Message written on a postcard of the Venus de Milo that he sent to his young niece

20 Nobody cares much at heart about Titian, only there is a strange undercurrent of everlasting murmur about his name, which means the deep consent of all great men that he is greater than they.

John Ruskin (1819–1900) British art critic and writer.
The Two Paths, Lecture II

21 If Botticelli were alive today he'd be working for *Vogue*.

Peter Ustinov (1921–) British actor.
The Observer, 'Sayings of the Week', 21 Oct 1962

22 No I ask it for the knowledge of a lifetime.

James Whistler (1834–1903) US painter.
Replying to the taunt, during the Ruskin trial, that he was asking a fee of 200 guineas for two days' painting
Lives of the Wits (H. Pearson)

ARTS

1 Every man's work, whether it be literature or music or pictures or architecture or anything else, is always a portrait of himself.

Samuel Butler (1835–1902) British writer.
The Way of All Flesh, Ch. 14

2 The artistic temperament is a disease that afflicts amateurs.
G. K. Chesterton (1874–1936) British writer.
Heretics, Ch. 17

3 No poet, no artist of any sort, has his complete meaning alone. His significance, his appreciation is the appreciation of his relation to the dead poets and artists.
T. S. Eliot (1888–1965) US-born British poet and dramatist.
Tradition and the Individual Talent

4 Yes, the work comes out more beautiful from a material that resists the process, verse, marble, onyx, or enamel.
Théophile Gautier (1811–72) French poet and critic.
L'Art

5 The excellence of every art is its intensity, capable of making all disagreeables evaporate, from their being in close relationship with beauty and truth.
John Keats (1795–1821) British poet.
Letter to G. and T. Keats, 21 Dec 1817

6 The whole of art is an appeal to a reality which is not without us but in our minds.
Desmond MacCarthy (1877–1952) British writer and theatre critic.
Theatre, 'Modern Drama'

7 Music begins to atrophy when it departs too far from the dance . . . poetry begins to atrophy when it gets too far from music.
Ezra Pound (1885–1972) US poet.
ABC of Reading, 'Warning'

8 The secret of the arts is to correct nature.
Voltaire (François-Marie Arouet; 1694–1778) French writer.
Épîtres, 'À M. de Verrière'

ASSASSINATION

See also killing, murder

1 Assassination has never changed the history of the world.
Benjamin Disraeli (1804–81) British statesman.
Speech, House of Commons, 1 May 1865

2 My fellow citizens, the President is dead, but the Government lives and God Omnipotent reigns.
James A. Garfield (1831–81) US statesman.
Speech following the assassination of Lincoln

3 They really are bad shots.
Charles De Gaulle (1890–1970) French general and statesman.
Remark after narrowly escaping death in an assassination attempt
Ten First Ladies of the World (Pauline Frederick)

4 Will no one rid me of this turbulent priest?
Henry II (1133–89) King of England.
Referring to Thomas Becket, Archbishop of Canterbury; four of Henry's household knights took these words literally, hur-

ried to Canterbury, and killed Becket in the cathedral (Dec 1170)
Attrib.

5 Assassination is the extreme form of censorship.
George Bernard Shaw (1856–1950) Irish dramatist and critic.
The Shewing-Up of Blanco Posnet, 'The Limits of Toleration'

ASTRONOMY

See also moon, space, stars, sun, universe

1 There is one glory of the sun, and another glory of the moon, and another glory of the stars: for one star differeth from another star in glory.
Bible: I Corinthians
15:41–42

2 . . . in my studies of astronomy and philosophy I hold this opinion about the universe, that the Sun remains fixed in the centre of the circle of heavenly bodies, without changing its place; and the Earth, turning upon itself, moves round the Sun.
Galileo Galilei (1564–1642) Italian scientist.
Letter to Cristina di Lorena, 1615

3 *Eppur si muove.*
Yet it moves.
Galileo Galilei
Referring to the Earth. Remark supposedly made after his recantation (1632) of belief in the Copernican system
Attrib.

4 Astronomy teaches the correct use of the sun and the planets.
Stephen Leacock (1869–1944) English-born Canadian economist and humorist.
Literary Lapses, 'A Manual of Education'

ATHEISM

See also God, religion

1 An atheist is one point beyond the devil.
Proverb

2 God never wrought miracle to convince atheism, because his ordinary works convince it.
Francis Bacon (1561–1626) English philosopher.
Essays, 'Of Atheism'

3 For none deny there is a God, but those for whom it maketh that there were no God.
Francis Bacon
Essays, 'Of Atheism'

4 I am an atheist still, thank God.
Luis Buñuel (1900–83) Spanish film director.
Luis Buñuel: an Introduction (Ado Kyrou)

5 An atheist is a man who has no invisible means of support.
Harry Emerson Fosdick (1878–1969) US baptist minister.
Attrib.

6 Perhaps if I wanted to be understood or to understand I would bamboozle myself into belief, but I am a reporter; God exists only for leader-writers.
Graham Greene (1904–) British novelist.
The Quiet American

7 If you don't find a God by five o'clock this afternoon you must leave the college.
Benjamin Jowett (1817–93) British theologian.
Responding to a conceited young student's assertion that he could find no evidence for a God
Attrib.

8 He was an embittered atheist (the sort of atheist who does not so much disbelieve in God as personally dislike Him).
George Orwell (Eric Blair; 1903–50) British novelist.
Down and Out in Paris and London, Ch. 30

9 It has been said that the highest praise of God consists in the denial of Him by the atheist, who finds creation so perfect that he can dispense with a creator.
Marcel Proust (1871–1922) French novelist.
À la recherche du temps perdu: Le Côté de Guermantes

AUDIENCES

1 Long experience has taught me that in England nobody goes to the theatre unless he or she has bronchitis.
James Agate (1877–1947) British theatre critic.
See also Artur SCHNABEL
Ego, 6

2 Ladies and gentlemen, unless the play is stopped, the child cannot possibly go on.
John Philip Kemble (1757–1823) British tragic actor.
Announcement to the audience when the play he was in was continually interrupted by a child crying
A Book of Anecdotes (D. George)

3 Those people on the stage are making such a noise I can't hear a word you're saying.
Henry Taylor Parker (1867–1934) US music critic.
Rebuking some talkative members of an audience, near whom he was sitting
The Humor of Music (L. Humphrey)

4 A nice respectable, middle-class, middle-aged maiden lady, with time on her hands and the money to help her pass it . . . Let us call her Aunt Edna . . . Aunt Edna is universal, and to those who feel that all the problems of the modern theatre might be saved by her liquidation, let me add that . . . She is also immortal.
Terence Rattigan (1911–77) British dramatist.
Collected Plays, Vol II, Preface

5 I know two kinds of audience only – one coughing and one not coughing.
Artur Schnabel (1882–1951) Austrian concert pianist.
See also James AGATE
My Life and Music, Pt. II, Ch. 10

6 I quite agree with you, sir, but what can two do against so many?
George Bernard Shaw (1856–1950) Irish dramatist and critic.
Responding to a solitary hiss heard amongst the applause at the first performance of *Arms and the Man* in 1894
Oxford Book of Literary Anecdotes

AUTHORITARIANISM

See also tyranny

1 *Roma locuta est; causa finita est.*
Rome has spoken; the case is concluded.
St Augustine of Hippo (354–430) Bishop of Hippo.
Sermons, Bk. I

2 Then cometh the end, when he shall have delivered up the kingdom to God, even the Father; when he shall have put down all rule and all authority and power.
For he must reign, till he hath put all enemies under his feet.
The last enemy that shall be destroyed is death.
Bible: I Corinthians
15:24–26

3 Dictators ride to and fro upon tigers which they dare not dismount. And the tigers are getting hungry.
Winston Churchill (1874–1965) British statesman.
While England Slept

4 I will have this done, so I order it done; let my will replace reasoned judgement.
Juvenal (Decimus Junius Juvenalis; 60–130 AD) Roman satirist.
Satires, VI

5 Big Brother is watching you.
George Orwell (Eric Blair; 1903–50) British novelist.
Nineteen Eighty-Four

6 I am painted as the greatest little dictator, which is ridiculous – you always take some consultations.
Margaret Thatcher (1925–) British politician and prime minister.
The Times, 1983

7 I don't mind how much my ministers talk – as long as they do what I say.
Margaret Thatcher
The Times, 1987

8 As for being a General, well, at the age of four with paper hats and wooden swords we're all Generals. Only some of us never grow out of it.
Peter Ustinov (1921–) British actor.
Romanoff and Juliet, I

AUTUMN

See months, seasons

B

BABIES

See also birth, children

1 There is no more sombre enemy of good art than the pram in the hall.
Cyril Connolly (1903–74) British journalist.
Enemies of Promise, Ch. 3

2 Every baby born into the world is a finer one than the last.
Charles Dickens (1812–70) British novelist.
Nicholas Nickleby, Ch. 36

3 These wretched babies don't come until they are ready.
Queen Elizabeth II (1926–   ) Queen of the United Kingdom.
Remark, Aug 1988

4 Other people's babies –
That's my life!
Mother to dozens,
And nobody's wife.
A. P. Herbert (1890–1971) British writer and politician.
A Book of Ballads, 'Other People's Babies'

5 A loud noise at one end and no sense of responsibility at the other.
Ronald Knox (1888–1957) British Roman Catholic priest.
Attrib.

6 Sweetes' li'l' feller,
Everybody knows;
Dunno what to call 'im,
But he's mighty lak' a rose!
Frank L. Stanton (1857–1927) US journalist and poet.
Sweetes' Li'l' Feller

BEAUTY

See also admiration, appearance, compliments

1 A good face is a letter of recommendation.
Proverb

2 Beauty is only skin-deep.
Proverb

3 Beauty is potent but money is omnipotent.
Proverb

4 Small is beautiful.
Proverb

5 My Love in her attire doth show her wit,
It doth so well become her:
For every season she hath dressings fit,
For winter, spring, and summer.
No beauty she doth miss,
When all her robes are on;
But beauty's self she is,
When all her robes are gone.
Anonymous
Madrigal

6 You know, you can only perceive real beauty in a person as they get older.
Anouk Aimee (1932–   ) French actress.
Remark, Aug 1988

7 There is no excellent beauty that hath not some strangeness in the proportion.
Francis Bacon (1561–1626) English philosopher.
Essays, 'Of Beauty'

8 Beauty and the lust for learning have yet to be allied.
Max Beerbohm (1872–1956) British writer.
Zuleika Dobson, Ch. 7

9 Exuberance is Beauty.
William Blake (1757–1827) British poet.
The Marriage of Heaven and Hell, 'Proverbs of Hell'

10 For beauty being the best of all we know
Sums up the unsearchable and secret aims
Of nature.
Robert Bridges (1844–1930) British poet.
The Growth of Love

11 Beauty sat with me all the summer day,
Awaiting the sure triumph of her eye;
Nor mark'd I till we parted, how, hard by,
Love in her train stood ready for his prey.
Robert Bridges
The Growth of Love

12 It is better to be first with an ugly woman than the hundredth with a beauty.
Pearl Buck (1892–1973) US novelist.
The Good Earth, Ch. 1

13 Beauty in distress is much the most affecting beauty.
Edmund Burke (1729–97) British politician.
On the Sublime and Beautiful, Pt. III

14 She walks in beauty, like the night
Of cloudless climes and starry skies;
And all that's best of dark and bright
Meet in her aspect and her eyes.
Lord Byron (1788–1824) British poet.
She Walks in Beauty

15 SONYA. I'm not beautiful.
HELEN. You have lovely hair.
SONYA. No, when a woman isn't beautiful, people always say, 'You have lovely eyes, you have lovely hair.'
Anton Chekhov (1860–1904) Russian dramatist.
Uncle Vanya, III

16 There is nothing ugly; *I never saw an ugly thing in my life:* for let the form of an object be what it may, – light, shade, and perspective will always make it beautiful.
John Constable (1776–1837) British landscape painter.
Letter to John Fisher, 23 Oct 1821

17 Love built on beauty, soon as beauty, dies.
John Donne (1573–1631) English poet.
Elegies, 2, 'The Anagram'

18 One girl can be pretty – but a dozen are only a chorus.
F. Scott Fitzgerald (1896–1940) US novelist.
The Last Tycoon

19 Against the beautiful and the clever and the successful, one can wage a pitiless war, but not against the unattractive.
Graham Greene (1904–   ) British novelist.
The Heart of the Matter

20 Glory be to God for dappled things –
For skies of couple-colour as a brindled cow;
For rose-moles all in stipple upon trout that swim.
Gerard Manley Hopkins (1844–99) British Jesuit and poet.
Pied Beauty

21 Beauty in things exists in the mind which contemplates them.
David Hume (1711–76) Scottish philosopher.
Essays, 'Of Tragedy'

22 Beauty is altogether in the eye of the beholder.
Margaret Wolfe Hungerford (c. 1855–97) Irish novelist.
Also attributed to the US soldier and writer Lew Wallace (1827–1905)
Molly Bawn

23 A thing of beauty is a joy for ever:
Its loveliness increases; it will never
Pass into nothingness; but still will keep
A bower quiet for us, and a sleep
Full of sweet dreams, and health, and quiet breathing.
John Keats (1795–1821) British poet.
Endymion, I

24 'Beauty is truth, truth beauty,' – that is all
Ye know on earth, and all ye need to know.
John Keats
Ode on a Grecian Urn

25 Was this the face that launch'd a thousand ships
And burnt the topless towers of Ilium?
Sweet Helen, make me immortal with a kiss.
Christopher Marlowe (1564–93) English dramatist.
Doctor Faustus, V:1

26 Oh, thou art fairer than the evening air
Clad in the beauty of a thousand stars.
Christopher Marlowe
Doctor Faustus, V:1

27 You're the most beautiful woman I've ever seen, which doesn't say much for you.
Groucho Marx (Julius Marx; 1895–1977) US comedian.
Animal Crackers

28 Beauty stands
In the admiration only of weak minds
Led captive.
John Milton (1608–74) English poet.
Paradise Regained, Bk. II

29 I hate that aesthetic game of the eye and the mind, played by these connoisseurs, these mandarins who 'appreciate' beauty. What *is* beauty, anyway? There's no such thing. I never 'appreciate', any more than I 'like'. I love or I hate.
Pablo Picasso (1881–1973) Spanish painter.
Life with Picasso (Françoise Gilot and Carlton Lake), Ch. 2

30 And when I told them how beautiful you are
They didn't believe me! They didn't believe me!
M. E. Rourke (20th century) US songwriter and lyricist.
They Didn't Believe Me (song)

31 There are no ugly women, only lazy ones.
Helena Rubinstein (1882–1965) Polish-born US cosmetics manufacturer.
My Life for Beauty, Pt. II, Ch. 1

32 All she has to do is to walk around and about Georgie White's stage with only a few light bandages on, and everybody considers her very beautiful, especially from the neck down.
Damon Runyon (1884–1946) US writer.
Furthermore, 'A Very Honourable Guy'

33 Remember that the most beautiful things in the world are the most useless, peacocks and lilies for instance.
John Ruskin (1819–1900) British art critic and writer.
The Stones of Venice, Vol. I, Ch. 2

34 I always say beauty is only sin deep.
Saki (Hector Hugh Munro; 1870–1916) British writer.
Reginald's Choir Treat

35 Beauty itself doth of itself persuade
The eyes of men without an orator.
William Shakespeare (1564–1616) English dramatist.
The Rape of Lucrece, I

36 From fairest creatures we desire increase,
That thereby beauty's rose might never die.
William Shakespeare
Sonnet 1

37 For she was beautiful – her beauty made
The bright world dim, and everything beside
Seemed like the fleeting image of a shade.
Percy Bysshe Shelley (1792–1822) British poet.
The Witch of Atlas, XII

38 Half light, half shade,
She stood, a sight to make an old man young.
Alfred, Lord Tennyson (1809–92) British poet.
The Gardener's Daughter

39 But Lancelot mused a little space;
He said, 'She has a lovely face;
God in his mercy lend her grace,
The Lady of Shalott.'
Alfred, Lord Tennyson
The Lady of Shalott, Pt. IV

40 A woman of so shining loveliness
That men threshed corn at midnight by a
tress,
A little stolen tress.
W. B. Yeats (1865–1939) Irish poet.
The Secret Rose

41 All changed, changed utterly:
A terrible beauty is born.
W. B. Yeats
Easter 1916

BED

See also idleness, rest, sleep

1 Early to bed and early to rise, makes a man
healthy, wealthy and wise.
Proverb

2 Go to bed with the lamb, and rise with the
lark.
Proverb

3 I'm Burlington Bertie:
I rise at ten-thirty.
W. F. Hargreaves (1846–1919) British songwriter.
Burlington Bertie

4 I have, all my life long, been lying till noon;
yet I tell all young men, and tell them with
great sincerity, that nobody who does not
rise early will ever do any good.
Samuel Johnson (1709–84) British lexicographer.
Tour to the Hebrides (J. Boswell)

5 O! it's nice to get up in the mornin',
But it's nicer to stay in bed.
Harry Lauder (Hugh MacLennon; 1870–1950) Scottish
music-hall artist.
Song

6 It was such a lovely day I thought it was a
pity to get up.
W. Somerset Maugham (1874–1965) British novelist.
Our Betters, II

7 And so to bed.
Samuel Pepys (1633–1703) English diarist.
Diary, 6 May 1660 and *passim*

8 Not to be abed after midnight is to be up
betimes.
William Shakespeare (1564–1616) English dramatist.
Twelfth Night, II:3

9 Early to rise and early to bed makes a male
healthy and wealthy and dead.
James Thurber (1894–1961) US humorist.
Fables for Our Time, 'The Shrike and the Chipmunks'

BEGINNING

See also prophecy

1 A journey of a thousand leagues begins with
a single step.
Chinese Proverb

2 Fingers were made before forks, and hands
before knives.
Proverb

3 From small beginnings come great things.
Proverb

4 Great oaks from little acorns grow.
Proverb

5 The first step is the hardest.
Proverb

6 No task is a long one but the task on which
one dare not start. It becomes a nightmare.
Charles Baudelaire (1821–67) French poet.
My Heart Laid Bare

7 She looked at him, as one who awakes:
The past was a sleep, and her life began.
Robert Browning (1812–89) British poet.
The Statue and the Bust

8 The distance doesn't matter; it is only the
first step that is difficult.
Marquise du Deffand (Marie de Vichy-Chamrond; 1697–
1780) French noblewoman.
Referring to the legend of St Denis, who is traditionally believed to have carried his severed head for six miles after his
execution
Letter to d'Alembert, 7 July 1763

9 From today and from this place there begins
a new epoch in the history of the world.
Goethe (1749–1832) German poet and dramatist.
On witnessing the victory of the French at the battle of Valmy
The Story of Civilization (W. Durant), Vol. II

10 'Tis always morning somewhere in the world.
Richard Henry Horne (1803–84) English writer.
Orion, Bk III, Ch. 2

11 There is an old saying 'well begun is half
done' – 'tis a bad one. I would use instead –
Not begun at all until half done.
John Keats (1795–1821) British poet.
Letter, 1817

12 We stand today on the edge of a new
frontier.
John Fitzgerald Kennedy (1917–63) US statesman.
Said on his nomination as Presidential candidate
Speech, Democratic Party Convention, 15 July 1960

13 Are you sitting comfortably? Then I'll begin.
Julia S. Lang (1921–) British broadcaster.
Introduction to the story in *Listen with Mother*

BELIEF

See also faith, religion

1 Believe nothing of what you hear, and only
half of what you see.
Proverb

2 Seeing is believing.
Proverb

3 Vain are the thousand creeds
That move men's hearts: unutterably vain;

Worthless as wither'd weeds.
Emily Brontë (1818–48) British novelist.
Last Lines

4 If Jesus Christ were to come to-day, people would not even crucify him. They would ask him to dinner, and hear what he had to say, and make fun of it.
Thomas Carlyle (1795–1881) Scottish historian and essayist.
Carlyle at his Zenith (D. A. Wilson)

5 *Action will furnish belief,* – but will that belief be the true one?
This is the point, you know.
Arthur Hugh Clough (1819–61) British poet.
Amours de voyage, V

6 Believe it or not.
R. L. Ripley (1893–1949) US writer.
Title of newspaper column

7 I believe because it is impossible.
Tertullian (c. 160–225 AD) Carthaginian father of the church.
The usual misquotation of 'It is certain because it is impossible.'
De Carne Christi, V

8 If there were a verb meaning 'to believe falsely', it would not have any significant first person, present indicative.
Ludwig Wittgenstein (1889–1951) Austrian philosopher.
A Certain World (W. H. Auden)

BEQUESTS

1 When you have told anyone you have left him a legacy the only decent thing to do is to die at once.
Samuel Butler (1835–1902) British writer.
Samuel Butler: A Memoir (Festing Jones), Vol. 2

2 I'm sorry to hear that, sir, you don't happen to have the shilling about you now, do you?
Tom Sheridan (1775–1817) Son of the dramatist Richard Brinsley Sheridan.
To his father, on learning that he was to be cut off in his will with a shilling
The Fine Art of Political Wit (L. Harris)

3 The man who leaves money to charity in his will is only giving away what no longer belongs to him.
Voltaire (François-Marie Arouet; 1694–1778) French writer.
Letter, 1769

BETRAYAL

See also treason

1 And forthwith he came to Jesus, and said, Hail, master; and kissed him.
And Jesus said unto him, Friend, wherefore art thou come? Then came they, and laid hands on Jesus, and took him.
Bible: Matthew
26:49–50

2 Just for a handful of silver he left us,
Just for a riband to stick in his coat.
Robert Browning (1812–89) British poet.
The Lost Leader

3 I hate the idea of causes, and if I had to choose between betraying my country and betraying my friend, I hope I should have the guts to betray my country.
E. M. Forster (1879–1970) British novelist.
Two Cheers for Democracy, 'What I Believe'.

4 I'm waiting for the cock to crow.
William Morris Hughes (1864–1952) Australian statesman.
Said in parliament, after being viciously critized by a member of his own party
The Fine Art of Political Wit (L. Harris)

5 He . . . felt towards those whom he had deserted that peculiar malignity which has, in all ages, been characteristic of apostates.
Lord Macaulay (1800–59) British historian.
History of England, Vol. I, Ch. 1

6 I let down my friends, I let down my country. I let down our system of government.
Richard Milhous Nixon (1913–) US president.
The Observer, 'Sayings of the Week', 8 May 1977

7 *Et tu, Brute?*
You too, Brutus?
William Shakespeare (1564–1616) English dramatist.
Said by Julius Caesar
Julius Caesar, III:1

BIBLE

See also religion

1 He will find one English book and one only, where, as in the *Iliad* itself, perfect plainness of speech is allied with perfect nobleness; and that book is the Bible.
Matthew Arnold (1822–88) British poet and critic.
On Translating Homer

2 Candidates should not attempt more than six of these.
Hilaire Belloc (1870–1953) French-born British poet.
Suggested addition to the Ten Commandments
Attrib.

3 There's a great text in Galatians,
Once you trip on it, entails
Twenty-nine distinct damnations,
One sure, if another fails.
Robert Browning (1812–89) British poet.
Soliloquy of the Spanish Cloister

4 It's just called 'The Bible' now. We dropped the word 'Holy' to give it a more mass-market appeal.
Editor, Hodder & Stoughton
The Daily Telegraph, 30 Dec 1989

5 I have spent a lot of time searching through the Bible for loopholes.

W. C. Fields (1880–1946) US actor.
Said during his last illness
Attrib.

6 We have used the Bible as if it was a constable's handbook – an opium-dose for keeping beasts of burden patient while they are being overloaded.

Charles Kingsley (1819–75) British writer.
Letters to the Chartists, 2

7 The English Bible, a book which, if everything else in our language should perish, would alone suffice to show the whole extent of its beauty and power.

Lord Macaulay (1800–59) British historian.
Essays and Biographies, 'John Dryden'. *Edinburgh Review*

8 The number one book of the ages was written by a committee, and it was called The Bible.

Louis B. Mayer (1885–1957) Russian-born US film producer.
Comment to writers who had objected to changes in their work
The Filmgoer's Book of Quotes (Leslie Halliwell)

9 There's a Bible on that shelf there. But I keep it next to Voltaire – poison and antidote.

Bertrand Russell (1872–1970) British philosopher.
Kenneth Harris Talking To: 'Bertrand Russell' (Kenneth Harris)

10 The Bible is literature, not dogma.

George Santayana (1863–1952) US philosopher.
Introduction to the Ethics of Spinoza

11 LORD ILLINGWORTH. The Book of Life begins with a man and a woman in a garden.

MRS ALLONBY. It ends with Revelations.

Oscar Wilde (1854–1900) Irish-born British dramatist.
A Woman of No Importance, I

BIOGRAPHY

1 The Art of Biography
Is different from Geography.
Geography is about Maps,
But Biography is about Chaps.

Edmund Clerihew Bentley (1875–1956) British writer.
Biography for Beginners

2 A well-written Life is almost as rare as a well-spent one.

Thomas Carlyle (1795–1881) Scottish historian and essayist.
Critical and Miscellaneous Essays, 'Richter'

3 History is the essence of innumerable biographies.

Thomas Carlyle
Critical and Miscellaneous Essays, 'History'

4 Campbell has added another terror to death.

John Singleton Copley (1772–1863) US-born British lawyer.
Referring to Lord Campbell's controversial *Lives of the Lord*

Chancellors (1845–47), from which Lyndhurst was excluded because he was still alive

5 There is properly no history; only biography.

Ralph Waldo Emerson (1803–82) US poet and essayist.
Essays, 'History'

6 Just how difficult it is to write biography can be reckoned by anybody who sits down and considers just how many people know the real truth about his or her love affairs.

Rebecca West (Cicely Isabel Fairfield; 1892–1983) British novelist and journalist.
Vogue magazine

BIRDS

1 That's the wise thrush; he sings each song twice over,
Lest you should think he never could recapture
The first fine careless rapture!

Robert Browning (1812–89) British poet.
Home Thoughts from Abroad

2 With my cross-bow
I shot the albatross.

Samuel Taylor Coleridge (1772–1834) British poet.
The Rime of the Ancient Mariner, I

3 It was the Rainbow gave thee birth,
And left thee all her lovely hues.

W. H. Davies (1871–1940) British poet.
The Kingfisher

4 On a tree by a river a little tom-tit
Sang 'Willow, titwillow, titwillow!'

W. S. Gilbert (1836–1911) British dramatist.
The Mikado, II

5 Thou wast not born for death, immortal Bird!
No hungry generations tread thee down;
The voice I hear this passing night was heard
In ancient days by emperor and clown:
Perhaps the self-same song that found a path
Through the sad heart of Ruth, when sick for home,
She stood in tears amid the alien corn;
The same that oft-times hath
Charm'd magic casements, opening on the foam
Of perilous seas, in faery lands forlorn.

John Keats (1795–1821) British poet.
Ode to a Nightingale

6 Ye living lamps, by whose dear light
The nightingale does sit so late,
And studying all the summer night,
Her matchless songs does meditate.

Andrew Marvell (1621–78) English poet.
The Mower to the Glow-worms

7 A Nightingale Sang in Berkeley Square.

Eric Maschwitz (20th century) British songwriter.
Song title

8 To hear the lark begin his flight,
And singing startle the dull night,
From his watch-tower in the skies,

Till the dappled dawn doth rise.
John Milton (1608–74) English poet.
L'Allegro

9 Sweet bird, that shunn'st the noise of folly,
Most musical, most melancholy!
John Milton
Referring to the nightingale
Il Penseroso

10 Hail to thee, blithe Spirit!
Bird thou never wert,
That from Heaven, or near it,
Pourest thy full heart
In profuse strains of unpremeditated art.
Percy Bysshe Shelley (1792–1822) British poet.
To a Skylark

11 Ethereal minstrel! pilgrim of the sky!
Dost thou despise the earth where cares
abound?
William Wordsworth (1770–1850) British poet.
To a Skylark

12 O Nightingale, thou surely art
A creature of a 'fiery heart'.
William Wordsworth
O Nightingale

13 The pious bird with the scarlet breast,
Our little English robin.
William Wordsworth
The Redbreast chasing the Butterfly

14 Thrice welcome, darling of the spring!
Even yet thou art to me
No bird, but an invisible thing,
A voice, a mystery.
William Wordsworth
To the Cuckoo

BIRTH

See also babies, life and death

1 A woman when she is in travail hath sorrow,
because her hour is come: but as soon as
she is delivered of the child, she
remembereth no more the anguish, for joy
that a man is born into the world.
Bible: John
16:21

2 For all men have one entrance into life, and
the like going out.
Bible: Wisdom
7:6

3 My mother groan'd, my father wept,
Into the dangerous world I leapt;
Helpless, naked, piping loud,
Like a fiend hid in a cloud.
William Blake (1757–1827) British poet.
Songs of Experience, 'Infant Sorrow'

4 For man's greatest crime is to have been
born.
Pedro Calderón de la Barca (1600–81) Spanish
dramatist.
La Vida es Sueño, I

5 The history of man for the nine months
preceding his birth would, probably, be far
more interesting and contain events of
greater moment than all the three-score and
ten years that follow it.
Samuel Taylor Coleridge (1772–1834) British poet.
Miscellanies, Aesthetic and Literary

6 If men had to have babies they would only
ever have one each.
Diana, Princess of Wales (1961–) Wife of Prince
Charles.
The Observer, 'Sayings of the Week', 29 July 1984

7 Birth may be a matter of a moment. But it is
a unique one.
Frédérick Leboyer (1918–) French obstetrician.
Birth Without Violence

8 I'll simply say here that I was born Beatrice
Gladys Lillie at an extremely tender age
because my mother needed a fourth at
meals.
Beatrice Lillie (Constance Sylvia Munston, Lady Peel;
1898–1989) Canadian-born British actress.
Every Other Inch a Lady, Ch. 1

9 MACBETH. I bear a charmed life, which must not
yield
To one of woman born.
MACDUFF. Despair thy charm;
And let the angel whom thou still hast serv'd
Tell thee Macduff was from his mother's womb
Untimely ripp'd.
William Shakespeare (1564–1616) English dramatist.
Macbeth, V:8

10 The explanation is quite simple. I wished to
be near my mother.
James Whistler (1834–1903) US painter.
Explaining to a snobbish lady why he had been born in such an
unfashionable place as Lowell, Massachusetts
Attrib.

BITTERNESS

1 The dupe of friendship, and the fool of love;
have I not reason to hate and to despise
myself? Indeed I do; and chiefly for not
having hated and despised the world enough.
William Hazlitt (1778–1830) British essayist.
On the Pleasure of Hating

2 It is very difficult to get up resentment
towards persons whom one has never seen.
Cardinal Newman (1801–90) British theologian.
Apologia pro Vita Sua (1864), 'Mr Kingsley's Method of Dispu-
tation'

3 He gave a deep sigh – I saw the iron enter
into his soul!
Laurence Sterne (1713–68) Irish-born British writer.
A Sentimental Journey, 'The Captive. Paris'

BLESSING

See also prayer

1 Matthew, Mark, Luke and John,
   The bed be blest that I lie on.
   Thomas Ady (17th century) English poet.
   A Candle in the Dark

2 I see the moon,
   And the moon sees me;
   God bless the moon,
   And God bless me.
   Anonymous
   Gammer Gurton's Garland

3 Thank you, sister. May you be the mother of
   a bishop!
   Brendan Behan (1923–64) Irish playwright.
   Said to a nun nursing him on his deathbed
   Attrib.

4 The Lord bless thee, and keep thee:
   The Lord make his face shine upon thee, and
   be gracious unto thee:
   The Lord lift up his countenance upon thee,
   and give thee peace.
   Bible: Numbers
   6:24–26

5 And the peace of God, which passeth all
   understanding, shall keep your hearts and
   minds through Christ Jesus.
   Bible: Philippians
   4:7

6 'God bless us every one!' said Tiny Tim, the
   last of all.
   Charles Dickens (1812–70) British novelist.
   A Christmas Carol

BLINDNESS

See also disability

1 A nod is as good as a wink to a blind horse.
   Proverb

2 How reconcile this world of fact with the
   bright world of my imagining? My darkness
   has been filled with the light of intelligence,
   and behold, the outer day-light world was
   stumbling and groping in social blindness.
   Helen Keller (1880–1968) US writer and lecturer.
   The Cry for Justice (ed. Upton Sinclair)

3 Ask for this great deliverer now, and find
   him
   Eyeless in Gaza at the mill with slaves.
   John Milton (1608–74) English poet.
   Samson Agonistes

4 O dark, dark, dark, amid the blaze of noon,
   Irrecoverably dark, total eclipse,
   Without all hope of day!
   John Milton
   Samson Agonistes

5 When I consider how my light is spent

Ere half my days in this dark world and wide,
And that one talent which is death to hide
Lodged with me useless.
John Milton
Sonnet: 'On his Blindness'

6 He clapped the glass to his sightless eye,
   And 'I'm damned if I see it', he said.
   Henry John Newbolt (1862–1938) British poet.
   Referring to Lord Nelson at the Battle of Copenhagen
   Admirals All

7 And so I betake myself to that course, which
   is almost as much as to see myself go into
   my grave – for which, and all the
   discomforts that will accompany my being
   blind, the good God prepare me!
   Samuel Pepys (1633–1703) English diarist.
   The closing words of Pepys's *Diary*; he lived another 34 years
   and did not go blind
   Diary, 31 May 1669

BOASTS

1 I have done almost every human activity
   inside a taxi which does not require main
   drainage.
   Alan Brien (1925–) British critic.
   Punch, 5 July 1972

2 CAPTAIN. I'm never, never sick at sea!
   ALL. What never?
   CAPTAIN. No, never!
   ALL. What, *never*?
   CAPTAIN. Hardly ever!
   W. S. Gilbert (1836–1911) British dramatist.
   HMS Pinafore, I

3 All my shows are great. Some of them are
   bad. But they are all great.
   Lew Grade (Lewis Winogradsky; 1906–) British film
   and TV producer.
   Attrib.

4 If, drunk with sight of power, we loose
   Wild tongues that have not Thee in awe,
   Such boastings as the Gentiles use,
   Or lesser breeds without the Law.
   Rudyard Kipling (1865–1936) Indian-born British writer.
   Recessional

5 I can piss the old boy in the snow.
   Max Liebermann (1847–1935) German painter.
   Remark to an artist who said he could not draw General Paul
   von Hindenburg's face
   Conversations with Stravinsky (Igor Stravinsky and Robert
   Craft)

6 And when we open our dykes, the waters
   are ten feet deep.
   Wilhelmina (1880–1962) Queen of the Netherlands.
   Replying to a boast by Wilhelm II that his guardsmen were all
   seven feet tall
   Attrib.

BOATS

See also navy, sea

1 There's something wrong with our bloody ships today.
Earl Beatty (1871–1936) British admiral.
Remark during Battle of Jutland, 30 May 1916
Attrib.

2 All rowed fast but none so fast as stroke.
Desmond Coke (1879–1931) British writer.
Popular misquotation, derived from the passage: 'His blade struck the water a full second before any other . . . until . . . as the boats began to near the winning post, his own was dipping into the water *twice* as often as any other.'
Sandford of Merton

3 As idle as a painted ship
Upon a painted ocean.
Samuel Taylor Coleridge (1772–1834) British poet.
The Rime of the Ancient Mariner, I

4 Jolly boating weather,
And a hay harvest breeze,
Blade on the feather,
Shade off the trees
Swing, swing together
With your body between your knees.
William Johnson Cory (1823–92) British schoolmaster and poet.
Eton Boating Song

5 Fair stood the wind for France
When we our sails advance.
Michael Drayton (1563–1631) English poet.
Agincourt

6 For you dream you are crossing the Channel, and tossing about in a steamer from Harwich Which is something between a large bathing machine and a very small second-class carriage.
W. S. Gilbert (1836–1911) British dramatist.
Iolanthe, II

7 There is nothing – absolutely nothing – half so much worth doing as simply messing about in boats.
Kenneth Grahame (1859–1932) Scottish writer.
The Wind in the Willows, Ch. 1

8 The little ships, the unforgotten Homeric catalogue of *Mary Jane* and *Peggy IV*, of *Folkestone Belle*, *Boy Billy*, and *Ethel Maud*, of *Lady Haig* and *Skylark* . . . the little ships of England brought the Army home.
Philip Guedalla (1889–1944) British writer.
Referring to the evacuation of Dunkirk
Mr. Churchill

9 No man will be a sailor who has contrivance enough to get himself into a jail; for being in a ship is being in a jail, with the chance of being drowned . . . A man in a jail has more room, better food, and commonly better company.
Samuel Johnson (1709–84) British lexicographer.
Life of Johnson (J. Boswell), Vol. I

10 I'd like to get you
On a slow boat to China.
Frank Loesser (1910–69) US songwriter.
Slow Boat to China

11 It was the schooner Hesperus,
That sailed the wintry sea;
And the skipper had taken his little daughter,
To bear him company.
Henry Wadsworth Longfellow (1807–82) US poet.
The Wreck of the Hesperus

12 Quinquireme of Nineveh from distant Ophir
Rowing home to haven in sunny Palestine,
With a cargo of ivory,
And apes and peacocks,
Sandalwood, cedarwood, and sweet white wine.
John Masefield (1878–1967) British poet.
Cargoes

13 Dirty British coaster with a salt-caked smoke stack,
Butting through the Channel in the mad March days,
With a cargo of Tyne coal,
Road-rail, pig-lead,
Firewood, iron-ware, and cheap tin trays.
John Masefield
Cargoes

14 Now the sunset breezes shiver,
And she's fading down the river,
But in England's song for ever
She's the Fighting Téméraire.
Henry John Newbolt (1862–1938) British poet.
The Fighting Téméraire

15 Only fools and passengers drink at sea.
Alan John Villiers (1903–) Australian naval commander.
The Observer, 'Sayings of the Week', 28 Apr 1957

BOLDNESS

See courage, danger, frankness, impertinence

BOOKS

See also criticism, fiction, literature, novels, publishing, reading, writing

1 Books and friends should be few but good.
Proverb

2 Some books are undeservedly forgotten; none are undeservedly remembered.
W. H. Auden (1907–73) British poet.
The Dyer's Hand, 'Reading'

3 Some books are to be tasted, others to be swallowed, and some few to be chewed and digested.
Francis Bacon (1561–1626) English philosopher.
Essays, 'Of Studies'

4 Books must follow sciences, and not sciences books.
Francis Bacon
Proposition touching Amendment of Laws

5 It is all very well to be able to write books, but can you waggle your ears?
J. M. Barrie (1860–1937) British novelist and dramatist.
Speaking to H. G. Wells
Barrie: The Story of A Genius (J. A. Hamerton)

6 When I am dead, I hope it may be said:
'His sins were scarlet, but his books were read.'
Hilaire Belloc (1870–1953) French-born British poet.
Epigrams, 'On His Books'

7 Child! do not throw this book about;
Refrain from the unholy pleasure
Of cutting all the pictures out!
Preserve it as your chiefest treasure.
Hilaire Belloc
The Bad Child's Book of Beasts, 'Dedication'

8 And further, by these, my son, be admonished: of making many books there is no end; and much study is a weariness of the flesh.
Bible: Ecclesiastes
12:12

9 I keep my books at the British Museum and at Mudie's.
Samuel Butler (1835–1902) British writer.
The Humour of Homer, 'Ramblings in Cheapside'

10 'Tis pleasant, sure, to see one's name in print;
A book's a book, although there's nothing in't.
Lord Byron (1788–1824) British poet.
English Bards and Scotch Reviewers

11 A good book is the purest essence of a human soul.
Thomas Carlyle (1795–1881) Scottish historian and essayist.
Speech made in support of the London Library
Carlyle and the London Library (F. Harrison)

12 'What is the use of a book,' thought Alice, 'without pictures or conversation?'
Lewis Carroll (Charles Lutwidge Dodgson; 1832–98) British writer.
Alice's Adventures in Wonderland, Ch. 1

13 Go, litel book, go litel myn tragedie.
O moral Gower, this book I directe To thee.
Geoffrey Chaucer (c. 1342–1400) English poet.
Troilus and Criseyde, 5

14 Due attention to the inside of books, and due contempt for the outside, is the proper relation between a man of sense and his books.
Earl of Chesterfield (1694–1773) English statesman.
Letter to his son, 10 Jan 1749

15 Books cannot always please, however good; Minds are not ever craving for their food.
George Crabbe (1754–1832) British poet.
The Borough, 'Schools'

16 Books, we are told, propose to *instruct* or to *amuse*. Indeed! . . . The true antithesis to knowledge, in this case, is not *pleasure*, but *power*. All that is literature seeks to communicate power; all that is not literature, to communicate knowledge.
Thomas De Quincey (1785–1859) British writer.
Letters to a Young Man

17 A book is not harmless merely because no one is consciously offended by it.
T. S. Eliot (1888–1965) US-born British poet and dramatist.
Religion and Literature

18 Books are made not like children but like pyramids . . . and they're just as useless! and they stay in the desert! . . . Jackals piss at their foot and the bourgeois climb up on them.
Gustave Flaubert (1821–80) French novelist.
Letter to Ernest Feydeau, 1857

19 Learning hath gained most by those books by which the printers have lost.
Thomas Fuller (1608–61) English historian.
The Holy State and the Profane State

20 A book may be amusing with numerous errors, or it may be very dull without a single absurdity.
Oliver Goldsmith (1728–74) Irish-born British writer.
The Vicar of Wakefield, Advertisement

21 Few books today are forgivable.
R. D. Laing (1927–89) British psychiatrist.
The Politics of Experience, Introduction

22 Get stewed:
Books are a load of crap.
Philip Larkin (1922–85) British poet.
A Study of Reading Habits

23 To every man who struggles with his own soul in mystery, a book that is a book flowers once, and seeds, and is gone.
D. H. Lawrence (1885–1930) British novelist.
Phoenix, 'A Bibliography of D.H.L.'

24 Never judge a cover by its book.
Fran Lebowitz (1950–) US writer.
Metropolitan Life

25 There can hardly be a stranger commodity in the world than books. Printed by people who don't understand them; sold by people who don't understand them; bound, criticized and read by people who don't understand them; and now even written by people who don't understand them.
Georg Christoph Lichtenberg (1742–99) German physicist and writer.
Aphorisms

26 In recommending a book to a friend the less said the better. The moment you praise a book too highly you awaken resistance in your listener.
Henry Miller (1891–1980) US novelist.
The Books In My Life

27 Who kills a man kills a reasonable creature,

God's image; but he who destroys a good book, kills reason itself, kills the image of God, as it were in the eye.

John Milton (1608–74) English poet.
Areopagitica

28 A good book is the precious life-blood of a master spirit, embalmed and treasured up on purpose to a life beyond life.

John Milton
Areopagitica

29 The books one reads in childhood, and perhaps most of all the bad and good bad books, create in one's mind a sort of false map of the world, a series of fabulous countries into which one can retreat at odd moments throughout the rest of life, and which in some cases can even survive a visit to the real countries which they are supposed to represent.

George Orwell (Eric Blair; 1903–50) British novelist.
Riding Down from Bangor

30 At last, an unprintable book that is readable.

Ezra Pound (1885–1972) US poet.
Referring to *Tropic of Cancer* by Henry Miller

31 An anthology is like all the plums and orange peel picked out of a cake.

Walter Raleigh (1861–1922) British scholar.
Letter to Mrs Robert Bridges, 15 Jan 1915

32 I have known her pass the whole evening without mentioning a single book, or *in fact anything unpleasant* at all.

Henry Reed (1914–86) British poet and dramatist.
A Very Great Man Indeed

33 When a new book is published, read an old one.

Samuel Rogers (1763–1855) British poet.
Attrib.

34 We all know that books burn – yet we have the greater knowledge that books cannot be killed by fire. People die, but books never die. No man and no force can abolish memory . . . In this war, we know, books are weapons.

Franklin D. Roosevelt (1882–1945) US Democratic president.
Message to American Booksellers Association, 23 Apr 1942

35 If a book is worth reading, it is worth buying.

John Ruskin (1819–1900) British art critic and writer.
Sesame and Lilies, 'Of Kings' Treasuries'

36 All books are divisible into two classes, the books of the hour, and the books of all time.

John Ruskin
Sesame and Lilies, 'Of Kings' Treasuries'

37 How long most people would look at the best book before they would give the price of a large turbot for it!

John Ruskin
Sesame and Lilies, 'Of Kings' Treasuries'

38 A library is thought in cold storage.

Herbert Samuel (1870–1963) British Liberal statesman.
A Book of Quotations

39 Children . . . have no use for psychology. They detest sociology. They still believe in God, the family, angels, devils, witches, goblins, logic, clarity, punctuation, and other such obsolete stuff . . . When a book is boring, they yawn openly. They don't expect their writer to redeem humanity, but leave to adults such childish illusions.

Isaac Bashevis Singer (1904–) Polish-born US writer.
Speech on receiving the Nobel Prize for Literature
The Observer, 17 Dec 1978

40 A best-seller is the gilded tomb of a mediocre talent.

Logan Pearsall Smith (1865–1946) US writer.
Afterthoughts, 'Art and Letters'

41 No furniture so charming as books.

Sydney Smith (1771–1845) British clergyman and essayist.
Memoir (Lady Holland)

42 Books are good enough in their own way, but they are a mighty bloodless substitute for life.

Robert Louis Stevenson (1850–94) Scottish writer.
Virginibus Puerisque

43 My brother-in-law wrote an unusal murder story. The victim got killed by a man from another book.

Robert Sylvester (1907–75) US writer.

44 A good book is the best of friends, the same to-day and for ever.

Martin Farquhar Tupper (1810–89) British writer.
Proverbial Philosophy, 'Of Reading'

45 Books, I don't know what you see in them . . . I can understand a person reading them, but I can't for the life of me see why people have to write them.

Peter Ustinov (1921–) British actor.
Photo-Finish

46 There is no such thing as a moral or an immoral book. Books are well written, or badly written.

Oscar Wilde (1854–1900) Irish-born British dramatist.
The Picture of Dorian Gray, Preface

BOOK, SONG, AND PLAY TITLES

1 Who's Afraid of Virginia Woolf?

Edward Albee (1928–) US dramatist.
Play title

2 Lucky Jim.

Kingsley Amis (1922–) British novelist.
Title of novel

3 The Ugly Duckling.

Hans Christian Andersen (1805–75) Danish writer.
Story title

4 Eating People Is Wrong.

Malcolm Bradbury (1932–) British academic, novelist, and critic.
From a song 'The Reluctant Cannibal' by Michael Flanders and Donald Swann
Book title

5 Room at the Top.

John Braine (1922–86) British novelist.
From Daniel Webster's remark 'There is always room at the top'
Book title

6 Tender Is the Night.

F. Scott Fitzgerald (1896–1940) US novelist.
From the 'Ode to a Nightingale' (John Keats): 'Already with thee! tender is the night'
Book title

7 When the Kissing Had to Stop.

Constantine FitzGibbon
From 'A Toccata at Galuppi's' (Robert Browning): 'What of soul was left, I wonder, when the kissing had to stop'
Book title

8 Diamonds Are Forever.

Ian Fleming (1908–64) British writer.
From the advertising slogan 'A Diamond is Forever' for De Beers Consolidated Mines
Book title

9 'Tis Pity She's a whore.

John Ford (c. 1586–c. 1640) English dramatist.
Play title

10 Goodbye to All That.

Robert Graves (1895–1985) British poet.
Book title

11 A Woman Killed with Kindness.

Thomas Heywood (c. 1574–1641) English dramatist.
Play title

12 The Light that Failed.

Rudyard Kipling (1865–1936) Indian-born British writer.
Novel title

13 Shoot all the bluejays you want, if you can hit 'em, but remember it's a sin to kill a mockingbird.

Harper Lee (1926–) US writer.
To Kill a Mockingbird, Pt. II, Ch. 10

14 Sergeant Pepper's Lonely Hearts Club Band.

John Lennon (1940–80) British rock singer.
Song title (with Paul McCartney)

15 None But the Lonely Heart.

Richard Llewellyn (1907–83) British writer.
Adapted from the English title of Tchaikovsky's song 'None But the Weary Heart' (original words by Goethe)
Book title

16 Of Human Bondage.

W. Somerset Maugham (1874–1965) British novelist and doctor.
From the title of one of the books in *Ethics* (Spinoza)
Book title

17 The Moon and Sixpence.

W. Somerset Maugham
From a review of his novel *Of Human Bondage*, 'Like so many young men, was so busy yearning for the moon that he never saw the sixpence at his feet'. (*Times Literary Supplement*)
Book title

18 The Heart Is a Lonely Hunter.

Carson McCullers (1917–67) US novelist.
From the poem 'The Lonely Hunter' (William Sharp): 'My heart is a lonely hunter that hunts on a lonely hill'
Book title

19 Gone With the Wind.

Margaret Mitchell (1909–49) US novelist.
From the poem *Non Sum Qualis Eram* (Ernest Dowson): 'I have forgot much, Cynara! Gone with the wind...'
Book title

20 The Moon's a Balloon.

David Niven (1909–83) British actor.
From e. e. cummings, '&': 'Who knows if the moon's a balloon, coming out of a keen city in the sky – filled with pretty people?'
Book title

21 A Dance to the Music of Time.

Anthony Powell (1905–) British novelist.
From the name of a painting by Nicolas Poussin
Book title

22 A Bridge Too Far.

Cornelius Ryan
Lieut. General Sir Frederick Browning said to Field Marshal Montgomery 'But, sir, we may be going a bridge too far'; referring to the airborne attack to capture eleven bridges over the Rhine, including the bridge at Arnhem, prior to the invasion of Germany (1944)
Book title

23 Fanny by Gaslight.

Michael Sadleir (1888–1957) British author.
Book title

24 Look Homeward, Angel!

Thomas Wolfe (1900–38) US novelist.
From 'Lycidas' by John Milton
Book title

BOREDOM

See also bores

1 Nothing happens, nobody comes, nobody goes, it's awful!

Samuel Beckett (1906–89) Irish novelist and dramatist.
Waiting for Godot, I

2 I wanted to be bored to death, as good a way to go as any.

Peter De Vries (1910–) US novelist.
Comfort me with Apples, Ch. 17

3 You ought not to be ashamed of being bored. What you ought to be ashamed of is being boring.

Lord Hailsham (1907–) British Conservative politician.
The Observer, 'Sayings of the Week', 12 Oct 1975

4 Symmetry is tedious, and tedium is the very basis of mourning. Despair yawns.

Victor Hugo (1802–85) French writer.
Les Misérables, Vol. II, Bk. IV, Ch. 1

5 The effect of boredom on a large scale in

history is underestimated. It is a main cause of revolutions, and would soon bring to an end all the static Utopias and the farmyard civilization of the Fabians.

Dean Inge (1860–1954) British churchman.
The End of an Age, Ch. 6

6 Is not life a hundred times too short for us to bore ourselves?

Friedrich Wilhelm Nietzsche (1844–1900) German philosopher.
Jenseits von Gut und Böse

7 When you're bored with yourself, marry and be bored with someone else.

David Pryce-Jones (1936–) British author and critic.
Owls and Satyrs

BORES

See also boredom

1 *Bore*, n. A person who talks when you wish him to listen.

Ambrose Bierce (1842–?1914) US writer and journalist.
The Devil's Dictionary

2 Society is now one polish'd horde,
Form'd of two mighty tribes, the *Bores* and *Bored*.

Lord Byron (1788–1824) British poet.
Don Juan, XIII

3 Sir, you are like a pin, but without either its head or its point.

Douglas William Jerrold (1803–57) British dramatist.
Speaking to a small thin man who was boring him
Attrib.

4 He is not only a bore but he bores for England.

Malcolm Muggeridge (1903–) British writer.
Referring to Sir Anthony Eden
In *Newstatesmanship* (E. Hyams), 'Boring for England'

5 A bore is a man who, when you ask him how he is, tells you.

Bert Leston Taylor (1866–1921) US journalist.
Attrib.

6 Somebody's boring me, I think it's me.

Dylan Thomas (1914–53) Welsh poet.
Remark made after he had been talking continuously for some time
Four Absentees (Rayner Heppenstall)

7 He is an old bore; even the grave yawns for him.

Herbert Beerbohm Tree (1853–1917) British actor and theatre manager.
Referring to Israel Zangwill
Beerbohm Tree (Hesketh Pearson)

8 A healthy male adult bore consumes each year one and a half times his own weight in other people's patience.

John Updike (1932–) US novelist.
Assorted Prose, 'Confessions of a Wild Bore'

9 Dear Frank, we believe you; you have dined in every house in London – *once*.

Oscar Wilde (1854–1900) Irish-born British dramatist.
Interrupting Frank Harris's interminable account of the houses he had dined at
Attrib.

BORROWING

1 Borrowed garments never fit well.

Proverb

2 I don't trust a bank that would lend money to such a poor risk.

Robert Benchley (1889–1945) US humorist.
To a bank that granted his request for a loan
Attrib.

3 Be not made a beggar by banqueting upon borrowing, when thou hast nothing in thy purse: for thou shalt lie in wait for thine own life, and be talked on.

Bible: Ecclesiasticus
18:33

4 One of the mysteries of human conduct is why adult men and women all over England are ready to sign documents which they do not read, at the behest of canvassers whom they do not know, binding them to pay for articles which they do not want, with money which they have not got.

Gerald Hurst (1877–1957) British writer and judge.
Closed Chapters

5 The human species, according to the best theory I can form of it, is composed of two distinct races, the men who borrow, and the men who lend.

Charles Lamb (1775–1834) British essayist.
Essays of Elia, 'The Two Races of Men'

6 Borrowers of books – those mutilators of collections, spoilers of the symmetry of shelves, and creators of odd volumes.

Charles Lamb
Essays of Elia, 'The Two Races of Men'

7 Not everyone is a debtor who wishes to be; not everyone who wishes makes creditors.

François Rabelais (1483–1553) French satirist.
Pantagruel, Bk. III, Ch. 3

8 Neither a borrower nor a lender be;
For loan oft loses both itself and friend,
And borrowing dulls the edge of husbandry.
This above all: to thine own self be true,
And it must follow, as the night the day,
Thou canst not then be false to any man.

William Shakespeare (1564–1616) English dramatist.
Hamlet, I:3

9 Thank God, that's settled.

Richard Brinsley Sheridan (1751–1816) British dramatist.
Handing one of his creditors an IOU
Wit, Wisdom, and Foibles of the Great (C. Shriner)

10 It is not my interest to pay the principal, nor my principle to pay the interest.

Richard Brinsley Sheridan
To his tailor when he requested the payment of a debt, or of the interest on it at least
Attrib.

11 My dear fellow, be reasonable; the sum you ask me for is a very considerable one, whereas I only ask you for twenty-five pounds.

Richard Brinsley Sheridan
On being refused a further loan of £25 from a friend to whom he already owed £500
Literary and Scientific Anecdotes (W. Keddie)

12 Let us all be happy, and live within our means, even if we have to borrer the money to do it with.

Artemus Ward (Charles Farrar Browne; 1834–67) US humorous writer.
Science and Natural History

13 I don't owe a penny to a single soul – not counting tradesmen, of course.

P. G. Wodehouse (1881–1975) British humorous novelist.
My Man Jeeves, 'Jeeves and the Hard-Boiled Egg'

BREVITY

See also sermons, speeches, verbosity

1 Good things, when short, are twice as good.

Baltasar Gracián (1601–58) Spanish writer.
The Art of Worldly Wisdom

2 I strive to be brief, and I become obscure.

Horace (Quintus Horatius Flaccus; 65–8 BC) Roman poet.
Ars Poetica

3 ?

Victor Hugo (1802–85) French writer.
The entire contents of a telegram sent to his publishers asking how *Les Misérables* was selling; the reply was '!'
The Literary Life (R. Hendrickson)

4 But the shortest works are always the best.

Jean de La Fontaine (1621–95) French poet.
Fables, X, 'Les Lapins'

5 Brevity is the soul of lingerie.

Dorothy Parker (1893–1967) US writer.
While Rome Burns (Alexander Woollcott)

6 Trust the man who hesitates in his speech and is quick and steady in action, but beware of long arguments and long beards.

George Santayana (1863–1952) US philosopher.
Soliloquies in England, 'The British Character'

7 Brevity is the soul of wit.

William Shakespeare (1564–1616) English dramatist.
Hamlet, II:2

8 Men of few words are the best men.

William Shakespeare
Henry V, III:2

9 Nurse unupblown.

Evelyn Waugh (1903–66) British novelist.
Cable sent after he had failed, while a journalist serving in Ethiopia, to substantiate a rumour that an English nurse had been blown up in an Italian air raid
Our Marvelous Native Tongue (R. Claiborne)

BRIBERY

See also corruption

1 When their lordships asked Bacon
How many bribes he had taken
He had at least the grace
To get very red in the face.

Edmund Clerihew Bentley (1875–1956) British writer.
Baseless Biography

2 To a shower of gold most things are penetrable.

Thomas Carlyle (1795–1881) Scottish historian and essayist.
History of the French Revolution, Pt. I, Bk. III, Ch. 7

3 I have often noticed that a bribe . . . has that effect – it changes a relation. The man who offers a bribe gives away a little of his own importance; the bribe once accepted, he becomes the inferior, like a man who has paid for a woman.

Graham Greene (1904–) British novelist.
The Comedians, Pt. I, Ch. 4

4 Though authority be a stubborn bear, yet he is oft led by the nose with gold.

William Shakespeare (1564–1616) English dramatist.
The Winter's Tale, IV:3

BRITAIN

See also British, British Empire, England, Ireland, patriotism, Scotland, Wales

1 Great Britain has lost an Empire and has not yet found a role.

Dean Acheson (1893–1971) US lawyer and statesman.
Speech, Military Academy, West Point, 5 Dec 1962

2 A nation of shop-keepers are very seldom so disinterested.

Samuel Adams (1722–1803) US revolutionary leader.
Referring to Britain, following the Declaration of Independence, 4 July 1776
Speech, Philadelphia, 1 Aug 1776

3 You must not miss Whitehall. At one end you will find a statue of one of our kings who was beheaded; at the other the monument to the man who did it. This is just an example of our attempts to be fair to everybody.

Edward Appleton (1892–1965) British physicist.
Referring to Charles I and Cromwell
Speech, Stockholm, 1 Jan 1948

4 Land of Hope and Glory, Mother of the Free,
How shall we extol thee, who are born of thee?
Wider still and wider shall thy bounds be set;

God who made thee mighty, make thee mightier yet.

A. C. Benson (1862–1925) British writer.
Land of Hope and Glory

5 Britain has lived for too long on borrowed time, borrowed money and even borrowed ideas.

James Callaghan (1912–) British politician and prime minister.
The Observer, 'Sayings of the Week', 3 Oct 1976

6 God save our Gracious King,
Long live our noble King,
God save the King.
Send him victorious,
Happy and glorious.

Henry Carey (c. 1690–1743) English poet and musician.
God Save the King

7 When the British warrior queen,
Bleeding from the Roman rods,
Sought, with an indignant mien,
Counsel of her country's gods.

William Cowper (1731–1800) British poet.
Boadicea

8 Britain is not a country that is easily rocked by revolution . . . In Britain our institutions evolve. We are a Fabian Society writ large.

William Hamilton (1917–) Scottish MP.
My Queen and I, Ch. 9

9 We may be a small island, but we are not a small people.

Edward Heath (1916–) British politician and prime minister.
The Observer, 'Sayings of the Week', 21 June 1970

10 Sir, it is not so much to be lamented that Old England is lost, as that the Scotch have found it.

Samuel Johnson (1709–84) British lexicographer.
Life of Johnson (J. Boswell), Vol. III

11 This is a very fine country to be acutely ill or injured in, but take my advice and do not be old and frail or mentally ill here – at least not for a few years. This is definitely not a good country to be deaf or blind in either.

Keith Joseph (1918–) British politician.
The Observer, 'Sayings of the Week', 1 July 1973

12 Once, when a British Prime Minister sneezed, men half a world away would blow their noses. Now when a British Prime Minister sneezes nobody else will even say 'Bless You'.

Bernard Levin (1928–) British journalist.
The Times, 1976

13 When Britain first, at heaven's command,
Arose from out the azure main,
This was the charter of the land,
And guardian angels sung this strain:
'Rule, Britannia, rule the waves;
Britons never will be slaves.'

James Thomson (1700–48) British poet.
Alfred: a Masque, Act II

14 I should like to help Britain to become a Third Programme country.

Ellen Cicely Wilkinson (1891–1947) British feminist and politician.
The Observer, 'Sayings of the Week', 2 Feb 1947

BRITISH

See also Britain, English, Irish, Scots, Welsh

1 A young Scotsman of your ability let loose upon the world with £300, what could he not do? It's almost appalling to think of; especially if he went among the English.

J. M. Barrie (1860–1937) British novelist and dramatist.
What Every Woman Knows, I

2 There are no countries in the world less known by the British than these selfsame British Islands.

George Henry Borrow (1803–81) British writer.
Lavengro, Preface

3 The British love permanence more than they love beauty.

Hugh Casson (1910–) British architect.
The Observer, 'Sayings of the Week', 14 June 1964

4 It must be owned, that the Graces do not seem to be natives of Great Britain; and I doubt, the best of us here have more of rough than polished diamond.

Earl of Chesterfield (1694–1773) English statesman.
Letter to his son, 18 Nov 1748

5 The maxim of the British people is 'Business as usual'.

Winston Churchill (1874–1965) British statesman.
Speech, Guildhall, 9 Nov 1914

6 They are the only people who like to be told how bad things are – who like to be told the worst.

Winston Churchill
Speech, 1921

7 Of all noxious animals, too, the most noxious is a tourist. And of all tourists the most vulgar, ill-bred, offensive and loathsome is the British tourist.

Francis Kilvert (1840–79) British diarist and clergyman.
Diary, 5 Apr 1870

8 The spread of personal ownership is in harmony with the deepest instincts of the British people. Few changes have done more to create one nation.

Nigel Lawson (1932–) British Conservative politician.
Speech, Jan 1988

9 It is beginning to be hinted that we are a nation of amateurs.

Lord Rosebery (1847–1929) British statesman.
Rectorial Address, Glasgow, 16 Nov 1900

10 Other nations use 'force'; we Britons alone use 'Might'.

Evelyn Waugh (1903–66) British novelist.
Scoop, Bk. II, Ch. 5

BRITISH EMPIRE

1 The loss of India would mark and consummate the downfall of the British Empire. That great organism would pass at a stroke out of life into history. From such a catastrophe there could be no recovery.
Winston Churchill (1874–1965) British statesman.
Speech to Indian Empire Society, London, 12 Dec 1930

2 I have not become the King's First Minister in order to preside over the liquidation of the British Empire.
Winston Churchill
Speech, Mansion House, 10 Nov 1942

3 It is only when you get to see and realize what India is – that she is the strength and the greatness of England – it is only then that you feel that every nerve a man may strain, every energy he may put forward, cannot be devoted to a nobler purpose than keeping tight the cords that hold India to ourselves.
Lord Curzon (1859–1925) British politician.
Speech, Southport, 15 Mar 1893

4 How is the Empire?
George V (1865–1936) King of the United Kingdom.
Last words
The Times, 21 Jan 1936

5 'Can't' will be the epitaph of the British Empire – unless we wake up in time.
Oswald Mosley (1896–1980) British politician.
Speech, Manchester, 9 Dec 1937

6 His Majesty's dominions, on which the sun never sets.
Christopher North (John Wilson; 1785–1854) Scottish writer.
Noctes Ambrosianae, 20 Apr 1829

7 The Empire is a Commonwealth of Nations.
Lord Rosebery (1847–1929) British statesman.
Speech, Adelaide, 18 Jan 1884

8 We the English seem, as it were, to have conquered and peopled half the world in a fit of absence of mind.
John Robert Seeley (1834–95) British historian.
The Expansion of England, I

BUREAUCRACY

1 A memorandum is written not to inform the reader but to protect the writer.
Dean Acheson (1893–1971) US lawyer and statesman.
Attrib.

2 The best way to kill an idea is to take it to a meeting.
Anonymous

3 I'm surprised that a government organization could do it that quickly.
Jimmy Carter (1924–) US statesman and president.
Visiting Egypt, when told that it took twenty years to build the Great Pyramid
Presidential Anecdotes (P. Boller)

4 A committee is a cul-de-sac down which ideas are lured and then quietly strangled.
Barnett Cocks (1907–) British political writer.
New Scientist, 1973

5 Whatever was required to be done, the Circumlocution Office was beforehand with all the public departments in the art of perceiving – HOW NOT TO DO IT.
Charles Dickens (1812–70) British novelist.
Little Dorrit, Bk. I, Ch. 10

6 A Royal Commission is a broody hen sitting on a china egg.
Michael Foot (1913–) British Labour politician and journalist.
Speech, House of Commons, 1964

7 A difficulty for every solution.
Herbert Samuel (1870–1963) British Liberal statesman.
Referring to the Civil Service
Attrib.

8 The working of great institutions is mainly the result of a vast mass of routine, petty malice, self interest, carelessness, and sheer mistake. Only a residual fraction is thought.
George Santayana (1863–1952) US philosopher.
The Crime of Galileo

9 My life's been a meeting, Dad, one long meeting. Even on the few committees I don't yet belong to, the agenda winks at me when I pass.
Gwyn Thomas (1913–81) British writer.
The Keep, I

10 The British civil service . . . is a beautifully designed and effective braking mechanism.
Shirley Williams (1930–) British politician.
Speech, Royal Institute of Public Administration, 11 Feb 1980

BUSINESS

See also capitalism

1 In Dublin's fair city, where the girls are so pretty,
I first set my eyes on sweet Molly Malone,
As she wheeled her wheelbarrow, through streets broad and narrow,
Crying, Cockles and mussels! alive, alive, O!

She was a fishmonger, but sure 'twas no wonder,
For so were her father and mother before.
Anonymous
Cockles and Mussels

2 Today's sales should be better than yesterday's – and worse than tomorrow's.
Anonymous

3 Who will change old lamps for new ones? . . . new lamps for old ones?
The Arabian Nights (c. 1500) A collection of tales from the East.
The History of Aladdin

4 You ask me what it is I do. Well actually, you know,
I'm partly a liaison man and partly P.R.O.
Essentially I integrate the current export drive
And basically I'm viable from ten o'clock till five.
John Betjeman (1906–84) British poet.
Executive

5 Here's the rule for bargains: 'Do other men, for they would do you.' That's the true business precept.
Charles Dickens (1812–70) British novelist.
Martin Chuzzlewit, Ch. 11

6 Whenever you see a successful business, someone once made a courageous decision.
Peter F. Drucker

7 The longest word in the English language is the one following the phrase: 'And now a word from our sponsor.'
Hal Eaton

8 A business that makes nothing but money is a poor kind of business.
Henry Ford (1863–1947) US car manufacturer.
Interview

9 No nation was ever ruined by trade.
Benjamin Franklin (1706–90) US scientist and statesman.
Essays, 'Thoughts on Commercial Subjects'

10 Remember that time is money.
Benjamin Franklin
Advice to a Young Tradesman

11 The salary of the chief executive of the large corporation is not a market award for achievement. It is frequently in the nature of a warm personal gesture by the individual to himself.
John Kenneth Galbraith (1908–) US economist.
Annals of an Abiding Liberal

12 Where wealth and freedom reign, contentment fails,
And honour sinks where commerce long prevails.
Oliver Goldsmith (1728–74) Irish-born British writer.
The Traveller

13 Cherry ripe, ripe, ripe, I cry.
Full and fair ones; come and buy.
Robert Herrick (1591–1674) English poet.
Hesperides, 'Cherry Ripe'

14 When you are skinning your customers, you should leave some skin on to grow so that you can skin them again.
Nikita Khrushchev (1894–1971) Soviet statesman.
Said to British businessmen
The Observer, 'Sayings of the Week', 28 May 1961

15 He is the only man who is for ever apologizing for his occupation.
H. L. Mencken (1880–1956) US journalist.
Referring to the businessman
Prejudices, 'Types of Men'

16 A friendship founded on business is better than a business founded on friendship.
John D. Rockefeller (1839–1937) US industrialist.

17 A dinner lubricates business.
William Scott (1745–1836) British jurist.
Life of Johnson (J. Boswell), 1791

18 The customer is always right.
H. Gordon Selfridge (1857–1947) US-born businessman.
Slogan adopted at his shops

19 A snapper-up of unconsidered trifles.
William Shakespeare (1564–1616) English dramatist.
The Winter's Tale, IV:2

20 The big print giveth and the fine print taketh away.
J. Fulton Sheen (1895–1979) US Roman Catholic archbishop.
Referring to his contract for a television appearance
Attrib.

21 People of the same trade seldom meet together but the conversation ends in a conspiracy against the public, or in some diversion to raise prices.
Adam Smith (1723–90) Scottish economist.
The Wealth of Nations

22 You never expected justice from a company, did you? They have neither a soul to lose nor a body to kick.
Sydney Smith (1771–1845) British clergyman and essayist.
Memoir (Lady Holland)

23 I have heard of a man who had a mind to sell his house, and therefore carried a piece of brick in his pocket, which he shewed as a pattern to encourage purchasers.
Jonathan Swift (1667–1745) Irish-born Anglican priest and writer.
The Drapier's Letters, 2 (4 Aug 1724)

24 It's just like having a licence to print your own money.
Lord Thomson of Fleet (1894–1976) Canadian-born British newspaper proprietor.
Speaking about commercial television
Attrib.

25 All business sagacity reduces itself in the last analysis to a judicious use of sabotage.
Thorstein Bunde Veblen (1857–1929) US social scientist.
The Nature of Peace

26 If Max gets to Heaven he won't last long. He will be chucked out for trying to pull off a merger between Heaven and Hell . . . after having secured a controlling interest in key

subsidiary companies in both places, of course.
H. G. Wells (1866–1946) British writer.
Referring to Lord Beaverbrook
Beaverbrook (A. J. P. Taylor)

27 The trouble with the profit system has always been that it was highly unprofitable to most people.
Elwyn Brooks White (1899–1985) US journalist and humorist.
Attrib.

28 For many years I thought what was good for

our country was good for General Motors, and vice versa.
Charles Erwin Wilson (1890–1961) US engineer.
Said in testimony to the Senate Armed Services Committee, Jan 1953
Attrib.

29 Business underlies everything in our national life, including our spiritual life. Witness the fact that in the Lord's Prayer the first petition is for daily bread. No one can worship God or love his neighbour on an empty stomach.
Woodrow Wilson (1856–1925) US statesman.
Speech, New York, 1912

C

CAMBRIDGE

See also England, Oxford

1 Oxford is on the whole more attractive than Cambridge to the ordinary visitor; and the traveller is therefore recommended to visit Cambridge first, or to omit it altogether if he cannot visit both.
Karl Baedeker (1801–59) German publisher.
Baedeker's Great Britain, 'From London to Oxford'

2 For Cambridge people rarely smile,
Being urban, squat, and packed with guile.
Rupert Brooke (1887–1915) British poet.
The Old Vicarage, Grantchester

3 The King to Oxford sent a troop of horse,
For Tories own no argument but force:
With equal skill to Cambridge books he sent,
For Whigs admit no force but argument.
William Browne (1692–1774) English physician.
A reply to TRAPP
Literary Anecdotes (Nichols), Vol. III

4 Spring and summer did happen in Cambridge almost every year.
Vladimir Nabokov (1899–1977) Russian-born US novelist.
The Real Life of Sebastian Knight, Ch. 5

5 This is the city of perspiring dreams.
Frederic Raphael (1931–) British author.
The Glittering Prizes: An Early Life, III

6 The King, observing with judicious eyes
The state of both his universities,
To Oxford sent a troop of horse, and why?
That learned body wanted loyalty;
To Cambridge books, as very well discerning
How much that loyal body wanted learning.
Joseph Trapp (1679–1747) English churchman and academic.
Written after George I donated the Bishop of Ely's library to Cambridge; for a reply see BROWNE
Literary Anecdotes (Nichols), Vol. III

CANNIBALISM

1 Eating people is wrong.
Michael Flanders (1922–75) British comedian and songwriter.
The Reluctant Cannibal

2 The better sort of Ishmaelites have been Christian for many centuries and will not publicly eat human flesh uncooked in Lent, without special and costly dispensation from their bishop.
Evelyn Waugh (1903–66) British novelist.
Scoop, Bk. II, Ch. 1

CAPITALISM

See also business

1 It is closing time in the gardens of the West.
Cyril Connolly (1903–74) British journalist.
The Condemned Playground

2 Property has its duties as well as its rights.
Thomas Drummond (1797–1840) British engineer and statesman.
Letter to the Earl of Donoughmore, 22 May 1838

3 If I had to give a definition of capitalism I would say: the process whereby American girls turn into American women.
Christopher Hampton (1946–) British writer and dramatist.
Savages, Sc. 16

4 It is the unpleasant and unacceptable face of capitalism but one should not suggest that the whole of British industry consists of practices of this kind.
Edward Heath (1916–) British politician and prime minister.
Referring to the Lonrho Affair
Speech, House of Commons, 15 May 1973

5 . . . militarism . . . is one of the chief

bulwarks of capitalism, and the day that militarism is undermined, capitalism will fail.
Helen Keller (1880–1968) US writer and lecturer.
The Story of My Life

6 We cannot remove the evils of capitalism without taking its source of power: ownership.
Neil Kinnock (1942–) British politician.
Tribune, 1975

7 Under capitalism we have a state in the proper sense of the word, that is, a special machine for the suppression of one class by another.
Lenin (Vladimir Ilich Ulyanov; 1870–1924) Russian revolutionary leader.
The State and Revolution, Ch. 5

8 Not every problem someone has with his girlfriend is necessarily due to the capitalist mode of production.
Herbert Marcuse (1898–1979) German-born US philosopher.
The Listener

9 Capitalist production begets, with the inexorability of a law of nature, its own negation.
Karl Marx (1818–83) German philosopher and revolutionary.
Das Kapital, Ch. 15

10 Man is the only creature that consumes without producing.
George Orwell (Eric Blair; 1903–50) British novelist.
Animal Farm, Ch. 1

11 I have gone to war too . . . I am going to fight capitalism even if it kills me. It is wrong that people like you should be comfortable and well fed while all around you people are starving.
Sylvia Pankhurst (1882–1960) British suffragette.
The Fighting Pankhursts (David Mitchell)

12 Property is theft.
Pierre Joseph Proudhon (1809–65) French socialist.
Qu'est-ce que la Propriété?, Ch. 1

13 Property is organised robbery.
George Bernard Shaw (1856–1950) Irish dramatist and critic.
Major Barbara, Preface

14 Lenin was the first to discover that capitalism 'inevitably' caused war; and he discovered this only when the First World War was already being fought. Of course he was right. Since every great state was capitalist in 1914, capitalism obviously 'caused' the First World War; but just as obviously it had 'caused' the previous generation of Peace.
A. J. P. Taylor (1906–) British historian.
The Origins of the Second World War, Ch. 6

15 The public be damned. I am working for my stockholders.
William Henry Vanderbilt (1821–85) US railway chief.
Refusing to speak to a reporter, who was seeking to find out his views on behalf of the public

CATHOLICISM

See also Christianity, Protestantism, religion

1 A priest is a man who is called Father by everyone except his own children who are obliged to call him Uncle.
Italian proverb

2 *Ad majorem Dei gloriam.*
To the greater glory of God.
Anonymous
Motto of the Jesuits

3 I expect you know my friend Evelyn Waugh, who, like you, your Holiness, is a Roman Catholic.
Randolph Churchill (1911–68) British political journalist.
Remark made during an audience with the Pope

4 I have a Catholic soul, but a Lutheran stomach.
Erasmus (1466–1536) Dutch humanist, scholar, and writer.
Replying to criticism of his failure to fast during Lent
Dictionnaire Encyclopédique

5 The Papacy is not other than the Ghost of the deceased Roman Empire, sitting crowned upon the grave thereof.
Thomas Hobbes (1588–1679) English philosopher.
Leviathan, Pt. IV, Ch. 37

6 There is no idolatry in the Mass. They believe God to be there, and they adore him.
Samuel Johnson (1709–84) British lexicographer.
Life of Johnson (J. Boswell), Vol. II

7 We know these new English Catholics. They are the last words in Protest. They are Protestants protesting against Protestantism.
D. H. Lawrence (1885–1930) British novelist.
Phoenix, 'Review of Eric Gill, *Art Nonsense*'

8 Since God has given us the papacy, let us enjoy it.
Leo X (Giovanni de' Medici; 1475–1521) Pope (1513–21).
Men of Art (T. Craven)

9 I was fired from there, finally, for a lot of things, among them my insistence that the Immaculate Conception was spontaneous combustion.
Dorothy Parker (1893–1967) US writer.
Writers at Work, First Series (Malcolm Cowley)

10 The Pope! How many divisions has *he* got?
Joseph Stalin (J. Dzhugashvili; 1879–1953) Soviet statesman.
When urged by Pierre Laval to tolerate Catholicism in the USSR to appease the Pope, 13 May 1935
The Second World War (W. S. Churchill), Vol. I, Ch. 8

11 Becoming an Anglo-Catholic must surely be a

sad business – rather like becoming an amateur conjurer.

John St Loe Strachey (1901–63) British politician.
The Coming Struggle for Power, Pt. III, Ch. 11

12 'God knows how you Protestants can be expected to have any sense of direction,' she said. 'It's different with us. I haven't been to mass for years, I've got every mortal sin on my conscience, but I know when I'm doing wrong. I'm still a Catholic.

Angus Wilson (1913–) British novelist.
The Wrong Set, 'Significant Experience'

CATS

See also animals

1 Cruel, but composed and bland,
Dumb, inscrutable and grand,
So Tiberius might have sat,
Had Tiberius been a cat.

Matthew Arnold (1822–88) British poet and critic.
Poor Matthias

2 Macavity, Macavity, there's no one like Macavity,
There never was a Cat of such deceitfulness and suavity.
He always has an alibi, and one or two to spare:
At whatever time the deed took place – MACAVITY WASN'T THERE!

T. S. Eliot (1888–1965) US-born British poet and dramatist.
Macavity: The Mystery Cat

3 I have noticed that what cats most appreciate in a human being is not the ability to produce food which they take for granted – but his or her entertainment value.

Geoffrey Household (1900–88) British writer.
Rogue Male

4 When I observed he was a fine cat, saying, 'why yes, Sir, but I have had cats whom I liked better than this'; and then as if perceiving Hodge to be out of countenance, adding, 'but he is a very fine cat, a very fine cat indeed.'

Samuel Johnson (1709–84) British lexicographer.
Life of Johnson (J. Boswell), Vol. IV

5 If a fish is the movement of water embodied, given shape, then cat is a diagram and pattern of subtle air.

Doris Lessing (1919–) British novelist.
Particularly Cats, Ch. 2

6 When I play with my cat, who knows whether she is not amusing herself with me more than I with her?

Michel de Montaigne (1533–92) French essayist.
Essais, II

7 If a dog jumps onto your lap it is because he is fond of you; but if a cat does the same thing it is because your lap is warmer.

A. N. Whitehead (1861–1947) British philosopher.
Dialogues

CAUTION

See also prudence

1 Better be safe than sorry.
Proverb

2 Don't put all your eggs in one basket.
Proverb

3 He that fights and runs away, may live to fight another day.
Proverb

4 He who sups with the devil should have a long spoon.
Proverb

5 If you trust before you try, you may repent before you die.
Proverb

6 Keep your mouth shut and your eyes open.
Proverb

7 Keep your weather-eye open.
Proverb

8 Look before you leap.
Proverb

9 And all should cry, Beware! Beware!
His flashing eyes, his floating hair!
Weave a circle round him thrice,
And close your eyes with holy dread,
For he on honey-dew hath fed,
And drunk the milk of Paradise.

Samuel Taylor Coleridge (1772–1834) British poet.
Kubla Khan

10 Chi Wen Tzu always thought three times before taking action. Twice would have been quite enough.

Confucius (K'ung Fu-tzu; 551–479 BC) Chinese philosopher.
Analects

11 Take example by your father, my boy, and be very careful o' vidders all your life.

Charles Dickens (1812–70) British novelist.
Pickwick Papers, Ch. 13

12 Don't go into Mr McGregor's garden: your Father had an accident there; he was put in a pie by Mrs McGregor.

Beatrix Potter (1866–1943) British children's writer.
The Tale of Peter Rabbit

13 The only way to be absolutely safe is never to try anything for the first time.

Magnus Pyke (1908–) British scientist, television personality, and writer.
BBC radio programme

CENSORSHIP

See also pornography, prudery

1 Whenever books are burned men also in the end are burned.
Heinrich Heine (1797–1856) German poet and writer.
Almansor

2 There is in our hands as citizens an instrument to mould the minds of the young and to create great and good and noble citizens for the future.
Edward Shortt (1862–1935) Home Secretary (1919–22); President of the British Board of Film Censors (1929–35). Referring to the British Board of Film Censors
Remark, 1929

3 Censorship is more depraving and corrupting than anything pornography can produce. ↲
Tony Smythe (1938–) Chairman of the National Council for Civil Liberties, Great Britain.
The Observer, 'Sayings of the Week', 18 Sept 1972

4 God forbid that any book should be banned. The practice is as indefensible as infanticide.
Rebecca West (Cicely Isabel Fairfield; 1892–1983) British novelist and journalist.
The Strange Necessity, 'The Tosh Horse'

CERTAINTY

See also self-confidence

1 If a man will begin with certainties, he shall end in doubts, but if he will be content to begin with doubts, he shall end in certainties.
Francis Bacon (1561–1626) English philosopher.
The Advancement of Learning, Bk. I, Ch. 5

2 Of that there is no manner of doubt –
No probable, possible shadow of doubt –
No possible doubt whatever.
W. S. Gilbert (1836–1911) British dramatist.
The Gondoliers, I

CHANCE

See also accident, luck, opportunity

1 Throw out a sprat to catch a mackerel.
Proverb

2 I returned, and saw under the sun, that the race is not to the swift, nor the battle to the strong, neither yet bread to the wise, nor yet riches to men of understanding, nor yet favour to men of skill; but time and chance happeneth to them all.
For man also knoweth not his time: as the fishes that are taken in an evil net, and as the birds that are caught in the snare; so are the sons of men snared in an evil time, when it falleth suddenly upon them.
Bible: Ecclesiastes
9:11–12

3 I shot an arrow into the air,

It fell to earth, I knew not where.
Henry Wadsworth Longfellow (1807–82) US poet.
The Arrow and the Song

4 Accidental and fortuitous concurrence of atoms.
Lord Palmerston (1784–1865) British statesman.
Speech, House of Commons, 1857

5 When you take the bull by the horns . . . what happens is a toss up.
William Pett Ridge (1860–1930) British novelist.
Love at Paddington Green, Ch. 4

CHANGE

See also conservatism, constancy, progress, transience

1 Can the Ethiopian change his skin, or the leopard his spots? then may ye also do good, that are accustomed to do evil.
Bible: Jeremiah
13:23

2 All reform except a moral one will prove unavailing.
Thomas Carlyle (1795–1881) Scottish historian and essayist.
Critical and Miscellaneous Essays, 'Corn Law Rhymes'

3 The time's come: there's a terrific thunder-cloud advancing upon us, a mighty storm is coming to freshen us up. . . . It's going to blow away all this idleness and indifference, and prejudice against work. . . . I'm going to work, and in twenty-five or thirty years' time every man and woman will be working.
Anton Chekhov (1860–1904) Russian dramatist.
Three Sisters, I

4 Variety's the very spice of life
That gives it all its flavour.
William Cowper (1731–1800) British poet.
The Task

5 Most women set out to try to change a man, and when they have changed him they do not like him.
Marlene Dietrich (Maria Magdalene von Losch; 1904–) German-born film star.
Attrib.

6 Come mothers and fathers
Throughout the land
And don't criticize
What you can't understand.
Bob Dylan (Robert Allen Zimmerman; 1941–) US popular singer.
The Times They Are A-Changin'

7 Man is so made that he can only find relaxation from one kind of labour by taking up another.
Anatole France (Jacques Anatole François Thibault; 1844–1924) French writer.
The Crime of Sylvestre Bonnard

8 One must never lose time in vainly regretting the past nor in complaining about the changes

which cause us discomfort, for change is the very essence of life.
Anatole France
Attrib.

9 Everything flows and nothing stays.
Heraclitus (c. 535 – c. 475 BC) Greek philosopher.
Cratylus (Plato), 402a

10 You can't step into the same river twice.
Heraclitus
Cratylus (Plato), 402a

11 Change is not made without inconvenience, even from worse to better.
Richard Hooker (c. 1554 – 1600) English theologian.
English Dictionary (Johnson), Preface

12 There is a certain relief in change, even though it be from bad to worse; as I have found in travelling in a stage-coach, that it is often a comfort to shift one's position and be bruised in a new place.
Washington Irving (1783 – 1859) US writer.
Tales of a Traveller, 'To the Reader'

13 An old Dutch farmer, who remarked to a companion once that it was not best to swap horses in mid-stream.
Abraham Lincoln (1809 – 65) US statesman.
Speech, 9 June 1864

14 Well, I find that a change of nuisances is as good as a vacation.
David Lloyd George (1863 – 1945) British Liberal statesman.
On being asked how he maintained his cheerfulness when beset by numerous political obstacles
Attrib.

15 The wind of change is blowing through the continent. Whether we like it or not, this growth of national consciousness is a political fact.
Harold Macmillan (1894 – 1986) British politician and prime minister.
Speech, South African Parliament, 3 Feb 1960

16 At last he rose, and twitched his mantle blue: To-morrow to fresh woods, and pastures new.
John Milton (1608 – 74) English poet.
Lycidas

17 Poor old Daddy – just one of those sturdy old plants left over from the Edwardian Wilderness, that can't understand why the sun isn't shining any more.
John Osborne (1929 –) British dramatist.
Look Back in Anger, II.2

18 Through all the changing scenes of life.
Nahum Tate (1652 – 1715) Irish-born English poet.
New Version of the Psalms, 'Through all the Changing'

19 And slowly answer'd Arthur from the barge: 'The old order changeth, yielding place to new, And God fulfils himself in many ways.'
Alfred, Lord Tennyson (1809 – 92) British poet.
Idylls of the King, 'The Passing of Arthur'

CHARACTER

1 Monday's child is fair of face, Tuesday's child is full of grace; Wednesday's child is full of woe, Thursday's child has far to go; Friday's child is loving and giving, Saturday's child works hard for its living; and the child that's born on the Sabbath day, is fair and wise and good and gay.
Proverb

2 If you wish to know what a man is, place him in authority.
Yugoslav Proverb

3 Every man is as Heaven made him, and sometimes a great deal worse.
Miguel de Cervantes (1547 – 1616) Spanish novelist.
Don Quixote, Pt. II, Ch. 4

4 He was as fresh as is the month of May.
Geoffrey Chaucer (c. 1342 – 1400) English poet.
Referring to the squire
The Canterbury Tales, Prologue

5 Souninge in moral vertu was his speche, And gladly wolde he lerne, and gladly teche.
Geoffrey Chaucer
Referring to the clerk
The Canterbury Tales, Prologue

6 From a timid, shy girl I had become a woman of resolute character, who could not longer be frightened by the struggle with troubles.
Anna Dostoevsky (1846 – 1918) Russian diarist and writer.
Dostoevsky Portrayed by His Wife

7 What e'r he did was done with so much ease,
In him alone, 'twas Natural to please.
John Dryden (1631 – 1700) British poet and dramatist.
Absalom and Achitophel, I

8 A patronizing disposition always has its meaner side.
George Eliot (Mary Ann Evans; 1819 – 80) British novelist.
Adam Bede

9 I am a man for whom the outside world exists.
Théophile Gautier (1811 – 72) French poet and critic.
Journal des Goncourt, 1 May 1857

10 Talent develops in quiet places, character in the full current of human life.
Goethe (1749 – 1832) German poet and dramatist.
Torquato Tasso, I

11 Strong enough to answer back to desires, to despise distinctions, and a whole man in himself, polished and well-rounded.
Horace (Quintus Horatius Flaccus; 65 – 8 BC) Roman poet.
Satires, II

12 A tart temper never mellows with age, and a

sharp tongue is the only edged tool that grows keener with constant use.
Washington Irving (1783–1859) US writer.
The Sketch Book, 'Rip Van Winkle'

13 What is character but the determination of incident? What is incident but the illustration of character?
Henry James (1843–1916) US novelist.
Partial Portraits, 'The Art of Fiction'

14 He was a vicious man, but very kind to me. If you call a dog *Hervey*, I shall love him.
Samuel Johnson (1709–84) British lexicographer.
Life of Johnson (J. Boswell), Vol. I

15 A very unclubable man.
Samuel Johnson
Referring to Sir John Hawkins
Life of Johnson (J. Boswell), Vol. I

16 I recognize that I am made up of several persons and that the person that at the moment has the upper hand will inevitably give place to another. But which is the real one? All of them or none?
W. Somerset Maugham (1874–1965) British novelist.
A Writer's Notebook

17 It is with narrow-souled people as with narrow-necked bottles: the less they have in them, the more noise they make in pouring it out.
Alexander Pope (1688–1744) British poet.
Thoughts on Various Subjects

18 Children with Hyacinth's temperament don't know better as they grow older; they merely know more.
Saki (Hector Hugh Munro; 1870–1916) British writer.
Hyacinth

19 There is no such thing as psychological. Let us say that one can improve the biography of the person.
Jean-Paul Sartre (1905–80) French writer.
The Divided Self (R. D. Laing), Ch. 8

20 A certain person may have, as you say, a wonderful presence: I do not know. What I do know is that he has a perfectly delightful absence.
Idries Shah (1924–) British author.
Reflections, 'Presence and Absence'

21 His life was gentle; and the elements
So mix'd in him that Nature might stand up
And say to all the world 'This was a man!'
William Shakespeare (1564–1616) English dramatist.
Referring to Brutus
Julius Caesar, V:5

22 A man of great common sense and good taste, – meaning thereby a man without originality or moral courage.
George Bernard Shaw (1856–1950) Irish dramatist and critic.
Referring to Julius Caesar
Caesar and Cleopatra, Notes

23 I'm not hard – I'm frightfully soft. But I will not be hounded.
Margaret Thatcher (1925–) British politician and prime minister.
Daily Mail, 1972

24 He is a man of brick. As if he was born as a baby literally of clay and decades of exposure have baked him to the colour and hardness of brick.
John Updike (1932–) US novelist.
Rabbit, Run

25 There aren't many left like him nowadays, what with education and whisky the price it is.
Evelyn Waugh (1903–66) British novelist.
Decline and Fall, Pt. I, Ch. 7

26 I've met a lot of hardboiled eggs in my time, but you're twenty minutes.
Billy Wilder (Samuel Wilder; 1906–) Austrian-born US film director.
Ace in the Hole

CHARITY

See also generosity, help, parasites

1 Charity begins at home.
Proverb

2 The living need charity more than the dead.
George Arnold (1834–65) US poet and humorist.
The Jolly Old Pedagogue

3 In charity there is no excess.
Francis Bacon (1561–1626) English philosopher.
Essays, 'Of Goodness, and Goodness of Nature'

4 Feed the World
Let them know it's Christmas.
Band Aid
Song written to raise money for the relief of famine in Ethiopia
Do They Know It's Christmas?

5 Don't bother to thank me. I know what a perfectly ghastly season it's been for you Spanish dancers.
Tallulah Bankhead (1903–68) US actress.
Said on dropping fifty dollars into a tambourine held out by a Salvation Army collector
With Malice Toward All (D. Hermann)

6 Though I speak with the tongues of men and of angels, and have not charity, I am become as sounding brass, or a tinkling cymbal.
And though I have the gift of prophecy, and understand all mysteries, and all knowledge; and though I have all faith, so that I could remove mountains, and have not charity, I am nothing.
And though I bestow all my goods to feed the poor, and though I give my body to be burned, and have not charity, it profiteth me nothing.
Charity suffereth long, and is kind; charity en-

vieth not; charity vaunteth not itself, is not puffed up,

Doth not behave itself unseemly, seeketh not her own, is not easily provoked, thinketh no evil;

Rejoiceth not in iniquity, but rejoiceth in the truth;

Beareth all things, believeth all things, hopeth all things, endureth all things.

Charity never faileth: but whether there be prophecies, they shall fail; whether there be tongues, they shall cease; whether there be knowledge, it shall vanish away.

For we know in part, and we prophesy in part. But when that which is perfect is come, then that which is in part shall be done away.

When I was a child, I spake as a child, I understood as a child, I thought as a child: but when I became a man, I put away childish things.

For now we see through a glass, darkly; but then face to face: now I know in part; but then shall I know even as also I am known.

And now abideth faith, hope, charity, these three; but the greatest of these is charity.

Bible: I Corinthians
13:1–13

7 Now as touching things offered unto idols, we know that we all have knowledge. Knowledge puffeth up, but charity edifieth.

Bible: I Corinthians
8:1

8 But a certain Samaritan, as he journeyed, came where he was: and when he saw him, he had compassion on him,

And went to him, and bound up his wounds, pouring in oil and wine, and set him on his own beast, and brought him to an inn, and took care of him.

And on the morrow when he departed, he took out two pence, and gave them to the host, and said unto him, Take care of him; and whatsoever thou spendest more, when I come again, I will repay thee.

Bible: Luke
10:33–35

9 All our doings without charity are nothing worth.

The Book of Common Prayer
Collect, Quinquagesima Sunday

10 Charity begins at home, is the voice of the world.

Thomas Browne (1605–82) English physician and writer.
Religio Medici, Pt. II

11 I have always heard, Sancho, that doing good to base fellows is like throwing water into the sea.

Miguel de Cervantes (1547–1616) Spanish novelist.
Don Quixote, Pt. I, Ch. 23

12 Charity is the power of defending that which we know to be indefensible. Hope is the

power of being cheerful in circumstances which we know to be desperate.

G. K. Chesterton (1874–1936) British writer.
Heretics, Ch. 12

13 No people do so much harm as those who go about doing good.

Mandell Creighton (1843–1901) British churchman.
Life

14 I'm not interested in the bloody system! Why has he no food? Why is he starving to death?

Bob Geldof (1952–) Irish rock musician.
The Observer, 'Sayings of the Week', 27 Oct 1985

15 She's the sort of woman who lives for others – you can always tell the others by their hunted expression.

C. S. Lewis (1898–1963) British academic and writer.
The Screwtape Letters

16 In the field of world policy; I would dedicate this nation to the policy of the good neighbor.

Franklin D. Roosevelt (1882–1945) US Democratic president.
First Inaugural Address, 4 Mar 1933

17 When they will not give a doit to relieve a lame beggar, they will lay out ten to see a dead Indian.

William Shakespeare (1564–1616) English dramatist.
The Tempest, II:2

18 If you see anybody fallen by the wayside and lying in the ditch, it isn't much good climbing into the ditch and lying by his side.

H. R. L. Sheppard (1880–1937) British clergyman.
Dick Sheppard (Carolyn Scott)

19 The white man knows how to make everything, but he does not know how to distribute it.

Sitting Bull (c. 1834–90) US Sioux Indian chief.
Attrib.

20 You find people ready enough to do the Samaritan, without the oil and twopence.

Sydney Smith (1771–1845) British clergyman and essayist.
Memoir (Lady Holland)

21 To keep a lamp burning we have to keep putting oil in it.

Mother Teresa (Agnes Gonxha Bojaxhui; 1910–) Yugoslavian missionary in Calcutta.
Time, 'Saints Among Us', 29 Dec 1975

22 As for doing good, that is one of the professions which are full.

Henry David Thoreau (1817–62) US writer.
Walden, 'Economy'

23 I have always depended on the kindness of strangers.

Tennessee Williams (1911–83) US dramatist.
A Streetcar Named Desire, II:3

CHARM

1 It's a sort of bloom on a woman. If you have

it, you don't need to have anything else; and
if you don't have it, it doesn't much matter
what else you have.

J. M. Barrie (1860–1937) British novelist and dramatist.
What Every Woman Knows, I

2 All charming people have something to
conceal, usually their total dependence on the
appreciation of others.

Cyril Connolly (1903–74) British journalist.
Enemies of Promise, Ch. 16

3 Oozing charm from every pore,
He oiled his way around the floor.

Alan Jay Lerner (1918–86) US songwriter.
My Fair Lady, II:1

4 It is absurd to divide people into good and
bad. People are either charming or tedious.

Oscar Wilde (1854–1900) Irish-born British dramatist.
Lady Windermere's Fan, I

CHAUCER

1 Chaucer notwithstanding the praises
bestowed on him. I think obscene and
contemptible; he owes his celebrity merely to
his antiquity.

Lord Byron (1788–1824) British poet.
Attrib.

2 Chaucer, I confess, is a rough diamond; and
must be polished e'er he shines.

John Dryden (1631–1700) British poet and dramatist.
Preface to the Fables

3 I read Chaucer still with as much pleasure as
any of our poets. He is a master of manners
and of description and the first tale-teller in
the true enlivened, natural way.

Alexander Pope (1688–1744) British poet.
Attrib.

4 Mr. C. had talent, but he couldn't spel. No
man has a right to be a lit'rary man onless he
knows how to spel. It is a pity that Chawcer,
who had geneyus, was so unedicated. He's
the wus speller I know of.

Artemus Ward (Charles Farrar Browne; 1834–67) US
humorous writer.
Chaucer's Poems

CHILDREN

See also babies, family, innocence of childhood, youth

1 Spare the rod and spoil the child.
Proverb

2 There's only one pretty child in the world,
and every mother has it.
Proverb

3 It was no wonder that people were so
horrible when they started life as children.

Kingsley Amis (1922–) British novelist.
One Fat Englishman, Ch. 14

4 Only those in the last stage of disease could

believe that children are true judges of
character.

W. H. Auden (1907–73) British poet.
The Orators, 'Journal of an Airman'

5 Children sweeten labours, but they make
misfortunes more bitter.

Francis Bacon (1561–1626) English philosopher.
Essays, 'Of Parents and Children'

6 Children have never been very good at
listening to their elders, but they have never
failed to imitate them.

James Baldwin (1924–87) US writer.
Esquire, 1960

7 I am married to Beatrice Salkeld, a painter.
We have no children, except me.

Brendan Behan (1923–64) Irish playwright.
Attrib.

8 I wish I'd been a mixed infant.

Brendan Behan
The Hostage, II

9 Alas! That such affected tricks
Should flourish in a child of six!

Hilaire Belloc (1870–1953) French-born British poet.
Cautionary Tales, 'Godolphin Horne'

10 A trick that everyone abhors
In little girls is slamming doors.

Hilaire Belloc
Cautionary Tales, 'Rebecca'

11 Desire not a multitude of unprofitable
children, neither delight in ungodly sons.

Bible: Ecclesiasticus
16:1

12 But when Jesus saw it, he was much
displeased, and said unto them. Suffer the
little children to come unto me, and forbid
them not: for of such is the kingdom of God.

Bible: Mark
10:14

13 Verily I say unto you, Except ye be
converted, and become as little children, ye
shall not enter into the kingdom of heaven.

Bible: Matthew
18:3

14 And whoso shall receive one such little child
in my name receiveth me.
But whoso shall offend one of these little ones
which believe in me, it were better for him
that a millstone were hanged about his neck,
and that he were drowned in the depth of
the sea.

Bible: Matthew
18:5–6

15 He that spareth his rod hateth his son: but
he that loveth him chasteneth him betimes.

Bible: Proverbs
13:24

16 You can do anything with children if you only play with them.
Bismarck (1815–98) German statesman.
Attrib.

17 'Twas on a Holy Thursday, their innocent faces clean,
The children walking two and two, in red and blue and green.
William Blake (1757–1827) British poet.
Songs of Innocence, 'Holy Thursday'

18 There is no finer investment for any community than putting milk into babies.
Winston Churchill (1874–1965) British statesman.
Radio Broadcast, 21 Mar 1943

19 Boys do not grow up gradually. They move forward in spurts like the hands of clocks in railway stations.
Cyril Connolly (1903–74) British journalist.
Enemies of Promise, Ch. 18

20 It is only rarely that one can see in a little boy the promise of a man, but one can almost always see in a little girl the threat of a woman.
Alexandre Dumas, fils (1824–95) French writer.
Attrib.

21 Anybody who hates children and dogs can't be all bad.
W. C. Fields (1880–1946) US actor.
Attrib.

22 To bear many children is considered not only a religious blessing but also an investment. The greater their number, some Indians reason, the more alms they can beg.
Indira Gandhi (1917–84) Indian stateswoman.
New York Review of Books, 'Indira's Coup' (Oriana Fallaci)

23 Three little maids from school are we,
Pert as a school-girl well can be,
Filled to the brim with girlish glee.
W. S. Gilbert (1836–1911) British dramatist.
The Mikado, I

24 Look at little Johnny there,
Little Johnny Head-in-Air.
Heinrich Hoffman (1809–74) German writer.
Struwwelpeter, 'Johnny Head-in-Air'

25 Anything to me is sweeter
Than to see Shock-headed Peter.
Heinrich Hoffman
Struwwelpeter, 'Shock-headed Peter'

26 The business of being a child interests a child not at all. Children very rarely play at being other children.
David Holloway (1924–) Literary editor.
The Daily Telegraph, 15 December 1966

27 One of the most obvious facts about grown-ups to a child is that they have forgotten what it is like to be a child.
Randall Jarrell (1914–65) US author.
Third Book of Criticism

28 A child deserves the maximum respect; if you ever have something disgraceful in mind, don't ignore your son's tender years.
Juvenal (Decimus Junius Juvenalis; 60–130 AD) Roman satirist.
Satires, XIV

29 The real menace in dealing with a five-year-old is that in no time at all you begin to sound like a five-year-old.
Jean Kerr (1923–) US dramatist.
Please Don't Eat the Daisies

30 At every step the child should be allowed to meet the real experiences of life; the thorns should never be plucked from his roses.
Ellen Key (Karolina Sofia Key; 1849–1926) Swedish writer.
The Century of the Child, Ch. 3

31 Boys are capital fellows in their own way, among their mates; but they are unwholesome companions for grown people.
Charles Lamb (1775–1834) British essayist.
Essays of Elia, 'The Old and the New Schoolmaster'

32 A child's a plaything for an hour.
Mary Lamb (1764–1847) Sister of Charles Lamb.
Parental Recollections

33 Kids haven't changed much, but parents seem increasingly unhappy with the child raising phase of their lives.
Penelope Leach British writer and child-care specialist.
Remark, Oct 1988

34 Where are the children I might have had? You may suppose I might have wanted them. Drowned to the accompaniment of the rattling of a thousand douche bags.
Malcolm Lowry (1909–57) British novelist.
Under the Volcano, Ch. 10

35 Part of the reason for the ugliness of adults, in a child's eyes, is that the child is usually looking upwards, and few faces are at their best when seen from below.
George Orwell (Eric Blair; 1903–50) British novelist.
Essays

36 The nice thing about having relatives' kids around is that they go home.
Cliff Richard (1940–) British pop singer.
Remark, Nov 1988

37 Parents learn a lot from their children about coping with life.
Muriel Spark (1918–) British novelist.
The Comforters, Ch. 6

38 There are only two things a child will share willingly – communicable diseases and his mother's age.
Dr Benjamin Spock (1903–) US pediatrician and psychiatrist.
Attrib.

39 I have a big house – and I hide a lot.
Mary Ure (1933–75) British actress.
Explaining how she coped with her large family of children
Attrib.

40 Never have children, only grandchildren.
Gore Vidal (1925–) US novelist.
Two Sisters

41 The English are growing demented about children. When I was a boy the classroom had icicles inside every window at this time of year. We were savagely beaten three times a week . . .
Auberon Waugh (1939–) British novelist.
The Diaries of Auberon Waugh 1976–1985, 'January 25, 1979'

42 A food is not necessarily essential just because your child hates it.
Katherine Whitehorn (1926–) British journalist.
How to Survive Children

CHIVALRY

See also courtesy

1 A gentleman is any man who wouldn't hit a woman with his hat on.
Fred Allen (1894–1956) US comedian.
Attrib.

2 Even nowadays a man can't step up and kill a woman without feeling just a bit unchivalrous.
Robert Benchley (1889–1945) US humorist.
Chips off the Old Benchley, 'Down in Front'

3 Somebody has said, that a king may make a nobleman, but he cannot make a gentleman.
Edmund Burke (1729–97) British politician.
Letter to William Smith, 29 Jan 1795

4 He was a verray parfit gentil knight.
Geoffrey Chaucer (c. 1342–1400) English poet.
Referring to the knight
The Canterbury Tales, Prologue

5 Madame, I would have given you another!
Alfred Jarry (1873–1907) French surrealist dramatist.
On being reprimanded by a woman for firing his pistol in the vicinity of her child, who might have been killed
Recollections of a Picture Dealer (A. Vollard)

6 Some say that the age of chivalry is past, that the spirit of romance is dead. The age of chivalry is never past, so long as there is a wrong left unredressed on earth.
Charles Kingsley (1819–75) British writer.
Life (Mrs C. Kingsley), Vol. II, Ch. 28

7 For he's one of Nature's Gentlemen, the best of every time.
W. J. Linton (1812–97) British writer.
Nature's Gentleman

8 It is almost a definition of a gentleman to say that he is one who never inflicts pain.
Cardinal Newman (1801–90) British theologian.
The Idea of a University, 'Knowledge and Religious Duty'

9 O, young Lochinvar is come out of the west,

Through all the wide Border his steed was the best.
Walter Scott (1771–1832) Scottish novelist.
Marmion, V

10 So faithful in love, and so dauntless in war, There never was knight like the young Lochinvar.
Walter Scott
Marmion, V

11 A bow-shot from her bower-eaves, He rode between the barley-sheaves, The sun came dazzling thro' the leaves And flamed upon the brazen graves Of bold Sir Lancelot.
Alfred, Lord Tennyson (1809–92) British poet.
The Lady of Shalott, Pt. III

CHOICE

1 Any colour, so long as it's black.
Henry Ford (1863–1947) US car manufacturer.
Referring to the colour options offered for the Model-T Ford car
Attrib.

2 Two roads diverged in a wood, and I – I took the one less traveled by, And that has made all the difference.
Robert Frost (1875–1963) US poet.
The Road Not Taken

3 More ways of killing a cat than choking her with cream.
Charles Kingsley (1819–75) British writer.
Westward Ho!, Ch. 20

4 We have to believe in free will. We've got no choice.
Isaac Bashevis Singer (1904–) Polish-born US writer.
The Times, 21 June 1982

5 The American Standard translation *orders* men to triumph over sin, and you can call sin ignorance. The King James translation makes a promise in 'Thou shalt', meaning that men will surely triumph over sin. But the Hebrew word, the word *timshel* – 'Thou mayest' – that gives a choice. It might be the most important word in the world. That says the way is open. . . . For if 'Thou mayest' – it is also true that 'Thou mayest not'.
John Steinbeck (1902–68) US novelist
Referring to Genesis, 4:7
East of Eden, Ch. 24

CHRISTIANITY

See also Catholicism, Protestantism, religion

1 There is a green hill far away, Without a city wall, Where the dear Lord was crucified, Who died to save us all.
C. F. Alexander (1818–95) British hymn writer.
There is a Green Hill Far Away

2 'Christianity, of course but why journalism?'
Arthur Balfour (1848–1930) British statesman.
In reply to Frank Harris's remark, '. . . all the faults of the age
come from Christianity and journalism'
Autobiography (Margot Asquith), Ch. 10

3 Onward, Christian soldiers,
Marching as to war,
With the Cross of Jesus
Going on before.
Sabine Baring-Gould (1834–1924) British author and
hymn writer.
Onward Christian Soldiers

4 Beware lest any man spoil you through
philosophy and vain deceit, after the tradition
of men, after the rudiments of the world, and
not after Christ.
Bible: Colossians
2:8

5 Where there is neither Greek nor Jew,
circumcision nor uncircumcision, Barbarian,
Scythian, bond nor free; but Christ is all, and
in all.
Bible: Colossians
3:11

6 Take heed to yourselves, that your heart be
not deceived, and ye turn aside, and serve
other gods, and worship them.
Bible: Deuteronomy
11:16

7 There is neither Jew nor Greek, there is
neither bond nor free, there is neither male
nor female: for ye are all one in Christ Jesus.
Bible: Galatians
3:28

8 But the fruit of the Spirit is love, joy, peace,
longsuffering, gentleness, goodness, faith,
Meekness, temperance: against such there is
no law.
Bible: Galatians
5:22–23

9 Therefore the Lord himself shall give you a
sign; Behold, a virgin shall conceive, and
bear a son, and shall call his name Immanuel.
Butter and honey shall he eat, that he may
know to refuse the evil, and choose the good.
Bible: Isaiah
7:14–15

10 He shall feed his flock like a shepherd: he
shall gather the lambs with his arm, and
carry them in his bosom, and shall gently
lead those that are with young.
Bible: Isaiah
40:11

11 He it is, who coming after me is preferred
before me, whose shoe's latchet I am not
worthy to unloose.
Bible: John
1:27

12 The next day John seeth Jesus coming unto
him, and saith, Behold the Lamb of God,
which taketh away the sin of the world.
Bible: John
1:29

13 For God so loved the world, that he gave his
only begotten Son, that whosoever believeth
in him should not perish, but have everlasting
life.
Bible: John
3:16

14 Then spake Jesus again unto them, saying, I
am the light of the world: he that followeth
me shall not walk in darkness, but shall have
the light of life.
Bible: John
8:12

15 I am the good shepherd: the good shepherd
giveth his life for the sheep.
Bible: John
10:11

16 Jesus said unto her, I am the resurrection,
and the life: he that believeth in me, though
he were dead, yet shall he live.
Bible: John
11:25

17 Jesus saith unto him, I am the way, the
truth, and the life: no man cometh unto the
Father, but by me.
Bible: John
14:6

18 Come unto me, all ye that labour and are
heavy laden, and I will give you rest.
Take my yoke upon you, and learn of me; for I
am meek and lowly in heart: and ye shall find
rest unto your souls.
For my yoke is easy, and my burden is light.
Bible: Matthew
11:28–30

19 Then said Jesus unto his disciples, If any man
will come after me, let him deny himself, and
take up his cross, and follow me.
Bible: Matthew
16:24

20 How very hard it is
To be a Christian!
Robert Browning (1812–89) British poet.
Easter-Day, I

21 It was just one of those parties which got out
of hand.
Lenny Bruce (1925–66) US comedian.
Referring to the Crucifixion
The Guardian, 10 May 1979

22 He who begins by loving Christianity better
than Truth will proceed by loving his own
sect or church better than Christianity, and
end by loving himself better than all.
Samuel Taylor Coleridge (1772–1834) British poet.
Aids to Reflection: Moral and Religious Aphorisms

23 His Christianity was muscular.

Benjamin Disraeli (1804–81) British statesman.
Endymion, Bk. 1, Ch. 14

24 Christianity has done a great deal for love by making a sin of it.

Anatole France (Jacques Anatole François Thibault; 1844–1924) French writer.
The Garden of Epicurus

25 What about it? Do you want to crucify the boy?

Lew Grade (Lewis Winogradsky; 1906–) British film and TV producer.
Referring to the revelation that an actor portraying Christ on television was living with a woman to whom he was not married
Attrib.

26 Christianity is part of the Common Law of England.

Matthew Hale (1609–76) English judge.
Historia Placitorum Coronae (ed. Sollom Emlyn)

27 Tell me the old, old story
Of unseen things above,
Of Jesus and His glory
Of Jesus and His love.

Katherine Hankey (1834–1911) British hymn writer.
Tell Me the Old, Old Story

28 A local cult called Christianity.

Thomas Hardy (1840–1928) British novelist.
The Dynasts, I:6

29 The Christian religion not only was at first attended with miracles, but even at this day cannot be believed by any reasonable person without one. Mere reason is insufficient to convince us of its veracity: and whoever is moved by faith to assent to it, is conscious of a continued miracle in his own person, which subverts all the principles of his understanding, and gives him a determination to believe what is most contrary to custom and experience.

David Hume (1711–76) Scottish philosopher.
Essays, 'Of Miracles'

30 Christianity accepted as given a metaphysical system derived from several already existing and mutually incompatible systems.

Aldous Huxley (1894–1964) British novelist.
Grey Eminence, Ch. 3

31 There must be several young women who would render the Christian life intensely difficult to him if only you could persuade him to marry one of them.

C. S. Lewis (1898–1963) British academic and writer.
The Screwtape Letters

32 Ride on! ride on in majesty!
In lowly pomp ride on to die.

Henry Hart Milman (1791–1868) British poet and historian.
Ride On

33 Fight the good fight with all thy might,

Christ is thy strength and Christ thy right,
Lay hold on life, and it shall be
Thy joy and crown eternally.

John Monsell (1811–75) British hymn writer.
Hymn

34 No kingdom has ever had as many civil wars as the kingdom of Christ.

Baron de Montesquieu (1689–1755) French writer.
Lettres persanes

35 I call Christianity the one great curse, the one enormous and innermost perversion, the one great instinct of revenge, for which no means are too venomous, too underhand, too underground and too petty – I call it the one immortal blemish of mankind.

Friedrich Wilhelm Nietzsche (1844–1900) German philosopher.
The Antichrist

36 Christianity has made of death a terror which was unknown to the gay calmness of the Pagan.

Ouida (Marie Louise de la Ramée; 1839–1908) British novelist.
The Failure of Christianity

37 All hail, the power of Jesus' name!
Let angels prostrate fall.

Edward Perronet (1726–92) British hymn writer.
Hymn

38 Whether you think Jesus was God or not, you must admit that he was a first-rate political economist.

George Bernard Shaw (1856–1950) Irish dramatist and critic.
Androcles and the Lion, Preface, 'Jesus as Economist'

39 Who dreamed that Christ has died in vain?
He walks again on the Seas of Blood,
He comes in the terrible Rain.

Edith Sitwell (1887–1964) British poet and writer.
The Shadow of Cain

40 The Church's one foundation
Is Jesus Christ her Lord;
She is His new creation
By water and the Word.

Samuel. J. Stone (1839–1901) US hymn writer.
Hymn

41 Well, you might try getting crucified and rising again on the third day.

Talleyrand (Charles Maurice de Talleyrand-Périgord; 1754–1838) French politician.
Giving his opinion upon what action might impress the French peasantry
Attrib.

42 Christianity is the most materialistic of all great religions.

William Temple (1881–1944) British churchman.
Reading in St John's Gospel, Vol. I, Introduction

43 And so the Word had breath, and wrought
With human hands the creed of creeds
In loveliness of perfect deeds,

More strong than all poetic thought.
Alfred, Lord Tennyson (1809–92) British poet.
In Memoriam A.H.H., XXXVI

44 The blood of the martyrs is the seed of the Church.
Tertullian (c. 160–225 AD) Carthaginian father of the church.
Traditional misquotation: more accurately, 'Our numbers increase as often as you cut us down: the blood of Christians is the seed.'
Apologeticus, L

45 See how these Christians love one another.
Tertullian
Apologeticus, XXXIX

46 Fraser . . . left his children unbaptized – his wife did it secretly in the washing basin.
Virginia Woolf (1882–1941) British novelist.
Jacob's Room, Ch. 9

CHRISTMAS

See also Christianity

1 I have often thought, says Sir Roger, it happens very well that Christmas should fall out in the Middle of Winter.
Joseph Addison (1672–1719) British essayist.
The Spectator, 269

2 Once in royal David's city
Stood a lowly cattle shed,
Where a Mother laid her Baby
In a manger for His bed:
Mary was that Mother mild,
Jesus Christ her little Child.
C. F. Alexander (1818–95) British hymn writer.
Once in Royal David's City

3 As I sat on a sunny bank,
On Christmas Day in the morning,
I spied three ships come sailing by.
Anonymous
As I sat on a Sunny Bank

4 God rest you merry, gentlemen,
Let nothing you dismay.
Anonymous
God Rest you Merry

5 The holly and the ivy,
When they are both full grown,
Of all the trees that are in the wood,
The holly bears the crown.
The rising of the sun
And the running of the deer,
The playing of the merry organ,
Sweet singing in the choir.
Anonymous
The Holly and the Ivy

6 For unto us a child is born, unto us a son is given: and the government shall be upon his shoulder: and his name shall be called Wonderful, Counsellor, The mighty God, The everlasting Father, The Prince of Peace.
Of the increase of his government and peace

there shall be no end, upon the throne of David, and upon his kingdom, to order it, and to establish it with judgment and with justice from henceforth even for ever. The zeal of the Lord of hosts will perform this.
Bible: Isaiah
9:6–7

7 And she brought forth her firstborn son, and wrapped him in swaddling clothes, and laid him in a manger; because there was no room for them in the inn.
Bible: Luke
2:7

8 And there were in the same country shepherds abiding in the field, keeping watch over their flock by night.
And, lo, the angel of the Lord came upon them, and the glory of the Lord shone round about them: and they were sore afraid.
And the angel said unto them, Fear not: for, behold, I bring you good tidings of great joy, which shall be to all people.
Bible: Luke
2:8–10

9 Now when Jesus was born in Bethlehem of Judaea in the days of Herod the king, behold, there came wise men from the east to Jerusalem,
Saying, Where is he that is born King of the Jews? for we have seen his star in the east, and are come to worship him.
When Herod the king had heard these things, he was troubled, and all Jerusalem with him.
Bible: Matthew
2:1–3

10 And when they were come into the house, they saw the young child with Mary his mother, and fell down, and worshipped him: and when they had opened their treasures, they presented unto him gifts; gold, and frankincense, and myrrh.
And being warned of God in a dream that they should not return to Herod, they departed into their own country another way.
Bible: Matthew
2:11–12

11 O little town of Bethlehem,
How still we see thee lie;
Above thy deep and dreamless sleep
The silent stars go by.
Phillips Brooks (1835–93) US Episcopal bishop.
O Little Town of Bethlehem

12 Christians awake, salute the happy morn,
Whereon the Saviour of the world was born.
John Byrom (1692–1763) British poet and hymn writer.
Hymn for Christmas Day

13 Fortified in their front parlours, at Yuletide men
    are the more murderous. Drunk, they defy battle-

axes, bellow of whale-bone and dung.
Geoffrey Hill (1932–   ) British poet.
Mercian Hymns, XXVI, 'Offa's Bestiary'

14 'Twas the night before Christmas, when all through the house
Not a creature was stirring, not even a mouse;
The stockings were hung by the chimney with care,
In hopes that St Nicholas soon would be there.
Clement Clarke Moore (1779–1863) US writer.
In Troy Sentinel, 23 Dec 1823, 'A Visit from St. Nicholas'

15 Good King Wenceslas looked out,
On the Feast of Stephen;
When the snow lay round about,
Deep and crisp and even.
John Mason Neale (1818–66) British churchman.
Good King Wenceslas

16 O come all ye faithful,
Joyful and triumphant,
O come ye, O come ye to Bethlehem.
Frederick Oakeley (1802–80) British churchman.
Translated from the Latin hymn, Adeste Fideles
O Come All Ye Faithful

17 It came upon the midnight clear,
That glorious song of old,
From Angels bending near the earth
To touch their harps of gold;
'Peace on the earth; good will to man
From Heaven's all gracious King.'
The world in solemn stillness lay
To hear the angels sing.
E. H. Sears (1810–76) US clergyman.
That Glorious Song of Old

18 While shepherds watch'd their flocks by night,
All seated on the ground,
The Angel of the Lord came down,
And Glory shone around.
Nahum Tate (1652–1715) Irish-born English poet.
Supplement to the New Version of the Psalms, 'While Shepherds Watched'

19 At Christmas play and make good cheer,
For Christmas comes but once a year.
Thomas Tusser (1524–80) English farmer.
Five Hundred Points of Good Husbandry, 'The Farmer's Daily Diet'

20 To perceive Christmas through its wrapping becomes more difficult with every year.
Elwyn Brooks White (1899–1985) US journalist and humorist.
The Second Tree from the Corner

CHURCH

See also clergy, religion

1 And I say also unto thee, That thou art Peter, and upon this rock I will build my church; and the gates of hell shall not prevail against it.
And I will give unto thee the keys of the kingdom of heaven: and whatsoever thou shalt bind on earth shall be bound in heaven: and whatsoever thou shalt loose on earth shall be loosed in heaven.
Bible: Matthew
16:18–19

2 For where two or three are gathered together in my name, there am I in the midst of them.
Bible: Matthew
18:20

3 And of all plagues with which mankind are curst,
Ecclesiastic tyranny's the worst.
Daniel Defoe (1660–1731) British journalist and writer.
The True-Born Englishman, Pt. II

4 It is hard to tell where MCC ends and the Church of England begins.
J. B. Priestley (1894–1984) British novelist.
New Statesman, 20 July 1962, 'Topside Schools'

5 The Church exists for the sake of those outside it.
William Temple (1881–1944) British churchman.
Attrib.

CHURCHILL

See also politicians, World War II

1 It hasn't taken Winston long to get used to American ways. He hadn't been an American citizen for three minutes before attacking an ex-secretary of state!
Dean Acheson (1893–1971) US lawyer and statesman.
At a ceremony in 1963 to make Churchill an honorary American citizen, Churchill obliquely attacked Acheson's reference to Britain losing an empire
Randolph Churchill (K. Halle)

2 Then comes Winston with his hundred-horse-power mind and what can I do?
Stanley Baldwin (1867–1947) British statesman.
Stanley Baldwin (G. M. Young), Ch. 11

3 I thought he was a young man of promise; but it appears he was a young man of promises.
Arthur Balfour (1848–1930) British statesman.
Said of Winston Churchill on his entry into politics, 1899
Winston Churchill (Randolph Churchill), Vol. I

4 He is a man suffering from petrified adolescence.
Aneurin Bevan (1897–1960) British Labour politician.
Aneurin Bevan (Vincent Brome), Ch. 11

5 The nation had the lion's heart. I had the luck to give the roar.
Winston Churchill (1874–1965) British statesman.
Said on his 80th birthday

6 The first time you meet Winston you see all his faults and the rest of your life you spend in discovering his virtues.
Lady Constance Lytton (1869–1923) British suffragette.
Edward Marsh (Christopher Hassall), Ch. 7

7 Winston has devoted the best years of his life to preparing his impromptu speeches.
F. E. Smith (1872–1930) British lawyer and politician.
Attrib.

8 Simply a radio personality who outlived his prime.
Evelyn Waugh (1903–66) British novelist.
Evelyn Waugh (Christopher Sykes)

CINEMA

See also Goldwynisms

1 If my books had been any worse I should not have been invited to Hollywood, and if they had been any better I should not have come.
Raymond Chandler (1888–1959) US novelist.
The Life of Raymond Chandler (F. MacShane)

2 I was born at the age of twelve on a Metro-Goldwyn-Mayer lot.
Judy Garland (Frances Gumm; 1922–69) US film star.
The Observer, 'Sayings of the Week', 18 Feb 1951

3 I like a film to have a beginning, a middle and an end, but not necessarily in that order.
Jean-Luc Godard (1930–) French film director.
Attrib.

4 Photography is truth. And cinema is truth twenty-four times a second.
Jean-Luc Godard
Le Petit Soldat

5 Why should people go out and pay money to see bad films when they can stay at home and see bad television for nothing?
Samuel Goldwyn (Samuel Goldfish; 1882–1974) Polish-born US film producer.
The Observer, 'Sayings of the Week', 9 Sept 1956

6 A wide screen just makes a bad film twice as bad.
Samuel Goldwyn
Attrib.

7 The very meaninglessness of life forces man to create his own meaning. If it can be written or thought, it can be filmed.
Stanley Kubrick (1928–) US film director.
Halliwell's Filmgoer's and Video Viewer's Companion

8 In Hollywood, if you don't have happiness you send out for it.
Rex Reed (1938–) US columnist and actor.
Colombo's Hollywood, 'Hollywood the Bad' (J. R. Colombo)

9 They only got two things right, the camels and the sand.
Lowell Thomas (1892–1981) US author and broadcaster.
Referring to the film *Lawrence of Arabia*
Obituary, *The Times*, 29 Aug 1981

10 Take that black box away. I can't act in front of it.
Herbert Beerbohm Tree (1853–1917) British actor and theatre manager.
Objecting to the presence of the camera while performing in a silent film
Hollywood: The Pioneers (K. Brownlow)

11 Thanks to the movies, gunfire has always sounded unreal to me, even when being fired at.
Peter Ustinov (1921–) British actor.
Dear Me, Ch. 7

12 Westerns are closer to art than anything else in the motion picture business.
John Wayne (Marion Michael Morrison; 1907–79) US film actor.
Halliwell's Filmgoer's and Video Viewer's Companion

13 Me? Tarzan?
Johnny Weissmuller (1904–84) US swimmer and film actor.
Reacting to an invitation to play Tarzan
Attrib.

14 When you get the personality, you don't need the nudity.
Mae West (1892–1980) US actress.
The Observer, 'Sayings of the Week', 4 Aug 1968

CIVILIZATION

See also culture

1 Civilization is a method of living, an attitude of equal respect for all men.
Jane Addams (1860–1935) US social worker.
Speech, Honolulu, 1933

2 I wish I could bring Stonehenge to Nyasaland to show there was a time when Britain had a savage culture.
Hastings Banda (1906–) Malawi statesman.
The Observer, 'Sayings of the Week', 10 Mar 1963

3 The three great elements of modern civilization, Gunpowder, Printing, and the Protestant Religion.
Thomas Carlyle (1795–1881) Scottish historian and essayist.
Critical and Miscellaneous Essays, 'The State of German Literature'

4 The modern world . . . has no notion except that of simplifying something by destroying nearly everything.
G. K. Chesterton (1874–1936) British writer.
All I Survey

5 In essence the Renaissance was simply the green end of one of civilization's hardest winters.
John Fowles (1926–) British novelist.
The French Lieutenant's Woman, Ch. 10

6 I think it would be a good idea.
Mahatma Gandhi (Mohandas Karamchand Gandhi; 1869–1948) Indian national leader.
On being asked for his view on Western civilization
Attrib.

7 There is precious little in civilization to appeal to a Yeti.

Edmund Hillary (1919–) New Zealand mountaineer.
The Observer, 'Sayings of the Week', 3 June 1960

8 As civilization advances, poetry almost necessarily declines.

Lord Macaulay (1800–59) British historian.
Literary Essays Contributed to the 'Edinburgh Review', 'Milton'

9 The degree of a nation's civilization is marked by its disregard for the necessities of existence.

W. Somerset Maugham (1874–1965) British novelist.
Our Betters, I

CLARITY

See also communication, confusion

1 Oh! rather give me commentators plain,
Who with no deep researches vex the brain;
Who from the dark and doubtful love to run,
And hold their glimmering tapers to the sun.

George Crabbe (1754–1832) British poet.
The Parish Register, 'Baptisms'

2 It's odd how people waiting for you stand out far less clearly than people you are waiting for.

Jean Giraudoux (1882–1944) French dramatist.
Tiger at the Gates, I

3 When man's whole frame is obvious to a flea.

Alexander Pope (1688–1744) British poet.
The Dunciad, IV

CLASS

See also aristocracy, equality, public, snobbery

1 There's one law for the rich, and another for the poor.

Proverb

2 You can measure the social caste of a person by the distance between the husband's and wife's apartments.

Alfonso XIII (1886–1941) Spanish monarch.
Attrib.

3 I often, therefore, when I want to distinguish clearly the aristocratic class from the Philistines proper, or middle class, name the former, in my own mind *the Barbarians*.

Matthew Arnold (1822–88) British poet and critic.
Culture and Anarchy, Ch. 3

4 When Adam delved and Eve span,
Who was then the gentleman?

John Ball (d. 1381) English priest.
Text of sermon

5 Yet it is better to drop thy friends, O my daughter, than to drop thy 'H's'.

C. S. Calverley (1831–84) British poet.
Proverbial Philosophy, 'Of Friendship'

6 One of those refined people who go out to sew for the rich because they cannot bear contact with the poor.

Colette (1873–1954) French novelist.
The Other One

7 Servants should not be ill. We have quite enough illnesses of our own without them adding to the symptoms.

Lady Diana Cooper (1892–1986) British actress and writer.
Diana Cooper (Philip Ziegler)

8 He bade me observe it, and I should always find, that the calamities of life were shared among the upper and lower part of mankind; but that the middle station had the fewest disasters.

Daniel Defoe (1660–1731) British journalist and writer.
Robinson Crusoe, Pt. I

9 O let us love our occupations,
Bless the squire and his relations,
Live upon our daily rations,
And always know our proper stations.

Charles Dickens (1812–70) British novelist.
The Chimes, '2nd Quarter'

10 He differed from the healthy type that was essentially middle-class – he never seemed to perspire.

F. Scott Fitzgerald (1896–1940) US novelist.
This Side of Paradise, Bk. I, Ch. 2

11 All shall equal be.
The Earl, the Marquis, and the Dook,
The Groom, the Butler, and the Cook,
The Aristocrat who banks with Coutts,
The Aristocrat who cleans the boots.

W. S. Gilbert (1836–1911) British dramatist.
The Gondoliers, I

12 He combines the manners of a Marquis with the morals of a Methodist.

W. S. Gilbert
Ruddigore, I

13 Bow, bow, ye lower middle classes!
Bow, bow, ye tradesmen, bow, ye masses!

W. S. Gilbert
Iolanthe, I

14 All the world over, I will back the masses against the classes.

William Ewart Gladstone (1809–98) British statesman.
Speech, Liverpool, 28 June 1886

15 Dialect words – those terrible marks of the beast to the truly genteel.

Thomas Hardy (1840–1928) British novelist.
The Mayor of Casterbridge, Ch. 20

16 '*Bourgeois*,' I observed, 'is an epithet which the riff-raff apply to what is respectable, and the aristocracy to what is decent'.

Anthony Hope (Sir Anthony Hope Hawkins; 1863–1933) British novelist.
The Dolly Dialogues

17 You may be the most liberal Liberal

Englishman, and yet you cannot fail to see the categorical difference between the responsible and the irresponsible classes.

D. H. Lawrence (1885–1930) British novelist.
Kangaroo, Ch. 1

18 A Social-Democrat must never forget that the proletariat will inevitably have to wage a class struggle for Socialism even against the most democratic and republican bourgeoisie and petty bourgeoisie.

Lenin (Vladimir Ilich Ulyanov; 1870–1924) Russian revolutionary leader.
The State and Revolution, Ch. 10

19 An Englishman's way of speaking absolutely classifies him
The moment he talks he makes some other Englishman despise him.

Alan Jay Lerner (1918–86) US songwriter.
My Fair Lady, I:1

20 I'm not interested in classes . . . Far be it from me to foster inferiority complexes among the workers by trying to make them think they belong to some special class. That has happened in Europe but it hasn't happened here yet.

John Llewellyn Lewis (1880–1969) US labour leader.
The Coming of the New Deal (A. M. Schlesinger, Jnr), Pt. 7, Ch. 25

21 Said Marx: 'Don't be snobbish, we seek to abolish
The 3rd Class, not the 1st.'

Christopher Logue (1926–   ) British poet and dramatist.
Christopher Logue's ABC, 'M'

22 The history of all hitherto existing society is the history of class struggles.

Karl Marx (1818–83) German philosopher and revolutionary.
The Communist Manifesto, 1

23 The one class you do *not* belong to and are not proud of at all is the lower-middle class. No one ever describes himself as belonging to the lower-middle class.

George Mikes (1912–87) Hungarian-born British writer.
How to be Inimitable

24 Only on the third class tourist class passengers' deck was it a sultry overcast morning, but then if you do things on the cheap you must expect these things.

Spike Milligan (1918–   ) British comic actor and author.
A Dustbin of Milligan

25 We have nothing to lose but our aitches.

George Orwell (Eric Blair; 1903–50) British novelist.
Referring to the middle classes
The Road to Wigan Pier, Ch. 13

26 I don't think one 'comes down' from Jimmy's university. According to him, it's not even red brick, but white tile.

John Osborne (1929–   ) British dramatist.
Look Back in Anger, II:1

27 You can be in the Horse Guards and still be common, dear.

Terence Rattigan (1911–77) British dramatist.
Separate Tables: 'Table Number Seven'

28 U and Non-U, An Essay in Sociological Linguistics.

Alan Strode Campbell Ross (1907–78) British professor of linguistics.
Essay title, *Noblesse Oblige*, 1956

29 There are two classes in good society in England. The equestrian classes and the neurotic classes.

George Bernard Shaw (1856–1950) Irish dramatist and critic.
Heartbreak House

30 I am a gentleman. I live by robbing the poor.

George Bernard Shaw
Man and Superman

31 I have to live for others and not for myself; that's middle class morality.

George Bernard Shaw
Pygmalion

32 It is impossible for one class to appreciate the wrongs of another.

Elizabeth Stanton (1815–1902) US suffragette.
History of Woman Suffrage (with Susan B. Anthony and Mathilda Gage), Vol. I

33 The charm of Britain has always been the ease with which one can move into the middle class.

Margaret Thatcher (1925–   ) British politician and prime minister.
The Observer, 'Sayings of the Week', 27 Oct 1974

34 The ship follows Soviet custom: it is riddled with class distinctions so subtle, it takes a trained Marxist to appreciate them.

Paul Theroux (1941–   ) US-born writer.
The Great Railway Bazaar, Ch. 30

35 For generations the British bourgeoisie have spoken of themselves as gentlemen, and by that they have meant, among other things, a self-respecting scorn of irregular perquisites. It is the quality that distinguishes the gentleman from both the artist and the aristocrat.

Evelyn Waugh (1903–66) British novelist.
Decline and Fall, Pt. I, Ch. 6

36 No writer before the middle of the 19th century wrote about the working classes other than as grotesque or as pastoral decoration. Then when they were given the vote certain writers started to suck up to them.

Evelyn Waugh
Interview
Paris Review, 1963

37 Bricklayers kick their wives to death, and dukes betray theirs; but it is among the small

clerks and shopkeepers nowadays that it comes most often to the cutting of throats.
H. G. Wells (1866–1946) British writer.
Short Stories, 'The Purple Pileus'

38 Margaret Thatcher's great strength seems to be the better people know her, the better they like her. But, of course, she has one great disadvantage – she is a daughter of the people and looks trim, as the daughters of the people desire to be. Shirley Williams has such an advantage over her because she's a member of the upper-middle class and can achieve that kitchen-sink-revolutionary look that one cannot get unless one has been to a really good school.
Rebecca West (Cicely Isabel Fairfield; 1892–1983) British novelist and journalist.
Said in an interview with Jilly Cooper
The Sunday Times, 25 July 1976

39 Really, if the lower orders don't set us a good example, what on earth is the use of them?
Oscar Wilde (1854–1900) Irish-born British dramatist.
The Importance of Being Earnest, I

40 The constitution does not provide for first and second class citizens.
Wendell Lewis Willkie (1892–1944) US lawyer and businessman.
An American Programme, Ch. 2

CLASSICS

1 They were a tense and peculiar family, the Oedipuses, weren't they?
Max Beerbohm (1872–1956) British writer.
Max: A Biography (D. Cecil)

2 So they told me how Mr Gladstone read Homer for fun, which I thought served him right.
Winston Churchill (1874–1965) British statesman.
My Early Life, Ch. 2

3 Nor can I do better, in conclusion, than impress upon you the study of Greek literature which not only elevates above the vulgar herd, but leads not infrequently to positions of considerable emolument.
Thomas Gaisford (1799–1855) British classicist.
Christmas Day Sermon at Oxford
Reminiscences of Oxford (Revd W. Tuckwell)

4 To the Greeks the Muse gave native wit, to the Greeks the gift of graceful eloquence.
Horace (Quintus Horatius Flaccus; 65–8 BC) Roman poet.
Ars Poetica

5 Thou hadst small Latin, and less Greek.
Ben Jonson (1573–1637) English dramatist.
To the Memory of William Shakespeare

6 The classics are only primitive literature. They belong in the same class as primitive machinery and primitive music and primitive medicine.
Stephen Leacock (1869–1944) English-born Canadian economist and humorist.
Homer and Humbug

7 Every man with a belly full of the classics is an enemy of the human race.
Henry Miller (1891–1980) US novelist.
Tropic of Cancer, 'Dijon'

8 Nobody can say a word against Greek: it stamps a man at once as an educated gentleman.
George Bernard Shaw (1856–1950) Irish dramatist and critic.
Major Barbara, I

9 We were taught as the chief subjects of instruction Latin and Greek. We were taught very badly because the men who taught us did not habitually use either of these languages.
H. G. Wells (1866–1946) British writer.
The New Machiavelli, Bk. I., Ch. 3

CLASSIFICATION

See also generalizations

1 One of the unpardonable sins, in the eyes of most people, is for a man to go about unlabelled. The world regards such a person as the police do an unmuzzled dog, not under proper control.
T. H. Huxley (1825–95) British biologist.
Evolution and Ethics

2 The young Cambridge group, the group that stood for 'freedom' and flannel trousers and flannel shirts open at the neck, and a well-bred sort of emotional anarchy, and a whispering, murmuring sort of voice, and an ultra-sensitive sort of manner.
D. H. Lawrence (1885–1930) British novelist.
Lady Chatterley's Lover, Ch. 1

3 Decades have a delusive edge to them. They are not, of course, really periods at all, except as any other ten years would be. But we, looking at them, are caught by the different name each bears, and give them different attributes, and tie labels on them, as if they were flowers in a border.
Rose Macaulay (1889–1958) British writer.
Told by an Idiot, Pt. II, Ch. 1

CLEANNESS

1 Bath twice a day to be really clean, once a day to be passably clean, once a week to avoid being a public menace.
Anthony Burgess (John Burgess Wilson; 1917–) British novelist.
Mr Enderby, Pt. I, Ch. 2

2 MR PRITCHARD. I must dust the blinds and then I must raise them.

MRS OGMORE-PRITCHARD. And before you let the sun in, mind it wipes its shoes.
Dylan Thomas (1914–53) Welsh poet.
Under Milk Wood

3 Have you ever taken anything out of the clothes basket because it had become, relatively, the cleaner thing?
Katherine Whitehorn (1926–) British journalist.
The Observer, 'On Shirts', 1964

CLERGY

See also Church, religion

1 I always like to associate with a lot of priests because it makes me understand anti-clerical things so well.
Hilaire Belloc (1870–1953) French-born British poet.
Letter to E. S. P. Haynes, 9 Nov 1909

2 This is a true saying, If a man desire the office of a bishop, he desireth a good work. A bishop then must be blameless, the husband of one wife, vigilant, sober, of good behaviour, given to hospitality, apt to teach; Not given to wine, no striker, not greedy of filthy lucre; but patient, not a brawler, not covetous.
Bible: I Timothy
3:1–3

3 As for the British churchman, he goes to church as he goes to the bathroom, with the minimum of fuss and no explanation if he can help it.
Ronald Blythe (1922–) British author.
The Age of Illusion

4 Make him a bishop, and you will silence him at once.
Earl of Chesterfield (1694–1773) English statesman.
When asked what steps might be taken to control the evangelical preacher George Whitefield
Attrib.

5 It is no accident that the symbol of a bishop is a crook, and the sign of an archbishop is a double-cross.
Dom Gregory Dix (1901–52) British monk.
Letter to *The Times*, 3 Dec 1977 (Francis Bown)

6 For clergy are men as well as other folks.
Henry Fielding (1707–54) British novelist.
Joseph Andrews, Bk II, Ch. 6

7 That whisky priest, I wish we had never had him in the house.
Graham Greene (1904–) British novelist.
The Power and the Glory, Pt. I

8 In old time we had treen chalices and golden priests, but now we have treen priests and golden chalices.
John Jewel (1522–71) English bishop.
Certain Sermons Preached Before the Queen's Majesty

9 A man who is good enough to go to heaven, is good enough to be a clergyman.
Samuel Johnson (1709–84) British lexicographer.
Life of Johnson (J. Boswell), Vol. II

10 Damn it all, another Bishop dead, – I verily believe they die to vex me.
Lord Melbourne (1779–1848) British statesman.
Attrib.

11 How can a bishop marry? How can he flirt? The most he can say is, 'I will see you in the vestry after service.'
Sydney Smith (1771–1845) British clergyman and essayist.
Memoir (Lady Holland)

12 I never saw, heard, nor read, that the clergy were beloved in any nation where Christianity was the religion of the country. Nothing can render them popular, but some degree of persecution.
Jonathan Swift (1667–1745) Irish-born Anglican priest and writer.
Thoughts on Religion

13 There is a certain class of clergyman whose mendicity is only equalled by their mendacity.
Frederick Temple (1821–1902) British churchman.
Remark at a meeting of the Ecclesiastical Commissioners
Years of Endeavour (Sir George Leveson Gower)

14 But the churchmen fain would kill their church,
As the churches have kill'd their Christ.
Alfred, Lord Tennyson (1809–92) British poet.
Maud, V

15 If I were a cassowary
On the plains of Timbuctoo,
I would eat a missionary,
Cassock, band, and hymn-book too.
Samuel Wilberforce (1805–73) British churchman.
Also attrib. to W. M. Thackeray
Attrib.

CLOCKS

1 My poor fellow, why not carry a watch?
Herbert Beerbohm Tree (1853–1917) British actor and theatre manager.
Remark made to a man carrying a grandfather clock
Beerbohm Tree (Hesketh Pearson)

2 My grandfather's clock was too large for the shelf.
So it stood ninety years on the floor.
Henry Clay Work (1832–84) US songwriter.
Grandfather's Clock

3 But it stopped short – never to go again –
When the old man died.
Henry Clay Work
Grandfather's Clock

CLOTHES

See also appearance, beauty, fashion, nakedness

1 It is not only fine feathers that make fine birds.
Aesop (6th century BC) Reputed Greek writer of fables.
Fables, 'The Jay and the Peacock'

2 She just wore
Enough for modesty – no more.
Robert Williams Buchanan (1841–1901) British poet and writer.
White Rose and Red, I

3 I go to a better tailor than any of you and pay more for my clothes. The only difference is that you probably don't sleep in yours.
Clarence Seward Darrow (1857–1938) US lawyer.
Reply when teased by reporters about his appearance
2500 Anecdotes (E. Fuller)

4 'Good heavens!' said he, 'if it be our clothes alone which fit us for society, how highly we should esteem those who make them.'
Marie Ebner von Eschenbach (1830–1916) Austrian writer.
The Two Countesses

5 The sense of being well-dressed gives a feeling of inward tranquillity which religion is powerless to bestow.
C. F. Forbes (1817–1911) British writer.
Social Aims (Emerson)

6 Those who make their dress a principal part of themselves, will, in general, become of no more value than their dress.
William Hazlitt (1778–1830) British essayist.
On the Clerical Character

7 A sweet disorder in the dress
Kindles in clothes a wantonness.
Robert Herrick (1591–1674) English poet.
Hesperides, 'Delight in Disorder'

8 Whenas in silks my Julia goes
Then, then (methinks) how sweetly flows
That liquefaction of her clothes.
Robert Herrick
Hesperides, 'Upon Julia's Clothes'

9 Fine clothes are good only as they supply the want of other means of procuring respect.
Samuel Johnson (1709–84) British lexicographer.
Life of Johnson (J. Boswell), Vol. II

10 The uniform 'e wore
Was nothin' much before,
An' rather less than 'arf o' that be'ind.
Rudyard Kipling (1865–1936) Indian-born British writer.
Gunga Din

11 How do you look when I'm sober?
Ring Lardner Jnr (1885–1933) American humorist.
Speaking to a flamboyantly dressed stranger who walked into the club where he was drinking
Ring (J. Yardley)

12 Brevity is the soul of lingerie.
Dorothy Parker (1893–1967) US writer.
While Rome Burns (Alexander Woollcott)

13 Where did you get that hat?
Where did you get that tile?
James Rolmaz (19th century) British songwriter.
Where Did You Get That Hat?

14 Not a gentleman; dresses too well.
Bertrand Russell (1872–1970) British philosopher.
Referring to Anthony Eden
Six Men (A. Cooke)

15 His socks compelled one's attention without losing one's respect.
Saki (Hector Hugh Munro; 1870–1916) British writer.
Ministers of Grace

16 Costly thy habit as thy purse can buy,
But not express'd in fancy; rich, not gaudy;
For the apparel oft proclaims the man.
William Shakespeare (1564–1616) English dramatist.
Hamlet, I:3

17 The only man who really needs a tail coat is a man with a hole in his trousers.
John Taylor (20th century) The editor of the *Tailor and Cutter*.
The Observer, 'Shouts and Murmurs'

18 You can say what you like about long dresses, but they cover a multitude of shins.
Mae West (1892–1980) US actress.
Peel Me a Grape (J. Weintraub)

19 Hats divide generally into three classes: offensive hats, defensive hats, and shrapnel.
Katherine Whitehorn (1926–   ) British journalist.
Shouts and Murmurs, 'Hats'

20 Then the little man wears a shocking bad hat.
Duke of York and Albany (1763–1827) The second son of George III.
Referring to Horace Walpole
Attrib.

COLD WAR

1 Let us not be deceived – we are today in the midst of a cold war.
Bernard Baruch (1870–1965) US financier and presidential adviser.
Speech, South Carolina Legislature, 16 Apr 1947

2 An iron curtain has descended across the Continent.
Winston Churchill (1874–1965) British statesman.
The phrase 'iron curtain' was originally coined by Joseph Goebbels
Address, Westminster College, Fulton, USA, 5 Mar 1946

3 Now we are in a period which I can characterize as a period of cold peace.
Trygve Lie (1896–1968) Norwegian lawyer.
The Observer, 'Sayings of the Week', 21 Aug 1949

COMFORT

See also endurance, sympathy

1 The crash of the whole solar and stellar systems could only kill you once.
Thomas Carlyle (1795–1881) Scottish historian and essayist.
Letter to John Carlyle, 1831

2 For this relief much thanks. 'Tis bitter cold, And I am sick at heart.
William Shakespeare (1564–1616) English dramatist.
Hamlet, I:1

3 I beg cold comfort.
William Shakespeare
King John, V:7

4 Like a bridge over troubled water, I will ease your mind.
Paul Simon (1942–) US singer.
Bridge Over Troubled Water

COMMITMENT

1 In for a penny, in for a pound.
Proverb

2 Never do things by halves.
Proverb

3 One cannot be a part-time nihilist.
Albert Camus (1913–60) French existentialist writer.
The Rebel

4 Catholics and Communists have committed great crimes, but at least they have not stood aside, like an established society, and been indifferent. I would rather have blood on my hands than water like Pilate.
Graham Greene (1904–) British novelist.
The Comedians, Pt. III, Ch. 4

5 I love being at the centre of things.
Margaret Thatcher (1925–) British politician and prime minister.
Reader's Digest, 1984

6 Miss Madeleine Philips was making it very manifest to Captain Douglas that she herself was a career; that a lover with any other career in view need not – as the advertisements say – apply.
H. G. Wells (1866–1946) British writer.
Bealby, Pt. V, Ch. 5

COMMUNICATION

See also clarity, conversation, language, letter-writing, speech

1 Only connect!
E. M. Forster (1879–1970) British novelist.
Howards End, Epigraph

2 Unless one is a genius, it is best to aim at being intelligible.
Anthony Hope (Sir Anthony Hope Hawkins; 1863–1933) British novelist.
The Dolly Dialogues

3 The medium is the message. This is merely to say that the personal and social consequences of any medium . . . result from the new scale that is introduced into our affairs by each extension of ourselves or by any new technology.
Marshall McLuhan (1911–81) Canadian sociologist.
Understanding Media, Ch. 1

4 What have we to say to India?
John Ruskin (1819–1900) British art critic and writer.
Referring to the completion of the British-Indian cable
Attrib.

COMMUNISM

See also Marxism, Russia, socialism

1 Its relationship to democratic institutions is that of the death watch beetle – it is not a Party, it is a conspiracy.
Aneurin Bevan (1897–1960) British Labour politician.
Referring to the Communist Party
Tribune

2 Socialism with a human face.
Alexander Dubček (1921–) Czechoslovak statesman.
A resolution by the party group in the Ministry of Foreign Affairs, in 1968, referred to Czechoslovak foreign policy acquiring 'its own defined face'
Attrib.

3 Every year humanity takes a step towards Communism. Maybe not you, but at all events your grandson will surely be a Communist.
Nikita Khrushchev (1894–1971) Soviet statesman.
Said to Sir William Hayter, June 1956

4 Communism is Soviet power plus the electrification of the whole country.
Lenin (Vladimir Ilich Ulyanov; 1870–1924) Russian revolutionary leader.
Political slogan of 1920, promoting the programme of electrification

5 There's no such thing in Communist countries as a load of old cod's wallop, the cod's wallop is always fresh made.
Robert Morley (1908–) British actor.
Punch, 20 Feb 1974

6 Communism is like prohibition, it's a good idea but it won't work.
Will Rogers (1879–1935) US actor and humorist.
Autobiography, Nov 1927

7 For us in Russia communism is a dead dog, while, for many people in the West, it is still a living lion.
Alexander Solzhenitsyn (1918–) Soviet novelist.
The Listener, 15 Feb 1979

8 Every communist has a fascist frown, every fascist a communist smile.
Muriel Spark (1918–) British novelist.
The Girls of Slender Means, Ch. 4

9 The party is the rallying-point for the best elements of the working class.
Joseph Stalin (J. Dzhugashvili; 1879–1953) Soviet statesman.
Attrib.

10 Communism continued to haunt Europe as a spectre – a name men gave to their own fears and blunders. But the crusade against Communism was even more imaginary than the spectre of Communism.
A. J. P. Taylor (1906–) British historian.
The Origins of the Second World War, Ch. 2

11 Lenin's method leads to this: the party organization at first substitutes itself for the party as a whole. Then the central committee substitutes itself for the party organization, and finally a single dictator substitutes himself for the central committee.
Leon Trotsky (Lev Davidovich Bronstein; 1879–1940) Russian revolutionary.
The Communist Parties of Western Europe (N. McInnes), Ch. 3

COMPLAINTS

1 We have first raised a dust and then complain we cannot see.
Bishop Berkeley (1685–1753) Irish churchman and philosopher.
Principles of Human Knowledge, Introduction

2 The world is disgracefully managed, one hardly knows to whom to complain.
Ronald Firbank (1886–1926) British novelist.
Vainglory

3 If you are foolish enough to be contented, don't show it, but grumble with the rest.
Jerome K. Jerome (1859–1927) British humorist.
Idle Thoughts of an Idle Fellow

4 Nay, Madam, when you are declaiming, declaim; and when you are calculating, calculate.
Samuel Johnson (1709–84) British lexicographer.
Commenting on Mrs Thrale's discourse on the price of children's clothes
Life of Johnson (J. Boswell), Vol. III

5 I want to register a complaint. Do you know who sneaked into my room at three o'clock this morning?
– Who?
Nobody, and that's my complaint.
Groucho Marx (Julius Marx; 1895–1977) US comedian.
Monkey Business

COMPLIMENTS

See also admiration, beauty, flattery, love, praise

1 She isn't a bad bit of goods, the Queen! I wish all the fleas in my bed were as good.
Miguel de Cervantes (1547–1616) Spanish novelist.
Don Quixote, Pt. I, Ch. 30

2 She is Venus when she smiles;

But she's Juno when she walks,
And Minerva when she talks.
Ben Jonson (1573–1637) English dramatist.
The Underwood, 'Celebration of Charis, V. His Discourse with Cupid'

3 Your eyes shine like the pants of my blue serge suit.
Groucho Marx (Julius Marx; 1895–1977) US comedian.
The Cocoanuts

4 Shall I compare thee to a summer's day?
Thou art more lovely and more temperate.
Rough winds do shake the darling buds of May,
And summer's lease hath all too short a date.
William Shakespeare (1564–1616) English dramatist.
Sonnet 18

5 Won't you come into the garden? I would like my roses to see you.
Richard Brinsley Sheridan (1751–1816) British dramatist.
Said to a young lady
Attrib. in *The Perfect Hostess*

6 She would rather light candles than curse the darkness, and her glow has warmed the world.
Adlai Stevenson (1900–65) US statesman.
Referring to Eleanor Roosevelt
Address, United Nations General Assembly, 9 Nov 1962

7 What, when drunk, one sees in other women, one sees in Garbo sober.
Kenneth Tynan (1927–80) British theatre critic.
The Sunday Times, 25 Aug 1963

8 Of this blest man, let his just praise be given,
Heaven was in him, before he was in heaven.
Izaak Walton (1593–1683) English writer.
Referring to Dr Richard Sibbes
Written in a copy of *Returning Backslider* by Richard Sibbes

9 Roses are flowering in Picardy,
But there's never a rose like you.
Frederic Edward Weatherly (1848–1929) British lawyer and songwriter.
Roses of Picardy

COMPOSERS

See musicians

COMPROMISE

1 It takes two to tango.
Proverb

2 We know what happens to people who stay in the middle of the road. They get run over.
Aneurin Bevan (1897–1960) British Labour politician.
The Observer, 9 Dec 1953

3 For the flesh lusteth against the Spirit, and the Spirit against the flesh: and these are

contrary the one to the other: so that ye cannot do the things that ye would.
Bible: Galatians
5:17

4 All government, indeed every human benefit and enjoyment, every virtue, and every prudent act, is founded on compromise and barter.
Edmund Burke (1729–97) British politician.
Speech on Conciliation with America (House of Commons, 22 Mar 1775)

5 Compromise used to mean that half a loaf was better than no bread. Among modern statesmen it really seems to mean that half a loaf is better than a whole loaf.
G. K. Chesterton (1874–1936) British writer.
What's Wrong with the World

CONCEIT

See also arrogance, boasts, egotism, pride

1 I'm the greatest!
Muhammad Ali (Cassius Clay; 1942–) US boxer.
Remark, often said after his fights

2 A man . . . must have a very good opinion of himself when he asks people to leave their own fireside, and encounter such a day as this, for the sake of coming to see him. He must think himself a most agreeable fellow.
Jane Austen (1775–1817) British novelist.
Emma, Ch. 13

3 It was prettily devised of Aesop, 'The fly sat upon the axletree of the chariot-wheel and said, what a dust do I raise.'
Francis Bacon (1561–1626) English philosopher.
Essays, 'Of Vain-Glory'

4 To give an accurate and exhaustive account of that period would need a far less brilliant pen than mine.
Max Beerbohm (1872–1956) British writer.
1880

5 If ever he went to school without any boots it was because he was too big for them.
Ivor Bulmer-Thomas (1905–) British writer and politician.
Referring to Harold Wilson
Remark, Conservative Party Conference, 1949

6 Vanity plays lurid tricks with our memory.
Joseph Conrad (Teodor Josef Konrad Korzeniowski; 1857–1924) Polish-born British novelist.
Lord Jim

7 I know he is, and he adores his maker.
Benjamin Disraeli (1804–81) British statesman.
Replying to a remark made in defence of John Bright that he was a self-made man; often also attrib. to Bright referring to Disraeli
The Fine Art of Political Wit (L. Harris)

8 We are so vain that we even care for the opinion of those we don't care for.
Marie Ebner von Eschenbach (1830–1916) Austrian writer.
Aphorism

9 I am the Captain of the *Pinafore*;
And a right good captain too!
W. S. Gilbert (1836–1911) British dramatist.
HMS Pinafore, I

10 I have a left shoulder-blade that is a miracle of loveliness. People come miles to see it. My right elbow has a fascination that few can resist.
W. S. Gilbert
The Mikado, II

11 All my shows are great. Some of them are bad. But they are all great.
Lew Grade (Lewis Winogradsky; 1906–) British film and TV producer.
The Observer, 'Sayings of the Week', 14 Sept 1975

12 Conceit is the finest armour a man can wear.
Jerome K. Jerome (1859–1927) British humorist.
Idle Thoughts of an Idle Fellow

13 He fell in love with himself at first sight and it is a passion to which he has always remained faithful. Self-love seems so often unrequited.
Anthony Powell (1905–) British novelist.
A Dance to the Music of Time: The Acceptance World, Ch. 1

14 Self-love is the greatest of all flatterers.
Duc de la Rochefoucauld (1613–80) French writer.
Maximes, 2

15 Besides Shakespeare and me, who do you think there is?
Gertrude Stein (1874–1946) US writer.
Speaking to a friend she considered knew little about literature
Charmed Circle (J. Mellow)

16 The Jews have produced only three originative geniuses: Christ, Spinoza, and myself.
Gertrude Stein
Charmed Circle (J. Mellow)

17 Vanity dies hard; in some obstinate cases it outlives the man.
Robert Louis Stevenson (1850–94) Scottish writer.
Prince Otto

18 I think, historically, the term 'Thatcherism' will be seen as a compliment.
Margaret Thatcher (1925–) British politician and prime minister.
Remark, Oct 1985

19 I think I have become a bit of an institution – you know, the sort of thing people expect to see around the place.
Margaret Thatcher
Remark, July 1987

20 He would like to destroy his old diaries and to appear before his children and the public

only in his patriarchal robes. His vanity is
immense!

Sophie Tolstoy (1844–1919) Russian writer.
A Diary of Tolstoy's Wife, 1860–1891

21 Isn't it? I know in my case I would grow
intolerably conceited.

James Whistler (1834–1903) US painter.
Replying to the pointed observaton that it was as well that we
do not not see ourselves as others see us
The Man Whistler (H. Pearson)

22 A LADY. I only know of two painters in the
world: yourself and Velasquez.
WHISTLER. Why drag in Velasquez?

James Whistler
Whistler Stories (D. Seitz)

23 No, no, Oscar, you forget. When you and I
are together we never talk about anything
except me.

James Whistler
Cable replying to Oscar Wilde's message: 'When you and I
are together we never talk about anything except ourselves'
The Gentle Art of Making Enemies

24 I cannot tell you that, madam. Heaven has
granted me no offspring.

James Whistler
Replying to a lady who had inquired whether he thought ge-
nius hereditary
Whistler Stories (D. Seitz)

25 Nothing, except my genius.

Oscar Wilde (1854–1900) Irish-born British dramatist.
Replying to a US customs official on being asked if he had any-
thing to declare
Attrib.

26 To love oneself is the beginning of a lifelong
romance.

Oscar Wilde
An Ideal Husband, III

27 Who am I to tamper with a masterpiece?

Oscar Wilde
Refusing to make alterations to one of his own plays
Attrib.

CONFLICT

See also opposites

1 Attack is the best form of defence.
Proverb

2 Fight fire with fire.
Proverb

3 He who lives by the sword dies by the
sword.
Proverb

4 Without Contraries is no progression.
Attraction and Repulsion, Reason and
Energy, Love and Hate, are necessary to
Human existence.

William Blake (1757–1827) British poet.
The Marriage of Heaven and Hell, 'The Argument'

5 No, when the fight begins within himself,

A man's worth something.

Robert Browning (1812–89) British poet.
Bishop Blougram's Apology

6 Two souls dwell, alas! in my breast.

Goethe (1749–1832) German poet and dramatist.
Faust, Pt. I

7 Two loves I have, of comfort and despair,
Which like two spirits do suggest me still;
The better angel is a man right fair,
The worser spirit a woman colour'd ill.

William Shakespeare (1564–1616) English dramatist.
Sonnet 144

CONFORMITY

See also orthodoxy

1 Who spits against the wind, it falls in his
face.
Proverb

2 When in Rome, live as the Romans do: when
elsewhere, live as they live elsewhere.

St Ambrose (c. 339–397) Bishop of Milan.
Advice to St Augustine

3 Take the tone of the company you are in.

Earl of Chesterfield (1694–1773) English statesman.
Letter to his son, 9 Oct 1747

4 Whoso would be a man must be a
nonconformist.

Ralph Waldo Emerson (1803–82) US poet and essayist.
Essays, 'Self-Reliance'

5 Uniformity isn't bad, as some people still
think, because if the quality is good, it
satisfies. People are never happy who want
change.

L. P. Hartley (1895–1972) British novelist.
Facial Justice, Ch. 13

6 Why do you have to be a nonconformist like
everybody else?

James Thurber (1894–1961) US humorist.
Attrib. Actually a cartoon caption by Stan Hunt in the *New
Yorker*

CONFUSION

1 Well, my deliberate opinion is – it's a jolly
strange world.

Arnold Bennett (1867–1931) British novelist.
The Title, I

2 I can't say I was ever lost, but I was
bewildered once for three days.

Daniel Boone (1734–1820) US pioneeer.
Reply when asked if he had ever been lost
Attrib.

3 'Curiouser and curiouser!' cried Alice.

Lewis Carroll (Charles Lutwidge Dodgson; 1832–98)
British writer.
Alice's Adventures in Wonderland, Ch. 2

4 This world is very odd we see,
We do not comprehend it;

But in one fact we all agree,
God won't, and we can't mend it.
Arthur Hugh Clough (1819–61) British poet.
Dipsychus, Bk. II

5   Bewitched, Bothered and Bewildered.
Lorenz Hart (1895–1943) US songwriter.
From the musical *Babes in Arms*
Song title

6   I had nothing to offer anybody except my
own confusion.
Jack Kerouac (1922–69) US novelist.
On the Road, Pt. II

7   I don't want you to think I'm not incoherent.
Harold W. Ross (1892–1951) US journalist.
The Years with Ross (James Thurber)

8   For mine own part, it was Greek to me.
William Shakespeare (1564–1616) English dramatist.
Julius Caesar, I:2

9   That blessed mood,
In which the burthen of the mystery,
In which the heavy and the weary weight
Of all this unintelligible world,
Is lightened.
William Wordsworth (1770–1850) British poet.
Lines composed a few miles above Tintern Abbey

CONSCIENCE

See also integrity

1   Conscience, I say, not thine own, but of the
other: for why is my liberty judged of
another man's conscience?
Bible: I Corinthians
10:29

2   Conscience is the internal perception of the
rejection of a particular wish operating within
us.
Sigmund Freud (1856–1939) Austrian psychoanalyst.
Totem and Taboo

3   Conscience is a coward, and those faults it
has not strength enough to prevent it seldom
has justice enough to accuse.
Oliver Goldsmith (1728–74) Irish-born British writer.
The Vicar of Wakefield, Ch. 13

4   Conscience is the inner voice that warns us
somebody may be looking.
H. L. Mencken (1880–1956) US journalist.
A Mencken Chrestomathy

5   Thus conscience does make cowards of us
all;
And thus the native hue of resolution
Is sicklied o'er with the pale cast of thought.
William Shakespeare (1564–1616) English dramatist.
Hamlet, III:1

CONSERVATION

See also ecology, environment

1   I gave my beauty and my youth to men. I
am going to give my wisdom and experience
to animals.
Brigitte Bardot (1934–) French film actress.
Referring to her animal-rights campaign
The Guardian, 1987

2   Contrary to popular mythology, it is not my
Department's mission in life to tarmac over
the whole of England.
Paul Channon (1935–) British politician.
Speech, Sept 1988

3   Population growth is the primary source of
environmental damage.
Jacques Cousteau (1910–) French naval officer and
underwater explorer.
Remark, Jan 1989

4   Trees are poems that the earth writes upon
the sky. We fell them down and turn them
into paper that we may record our
emptiness.
Kahil Gibran (1833–1931) Lebanese mystic and poet.
Sand and Foam

5   Green politics is not about being far left or
far right, but far-sighted.
David Icke (1952–) Green Party spokesman.
Speech, Green Party conference, Sept 1989

6   The biggest waste of water in the country by
far is when you spend half a pint and flush
two gallons.
Prince Philip (1921–) The consort of Queen Elizabeth
II.
Speech, 1965

7   Simply having a convention which says you
must not make species extinct does not make
a blind bit of difference.
Prince Philip
Referring to the UN treaty on world conservation, Mar 1989
The Sunday Correspondent, 31 Dec, 1989

8   Our English countryside is one of the most
heavily man-made habitats in Europe. To
make it into a green museum would be to
belie its whole history.
Nicholas Ridley (1929–) British politician.
Speech, Nov 1988

CONSERVATISM

See also change

1   All conservatism is based upon the idea that
if you leave things alone you leave them as
they are. But you do not. If you leave a
thing alone you leave it to a torrent of
change.
G. K. Chesterton (1874–1936) British writer.
Orthodoxy, Ch. 7

2   I love everything that's old: old friends, old
times, old manners, old books, old wine.
Oliver Goldsmith (1728–74) Irish-born British writer.
She Stoops to Conquer, I

3 You can't teach the old maestro a new tune.
Jack Kerouac (1922–69) US novelist.
On the Road, Pt. I

4 I do not know which makes a man more conservative – to know nothing but the present, or nothing but the past.
John Maynard Keynes (1883–1946) British economist.
The End of Laisser-Faire, I

5 What is conservatism? Is it not adherence to the old and tried, against the new and untried?
Abraham Lincoln (1809–65) US statesman.
Speech, 27 Feb 1860

6 You can't teach an old dogma new tricks.
Dorothy Parker (1893–1967) US writer.
Wit's End (R. E. Drennan)

7 The radical invents the views. When he has worn them out, the conservative adopts them.
Mark Twain (Samuel Langhorne Clemens; 1835–1910) US writer.
Notebooks

CONSTANCY

See also change, conservatism

1 A foolish consistency is the hobgoblin of little minds, adored by little statesmen and philosophers and divines. With consistency a great soul has simply nothing to do.
Ralph Waldo Emerson (1803–82) US poet and essayist.
Essays, 'Self-reliance'

2 Consistency is contrary to nature, contrary to life. The only completely consistent people are the dead.
Aldous Huxley (1894–1964) British novelist.
Do What you Will

3 *Plus ça change, plus c'est la même chose.*
The more things change, the more they stay the same.
Alphonse Karr (1808–90) French writer.
Les Guêpes, Jan 1849

4 For men may come and men may go
But I go on for ever.
Alfred, Lord Tennyson (1809–92) British poet.
The Brook

5 Still glides the Stream, and shall for ever glide;
The Form remains, the Function never dies.
William Wordsworth (1770–1850) British poet.
The River Duddon, 'After-Thought'

CONTEMPT

See also ridicule

1 She was nothing more than a mere good-tempered, civil and obliging young woman; as such we could scarcely dislike her – she was only an Object of Contempt.
Jane Austen (1775–1817) British novelist.
Love and Friendship

2 'You threaten us, fellow? Do your worst,
Blow your pipe there till you burst!'
Robert Browning (1812–89) British poet.
The Pied Piper of Hamelin

3 He looked at me as if I was a side dish he hadn't ordered.
Ring Lardner Jnr (1885–1933) American humorist.
Referring to W. H. Taft, US president (1909–13)
The Home Book of Humorous Quotations (A. K. Adams)

CONTENTMENT

See also happiness, satisfaction

1 Live with the gods. And he does so who constantly shows them that his soul is satisfied with what is assigned to him.
Marcus Aurelius (121–180 AD) Roman emperor.
Meditations, Bk. V, Ch. 27

2 Sweet Stay-at-Home, sweet Well-content.
W. H. Davies (1871–1940) British poet.
Sweet Stay-at-Home

3 Here with a Loaf of Bread beneath the Bough,
A Flask of Wine, a Book of Verse – and Thou
Beside me singing in the Wilderness –
And Wilderness is Paradise enow.
Edward Fitzgerald (1809–83) British poet.
The Rubáiyát of Omar Khayyám

4 Notwithstanding the poverty of my outside experience, I have always had a significance for myself, and every chance to stumble along my straight and narrow little path, and to worship at the feet of my Deity, and what more can a human soul ask for?
Alice James (1848–92) US diarist.
The Diary of Alice James (ed. Leon Edel)

5 If I had not been born Perón, I would have liked to be Perón.
Juan Perón (1895–1974) Argentine statesman.
The Observer, 'Sayings of the Week', 21 Feb 1960

6 Nought's had, all's spent,
Where our desire is got without content.
'Tis safer to be that which we destroy,
Than by destruction dwell in doubtful joy.
William Shakespeare (1564–1616) English dramatist.
Macbeth, III:2

7 O, this life
Is nobler than attending for a check,
Richer than doing nothing for a bribe,
Prouder than rustling in unpaid-for silk.
William Shakespeare
Cymbeline, III:3

CONTRACEPTION

See also sex

1 Vasectomy means not ever having to say you're sorry.
Larry Adler (1914–   ) US harmonica player and entertainer.
Attrib.

2 I want to tell you a terrific story about oral contraception. I asked this girl to sleep with me and she said 'no'.
Woody Allen (Allen Stewart Konigsberg; 1935–   ) US film actor.
Woody Allen: Clown Prince of American Humor (Adler and Feinman), Ch. 2

3 He no play-a da game. He no make-a da rules!
Earl Butz (1909–   ) US politician.
Referring to the Pope's strictures against contraception
Remark, 1974

4 The command 'Be fruitful and multiply was promulgated according to our authorities, when the population of the world consisted of two people.
Dean Inge (1860–1954) British churchman.
More Lay Thoughts of a Dean

5 It is now quite lawful for a Catholic woman to avoid pregnancy by a resort to mathematics, though she is still forbidden to resort to physics and chemistry.
H. L. Mencken (1880–1956) US journalist.
Notebooks, 'Minority Report'

6 Contraceptives should be used on every conceivable occasion.
Spike Milligan (1918–   ) British comic actor and author.
The Last Goon Show of All

7 Skullion had little use for contraceptives at the best of times. Unnatural, he called them, and placed them in the lower social category of things along with elastic-sided boots and made-up bow ties. Not the sort of attire for a gentleman.
Tom Sharpe (1928–   ) British novelist.
Porterhouse Blue, Ch. 9

8 Protestant women may take the Pill. Roman Catholic women must keep taking the *Tablet*.
Irene Thomas (1920–   ) British writer.
The Tablet is a British Roman Catholic newspaper
Attrib.

CONVERSATION

See also speech

1 Although there exist many thousand subjects for elegant conversation, there are persons who cannot meet a cripple without talking about feet.
Chinese proverb

2 I have but ninepence in ready money, but I can draw for a thousand pounds.
Joseph Addison (1672–1719) British essayist.
Comparing his ability to make conversation and to write
Life of Johnson (Boswell)

3 JOHNSON. Well, we had a good talk.
BOSWELL. Yes, Sir; you tossed and gored several persons.
James Boswell (1740–95) Scottish lawyer and writer.
Life of Johnson, Vol. II

4 Questioning is not the mode of conversation among gentlemen.
Samuel Johnson (1709–84) British lexicographer.
Life of Johnson (J. Boswell), Vol. II

5 That is the happiest conversation where there is no competition, no vanity but a calm quiet interchange of sentiments.
Samuel Johnson
Life of Johnson (J. Boswell), Vol. II

6 Beware of the conversationalist who adds 'in other words'. He is merely starting afresh.
Robert Morley (1908–   ) British actor.
The Observer, 'Sayings of the Week', 6 Dec 1964

7 Ideal conversation must be an exchange of thought, and not, as many of those who worry most about their shortcomings believe, an eloquent exhibition of wit or oratory.
Emily Post (1873–1960) US writer.
Etiquette, Ch. 6

8 Conversation has a kind of charm about it, an insinuating and insidious something that elicits secrets from us just like love or liquor.
Seneca (c. 4 BC–65 AD) Roman author.
Epistles

9 Teas,
Where small talk dies in agonies.
Percy Bysshe Shelley (1792–1822) British poet.
Peter Bell the Third

10 There is no such thing as conversation. It is an illusion. There are intersecting monologues, that is all.
Rebecca West (Cicely Isabel Fairfield; 1892–1983) British novelist and journalist.
There Is No Conversation, Ch. 1

11 A good listener is not someone who has nothing to say. A good listener is a good talker with a sore throat.
Katherine Whitehorn (1926–   ) British journalist.
Attrib.

CORRUPTION

See also bribery, decline

1 Among a people generally corrupt, liberty cannot long exist.
Edmund Burke (1729–97) British politician.
Letter to the Sheriffs of Bristol, 1777

2 Corruption, the most infallible symptom of constitutional liberty.
Edward Gibbon (1737–94) British historian.
Decline and Fall of the Roman Empire, Ch. 21

3 The hungry sheep look up, and are not fed,
But, swoln with wind and the rank mist they draw,
Rot inwardly, and foul contagion spread.
John Milton (1608–74) English poet.
Lycidas

4 As killing as the canker to the rose.
John Milton
Lycidas

5 All things can corrupt perverted minds.
Ovid (Publius Ovidius Naso; 43 BC–17 AD) Roman poet.
Tristia, Bk. II

6 Any institution which does not suppose the people good, and the magistrate corruptible is evil.
Robespierre (1758–94) French lawyer and revolutionary.
Déclaration des Droits de l'homme, 24 Apr 1793

7 Something is rotten in the state of Denmark.
William Shakespeare (1564–1616) English dramatist.
Hamlet, I:4

8 For sweetest things turn sourest by their deeds:
Lilies that fester smell far worse than weeds.
William Shakespeare
Sonnet 94

9 A reformer is a guy who rides through a sewer in a glass-bottomed boat.
James J. Walker (1881–1946) US politician.
Speech, New York, 1928

10 All those men have their price.
Robert Walpole (1676–1745) British statesman.
Memoirs of Sir Robert Walpole (W. Coxe)

COSMETICS

See also appearance

1 Most women are not so young as they are painted.
Max Beerbohm (1872–1956) British writer.
A Defence of Cosmetics

2 Wherever one wants to be kissed.
Coco Chanel (1883–1971) French dress designer.
When asked where one should wear perfume
Coco Chanel, Her Life, Her Secrets (Marcel Haedrich)

3 In the factory we make cosmetics. In the store we sell hope.
Charles Revson (1906–75) US business tycoon.
Fire and Ice (A. Tobias)

COUNTRYSIDE

See also agriculture, ecology, flowers, Nature, trees

1 I nauseate walking; 'tis a country diversion, I

loathe the country and everything that relates to it.
William Congreve (1670–1729) British Restoration dramatist.
The Way of the World, IV:4

2 God made the country, and man made the town.
William Cowper (1731–1800) British poet.
The Task

3 Ever charming, ever new,
When will the landscape tire the view?
John Dyer (1700–58) British poet.
Grongar Hill

4 There is nothing good to be had in the country, or, if there is, they will not let you have it.
William Hazlitt (1778–1830) British essayist.
Observations on Wordsworth's 'Excursion'

5 When I am in the country I wish to vegetate like the country.
William Hazlitt
On Going a Journey

6 Here of a Sunday morning
My love and I would lie,
And see the coloured counties,
And hear the larks so high
About us in the sky.
A. E. Housman (1859–1936) British scholar and poet.
A Shropshire Lad, 'Bredon Hill'

7 It must be generations since anyone but highbrows lived in this cottage . . . I imagine most of the agricultural labourers round here commute from London.
Anthony Powell (1905–) British novelist.
A Dance to the Music of Time: The Kindly Ones, Ch. 2

8 O, Brignal banks are wild and fair,
And Gretna woods are green,
And you may gather garlands there
Would grace a summer queen.
Walter Scott (1771–1832) Scottish novelist.
Rokeby, III

9 Under the greenwood tree
Who loves to lie with me,
And turn his merry note
Unto the sweet bird's throat,
Come hither, come hither, come hither.
Here shall he see
No enemy
But winter and rough weather.
William Shakespeare (1564–1616) English dramatist.
As You Like It, II:5

10 Anybody can be good in the country.
Oscar Wilde (1854–1900) Irish-born British dramatist.
The Picture of Dorian Gray, Ch. 19

COURAGE

See also endurance, heroism, patriotism

1 The sons of the prophet were brave men and bold,
And quite unaccustomed to fear,
But the bravest by far in the ranks of the Shah
Was Abdul the Bulbul Amir.
Anonymous
Abdul the Bulbul Amir

2 Because of my title, I was the first to enter here. I shall be the last to go out.
Duchesse d'Alençon (d. 1897) Bavarian-born duchess.
Refusing help during a fire, 4 May 1897, at a charity bazaar in Paris. She died along with 120 others
Attrib.

3 No coward soul is mine,
No trembler in the world's storm-troubled sphere:
I see Heaven's glories shine,
And faith shines equal, arming me from fear.
Emily Brontë (1818–48) British novelist.
Last Lines

4 Perhaps your fear in passing judgement is greater than mine in receiving it.
Giordano Bruno (1548–1600) Italian philosopher.
Said to the cardinals who excommunicated him, 8 Feb 1600
Attrib.

5 And though hard be the task,
'Keep a stiff upper lip.'
Phoebe Cary (1824–71) US poet.
Keep a Stiff Upper Lip

6 Down these mean streets a man must go who is not himself mean; who is neither tarnished nor afraid.
Raymond Chandler (1888–1959) US novelist.
The Simple Art of Murder

7 The Red Badge of Courage.
Stephen Crane (1871–1900) US writer.
Title of novel

8 Boldness, and again boldness, and always boldness!
Georges Jacques Danton (1759–94) French political activist.
Speech, French Legislative Committee, 2 Sept 1792

9 Oliver Twist has asked for more.
Charles Dickens (1812–70) British novelist.
Oliver Twist, Ch. 2

10 I'll bell the cat.
Archibald Douglas (1449–1514) Scottish nobleman.
Of his proposed capture of Robert Cochrane (executed 1482); the phrase 'bell the cat' was earlier used by Eustache Deschamps in his *Ballade: Le Chat et les souris*

11 None but the Brave deserves the Fair.
John Dryden (1631–1700) British poet and dramatist.
Alexander's Feast

12 Courage is the price that Life exacts for granting peace.
Amelia Earhart (1898–1937) US flyer.
Courage

13 Come cheer up, my lads! 'tis to glory we steer,
To add something more to this wonderful year;
To honour we call you, not press you like slaves,
For who are so free as the sons of the waves?
Heart of oak are our ships,
Heart of oak are our men:
We always are ready;
Steady, boys, steady;
We'll fight and we'll conquer again and again.
David Garrick (1717–79) British actor and manager.
Heart of Oak

14 The boy stood on the burning deck
Whence all but he had fled;
The flame that lit the battle's wreck
Shone round him o'er the dead.
Felicia Dorothea Hemans (1793–1835) British poet.
Casabianca

15 It is better to be the widow of a hero than the wife of a coward.
Dolores Ibarruri (1895–1989) Spanish politician.
Speech, Valencia, 1936

16 If the creator had a purpose in equipping us with a neck, he surely meant us to stick it out.
Arthur Koestler (1905–83) Hungarian-born British writer.
Encounter, May 1970

17 Then out spake brave Horatius,
The Captain of the Gate:
'To every man upon this earth
Death cometh soon or late.
And how can man die better
Than facing fearful odds,
For the ashes of his fathers,
And the temples of his Gods?'
Lord Macaulay (1800–59) British historian.
Lays of Ancient Rome, 'Horatius', 27

18 The stubborn spear-men still made good
Their dark impenetrable wood,
Each stepping where his comrade stood,
The instant that he fell.
Walter Scott (1771–1832) Scottish novelist.
Marmion, VI

19 Once more unto the breach, dear friends, once more;
Or close the wall up with our English dead.
William Shakespeare (1564–1616) English dramatist.
Henry V, III:1

20 He was a bold man that first eat an oyster.
Jonathan Swift (1667–1745) Irish-born Anglican priest and writer.
Polite Conversation, Dialogue 2

21 Half a league, half a league,
Half a league onward,
All in the valley of Death
Rode the six hundred.
Alfred, Lord Tennyson (1809–92) British poet.
The Charge of the Light Brigade

22 Into the jaws of Death,

Into the mouth of Hell.
Alfred, Lord Tennyson
The Charge of the Light Brigade

23 Fortune favours the brave.
Terence (Publius Terentius Afer; c. 190–159 BC) Roman poet.
Phormio

24 The three-o'-clock in the morning courage, which Bonaparte thought was the rarest.
Henry David Thoreau (1817–62) US writer.
Walden, 'Sounds'

COURTESY

See also chivalry, etiquette, manners, respect

1 Civility costs nothing.
Proverb

2 If a man be gracious and courteous to strangers, it shews he is a citizen of the world.
Francis Bacon (1561–1626) English philosopher.
Essays, 'Of Goodness and Goodness of Nature'

3 The English are polite by telling lies. The Americans are polite by telling the truth.
Malcolm Bradbury (1932–) British academic and novelist.
Stepping Westward, Bk. II, Ch. 5

4 Courtesy is not dead – it has merely taken refuge in Great Britain.
Georges Duhamel (1884–1966) French writer.
The Observer, 'Sayings of Our Times', 31 May 1953

COWARDICE

See also self-preservation

1 Probably a fear we have of facing up to the real issues. Could you say we were guilty of Noël Cowardice?
Peter De Vries (1910–) US novelist.
Comfort me with Apples, Ch. 8

2 None but a coward dares to boast that he has never known fear.
Marshal Foch (1851–1929) French soldier.
Attrib.

3 He led his regiment from behind
He found it less exciting.
W. S. Gilbert (1836–1911) British dramatist.
The Gondoliers, I

4 When the foeman bares his steel,
Tarantara! tarantara!
We uncomfortable feel.
W. S. Gilbert
The Pirates of Penzance, II

5 To a surprising extent the war-lords in shining armour, the apostles of the martial virtues, tend not to die fighting when the time comes. History is full of ignominious getaways by the great and famous.
George Orwell (Eric Blair; 1903–50) British novelist.
Who Are the War Criminals?

6 The summer soldier and the sunshine patriot will, in this crisis, shrink from the service of their country.
Thomas Paine (1737–1809) British writer.
Pennsylvania Journal, 'The American Crisis'

7 Some craven scruple
Of thinking too precisely on th' event.
William Shakespeare (1564–1616) English dramatist.
Hamlet, IV:4

8 I dare not fight; but I will wink and hold out mine iron.
William Shakespeare
Henry V, II:1

9 Cowards die many times before their deaths:
The valiant never taste of death but once.
William Shakespeare
Julius Caesar, II:2

CREATION

1 The Hand that made us is divine.
Joseph Addison (1672–1719) British essayist.
The Spectator, 465

2 In the beginning God created the heaven and the earth.
And the earth was without form, and void; and darkness was upon the face of the deep. And the Spirit of God moved upon the face of the waters.
And God said, Let there be light: and there was light.
And God saw the light, that it was good: and God divided the light from the darkness.
And God called the light Day, and the darkness he called Night. And the evening and the morning were the first day.
Bible: Genesis
1:1–5

3 And God called the dry land Earth; and the gathering together of the waters called he Seas: and God saw that it was good.
And God said, Let the earth bring forth grass, the herb yielding seed, and the fruit tree yielding fruit after his kind, whose seed is in itself, upon the earth: and it was so.
Bible: Genesis
1:10–11

4 And God made two great lights: the greater light to rule the day, and the lesser light to rule the night: he made the stars also.
Bible: Genesis
1:16

5 And God said, Let the earth bring forth the living creature after his kind, cattle, and

creeping thing, and beast of the earth after his kind: and it was so.
Bible: Genesis
1:24

6 And God said, Let us make man in our image, after our likeness: and let them have dominion over the fish of the sea, and over the fowl of the air, and over the cattle, and over all the earth, and over every creeping thing that creepeth upon the earth.
So God created man in his own image, in the image of God created he him; male and female created he them.
And God blessed them, and God said unto them, Be fruitful, and multiply, and replenish the earth, and subdue it: and have dominion over the fish of the sea, and over the fowl of the air, and over every living thing that moveth upon the earth.
Bible: Genesis
1:26–28

7 When the stars threw down their spears,
And watered heaven with their tears,
Did he smile his work to see?
Did he who made the Lamb make thee?
William Blake (1757–1827) British poet.
Songs of Experience, 'The Tiger'

8 Little Lamb, who made thee?
Dost thou know who made thee?
William Blake
Songs of Innocence, 'The Lamb'

9 Whan that the month in which the world bigan,
That highte March, whan God first maked man.
Geoffrey Chaucer (c. 1342–1400) English poet.
The Canterbury Tales, 'The Nun's Priest's Tale'

10 'Who *is* the Potter, pray, and who the Pot?'
Edward Fitzgerald (1809–83) British poet.
The Rubáiyát of Omar Khayyám

11 I cannot forgive Descartes; in all his philosophy he did his best to dispense with God. But he could not avoid making Him set the world in motion with a flip of His thumb; after that he had no more use for God.
Blaise Pascal (1623–62) French philosopher and mathematician.
Pensées, II

12 For suddenly it was clear to me that virtue in the creator is not the same as virtue in the creature. For the creator, if he should love his creature, would be loving only a part of himself; but the creature, praising the creator, praises an infinity beyond himself.
Olaf Stapledon (1886–1950) British philosopher and science-fiction writer.
Star Maker, Ch. 13

13 'Do you know who made you?' 'Nobody, as I knows on,' said the child, with a short laugh ... 'I 'spect I grow'd.'
Harriet Beecher Stowe (1811–96) US novelist.
Uncle Tom's Cabin, Ch. 20

14 Which beginning of time according to our Chronologie, fell upon the entrance of the night preceding the twenty third day of *Octob.,* in the year of the Julian Calendar, 710.
James Ussher (1581–1656) Irish churchman.
Referring to the Creation, as described in Genesis, which, he had calculated, took place on 22 Oct 4004 BC
The Annals of the World

15 God made everything out of nothing. But the nothingness shows through.
Paul Valéry (1871–1945) French poet and writer.
Mauvaises Pensées et autres

16 The art of creation
is older than the art of killing.
Andrei Voznesensky (1933–) Soviet poet.
Poem with a Footnote

CRICKET

See also sport and games

1 It's not in support of cricket but as an earnest protest against golf.
Max Beerbohm (1872–1956) British writer.
Said when giving a shilling towards W. G. Grace's testimonial
Carr's Dictionary of Extraordinary English Cricketers

2 I do love cricket – it's so very English.
Sarah Bernhardt (Sarah Henriette Rosine Bernard; 1844–1923) French actress.
On seeing a game of football
Nijinsky (R. Buckle)

3 They came to see me bat not to see you bowl.
W. G. Grace (1848–1915) British doctor and cricketer.
Refusing to leave the crease after being bowled first ball in front of a large crowd
Attrib.

4 It's more than a game. It's an institution.
Thomas Hughes (1822–96) British novelist.
Referring to cricket
Tom Brown's Schooldays, Pt. II, Ch. 7

5 There's a breathless hush in the Close tonight –
Ten to make and the match to win –
A bumping pitch and a blinding light,
An hour to play and the last man in.
Henry John Newbolt (1862–1938) British poet.
Vitaî Lampada

6 I tend to believe that cricket is the greatest thing that God ever created on earth ... certainly greater than sex, although sex isn't too bad either.
Harold Pinter (1930–) British dramatist.
The Observer, 5 Oct 1980

7 I have always looked upon cricket as organised loafing.

William Temple (1881–1944) British churchman.
Address to parents when headmaster of Repton School

8 If the French noblesse had been capable of playing cricket with their peasants, their chateaux would never have been burnt.

George Macaulay Trevelyan (1876–1962) British historian.
English Social History, Ch. XIII

9 It requires one to assume such indecent postures.

Oscar Wilde (1854–1900) Irish-born British dramatist.
Explaining why he did not play cricket
Attrib.

CRIME

See also murder, theft

1 And surely your blood of your lives will I require; at the hand of every beast will I require it, and at the hand of man; at the hand of every man's brother will I require the life of man.
Whoso sheddeth man's blood, by man shall his blood be shed: for in the image of God made he man.

Bible: Genesis
9:5–6

2 How many crimes committed merely because their authors could not endure being wrong!

Albert Camus (1913–60) French existentialist writer.
The Fall

3 He is the Napoleon of crime.

Arthur Conan Doyle (1856–1930) British writer.
Referring to Professor Moriarty
The Final Problem

4 If poverty is the mother of crime, stupidity is its father.

Jean de La Bruyère (1645–96) French satirist.
Les Caractères

5 Crime, like virtue, has its degrees.

Jean Racine (1639–99) French dramatist.
Phèdre, IV:2

6 I came to the conclusion many years ago that almost all crime is due to the repressed desire for aesthetic expression.

Evelyn Waugh (1903–66) British novelist.
Decline and Fall, Pt. III, Ch. 1

CRITICISM

See also actors, compliments, insults, poets, writers

1 I am bound by my own definition of criticism: a disinterested endeavour to learn and propagate the best that is known and thought in the world.

Matthew Arnold (1822–88) British poet and critic.
Essays in Criticism, First Series, 'Functions of Criticism at the Present Time'

2 There is less in this than meets the eye.

Tallulah Bankhead (1903–68) US actress.
Referring to a revival of a play by Maeterlinck
Shouts and Murmurs (A. Woollcott), 'Capsule Criticism'

3 Too much counterpoint; what is worse, Protestant counterpoint.

Thomas Beecham (1879–1961) British conductor.
Said of J. S. Bach
The Guardian, 8 Mar 1971

4 Of all fatiguing, futile, empty trades, the worst, I suppose, is writing about writing.

Hilaire Belloc (1870–1953) French-born British poet.
The Silence of the Sea

5 Criticism of a long-running play; the text is: 'Jesus Christ the same yesterday, and today, and for ever'.

Robert Benchley (1889–1945) US humorist.
Attrib.

6 And why beholdest thou the mote that is in thy brother's eye, but considerest not the beam that is in thine own eye?

Bible: Matthew
7:3

7 He who discommendeth others obliquely commendeth himself.

Thomas Browne (1605–82) English physician and writer.
Christian Morals, Pt. I

8 A great deal of contemporary criticism reads to me like a man saying: 'Of course I do not like green cheese: I am very fond of brown sherry.'

G. K. Chesterton (1874–1936) British writer.
All I Survey

9 To see him act, is like reading Shakespeare by flashes of lightning.

Samuel Taylor Coleridge (1772–1834) British poet.
Referring to Kean
Table Talk

10 I never realized before that Albert married beneath him.

Noël Coward (1899–1973) British dramatist.
After seeing a certain actress in the role of Queen Victoria
Tynan on Theatre (K. Tynan)

11 This paper will no doubt be found interesting by those who take an interest in it.

John Dalton (1766–1844) British scientist.
Said on many occasions when chairing scientific meetings
Attrib.

12 If you hear that someone is speaking ill of you, instead of trying to defend yourself you should say: 'He obviously does not know me very well, since there are so many other faults he could have mentioned'.

Epictetus (c. 60–110 AD) Stoic philosopher.
Enchiridion

13 He played the King as though under

momentary apprehension that someone else was about to play the ace.

Eugene Field (1850–95) US poet and journalist.
Referring to Creston Clarke's performance in the role of King Lear
Attrib.

14 It is not good enough to spend time and ink in describing the penultimate sensations and physical movements of people getting into a state of rut, we all know them too well.

John Galsworthy (1867–1933) British novelist.
Referring to D. H. Lawrence's *Sons and Lovers*
Letter to Edward Garnett, 13 Apr 1914

15 Funny without being vulgar.

W. S. Gilbert (1836–1911) British dramatist.
Referring to Sir Henry Irving's *Hamlet*
Attrib.

16 My dear chap! Good isn't the word!

W. S. Gilbert
Speaking to an actor after he had given a poor performance
Attrib.

17 We were as nearly bored as enthusiasm would permit.

Edmund Gosse (1849–1928) British writer and critic.
Referring to a play by Swinburne
Biography of Edward Marsh (C. Hassall)

18 There are two things which I am confident I can do very well: one is an introduction to any literary work, stating what it is to contain, and how it should be executed in the most perfect manner; the other is a conclusion, shewing from various causes why the execution has not been equal to what the author promised to himself and to the public.

Samuel Johnson (1709–84) British lexicographer.
Life of Johnson (J. Boswell), Vol. I

19 It is burning a farthing candle at Dover, to shew light at Calais.

Samuel Johnson
Referring to the impact of Sheridan's works upon the English language
Life of Johnson (J. Boswell), Vol. I

20 You *may* abuse a tragedy, though you cannot write one. You may scold a carpenter who has made you a bad table, though you cannot make a table. It is not your trade to make tables.

Samuel Johnson
Referring to the qualifications needed to indulge in literary criticism
Life of Johnson (J. Boswell), Vol. I

21 This man I thought had been a Lord among wits; but, I find, he is only a wit among Lords.

Samuel Johnson
Referring to Lord Chesterfield
Life of Johnson (J. Boswell), Vol. I

22 They teach the morals of a whore, and the manners of a dancing master.

Samuel Johnson
Referring to Lord Chesterfield's *Letters*
Life of Johnson (J. Boswell), Vol. I

23 Yes, Sir, many men, many women, and many children.

Samuel Johnson
When asked by Dr Blair whether any man of their own time could have written the poems of Ossian
Life of Johnson (J. Boswell), Vol. I

24 Difficult do you call it, Sir? I wish it were impossible.

Samuel Johnson
On hearing a famous violinist
Johnsonian Miscellanies (ed. G. B. Hill), Vol. II

25 They are forced plants, raised in a hot-bed; and they are poor plants; they are but cucumbers after all.

Samuel Johnson
Referring to Gray's *Odes*
Life of Johnson (J. Boswell), Vol. IV

26 The pleasure of criticizing robs us of the pleasure of being moved by some very fine things.

Jean de La Bruyère (1645–96) French satirist.
Les Caractères

27 They are great parables, the novels, but false art. They are only parables. All the people are *fallen angels* – even the dirtiest scrubs. This I cannot stomach. People are not fallen angels, they are merely people.

D. H. Lawrence (1885–1930) British novelist.
Referring to the novels of Dostoyevsky
Letter to J. Middleton Murray and Katherine Mansfield, 17 Feb 1916

28 His verse exhibits . . . something that is rather like Keats's vulgarity with a Public School accent.

F. R. Leavis (1895–1978) British literary critic.
Referring to Rupert Brooke
New Bearings in English Poetry, Ch. 2

29 I cried all the way to the bank.

Liberace (Wladzin Valentino Liberace; 1919–87) US pianist and showman.
Said when asked whether he minded being criticized
Liberace: An Autobiography, Ch. 2

30 People who like this sort of thing will find this is the sort of thing they like.

Abraham Lincoln (1809–65) US statesman.
A comment on a book
Attrib.

31 His writing bears the same relation to poetry which a Turkey carpet bears to a picture. There are colours in the Turkey carpet out of which a picture might be made. There are words in Mr Montgomery's writing which, when disposed in certain orders and combinations, have made, and will make again, good poetry. But, as they now stand, they seem to be put together on principle in such a manner as to give no image of anything 'in the heavens above, or in the earth beneath, or in the waters under the earth'.

Lord Macaulay (1800–59) British historian.
Literary Essays Contributed to the 'Edinburgh Review', 'Mr. Robert Montgomery's Poems'

32 It was a book to kill time for those who like it better dead.

Rose Macaulay (1889–1958) British writer.
Attrib.

33 I was so long writing my review that I never got around to reading the book.

Groucho Marx (Julius Marx; 1895–1977) US comedian.
Attrib.

34 People ask you for criticism, but they only want praise.

W. Somerset Maugham (1874–1965) British novelist.
Of Human Bondage, Ch. 50

35 Yea, marry, now it is somewhat, for now it is rhyme; before, it was neither rhyme nor reason.

Thomas More (1478–1535) English lawyer and scholar.
On reading an unremarkable book recently rendered into verse by a friend of his
Apophthegms (Bacon), 287

36 Prolonged, indiscriminate reviewing of books involves constantly *inventing* reactions towards books about which one has no spontaneous feelings whatever.

George Orwell (Eric Blair; 1903–50) British novelist.
Confessions of a Book Reviewer

37 She ran the whole gamut of the emotions from A to B.

Dorothy Parker (1893–1967) US writer.
Referring to a performance by Katharine Hepburn on Broadway
Attrib.

38 This is not a novel to be tossed aside lightly. It should be thrown with great force.

Dorothy Parker
Book review
Wit's End (R. E. Dremman)

39 'Tis hard to say, if greater want of skill
Appear in writing or in judging ill.

Alexander Pope (1688–1744) British poet.
An Essay on Criticism

40 Damn with faint praise, assent with civil leer,
And, without sneering, teach the rest to sneer.

Alexander Pope
Epistle to Dr. Arbuthnot

41 I never read anything concerning my work. I feel that criticism is a letter to the public which the author, since it is not directed to him, does not have to open and read.

Rainer Maria Rilke (1875–1926) Austrian poet.
Letters

42 Very good, but it has its *longueurs*.

Antoine de Rivarol (1753–1801) French writer and wit.
Giving his opinion of a couplet by a mediocre poet
Das Buch des Lachens (W. Scholz)

43 The Stealthy School of Criticism.

Dante Gabriel Rossetti (1828–82) British painter and poet.
Letter to the *Athenaeum*, 1871

44 Wagner has lovely moments but awful quarters of an hour.

Gioacchino Rossini (1792–1868) Italian operatic composer.
Remark made to Emile Naumann, April 1867
Italienische Tondichter (Naumann)

45 I have seen, and heard, much of Cockney impudence before now; but never expected to hear a coxcomb ask two hundred guineas for flinging a pot of paint in the public's face.

John Ruskin (1819–1900) British art critic and writer.
On Whistler's painting 'Nocturne in Black and Gold'
Letter, 18 June 1877

46 For I am nothing if not critical.

William Shakespeare (1564–1616) English dramatist.
Othello, II:1

47 It does not follow . . . that the right to criticize Shakespeare involves the power of writing better plays. And in fact . . . I do not profess to write better plays.

George Bernard Shaw (1856–1950) Irish dramatist and critic.
Three Plays for Puritans, Preface

48 It is disappointing to report that George Bernard Shaw appearing as George Bernard Shaw is sadly miscast in the part. Satirists should be heard and not seen.

Robert E. Sherwood (1896–1955) US writer and dramatist.
Reviewing a Shaw play

49 It had only one fault. It was kind of lousy.

James Thurber (1894–1961) US humorist.
Remark made about a play
Attrib.

50 A strange, horrible business, but I suppose good enough for Shakespeare's day.

Victoria (1819–1901) Queen of the United Kingdom.
Giving her opinion of *King Lear*
Living Biographies of Famous Rulers (H. Thomas)

51 I do not think this poem will reach its destination.

Voltaire (François-Marie Arouet; 1694–1778) French writer.
Reviewing Rousseau's poem 'Ode to Posterity'
Attrib.

52 As far as criticism is concerned, we don't resent that unless it is absolutely biased, as it is in most cases.

John Vorster (Balthazar Johannes Vorster; 1915–83) South African politician.
The Observer, 'Sayings of the Week', 9 Nov 1969

53 You have riches and freedom here but I feel

no sense of faith or direction. You have so many computers, why don't you use them in the search for love?

Lech Walesa (1943–) Polish trade unionist.
Speech, Dec 1988

54 My dear fellow a unique evening! I wouldn't have left a turn unstoned.

Arthur Wimperis (1874–1953) British screenwriter.
Replying when asked his opinion of a vaudeville show
Fifty Years of Vaudeville (E. Short)

55 I saw it at a disadvantage – the curtain was up.

Walter Winchell (1879–1972) US journalist.
Referring to a show starring Earl Carroll
Come to Judgment (A. Whiteman)

56 Trivial personalities decomposing in the eternity of print.

Virginia Woolf (1882–1941) British novelist.
The Common Reader, 'Jane Eyre'

57 *Middlemarch*, the magnificent book which with all its imperfections is one of the few English novels for grown up people.

Virginia Woolf
The Common Reader, 'George Eliot'

58 He is all blood, dirt and sucked sugar stick.

W. B. Yeats (1865–1939) Irish poet.
Referring to Wilfred Owen
Letters on Poetry to Dorothy Wellesley, Letter, 21 Dec 1936

CRITICS

1 I will try to account for the degree of my aesthetic emotion. That, I conceive, is the function of the critic.

Clive Bell (1881–1964) British art critic.
Art, Pt. II, Ch. 3

2 A man must serve his time to every trade Save censure – critics all are ready made.

Lord Byron (1788–1824) British poet.
English Bards and Scotch Reviewers

3 Reviewers are usually people who would have been poets, historians, biographers, . . . if they could; they have tried their talents at one or at the other, and have failed; therefore they turn critics.

Samuel Taylor Coleridge (1772–1834) British poet.
Lectures on Shakespeare and Milton, I

4 I make my pictures for people, not for critics.

Cecil B. de Mille (1881–1959) US film producer and director.
Halliwell's Filmgoer's and Video Viewer's Companion

5 A good critic is one who narrates the adventures of his mind among masterpieces.

Anatole France (Jacques Anatole François Thibault; 1844–1924) French writer.
The Literary Life, Preface

6 I sometimes think
His critical judgement is so exquisite

It leaves us nothing to admire except his opinion.

Christopher Fry (1907–) British dramatist.
The Dark is Light Enough, II

7 Asking a working writer what he thinks about critics is like asking a lamp-post how it feels about dogs.

Christopher Hampton (1946–) British writer and dramatist.
The Sunday Times Magazine, 16 Oct 1977

8 What is a modern poet's fate?
To write his thoughts upon a slate;
The critic spits on what is done,
Gives it a wipe – and all is gone.

Thomas Hood (1799–1845) British poet.
Alfred Lord Tennyson, A Memoir (Hallam Tennyson), Vol. II, Ch. 3

9 Critics are more malicious about poetry than about other books – maybe because so many manqué poets write reviews.

Elizabeth Jennings (1926–) British poet.
Remark, Dec 1987

10 There is a certain race of men that either imagine it their duty, or make it their amusement, to hinder the reception of every work of learning or genius, who stand as sentinels in the avenues of fame, and value themselves upon giving Ignorance and Envy the first notice of a prey.

Samuel Johnson (1709–84) British lexicographer.
The Rambler

11 A fly, Sir, may sting a stately horse and make him wince; but one is but an insect, and the other is a horse still.

Samuel Johnson
Life of Johnson (J. Boswell), Vol. I

12 Dear Roger Fry whom I love as a man but detest as a movement.

Edward Howard Marsh (1872–1953) British civil servant and writer.
Roger Fry (1866–1934) was an artist and art critic, who championed the postimpressionists
Edward Marsh (Christopher Hassall), Ch. 11

13 Insects sting, not from malice, but because they want to live. It is the same with critics – they desire our blood, not our pain.

Friedrich Wilhelm Nietzsche (1844–1900) German philosopher.
Miscellaneous Maxims and Reflections

14 Nor in the critic let the man be lost.

Alexander Pope (1688–1744) British poet.
An Essay on Criticism

15 They will review a book by a writer much older than themselves as if it were an over-ambitious essay by a second-year student . . . It is the little dons I complain about, like so many corgis trotting up, hoping to nip your ankles.

J. B. Priestley (1894–1984) British novelist.
Outcries and Asides

16 The greater part of critics are parasites, who, if nothing had been written, would find nothing to write.
J. B. Priestley
Outcries and Asides

17 I doubt that art needed Ruskin any more than a moving train needs one of its passengers to shove it.
Tom Stoppard (1937–) Czech-born British dramatist.
Times Literary Supplement, 3 June 1977

18 I had another dream the other day about music critics. They were small and rodent-like with padlocked ears, as if they had stepped out of a painting by Goya.
Igor Stravinsky (1882–1971) Russian-born US composer.
The Evening Standard, 29 Oct 1969

19 A whipper-snapper of criticism who quoted dead languages to hide his ignorance of life.
Herbert Beerbohm Tree (1853–1917) British actor and theatre manager.
Referring to A. B. Walkley
Beerbohm Tree (Hesketh Pearson)

20 A critic is a man who knows the way but can't drive the car.
Kenneth Tynan (1927–80) British theatre critic.
New York Times Magazine, 9 Jan 1966

21 A good drama critic is one who perceives what is happening in the theatre of his time. A great drama critic also perceives what is not happening.
Kenneth Tynan
Tynan Right and Left, Foreword

CRUELTY

See also hurt, nastiness, violence

1 The wish to hurt, the momentary intoxication with pain, is the loophole through which the pervert climbs into the minds of ordinary men.
Jacob Bronowski (1908–74) British scientist and writer.
The Face of Violence, Ch. 5

2 Man's inhumanity to man
Makes countless thousands mourn!
Robert Burns (1759–96) Scottish poet.
Man was Made to Mourn

3 Fear is the parent of cruelty.
J. A. Froude (1818–94) British historian.
Short Studies on Great Subjects, 'Party Politics'

4 A cruel story runs on wheels, and every hand oils the wheels as they run.
Ouida (Marie Louise de la Ramée; 1839–1908) British novelist.
Wisdom, Wit and Pathos, 'Moths'

5 Whipping and abuse are like laudanum: You have to double the dose as the sensibilities decline.
Harriet Beecher Stowe (1811–96) US novelist.
Uncle Tom's Cabin, Ch. 20

CULTURE

See also civilization, philistinism

1 Culture, the acquainting ourselves with the best that has been known and said in the world, and thus with the history of the human spirit.
Matthew Arnold (1822–88) British poet and critic.
Literature and Dogma, Preface

2 Culture is the passion for sweetness and light, and (what is more) the passion for making them prevail.
Matthew Arnold
Literature and Dogma, Preface

3 Culture is an instrument wielded by professors to manufacture professors, who when their turn comes will manufacture professors.
Simone Weil (1909–43) French philosopher.
The Need for Roots

4 Mrs Ballinger is one of the ladies who pursue Culture in bands, as though it were dangerous to meet it alone.
Edith Wharton (1862–1937) US novelist.
Xingu, Ch. 1

CURIOSITY

See also interfering, wonder

1 Ask no questions and hear no lies.
Proverb

2 Curiosity killed the cat.
Proverb

3 Be not curious in unnecessary matters: for more things are shewed unto thee than men understand
Bible: Ecclesiasticus
3:23

4 'If everybody minded their own business,' the Duchess said in a hoarse growl, 'the world would go round a deal faster than it does.'
Lewis Carroll (Charles Lutwidge Dodgson; 1832–98) British writer.
Alice's Adventures in Wonderland, Ch. 6

5 There is no such thing on earth as an uninteresting subject; the only thing that can exist is an uninterested person.
G. K. Chesterton (1874–1936) British writer.
Heretics, Ch. 1

6 The world is but a school of inquiry.
Michel de Montaigne (1533–92) French essayist.
Essais, III

7 I ofen looked up at the sky an' assed meself the question – what is the stars, what is the stars?
Sean O'Casey (1884–1964) Irish dramatist.
Juno and the Paycock, I

8 Curiosity will conquer fear even more than bravery will.
James Stephens (1882–1950) Irish novelist.
The Crock of Gold

9 Disinterested intellectual curiosity is the life blood of real civilisation.
George Macaulay Trevelyan (1876–1962) British historian.
English Social History, Preface

CURSES

1 A plague o' both your houses!
They have made worms' meat of me.
William Shakespeare (1564–1616) English dramatist.
Romeo and Juliet, III:1

2 Curses are like young chickens, they always come home to roost.
Robert Southey (1774–1843) British poet.
The Curse of Kehama, Motto

3 'The curse is come upon me,' cried
The Lady of Shalott.
Alfred, Lord Tennyson (1809–92) British poet.
The Lady of Shalott, Pt. III

4 She has heard a whisper say,
A curse is on her if she stay
To look down to Camelot.
Alfred, Lord Tennyson
The Lady of Shalott, Pt. II

CUSTOM

See also habit

1 *O tempora! O mores!*
What times! What customs!
Cicero (106–43 BC) Roman orator and statesman.
In Catilinam, I

2 Custom, then, is the great guide of human life.
David Hume (1711–76) Scottish philosopher.
An Enquiry Concerning Human Understanding

3 But to my mind, though I am native here
And to the manner born, it is a custom
More honour'd in the breach than the observance.
William Shakespeare (1564–1616) English dramatist.
Hamlet, I:4

4 Custom calls me to't.
What custom wills, in all things should we do't,
The dust on antique time would lie unswept,
And mountainous error be too highly heap'd
For truth to o'erpeer.
William Shakespeare
Coriolanus, II:3

CYNICISM

1 One is not superior merely because one sees the world in an odious light.
Vicomte de Chateaubriand (1768–1848) French diplomat and writer.
Attrib.

2 Cynicism is an unpleasant way of saying the truth.
Lillian Hellman (1905–84) US dramatist.
The Little Foxes, I

3 A cynic is a man who, when he smells flowers, looks around for a coffin.
H. L. Mencken (1880–1956) US journalist.
Attrib.

4 Cynicism is humour in ill-health.
H. G. Wells (1866–1946) British writer.
Short Stories, 'The Last Trump'

5 A man who knows the price of everything and the value of nothing.
Oscar Wilde (1854–1900) Irish-born British dramatist.
A cynic
Lady Windermere's Fan, III

D

DAMNATION

See also devil, hell

1 Blot out his name, then, record one lost soul more,
One task more declined, one more footpath untrod,
One more devils'-triumph and sorrow for angels,
One wrong more to man, one more insult to God!
Robert Browning (1812–89) British poet.
The Lost Leader

2 You will be damned if you do – And you will be damned if you don't.
Lorenzo Dow (1777–1834) British churchman.
Speaking of Calvinism
Reflections on the Love of God

3 Now hast thou but one bare hour to live,
And then thou must be damn'd perpetually!
Stand still, you ever-moving spheres of heaven,
That time may cease, and midnight never come.
Christopher Marlowe (1564–93) English dramatist.
Doctor Faustus, V:2

4 Ugly hell, gape not! come not, Lucifer!

I'll burn my books!
Christopher Marlowe
Doctor Faustus, V:2

DANCING

1 On with the dance! let joy be unconfined;
No sleep till morn, when Youth and Pleasure meet
To chase the glowing Hours with flying feet.
Lord Byron (1788–1824) British poet.
Childe Harold's Pilgrimage, III

2 Will you, won't you, will you, won't you, will you join the dance?
Lewis Carroll (Charles Lutwidge Dodgson; 1832–98) British writer.
Alice's Adventures in Wonderland, Ch. 10

3 Dance, dance, dance little lady.
Noël Coward (1899–1973) British dramatist.
Title of song

4 I have discovered the dance. I have discovered the art which has been lost for two thousand years.
Isadora Duncan (1878–1927) US dancer.
My Life

5 Any time you're Lambeth way,
Any evening, any day,
You'll find us all doin' the Lambeth walk.
Douglas Furber (1885–1961) British songwriter.
Doin' the Lambeth Walk

6 My men, like satyrs grazing on the lawns,
Shall with their goat-feet dance an antic hay.
Christopher Marlowe (1564–93) English dramatist.
Edward the Second, I:1

7 Come, and trip it as you go
On the light fantastic toe.
John Milton (1608–74) English poet.
L'Allegro

8 . . . although one may fail to find happiness in theatrical life, one never wishes to give it up after having once tasted its fruits. To enter the School of the Imperial Ballet is to enter a convent whence frivolity is banned, and where merciless discipline reigns.
Anna Pavlova (1881–1931) Russian ballet dancer.
Pavlova: A Biography (ed. A. H. Franks), 'Pages of My Life'

DANGER

1 Any port in a storm.
Proverb

2 If you play with fire you get burnt.
Proverb

3 Defend us from all perils and dangers of this night.
The Book of Common Prayer
Morning Prayer, Prayer of St Chrysostom

4 Dangers by being despised grow great.
Edmund Burke (1729–97) British politician.
Speech, House of Commons, 11 May 1792

5 Of course I realized there was a measure of danger. Obviously I faced the possibility of not returning when first I considered going. Once faced and settled there really wasn't any good reason to refer to it.
Amelia Earhart (1898–1937) US flyer.
Referring to her flight in the 'Friendship'
20 Hours: 40 Minutes – Our Flight in the Friendship, Ch. 5

6 Believe me! The secret of reaping the greatest fruitfulness and the greatest enjoyment from life is to *live dangerously!*
Friedrich Wilhelm Nietzsche (1844–1900) German philosopher.
Die Fröhliche Wissenschaft, Bk. IV

7 There's a snake hidden in the grass.
Virgil (Publius Vergilius Maro; 70–19 BC) Roman poet.
Eclogue, Bk. III

DAY

1 Now the day is over,
Night is drawing nigh,
Shadows of the evening
Steal across the sky.
Sabine Baring-Gould (1834–1924) British author and hymn writer.
The Evening Hymn

2 The day begins to droop, –
Its course is done:
But nothing tells the place
Of the setting sun.
Robert Bridges (1844–1930) British poet.
Winter Nightfall

3 Where the quiet-coloured end of evening smiles,
Miles and miles.
Robert Browning (1812–89) British poet.
Love among the Ruins, I

4 The day Thou gavest, Lord, is ended,
The darkness falls at Thy behest.
John Ellerton (1826–93) British churchman.
A Liturgy for Missionary Meetings

5 Awake! for Morning in the Bowl of Night
Has flung the Stone that puts the Stars to Flight:
And Lo! the Hunter of the East has caught
The Sultan's Turret in a Noose of Light.
Edward Fitzgerald (1809–83) British poet.
The Rubáiyát of Omar Khayyám

6 The Curfew tolls the knell of parting day,
The lowing herd winds slowly o'er the lea,
The plowman homeward plods his weary way,
And leaves the world to darkness and to me.
Thomas Gray (1716–71) British poet.
Elegy Written in a Country Churchyard

7 Oh, what a beautiful morning!

Oh, what a beautiful day!
Oscar Hammerstein (1895–1960) US lyricist.
From the musical *Oklahoma*
Oh, What a Beautiful Morning

8 Sweet day, so cool, so calm, so bright,
The bridal of the earth and sky.
George Herbert (1593–1633) English poet.
Virtue

9 The candles burn their sockets,
The blinds let through the day,
The young man feels his pockets
And wonders what's to pay.
A. E. Housman (1859–1936) British scholar and poet.
Last Poems, 'Eight O'Clock'

10 Under the opening eye-lids of the morn.
John Milton (1608–74) English poet.
Lycidas

11 Now came still Evening on, and Twilight grey
Had in her sober livery all things clad.
John Milton
Paradise Lost, Bk. IV

12 Midnight brought on the dusky hour
Friendliest to sleep and silence.
John Milton
Paradise Lost, Bk. V

13 Three o'clock is always too late or too early
for anything you want to do.
Jean-Paul Sartre (1905–80) French writer.
Nausea

DEATH

See also afterlife, assassination, drowning, epitaphs, equality in death, execution, funerals, killing, last words, life and death, love and death, memorials, mortality, mourning, murder, obituaries, posterity, suicide

1 A man can die but once.
Proverb

2 A piece of churchyard fits everybody.
Proverb

3 As soon as man is born he begins to die.
Proverb

4 Dead men tell no tales.
Proverb

5 Death defies the doctor.
Proverb

6 Death is the great leveller.
Proverb

7 Fear of death is worse than death itself.
Proverb

8 Never speak ill of the dead.
Proverb

9 Nothing is certain but death and taxes.
Proverb

10 The good die young.
Proverb

11 The old man has his death before his eyes;
the young man behind his back.
Proverb

12 There will be sleeping enough in the grave.
Proverb

13 It's not that I'm afraid to die. I just don't
want to be there when it happens.
Woody Allen (Allen Stewart Konigsberg; 1935–) US film actor.
Without Feathers, 'Death (A Play)'

14 God grants an easy death only to the just.
Svetlana Alliluyeva (1926–) Russian writer; daughter of Joseph Stalin.
Twenty Letters to a Friend

15 As Amr lay on his death-bed a friend said to
him: 'You have often remarked that you
would like to find an intelligent man at the
point of death, and to ask him what his
feelings were. Now I ask *you* that question.
Amr replied, 'I feel as if heaven lay close
upon the earth and I between the two,
breathing through the eye of a needle.'
Amr Ibn Al-As (d. 664) Arab conqueror of Egypt.
The Harvest of a Quiet Eye (Alan L. Mackay)

16 O Death, where is thy sting-a-ling-a-ling,
O Grave, thy victoree?
The bells of hell go ting-a-ling-a-ling
For you but not for me.
Anonymous
Song of World War I

17 Swing low sweet chariot,
Comin' for to carry me home,
I looked over Jordan an' what did I see?
A band of Angels coming after me,
Comin' for to carry me home.
Anonymous
Swing Low, Sweet Chariot

18 He's gone to join the majority.
Petronius Arbiter (1st century AD) Roman satirist.
Referring to a dead man
Satyricon: Cena Trimalchionis, 42

19 Now he is dead! Far hence he lies
In the lorn Syrian town;
And on his grave, with shining eyes,
The Syrian stars look down.
Matthew Arnold (1822–88) British poet and critic.
Obermann Once More

20 I have often thought upon death, and I find it
the least of all evils.
Francis Bacon (1561–1626) English philosopher.
An Essay on Death

21 I do not believe that any man fears to be
dead, but only the stroke of death.
Francis Bacon
An Essay on Death

22 Men fear death, as children fear to go in the

dark; and as that natural fear in children is increased with tales, so is the other.
Francis Bacon
Essays, 'Of Death'

23 It is natural to die as to be born; and to a little infant, perhaps, the one is as painful as the other.
Francis Bacon
Essays, 'Of Death'

24 To die will be an awfully big adventure.
J. M. Barrie (1860–1937) British novelist and dramatist.
Peter Pan, III

25 Graveyards have a morbid reputation. Many people associate them with death.
Bishop of Bath and Wells (1935–   ) British churchman.
Remark, Apr 1988

26 What I like about Clive
Is that he is no longer alive.
There is a great deal to be said
For being dead.
Edmund Clerihew Bentley (1875–1956) British writer.
Biography for Beginners

27 The physician cutteth off a long disease; and he that is today a king tomorrow shall die.
Bible: Ecclesiasticus
10:10

28 Behold, I shew you a mystery; We shall not all sleep, but we shall all be changed,
In a moment, in the twinkling of an eye, at the last trump: for the trumpet shall sound, and the dead shall be raised incorruptible, and we shall be changed.
For this corruptible must put on incorruption, and this mortal must put on immortality.
So when this corruptible shall have put on incorruption, and this mortal shall have put on immortality, then shall be brought to pass the saying that is written, Death is swallowed up in victory.
O death, where is thy sting? O grave, where is thy victory?
Bible: I Corinthians
15:51–55

29 For all flesh is as grass, and all the glory of man as the flower of grass. The grass withereth, and the flower thereof falleth away.
Bible: I Peter
1:23–24

30 Lord, now lettest thou thy servant depart in peace, according to thy word:
For mine eyes have seen thy salvation,
Which thou hast prepared before the face of all people;
A light to lighten the Gentiles, and the glory of thy people Israel.
Bible: Luke
2:29–32

31 And I looked, and behold a pale horse: and his name that sat on him was Death, and Hell followed with him. And power was given unto them over the fourth part of the earth, to kill with sword, and with hunger, and with death, and with the beasts of the earth.
Bible: Revelations
6:8

32 Its visits,
Like those of angels, short, and far between.
Robert Blair (1699–1746) Scottish poet.
The Grave

33 In the hour of death, and in the day of judgement.
The Book of Common Prayer
Morning Prayer, Prayer of St Chrysostom

34 Any amusing deaths lately?
Maurice Bowra (1898–1971) British scholar.
Attrib.

35 For I say, this is death, and the sole death,
When a man's loss comes to him from his gain,
Darkness from light, from knowledge ignorance,
And lack of love from love made manifest.
Robert Browning (1812–89) British poet.
A Death in the Desert

36 It is important what a man still plans at the end. It shows the measure of injustice in his death.
Elias Canetti (1905–   ) Bulgarian-born novelist.
The Human Province

37 Days and moments quickly flying,
Blend the living with the dead;
Soon will you and I be lying
Each within our narrow bed.
Edward Caswall (1814–78) British hymn writer.
Hymn

38 He had been, he said, a most unconscionable time dying; but he hoped that they would excuse it.
Charles II (1630–85) King of England.
History of England (Macaulay), Vol. I, Ch. 4

39 Alack he's gone the way of all flesh.
William Congreve (1670–1729) British Restoration dramatist.
Squire Bickerstaff Detected, attrib.

40 We perish'd, each alone:
But I beneath a rougher sea,
And whelm'd in deeper gulphs than he.
William Cowper (1731–1800) British poet.
The Castaway

41 He'd make a lovely corpse.
Charles Dickens (1812–70) British novelist.
Martin Chuzzlewit, Ch. 25

42 Because I could not stop for Death,
He kindly stopped for me;
The carriage held but just ourselves

And Immortality.
Emily Dickinson (1830–86) US poet.
The Chariot

43 Our journey had advanced;
Our feet were almost come
To that odd fork in Being's road,
Eternity by term.
Emily Dickinson
Our Journey had Advanced

44 Death be not proud, though some have called thee
Mighty and dreadful, for, thou art not so.
John Donne (1573–1631) English poet.
Holy Sonnets, 10

45 Any man's death diminishes me, because I am involved in Mankind; And therefore never send to know for whom the bell tolls; it tolls for thee.
John Donne
Devotions, 17

46 Sin brought death, and death will disappear with the disappearance of sin.
Mary Baker Eddy (1821–1910) US religious leader.
Science and Health, with Key to the Scriptures

47 So death, the most terrifying of ills, is nothing to us, since so long as we exist, death is not with us; but when death comes, then we do not exist. It does not then concern either the living or the dead, since for the former it is not, and the latter are no more.
Epicurus (341–270 BC) Greek philosopher.
Letter to Menoeceus

48 Death is my neighbour now.
Edith Evans (1888–1976) British actress.
Said a week before her death
BBC radio interview, 14 Oct 1976

49 It hath been often said, that it is not death, but dying, which is terrible.
Henry Fielding (1707–54) British novelist.
Amelia, Bk. III, Ch. 4

50 Strange, is it not? that of the myriads who Before us pass'd the door of Darkness through,
Not one returns to tell us of the Road,
Which to discover we must travel too.
Edward Fitzgerald (1809–83) British poet.
The Rubáiyát of Omar Khayyám

51 He hath shook hands with time.
John Ford (c. 1586–c. 1640) English dramatist.
The Broken Heart, V:2

52 Death destroys a man, the idea of Death saves him.
E. M. Forster (1879–1970) British novelist.
Howards End, Ch. 27

53 Dere's no more work for poor old Ned,

He's gone whar de good niggers go.
Stephen Foster (1826–64) US composer of popular songs.
Uncle Ned

54 If Mr Selwyn calls again, shew him up: if I am alive I shall be delighted to see him; and if I am dead he would like to see me.
Henry Fox (1705–74) British politician.
Said during his last illness. George Selwyn was known for his morbid fascination for dead bodies
George Selwyn and his Contemporaries (J. H. Jesse), Vol. III

55 Something lingering, with boiling oil in it, I fancy.
W. S. Gilbert (1836–1911) British dramatist.
The Mikado, II

56 I am told he makes a very handsome corpse, and becomes his coffin prodigiously.
Oliver Goldsmith (1728–74) Irish-born British writer.
The Good-Natured Man, I

57 Can storied urn or animated bust
Back to its mansion call the fleeting breath?
Can honour's voice provoke the silent dust,
Or flatt'ry soothe the dull cold ear of death?
Thomas Gray (1716–71) British poet.
Elegy Written in a Country Churchyard

58 Here rests his head upon the lap of Earth
A youth to fortune and to fame unknown.
Fair Science frown'd not on his humble birth,
And Melancholy mark'd him for her own.
Thomas Gray
Elegy Written in a Country Churchyard

59 Grieve not that I die young. Is it not well
To pass away ere life hath lost its brightness?
Lady Flora Hastings (1806–39) British poet.
Swan Song

60 Death is still working like a mole,
And digs my grave at each remove.
George Herbert (1593–1633) English poet.
Grace

61 Anno domini – that's the most fatal complaint of all in the end.
James Hilton (1900–54) British novelist.
Good-bye, Mr Chips, Ch. 1

62 Death . . . It's the only thing we haven't succeeded in completely vulgarizing.
Aldous Huxley (1894–1964) British novelist.
Eyeless in Gaza, Ch. 31

63 Our civilization is founded on the shambles, and every individual existence goes out in a lonely spasm of helpless agony.
William James (1842–1910) US psychologist and philosopher.
Varieties of Religious Experience

64 Who doesn't regret Lazarus was not
Questioned about after-lives? Of course
He only reached death's threshold. I fear what
Dark exercises may with cunning powers

Do when I am brought To my conclusion.
Elizabeth Jennings (1926–) British poet and writer.
The Fear of Death

65 I die because I do not die.
St John of the Cross (Juan de Yepes y Alvarez; 1542–91) Spanish churchman and poet.
Coplas del alma que pena por ver a dios

66 It matters not how a man dies, but how he lives. The act of dying is not of importance, it lasts so short a time.
Samuel Johnson (1709–84) British lexicographer.
Life of Johnson (J. Boswell), Vol. II

67 I am able to follow my own death step by step. Now I move softly towards the end.
Pope John XXIII (Angelo Roncalli; 1881–1963) Italian churchman.
Remark made two days before he died
The Guardian, 3 June 1963

68 Above ground I shall be food for kites; below I shall be food for mole-crickets and ants. Why rob one to feed the other?
Juang-zu (4th century BC) Chinese Taoist philosopher.
When asked on his deathbed what his wishes were regarding the disposal of his body
Famous Last Words (B. Conrad)

69 All right, my lord creator, Don Miguel, you too will die and return to the nothing whence you came. God will cease to dream you!
Miguel de Unamuno y Jugo (1864–1936) Spanish writer.
Mist

70 Darkling I listen; and, for many a time
I have been half in love with easeful Death,
Call'd him soft names in many a mused rhyme,
To take into the air my quiet breath;
Now more than ever seems it rich to die,
To cease upon the midnight with no pain,
While thou art pouring forth thy soul abroad
In such an ecstasy!
John Keats (1795–1821) British poet.
Ode to a Nightingale

71 I shall soon be laid in the quiet grave – thank God for the quiet grave – O! I can feel the cold earth upon me – the daisies growing over me – O for this quiet – it will be my first.
John Keats
In a letter to John Taylor by Joseph Severn, 6 Mar 1821

72 Teach me to live, that I may dread
The grave as little as my bed.
Thomas Ken (1637–1711) English bishop.
An Evening Hymn

73 In the long run we are all dead.
John Maynard Keynes (1883–1946) British economist.
Collected Writings, 'A Tract on Monetary Reform'

74 That is the road we all have to take – over the Bridge of Sighs into eternity.
Soren Kierkegaard (1813–55) Danish philosopher.
Kierkegaard Anthology (Auden)

75 O pity the dead that are dead, but cannot make
the journey, still they moan and beat
against the silvery adamant walls of life's exclusive city.
D. H. Lawrence (1885–1930) British novelist.
The Houseless Dead

76 The dead don't die. They look on and help.
D. H. Lawrence
Letter

77 I detest life-insurance agents. They always argue that I shall some day die, which is not so.
Stephen Leacock (1869–1944) English-born Canadian economist and humorist.
Literary Lapses

78 There is a Reaper whose name is Death,
And, with his sickle keen,
He reaps the bearded grain at a breath,
And the flowers that grow between.
Henry Wadsworth Longfellow (1807–82) US poet.
The Reaper and the Flowers

79 It is the only disease you don't look forward to being cured of.
Herman J. Mankiewicz (1897–1953) US journalist and screenwriter.
Referring to death
Citizen Kane

80 Cut is the branch that might have grown full straight,
And burned is Apollo's laurel-bough,
That sometime grew within this learned man.
Christopher Marlowe (1564–93) English dramatist.
Doctor Faustus, Epilogue

81 The grave's a fine and private place,
But none, I think, do there embrace.
Andrew Marvell (1621–78) English poet.
To His Coy Mistress

82 Either he's dead or my watch has stopped.
Groucho Marx (Julius Marx; 1895–1977) US comedian.
A Day at the Races

83 My husband is dead.
 – I'll bet he's just using that as an excuse.
I was with him to the end.
 – No wonder he passed away.
I held him in my arms and kissed him.
 – So it was murder!
Groucho Marx
Duck Soup

84 Dying is a very dull, dreary affair. And my advice to you is to have nothing whatever to do with it.
W. Somerset Maugham (1874–1965) British novelist.
Escape from the Shadows (Robin Maugham)

85 Alas! Lord and Lady Dalhousie are dead, and buried at last,

Which causes many people to feel a little downcast.

William McGonagall (1830–1902) Scottish poet.
The Death of Lord and Lady Dalhousie

86 Whom the gods love dies young.

Menander (c. 341–c. 290 BC) Greek dramatist.
Dis Exapaton

87 One dies only once, and it's for such a long time!

Molière (Jean Baptiste Poquelin; 1622–73) French dramatist.
Le Dépit amoureux, V:3

88 Oh well, no matter what happens, there's always death.

Napoleon I (Napoleon Bonaparte; 1769–1821) French emperor.
Attrib.

89 And in the happy no-time of his sleeping
Death took him by the heart.

Wilfred Owen (1893–1918) British poet.
Asleep

90 It costs me never a stab nor squirm
To tread by chance upon a worm.
'Aha, my little dear,' I say,
'Your clan will pay me back one day.'

Dorothy Parker (1893–1967) US writer.
Sunset Gun, 'Thought for a Sunshiny Morning'

91 She closed her eyes; and in sweet slumber lying
her spirit tiptoed from its lodging-place.
It's folly to shrink in fear, if this is dying;
for death looked lovely in her lovely face.

Petrarch (Francesco Petrarca; 1304–74) Italian poet.
Triumphs

92 The surgeon is quiet, he does not speak.
He has seen too much death, his hands are full of it.

Sylvia Plath (1932–63) US poet and writer.
Winter Trees, 'The Courage of Shutting-Up'

93 I mount! I fly!
O grave! where is thy victory?
O death! where is thy sting?

Alexander Pope (1688–1744) British poet.
The Dying Christian to his Soul

94 Here am I, dying of a hundred good symptoms.

Alexander Pope
Anecdotes by and about Alexander Pope (Joseph Spence)

95 How often are we to die before we go quite off this stage? In every friend we lose a part of ourselves, and the best part.

Alexander Pope
Letter to Jonathan Swift, 5 Dec 1732

96 The hero is strangely akin to those who die young.

Rainer Maria Rilke (1875–1926) Austrian poet.
Duineser Elegien, VI

97 I shall have more to say when I am dead.

Edwin Arlington Robinson (1869–1935) US poet.
John Brown

98 When I am dead, my dearest,
Sing no sad songs for me;
Plant thou no roses at my head,
Nor shady cypress tree:
Be the green grass above me
With showers and dewdrops wet;
And if thou wilt, remember,
And if thou wilt, forget.

Christina Rossetti (1830–74) British poet.
When I am Dead

99 He who pretends to look on death without fear lies. All men are afraid of dying, this is the great law of sentient beings, without which the entire human species would soon be destroyed.

Jean Jacques Rousseau (1712–78) French philosopher.
Julie, or the New Eloise

100 To that dark inn, the grave!

Walter Scott (1771–1832) Scottish novelist.
The Lord of the Isles, VI

101 His morning walk was beneath the elms in the churchyard; 'for death,' he said, 'had been his next-door neighbour for so many years, that he had no apology for dropping the acquaintance.'

Walter Scott
The Legend of Montrose, Introduction

102 I have a rendezvous with Death
At some disputed barricade.

Alan Seeger (1888–1916) US poet.
I Have a Rendezvous with Death

103 The rest is silence.

William Shakespeare (1564–1616) English dramatist.
Hamlet, V:2

104 Why, he that cuts off twenty years of life
Cuts off so many years of fearing death.

William Shakespeare
Julius Caesar, III:1

105 O mighty Caesar! dost thou lie so low?
Are all thy conquests, glories, triumphs, spoils,
Shrunk to this little measure?

William Shakespeare
Julius Caesar, III:1

106 Ay, but to die, and go we know not where;
To lie in cold obstruction, and to rot;
This sensible warm motion to become
A kneaded clod; and the delighted spirit
To bathe in fiery floods or to reside
In thrilling region of thick-ribbed ice.

William Shakespeare
Measure for Measure, III:1

107 Full fathom five thy father lies;
Of his bones are coral made;
Those are pearls that were his eyes;
Nothing of him that doth fade

But doth suffer a sea-change
Into something rich and strange.
William Shakespeare
The Tempest, I:2

108 He that dies pays all debts.
William Shakespeare
The Tempest, III:2

109 Nothing in his life
Became him like the leaving it: he died
As one that had been studied in his death
To throw away the dearest thing he ow'd
As 'twere a careless trifle.
William Shakespeare
Macbeth, I:4

110 But thoughts, the slaves of life, and life, time's fool,
And time, that takes survey of all the world,
Must have a stop.
William Shakespeare
Henry IV, Part One, V:4

111 His nose was as sharp as a pen, and 'a babbl'd of green fields.
William Shakespeare
Referring to Falstaff on his deathbed
Henry V, II:3

112 I care not; a man can die but once; we owe God a death.
William Shakespeare
Henry IV, Part Two, III:2

113 Death is the veil which those who live call life:
They sleep, and it is lifted.
Percy Bysshe Shelley (1792–1822) British poet.
Prometheus Unbound, III

114 It is a modest creed, and yet
Pleasant if one considers it,
To own that death itself must be,
Like all the rest, a mockery.
Percy Bysshe Shelley
The Sensitive Plant, III

115 I cannot forgive my friends for dying: I do not find these vanishing acts of theirs at all amusing.
Logan Pearsall Smith (1865–1946) US writer.
Trivia

116 I do really think that death will be marvellous
. . . If there wasn't death, I think you couldn't go on.
Stevie Smith (Florence Margaret Smith; 1902–71) British poet.
The Observer, 9 Nov 1969

117 The whole of his life had prepared Podduyev for living, not for dying.
Alexander Solzhenitsyn (1918–) Soviet novelist.
Cancer Ward, Pt. I, Ch. 8

118 Sleep after toil, port after stormy seas,

Ease after war, death after life does greatly please.
Edmund Spenser (1552–99) English poet.
The Faerie Queene, I:9

119 Under the wide and starry sky
Dig the grave and let me lie.
Glad did I live and gladly die,
– And I laid me down with a will.
This is the verse you grave for me:
'Here he lies where he longed to be;
Home is the sailor, home from sea,
 And the hunter home from the hill.'
Robert Louis Stevenson (1850–94) Scottish writer.
Underwoods, Bk. I, 'Requiem'

120 Even so, in death the same unknown will appear as ever known to me. And because I love this life, I know I shall love death as well.
The child cries out when from the right breast the mother takes it away, in the very next moment to find in the left one its consolation.
Rabindranath Tagore (1861–1941) Indian poet and philosopher.
Gitanjali

121 Row upon row with strict impunity
The headstones yield their names to the element.
Allen Tate (1899–1979) US poet.
Ode to the Confederate Dead

122 A day less or more
At sea or ashore,
We die – does it matter when?
Alfred, Lord Tennyson (1809–92) British poet.
The Revenge, XI

123 I, born of flesh and ghost, was neither
A ghost nor man, but mortal ghost.
And I was struck down by death's feather.
Dylan Thomas (1914–53) Welsh poet.
Before I knocked

124 After the first death, there is no other.
Dylan Thomas
A Refusal to Mourn the Death, by Fire, of a Child in London

125 Do not go gentle into that good night,
Old age should burn and rave at close of day;
Rage, rage, against the dying of the light.
Dylan Thomas
Do not go gentle into that good night

126 There is not any book
Or face of dearest look
That I would not turn from now
To go into the unknown
I must enter, and leave, alone,
I know not how.
Edward Thomas (1878–1917) British poet.
Lights Out

127 Go and try to disprove death. Death will disprove you, and that's all!
Ivan Turgenev (1818–83) Russian novelist.
Fathers and Sons, Ch. 27

128 While I thought that I was learning how to live, I have been learning how to die.
Leonardo da Vinci (1452–1519) Italian artist.
Notebooks

129 There's no repentance in the grave.
Isaac Watts (1674–1748) English theologian and hymn writer.
Divine Songs for Children, 'Solemn Thoughts of God and Death'

130 For he who lives more lives than one
More deaths than one must die.
Oscar Wilde (1854–1900) Irish-born British dramatist.
The Ballad of Reading Gaol, III:37

131 Dead! and . . . never called me mother.
Mrs Henry Wood (1814–87) British novelist.
East Lynne (dramatized version; the words do not occur in the novel)

132 Three years she grew in sun and shower,
Then Nature said, 'A lovelier flower
On earth was never sown;
This child I to myself will take;
She shall be mine, and I will make
A Lady of my own.
William Wordsworth (1770–1850) British poet.
Three Years she Grew

133 We are laid asleep
In body, and become a living soul:
While with an eye made quiet by the power
Of harmony, and the deep power of joy,
We see into the life of things.
William Wordsworth
Lines composed a few miles above Tintern Abbey

DEBAUCHERY

See also animalism, lust, pleasure, sex

1 A fool bolts pleasure, then complains of moral indigestion.
Minna Antrim (1861–?) US writer.
Naked Truth and Veiled Allusions

2 A great many people have come up to me and asked how I manage to get so much work done and still keep looking so dissipated.
Robert Benchley (1889–1945) US humorist.
Chips off the Old Benchley, 'How to Get Things Done'

3 *Debauchee*, n. One who has so earnestly pursued pleasure that he has had the misfortune to overtake it.
Ambrose Bierce (1842–?1914) US writer and journalist.
The Devil's Dictionary

4 So, we'll go no more a roving
So late into the night,
Though the heart be still as loving,

And the moon be still as bright.
Lord Byron (1788–1824) British poet.
So, we'll go no more a roving

5 I've over-educated myself in all the things I shouldn't have known at all.
Noël Coward (1899–1973) British dramatist.
Wild Oats

6 No one ever suddenly became depraved.
Juvenal (Decimus Junius Juvenalis; 60–130 AD) Roman satirist.
Satires, II

7 We're poor little lambs who've lost our way,
Baa! Baa! Baa!
We're little black sheep who've gone astray,
Baa-aa-aa!
Gentleman-rankers on the spree,
Damned from here to Eternity,
God ha' mercy on such as we,
Baa! Yah! Bah!
Rudyard Kipling (1865–1936) Indian-born British writer.
Gentleman-Rankers

8 Home is heaven and orgies are vile
But you need an orgy, once in a while.
Ogden Nash (1902–71) US poet.
Home, 99.44100% Sweet Home

9 Once: a philosopher; twice: a pervert!
Voltaire (François-Marie Arouet; 1694–1778) French writer.
Turning down an invitation to an orgy, having attended one the previous night for the first time
Attrib.

DECEPTION

See also appearances, hypocrisy, insincerity, lying

1 To deceive oneself is very easy.
Proverb

2 Beware of false prophets, which come to you in sheep's clothing, but inwardly they are ravening wolves.
Bible: Matthew
7:15

3 Almost every man wastes part of his life in attempts to display qualities which he does not possess, and to gain applause which he cannot keep.
Samuel Johnson (1709–84) British lexicographer.
The Rambler

4 You can fool some of the people all the time and all the people some of the time; but you can't fool all the people all the time.
Abraham Lincoln (1809–65) US statesman.
Attrib.

5 False face must hide what the false heart doth know.
William Shakespeare (1564–1616) English dramatist.
Macbeth, I:7

6 You can fool too many of the people too much of the time.

James Thurber (1894–1961) US humorist.
Fables for Our Time, 'The Owl Who Was God'

7 I have invented an invaluable permanent invalid called Bunbury, in order that I may be able to go down into the country whenever I choose.

Oscar Wilde (1854–1900) Irish-born British dramatist.
The Importance of Being Earnest, I

DECISION

See also determination

1 Tender-handed stroke a nettle,
And it stings you for your pains;
Grasp it like a man of mettle,
And it soft as silk remains.

Aaron Hill (1685–1750) British poet and dramatist.
Verses Written on Window

2 Like all weak men he laid an exaggerated stress on not changing one's mind.

W. Somerset Maugham (1874–1965) British novelist.
Of Human Bondage, Ch. 37

3 If someone tells you he is going to make 'a realistic decision', you immediately understand that he has resolved to do something bad.

Mary McCarthy (1912–89) US novelist.
On the Contrary

DECLINE

1 And though the Van Dycks have to go
And we pawn the Bechstein grand,
We'll stand by the Stately Homes of England.

Noël Coward (1899–1973) British dramatist.
Operette, The Stately Homes of England

2 That's Why the Lady Is a Tramp.

Lorenz Hart (1895–1943) US songwriter.
From the musical *Babes in Arms*
Song title

3 It is the logic of our times,
No subject for immortal verse –
That we who lived by honest dreams
Defend the bad against the worse.

C. Day Lewis (1904–72) British poet.
Where are the War Poets?

4 From morn
To noon he fell, from noon to dewy eve,
A summer's day, and with the setting sun
Dropped from the zenith, like a falling star.

John Milton (1608–74) English poet.
Paradise Lost, Bk. I

5 Macmillan seemed, in his very person, to embody the national decay he supposed himself to be confuting. He exuded a flavour of moth-balls.

Malcolm Muggeridge (1903–) British writer.
Tread Softly For You Tread on My Jokes, 'England, whose England'

6 It is only a step from the sublime to the ridiculous.

Napoleon I (Napoleon Bonaparte; 1769–1821) French emperor.
Remark following the retreat from Moscow, 1812
Attrib.

7 We have on our hands a sick man – a very sick man.

Nicholas I (1796–1855) Tsar of Russia.
Referring to Turkey, the 'sick man of Europe'; said to Sir G. H. Seymour, British envoy to St Petersburg, Jan 1853
Attrib.

8 Now there are fields where Troy once was.

Ovid (Publius Ovidius Naso; 43 BC–17 AD) Roman poet.
Heroides, Bk. I

9 There may have been disillusionments in the lives of the medieval saints, but they would scarcely have been better pleased if they could have foreseen that their names would be associated nowadays chiefly with racehorses and the cheaper clarets.

Saki (Hector Hugh Munro; 1870–1916) British writer.
Reginald at the Carlton

10 I shall be like that tree; I shall die from the top.

Jonathan Swift (1667–1745) Irish-born Anglican priest and writer.
Predicting his own mental decline on seeing a tree with a withered crown
Lives of the Wits (H. Pearson)

11 I dreamed there would be Spring no more,
That Nature's ancient power was lost.

Alfred, Lord Tennyson (1809–92) British poet.
In Memoriam A.H.H., LXIX

12 The difference between our decadence and the Russians' is that while theirs is brutal, ours is apathetic.

James Thurber (1894–1961) US humorist.
The Observer, 'Sayings of the Week', 5 Feb 1961

13 I started at the top and worked my way down.

Orson Welles (1915–85) US film actor.
The Filmgoer's Book of Quotes (Leslie Halliwell)

14 Plain living and high thinking are no more.

William Wordsworth (1770–1850) British poet.
Sonnets, 'O friend! I know not'

15 Milton! thou shouldst be living at this hour:
England hath need of thee; she is a fen
Of stagnant waters: altar, sword, and pen,
Fireside, the heroic wealth of hall and bower,
Have forfeited their ancient English dower
Of inward happiness.

William Wordsworth
Sonnets, 'Milton! thou shouldst'

DEFEAT

See also loss

1 'Tis better to have fought and lost,

Than never to have fought at all.
Arthur Hugh Clough (1819–61) British poet.
Peschiera

2 Of all I had, only honour and life have been spared.
Francis I (1494–1547) King of France.
Referring to his defeat at the Battle of Pavia, 24 Feb 1525; usually misquoted as 'All is lost save honour.'
Letter to Louise of Savoy (his mother), 1525

3 A man can be destroyed but not defeated.
Ernest Hemingway (1899–1961) US novelist.
The Old Man and the Sea

4 Woe to the vanquished.
Livy (Titus Livius; 59 BC–17 AD) Roman historian.
History, V:48

5 When I am dead and opened, you shall find 'Calais' lying in my heart.
Mary I (1516–58) Queen of England.
Chronicles (Holinshed), III

6 Every man meets his Waterloo at last.
Wendell Phillips (1811–84) US reformer.
Speech, Brooklyn, 1 Nov 1859

7 Well, I have one consolation, No candidate was ever elected ex-president by such a large majority!
William Howard Taft (1857–1930) US statesman.
Referring to his disastrous defeat in the 1912 presidential election
Attrib.

8 It is the beginning of the end.
Talleyrand (Charles Maurice de Talleyrand-Périgord; 1754–1838) French politician.
Referring to Napoleon's defeat at Borodino, 1813
Attrib.

9 Another year! – another deadly blow!
Another mighty empire overthrown!
And we are left, or shall be left, alone.
William Wordsworth (1770–1850) British poet.
Napoleon defeated Prussia at the Battles of Jena and Anerstädt, 14 Oct 1806
Sonnets, 'Another year!'

DELUSION

1 But yet the light that led astray
Was light from Heaven.
Robert Burns (1759–96) Scottish poet.
The Vision

2 Take care, your worship, those things over there are not giants but windmills.
Miguel de Cervantes (1547–1616) Spanish novelist.
Don Quixote, Pt. I, Ch. 8

3 Didn't I tell you, Don Quixote, sir, to turn back, for they were not armies you were going to attack, but flocks of sheep?
Miguel de Cervantes
Don Quixote, Pt. I, Ch. 18

4 Take the life-lie away from the average man

and straight away you take away his happiness.
Henrik Ibsen (1828–1906) Norwegian dramatist.
The Wild Duck, V

5 Many people have delusions of grandeur but you're deluded by triviality.
Eugène Ionesco (1912–) French dramatist.
Exit the King

DEMOCRACY

See also class, government, majority, public, republic

1 Democracy means government by discussion but it is only effective if you can stop people talking.
Clement Attlee (1883–1967) British statesman and Labour prime minister.
Anatomy of Britain (Anthony Sampson)

2 One man shall have one vote.
John Cartwright (1740–1824) British writer.
People's Barrier Against Undue Influence

3 Democracy means government by the uneducated, while aristocracy means government by the badly educated.
G. K. Chesterton (1874–1936) British writer.
New York Times, 1 Feb 1931

4 Some comrades apparently find it hard to understand that democracy is just a slogan.
Mikhail Gorbachov (1931–) Soviet statesman.
The Observer, 'Sayings of the Week', 1 Feb 1987

5 Democracy can't work. Mathematicians, peasants, and animals, that's all there is – so democracy, a theory based on the assumption that mathematicians and peasants are equal, can never work. Wisdom is not additive; its maximum is that of the wisest man in a given group.
Robert Heinlein (1907–88) US science-fiction writer.
Glory Road, Ch. 20

6 Democracy is only an experiment in government, and it has the obvious disadvantage of merely counting votes instead of weighing them.
Dean Inge (1860–1954) British churchman.
Possible Recovery?

7 The vote is the most powerful instrument ever devised by man for breaking down injustice and destroying the terrible walls which imprison men because they are different from other men.
Lyndon B. Johnson (1908–73) US statesman.
Address on signing Voting Rights Bill, Washington, DC, 6 Aug 1965

8 No man is good enough to govern another man without that other's consent.
Abraham Lincoln (1809–65) US statesman.
Speech, 1854

9 The ballot is stronger than the bullet.
Abraham Lincoln
Speech, 19 May 1856

10 This country, with its institutions, belongs to the people who inhabit it. Whenever they shall grow weary of the existing government, they can exercise their constitutional right of amending it, or their revolutionary right to dismember or overthrow it.
Abraham Lincoln
First Inaugural Address, 4 Mar 1861

11 ... that government of the people, by the people, and for the people, shall not perish from the earth.
Abraham Lincoln
Speech, 19 Nov 1863, dedicating the national cemetery on the site of the Battle of Gettesburg

12 Man's capacity for evil makes democracy necessary and man's capacity for good makes democracy possible.
Reinhold Niebuhr (1892–1971) US churchman.
Quoted by Anthony Wedgwood Benn in *The Times*, 18 Jul 1977

13 Democracy passes into despotism.
Plato (429–347 BC) Greek philosopher.
Republic, Bk. 8

14 I think if the people of this country can be reached with the truth, their judgment will be in favor of the many, as against the privileged few.
Eleanor Roosevelt (1884–1962) US writer and lecturer.
Ladies' Home Journal

15 We must be the great arsenal of democracy.
Franklin D. Roosevelt (1882–1945) US Democratic president.
Broadcast address to Forum on Current Problems, 29 Dec 1940

16 We must be thoroughly democratic and patronise everybody without distinction of class.
George Bernard Shaw (1856–1950) Irish dramatist and critic.
John Bull's Other Island

17 It's not the voting that's democracy; it's the counting.
Tom Stoppard (1937–) Czech-born British dramatist.
Jumpers

18 A committee should consist of three men, two of whom are absent.
Herbert Beerbohm Tree (1853–1917) British actor and theater manager.
Beerbohm Tree (H. Pearson)

19 I shall not vote because I do not aspire to advise my sovereign on the choice of her servants.
Evelyn Waugh (1903–66) British novelist.
A Little Order

20 Democracy means simply the bludgeoning of the people by the people for the people.
Oscar Wilde (1854–1900) Irish-born British dramatist.
The Soul of Man under Socialism

21 The world must be made safe for democracy.
Woodrow Wilson (1856–1925) US statesman.
Address to Congress, asking for a declaration of war 2 Apr 1917

DENIAL

1 I am the spirit that always denies.
Goethe (1749–1832) German poet and dramatist.
Faust, Pt. I

2 No, I am no one's contemporary – ever. That would have been above my station ... How I loathe that other with my name. He certainly never was me.
Osip Mandelstam (1891–1938) Russian poet.
Poems, No. 141

3 I am not a crook.
Richard Milhous Nixon (1913–) US president.
Attrib., 17 Nov 1973

4 He would, wouldn't he?
Mandy Rice-Davies (1944–) British call girl.
Of Lord Astor, when told that he had repudiated her evidence at the trial of Stephen Ward, 29 June 1963

DEPARTURE

See also dismissal, parting

1 Come, dear children, let us away; Down and away below.
Matthew Arnold (1822–88) British poet and critic.
The Forsaken Merman

2 She left lonely for ever The kings of the sea.
Matthew Arnold
The Forsaken Merman

3 Once I leave, I leave. I am not going to speak to the man on the bridge, and I am not going to spit on the deck.
Stanley Baldwin (1867–1947) British statesman.
Statement to the Cabinet, 28 May 1937

4 Adieu, adieu! my native shore Fades o'er the waters blue.
Lord Byron (1788–1824) British poet.
Childe Harold's Pilgrimage, I

5 My native Land – Good Night!
Lord Byron
Childe Harold's Pilgrimage, I

6 Let us go then, you and I, When the evening is spread out against the sky Like a patient etherized upon a table.
T. S. Eliot (1888–1965) US-born British poet and dramatist.
The Love Song of J. Alfred Prufrock

7 And they are gone: aye, ages long ago

These lovers fled away into the storm.
John Keats (1795–1821) British poet.
The Eve of Saint Agnes, XLII

8 She's leaving home after living alone for so
many years.
John Lennon (1940–80) British rock musician.
She's Leaving Home (with Paul McCartney)

DESIGN

See also art

1 Demand bare walls in your bedroom, your
living room and your dining room. Built-in
furniture takes the place of much of the
furniture which is expensive to buy . . .
Demand concealed or diffused lighting.
Demand a vacuum cleaner. Buy only practical
furniture and never buy 'decorative' pieces. If
you want to see bad taste, go into the
houses of the rich. Put only a few pictures
on your walls and none but good ones.
Le Corbusier (Charles-Édouard Jeanneret; 1887–1965)
French architect.

2 A machine for living in.
Le Corbusier
Referring to a house
Towards a New Architecture

3 It is not this or that tangible steel or brass
machine which we want to get rid of, but the
great intangible machine of commercial tyranny
which oppresses the lives of us all.
William Morris (1834–96) British designer, artist, and poet.

4 Nothing should be made by man's labour
which is not worth making or which must be
made by labour degrading to the makers.
William Morris

5 Art will make our streets as beautiful as the
woods, as elevating as the mountain-side: it
will be a pleasure and a rest, and not a
weight upon the spirits to come from the
open country into a town. Every man's house
will be fair and decent, soothing to his mind
and helpful to his work.
William Morris

6 Today industrial design has put murder on a
mass-production basis.
Victor Papanek
Design for the Real World

7 It will be a great day when cutlery and
furniture designs (to name but two) swing
like the Supremes.
Michael Wolff

8 The tall modern office building is the machine

pure and simple . . . the engine, the motor
and the battleship the works of the century.
Frank Lloyd Wright (1869–1959) US architect.

DESIRE

See also hunger, lust, thirst

1 Give me my golf clubs, fresh air and a
beautiful partner, and you can keep my golf
clubs and the fresh air.
Jack Benny (Benjamin Kublesky; 1894–1974) US actor.
Attrib.

2 Those who restrain Desire, do so because
theirs is weak enough to be restrained.
William Blake (1757–1827) British poet.
The Marriage of Heaven and Hell, 'Those who restrain
Desire . . . '

3 Sooner murder an infant in its cradle than
nurse unacted desires.
William Blake
The Marriage of Heaven and Hell, 'Proverbs of Hell'

4 Man's Desires are limited by his Perceptions;
none can desire what he has not perceived.
William Blake
There is no Natural Religion

5 A sight to dream of, not to tell!
Samuel Taylor Coleridge (1772–1834) British poet.
Christabel, I

6 O, she is the antidote to desire.
William Congreve (1670–1729) British Restoration
dramatist.
The Way of the World, IV:14

7 Someday I'll wish upon a star.
E. Y. Harburg (1896–1981) US songwriter.
From the musical *The Wizard of Oz*
Over the Rainbow

8 Somewhere over the rainbow,
Way up high:
There's a land that I heard of
Once in a lullaby.
E. Y. Harburg
From the musical *The Wizard of Oz*
Over the Rainbow

9 Ship me somewheres east of Suez, where
the best is like the worst,
Where there aren't no Ten Commandments,
an' a man can raise a thirst:
For the temple-bells are callin', an' it's there
that I would be –
By the old Moulmein Pagoda, looking lazy at
the sea.
Rudyard Kipling (1865–1936) Indian-born British writer.
The Road to Mandalay

10 All I want is a room somewhere,
Far away from the cold night air;
With one enormous chair . . .
Oh, wouldn't it be loverly?
Alan Jay Lerner (1918–86) US songwriter.
My Fair Lady, I:1

11 There is wishful thinking in Hell as well as on earth.
C. S. Lewis (1898–1963) British academic and writer.
The Screwtape Letters, Preface

12 There is nothing like desire for preventing the thing one says from bearing any resemblance to what one has in mind.
Marcel Proust (1871–1922) French novelist.
À la recherche du temps perdu: Le Côté de Guermantes

13 Appetite comes with eating.
François Rabelais (1483–1553) French satirist.
Gargantua, Bk. I, Ch. 5

14 That she belov'd knows nought that knows not this:
Men prize the thing ungain'd more than it is.
William Shakespeare (1564–1616) English dramatist.
Troilus and Cressida, I:2

15 There are two tragedies in life. One is to lose your heart's desire. The other is to gain it.
George Bernard Shaw (1856–1950) Irish dramatist and critic.
Man and Superman, IV

16 Desire is the very essence of man.
Benedict Spinoza (Baruch de Spinoza; 1632–77) Dutch philosopher.
Ethics

17 As soon as you stop wanting something you get it. I've found that to be absolutely axiomatic.
Andy Warhol (Andrew Warhola; 1926–87) US pop artist.
Attrib.

18 And pluck till time and times are done
The silver apples of the moon
The golden apples of the sun.
W. B. Yeats (1865–1939) Irish poet.
The Song of Wandering Aengus

DESPAIR

See also sorrow

1 And about the ninth hour Jesus cried with a loud voice, saying, Eli, Eli, lama sabachthani? that is to say, My God, my God, why hast thou forsaken me?
Bible: Matthew
27:46

2 The name of the slough was Despond.
John Bunyan (1628–88) English writer.
The Pilgrim's Progress, Pt. I

3 A castle called Doubting Castle, the owner whereof was Giant Despair.
John Bunyan
The Pilgrim's Progress, Pt. I

4 Not, I'll not, carrion comfort, Despair, not feast on thee;
Not untwist – slack they may be – these last strands of man

In me or, most weary, cry *I can no more*. I can;
Can something, hope, wish day come, not choose not to be.
Gerard Manley Hopkins (1844–99) British Jesuit and poet.
Carrion Comfort

5 Don't despair, not even over the fact that you don't despair.
Franz Kafka (1883–1924) Czech novelist.
Diary

6 The mass of men lead lives of quiet desperation.
Henry David Thoreau (1817–62) US writer.
Walden, 'Economy'

DESTINY

See also purpose

1 What must be, must be.
Proverb

2 Whatever may happen to you was prepared for you from all eternity; and the implication of causes was from eternity spinning the thread of your being.
Marcus Aurelius (121–180 AD) Roman emperor.
Meditations, Bk. X, Ch. 5

3 Everything that happens happens as it should, and if you observe carefully, you will find this to be so.
Marcus Aurelius
Meditations, Bk. IV, Ch. 10

4 I felt as if I were walking with destiny, and that all my past life had been but a preparation for this hour and this trial.
Winston Churchill (1874–1965) British statesman.
The Gathering Storm, Ch. 38

5 Which brings me to my conclusion upon Free Will and Predestination, namely – let the reader mark it – that they are identical.
Winston Churchill
My Early Life, Ch. 3

6 'Tis all a Chequer-board of Nights and Days
Where Destiny with Men for Pieces plays:
Hither and thither moves, and mates, and slays,
And one by one back in the Closet lays.
Edward Fitzgerald (1809–83) British poet.
The Rubáiyát of Omar Khayyám, XLIX

7 The Moving Finger writes; and, having writ,
Moves on: nor all thy Piety nor Wit
Shall lure it back to cancel half a Line,
Nor all thy Tears wash out a Word of it.
Edward Fitzgerald
The Rubáiyát of Omar Khayyám, LI

8 And that inverted Bowl we call The Sky,
Whereunder crawling coop't we live and die,
Lift not thy hands to *It* for help – for It

Rolls impotently on as Thou or I.
Edward Fitzgerald
The Rubáiyát of Omar Khayyám, LII

9 Drink! for you know not whence you came,
nor why:
Drink! for you know not why you go, nor
where.
Edward Fitzgerald
The Rubáiyát of Omar Khayyám, LXXIV

10 Tempt not the stars, young man, thou canst
not play
With the severity of fate.
John Ford (c. 1586 – c. 1640) English dramatist.
The Broken Heart, I:3

11 I go the way that Providence dictates with
the assurance of a sleepwalker.
Adolf Hitler (1889 – 1945) German dictator.
Referring to his successful re-occupation of the Rhineland, despite advice against the attempt
Speech, Munich, 15 Mar 1936

12 Do not try to find out – we're forbidden to
know – what end the gods have in store for
me, or for you.
Horace (Quintus Horatius Flaccus; 65 – 8 BC) Roman poet.
Odes, I

13 Who can foretell for what high cause
This darling of the Gods was born?
Andrew Marvell (1621 – 78) English poet.
The Picture of Little T.C. in a Prospect of Flowers

14 And yet the order of the acts is planned,
The way's end destinate and unconcealed.
Alone. Now is the time of Pharisees.
To live is not like walking through a field.
Boris Pasternak (1890 – 1960) Russian Jewish poet and
novelist.
Hamlet (trans. Henry Kamen)

15 We may become the makers of our fate
when we have ceased to pose as its
prophets.
Karl Popper (1902 –   ) Austrian-born British philosopher.
The Observer, 28 Dec 1975

16 Man never found the deities so kindly
As to assure him that he'd live tomorrow.
François Rabelais (1483 – 1553) French satirist.
Pantagruel, Bk. III, Ch. 2

17 Fate sits on these dark battlements, and
frowns;
And as the portals open to receive me,
Her voice, in sullen echoes, through the
courts,
Tells of a nameless deed.
Ann Radcliffe (1764 – 1823) British novelist.
The Mysteries of Udolpho

18 There's a divinity that shapes our ends,
Rough-hew them how we will.
William Shakespeare (1564 – 1616) English dramatist.
Hamlet, V:2

19 As flies to wanton boys are we to th' gods –
They kill us for their sport.
William Shakespeare
King Lear, IV:1

20 The ancient saying is no heresy:
Hanging and wiving goes by destiny.
William Shakespeare
The Merchant of Venice, II:9

21 One God, one law, one element,
And one far-off divine event,
To which the whole creation moves.
Alfred, Lord Tennyson (1809 – 92) British poet.
In Memoriam A.H.H., CXXXI

22 I embrace the purpose of God and the doom
assigned.
Alfred, Lord Tennyson
Maud, III

23 We are merely the stars' tennis-balls, struck
and bandied
Which way please them.
John Webster (1580 – 1625) English dramatist.
The Duchess of Malfi, V:4

24 Every bullet has its billet.
William III (1650 – 1702) King of England.
Journal (John Wesley), 6 June 1765

DETERMINATION

See also decision, endurance, inflexibility, persistence, stubbornness

1 He who hesitates is lost.
Proverb

2 Where there's a will there's a way.
Proverb

3 Don't listen to anyone who tells you that you
can't do this or that. That's nonsense. Make
up your mind, you'll never use crutches or a
stick, then have a go at everything. Go to
school, join in all the games you can. Go
anywhere you want to. But never, never let
them persuade you that things are too
difficult or impossible.
Douglas Bader (1910 – 82) British fighter pilot.
Speaking to a fourteen-year-old boy who had had a leg amputated after a road accident
Flying Colours (Laddie Lucas)

4 There is no such thing as a great talent
without great will-power.
Honoré de Balzac (1799 – 1850) French novelist.
La Muse du département

5 Let us determine to die here, and we will
conquer.
There is Jackson standing like a stone wall.
Rally behind the Virginians.
Barnard Elliot Bee (1824 – 61) US soldier.
Said at the First Battle of Bull Run, 1861; hence Gen Thomas
Jackson's nickname, 'Stonewall Jackson'
Reminiscences of Metropolis (Poore), II

6 We will not go to Canossa.

Bismarck (1815–98) German statesman.
A declaration of his anti-Roman Catholic policy; the Emperor Henry IV had submitted to Pope Gregory VII at Canossa, N. Italy, in 1077
Speech, Reichstag, 14 May 1872

7 The spirit burning but unbent,
May writhe, rebel – the weak alone repent!

Lord Byron (1788–1824) British poet.
The Corsair, II

8 I purpose to fight it out on this line, if it takes all summer.

Ulysses Simpson Grant (1822–85) US general.
Dispatch to Washington, 11 May 1864

9 I will be conquered; I will not capitulate.

Samuel Johnson (1709–84) British lexicographer.
Referring to his illness
Life of Johnson (J. Boswell), Vol. IV

10 I have not yet begun to fight.

John Paul Jones (1747–92) Scottish-born US naval commander.
Retort when informed his ship was sinking
Life and Letters of J. P. Jones (De Koven), Vol. I

11 I shall return.

Douglas Macarthur (1880–1964) US general.
Message (11 Mar 1942) on leaving for Australia from Corregidor Island (Philippines), which he had been defending against the Japanese

12 What though the field be lost?
All is not lost – the unconquerable will,
And study of revenge, immortal hate,
And courage never to submit or yield:
And what is else not to be overcome?

John Milton (1608–74) English poet.
Paradise Lost, Bk. I

13 Look for me by moonlight;
Watch for me by moonlight;
I'll come to thee by moonlight, though hell should bar the way!

Alfred Noyes (1880–1958) British poet.
The Highwayman

14 *Ils ne passeront pas.*
They shall not pass.

Marshal Pétain (1856–1951) French marshal.
Attrib; probably derived from General R.-G. Nivelle's Order of the Day, *'Vous ne les laisserez pas passer'* (June 1916). It is also attributed to the Spanish politician Dolores Ibarruri.

15 We are not now that strength which in old days
Moved earth and heaven; that which we are, we are;
One equal temper of heroic hearts,
Made weak by time and fate, but strong in will
To strive, to seek, to find, and not to yield.

Alfred, Lord Tennyson (1809–92) British poet.
Ulysses

DEVIL

See also damnation, hell

1 The devil is not so black as he is painted.

Proverb

2 And he said unto them, I beheld Satan as lightning fall from heaven.

Bible: Luke
10:18

3 And he asked him, What is thy name? And he answered, saying. My name is Legion: for we are many.

Bible: Mark
5:9

4 And there was war in heaven: Michael and his angels fought against the dragon; and the dragon fought and his angels,
And prevailed not; neither was their place found any more in heaven.
And the great dragon was cast out, that old serpent, called the Devil, and Satan, which deceiveth the whole world: he was cast out into the earth, and his angels were cast out with him.

Bible: Revelations
12:7–9

5 And that no man might buy or sell, save he that had the mark, or the name of the beast, or the number of his name.
Here is wisdom. Let him that hath understanding count the number of the beast: for it is the number of a man; and his number is Six hundred threescore and six.

Bible: Revelations
13:17–18

6 O Thou! Whatever title suit thee –
Auld Hornie, Satan, Nick, or Clootie.

Robert Burns (1759–96) Scottish poet.
Address to the Devil

7 Wherever God erects a house of prayer,
The Devil always builds a chapel there;
And 'twill be found, upon examination,
The latter has the largest congregation.

Daniel Defoe (1660–1731) British journalist and writer.
The True-Born Englishman, Pt. I

8 It is so stupid of modern civilization to have given up believing in the devil when he is the only explanation of it.

Ronald Knox (1888–1957) British Roman Catholic priest.
Let Dons Delight

9 It is no good casting out devils. They belong to us, we must accept them and be at peace with them.

D. H. Lawrence (1885–1930) British novelist.
Phoenix, 'The Reality of Peace'

10 High on a throne of royal state, which far
Outshone the wealth of Ormus and of Ind,
Or where the gorgeous East with richest hand
Showers on her kings barbaric pearl and gold,
Satan exalted sat, by merit raised

To that bad eminence.
John Milton (1608–74) English poet.
Paradise Lost, Bk. II

11 Sometimes
The Devil is a gentleman.
Percy Bysshe Shelley (1792–1822) British poet.
Peter Bell the Third

DIARIES

1 Let diaries, therefore, be brought in use.
Francis Bacon (1561–1626) English philosopher.
Essays, 'Of Travel'

2 Only good girls keep diaries. Bad girls don't have the time.
Tallulah Bankhead (1903–68) US actress.
Attrib.

3 With the publication of his Private Papers in 1952, he committed suicide 25 years after his death.
Lord Beaverbrook (1879–1964) British newspaper owner and politician.
Referring to Earl Haig
Men and Power

4 I do not keep a diary. Never have. To write a diary every day is like returning to one's own vomit.
Enoch Powell (1912–) British politician.
Sunday Times, 6 Nov 1977

5 What is a diary as a rule? A document useful to the person who keeps it, dull to the contemporary who reads it, invaluable to the student, centuries afterwards, who treasures it!
Ellen Terry (1847–1928) British actress.
The Story of My Life, Ch. 14

6 I never travel without my diary. One should always have something sensational to read in the train.
Oscar Wilde (1854–1900) Irish-born British dramatist.
The Importance of Being Earnest, II

DICKENS

See also criticism, writers

1 We were put to Dickens as children but it never quite took. That unremitting humanity soon had me cheesed off.
Alan Bennett (1934–) British playwright.
The Old Country, II

2 It does not matter that Dickens' world is not life-like; it is alive.
Lord Cecil (1902–86) British writer and critic.
Early Victorian Novelists

3 Of Dickens's style it is impossible to speak in praise. It is jerky, ungrammatical, and

created by himself in defiance of rules . . . No young novelist should ever dare to imitate the style of Dickens.
Anthony Trollope (1815–82) British novelist.
Autobiography

4 One would have to have a heart of stone to read the death of Little Nell without laughing.
Oscar Wilde (1854–1900) Irish-born British dramatist.
Lecturing upon Dickens
Lives of the Wits (H. Pearson)

DIFFERENCE

See also individuality, opposites, similarity, taste

1 Every man after his fashion.
Proverb

2 Every one to his taste.
Proverb

3 One man's meat is another man's poison.
Proverb

4 There is more than one way to skin a cat.
Proverb

5 There is no accounting for tastes.
Proverb

6 There's nowt so queer as folk.
Proverb

7 All colours will agree in the dark.
Francis Bacon (1561–1626) English philosopher.
Essays, 'Of Unity in Religion'

8 If we cannot now end our differences, at least we can help make the world safe for diversity.
John Fitzgerald Kennedy (1917–63) US statesman.
Speech, American University (Washington, DC), 10 June 1963

DIPLOMACY

See also tact

1 It is better for aged diplomats to be bored than for young men to die.
Warren Austin (1877–1962) US politician and diplomat.
When asked if he got tired during long debates at the UN
Attrib.

2 There are three groups that no British Prime Minister should provoke: the Vatican, the Treasury and the miners.
Stanley Baldwin (1867–1947) British statesman.
A similar remark is often attributed to Harold Macmillan
Attrib.

3 An honest broker.
Bismarck (1815–98) German statesman.
His professed role in the diplomacy of 1878, including the Congress of Berlin
Speech, Reichstag, 19 Feb 1878

4 The healthy bones of a single Pomeranian grenadier.
Bismarck
A price too high for Germany to pay regarding the Eastern Question
Speech, Reichstag, 5 Dec 1876

5 To jaw-jaw is better than to war-war.
Winston Churchill (1874–1965) British statesman.
Speech, Washington, 26 June 1954

6 An appeaser is one who feeds a crocodile – hoping that it will eat him last.
Winston Churchill
Attrib.

7 When you have to kill a man it costs nothing to be polite.
Winston Churchill
Justifying the fact that the declaration of war against Japan was made in the usual diplomatic language
The Grand Alliance

8 America has all that Russia has not. Russia has things America has not. Why will America not reach out a hand to Russia, as I have given my hand?
Isadora Duncan (1878–1927) US dancer.
Speaking in support of Russia following the 1917 Revolution
Speech, Symphony Hall, Boston, 1922

9 REPORTER: If Mr Stalin dies, what will be the effect on international affairs?
EDEN: That is a good question for you to ask, not a wise question for me to answer.
Anthony Eden (1897–1977) British statesman.
Interview on board the *Queen Elizabeth*, 4 Mar 1953

10 Treaties are like roses and young girls – they last while they last.
Charles De Gaulle (1890–1970) French general and statesman.
Attrib.

11 I met the great little man, the man who can be silent in several languages.
James Guthrie Harbord (1866–1947) US general.
Referring to Colonel House
Mr Wilson's War (John Dos Passos), Ch. 3

12 Official dignity tends to increase in inverse ratio to the importance of the country in which the office is held.
Aldous Huxley (1894–1964) British novelist.
Beyond the Mexique Bay

13 The great nations have always acted like gangsters, and the small nations like prostitutes.
Stanley Kubrick (1928–) US film director.
The Guardian, 5 June 1963

14 All diplomacy is a continuation of war by other means.
Chou En Lai (1898–1976) Chinese statesman.

15 *La cordiale entente qui existe entre mon gouvernement et le sien.*

The friendly understanding that exists between my government and hers.
Louis Philippe (1773–1850) King of France.
Referring to an informal understanding reached between Britain and France in 1843. The more familiar phrase, 'entente cordiale', was first used in 1844
Speech, 27 Dec 1843

16 The reluctant obedience of distant provinces generally costs more than it is worth.
Lord Macaulay (1800–59) British historian.
Historical Essays Contributed to the 'Edinburgh Review', 'Lord Mahon's War of the Succession'

17 Let them especially put their demands in such a way that Great Britain could say that she supported both sides.
Ramsey MacDonald (1866–1937) British statesman and prime minister.
Referring to France and Germany
The Origins of the Second Word War (A. J. P. Taylor), Ch. 3

18 Austria will astound the world with the magnitude of her ingratitude.
Prince Schwarzenberg (1800–52) Austrian statesman.
On being asked whether Austria was under any obligation to Russia for help received previously
The Fall of the House of Habsburg (E. Crankshaw)

19 A diplomat these days is nothing but a head-waiter who's allowed to sit down occasionally.
Peter Ustinov (1921–) British actor.
Romanoff and Juliet, I

20 No nation is fit to sit in judgement upon any other nation.
Woodrow Wilson (1856–1925) US statesman.
Address, Apr 1915

21 An ambassador is an honest man sent to lie abroad for the good of his country.
Henry Wotton (1568–1639) English poet and diplomat.
Life (Izaak Walton)

DISABILITY

See also blindness

1 If there are any of you at the back who do not hear me, please don't raise your hands because I am also nearsighted.
W. H. Auden (1907–73) British poet.
Starting a lecture in a large hall
In *Book of the Month Club News*, Dec 1946

2 I'm a coloured, one-eyed Jew.
Sammy Davis Jnr (1925–) US singer.
When asked what his handicap was during a game of golf
Attrib.

DISAPPOINTMENT

See also disillusion, expectation

1 Unhappiness is best defined as the difference between our talents and our expectations.
Edward de Bono (1933–) British physician and writer.
The Observer, 'Sayings of the Week', 12 June 1977

2 The best laid schemes o' mice an' men

Gang aft a-gley,
An' lea'e us nought but grief an' pain
For promis'd joy.
Robert Burns (1759–96) Scottish poet.
To a Mouse

3 Mountains will heave in childbirth, and a silly
little mouse will be born.
Horace (Quintus Horatius Flaccus; 65–8 BC) Roman poet.
Ars Poetica

4 A mountain in labour shouted so loud that
everyone, summoned by the noise, ran up
expecting that she would be delivered of a
city bigger than Paris; she brought forth a
mouse.
Jean de La Fontaine (1621–95) French poet.
Fables, V, 'La Montagne qui accouche'

5 Levin wanted friendship and got friendliness;
he wanted steak and they offered spam.
Bernard Malamud (1914–86) US novelist.
A New Life, VI

6 Look in my face; my name is Might-have-
been.
I am also called No-more, Too-late, Farewell.
Dante Gabriel Rossetti (1828–82) British painter and
poet.
The House of Life, 'A Superscription'

7 Oh, I wish that God had not given me what I
prayed for! It was not so good as I thought.
Johanna Spyri (1827–1901) Swiss writer.
Heidi, Ch. 11

8 He said that he was too old to cry, but it
hurt too much to laugh.
Adlai Stevenson (1900–65) US statesman.
Said after losing an election, quoting a story told by Abraham
Lincoln
Speech, 5 Nov 1952

DISASTER

See also accidents

1 Bad news travels fast.
Proverb

2 Let us hope . . . that a kind of Providence will
put a speedy end to the acts of God under
which we have been labouring.
Peter De Vries (1910–) US novelist.
The Mackerel Plaza, Ch. 3

3 An Act of God was defined as *something
which no reasonable man could have expected.*
A. P. Herbert (1890–1971) British writer and politician.
Uncommon Law

4 Beautiful Railway Bridge of the Silv'ry Tay!
Alas, I am very sorry to say
That ninety lives have been taken away
On the last Sabbath day of 1879,
Which will be remember'd for a very long time.
William McGonagall (1830–1902) Scottish poet.
The Tay Bridge Disaster

DISCONTENT

See also envy

1 And sigh that one thing only has been lent
To youth and age in common – discontent.
Matthew Arnold (1822–88) British poet and critic.
Youth's Agitations

2 The idiot who praises, with enthusiastic tone,
All centuries but this, and every country but
his own.
W. S. Gilbert (1836–1911) British dramatist.
The Mikado, I

3 So have I loitered my life away, reading
books, looking at pictures, going to plays,
hearing, thinking, writing on what pleased me
best. I have wanted only one thing to make
me happy, but wanting that have wanted
everything.
William Hazlitt (1778–1830) British essayist.
English Literature, Ch. XVII, 'My First Acquaintance with
Poets'

4 How is it, Maecenas, that no one lives
contented with his lot, whether he has
planned it for himself or fate has flung him
into it, but yet he praises those who follow
different paths?
Horace (Quintus Horatius Flaccus; 65–8 BC) Roman poet.
Satires, I

5 Ever let the fancy roam,
Pleasure never is at home.
John Keats (1795–1821) British poet.
Fancy, I

6 I am sick o' wastin' leather on these gritty
pavin'-stones,
An' the blasted English drizzle wakes the fever
in my bones;
Tho' I walks with fifty 'ousemaids outer Chel-
sea to the Strand,
An' they talks a lot o' lovin', but wot do they
understand?
Beefy face an' grubby 'and –
Law! Wot do they understand?
I've a neater, sweeter maiden in a cleaner,
greener land!
Rudyard Kipling (1865–1936) Indian-born British writer.
The Road to Mandalay

7 He disdains all things above his reach, and
preferreth all countries before his own.
Thomas Overbury (1581–1613) English poet.
Miscellaneous Works, 'An Affectate Traveller'

8 When in disgrace with fortune and men's
eyes
I all alone beweep my outcast state,
And trouble deaf heaven with my bootless
cries,
And look upon myself, and curse my fate,
Wishing me like to one more rich in hope
Featur'd like him, like him with friends
possess'd,
Desiring this man's art, and that man's scope,

With what I most enjoy contented least.
William Shakespeare (1564–1616) English dramatist.
Sonnet 29

9 While not exactly disgruntled, he was far from feeling gruntled.
P. G. Wodehouse (1881–1975) British humorous novelist.
The Code of the Woosters

10 I'd rather be
A Pagan suckled in a creed outworn;
So might I, standing on this pleasant lea,
Have glimpses that would make me less forlorn;
Have sight of Proteus rising from the sea;
Or hear Old Triton blow his wreathed horn.
William Wordsworth (1770–1850) British poet.
Sonnets, 'The world is too much with us'

DISCOVERY

See also exploration, science, space

1 *Eureka!*
I have found it!
Archimedes (c. 287–212 BC) Greek mathematician.
An exclamation of joy supposedly uttered as, stepping into a bath and noticing the water overflowing, he saw the answer to a problem and began the train of thought that led to his principle of buoyancy
Attrib.

2 Look, stranger, at this island now
The leaping light for your delight discovers.
W. H. Auden (1907–73) British poet.
Look, Stranger

3 They are ill discoverers that think there is no land, when they can see nothing but sea.
Francis Bacon (1561–1626) English philosopher.
The Advancement of Learning, Bk. II, Ch. 7

4 God could cause us considerable embarrassment by revealing all the secrets of nature to us: we should not know what to do for sheer apathy and boredom.
Goethe (1749–1832) German poet and dramatist.
Memoirs (Riemer)

5 Then felt I like some watcher of the skies
When a new planet swims into his ken;
Or like stout Cortez when with eagle eyes
He star'd at the Pacific – and all his men
Look'd at each other with a wild surmise –
Silent, upon a peak in Darien.
John Keats (1795–1821) British poet.
On first looking into Chapman's Homer

6 I do not know what I may appear to the world, but to myself I seem to have been only like a boy playing on the sea-shore, and diverting myself in now and then finding a smoother pebble or a prettier shell than ordinary, whilst the great ocean of truth lay all undiscovered before me.
Isaac Newton (1642–1727) British scientist.
Isaac Newton (L. T. More)

7 The people – could you patent the sun?
Jonas E. Salk (1914–) US virologist.
On being asked who owned the patent on his polio vaccine
Famous Men of Science (S. Bolton)

8 Discovery consists of seeing what everybody has seen and thinking what nobody has thought.
Albert Szent-Györgyi (1893–1986) Hungarian-born US biochemist.
The Scientist Speculates (I. J. Good)

DISEASE

1 A disease known is half cured.
Proverb

2 'Pray, Mr. Abernethy, what is a cure for gout' was the question of an indolent and luxurious citizen.
'Live upon sixpence a day – and earn it,' was the cogent reply.
John Abernethy (1764–1831) English surgeon.
Medical Portrait Gallery, Vo. II (Thomas J. Pettigrew)

3 We are led to think of diseases as isolated disturbances in a healthy body, not as the phases of certain periods of bodily development.
Sir Clifford Allbutt (1836–1925)
Bulletin of the New York Academy of Medicine, 4:1000, 1928 (F. H. Garrison)

4 Screw up the vise as tightly as possible – you have rheumatism; give it another turn, and that is gout.
Anonymous

5 Once I am sure a patient has terminal cancer I tell them straight, I say, 'Its time to go visit with the grand-children.' They seem to appreciate it.
Anonymous
Said by a doctor from New Mexico
The Encyclopedia of Alternative Medicine and Self-Help (ed. Malcolm Hulke)

6 Before this strange disease of modern life,
With its sick hurry, its divided aims.
Matthew Arnold
The Scholar Gipsy

7 Only those in the last stage of disease could believe that children are true judges of character.
W. H. Auden (1907–73) British poet.
The Orators, 'Journal of an Airman'

8 Cure the disease and kill the patient.
Francis Bacon (1561–1626) English philosopher.
Essays, 'Of Friendship'

9 The remedy is worse than the disease.
Francis Bacon
Essays, 'Of Seditions and troubles'

10 GOUT, n. A physician's name for the rheumatism of a rich patient.
Ambrose Bierce (1842–c. 1914) US writer and journalist.
The Devil's Dictionary

11 Diseases crucify the soul of man, attenuate our bodies, dry them, wither them, shrivel them up like old apples make them so many anatomies.
Robert Burton (1577–1640) English scholar and churchman.
The Anatomy of Melancholy, 1

12 Evil comes at leisure like the disease; good comes in a hurry like the doctor.
G. K. Chesterton (1874–1936) British writer.
The Man who was Orthodox

13 Life is an incurable disease.
Abraham Cowley (1618–67) English poet.
To Dr Scarborough

14 There is a dread disease which so prepares its victim, as it were, for death . . . a disease in which death and life are so strangely blended, that death takes a glow and hue of life, and life the gaunt and grisly form of death – a disease which medicine never cured, wealth warded off, or poverty could boast exemption from – which sometimes moves in giant strides, and sometimes at a tardy sluggish pace, but, slow or quick, is ever sure and certain.
Charles Dickens (1812–70) British novelist.
Nicholas Nickleby, Ch. 49

15 Epidemics have often been more influential than statesman and soldiers in shaping the course of political history, and diseases may also colour the moods of civilizations.
René and Jean Dubos (1901– ; 1918–)
The White Plague, Ch. 5

16 Disease is an experience of mortal mind. It is fear made manifest on the body.
Mary Baker Eddy (1821–1910) US religious reader and scientist.
Science and Health, Ch. 14

17 To think that a bottle of wine or a truffled pâté, or even a glass of beer, instead of being absorbed and eliminated by the system in the usual manner, should mine its way through the thighs, knees, calves, ankles, and instep, to explode at last in a fiery volcano in one's great toe, seems a mirth-provoking phenomenon to all but him who is immediately concerned.
George Herman Ellwanger (fl. 1897)
Meditations on Gout, 'The Malady'

18 Time had robbed her of her personal charms, and that scourge of the human race, the gout, was racking her bones and sinews.
Hannah Farnham Lee (1780–1865)
Referring to Catherine de Medici
The Huguenots in France and America

19 Many a diabetic has stayed alive by stealing the bread denied him by his doctor.
Martin H. Fischer (1879–1962)
Fischerisms (Howard Fabing and Ray Marr)

20 Cancer's a Funny Thing:
I wish I had the voice of Homer
To sing of rectal carcinoma,
Which kills a lot more chaps, in fact,
Than were bumped off when Troy
was sacked . . .
J. B. S. Haldane (1892–1964) British geneticist.
Written while mortally ill with cancer
JBS (Ronald Clark)

21 If gentlemen love the pleasant titillation of the gout, it is all one to the Town Pump.
Nathaniel Hawthorne (1804–64) US writer.
The Town Pump

22 Some people are so sensitive they feel snubbed if an epidemic overlooks them.
Frank (Kin) Hubbard (1868–1930) US humorist and journalist.
Abe Martin's Broadcast

23 Gout is to the arteries what rheumatism is to the heart.
Henri Huchard (1844–1910)
Lancet, 1:164, 1967 (D. Evan Bedford)

24 We're all going to go crazy, living this epidemic every minute, while the rest of the world goes on out there, all around us, as if nothing is happening, going on with their own lives and not knowing what it's like, what we're going through. We're living through war, but where they're living it's peacetime, and we're all in the same country.
Larry Kramer (1935–) US dramatist and novelist.
The Normal Heart

25 It is the only disease you don't look forward to being cured of.
Herman J. Mankiewicz (1897–1953) US journalist and screenwriter.
Referring to death
Citizen Kane

26 While there are several chronic diseases more destructive to life than cancer, none is more feared.
Charles H. Mayo (1865–1939) US physician.
Annals of Surgery, 83:357, 1926

27 Fever the eternal reproach to the physicians.
John Milton (1608–74) English poet.
Paradise Lost, Bk. XI

28 I have Bright's disease and he has mine.
S. J. Perelman
Attrib.

29 The Muse but serv'd to ease some friend, not Wife,
To help me through this long disease, my life.
Alexander Pope (1688–1744) British poet.
Epistle to Dr. Arbuthnot

30 Cur'd yesterday of my disease,
I died last night of my physician.
Matthew Prior (1664–1721) British poet.
The Remedy Worse than the Disease

31 Diseases are the tax on pleasures.
John Ray (1627–1705) English naturalist.
English Proverbs

32 The diseases which destroy a man are no less natural than the instincts which preserve him.
George Santayana (1863–1952) Spanish-born US philosopher, poet, and critic.
Dialogues in Limbo, 3

33 Preachers say, Do as I say, not as I do. But if the physician had the same disease upon him that I have, and he should bid me do one thing, and himself do quite another, could I believe him?
John Selden (1584–1654) English historian.
Table Talk

34 Disease is not of the body but of the place.
Seneca (c. 4 BC–65 AD) Roman writer.
Epistulae ad Lucilium

35 Not even remedies can master incurable diseases.
Seneca
Epistulae ad Lucilium

36 The development of industry has created many new sources of danger. Occupational diseases are socially different from other diseases, but not biologically.
Henry E. Sigerist (1891–1957)
Journal of the History of Medicine and Allied Sciences, 13:214, 1958

37 The man of the present day would far rather believe that disease is connected only with immediate causes for the fundamental tendency in the modern view of life is always to seek what is more convenient.
Rudolf Steiner (1861–1925) Austrian philosopher, founder of anthroposophy.
The Manifestations of Karma, Lecture III

38 The old saw is that 'if you drink wine you have the gout and if you do not drink wine the gout will have you.'
Thomas Sydenham (1624–89)
Works, 'A Treatise on Gout and Dropsy'

39 Decay and disease are often beautiful, like the pearly tear of the shellfish and the hectic glow of consumption.
Henry David Thoreau (1817–62) US writer.
Journal, 11 June 1852

40 The art of medicine consists of amusing the patient while Nature cures the disease.
Voltaire (1694–1788) French writer.
Attrib.

41 I would like to remind those responsible for the treatment of tuberculosis that Keats wrote his best poems while dying of this disease. In my opinion he would never have

done so under the influence of modern chemotherapy.
Arthur M. Walker (1896–1955)
Walkerisms (Julius L. Wilson)

DISILLUSION

See also disappointment, innocence of childhood

1 The price one pays for pursuing any profession or calling is an intimate knowledge of its ugly side.
James Baldwin (1924–87) US writer.
Nobody Knows My Name

2 If you live long enough, you'll see that every victory turns into a defeat.
Simone de Beauvoir (1908–86) French writer.
Tous les hommes sont mortels

3 The coach has turned into a pumpkin and the mice have all run away.
Ladybird Johnson (1912–   ) Wife of Lyndon B. Johnson.
Said after Lyndon Johnson gave up the presidency
The Vantage Point (Lyndon B. Johnson)

4 I have protracted my work till most of those whom I wished to please have sunk into the grave; and success and miscarriage are empty sounds.
Samuel Johnson (1709–84) British lexicographer.
Dictionary of the English Language

5 One stops being a child when one realizes that telling one's trouble does not make it better.
Cesare Pavese (1908–50) Italian novelist and poet.
The Business of Living: Diaries 1935–50

DISMISSAL

See also departure

1 You have sat too long here for any good you have been doing. Depart, I say, and let us have done with you. In the name of God, *go!*
Leopold Amery (1873–1955) British statesman.
Said to Neville Chamberlain using Cromwell's words
Speech, House of Commons, May 1940

2 You have delighted us long enough.
Jane Austen (1775–1817) British novelist.
Pride and Prejudice, Ch. 18

3 It is not fit that you should sit here any longer! . . . you shall now give place to better men.
Oliver Cromwell (1599–1658) English soldier and statesman.
Speech to the Rump Parliament, 22 Jan 1655

4 Take away that fool's bauble, the mace.
Oliver Cromwell
Speech dismissing Parliament, 20 Apr 1653

5 Go, and never darken my towels again!
Groucho Marx (Julius Marx; 1895–1977) US comedian.
Duck Soup

6 There comes a time in every man's life when he must make way for an older man.

Reginald Maudling (1917–77) British politician.
Remark made on being replaced in the shadow cabinet by John Davies, his elder by four years
The Guardian, 20 Nov 1976

7 We Don't Want To Lose You But We Think You Ought To Go.

Paul Alfred Rubens (1875–1917) British dramatist and songwriter.
Title of song

8 Stand not upon the order of your going, But go at once.

William Shakespeare (1564–1616) English dramatist.
Macbeth, III:4

9 Dropping the pilot.

John Tenniel (1820–1914) British illustrator and cartoonist.
Caption of a cartoon. The cartoon refers to Bismarck's resignation portraying him as a ship's pilot walking down the gangway of the ship while Wilhelm II watches from the deck
Punch, 29 Mar 1890

DOCTORS

See also disease, drugs, health and healthy living, illness, medicine, remedies

1 I am dying with the help of too many physicians.

Alexander the Great (356–323 BC) King of Macedon.
Attrib.

2 And he said unto them, Ye will surely say unto me this proverb, Physician, heal thyself: whatsoever we have heard done in Capernaum, do also here in thy country.

Bible: Luke
4:23

3 The doctor found, when she was dead, Her last disorder mortal.

Oliver Goldsmith (1728–74) Irish-born British writer.
Elegy on Mrs. Mary Blaize

4 I suppose one has a greater sense of intellectual degradation after an interview with a doctor than from any human experience.

Alice James (1848–92) US diarist.
The Diary of Alice James (ed. Leon Edel), 27 Sept 1890

5 It is incident to physicians, I am afraid, beyond all other men, to mistake subsequence for consequence.

Samuel Johnson (1709–84) British lexicographer.
Life of Johnson (J. Boswell), Vol. I

6 Who shall decide when doctors disagree?

Alexander Pope (1688–1744) British poet.
Moral Essays, III

7 Cur'd yesterday of my disease, I died last night of my physician.

Matthew Prior (1664–1721) British poet.
The Remedy Worse than the Disease

8 First they get *on*, then they get *honour*, then they get *honest*.

Humphrey Rolleston (1862–1944) British physician.
Referring to physicians
Confessions of an Advertising Man (David Ogilvy)

9 Physicians are like kings, – they brook no contradiction.

John Webster (1580–1625) English dramatist.
The Duchess of Malfi, V:2

DOGS

See also animals

1 A huge dog, tied by a chain, was painted on the wall and over it was written in capital letters 'Beware of the dog.'

Petronius Arbiter (1st century AD) Roman satirist.
Latin, *Cave canem*
Satyricon: Cena Trimalchionis, 29

2 The woman who is really kind to dogs is always one who has failed to inspire sympathy in men.

Max Beerbohm (1872–1956) British writer.
Zuleika Dobson

3 It's the one species I wouldn't mind seeing vanish from the face of the earth. I wish they were like the White Rhino – six of them left in the Serengeti National Park, and all males.

Alan Bennett (1934–) British playwright.
Referring to dogs
Getting On, I

4 The great pleasure of a dog is that you may make a fool of yourself with him and not only will he not scold you, he will make a fool of himself too.

Samuel Butler (1835–1902) British writer.
Notebooks

5 'Tis sweet to hear the watch-dog's honest bark
Bay deep-mouthed welcome as we draw near home;
'Tis sweet to know there is an eye will mark
Our coming, and look brighter when we come.

Lord Byron (1788–1824) British poet.
Don Juan, I

6 Anybody who hates children and dogs can't be all bad.

W. C. Fields (1880–1946) US actor.
Attrib.

7 The dog, to gain some private ends, Went mad and bit the man.

Oliver Goldsmith (1728–74) Irish-born British writer.
Elegy on the Death of a Mad Dog

8 The man recovered of the bite, The dog it was that died.

Oliver Goldsmith
Elegy on the Death of a Mad Dog

9 Stop running those dogs on your page. I

wouldn't have them peeing on my cheapest rug.

William Randolph Hearst (1863–1951) US newspaper owner.
Referring to the publication of Thurber's drawings by one of his editors
The Years with Ross (James Thurber)

10 A door is what a dog is perpetually on the wrong side of.

Ogden Nash (1902–71) US poet.
A Dog's Best Friend Is His Illiteracy

11 I am His Highness' dog at Kew;
Pray tell me sir, whose dog are you?

Alexander Pope (1688–1744) British poet.
On the collar of a dog given to Frederick, Prince of Wales

12 That indefatigable and unsavoury engine of pollution, the dog.

John Sparrow (1906–) British lawyer and academic.
Letter to *The Times*, 30 Sep 1975

13 I loathe people who keep dogs. They are cowards who haven't got the guts to bite people themselves.

August Strindberg (1849–1912) Swedish dramatist.
A Madman's Diary

14 Daddy wouldn't buy me a bow-wow, bow-wow.
I've got a little cat
And I'm very fond of that.

Joseph Tabrar (20th century) US songwriter.
Daddy Wouldn't Buy Me A Bow-wow (song)

DOOMSDAY

1 That at what time ye hear the sound of the cornet, flute, harp, sackbut, psaltery, dulcimer, and all kinds of musick, ye fall down and worship the golden image that Nebuchadnezzar the king hath set up:
And whoso falleth not down and worshippeth shall the same hour be cast into the midst of a burning fiery furnace.

Bible: Daniel
3:5–6

2 Immediately after the tribulation of those days shall the sun be darkened, and the moon shall not give her light, and the stars shall fall from heaven, and the powers of the heavens shall be shaken:
And then shall appear the sign of the Son of man in heaven: and then shall all the tribes of the earth mourn, and they shall see the Son of man coming in the clouds of heaven with power and great glory.
And he shall send his angels with a great sound of a trumpet, and they shall gather together his elect from the four winds, from one end of heaven to the other.

Bible: Matthew
24:29–31

3 'Tis the Last Judgment's fire must cure this place,

Calcine its clods and set my prisoners free.

Robert Browning (1812–89) British poet.
Childe Roland to the Dark Tower Came, XI

4 Don't wait for the Last Judgement. It takes place every day.

Albert Camus (1913–60) French existentialist writer.
The Fall

5 When all the world dissolves,
And every creature shall be purified,
All place shall be hell that is not heaven.

Christopher Marlowe (1564–93) English dramatist.
Doctor Faustus, II:1

DOUBT

See also indecision, scepticism, uncertainty

1 If a man will begin with certainties, he shall end in doubts, but if he will be content to begin with doubts, he shall end in certainties.

Francis Bacon (1561–1626) English philosopher.
The Advancement of Learning, Bk. I, Ch. 5

2 And immediately Jesus stretched forth his hand, and caught him, and said unto him, O thou of little faith, wherefore didst thou doubt?

Bible: Matthew
14:31

3 He who shall teach the child to doubt
The rotting grave shall ne'er get out.

William Blake (1757–1827) British poet.
Auguries of Innocence

4 All we have gained then by our unbelief
Is a life of doubt diversified by faith,
For one of faith diversified by doubt:
We called the chess-board white, – we call it black.

Robert Browning (1812–89) British poet.
Bishop Blougram's Apology

5 His doubts are better than most people's certainties.

Lord Hardwicke (1690–1764) English judge.
Referring to Dirleton's *Doubts*
Life of Johnson (J. Boswell)

6 Negative Capability, that is, when a man is capable of being in uncertainties, mysteries, doubts, without any irritable reaching after fact and reason.

John Keats (1795–1821) British poet.
Letter to G. and T. Keats, 21 Dec 1817

7 The trouble with the world is that the stupid are cocksure and the intelligent full of doubt.

Bertrand Russell (1872–1970) British philosopher.
Autobiography

8 Those obstinate questionings
Of sense and outward things,
Fallings from us, vanishings;
Blank misgivings of a Creature
Moving about in worlds not realised,
High instincts before which our mortal nature

Did tremble like a guilty thing surprised.
William Wordsworth (1770–1850) British poet.
Ode. Intimations of Immortality, IX

DREAMS

1 Dreams and predictions ought to serve but for winter talk by the fireside.
Francis Bacon (1561–1626) English philosopher.
Essays, 'Of Prophecies'

2 It was a dream of perfect bliss,
Too beautiful to last.
Thomas Haynes Bayly (1797–1839) British writer.
It was a Dream

3 So I awoke, and behold it was a dream.
John Bunyan (1628–88) English writer.
The Pilgrim's Progress, Pt. I

4 I do not know whether I was then a man dreaming I was a butterfly, or whether I am now a butterfly dreaming I am a man.
Chuang Tse (*or* Zhuangzi; c. 369–286 BC) Chinese philosopher.
Chuang Tse (H. A. Giles), Ch. 2

5 The people's prayer, the glad diviner's theme,
The young men's vision, and the old men's dream!
John Dryden (1631–1700) British poet and dramatist.
Absalom and Achitophel, I

6 Last night I dreamt I went to Manderley again.
Daphne Du Maurier (1907–89) British novelist.
Rebecca, Ch. 1

7 Underneath the arches
We dream our dreams away.
Bud Flanagan (Robert Winthrop; 1896–1968) British comedian.
Underneath the Arches

8 Castles in the air – they're so easy to take refuge in. So easy to build, too.
Henrik Ibsen (1828–1906) Norwegian dramatist.
The Master Builder, III

9 Alas, all the castles I have, are built with air, thou know'st.
Ben Jonson (1573–1637) English dramatist.
Eastward Ho, II:2

10 All men dream: but not equally. Those who dream by night in the dusty recesses of their minds wake in the day to find that it was vanity: but the dreamers of the day are dangerous men, for they may act their dream with open eyes, to make it possible.
T. E. Lawrence (1888–1935) British soldier and writer.
Seven Pillars of Wisdom, Ch. 1

11 Abou Ben Adhem (may his tribe increase!)
Awoke one night from a deep dream of peace,
And saw, within the moonlight in his room,

Making it rich, and like a lily in bloom,
An angel writing in a book of gold: – ...
Leigh Hunt (1784–1859) British poet.
Abou Ben Adhem and the Angel

12 Many's the long night I've dreamed of cheese – toasted, mostly.
Robert Louis Stevenson (1850–94) Scottish writer.
Treasure Island, Ch. 15

13 Dreams are true while they last, and do we not live in dreams?
Alfred, Lord Tennyson (1809–92) British poet.
The Higher Pantheism

14 I have spread my dreams under your feet.
Tread softly because you tread on my dreams.
W. B. Yeats (1865–1939) Irish poet.
He wishes For The Cloths of Heaven

DRINKS

See also alcohol, drunkenness, water

1 The infusion of a China plant sweetened with the pith of an Indian cane.
Joseph Addison (1672–1719) British essayist.
The Spectator, 69

2 I the Trinity illustrate,
Drinking watered orange-pulp –
In three sips the Arian frustrate;
While he drains his at one gulp.
Robert Browning (1812–89) British poet.
Soliloquy of the Spanish Cloister

3 I am willing to taste any drink once.
James Cabell (1879–1958) US novelist and journalist.
Jurgen, Ch. 1

4 While the bubbling and loud-hissing urn
Throws up a steamy column, and the cups,
That cheer but not inebriate, wait on each,
So let us welcome peaceful evening in.
William Cowper (1731–1800) British poet.
The Task

5 Tea for Two, and Two for Tea.
Otto Harback (1873–1963) US dramatist.
From the musical *No! No! Nanette*
Song title

6 Coffee which makes the politician wise,
And see through all things with his half-shut eyes.
Alexander Pope (1688–1744) British poet.
The Rape of the Lock, III

7 Here thou great Anna! whom three realms obey,
Dost sometimes counsel take – and sometimes Tea.
Alexander Pope
The Rape of the Lock, III

8 Our trouble is that we drink too much tea. I see in this the slow revenge of the Orient, which has diverted the Yellow River down our throats.

J. B. Priestley (1894–1984) British novelist.
The Observer, 'Sayings of the Week', 15 May 1949

9 I think it must be so, for I have been drinking it for sixty-five years and I am not dead yet.

Voltaire (François-Marie Arouet; 1694–1778) French writer.
On learning that coffee was considered a slow poison
Attrib.

DROWNING

See also death

1 The western tide crept up along the sand,
And o'er and o'er the sand,
And round and round the sand,
As far as eye could see.
The rolling mist came down and hid the land:
And never home came she.

Charles Kingsley (1819–75) British writer.
The Sands of Dee

2 O Lord, methought what pain it was to drown,
What dreadful noise of waters in my ears,
What sights of ugly death within my eyes!

William Shakespeare (1564–1616) English dramatist.
Richard III, I:4

3 Nobody heard him, the dead man,
But still he lay moaning:
I was much further out than you thought
And not waving but drowning.

Stevie Smith (Florence Margaret Smith; 1902–71) British poet.
Not Waving But Drowning

DRUGS

1 A drug is that substance which, when injected into a rat, will produce a scientific report.

Anonymous

2 Hark! The herald angels sing
Beecham's pills are just the thing.
Peace on earth and mercy mild;
Two for man and one for child.

Anonymous
Apparently the result of a Beecham's advertisement in a hymnbook

3 Thou hast the keys of Paradise, oh, just, subtle, and mighty opium!

Thomas De Quincey (1785–1859) British essayist and critic.
Confessions of an English Opium-Eater, Pt. II

4 Alarmed successively by every fashionable medical terror of the day, she dosed her children with every specific which was publicly advertised or privately recommended. No creatures of their age had taken such quantities of Ching's lozenges, Godbold's

elixir, or Dixon's anti-bilious pills. The consequence was, that the dangers, which had at first been imaginary, became real: these little victims of domestic medicine never had a day's health: they looked, and were, more dead than alive.

Maria Edgeworth (1767–1849) British novelist.
Patronage

5 A man who cannot work without his hypodermic needle is a poor doctor. The amount of narcotic you use is inversely proportional to your skill.

Martin H. Fischer (1879–1962)
Fischerisms (Howard Fabing and Ray Marr)

6 Half the modern drugs could well be thrown out the window except that the birds might eat them.

Martin H. Fischer
Fischerisms (Howard Fabing and Ray Marr)

7 A hundred doses of happiness are not enough: send to the drug-store for another bottle – and, when that is finished, for another . . . There can be no doubt that, if tranquillizers could be bought as easily and cheaply as aspirin they would be consumed, not by the billions, as they are at present, but by the scores and hundreds of billions. And a good, cheap stimulant would be almost as popular.

Aldous Huxley (1894–1963) British writer.
Brave New World Revisited, Ch. 8

8 What is dangerous about the tranquillizer is that whatever peace of mind they bring is a packaged peace of mind. Where you buy a pill and buy peace with it, you get conditioned to cheap solutions instead of deep ones.

Max Lerner (1902–) Russian-born US teacher, editor, and journalist.
The Unfinished Country, 'The Assault on the Mind'

9 I will lift up mine eyes unto the pills. Almost everyone takes them, from the humble aspirin to the multi-coloured, king-sized three deckers, which put you to sleep, wake you up, stimulate and soothe you all in one. It is an age of pills.

Malcolm Muggeridge (1903–) British writer and editor.
The New Statesman, 3 Aug 1962

10 Two great European narcotics, alcohol and Christianity.

Friedrich Wilhelm Nietzsche (1844–1900) German philosopher.
The Twilight of the Idols, 'Things the Germans Lack'

11 Imperative drugging – the ordering of medicine in any and every malady – is no longer regarded as the chief function of the doctor.

William Osler
Aequanimitas, with Other Addresses, 'Medicine in the Nineteenth Century'

12 The treatment with poison medicines comes from the West.
Huang Ti (The Yellow Emperor, 2697 BC – 2597 BC)
Nei Ching Su Wen, Bk. 4

13 I owe my reputation to the fact that I use digitalis in doses the text books say are dangerous and in cases that the text books say are unsuitable.
Karel Frederik Wençkebach (1864 – 1940)
Lancet, 2:633, 1937

DRUNKENNESS

See also alcohol

1 There are more old drunkards than old doctors.
Proverb

2 His mouth has been used as a latrine by some small animal of the night.
Kingsley Amis (1922 –) British novelist.
Describing a hangover
Lucky Jim

3 Come landlord, fill the flowing bowl,
Until it doth run over . . .
For tonight we'll merry, merry be,
Tomorrow we'll be sober.
Anonymous
Come, Landlord, Fill the Flowing Bowl

4 What shall we do with the drunken sailor
Early in the morning?
Hoo-ray and up she rises
Early in the morning.
Anonymous
What shall we do with the Drunken Sailor?

5 Ha, ha, ha, you and me,
Little brown jug, don't I love thee!
Anonymous
The Little Brown Jug

6 One reason I don't drink is that I want to know when I am having a good time.
Nancy Astor (1879 – 1964) American-born British politician.
Attrib.

7 For when the wine is in, the wit is out.
Thomas Becon (1512 – 67) English Protestant churchman.
Catechism, 375

8 Others mocking said, These men are full of new wine.
Bible: Acts
2:13

9 Wine is a mocker, strong drink is raging: and whosoever is deceived thereby is not wise.
Bible: Proverbs
20:1

10 Man, being reasonable, must get drunk;
The best of life is but intoxication.
Lord Byron (1788 – 1824) British poet.
Don Juan, II

11 It's my opinion, sir, that this meeting is drunk.
Charles Dickens (1812 – 70) British novelist.
Pickwick Papers, Ch. 33

12 I am as sober as a Judge.
Henry Fielding (1707 – 54) British novelist.
Don Quixote in England, III:14

13 If merely 'feeling good' could decide, drunkenness would be the supremely valid human experience.
William James (1842 – 1910) US psychologist and philosopher.
Varieties of Religious Experience

14 A branch of the sin of drunkenness, which is the root of all sins.
James I (1566 – 1625) King of England.
A Counterblast to Tobacco

15 A man who exposes himself when he is intoxicated, has not the art of getting drunk.
Samuel Johnson (1709 – 84) British lexicographer.
Life of Johnson (J. Boswell), Vol. III

16 Better sleep with a sober cannibal than a drunken Christian.
Herman Melville (1819 – 91) US novelist.
Moby Dick, Ch. 3

17 I am as drunk as a lord, but then, I am one, so what does it matter?
Bertrand Russell (1872 – 1970) British philosopher.
Bertrand Russell, Philosopher of the Century (Ralph Schoenman)

18 No, thank you, I was born intoxicated.
George William Russell (1867 – 1935) Irish poet and dramatist.
Refusing a drink that was offered him
10,000 Jokes, Toasts, and Stories (L. Copeland)

19 But I'm not so think as you drunk I am.
John Collings Squire (1884 – 1958) British journalist.
Ballade of Soporific Absorption

20 Come, Robert, you shall drink twice while I drink once, for I cannot permit the son in his sober senses to witness the intoxication of his father.
Horace Walpole (1717 – 97) British writer.
Explaining why he filled his son's glass twice for every glass he drank himself
Attrib.

DUTY

See also obligation

1 From a very early age, I had imbibed the opinion, that it was every man's duty to do all that lay in his power to leave his country as good as he had found it.
William Cobbett (1763 – 1835) British journalist and writer.
Political Register, 22 Dec 1832

2 Do your duty and leave the rest to the Gods.
Pierre Corneille (1606 – 84) French dramatist.
Horace, II:8

3 England expects every man will do his duty.
Lord Nelson (1758–1805) British admiral.
Signal hoisted prior to the Battle of Trafalgar, 1805

4 When a stupid man is doing something he is ashamed of, he always declares that it is his duty.
George Bernard Shaw (1856–1950) Irish dramatist and critic.

Caesar and Cleopatra, III

5 Sunset and evening star,
And one clear call for me!
And may there be no moaning of the bar
When I put out to sea.
Alfred, Lord Tennyson (1809–92) British poet.
Crossing the Bar

E

ECOLOGY

See also conservation, environment

1 Over increasingly large areas of the United States, spring now comes unheralded by the return of the birds, and the early mornings are strangely silent where once they were filled with the beauty of bird song.
Rachel Carson (1907–64) US biologist.
The Silent Spring

2 As cruel a weapon as the cave man's club, the chemical barrage has been hurled against the fabric of life.
Rachel Carson
The Silent Spring

3 Man has been endowed with reason, with the power to create, so that he can add to what he's been given. But up to now he hasn't been a creator, only a destroyer. Forests keep disappearing, rivers dry up, wild life's become extinct, the climate's ruined and the land grows poorer and uglier every day.
Anton Chekhov (1860–1904) Russian dramatist.
Uncle Vanya, I

4 It will be said of this generation that it found England a land of beauty and left it a land of beauty spots.
Cyril Joad (1891–1953) British writer and broadcaster.
The Observer, 'Sayings of Our Times', 31 May 1953

5 We are living beyond our means. As a people we have developed a life-style that is draining the earth of its priceless and irreplaceable resources without regard for the future of our children and people all around the world.
Margaret Mead (1901–78) US anthropologist.
Redbook, 'The Energy Crisis – Why Our World Will Never Again Be the Same.'

6 The Irish Sea is naturally radioactive, the Sellafield discharges are less radioactive than the sea they are discharged into.
Cecil Parkinson (1931–) British politician.
Speech, Nov 1987

7 We are wealthy and wasteful but this can't go on. If we don't eat dog biscuits, we could end up eating our dog instead.
Magnus Pyke (1908–) British scientist, television personality, and writer.
The Observer, 'Sayings of the Week', 12 Jan 1975

8 Had we gone the way of France and got 60 per cent of our electricity from nuclear power, we should not have environmental problems.
Margaret Thatcher (1925–) British politician and prime minister.
Speech, Oct 1988

9 To the average British farmer, organic farming is about as relevant as caviar and a flight on Concorde.
Oliver Walston (1941–)
Speech, Jan 1989

ECONOMICS

1 Don't spoil the ship for a ha'porth of tar.
Proverb

2 A budget is a method of worrying before you spend instead of afterwards.
Anonymous

3 John Stuart Mill
By a mighty effort of will
Overcame his natural bonhomie
And wrote 'Principles of Political Economy'.
Edmund Clerihew Bentley (1875–1956) British writer.
Biography for Beginners

4 Respectable Professors of the Dismal Science.
Thomas Carlyle (1795–1881) Scottish historian and essayist.
Referring to economists
Latter-Day Pamphlets, 1

5 Provided that the City of London remains as at present, the Clearing-house of the World.
Joseph Chamberlain (1836–1914) British politician.
Speech, Guildhall, London, 19 Jan 1904

6 I am not prepared to accept the economics of a housewife.
Jacques Chirac (1932–) French politician.
Referring to Margaret Thatcher
Remark, July 1987

7 Annual income twenty pounds, annual expenditure nineteen nineteen six, result happiness. Annual income twenty pounds, annual expenditure twenty pounds ought and six, result misery.
Charles Dickens (1812–70) British novelist.
David Copperfield, Ch. 12

8 If freedom were not so economically efficient it certainly wouldn't stand a chance.
Milton Friedman (1912–) US economist.
Remark, Mar 1987

9 When every blessed thing you hold
Is made of silver, or of gold,
You long for simple pewter.
When you have nothing else to wear
But cloth of gold and satins rare,
For cloth of gold you cease to care –
Up goes the price of shoddy.
W. S. Gilbert (1836–1911) British dramatist.
The Gondoliers, I

10 Having a little inflation is like being a little pregnant.
Leon Henderson (1895–1986) US economist.
Attrib.

11 I will not be a party to debasing the currency.
John Maynard Keynes (1883–1946) British economist.
On refusing to pay more than a small tip on having his shoes polished, whilst on a visit to Africa
John Maynard Keynes (C. Hession)

12 Economics is a subject that does not greatly respect one's wishes.
Nikita Khrushchev (1894–1971) Soviet statesman.
Attrib.

13 Inflation in the Sixties was a nuisance to be endured, like varicose veins or French foreign policy.
Bernard Levin (1928–) British journalist.
The Pendulum Years, 'Epilogue'

14 One nanny said, 'Feed a cold'; she was a neo-Keynesian. Another nanny said, 'Starve a cold'; she was a monetarist.
Harold Macmillan (1894–1986) British politician and prime minister.
Maiden speech, House of Lords, 1984

15 Population, when unchecked, increases in a geometrical ratio. Subsistence only increases in an arithmetical ratio.
Thomas Robert Malthus (1766–1834) British clergyman and economist.
Essays on the Principle of Population

16 A nation is not in danger of financial disaster merely because it owes itself money.
Andrew William Mellon (1855–1937) US financier.
Attrib.

17 In the days when the nation depended on agriculture for its wealth it made the Lord Chancellor sit on a woolsack to remind him where the wealth came from. I would like to suggest we remove that now and make him sit on a crate of machine tools.
Prince Philip (1921–) The consort of Queen Elizabeth II.
Speech, Aug 1986

18 Recession is when a neighbour loses his job; depression is when you lose yours.
Ronald Reagan (1911–) US politician and president.
The Observer, 'Sayings of the Week', 26 Oct 1980

19 If all economists were laid end to end, they would not reach a conclusion.
George Bernard Shaw (1856–1950) Irish dramatist and critic.
Attrib.

20 Give me a one-handed economist! All my economists say, 'on the one hand . . . on the other'.
Harry S. Truman (1884–1972) US statesman.
Presidential Anecdotes (P. Boller)

21 From now, the pound is worth 14 per cent or so less in terms of other currencies. It does not mean, of course, that the pound here in Britain, in your pocket or purse or in your bank, has been devalued.
Harold Wilson (1916–) British politician and prime minister.
Speech after devaluation of the pound, 20 Nov 1967

22 One man's wage rise is another man's price increase.
Harold Wilson
The Observer, 'Sayings of the Week', 11 Jan 1970

EDITORS

See also books, journalism, newspapers, publishing

1 Where were you fellows when the paper was blank?
Fred Allen (1894–1956) US comedian.
Said to writers who heavily edited one of his scripts
Attrib.

2 He made righteousness readable.
James Bone (1872–1962) British journalist.
Referring to C. P. Scott, former editor of *The Manchester Guardian*
Attrib.

3 An editor is one who separates the wheat from the chaff and prints the chaff.
Adlai Stevenson (1900–65) US statesman.
The Stevenson Wit

EDUCATION

See also academics, classics, examinations, indoctrination, learning, punishment

1 Soon learnt, soon forgotten.
Proverb

2 What we must look for here is, first, religious and moral principles; secondly, gentlemanly conduct; thirdly, intellectual ability.
Thomas Arnold (1795–1842) British educator.
Address to the Scholars at Rugby

3 My object will be, if possible to form

Christian men, for Christian boys I can
scarcely hope to make.
Thomas Arnold
Letter on appointment as Headmaster of Rugby, 1828

4   Universities incline wits to sophistry and
affectation.
Francis Bacon (1561–1626) English philosopher.
Valerius Terminus of the Interpretation of Nature, Ch. 26

5   Studies serve for delight, for ornament, and
for ability.
Francis Bacon
Essays, 'Of Studies'

6   It is Oxford that has made me insufferable.
Max Beerbohm (1872–1956) British writer.
More, 'Going back to School'

7   The dread of beatings,
Dread of Being Late
And greatest dread of all, the dread of games.
John Betjeman (1906–84) British poet.
Summoned by Bells

8   The true University of these days is a
collection of books.
Thomas Carlyle (1795–1881) Scottish historian and
essayist.
Heroes and Hero-Worship, 'The Hero as Man of Letters'

9   'Reeling and Writhing, of course, to begin
with,' the Mock Turtle replied; 'and then the
different branches of Arithmetic – Ambition,
Distraction, Uglification, and Derision.'
Lewis Carroll (Charles Lutwidge Dodgson; 1832–98)
British writer.
Alice's Adventures in Wonderland, Ch. 9

10 His English education at one of the great
public schools had preserved his intellect
perfectly and permanently at the stage of
boyhood.
G. K. Chesterton (1874–1936) British writer.
The Man Who Knew Too Much

11 Education is simply the soul of a society as it
passes from one generation to another.
G. K. Chesterton
The Observer, 'Sayings of the Week', 6 July 1924

12 Headmasters have powers at their disposal
with which Prime Ministers have never yet
been invested.
Winston Churchill (1874–1965) British statesman.
My Early Life, Ch. 2

13 The ape-like virtues without which no one
can enjoy a public school.
Cyril Connolly (1903–74) British journalist.
Enemies of Promise, Ch. 1

14 When he has learnt that bottinney means a
knowledge of plants, he goes and knows 'em.
That's our system, Nickleby; what do you
think of it?
Charles Dickens (1812–70) British novelist.
Said by Mr Squeers
Nicholas Nickleby, Ch. 8

15 I pay the schoolmaster, but 'tis the
schoolboys that educate my son.
Ralph Waldo Emerson (1803–82) US poet and essayist.
Journal

16 Public schools are the nurseries of all vice
and immorality.
Henry Fielding (1707–54) British novelist.
Joseph Andrews, Bk. III, Ch. 5

17 It is not that the Englishman can't feel – it is
that he is afraid to feel. He has been taught
at his public school that feeling is bad form.
He must not express great joy or sorrow, or
even open his mouth too wide when he talks
– his pipe might fall out if he did.
E. M. Forster (1879–1970) British novelist.
Abinger Harvest, 'Notes on the English character'

18 They go forth into it with well-developed
bodies, fairly developed minds, and
undeveloped hearts.
E. M. Forster
Referring to public schoolboys going into the world
Abinger Harvest, 'Notes on the English Character'

19 Spoon feeding in the long run teaches us
nothing but the shape of the spoon.
E. M. Forster
The Observer, 'Sayings of the Week', 7 Oct 1951

20 To the University of Oxford I acknowledge
no obligation; and she will as cheerfully
renounce me for a son, as I am willing to
disclaim her for a mother. I spent fourteen
months at Magdalen College: they proved the
fourteen months the most idle and
unprofitable of my whole life.
Edward Gibbon (1737–94) British historian.
Autobiography

21 Education made us what we are.
Claude-Adrien Helvétius (1715–71) French philosopher.
Discours XXX, Ch. 30

22 And seek for truth in the groves of
Academe.
Horace (Quintus Horatius Flaccus; 65–8 BC) Roman poet.
Epistles, II

23 You sought the last resort of feeble minds
with classical educations. You became a
schoolmaster.
Aldous Huxley (1894–1964) British novelist.
Antic Hay

24 Some experience of popular lecturing had
convinced me that the necessity of making
things plain to uninstructed people was one of
the very best means of clearing up the
obscure corners in one's own mind.
T. H. Huxley (1825–95) British biologist.
Man's Place in Nature, Preface

25 Any attempt to reform the university without
attending to the system of which it is an
integral part is like trying to do urban

renewal in New York City from the twelfth storey up.

Ivan Illich (1926–) Austrian sociologist.
Deschooling Society, Ch. 3

26 It is no matter what you teach them first, any more than what leg you shall put into your breeches first.

Samuel Johnson (1709–84) British lexicographer.
Life of Johnson (J. Boswell), Vol. I

27 There is now less flogging in our great schools than formerly, but then less is learned there; so that what the boys get at one end they lose at the other.

Samuel Johnson
Life of Johnson (J. Boswell), Vol. II

28 I find the three major administrative problems on a campus are sex for the students, athletics for the alumni and parking for the faculty.

Clark Kerr (1911–) US educator.
Time, 17 Nov 1958

29 Nothing would more effectively further the development of education than for all flogging pedagogues to learn to educate with the head instead of with the hand.

Ellen Key (Karolina Sofia Key; 1849–1926) Swedish writer.
The Century of the Child, Ch. 3

30 If every day in the life of a school could be the last day but one, there would be little fault to find with it.

Stephen Leacock (1869–1944) English-born Canadian economist and humorist.
College Days, 'Memories and Miseries of a Schoolmaster'

31 Four times, under our educational rules, the human pack is shuffled and cut – at eleven-plus, sixteen-plus, eighteen-plus and twenty-plus – and happy is he who comes top of the deck on each occasion, but especially the last. This is called Finals, the very name of which implies that nothing of importance can happen after it. The British postgraduate student is a lonely forlorn soul . . . for whom nothing has been real since the Big Push.

David Lodge (1935–) British author.
Changing Places, Ch. 1

32 Universities are the cathedrals of the modern age. They shouldn't have to justify their existence by utilitarian criteria.

David Lodge
Nice Work IV

33 If you educate a man you educate a person, but if you educate a woman you educate a family.

Ruby Manikan (20th century) Indian Church leader.
The Observer, 'Sayings of the Week', 30 Mar 1947

34 A gentleman need not know Latin, but he should at least have forgotten it.

Brander Matthews (1852–1929) US writer.
Attrib.

35 A whale ship was my Yale College and my Harvard.

Herman Melville (1819–91) US novelist.
Moby Dick, Ch. 24

36 One tongue is sufficient for a woman.

John Milton (1608–74) English poet.
On being asked whether he would allow his daughters to learn foreign languages
Attrib.

37 And if education is always to be conceived along the same antiquated lines of a mere transmission of knowledge, there is little to be hoped from it in the bettering of man's future. For what is the use of transmitting knowledge if the individual's total development lags behind?

Maria Montessori (1870–1952) Italian doctor and educationalist.
The Absorbent Mind

38 We teachers can only help the work going on, as servants wait upon a master.

Maria Montessori
The Absorbent Mind

39 Discussion in class, which means letting twenty young blockheads and two cocky neurotics discuss something that neither their teacher nor they know.

Vladimir Nabokov (1899–1977) Russian-born US novelist.
Pnin, Ch. 6

40 Every schoolmaster after the age of 49 is inclined to flatulence, is apt to swallow frequently, and to puff.

Harold Nicolson (1886–1968) British writer.
The Old School

41 The schoolteacher is certainly underpaid as a childminder, but ludicrously overpaid as an educator.

John Osborne (1929–) British dramatist.
The Observer, 'Sayings of the Week', 21 July 1985

42 School yourself to demureness and patience. Learn to innure yourself to drudgery in science. Learn, compare, collect the facts.

Ivan Pavlov (1849–1936) Russian physiologist.
Bequest to the Academic Youth of Soviet Russia, 27 Feb 1936

43 He was sent, as usual, to a public school, where a little learning was painfully beaten into him, and from thence to the university, where it was carefully taken out of him.

Thomas Love Peacock (1785–1866) British novelist.
Nightmare Abbey, Ch. 1

44 'Tis education forms the common mind, Just as the twig is bent, the tree's inclined.

Alexander Pope (1688–1744) British poet.
Moral Essays, I

45 Girls and boys grow up more normally together than apart.

Daphne Rae Wife of the Headmaster of Westminster School.
Remark, May 1988

46 A man who has never gone to school may

steal from a freight car, but if he has a university education he may steal the whole railroad.
Franklin D. Roosevelt (1882–1945) US Democratic president.
Attrib.

47 But, good gracious, you've got to educate him first.
You can't expect a boy to be vicious till he's been to a good school.
Saki (Hector Hugh Munro; 1870–1916) British writer.
Reginald in Russia

48 For every person wishing to teach there are thirty not wanting to be taught.
W. C. Sellar (1898–1951) British humorous writer.
And Now All This

49 No profit grows where is no pleasure ta'en;
In brief, sir, study what you most affect.
William Shakespeare (1564–1616) English dramatist.
The Taming of the Shrew, I:1

50 A learned man is an idler who kills time by study.
George Bernard Shaw (1856–1950) Irish dramatist and critic.
Man and Superman

51 There is nothing on earth intended for innocent people so horrible as a school. It is in some respects more cruel than a prison. In a prison, for example, you are not forced to read books written by the warders and the governor.
George Bernard Shaw
Parents and Children

52 He who can, does. He who cannot, teaches.
George Bernard Shaw
Man and Superman, 'Maxims for Revolutionists'

53 Indeed one of the ultimate advantages of an education is simply coming to the end of it.
B. F. Skinner (1904–) US psychologist.
The Technology of Teaching

54 Education is what survives when what has been learnt has been forgotten.
B. F. Skinner
New Scientist, 21 May 1964, 'Education in 1984'

55 To me education is a leading out of what is already there in the pupil's soul. To Miss Mackay it is a putting in of something that is not there, and that is not what I call education, I call it intrusion. . . .
Muriel Spark (1918–) British novelist.
The Prime of Miss Jean Brodie, Ch. 2

56 Soap and education are not as sudden as a massacre, but they are more deadly in the long run.
Mark Twain (Samuel Langhorne Clemens; 1835–1910) US writer.
The Facts concerning the Recent Resignation

57 People at the top of the tree are those without qualifications to detain them at the bottom.
Peter Ustinov (1921–) British actor.
Attrib.

58 I expect you'll be becoming a schoolmaster sir. That's what most of the gentlemen does sir, that gets sent down for indecent behaviour.
Evelyn Waugh (1903–66) British novelist.
Decline and Fall, Prelude

59 We class schools you see, into four grades: Leading School, First-rate School, Good School, and School.
Evelyn Waugh
Decline and Fall, Pt. I, Ch. 1

60 We schoolmasters must temper discretion with deceit.
Evelyn Waugh
Decline and Fall, Pt. I, Ch. 1

61 That's the public-school system all over. They may kick you out, but they never let you down.
Evelyn Waugh
Decline and Fall, Pt. I, Ch. 3

62 Anyone who has been to an English public school will always feel comparatively at home in prison.
Evelyn Waugh
Decline and Fall, Pt. III, Ch. 4

63 Assistant masters came and went. . . Some liked little boys too little and some too much.
Evelyn Waugh
A Little Learning

64 The battle of Waterloo was won on the playing fields of Eton.
Duke of Wellington (1769–1852) British general and statesman.
Attrib.

65 A very large part of English middle-class education is devoted to the training of servants . . . In so far as it is, by definition, the training of upper servants, it includes, of course, the instilling of that kind of confidence which will enable the upper servants to supervise and direct the lower servants.
Raymond Henry Williams (1921–88) British academic and writer.
Culture and Society, Ch. 3

EFFORT

See also work

1 If a job's worth doing, it's worth doing well.
Proverb

2 Energy is Eternal Delight.
William Blake (1757–1827) British poet.
The Marriage of Heaven and Hell, 'The Voice of the Devil'

3 I have nothing to offer but blood, toil, tears and sweat.
Winston Churchill (1874–1965) British statesman.
On becoming prime minister
Speech, House of Commons, 13 May 1940

4 A world where nothing is had for nothing.
Arthur Hugh Clough (1819–61) British poet.
The Bothie of Tober-na-Vuolich, Bk. VIII, Ch. 5

5 As is the case in all branches of art, success depends in a very large measure upon individual initiative and exertion, and cannot be achieved except by dint of hard work.
Anna Pavlova (1881–1931) Russian ballet dancer.
Pavlova: A Biography (ed. A. H. Franks), 'Pages of My Life'

6 And here is the lesson I learned in the army. If you want to do a thing badly, you have to work at it as though you want to do it well.
Peter Ustinov (1921–) British actor.
Dear Me, Ch. 8

7 Please do not shoot the pianist. He is doing his best.
Oscar Wilde (1854–1900) Irish-born British dramatist.
Impressions of America, 'Leadville'

EGOTISM

See also arrogance, conceit, pride, selfishness

1 Against whom?
Alfred Adler (1870–1937) Austrian psychiatrist.
Said when he heard that an egocentric had fallen in love
Some of My Best Friends (J. Bishop), 'Exponent of the Soul'

2 No poet or novelist wishes he were the only one who ever lived, but most of them wish they were the only one alive, and quite a number fondly believe their wish has been granted.
W. H. Auden (1907–73) British poet.
The Dyer's Hand, 'Writing'

3 *Egotist*, n. A person of low taste, more interested in himself than in me.
Ambrose Bierce (1842–?1914) US writer and journalist.
The Devil's Dictionary

4 Someone said of a very great egotist: 'He would burn your house down to cook himself a couple of eggs.'
Nicolas Chamfort (1741–94) French writer.
Caractères et anecdotes

5 An author who speaks about his own books is almost as bad as a mother who talks about her own children.
Benjamin Disraeli (1804–81) British statesman.
Speech in Glasgow, 19 Nov 1873

6 If the Almighty himself played the violin, the credits would still read 'Rubinstein, God, and Piatigorsky', in that order.
Jascha Heifetz (1901–87) Russian-born US violinist.
Whenever Heifetz played in trios with Arthur Rubinstein (piano) and Gregor Piatigorsky (cello), Rubinstein always got top billing
Los Angeles Times, 29 Aug 1982

7 One had rather malign oneself than not speak of oneself at all.
Duc de la Rochefoucauld (1613–80) French writer.
Maximes, 138

8 As who should say 'I am Sir Oracle,
And when I ope my lips let no dog bark'.
William Shakespeare (1564–1616) English dramatist.
The Merchant of Venice, I:1

9 A pompous woman of his acquaintance, complaining that the head-waiter of a restaurant had not shown her and her husband immediately to a table, said, 'We had to tell him who we were.' Gerald, interested, enquired, 'And who were you?'
Edith Sitwell (1887–1964) British poet and writer.
Taken Care Of, Ch. 15

10 No man thinks there is much ado about nothing when the ado is about himself.
Anthony Trollope (1815–82) British novelist.
The Bertrams, Ch. 27

11 I am the only person in the world I should like to know thoroughly.
Oscar Wilde (1854–1900) Irish-born British dramatist.
Lady Windermere's Fan, II

EMBARRASSMENT

1 The question about everything was, would it bring a blush to the cheek of a young person?
Charles Dickens (1812–70) British novelist.
Pondered by Mr Podsnap
Our Mutual Friend, Bk. I, Ch. 11

2 Man is the only animal that blushes. Or needs to.
Mark Twain (Samuel Langhorne Clemens; 1835–1910) US writer.
Following the Equator, heading of Ch. 27

EMOTION

See also passion, sentimentality

1 There is a road from the eye to the heart that does not go through the intellect.
G. K. Chesterton (1874–1936) British writer.
The Defendant

2 'There are strings', said Mr Tappertit, 'in the human heart that had better not be wibrated.'
Charles Dickens (1812–70) British novelist.
Barnaby Rudge, Ch. 22

3 Grief and disappointment give rise to anger, anger to envy, envy to malice, and malice to grief again, till the whole circle be completed.
David Hume (1711–76) Scottish philosopher.
A Treatise of Human Nature

4 The intellect is always fooled by the heart.
Duc de la Rochefoucauld (1613–80) French writer.
Maximes, 102

5 Light breaks where no sun shines;

Where no sea runs, the waters of the heart
Push in their tides.
Dylan Thomas (1914–53) Welsh poet.
Light breaks where no sun shines

6 Pure and complete sorrow is as impossible as
pure and complete joy.
Leo Tolstoy (1828–1910) Russian writer.
War and Peace, Bk. XV, Ch. 1

ENDING

1 All good things must come to an end.
Proverb

2 All's well that ends well.
Proverb

3 This is the way the world ends
Not with a bang but a whimper.
T. S. Eliot (1888–1965) US-born British poet and
dramatist.
The Hollow Men

4 We'll to the woods no more,
The laurels all are cut.
A. E. Housman (1859–1936) British scholar and poet.
Last Poems, Introductory

5 That but this blow
Might be the be-all and the end-all here –
But here upon this bank and shoal of time –
We'd jump the life to come.
William Shakespeare (1564–1616) English dramatist.
Macbeth, I:7

6 The bright day is done,
And we are for the dark.
William Shakespeare
Antony and Cleopatra, V:2

7 Ring out, wild bells, to the wild sky,
The flying cloud, the frosty light:
The year is dying in the night;
Ring out, wild bells, and let him die.
Alfred, Lord Tennyson (1809–92) British poet.
In Memoriam A.H.H., CVI

ENDURANCE

See also comfort, courage, determination, misfortune, suffering

1 Even a worm will turn.
Proverb

2 The last straw breaks the camel's back.
Proverb

3 What can't be cured, must be endured.
Proverb

4 Nothing happens to any man that he is not
formed by nature to bear.
Marcus Aurelius (121–180 AD) Roman emperor.
Meditations, Bk. V, Ch. 18

5 Through the night of doubt and sorrow
Onward goes the pilgrim band,

Singing songs of expectation,
Marching to the Promised Land.
Sabine Baring-Gould (1834–1924) British author and
hymn writer.
Through the Night of Doubt and Sorrow

6 In the fell clutch of circumstance,
I have not winced nor cried aloud;
Under the bludgeonings of chance
My head is bloody, but unbowed.
William Ernest Henley (1849–1903) British writer.
Echoes, IV, 'Invictus. In Mem. R.T.H.B.'

7 . . . we could never learn to be brave and
patient, if there were only joy in the world.
Helen Keller (1880–1968) US writer and lecturer.
Atlantic Monthly (May 1890)

8 Job endured everything – until his friends
came to comfort him, then he grew
impatient.
Soren Kierkegaard (1813–55) Danish philosopher.
Journal

9 Sorrow and silence are strong, and patient
endurance is godlike.
Henry Wadsworth Longfellow (1807–82) US poet.
Evangeline

10 Know how sublime a thing it is
To suffer and be strong.
Henry Wadsworth Longfellow
The Light of Stars

11 The weariest nights, the longest days,
sooner or later must perforce come to an
end.
Baroness Orczy (1865–1947) British novelist.
The Scarlet Pimpernel, Ch. 22

12 No pain, no palm; no thorns, no throne; no
gall, no glory; no cross, no crown.
William Penn (1644–1718) English preacher.
No Cross, No Crown

13 The Muse but serv'd to ease some friend,
not Wife,
To help me through this long disease, my life.
Alexander Pope (1688–1744) British poet.
Epistle to Dr. Arbuthnot

14 The pain passes, but the beauty remains.
Pierre Auguste Renoir (1841–1919) French
impressionist painter.
Explaining why he still painted when his hands were twisted
with arthritis
Attrib.

15 Does the road wind up-hill all the way?
Yes, to the very end.
Will the day's journey take the whole long day?
From morn to night, my friend.
Christina Rossetti (1830–74) British poet.
Up-Hill

16 Had we lived, I should have had a tale to tell
of the hardihood, endurance, and courage of
my companions which would have stirred the

heart of every Englishman. These rough notes and our dead bodies must tell the tale.
Captain Robert Falcon Scott (1868–1912) British explorer.
Message to the Public

17 Men must endure
Their going hence, even as their coming hither:
Ripeness is all.
William Shakespeare (1564–1616) English dramatist.
King Lear, V:2

18 For there was never yet philosopher
That could endure the toothache patiently.
William Shakespeare
Much Ado About Nothing, V:1

19 Let's talk sense to the American people. Let's tell them the truth, that there are no gains without pains.
Adlai Stevenson (1900–65) US statesman.
Speech, Chicago, 26 July 1952

20 If you can't stand the heat, get out of the kitchen.
Harry S. Truman (1884–1972) US statesman.
Perhaps proverbial in origin, possibly echoes the expression 'kitchen cabinet'
Mr Citizen, Ch. 15

21 O you who have borne even heavier things, God will grant an end to these too.
Virgil (Publius Vergilius Maro; 70–19 BC) Roman poet.
Aeneid, Bk. I

22 Maybe one day we shall be glad to remember even these hardships.
Virgil
Aeneid, Bk. I

23 I sing of arms and the man who first from the shores
of Troy came destined an exile to Italy and the Lavinian beaches, much buffeted he on land and on
the deep by force of the gods because of fierce Juno's never-forgetting anger.
Virgil
Referring to Aeneas
Aeneid, Bk. I

24 Much in sorrow, oft in woe,
Onward, Christians, onward go.
Henry Kirke White (1785–1806) British poet.
A hymn, better known in its later form, 'Oft in danger, oft in woe'

ENEMIES

1 Better a thousand enemies outside the house than one inside.
Arabic proverb
Proverb

2 But I say unto you, That ye resist not evil: but whosoever shall smite thee on thy right cheek, turn to him the other also.
And if any man will sue thee at the law, and

take away thy coat, let him have thy cloke also.
And whosoever shall compel thee to go a mile, go with him twain.
Bible: Matthew
5:39–41

3 But I say unto you, Love your enemies, bless them that curse you, do good to them that hate you, and pray for them which despitefully use you, and persecute you;
That ye may be the children of your Father which is in heaven: for he maketh his sun to rise on the evil and on the good, and sendeth rain on the just and on the unjust.
For if ye love them which love you, what reward have ye? do not even the publicans the same?
Bible: Matthew
5:44–46

4 Even a paranoid can have enemies.
Henry Kissinger (1923–) German-born US politician and diplomat.
Time, 24 Jan 1977

5 They made peace between us; we embraced, and we have been mortal enemies ever since.
Alain-René Lesage (1668–1747) French writer.
Le Diable boiteux, Ch. 3

6 You must hate a Frenchman as you hate the devil.
Lord Nelson (1758–1805) British admiral.
Life of Nelson (Southey), Ch. 3

7 The only good Indians I ever saw were dead.
Philip H. Sheridan (1831–88) US general.
The People's Almanac 2 (D. Wallechinsky)

8 He makes no friend who never made a foe.
Alfred, Lord Tennyson (1809–92) British poet.
Idylls of the King, 'Lancelot and Elaine'

9 I should be like a lion in a cave of savage Daniels.
Oscar Wilde (1854–1900) Irish-born British dramatist.
Explaining why he would not be attending a function at a club whose members were hostile to him
Attrib.

ENGLAND

See also Britain, Cambridge, English, London, Oxford, patriotism

1 Oh! who can ever be tired of Bath?
Jane Austen (1775–1817) British novelist.
Northanger Abbey, Ch. 10

2 One has no great hopes from Birmingham. I always say there is something direful in the sound.
Jane Austen
Emma, Ch. 36

3 When you think about the defence of England you no longer think of the chalk cliffs of

Dover. You think of the Rhine. That is
where our frontier lies to-day.

Stanley Baldwin (1867–1947) British statesman.
Speech, House of Commons, 30 July 1934

4 Come, friendly bombs, and fall on Slough
It isn't fit for humans now.
There isn't grass to graze a cow
Swarm over, Death!

. . .

Come, friendly bombs, and fall on Slough
To get it ready for the plough.
The cabbages are coming now:
The earth exhales.

John Betjeman (1906–84) British poet.
Slough

5 And did those feet in ancient time
Walk upon England's mountains green?
And was the holy lamb of God
On England's pleasant pastures seen?

. . .

I will not cease from mental fight,
Nor shall my sword sleep in my hand,
Till we have built Jerusalem
In England's green and pleasant land.

William Blake (1757–1827) British poet.
Better known as the hymn 'Jerusalem', with music by Sir Hu-
bert Parry; not to be confused with Blake's longer poem
Jerusalem
Milton, Preface

6 England is the mother of parliaments.

John Bright (1811–89) British radical politician.
Speech, Birmingham, 18 Jan 1865

7 For England's the one land, I know,
Where men with Splendid Hearts may go;
And Cambridgeshire, of all England,
The shire for Men who Understand.

Rupert Brooke (1887–1915) British poet.
The Old Vicarage, Grantchester

8 Oh, to be in England
Now that April's there.

Robert Browning (1812–89) British poet.
Home Thoughts from Abroad

9 Without class differences, England would
cease to be the living theatre it is.

Anthony Burgess (John Burgess Wilson; 1917–)
British novelist.
The Observer, 'Sayings of the Week', 26 May 1985

10 In England there are sixty different religions,
and only one sauce.

Domenico Caracciolo (1715–89) Governor of Sicily.
Attrib.

11 This could have occurred nowhere but in
England, where men and sea interpenetrate,
so to speak.

Joseph Conrad (Teodor Josef Konrad Korzeniowski;
1857–1924) Polish-born British novelist.
Youth

12 Very flat, Norfolk.

Noël Coward (1899–1973) British dramatist.
Private Lives

13 Regions Caesar never knew
Thy posterity shall sway,
Where his eagles never flew,
None invincible as they.

William Cowper (1731–1800) British poet.
Boadicea

14 There are many things in life more
worthwhile than money. One is to be brought
up in this our England which is still the envy
of less happy lands.

Lord Denning (1899–) British judge.
The Observer, 'Sayings of the Week', 4 Aug 1968

15 Kent, sir – everybody knows Kent – apples,
cherries, hops and women.

Charles Dickens (1812–70) British novelist.
Pickwick Papers, Ch. 2

16 The Continent will not suffer England to be
the workshop of the world.

Benjamin Disraeli (1804–81) British statesman.
Speech, House of Commons, 15 Mar 1838

17 England is the paradise of women, the
purgatory of men, and the hell of horses.

John Florio (c. 1553–1625) English lexicographer.
Second Fruits

18 Living in England, provincial England, must
be like being married to a stupid but
exquisitely beautiful wife.

Margaret Halsey (1910–) US writer.
With Malice Toward Some

19 All of Stratford, in fact, suggests powdered
history –add hot water and stir and you have
a delicious, nourishing Shakespeare.

Margaret Halsey
With Malice Toward Some

20 Dr Johnson's morality was as English an
article as a beefsteak.

Nathaniel Hawthorne (1804–64) US novelist and writer.
Our Old Home, 'Lichfield and Uttoxeter'

21 Pass a law to give every single wingeing
bloody Pommie his fare home to England.
Back to the smoke and the sun shining ten
days a year and shit in the streets. Yer can
have it.

Thomas Keneally (1935–) Australian novelist.
The Chant of Jimmy Blacksmith

22 Winds of the World, give answer! They are
whimpering to and fro –
And what should they know of England who
only England know?

Rudyard Kipling (1865–1936) Indian-born British writer.
The English Flag

23 It was one of those places where the spirit of
aboriginal England still lingers, the old savage
England, whose last blood flows still in a few
Englishmen, Welshmen, Cornishmen.

D. H. Lawrence (1885–1930) British novelist.
St Mawr

24 And suddenly she craved again for the more

absolute silence of America. English stillness was so soft, like an inaudible murmur of voices, of presences.
D. H. Lawrence
St Mawr

25 In an English ship, they say, it is poor grub, poor pay, and easy work; in an American ship, good grub, good pay, and hard work. And this is applicable to the working populations of both countries.
Jack London (1876–1916) US novelist.
The People of the Abyss, Ch. 20

26 In no country, I believe, are the marriage laws so iniquitous as in England, and the conjugal relation, in consequence, so impaired.
Harriet Martineau (1802–76) British writer.
Society in America, Vol. III, 'Marriage'

27 In England there is only silence or scandal.
André Maurois (Émile Herzog; 1885–1967) French writer.
Attrib.

28 When people say England, they sometimes mean Great Britain, sometimes the United Kingdom, sometimes the British Isles, – but never England.
George Mikes (1912–87) Hungarian-born British writer.
How to be an Alien

29 It was twenty-one years ago that England and I first set foot on each other. I came for a fortnight; I have stayed ever since.
George Mikes
How to be Inimitable

30 A family with the wrong members in control – that, perhaps, is as near as one can come to describing England in a phrase.
George Orwell (Eric Blair; 1903–50) British novelist.
The Lion and the Unicorn, 'The Ruling Class'

31 There can hardly be a town in the South of England where you could throw a brick without hitting the niece of a bishop.
George Orwell
The Road to Wigan Pier, Ch. 7

32 Damn you, England. You're rotting now, and quite soon you'll disappear.
John Osborne (1929–) British dramatist.
Letter in *Tribune*, Aug 1961

33 There'll always be an England
While there's a country lane,
Wherever there's a cottage small
Beside a field of grain.
Clarke Ross Parker (1914–74) British songwriter.
There'll Always Be an England

34 The real fact is that I could no longer stand their eternal cold mutton.
Cecil Rhodes (1853–1902) South African statesman.
Explaining why he had left his friends in England and come to South Africa
Cecil Rhodes (G. le Sueur)

35 England is the paradise of individuality, eccentricity, heresy, anomalies, hobbies, and humours.
George Santayana (1863–1952) US philosopher.
Soliloquies in England, 'The British Character'

36 This royal throne of kings, this sceptred isle,
This earth of majesty, this seat of Mars,
This other Eden, demi-paradise,
This fortress built by Nature for herself
Against infection and the hand of war,
This happy breed of men, this little world,
This precious stone set in the silver sea,
Which serves it in the office of a wall,
Or as a moat defensive to a house,
Against the envy of less happier lands;
This blessed plot, this earth, this realm, this England,
This nurse, this teeming womb of royal kings,
Fear'd by their breed, and famous by their birth.
William Shakespeare (1564–1616) English dramatist.
Richard II, II:1

37 Well, I cannot last ever; but it was always yet the trick of our English nation, if they have a good thing, to make it too common.
William Shakespeare
Henry IV, Part Two, I:2

38 The English take their pleasures sadly after the fashion of their country.
Duc de Sully (1560–1641) French statesman.
Memoirs

39 They say that men become attached even to Widnes.
A. J. P. Taylor (1906–) British historian.
The Observer, 15 Sept 1963

40 Yes. I remember Adlestrop –
The name, because one afternoon
Of heat the express train drew up there
Unwontedly. It was late June.
Edward Thomas (1878–1917) British poet.
Adlestrop

41 You never find an Englishman among the underdogs – except in England of course.
Evelyn Waugh (1903–66) British novelist.
The Loved One

ENGLISH

See also British, nationality

1 An Englishman's home is his castle.
Proverb

2 An Englishman's word is his bond.
Proverb

3 That typically English characteristic for which there is no English name – *esprit de corps*.
Frank Ezra Adcock (1886–1968) British classicist.
Presidential address

4 The English instinctively admire any man who has no talent and is modest about it.

James Agate (1877–1947) British theatre critic.
Attrib.

5 But of all nations in the world the English are perhaps the least a nation of pure philosophers.

Walter Bagehot (1826–77) British economist and journalist.
The English Constitution, 'The Monarchy'

6 I like the English. They have the most rigid code of immorality in the world.

Malcolm Bradbury (1932–) British academic and novelist.
Eating People is Wrong, Ch. 5

7 The wish to spread those opinions that we hold conducive to our own welfare is so deeply rooted in the English character that few of us can escape its influence.

Samuel Butler (1835–1902) British writer.
Erewhon, Ch. 20

8 The most dangerous thing in the world is to make a friend of an Englishman, because he'll come sleep in your closet rather than spend 10s on a hotel.

Truman Capote (1924–84) US novelist.
The Observer, 'Sayings of the Week', 24 Mar 1968

9 Thirty millions, mostly fools.

Thomas Carlyle (1795–1881) Scottish historian and essayist.
When asked what the population of England was
Attrib.

10 He's an Anglo-Saxon Messenger – and those are Anglo-Saxon attitudes.

Lewis Carroll (Charles Lutwidge Dodgson; 1832–98) British writer.
Through the Looking-Glass, Ch. 7

11 All the faces here this evening seem to be bloody Poms.

Charles, Prince of Wales (1948–) Eldest son of Elizabeth II.
Remark at Australia Day dinner, 1973

12 Smile at us, pay us, pass us; but do not quite forget.
For we are the people of England, that never have spoken yet.

G. K. Chesterton (1874–1936) British writer.
The Secret People

13 It is said, I believe, that to behold the Englishman at his *best* one should watch him play tip-and-run.

Ronald Firbank (1886–1926) British novelist.
The Flower Beneath the Foot, Ch. 14

14 *Non Angli sed Angeli*
Not Angles, but angels.

Gregory I (540–604) Pope and saint.
Attrib.

15 . . . it takes a great deal to produce ennui in

an Englishman and if you do, he only takes it as convincing proof that you are well-bred.

Margaret Halsey (1910–) US writer.
With Malice Toward Some

16 The attitude of the English . . . toward English history reminds one a good deal of the attitude of a Hollywood director toward love.

Margaret Halsey
With Malice Toward Some

17 . . . the English think of an opinion as something which a decent person, if he has the misfortune to have one, does all he can to hide.

Margaret Halsey
With Malice Toward Some

18 The English (it must be owned) are rather a foul-mouthed nation.

William Hazlitt (1778–1830) British essayist.
On Criticism

19 The Englishman never enjoys himself except for a noble purpose.

A. P. Herbert (1890–1971) British writer and politician.
Uncommon Law

20 When two Englishmen meet, their first talk is of the weather.

Samuel Johnson (1709–84) British lexicographer.
The Idler

21 The English people on the whole are surely the *nicest* people in the world, and everyone makes everything so easy for everybody else, that there is almost nothing to resist at all.

D. H. Lawrence (1885–1930) British novelist.
Dull London

22 England is . . . a country infested with people who love to tell us what to do, but who very rarely seem to know what's going on.

Colin MacInnes (1914–76) British novelist.
England, Half English, 'Pop Songs and Teenagers'

23 An Englishman, even if he is alone, forms an orderly queue of one.

George Mikes (1912–87) Hungarian-born British writer.
How to be an Alien

24 Continental people have sex life; the English have hot-water bottles.

George Mikes
How to be an Alien

25 English women are elegant until they are ten years old, and perfect on grand occasions.

Nancy Mitford (1904–73) British writer.
The Wit of Women (L. and M. Cowan)

26 The English are busy; they don't have time to be polite.

Baron de Montesquieu (1689–1755) French writer.
Pensées diverses

27 It has to be admitted that we English have

sex on the brain, which is a very unsatisfactory place to have it.

Malcolm Muggeridge (1903–) British writer.
The Observer, 'Sayings of the Decade', 1964

28 England is a nation of shopkeepers.

Napoleon I (Napoleon Bonaparte; 1769–1821) French emperor.
Attrib.

29 To be an Englishman is to belong to the most exclusive club there is.

Ogden Nash (1902–71) US poet.
England Expects

30 But Lord! to see the absurd nature of Englishmen, that cannot forbear laughing and jeering at everything that looks strange.

Samuel Pepys (1633–1703) English diarist.
Diary, 27 Nov 1662

31 Remember that you are an Englishman, and have consequently won first prize in the lottery of life.

Cecil Rhodes (1853–1902) South African statesman.
Dear Me (Peter Ustinov), Ch. 4

32 The English have no respect for their language, and will not teach their children to speak it . . . It is impossible for an Englishman to open his mouth, without making some other Englishman despise him.

George Bernard Shaw (1856–1950) Irish dramatist and critic.
Pygmalion, Preface

33 I think for my part one half of the nation is mad – and the other not very sound.

Tobias Smollett (1721–71) British novelist.
The Adventures of Sir Launcelot Greaves, Ch. 6

34 I cannot but conclude the bulk of your natives to be the most pernicious race of little odious vermin that nature ever suffered to crawl upon the surface of the earth.

Jonathan Swift (1667–1745) Irish-born Anglican priest and writer.
Gulliver's Travels, 'Voyage to Brobdingnag', Ch. 6

35 The national sport of England is obstacle-racing. People fill their rooms with useless and cumbersome furniture, and spend the rest of their lives in trying to dodge it.

Herbert Beerbohm Tree (1853–1917) British actor and theatre manager.
Beerbohm Tree (Hesketh Pearson)

ENTHUSIASM

1 How can I take an interest in my work when I don't like it?

Francis Bacon (1909–) British painter.
Francis Bacon (Sir John Rothenstein)

2 It is unfortunate, considering that enthusiasm moves the world, that so few enthusiasts can be trusted to speak the truth.

Arthur Balfour (1848–1930) British statesman.
Letter to Mrs Drew, 1918

3 Nothing is so contagious as enthusiasm. . . . It is the genius of sincerity and truth accomplishes no victories without it.

Edward Bulwer-Lytton (1803–73) British novelist and politician.
Dale Carnegie's Scrapbook

4 Nothing great was ever achieved without enthusiasm.

Ralph Waldo Emerson (1803–82) US poet and essayist.
Essays, 'Circles'

5 The love of life is necessary to the vigorous prosecution of any undertaking.

Samuel Johnson (1709–84) British lexicographer.
The Rambler

6 Don't clap too hard – it's a very old building.

John Osborne (1929–) British dramatist.
The Entertainer

7 Every man loves what he is good at.

Thomas Shadwell (1642–92) English dramatist.
A True Widow, V:1

8 To business that we love we rise betime,
And go to't with delight.

William Shakespeare (1564–1616) English dramatist.
Antony and Cleopatra, IV:4

ENVIRONMENT

See also conservation, ecology

1 One cannot assess in terms of cash or exports and imports an imponderable thing like the turn of a lane or an inn or a church tower or a familiar skyline.

John Betjeman (1906–84) British poet.
On siting a new London airport at Wing
The Observer, 'Sayings of the Week', 20 July 1969

2 They improvidentially piped growing volumes of sewage into the sea, the healing virtues of which were advertised on every railway station.

Robert Cecil (1913–) British writer.
Referring to seaside resorts
Life in Edwardian England

3 If sunbeams were weapons of war, we would have had solar energy long ago.

George Porter (1920–) British chemist.
The Observer, 'Sayings of the Week', 26 Aug 1973

4 The emergence of intelligence, I am convinced, tends to unbalance the ecology. In other words, intelligence is the great polluter. It is not until a creature begins to manage its environment that nature is thrown into disorder.

Clifford D. Simak (1904–) US journalist.
Shakespeare's Planet

ENVY

See also discontent, jealousy

1 Better be envied than pitied.
Proverb

2 The rich man has his motor car,
His country and his town estate.
He smokes a fifty-cent cigar
And jeers at Fate.
F. P. Adams (1881–1960) US journalist.
The Rich Man

3 Yet though my lamp burns low and dim,
Though I must slave for livelihood –
Think you that I would change with him?
You bet I would!
F. P. Adams
The Rich Man

4 I am sure the grapes are sour.
Aesop (6th century BC) Reputed Greek writer of fables.
Fables, 'The Fox and the Grapes'

5 Nearly every man in the city wants a farm
until he gets it.
Jacob M. Braude

6 Fools may our scorn, not envy raise,
For envy is a kind of praise.
John Gay (1685–1732) English poet and dramatist.
Fables

7 The man with toothache thinks everyone
happy whose teeth are sound.
George Bernard Shaw (1856–1950) Irish dramatist and
critic.
Man and Superman

8 Whenever a friend succeeds, a little
something in me dies.
Gore Vidal (1925–) US novelist.
The Sunday Times Magazine, 16 Sept 1973

9 Never having been able to succeed in the
world, he took his revenge by speaking ill of
it.
Voltaire (François-Marie Arouet; 1694–1778) French
writer.
Zadig, Ch. 4

EPITAPHS

See also memorials, obituaries

1 She sleeps alone at last.
Robert Benchley (1889–1945) US humorist.
Suggested epitaph for an actress
Attrib.

2 Their name, their year, spelt by the
unlettered muse,
The place of fame and elegy supply:
On many a holy text around she strews,
That teach the rustic moralist to die.
Thomas Gray (1716–71) British poet.
Elegy Written in a Country Churchyard

3 In lapidary inscriptions a man is not upon
oath.
Samuel Johnson (1709–84) British lexicographer.
Life of Johnson (J. Boswell), Vol. II

4 Nowhere probably is there more true feeling,
and nowhere worse taste, than in a
churchyard – both as regards the monuments
and the inscriptions. Scarcely a word of true
poetry anywhere.
Benjamin Jowett (1817–93) British theologian.
Letters of B. Jowett (Abbott and Campbell)

Some actual and literary examples

5 Hereabouts died a very gallant gentleman,
Captain L. E. G. Oates of the Inniskilling
Dragoons. In March 1912, returning from the
Pole, he walked willingly to his death in a
blizzard, to try and save his comrades, beset
by hardships.
E. L. Atkinson (1882–1929) British naval officer.
Epitaph on memorial in the Antarctic

6 I've played everything but the harp.
When asked what words he would like engraved on his
tombstone
Lionel Barrymore (1848–1954) US actor.
Attrib.

7 When Sir Joshua Reynolds died
All Nature was degraded;
The King dropped a tear in the Queen's ear,
And all his pictures faded.
William Blake (1757–1827) British poet.
On Art and Artists

8 With death doomed to grapple,
Beneath this cold slab, he
Who lied in the chapel
Now lies in the Abbey.
Lord Byron (1788–1824) British poet.
Epitaph for William Pitt

9 Here Skugg
Lies snug
As a bug
In a rug.
Benjamin Franklin (1706–90) US scientist and statesman.
Letter to Georgiana Shipley, 26 Sept 1772
An epitaph for a squirrel, 'skugg' being a dialect name for the
animal

10 The body of
Benjamin Franklin, printer,
(Like the cover of an old book,
Its contents worn out,
And stript of its lettering and gilding)
Lies here, food for worms!
Yet the work itself shall not be lost,
For it will, as he believed, appear once more
In a new
And more beautiful edition,
Corrected and amended
By its Author!
Benjamin Franklin
Suggestion for his own epitaph

11 Here rests his head upon the lap of Earth
A youth to fortune and to fame unknown.
Fair Science frown'd not on his humble birth,

And Melancholy mark'd him for her own.
Thomas Gray (1716–71) British poet.
Elegy Written in a Country Churchyard

12 He gave to Mis'ry all he had, a tear,
He gain'd from Heav'n ('twas all he wish'd) a
friend.
Thomas Gray
Elegy Written in a Country Churchyard

13 John Brown's body lies a-mouldering in the
grave,
His soul is marching on!
Charles Sprague Hall (19th century) US songwriter.
John Brown's Body
The song commemorates the American hero who died in the
cause of abolishing slavery

14 To Oliver Goldsmith, A Poet, Naturalist, and
Historian, who left scarcely any style of
writing untouched, and touched none that he
did not adorn.
Samuel Johnson (1709–84) British lexicographer.
Life of Johnson (J. Boswell), Vol. III
Epitaph on Goldsmith

15 Over my dead body!
George S. Kaufman (1889–1961) US dramatist.
The Algonquin Wits (R. Drennan)
On being asked to suggest his own epitaph

16 Here lies one whose name was writ in water.
John Keats (1795–1821) British poet.
Life of Keats (Lord Houghton), Ch. 2
Suggesting his own epitaph (recalling a line from *Philaster* by
Beaumont and Fletcher)

17 'There is a report that Piso is dead; it is a
great loss; he was an honest man, who
deserved to live longer; he was intelligent
and agreeable, resolute and courageous, to
be depended upon, generous and faithful.'
Add: 'provided he is really dead'.
Jean de La Bruyère (1645–96) French satirist.
Les Caractères

18 Go, stranger, and tell the Lacedaemonians
that here we lie, obedient to their
commands.
Leonidas (d. 480 BC) King of Sparta.
Epitaph over the tomb in which he and his followers were buried after their defeat at Thermopylae

19 Malcolm Lowry
Late of the Bowery
His prose was flowery
And often glowery
He lived, nightly, and drank, daily,
And died playing the ukulele.
Malcolm Lowry (1909–57) British novelist.
Epitaph

20 Beneath this slab
John Brown is stowed.
He watched the ads
And not the road.
Ogden Nash (1902–71) US poet.
Lather as You Go

21 For all the Brothers were valiant, and all the
Sisters virtuous.
Margaret, Duchess of Newcastle (1624–74) Second
wife of William Cavendish.
Epitaph in Westminster Abbey

22 He lies below, correct in cypress wood,
And entertains the most exclusive worms.
Dorothy Parker (1893–1967) US writer.
Epitaph for a Very Rich Man

23 The poor son-of-a-bitch!
Dorothy Parker
Thalberg: Life and Legend (B. Thomas)
Quoting from *The Great Gatsby* on paying her last respects to
F. Scott Fitzgerald

24 In wit a man; simplicity a child.
Alexander Pope (1688–1744) British poet.
Epitaph on Mr. Gay

25 At last God caught his eye.
Suggested epitaph for a head waiter
Harry Secombe (1921–) Welsh singer, actor, and
comedian.
In *Punch*, May 1962

26 Alas, poor Yorick! I knew him, Horatio: a
fellow of infinite jest, of most excellent fancy.
William Shakespeare (1564–1616) English dramatist.
Hamlet, V:1

27 *Si monumentum requiris, circumspice.*
If you seek my monument, look around you.
Sir Christopher Wren (1632–1723) English architect.
Inscription in St Paul's Cathedral, London

28 Under bare Ben Bulben's head
In Drumcliff churchyard Yeats is laid . . .
On limestone quarried near the spot
By his command these words are cut:
W. B. Yeats (1865–1939) Irish poet.
Under Ben Bulben, VI

Some anonymous examples

29 All who come my grave to see
Avoid damp beds and think of me.
Epitaph of Lydia Eason, St Michael's, Stoke

30 Beneath this stone, in hope of Zion,
Doth lie the landlord of the 'Lion'.
His son keeps on the business still,
Resign'd unto the Heavenly will.
Epitaph, Upton-on-Severn churchyard

31 Here lie I and my four daughters,
Killed by drinking Cheltenham waters.
Had we but stick to Epsom salts,
We wouldn't have been in these here vaults.
Cheltenham Waters

32 Here lie I by the chancel door;
They put me here because I was poor.
The further in, the more you pay,
But here lie I as snug as they.
Epitaph, Devon churchyard

33 Here lies a man who was killed by lightning;

He died when his prospects seemed to be
brightening.
He might have cut a flash in this world of
trouble,
But the flash cut him, and he lies in the
stubble.
Epitaph, Torrington, Devon

34 Here lies a valiant warrior
Who never drew a sword;
Here lies a noble courtier
Who never kept his word;
Here lies the Earl of Leicester
Who governed the estates
Whom the earth could never living love,
And the just heaven now hates.
Attrib. to Ben Jonson in *Collection of Epitaphs* (Tissington),
1857

35 Here lies father and mother and sister and I,
We all died within the space of one short year;
They all be buried at Wimble, except I,
And I be buried here.
Epitaph, Staffordshire churchyard

36 Here lies Fred,
Who was alive and is dead:
Had it been his father,
I had much rather;
Had it been his brother,
Still better than another;
Had it been his sister,
No one would have missed her;
Had it been the whole generation,
Still better for the nation:
But since 'tis only Fred,
Who was alive and is dead, –
There's no more to be said.
Referring to Frederick, Prince of Wales (d. 1751), eldest son
of George II and father of George III
Memoirs of George II (Horace Walpole)

37 Here lies my wife,
Here lies she;
Hallelujah!
Hallelujee!
Epitaph, Leeds churchyard

38 Here lies the body of Mary Ann Lowder,
She burst while drinking a seidlitz powder.
Called from the world to her heavenly rest,
She should have waited till it effervesced.
Epitaph

39 Here lies the body of Richard Hind,
Who was neither ingenious, sober, nor kind.
Epitaph

40 Here lies Will Smith – and, what's something
rarish,
He was born, bred, and hanged, all in the same
parish.
Epitaph

41 Mary Ann has gone to rest,
Safe at last on Abraham's breast,
Which may be nuts for Mary Ann,
But is certainly rough on Abraham.
Epitaph

42 My sledge and anvil lie declined
My bellows too have lost their wind
My fire's extinct, my forge decayed,
And in the Dust my Vice is laid
My coals are spent, my iron's gone
My Nails are Drove, My Work is done.
An epitaph to William Strange, blacksmith, died 6 June 1746
and buried in Nettlebed churchyard

43 Sacred to the memory of
Captain Anthony Wedgwood
Accidentally shot by his gamekeeper
Whilst out shooting
"Well done thou good and faithful servant"
Epitaph

44 Stranger! Approach this spot with gravity!
John Brown is filling his last cavity.
Epitaph of a dentist

45 This the grave of Mike O'Day
Who died maintaining his right of way.
His right was clear, his will was strong.
But he's just as dead as if he'd been wrong.
Epitaph

46 Warm summer sun shine kindly here:
Warm summer wind blow softly here:
Green sod above lie light, lie light:
Good-night, Dear Heart: good-night, good-
night.
Memorial to Clorinda Haywood, St Bartholomew's, Edgbaston

EQUALITY

See also class, feminism, human rights

1 A cat may look at a king.
Proverb

2 All cats are grey in the dark.
Proverb

3 Equality may perhaps be a right, but no
power on earth can ever turn it into a fact.
Honoré de Balzac (1799–1850) French novelist.
La Duchesse de Langeais

4 From the point of view of sexual morality the
aeroplane is valuable in war in that it
destroys men and women in equal numbers.
Ernest William Barnes (1874–1953) British clergyman
and mathematician.
Rise of Christianity

5 What makes equality such a difficult business
is that we only want it with our superiors.
Henry Becque (1837–99) French dramatist.
Querelles littéraires

6 All service ranks the same with God –
With God, whose puppets, best and worst,
Are we: there is no last or first.
Robert Browning (1812–89) British poet.
Pippa Passes, Pt. I

7 The terrorist and the policeman both come from the same basket.

Joseph Conrad (Teodor Josef Konrad Korzeniowski; 1857–1924) Polish-born British novelist.
The Secret Agent, Ch. 4

8 The majestic egalitarianism of the law, which forbids rich and poor alike to sleep under bridges, to beg in the streets, and to steal bread.

Anatole France (Jacques Anatole François Thibault; 1844–1924) French writer.
The Red Lily, Ch. 7

9 Men are made by nature unequal. It is vain, therefore, to treat them as if they were equal.

J. A. Froude (1818–94) British historian.
Short Studies on Great Subjects, 'Party Politics'

10 That all men are equal is a proposition to which, at ordinary times, no sane individual has ever given his assent.

Aldous Huxley (1894–1964) British novelist.
Proper Studies

11 A just society would be one in which liberty for one person is constrained only by the demands created by equal liberty for another.

Ivan Illich (1926–) Austrian sociologist.
Tools for Conviviality

12 His foreparents came to America in immigrant ships. My foreparents came to America in slave ships. But whatever the original ships, we are both in the same boat tonight.

Jesse Jackson (1941–) US Black statesman.
Speech, July 1988

13 Your levellers wish to level *down* as far as themselves; but they cannot bear levelling *up* to themselves.

Samuel Johnson (1709–84) British lexicographer.
Life of Johnson (J. Boswell), Vol. I

14 It is better that some should be unhappy than that none should be happy, which would be the case in a general state of equality.

Samuel Johnson
Life of Johnson (J. Boswell), Vol. III

15 I have a dream that one day this nation will rise up, live out the true meaning of its creed: we hold these truths to be self-evident, that all men are created equal.

Martin Luther King (1929–68) US Black civil-rights leader.
He used the words 'I have a dream' in a number of speeches
Speech, Washington, 27 Aug 1963

16 Never descend to the ways of those above you.

George Mallaby (1902–78) British diplomat and writer.
From My Level

17 The cry of equality pulls everyone down.

Iris Murdoch (1919–) Irish-born British novelist.
Remark, Sept 1987

18 All animals are equal but some animals are more equal than others.

George Orwell (Eric Blair; 1903–50) British novelist.
Animal Farm, Ch. 10

19 EQUALITY . . . is the thing. It is the only true and central premise from which constructive ideas can radiate freely and be operated without prejudice.

Mervyn Peake (1911–68) British novelist.
Titus Groan, 'The Sun goes down'

20 In America everybody is of the opinion that he has no social superiors, since all men are equal, but he does not admit that he has no social inferiors.

Bertrand Russell (1872–1970) British philosopher.
Unpopular Essays

21 I think the King is but a man as I am: the violet smells to him as it doth to me.

William Shakespeare (1564–1616) English dramatist.
Henry V, IV:1

22 Hath not a Jew eyes? Hath not a Jew hands, organs, dimensions, senses, affections, passions, fed with the same food, hurt with the same weapons, subject to the same diseases, healed by the same means, warmed and cooled by the same winter and summer, as a Christian is? If you prick us, do we not bleed? If you tickle us, do we not laugh? If you poison us, do we not die? And if you wrong us, shall we not revenge?

William Shakespeare
The Merchant of Venice, III:1

23 This is a movie, not a lifeboat.

Spencer Tracy (1900–67) US film star.
Defending his demand for equal billing with Katherine Hepburn
Attrib.

24 Everybody should have an equal chance – but they shouldn't have a flying start.

Harold Wilson (1916–) British politician and prime minister.
The Observer, 'Sayings of the Year', 1963

25 Whatever women do, they must do it twice as well as men to be thought half as good. Luckily, this is not difficult.

Charlotte Witton
Attrib.

Equality in death

See also death

26 It comes equally to us all, and makes us all equal when it comes. The ashes of an Oak in the Chimney, are no epitaph of that Oak, to tell me how high or how large that was; It tells me not what flocks it sheltered while it stood, nor what men it hurt when it fell. The dust of great persons' graves is speechless too, it says nothing, it distinguishes nothing.

John Donne (1573–1631) English poet.
Sermons, XV

27 Now at last our child is just like all children.

Charles De Gaulle (1890–1970) French general and statesman.
On the death of his retarded daughter Anne
Ten First Ladies of the World (Pauline Frederick)

28 Pale Death kicks his way equally into the cottages of the poor and the castles of kings.

Horace (Quintus Horatius Flaccus; 65–8 BC) Roman poet.
Odes, I

29 A heap of dust alone remains of thee;
'Tis all thou art, and all the proud shall be!

Alexander Pope (1688–1744) British poet.
Elegy to the Memory of an Unfortunate Lady

ESCAPE

1 I bet you a hundred bucks he ain't in here.

Charles Bancroft Dillingham (1868–1934) US theatrical manager.
Referring to the escapologist Harry Houdini; said at his funeral, while carrying his coffin
Attrib.

2 He can run, but he can't hide.

Joe Louis (Joseph Louis Barrow; 1914–81) US boxer.
Referring to the speed for which his coming opponent, Billy Conn, was renowned
Attrib.

ETERNITY

See also immortality, time

1 Kiss till the cow comes home.

Francis Beaumont (1584–1616) English dramatist.
Scornful Lady, II:2

2 As it was in the beginning, is now, and ever shall be: world without end.

The Book of Common Prayer
Morning Prayer, Gloria

3 Thou, silent form, dost tease us out of thought
As doth eternity: Cold Pastoral!

John Keats (1795–1821) British poet.
Ode on a Grecian Urn

4 Eternity's a terrible thought. I mean, where's it going to end?

Tom Stoppard (1937–) Czech-born British dramatist.
Rosencrantz and Guildenstern Are Dead, II

ETIQUETTE

See also manners

1 Phone for the fish knives Norman,
As Cook is a little unnerved;
You kiddies have crumpled the serviettes
And I must have things daintily served.

John Betjeman (1906–84) British poet.
How to get on in Society

2 It is necessary to clean the teeth frequently, more especially after meals, but not on any account with a pin, or the point of a penknife, and it must never be done at table.

St Jean Baptiste de la Salle (1651–1719)
The Rules of Christian Manners and Civility, I

3 'It is very pleasant dining with a bachelor,' said Miss Matty, softly, as we settled ourselves in the counting-house. 'I only hope it is not improper; so many pleasant things are!'

Elizabeth Gaskell (1810–65) British novelist.
Cranford, Ch. 4

4 It's all right, Arthur, the white wine came up with the fish.

Herman J. Mankiewicz (1897–1953) US journalist and screenwriter.
After vomiting at the table of a fastidious host
Attrib.

5 We could not lead a pleasant life,
And 'twould be finished soon,
If peas were eaten with the knife,
And gravy with the spoon.
Eat slowly: only men in rags
And gluttons old in sin
Mistake themselves for carpet bags
And tumble victuals in.

Walter Raleigh (1861–1922) British scholar.
Laughter from a Cloud, 'Stans puer ad mensam'

6 'How did you think I managed at dinner, Clarence?' 'Capitally!' 'I had a knife and two forks left at the end,' she said regretfully.

William Pett Ridge (1860–1930) British novelist.
Love at Paddington Green, Ch. 6

7 I think she must have been very strictly brought up, she's so desperately anxious to do the wrong thing correctly.

Saki (Hector Hugh Munro; 1870–1916) British writer.
Reginald on Worries

EUROPE

See also Britain, England, France, Germany, Ireland, Russia, Scotland, Switzerland, Venice, Wales

1 Rome's just a city like anywhere else. A vastly overrated city, I'd say. It trades on belief just as Stratford trades on Shakespeare.

Anthony Burgess (John Burgess Wilson; 1917–) British novelist.
Mr Enderby, Pt. II, Ch. 2

2 But the age of chivalry is gone. That of sophisters, economists, and calculators, has succeeded; and the glory of Europe is extinguished for ever.

Edmund Burke (1729–97) British politician.
Reflections on the Revolution in France

3 The isles of Greece, the isles of Greece!
Where burning Sappho loved and sung,
Where grew the arts of war and peace,
Where Delos rose, and Phoebus sprung!
Eternal summer gilds them yet,

But all, except their sun, is set.
Lord Byron (1788–1824) British poet.
Don Juan, III

4 The mountains look on Marathon –
And Marathon looks on the sea:
And musing there an hour alone,
I dream'd that Greece might still be free.
Lord Byron
Don Juan, III

5 While stands the Coliseum, Rome shall stand;
When falls the Coliseum, Rome shall fall;
And when Rome falls – the World.
Lord Byron
Childe Harold's Pilgrimage, IV

6 We must build a kind of United States of
Europe.
Winston Churchill (1874–1965) British statesman.
Speech, Zurich, 19 Sept 1946

7 Apart from cheese and tulips, the main
product of the country is advocaat, a drink
made from lawyers.
Alan Coren (1938–) British humorist and writer.
Referring to Holland
The Sanity Inspector, 'All You Need to Know about Europe'

8 Holland . . . lies so low they're only saved by
being dammed.
Thomas Hood (1799–1845) British poet.
Up the Rhine

9 It's not enough to be Hungarian, you must
have talent too.
Alexander Korda (Sandor Kellner; 1893–1956)
Hungarian-born British film director.
Alexander Korda (K. Kulik)

10 In Western Europe there are now only small
countries – those that know it and those that
don't know it yet.
Théo Lefèvre (1914–73) Belgian prime minister.
The Observer, 'Sayings of the Year', 1963

11 I am inclined to notice the ruin in things,
perhaps because I was born in Italy.
Arthur Miller (1915–) US dramatist.
A View from the Bridge, I

12 Austria is Switzerland speaking pure German
and with history added.
J. E. Morpurgo (1918–) British writer and academic.
The Road to Athens

13 Providence has given to the French the
empire of the land, to the English that of the
sea, and to the Germans that of the air.
Jean Paul Richter (Johann Paul Friedrich Richter; 1763–
1825) German novelist.
Quoted by Thomas Carlyle

14 The people of Crete unfortunately make
more history than they can consume locally.
Saki (Hector Hugh Munro; 1870–1916) British writer.
The Jesting of Arlington Stringham

15 We are part of the community of Europe and
we must do our duty as such.
Marquess of Salisbury (1830–1903) British statesman.
Speech, Caernarvon, 11 Apr 1888

16 We're from Madeira, but perfectly
respectable, so far.
George Bernard Shaw (1856–1950) Irish dramatist and
critic.
You Never Can Tell, I

17 Let there be light! said Liberty,
And like sunrise from the sea,
Athens arose!
Percy Bysshe Shelley (1792–1822) British poet.
Hellas, I

18 This going into Europe will not turn out to
be the thrilling mutual exchange supposed. It
is more like nine middle-aged couples with
failing marriages meeting in a darkened
bedroom in a Brussels hotel for a Group
Grope.
E. P. Thompson (1924–) British historian.
On the Europe debate, *Sunday Times*, 27 Apr 1975

19 Every place I look at I work out the cubic
feet, and I say it will make a good warehouse
or it won't. Can't help myself. One of the
best warehouses I ever see was the Vatican
in Rome.
Arnold Wesker (1932–) British dramatist.
Chips with Everything, I:6

20 That Europe's nothin' on earth but a great
big auction, that's all it is.
Tennessee Williams (1911–83) US dramatist.
Cat on a Hot Tin Roof, I

EVIL

See also good and evil, sin, vice

1 *Honi soit qui mal y pense.*
Evil be to him who evil thinks.
Anonymous
Motto for the Order of the Garter

2 It takes a certain courage and a certain
greatness even to be truly base.
Jean Anouilh (1910–87) French dramatist.
Ardele

3 Wherefore I praised the dead which are
already dead more than the living which are
yet alive.
Yea, better is he than both they, which hath
not yet been, who hath not seen the evil work
that is done under the sun.
Bible: Ecclesiastes
4:2–3 sun

4 But evil men and seducers shall wax worse
and worse, deceiving, and being deceived.
Bible: II Timothy
3:13

5 And this is the condemnation, that light is
come into the world, and men loved darkness

rather than light, because their deeds were evil.
Bible: John
3:19

6 I never saw a brute I hated so;
He must be wicked to deserve such pain.
Robert Browning (1812–89) British poet.
Childe Roland to the Dark Tower Came, XIV

7 The belief in a supernatural source of evil is not necessary; men alone are quite capable of every wickedness.
Joseph Conrad (Teodor Josef Konrad Korzeniowski; 1857–1924) Polish-born British novelist.
Under Western Eyes, Part 2

8 There's a young man hid with me, in comparison with which young man I am a Angel. That young man hears the words I speak. That young man has a secret way pecooliar to himself, of getting at a boy, and at his heart, and at his liver.
Charles Dickens (1812–70) British novelist.
Said by Magwitch
Great Expectations, Ch. 1

9 Something nasty in the woodshed.
Stella Gibbons (1902–89) British poet and novelist.
Cold Comfort Farm

10 But evil is wrought by want of thought,
As well as want of heart!
Thomas Hood (1799–1845) British poet.
The Lady's Dream

11 He who passively accepts evil is as much involved in it as he who helps to perpetrate it.
Martin Luther King (1929–68) US Black civil-rights leader.
Stride Towards Freedom

12 Farewell remorse! All good to me is lost;
Evil, be thou my Good.
John Milton (1608–74) English poet.
Paradise Lost, Bk. IV

13 Take thy beak from out my heart, and take thy form from off my door!
Quoth the Raven, 'Nevermore.'
Edgar Allan Poe (1809–49) US poet and writer.
The Raven

14 There is scarcely a single man sufficiently aware to know all the evil he does.
Duc de la Rochefoucauld (1613–80) French writer.
Maximes, 269

15 She is a smart old broad. It is a pity she is so nefarious.
Damon Runyon (1884–1946) US writer.
Runyon à la carte, 'Broadway Incident'

16 Friends, Romans, countrymen, lend me your ears
I come to bury Caesar, not to praise him.
The evil that men do lives after them;

The good is oft interred with their bones.
William Shakespeare (1564–1616) English dramatist.
Julius Caesar, III:2

EVOLUTION

See also survival

1 Descended from the apes? My dear, we will hope it is not true. But if it is, let us pray that it may not become generally known.
Anonymous
Remark by the wife of a canon of Worcester Cathedral
Man's Most Dangerous Myth, The Fallacy of Race (F. Ashley Montagu)

2 From an evolutionary point of view, man has stopped moving, if he ever did move.
Pierre Teilhard de Chardin (1881–1955) French Jesuit and palaeontologist.
The Phenomenon of Man, Postscript

3 Man is developed from an ovule, about the 125th of an inch in diameter, which differs in no respect from the ovules of other animals.
Charles Darwin (1809–82) British life scientist.
The Descent of Man, Ch. 1

4 We must, however, acknowledge, as it seems to me, that man with all his noble qualities, still bears in his bodily frame the indelible stamp of his lowly origin.
Charles Darwin
Closing words
Descent of Man, Ch. 21

5 We will now discuss in a little more detail the struggle for existence.
Charles Darwin
Origin of Species, Ch. 3

6 I have called this principle, by which each slight variation, if useful, is preserved, by the term of Natural Selection.
Charles Darwin
Origin of Species, Ch. 3

7 The expression often used by Mr Herbert Spencer of the Survival of the Fittest is more accurate, and is sometimes equally convenient.
Charles Darwin
Origin of Species, Ch. 3

8 The question is this: Is man an ape or an angel? I, my lord, am on the side of the angels.
Benjamin Disraeli (1804–81) British statesman.
Speech, 25 Nov 1864

9 Philip is a living example of natural selection. He was as fitted to survive in this modern world as a tapeworm in an intestine.
William Golding (1911–) British novelist.
Free Fall, Ch. 2

10 I asserted – and I repeat – that a man has no reason to be ashamed of having an ape for his grandfather. If there were an ancestor whom I should feel shame in recalling it would rather be a *man* – a man of restless and versatile intellect – who, not content with an equivocal success in his own sphere of activity, plunges into scientific questions with which he has no real acquaintance, only to obscure them by an aimless rhetoric, and distract the attention of his hearers from the real point at issue by eloquent digressions and skilled appeals to religious prejudice.

T. H. Huxley (1825–95) British biologist.
Replying to Bishop WILBERFORCE in the debate on Darwin's theory of evolution at the meeting of the British Association at Oxford. No transcript was taken at the time; the version above is commonly quoted. After hearing Wilberforce's speech, and before rising himself, Huxley is said to have remarked, 'The Lord has delivered him into my hands!'
Speech, 30 June 1860

11 And, in conclusion, I would like to ask the gentleman . . . whether the ape from which he is descended was on his grandmother's or his grandfather's side of the family.

Samuel Wilberforce (1805–73) British churchman.
See T. H. HUXLEY
Speech, 30 June 1860

EXAMINATIONS

See also education

1 Examinations are formidable even to the best prepared, for the greatest fool may ask more than the wisest man can answer.

Charles Caleb Colton (?1780–1832) British clergyman and writer.
Lacon, Vol. II

2 Do not on any account attempt to write on both sides of the paper at once.

W. C. Sellar (1898–1951) British humorous writer.
1066 And All That, Test Paper 5

3 If silicon had been a gas I should have been a major-general.

James Whistler (1834–1903) US painter.
Referring to his failure in a West Point chemistry examination
English Wits (L. Russell)

EXAMPLE

1 Practise what you preach.
Proverb

2 Example is the school of mankind, and they will learn at no other.

Edmund Burke (1729–97) British politician.
Letters on a Regicide Peace, letter 1

3 Do as you would be done by is the surest method that I know of pleasing.

Earl of Chesterfield (1694–1773) English statesman.
Letter to his son, 16 Oct 1747

4 What you do not want done to yourself, do not do to others.

Confucius (K'ung Fu-tzu; 551–479 BC) Chinese philosopher.
Analects

5 Men are not hanged for stealing horses, but that horses may not be stolen.

George Saville (1633–95) English statesman.
Political, Moral and Miscellaneous Thoughts and Reflections

6 A precedent embalms a principle.

William Scott (1745–1836) British jurist.
An opinion given while Advocate-General
Attrib.; also quoted by Benjamin Disraeli (1848)

7 Preachers say, Do as I say, not as I do. But if the physician had the same disease upon him that I have, and he should bid me do one thing, and himself do quite another, could I believe him?

John Selden (1584–1654) English historian.
Table Talk

8 Do not, as some ungracious pastors do,
Show me the steep and thorny way to heaven,
Whiles, like a puff'd and reckless libertine,
Himself the primrose path of dalliance treads
And recks not his own rede.

William Shakespeare (1564–1616) English dramatist.
Hamlet, I:3

9 *Dans ce pays-ci, il est bon de tuer de temps en temps un amiral pour encourager les autres.*
In this country it is good to kill an admiral from time to time, to encourage the others.

Voltaire (François-Marie Arouet; 1694–1778) French writer.
Referring to England: Admiral Byng was executed for failing to defeat the French at Minorca (1757)
Candide, Ch. 23

EXCELLENCE

See also superiority

1 Whatever is worth doing at all is worth doing well.

Earl of Chesterfield (1694–1773) English statesman.
Letter to his son, 10 Mar 1746

2 The danger chiefly lies in acting well,
No crime's so great as daring to excel.

Charles Churchill (1731–64) British poet.
Epistle to William Hogarth

3 If you had been mine when you were seven you would have been the crème de la crème.

Muriel Spark (1918–) British novelist.
The Prime of Miss Jean Brodie, Ch. 2

4 The best is the enemy of the good.

Voltaire (François-Marie Arouet; 1694–1778) French writer.
Dictionnaire philosophique, 'Art dramatique'

EXCESS

See also extravagance, moderation

1 *L'embarras des richesses.*
A superfluity of good things.

Abbé Lénor Jean d'Allainval (1700–53) French dramatist.
Play title

2 What fun it would be to be poor, as long as one was *excessively* poor! Anything in excess is most exhilarating.
Jean Anouilh (1910–87) French dramatist.
Ring Round the Moon

3 The road of excess leads to the palace of Wisdom.
William Blake (1757–1827) British poet.
The Marriage of Heaven and Hell, 'Proverbs of Hell'

4 I would remind you that extremism in the defence of liberty is no vice. And let me remind you also that moderation in the pursuit of justice is no virtue!
Barry Goldwater (1909–) US politician.
Speech, San Francisco, 17 July 1964

5 No part of the walls is left undecorated. From everywhere the praise of the Lord is drummed into you.
Nikolaus Pevsner (Bernhard Leon; 1902–83) German-born British art historian.
London, except the Cities of London and Westminster

6 In baiting a mouse-trap with cheese, always leave room for the mouse.
Saki (Hector Hugh Munro; 1870–1916) British writer.
The Square Egg

7 'Tis not the drinking that is to be blamed, but the excess.
John Selden (1584–1654) English historian.
Table Talk

8 The lady doth protest too much, methinks.
William Shakespeare (1564–1616) English dramatist.
Hamlet, III:2

9 Well said; that was laid on with a trowel.
William Shakespeare
As You Like It, I:2

10 To gild refined gold, to paint the lily,
To throw a perfume on the violet,
To smooth the ice, or add another hue
Unto the rainbow, or with taper-light
To seek the beauteous eye of heaven to garnish,
Is wasteful and ridiculous excess.
William Shakespeare
King John, IV:2

11 Heat not a furnace for your foe so hot
That it do singe yourself. We may outrun
By violent swiftness that which we run at,
And lose by over-running.
William Shakespeare
Henry VIII, I:1

12 It out-herods Herod.
William Shakespeare
Hamlet, III:2

13 Extreme *busyness*, whether at school or college, kirk or market, is a symptom of deficient vitality.
Robert Louis Stevenson (1850–94) Scottish writer.
Virginibus Puerisque

14 Battering the gates of heaven with storms of prayer.
Alfred, Lord Tennyson (1809–92) British poet.
St Simeon Stylites

15 Moderation is a fatal thing, Lady Hunstanton. Nothing succeeds like excess.
Oscar Wilde (1854–1900) Irish-born British dramatist.
A Woman of No Importance, III

EXECUTION

See also last words, martyrdom, punishment

1 It's time for me to enjoy another pinch of snuff. Tomorrow my hands will be bound, so as to make it impossible.
Jean Sylvain Bailly (1736–93) French astronomer.
Said on the evening before his execution
Anekdotenschatz (H. Hoffmeister)

2 And almost all things are by the law purged with blood; and without shedding of blood is no remission.
Bible: Hebrews
9:22

3 And when they were come to the place, which is called Calvary, there they crucified him, and the malefactors, one on the right hand, and the other on the left.
Bible: Luke
23:33

4 I die a Christian, according to the Profession of the Church of England, as I found it left me by my Father.
Charles I (1600–49) King of England.
Speech on the scaffold, 30 Jan 1649

5 Thou wilt show my head to the people: it is worth showing.
Georges Jacques Danton (1759–94) French political activist.
Said as he mounted the scaffold, 5 Apr 1794
French Revolution (Carlyle), Bk. VI, Ch. 2

6 It is a far, far, better thing that I do, than I have ever done; it is a far, far, better rest that I go to, than I have ever known.
Charles Dickens (1812–70) British novelist.
Said by Sydney Carton
A Tale of Two Cities, Bk. II, Ch. 15

7 To die for faction is a common evil,
But to be hanged for nonsense is the Devil.
John Dryden (1631–1700) British poet and dramatist.
Absalom and Achitophel, II

8 Son of Saint Louis, ascend to heaven.
Abbé Edgeworth de Firmont (1745–1807) Irish-born confessor to Louis XVI.
Said to Louis XVI as he climbed up to the guillotine
Attrib.

9 Let them bestow on every airth a limb;
Then open all my veins, that I may swim
To thee, my Maker! in that crimson lake;
Then place my parboiled head upon a stake –
Scatter my ashes – strew them in the air; –

Lord! since thou know'st where all these at-
oms are,
I'm hopeful thou'lt recover once my dust,
And confident thou'lt raise me with the just.
James Graham (1612–50) Scottish general.
Lines written on the window of his jail the night before his
execution

10 And have they fixed the where and when?
And shall Trelawny die?
Here's twenty thousand Cornish men
Will know the reason why!
R. S. Hawker (1803–75) British poet.
Referring to the imprisonment (1688) of Trelawny, Bishop of
Bristol, by James II
Song of the Western Men

11 They hang us now in Shrewsbury jail:
The whistles blow forlorn,
And trains all night groan on the rail
To men that die at morn.
A. E. Housman (1859–1936) British scholar and poet.
A Shropshire Lad, 'Reveillé'

12 Depend upon it, Sir, when a man knows he
is to be hanged in a fortnight, it concentrates
his mind wonderfully.
Samuel Johnson (1709–84) British lexicographer.
Life of Johnson (J. Boswell), Vol. III

13 If we are to abolish the death penalty, I
should like to see the first step taken by our
friends the murderers.
Alphonse Karr (1808–90) French writer.
Les Guêpes, Jan 1849

14 'For they're hangin' Danny Deever, you can
hear the Dead March play,
The Regiment's in 'ollow square – they're
hangin' 'im to-day;
They've taken of 'is buttons off an' cut 'is
stripes away,
An' they're hangin' Danny Deever in the
mornin'.'
Rudyard Kipling (1865–1936) Indian-born British writer.
Danny Deever

15 Be of good comfort, Master Ridley, and play
the man; we shall this day light such a
candle, by God's grace, in England as I trust
shall never be put out.
Hugh Latimer (1485–1555) English churchman.
Said to Nicholas Ridley as they were about to be burnt at the
stake for heresy
Famous Last Words (B. Conrad)

16 He nothing common did or mean
Upon that memorable scene,
But with his keener eye
The axe's edge did try.
Andrew Marvell (1621–78) English poet.
Referring to the execution of Charles I
An Horatian Ode upon Cromwell's Return from Ireland

17 Do not hack me as you did my Lord Russell.
Duke of Monmouth (1649–85) An illegitimate son of
Charles II.
Said to the headsman before his execution
History of England (Macaulay), Vol. I, Ch. 5

18 I pray you, Master Lieutenant, see me safe
up, and for coming down let me shift for
myself.
Thomas More (1478–1535) English lawyer and scholar.
On climbing onto the scaffold prior to his execution
Life of Sir Thomas More (William Roper)

19 Pluck up thy spirits, man, and be not afraid
to do thine office; my neck is very short;
take heed therefore thou strike not awry, for
saving of thine honesty.
Thomas More
Said to the headsman
Life of Sir Thomas More (Roper)

20 This hath not offended the king.
Thomas More
Said as he drew his beard aside before putting his head on the
block

21 The sight of it gave me infinite pleasure, as
it proved that I was in a civilized society.
Mungo Park (1771–1806) Scottish explorer.
Remark on finding a gibbet in an unexplored part of Africa
Attrib.

22 I went out to Charing Cross, to see Major-
general Harrison hanged, drawn, and
quartered; which was done there, he looking
as cheerful as any man could do in that
condition.
Samuel Pepys (1633–1703) English diarist.
Diary, 13 Oct 1660

23 The world itself is but a large prison, out of
which some are daily led to execution.
Walter Raleigh (1554–1618) English explorer.
Said after his trial for treason, 1603
Attrib.

24 So the heart be right, it is no matter which
way the head lies.
Walter Raleigh
On laying his head on the executioner's block
Attrib.

25 Tis a sharp remedy, but a sure one for all
ills.
Walter Raleigh
Referring to the executioner's axe just before he was
beheaded
Attrib.

26 If you give me six lines written by the most
honest man, I will find something in them to
hang him.
Cardinal Richelieu (1585–1642) French statesman.
Exact wording uncertain
Attrib.

27 'O liberté! O liberté! Que de crimes on commet
en ton nom!'
Oh liberty! Oh liberty! What crimes are com-
mitted in thy name!
Madame Roland (1754–93) French revolutionary.
Said as she mounted the steps of the guillotine
Attrib.

28 Then, with that faint fleeting smile playing
about his lips, he faced the firing squad;

erect and motionless, proud and disdainful, Walter Mitty, the undefeated, inscrutable to the last.

James Thurber (1894–1961) US humorist.
My World and Welcome to It, 'The Secret Life of Walter Mitty'

EXISTENCE

1 Dear Sir, Your astonishment's odd:
I am always about in the Quad.
And that's why the tree
Will continue to be,
Since observed by Yours faithfully, God.

Anonymous
The response to KNOX's limerick

2 Let us be moral. Let us contemplate existence.

Charles Dickens (1812–70) British novelist.
Martin Chuzzlewit, Ch. 10

3 As far as we can discern, the sole purpose of human existence is to kindle a light in the darkness of mere being.

Carl Gustav Jung (1875–1961) Swiss psychoanalyst.
Memories, Dreams, Reflections, Ch. 11

4 There once was a man who said 'God
Must think it exceedingly odd
If he find that this tree
Continues to be
When there's no one about in the Quad.'

Ronald Knox (1888–1957) British Roman Catholic priest.
For a reply, *see* ANONYMOUS
Attrib.

5 I know perfectly well that I don't want to do anything; to do something is to create existence – and there's quite enough existence as it is.

Jean-Paul Sartre (1905–80) French writer.
Nausea

EXPECTATION

See also anticipation, disappointment, hope

1 As I know more of mankind I expect less of them, and am ready now to call a man *a good man*, upon easier terms than I was formerly.

Samuel Johnson (1709–84) British lexicographer.
Life of Johnson (J. Boswell), Vol. IV

2 Dear Mary, We all knew you had it in you.

Dorothy Parker (1893–1967) US writer.
Telegram sent to a friend on the successful outcome of her much-publicized pregnancy

3 'Blessed is the man who expects nothing, for he shall never be disappointed' was the ninth beatitude.

Alexander Pope (1688–1744) British poet.
Letter to Fortescue, 23 Sept 1725

4 See yon pale stripling! when a boy,
A mother's pride, a father's joy!

Walter Scott (1771–1832) Scottish novelist.
Rokeby, III

5 Gomer Owen who kissed her once by the pig-sty when she wasn't looking and never kissed her again although she was looking all the time.

Dylan Thomas (1914–53) Welsh poet.
Under Milk Wood

6 This suspense is terrible. I hope it will last.

Oscar Wilde (1854–1900) Irish-born British dramatist.
The Importance of Being Earnest, III

EXPEDIENCY

1 And my parents finally realize that I'm kidnapped and they snap into action immediately: they rent out my room.

Woody Allen (Allen Stewart Konigsberg; 1935–) US film actor.
Woody Allen and His Comedy (E. Lax)

2 I would rather be an opportunist and float than go to the bottom with my principles round my neck.

Stanley Baldwin (1867–1947) British statesman.
Attrib.

3 Nobody is forgotten when it is convenient to remember him.

Benjamin Disraeli (1804–81) British statesman.
Attrib.

4 You can't learn too soon that the most useful thing about a principle is that it can always be sacrificed to expediency.

W. Somerset Maugham (1874–1965) British novelist.
The Circle, III

5 Death and taxes and childbirth! There's never any convenient time for any of them!

Margaret Mitchell (1909–49) US novelist.
Gone with the Wind

6 No man is justified in doing evil on the ground of expediency.

Theodore Roosevelt (1858–1919) US Republican president.
The Strenuous Life

7 Well, a widow, I see, is a kind of sinecure.

William Wycherley (1640–1716) English dramatist.
The Plain Dealer, V:3

EXPERIENCE

See also history, past

1 A young physician fattens the churchyard.
Proverb

2 Experience is the best teacher.
Proverb

3 Experience is the mother of wisdom.
Proverb

4 Live and learn.
Proverb

5 Practice makes perfect.
Proverb

6 Experience is a good teacher, but she sends in terrific bills.

Minna Antrim (1861–?) US writer.
Naked Truth and Veiled Allusions

7 One should try everything once, except incest and folk-dancing.

Arnold Bax (1883–1953) British composer.
Farewell to My Youth

8 You will think me lamentably crude: my experience of life has been drawn from life itself.

Max Beerbohm (1872–1956) British writer.
Zuleika Dobson, Ch. 7

9 Experience isn't interesting till it begins to repeat itself – in fact, till it does that, it hardly *is* experience.

Elizabeth Bowen (1899–1973) Irish novelist.
The Death of the Heart, Pt. I, Ch. 1

10 When all is said and done, no literature can outdo the cynicism of real life; you won't intoxicate with one glass someone who has already drunk up a whole barrel.

Anton Chekhov (1860–1904) Russian dramatist.
Letter, 1887

11 If men could learn from history, what lessons it might teach us! But passion and party blind our eyes and the light which experience gives is a lantern on the stern, which shines only on the waves behind us!

Samuel Taylor Coleridge (1772–1834) British poet.
Recollections (Allsop)

12 An experience of women which extends over many nations and three continents.

Arthur Conan Doyle (1856–1930) British writer.
The Sign of Four

13 How many roads must a man walk down Before you call him a man?

Bob Dylan (Robert Allen Zimmerman; 1941–) US popular singer.
Blowin' in the Wind

14 What experience and history teach is this – that people and governments never have learned anything from history, or acted on principles deduced from it.

Hegel (1770–1831) German philosopher.
Philosophy of History, Introduction

15 A moment's insight is sometimes worth a life's experience.

Oliver Wendell Holmes (1809–94) US writer.
The Professor at the Breakfast Table, Ch. 10

16 Experience is never limited, and it is never complete; it is an immense sensibility, a kind of huge spider-web of the finest silken threads suspended in the chamber of consciousness, and catching every air-borne particle in its tissue.

Henry James (1843–1916) US novelist.
Partial Portraits, 'The Art of Fiction'

17 Nothing ever becomes real till it is experienced – even a proverb is no proverb to you till your life has illustrated it.

John Keats (1795–1821) British poet.
Letter to George and Georgiana Keats, 19 Mar 1819

18 He was what I often think is a dangerous thing for a statesman to be – a student of history; and like most of those who study history, he learned from the mistakes of the past how to make new ones.

A. J. P. Taylor (1906–) British historian.
Referring to Napoleon III
The Listener, 6 June 1963

19 Nourishing a youth sublime
With the fairy tales of science, and the long result of Time.

Alfred, Lord Tennyson (1809–92) British poet.
Locksley Hall

20 All experience is an arch wherethro'
Gleams that untravelled world, whose margin fades
For ever and for ever when I move.

Alfred, Lord Tennyson
Ulysses

21 You don't set a fox to watching the chickens just because he has a lot of experience in the hen house.

Harry S. Truman (1884–1972) US statesman.
Referring to Vice-President Nixon's nomination for President
Speech, 30 Oct 1960

22 I have learned
To look on nature, not as in the hour
Of thoughtless youth; but hearing often-times
The still, sad music of humanity.

William Wordsworth (1770–1850) British poet.
Lines composed a few miles above Tintern Abbey

EXPERTS

1 By studying the masters – not their pupils.

Niels Henrik Abel (1809–29) Norwegian mathematician.
When asked how he had become a great mathematician so quickly
Men of Mathematics (E. T. Bell)

2 An expert is a man who has made all the mistakes, which can be made, in a very narrow field.

Niels Bohr (1885–1962) Danish physicist.
Attrib.

3 An expert is someone who knows some of the worst mistakes that can be made in his subject, and how to avoid them.

Werner Heisenberg (1901–76) German physicist.
Physics and Beyond

4 An accomplished man to his finger-tips.

Horace (Quintus Horatius Flaccus; 65–8 BC) Roman poet.
Satires, I

5 Specialist – A man who knows more and more about less and less.

William James Mayo (1861–1934) US surgeon.
Also attributed to Nicholas Butler

6 The trouble with specialists is that they tend to think in grooves.

Elaine Morgan (1920–) British writer.
The Descent of Woman, Ch. 1

EXPLANATIONS

1 I am one of those unfortunates to whom death is less hideous than explanations.

Wyndham Lewis (1891–1969) British journalist and writer.
Welcome to All This

2 There is occasions and causes why and wherefore in all things.

William Shakespeare (1564–1616) English dramatist.
Henry V, V:1

EXPLOITATION

1 Thus the devil played at chess with me, and yielding a pawn, thought to gain a queen of me, taking advantage of my honest endeavours.

Thomas Browne (1605–82) English physician and writer.
Religio Medici, Pt. I

2 Mortals, whose pleasures are their only care, First wish to be imposed on, and then are.

William Cowper (1731–1800) British poet.
The Progress of Error

3 I should be trading on the blood of my men.

Robert E. Lee (1807–70) US general.
Refusing to write his memoirs
Nobody Said It Better (M. Ringo)

EXPLORATION

See also discovery

1 The fair breeze blew, the white foam flew, The furrow followed free;
We were the first that ever burst
Into that silent sea.

Samuel Taylor Coleridge (1772–1834) British poet.
The Rime of the Ancient Mariner, II

2 Go West, young man, and grow up with the country.

Horace Greeley (1811–72) US politician and journalist.
Also attributed to the US writer John Soule (1815–91), *Terre Haute* (Indiana) *Express*, 1851
Hints toward Reform

3 Nothing easier. One step beyond the pole,

you see, and the north wind becomes a south one.

Robert Edwin Peary (1856–1920) US explorer.
Explaining how he knew he had reached the North Pole
Attrib.

EXTRAVAGANCE

See also excess, luxury, money, ostentation, thrift, waste

1 Riches are for spending.

Francis Bacon (1561–1626) English philosopher.
Essays, 'Of Expense'

2 All progress is based upon a universal innate desire on the part of every organism to live beyond its income.

Samuel Butler (1835–1902) British writer.
Notebooks

3 He sometimes forgets that he is Caesar, but I always remember that I am Caesar's daughter.

Julia (39 BC–14 AD) Daughter of Augustus.
Replying to suggestions that she should live in the simple style of her father, which contrasted with her own extravagance
Saturnalia (Macrobius)

4 All decent people live beyond their incomes nowadays, and those who aren't respectable live beyond other people's. A few gifted individuals manage to do both.

Saki (Hector Hugh Munro; 1870–1916) British writer.
The Match-Maker

5 I suppose that I shall have to die beyond my means.

Oscar Wilde (1854–1900) Irish-born British dramatist.
When told that an operation would be expensive. He is also believed to have said 'I am dying beyond my means' on accepting a glass of champagne as he lay on his deathbed
Life of Wilde (Sherard)

EYES

See also appearance

1 It needs no dictionary of quotations to remind me that the eyes are the windows of the soul.

Max Beerbohm (1872–1956) British writer.
Zuleika Dobson, Ch. 4

2 Jeepers Creepers – where'd you get them peepers?

Johnny Mercer (1909–76) US lyricist and composer.
Jeepers Creepers

3 Out vile jelly!
Where is thy lustre now?

William Shakespeare (1564–1616) English dramatist.
Spoken by Cornwall as he puts out Gloucester's remaining eye
King Lear, III:7

F

FACTS

See also truth

1 Now, what I want is Facts . . . Facts alone are wanted in life.
Charles Dickens (1812–70) British novelist.
Hard Times, Bk. I, Ch. 1

2 Facts do not cease to exist because they are ignored.
Aldous Huxley (1894–1964) British novelist.
Proper Studies

3 Facts speak louder than statistics.
Geoffrey Streatfield (1897–1978) British lawyer.
The Observer, 'Sayings of the Week', 19 Mar 1950

FAILURE

See also success

1 A miss is as good as a mile.
Proverb

2 She knows there's no success like failure
And that failure's no success at all.
Bob Dylan (Robert Allen Zimmerman; 1941–) US popular singer.
Love Minus Zero No Limit

3 Here lies Joseph, who failed in everything he undertook.
Joseph II (1741–90) Holy Roman Emperor.
Suggesting his own epitaph when reflecting upon the disappointment of his hopes for reform

4 Show me a good and gracious loser and I'll show you a failure.
Knute Rockne (1888–1931) US football coach.

FAIRIES

See also supernatural

1 Every time a child says 'I don't believe in fairies' there is a little fairy somewhere that falls down dead.
J. M. Barrie (1860–1937) British novelist and dramatist.
Peter Pan, I

2 When the first baby laughed for the first time, the laugh broke into a thousand pieces and they all went skipping about, and that was the beginning of fairies.
J. M. Barrie

3 There are fairies at the bottom of our garden.
Rose Fyleman (1877–1957) British writer.
Fairies and Chimneys

FAITH

See also belief, faithfulness, God, religion, trust

1 Faith will move mountains.
Proverb

2 By faith the walls of Jericho fell down, after they were compassed about seven days.
Bible: Hebrews
11:30

3 Now faith is the substance of things hoped for, the evidence of things not seen.
Bible: Hebrews
11:1

4 These all died in faith, not having received the promises, but having seen them afar off, and were persuaded of them, and embraced them, and confessed that they were strangers and pilgrims on the earth.
Bible: Hebrews
11:13

5 For we walk by faith, not by sight.
Bible: II Corinthians
5:7

6 For I am now ready to be offered, and the time of my departure is at hand.
I have fought a good fight, I have finished my course, I have kept the faith:
Henceforth there is laid up for me a crown of righteousness, which the Lord, the righteous judge, shall give me at that day: and not to me only, but unto all them also that love his appearing.
Bible: II Timothy
4:6–8

7 Even so faith, if it hath not works, is dead, being alone.
Bible: James
2:17

8 And Jesus said unto them, I am the bread of life: he that cometh to me shall never hunger; and he that believeth on me shall never thirst.
Bible: John
6:35

9 I feel no need for any other faith than my faith in human beings.
Pearl Buck (1892–1973) US novelist.
I Believe

10 The prayer that reforms the sinner andheals the sick is an absolute faith that all things are possible to God – a spiritual understanding of Him, an unselfed love.
Mary Baker Eddy (1821–1910) US religious leader.
Science and Health, with Key to the Scriptures

11 And I said to the man who stood at the gate of the year: 'Give me a light that I may tread safely into the unknown'. And he replied: 'Go out into the darkness and put your hand into

the hand of God. That shall be to you better than light and safer than a known way.'
Minnie Louise Haskins (1875–1957) US writer.
Remembered because it was quoted by George VI in his Christmas broadcast, 1939
The Desert, Introduction

12 My dear child, you must believe in God in spite of what the clergy tell you.
Benjamin Jowett (1817–93) British theologian.
Autobiography (Asquith), Ch. 8

13 Booth died blind and still by faith he trod, Eyes still dazzled by the ways of God.
Vachel Lindsay (1879–1931) US poet.
General William Booth Enters Heaven

14 Faith may be defined briefly as an illogical belief in the occurrence of the improbable.
H. L. Mencken (1880–1956) US journalist.
Prejudices, 'Types of Men'

15 It takes a long while for a naturally trustful person to reconcile himself to the idea that after all God will not help him.
H. L. Mencken
Notebooks, 'Minority Report'

16 Lead, kindly Light, amid the encircling gloom, Lead thou me on;
The night is dark, and I am far from home, Lead thou me on.
Cardinal Newman (1801–90) British theologian.
Lead Kindly Light

17 Even such is Time, that takes in trust Our youth, our joys, our all we have, And pays us but with age and dust; Who in the dark and silent grave, When we have wandered all our ways, Shuts up the story of our days; But from this earth, this grave, this dust, My God shall raise me up, I trust.
Walter Raleigh (1554–1618) English explorer.
Written on the night before his execution
Attrib.

18 'Tis not the dying for a faith that's so hard, Master Harry – every man of every nation has done that – 'tis the living up to it that is difficult.
William Makepeace Thackeray (1811–63) British novelist.
Henry Esmond, Ch. 6

19 Faith consists in believing when it is beyond the power of reason to believe. It is not enough that a thing be possible for it to be believed.
Voltaire (François-Marie Arouet; 1694–1778) French writer.
Questions sur l'encyclopédie

FAITHFULNESS

See also loyalty

1 It is better to be unfaithful than faithful without wanting to be.
Brigitte Bardot (1934–) French film actress.
The Observer, 'Sayings of the Week', 18 Feb 1968

2 Through perils both of wind and limb, Through thick and thin she follow'd him.
Samuel Butler (1612–80) English satirist.
Hudibras, Pt. II

3 I have been faithful to thee, Cynara! in my fashion.
Ernest Dowson (1867–1900) British lyric poet.
Non Sum Qualis Eram Bonae Sub Regno Cynarae

4 We only part to meet again.
Change, as ye list, ye winds; my heart shall be The faithful compass that still points to thee.
John Gay (1685–1732) English poet and dramatist.
Sweet William's Farewell

5 But I'm always true to you, darlin', in my fashion,
Yes, I'm always true to you, darlin', in my way.
Cole Porter (1893–1964) US songwriter.
Kiss Me, Kate, 'Always True to You in My Fashion'

FAME

See also popularity, posterity, reputation

1 A celebrity is a person who works hard all his life to become known, then wears dark glasses to avoid being recognized.
Fred Allen (1894–1956) US comedian.
Treadmill to Oblivion

2 Fame is like a river, that beareth up things light and swollen, and drowns things weighty and solid.
Francis Bacon (1561–1626) English philosopher.
Essays, 'Of Praise'

3 I should like one of these days to be so well known, so popular, so celebrated, so famous, that it would permit me . . . to break wind in society, and society would think it a most natural thing.
Honoré de Balzac (1799–1850) French novelist.
Attrib.

4 The celebrity is a person who is known for his well-knownness.
Daniel J. Boorstin (1914–) US writer.
The Image, 'From Hero to Celebrity: The Human Pseudo-event'

5 A best-seller was a book which somehow sold well simply because it was selling well.
Daniel J. Boorstin
The Image, 'From Shapes to Shadows: Dissolving Forms'

6 I awoke one morning and found myself famous.
Lord Byron (1788–1824) British poet.
Remark made after the publication of *Childe Harold's Pilgrimage* (1812)
Entry in Memoranda

7 Being a star has made it possible for me to get insulted in places where the average Negro could never hope to get insulted.
Sammy Davis Jnr (1925–) US singer.
Yes I Can

8 If a man make a better mouse-trap than his neighbour, though he build his house in the woods, the world will make a beaten path to his door.
Ralph Waldo Emerson (1803–82) US poet and essayist.
Attrib.

9 A big man has no time really to do anything but just sit and be big.
F. Scott Fitzgerald (1896–1940) US novelist.
This Side of Paradise, Bk. III, Ch. 2

10 Fame is sometimes like unto a kind of mushroom, which Pliny recounts to be the greatest miracle in nature, because growing and having no root.
Thomas Fuller (1608–61) English historian.
The Holy State and the Profane State

11 Fame is a powerful aphrodisiac.
Graham Greene (1904–) British novelist.
Radio Times, 10 Sept 1964

12 Every man has a lurking wish to appear considerable in his native place.
Samuel Johnson (1709–84) British lexicographer.
Letter to Sir Joshua Reynolds
Life of Johnson (J. Boswell), Vol. II

13 One of the drawbacks of Fame is that one can never escape from it.
Nellie Melba (Helen Porter Mitchell; 1861–1931) Australian soprano.
Melodies and Memories

14 Fame is the spur that the clear spirit doth raise
(That last infirmity of noble mind)
To scorn delights, and live laborious days.
John Milton (1608–74) English poet.
Lycidas

15 'What are you famous *for*?'
'For nothing. I am just famous.'
Iris Murdoch (1919–) Irish-born British novelist.
The Flight from the Enchanter

16 I'm never going to be famous . . . I don't do anything. Not one single thing. I used to bite my nails, but I don't even do that any more.
Dorothy Parker (1893–1967) US writer.
The Little Hours

17 If you have to tell them who you are, you aren't anybody.
Gregory Peck (1916–) US film star.
Remarking upon the failure of anyone in a crowded restaurant to recognize him
Pieces of Eight (S. Harris)

18 The more you are talked about, the more you will wish to be talked about. The condemned murderer who is allowed to see the account of his trial in the Press is indignant if he finds a newspaper which has reported it inadequately. . . . Politicians and literary men are in the same case.
Bertrand Russell (1872–1970) British philosopher.
Human Society in Ethics and Politics

19 Love of fame is the last thing even learned men can bear to be parted from.
Tacitus (c. 55–c. 120 AD) Roman historian.
Histories, IV, 6

20 To famous men all the earth is a sepulchre.
Thucydides (c. 460–c. 400 BC) Greek historian and general.
History of the Peloponnesian War, Bk. II, Ch. 43

21 The only man who wasn't spoilt by being lionized was Daniel.
Herbert Beerbohm Tree (1853–1917) British actor and theatre manager.
Beerbohm Tree (Hesketh Pearson)

22 When I pass my name in such large letters I blush, but at the same time instinctively raise my hat.
Herbert Beerbohm Tree
Beerbohm Tree (Hesketh Pearson)

23 In the future, everyone will be famous for 15 minutes.
Andy Warhol (Andrew Warhola; 1926–87) US pop artist.
Attrib.

24 There is only one thing in the world worse than being talked about, and that is not being talked about.
Oscar Wilde (1854–1900) Irish-born British dramatist.
The Picture of Dorian Gray, Ch. 1

FAMILIARITY

1 Familiarity breeds contempt.
Proverb

2 No man is a hero to his valet.
Anne-Marie Bigot de Cornuel (1605–94) French society hostess.
Lettres de Mlle Aïssé, 13 Aug 1728

3 I've grown accustomed to the trace
Of something in the air,
Accustomed to her face.
Alan Jay Lerner (1918–86) US songwriter.
My Fair Lady, II:6

4 I have been here before.
But when or how I cannot tell:
I know the grass beyond the door,
The sweet keen smell,
The sighing sound, the lights around the shore.
Dante Gabriel Rossetti (1828–82) British painter and poet.
Sudden Light

5 I like familiarity. In me it does not breed contempt. Only more familiarity.
Gertrude Stein (1874–1946) US writer.
Dale Carnegie's Scrapbook

6 He began to think the tramp a fine,

brotherly, generous fellow. He was also growing accustomed to something – shall I call it an olfactory bar – that had hitherto kept them apart.

H. G. Wells (1866–1946) British writer.
Bealby, Pt. VI, Ch. 3

FAMILY

See also ancestry, children, marriage

1 Blood is thicker than water.
Proverb

2 Every family has a skeleton in the cupboard.
Proverb

3 Like father, like son.
Proverb

4 The family that prays together stays together.
Proverb

5 There's a black sheep in every flock.
Proverb

6 Sir Walter, being strangely surprised and put out of his countenance at so great a table, gives his son a damned blow over the face. His son, as rude as he was, would not strike his father, but strikes over the face the gentleman that sat next to him and said 'Box about: 'twill come to my father anon'.
John Aubrey (1626–97) English antiquary.
Brief Lives, 'Sir Walter Raleigh'

7 He that hath wife and children hath given hostages to fortune; for they are impediments to great enterprises, either of virtue or mischief.
Francis Bacon (1561–1626) English philosopher.
See also LUCAN
Essays, 'Of Marriage and Single Life'

8 The joys of parents are secret, and so are their griefs and fears.
Francis Bacon
Essays, 'Of Parents and Children'

9 Fathers, provoke not your children to anger, lest they be discouraged.
Bible: Colossians
3:21

10 Behold, every one that useth proverbs shall use this proverb against thee, saying, As is the mother, so is her daughter.
Bible: Ezekiel
16:44–45

11 I love all my children, but some of them I don't like.
Lillian Carter (1902–83) The mother of Jimmy Carter.
In *Woman*, 9 Apr 1977

12 If one is not going to take the necessary precautions to avoid having parents one must undertake to bring them up.
Quentin Crisp (?1910–   ) Model, publicist, and writer.
The Naked Civil Servant

13 Fate chooses your relations, you choose your friends.
Jacques Delille (1738–1813) French abbé and poet.
Malheur et pitié, I

14 It is a melancholy truth that even great men have their poor relations.
Charles Dickens (1812–70) British novelist.
Bleak House, Ch. 28

15 What a marvellous place to drop one's mother-in-law!
Marshal Foch (1851–1929) French soldier.
Remark on being shown the Grand Canyon
Attrib.

16 The mother-child relationship is paradoxical and, in a sense, tragic. It requires the most intense love on the mother's side, yet this very love must help the child grow away from the mother and to become fully independent.
Erich Fromm (1900–80) US psychologist and philosopher.

17 My father was frightened of his mother. I was frightened of my father, and I'm damned well going to make sure that my children are frightened of me.
George V (1865–1936) King of the United Kingdom.
Attrib.

18 And so do his sisters, and his cousins and his aunts!
His sisters and his cousins,
Whom he reckons up by dozens,
And his aunts!
W. S. Gilbert (1836–1911) British dramatist.
HMS Pinafore, I

19 LEONTINE. An only son, sir, might expect more indulgence.
CROAKER. An only father, sir, might expect more obedience.
Oliver Goldsmith (1728–74) Irish-born British writer.
The Good-Natured Man, I

20 A person may be indebted for a nose or an eye, for a graceful carriage or a voluble discourse, to a great-aunt or uncle, whose existence he has scarcely heard of.
William Hazlitt (1778–1830) British essayist.
On Personal Character

21 Good families are generally worse than any others.
Anthony Hope (Sir Anthony Hope Hawkins; 1863–1933) British novelist.
The Prisoner of Zenda, Ch. 1

22 But there, everything has its drawbacks, as the man said when his mother-in-law died,

and they came down upon him for the funeral expenses.

Jerome K. Jerome (1859–1927) British humorist.
Three Men in a Boat, Ch. 3

23 A poor relation – is the most irrelevant thing in nature.

Charles Lamb (1775–1834) British essayist.
Last Essays of Elia, 'Poor Relations'

24 They fuck you up, your mum and dad.
They may not mean to, but they do.
They fill you with the faults they had
And add some extra, just for you.

Philip Larkin (1922–85) British poet.
This be the Verse

25 Far from being the basis of the good society, the family, with its narrow privacy and tawdry secrets, is the source of all our discontents.

Edmund Leach (1910–) British social anthropologist.
In the BBC Reith Lectures for 1967. Lecture reprinted in *The Listener*

26 I have a wife, I have sons: all of them hostages given to fate.

Lucan (Marcus Annaeus Lucanus; 39–65 AD) Roman poet.
See also BACON
Works, VII

27 A group of closely related persons living under one roof; it is a convenience, often a necessity, sometimes a pleasure, sometimes the reverse; but who first exalted it as admirable, an almost religious ideal?

Rose Macaulay (1889–1958) British writer.
The World My Wilderness, Ch. 20

28 You're a disgrace to our family name of Wagstaff, if such a thing is possible.

Groucho Marx (Julius Marx; 1895–1977) US comedian.
Horse Feathers

29 The sink is the great symbol of the bloodiness of family life. All life is bad, but family life is worse.

Julian Mitchell (1935–) British writer.
As Far as You Can Go, Pt. I, Ch. 1

30 I cumber you goode Margaret muche, but I woulde be sorye, if it shoulde be any lenger than to morrowe, for it is S. Thomas evin and the vtas of Sainte Peter and therefore to morowe longe I to goe to God, it were a daye very meete and conveniente for me. I neuer liked your maner towarde me better then when you kissed me laste for I loue when dougtherly loue and deere charitie hathe no laisor to looke to worldely curtesye. Fare well my deere childe and praye for me, and I shall for you and all your friendes that we maie merily meete in heaven.

Thomas More (1478–1535) English lawyer and scholar.
Last letter to Margaret Roper, his daughter, on the eve of his execution on 6 July 1535

31 Children aren't happy with nothing to ignore,

And that's what parents were created for.

Ogden Nash (1902–71) US poet.
The Parents

32 And Her Mother Came Too.

Ivor Novello (David Ivor Davies; 1893–1951) British actor, composer, and dramatist.
Title of song

33 Men are generally more careful of the breed of their horses and dogs than of their children.

William Penn (1644–1718) English preacher.
Some Fruits of Solitude, in Reflections and Maxims relating to the conduct of Humane Life, Pt. I, No 52

34 Parents are sometimes a bit of a disappointment to their children. They don't fulfil the promise of their early years.

Anthony Powell (1905–) British novelist.
A Buyer's Market

35 All men are brothers, but, thank God, they aren't all brothers-in-law.

Anthony Powell
A Dance to the Music of Time: At Lady Molly's, Ch. 4

36 For there is no friend like a sister
In calm or stormy weather;
To cheer one on the tedious way,
To fetch one if one goes astray,
To lift one if one totters down,
To strengthen whilst one stands.

Christina Rossetti (1830–74) British poet.
Goblin Market

37 Two mothers-in-law.

Lord John Russell (1792–1878) British statesman.
His answer when asked what he would consider a proper punishment for bigamy
Anekdotenschatz (H. Hoffmeister)

38 It is a wise father that knows his own child.

William Shakespeare (1564–1616) English dramatist.
The Merchant of Venice, II:2

39 That dear octopus from whose tentacles we never quite escape, nor in our innermost hearts never quite wish to.

Dodie Smith (1896–) British dramatist and novelist.
Dear Octopus

40 I wish either my father or my mother, or indeed both of them, as they were in duty both equally bound to it, had minded what they were about when they begot me.

Laurence Sterne (1713–68) Irish-born British writer.
Tristram Shandy

41 The greatest destroyer of peace is abortion because if a mother can kill her own child what is left for me to kill you and you to kill me? There is nothing between.

Mother Teresa (Agnes Gonxha Bojaxhui; 1910–) Yugoslavian missionary in Calcutta.
Nobel Peace Prize Lecture

42 If a man's character is to be abused, say

what you will, there's nobody like a relation to do the business.
William Makepeace Thackeray (1811–63) British novelist.
Vanity Fair, Ch. 19

43 All happy families resemble one another, each unhappy family is unhappy in its own way.
Leo Tolstoy (1828–1910) Russian writer.
Anna Karenina, Pt. I, Ch. 1

44 No man is responsible for his father. That is entirely his mother's affair.
Margaret Turnbull (fl. 1920s–1942) US writer.
Alabaster Lamps

45 Parents are the bones on which children sharpen their teeth.
Peter Ustinov (1921–) British actor.
Dear Me

46 Don't hold your parents up to contempt. After all, you are their son, and it is just possible that you may take after them.
Evelyn Waugh (1903–66) British novelist.
The Tablet, 9 May 1951

47 The thing that impresses me most about America is the way parents obey their children.
Duke of Windsor (1894–1972) King of the United Kingdom; abdicated 1936.
Look Magazine, 5 Mar 1957

48 It is no use telling me that there are bad aunts and good aunts. At the core they are all alike. Sooner or later, out pops the cloven hoof.
P. G. Wodehouse (1881–1975) British humorous novelist.
The Code of the Woosters

FANATICISM

1 Defined in psychological terms, a fanatic is a man who consciously over-compensates a secret doubt.
Aldous Huxley (1894–1964) British novelist.
Vulgarity in Literature, Ch. 4

2 Fanatics have their dreams, wherewith they weave
A paradise for a sect.
John Keats (1795–1821) British poet.
The Fall of Hyperion, I

3 You are never dedicated to something you have complete confidence in. No one is fanatically shouting that the sun is going to rise tomorrow. They *know* it's going to rise tomorrow. When people are fanatically dedicated to political or religious faiths or any other kind of dogmas or goals, it's always because these dogmas or goals are in doubt.
Robert T. Pirsig (1928–) US writer.
Zen and the Art of Motorcycle Maintenance, Pt. II, Ch. 13

FASCISM

See also Hitler, Nazism

1 I should be pleased, I suppose, that Hitler has carried out a revolution on our lines. But they are Germans. So they will end by ruining our idea.
Benito Mussolini (1883–1945) Italian dictator.
Benito Mussolini (C. Hibbert), Pt. II, Ch. 1

2 Fascism is a religion; the twentieth century will be known in history as the century of Fascism.
Benito Mussolini
On Hitler's seizing power
Sawdust Caesar (George Seldes), Ch. 24

3 Fascism is not an article for export.
Benito Mussolini
Report in the German press, 1932

4 Every communist has a fascist frown, every fascist a communist smile.
Muriel Spark (1918–) British novelist.
The Girls of Slender Means, Ch. 4

5 Fascism means war.
John St Loe Strachey (1901–63) British politician.
Slogan, 1930s

FASHION

See also clothes

1 Fashion is architecture: it is a matter of proportions.
Coco Chanel (1883–1971) French dress designer.
Coco Chanel, Her Life, Her Secrets (Marcel Haedrich)

2 One had as good be out of the world, as out of the fashion.
Colley Cibber (1671–1757) British actor and dramatist.
Love's Last Shift, II

3 I walk down the Strand
With my gloves on my hand,
And I walk down again
With them off.
W. F. Hargreaves (1846–1919) British songwriter.
Burlington Bertie

4 There are few who would not rather be taken in adultery than in provincialism.
Aldous Huxley (1894–1964) British novelist.
Antic Hay, Ch. 10

5 Her frocks are built in Paris but she wears them with a strong English accent.
Saki (Hector Hugh Munro; 1870–1916) British writer.
Reginald on Women

6 For an idea ever to be fashionable is ominous, since it must afterwards be always old-fashioned.
George Santayana (1863–1952) US philosopher.
Winds of Doctrine, 'Modernism and Christianity'

7 Fashions, after all, are only induced epidemics.

George Bernard Shaw (1856–1950) Irish dramatist and critic.
Doctor's Dilemma, Preface

8 A love of fashion makes the economy go round.

Liz Tilberis (1947–) Editor of Vogue.
Remark, Aug 1987

FEAR

---

1 It is a miserable state of mind to have few things to desire and many things to fear.

Francis Bacon (1561–1626) English philosopher.
Essays, 'Of Empire'

2 For God hath not given us the spirit of fear; but of power, and of love, and of a sound mind.

Bible: II Timothy
1:7

3 There is no fear in love; but perfect love casteth out fear: because fear hath torment. He that feareth is not made perfect in love.

Bible: I John
4:18

4 Fear has many eyes and can see things underground.

Miguel de Cervantes (1547–1616) Spanish novelist.
Don Quixote, Pt. I, Ch. 20

5 You may take the most gallant sailor, the most intrepid airman, or the most audacious soldier, put them at a table together – what do you get? *The sum of their fears.*

Winston Churchill (1874–1965) British statesman.
Talking about the Chiefs of Staffs system, 16 Nov 1943
The Blast of War (H. Macmillan), Ch. 16

6 Like one, that on a lonesome road
Doth walk in fear and dread,
And having once turned round walks on,
And turns no more his head;
Because he knows, a frightful fiend
Doth close behind him tread.

Samuel Taylor Coleridge (1772–1834) British poet.
The Rime of the Ancient Mariner, VI

7 I'm not frightened of the darkness outside. It's the darkness inside houses I don't like.

Shelagh Delaney (1939–) British dramatist.
A Taste of Honey, I:1

8 I wants to make your flesh creep.

Charles Dickens (1812–70) British novelist.
Pickwick Papers, Ch. 8

9 And I will show you something different from either
Your shadow at morning striding behind you,
Or your shadow at evening rising to meet you
I will show you fear in a handful of dust.

T. S. Eliot (1888–1965) US-born British poet and dramatist.
The Waste Land, 'The Burial of the Dead'

10 Let me assert my firm belief that the only thing we have to fear is fear itself.

Franklin D. Roosevelt (1882–1945) US Democratic president.
First Inaugural Address, 4 Mar 1933

11 I had else been perfect,
Whole as the marble, founded as the rock,
As broad and general as the casing air,
But now I am cabin'd, cribb'd, confin'd, bound in
To saucy doubts and fears.

William Shakespeare (1564–1616) English dramatist.
Macbeth, II:4

12 A lion among ladies is a most dreadful thing; for there is not a more fearful wild-fowl than your lion living.

William Shakespeare
A Midsummer Night's Dream, III:1

13 Fear lent wings to his feet.

Virgil (Publius Vergilius Maro; 70–19 BC) Roman poet.
Aeneid, Bk. VIII

14 He had one peculiar weakness; he had faced death in many forms but he had never faced a dentist. The thought of dentists gave him just the same sick horror as the thought of Socialism.

H. G. Wells (1866–1946) British writer.
Bealby, Pt. VIII, Ch. 1

15 By night an atheist half believes a God.

Edward Young (1683–1765) British poet.
Night Thoughts

FEMINISM

See also equality, sexes, woman's role, women

Those in favour

1 Old-fashioned ways which no longer apply to changed conditions are a snare in which the feet of women have always become readily entangled.

Jane Addams (1860–1935) US social worker.
In *Newer Ideals of Peace*, 'Utilization of Women in City Government'

2 Men their rights and nothing more; women their rights and nothing less.

Susan B. Anthony (1820–1906) US editor.
The Revolution, Motto

3 ... there never will be complete equality until women themselves help to make laws and elect lawmakers.

Susan B. Anthony
In *The Arena*, (May 1897) 'The Status of Women, Past, Present and Future'

4 From a timid, shy girl I had become a woman of resolute character, who could not longer be frightened by the struggle with troubles.

Anna Dostoevsky (1846–1918) Russian diarist and writer.
Dostoevsky Portrayed by His Wife

5 The extension of women's rights is the basic principle of all social progress.

Charles Fourier (1772–1837) French social reformer.
Théorie des Quatre Mouvements

6 Where young boys plan for what they will achieve and attain, young girls plan for whom they will achieve and attain.

Charlotte Perkins Gilman (1860–1935) US writer.
Women and Economics, Ch. 5

7 A woman needs a man like a fish needs a bicycle.

Graffiti

8 Mother is the dead heart of the family, spending father's earnings on consumer goods to enhance the environment in which he eats, sleeps and watches the television.

Germaine Greer (1939–   ) Australian-born British writer and feminist.
The Female Eunuch

9 Women fail to understand how much men hate them.

Germaine Greer
The Female Eunuch

10 I know you do not make the laws but I also know that you are the wives and mothers, the sisters and daughters of those who do.

Angelina Grimké (1805–79) US writer and reformer.
The Anti-Slavery Examiner (Sep 1836), 'Appeal to the Christian Women of the South'

11 . . . the emancipation of women is practically the greatest egoistic movement of the nineteenth century, and the most intense affirmation of the right of the self that history has yet seen . . .

Ellen Key (Karolina Sofia Key; 1849–1926) Swedish writer.
The Century of the Child, Ch. 2

12 Can anything be more absurd than keeping women in a state of ignorance, and yet so vehemently to insist on their resisting temptation?

Vicesimus Knox (1752–1821) British essayist.
Liberal Education, Vol. I, 'On the Literary Education of Women'

13 It is ironic that the wife who made Britain great again, and who is the leader of the Western World, has to get her husband to sign her tax form.

Jacqui Lait
Referring to Margaret Thatcher
Speech, Oct 1987

14 Other books have been written by men physicians . . . One would suppose in reading them that women possess but one class of physical organs, and that these are always diseased. Such teaching is pestiferous, and tends to cause and perpetuate the very evils it professes to remedy.

Mary Ashton Livermore (c. 1820–1905) US writer.
What Shall We Do with Our Daughters?, Ch. 2

15 I'm furious about the Women's Liberationists. They keep getting up on soapboxes and proclaiming that women are brighter than men. That's true, but it should be kept very quiet or it ruins the whole racket.

Anita Loos (1891–1981) US novelist.
The Observer, 'Sayings of the Year', 30 Dec 1973

16 . . . is it to be understood that the principles of the Declaration of Independence bear no relation to half of the human race?

Harriet Martineau (1802–76) British writer.
Society in America, Vol. III, 'Marriage'

17 The most important thing women have to do is to stir up the zeal of women themselves.

John Stuart Mill (1806–73) British philosopher.
Letter to Alexander Bain, 14 July 1869

18 . . . the rumblings of women's liberation are only one pointer to the fact that you already have a discontented work force. And if conditions continue to lag so far behind the industrial norm and the discomfort increases, you will find . . . that you will end up with an inferior product.

Elaine Morgan (1920–   ) British writer.
The Descent of Woman, Ch. 11

19 No *man*, not even a doctor, ever gives any other definition of what a nurse should be than this – "devoted and obedient." This definition would do just as well for a porter. It might even do for a horse. It would not do for a policeman.

Florence Nightingale (1820–1910) British nurse.
Notes on Nursing

20 The vote, I thought, means nothing to women. We should be armed.

Edna O'Brien (1936–   ) Irish novelist.
Quoted as epigraph to *Fear of Flying* (Erica Jong), Ch. 16

21 . . . if civilisation is to advance at all in the future, it must be through the help of women, women freed of their political shackles, women with full power to work their will in society. It was rapidly becoming clear to my mind that men regarded women as a servant class in the community, and that women were going to remain in the servant class until they lifted themselves out of it.

Emmeline Pankhurst (1858–1928) British suffragette.
My Own Story

22 Women had always fought for men, and for their children. Now they were ready to fight for their own human rights. Our militant movement was established.

Emmeline Pankhurst
My Own Story

23 We have taken this action, because as women . . . we realize that the condition of our sex is so deplorable that it is our duty even to break the law in order to call attention to the reasons why we do so.
Emmeline Pankhurst
Shoulder to Shoulder (ed. Midge Mackenzie)
Speech in court, 21 Oct 1908

24 The prolonged slavery of women is the darkest page in human history.
Elizabeth Stanton (1815–1902) US suffragette.
History of Woman Suffrage (with Susan B. Anthony and Mathilda Gage), Vol. I

25 Womanhood is the great fact in her life; wifehood and motherhood are but incidental relations.
Elizabeth Stanton
History of Woman Suffrage (with Susan B. Anthony and Mathilda Gage), Vol. I

26 *Declaration of Sentiments:* . . . We hold these truths to be self-evident: that all men and women are created equal . . .
Elizabeth Stanton
History of Woman Suffrage (with Susan B. Anthony and Mathilda Gage), Vol. I

27 People call me a feminist whenever I express sentiments that differentiate me from a doormat or a prostitute.
Rebecca West (Cicely Isabel Fairfield; 1892–1983) British novelist and journalist.
Attrib.

28 Women have always been the guardians of wisdom and humanity which makes them natural, but usually secret, rulers. The time has come for them to rule openly, but together with and not against men.
Charlotte Wolff (1904–86) German-born British writer.
Bisexuality: A Study, Ch. 2

29 Women have served all these centuries as looking-glasses possessing the magic and delicious power of reflecting the figure of man at twice its natural size.
Virginia Woolf (1882–1941) British novelist.
A Room of One's Own

30 The *divine right* of husbands, like the divine right of kings, may, it is hoped, in this enlightened age, be contested without danger.
Mary Wollstonecraft 1759–97) British writer.
A Vindication of the Rights of Woman, Ch. 3

31 I do not wish them to have power over men; but over themselves.
Mary Wollstonecraft
A Vindication of the Rights of Woman, Ch. 4
Referring to women

Those against

32 There is a tide in the affairs of women,

Which, taken at the flood, leads – God knows where.
Lord Byron (1788–1824) British poet.
Don Juan, VI

33 Nothing would induce me to vote for giving women the franchise. I am not going to be henpecked into a question of such importance.
Winston Churchill (1874–1963) British statesman.
The Amazing Mr Churchill (Robert Lewis Taylor)

34 The great question . . . which I have not been able to answer, despite my thirty years of research into the feminine soul, is 'What does a woman want'?
Sigmund Freud (1856–1939) Austrian psychoanalyst.
Psychiatry in American Life (Charles Rolo)

35 The First Blast of the Trumpet Against the Monstrous Regiment of Women.
John Knox (c. 1514–72) Scottish religious reformer.
Title of Pamphlet, 1558

36 Women's Liberation is just a lot of foolishness. It's the men who are discriminated against. They can't bear children. And no one's likely to do anything about that.
Golda Meir (1898–1978) Russian-born Israeli stateswoman.
Attrib.

37 The only good thing about Hammerfall, women's lib was dead milliseconds after Hammerstrike.
Larry Niven (1938–) US science-fiction writer.
'Hammerfall' was a fictional collision in the late 1970s between the Earth and a large comet that destroyed civilization
Lucifer's Hammer, Pt. III (with Jerry Pournelle)

38 Give women the vote, and in five years there will be a crushing tax on bachelors.
George Bernard Shaw (1856–1950) Irish dramatist and critic.
Man and Superman, Preface

39 The Queen is most anxious to enlist every one who can speak or write to join in checking this mad, wicked folly of 'Woman's Rights', with all its attendant horrors, on which her poor feeble sex is bent, forgetting every sense of womanly feeling and propriety.
Victoria (1819–1901) Queen of the United Kingdom.
Letter to Sir Theodore Martin, 29 May 1870

40 The thought could not be avoided that the best home for a feminist was in another person's lab.
James Dewey Watson (1928–) US geneticist.
The Double Helix, Ch. 2

…and a final word

41 The battle for women's rights has been
largely won.
Margaret Thatcher (1925–   ) British politician and prime
minister.
The Guardian, 1982

42 I do, and I also wash and iron them.
Denis Thatcher (1915–   ) British businessman married to
Margaret Thatcher.
Times (Los Angeles), 21 Apr 1981
Replying to the question "Who wears the pants in this house?"

43 WOMEN'S RIGHTS NOW
Followed by
Yes Dear
Exchange of graffiti

FICTION

See also books, literature, novels, writing

1 Science fiction is no more written for
scientists than ghost stories are written for
ghosts.
Brian Aldiss (1925–   ) British science-fiction writer.
Penguin Science Fiction, Introduction

2 Sometimes I don't know whether Zelda and I
are real or whether we are characters in one
of my novels.
F. Scott Fitzgerald (1896–1940) US novelist.
Said of himself and his wife
A Second Flowering (Malcolm Cowley)

3 There are many reasons why novelists write,
but they all have one thing in common – a
need to create an alternative world.
John Fowles (1926–   ) British novelist.
The Sunday Times Magazine, 2 Oct 1977

4 Casting my mind's eye over the whole of
fiction, the only absolutely original creation I
can think of is Don Quixote.
W. Somerset Maugham (1874–1965) British novelist.
10 Novels and Their Authors, Ch. 1

FIRE

1 All things, oh priests, are on fire . . . The eye
is on fire; forms are on fire; eye-
consciousness is on fire; impressions received
by the eye are on fire.
Buddha (Gautama Siddhartha; c. 563–c. 483 BC) Indian
religious teacher.
The Fire Sermon

2 Billy, in one of his nice new sashes,
Fell in the fire and was burnt to ashes;
Now, although the room grows chilly,
I haven't the heart to poke poor Billy.
Harry Graham (1874–1936) British writer.
Ruthless Rhymes for Heartless Homes, 'Tender-Heartedness'

3 Whatsoever might be the extent of the
private calamity, I hope it will not interfere
with the public business of the country.
Richard Brinsley Sheridan (1751–1816) British
dramatist.
On learning, whilst in the House of Commons, that his Drury
Lane Theatre was on fire
Memoirs of the Life of the Rt. Hon. Richard Brinsley Sheridan
(T. Moore)

4 A man may surely be allowed to take a glass
of wine by his own fireside.
Richard Brinsley Sheridan
As he sat in a coffeehouse watching his theatre burn down
Memoirs of the Life of the Rt. Hon. Richard Brinsley Sheridan
(T. Moore)

5 Arson, after all, is an artificial crime . . . A
large number of houses deserve to be burnt.
H. G. Wells (1866–1946) British writer.
The History of Mr Polly, Pt. X, Ch. 1

FIRST IMPRESSIONS

1 First impressions are the most lasting.
Proverb

2 There is a lady sweet and kind,
Was never face so pleased my mind;
I did but see her passing by,
And yet I love her till I die.
Anonymous
Passing By

3 Harris, I am not well; pray get me a glass of
brandy.
George IV (1762–1830) King of the United Kingdom.
On seeing Caroline of Brunswick for the first time
Diaries (Earl of Malmesbury)

4 You have sent me a Flanders mare.
Henry VIII (1491–1547) King of England.
Said on meeting his fourth wife, Anne of Cleves, for the first
time
Attrib.

5 First feelings are always the most natural.
Louis XIV (1638–1715) French king.
Repeated by Mme de Sévigné

6 Who ever loved, that loved not at first sight?
Christopher Marlowe (1564–93) English dramatist.
Hero and Leander, I

7 Mistrust first impulses; they are nearly
always good.
Talleyrand (Charles Maurice de Talleyrand-Périgord;
1754–1838) French politician.
Sometimes attrib. to Count Montrond
Attrib.

FISHING

See also sport and games

1 Fly fishing may be a very pleasant
amusement; but angling or float fishing I can
only compare to a stick and a string, with a
worm at one end and a fool at the other.
Samuel Johnson (1709–84) British lexicographer.
Attrib. in *Instructions to Young Sportsmen* (Hawker)

2 Angling is somewhat like poetry, men are to be born so.
Izaak Walton
The Compleat Angler, Ch. 1

3 Let the blessing of St Peter's Master be . . . upon all that are lovers of virtue; and dare trust in His providence; and be quiet; and go a-Angling.
Izaak Walton
The Compleat Angler, Ch. 21

4 Angling may be said to be so like the mathematics, that it can never be fully learnt.
Izaak Walton
The Compleat Angler, Epistle to the Reader

5 We may say of angling as Dr Boteler said of strawberries, 'Doubtless God could have made a better berry, but doubtless God never did.'
Izaak Walton
The Compleat Angler, Ch. 5

FLATTERY

See also compliments, insincerity, praise, servility

1 Imitation is the sincerest form of flattery.
Proverb

2 It is happy for you that you possess the talent of flattering with delicacy. May I ask whether these pleasing attentions proceed from the impulse of the moment, or are the result of previous study?
Jane Austen (1775–1817) British novelist.
Pride and Prejudice, Ch. 14

3 A rich man's joke is always funny.
Thomas Edward Brown (1830–97) British poet.
The Doctor

4 Every woman is infallibly to be gained by every sort of flattery, and every man by one sort or other.
Earl of Chesterfield (1694–1773) English statesman.
Letter to his son, 16 Mar 1752

5 Madam, before you flatter a man so grossly to his face, you should consider whether or not your flattery is worth his having.
Samuel Johnson (1709–84) British lexicographer.
Diary and Letters (Mme D'Arblay), Vol. I, Ch. 2

6 Be advised that all flatterers live at the expense of those who listen to them.
Jean de La Fontaine (1621–95) French poet.
Fables, I, 'Le Corbeau et le Renard'

7 I will praise any man that will praise me.
William Shakespeare (1564–1616) English dramatist.
Antony and Cleopatra, II:6

8 Flattery is all right so long as you don't inhale.
Adlai Stevenson (1900–65) US statesman.
Attrib.

9 'Tis an old maxim in the schools,
That flattery's the food of fools;
Yet now and then your men of wit
Will condescend to take a bit.
Jonathan Swift (1667–1745) Irish-born Anglican priest and writer.
Cadenus and Vanessa

FLOWERS

See also gardens

1 She wore a wreath of roses,
The night that first we met.
Thomas Haynes Bayly (1797–1839) British writer.
She Wore a Wreath of Roses

2 Just now the lilac is in bloom
All before my little room.
Rupert Brooke (1887–1915) British poet.
The Old Vicarage, Grantchester

3 Tiptoe through the tulips with me.
Al Dubin (20th century) US songwriter.
From the musical, *Gold Diggers of Broadway*
Tiptoe Through the Tulips

4 I sometimes think that never blows so red
The Rose as where some buried Caesar bled;
That every Hyacinth the Garden wears
Dropt in her Lap from some once lovely Head.
Edward Fitzgerald (1809–83) British poet.
The Rubáiyát of Omar Khayyám (1st edn.), XVIII

5 Their smiles,
Wan as primroses gather'd at midnight
By chilly finger'd spring.
John Keats (1795–1821) British poet.
Endymion, IV

6 Good God, I forgot the violets!
Walter Savage Landor (1775–1864) British poet and writer.
Having thrown his cook out of an open window onto the flowerbed below
Irreverent Social History (F. Muir)

7 And I will make thee beds of roses
And a thousand fragrant posies.
Christopher Marlowe (1564–93) English dramatist.
The Passionate Shepherd to his Love

8 Gather the flowers, but spare the buds.
Andrew Marvell (1621–78) English poet.
The Picture of Little T.C. in a Prospect of Flowers

9 'Tis the last rose of summer
Left blooming alone;
All her lovely companions
Are faded and gone.
Thomas Moore (1779–1852) Irish poet.
Irish Melodies, ''Tis the Last Rose'

10 Say it with flowers.
Patrick O'Keefe (1872–1934) US advertising agent.
Slogan for Society of American Florists

11 They are for prima donnas or corpses – I am neither.
Arturo Toscanini (1867–1957) Italian conductor.
Refusing a floral wreath at the end of a performance
The Elephant that Swallowed a Nightingale (C. Galtey)

12 But as we went along there were more and yet more and there at last under the boughs of the trees, we saw that there was a long belt of them along the shore, about the breadth of a country turnpike road. I never saw daffodils so beautiful they grew among the mossy stones about and about them, some rested their heads upon these stones as on pillow for weariness and the rest tossed and reeled and danced and seemed as if they verily laughed with the wind that blew upon them over the lake.
Dorothy Wordsworth (1771–1855) British diarist and sister of William Wordsworth.
The Grasmere Journals, 15 Apr 1802

13 Thou unassuming common-place
Of Nature.
William Wordsworth (1770–1850) British poet.
To the Daisy

14 I wandered lonely as a cloud
That floats on high o'er vales and hills,
When all at once I saw a crowd,
A host, of golden daffodils.
William Wordsworth
I Wandered Lonely as a Cloud

FLYING

See also travel

1 Had I been a man I might have explored the Poles or climbed Mount Everest, but as it was my spirit found outlet in the air. . . .
Amy Johnson (1903–41) British flyer.
Myself When Young (ed. Margot Asquith)

2 I feel about airplanes the way I feel about diets. It seems to me that they are wonderful things for other people to go on.
Jean Kerr (1923–) US dramatist.
The Snake Has All the Lines, 'Mirror, Mirror, on the Wall'

3 There are only two emotions in a plane: boredom and terror.
Orson Welles (1915–85) US film actor.
The Observer, 'Sayings of the Week', 12 May 1985

4 Nor law, nor duty bade me fight,
Nor public men, nor cheering crowds,
A lonely impulse of delight
Drove to this tumult in the clouds;
I balanced all, brought all to mind,
The years to come seemed waste of breath,
A waste of breath the years behind
In balance with this life, this death.
W. B. Yeats (1865–1939) Irish poet.
An Irish Airman Foresees his Death

FOOD

See also etiquette, greed, obesity

1 A meal without flesh is like feeding on grass.
Proverb

2 An apple-pie without some cheese is like a kiss without a squeeze.
Proverb

3 Bread is the staff of life.
Proverb

4 Eat to live and not live to eat.
Proverb

5 The nearer the bone, the sweeter the flesh.
Proverb

6 I always eat peas with honey
I've done it all my life,
They do taste kind of funny,
But it keeps them on the knife.
Anonymous
Peas

7 'Oh, my Friends, be warned by me,
That Breakfast, Dinner, Lunch and Tea
Are all the Human Frame requires . . .'
With that the Wretched Child expires.
Hilaire Belloc (1870–1953) French-born British poet.
Cautionary Tales, 'Henry King'

8 The Chief Defect of Henry King
Was chewing little bits of String.
Hilaire Belloc
Cautionary Tales, 'Henry King'

9 I know what I wanted to ask you;
Is trifle sufficient for sweet?
John Betjeman (1906–84) British poet.
How to get on in Society

10 I'm a man
More dined against than dining.
Maurice Bowra (1898–1971) British scholar.
Summoned by Bells (J. Betjeman)

11 Some hae meat, and canna eat,
And some wad eat that want it,
But we hae meat and we can eat,
And sae the Lord be thankit.
Robert Burns (1759–96) Scottish poet.
The Selkirk Grace

12 The Queen of Hearts, she made some tarts,
All on a summer day:
The Knave of Hearts, he stole those tarts,
And took them quite away!
Lewis Carroll (Charles Lutwidge Dodgson; 1832–98) British writer.
Alice's Adventures in Wonderland, Ch. 11

13 Soup of the evening, beautiful Soup!
Lewis Carroll
Said by the Mock Turtle
Alice's Adventures in Wonderland, Ch. 10

14 The right diet directs sexual energy into the parts that matter.
Barbara Cartland (1902–) British romantic novelist.
Remark, Jan 1981

15 Don't eat too many almonds; they add weight to the breasts
Colette (1873–1954) French novelist.
Gigi

16 Do you *know* what breakfast cereal is made of? It's made of all those little curly wooden shavings you find in pencil sharpeners!
Roald Dahl (1916–) British writer.
Charlie and the Chocolate Factory, Ch. 27

17 Bouillabaisse is only good because cooked by the French, who, if they cared to try, could produce an excellent and nutritious substitute out of cigar stumps and empty matchboxes.
Norman Douglas (1868–1952) British novelist.
Siren Land, 'Rain on the Hills'

18 The winter evening settles down
With smell of steaks in passageways.
T. S. Eliot (1888–1965) US-born British poet and dramatist.
Preludes

19 The way to a man's heart is through his stomach.
Fanny Fern (1811–72) US writer.
Willis Parton

20 Oh! The roast beef of England.
And old England's roast beef.
Henry Fielding (1707–54) British novelist.
The Grub Street Opera, III:3

21 With my little stick of Blackpool rock,
Along the Promenade I stroll.
It may be sticky but I never complain,
It's nice to have a nibble at it now and again.
George Formby (1905–61) British comedian.
With My Little Stick of Blackpool Rock

22 Take your hare when it is cased . . .
Hannah Glasse (18th century) English writer.
Often misquoted as, 'First catch your hare'
The Art of Cookery Made Plain and Easy, Ch. 1

23 The best number for a dinner party is two – myself and a dam' good head waiter.
Nubar Gulbenkian (1896–1972) Turkish oil magnate.
Attrib.

24 But one day, one cold winter's day,
He screamed out, 'Take the soup away!'
Heinrich Hoffman (1809–74) German writer.
Struwwelpeter, 'Augustus'

25 The British hamburger thus symbolised, with savage neatness, the country's failure to provide its ordinary people with food which did anything more for them than sustain life.
Clive James (1939–) Writer and broadcaster, born in Australia.
Falling Towards England, Ch. 17

26 This was a good dinner enough, to be sure; but it was not a dinner to *ask* a man to.
Samuel Johnson (1709–84) British lexicographer.
Life of Johnson (J. Boswell), Vol. I

27 It is as bad as bad can be: it is ill-fed, ill-killed, ill-kept, and ill-drest.
Samuel Johnson
About the roast mutton at an inn
Life of Johnson (J. Boswell), Vol. IV

28 A cucumber should be well sliced, and dressed with pepper and vinegar, and then thrown out, as good for nothing.
Samuel Johnson
Tour to the Hebrides (J. Boswell)

29 I hate a man who swallows it, affecting not to know what he is eating. I suspect his taste in higher matters.
Charles Lamb (1775–1834) British essayist.
Referring to food
Essays of Elia, 'Grace before Meat'

30 Any two meals at a boarding-house are together less than two square meals.
Stephen Leacock (1869–1944) English-born Canadian economist and humorist.
Literary Lapses, 'Boarding-House Geometry'

31 They dined on mince, and slices of quince,
Which they ate with a runcible spoon;
And hand in hand, on the edge of the sand,
They danced by the light of the moon.
Edward Lear (1812–88) British artist and writer.
The Owl and the Pussy-Cat

32 Food is an important part of a balanced diet.
Fran Lebowitz (1950–) US writer.
Metropolitan Life, 'Food for Thought and Vice Versa'

33 This piece of cod passes all understanding.
Edwin Lutyens (1869–1944) British architect.
Comment made in a restaurant
Attrib.

34 It's a very odd thing –
As odd as can be –
That whatever Miss T eats
Turns into Miss T.
Walter De La Mare (1873–1956) British poet.
Miss T

35 Many children are suffering from muesli-belt malnutrition.
Professor Vincent Marks British nutritionist.
Remark, June 1986

36 To eat well in England you should have breakfast three times a day.
W. Somerset Maugham (1874–1965) British novelist.
Attrib.

37 Kissing don't last: cookery do!
George Meredith (1828–1909) British novelist.
The Ordeal of Richard Feverel, Ch. 28

38 One should eat to live, not live to eat.
Molière (Jean Baptiste Poquelin; 1622–73) French dramatist.
L'Avare, III:2

39 Some breakfast food manufacturer hit upon the simple notion of emptying out the leavings of carthorse nosebags, adding a few other things like unconsumed portions of chicken layer's mash, and the sweepings of racing stables, packing the mixture in little bags and selling them in health food shops.
Frank Muir (1920–) British writer and broadcaster.
Upon My Word!

40 An army marches on its stomach.
Napoleon I (Napoleon Bonaparte; 1769–1821) French emperor.
Attrib.

41 I think I could eat one of Bellamy's veal pies.
William Pitt the Younger (1759–1806) British statesman.
Last words
Attrib.

42 The vulgar boil, the learned roast an egg.
Alexander Pope (1688–1744) British poet.
Satires and Epistles of Horace Imitated, Bk II

43 To the old saying that man built the house but woman made of it a 'home' might be added the modern supplement that woman accepted cooking as a chore but man has made of it a recreation.
Emily Post (1873–1960) US writer.
Etiquette, Ch. 34

44 Dinner at the Huntercombes' possessed 'only two dramatic features – the wine was a farce and the food a tragedy'.
Anthony Powell (1905–) British novelist.
A Dance to the Music of Time: The Acceptance World, Ch. 4

45 Great restaurants are, of course, nothing but mouth-brothels. There is no point in going to them if one intends to keep one's belt buckled.
Frederic Raphael (1931–) British author.
The Sunday Times Magazine, 25 Sep 1977

46 The thought of two thousand people crunching celery at the same time horrified me.
George Bernard Shaw (1856–1950) Irish dramatist and critic.
Explaining why he had turned down an invitation to a vegetarian gala dinner
The Greatest Laughs of All Time (G. Lieberman)

47 Yes, cider and tinned salmon are the staple diet of the agricultural classes.
Evelyn Waugh (1903–66) British novelist.
Scoop, Bk. I, Ch. 1

48 I saw him even now going the way of all flesh, that is to say towards the kitchen.
John Webster (1580–1625) English dramatist.
Westward Hoe, II:2

49 You breed babies and you eat chips with everything.
Arnold Wesker (1932–) British dramatist.
Chips with Everything, I:2

50 If I had the choice between smoked salmon and tinned salmon, I'd have it tinned. With vinegar.
Harold Wilson (1916–) British politician and prime minister.
The Observer, 'Sayings of the Week,' 11 Nov 1962

FOOLISHNESS

See also gullibility, ignorance, stupidity, wisdom and foolishness

1 A fool and his money are soon parted.
Proverb

2 A fool at forty is a fool indeed.
Proverb

3 A fool believes everything.
Proverb

4 Better be a fool than a knave.
Proverb

5 Empty vessels make the greatest sound.
Proverb

6 Fools build houses, and wise men buy them.
Proverb

7 Fools live poor to die rich.
Proverb

8 There's no fool like an old fool.
Proverb

9 Give not that which is holy unto the dogs, neither cast ye your pearls before swine, lest they trample them under their feet, and turn again and rend you.
Bible: Matthew
7:6

10 Answer a fool according to his folly, lest he be wise in his own conceit.
Bible: Proverbs
26:5

11 The world is made up for the most part of fools and knaves.
Duke of Buckingham (1628–87) English politician.
To Mr Clifford, on his Humane Reason

12 He's a muddle-headed fool, with frequent lucid intervals.
Miguel de Cervantes (1547–1616) Spanish novelist.
Sancho Panza describing Don Quixote
Don Quixote, Pt. II, Ch. 18

13 The wisest fool in Christendom.
Henri IV (1553–1610) King of France.
Referring to James I of England
Attrib.

14 Mix a little foolishness with your serious plans: it's lovely to be silly at the right moment.
Horace (Quintus Horatius Flaccus; 65–8 BC) Roman poet.
Odes, IV

15 Fools are in a terrible, overwhelming majority, all the wide world over.
Henrik Ibsen (1828–1906) Norwegian dramatist.
An Enemy of the People, IV

16 You cannot fashion a wit out of two half-wits.
Neil Kinnock (1942–) British politician.
The Times, 1983

17 No creature smarts so little as a fool.
Alexander Pope (1688–1744) British poet.
Epistle to Dr. Arbuthnot

18 Lord, what fools these mortals be!
William Shakespeare (1564–1616) English dramatist.
A Midsummer Night's Dream, III:2

19 He was a bold man that first eat an oyster.
Jonathan Swift (1667–1745) Irish-born writer.
Polite conversation, Dialogue 2

FOOTBALL

See also sport and games

1 Professional football is no longer a game. It's a war. And it brings out the same primitive instincts that go back thousands of years.
Malcolm Allison British football manager.
The Observer, 'Sayings of the Week', 14 Mar 1973

2 I do love cricket – it's so very English.
Sarah Bernhardt (Sarah Henriette Rosine Bernard; 1844–1923) French actress.
On seeing a game of football
Nijinsky (R. Buckle)

3 The goal stands up, the keeper
Stands up to keep the goal.
A. E. Housman (1859–1936) British scholar and poet.
A Shropshire Lad, 'Bredon Hill'

4 I loathed the game . . . it was very difficult for me to show courage at it. Football, it seemed to me, is not really played for the pleasure of kicking a ball about, but is a species of fighting.
George Orwell (Eric Blair; 1903–50) British novelist.
Such, Such Were The Joys

5 The streets were full of footballs.
Samuel Pepys (1633–1703) English diarist.
Diary, 2 Jan 1665

6 A man who had missed the last home match of 't 'United' had to enter social life on tiptoe in Bruddersford.
J. B. Priestley (1894–1984) British novelist.
The Good Companions

7 Football isn't a matter of life and death – it's much more important than that.
Bill Shankly (1914–81) British football manager.
Attrib.

8 Footeball . . . causeth fighting, brawling, contention, quarrel picking, murder, homicide and great effusion of bloode, as daily experience teacheth.
Philip Stubbes (fl. 1583–91) English puritan pamphleteer.
Anatomie of Abuses

9 I will not permit thirty men to travel four hundred miles to agitate a bag of wind.
Andrew Dickson White (1832–1918) US educationalist.
Refusing to allow the Cornell American football team to visit Michigan to play a match
The People's Almanac (D. Wallechinsky)

FORCE

See also oppression, power politics, violence

1 Force is not a remedy.
John Bright (1811–89) British radical politician.
Speech, Birmingham, 16 Nov 1880

2 The use of force alone is but *temporary*. It may subdue for a moment; but it does not remove the necessity of subduing again: and a nation is not governed, which is perpetually to be conquered.
Edmund Burke (1729–97) British politician.
Speech on Conciliation with America (House of Commons, 22 Mar 1775)

FORGIVENESS

1 Forgive and forget.
Proverb

2 Let bygones be bygones.
Proverb

3 Come now, and let us reason together, saith the Lord: though your sins be as scarlet, they shall be as white as snow; though they be red like crimson, they shall be as wool.
Bible: Isaiah
1:18

4 Then said Jesus, Father, forgive them; for they know not what they do. And they parted his raiment, and cast lots.
Bible: Luke
23:34

5 Wherefore I say unto thee, Her sins, which are many, are forgiven; for she loved much: but to whom little is forgiven, the same loveth little.
Bible: Luke
7:47

6 Then came Peter to him, and said, Lord, how oft shall my brother sin against me, and I forgive him? till seven times?
Jesus saith unto him, I say not unto thee, Until seven times: but, Until seventy times seven.
Bible: Matthew
18:21–22

7 The cut worm forgives the plough.
William Blake (1757–1827) British poet.
The Marriage of Heaven and Hell, 'Proverbs of Hell'

8 The women pardoned all except her face.
Lord Byron (1788–1824) British poet.
Don Juan, V

9 It is the government that should ask me for a pardon.
Eugene Victor Debs (1855–1926) US trade unionist, socialist, and pacifist.
When released from prison (1921) on the orders of President Harding after being jailed for sedition (1918)
The People's Almanac (D. Wallechinsky)

10 Once a woman has forgiven her man, she must not reheat his sins for breakfast.
Marlene Dietrich (Maria Magdalene von Losch; 1904–) German-born film star.
Marlene Dietrich's ABC

11 God may pardon you, but I never can.
Elizabeth I (1533–1603) Queen of England.
To the Countess of Nottingham
History of England under the House of Tudor (Hume), Vol. II, Ch. 7

12 Only lies and evil come from letting people off...
Iris Murdoch (1919–) Irish-born British novelist.
A Severed Head

13 To err is human, to forgive, divine.
Alexander Pope (1688–1744) British poet.
An Essay on Criticism

14 Beware of the man who does not return your blow: he neither forgives you nor allows you to forgive yourself.
George Bernard Shaw (1856–1950) Irish dramatist and critic.
Man and Superman, 'Maxims for Revolutionists'

15 The stupid neither forgive nor forget; the naive forgive and forget; the wise forgive but do not forget.
Thomas Szasz (1920–) US psychiatrist.
The Second Sin

16 I bear no ill-will against those responsible for this. That sort of talk will not bring her back to life. I know there has to be a plan even though we might not understand it. God is good and we shall meet again.
Gordon Wilson Retired businessman.
Speaking of the murder of his daughter, Marie Wilson, in an IRA bombing at the Enniskillen Remembrance Day service, 8 Nov 1987

FRANCE

See also Europe, French Revolution, Paris

1 All Gaul is divided into three parts.
Julius Caesar (100–44 BC) Roman general and statesman.
De Bello Gallico, Vol. I, Ch. 1

2 France was a long despotism tempered by epigrams.
Thomas Carlyle (1795–1881) Scottish historian and essayist.
History of the French Revolution, Pt. I, Bk. I, Ch. 1

3 They are short, blue-vested people who carry their own onions when cycling abroad, and have a yard which is 3.37 inches longer than other people's.
Alan Coren (1938–) British humorist and writer.
The Sanity Inspector, 'All You Need to Know about Europe'

4 There's always something fishy about the French.
Noël Coward (1899–1973) British dramatist.
Conversation Piece, I:6

5 Bouillabaisse is only good because cooked by the French, who, if they cared to try, could produce an excellent and nutritious substitute out of cigar stumps and empty matchboxes.
Norman Douglas (1868–1952) British novelist.
Siren Land, 'Rain on the Hills'

6 The French will only be united under the threat of danger. Nobody can simply bring together a country that has 265 kinds of cheese.
Charles De Gaulle (1890–1970) French general and statesman.
Speech, 1951

7 I hate the French because they are all slaves, and wear wooden shoes.
Oliver Goldsmith (1728–74) Irish-born British writer.
Essays, 'Distresses of a Common Soldier'

8 The best thing I know between France and England is – the sea.
Douglas William Jerrold (1803–57) British dramatist.
Wit and Opinions of Douglas Jerrold, 'The Anglo-French Alliance'

9 A Frenchman must be always talking, whether he knows anything of the matter or not; an Englishman is content to say nothing, when he has nothing to say.
Samuel Johnson (1709–84) British lexicographer.
Life of Johnson (J. Boswell), Vol. IV

10 *Allons, enfants, de la patrie,*
Le jour de gloire est arrivé.
Come, children of our native land,
The day of glory has arrived.
Rouget de Lisle (Claude Joseph Rouget de Lisle; 1760–1836) French military engineer and composer.
La Marseillaise (French national anthem)

11 Yet, who can help loving the land that has taught us
Six hundred and eighty-five ways to dress eggs?
Thomas Moore (1779–1852) Irish poet.
The Fudge Family in Paris

12 There's something Vichy about the French.
Ivor Novello (David Ivor Davies; 1893–1951) British actor, composer, and dramatist.
Ambrosia and Small Beer (Edward Marsh), Ch. 4

13 A mademoiselle from Armenteers,
She hasn't been kissed for forty years,
Hinky, dinky, par-lee-voo.
Edward Rowland (20th century) British songwriter.
Armentières was completely destroyed (1918) in World War I
Mademoiselle from Armentières (song)

14 They are a loyal, a gallant, a generous, an ingenious, and good-temper'd people as is under heaven – if they have a fault, they are too *serious*.

Laurence Sterne (1713–68) Irish-born British writer.
A Sentimental Journey, 'The Character. Versailles'

15 I do not dislike the French from the vulgar antipathy between neighbouring nations, but for their insolent and unfounded airs of superiority.

Horace Walpole (1717–97) British writer.
Letter to Hannah More, 14 Oct 1787

16 France is a country where the money falls apart in your hands and you can't tear the toilet paper.

Billy Wilder (Samuel Wilder; 1906–) Austrian-born US film director.
Attrib.

FRANKNESS

See also honesty, sincerity, truth

1 But of all plagues, good Heaven, thy wrath can send,
Save me, oh, save me, from the candid friend.

George Canning (1770–1827) British statesman.
New Morality

2 I have two very cogent reasons for not printing any list of subscribers; – one, that I have lost all the names, – the other, that I have spent all the money.

Samuel Johnson (1709–84) British lexicographer.
Referring to subscribers to his *Dictionary of the English Language*
Life of Johnson (J. Boswell), Vol. IV

3 The great consolation in life is to say what one thinks.

Voltaire (François-Marie Arouet; 1694–1778) French writer.
Letter, 1765

4 On an occasion of this kind it becomes more than a moral duty to speak one's mind. It becomes a pleasure.

Oscar Wilde (1854–1900) Irish-born British dramatist.
The Importance of Being Earnest, II

FREEDOM

See also human rights, imprisonment

1 I'll have a fling.

Francis Beaumont (1584–1616) English dramatist.
Rule a Wife and have a Wife, III:5

2 My policy is to be able to take a ticket at Victoria Station and go anywhere I damn well please.

Ernest Bevin (1881–1951) British trade-union leader and politician.
The Spectator, 20 Apr 1951

3 Conscience, I say, not thine own, but of the other: for why is my liberty judged of another man's conscience?

Bible: I Corinthians
10:29

4 So free we seem, so fettered fast we are!

Robert Browning (1812–89) British poet.
Andrea del Sarto

5 Liberty, too, must be limited in order to be possessed.

Edmund Burke (1729–97) British politician.
Letter to the Sheriffs of Bristol, 1777

6 Hereditary bondsmen! know ye not
Who would be free themselves must strike the blow?

Lord Byron (1788–1824) British poet.
Childe Harold's Pilgrimage, I

7 England may as well dam up the waters from the Nile with bulrushes as to fetter the step of Freedom, more proud and firm in this youthful land.

Lydia M. Child (1802–80) US abolitionist campaigner.
The Rebels, Ch. 4

8 But what is Freedom? Rightly understood,
A universal licence to be good.

Hartley Coleridge (1796–1849) British poet.
Liberty

9 The condition upon which God hath given liberty to man is eternal vigilance.

John Philpot Curran (1750–1817) Irish judge.
Speech on the Right of Election of Lord Mayor of Dublin, 10 July 1790

10 Yes, 'n' how many years can some people exist
Before they're allowed to be free?
Yes, 'n' how many times can a man turn his head,
Pretending he just doesn't see?
The answer, my friend, is blowin' in the wind.

Bob Dylan (Robert Allen Zimmerman; 1941–) US popular singer.
Blowin' in the Wind

11 My people and I have come to an agreement which satisfies us both. They are to say what they please, and I am to do what I please.

Frederick the Great (1712–86) King of Prussia.
Attrib.

12 This is Liberty-Hall, gentlemen.

Oliver Goldsmith (1728–74) Irish-born British writer.
She Stoops to Conquer, II

13 *Laissez faire, laissez passer.*
Liberty of action, liberty of movement.

Jean Claude Vincent de Gournay (1712–59) French economist.
Speech, Sept 1758

14 Power is so apt to be insolent and Liberty to be saucy, that they are seldom upon good Terms.

Lord Halifax (1633–95) English statesman.
Political, Moral, and Miscellaneous Thoughts and Reflections

15 The love of liberty is the love of others; the love of power is the love of ourselves.
William Hazlitt (1778–1830) British essayist.
The Times, 1819

16 I know not what course others may take; but as for me, give me liberty or give me death.
Patrick Henry (1736–99) US statesman.
Speech, Virginia Convention, 23 Mar 1775

17 I struck the board, and cried, 'No more;
I will abroad.'
What, shall I ever sigh and pine?
My lines and life are free; free as the road,
Loose as the wind, as large as store.
George Herbert (1593–1633) English poet.
The Collar

18 'Painters and poets alike have always had licence to dare anything.' We know that, and we both claim and allow to others in their turn this indulgence.
Horace (Quintus Horatius Flaccus; 65–8 BC) Roman poet.
Ars Poetica

19 *Nullius addictus iurare in verba magistri,*
Quo me cumque rapit tempestas, deferor hospes.
Not bound to swear allegiance to any master, wherever the wind takes me I travel as a visitor.
Horace
Nullius in verba is the motto of the Royal Society
Epistles, I

20 A man should never put on his best trousers when he goes out to battle for freedom and truth.
Henrik Ibsen (1828–1906) Norwegian dramatist.
An Enemy of the People, V

21 The tree of liberty must be refreshed from time to time with the blood of patriots and tyrants. It is its natural manure.
Thomas Jefferson (1743–1826) US statesman.
Letter to W. S. Smith, 13 Nov 1787

22 I have got no further than this: Every man has a right to utter what he thinks truth, and every other man has a right to knock him down for it. Martyrdom is the test.
Samuel Johnson (1709–84) British lexicographer.
Life of Johnson (J. Boswell), Vol. IV

23 The Liberty of the press is the *Palladium* of all the civil, political and religious rights of an Englishman.
Junius An unidentified writer of letters (1769–72) to the *London Public Advertiser*.
Letters, 'Dedication'

24 It's often safer to be in chains than to be free.
Franz Kafka (1883–1924) Czech novelist.
The Trial, Ch. 8

25 Freedom's just another word for nothing left to lose.
Kris Kristofferson (1936–) US film actor and folk musician.
Me and Bobby McGee

26 It is true that liberty is precious – so precious that it must be rationed.
Lenin (Vladimir Ilich Ulyanov; 1870–1924) Russian revolutionary leader.
Attrib.

27 I intend no modification of my oft-expressed personal wish that all men everywhere could be free.
Abraham Lincoln (1809–65) US statesman.
Letter to Horace Greeley, 22 Aug 1862

28 Those who deny freedom to others, deserve it not for themselves.
Abraham Lincoln
Speech, 19 May 1856

29 Many politicians of our time are in the habit of laying it down as a self-evident proposition, that no people ought to be free till they are fit to use their freedom. The maxim is worthy of the fool in the old story, who resolved not to go into the water till he had learnt to swim. If men are to wait for liberty till they become wise and good in slavery, they may indeed wait for ever.
Lord Macaulay (1800–59) British historian.
Literary Essays Contributed to the 'Edinburgh Review', 'Milton',

30 It would be better that England should be free than that England should be compulsorily sober.
William Connor Magee (1821–91) British clergyman.
Speech on the Intoxicating Liquor Bill, House of Lords, 2 May 1872

31 I cannot and will not give any undertaking at a time when I, and you, the people, are not free. Your freedom and mine cannot be separated.
Nelson Mandela (1918–) South African lawyer and politician.
Message read by his daughter to a rally in Soweto, 10 Feb 1985

32 Letting a hundred flowers blossom and a hundred schools of thought contend is the policy for promoting the progress of the arts and the sciences.
Mao Tse-Tung (1893–1976) Chinese communist leader.
Quotations from Chairman Mao Tse-Tung, Ch. 32

33 The liberty of the individual must be thus far limited; he must not make himself a nuisance to other people.
John Stuart Mill (1806–73) British philosopher.
On Liberty, Ch. 3

34 None can love freedom heartily, but good men; the rest love not freedom, but licence.
John Milton (1608–74) English poet.
Tenure of Kings and Magistrates

35 Liberty is the right to do everything which the laws allow.
Baron de Montesquieu (1689–1755) French writer.
L'Esprit des lois

36 Before the organization of the Blackshirt movement free speech did not exist in this country.
Oswald Mosley (1896–1980) British politician.
Selections from the *New Statesman, This England*, Pt. I

37 My government will protect all liberties but one – the liberty to do away with other liberties.
Gustavo Diaz Ordaz (1911–   ) President of Mexico (1964–1970).
Inaugural speech

38 Freedom is the right to tell people what they do not want to hear.
George Orwell (Eric Blair; 1903–50) British novelist.
The Road to Wigan Pier

39 I sometimes think that the price of liberty is not so much eternal vigilance as eternal dirt.
George Orwell
The Road to Wigan Pier, Ch. 4

40 We must plan for freedom, and not only for security, if for no other reason than that only freedom can make security secure.
Karl Popper (1902–   ) Austrian-born British philosopher.
The Open Society and Its Enemies

41 Now: heaven knows, anything goes.
Cole Porter (1893–1964) US songwriter.
Anything Goes, title song

42 *Laissez faire, laissez passer.*
Let it be, let it pass.
François Quesnay (1694–1774) French economist.
Attrib.

43 In their rules there was only one clause: Do what you will.
François Rabelais (1483–1553) French satirist.
Referring to the fictional Abbey of Thélème
Gargantua, Bk. I, Ch. 57

44 *'O liberté! O liberté! Que de crimes on commet en ton nom!'*
Oh liberty! Oh liberty! What crimes are committed in thy name!
Madame Roland (1754–93) French revolutionary.
Said as she mounted the steps of the guillotine at her execution
Attrib.

45 Man was born free and everywhere he is in chains.
Jean Jacques Rousseau (1712–78) French philosopher.
Du contrat social, Ch. 1

46 No human being, however great, or powerful, was ever so free as a fish.
John Ruskin (1819–1900) British art critic and writer.
The Two Paths, Lecture V

47 Man is condemned to be free.
Jean-Paul Sartre (1905–80) French writer.
Existentialism is a Humanism

48 You took my freedom away a long time ago and you can't give it back because you haven't got it yourself.
Alexander Solzhenitsyn (1918–   ) Soviet novelist.
The First Circle, Ch. 17

49 My definition of a free society is a society where it is safe to be unpopular.
Adlai Stevenson (1900–65) US statesman.
Speech, Detroit, Oct. 1952

50 It is by the goodness of God that in our country we have those three unspeakably precious things: freedom of speech, freedom of conscience, and the prudence never to practise either of them.
Mark Twain (Samuel Langhorne Clemens; 1835–1910) US writer.
Following the Equator, heading of Ch. 20

51 I disapprove of what you say, but I will defend to the death your right to say it.
Voltaire (François-Marie Arouet; 1694–1778) French writer.
Attrib.

52 Me this unchartered freedom tires;
I feel the weight of chance-desires:
My hopes no more must change their name,
I long for a repose that ever is the same.
William Wordsworth (1770–1850) British poet.
Ode to Duty

53 We must be free or die, who speak the tongue
That Shakespeare spake; the faith and morals hold
Which Milton held.
William Wordsworth
Sonnets, 'It is not to be thought of'

54 Two voices are there; one is of the sea,
One of the mountains; each a mighty voice:
In both from age to age thou didst rejoice,
They were thy chosen music, Liberty!
William Wordsworth
Sonnets, 'Two voices are there'

FRENCH REVOLUTION

See also France, revolution

1 It was the best of times, it was the worst of times, it was the age of wisdom, it was the age of foolishness, it was the epoch of belief, it was the epoch of incredulity, it was the season of Light, it was the season of Darkness, it was the spring of hope, it was the winter of despair, we had everything before us, we had nothing before us, we

were all going direct to Heaven, we were all going direct the other way.
Charles Dickens (1812–70) British novelist.
The opening words of the book
A Tale of Two Cities, Bk. I, Ch. 1

2 How much the greatest event it is that ever happened in the world! and how much the best!
Charles James Fox (1749–1806) British Whig politician.
Referring to the fall of the Bastille, 14 July 1789
Letter to Fitzpatrick, 30 July 1789

3 Bliss was it in that dawn to be alive,
But to be young was very heaven!
William Wordsworth (1770–1850) British poet.
The Prelude, XI

4 That which sets
. . . The budding rose above the rose full blown.
William Wordsworth
The Prelude, XI

5 Not in Utopia, – subterranean fields, –
Or some secreted island, Heaven knows where!
But in the very world, which is the world
Of all of us, – the place where, in the end,
We find our happiness, or not at all!
William Wordsworth
The Prelude, XI

FRIENDS

See also enemies, friendship

1 Books and friends should be few but good.
Proverb

2 Forsake not an old friend; for the new is not comparable to him: a new friend is as new wine; when it is old, thou shalt drink it with pleasure.
Bible: Ecclesiasticus
9:10

3 Cost his enemies a long repentance,
And made him a good friend, but bad acquaintance.
Lord Byron (1788–1824) British poet.
Don Juan, III

4 Tell me what company thou keepest, and I'll tell thee what thou art.
Miguel de Cervantes (1547–1616) Spanish novelist.
Don Quixote, Pt. II, Ch. 23

5 Have no friends not equal to yourself.
Confucius (K'ung Fu-tzu; 551–479 BC) Chinese philosopher.
Analects

6 Fate chooses your relations, you choose your friends.
Jacques Delille (1738–1813) French abbé and poet.
Malheur et pitié, I

7 A Friend may well be reckoned the masterpiece of Nature.
Ralph Waldo Emerson (1803–82) US poet and essayist.
Essays, 'Friendship'

8 *Changez vos amis.*
Change your friends.
Charles De Gaulle (1890–1970) French general and statesman.
Replying to the complaint by Jacques Soustelle that he was being attacked by his own friends
Attrib.

9 If a man does not make new acquaintance as he advances through life, he will soon find himself left alone. A man, Sir, should keep his friendship in constant repair.
Samuel Johnson (1709–84) British lexicographer.
Life of Johnson (J. Boswell), Vol. I

10 I get by with a little help from my friends.
John Lennon (1940–80) British rock musician.
With a Little Help from My Friends (with Paul McCartney)

11 He's an oul' butty o' mine – oh, he's a darlin' man, a daarlin' man.
Sean O'Casey (1884–1964) Irish dramatist.
Juno and the Paycock, I

12 It is more shameful to distrust one's friends than to be deceived by them.
Duc de la Rochefoucauld (1613–80) French writer.
Maximes, 84

13 A friend should bear his friend's infirmities,
But Brutus makes mine greater than they are.
William Shakespeare (1564–1616) English dramatist.
Julius Caesar, IV:3

14 If it is abuse – why one is always sure to hear of it from one damned good-natured friend or other!
Richard Brinsley Sheridan (1751–1816) British dramatist.
The Critic, I

15 Associate yourself with men of good quality if you esteem your own reputation; for 'tis better to be alone than in bad company.
George Washington (1732–99) US statesman.
Rules of Civility

FRIENDSHIP

See also friends, love and friendship

1 A friend in need is a friend indeed.
Proverb

2 A good friend is my nearest relation.
Proverb

3 A hedge between keeps friendship green.
Proverb

4 God defend me from my friends; from my enemies I can defend myself.
Proverb

5 Love is blind; friendship closes its eyes.
Proverb

6 The best of friends must part.
Proverb

7 There is no such thing as a free lunch.
Anonymous
Often attributed to Milton Friedman

8 Two are better than one; because they have a good reward for their labour.
For if they fall, the one will lift up his fellow: but woe to him that is alone when he falleth; for he hath not another to help him up.
Bible: Ecclesiastes
4:9–10

9 Saul and Jonathan were lovely and pleasant in their lives, and in their death they were not divided: they were swifter than eagles, they were stronger than lions.
Bible: II Samuel
1:23–24

10 I've noticed your hostility towards him . . . I ought to have guessed you were friends.
Malcolm Bradbury (1932–) British academic and novelist.
The History Man, Ch. 7

11 I don't trust him. We're friends.
Bertolt Brecht (1898–1956) German dramatist.
Mother Courage, III

12 Should auld acquaintance be forgot,
And never brought to min'?
Robert Burns (1759–96) Scottish poet.
Auld Lang Syne

13 We'll tak a cup o' kindness yet,
For auld lang syne.
Robert Burns
Auld Lang Syne

14 Two may talk together under the same roof for many years, yet never really meet; and two others at first speech are old friends.
Mary Catherwood (1847–1901) US writer.
Mackinac and Lake Stories, 'Marianson'

15 A woman can become a man's friend only in the following stages – first an acquaintance, next a mistress, and only then a friend.
Anton Chekhov (1860–1904) Russian dramatist.
Uncle Vanya, II

16 There is nothing in the world I wouldn't do for Hope, and there is nothing he wouldn't do for me . . . We spend our lives doing nothing for each other.
Bing Crosby (Harry Lillis; 1904–77) US singer.
Referring to Bob Hope
The Observer, 'Sayings of the Week', 7 May 1950

17 It is not so much our friends' help that helps

us as the confident knowledge that they will help us.
Epicurus (341–270 BC) Greek philosopher.

18 These are called the pious frauds of friendship.
Henry Fielding (1707–54) British novelist.
Amelia, Bk. III, Ch. 4

19 Always, Sir, set a high value on spontaneous kindness. He whose inclination prompts him to cultivate your friendship of his own accord, will love you more than one whom you have been at pains to attach to you.
Samuel Johnson (1709–84) British lexicographer.
Life of Johnson (J. Boswell), Vol. IV

20 Sir, I look upon every day to be lost, in which I do not make a new acquaintance.
Samuel Johnson
Life of Johnson (J. Boswell), Vol. IV

21 Greater love than this, he said, no man hath that a man lay down his wife for a friend. Go thou and do likewise. Thus, or words to that effect, saith Zarathustra, sometime regius professor of French letters to the University of Oxtail.
James Joyce (1882–1941) Irish novelist.
Ulysses

22 Friendship is unnecessary, like philosophy, like art . . . . It has no survival value; rather it is one of those things that give value to survival.
C. S. Lewis (1898–1963) British academic and writer.
The Four Loves, Friendship

23 That the world will never be quite – what a cliché – the same again
Is what we only learn by the event
When a friend dies out on us and is not there
To share the periphery of a remembered scent.
Louis MacNiece (1907–63) Irish-born British poet.
Tam Cari Capitis

24 Two buttocks of one bum.
T. Sturge Moore (1870–1944) British poet and illustrator.
Referring to Hilaire Belloc and G. K. Chesterton

25 A true bond of friendship is usually only possible between people of roughly equal status. This equality is demonstrated in many indirect ways, but it is reinforced in face-to-face encounters by a matching of the posture of relaxation or alertness.
Desmond Morris (1928–) British biologist.
Manwatching, 'Postural Echo'

26 To like and dislike the same things, that is indeed true friendship.
Sallust (Gaius Sallustius Crispus; c. 86–c. 34 BC) Roman historian and politician.
Bellum Catilinae

27 I might give my life for my friend, but he had better not ask me to do up a parcel.
Logan Pearsall Smith (1865–1946) US writer.
Trivia

FUNERALS

See also death

1 Most of the people who will walk after me will be children, so make the beat keep time with short steps.
Hans Christian Andersen (1805–75) Danish writer.
Planning the music for his funeral
Hans Christian Andersen (R. Godden)

2 This is the last time that I will take part as an amateur.
Daniel-François-Esprit Auber (1782–1871) French composer.
Said at a funeral
Das Buch des Lachens (W. Scholz)

3 When we attend the funerals of our friends we grieve for them, but when we go to those of other people it is chiefly our own deaths that we mourn for.
Gerald Brenan (Edward Fitzgerald Brenan; 1894–1987) British writer.
Thoughts in a Dry Season, 'Death'

4 'If you don't go to other men's funerals,' he told Father stiffly, 'they won't go to yours.'
Clarence Shepard Day (1874–1935) US writer.
Life With Father, 'Father plans'

5 I bet you a hundred bucks he ain't in here.
Charles Bancroft Dillingham (1868–1934) US theatrical manager.
Referring to the escapologist Harry Houdini; said at his funeral, while carrying his coffin
Attrib.

6 When I die I want to decompose in a barrel of porter and have it served in all the pubs in Dublin.
J. P. Donleavy (1926–) US novelist.
The Ginger Man

7 Why should I go? She won't be there.
Arthur Miller (1915–) US dramatist.
When asked if he would attend Marilyn Monroe's funeral
Attrib.

8 It proves what they say, give the public what they want to see and they'll come out for it.
Red Skelton (Richard Bernard Skelton; 1913–) US actor and comedian.
Said while attending the funeral in 1958 of Hollywood producer Harry Cohn. It has also been attributed to Samuel Goldwyn while attending Louis B. Mayer's funeral in 1957

9 How Henry would have loved it!
Ellen Terry (1847–1928) British actress.
Referring to Sir Henry Irving's funeral
Yesterdays (Robert Hitchens)

10 Not a drum was heard, not a funeral note,
As his corse to the rampart we hurried.
Charles Wolfe (1791–1823) Irish poet.
The Burial of Sir John Moore at Corunna, I

11 We carved not a line, and we raised not a stone –
But we left him alone with his glory.
Charles Wolfe
The Burial of Sir John Moore at Corunna, VIII

FUTILITY

See also purpose

1 Why buy a cow when milk is so cheap?
Proverb

2 Why keep a dog and bark yourself?
Proverb

3 You can't get blood out of a stone.
Proverb

4 Don't curse the darkness – light a candle.
Chinese Proverb

5 Mock on, mock on, Voltaire, Rousseau;
Mock on, mock on; 'tis all in vain!
You throw the sand against the wind,
And the wind blows it back again.
William Blake (1757–1827) British poet.
Mock on, mock on, Voltaire, Rousseau

6 It's but little good you'll do a-watering the last year's crop.
George Eliot (Mary Ann Evans; 1819–80) British novelist.
Adam Bede

7 He is very fond of making things which he does not want, and then giving them to people who have no use for them.
Anthony Hope (Sir Anthony Hope Hawkins; 1863–1933) British novelist.
The Dolly Dialogues

8 He's a real Nowhere Man,
Sitting in his Nowhere Land,
Making all his nowhere plans for nobody.
Doesn't have a point of view,
Knows not where he's going to,
Isn't he a bit like you and me?
John Lennon (1940–80) British rock musician.
Nowhere Man (with Paul McCartney)

9 'Tis not necessary to light a candle to the sun.
Algernon Sidney (1622–83) English statesman.
Discourses concerning Government, Ch. 2

10 People talking without speaking,
People listening without hearing,
People writing songs that voices never shared.
Paul Simon (1942–) US singer.
Sound of Silence

11 All dressed up, with nowhere to go.
William Allen White (1868–1944) US writer.
Referring to the Progressive Party, after Theodore Roosevelt's withdrawal from the 1916 US Presidential election

FUTURE

See also past, present, promises, prophecy, time

1 Years hence, perhaps, may dawn an age,
More fortunate, alas! than we,
Which without hardness will be sage,
And gay without frivolity.
Matthew Arnold (1822–88) British poet and critic.
The Grande Chartreuse

2 I have a vision of the future, chum.
The workers' flats in fields of soya beans
Tower up like silver pencils.
John Betjeman (1906–84) British poet.

3 Boast not thyself of tomorrow; for thou
knowest not what a day may bring forth.
Bible: Proverbs
27:1

4 *Future*, n That period of time in which our
affairs prosper, our friends are true and our
happiness is assured.
Ambrose Bierce (1842–?1914) US writer and journalist.
The Devil's Dictionary

5 Not a future. At least not in Europe.
America's different, of course, but America's
really only a kind of Russia. You've no idea
how pleasant it is not to have any future. It's
like having a totally efficient contraceptive.
Anthony Burgess (John Burgess Wilson; 1917–)
British novelist.
Honey for the Bears, Pt. II, Ch. 6

6 I never think of the future. It comes soon
enough.
Albert Einstein (1879–1955) German-born US physicist.
Interview, 1930

7 I have seen the future and it works.
Lincoln Steffens (1866–1936) US journalist.
Speaking to Bernard Baruch after visiting the Soviet Union,
1919
Autobiography, Ch. 18

8 The future is made of the same stuff as the
present.
Simone Weil (1909–43) French philosopher.
On Science, Necessity, and the Love of God (ed. Richard Rees),
'Some Thoughts on the Love of God'

G

GARDENS

See also flowers

1 Mary, Mary, quite contrary,
How does your garden grow?
With silver bells and cockle shells,
And pretty maids all in a row.
Anonymous
Tommy Thumb's Pretty Song Book

2 God Almighty first planted a garden. And
indeed it is the purest of human pleasures.
Francis Bacon (1561–1626) English philosopher.
Essays, 'Of Gardens'

3 But there went up a mist from the earth, and
watered the whole face of the ground.
And the Lord God formed man of the dust of
the ground, and breathed into his nostrils the
breath of life; and man became a living soul.
And the Lord God planted a garden eastward
in Eden; and there he put the man whom he
had formed.
And out of the ground made the Lord God to
grow every tree that is pleasant to the sight,
and good for food; the tree of life also in the
midst of the garden, and the tree of knowledge of good and evil.
And a river went out of Eden to water the
garden.
Bible: Genesis
2:6–10

4 A garden is a lovesome thing, God wot!
Thomas Edward Brown (1830–97) British poet.
My Garden

5 To get the best results you must talk to your
vegetables.
Charles, Prince of Wales (1948–) Eldest son of
Elizabeth II.
The Observer, 'Sayings of the Week', 28 Sept 1986

6 God the first garden made, and the first city
Cain.
Abraham Cowley (1618–67) English poet.
The Garden

7 The kiss of sun for pardon,
The song of the birds for mirth –
One is nearer God's Heart in a garden
Than anywhere else on earth.
Dorothy Gurney (1858–1932) British poet.
The Lord God Planted a Garden

8 Oh, Adam was a gardener, and God who
made him sees
That half a proper gardener's work is done up-
on his knees,
So when your work is finished, you can wash
your hands and pray
For the Glory of the Garden, that it may not
pass away!
Rudyard Kipling (1865–1936) Indian-born British writer.
The Glory of the Garden

9 A little thin, flowery border, round, neat, not
gaudy.
Charles Lamb (1775–1834) British essayist.
Letter to Wordsworth, June 1806

10 I have a garden of my own,
But so with roses overgrown,
And lilies, that you would it guess

To be a little wilderness.
Andrew Marvell (1621–78) English poet.
The Nymph Complaining for the Death of her Fawn

GENERALIZATIONS

See also classification

1 To generalize is to be an idiot.
William Blake (1757–1827) British poet.
Life of Blake (Gilchrist)

2 All generalizations are dangerous, even this one.
Alexandre Dumas, fils (1824–95) French writer.
Attrib.

3 Any general statement is like a cheque drawn on a bank. Its value depends on what is there to meet it.
Ezra Pound (1885–1972) US poet.
ABC of Reading, Ch. 2

GENEROSITY

See also charity, gifts, kindness, parasites

1 A bit of fragrance always clings to the hand that gives you roses.
Chinese Proverb

2 Every man according as he purposeth in his heart, so let him give; not grudgingly, or of necessity: for God loveth a cheerful giver.
Bible: II Corinthians
9:7

3 Heal the sick, cleanse the lepers, raise the dead, cast out devils: freely ye have received, freely give.
Bible: Matthew
10:8

4 Experience was to be taken as showing that one might get a five-pound note as one got a light for a cigarette; but one had to check the friendly impulse to ask for it in the same way.
Henry James (1843–1916) US novelist.
The Awkward Age

5 In the first place, I have only five guineas in my pocket; and in the second, they are very much at your service.
Lord Peterborough (1658–1735) English military and naval commander.
Persuading an angry mob that he was not the Duke of Marlborough, notorious for his meanness
Dictionary of National Biography

GENIUS

See also talent, talent and genius

1 Genius is an infinite capacity for taking pains.
Proverb

2 Genius (which means transcendent capacity of taking trouble, first of all).
Thomas Carlyle (1795–1881) Scottish historian and essayist.
Frederick the Great, Vol. IV, Ch. 3

3 I'm going to live forever. Geniuses don't die.
Salvador Dali (1904–89) Spanish painter.
Remark, July 1986

4 Great Wits are sure to Madness near alli'd
And thin Partitions do their Bounds divide.
John Dryden (1631–1700) British poet and dramatist.
Absalom and Achitophel, I

5 Genius is one per cent inspiration and ninety-nine per cent perspiration.
Thomas Edison (1847–1931) US inventor.
Attrib.

6 True genius walks along a line, and, perhaps, our greatest pleasure is in seeing it so often near falling, without being ever actually down.
Oliver Goldsmith (1728–74) Irish-born British writer.
The Bee, 'The Characteristics of Greatness'

7 The true genius is a mind of large general powers, accidentally determined to some particular direction.
Samuel Johnson (1709–84) British lexicographer.
Lives of the English Poets, 'Cowley'

8 A genius! For thirty-seven years I've practiced fourteen hours a day, and now they call me a genius!
Pablo Sarasate (1844–1908) Spanish violinist and composer.
On being hailed as a genius by a critic
Attrib.

9 When a true genius appears in the world, you may know him by this sign, that the dunces are all in confederacy against him.
Jonathan Swift (1667–1745) Irish-born Anglican priest and writer.
Thoughts on Various Subjects

GERMANY

See also Europe, Hitler, Nazism, World War II

1 Hamelin Town's in Brunswick,
By famous Hanover city;
The river Weser, deep and wide,
Washes its wall on the southern side;
A pleasanter spot you never spied.
Robert Browning (1812–89) British poet.
The Pied Piper of Hamelin

2 Don't let's be beastly to the Germans.
Noël Coward (1899–1973) British dramatist.
Title of song

3 *Deutschland, Deutschland über alles.*
Germany, Germany before all else.
Heinrich Hoffmann von Fallersleben (1798–1876) German poet.
German national anthem

4 Germany will be either a world power or will not be at all.
Adolf Hitler (1889–1945) German dictator.
Mein Kampf, Ch. 14

5 How appallingly thorough these Germans always managed to be, how emphatic! In sex no less than in war – in scholarship, in science. Diving deeper than anyone else and coming up muddier.
Aldous Huxley (1894–1964) British novelist.

6 All free men, wherever they may live, are citizens of Berlin. And therefore, as a free man, I take pride in the words *Ich bin ein Berliner.*
John Fitzgerald Kennedy (1917–63) US statesman.
Speech, City Hall, West Berlin, 26 June 1963

7 America . . . is the prize amateur nation of the world. Germany is the prize professional nation.
Woodrow Wilson (1856–1925) US statesman.
Speech, Aug 1917
Mr Wilson's War (John Dos Passos), Pt. III, Ch. 13

GIFTS

See also generosity, materialism

1 Every good gift and every perfect gift is from above, and cometh down from the Father of lights, with whom is no variableness, neither shadow of turning.
Bible: James
1:17

2 Heal the sick, cleanse the lepers, raise the dead, cast out devils: freely ye have received, freely give.
Bible: Matthew
10:8

3 'They gave it me,' Humpty Dumpty continued thoughtfully, . . . 'for an un-birthday present.'
Lewis Carroll (Charles Lutwidge Dodgson; 1832–98) British writer.
Through the Looking-Glass, Ch. 6

4 The manner of giving is worth more than the gift.
Pierre Corneille (1606–84) French dramatist.
Le Menteur, I:1

5 If one doesn't get birthday presents it can remobilize very painfully the persecutory anxiety which usually follows birth.
Henry Reed (1914–86) British poet and dramatist.
The Primal Scene, as it were

GLORY

1 Fools! For I also had my hour;
One far fierce hour and sweet;
There was a shout about my ears,
And palms before my feet.
G. K. Chesterton (1874–1936) British writer.
The Donkey

2 May God deny you peace but give you glory!
Miguel de Unamuno y Jugo (1864–1936) Spanish writer.
Closing words
The Tragic Sense of Life

3 *Sic transit gloria mundi.*
Thus the glory of the world passes away.
Thomas à Kempis (Thomas Hemmerken; c. 1380–1471) German monk.
The Imitation of Christ, I

4 Wi' a hundred pipers an' a', an' a'.
Carolina Nairne (1766–1845) Scottish songwriter.
A romantic glorification of the 1745 Jacobite Rebellion
The Hundred Pipers

5 'Hurrah! hurrah! we bring the Jubilee!
Hurrah! hurrah! the flag that makes you free!'
So we sang the chorus from Atlanta to the sea
As we were marching through Georgia.
Henry Clay Work (1832–84) US songwriter.
Commemorating the march (Nov–Dec 1864) by a Union army under General Sherman through Confederate Georgia
Marching Through Georgia

GOD

See also atheism, creation, faith, prayer, religion

1 God be in my head,
And in my understanding;
God be in my eyes,
And in my looking;
God be in my mouth,
And in my speaking;
God be in my heart,
And in my thinking;
God be at my end,
And at my departing.
Anonymous
Sarum Missal

2 Every man thinks God is on his side. The rich and powerful know that he is.
Jean Anouilh (1910–87) French dramatist.
The Lark

3 It were better to have no opinion of God at all, than such an opinion as is unworthy of him.
Francis Bacon (1561–1626) English philosopher.
Essays, 'Of Superstition'

4 Then Peter opened his mouth, and said, Of a truth I perceive that God is no respecter of persons.
Bible: Acts
10:34

5 For in him we live, and move, and have our being; as certain also of your own poets have said, For we are also his offspring.
Bible: Acts
17:28

6 Seek him that maketh the seven stars and Orion, and turneth the shadow of death into the morning, and maketh the day dark with

night: that calleth for the waters of the sea, and poureth them out upon the face of the earth: The Lord is his name.
Bible: Amos
5:8

7 And he changeth the times and the seasons: he removeth kings, and setteth up kings: he giveth wisdom unto the wise, and knowledge to them that know understanding:
He revealeth the deep and secret things: he knoweth what is in the darkness, and the light dwelleth with him.
Bible: Daniel
2:21–22

8 Be strong and of a good courage, fear not, nor be afraid of them: for the Lord thy God, he it is that doth go with thee; he will not fail thee, nor forsake thee.
Bible: Deuteronomy
31:6

9 Let us hear the conclusion of the whole matter: Fear God, and keep his commandments: for this is the whole duty of man.
Bible: Ecclesiastes
12:13

10 I am the Lord thy God, which have brought thee out of the land of Egypt, out of the house of bondage.
Thou shalt have no other gods before me.
Thou shalt not make unto thee any graven image, or any likeness of any thing that is in heaven above, or that is in the earth beneath, or that is in the water under the earth:
Thou shalt not bow down thyself to them, nor serve them: for Lord thy God am a jealous God, visiting the iniquity of the fathers upon the children unto the third and fourth generation of them that hate me;
And shewing mercy unto thousands of them that love me, and keep my commandments.
Thou shalt not take the name of the Lord thy God in vain; for the Lord will not hold him guiltless that taketh his name in vain.
Remember the sabbath day, to keep it holy.
Six days shalt thou labour, and do all thy work:
But the seventh day is the sabbath of the Lord thy God: in it thou shalt not do any work, thou, nor thy son, nor thy daughter, thy manservant, nor thy maidservant, nor thy cattle, nor thy stranger that is within thy gates:
For in six days the Lord made heaven and earth, the sea, and all that in them is, and rested the seventh day: wherefore the Lord blessed the sabbath day, and hallowed it.
Honour thy father and thy mother: that thy days may be long upon the land which the Lord thy God giveth thee.
Thou shalt not kill.
Thou shalt not commit adultery.
Thou shalt not steal.

Thou shalt not bear false witness against thy neighbour.
Thou shalt not covet thy neighbour's house, thou shalt not covet thy neighbour's wife, nor his manservant, nor his maidservant, nor his ox, nor his ass, nor any thing that is thy neighbour's.
Bible: Exodus
20:2–17

11 And he said, Thou canst not see my face: for there shall no man see me, and live.
Bible: Exodus
33:20

12 For the kingdom of God is not in word, but in power.
Bible: I Corinthians
4:20

13 And he said, Go forth, and stand upon the mount before the Lord. And, behold, the Lord passed by, and a great and strong wind rent the mountains, and brake in pieces the rocks before the Lord; but the Lord was not in the wind: and after the wind an earthquake; but the Lord was not in the earthquake:
And after the earthquake a fire; but the Lord was not in the fire: and after the fire a still small voice.
Bible: I Kings
19:11–12

14 Man has learned to cope with all questions of importance without recourse to God as a working hypothesis.
Dietrich Bonhoeffer (1906–45) German theologian.
Letters and Papers from Prison, 8 June 1944

15 A God who let us prove his existence would be an idol.
Dietrich Bonhoeffer
No Rusty Swords

16 God's gifts put man's best gifts to shame.
Elizabeth Barrett Browning (1806–61) British poet.
Sonnets from the Portuguese, XXVI

17 Thou shalt have one God only; who
Would be at the expense of two?
Arthur Hugh Clough (1819–61) British poet.
The Latest Decalogue, 1

18 God moves in a mysterious way
His wonders to perform;
He plants his footsteps in the sea,
And rides upon the storm.
William Cowper (1731–1800) British poet.
Olney Hymns, 35

19 It is the final proof of God's omnipotence that he need not exist in order to save us.
Peter De Vries (1910–) US novelist.
The Mackerel Plaza, Ch. 2

20 What sort of God are we portraying and believing in if we insist on what I will nickname 'the divine laser beam' type of

miracle as the heart and basis of the Incarnation and Resurrection?

Bishop of Durham (1925–) British churchman.
Speech, July 1986

21 God is subtle but he is not malicious.

Albert Einstein (1879–1955) German-born US physicist.
Inscribed over the fireplace in the Mathematical Institute, Princeton. It refers to Einstein's objection to the quantum theory
Albert Einstein (Carl Seelig), Ch. 8

22 At bottom God is nothing more than an exalted father.

Sigmund Freud (1856–1939) Austrian psychoanalyst.
Totem and Taboo

23 O worship the King, all glorious above!
O gratefully sing his power and his love!
Our Shield and Defender – the Ancient of Days,
Pavilioned in splendour, and girded with praise.

Robert Grant (1779–1838) British hymn writer.
Hymn

24 Holy, holy, holy, Lord God Almighty!
Early in the morning our song shall rise to thee.

Reginald Heber (1783–1826) British bishop and hymn writer.
Holy, Holy, Holy

25 The world is charged with the grandeur of God.

Gerard Manley Hopkins (1844–99) British Jesuit and poet.
God's Grandeur

26 Mine eyes have seen the glory of the coming of the Lord:
He is trampling out the vintage where the grapes of wrath are stored.

Julia Ward Howe (1819–1910) US writer.
Battle Hymn of the American Republic

27 Operationally, God is beginning to resemble not a ruler but the last fading smile of a cosmic Cheshire cat.

Julian Huxley (1887–1975) British biologist.
Religion without Revelation

28 The chess-board is the world; the pieces are the phenomena of the universe; the rules of the game are what we call the laws of Nature. The player on the other side is hidden from us. We know that his play is always fair, just, and patient. But also we know, to our cost, that he never overlooks a mistake, or makes the smallest allowance for ignorance.

T. H. Huxley (1825–95) British biologist.
Lay Sermons, 'A Liberal Education'

29 An honest God is the noblest work of man.

Robert G. Ingersoll (1833–99) US lawyer and agnostic.
Gods

30 Man proposes but God disposes.

Thomas à Kempis (Thomas Hemmerken; c. 1380–1471) German monk.
The Imitation of Christ, I

31 A man with God is always in the majority.

John Knox (c. 1514–72) Scottish religious reformer.
Inscription, Reformation Monument, Geneva, Switzerland

32 What God does, He does well.

Jean de La Fontaine (1621–95) French poet.
Fables, IX, 'Le Gland et la Citrouille'

33 I have no need of that hypothesis.

Marquis de Laplace (1749–1827) French mathematician and astronomer.
On being asked by Napoleon why he had made no mention of God in his book about the universe, *Mécanique céleste*
Men of Mathematics (E. Bell)

34 Though the mills of God grind slowly, yet they grind exceeding small;
Though with patience He stands waiting, with exactness grinds He all.

Friedrich von Logau (1604–55) German poet and writer.
Sinngedichte, III

35 God is the immemorial refuge of the incompetent, the helpless, the miserable. They find not only sanctuary in His arms, but also a kind of superiority, soothing to their macerated egos; He will set them above their betters.

H. L. Mencken (1880–1956) US journalist.
Notebooks, 'Minority Report'

36 There's a Friend for little children
Above the bright blue sky,
A Friend who never changes,
Whose love will never die.

Albert Midlane (1825–1909) British hymn writer.
Hymn

37 Let us with a gladsome mind
Praise the Lord, for he is kind,
For his mercies ay endure,
Ever faithful, ever sure.

John Milton (1608–74) English poet.
Psalm

38 What in me is dark
Illumine, what is low raise and support;
That, to the height of this great argument,
I may assert Eternal Providence,
And justify the ways of God to men.

John Milton
Paradise Lost, Bk. I

39 God is dead: but considering the state the species Man is in, there will perhaps be caves, for ages yet, in which his shadow will be shown.

Friedrich Wilhelm Nietzsche (1844–1900) German philosopher.
Die Fröhliche Wissenschaft, Bk. III

40 God is a gentleman. He prefers blondes.

Joe Orton (1933–67) British dramatist.
Loot, II

41 One on God's side is a majority.
Wendell Phillips (1811–84) US reformer.
Speech, Brooklyn, 1 Nov 1859

42 God is really only another artist. He invented the giraffe, the elephant, and the cat. He has no real style, He just goes on trying other things.
Pablo Picasso (1881–1973) Spanish painter.
Life with Picasso Ch. 1 (Françoise Gilot and Carlton Lake),

43 God can stand being told by Professor Ayer and Marghanita Laski that He doesn't exist.
J. B. Priestley (1894–1984) British novelist.
The Listener, 1 July 1965, 'The BBC's Duty to Society'

44 Write down that they hope they serve God; and write God first; for God defend but God should go before such villains!
William Shakespeare (1564–1616) English dramatist.
Much Ado About Nothing, IV:2

45 But already it is time to depart, for me to die, for you to go on living; which of us takes the better course, is concealed from anyone except God.
Socrates (469–399 BC) Athenian philosopher.
Apology (Plato)

46 In the days of my youth I remembered my God!
And He hath not forgotten my age.
Robert Southey (1774–1843) British poet.
The Old Man's Comforts, and how he Gained them

47 Yet her conception of God was certainly not orthodox. She felt towards Him as she might have felt towards a glorified sanitary engineer; and in some of her speculations she seems hardly to distinguish between the Deity and the Drains.
Lytton Strachey (1880–1932) British writer.
Eminent Victorians, 'Florence Nightingale'

48 It is a mistake to assume that God is interested only, or even chiefly, in religion.
William Temple (1881–1944) British churchman.
Attrib.

49 If God did not exist, it would be necessary to invent Him.
Voltaire (François-Marie Arouet; 1694–1778) French writer.
Épîtres, 'À l'auteur du livre des trois Imposteurs'

50 If God made us in His image, we have certainly returned the compliment.
Voltaire
Le Sottisier

GOLDWYNISMS

Sayings attributed to Samuel Goldwyn (Samuel Goldfish; 1882–1974). Most are apocryphal. *See also* cinema, mixed metaphors

1 Let's have some new clichés.
The Observer, 'Sayings of the Week', 24 Oct 1948

2 Too caustic? To hell with cost; we'll make the picture anyway.

3 We're overpaying him but he's worth it.

4 What we want is a story that starts with an earthquake and works its way up to a climax.

5 I am willing to admit that I may not always be right, but I am never wrong.

6 I don't care if it doesn't make a nickel, I just want every man, woman, and child in America to see it!
Referring to his film *The Best Years of Our Lives*

7 A wide screen just makes a bad film twice as bad.

8 For years I have been known for saying 'Include me out'; but today I am giving it up for ever.
Address, Balliol College, Oxford, 1 Mar 1945

9 In two words: im - possible.
Attrib.

10 Anybody who goes to see a psychiatrist ought to have his head examined.

11 Every director bites the hand that lays the golden egg.

12 I'll give you a definite maybe.

13 A verbal contract isn't worth the paper it's written on.

14 You ought to take the bull between the teeth.

15 We have all passed a lot of water since then.

16 I read part of it all the way through.

17 If Roosevelt were alive he'd turn in his grave.

18 It's more than magnificent – it's mediocre.

19 'Why only twelve?' 'That's the original number.' 'Well, go out and get thousands.'
Referring to the number of disciples whilst filming a scene for *The Last Supper*

20 Yes, I'm going to have a bust made of them.
Replying to an admiring comment about his wife's hands

21 Tell me, how did you love my picture?

22 I don't want any yes-men around me. I want everybody to tell me the truth even if it costs them their jobs.

GOLF

See also sport and games

1 It's not in support of cricket but as an earnest protest against golf.
Max Beerbohm (1872–1956) British writer.
Said when giving a shilling towards W. G. Grace's testimonial
Carr's Dictionary of Extraordinary English Cricketers

2 Golf may be played on Sunday, not being a game within the view of the law, but being a form of moral effort.
Stephen Leacock (1869–1944) English-born Canadian economist and humorist.
Other Fancies, 'Why I refuse to play Golf'

3 All I've got against it is that it takes you so far from the club house.
Eric Linklater (1889–1974) Scottish novelist.
Referring to golf
Poet's Pub, Ch. 3

GOOD

See also good and evil, righteousness, virtue

1 Men have never been good, they are not good, they never will be good.
Karl Barth (1886–1968) Swiss Protestant theologian.
Time, 12 Apr 1954

2 He who would do good to another must do it in Minute Particulars.
General Good is the plea of the scoundrel, hypocrite, and flatterer.
William Blake (1757–1827) British poet.
Jerusalem

3 *Summum bonum.*
The greatest good.
Cicero (106–43 BC) Roman orator and statesman.
De Officiis, I

4 Nice guys finish last.
Leo Durocher (1905–) US baseball player.
Attrib.

5 What is a weed? A plant whose virtues have not been discovered.
Ralph Waldo Emerson (1803–82) US poet and essayist.
Fortune of the Republic

6 Would to God that we might spend a single day really well!
Thomas à Kempis (Thomas Hemmerken; c. 1380–1471) German monk.
The Imitation of Christ, I

7 Teach us delight in simple things,
And mirth that has no bitter springs;
Forgiveness free of evil done,
And love to all men 'neath the sun!
Rudyard Kipling (1865–1936) Indian-born British writer.
The Children's Song

8 The greatest pleasure I know, is to do a good action by stealth, and to have it found out by accident.
Charles Lamb (1775–1834) British essayist.
The Athenaeum, 'Table Talk by the late Elia', 4 Jan 1834

9 Goodness does not more certainly make men happy than happiness makes them good.
Walter Savage Landor (1775–1864) British poet and writer.
Imaginary Conversations, 'Lord Brooke and Sir Philip Sidney'

10 Dowel, Dobet and Dobest.
William Langland (c. 1330–c. 1400) English poet.
Do well, Do better, and Do Best: three concepts central to the search for Truth in *Piers Plowman*, in which they appear as allegorical characters
The Vision of Piers Plowman

11 Much benevolence of the passive order may be traced to a disinclination to inflict pain upon oneself.
George Meredith (1828–1909) British novelist.
Vittoria, Ch. 42

12 Abashed the devil stood,
And felt how awful goodness is.
John Milton (1608–74) English poet.
Paradise Lost, Bk. IV

13 The good is the beautiful.
Plato (429–347 BC) Greek philosopher.
Lysis

14 Do good by stealth, and blush to find it fame.
Alexander Pope (1688–1744) British poet.
Epilogue to the Satires, Dialogue I

15 How far that little candle throws his beams!
So shines a good deed in a naughty world.
William Shakespeare (1564–1616) English dramatist.
The Merchant of Venice, V:1

16 Nothing can harm a good man, either in life or after death.
Socrates (469–399 BC) Athenian philosopher.
Apology (Plato)

17 – My goodness those diamonds are lovely!
Goodness had nothing whatever to do with it.
Mae West (1892–1980) US actress.
Used in 1959 as the title of the first volume of her autobiography
Diamond Lil, film 1932

18 You shouldn't say it is not good. You should say you do not like it; and then, you know, you're perfectly safe.
James Whistler (1834–1903) US painter.
Whistler Stories (D. Seitz)

GOOD AND EVIL

See also evil, good, virtue and vice

1 There is so much good in the worst of us,
And so much bad in the best of us,
That it hardly becomes any of us
To talk about the rest of us.
Anonymous
Good and Bad

2 Evil comes at leisure like the disease; good comes in a hurry like the doctor.
G. K. Chesterton (1874–1936) British writer.
The Man who was Orthodox

3 The good die early, and the bad die late.
Daniel Defoe (1660–1731) British journalist and writer.
Character of the late Dr. Annesley

4 The web of our life is of a mingled yarn, good and ill together.
William Shakespeare (1564–1616) English dramatist.
All's Well that Ends Well, IV:3

5 The good die first,
And they whose hearts are dry as summer dust
Burn to the socket.
William Wordsworth (1770–1850) British poet.
The Excursion

GOSSIP

See also secrecy

1 A tale never loses in the telling.
Proverb

2 Don't wash your dirty linen in public.
Proverb

3 No names, no pack-drill.
Proverb

4 There's no smoke without fire.
Proverb

5 Throw dirt enough, and some will stick.
Proverb

6 Walls have ears.
Proverb

7 How these curiosities would be quite forgot, did not such idle fellows as I am put them down.
John Aubrey (1626–97) English antiquary.
Brief Lives, 'Venetia Digby'

8 No one gossips about other people's secret virtues.
Bertrand Russell (1872–1970) British philosopher.
On Education

9 Her first economic drive will be to replace X-ray by hearsay.
Gwyn Thomas (1913–81) British writer.
The Keep, II

10 I remember that a wise friend of mine did usually say, 'that which is everybody's business is nobody's business'.
Izaak Walton (1593–1683) English writer.
The Compleat Angler, Ch. 2

GOVERNMENT

See also democracy, Houses of Parliament, monarchy, opposition, politicians, politics

1 I will undoubtedly have to seek what is happily known as gainful employment, which I am glad to say does not describe holding public office.
Dean Acheson (1893–1971) US lawyer and statesman.
Remark made on leaving his post as secretary of state, 1952; he subsequently returned to private legal practice

2 The danger is not that a particular class is unfit to govern. Every class is unfit to govern.
Lord Acton (1834–1902) British historian.
Letter to Mary Gladstone, 1881

3 Whose Finger do you want on the Trigger When the World Situation Is So Delicate?
Anonymous
Headline from the *Daily Mirror* on the day before the General Election, Oct 1951
Publish and Be Damned (Hugh Cudlipp), 1953

4 Where some people are very wealthy and others have nothing, the result will be either extreme democracy or absolute oligarchy, or despotism will come from either of those excesses.
Aristotle (384–322 BC) Greek philosopher.
Politics, Bk. IV

5 One to mislead the public, another to mislead the Cabinet, and the third to mislead itself.
Herbert Henry Asquith (1852–1928) British statesman.
Explaining why the War Office kept three sets of figures
The Price of Glory (Alastair Horne), Ch. 2

6 The object of government in peace and in war is not the glory of rulers or of races, but the happiness of the common man.
Lord Beveridge (1879–1963) British economist.
Social Insurance

7 Too bad all the people who know how to run the country are busy driving cabs and cutting hair.
George Burns (1896–) US comedian.

8 A small acquaintance with history shows that all Governments are selfish and the French Governments more selfish than most.
David Eccles (1904–) British politician.
The Observer, 'Sayings of the Year', 29 Dec 1962

9 He was uniformly of an opinion which, though not a popular one, he was ready to aver, that the right of governing was not property but a trust.
Charles James Fox (1749–1806) British Whig politician.
Referring to William Pitt's plans for parliamentary reform
C.J. Fox (J. L. Hammond)

10 The principles of a free constitution are irrecoverably lost, when the legislative power is nominated by the executive.
Edward Gibbon (1737–94) British historian.
Decline and Fall of the Roman Empire, Ch. 3

11 A government that is big enough to give you all you want is big enough to take it all away.
Barry Goldwater (1909–) US politician.
Bachman's Book of Freedom Quotations (M. Ivens and R. Dunstan)

12 They that are discontented under *monarchy*, call it *tyranny* ; and they that are displeased with *aristocracy*, call it *oligarchy*: so also, they which find themselves grieved under a *democracy*, call it *anarchy*, which signifies the want of government; and yet I think no man believes, that want of government, is any new kind of government.
Thomas Hobbes (1588–1679) English philosopher.
Leviathan, Pt. II, Ch. 19

13 I would not give half a guinea to live under one form of government rather than another. It is of no moment to the happiness of an individual.
Samuel Johnson (1709–84) British lexicographer.
Life of Johnson (J. Boswell), Vol. II

14 Any cook should be able to run the country.
Lenin (Vladimir Ilich Ulyanov; 1870–1924) Russian revolutionary leader.
The First Circle (Alexander Solzhenitsyn)

15 What is our task? To make Britain a fit country for heroes to live in.
David Lloyd George (1863–1945) British Liberal statesman.
Speech, 24 Nov 1918

16 The Commons, faithful to their system, remained in a wise and masterly inactivity.
James Mackintosh (1765–1832) Scottish lawyer, philosopher, and historian.
Vindiciae Gallicae

17 Every country has the government it deserves.
Joseph de Maistre (1753–1821) French monarchist.
Lettres et Opuscules Inédits, 15 Aug 1811

18 The worst government is the most moral. One composed of cynics is often very tolerant and human. But when fanatics are on top there is no limit to oppression.
H. L. Mencken (1880–1956) US journalist.
Notebooks, 'Minority Report'

19 One day the don't-knows will get in, and then where will we be?
Spike Milligan (1918–) British comic actor and author.
Attributed remark made about a pre-election poll

20 Do you not know, my son, with how little wisdom the world is governed?
Axel Oxenstierna (1583–1654) Swedish statesman.
Letter to his son, 1648

21 Government, even in its best state, is but a necessary evil; in its worst state, an intolerable one.
Thomas Paine (1737–1809) British writer.
Common Sense, Ch. 1

22 As to religion, I hold it to be the indispensable duty of government to protect all conscientious professors thereof, and I

know of no other business which government hath to do therewith.
Thomas Paine
Common Sense, Ch. 4

23 We live under a government of men and morning newspapers.
Wendell Phillips (1811–84) US reformer.
Address: The Press

24 I don't make jokes – I just watch the government and report the facts.
Will Rogers (1879–1935) US actor and humorist.
Saturday Review, 'A Rogers Thesaurus', 25 Aug 1962

25 Hansard is history's ear, already listening.
Herbert Samuel (1870–1963) British Liberal statesman.
The Observer, 'Sayings of the Week', 18 Dec 1949

26 Parliament is the longest running farce in the West End.
Cyril Smith (1928–) British Liberal politician.
The Times, 23 Sept 1977

27 It would be desirable if every government, when it comes to power, should have its old speeches burned.
Philip Snowden (1864–1937) British politician.
Biography (C. E. Bechafer Roberts)

28 Accidentally.
Talleyrand (Charles Maurice de Talleyrand-Périgord; 1754–1838) French politician.
Replying, during the reign of Louis Philippe, to the query 'How do you think this government will end?'
The Wheat and the Chaff (F. Mitterand)

29 Governments needs to have both shepherds and butchers.
Voltaire (François-Marie Arouet; 1694–1778) French writer.
Notebooks

30 Many people consider the things which government does for them to be social progress, but they consider the things government does for others as socialism.
Earl Warren (1891–1971) US lawyer.
Peter's Quotations (Laurence J. Peter)

31 The people's government, made for the people, made by the people, and answerable to the people.
Daniel Webster (1782–1852) US statesman.
Second speech on Foote's resolution, 26 Jan 1830

32 If people behaved in the way nations do they would all be put in straitjackets.
Tennessee Williams (1911–83) US dramatist.
BBC interview

GRAMMAR

See also language, words

1 'Whom are you?' said he, for he had been to night school.
George Ade (1866–1944) US dramatist and humorist.
Bang! Bang!: The Steel Box

2 When I split an infinitive, god damn it, I split it so it stays split.
Raymond Chandler (1888–1959) US novelist.
Letter to his English publisher

3 By being so long in the lowest form I gained an immense advantage over the cleverest boys . . . I got into my bones the essential structure of the normal British sentence – which is a noble thing.
Winston Churchill (1874–1965) British statesman.
My Early Life, Ch. 2

4 This is the sort of English up with which I will not put.
Winston Churchill
The story is that Churchill wrote the comment in the margin of a report in which a Civil Servant had used an awkward construction to avoid ending a sentence with a preposition. An alternative version substitutes 'bloody nonsense' for 'English'
Plain Words (E. Gowers), Ch. 9

5 I will not go down to posterity talking bad grammar.
Benjamin Disraeli (1804–81) British statesman.
Remark made when correcting proofs of his last parliamentary speech, 31 Mar 1881
Disraeli (Blake), Ch. 32

6 Grammar, which can govern even kings.
Molière (Jean Baptiste Poquelin; 1622–73) French dramatist.
Les Femmes savantes, II:6

7 I am the Roman Emperor, and am above grammar.
Sigismund (1368–1437) Holy Roman Emperor.
Responding to criticism of his Latin
Attrib.

8 Why care for grammar as long as we are good?
Artemus Ward (Charles Farrar Browne; 1834–67) US humorous writer.
Pyrotechny

9 Subjunctive to the last, he preferred to ask, 'And that, sir, would be the Hippodrome?'
Alexander Woollcott (1887–1943) US journalist.
While Rome Burns, 'Our Mrs Parker'

GRATITUDE

1 There are minds so impatient of inferiority that their gratitude is a species of revenge, and they return benefits, not because recompense is a pleasure, but because obligation is a pain.
Samuel Johnson (1709–84) British lexicographer.
The Rambler

2 When the messenger who carried the last sheet to Millar returned, Johnson asked him, 'Well, what did he say?' – 'Sir (answered the messenger), he said, thank God I have done

with him.' – 'I am glad (replied Johnson, with a smile) that he thanks God for anything.'
Samuel Johnson
After the final page of his *Dictionary* had been delivered
Life of Johnson (J. Boswell)

3 Thank me no thankings, nor proud me no prouds.
William Shakespeare (1564–1616) English dramatist.
Romeo and Juliet, III:5

GREATNESS

1 A truly great man never puts away the simplicity of a child.
Chinese proverb

2 The dullard's envy of brilliant men is always assuaged by the suspicion that they will come to a bad end.
Max Beerbohm (1872–1956) British writer.
Zuleika Dobson

3 Great men are but life-sized. Most of them, indeed, are rather short.
Max Beerbohm
And Even Now

4 Great things are done when men and mountains meet;
This is not done by jostling in the street.
William Blake (1757–1827) British poet.
Gnomic Verses

5 Nothing grows well in the shade of a big tree.
Constantin Brancusi (1876–1957) Romanian sculptor.
Refusing Rodin's invitation to work in his studio
Compton's Encyclopedia

6 No great man lives in vain. The history of the world is but the biography of great men.
Thomas Carlyle (1795–1881) Scottish historian and essayist.
Heroes and Hero-Worship, 'The Hero as Divinity'

7 To be great is to be misunderstood.
Ralph Waldo Emerson (1803–82) US poet and essayist.
Essays, 'Self-Reliance'

8 The world's great men have not commonly been great scholars, nor great scholars great men.
Oliver Wendell Holmes (1809–94) US writer.
The Autocrat of the Breakfast Table, Ch. 6

9 If I am a great man, then a good many of the great men of history are frauds.
Bonar Law (1858–1923) British statesman.
Attrib.

10 You are one of the forces of nature.
Jules Michelet (1798–1874) French historian.
From a letter received by Dumas
Memoirs, Vol. VI, Ch. 138 (Alexandre Dumas)

11 To be alone is the fate of all great minds – a

fate deplored at times, but still always chosen as the less grievous of two evils.
Arthur Schopenhauer (1788–1860) German philosopher.
Aphorismen zur Lebensweisheit

12 Some are born great, some achieve greatness, and some have greatness thrust upon 'em.
William Shakespeare (1564–1616) English dramatist.
Twelfth Night, II:5

13 'My name is Ozymandias, king of kings:
Look on my works, ye Mighty, and despair!'
Percy Bysshe Shelley (1792–1822) British poet.
Ozymandias

14 Oh, Vanity of vanities!
How wayward the decrees of Fate are;
How very weak the very wise,
How very small the very great are!
William Makepeace Thackeray (1811–63) British novelist.
Vanitas Vanitatum

15 A great city is that which has the greatest men and women.
Walt Whitman (1819–92) US poet.
Song of the Broad-Axe, 5

GREED

See also food, materialism, obesity

1 Give him an inch and he'll take a yard.
Proverb

2 Kill not the goose that lays the golden egg.
Proverb

3 The eye is bigger than the belly.
Proverb

4 Beware that you do not lose the substance by grasping at the shadow.
Aesop (6th century BC) Reputed Greek writer of fables.
Fables, 'The Dog and the Shadow'

5 But answer came there none –
And this was scarcely odd because
They'd eaten every one.
Lewis Carroll (Charles Lutwidge Dodgson; 1832–98) British writer.
Through the Looking-Glass, Ch. 4

6 Gluttony is an emotional escape, a sign something is eating us.
Peter De Vries (1910–) US novelist.
Comfort me with Apples, Ch. 7

7 The mountain sheep are sweeter,
But the valley sheep are fatter;
We therefore deemed it meeter
To carry off the latter.
Thomas Love Peacock (1785–1866) British novelist.
The Misfortunes of Elphin, Ch. 11, 'The War-Song of Dinas Vawr'

8 These citizens are always willing to bet that what Nicely-Nicely dies of will be over-feeding and never anything small like

pneumonia, for Nicely-Nicely is known far and wide as a character who dearly loves to commit eating.
Damon Runyon (1884–1946) US writer.
Take it Easy, 'Lonely Heart'

9 Wealth is like sea-water; the more we drink, the thirstier we become; and the same is true of fame.
Arthur Schopenhauer (1788–1860) German philosopher.
Parerga and Paralipomena

10 People will swim through shit if you put a few bob in it.
Peter Sellers (1925–80) British comic actor.
Halliwell's Filmgoer's and Video Viewer's Companion

11 He hath eaten me out of house and home.
William Shakespeare (1564–1616) English dramatist.
Henry IV, Part Two, II:1

GREETINGS

1 *Atque in perpetuum, frater, ave atque vale.*
And for ever, brother, hail and farewell!
Catullus (c. 84–c. 54 BC) Roman poet.
Carmina, CI

2 Wery glad to see you indeed, and hope our acquaintance may be a long 'un, as the gen'l'm'n said to the fi' pun' note.
Charles Dickens (1812–70) British novelist.
Pickwick Papers, Ch. 25

3 Dr Livingstone, I presume?
Henry Morton Stanley (1841–1904) British explorer.
On finding David Livingstone at Ujiji on Lake Tanganyika, Nov 1871
How I found Livingstone, Ch. 11

4 Lafayette, we are here!
C. E. Stanton (1859–1933) US colonel.
The Marquis de Lafayette (1757–1834) aided the colonists in the US War of Independence
Address at Lafayette's grave, Paris, 4 July 1917

GUIDANCE

See also leadership

1 Everyman, I will go with thee, and be thy guide.
In thy most need to go by thy side.
Anonymous
Everyman Pt. 1

2 Wandering in a vast forest at night, I have only a faint light to guide me. A stranger appears and says to me: 'My friend, you should blow out your candle in order to find your way more clearly.' This stranger is a theologian.
Denis Diderot (1713–84) French writer.
Addition aux Pensées philosophiques

3 A little onward lend thy guiding hand
To these dark steps, a little further on.
John Milton (1608–74) English poet.
Samson Agonistes

GUILT

See also conscience, regret

1 It is quite gratifying to feel guilty if you haven't done anything wrong: how noble! Whereas it is rather hard and certainly depressing to admit guilt and to repent.
Hannah Arendt (1906–75) German-born US philosopher and historian.
Eichmann in Jerusalem, Ch. 15

2 Alone, alone, about the dreadful wood
Of conscious evil runs a lost mankind,
Dreading to find its Father.
W. H. Auden (1907–73) British poet.
For the Time Being, 'Chorus'

3 When Pilate saw that he could prevail nothing, but that rather a tumult was made, he took water, and washed his hands before the multitude, saying, I am innocent of the blood of this just person: see ye to it.
Then answered all the people, and said, His blood be on us, and on our children.
Bible: Matthew
27:24–25

4 The many men, so beautiful!
And they all dead did lie:
And a thousand thousand slimy things
Lived on; and so did I.
Samuel Taylor Coleridge (1772–1834) British poet.
The Rime of the Ancient Mariner, IV

5 Love bade me welcome; yet my soul drew back,
Guilty of dust and sin.
George Herbert (1593–1633) English poet.
Love

6 You will put on a dress of guilt
and shoes with broken high ideals.
Roger McGough (1937–) British poet.
Comeclose and Sleepnow

7 I am in blood
Stepp'd in so far that, should I wade no more,
Returning were as tedious as go o'er.
William Shakespeare (1564–1616) English dramatist.
Macbeth, III:4

8 Out, damned spot! out, I say!
William Shakespeare
Macbeth, V:1

9 Here's the smell of the blood still. All the perfumes of Arabia will not sweeten this little hand.
William Shakespeare
Macbeth, V:1

GULLIBILITY

See also foolishness, impressionability

1 There's a sucker born every minute.
Phineas Barnum (1810–91) US showman.
Attrib.

2 When lovely woman stoops to folly,
And finds too late that men betray,
What charm can soothe her melancholy,
What art can wash her guilt away?
Oliver Goldsmith (1728–74) Irish-born British writer.
The Vicar of Wakefield, Ch. 9

H

HABIT

See also custom

1 Old habits die hard.
Proverb

2 Habit is a great deadener.
Samuel Beckett (1906–89) Irish novelist and dramatist.
Waiting for Godot, III

3 Curious things, habits. People themselves never knew they had them.
Agatha Christie (1891–1976) British detective-story writer.
Witness for the Prosecution

4 Men's natures are alike; it is their habits that carry them far apart.
Confucius (K'ung Fu-tzu; 551–479 BC) Chinese philosopher.
Analects

5 Cultivate only the habits that you are willing should master you.
Elbert Hubbard (1856–1915) US writer.
Attrib.

6 They do those little personal things people sometimes do when they think they are alone in railway carriages; things like smelling their own armpits.
Jonathan Miller (1934–) British doctor and television and stage director.
Beyond the Fringe

HALF MEASURES

1 Two half-truths do not make a truth, and two half-cultures do not make a culture.
Arthur Koestler (1905–83) Hungarian-born British writer.
The Ghost in the Machine, Preface

2 I'm not really a Jew; just Jew-ish, not the whole hog.
Jonathan Miller (1934–) British doctor and television and stage director.
Beyond the Fringe

HAPPINESS

See also contentment, laughter, pleasure

1 One joy scatters a hundred griefs.
Chinese proverb

2 If you haven't been happy very young, you can still be happy later on, but it's much harder. You need more luck.
Simone de Beauvoir (1908–86) French writer.
The Observer, 'Sayings of the Week', 19 May 1975

3 The greatest happiness of the greatest number is the foundation of morals and legislation.
Jeremy Bentham (1748–1832) British philosopher.
The Commonplace Book

4 There was a jolly miller once,
Lived on the river Dee;
He worked and sang from morn till night;
No lark more blithe than he.
Isaac Bickerstaffe (c. 1735–c. 1812) Irish dramatist.
Love in a Village, I

5 When the green woods laugh with
the voice of joy.
William Blake (1757–1827) British poet.
Songs of Innocence, 'Laughing song'

6 In every adversity of fortune, to have been happy is the most unhappy kind of misfortune.
Boethius (c. 480–524) Roman statesman, philosopher, and scholar.
The Consolation of Philosophy

7 Happiness is a mystery like religion, and should never be rationalized.
G. K. Chesterton (1874–1936) British writer.
Heretics, Ch. 7

8 To marvel at nothing is just about the one and only thing, Numicius, that can make a man happy and keep him that way.
Horace (Quintus Horatius Flaccus; 65–8 BC) Roman poet.
Epistles, I

9 Not the owner of many possessions will you be right to call happy: he more rightly deserves the name of happy who knows how to use the gods' gifts wisely and to put up with rough poverty, and who fears dishonour more than death.
Horace
Odes, IV

10 That action is best, which procures the greatest happiness for the greatest numbers.
Francis Hutcheson (1694–1746) Scottish philosopher.
Inquiry into the Original of our Ideas of Beauty and Virtue, Treatise II, 'Concerning Moral Good and Evil'

11 Happiness is like coke - something you get as a by-product in the process of making something else.
Aldous Huxley (1894–1964) British novelist.
Point Counter Point

12 That all who are happy, are equally happy, is not true. A peasant and a philosopher may be equally *satisfied*, but not equally *happy*. Happiness consists in the multiplicity of agreeable consciousness.
Samuel Johnson (1709–84) British lexicographer.
Life of Johnson (J. Boswell), Vol. II

13 . . . because happiness is not an ideal of reason but of imagination.
Immanuel Kant (1724–1804) German philosopher.
Grundlegung zur Metaphysik der Sitten, II

14 Ask yourself whether you are happy, and you cease to be so.
John Stuart Mill (1806–73) British philosopher.
Autobiography, Ch. 5

15 When a small child . . . I thought that success spelled happiness. I was wrong. Happiness is like a butterfly which appears and delights us for one brief moment, but soon flits away.
Anna Pavlova (1881–1931) Russian ballet dancer.
Pavlova: A Biography (ed. A. H. Franks), 'Pages of My Life'

16 And we suddenly know, what heaven we're in,
When they begin the beguine.
Cole Porter (1893–1964) US songwriter.
Jubilee, 'Begin the Beguine'

17 We are never so happy nor so unhappy as we imagine.
Duc de la Rochefoucauld (1613–80) French writer.
Maximes, 49

18 Happiness is not best achieved by those who seek it directly.
Bertrand Russell (1872–1970) British philosopher.
Mysticism and Logic

19 Every time I talk to a savant I feel quite sure that happiness is no longer a possibility. Yet when I talk with my gardener, I'm convinced of the opposite.
Bertrand Russell
Attrib.

20 To be without some of the things you want is an indispensable part of happiness.
Bertrand Russell
Attrib.

21 One is happy as a result of one's own efforts, once one knows the necessary ingredients of happiness – simple tastes, a certain degree of courage, self denial to a point, love of work, and, above all, a clear conscience. Happiness is no vague dream, of that I now feel certain.
George Sand (Aurore Dupin, Baronne Dudevant; 1804–76) French novelist.
Correspondence, Vol. V

22 Happiness is the only sanction of life; where happiness fails, existence remains a mad and lamentable experiment.
George Santayana (1863–1952) US philosopher.
The Life of Reason

23 Happiness? That's nothing more than health and a poor memory.
Albert Schweitzer (1875–1965) French Protestant theologian, philosopher, physician and musician.
Attrib.

24 A lifetime of happiness: no man alive could bear it: it would be hell on earth.
George Bernard Shaw (1856–1950) Irish dramatist and critic.
Man and Superman, I

25 Mankind are always happy for having been happy, so that if you make them happy now, you make them happy twenty years hence by the memory of it.
Sydney Smith (1771–1845) British clergyman and essayist.
Elementary Sketches of Moral Philosophy

26 A man is happy so long as he choose to be happy and nothing can stop him.
Alexander Solzhenitsyn (1918–) Soviet novelist.
Cancer Ward

27 There is no duty we so much underrate as the duty of being happy.
Robert Louis Stevenson (1850–94) Scottish writer.
Virginibus Puerisque

28 Happiness is an imaginary condition, formerly often attributed by the living to the dead, now usually attributed by adults to children, and by children to adults.
Thomas Szasz (1920–) US psychiatrist.
The Second Sin

29 If you want to be happy, be.
Leo Tolstoy (1828–1910) Russian writer.
Kosma Prutkov

30 Happiness is no laughing matter.
Richard Whately (1787–1863) British churchman.
Apohthegms

31 Happy Days Are Here Again.
Jack Yellen (b. 1892) US lyricist.
Used by Roosevelt as a campaign song in 1932
Song title

32 For the good are always the merry,
Save by an evil chance,
And the merry love the fiddle,
And the merry love to dance
W. B. Yeats (1865–1939) Irish poet.
The Fiddler of Dooney

33 The hell with it. Who never knew the price of happiness will not be happy.
Yevgeny Yevtushenko (1933–) Soviet poet.
Lies

HASTE

See also impetuosity

1 Don't throw the baby out with the bathwater.
Proverb

2 First come, first served.
Proverb

3 Haste makes waste.
Proverb

4 More haste, less speed.
Proverb

5 'Will you walk a little faster?' said a whiting to a snail,
'There's a porpoise close behind us, and he's treading on my tail.'
Lewis Carroll (Charles Lutwidge Dodgson; 1832–98) British writer.
Alice's Adventures in Wonderland, Ch. 10

6 In skating over thin ice, our safety is in our speed.
Ralph Waldo Emerson (1803–82) US poet and essayist.
Essays, 'Prudence'

7 Slow and steady wins the race.
Robert Lloyd (1733–64) British poet.
The Hare and the Tortoise

8 For fools rush in where angels fear to tread.
Alexander Pope (1688–1744) British poet.
An Essay on Criticism

9 Never before have we had so little time in which to do so much.
Franklin D. Roosevelt (1882–1945) US Democratic president.
Radio address, 23 Feb 1942

10 If it were done when 'tis done, then 'twere well
It were done quickly.
William Shakespeare (1564–1616) English dramatist.
Macbeth, I:7

11 Wisely and slow; they stumble that run fast.
William Shakespeare
Romeo and Juliet, II:3

12 Hurry! I never hurry. I have no time to hurry.
Igor Stravinsky (1882–1971) Russian-born US composer.
Responding to his publisher's request that he hurry his completion of a composition
Attrib.

HATE

See also bitterness, love and hate

1 I do not love thee, Doctor Fell,
The reason why I cannot tell;
But this alone I know full well,
I do not love thee, Doctor Fell.
Thomas Brown (1663–1704) English satirist.
Translation of Martial's *Epigrams*

2 Gr-r-r- there go, my heart's abhorrence!
Water your damned flower-pots, do!
Robert Browning (1812–89) British poet.
Soliloquy of the Spanish Cloister

3 I am free of all prejudice. I hate everyone
equally.
W. C. Fields (1880–1946) US actor.
Attrib.

4 We can scarcely hate any one that we know.
William Hazlitt (1778–1830) British essayist.
On Criticism

5 If you hate a person, you hate something in
him that is part of yourself. What isn't part of
ourselves doesn't disturb us.
Hermann Hesse (1877–1962) German novelist and poet.
Demian, Ch. 6

6 With a heavy step Sir Matthew left the room
and spent the morning designing mausoleums
for his enemies.
Eric Linklater (1889–1974) Scottish novelist.
Juan in America, Prologue

7 Few people can be happy unless they hate
some other person, nation or creed.
Bertrand Russell (1872–1970) British philosopher.
Attrib.

8 An intellectual hatred is the worst.
W. B. Yeats (1865–1939) Irish poet.
A Prayer for My Daughter

HEALTH AND HEALTHY LIVING

See also doctors, illness, medicine, remedies

1 An apple a day keeps the doctor away.
Proverb

2 Health is better than wealth.
Proverb

3 It is a fact that not once in all my life have I
gone out for a walk. I have been taken out
for walks; but that is another matter.
Max Beerbohm (1872–1956) British writer.
Going Out of a Walk

4 I answer 20 000 letters a year and so many
couples are having problems because they
are not getting the right proteins and
vitamins.
Barbara Cartland (1902–) British romantic novelist.
The Observer, 'Sayings of the Week', 31 Aug 1986

5 The strongest possible piece of advice I
would give to any young woman is: Don't
screw around, and don't smoke.
Edwina Currie (1946–) British politician.
The Observer, 'Sayings of the Week', 3 Apr 1988

6 Exercise is bunk. If you are healthy, you
don't need it: if you are sick you shouldn't
take it.
Henry Ford (1863–1947) US car manufacturer.
Attrib.

7 A wise man ought to realize that health is his
most valuable possession.
Hippocrates (c. 460 –c. 377 BC) Greek physician.
A Regimen for Health, 9

8 One swears by wholemeal bread, one by
sour milk; vegetarianism is the only road to
salvation of some, others insist not only on
vegetables alone, but on eating those raw. At
one time the only thing that matters is
calories; at another time they are crazy about
vitamins or about roughage.
The scientific truth may be put quite briefly;
eat moderately, having an ordinary mixed diet,
and don't worry.
Robert Hutchison (1871–1960)
Newcastle Medical Journal, Vol. 12, 1932

9 Vegetarianism is harmless enough, though it
is apt to fill a man with wind and self
righteousness.
Robert Hutchison
Attrib.

10 *Orandum est ut sit mens sana in corpore
sano.*
Your prayer must be for a sound mind in a
sound body.
Juvenal (Decimus Junius Juvenalis; 60–130 AD) Roman
satirist.
Satires, X

11 Some breakfast food manufacturer hit upon
the simple notion of emptying out the
leavings of carthorse nosebags, adding a few
other things like unconsumed portions of
chicken layer's mash, and the sweepings of
racing stables, packing the mixture in little
bags and selling them in health food shops.
Frank Muir (1920–) British writer and broadcaster.
Upon My Word!

12 Look to your health: and if you have it,
praise God, and value it next to a good
conscience; for health is the second blessing
that we mortals are capable of; a blessing
that money cannot buy.
Izaak Walton (1593–1683) English writer.
The Compleat Angler, Pt. I, Ch. 21

HEAVEN

See also afterlife

1 And he dreamed, and behold a ladder set up
on the earth, and the top of it reached to
heaven: and behold the angels of God
ascending and descending on it.
Bible: Genesis
28:12

2 And Jacob awaked out of his sleep, and he
said, Surely the Lord is in this place; and I
knew it not.
And he was afraid, and said, How dreadful is

this place! this is none other but the house of God, and this is the gate of heaven.
Bible: Genesis
28:16–17

3 In my Father's house are many mansions: if it were not so, I would have told you. I go to prepare a place for you.
Bible: John
14:2

4 Then let him receive the new knowledge and wait us,
Pardoned in heaven, the first by the throne!
Robert Browning (1812–89) British poet.
The Lost Leader

5 Probably no invention came more easily to man than Heaven.
Georg Christoph Lichtenberg (1742–99) German physicist and writer.
Aphorisms

6 A heav'n on earth.
John Milton (1608–74) English poet.
Paradise Lost, Bk. IV

7 Glorious things of thee are spoken,
Zion, city of our God.
John Newton (1725–1807) British hymn writer.
Glorious Things

8 It may be only glory that we seek here, but I persuade myself that, as long as we remain here, that is right. Another glory awaits us in heaven and he who reaches there will not wish even to think of earthly fame.
Petrarch (1304–74) Italian poet.
Secretum

9 For observe, that to hope for Paradise is to live in Paradise, a very different thing from actually getting there.
Vita Sackville-West (Victoria Sackville-West; 1892–1962) British poet and novelist.
Passenger to Tehran, Ch. 1

10 I expect no very violent transition.
Catharine Maria Sedgwick (1789–1867) US writer.
Comparing heaven with her home-town of Stockbridge, Massachussetts
Edie (Jean Stein)

11 If you go to Heaven without being naturally qualified for it you will not enjoy yourself there.
George Bernard Shaw (1856–1950) Irish dramatist and critic.
Man and Superman

12 Heaven, as conventionally conceived, is a place so inane, so dull, so useless, so miserable, that nobody has ever ventured to describe a whole day in heaven, though plenty of people have described a day at the seaside.
George Bernard Shaw
Misalliance, Preface

13 Shall shine the traffic of Jacob's ladder

Pitched between Heaven and Charing Cross.
Francis Thompson (1859–1907) British poet.
The Kingdom of God

14 Grant me paradise in this world; I'm not so sure I'll reach it in the next.
Tintoretto (Jacopo Robusti; 1518–94) Venetian painter.
Arguing that he be allowed to paint the *Paradiso* at the doge's palace in Venice, despite his advanced age
Attrib.

15 There is a happy land,
Far, far away,
Where saints in glory stand,
Bright, bright as day.
Andrew John Young (1885–1971) Scottish poet.
There is a Happy Land

HELL

See also damnation, devil

1 Every wolf's and lion's howl
Raises from Hell a human soul.
William Blake (1757–1827) British poet.
Auguries of Innocence

2 Abandon hope, all ye who enter here.
Dante (1265–1321) Italian poet.
The inscription at the entrance to Hell
Divine Comedy, Inferno, III

3 Hell is oneself;
Hell is alone, the other figures in it
Merely projections. There is nothing to escape from
And nothing to escape to. One is always alone.
T. S. Eliot (1888–1965) US-born British poet and dramatist.
The Cocktail Party, I:3

4 Long is the way
And hard, that out of hell leads up to light.
John Milton (1608–74) English poet.
Paradise Lost, Bk. II

5 Which way I fly is Hell; myself am Hell;
And, in the lowest deep, a lower deep
Still threat'ning to devour me opens wide,
To which the Hell I suffer seems a Heaven.
John Milton
Paradise Lost, Bk. IV

6 Hell is other people.
Jean-Paul Sartre (1905–80) French writer.
Huis clos

7 The way down to Hell is easy.
Virgil (Publius Vergilius Maro; 70–19 BC) Roman poet.
Aeneid, Bk. VI

HELP

See also charity, support

1 Every little helps.
Proverb

2 Many hands make light work.
Proverb

3 One good turn deserves another.
Proverb

4 Scratch my back and I'll scratch yours.
Proverb

5 Too many cooks spoil the broth.
Proverb

6 Two heads are better than one.
Proverb

7 People must help one another; it is nature's law.
Jean de La Fontaine (1621–95) French poet.
Fables, VIII, 'L'Âne et le Chien'

HEROISM

See also courage, endurance, patriotism, war

1 Some talk of Alexander, and some of Hercules,
Of Hector and Lysander, and such great names as these;
But of all the world's brave heroes there's none that can compare
With a tow, row, row, row, row, row for the British Grenadier.
Anonymous
The British Grenadiers

2 They died to save their country and they only saved the world.
Hilaire Belloc (1870–1953) French-born British poet.
The English Graves

3 ANDREA. Unhappy the land that has no heroes.
GALILEO. No, unhappy the land that needs heroes.
Bertolt Brecht (1898–1956) German dramatist.
Galileo, 13

4 In short, he was a perfect cavaliero,
And to his very valet seem'd a hero.
Lord Byron (1788–1824) British poet.
Beppo

5 Every hero becomes a bore at last.
Ralph Waldo Emerson (1803–82) US poet and essayist.
Representative Men, 'Uses of Great Men'

6 Being a hero is about the shortest-lived profession on earth.
Will Rogers (1879–1935) US actor and humorist.
Saturday Review, 'A Rogers Thesaurus', 25 Aug 1962

HISTORIANS

See also history

1 A good historian is timeless; although he is a patriot, he will never flatter his country in any respect.
François Fénelon (1651–1715) French writer and prelate.
Letter to M. Dacier

2 The historian must have . . . some conception of how men who are not historians behave. Otherwise he will move in a world of the dead.
E. M. Forster (1879–1970) British novelist.
Abinger Harvest, 'Captain Edward Gibbon'

3 Great abilities are not requisite for an Historian . . . Imagination is not required in any high degree.
Samuel Johnson (1709–84) British lexicographer.
Life of Johnson (J. Boswell), Vol. I

4 History is too serious to be left to historians.
Iain Macleod (1913–70) British politician.
The Observer, 'Sayings of the Week', 16 July 1961

5 And even I can remember
A day when the historians left blanks in their writings,
I mean for things they didn't know.
Ezra Pound (1885–1972) US poet.
Cantos, XIII

6 A historian is a prophet in reverse.
Friedrich von Schlegel (1772–1829) German diplomat, writer, and critic.
Das Athenäum

7 Historians are like deaf people who go on answering questions that no one has asked them.
Leo Tolstoy (1828–1910) Russian writer.
A Discovery of Australia, 'Being an Historian' (Manning Clark)

HISTORY

See also experience, historians, past

1 History repeats itself.
Proverb

2 History is the sum total of the things that could have been avoided.
Konrad Adenauer (1876–1967) German statesman.

3 Political history is far too criminal and pathological to be a fit subject of study for the young. Children should acquire their heroes and villains from fiction.
W. H. Auden (1907–73) British poet.
A Certain World

4 Man is a history-making creature who can neither repeat his past nor leave it behind.
W. H. Auden
The Dyer's Hand, 'D. H. Lawrence'

5 All things from eternity are of like forms and come round in a circle.
Marcus Aurelius (121–180 AD) Roman emperor.
Meditations, Bk. II, Ch. 14

6 History does not repeat itself. Historians repeat each other.
Arthur Balfour (1848–1930) British statesman.
Attrib.

7 History is the essence of innumerable biographies.

Thomas Carlyle (1795–1881) Scottish historian and essayist.
Critical and Miscellaneous Essays, 'History'

8 No great man lives in vain. The history of the world is but the biography of great men.

Thomas Carlyle
Heroes and Hero-Worship, 'The Hero as Divinity'

9 The history of every country begins in the heart of a man or woman.

Willa Cather (1873–1947) US writer and poet.
O Pioneers!, Pt. II, Ch. 4

10 History is philosophy teaching by examples.

Dionysius of Halicarnassus (40–8 BC) Greek historian.
Ars rhetorica, XI:2

11 History is an endless repetition of the wrong way of living.

Lawrence Durrell (1912–) British novelist.
The Listener, 1978

12 There is properly no history; only biography.

Ralph Waldo Emerson (1803–82) US poet and essayist.
Essays, 'History'

13 History is more or less bunk. It's tradition. We don't want tradition. We want to live in the present and the only history that is worth a tinker's damn is the history we make today.

Henry Ford (1863–1947) US car manufacturer.
Chicago Tribune, 25 May 1916

14 There are moments in history when brooding tragedy and its dark shadows can be lightened by recalling great moments of the past.

Indira Gandhi (1917–84) Indian stateswoman.
Letter to Richard Nixon, 16 Dec 1971

15 History never looks like history when you are living through it. It always looks confusing and messy, and it always feels uncomfortable.

John W. Gardner (1912–) US writer.
No Easy Victories

16 His reign is marked by the rare advantage of furnishing very few materials for history; which is, indeed, little more than the register of the crimes, follies, and misfortunes of mankind.

Edward Gibbon (1737–94) British historian.
Referring to the reign of Antoninus Pius
Decline and Fall of the Roman Empire, Ch. 3

17 What we know of the past is mostly not worth knowing. What is worth knowing is mostly uncertain. Events in the past may roughly be divided into those which probably never happened and those which do not matter.

Dean Inge (1860–1954) British churchman.
Assessments and Anticipations, 'Prognostications'

18 It takes a great deal of history to produce a little literature.

Henry James (1843–1916) US novelist.
Life of Nathaniel Hawthorne, Ch. 1

19 'History', Stephen said, 'is a nightmare from which I am trying to awake'.

James Joyce (1882–1941) Irish novelist.
Ulysses

20 Hegel says somewhere that all great events and personalities in world history reappear in one fashion or another. He forgot to add: the first time as tragedy, the second as farce.

Karl Marx (1818–83) German philosopher and revolutionary.
The Eighteenth Brumaire of Louis Napoleon

21 It is impossible to write ancient history because we do not have enough sources, and impossible to write modern history because we have far too many.

Charles Pierre Péguy (1873–1914) French writer.
Clio

22 There is no history of mankind, there are only many histories of all kinds of aspects of human life. And one of these is the history of political power. This is elevated into the history of the world.

Karl Popper (1902–) Austrian-born British philosopher.
The Open Society and Its Enemies

23 Progress, far from consisting in change, depends on retentiveness. Those who cannot remember the past are condemned to repeat it.

George Santayana (1863–1952) US philosopher.
The Life of Reason

24 I have looked upon the face of Agamemnon.

Heinrich Schliemann (1822–90) German archaeologist.
On discovering a gold death mask at an excavation in Mycenae
The Story of Civilization (W. Durant), Vol. 2

25 History is past politics, and politics present history.

John Robert Seeley (1834–95) British historian.
Quoting the historian E. A. Freeman
The Growth of British Policy

26 Hindsight is always twenty-twenty.

Billy Wilder (Samuel Wilder; 1906–) Austrian-born US film director.
Attrib.

27 The Cavaliers (Wrong but Wromantic) and the Roundheads (Right but Repulsive).

W. C. Sellar (1898–1951) British humorous writer.
1066 And All That

28 1066 And All That.

W. C. Sellar
Book title

29 The Roman Conquest was, however, a *Good Thing*, since the Britons were only natives at the time.

W. C. Sellar
1066 And All That

30 Napoleon's armies used to march on their stomachs, shouting: 'Vive l'intérieur!'
W. C. Sellar
1066 And All That

31 America became top nation and history came to a full stop.
W. C. Sellar
1066 And All That

32 When in the chronicle of wasted time
I see descriptions of the fairest wights.
William Shakespeare (1564–1616) English dramatist.
Sonnet 106

33 History gets thicker as it approaches recent times.
A. J. P. Taylor (1906–   ) British historian.
English History, 1914–1945, Bibliography

34 All our ancient history, as one of our wits remarked, is no more than accepted fiction.
Voltaire (François-Marie Arouet; 1694–1778) French writer.
Jeannot et Colin

35 Indeed, history is nothing more than a tableau of crimes and misfortunes.
Voltaire
L'Ingénu, Ch. 10

36 Anything but history, for history must be false.
Robert Walpole (1676–1745) British statesman.
Walpoliana

37 The greater part of what passes for diplomatic history is little more than the record of what one clerk said to another clerk.
George Malcolm Young (1882–1959) British historian.
Victorian England: Portrait of an Age

HITLER

See also fascism, Germany, Nazism, World War II

1 The people Hitler never understood, and whose actions continued to exasperate him to the end of his life, were the British.
Alan Bullock (1914–   ) British academic and historian.
Hitler, A Study in Tyranny, Ch. 8

2 Hitler showed surprising loyalty to Mussolini, but it never extended to trusting him.
Alan Bullock
Hitler, A Study in Tyranny, Ch. 11

3 I have only one purpose, the destruction of Hitler, and my life is much simplified thereby. If Hitler invaded Hell I would make at least a favourable reference to the Devil in the House of Commons.
Winston Churchill (1874–1965) British statesman.
The Grand Alliance

4 The Italians will laugh at me; every time

Hitler occupies a country he sends me a message.
Benito Mussolini (1883–1945) Italian dictator.
Hitler (Alan Bullock), Ch. 8

5 That garrulous monk.
Benito Mussolini
Referring to Hitler
The Second World War (W. Churchill)

6 I wouldn't believe Hitler was dead, even if he told me so himself.
Hjalmar Schacht (1877–1970) German banker.
Attrib.

7 A racing tipster who only reached Hitler's level of accuracy would not do well for his clients.
A. J. P. Taylor (1906–   ) British historian.
The Origins of the Second World War, Ch. 7

8 Germany was the cause of Hitler just as much as Chicago is responsible for the *Chicago Tribune*.
Alexander Woollcott (1887–1943) US writer and critic.
Woollcott died after the broadcast
Radio broadcast, 1943

HOME

See also homesickness, travel

1 East, west, home's best.
Proverb

2 Home is where the heart is.
Proverb

3 Home is home, though it be never so homely.
John Clarke (fl. 1639) English scholar.
Paroemiologia Anglo-Latina

4 Home is the place where, when you have to go there,
They have to take you in.
Robert Frost (1875–1963) US poet.
The Death of the Hired Man

5 In fact there was but one thing wrong with the Babbitt house; it was not a home.
Sinclair Lewis (1885–1951) US novelist.
Babbitt, Ch. 2

6 A man travels the world over in search of what he needs and returns home to find it.
George Moore (1852–1933) Irish writer and art critic.
The Brook Kerith, Ch. 11

7 Mid pleasures and palaces though we may roam,
Be it ever so humble, there's no place like home;
 . . .
Home, home, sweet, sweet home!
There's no place like home! there's no place like home!
John Howard Payne (1791–1852) US actor and dramatist.
Clari, or the Maid of Milan

8 Home-keeping youth have ever homely wits.
William Shakespeare (1564–1616) English dramatist.
The Two Gentlemen of Verona, I:1

9 Seek home for rest,
For home is best.
Thomas Tusser (1524–80) English farmer.
Five Hundred Points of Good Husbandry, 'Instructions to Housewifery'

HOMESICKNESS

See also home, nostalgia

1 They say there's bread and work for all,
And the sun shines always there:
But I'll not forget old Ireland,
Were it fifty times as fair.
Helen Selina Blackwood (1807–67) British poet.
Lament of the Irish Emigrant

2 Weep no more, my lady,
Oh! weep no more today!
We will sing one song for the old Kentucky Home,
For the old Kentucky Home far away.
Stephen Foster (1826–64) US composer of popular songs.
My Old Kentucky Home

3 'Way down upon de Swanee Ribber,
Far, far away,
Dere's where my heart is turning ebber:
Dere's where de old folks stay.
All up and down de whole creation
Sadly I roam,
Still longing for de old plantation,
And for de old folks at home.
Stephen Foster
Old Folks at Home

4 Oh give me a home where the buffalo roam,
Where the deer and the antelope play,
Where seldom is heard a discouraging word
And the skies are not cloudy all day.
Brewster Higley (19th century) US songwriter.
Home on the Range

5 The accent of one's birthplace lingers in the mind and in the heart as it does in one's speech.
Duc de la Rochefoucauld (1613–80) French writer.
Maximes, 342

6 Breathes there the man, with soul so dead,
Who never to himself hath said,
This is my own, my native land!
Whose heart hath ne'er within him burn'd,
As home his footsteps he hath turn'd
From wandering on a foreign strand!
Walter Scott (1771–1832) Scottish novelist.
The Lay of the Last Minstrel, VI

7 In home-sickness you must keep moving – it is the only disease that does not require rest.
H. de Vere Stacpoole (1863–1931) Irish-born novelist.
The Bourgeois

8 Good-bye Piccadilly, Farewell Leicester Square;
It's a long, long way to Tipperary, but my heart's right there!
Harry Williams (1874–1924) British songwriter.
Written with Jack Judge (1878–1938)
It's a Long Way to Tipperary

9 I travelled among unknown men
In lands beyond the sea;
Nor, England! did I know till then
What love I bore to thee.
William Wordsworth (1770–1850) British poet.
I Travelled among Unknown Men

HOMOSEXUALITY

See also sex

1 But the men of Sodom were wicked and sinners before the Lord exceedingly.
Bible: Genesis
13:13

2 I became one of the stately homos of England.
Quentin Crisp (?1910–   ) Model, publicist, and writer.
The Naked Civil Servant

3 The . . . problem which confronts homosexuals is that they set out to win the love of a 'real' man. If they succeed, they fail. A man who 'goes with' other men is not what they would call a real man.
Quentin Crisp
The Naked Civil Servant

4 I am the Love that dare not speak its name.
Lord Alfred Douglas (1870–1945) British writer and poet.
Two Loves

5 The 'homo' is the legitimate child of the 'suffragette'.
Wyndham Lewis (1882–1957) British novelist.
The Art of Being Ruled, Pt. VIII, Ch. 4

6 Well, he looks like a man.
Abraham Lincoln (1809–65) US statesman.
On catching sight of Walt Whitman for the first time
Attrib.

7 This sort of thing may be tolerated by the French, but we are British – thank God.
Lord Montgomery (1887–1976) British field marshal.
Comment on a bill to relax the laws against homosexuals
Daily Mail, 27 May 1965

8 If Michelangelo had been straight, the Sistine Chapel would have been wallpapered.
Robin Tyler US comedienne.
Speech to gay-rights rally, Washington, 9 Jan 1988

HONESTY

See also frankness, integrity, sincerity, truth

1 An honest man's word is as good as his bond.
Proverb

2 Honesty is the best policy.
Proverb

3 It is impossible that a man who is false to his friends and neighbours should be true to the public.
Bishop Berkeley (1685–1753) Irish churchman and philosopher.
Maxims Concerning Patriotism

4 You see, I always divide people into two groups. Those who live by what they know to be a lie, and those who live by what they believe, falsely, to be the truth.
Christopher Hampton (1946–) British writer and dramatist.
The Philanthropist, Sc. 6

5 Though I be poor, I'm honest.
Thomas Middleton (1580–1627) English dramatist.
The Witch, III:2

6 To make your children *capable of honesty* is the beginning of education.
John Ruskin (1819–1900) British art critic and writer.
Time and Tide, Letter VIII

7 To be honest, as this world goes, is to be one man pick'd out of ten thousand.
William Shakespeare (1564–1616) English dramatist.
Hamlet, II:2

8 I thank God I am as honest as any man living that is an old man and no honester than I.
William Shakespeare
Much Ado About Nothing, III:5

9 Though I am not naturally honest, I am so sometimes by chance.
William Shakespeare
The Winter's Tale, IV:3

10 Father, I cannot tell a lie. I did it with my little hatchet.
George Washington (1732–99) US statesman.
Attrib.

11 Honesty is the best policy; but he who is governed by that maxim is not an honest man.
Richard Whately (1787–1863) British churchman.
Apophthegms

12 It is a terrible thing for a man to find out suddenly that all his life he has been speaking nothing but the truth.
Oscar Wilde (1854–1900) Irish-born British dramatist.
The Importance of Being Earnest, III

13 If you do not tell the truth about yourself you cannot tell it about other people.
Virginia Woolf (1882–1941) British novelist.
The Moment and Other Essays

HONOUR

See also titles

1 And they were offended in him. But Jesus said unto them, A prophet is not without honour, save in his own country, and in his own house.
Bible: Matthew
13:57

2 That chastity of honour, that felt a stain like a wound.
Edmund Burke (1729–97) British politician.
Reflections on the Revolution in France

3 Remember, men, we're fighting for this woman's honour; which is probably more than she ever did.
Groucho Marx (Julius Marx; 1895–1977) US comedian.
Duck Soup

4 Honour pricks me on. Yea, but how if honour prick me off when I come on? How then? Can honour set to a leg? No. Or an arm? No. Or take away the grief of a wound? No. Honour hath no skill in surgery, then? No. What is honour? A word. What is in that word? Honour. What is that honour? Air.
William Shakespeare (1564–1616) English dramatist.
Henry IV, Part One, V:1

5 For Brutus is an honourable man;
So are they all, all honourable men.
William Shakespeare
Julius Caesar, III:2

6 I once had a sparrow alight upon my shoulder for a moment while I was hoeing in a village garden, and I felt that I was more distinguished by that circumstance than I should have been by any epaulet I could have worn.
Henry David Thoreau (1817–62) US writer.
Walden, 'Winter Visitors'

7 Brothers all
In honour, as in one community,
Scholars and gentlemen.
William Wordsworth (1770–1850) British poet.
The Prelude, IX

HOPE

See also ambition, desire, expectation, optimism

1 A drowning man will clutch at a straw.
Proverb

2 Hope for the best.
Proverb

3 It is a long lane that has no turning.
Proverb

4 Still nursing the unconquerable hope,
Still clutching the inviolable shade.
Matthew Arnold (1822–88) British poet and critic.
The Scholar Gipsy

5 Charity is the power of defending that which we know to be indefensible. Hope is the power of being cheerful in circumstances which we know to be desperate.
G. K. Chesterton (1874–1936) British writer.
Heretics, Ch. 12

6 While there is life, there's hope,' he cried; 'Then why such haste?' so groaned and died.
John Gay (1685–1732) English poet and dramatist.
Fables

7 After all, tomorrow is another day.
Margaret Mitchell (1909–49) US novelist.
The closing words of the book
Gone with the Wind

8 Hope springs eternal in the human breast; Man never is, but always to be blest.
Alexander Pope (1688–1744) British poet.
An Essay on Man, I

9 For hope is but the dream of those that wake.
Matthew Prior (1664–1721) British poet.
Solomon, II

10 The miserable have no other medicine But only hope.
William Shakespeare (1564–1616) English dramatist.
Measure for Measure, III:1

HORSES

See also animals, hunting, sport and games

1 When I appear in public people expect me to neigh, grind my teeth, paw the ground and swish my tail – none of which is easy.
Princess Anne (1950–) The Princess Royal, only daughter of Elizabeth II.
The Observer, 'Sayings of the Week', 22 May 1977

2 I know two things about the horse, And one of them is rather coarse.
Anonymous
The Horse

3 I sprang to the stirrup, and Joris, and he; I galloped, Dirck galloped, we galloped all three.
Robert Browning (1812–89) British poet.
How they brought the Good News from Ghent to Aix

4 As lene was his hors as is a rake.
Geoffrey Chaucer (c. 1342–1400) English poet.
The Canterbury Tales, Prologue

5 The blue ribbon of the turf.
Benjamin Disraeli (1804–81) British statesman.
Describing the Derby
Life of Lord George Bentinck, Ch. 26

6 Gwine to run all night! Gwine to run all day! I bet my money on the bob-tail nag. Somebody bet on the bay.
Stephen Foster (1826–64) US composer of popular songs.
Camptown Races

7 They say princes learn no art truly, but the art of horsemanship. The reason is, the brave beast is no flatterer. He will throw a prince as soon as his groom.
Ben Jonson (1573–1637) English dramatist.
Timber, or Discoveries made upon Men and Matter

8 It takes a good deal of physical courage to ride a horse. This, however, I have. I get it at about forty cents a flask, and take it as required.
Stephen Leacock (1869–1944) English-born Canadian economist and humorist.
Literary Lapses, 'Reflections on Riding'

9 To confess that you are totally Ignorant about the Horse, is social suicide: you will be despised by everybody, especially the horse.
W. C. Sellar (1898–1951) British humorous writer.
Horse Nonsense

10 A horse! a horse ! my kingdom for a horse.
William Shakespeare (1564–1616) English dramatist.
Richard III, V:4

11 I have endured the Sandhurst riding-school, I have galloped for an impetuous general, I have been steward at regimental races, but none of these feats have altered my opinion that the horse, as a means of locomotion, is obsolete.
E. . Somerville (1858–1949) Irish writer.
Experiences of an Irish R.M., 'Great-Uncle McCarthy'

HOSPITALITY

1 A constant guest is never welcome.
Proverb

2 Fish and guests smell in three days.
Proverb

3 The first day a guest, the second day a guest, the third day a calamity.
Indian proverb

4 The guest who outstays his fellow-guests loses his overcoat.
Chinese proverb

5 I'd rather be a host than a guest. As Beerbohm wonderfully observed, a happy host makes a sad guest.
Harold Acton (1904–) British writer.
The Times, 18 Apr 1970

6 Let brotherly love continue. Be not forgetful to entertain strangers: for thereby some have entertained angels unawares.
Bible: Hebrews
13:1–2

HOUSES

See also architecture, home, stately homes

1 Houses are built to live in and not to look

on; therefore let use be preferred before uniformity, except where both may be had.
Francis Bacon (1561–1626) English philosopher.
Essays, 'Of Building'

2 A hundred and fifty accurate reproductions of Anne Hathaway's cottage, each complete with central heating and garage.
Osbert Lancaster (1908–86) British cartoonist.
Pillar to Post, 'Stockbrokers Tudor'

3 A house is a machine for living in.
Le Corbusier (Charles-Édouard Jeanneret; 1887–1965) Swiss-born French architect.
Towards an Architecture

4 They're all made out of ticky-tacky, and they all look just the same.
Malvina Reynolds (1900–78) US folksinger and songwriter.
Song describing a housing scheme built in the hills south of San Francisco
Little Boxes

5 It's 'aving 'ouses built by men, I believe, makes all the work and trouble.
H. G. Wells (1866–1946) British writer.
Kipps, Bk. III, Ch. 1

HOUSES OF PARLIAMENT

See also aristocracy, government, politics

1 This is a rotten argument, but it should be good enough for their lordships on a hot summer afternoon.
Anonymous
A note on a ministerial brief read out by mistake in the House of Lords
The Way the Wind Blows (Lord Home), 1976

2 The House of Lords is like a glass of champagne that has stood for five days.
Clement Attlee (1883–1967) British statesman and Labour prime minister.
Attrib.

3 A severe though not unfriendly critic of our institutions said that 'the cure for admiring the House of Lords was to go and look at it.'
Walter Bagehot (1826–77) British economist and journalist.
The English Constitution, 'The House of Lords'

4 A lot of hard-faced men who look as if they had done very well out of the war.
Stanley Baldwin (1867–1947) British statesman.
Referring to the first House of Commons elected after World War I (1918)
Economic Consequences of the Peace (J. M. Keynes), Ch. 5

5 The House of Lords is the British Outer Mongolia for retired politicians.
Tony Benn (1925–) British politician.
Speech, 11 Feb 1962

6 Better than a play.
Charles II (1630–85) King of England.
Referring to House of Lords debate on the Divorce Bill
Attrib.

7 I think . . . that it is the best club in London.
Charles Dickens (1812–70) British novelist.
Mr Tremlow describing the House of Commons
Our Mutual Friend, Bk. II, Ch. 3

8 I am dead: dead, but in the Elysian fields.
Benjamin Disraeli (1804–81) British statesman.
Said on his move to the House of Lords
Attrib.

9 The House of Lords is a model of how to care for the elderly.
Frank Field (1942–) British politician.
The Observer, 24 May 1981

10 The House of Peers, throughout the war,
Did nothing in particular,
And did it very well.
W. S. Gilbert (1836–1911) British dramatist.
Iolanthe, II

11 I have neither eye to see, nor tongue to speak here, but as the House is pleased to direct me.
William Lenthall (1591–1662) English parliamentarian.
Said on 4 Jan 1642 in the House of Commons when asked by Charles I if he had seen five MPs whom the King wished to arrest. It was a succinct restatement of the Speaker's traditional role
Historical Collections (Rushworth)

12 Mr Balfour's Poodle.
David Lloyd George (1863–1945) British Liberal statesman.
Referring to the House of Lords and its in-built Conservative majority; said in reply to a claim that it was 'the watchdog of the nation'
Remark, House of Commons, 26 June 1907

13 Every man has a House of Lords in his own head. Fears, prejudices, misconceptions – those are the peers, and they are hereditary.
David Lloyd George
Speech, Cambridge, 1927

14 The British, being brought up on team games, enter their House of Commons in the spirit of those who would rather be doing something else. If they cannot be playing golf or tennis, they can at least pretend that politics is a game with very similar rules.
Cyril Northcote Parkinson (1919–) British historian and writer.
Parkinson's Law, Ch. 2

15 The House of Lords must be the only institution in the world which is kept efficient by the persistent absenteeism of most of its members.
Herbert Samuel (1870–1963) British Liberal statesman.
News Review, 5 Feb 1948

16 A life peer is like a mule – no pride of ancestry, no hope of posterity.
Lord Shackleton (1911–) British politician, businessman, and life peer.
Attrib.

17 The House of Lords is a perfect eventide home.
Mary Stocks (1891–1975) British politician and writer.
The Observer, 'Sayings of the Week', 4 Oct 1970

18 The House of Lords, an illusion to which I have never been able to subscribe – responsibility without power, the prerogative of the eunuch throughout the ages.
Tom Stoppard (1937–) Czech-born British dramatist.
Lord Malquist and Mr Moon, Pt. VI, Ch. 1

19 You must build your House of Parliament upon the river: so . . . that the populace cannot exact their demands by sitting down round you.
Duke of Wellington (1769–1852) British general and statesman.
Words on Wellington (Sir William Fraser)

HOUSEWORK

See also woman's role

1 Housekeeping ain't no joke.
Louisa May Alcott (1832–88) US novelist.
Little Women, Pt. I

2 Our motto: Life is too short to stuff a mushroom.
Shirley Conran (1932–) Designer and journalist.
Superwoman, Epigraph

3 There was no need to do any housework at all. After the first four years the dirt doesn't get any worse.
Quentin Crisp (?1910–) Model, publicist, and writer.
The Naked Civil Servant

4 Cleaning your house while your kids are still growing
Is like shoveling the walk before it stops snowing.
Phyllis Diller (1917–) US writer and comedienne.
Phyllis Diller's Housekeeping Hints

5 I do, and I also wash and iron them.
Denis Thatcher (1915–) British businessman married to Mrs Margaret Thatcher.
Replying to the question 'Who wears the pants in this house?'
Times (Los Angeles), 21 Apr 1981

HUMAN CONDITION

See also human nature, life, mankind

1 A wanderer is man from his birth.
He was born in a ship
On the breast of the river of Time.
Matthew Arnold (1822–88) British poet and critic.
The Future

2 Thou hast created us for Thyself, and our heart is not quiet until it rests in Thee.
St Augustine of Hippo (354–430) Bishop of Hippo.
Confessions, Bk. I, Ch. 1

3 Man that is born of a woman is of few days, and full of trouble.
Bible: Job
14:1

4 We mortals cross the ocean of this world
Each in his average cabin of a life.
Robert Browning (1812–89) British poet.
Bishop Blougram's Apology

5 The human race, to which so many of my readers belong.
G. K. Chesterton (1874–1936) British writer.
The Napoleon of Notting Hill, Vol. I, Ch. 1

6 If God were suddenly condemned to live the life which he has inflicted on men, He would kill Himself.
Alexandre Dumas, fils (1824–95) French writer.
Pensées d'album

7 Every man is wanted, and no man is wanted much.
Ralph Waldo Emerson (1803–82) US poet and essayist.
Essays, 'Nominalist and Realist'

8 The world is a beautiful place
to be born into
if you don't mind some people dying
all the time
or maybe only starving
some of the time
which isn't half so bad
if it isn't you.
Laurence Ferlinghetti (1919–) US poet.
Pictures of the Gone World

9 Oh wearisome condition of humanity!
Born under one law, to another bound.
Fulke Greville (1554–1628) English poet and politician.
Mustapha, V:6

10 The condition of man . . . is a condition of war of everyone against everyone.
Thomas Hobbes (1588–1679) English philosopher.
Leviathan, Pt. I, Ch. 4

11 No arts; no letters; no society; and which is worst of all, continual fear and danger of violent death; and the life of man, solitary, poor, nasty, brutish, and short.
Thomas Hobbes
Leviathan, Pt. I, Ch. 13

12 Fade far away, dissolve, and quite forget
What thou among the leaves hast never known,
The weariness, the fever, and the fret,
Here, where men sit and hear each other groan.
John Keats (1795–1821) British poet.
Ode to a Nightingale

13 You come into the world alone, you go out

alone. In between it's nice to know a few people, but being alone is a fundamental quality of human life, depressing as that is.
Helen Mirren (1945–) British actress.
Remark, Jan 1989

14 Created half to rise, and half to fall;
Great lord of all things, yet a prey to all;
Sole judge of truth, in endless error hurl'd;
The glory, jest, and riddle of the world!
Alexander Pope (1688–1744) British poet.
An Essay on Man, II

15 Brief and powerless is Man's life; on him and all his race the slow, sure doom falls pitiless and dark.
Bertrand Russell (1872–1970) British philosopher.
Mysticism and Logic, 'A Free Man's Worship'

16 Farewell, a long farewell, to all my greatness!
This is the state of man: to-day he puts forth
The tender leaves of hopes: to-morrow blossoms
And bears his blushing honours thick upon him;
The third day comes a frost, a killing frost,
And when he thinks, good easy man, full surely
His greatness is a-ripening, nips his root,
And then he falls, as I do.
William Shakespeare (1564–1616) English dramatist.
Henry VIII, III:2

17 All the world's a stage,
And all the men and women merely players;
They have their exits and their entrances;
And one man in his time plays many parts,
His acts being seven ages.
William Shakespeare
As You Like It, II:7

18 When we are born, we cry that we are come
To this great stage of fools.
William Shakespeare
King Lear, IV:6

19 We have to believe in free-will. We've got no choice.
Isaac Bashevis Singer (1904–) Polish-born US writer.
The Times, 21 June 1982

20 But what am I?
An infant crying in the night:
An infant crying for the light:
And with no language but a cry.
Alfred, Lord Tennyson (1809–92) British poet.
In Memoriam A.H.H., LIV

21 All men should strive to learn before they die
What they are running from, and to, and why.
James Thurber (1894–1961) American humorist.
Attrib.

22 For what human ill does not dawn seem to be an alternative?
Thornton Wilder (1897–1975) US novelist and dramatist.
The Bridge of San Luis Rey

HUMAN NATURE

See also mankind

1 Human nature is so well disposed towards those who are in interesting situations, that a young person, who either marries or dies, is sure to be kindly spoken of.
Jane Austen (1775–1817) British novelist.
Emma, Ch. 22

2 A man's nature runs either to herbs, or to weeds; therefore let him seasonably water the one, and destroy the other.
Francis Bacon (1561–1626) English philosopher.
Essays, 'Of Nature in Men'

3 There is in human nature generally more of the fool than of the wise.
Francis Bacon
Essays, 'Of Boldness'

4 Nature is often hidden, sometimes overcome, seldom extinguished.
Francis Bacon
Essays, 'Of Nature in Men'

5 Nature, to be commanded, must be obeyed.
Francis Bacon
Novum Organum

6 Pleasant people are just as real as horrible people.
John Braine (1922–86) British novelist.
Remark, Apr 1983

7 When dealing with people, let us remember we are not dealing with creatures of logic. We are dealing with creatures of emotion, creatures bristling with prejudices and motivated by pride and vanity.
Dale Carnegie (1888–1955) US lecturer and writer.
Dale Carnegie's Scrapbook

8 I got disappointed in human nature as well and gave it up because I found it too much like my own.
J. P. Donleavy (1926–) US novelist.
Fairy Tales of New York

9 A man so various, that he seem'd to be
Not one, but all Mankind's Epitome.
Stiff in Opinions, always in the wrong;
Was Everything by starts, and Nothing long.
John Dryden (1631–1700) British poet and dramatist.
Absalom and Achitophel, I

10 A person seldom falls sick, but the bystanders are animated with a faint hope that he will die.
Ralph Waldo Emerson (1803–82) US poet and essayist.
Conduct of Life, 'Considerations by the Way'

11 Looks like whatever you try to do, somebody jumps up and hollers and raises cain – then the feller next to him jumps up and hollers how much he likes it.
Woody Guthrie (1912–67) US folk singer.
My Beat: An Intimate Volume of Shop Talk (Howard Taubman)

12 You may drive out nature with a pitchfork, yet she'll be constantly running back.
Horace (Quintus Horatius Flaccus; 65–8 BC) Roman poet.
Epistles, I

13 Most human beings have an almost infinite capacity for taking things for granted.
Aldous Huxley (1894–1964) British novelist.
Themes and Variations

14 We need more understanding of human nature, because the only real danger that exists is man himself . . . We know nothing of man, far too little. His psyche should be studied because we are the origin of all coming evil.
Carl Gustav Jung (1875–1961) Swiss psychoanalyst.
BBC television interview

15 Out of the crooked timber of humanity no straight thing can ever be made.
Immanuel Kant (1724–1804) German philosopher.
Idee zu einer allgemeinen Geschichte in weltbürgerlicher Absicht

16 Scenery is fine – but human nature is finer.
John Keats (1795–1821) British poet.
Letter to Benjamin Bailey, 13 Mar 1818

17 Upon the whole I dislike mankind: whatever people on the other side of the question may advance, they cannot deny that they are always surprised at hearing of a good action and never of a bad one.
John Keats
Letter, 1820

18 No absolute is going to make the lion lie down with the lamb unless the lamb is inside.
D. H. Lawrence (1885–1930) British novelist.
The Later D. H. Lawrence

19 Observe diners arriving at any restaurant and you will see them make a bee-line for the wall-seats. No one ever voluntarily selects a centre table in an open space. Open seating positions are only taken when all the wall-seats are already occupied. This dates back to a primeval feeding practice of avoiding sudden attack during the deep concentration involved in consuming food.
Desmond Morris (1928–) British biologist.
Manwatching, 'Feeding Behaviour'

20 In the misfortune of our best friends we always find something which is not displeasing to us.
Duc de la Rochefoucauld (1613–80) French writer.
Maximes, 99

21 'Tis the way of all flesh.
Thomas Shadwell (1642–92) English dramatist.
The Sullen Lovers, V:2

22 It is part of human nature to hate the man you have hurt.
Tacitus (c. 55–c. 120 AD) Roman historian.
Agricola, 42

23 It is not the ape, nor the tiger in man that I fear, it is the donkey.
William Temple (1881–1944) British churchman.
Attrib.

24 . . . use thought only to justify their injustices, and speech only to conceal their thoughts.
Voltaire (François-Marie Arouet; 1694–1778) French writer.
Referring to men
Dialogue, 'Le Chapon et la poularde'

25 The earth does not argue,
Is not pathetic, has no arrangements,
Does not scream, haste, persuade, threaten, promise,
Makes no discriminations, has no conceivable failures,
Closes nothing, refuses nothing, shuts none out.
Walt Whitman (1819–92) US poet.
To the sayers of words

HUMAN RIGHTS

See also equality, freedom, race

1 All human beings are born free and equal in dignity and rights.
Anonymous
Universal Declaration of Human Rights (1948), Article 1

2 *Liberté! Égalité! Fraternité!*
Freedom! Equality! Brotherhood!
Anonymous
Motto for French Revolutionaries

3 We hold these truths to be self-evident: that all men are created equal; that they are endowed by their Creator with certain unalienable rights; that among these are life, liberty, and the pursuit of happiness.
Thomas Jefferson (1743–1826) US statesman.
Declaration of American Independence, 4 July 1776

4 We look forward to a world founded upon four essential human freedoms. The first is freedom of speech and expression – everywhere in the world. The second is freedom of every person to worship God in his own way – everywhere in the world. The third is freedom from want . . . everywhere in the world. The fourth is freedom from fear . . . anywhere in the world.
Franklin D. Roosevelt (1882–1945) US Democratic president.
Speech to Congress, 6 Jan 1941

5 Freedom is an indivisible word. If we want to enjoy it, and fight for it, we must be prepared to extend it to everyone, whether they are rich or poor, whether they agree with us or not, no matter what their race or the colour of their skin.
Wendell Lewis Willkie (1892–1944) US lawyer and businessman.
One World, Ch. 13

HUMILITY

See also service, servility

1 Blessed are the meek: for they shall inherit the earth.
Bible: Matthew
5:5

2 Humility is only doubt,
And does the sun and moon blot out.
William Blake (1757–1827) British poet.
The Everlasting Gospel

3 I do not consider it an insult but rather a compliment to be called an agnostic. I do not pretend to know where many ignorant men are sure.
Clarence Seward Darrow (1857–1938) US lawyer.
Remark during the trial (1925) of John Scopes for teaching the theory of evolution in school

4 It is difficult to be humble. Even if you aim at humility, there is no guarantee that when you have attained the state you will not be proud of the feat.
Bonamy Dobrée (1891–1974) British scholar and writer.
John Wesley

5 Less than the dust beneath thy chariot wheel,
Less than the weed that grows beside thy door,
Less than the rust that never stained thy sword,
Less than the need thou hast in life of me,
Even less am I.
Laurence Hope (Mrs M. H. Nicolson; 1804–1905) British poet and songwriter.
The Garden of Kama and other Love Lyrics from India, 'Less than the Dust'

6 The meek do not inherit the earth unless they are prepared to fight for their meekness.
H. J. Laski (1893–1950) British political theorist.
Attrib.

7 The humble and meek are thirsting for blood.
Joe Orton (1933–67) British dramatist.
Funeral Games, I

8 Because there's no fourth class.
George Santayana (1863–1952) US philosopher.
On being asked why he always travelled third class
Living Biographies of the Great Philosophers (H. Thomas)

9 I too had thoughts once of being an intellectual, but I found it too difficult.
Albert Schweitzer (1875–1965) French Protestant theologian, philosopher, physician, and musician.
Remark made to an African who refused to perform a menial task on the grounds that he was an intellectual
Attrib.

10 Take physic, pomp;
Expose thyself to feel what wretches feel.
William Shakespeare (1564–1616) English dramatist.
King Lear, III:4

11 We have the highest authority for believing that the meek shall inherit the Earth; though I have never found any particular corroboration of this aphorism in the records of Somerset House.
F. E. Smith (1872–1930) British lawyer and politician.
Contemporary Personalities, 'Marquess Curzon'

12 This is not for me. The honour is for the poor.
Mother Teresa (Agnes Gonxha Bojaxhui; 1910–) Yugoslavian missionary in Calcutta.
Said on receiving the Order of Merit, 24 Nov 1983
The Sunday Times, 3 Dec 1989

13 When I survey the wondrous Cross,
On which the Prince of Glory died,
My richest gain I count but loss
And pour contempt on all my pride.
Isaac Watts (1674–1748) English theologian and hymn writer.
When I Survey the Wondrous Cross

14 Gentle Jesus, meek and mild,
Look upon a little child;
Pity my simplicity,
Suffer me to come to thee.
Charles Wesley (1707–88) British religious leader.
Hymns and Sacred Poems

HUMOUR

See also laughter, nonsense, puns

On the subject

1 I have a fine sense of the ridiculous, but no sense of humour.
Edward Albee (1928–) US dramatist.
Who's Afraid of Virginia Woolf?, I

2 The marvellous thing about a joke with a double meaning is that it can only mean one thing.
Ronnie Barker (1929–) British comedian.
Sauce, 'Daddie's Sauce'

3 The world would not be in such a snarl, had Marx been Groucho instead of Karl.
Irving Berlin (Israel Baline; 1888–1989) US composer.
Telegram to Groucho Marx on his seventy-first birthday

4 It's a good deed to forget a poor joke.
Brendan Bracken (1901–58) British newspaper publisher and politician.
The Observer, 'Sayings of the Week', 17 Oct 1943

5 All I need to make a comedy is a park, a policeman and a pretty girl.
Charlie Chaplin (Sir Charles Spencer C.; 1889–1977) British film actor.
My Autobiography

6 I remain just one thing, and one thing only – and that is a clown.
It places me on a far higher plane than any politician.
Charlie Chaplin
The Observer, 'Sayings of the Week', 17 June 1960

7 A joke's a very serious thing.
Charles Churchill (1731–64) British poet.
The Ghost, Bk. IV

8 Men will confess to treason, murder, arson, false teeth, or a wig. How many of them will own up to a lack of humour?
Frank More Colby (1865–1925) US editor.
Essays, I

9 No mind is thoroughly well organized that is deficient in a sense of humour.
Samuel Taylor Coleridge (1772–1834) British poet.
Table Talk

10 Total absence of humour renders life impossible.
Colette (1873–1954) French novelist.
Chance Acquaintances

11 A different taste in jokes is a great strain on the affections.
George Eliot (Mary Ann Evans; 1819–80) British novelist.
Daniel Deronda

12 Comedy, like sodomy, is an unnatural act.
Marty Feldman (1933–83) British comedian.
The Times, 9 June 1969

13 As for the Freudian, it is a very low, Central European sort of humour.
Robert Graves (1895–1985) British poet and novelist.
Occupation: Writer

14 Funny peculiar, or funny ha-ha?
Ian Hay (John Hay Beith; 1876–1952) British novelist and dramatist.
The Housemaster, III

15 His foe was folly and his weapon wit.
Anthony Hope (Sir Anthony Hope Hawkins; 1863–1933) British novelist.
Written for the inscription on the memorial to W. S. Gilbert, Victoria Embankment, London

16 Every man has, some time in his life, an ambition to be a wag.
Samuel Johnson (1709–84) British lexicographer.
Diary and Letters (Mme D'Arblay), Vol. III, Ch. 46

17 The essence of any blue material is timing. If you sit on it, it becomes vulgar.
Danny La Rue (Daniel Patrick Carroll; 1928–) British entertainer.
Attrib.

18 The coarse joke proclaims that we have here an animal which finds its own animality either objectionable or funny.
C. S. Lewis (1898–1963) British academic and writer.
Miracles

19 Impropriety is the soul of wit.
W. Somerset Maugham (1874–1965) British novelist.
The Moon and Sixpence, Ch. 4

20 It is not for nothing that, in the English language alone, to accuse someone of trying to be funny is highly abusive.
Malcolm Muggeridge (1903–) British writer.
Tread Softly For You Tread on My Jokes

21 Attic wit.
Pliny the Elder (Gaius Plinius Secundus; 23–79 AD) Roman scholar.
Natural History, II

22 True wit is nature to advantage dress'd;
What oft was thought, but ne'er so well express'd.
Alexander Pope (1688–1744) British poet.
An Essay on Criticism

23 Comedy, we may say, is society protecting itself – with a smile.
J. B. Priestley (1894–1984) British novelist.
George Meredith

24 A comedian can only last till he either takes himself serious or his audience takes him serious.
Will Rogers (1879–1935) US actor and humorist.
Newspaper article, 1931

25 Everything is funny, as long as it's happening to somebody else.
Will Rogers
The Illiterate Digest

26 I am not only witty in myself, but the cause that wit is in other men. I do here walk before thee like a sow that hath overwhelm'd all her litter but one.
William Shakespeare (1564–1616) English dramatist.
Henry IV, Part Two, I:2

27 A jest's prosperity lies in the ear
Of him that hears it, never in the tongue
Of him that makes it.
William Shakespeare
Love's Labour's Lost, V:2

28 It's hard to be funny when you have to be clean.
Mae West (1892–1980) US actress.
The Wit and Wisdom of Mae West (ed. J. Weintraub)

Some examples

29 There's a wonderful family called Stein,
There's Gert and there's Epp and there's Ein;
Gert's poems are bunk,
Epp's statues are junk,
And no one can understand Ein.
Anonymous

30 Little Willy from his mirror
Licked the mercury right off,
Thinking in his childish error,
It would cure the whooping cough.
At the funeral his mother
Smartly said to Mrs Brown:
'Twas a chilly day for Willie
When the mercury went down'.
Anonymous
Willie's Epitaph

31 There was an old man from Darjeeling,
Who boarded a bus bound for Ealing,
He saw on the door:
'Please don't spit on the floor',
So he stood up and spat on the ceiling.
Anonymous

32 I do most of my work sitting down; that's
where I shine.
Robert Benchley (1889–1945) US humorist.
Attrib.

33 No visit to Dove Cottage, Grasmere, is
complete without examining the outhouse
where Hazlitt's father, a Unitarian minister of
strong liberal views, attempted to put his
hand up Dorothy Wordsworth's skirt.
Alan Coren (1938–) British humorist and writer.
All Except the Bastard, 'Bohemia'

34 Dear 338171 (May I call you 338?).
Noël Coward (1899–1973) British dramatist.
Starting a letter to T. E. Lawrence who had retired from pub-
lic life to become Aircraftsman Brown, 338171
Letters to T. E. Lawrence

35 Miss Bolo rose from the table considerably
agitated, and went straight home, in a flood
of tears and a Sedan chair.
Charles Dickens (1812–70) British novelist.
Pickwick Papers, Ch. 35

36 It . . . was full of dry rot. An unkind visitor
said the only reason Menabilly still stood was
that the woodworm obligingly held hands.
Daphne Du Maurier (1907–89) British novelist.
Interview – referring to her own house in Cornwall upon
which Manderley in *Rebecca* was based

37 Wembley, adj. Suffering from a vague
malaise. 'I feel a bit w. this morning.'
Paul Jennings (1918–) British humorous writer.
The Jenguin Pennings, 'Ware, Wye, Watford'

38 The desire of the moth for the star.
James Joyce (1882–1941) Irish novelist.
Commenting on the interruption of a music recital when a moth
flew into the singer's mouth
James Joyce (R. Ellmann)

39 'When I makes tea I makes tea,' as old
mother Grogan said. 'And when I makes
water I makes water'.
James Joyce
Ulysses

40 The landlady of a boarding-house is a
parallelogram – that is, an oblong angular
figure, which cannot be described, but which
is equal to anything.
Stephen Leacock (1869–1944) English-born Canadian
economist and humorist.
Literary Lapses, 'Boarding-House Geometry'

41 One morning I shot an elephant in my
pajamas.
How he got into my pajamas I'll never know.
Groucho Marx (Julius Marx; 1895–1977) US comedian.
Animal Crackers

42 I could dance with you till the cows come
home. Better still, I'll dance with the cows
and *you* come home.
Groucho Marx
Duck Soup

43 Go – and never darken my towels again.
Groucho Marx
Duck Soup

44 I don't have a photograph, but you can have
my footprints. They are upstairs in my
socks.
Groucho Marx
A Night At the Opera

45 The strains of Verdi will come back to you
tonight, and Mrs Claypool's cheque will come
back to you in the morning.
Groucho Marx
A Night at the Opera

46 Please accept my resignation. I don't want to
belong to any club that will accept me as a
member.
Groucho Marx
Resigning from the Friar's Club in Hollywood
Attrib.

47 Dr Strabismus (Whom God Preserve) of
Utrecht is carrying out research work with a
view to crossing salmon with mosquitoes. He
says it will mean a bite every time for
fishermen.
J. B. Morton (1893–1979) British journalist.
By the Way, 'January Tail-piece'

48 Oh, don't worry about Alan . . . Alan will
always land on somebody's feet.
Dorothy Parker (1893–1967) US writer.
Said of her husband on the day their divorce became final
You Might As Well Live (J. Keats), Pt. IV, Ch. 1

49 He bit his lip in a manner which immediately
awakened my maternal sympathy, and I
helped him bite it.
S. J. Perelman (1904–79) US humorous writer.
Crazy Like a Fox, 'The Love Decoy'

50 I have Bright's disease and he has mine.
S. J. Perelman
(Bennet Cerf)

51 A case of the tail dogging the wag.
S. J. Perelman
Having escaped with some difficulty from the persistent atten-
tions of some prostitutes in the street
Another Almanac of Words at Play (W. Epsy)

52 The cook was a good cook, as cooks go; and
as cooks go she went.
Saki (Hector Hugh Munro; 1870–1916) British writer.
Reginald on Besetting Sins

53 Napoleon's armies used to march on their
stomachs, shouting: 'Vive l'intérieur!'
W. C. Sellar (1898–1951) British humorous writer.
1066 And All That

54 You wait here and I'll bring the etchings down.
James Thurber (1894–1961) US humorist.
Cartoon caption

55 Wall is the name – Max Wall. My father was the Great Wall of China. He was a brick.
Max Wall (1908–) British comedian.
Opening line of one of his acts

56 He spoke with a certain what-is-it in his voice, and I could see that, if not actually disgruntled, he was far from being gruntled.
P. G. Wodehouse (1881–1975) British humorous novelist.
The Code of the Woosters

HUNGER

See also desire, food, thirst

1 Hunger is the best sauce.
Proverb

2 Poverty is an anomaly to rich people. It is very difficult to make out why people who want dinner do not ring the bell.
Walter Bagehot (1826–77) British economist and journalist.
Literary Studies, II

3 When he told men to love their neighbour, their bellies were full. Nowadays things are different.
Bertolt Brecht (1898–1956) German dramatist.
Mother Courage, II

4 The best sauce in the world is hunger.
Miguel de Cervantes (1547–1616) Spanish novelist.
Don Quixote, Pt. II, Ch. 5

5 If only it were as easy to banish hunger by rubbing the belly as it is to masturbate.
Diogenes (412–322 BC) Greek philosopher.
Lives and Opinions of Eminent Philosophers (Diogenes Laertius)

6 They that die by famine die by inches.
Matthew Henry (1662–1714) English nonconformist minister.
Exposition of the Old and New Testaments

7 The war against hunger is truly mankind's war of liberation.
John Fitzgerald Kennedy (1917–63) US statesman.
Speech, World Food Congress, 4 June 1963

8 A hungry stomach has no ears.
Jean de La Fontaine (1621–95) French poet.
Fables, IX, 'Le Milan et le Rossignol'

9 I came home . . . hungry as a hunter.
Charles Lamb (1775–1834) British essayist.
Letter to Coleridge, Apr 1800

10 Let them eat cake.
Marie-Antoinette (1755–93) Queen of France.
On being told that the people had no bread to eat; in fact she was repeating a much older saying
Attrib.

HUNTING

See also sport and games

1 Spirits of well-shot woodcock, partridge, snipe
Flutter and bear him up the Norfolk sky.
John Betjeman (1906–84) British poet.
Death of King George V

2 Detested sport,
That owes its pleasures to another's pain.
William Cowper (1731–1800) British poet.
The Task

3 Wild animals never kill for sport. Man is the only one to whom the torture and death of his fellow-creatures is amusing in itself.
J. A. Froude (1818–94) British historian.
Oceana, Ch. 5

4 D'ye ken John Peel with his coat so gay?
D'ye ken John Peel at the break of the day?
D'ye ken John Peel when he's far far away
With his hounds and his horn in the morning?

'Twas the sound of his horn called me from my bed,
And the cry of his hounds has me oft-times led;
For Peel's view-hollo would waken the dead,
Or a fox from his lair in the morning.
John Woodcock Graves (1795–1886) British poet, huntsman, and songwriter.
John Peel

5 It is very strange, and very melancholy, that the paucity of human pleasures should persuade us ever to call hunting one of them.
Samuel Johnson (1709–84) British lexicographer.
Johnsonian Miscellanies (ed. G. B. Hill), Vol. I

6 It isn't mere convention. Everyone can see that the people who hunt are the right people and the people who don't are the wrong ones.
George Bernard Shaw (1856–1950) Irish dramatist and critic.
Heartbreak House

7 But He was never, well,
What I call
A Sportsman;
For forty days
He went out into the desert
– And never shot anything.
Osbert Sitwell (1892–1969) British writer.
Old Fashioned Sportsmen

8 The English country gentleman galloping after a fox – the unspeakable in full pursuit of the uneatable.
Oscar Wilde (1854–1900) Irish-born British dramatist.
A Woman of No Importance, I

HURT

See also cruelty, insensitivity, nastiness, suffering

1 Those have most power to hurt us that we love.

Francis Beaumont (1584–1616) English dramatist.
The Maid's Tragedy, V:6

2 Mrs Montagu has dropt me. Now, Sir, there are people whom one should like very well to drop, but would not wish to be dropped by.

Samuel Johnson (1709–84) British lexicographer.
Life of Johnson (J. Boswell), Vol. IV

3 It takes your enemy and your friend, working together, to hurt you to the heart; the one to slander you and the other to get the news to you.

Mark Twain (Samuel Langhorne Clemens; 1835–1910) US writer.
Following the Equator

4 We flatter those we scarcely know,
We please the fleeting guest,
And deal full many a thoughtless blow
To those who love us best.

Ella Wheeler Wilcox (1850–1919) US poet.
Life's Scars

HYPOCHONDRIA

1 I never read a patent medicine advertisement without being impelled to the conclusion that I am suffering from the particular disease therein dealt with in its most virulent form.

Jerome K. Jerome (1859–1927) British humorist.
Three Men in a Boat, Ch. 1

2 People who are always taking care of their health are like misers, who are hoarding a treasure which they have never spirit enough to enjoy.

Laurence Sterne (1713–68) Irish-born British writer.
Attrib.

3 The imaginary complaints of indestructible old ladies.

Elwyn Brooks White (1899–1985) US journalist and humorist.
Harper's Magazine, Nov 1941

HYPOCRISY

See also example, insincerity

1 All are not saints that go to church.
Proverb

2 It is the wisdom of the crocodiles, that shed tears when they would devour.

Francis Bacon (1561–1626) English philosopher.
Essays, 'Of Wisdom for a Man's Self'

3 Woe unto you, scribes and Pharisees, hypocrites! for ye are like unto whited sepulchres, which indeed appear beautiful outward, but are within full of dead men's bones, and of all uncleanness.

Bible: Matthew
23:27

4 Prisons are built with stones of Law, brothels with bricks of Religion.

William Blake (1757–1827) British poet.
The Marriage of Heaven and Hell, 'Proverbs of Hell'

5 God be thanked, the meanest of his creatures
Boasts two soul-sides, one to face the world with,
One to show a woman when he loves her!

Robert Browning (1812–89) British poet.
One Word More, XVII

6 Man is the only animal that can remain on friendly terms with the victims he intends to eat until he eats them.

Samuel Butler (1835–1902) British writer.
Notebooks

7 The smyler with the knyf under the cloke.

Geoffrey Chaucer (c. 1342–1400) English poet.
The Canterbury Tales, 'The Knight's Tale'

8 We ought to see far enough into a hypocrite to see even his sincerity.

G. K. Chesterton (1874–1936) British writer.
Heretics, Ch. 5

9 The book written against fame and learning has the author's name on the title-page.

Ralph Waldo Emerson (1803–82) US poet and essayist.
Journal

10 Man is the only animal that learns by being hypocritical. He pretends to be polite and then, eventually, he *becomes* polite.

Jean Kerr (1923–) US dramatist.
Finishing Touches

11 Hypocrisy is the most difficult and nerve-racking vice that any man can pursue; it needs an unceasing vigilance and a rare detachment of spirit. It cannot, like adultery or gluttony, be practised at spare moments; it is a whole-time job.

W. Somerset Maugham (1874–1965) British novelist.
Cakes and Ale, Ch. 1

12 For neither man nor angel can discern Hypocrisy, the only evil that walks Invisible, except to God alone.

John Milton (1608–74) English poet.
Paradise Lost, Bk. III

13 Ancient sculpture is the true school of modesty. But where the Greeks had modesty, we have cant; where they had poetry, we have cant; where they had patriotism, we have cant; where they had anything that exalts, delights, or adorns humanity, we have nothing but cant, cant, cant.

Thomas Love Peacock (1785–1866) British novelist.
Crotchet Castle, Ch. 7

14 Hypocrisy is the homage paid by vice to virtue.

Duc de la Rochefoucauld (1613–80) French writer.
Maximes, 218

15 Well, whiles I am a beggar, I will rail
And say there is no sin but to be rich;
And being rich, my virtue then shall be
To say there is no vice but beggary.
William Shakespeare (1564–1616) English dramatist.
King John, II:1

16 Come not, when I am dead,
To drop thy foolish tears upon my grave,
To trample round my fallen head,
And vex the unhappy dust thou wouldst not
save.
Alfred, Lord Tennyson (1809–92) British poet.
Come Not, When I Am Dead

17 I sit on a man's back, choking him and
making him carry me, and yet assure myself
and others that I am very sorry for him and
wish to ease his lot by all possible means –
except by getting off his back.
Leo Tolstoy (1828–1910) Russian writer.
What Then Must We Do?, Ch. 16

18 I hope you have not been leading a double
life, pretending to be wicked and being really
good all the time. That would be hypocrisy.
Oscar Wilde (1854–1900) Irish-born British dramatist.
The Importance of Being Earnest, II

19 A Christian is a man who feels
Repentance on a Sunday
For what he did on Saturday
And is going to do on Monday.
Thomas Russell Ybarra (b. 1880) Venezuelan-born US
writer.
The Christian

I

IDEALISM

1 If a man hasn't discovered something that he
would die for, he isn't fit to live.
Martin Luther King (1929–68) US Black civil-rights
leader.
Speech, Detroit, 23 June 1963

2 If you can talk with crowds and keep your
virtue,
Or walk with Kings – nor lose the common
touch,
If neither foes nor loving friends can hurt you,
If all men count with you, but none too much;
If you can fill the unforgiving minute
With sixty seconds' worth of distance run,
Yours is the Earth and everything that's in it,
And – which is more – you'll be a Man my
son!
Rudyard Kipling (1865–1936) Indian-born British writer.
If

3 Ideal mankind would abolish death, multiply
itself million upon million, rear up city upon
city, save every parasite alive, until the
accumulation of mere existence is swollen to
a horror.
D. H. Lawrence (1885–1930) British novelist.
St Mawr

4 An idealist is one who, on noticing that a
rose smells better than a cabbage, concludes
that it will also make better soup.
H. L. Mencken (1880–1956) US journalist.
Sententiae

5 Do not despair
For Johnny head-in-air;
He sleeps as sound
As Johnny underground.
John Sleigh Pudney (1909–77) British poet and writer.
For Johnny

6 A radical is a man with both feet firmly
planted in the air.
Franklin D. Roosevelt (1882–1945) US Democratic
president.
Broadcast, 26 Oct 1939

7 Those who have never dwelt in tents have
no idea either of the charm or of the
discomfort of a nomadic existence. The
charm is purely romantic, and consequently
very soon proves to be fallacious.
Vita Sackville-West (Victoria Sackville-West; 1892–1962)
British poet and novelist.
Twelve Days, Ch. 6

8 If a woman like Eva Peron with no ideals can
get that far, think how far I can go with all
the ideals that I have.
Margaret Thatcher (1925–   ) British politician and prime
minister.
The Sunday Times, 1980

IDEAS

See also opinions, theory

1 What was once thought can never be
unthought.
Friedrich Dürrenmatt (1921–   ) Swiss writer.
The Physicists

2 A stand can be made against invasion by an
army; no stand can be made against invasion
by an idea.
Victor Hugo (1802–85) French writer.
Histoire d'un Crime, 'La Chute'

3 Many ideas grow better when transplanted
into another mind than in the one where they
sprang up.
Oliver Wendell Holmes Jnr (1841–1935) US jurist.

4 Society goes on and on and on. It is the
same with ideas.
Ramsey MacDonald (1866–1937) British statesman and
prime minister.
Speech, 1935

5 An idea isn't responsible for the people who believe in it.
Don Marquis (1878–1937) US journalist.
New York Sun

6 A society made up of individuals who were all capable of original thought would probably be unendurable. The pressure of ideas would simply drive it frantic.
H. L. Mencken (1880–1956) US journalist.
Notebooks, 'Minority Report'

IDLENESS

See also bed, laziness, leisure, unemployment

1 The devil finds work for idle hands to do.
Proverb

2 The dreadful burden of having nothing to do.
Nicolas Boileau (1636–1711) French writer.
Épitres, XI

3 Idleness is only the refuge of weak minds.
Earl of Chesterfield (1694–1773) English statesman.
Letter to his son, 20 July 1749

4 What is this life if, full of care,
We have no time to stand and stare?
W. H. Davies (1871–1940) British poet.
Leisure

5 It is impossible to enjoy idling thoroughly unless one has plenty of work to do.
Jerome K. Jerome (1859–1927) British humorist.
Idle Thoughts of an Idle Fellow

6 I like work; it fascinates me. I can sit and look at it for hours. I love to keep it by me; the idea of getting rid of it nearly breaks my heart.
Jerome K. Jerome
Three Men in a Boat, Ch. 15

7 We would all be idle if we could.
Samuel Johnson (1709–84) British lexicographer.
Life of Johnson (J. Boswell), Vol. III

8 Young people ought not to be idle. It is very bad for them.
Margaret Thatcher (1925–) British politician and prime minister.
The Times, 1984

9 I am happiest when I am idle. I could live for months without performing any kind of labour, and at the expiration of that time I should feel fresh and vigorous enough to go right on in the same way for numerous more months.
Artemus Ward (Charles Farrar Browne; 1834–67) US humorous writer.
Pyrotechny

10 For Satan finds some mischief still
For idle hands to do.
Isaac Watts (1674–1748) English theologian and hymn writer.
Divine Songs for Children, 'Against Idleness and Mischief'

IGNORANCE

See also foolishness, innocence, innocence of childhood, stupidity

1 He that knows little, often repeats it.
Proverb

2 He that knows nothing, doubts nothing.
Proverb

3 What you don't know can't hurt you.
Proverb

4 Happy the hare at morning, for she cannot read
The Hunter's waking thoughts.
W. H. Auden (1907–73) British poet.
The Dog Beneath the Skin (with Christopher Isherwood)

5 She is an excellent creature, but she never can remember which came first, the Greeks or the Romans.
Benjamin Disraeli (1804–81) British statesman.
Referring to his wife
Attrib.

6 To each his suff'rings, all are men,
Condemn'd alike to groan;
The tender for another's pain,
Th' unfeeling for his own.
Yet ah! why should they know their fate?
Since sorrow never comes too late,
And happiness too swiftly flies.
Thought would destroy their paradise.
No more; where ignorance is bliss,
'Tis folly to be wise.
Thomas Gray (1716–71) British poet.
Ode on a Distant Prospect of Eton College

7 Alas, regardless of their doom,
The little victims play!
Thomas Gray
Ode on a Distant Prospect of Eton College

8 I wish you would read a little poetry sometimes. Your ignorance cramps my conversation.
Anthony Hope (Sir Anthony Hope Hawkins; 1863–1933) British novelist.
The Dolly Dialogues

9 Ignorance, madam, pure ignorance.
Samuel Johnson (1709–84) British lexicographer.
His reply on being questioned, by a lady reader of his *Dictionary*, why he had incorrectly defined 'pastern' as the 'knee' of a horse
Life of Johnson (J. Boswell), Vol. I

10 The ignorant man always adores what he cannot understand.
Cesare Lombroso (1853–1909) Italian criminologist.
The Man of Genius, Pt. III, Ch. 3

11 I count religion but a childish toy,
And hold there is no sin but ignorance.
Christopher Marlowe (1564–93) English dramatist.
The Jew of Malta, Prologue

12 From ignorance our comfort flows,

The only wretched are the wise.
Matthew Prior (1664–1721) British poet.
To the Hon. Charles Montague

13 He hath never fed of the dainties that are
bred in a book; he hath not eat paper, as it
were; he hath not drunk ink; his intellect is
not replenished.
William Shakespeare (1564–1616) English dramatist.
Love's Labour's Lost, IV:2

14 He that is robb'd, not wanting what is stol'n,
Let him not know't, and he's not robb'd at all.
William Shakespeare
Othello, III:3

15 What you don't know would make a great
book.
Sydney Smith (1771–1845) British clergyman and
essayist.
Memoir (Lady Holland)

16 Somebody else's ignorance is bliss.
Jack Vance (1916–) US writer.
Star King

17 Ignorance is like a delicate exotic fruit; touch
it, and the bloom is gone.
Oscar Wilde (1854–1900) Irish-born British dramatist.
The Importance of Being Earnest, I

ILLEGITIMACY

1 If you please, ma'am, it was a very little one.
Captain Frederick Marryat (1792–1848) British
novelist.
Said by the nurse to excuse the fact that she had had an illegiti-
mate baby
Mr. Midshipman Easy, Ch. 3

2 It serves me right for putting all my eggs in
one bastard.
Dorothy Parker (1893–1967) US writer.
Said on going into hospital to get an abortion
You Might as Well Live (J. Keats), Pt. II, Ch. 3

3 There are no illegitimate children – only
illegitimate parents.
Léon R. Yankwich US lawyer.
Decision, State District Court, Southern District of California,
Jun 1928, quoting columnist O. O. McIntyre

ILLNESS

See also disease, doctors, drugs, health and healthy living,
medicine, remedies

1 Across the wires the electric message came:
'He is no better, he is much the same.'
Alfred Austin (1835–1913) British poet.
Generally attrib. to Austin but there is no definite evidence
that he wrote it
On the Illness of the Prince of Wales

2 'Ye can call it influenza if ye like,' said Mrs
Machin. 'There was no influenza in my young
days. We called a cold a cold.'
Arnold Bennett (1867–1931) British novelist.
The Card, Ch. 8

3 My message to the businessmen of this
country when they go abroad on business is
that there is one thing above all they can
take with them to stop them catching Aids,
and that is the wife.
Edwina Currie (1946–) British politician.
The Observer, 'Sayings of the Week', 15 Feb 1987

4 Much of the world's work, it has been said,
is done by men who do not feel quite well.
Marx is a case in point.
John Kenneth Galbraith (1908–) US economist.
The Age of Uncertainty, Ch. 3

5 Every time you sleep with a boy you sleep
with all his old girlfriends.
Government-sponsored AIDS advertisement, 1987

6 Hungry Joe collected lists of fatal diseases
and arranged them in alphabetical order so
that he could put his finger without delay on
any one he wanted to worry about.
Joseph Heller (1923–) US novelist.
Catch-22, Ch. 17

7 For that old enemy the gout
Had taken him in toe!
Thomas Hood (1799–1845) British poet.
Lieutenant Luff

8 Indigestion is charged by God with enforcing
morality on the stomach.
Victor Hugo (1802–85) French writer.
Les Misérables, 'Fantine', Bk. III, Ch. 7

9 How few of his friends' houses would a man
choose to be at when he is sick.
Samuel Johnson (1709–84) British lexicographer.
Life of Johnson (J. Boswell), Vol. IV

10 Oh what can ail thee, knight at arms
Alone and palely loitering;
The sedge has wither'd from the lake,
And no birds sing.
John Keats (1795–1821) British poet.
La Belle Dame Sans Merci

11 How sickness enlarges the dimensions of a
man's self to himself.
Charles Lamb (1775–1834) British essayist.
Last Essays of Elia, 'The Convalescent'

12 I am only half there when I am ill, and so
there is only half a man to suffer. To suffer
in one's whole self is so great a violation,
that it is not to be endured.
D. H. Lawrence (1885–1930) British novelist.
Letter to Catherine Carswell, 16 Apr 1916

13 Too late for fruit, too soon for flowers.
Walter De La Mare (1873–1956) British poet.
On being asked, as he lay seriously ill, whether he would like
some fruit or flowers
Attrib.

14 Only do always in health what you have often
promised to do when you are sick.
Sigismund (1368–1437) Holy Roman Emperor.
His advice on achieving happiness
Biographiana, Vol. I

15 Illness is the night-side of life, a more onerous citizenship. Everyone who is born holds dual citizenship, in the kingdom of the well and in the kingdom of the sick. Although we all prefer to use only the good passport, sooner or later each of us is obliged, at least for a spell, to identify ourselves as citizens of that other place.

Susan Sontag (1933–) US novelist and essayist.
Illness as Metaphor

16 Most of the time we think we're sick, it's all in the mind.

Thomas Wolfe (1900–38) US novelist.
Look Homeward, Angel, Pt. I, Ch. 1

IMAGINATION

1 The primary imagination I hold to be the living power and prime agent of all human perception, and as a repetition in the finite mind of the eternal act of creation in the infinite I AM.

Samuel Taylor Coleridge (1772–1834) British poet.
Biographia Literaria, Ch. 13

2 The Fancy is indeed no other than a mode of memory emancipated from the order of time and space.

Samuel Taylor Coleridge
Biographia Literaria, Ch. 13

3 Art is ruled uniquely by the imagination.

Benedetto Croce (1866–1952) Italian philosopher.
Esthetic, Ch. 1

4 She has no imagination and that means no compassion.

Michael Foot (1913–) British Labour politician and journalist.
Referring to Margaret Thatcher
Attrib.

5 Were it not for imagination, Sir, a man would be as happy in the arms of a chambermaid as of a Duchess.

Samuel Johnson (1709–84) British lexicographer.
Life of Johnson (J. Boswell), Vol. III

6 I am certain of nothing but the holiness of the heart's affections and the truth of imagination – what the imagination seizes as beauty must be truth – whether it existed before or not.

John Keats (1795–1821) British poet.
Letter to Benjamin Bailey, 22 Nov 1817

7 Picture yourself in a boat on a river with tangerine trees and marmalade skies.
Somebody calls you, you answer quite slowly a girl with kaleidoscope eyes.

John Lennon (1940–80) British rock musician.
Lucy in the Sky with Diamonds (with Paul McCartney)

8 His imagination resembled the wings of an ostrich. It enabled him to run, though not to soar.

Lord Macaulay (1800–59) British historian.
Essays and Biographies, 'John Dryden'. *Edinburgh Review*

9 Imagination and fiction make up more than three quarters of our real life.

Simone Weil (1909–43) French philosopher.
Gravity and Grace

IMITATION

See also originality

1 A lotta cats copy the Mona Lisa, but people still line up to see the original.

Louis Armstrong (1900–71) US jazz trumpeter.
When asked whether he objected to people copying his style
Attrib.

2 Imitation is the sincerest form of flattery.

Charles Caleb Colton (?1780–1832) British clergyman and writer.
Lacon, Vol. I

3 When people are free to do as they please, they usually imitate each other.

Eric Hoffer (1902–83) US writer.
The Passionate State of Mind

4 A mere copier of nature can never produce anything great.

Joshua Reynolds (1723–92) British portrait painter.
Discourse to Students of the Royal Academy, 14 Dec 1770

5 He who resolves never to ransack any mind but his own, will be soon reduced, from mere barrenness, to the poorest of all imitations; he will be obliged to imitate himself, and to repeat what he has before often repeated.

Joshua Reynolds
Discourse to Students of the Royal Academy, 10 Dec 1774

6 Of all my verse, like not a single line;
But like my title, for it is not mine.
That title from a better man I stole;
Ah, how much better, had I stol'n the whole!

Robert Louis Stevenson (1850–94) Scottish writer.
Underwoods, Foreword

7 You will, Oscar, you will.

James Whistler (1834–1903) US painter.
Replying to Oscar Wilde's exclamation 'I wish I had said that!'
Attrib.

IMMORTALITY

See also eternity, mortality, posterity

1 I don't want to achieve immortality through my work . . . I want to achieve it through not dying.

Woody Allen (Allen Stewart Konigsberg; 1935–) US film actor.
Woody Allen and His Comedy (E. Lax)

2 No young man believes he shall ever die.

William Hazlitt (1778–1830) British essayist.
On the Feeling of Immortality in Youth

3 He had decided to live for ever or die in the attempt.
Joseph Heller (1923–) US novelist.
Catch-22, Ch. 3

4 I detest life-insurance agents; they always argue that I shall some day die, which is not so.
Stephen Leacock (1869–1944) English-born Canadian economist and humorist.
Literary Lapses, 'Insurance. Up to Date'

5 Stuck with placards for 'Deathless', that bitter beer that tastes sweet to its drinkers.
Rainer Maria Rilke (1875–1926) Austrian poet.
Duineser Elegien, X

6 We feel and know that we are eternal.
Benedict Spinoza (Baruch de Spinoza; 1632–77) Dutch philosopher.
Ethics

7 A slumber did my spirit seal;
I had no human fears:
She seemed a thing that could not feel
The touch of earthly years.

No motion has she now, no force;
She neither hears nor sees;
Rolled round in earth's diurnal course,
With rocks, and stones, and trees.
William Wordsworth (1770–1850) British poet.
A Slumber did my Spirit seal

IMPERFECTION

See also mistakes, perfection, weakness

1 Accidents will happen in the best regulated families.
Proverb

2 No man is infallible.
Proverb

3 To err is human.
Proverb

4 Watch and pray, that ye enter not into temptation: the spirit indeed is willing, but the flesh is weak.
Bible: Matthew
26:41

5 He has his talents, his vast and cultivated mind, his vivid imagination, his independence of soul and his high-souled principles of honour. But then – ah, these Buts! Saint Preux never kicked the fireirons, nor made puddings in his tea cup.
Jane Welsh Carlyle (1801–66) The wife of Thomas Carlyle.
Referring to her husband, Thomas Carlyle
Letter to a friend, July 1821

6 When you have faults, do not fear to abandon them.
Confucius (K'ung Fu-tzu; 551–479 BC) Chinese philosopher.
Analects

7 Even imperfection itself may have its ideal or perfect state.
Thomas De Quincey (1785–1859) British writer.
Murder Considered as one of the Fine Arts

8 We must touch his weaknesses with a delicate hand. There are some faults so nearly allied to excellence, that we can scarce weed out the fault without eradicating the virtue.
Oliver Goldsmith (1728–74) Irish-born British writer.
The Good-Natured Man, I

9 I'm aggrieved when sometimes even excellent Homer nods.
Horace (Quintus Horatius Flaccus; 65–8 BC) Roman poet.
Ars Poetica

10 People often say that, by pointing out to a man the faults of his mistress, you succeed only in strengthening his attachment to her, because he does not believe you; yet how much more so if he does!
Marcel Proust (1871–1922) French novelist.
À la recherche du temps perdu: Du côté de chez Swann

11 We only confess our little faults to persuade people that we have no large ones.
Duc de la Rochefoucauld (1613–80) French writer.
Maximes, 327

12 If we had no faults of our own, we would not take so much pleasure in noticing those of others.
Duc de la Rochefoucauld
Maximes, 31

13 Oh. I have got lots of human weaknesses, who hasn't?
Margaret Thatcher (1925–) British politician and prime minister.
The Times, 1983

14 We are none of us infallible – not even the youngest of us.
William Hepworth Thompson (1810–86) British academic.
Referring to G. W. Balfour, who was a junior fellow of Trinity College at the time
Collections and Recollections (G. W. E. Russell), Ch. 18

IMPERTINENCE

See also frankness, rudeness

1 He has to learn that petulance is not sarcasm, and that insolence is not invective.
Benjamin Disraeli (1804–81) British statesman.
Said of Sir C. Wood
Speech, House of Commons, 16 Dec 1852

2 Must! Is *must* a word to be addressed to princes? Little man, little man! thy father, if

he had been alive, durst not have used that word.
Elizabeth I (1533 – 1603) Queen of England.
Said to Robert Cecil, on her death bed
A Short History of the English People (J. R. Green), Ch. 7

3 The right people are rude. They can afford to be.
W. Somerset Maugham (1874 – 1965) British novelist.
Our Betters, II

4 JUDGE WILLIS. You are extremely offensive, young man.
F. E. SMITH. As a matter of fact, we both are, and the only difference between us is that I am trying to be, and you can't help it.
F. E. Smith (1872 – 1930) British lawyer and politician.
Frederick Elwin, Earl of Birkenhead (Lord Birkenhead), Vol. I, Ch. 9

IMPETUOSITY

See also haste, spontaneity

1 In me the need to talk is a primary impulse, and I can't help saying right off what comes to my tongue.
Miguel de Cervantes (1547 – 1616) Spanish novelist.
Don Quixote, Pt. I, Ch. 30

2 There are some who speak one moment before they think.
Jean de La Bruyère (1645 – 96) French satirist.
Les Caractères

3 Celerity is never more admir'd
Than by the negligent.
William Shakespeare (1564 – 1616) English dramatist.
Antony and Cleopatra, III:7

4 A youth to whom was given
So much of earth – so much of heaven,
And such impetuous blood.
William Wordsworth (1770 – 1850) British poet.
Ruth

IMPORTANCE

See also triviality

1 Not to be sneezed at.
George Colman, the Younger (1762 – 1836) British dramatist.
Heir-at-Law, II:1

2 In heaven an angel is nobody in particular.
George Bernard Shaw (1856 – 1950) Irish dramatist and critic.
Man and Superman, 'Maxims for Revolutionists'

3 Art and religion first; then philosophy; lastly science. That is the order of the great subjects of life, that's their order of importance.
Muriel Spark (1918 –) British novelist.
The Prime of Miss Jean Brodie, Ch. 2

IMPOSSIBILITY

See possibility

IMPRESSIONABILITY

See also gullibility

1 She had
A heart – how shall I say? – too soon made glad,
Too easily impressed.
Robert Browning (1812 – 89) British poet.
My Last Duchess

2 Like a cushion, he always bore the impress of the last man who sat on him.
David Lloyd George (1863 – 1945) British Liberal statesman.
Referring to Lord Derby
Attrib. in *The Listener*, 7 Sep 1978. This remark is also credited to Earl Haig

3 Give me a girl at an impressionable age, and she is mine for life.
Muriel Spark (1918 –) British novelist.
The Prime of Miss Jean Brodie, Ch. 1

IMPRISONMENT

See also freedom, oppression, slavery

1 A robin redbreast in a cage
Puts all Heaven in a rage.
William Blake (1757 – 1827) British poet.
Auguries of Innocence

2 O! dreadful is the check – intense the agony
When the ear begins to hear, and the eye begins to see;
When the pulse begins to throb – the brain to think again –
The soul to feel the flesh, and the flesh to feel the chain.
Emily Brontë (1818 – 48) British novelist.
The Prisoner

3 She's only a bird in a gilded cage.
A. J. Lamb (1870 – 1928) British songwriter.
Song title

4 Stone walls do not a prison make,
Nor iron bars a cage.
Richard Lovelace (1618 – 58) English poet.
To Althea, from Prison

5 Forget the outside world. Life has different laws in here. This is Campland, an invisible country. It's not in the geography books, or the psychology books or the history books. This is the famous country where ninety-nine men weep while one laughs.
Alexander Solzhenitsyn (1918 –) Soviet novelist.
The Love-Girl and the Innocent, I:3

6 We think caged birds sing, when indeed they cry.
John Webster (1580 – 1625) English dramatist.
The White Devil, V:4

7 I never saw a man who looked
With such a wistful eye
Upon that little tent of blue
Which prisoners call the sky.
Oscar Wilde (1854–1900) Irish-born British dramatist.
The Ballad of Reading Gaol, I:3

8 The Governor was strong upon
The Regulations Act:
The Doctor said that Death was but
A scientific fact:
And twice a day the Chaplain called,
And left a little tract.
Oscar Wilde
The Ballad of Reading Gaol, III:3

9 Something was dead in each of us,
And what was dead was Hope.
Oscar Wilde
The Ballad of Reading Gaol, III:31

10 I know not whether Laws be right,
Or whether Laws be wrong;
All that we know who lie in gaol
Is that the wall is strong;
And that each day is like a year,
A year whose days are long.
Oscar Wilde
The Ballad of Reading Gaol, V:1

11 If this is the way Queen Victoria treats her
prisoners, she doesn't deserve to have any.
Oscar Wilde
Complaining at having to wait in the rain for transport to take
him to prison
Attrib.

IMPROVEMENT

See also progress

1 He so improved the city that he justly
boasted that he found it brick and left it
marble.
Augustus (63 BC – 14 AD) Roman emperor.
Referring to Rome
The Lives of the Caesars (Suetonius), 'Augustus'

2 I've got to admit it's getting better.
It's a little better all the time.
John Lennon (1940–80) British rock musician.
Getting Better (with Paul McCartney)

3 It is a stupidity second to none, to busy
oneself with the correction of the world.
Molière (Jean Baptiste Poquelin; 1622–73) French
dramatist.
Le Misanthrope, I:1

INATTENTION

1 Thank you for the manuscript; I shall lose no
time in reading it.
Benjamin Disraeli (1804–81) British statesman.
His customary reply to those who sent him unsolicited
manuscripts
Irreverent Social History (F. Muir)

2 That should assure us of at least forty-five
minutes of undisturbed privacy.
Dorothy Parker (1893–1967) US writer.
Pressing a button marked NURSE during a stay in hospital
The Algonquin Wits (R. Drennan)

3 Donsmanship . . . 'the art of criticizing without
actually listening'.
Stephen Potter (1900–69) British writer.
Lifemanship, Ch. 6

4 I murdered my grandmother this morning.
Franklin D. Roosevelt (1882–1945) US Democratic
president.
His habitual greeting to any guest at the White House he sus-
pected of paying no attention to what he said
Ear on Washington (D. McClellan)

INCOMPETENCE

1 This island is almost made of coal and
surrounded by fish. Only an organizing genius
could produce a shortage of coal and fish in
Great Britain at the same time.
Aneurin Bevan (1897–1960) British Labour politician.
Speech, Blackpool, 18 May 1945

2 The grotesque chaos of a Labour council – a
Labour council – hiring taxis to scuttle
around a city handing out redundancy notices
to its own workers.
Neil Kinnock (1942–) British politician.
Attacking militant members in Liverpool
Speech, Labour Party Conference, Bournemouth, 1985

3 He really deserves some sort of decoration
. . . a medal inscribed 'For Vaguery in the
Field'.
John Osborne (1929–) British dramatist.
Look Back in Anger, I

4 Work is accomplished by those employees
who have not yet reached their level of
incompetence.
Laurence J. Peter (1919–90) Canadian writer.
The Peter Principle

5 Madame, there you sit with that magnificent
instrument between your legs, and all you
can do is *scratch* it!
Arturo Toscanini (1867–1957) Italian conductor.
Rebuking an incompetent woman cellist
Attrib.

6 His ideas of first-aid stopped short at
squirting soda-water.
P. G. Wodehouse (1881–1975) British humorous
novelist.
My Man Jeeves, 'Doing Clarence a Bit of Good'

INDECISION

See also uncertainty

1 I will have nothing to do with a man who can
blow hot and cold with the same breath.
Aesop (6th century BC) Reputed Greek writer of fables.
Fables, 'The Man and the Satyr'

2 Nothing is so exhausting as indecision, and nothing is so futile.
Bertrand Russell (1872–1970) British philosopher.
Attrib.

3 I must have a prodigious quantity of mind; it takes me as much as a week, sometimes, to make it up.
Mark Twain (Samuel Langhorne Clemens; 1835–1910) US writer.
The Innocents Abroad, Ch. 7

INDEPENDENCE

See also self-reliance, society

1 I'm short enough and ugly enough to succeed on my own.
Woody Allen (Allen Stewart Konigsberg; 1935–) US film actor.
Play It Again Sam

2 When in the course of human events, it becomes necessary for one people to dissolve the political bonds which have connected them with another, and to assume among the powers of the earth the separate and equal station to which the laws of nature and of Nature's God entitle them, a decent respect to the opinions of mankind requires that they should declare the causes which impel them to the separation.
Thomas Jefferson (1743–1826) US statesman.
Declaration of Independence, Preamble

3 I think it much better that . . . every man paddle his own canoe.
Captain Frederick Marryat (1792–1848) British novelist.
Settlers in Canada, Ch. 8

INDIFFERENCE

See also insensitivity

1 But what is past my help is past my care.
Francis Beaumont (1584–1616) English dramatist.
With John Fletcher
The Double Marriage, I:1

2 Nothing is so fatal to religion as indifference, which is, at least, half infidelity.
Edmund Burke (1729–97) British politician.
Letter to William Smith, 29 Jan 1795

3 Sir, I view the proposal to hold an international exhibition at San Francisco with an equanimity bordering on indifference.
W. S. Gilbert (1836–1911) British dramatist.
Gilbert, His Life and Strife (Hesketh Pearson)

4 It's no go the picture palace, it's no go the stadium,
It's no go the country cot with a pot of pink geraniums,
It's no go the Government grants, it's no go the elections,

Sit on your arse for fifty years and hang your hat on a pension.
Louis MacNeice (1907–63) Irish-born British poet.
Bagpipe Music

5 At length the morn and cold indifference came.
Nicholas Rowe (1674–1718) English dramatist.
The Fair Penitent, I:1

6 I don't care a twopenny damn what becomes of the ashes of Napoleon Bonaparte.
Duke of Wellington (1769–1852) British general and statesman.
Attrib.

7 I hear it was charged against me that I sought to destroy institutions,
But really I am neither for nor against institutions.
Walt Whitman (1819–92) US poet.
I Hear It was Charged against Me

INDIVIDUALITY

See also difference, opinions, taste

1 Here's tae us wha's like us?
Gey few, and they're a' deid.
Anonymous
Scottish toast

2 Nature made him, and then broke the mould.
Ludovico Ariosto (1474–1533) Italian poet.
Referring to Charlemagne's paladin, Roland
Orlando furioso

3 It is the common wonder of all men, how among so many million of faces, there should be none alike.
Thomas Browne (1605–82) English physician and writer.
Religio Medici, Pt. II

4 We boil at different degrees.
Ralph Waldo Emerson (1803–82) US poet and essayist.
Society and Solitude, 'Eloquence'

INDOCTRINATION

See also education

1 Their teacher had advised them not to read Tolstoy novels, because they were very long and would easily confuse the clear ideas which they had learned from reading critical studies of him.
Alexander Solzhenitsyn (1918–) Soviet novelist.
The First Circle, Ch. 40

2 This universal, obligatory force-feeding with lies is now the most agonizing aspect of existence in our country – worse than all our material miseries, worse than any lack of civil liberties.
Alexander Solzhenitsyn
Letter to Soviet Leaders, 6

3 For us, the tasks of education in socialism were closely integrated with those of fighting.

Ideas that enter the mind under fire remain there securely and for ever.
Leon Trotsky (Lev Davidovich Bronstein; 1879–1940) Russian revolutionary.
My Life, Ch. 35

INDULGENCE

1 Love is a boy, by poets styl'd,
Then spare the rod, and spoil the child.
Samuel Butler (1612–80) English satirist.
Hudibras, Pt. II

2 Every luxury was lavished on you – atheism, breast-feeding, circumcision. I had to make my own way.
Joe Orton (1933–67) British dramatist.
Loot, I

INDUSTRIAL RELATIONS

See also diplomacy, strikes

1 British management doesn't seem to understand the importance of the human factor.
Charles, Prince of Wales (1948–) Eldest son of Elizabeth II.
Speech, Parliamentary and Scientific Committee lunch, 21 Feb 1979

2 Industrial relations are like sexual relations. It's better between two consenting parties.
Vic Feather (1908–76) British trade-union leader.
Guardian Weekly, 8 Aug 1976

3 It might be said that it is the ideal of the employer to have production without employees and the ideal of the employee is to have income without work.
E. F. Schumacher (1911–77) German-born economist.
The Observer, 'Sayings of the Week', 4 May 1975

INFERIORITY

See also equality, mediocrity

1 I just met X in the street, I stopped for a moment to exchange ideas, and now I feel like a complete idiot.
Heinrich Heine (1797–1856) German poet and writer.
Autant en apportent les mots (Pedrazzini)

2 Wherever an inferiority complex exists, there is a good reason for it. There is always something inferior there, although not just where we persuade ourselves that it is.
Carl Gustav Jung (1875–1961) Swiss psychoanalyst.
Interview, 1943

3 It is an infallible sign of the second-rate in nature and intellect to make use of everything and everyone.
Ada Beddington Leverson (1862–1933) British writer.
The Limit

4 There's no such thing as a bad Picasso, but some are less good than others.
Pablo Picasso (1881–1973) Spanish painter.
Come to Judgment (A. Whitman)

5 No one can make you feel inferior without your consent.
Eleanor Roosevelt (1884–1962) US writer and lecturer.
This is My Story

6 A king of shreds and patches.
William Shakespeare (1564–1616) English dramatist.
Hamlet, III:4

INFINITY

1 The Desire of Man being Infinite, the possession is Infinite, and himself Infinite.
William Blake (1757–1827) British poet.
There is no Natural Religion

2 I cannot help it; – in spite of myself, infinity torments me.
Alfred de Musset (1810–57) French dramatist and poet.
L'Espoir en Dieu

INFLEXIBILITY

See also determination, stubbornness

1 Whenever you accept our views we shall be in full agreement with you.
Moshe Dayan (1915–81) Israeli general.
Said to Cyrus Vance during Arab-Israeli negotiations
The Observer, 'Sayings of the Week', 14 Aug 1977

2 You cannot shake hands with a clenched fist.
Indira Gandhi (1917–84) Indian stateswoman.
Remark at a press conference, New Delhi, 19 Oct 1971

3 U-turn if you want to. The lady's not for turning.
Margaret Thatcher (1925–) British politician and prime minister.
Speech, Conservative Conference, 1980

4 Minds like beds always made up,
(more stony than a shore)
unwilling or unable.
William Carlos Williams (1883–1963) US poet.
Patterson, I, Preface

INFLUENCE

See also inspiration, power

1 Though Rome's gross yoke
Drops off, no more to be endured,
Her teaching is not so obscured
By errors and perversities,
That no truth shines athwart the lies.
Robert Browning (1812–89) British poet.
Christmas Eve, XI

2 How to Win Friends and Influence People.
Dale Carnegie (1888–1955) US lecturer and writer.
Book title

3 The proper time to influence the character of

a child is about a hundred years before he is born.
Dean Inge (1860–1954) British churchman.
The Observer, 21 June, 1929

4 We have met too late. You are too old for me to have any effect on you.
James Joyce (1882–1941) Irish novelist.
On meeting W. B. Yeats
James Joyce (R. Ellmann)

5 Practical men, who believe themselves to be quite exempt from any intellectual influences, are usually the slaves of some defunct economist. Madmen in authority, who hear voices in the air, are distilling their frenzy from some academic scribbler of a few years back.
John Maynard Keynes (1883–1946) British economist.
The General Theory of Employment, Interest and Money, Bk. VI, Ch. 24

6 The great man . . . walks across his century and leaves the marks of his feet all over it, ripping out the dates on his goloshes as he passes.
Stephen Leacock (1869–1944) English-born Canadian economist and humorist.
Literary Lapses, 'The Life of John Smith'

7 So you're the little woman who wrote the book that made this great war!
Abraham Lincoln (1809–65) US statesman.
Said on meeting Harriet Beecher Stowe, the author of *Uncle Tom's Cabin* (1852), which stimulated opposition to slavery before the US Civil War
Abraham Lincoln: The War Years (Carl Sandburg), Vol. II, Ch. 39

8 Athens holds sway over all Greece; I dominate Athens; my wife dominates me; our newborn son dominates her.
Themistocles (c. 528–462 BC) Athenian statesman.
Explaining an earlier remark to the effect that his young son ruled all Greece
Attrib.

9 The hand that rocks the cradle
Is the hand that rules the world.
William Ross Wallace (1819–81) US poet and songwriter.
John o'London's Treasure Trove

10 The man who can dominate a London dinner-table can dominate the world.
Oscar Wilde (1854–1900) Irish-born British dramatist.
Attrib. by R. Aldington in his edition of Wilde

INGRATITUDE

1 Never look a gift horse in the mouth.
Proverb

2 And having looked to government for bread, on the very first scarcity they will turn and bite the hand that fed them.
Edmund Burke (1729–97) British politician.
Thoughts and Details on Scarcity

3 Our gratitude to most benefactors is the same as our feeling for dentists who have pulled our teeth. We acknowledge the good they have done and the evil from which they have delivered us, but we remember the pain they occasioned and do not love them very much.
Nicolas Chamfort (1741–94) French writer.
Maximes et pensées

4 Blow, blow, thou winter wind,
Thou art not so unkind
As man's ingratitude.
William Shakespeare (1564–1616) English dramatist.
As You Like It, II:7

5 Ingratitude, thou marble-hearted fiend,
More hideous when thou show'st thee in a child
Than the sea-monster!
William Shakespeare
King Lear I:4

6 I hate ingratitude more in a man
Than lying, vainness, babbling drunkenness,
Or any taint of vice whose strong corruption
Inhabits our frail blood.
William Shakespeare
Twelfth Night, III:4

INJUSTICE

1 Give a dog a bad name and hang him.
Proverb

2 Those who have had no share in the good fortunes of the mighty often have a share in their misfortunes.
Bertolt Brecht (1898–1956) German dramatist.
The Caucasian Chalk Circle

3 When one has been threatened with a great injustice, one accepts a smaller as a favour.
Jane Welsh Carlyle (1801–66) The wife of Thomas Carlyle.
Journal, 21 Nov 1855

4 'No, no!' said the Queen. 'Sentence first – verdict afterwards.'
Lewis Carroll (Charles Lutwidge Dodgson; 1832–98) British writer.
Alice's Adventures in Wonderland, Ch. 12

5 I feel as a horse must feel when the beautiful cup is given to the jockey.
Edgar Degas (1834–1917) French artist.
On seeing one of his pictures sold at auction
Attrib.

6 To disarm the strong and arm the weak would be to change the social order which it's my job to preserve. Justice is the means by which established injustices are sanctioned.
Anatole France (Jacques Anatole François Thibault; 1844–1924) French writer.
Crainquebille

7 Undeservedly you will atone for the sins of your fathers.

Horace (Quintus Horatius Flaccus; 65–8 BC) Roman poet.
Odes, III

8 We was robbed!

Joe Jacobs (1896–1940) US boxing manager.
Complaining to the audience when the heavyweight title of Max Schmeling, whom he managed, was passed to Jack Sharkey
Attrib.

9 How could God do this to me after all I have done for him?

Louis XIV (1638–1715) French king.
On receiving news of the French army's defeat at the Battle of Blenheim
Saint-Simon at Versailles (L. Norton)

10 The government burns down whole cities while the people are forbidden to light lamps.

Mao Tse-Tung (1893–1976) Chinese communist leader.
Attrib.

11 That in the captain's but a choleric word Which in the soldier is flat blasphemy.

William Shakespeare (1564–1616) English dramatist.
Measure for Measure, II:2

12 I am a man More sinn'd against than sinning.

William Shakespeare
King Lear, III:2

13 He was quite sure that he had been wronged. Not to be wronged is to forgo the first privilege of goodness.

H. G. Wells (1866–1946) British writer.
Bealby, Pt. IV, Ch. 1

14 There is something utterly nauseating about a system of society which pays a harlot 25 times as much as it pays its Prime Minister, 250 times as much as it pays its Members of Parliament, and 500 times as much as it pays some of its ministers of religion.

Harold Wilson (1916–) British politician and prime minister.
Referring to the case of Christine Keeler
Speech, House of Commons, June 1963

INNOCENCE

See also conscience, ignorance

1 Now I am ashamed of confessing that I have nothing to confess.

Fanny Burney (Frances Burney D'Arblay; 1752–1840) British novelist.
Evelina, Letter 59

2 Now my innocence begins to weigh me down.

Jean Racine (1639–99) French dramatist.
Andromaque, III:1

Innocence of childhood

See also age, children, ignorance

3 'But the Emperor has nothing on at all!' cried a little child.

Hans Christian Andersen (1805–75) Danish writer.
The Emperor's New Clothes

4 No, it is not only our fate but our business to lose innocence, and once we have lost that, it is futile to attempt a picnic in Eden.

Elizabeth Bowen (1899–1973) Irish novelist.
In *Orion III*, 'Out of a Book'

5 Ralph wept for the end of innocence, the darkness of man's heart, and the fall through the air of the true, wise friend called Piggy.

William Golding (1911–) British novelist.
Lord of the Flies, Ch. 12

6 I remember, I remember,
The fir trees dark and high;
I used to think their slender tops
Were close against the sky:
It was a childish ignorance,
But now 'tis little joy
To know I'm farther off from heav'n
Than when I was a boy.

Thomas Hood (1799–1845) British poet.
I Remember

7 Credulity is the man's weakness, but the child's strength.

Charles Lamb (1775–1834) British essayist.
Essays of Elia, 'Witches and other Night Fears'

8 I'd the upbringing a nun would envy and that's the truth. Until I was fifteen I was more familiar with Africa than my own body.

Joe Orton (1933–67) British dramatist.
Entertaining Mr Sloane, I

9 And the wild boys innocent as strawberries.

Dylan Thomas (1914–53) Welsh poet.
The hunchback in the park

10 We live in our own world,
A world that is too small
For you to stoop and enter
Even on hands and knees,
The adult subterfuge.

R. S. Thomas
Song at the Year's Turning, 'Children's Song'

11 There was a time when meadow, grove, and stream,
The earth, and every common sight,
To me did seem
Apparelled in celestial light,
The glory and the freshness of a dream.

William Wordsworth (1770–1850) British poet.
Ode. Intimations of Immortality, I

INNOVATION

See also conservatism, novelty, originality, progress

1 He that will not apply new remedies must

expect new evils: for time is the greatest innovator.

Francis Bacon (1561–1626) English philosopher.
Essays, 'Of Innovations'

2 I once knew a chap who had a system of just hanging the baby on the clothes line to dry and he was greatly admired by his fellow citizens for having discovered a wonderful innovation on changing a diaper.

Damon Runyon (1884–1946) US writer.
Short Takes, 'Diaper Dexterity'

INNUENDO

See also meaning

1 There was an old man of Boulogne
Who sang a most topical song.
It wasn't the words
That frightened the birds,
But the horrible double-entendre.

Anonymous

2 I'm one of the ruins that Cromwell knocked about a bit.

Marie Lloyd (1870–1922) British music-hall singer.
Song title

3 Where more is meant than meets the ear.

John Milton (1608–74) English poet.
Il Penseroso

INSENSITIVITY

See also hurt, indifference

1 Miss Buss and Miss Beale
Cupid's darts do not feel.
How different from us,
Miss Beale and Miss Buss.

Anonymous
Written about the headmistresses of North London Collegiate School and Cheltenham Ladies' College, respectively

2 'There's been an accident' they said,
'Your servant's cut in half; he's dead!'
'Indeed!' said Mr Jones, 'and please
Send me the half that's got my keys.'

Harry Graham (1874–1936) British writer.
Ruthless Rhymes for Heartless Homes, 'Mr. Jones'

3 Just as the meanest and most vicious deeds require spirit and talent, so even the greatest deeds require a certain insensitiveness which on other occasions is called stupidity.

Georg Christoph Lichtenberg (1742–99) German physicist and writer.
Aphorisms

4 One would have to have a heart of stone to read the death of Little Nell without laughing.

Oscar Wilde (1854–1900) Irish-born British dramatist.
Lecturing upon Dickens
Lives of the Wits (H. Pearson)

INSIGNIFICANCE

See also triviality

1 There are some people who leave impressions not so lasting as the imprint of an oar upon the water.

Kate Chopin (1851–1904) US writer.
The Awakening, Ch. 34

2 She was one of those indispensables of whom one makes the discovery, when they are gone, that one can get on quite as well without them.

Aldous Huxley (1894–1964) British novelist.
Mortal Coils, 'Nuns at Luncheon'

INSINCERITY

See also hypocrisy

1 Experience teaches you that the man who looks you straight in the eye, particularly if he adds a firm handshake, is hiding something.

Clifton Fadiman (1904–) US writer.
Enter, Conversing

2 He who praises everybody praises nobody.

Samuel Johnson (1709–84) British lexicographer.
Life of Johnson (J. Boswell), Vol. III

3 Went to hear Mrs Turner's daughter . . . play on the harpsichon; but, Lord! it was enough to make any man sick to hear her; yet was I forced to commend her highly.

Samuel Pepys (1633–1703) English diarist.
Diary, 1 May 1663

4 Most friendship is feigning, most loving mere folly.

William Shakespeare (1564–1616) English dramatist.
As You Like It, II:7

INSPIRATION

1 A spur in the head is worth two in the heel.
Proverb

2 Ninety per cent of inspiration is perspiration.
Proverb

3 I dare not alter these things; they come to me from above.

Alfred Austin (1835–1913) British poet.
When accused of writing ungrammatical verse
A Number of People (E. Marsh)

4 That I make poetry and give pleasure (if I give pleasure) are because of you.

Horace (Quintus Horatius Flaccus; 65–8 BC) Roman poet.
Odes, IV

5 Biting my truant pen, beating myself for spite:
'Fool!' said my Muse to me, 'look in thy heart and write.'

Philip Sidney (1554–86) English poet and courtier.
Sonnet, *Astrophel and Stella*

6 I did not write it. God wrote it. I merely did his dictation.

Harriet Beecher Stowe (1811–96) US novelist.
Referring to *Uncle Tom's Cabin*
Attrib.

7 The true God, the mighty God, is the God of ideas.

Alfred de Vigny (1797–1863) French writer.
La Bouteille à la mer

INSULTS

See also actors, criticism, politicians, rudeness

1 Sticks and stones may break my bones, but words will never hurt me.
Proverb

2 I don't want you here – now sod off!

Princess Anne (1950–) The Princess Royal, only daughter of Elizabeth II.
Remark, Jan 1987

3 Lloyd George could not see a belt without hitting below it.

Margot Asquith (1865–1945) The second wife of Herbert Asquith.
The Autiobiography of Margot Asquith

4 She was a woman of mean understanding, little information, and uncertain temper.

Jane Austen (1775–1817) British novelist.
Pride and Prejudice, Ch. 1

5 I have known many an instance of a man writing a letter and forgetting to sign his name, but this is the only instance I have ever known of a man signing his name and forgetting to write the letter.

Henry Ward Beecher (1813–87) US Congregational minister.
Said on receiving a note containing the single word: 'Fool'
The Best Stories in the World (T. Masson)

6 Of course we all know that Morris was a wonderful all-round man, but the act of walking round him has always tired me.

Max Beerbohm (1872–1956) British writer.
Referring to William Morris
Conversations with Max (S. N. Behrman)

7 Come in, you Anglo-Saxon swine
And drink of my Algerian wine.
'Twill turn your eyeballs black and blue,
And damn well good enough for you.

Brendan Behan (1923–64) Irish playwright.
Painted as an advert on the window of a Paris café (the owner of which could not speak English)
My Life with Brendan (B. Behan)

8 So boring you fall asleep halfway through her name.

Alan Bennett (1934–) British playwright.
Referring to the Greek writer Arianna Stassinopoulos
The Observer, 18 Sept 1983

9 I mock thee not, though I by thee am mockèd;

Thou call'st me madman, but I call thee blockhead.

William Blake (1757–1827) British poet.
To Flaxman

10 If there is anyone here whom I have not insulted, I beg his pardon.

Johannes Brahms (1833–97) German composer.
Said on leaving a gathering of friends
Brahms (P. Latham)

11 Macaulay is well for a while, but one wouldn't *live* under Niagara.

Thomas Carlyle (1795–1881) Scottish historian and essayist.
Notebook (R. M. Milnes)

12 An injury is much sooner forgotten than an insult.

Earl of Chesterfield (1694–1773) English statesman.
Letter to his son, 9 Oct 1746

13 The only time in his life he ever put up a fight was when we asked him for his resignation.

Georges Clemenceau (1841–1929) French statesman.
Referring to Marshal Joffre
Here I Lie (A.M. Thomson)

14 The Cat, the Rat, and Lovell our dog
Rule all England under a hog.

William Collingbourne (d. 1484) English landowner.
The cat was Sir William Catesby; the rat Sir Richard Ratcliffe; the dog Lord Lovell, who had a dog on his crest. The wild boar refers to the emblem of Richard III
Chronicles (R. Holinshed), III

15 Your dexterity seems a happy compound of the smartness of an attorney's clerk and the intrigue of a Greek of the lower empire.

Benjamin Disraeli (1804–81) British statesman.
Speaking to Lord Palmerston
Attrib.

16 Good-morning, gentlemen both.

Elizabeth I (1533–1603) Queen of England.
When addressing a group of eighteen tailors
Sayings of Queen Elizabeth (Chamberlin)

17 A semi-house-trained polecat.

Michael Foot (1913–) British Labour politician and journalist.
Referring to Norman Tebbitt
Speech, House of Commons

18 Like being savaged by a dead sheep.

Denis Healey (1917–) British Labour politician.
Referring to the attack launched by Geoffrey Howe upon his Budget proposals
The Listener, 21 Dec 1978

19 Do you call that thing under your hat a head?

Ludwig Holberg (1684–1754) Danish dramatist.
Reply to the jibe, 'Do you call that thing on your head a hat?'
Anekdotenschatz (H. Hoffmeister)

20 In a disastrous fire in President Reagan's library both books were destroyed. And the

real tragedy is that he hadn't finished colouring one.
Jonathan Hunt (1938–) New Zealand politician.
The Observer, 30 Aug 1981

21 Sir, your wife, under pretence of keeping a bawdy-house, is a receiver of stolen goods.
Samuel Johnson (1709–84) British lexicographer.
An example of the customary badinage between travellers on the Thames
Life of Johnson (J. Boswell), Vol. IV

22 Calumnies are answered best with silence.
Ben Jonson (1573–1637) English dramatist.
Volpone, II:2

23 They travel best in gangs, hanging around like clumps of bananas, thick skinned and yellow.
Neil Kinnock (1942–) British politician.
Referring to Tory critics
The Observer, 'Sayings of the Week', 22 Feb 1987

24 She only went to Venice because somebody told her she could walk down the middle of the street.
Neil Kinnock
Referring to Margaret Thatcher who attended a meeting in Venice just before the 1987 election
Speech, Leeds, 9 June 1987

25 Play us a medley of your hit.
Oscar Levant (1906–72) US pianist and actor.
Replying to George Gershwin's barb 'If you had it all over again, would you fall in love with yourself?'
Attrib.

26 I'm sure he had a fork in the other.
Ada Beddington Leverson (1862–1933) British writer.
Reply when told by Oscar Wilde of a devoted *apache* (Parisian gangster) who used to follow him with a knife in one hand
Attrib.

27 When they circumcised Herbert Samuel they threw away the wrong bit.
David Lloyd George (1863–1945) British Liberal statesman.
Attrib. in *The Listener*, 7 Sept 1978

28 The answer is in the plural and they bounce.
Edwin Lutyens (1869–1944) British architect.
Attrib.

29 From the moment I picked up your book until I laid it down, I was convulsed with laughter. Some day I intend reading it.
Groucho Marx (Julius Marx; 1895–1977) US comedian.
The Last Laugh (S. J. Perelman)

30 I have forgotten more law than you ever knew, but allow me to say, I have not forgotten much.
John Maynard (1602–90) English judge.
Replying to Judge Jeffreys' suggestion that he was so old he had forgotten the law

31 And I don't feel the attraction of the

Kennedys at all . . . I don't think they are Christians; they may be Catholics but they are not Christians, in my belief anyway.
Mary McCarthy (1912–89) US novelist.
The Observer, 14 Oct 1979

32 Peel's smile: like the silver plate on a coffin.
Daniel O'Connell (1775–1847) Irish politician.
Referring to Sir Robert Peel; quoting J. P. Curran (1750–1817)
Hansard, 26 Feb 1835

33 I remember coming across him at the Grand Canyon and finding him peevish, refusing to admire it or even look at it properly. He was jealous of it.
J. B. Priestley (1894–1984) British novelist.
Referring to George Bernard Shaw
Thoughts In the Wilderness

34 Thou whoreson zed! thou unnecessary letter!
William Shakespeare (1564–1616) English dramatist.
King Lear, II:2

35 He has occasional flashes of silence, that make his conversation perfectly delightful.
Sydney Smith (1771–1845) British clergyman and essayist.
Referring to Lord Macaulay
Memoir (Lady Holland)

36 You silly moo.
Johnny Speight (1920–) British television scriptwriter.
Till Death Do Us Part

37 Okie use' to mean you was from Oklahoma. Now it means you're scum. Don't mean nothing itself, it's the way they say it.
John Steinbeck (1902–68) US novelist.
The Grapes of Wrath, Ch. 18

38 I dunno. Maybe it's that tally-ho lads attitude. You know, there'll always be an England, all that Empire crap they dish out. But I never could cop Poms.
Jeff Thomson Australian cricketer.
Remark, Oct 1987

39 It's too late to apologize.
Arturo Toscanini (1867–1957) Italian conductor.
Retort to the insult 'Nuts to you!' shouted at him by a player he had just ordered from the stage during rehearsal
The Humor of Music (L. Humphrey)

40 A triumph of the embalmer's art.
Gore Vidal (1925–) US novelist.
Referring to Ronald Reagan
The Observer, 26 Apr 1981

41 A typical triumph of modern science to find the only part of Randolph that was not malignant and remove it.
Evelyn Waugh (1903–66) British novelist.
Remarking upon the news that Randolph Churchill had had a noncancerous lung removed
Attrib.

42 Perhaps not, but then you can't call yourself a great work of nature.

James Whistler (1834–1903) US painter.
Responding to a sitter's complaint that his portrait was not a great work of art
Whistler Stories (D. Seitz)

43 I do not mind the Liberals, still less do I mind the Country Party, calling me a bastard. In some circumstances I am only doing my job if they do. But I hope you will not publicly call me a bastard, as some bastards in the Caucus have.

Gough Whitlam (1916–) Australian statesman.
Speech to the Australian Labor Party, 9 June 1974

44 You have Van Gogh's ear for music.

Billy Wilder (Samuel Wilder; 1906–) Austrian-born US film director.
Said to Cliff Osmond
Attrib.

45 I have always said about Tony that he immatures with age.

Harold Wilson (1916–) British politician and prime minister.
Referring to Anthony Wedgwood Benn
The Chariot of Israel

46 If I had had to choose between him and a cockroach as a companion for a walking-tour, the cockroach would have had it by a short head.

P. G. Wodehouse (1881–1975) British humorous novelist.
My Man Jeeves, 'The Spot of Art'

INTEGRITY

See also honesty, morality, principles, righteousness, self, sincerity

1 Be so true to thyself, as thou be not false to others.

Francis Bacon (1561–1626) English philosopher.
Essays, 'Of Wisdom for a Man's Self'

2 Caesar's wife must be above suspicion.

Julius Caesar (100–44 BC) Roman general and statesman.
Said in justification of his divorce from Pompeia, after she was unwittingly involved in a scandal
Lives, 'Julius Caesar' (Plutarch)

3 I cannot and will not cut my conscience to fit this year's fashions, even though I long ago came to the conclusion that I was not a political person and could have no comfortable place in any political group.

Lillian Hellman (1905–84) US dramatist.
Letter to the US House of Representatives Committee on Un-American Activities, *The Nation*, 31 May 1952

4 Integrity without knowledge is weak and useless, and knowledge without integrity is dangerous and dreadful.

Samuel Johnson (1709–84) British lexicographer.
Rasselas, Ch. 41

5 It is necessary to the happiness of man that he be mentally faithful to himself. Infidelity does not consist in believing, or in disbelieving, it consists in professing to believe what one does not believe.

Thomas Paine (1737–1809) British writer.
The Age of Reason, Pt. I

6 Neither a borrower nor a lender be;
For loan oft loses both itself and friend,
And borrowing dulls the edge of husbandry.
This above all: to thine own self be true,
And it must follow, as the night the day,
Thou canst not then be false to any man.

William Shakespeare (1564–1616) English dramatist.
Hamlet, I:3

7 My strength is as the strength of ten,
Because my heart is pure.

Alfred, Lord Tennyson (1809–92) British poet.
Sir Galahad

INTELLECT

See also intelligence, mind, thinking

1 We should take care not to make the intellect our god; it has, of course, powerful muscles, but no personality.

Albert Einstein (1879–1955) German-born US physicist.
Out of My Later Life, 51

2 The voice of the intellect is a soft one, but it does not rest till it has gained a hearing.

Sigmund Freud (1856–1939) Austrian psychoanalyst.
The Future of an Illusion

3 Man is an intellectual animal, and therefore an everlasting contradiction to himself. His senses centre in himself, his ideas reach to the ends of the universe; so that he is torn in pieces between the two, without a possibility of its ever being otherwise.

William Hazlitt (1778–1830) British essayist.
Characteristics

4 We are thinking beings, and we cannot exclude the intellect from participating in any of our functions.

William James (1842–1910) US psychologist and philosopher.
Varieties of Religious Experience

5 The highest intellects, like the tops of mountains, are the first to catch and to reflect the dawn.

Lord Macaulay (1800–59) British historian.
Historical Essays Contributed to the 'Edinburgh Review', 'Sir James Mackintosh'

6 The higher the voice the smaller the intellect.

Ernest Newman (1868–1959) British music critic.
Attrib.

7 Intellect is invisible to the man who has none.

Arthur Schopenhauer (1788–1860) German philosopher.
Aphorismen zur Lebensweisheit

INTELLECTUALS

See also academics

1 An intellectual is a man who doesn't know how to park a bike.
Spiro Agnew (1918–) US politician.
Attrib.

2 To the man-in-the-street, who, I'm sorry to say
Is a keen observer of life,
The word Intellectual suggests straight away
A man who's untrue to his wife.
W. H. Auden (1907–73) British poet.
Note on Intellectuals

3 I've been called many things, but never an intellectual.
Tallulah Bankhead (1903–68) US actress.
Tallulah, Ch. 15

4 Intellectuals are people who believe that ideas are of more importance than values. That is to say, their own ideas and other people's values.
Gerald Brenan (Edward Fitzgerald Brenan; 1894–1987) British writer.
Thoughts in a Dry Season, 'Life'

5 An intellectual is someone whose mind watches itself.
Albert Camus (1913–60) French existentialist writer.
Notebooks, 1935–42

6 You will hear more good things on the outside of a stagecoach from London to Oxford than if you were to pass a twelvemonth with the undergraduates, or heads of colleges, of that famous university.
William Hazlitt (1778–1830) British essayist.
The Ignorance of the Learned

7 The trouble with me is, I belong to a vanishing race. I'm one of the intellectuals.
Robert E. Sherwood (1896–1955) US writer and dramatist.
The Petrified Forest

8 Do you think it pleases a man when he looks into a woman's eyes and sees a reflection of the British Museum Reading Room?
Muriel Spark (1918–) British novelist.
The Wit of Women (L. and M. Cowan)

9 What is a highbrow? It is a man who has found something more interesting than women.
Edgar Wallace (1875–1932) British thriller writer.
Interview

INTELLIGENCE

See also intellect, knowledge, mind, perception, thinking, understanding, wisdom

1 The intelligent are to the intelligentsia what a man is to a gent.
Stanley Baldwin (1867–1947) British statesman.
Attrib.

2 I never heard tell of any clever man that came of entirely stupid people.
Thomas Carlyle (1795–1881) Scottish historian and essayist.
Speech, Edinburgh, 2 Apr 1886

3 One wants to mutter deeply that apart from having two good legs I also have two good degrees and it is just possible that I do know what I'm talking about.
Edwina Currie (1946–) British politician.
Remark, Nov 1986

4 A really intelligent man feels what other men only know.
Baron de Montesquieu (1689–1755) French writer.
Essai sur les causes qui peuvent affecter les esprits et les caractères

5 The more intelligence one has the more people one finds original. Commonplace people see no difference between men.
Blaise Pascal (1623–62) French philosopher and mathematician.
Pensées, I

6 The height of cleverness is to be able to conceal it.
Duc de la Rochefoucauld (1613–80) French writer.
Maximes, 245

7 Intelligence is quickness to apprehend as distinct from ability, which is capacity to act wisely on the thing apprehended.
A. N. Whitehead (1861–1947) British philosopher.
Dialogues, 135

8 All the unhappy marriages come from the husbands having brains. What good are brains to a man? They only unsettle him.
P. G. Wodehouse (1881–1975) British humorous novelist.
The Adventures of Sally

INTERRUPTIONS

1 On awaking he . . . instantly and eagerly wrote down the lines that are here preserved. At this moment he was unfortunately called out by a person on business from Porlock.
Samuel Taylor Coleridge (1772–1834) British poet.
Kubla Khan (preliminary note)

2 As I was saying the other day.
Luis Ponce de Léon (1527–91) Spanish monk.
Said on resuming a lecture interrupted by five years' imprisonment

3 Mr Wordsworth is never interrupted.
Mary Wordsworth (1770–1850) Wife of William Wordsworth.
Rebuking John Keats for interrupting a long monologue by William Wordsworth
Attrib.

INTRIGUE

1 Ay, now the plot thickens very much upon us.
Duke of Buckingham (1628–87) English politician.
The Rehearsal, III:1

2 Everybody was up to something, especially, of course, those who were up to nothing.
Noël Coward (1899–1973) British dramatist.
Future Indefinite

INTRODUCTIONS

1 'You look a little shy; let me introduce you to that leg of mutton,' said the Red Queen. 'Alice – Mutton; Mutton – Alice.'
Lewis Carroll (Charles Lutwidge Dodgson; 1832–98) British writer.
Through the Looking-Glass, Ch. 9

2 Do you suppose I could buy back my introduction to you?
Groucho Marx (Julius Marx; 1895–1977) US comedian.
Monkey Business

INVITATIONS

See also summons

1 'Will you walk into my parlour?' said a spider to a fly:
"Tis the prettiest little parlour that ever you did spy.'
Mary Howitt (1799–1888) British writer.
The Spider and the Fly

2 Come into the garden, Maud,
For the black bat, night, has flown,
Come into the garden, Maud,
I am here at the gate alone.
Alfred, Lord Tennyson (1809–92) British poet.
Maud, I

3 I always did like a man in uniform. And that one fits you grand. Why don't you come up sometime and see me?
Mae West (1892–1980) US actress.
Often misquoted as 'Come up and see me some time'
She Done Him Wrong, film 1933

IRELAND

See also Britain, Irish

1 I met wid Napper Tandy, and he took me by the hand,
And he said, 'How's poor ould Ireland, and how does she stand?'
She's the most disthressful country that iver yet was seen,
For they're hangin' men an' women there for the wearin' o' the Green.
Anonymous
The Wearin' o' the Green

2 A bit of shooting takes your mind off your troubles – it makes you forget the cost of living.
Brendan Behan (1923–64) Irish playwright.
The Hostage

3 Ulster will fight; Ulster will be right.
Lord Randolph Churchill (1849–95) British Conservative politician.
Letter, 7 May 1886

4 By yesterday morning British troops were patrolling the streets of Belfast. I fear that once Catholics and Protestants get used to our presence they will hate us more than they hate each other.
Richard Crossman (1907–74) British politician.
Diaries, 17 Aug 1969

5 Thus you have a starving population, an absentee aristocracy, and an alien Church, and in addition the weakest executive in the world. That is the Irish Question.
Benjamin Disraeli (1804–81) British statesman.
Speech, House of Commons, 16 Feb 1844

6 I never met anyone in Ireland who understood the Irish question, except one Englishman who had only been there a week.
Keith Fraser (1867–1935) British politician.
Speech, House of Commons, May 1919

7 Worth seeing? yes; but not worth going to see.
Samuel Johnson (1709–84) British lexicographer.
Referring to the Giant's Causeway
Life of Johnson (J. Boswell), Vol. III

8 Ireland is the old sow that eats her farrow.
James Joyce (1882–1941) Irish novelist.
A Portrait of the Artist as a Young Man, Ch. 5

9 It is a symbol of Irish art. The cracked looking glass of a servant.
James Joyce
Ulysses

10 The problem with Ireland is that it's a country full of genius, but with absolutely no talent.
Hugh Leonard (1926–) Irish dramatist.
Said during an interview
The Times, Aug 1977

11 The harp that once through Tara's halls
The soul of music shed,
Now hangs as mute on Tara's walls
As if that soul were fled. –
So sleeps the pride of former days,
So glory's thrill is o'er;
And hearts, that once beat high for praise,
Now feel that pulse no more.
Thomas Moore (1779–1852) Irish poet.
Irish Melodies, 'The Harp that Once'

12 It is a city where you can see a sparrow fall to the ground, and God watching it.
Conor Cruise O'Brien (1917–) Irish diplomat and writer.
Referring to Dublin
Attrib.

13 I will drive a coach and six horses through the Act of Settlement.
Stephen Rice (1637–1715) English politician.
State of the Protestants of Ireland (W. King), Ch. 3

14 The English should give Ireland home rule – and reserve the motion picture rights.
Will Rogers (1879–1935) US actor and humorist.
Autobiography (published posthumously)

15 Before Irish Home Rule is conceded by the Imperial Parliament, England as the predominant member of the three kingdoms will have to be convinced of its justice and equity.
Lord Rosebery (1847–1929) British statesman.
Speech, House of Lords, 11 Mar 1894

16 The moment the very name of Ireland is mentioned, the English seem to bid adieu to common feeling, common prudence, and common sense, and to act with the barbarity of tyrants, and the fatuity of idiots.
Sydney Smith (1771–1845) British clergyman and essayist.
The Letters of Peter Plymley

17 I would have liked to go to Ireland, but my grandmother would not let me. Perhaps she thought I wanted to take the little place.
Wilhelm II (1859–1941) King of Prussia and Emperor of Germany.
Queen Victoria was his grandmother
Carson (H. Montgomery Hyde), Ch. 9

IRISH

See also British, Ireland

1 Put an Irishman on the spit, and you can always get another Irishman to baste him.
Proverb

2 Other people have a nationality. The Irish and the Jews have a psychosis.
Brendan Behan (1923–64) Irish playwright.
Richard's Cork Leg, I

3 The English and Americans dislike only *some* Irish – the same Irish that the Irish themselves detest, Irish writers – the ones that *think*.
Brendan Behan
Richard's Cork Leg, I

4 Not in vain is Ireland pouring itself all over the earth . . . The Irish, with their glowing hearts and reverent credulity, are needed in this cold age of intellect and skepticism.
Lydia M. Child (1802–80) US abolitionist campaigner.
Letters from New York, Vol. I, No. 33, 8 Dec 1842

5 All races have produced notable economists, with the exception of the Irish who doubtless can protest their devotion to higher arts.
John Kenneth Galbraith (1908–   ) US economist.
The Age of Uncertainty, Ch. 1

6 Irish Americans are about as Irish as Black Americans are African.
Bob Geldof (1952–   ) Irish rock musician.
The Observer, 'Sayings of the Week', 22 Jun 1986

7 The Irish are a fair people; – they never speak well of one another.
Samuel Johnson (1709–84) British lexicographer.
Life of Johnson (J. Boswell), Vol. II

8 The Irish don't know what they want and are prepared to fight to the death to get it.
Sidney Littlewood (1895–1967) President of the Law Society.
Speech, 13 Apr 1961

IRREVOCABILITY

1 The die is cast.
Julius Caesar (100–44 BC) Roman general and statesman.
Said on crossing the Rubicon (49 BC) at the start of his campaign against Pompey
Attrib.

2 The Gods themselves cannot recall their gifts.
Alfred, Lord Tennyson (1809–92) British poet.
Tithonus

J

JEALOUSY

See also envy

1 For the ear of jealousy heareth all things: and the noise of murmurings is not hid.
Bible: Wisdom
1:10

2 Jealousy is no more than feeling alone among smiling enemies.
Elizabeth Bowen (1899–1973) Irish novelist.
The House in Paris

3 The others were only my wives. But you, my dear, will be my widow.
Sacha Guitry (1885–1957) French actor and dramatist.
Allaying his fifth wife's jealousy of his previous wives
Speaker's and Toastmaster's Handbook (J. Brawle)

4 The secret of my success is that no woman has ever been jealous of me.
Elsa Maxwell (1883–1963) US songwriter, broadcaster, and actress.
The Natives were Friendly (Noël Barber)

5 O, beware, my lord, of jealousy;
It is the green-ey'd monster which doth mock

The meat it feeds on.
William Shakespeare (1564–1616) English dramatist.
Othello, III:3

6 O curse of marriage,
That we can call these delicate creatures ours,
And not their appetites! I had rather be a toad,
And live upon the vapour of a dungeon,
Than keep a corner in the thing I love
For others' uses.
William Shakespeare
Othello, III:3

JEWS

See also Nazism, prejudice, racism, religion

1 Other people have a nationality. The Irish
and the Jews have a psychosis.
Brendan Behan (1923–64) Irish playwright.
Richard's Cork Leg, I

2 The gentleman will please remember that
when his half-civilized ancestors were hunting
the wild boar in Silesia, mine were princes of
the earth.
Judah Philip Benjamin (1811–84) US politician.
Replying to a senator of Germanic origin who had made an an-
tisemitic remark
Attrib.

3 Now the Lord had said unto Abram, Get
thee out of thy country, and from thy
kindred, and from thy father's house, unto a
land that I will shew thee:
And I will make of thee a great nation, and I
will bless thee, and make thy name great;
and thou shalt be a blessing:
And I will bless them that bless thee, and
curse him that curseth thee: and in thee shall
all families of the earth be blessed.
Bible: Genesis
12:1–3

4 How odd
Of God
To choose
The Jews.
William Norman Ewer (1885–1976) British writer.
For a reply see Cecil BROWNE
How Odd

5 But not so odd
As those who choose
A Jewish God,
But spurn the Jews.
Cecil Browne
In reply to EWER (above)

6 It is extremely difficult for a Jew to be
converted, for how can he bring himself to
believe in the divinity of – another Jew?
Heinrich Heine (1797–1856) German poet and writer.
Attrib.

7 For me this is a vital litmus test: no

intellectual society can flourish where a Jew
feels even slightly uneasy.
Paul Johnson (1928–) British editor.
The Sunday Times Magazine, 6 Feb 1977

8 The very best that is in the Jewish blood: a
faculty for pure disinterestedness, and warm,
physically warm love, that seems to make
the corpuscles of the blood glow.
D. H. Lawrence (1885–1930) British novelist.
Kangaroo, Ch. 6

9 Pessimism is a luxury that a Jew never can
allow himself.
Golda Meir (1898–1978) Russian-born Israeli
stateswoman.
The Observer, 'Sayings of the Year', 29 Dec 1974

10 There are not enough prisons and
concentration camps in Palestine to hold all
the Jews who are ready to defend their lives
and property.
Golda Meir
Speech, 2 May 1940

11 And furthermore did you know that behind
the discovery of America there was a Jewish
financier?
Mordecai Richler (1931–) Canadian novelist.
Cocksure, Ch. 24

12 Doctor, my doctor, what do you say – let's
put the id back in yid!
Philip Roth (1933–) US novelist.
Portnoy's Complaint

13 A Jewish man with parents alive is a fifteen-
year-old boy, and will remain a fifteen-year-
old boy till they die.
Philip Roth
Portnoy's Complaint

14 I believe that the Jews have made a
contribution to the human condition out of all
proportion to their numbers: I believe them
to be an immense people. Not only have they
supplied the world with two leaders of the
stature of Jesus Christ and Karl Marx, but
they have even indulged in the luxury of
following neither one nor the other.
Peter Ustinov (1921–) British actor.
Dear Me, Ch. 19

15 The law of dislike for the unlike will always
prevail. And whereas the unlike is normally
situated at a safe distance, the Jews bring
the unlike into the heart of *every milieu*, and
must there defend a frontier line as large as
the world.
Israel Zangwill (1864–1926) British writer.
Speeches, Articles and Letters, 'The Jewish Race'

JOURNALISM

See also editors, newspapers

1 Have you noticed that life, real honest to
goodness life, with murders and catastrophes

and fabulous inheritances, happens almost exclusively in newspapers?

Jean Anouilh (1910–87) French dramatist.
The Rehearsal

2 What the proprietorship of these papers is aiming at is power, and power without responsibility – the prerogative of the harlot through the ages.

Stanley Baldwin (1867–1947) British statesman.
Attacking the press barons Lords Rothermere and Beaverbrook. It was first used by KIPLING. *See also* DEVONSHIRE (10th Duke)
Speech, election rally, 18 Mar 1931

3 'Christianity, of course but why journalism?'

Arthur Balfour (1848–1930) British statesman.
In reply to Frank Harris's remark, '. . . all the faults of the age come from Christianity and journalism'
Autobiography (Margot Asquith), Ch. 10

4 Go out and speak for the inarticulate and the submerged.

Lord Beaverbrook (1879–1964) British newspaper owner and politician.
Somerset Maugham (E. Morgan)

5 Because he shakes hands with people's hearts.

Lord Beaverbrook
On being asked why the sentimental writer Godfrey Winn was paid so much
Somerset Maugham (E. Morgan)

6 If you want to make mischief come and work on my papers.

Lord Beaverbrook
Inviting Anthony Howard to join his staff
Radio Times, 27 June 1981

7 If I rescued a child from drowning, the Press would no doubt headline the story 'Benn grabs child'.

Tony Benn (1925–) British politician.
The Observer, 'Sayings of the Week', 2 Mar 1975

8 Journalists say a thing that they know isn't true, in the hope that if they keep on saying it long enough it will be true.

Arnold Bennett (1867–1931) British novelist.
The Title, II

9 No news is good news; no journalists is even better.

Nicolas Bentley (1907–78) British cartoonist and writer.
Attrib.

10 I read the newspaper avidly. It is my one form of continuous fiction.

Aneurin Bevan (1897–1960) British Labour politician.
The Observer, 'Sayings of the Week', 3 Apr 1960

11 When a dog bites a man that is not news, but when a man bites a dog that is news.

John B. Bogart (1845–1920) US journalist.
Sometimes attributed to Charles Dana and Amos Cummings
Attrib.

12 Journalism is the only job that requires no

degrees, no diplomas and no specialised knowledge of any kind.

Patrick Campbell (1913–80) British humorous writer and editor.
My Life and Easy Times

13 Journalism largely consists of saying 'Lord Jones is dead' to people who never knew Lord Jones was alive.

G. K. Chesterton (1874–1936) British writer.
Attrib.

14 Literature is the art of writing something that will be read twice; journalism what will be grasped at once.

Cyril Connolly (1903–74) British journalist.
Enemies of Promise, Ch. 3

15 I hesitate to say what the functions of the modern journalist may be; but I imagine that they do not exclude the intelligent anticipation of facts even before they occur.

Lord Curzon (1859–1925) British politician.
Speech, House of Commons, 29 Mar 1898

16 Good God, that's done it. He's lost us the tarts' vote.

Duke of Devonshire (1895–1950) Conservative politician.
Referring to Stanley BALDWIN's attack on newspaper proprietors; recalled by Harold Macmillan
Attrib.

17 I am myself a gentleman of the Press, and I bear no other scutcheon.

Benjamin Disraeli (1804–81) British statesman.
Speech, House of Commons, 18 Feb 1863

18 Blood sport is brought to its ultimate refinement in the gossip columns.

Bernard Ingham (1932–) British journalist.
The Observer, 'Sayings of the Week', 28 Dec 1986

19 Newspapers always excite curiosity. No one ever lays one down without a feeling of disappointment.

Charles Lamb (1775–1834) British essayist.
Last Essays of Elia, 'Detached Thoughts on Books and Reading'

20 On the whole I would not say that our Press is obscene. I would say that it trembles on the brink of obscenity.

Lord Longford (1905–) British politician and social reformer.
The Observer, 'Sayings of the Year', 1963

21 The gallery in which the reporters sit has become a fourth estate of the realm.

Lord Macaulay (1800–59) British historian.
Referring to the press gallery in the House of Commons
Historical Essays Contributed to the 'Edinburgh Review', 'Hallam's "Constitutional History"'

22 Once a newspaper touches a story, the facts are lost forever, even to the protagonists.

Norman Mailer (1923–) US writer.
The Presidential Papers

23 A good newspaper, I suppose, is a nation talking to itself.

Arthur Miller (1915–) US dramatist.
The Observer, 'Sayings of the Week', 26 Nov 1961

24 SIXTY HORSES WEDGED IN A CHIMNEY
The story to fit this sensational headline has not turned up yet.

J. B. Morton (1893–1979) British journalist.
The Best of Beachcomber, 'Mr Justice Cocklecarrot: Home Life'

25 A reporter is a man who has renounced everything in life but the world, the flesh, and the devil.

David Murray (1888–1962) British journalist.
The Observer, 'Sayings of the Week', 5 July 1931

26 We live under a government of men and morning newspapers.

Wendell Phillips (1811–84) US reformer.
Address: The Press

27 Its primary office is the gathering of news. At the peril of its soul it must see that the supply is not tainted. Neither in what it gives, nor in what it does not give, nor in the mode of presentation, must the unclouded face of truth suffer wrong. Comment is free but facts are sacred.

C. P. Scott (1846–1932) British journalist.
Manchester Guardian, 6 May 1926

28 He's someone who flies around from hotel to hotel and thinks the most interesting thing about any story is the fact that he has arrived to cover it.

Tom Stoppard (1937–) Czech-born British dramatist.
Referring to foreign correspondents
Night and Day, I

29 MILNE. No matter how imperfect things are, if you've got a free press everything is correctable, and without it everything is conceivable.
RUTH. I'm with you on the free press. It's the newspapers I can't stand.

Tom Stoppard
Night and Day, I

30 Freedom of the press in Britain is freedom to print such of the proprietor's prejudices as the advertisers don't object to.

Hannen Swaffer (1879–1962) British journalist.
Attrib.

31 Journalism – an ability to meet the challenge of filling the space.

Rebecca West (Cicely Isabel Fairfield; 1892–1983) British novelist and journalist.
The New York Herald Tribune, 22 April 1956

32 There is much to be said in favour of modern journalism. By giving us the opinions of the uneducated, it keeps us in touch with the ignorance of the community.

Oscar Wilde (1854–1900) Irish-born British dramatist.
The Critic as Artist, Pt. 2

33 You cannot hope
to bribe or twist,
thank God! the
British journalist.

But, seeing what
the man will do
unbribed, there's
no occasion to.

Humbert Wolfe (1886–1940) British poet.
The Uncelestial City, Bk. I, 'Over the Fire'

JUDGMENT

1 And this is the writing that was written, MENE, MENE, TEKEL, UPHARSIN.
This is the interpretation of the thing: MENE; God hath numbered thy kingdom, and finished it.
TEKEL; Thou art weighed in the balances, and art found wanting.
PERES; Thy kingdom is divided, and given to the Medes and Persians.

Bible: Daniel
5:25–28

2 Judge not, that ye be not judged.

Bible: Matthew
7:1

3 And why beholdest thou the mote that is in thy brother's eye, but considerest not the beam that is in thine own eye?

Bible: Matthew
7:3

4 And I saw a great white throne, and him that sat on it, from whose face the earth and the heaven fled away; and there was found no place for them.
And I saw the dead, small and great, stand before God; and the books were opened: and another book was opened, which is the book of life: and the dead were judged out of those things which were written in the books, according to their works.
And the sea gave up the dead which were in it; and death and hell delivered up the dead which were in them: and they were judged every man according to their works.

Bible: Revelations
20:11–13

5 No man can justly censure or condemn another, because indeed no man truly knows another.

Thomas Browne (1605–82) English physician and writer.
Religio Medici, Pt. II

6 Your representative owes you, not his industry only, but his judgement; and he betrays instead of serving you if he sacrifices it to your opinion.

Edmund Burke (1729–97) British politician.
Speech to the electors of Bristol, 3 Nov 1774

7 You shall judge of a man by his foes as well as by his friends.
Joseph Conrad (Teodor Josef Konrad Korzeniowski; 1857–1924) Polish-born British novelist.
Lord Jim, Ch. 34

8 Judge not the play before the play be done.
John Davies (1569–1626) English jurist.
Respice Finem

9 Force, if unassisted by judgement, collapses through its own mass.
Horace (Quintus Horatius Flaccus; 65–8 BC) Roman poet.
Odes, III

10 Let me remind you of the old maxim: people under suspicion are better moving than at rest, since at rest they may be sitting in the balance without knowing it, being weighed together with their sins.
Franz Kafka (1883–1924) Czech novelist.
The Trial, Ch. 8

11 Consider what you think justice requires, and decide accordingly. But never give your reasons; for your judgement will probably be right, but your reasons will certainly be wrong.
Lord Mansfield (1705–93) British judge and politician.
Advice given to a new colonial governor
Lives of the Chief Justices (Campbell), Ch. 40

12 Everyone complains of his memory, but no one complains of his judgement.
Duc de la Rochefoucauld (1613–80) French writer.
Maximes, 89

JUSTICE

See also injustice, judgment, law, lawyers

1 The place of justice is a hallowed place.
Francis Bacon (1561–1626) English philosopher.
Essays, 'Of Judicature'

2 When I came back to Dublin, I was court-martialled in my absence and sentenced to death in my absence, so I said they could shoot me in my absence.
Brendan Behan (1923–64) Irish playwright.
The Hostage, I

3 It is better that ten guilty persons escape than one innocent suffer.
William Blackstone (1723–80) British jurist.
Commentaries on the Laws of England, Bk. IV, Ch. 27

4 The rain it raineth on the just
And also on the unjust fella:
But chiefly on the just, because
The unjust steals the just's umbrella.
Charles Bowen (1835–94) British judge.
Sands of Time (Walter Sichel)

5 Trial by jury itself, instead of being a security to persons who are accused, will be a delusion, a mockery, and a snare.
Thomas Denman (1779–1854) British judge.
Judgment in O'Connell v The Queen, 4 Sept 1844

6 'It is my duty to warn you that it will be used against you,' cried the Inspector, with the magnificent fair play of the British criminal law.
Arthur Conan Doyle (1856–1930) British writer.
The Dancing Men

7 Let justice be done, though the world perish.
Ferdinand I (1503–64) Holy Roman Emperor.
Attrib.

8 Ah, colonel, all's fair in love and war, you know.
Nathan Bedford Forrest (1821–77) Confederate general.
Remark to a captured enemy officer who had been tricked into surrendering
A Civil War Treasury (B. Botkin)

9 Let no guilty man escape, if it can be avoided . . . No personal considerations should stand in the way of performing a public duty.
Ulysses Simpson Grant (1822–85) US general.
Referring to the Whiskey Ring
Indorsement of a letter, 29 July 1875

10 Justice should not only be done, but should manifestly and undoubtedly be seen to be done.
Gordon Hewart (1870–1943) British lawyer and politician.
The Chief (R. Jackson)

11 I have come to regard the law courts not as a cathedral but rather as a casino.
Richard Ingrams (1937–) British editor.
The Guardian, 30 July 1977

12 Consider, Sir, how should you like, though conscious of your innocence, to be tried before a jury for a capital crime, once a week.
Samuel Johnson (1709–84) British lexicographer.
Life of Johnson (J. Boswell), Vol. III

13 A lawyer has no business with the justice or injustice of the cause which he undertakes, unless his client asks his opinion, and then he is bound to give it honestly. The justice or injustice of the cause is to be decided by the judge.
Samuel Johnson
Tour to the Hebrides (J. Boswell)

14 Justice is the constant and perpetual wish to render to every one his due.
Justinian I (482–565 AD) Byzantine emperor.
Institutes, I

15 Justice is such a fine thing that we cannot pay too dearly for it.
Alain-René Lesage (1668–1747) French writer.
Crispin rival de son maître, IX

16 I'm arm'd with more than complete steel –
The justice of my quarrel.
Christopher Marlowe (1564–93) English dramatist.
Play also attributed to others
Lust's Dominion, IV:3

17 In England, Justice is open to all, like the Ritz hotel.
James Mathew (1830–1908) British judge.
Also attrib. to Lord Darling
Miscellany-at-Law (R. E. Megarry)

18 A judge is not supposed to know anything about the facts of life until they have been presented in evidence and explained to him at least three times.
Hubert Lister Parker (1900–72) Lord Chief Justice of England.
The Observer, 'Sayings of the Week', 12 Mar 1961

19 The hungry judges soon the sentence sign,
And wretches hang that jury-men may dine.
Alexander Pope (1688–1744) British poet.
The Rape of the Lock, III

20 The love of justice in most men is simply the fear of suffering injustice.
Duc de la Rochefoucauld (1613–80) French writer.
Maximes, 78

21 A man who is good enough to shed his blood for the country is good enough to be given a square deal afterwards. More than that no man is entitled to, and less than that no man shall have.
Theodore Roosevelt (1858–1919) US Republican president.
Speech at the Lincoln Monument, Springfield, Illinois, 4 June 1903

22 Haste still pays haste, and leisure answers leisure;
Like doth quit like, and Measure still for Measure.
William Shakespeare (1564–1616) English dramatist.
Measure for Measure, V:1

23 This is a British murder inquiry and some degree of justice must be seen to be more or less done.
Tom Stoppard (1937–) Czech-born British dramatist.
Jumpers, II

24 Under a government which imprisons any unjustly, the true place for a just man is also a prison.
Henry David Thoreau (1817–62) US writer.
Civil Disobedience

K

KILLING

See also assassination, death, murder, suicide

1 Euthanasia is a long, smooth-sounding word, and it conceals its danger as long, smooth words do, but the danger is there, nevertheless.
Pearl Buck (1892–1973) US novelist.
The Child Who Never Grew, Ch. 2

2 Thou shalt not kill; but needst not strive Officiously to keep alive.
Arthur Hugh Clough (1819–61) British poet.
The Latest Decalogue, 11

3 To save a man's life against his will is the same as killing him.
Horace (Quintus Horatius Flaccus; 65–8 BC) Roman poet.
Ars Poetica

4 To kill a human being is, after all, the least injury you can do him.
Henry James (1843–1916) US novelist.
My Friend Bingham

5 Killing
Is the ultimate simplification of life.
Hugh MacDiarmid (Christopher Murray Grieve; 1892–1978) Scottish poet.
England's Double Knavery

6 . . . there's no difference between one's killing and making decisions that will send others to kill. It's exactly the same thing, or even worse.
Golda Meir (1898–1978) Russian-born Israeli stateswoman.
L'Europeo (Oriana Fallaci)

7 Kill a man, and you are a murderer. Kill millions of men, and you are a conqueror. Kill everyone, and you are a god.
Jean Rostand (1894–1977) French biologist and writer.
Pensées d'un biologiste

8 Yet each man kills the thing he loves,
By each let this be heard,
Some do it with a bitter look,
Some with a flattering word.
The coward does it with a kiss,
The brave man with a sword!
Oscar Wilde (1854–1900) Irish-born British dramatist.
The Ballad of Reading Gaol, I:7

KINDNESS

See also charity, generosity

1 Recompense injury with justice, and recompense kindness with kindness.
Confucius (K'ung Fu-tzu; 551–479 BC) Chinese philosopher.
Analects

2 I love thee for a heart that's kind –
Not for the knowledge in thy mind.
W. H. Davies (1871–1940) British poet.
Sweet Stay-at-Home

3 One kind word can warm three winter months.
Japanese Proverb

4 Yet do I fear thy nature;
It is too full o' th' milk of human kindness

To catch the nearest way.
William Shakespeare (1564–1616) English dramatist.
Macbeth, I:5

5 This is a way to kill a wife with kindness.
William Shakespeare
The Taming of the Shrew, IV:1

6 So many gods, so many creeds,
So many paths that wind and wind,
While just the art of being kind
Is all the sad world needs.
Ella Wheeler Wilcox (1850–1919) US poet.
The World's Need

7 That best portion of a good man's life,
His little, nameless, unremembered acts
Of kindness and of love.
William Wordsworth (1770–1850) British poet.
Lines composed a few miles above Tintern Abbey

KISSING

1 What of soul was left, I wonder, when the
kissing had to stop?
Robert Browning (1812–89) British poet.
A Toccata of Galuppi's

2 Jenny kissed me when we met,
Jumping from the chair she sat in;
Time, you thief, who love to get
Sweets into your list, put that in:
Say I'm weary, say I'm sad,
Say that health and wealth have missed me,
Say I'm growing old, but add,
Jenny kissed me.
Leigh Hunt (1784–1859) British poet.
Writing about Jane Carlyle
Rondeau

3 Being kissed by a man who didn't wax his
moustache was –like eating an egg without
salt.
Rudyard Kipling (1865–1936) Indian-born British writer.
A similar remark is attributed to the US poet Madison Julius
Cawein (1865–1914)
Soldiers Three, 'The Gadsbys, Poor Dear Mamma'

4 A kiss without a moustache, they said then,
is like an egg without salt; I will add to it:
and it is like Good without Evil.
Jean-Paul Sartre (1905–80) French writer.
Words

KNOWLEDGE

See also learning, self-knowledge, wisdom

1 Knowledge is the mother of all virtue; all
vice proceeds from ignorance.
Proverb

2 Learning is a treasure which accompanies its
owner everywhere.
Chinese proverb

3 *Nam et ipsa scientia potestas est.*

Knowledge itself is power.
Francis Bacon (1561–1626) English philosopher.
Religious Meditations, 'Of Heresies'

4 I have taken all knowledge to be my
province.
Francis Bacon
Letter to Lord Burleigh, 1592

5 For all knowledge and wonder (which is the
seed of knowledge) is an impression of
pleasure in itself.
Francis Bacon
The Advancement of Learning, Bk. I, Ch. 1

6 For in much wisdom is much grief: and he
that increaseth knowledge increaseth sorrow.
Bible: Ecclesiastes
1:18

7 And the Lord God took the man, and put him
into the garden of Eden to dress it and to
keep it.
And the Lord God commanded the man, saying, Of every tree of the garden thou mayest
freely eat:
But of the tree of the knowledge of good and
evil, thou shalt not eat of it: for in the day
that thou eatest thereof thou shalt surely die.
Bible: Genesis
2:15–17

8 Now as touching things offered unto idols,
we know that we all have knowledge.
Knowledge puffeth up, but charity edifieth.
Bible: I Corinthians
8:1

9 There goes a woman who knows all the
things that can be taught and none of the
things that cannot be taught.
Coco Chanel (1883–1971) French dress designer.
Coco Chanel, Her Life, Her Secrets (Marcel Haedrich)

10 Learning without thought is labour lost;
thought without learning is perilous.
Confucius (K'ung Fu-tzu; 551–479 BC) Chinese
philosopher.
Analects

11 Knowledge dwells
In heads replete with thoughts of other men;
Wisdom in minds attentive to their own.
William Cowper (1731–1800) British poet.
The Task

12 A smattering of everything, and a knowledge
of nothing.
Charles Dickens (1812–70) British novelist.
Sketches by Boz, 'Tales', Ch. 3

13 A man should keep his little brain attic
stocked with all the furniture that he is likely
to use, and the rest he can put away in the
lumber room of his library, where he can get
it if he wants it.
Arthur Conan Doyle (1856–1930) British writer.
Five Orange Pips

14 For lust of knowing what should not be known,
We take the Golden Road to Samarkand.
James Elroy Flecker (1884–1915) British poet.
Hassan, V:2

15 I now want to know all things under the sun, and the moon, too. For all things are beautiful in themselves, and become more beautiful when known to man. Knowledge is Life with wings.
Kahil Gibran (1833–1931) Lebanese mystic and poet.
Beloved Prophet (ed. Virginia Hiln)

16 I am the very model of a modern Major-General,
I've information vegetable, animal and mineral,
I know the kings of England, and I quote the fights historical,
From Marathon to Waterloo, in order categorical.
W. S. Gilbert (1836–1911) British dramatist.
The Pirates of Penzance, I

17 In arguing too, the parson own'd his skill,
For e'en though vanquish'd, he could argue still;
While words of learned length, and thund'ring sound
Amazed the gazing rustics rang'd around,
And still they gaz'd, and still the wonder grew,
That one small head could carry all he knew.
Oliver Goldsmith (1728–74) Irish-born British writer.
The Deserted Village

18 The clever men at Oxford
Know all that there is to be knowed.
But they none of them know one half as much
As intelligent Mr Toad.
Kenneth Grahame (1859–1932) Scottish writer.
The Wind in the Willows, Ch. 10

19 It is the province of knowledge to speak and it is the privilege of wisdom to listen.
Oliver Wendell Holmes (1809–94) US writer.
The Poet at the Breakfast Table, Ch. 10

20 Knowledge is proportionate to being. . . .
You know in virtue of what you are.
Aldous Huxley (1894–1964) British novelist.
Time Must Have a Stop, Ch. 26

21 If a little knowledge is dangerous, where is the man who has so much as to be out of danger?
T. H. Huxley (1825–95) British biologist.
On Elementary Instruction in Physiology

22 There was never an age in which useless knowledge was more important than in our own.
Cyril Joad (1891–1953) British writer and broadcaster.
The Observer, 'Sayings of the Week', 30 Sept 1951

23 All knowledge is of itself of some value.

There is nothing so minute or inconsiderable, that I would not rather know it than not.
Samuel Johnson (1709–84) British lexicographer.
Life of Johnson (J. Boswell)

24 Integrity without knowledge is weak and useless, and knowledge without integrity is dangerous and dreadful.
Samuel Johnson
Rasselas, Ch. 41

25 In my early years I read very hard. It is a sad reflection, but a true one, that I knew almost as much at eighteen as I do now.
Samuel Johnson
Life of Johnson (J. Boswell), Vol. I

26 Knowledge is of two kinds. We know a subject ourselves, or we know where we can find information upon it.
Samuel Johnson
Life of Johnson (J. Boswell), Vol. II

27 A study of history shows that civilizations that abandon the quest for knowledge are doomed to disintegration.
Bernard Lovell (1913–) British astronomer and writer.
The Observer, 'Sayings of the Week', 14 May 1972

28 Knowledge advances by steps, and not by leaps.
Lord Macaulay (1800–59) British historian.
Essays and Biographies, 'History'. *Edinburgh Review*

29 We have learned the answers, all the answers:
It is the question that we do not know.
Archibald MacLeish (1892–1982) US poet and dramatist.
The Hamlet of A. Macleish

30 A little learning is a dangerous thing;
Drink deep, or taste not the Pierian spring:
There shallow draughts intoxicate the brain,
And drinking largely sobers us again.
Alexander Pope (1688–1744) British poet.
An Essay on Criticism

31 Our knowledge can only be finite, while our ignorance must necessarily be infinite.
Karl Popper (1902–) Austrian-born British philosopher.
Conjectures and Refutations

32 His had been an intellectual decision founded on his conviction that if a little knowledge was a dangerous thing, a lot was lethal.
Tom Sharpe (1928–) British novelist.
Porterhouse Blue, Ch. 18

33 These things shall be! A loftier race
Than e'er the world hath known shall rise,
With flame of freedom in their souls,
And light of knowledge in their eyes.
John Addington Symonds (1840–93) British art historian.
Hymn

34 Beware you be not swallowed up in books!

An ounce of love is worth a pound of knowledge.

John Wesley (1703–91) British religious leader.
Life of Wesley (R. Southey), Ch. 16

35 'I dunno,' Arthur said. 'I forget what I was taught. I only remember what I've learnt.'

Patrick White (1912–) British-born Australian novelist.
The Solid Mandala, Ch. 2

36 I have drunk ale from the Country of the Young
And weep because I know all things now.

W. B. Yeats (1865–1939) Irish poet.
He Thinks of his Past Greatness

L

LANGUAGE

See also class, communication, grammar, Goldwynisms, malapropisms, mixed metaphors, opera, pronunciation, speech, spoonerisms, style, words, writing

1 The Greeks Had a Word for It.

Zoë Akins (1886–1958) US dramatist.
Play title

2 Therefore is the name of it called Babel; because the Lord did there confound the language of all the earth: and from thence did the Lord scatter them abroad upon the face of all the earth.

Bible: Genesis
11:9

3 The cliché is dead poetry. English, being the language of an imaginative race, abounds in clichés, so that English literature is always in danger of being poisoned by its own secretions.

Gerald Brenan (Edward Fitzgerald Brenan; 1894–1987) British writer.
Thoughts in a Dry Season, 'Literature'

4 'Take some more tea,' the March Hare said to Alice, very earnestly.
'I've had nothing yet,' Alice replied in an offended tone, 'so I can't take more.'
'You mean you can't take *less*,' said the Hatter: 'it's very easy to take *more* than nothing.'

Lewis Carroll (Charles Lutwidge Dodgson; 1832–98) British writer.
Alice's Adventures in Wonderland, Ch. 7

5 A silly remark can be made in Latin as well as in Spanish.

Miguel de Cervantes (1547–1616) Spanish novelist.
The Dialogue of the Dogs

6 Well, frankly, the problem as I see it at this moment in time is whether I should just lie down under all this hassle and let them walk all over me, or whether I should just say OK, I get the message, and do myself in. I mean, let's face it, I'm in a no-win situation, and quite honestly, I'm so stuffed up to here with the whole stupid mess that I can tell you I've just got a good mind to take the easy way out. That's the bottom line. The only problem is, what happens if I find, when I've bumped myself off, there's some kind of . . . ah, you know, all that mystical stuff about when you die, you might find you're still – know what I mean?

Charles, Prince of Wales (1948–) Eldest son of Elizabeth II.
At the presentation of the Thomas Cranmer Schools Prize, 1989, suggesting a possible modern English version of Hamlet's soliloquy. The original version is:

To be, or not to be: that is the question:
Whether 'tis nobler in the mind to suffer
The slings and arrows of outrageous fortune,
Or to take arms against a sea of troubles,
And by opposing end them? To die: to sleep;
No more; and, by a sleep to say we end
The heartache and the thousand natural shocks
That flesh is heir to, 'tis a consummation
Devoutly to be wish'd. To die, to sleep;
To sleep: perchance to dream: aye, there's the rub;
For in that sleep of death what dreams may come
When we have shuffled off this mortal coil,
Must give us pause.

7 I speak Spanish to God, Italian to women, French to men, and German to my horse.

Charles V (1500–58) Holy Roman Emperor.
Attrib.

8 The one stream of poetry which is continually flowing is slang.

G. K. Chesterton (1874–1936) British writer.
The Defendant

9 All slang is metaphor, and all metaphor is poetry.

G. K. Chesterton
The Defendant

10 I don't hold with abroad and think that foreigners speak English when our backs are turned.

Quentin Crisp (?1910–) Model, publicist, and writer.
The Naked Civil Servant

11 Bring on the empty horses!

Michael Curtiz (1888–1962) Hungarian-born US film director.
Said during the filming of *The Charge of the Light Brigade*. Curtiz, who was not noted for his command of the English language, meant 'riderless horses'. When people laughed at his order he became very angry, shouting, 'You think I know fuck-nothing, when I know fuck-all!' David Niven used the remark as the title of his second volume of autobiography about his experiences in the film industry
Bring on the Empty Horses (David Niven)

12 Imagine the Lord talking French! Aside from a few odd words in Hebrew, I took it completely for granted that God had never spoken anything but the most dignified English.

Clarence Shepard Day (1874–1935) US writer.
Life With Father, 'Father interferes'

13 What is the prose for God?

Harley Granville-Barker (1877–1946) British actor and dramatist.
Waste, I

14 I have laboured to refine our language to grammatical purity, and to clear it from colloquial barbarisms, licentious idioms, and irregular combinations.

Samuel Johnson (1709–84) British lexicographer.
The Rambler

15 I am always sorry when any language is lost, because languages are the pedigree of nations.

Samuel Johnson
Tour to the Hebrides (J. Boswell)

16 I am not yet so lost in lexicography, as to forget that words are the daughters of earth, and that things are the sons of heaven. Language is only the instrument of science, and words are but the signs of ideas: I wish, however, that the instrument might be less apt to decay, and that signs might be permanent, like the things which they denote.

Samuel Johnson
Dictionary of the English Language

17 The baby doesn't understand English and the Devil knows Latin.

Ronald Knox (1888–1957) British Roman Catholic priest.
Said when asked to conduct a baptism service in English
Ronald Knox (Evelyn Waugh), Pt. I, Ch. 5

18 If the English language had been properly organized . . . then there would be a word which meant both 'he' and 'she', and I could write, 'If John or Mary comes heesh will want to play tennis,' which would save a lot of trouble.

A. A. Milne (1882–1956) British writer.
The Christopher Robin Birthday Book

19 Most of their discourse was about hunting, in a dialect I understand very little.

Samuel Pepys (1633–1703) English diarist.
Diary, 22 Nov 1663

20 I include 'pidgin-English' . . . even though I am referred to in that splendid language as 'Fella belong Mrs Queen'.

Prince Philip (1921–) The consort of Queen Elizabeth II.
Speech, English-Speaking Union Conference, Ottawa, 29 Oct 1958

21 Life is too short to learn German.

Richard Porson (1759–1808) British classicist.
Gryll Grange (T. L. Peacock), Ch. 3

22 Language grows out of life, out of its needs and experiences . . . *Language* and *knowledge* are indissolubly connected; they are interdependent. Good work in language presupposes and depends on a real knowledge of things.

Annie Sullivan (1866–1936) US teacher of the handicapped.
Speech, American Association to Promote the Teaching of Speech to the Deaf, July 1894

23 A foreign swear-word is practically inoffensive except to the person who has learnt it early in life and knows its social limits.

Paul Theroux (1941–) US-born writer.
Saint Jack, Ch. 12

24 The most attractive sentences are not perhaps the wisest, but the surest and soundest.

Henry David Thoreau (1817–62) US writer.
Journal, 1842

25 I am not like a lady at the court of Versailles, who said: 'What a dreadful pity that the bother at the tower of Babel should have got language all mixed up, but for that, everyone would always have spoken French.

Voltaire (François-Marie Arouet; 1694–1778) French writer.
Letter to Catherine the Great, Empress of Russia, 26 May 1767

26 We should constantly use the most common, little, easy words (so they are pure and proper) which our language affords.

John Wesley (1703–91) British religious leader.
Advice for preaching to 'plain people'
Attrib.

27 We dissect nature along lines laid down by our native language . . . Language is not simply a reporting device for experience but a defining framework for it.

Benjamin Lee Whorf (1897–1941) US linguist.
New Directions in the Study of Language (ed. Hoyer), 'Thinking in Primitive Communities'

LAST WORDS

Not always the actual last words said, but including remarks made when dying. Many are apocryphal, hence the fact that some people have more than one set of attributed 'last words'.
See also death, execution

1 A lot of people, on the verge of death, utter famous last words or stiffen into attitudes, as if the final stiffening in three days' time were not enough; they will have ceased to exist three days' hence, yet they still want to arouse admiration and adopt a pose and tell a lie with their last gasp.

Henry de Montherlant (1896–1972) French novelist.
Explicit Mysterium

Some examples

2 I inhabit a weak, frail, decayed tenement; battered by the winds and broken in on by the storms, and, from all I can learn, the landlord does not intend to repair.

John Quincy Adams (1767–1848) Sixth president of the USA.
Said during his last illness
Attrib.

3 See in what peace a Christian can die.

Joseph Addison (1672–1719) British essayist.

4 *Ave Caesar, morituri te salutant.*

Hail Caesar; those who are about to die salute you.

Anonymous
Greeting to the Roman Emperor by gladiators

5 Jakie, is it my birthday or am I dying?

Viscountess Nancy Astor (1879–1964) American-born British politician.
To her son on her death bed He replied: 'A bit of both, Mum'.

6 How were the receipts today in Madison Square Garden?

Phineas Taylor Barnum (1810–91) US showman.

7 I am ready to die for my Lord, that in my blood the Church may obtain liberty and peace.

Thomas Becket (c. 1118–79) English churchman.
One version of his last words
Vita S. Thomae, Cantuariensis Archiepiscopi et Martyris (Edward Grim)

8 Thank you, sister. May you be the mother of a bishop!

Brendan Behan (1923–64) Irish playwright.
Said to a nun nursing him on his deathbed
Attrib.

9 When Jesus therefore had received the vinegar, he said, It is finished: and he bowed his head, and gave up the ghost.

Bible: John
19:30

10 And when Jesus had cried with a loud voice, he said, Father, into thy hands I commend my spirit: and having said thus, he gave up the ghost.

Bible: Luke
23:46

11 Jesus, when he had cried again with a loud voice, yielded up the ghost.

And, behold, the veil of the temple was rent in twain from the top to the bottom; and the earth did quake, and the rocks rent;

And the graves were opened; and many bodies of the saints which slept arose.

Bible: Matthew
27:50–52

12 *Et tu, Brute?*

You too, Brutus?

Julius Caesar (100–44 BC) Roman general and statesman.

13 All right, then, I'll say it: Dante makes me sick.

Lope Félix de Vega Carpio (1562–1635) Spanish dramatist and poet.
On being informed he was about to die
Attrib.

14 I realize that patriotism is not enough. I must have no hatred or bitterness towards anyone.

Edith Cavell (1865–1915) British nurse.
Before her execution by the Germans in 1915

15 Let not poor Nelly starve.

Charles II (1630–85) King of England.
Referring to Nell Gwynne
Said on his death bed

16 Give Dayrolles a chair.

Earl of Chesterfield (1694–1773) English statesman.
Said on his deathbed when visited by his godson, Solomon Dayrolles
Last words

17 Nurse, it was I who discovered that leeches have red blood.

Baron Georges Cuvier (1769–1832) French zoologist.
On his deathbed when the nurse came to apply leeches
The Oxford Book of Death (D. Enright)

18 No, it is better not. She will only ask me to take a message to Albert.

Benjamin Disraeli (1804–81) British statesman.
On his deathbed, declining an offer of a visit from Queen Victoria

19 Shakespeare, I come!

Theodore Dreiser (1871–1945) US novelist.
His intended last words
The Constant Circle (S. Mayfield)

20 Goodbye, my friends, I go on to glory.

Isadora Duncan (1878–1927) US dancer.
She was strangled when her long scarf became entangled in the wheel of a sports car
Attrib.

21 My work is done. Why wait?

George Eastman (1854–1932) US inventor and industrialist.
His suicide note

22 All my possessions for a moment of time.

Elizabeth I (1533–1603) Queen of England.

23 I have no pain, dear mother, now;
But oh! I am so dry:
Just moisten poor Jim's lips once more;
And, mother, do not cry!

Edward Farmer (1809–76) British writer.
A typical sentimental verse of the time
The Collier's Dying Child

24 Now I'll have *eine kleine Pause.*

Kathleen Ferrier (1912–53) British contralto.
Said shortly before her death
Am I Too Loud? (Gerald Moore)

25 It is high time for me to depart, for at my

age I now begin to see things as they really are.
Bernard de Fontenelle (1657–1757) French philosopher.
Remark on his deathbed
Anekdotenschatz (H. Hoffmeister)

26 I feel nothing, apart from a certain difficulty in continuing to exist.
Bernard de Fontenelle
Remark on his deathbed
Famous Last Words (B. Conrad)

27 I die happy.
Charles James Fox (1749–1806) British Whig politician.
Life and Times of C. J. Fox (Russell), Vol. III

28 We are all going to Heaven, and Vandyke is of the company.
Thomas Gainsborough (1727–88) British painter.
Thomas Gainsborough (Boulton), Ch. 9

29 I don't mind if my life goes in the service of the nation. If I die today every drop of my blood will invigorate the nation.
Indira Gandhi (1917–84) Indian stateswoman.
Said the night before she was assassinated by Sikh militants, 30 Oct 1984
The Sunday Times, 3 Dec 1989

30 Bugger Bognor.
George V (1865–1936) King of the United Kingdom.
His alleged last words, when his doctor promised him he would soon be well enough to visit Bognor Regis

31 How is the Empire?
George V
Last words
The Times, 21 Jan 1936

32 We are as near to heaven by sea as by land.
Humphrey Gilbert (c. 1539–83) English navigator.
Remark made shortly before he went down with his ship *Squirrel*
A Book of Anecdotes (D. George)

33 *Mehr Licht!*
More light!
Goethe (1749–1832) German poet and dramatist.
Attrib. last words. In fact he asked for the second shutter to be opened, to allow more light in

34 Well, I've had a happy life.
William Hazlitt (1778–1830) British essayist.

35 You might make that a double.
Neville Heath (1917–46) British murderer.
Comment made when offered a drink before his execution
Attrib.

36 God will pardon me. It is His trade.
Heinrich Heine (1797–1856) German poet and writer.
Journal (Edmond and Charles Goncourt), 23 Feb 1863

37 Turn up the lights, I don't want to go home in the dark.
O. Henry (William Sidney Porter; 1862–1910) US short-story writer.
Quoting a popular song of the time
O. Henry (C. A. Smith), Ch. 9

38 I am about to take my last voyage, a great leap in the dark.
Thomas Hobbes (1588–1679) English philosopher.

39 If heaven had granted me five more years, I could have become a real painter.
Hokusai (1760–1849) Japanese painter.
Said on his deathbed
Famous Last Words (B. Conrad)

40 On the contrary!
Henrik Ibsen (1828–1906) Norwegian dramatist.
His nurse had just remarked that he was feeling a little better
True Remarkable Occurrences (J. Train)

41 So it has come at last, the distinguished thing.
Henry James (1843–1916) US novelist.
A Backward Glance (Edith Wharton), Ch. 14

42 Don't give up the ship.
James Lawrence (1781–1813) US naval officer.
As he lay dying in his ship, the US frigate *Chesapeake*, during the battle with the British frigate *Shannon*

43 It's all been rather lovely.
John Le Mesurier (1912–83) British actor.
The Times, 15 Nov 1983

44 Why are you weeping? Did you imagine that I was immortal?
Louis XIV (1638–1715) French king.
Noticing as he lay on his deathbed that his attendants were crying
Louis XIV (V. Cronin)

45 *Tête d'Armée.*
Chief of the Army.
Napoleon I (Napoleon Bonaparte; 1769–1821) French emperor.
Last words
Attrib.

46 I do not have to forgive my enemies, I have had them all shot.
Ramón Maria Narváez (1800–68) Spanish general and political leader.
Said on his deathbed, when asked by a priest if he forgave his enemies
Famous Last Words (B. Conrad)

47 Kiss me, Hardy.
Lord Nelson (1758–1805) British admiral.
Spoken to Sir Thomas Hardy, captain of the *Victory*, during the Battle of Trafalgar, 1805

48 I am just going outside and may be some time.
Captain Lawrence Oates (1880–1912) British soldier and explorer.
Before leaving the tent and vanishing into the blizzard on the ill-fated Antarctic expedition (1910–12). Oates was afraid that his lameness would slow down the others
Journal (R. F. Scott), 17 Mar 1912

49 Die, my dear Doctor, that's the last thing I shall do!
Lord Palmerston (1784–1865) British statesman.

50 I am curious to see what happens in the next world to one who dies unshriven.
Pietro Perugino (1446–1523) Italian painter.
Giving his reasons for refusing to see a priest as he lay dying
Attrib.

51 Oh, my country! How I leave my country!
William Pitt the Younger (1759–1806) British statesman.

52 I think I could eat one of Bellamy's veal pies.
William Pitt the Younger

53 I have not told half of what I saw.
Marco Polo (c. 1254–1324) Venetian traveller.
The Story of Civilization (W. Durant), Vol. I

54 I owe much; I have nothing; the rest I leave to the poor.
François Rabelais (1483–1553) French satirist.

55 Ring down the curtain, the farce is over.
François Rabelais

56 I am going in search of a great perhaps.
François Rabelais

57 I have a long journey to take, and must bid the company farewell.
Walter Raleigh (1554–1618) English explorer.
Sir Walter Raleigh (Edward Thompson), Ch. 26

58 So little done, so much to do.
Cecil Rhodes (1853–1902) South African statesman.

59 You can keep the things of bronze and stone and give me one man to remember me just once a year.
Damon Runyon (1884–1946) US writer.

60 Dear World, I am leaving you because I am bored. I am leaving you with your worries. Good luck.
George Sanders (1906–72) British film actor.
Suicide note

61 Everybody has got to die, but I have always believed an exception would be made in my case. Now what?
William Saroyan (1908–81) US dramatist.
Time, 16 Jan 1984

62 At last I am going to be well!
Paul Scarron (1610–60) French poet.
As he lay dying
Attrib.

63 Nonsense, they couldn't hit an elephant at this distance
John Sedgwick (1813–64) US general.
In response to a suggestion that he should not show himself over the parapet during the Battle of the Wilderness
Attrib.

64 Thank heavens the sun has gone in and I don't have to go out and enjoy it.
Logan Pearsall Smith (1865–1946) US writer.

65 Crito, we owe a cock to Aesculapius; please pay it and don't let it pass.
Socrates (469–399 BC) Athenian philosopher.
Before his execution by drinking hemlock
Phaedo (Plato), 118

66 Beautifully done.
Stanley Spencer (1891–1959) British artist.
Said to the nurse who had injected him, just before he died
Stanley Spencer, a Biography (Maurice Collis), Ch. 19

67 If this is dying, I don't think much of it.
Lytton Strachey (1880–1932) British writer.
Lytton Strachey (Michael Holroyd), Pt. V, Ch. 17

68 Ah, a German and a genius! a prodigy, admit him!
Jonathan Swift (1667–1745) Irish-born Anglican priest and writer.
Learning of the arrival of Handel

69 God bless ... God damn.
James Thurber (1894–1961) US humorist.

70 Even in the valley of the shadow of death, two and two do not make six.
Leo Tolstoy (1828–1910) Russian writer.
Refusing to reconcile himself with the Russian Orthodox Church as he lay dying

71 I have had no real gratification or enjoyment of any sort more than my neighbor on the next block who is worth only half a million.
William Henry Vanderbilt (1821–85) US railway chief.
Famous Last Words (B. Conrad)

72 Dear me, I believe I am becoming a god. An emperor ought at least to die on his feet.
Vespasian (9–79 AD) Roman emperor.
Lives of the Caesars (Suetonius)

73 Either that wall paper goes, or I do.
Oscar Wilde (1854–1900) Irish-born British dramatist.
As he lay dying in a drab Paris bedroom
Time, 16 Jan 1984

74 I expect I shall have to die beyond my means
Oscar Wilde
On accepting a glass of champagne on his deathbed

75 Now God be praised, I will die in peace.
James Wolfe (1727–59) British general.
After being mortally wounded at the Battle of Quebec, 1759
Historical Journal of Campaigns, 1757–60 (J. Knox), Vol. II

LAUGHTER

See also happiness, humour

1 Laugh and grow fat.
Proverb

2 Laugh before breakfast, you'll cry before supper.
Proverb

3 Laughter is the best medicine.
Proverb

4 I make myself laugh at everything, so that I do not weep.
Beaumarchais (1732–99) French dramatist.
Le Barbier de Séville, I:2

5 I said of laughter, It is mad: and of mirth, What doeth it?
Bible: Ecclesiastes
2:2

6 The most wasted of all days is that on which one has not laughed.
Nicolas Chamfort (1741–94) French writer.
Maximes et pensées

7 But laughter is weakness, corruption, the foolishness of our flesh.
Umberto Eco (1932–) Italian semiologist and writer.
The Name of the Rose

8 One must laugh before one is happy, or one may die without ever laughing at all.
Jean de La Bruyère (1645–96) French satirist.
Les Caractères

9 Laughter is pleasant, but the exertion is too much for me.
Thomas Love Peacock (1785–1866) British novelist.
Said by the Hon. Mr Listless
Nightmare Abbey, Ch. 5

10 Laugh, and the world laughs with you;
Weep, and you weep alone,
For the sad old earth must borrow its mirth,
But has trouble enough of its own.
Ella Wheeler Wilcox (1850–1919) US poet.
Solitude

LAW

See also crime, justice, lawyers

1 A judge knows nothing unless it has been explained to him three times.
Proverb

2 Every dog is allowed one bite.
Proverb

3 Every one is innocent until he is proved guilty.
Proverb

4 Possession is nine points of the law.
Proverb

5 The law does not concern itself about trifles.
Proverb

6 One of the Seven was wont to say: 'That laws were like cobwebs; where the small flies were caught, and the great brake through.'
Francis Bacon (1561–1626) English philosopher.
See also SHENSTONE; SOLON; SWIFT
Apothegms

7 The good of the people is the chief law.
Cicero (106–43 BC) Roman orator and statesman.
De Legibus, III

8 The Law of England is a very strange one; it cannot compel anyone to tell the truth. . . . But what the Law can do is to give you seven years for not telling the truth.
Lord Darling (1849–1936) British judge.
Lord Darling (D. Walker-Smith), Ch. 27

9 'If the law supposes that,' said Mr Bumble . . . , 'the law is a ass – a idiot.'
Charles Dickens (1812–70) British novelist.
Oliver Twist, Ch. 51

10 When I went to the Bar as a very young man,
(Said I to myself – said I),
I'll work on a new and original plan,
(Said I to myself – said I).
W. S. Gilbert (1836–1911) British dramatist.
Iolanthe, I

11 The Law is the true embodiment
Of everything that's excellent.
It has no kind of fault or flaw,
And I, my lords, embody the Law.
W. S. Gilbert
Iolanthe, I

12 There's no better way of exercising the imagination than the study of law. No poet ever interpreted nature as freely as a lawyer interprets truth.
Jean Giraudoux (1882–1944) French dramatist.
Tiger at the Gates, I

13 Laws grind the poor, and rich men rule the law.
Oliver Goldsmith (1728–74) Irish-born British writer.
The Traveller

14 I know no method to secure the repeal of bad or obnoxious laws so effective as their stringent execution.
Ulysses Simpson Grant (1822–85) US general.
Inaugural address, 4 Mar 1869

15 The Common Law of England has been laboriously built about a mythical figure – the figure of 'The Reasonable Man'.
A. P. Herbert (1890–1971) British writer and politician.
Uncommon Law

16 In *this* country, my Lords, . . . the individual subject . . . 'has nothing to do with the laws but to obey them.'
Bishop Samuel Horsley (1733–1806) British bishop.
House of Lords, 13 Nov 1795

17 Oh, Mr. President, do not let so great an achievement suffer from any taint of legality.
Philander Chase Knox (1853–1921) US lawyer and politician.
Responding to Theodore Roosevelt's request for legal justification of his acquisition of the Panama Canal Zone
Violent Neighbours (T. Buckley)

18 In university they don't tell you that the

greater part of the law is learning to tolerate fools.

Doris Lessing (1919–) British novelist.
Martha Quest, Pt. III, Ch. 2

19 No brilliance is needed in the law. Nothing but common sense, and relatively clean finger nails.

John Mortimer (1923–) British lawyer and dramatist.
A Voyage Round My Father, I

20 Laws were made to be broken.

Christopher North (John Wilson; 1785–1854) Scottish writer.
Noctes Ambrosianae, 24 May 1830

21 Let us consider the reason of the case. For nothing is law that is not reason.

John Powell (1645–1713) English judge.
Coggs v. Bernard, 2 Lord Raymond, 911

22 Every law is a contract between the king and the people and therefore to be kept.

John Selden (1584–1654) English historian.
Table Talk

23 Ignorance of the law excuses no man; not that all men know the law, but because 'tis an excuse every man will plead, and no man can tell how to confute him.

John Selden
Table Talk

24 Still you keep o' th' windy side of the law.

William Shakespeare (1564–1616) English dramatist.
Twelfth Night, III:4

25 Laws are generally found to be nets of such a texture, as the little creep through, the great break through, and the middle-sized are alone entangled in.

William Shenstone
See also BACON; SOLON; SWIFT
Essays on Men, Manners, and Things, 'On Politics'

26 Laws are like spider's webs: if some poor weak creature come up against them, it is caught; but a bigger one can break through and get away.

Solon (6th century BC) Athenian statesman.
See also BACON; SHENSTONE; SWIFT
Lives of the Eminent Philosophers (Diogenes Laertius), I

27 Laws are like cobwebs, which may catch small flies, but let wasps and hornets break through.

Jonathan Swift (1667–1745) Irish-born Anglican priest and writer.
See also BACON; SHENSTONE; SOLON
A Tritical Essay upon the Faculties of the Mind

LAWYERS

See also law

1 He that is his own lawyer has a fool for a client.

Proverb

2 A lawyer never goes to law himself.

Proverb

3 A lawyer's opinion is worth nothing unless paid for.

Proverb

4 Lawyers are the only persons in whom ignorance of the law is not punished.

Jeremy Bentham (1748–1832) British philosopher.
Attrib.

5 Woe unto you, lawyers! for ye have taken away the key of knowledge: ye entered not in yourselves, and them that were entering in ye hindered.

Bible: Luke
11:52

6 A client is fain to hire a lawyer to keep from the injury of other lawyers – as Christians that travel in Turkey are forced to hire Janissaries, to protect them from the insolencies of other Turks.

Samuel Butler (1835–1902) British writer.
Prose Observations

7 I do not care to speak ill of any man behind his back, but I believe the gentleman is an *attorney*.

Samuel Johnson (1709–84) British lexicographer.
Life of Johnson (J. Boswell), Vol. II

8 It is a very salutary check for a judge to realise that if he does say something silly it is liable to get into the papers.

Mr Justice Templeman (1920–) British judge.
Observer, 20 Aug 1978

LAZINESS

See also bed, idleness

1 I make no secret of the fact that I would rather lie on a sofa than sweep beneath it. But you have to be efficient if you're going to be lazy.

Shirley Conran (1932–) British designer and journalist.
Superwoman, 'The Reason Why'

2 Happy is the man with a wife to tell him what to do and a secretary to do it.

Lord Mancroft (1917–87) British businessman and writer.
The Observer, 'Sayings of the Week', 18 Dec 1966

3 For one person who dreams of making fifty thousand pounds, a hundred people dream of being left fifty thousand pounds.

A. A. Milne (1882–1956) British writer.
If I May, 'The Future'

4 It is better to have loafed and lost than never to have loafed at all.

James Thurber (1894–1961) US humorist.
Fables for Our Time, 'The Courtship of Arthur and Al'

5 'Tis the voice of the sluggard, I heard him complain:

'You have waked me too soon, I must slumber again.'

Isaac Watts (1674–1748) English theologian and hymn writer.
The Sluggard

LEADERSHIP

See also guidance

1 The trouble in modern democracy is that men do not approach to leadership until they have lost the desire to lead anyone.
Lord Beveridge (1879–1963) British economist.
The Observer, 'Sayings of the Week', 15 Apr 1934

2 And he shall rule them with a rod of iron; as the vessels of a potter shall they be broken to shivers: even as I received of my Father.
Bible: Revelations
2:27

3 I believe in benevolent dictatorship provided I am the dictator.
Richard Branson (1950–) British entrepreneur.
Remark, Nov 1984

4 Captains of industry.
Thomas Carlyle (1795–1881) Scottish historian and essayist.
Past and Present, Bk. IV, Ch. 4

5 As the Prime Minister put it to me . . . he saw his role as being that of Moses.
Peter Jay (1937–) British economist and broadcaster.
Referring to a conversation with James Callaghan
Guardian Weekly, 18 Sept 1977

6 Let me pass, I have to follow them, I am their leader.
Alexandre Auguste Ledru-Rollin (1807–74) French lawyer and politician.
Trying to force his way through a mob during the Revolution of 1848, of which he was one of the chief instigators. A similar remark is attributed to Bonar Law
The Fine Art of Political Wit (L. Harris)

7 A leader who doesn't hesitate before he sends his nation into battle is not fit to be a leader.
Golda Meir (1898–1978) Russian-born Israeli stateswoman.
As Good as Golda (ed. Israel and Mary Shenker)

8 No general in the midst of battle has a great discussion about what he is going to do if defeated.
David Owen (1938–) British politician.
The Observer, 'Sayings of the Week', 6 June 1987

LEARNING

See also education, knowledge

1 What we have to learn to do, we learn by doing.
Aristotle (384–322 BC) Greek philosopher.
Nicomachean Ethics, Bk. II

2 Miss not the discourse of the elders: for they also learned of their fathers, and of them thou shalt learn understanding, and to give answer as need requireth.
Bible: Ecclesiasticus
8:9

3 Read, mark, learn and inwardly digest.
The Book of Common Prayer
Collect, 2nd Sunday in Advent

4 An art can only be learned in the workshop of those who are winning their bread by it.
Samuel Butler (1835–1902) British writer.
Erewhon, Ch. 20

5 LIBOV ANDREEVNA. Are you still a student?
TROFIMOV. I expect I shall be a student to the end of my days.
Anton Chekhov (1860–1904) Russian dramatist.
The Cherry Orchard, I

6 . . . that is what learning is. You suddenly understand something you've understood all your life, but in a new way.
Doris Lessing (1919–) British novelist.
The Four-Gated City

7 He intended, he said, to devote the rest of his life to learning the remaining twenty-two letters of the alphabet.
George Orwell (Eric Blair; 1903–50) British novelist.
Animal Farm, Ch. 9

8 For where is any author in the world
Teaches such beauty as a woman's eye?
Learning is but an adjunct to oneself.
William Shakespeare (1564–1616) English dramatist.
Love's Labour's Lost, IV:3

9 Not with blinded eyesight poring over miserable books.
Alfred, Lord Tennyson (1809–92) British poet.
Locksley Hall

10 One impulse from a vernal wood
May teach you more of man,
Of moral evil and of good,
Than all the sages can.
William Wordsworth (1770–1850) British poet.
The Tables Turned

11 Some for renown, on scraps of learning dote,
And think they grow immortal as they quote.
Edward Young (1683–1765) British poet.
Love of Fame, I

LEISURE

See also idleness, merrymaking, pleasure, rest

1 The wisdom of a learned man cometh by opportunity of leisure: and he that hath little business shall become wise.
How can he get wisdom that holdeth the plough, and that glorieth in the goad, that driveth oxen, and is occupied in their labours, and whose talk is of bullocks?
Bible: Ecclesiasticus
38:24–25

2 Hey! Mr Tambourine Man, play a song for me.
I'm not sleepy and there is no place I'm going to.
Bob Dylan (Robert Allen Zimmerman; 1941–) US popular singer.
Mr Tambourine Man

3 If all the year were playing holidays, To sport would be as tedious as to work.
William Shakespeare (1564–1616) English dramatist.
Henry IV, Part One, I:2

4 Days off.
Spencer Tracy (1900–67) US film star.
Explaining what he looked for in a script
Attrib.

LETTER-WRITING

See also communication

1 . . . a habit the pleasure of which increases with practise, but becomes more urksome with neglect.
Abigail Adams (1744–1818) US feminist.
Letter to her daughter, 8 May 1808

2 When he wrote a letter, he would put that which was most material in the postscript, as if it had been a by-matter.
Francis Bacon (1561–1626) English philosopher.
Essays, 'Of Cunning'

3 His sayings are generally like women's letters; all the pith is in the postscript.
William Hazlitt (1778–1830) British essayist.
Referring to Charles Lamb
Conversations of Northcote

LEXICOGRAPHY

1 To finish is both a relief and a release from an extraordinarily pleasant prison.
Robert Burchfield (1923–) New Zealand editor.
On completing the supplements to the Oxford English Dictionary
The Observer, 'Sayings of the Week', 11 Sept 1986

2 Like Webster's Dictionary
We're Morocco bound.
Johnny Burke (1908–64) US songwriter.
Song, 'Road to Morocco' from the film *The Road to Morocco*

3 The responsibility of a dictionary is to record a language, not set its style.
Philip Babcock Gove (1902–72) US dictionary editor.
Letter to *Life Magazine*, 17 Nov 1961

4 But these were the dreams of a poet doomed at last to wake a lexicographer.
Samuel Johnson (1709–84) British lexicographer.
Dictionary of the English Language

5 *Dull.* 8. To make dictionaries is dull work.
Samuel Johnson
Dictionary of the English Language

6 *Lexicographer.* A writer of dictionaries, a harmless drudge.
Samuel Johnson
Dictionary of the English Language

7 I've been in *Who's Who*, and I know what's what, but this is the first time I ever made the dictionary.
Mae West (1892–1980) US actress.
On having a life-jacket named after her
Attrib.

LIBERALISM

1 To be absolutely honest, what I feel really bad about is that I don't feel worse. There's the ineffectual liberal's problem in a nutshell.
Michael Frayn (1933–) British journalist and writer.
The Observer, 8 Aug 1965

2 When a liberal is abused, he says: Thank God they didn't beat me. When he is beaten, he thanks God they didn't kill him. When he is killed, he will thank God that his immortal soul has been delivered from its mortal clay.
Lenin (Vladimir Ilich Ulyanov; 1870–1924) Russian revolutionary leader.
Lenin heard this characterization at a meeting, and repeated it with approval
The Government's Falsification of the Duma and the Tasks of the Social-Democrats, 'Proletary', Dec 1906.

3 A pleasant old buffer, nephew to a lord,
Who believed that the bank was mightier than the sword,
And that an umbrella might pacify barbarians abroad:
Just like an old liberal
Between the wars.
William Plomer (1903–73) South African poet and novelist.
Father and Son: 1939

LIBERTY

1 It is not our frowning battlements . . . or the strength of our gallant and disciplined army. These are not our reliance against a resumption of tyranny in our fair land. . . . Our defence is in the preservation of the spirit which prizes liberty as the heritage of all men, in all lands, everywhere.
Abraham Lincoln (1809–65) US statesman.
Speech, 11 Sept 1858

2 Liberty means responsibility. That is why most men dread it.
George Bernard Shaw (1856–1950) Irish dramatist and critic.

LIFE

See also afterlife, human condition, life and death, mortality, purpose, time, world-weariness

1 Life begins at forty.
Proverb

2 Life is just a bowl of cherries.
Proverb

3 Life is sweet.
Proverb

4 Is it so small a thing
To have enjoy'd the sun,
To have lived light in the spring,
To have loved, to have thought, to have done?
Matthew Arnold (1822–88) British poet and critic.
Empedocles on Etna

5 Before this strange disease of modern life,
With its sick hurry, its divided aims.
Matthew Arnold
The Scholar Gipsy

6 Who saw life steadily, and saw it whole:
The mellow glory of the Attic stage.
Matthew Arnold
Sonnets to a Friend

7 Remember that no man loses any other life
than this which he now lives, nor lives any
other than this which he now loses.
Marcus Aurelius (121–180 AD) Roman emperor.
Meditations, Bk. II, Ch. 14

8 The universe is transformation; our life is
what our thoughts make it.
Marcus Aurelius
Meditations, Bk. IV, Ch. 3

9 The present life of men on earth, O king, as
compared with the whole length of time
which is unknowable to us, seems to me to
be like this: as if, when you are sitting at
dinner with your chiefs and ministers, . . . one of the sparrows from
outside flew very quickly through the hall; as
if it came in one door and soon went out
through another. In that actual time it is
indoors it is not touched by the winter's
storm; but yet the tiny period of calm is over
in a moment, and having come out of the
winter it soon returns to the winter and slips
out of your sight. Man's life appears to be
more or less like this; and of what may
follow it, or what preceded it, we are
absolutely ignorant.
St Bede (The Venerable Bede; c. 673–735 AD) English
churchman and historian.
Ecclesiastical History of the English People, Bk. II, Ch. 13

10 Life is rather like a tin of sardines – we're
all of us looking for the key.
Alan Bennett (1934–   ) British playwright.
Beyond the Fringe

11 Your whole life is on the other side of the
glass. And there is nobody watching.
Alan Bennett
The Old Country, I

12 For everything that lives is holy, life delights
in life.
William Blake (1757–1827) British poet.
America

13 At last awake
From life, that insane dream we take
For waking now.
Robert Browning (1812–89) British poet.
Easter-Day, XIV

14 How good is man's life, the mere living! how
fit to employ
All the heart and the soul and the senses for
ever in joy!
Robert Browning
Saul, IX

15 Life is one long process of getting tired.
Samuel Butler (1835–1902) British writer.
Notebooks

16 Life is the art of drawing sufficient
conclusions from insufficient premises.
Samuel Butler
Notebooks

17 Life is a tragedy when seen in close-up, but
a comedy in long-shot.
Charlie Chaplin (Sir Charles Spencer C.; 1889–1977)
British film actor.
In *The Guardian*, Obituary, 28 Dec 1977

18 Life is a maze in which we take the wrong
turning before we have learnt to walk.
Cyril Connolly (1903–74) British journalist.
The Unquiet Grave

19 Life is an incurable disease.
Abraham Cowley (1618–67) English poet.
To Dr Scarborough

20 What a fine comedy this world would be if
one did not play a part in it!
Denis Diderot (1713–84) French writer.
Letters to Sophie Volland

21 People do not live nowadays – they get
about ten percent out of life.
Isadora Duncan (1878–1927) US dancer.
This Quarter Autumn, 'Memoirs'

22 'Put your shoes at the door, sleep, prepare
for life.'
The last twist of the knife.
T. S. Eliot (1888–1965) US-born British poet and
dramatist.
Rhapsody on a Windy Night

23 I have measured out my life with coffee
spoons.
T. S. Eliot
The Love Song of J. Alfred Prufrock

24 One thing is certain, that Life flies;
One thing is certain, and the Rest is Lies;
The Flower that once has blown for ever dies.
Edward Fitzgerald (1809–83) British poet.
The Rubáiyát of Omar Khayyám (1st edn.), XXVI

25 Life is a jest; and all things show it.
I thought so once; but now I know it.
John Gay (1685–1732) English poet and dramatist.
My Own Epitaph

26 Life's Little Ironies.

Thomas Hardy (1840–1928) British novelist.
Title of book of stories

27 Life is just one damned thing after another.

Elbert Hubbard (1856–1915) US writer.
A Thousand and One Epigrams

28 Life isn't all beer and skittles.

Thomas Hughes (1822–96) British novelist.
Tom Brown's Schooldays, Pt. I, Ch. 2

29 Live all you can; it's a mistake not to. It doesn't so much matter what you do in particular, so long as you have your life. If you haven't had that what *have* you had?

Henry James (1843–1916) US novelist.
The Ambassadors, Bk. V, Ch. 2

30 Life is like a sewer. What you get out of it depends on what you put into it.

Tom Lehrer (1928–) US university teacher and songwriter.
We Will all Go together When We Go

31 Life is what happens to you while you're busy making other plans.

John Lennon (1940–80) British rock musician.
Beautiful Boy

32 Our ingress into the world
Was naked and bare;
Our progress through the world
Is trouble and care.

Henry Wadsworth Longfellow (1807–82) US poet.
Tales of A Wayside Inn, 'The Student's Tale'

33 And thou wilt give thyself relief, if thou doest every act of thy life as if it were the last.

Marcus Aurelius (121–180 AD) Roman emperor.
Meditations, Bk. II, Ch. 5

34 Life to me is like boarding-house wallpaper. It takes a long time to get used to it, but when you finally do, you never notice that it's there. And then you hear the decorators are arriving.

Derek Marlowe (1938–) British writer.
A Dandy in Aspic

35 I've looked at life from both sides now
From win and lose and still somehow
It's life's illusions I recall
I really don't know life at all.

Joni Mitchell (1943–) US singer and songwriter.
Both Sides Now

36 There are three ingredients in the good life: learning, earning and yearning.

Christopher Darlington Morley (1890–1957) US writer.
Parnassus on Wheels, Ch. 10

37 Our lives are merely strange dark interludes in the electric display of God the Father.

Eugene O'Neill (1888–1953) US dramatist.
Strange Interlude

38 Most people get a fair amount of fun out of their lives, but on balance life is suffering and only the very young or the very foolish imagine otherwise.

George Orwell (Eric Blair; 1903–50) British novelist.
Shooting an Elephant

39 The vanity of human life is like a river, constantly passing away, and yet constantly coming on.

Alexander Pope (1688–1744) British poet.
Thoughts on Various Subjects

40 Life is not a spectacle or a feast; it is a predicament.

George Santayana (1863–1952) US philosopher.
The Perpetual Pessimist (Sagittarius and George)

41 It is only in the microscope that our life looks so big. It is an indivisible point, drawn out and magnified by the powerful lenses of Time and Space.

Arthur Schopenhauer (1788–1860) German philosopher.
Parerga and Paralipomena, 'The Vanity of Existence'

42 Life is as tedious as a twice-told tale
Vexing the dull ear of a drowsy man.

William Shakespeare (1564–1616) English dramatist.
King John, III:4

43 Tomorrow, and tomorrow, and tomorrow,
Creeps in this petty pace from day to day
To the last syllable of recorded time,
And all our yesterdays have lighted fools
The way to dusty death. Out, out, brief candle!
Life's but a walking shadow, a poor player,
That struts and frets his hour upon the stage,
And then is heard no more; it is a tale
Told by an idiot, full of sound and fury,
Signifying nothing.

William Shakespeare
Macbeth, V:5

44 And so, from hour to hour, we ripe and ripe,
And then, from hour to hour, we rot and rot;
And thereby hangs a tale.

William Shakespeare
As You Like It, II:7

45 Lift not the painted veil which those who live
Call life.

Percy Bysshe Shelley (1792–1822) British poet.
Lift not the Painted Veil

46 Life is a gamble, at terrible odds – if it was a bet, you wouldn't take it.

Tom Stoppard (1937–) Czech-born British dramatist.
Rosencrantz and Guildenstern Are Dead, III

47 As our life is very short, so it is very miserable, and
therefore it is well it is short.

Jeremy Taylor (1613–67) English Anglican theologian.
The Rule and Exercise of Holy Dying, Ch. 1

48 A life that moves to gracious ends
Thro' troops of unrecording friends,
A deedful life, a silent voice.

Alfred, Lord Tennyson (1809–92) British poet.
To – , after reading a Life and Letters

49 Oh, isn't life a terrible thing, thank God?

Dylan Thomas (1914–53) Welsh poet.
Under Milk Wood

50 For life is but a dream whose shapes return,
Some frequently, some seldom, some by night
And some by day.

James Thomson (1834–82) British poet.
The City of Dreadful Night, I

51 The world is a comedy to those who think, a
tragedy to those who feel.

Horace Walpole (1717–97) British writer.
Letter to Sir Horace Mann, 1769

52 I spent the afternoon musing on Life. If you
come to think of it, what a queer thing Life
is! So unlike anything else, don't you know, if
you see what I mean.

P. G. Wodehouse (1881–1975) British humorous
novelist.
My Man Jeeves, 'Rallying Round Old George'

53 When I think of all the books I have read,
and of the wise words I have heard spoken,
and of the anxiety I have given to parents
and grandparents, and of the hopes that I
have had, all life weighed in the scales of my
own life seems to me preparation for
something that never happens.

W. B. Yeats (1865–1939) Irish poet.
Autobiography

54 Never to have lived is best, ancient writers
say;
Never to have drawn the breath of life,
never to have looked into the eye of day
The second best's a gay goodnight and quickly
turn away.

W. B. Yeats
Oedipus at Colonus

LIFE AND DEATH

See also death, life

1 Every moment dies a man,
Every moment one and one sixteenth is born.

Charles Babbage (1792–1871) British mathematician.
A parody of TENNYSON's *Vision of Sin*
Letter to Tennyson

2 I call heaven and earth to record this day
against you, that I have set before you life
and death, blessing and cursing: therefore
choose life, that both thou and thy seed may
live.

Bible: Deuteronomy
30:19

3 This world nis but a thurghfare ful of wo,
And we ben pilgrimes, passinge to and fro;
Deeth is an ende of every worldly sore.

Geoffrey Chaucer (c. 1342–1400) English poet.
The Canterbury Tales, 'The Knight's Tale'

4 Birth, and copulation, and death.

That's all the facts when you come to brass
tacks.

T. S. Eliot (1888–1965) US-born British poet and
dramatist.
Sweeney Agonistes, 'Fragment of an Agon'

5 I came like Water, and like Wind I go.

Edward Fitzgerald (1809–83) British poet.
The Rubáiyát of Omar Khayyám (1st edn.), XXVIII

6 I believe that the struggle against death, the
unconditional and self-willed determination to
live, is the motive power behind the lives and
activities of all outstanding men.

Hermann Hesse (1877–1962) German novelist and poet.
Steppenwolf, 'Treatise on the Steppenwolf'

7 There are only three events in a man's life;
birth, life, and death; he is not conscious of
being born, he dies in pain, and he forgets to
live.

Jean de La Bruyère (1645–96) French satirist.
Les Caractères

8 I strove with none; for none was worth my
strife;
Nature I loved, and, next to Nature, Art;
I warmed both hands before the fire of life;
It sinks, and I am ready to depart.

Walter Savage Landor (1775–1864) British poet and
writer.
I Strove with None

9 Many men would take the death-sentence
without a whimper to escape the life-
sentence which fate carries in her other
hand.

T. E. Lawrence (1888–1935) British soldier and writer.
The Mint, Pt. I, Ch. 4

10 Life is a great surprise. I do not see why
death should not be an even greater one.

Vladimir Nabokov (1899–1977) Russian-born US novelist.
Pale Fire, 'Commentary'

11 There is no cure for birth and death save to
enjoy the interval.

George Santayana (1863–1952) US philosopher.
Soliloquies in England, 'War Shrines'

12 He hath awakened from the dream of life –
'Tis we, who lost in stormy visions, keep
With phantoms an unprofitable strife,
And in mad trance, strike with our spirit's knife
Invulnerable nothings.

Percy Bysshe Shelley (1792–1822) British poet.
Adonais, XXXIX

13 Every moment dies a man,
Every moment one is born.

Alfred, Lord Tennyson (1809–92) British poet.
For a parody, *see* BABBAGE
The Vision of Sin

14 Because there is no difference.

Thales (c. 624–547 BC) Greek philosopher and astronomer.
His reply when asked why he chose to carry on living after
saying there was no difference between life and death
The Story of Civilization (W. Durant), Vol. 2

LIMERICKS

A small selection

1 There's a wonderful family called Stein,
There's Gert and there's Epp and there's Ein;
Gert's poems are bunk,
Epp's statues are junk,
And no one can understand Ein.
Anonymous

2 There was a faith-healer of Deal,
Who said, 'Although pain isn't real,
If I sit on a pin
And it punctures my skin,
I dislike what I fancy I feel.'
Anonymous

3 There was an old man from Darjeeling,
Who boarded a bus bound for Ealing,
He saw on the door:
'Please don't spit on the floor,'
So he stood up and spat on the ceiling.
Anonymous

4 There was an old man of Boulogne
Who sang a most topical song.
It wasn't the words
That frightened the birds,
But the horrible double-entendre.
Anonymous

5 There was a young lady of Riga,
Who went for a ride on a tiger;
They returned from the ride
With the lady inside,
And a smile on the face of the tiger.
Anonymous

6 There was a young man of Japan
Whose limericks never would scan;
When they said it was so,
He replied, 'Yes, I know,
But I always try to get as many words into the
last line as ever I possibly can.'
Anonymous

7 There once was a man who said 'God
Must think it exceedingly odd
If he find that this tree
Continues to be
When there's no one about in the Quad.'
Ronald Knox (1888–1957) British Roman Catholic priest.
For a reply, see below
Atrrib.

8 Dear Sir, Your astonishment's odd:
I am always about in the Quad.
And that's why the tree
Will continue to be,
Since observed by Yours faithfully, God.
Anonymous
A reply to KNOX

9 There was an Old Man with a beard,
Who said, 'It is just as I feared! –
Two Owls and a Hen,
Four Larks and a Wren,
Have all built their nests in my beard!'
Edward Lear (1812–88) British artist and writer.
Book of Nonsense

LITERACY

See also reading, writing

1 The ratio of literacy to illiteracy is constant,
but nowadays the illiterates can read and
write.
Alberto Moravia (Alberto Pincherle; 1907–) Italian
novelist.
The Observer, 14 Oct 1979

2 To be a well-favoured man is the gift of
fortune; but to write and read comes by
nature.
William Shakespeare (1564–1616) English dramatist.
Much Ado About Nothing, III:3

LITERATURE

See also arts, books, criticism, fiction, novels, plays, poetry,
poetry and prose, poets, prose, reading, theatre, writers,
writing

1 Literature is the art of writing something that
will be read twice; journalism what will be
grasped at once.
Cyril Connolly (1903–74) British journalist.
Enemies of Promise, Ch. 3

2 A work that aspires, however humbly, to the
condition of art should carry its justification in
every line.
Joseph Conrad (Teodor Josef Konrad Korzeniowski;
1857–1924) Polish-born British novelist.
The Nigger of the Narcissus, Preface

3 The reading of all good books is like a
conversation with the finest men of past
centuries.
René Descartes (1596–1650) French philosopher.
Le Discours de la méthode

4 He knew everything about literature except
how to enjoy it.
Joseph Heller (1923–) US novelist.
Catch-22, Ch. 8

5 The proper study of mankind is books.
Aldous Huxley (1894–1963) British novelist.
Chrome Yellow

6 Literature flourishes best when it is half a
trade and half an art.
Dean Inge (1860–1954) British churchman.
The Victorian Age

7 It takes a great deal of history to produce a
little literature.
Henry James (1843–1916) US novelist.
Life of Nathaniel Hawthorne, Ch. 1

8 Was there ever yet anything written by mere
man that was wished longer by its readers,

excepting *Don Quixote, Robinson Crusoe,* and the *Pilgrim's Progress?*
Samuel Johnson (1709–84) British lexicographer.
Johnsonian Miscellanies (ed. G. B. Hill), Vol. I

9 *Sturm und Drang.*
Storm and stress.
Friedrich Maximilian von Klinger (1752–1831) German dramatist and novelist.
Used to designate a late 18th-century literary movement in Germany
Play title

10 Our American professors like their literature clear and cold and pure and very dead.
Sinclair Lewis (1885–1951) US novelist.
Speech, on receiving the Nobel Prize, 1930

11 Literature is mostly about having sex and not much about having children; life is the other way round.
David Lodge (1935–) British author.
The British Museum is Falling Down, Ch. 4

12 You understand *Epipsychidion* best when you are in love; *Don Juan* when anger is subsiding into indifference. Why not Strindberg when you have a temperature?
Desmond MacCarthy (1877–1952) British writer and theatre critic.
Theatre, 'Miss Julie and the Pariah'

13 Literature and butterflies are the two sweetest passions known to man.
Vladimir Nabokov (1899–1977) Russian-born US novelist.
Radio Times, Oct 1962

14 Literature is news that STAYS news.
Ezra Pound (1885–1972) US poet.
ABC of Reading, Ch. 2

15 Great Literature is simply language charged with meaning to the utmost possible degree.
Ezra Pound
How to Read

16 Romanticism is the art of presenting people with the literary works which are capable of affording them the greatest possible pleasure, in the present state of their customs and beliefs.
Classicism, on the other hand, presents them with the literature that gave the greatest possible pleasure to their great-grandfathers.
Stendhal (Henri Beyle; 1783–1842) French novelist.
Racine et Shakespeare, Ch. 3

17 Something that everybody wants to have read and nobody wants to read.
Mark Twain (Samuel Langhorne Clemens; 1835–1910) US writer.
Definition of a classic of literature
Speech at Nineteenth Century Club, New York, 20 Nov 1900

18 *'Language,* man!' roared Parsons; 'why, it's LITERATURE!'
H. G. Wells (1866–1946) British writer.
The History of Mr Polly, Pt. I, Ch. 3

19 Literature is the orchestration of platitudes.
Thornton Wilder (1897–1975) US novelist and dramatist.
Time magazine

LOGIC

See also philosophy

1 'Contrariwise,' continued Tweedledee, 'if it was so, it might be; and if it were so, it would be: but as it isn't, it ain't. That's logic.'
Lewis Carroll (Charles Lutwidge Dodgson; 1832–98) British writer.
Through the Looking-Glass, Ch. 4

2 You can only find truth with logic if you have already found truth without it.
G. K. Chesterton (1874–1936) British writer.
The Man who was Orthodox

3 Logical consequences are the scarecrows of fools and the beacons of wise men.
T. H. Huxley (1825–95) British biologist.
Science and Culture, 'On the Hypothesis that Animals are Automata'

4 The world is everything that is the case.
Ludwig Wittgenstein (1889–1951) Austrian philosopher.
Tractatus Logico-Philosophicus, Ch. 1

5 Logic must take care of itself.
Ludwig Wittgenstein
Tractatus Logico-Philosophicus, Ch. 5

LONDON

See also England

1 The streets of London are paved with gold.
Proverb

2 Oranges and lemons,
Say the bells of St Clement's.
You owe me five farthings,
Say the bells of St Martin's.
When will you pay me?
Say the bells of Old Bailey.
When I grow rich,
Say the bells of Shoreditch.
When will that be?
Say the bells of Stepney.
I'm sure I don't know,
Says the great bell at Bow.
Here comes a candle to light you to bed,
Here comes a chopper to chop off your head.
Tommy Thumb's Pretty Song Book

3 Nobody is healthy in London, nobody can be.
Jane Austen (1775–1817) British novelist.
Emma, Ch. 12

4 Let's all go down the Strand.
Harry Castling (19th century) British songwriter.
Song title

5 But what is to be the fate of the great wen of all?
William Cobbett (1763–1835) British journalist and writer.
A wen is a sebaceous cyst
Rural Rides

6 London, that great cesspool into which all the loungers of the Empire are irresistibly drained.
Arthur Conan Doyle (1856–1930) British writer.
A Study in Scarlet

7 Crowds without company, and dissipation without pleasure.
Edward Gibbon (1737–94) British historian.
Autobiography

8 The tourists who come to our island take in the Monarchy along with feeding the pigeons in Trafalgar Square.
William Hamilton (1917–) Scottish MP.
My Queen and I, Ch. 9

9 I think the full tide of human existence is at Charing-Cross.
Samuel Johnson (1709–84) British lexicographer.
Life of Johnson (J. Boswell), Vol. II

10 When a man is tired of London, he is tired of life; for there is in London all that life can afford.
Samuel Johnson
Life of Johnson (J. Boswell), Vol. III

11 London, that great sea, whose ebb and flow
At once is deaf and loud, and on the shore
Vomits its wrecks, and still howls on for more.
Percy Bysshe Shelley (1792–1822) British poet.
Letter to Maria Gisborne, I

12 Hell is a city much like London –
A populous and smoky city.
Percy Bysshe Shelley
Peter Bell the Third

13 Crossing Piccadilly Circus.
Joseph Thomson (1858–95) Scottish explorer.
His reply when asked by J. M. Barrie what was the most hazardous part of his expedition to Africa
J. M. Barrie (D. Dunbar)

14 Earth has not anything to show more fair:
Dull would he be of soul who could pass by
A sight so touching in its majesty:
The City now doth, like a garment, wear
The beauty of the morning; silent, bare,
Ships, towers, domes, theatres, and temples lie
Open unto the fields, and to the sky;
All bright and glittering in the smokeless air.
William Wordsworth (1770–1850) British poet.
Sonnets, 'Composed upon Westminster Bridge'

1 Oh! why does the wind blow upon me so wild? – It is because I'm nobody's child?
Phila Henrietta Case (fl. 1864) British poet.
Nobody's Child

2 A fav'rite has no friend.
Thomas Gray (1716–71) British poet.
Ode on the Death of a Favourite Cat

3 Pray that your loneliness may spur you into finding something to live for, great enough to die for.
Dag Hammarskjöld (1905–61) Swedish diplomat.
Diaries, 1951

4 Waits at the window, wearing the face that she keeps in a jar by the door
Who is it for? All the lonely people, where do they all come from?
All the lonely people, where do they all belong?
John Lennon (1940–80) British rock musician.
Eleanor Rigby (with Paul McCartney)

5 My heart is a lonely hunter that hunts on a lonely hill.
Fiona Macleod (William Sharp; 1856–1905) Scottish poet and writer.
The Lonely Hunter

6 To be alone is the fate of all great minds – a fate deplored at times, but still always chosen as the less grievous of two evils.
Arthur Schopenhauer (1788–1860) German philosopher.
Aphorismen zur Lebensweisheit

7 Loneliness and the feeling of being unwanted is the most terrible poverty.
Mother Teresa (Agnes Gonxha Bojaxhui; 1910–) Yugoslavian missionary in Calcutta.
Time, 'Saints Among Us', 29 Dec 1975

8 The hunchback in the park
A solitary mister
Propped between trees and water.
Dylan Thomas (1914–53) Welsh poet.
The Hunchback in the Park

9 She dwelt among the untrodden ways
Beside the springs of Dove,
A maid whom there were none to praise
And very few to love . . .
William Wordsworth (1770–1850) British poet.
She Dwelt Among the Untrodden Ways

10 The wind blows out of the gates of the day,
The wind blows over the lonely of heart,
And the lonely of heart is withered away.
W. B. Yeats (1865–1939) Irish poet.
The Land of Heart's Desire

LONELINESS

See also solitude

LONGEVITY

See also age, life, old age

1 Aging seems to be the only available way to live a long time.
Daniel-François-Esprit Auber (1782–1871) French composer.
Dictionnaire Encyclopédique (E. Guérard)

2 Get your room full of good air, then shut up the windows and keep it. It will keep for years. Anyway, don't keep using your lungs all the time. Let them rest.
Stephen Leacock (1869–1944) English-born Canadian economist and humorist.
Literary Lapses, 'How to Live to be 200'

3 If you live long enough, the venerability factor creeps in; you get accused of things you never did and praised for virtues you never had.
I. F. Stone (1907–) US writer and publisher.
Peter's Quotations (Laurence J. Peter)

LOSS

See also defeat, mourning

1 'Tis better to have loved and lost than never to have lost at all.
Samuel Butler (1835–1902) British writer.
The Way of All Flesh, Ch. 77

2 What's lost upon the roundabouts we pulls up on the swings!
Patrick Reginald Chalmers (1872–1942) British banker and novelist.
Green Days and Blue Days: Roundabouts and Swings

3 And much more am I sorrier for my good knights' loss than for the loss of my fair queen; for queens I might have enough, but such a fellowship of good knights shall never be together in no company.
Thomas Malory (1400–71) English writer.
Morte d'Arthur, Bk. XX, Ch. 9

4 There is a ghost
That eats handkerchiefs;
It keeps you company
On all your travels.
Christian Morgenstern (1871–1914) German poet.
Der Gingganz, 'Gespenst'

5 Where have all the flowers gone?
Young girls picked them every one.
Pete Seeger (1919–) US folksinger and songwriter.
Where Have All the Flowers Gone?

6 I've lost the only playboy of the western world.
John Millington Synge (1871–1909) Anglo-Irish dramatist.
The closing words
The Playboy of the Western World, III

7 I've lost one of my children this week.
Joseph Turner (1775–1851) British painter.
His customary remark following the sale of one of his paintings
Sketches of Great Painters (E. Chubb)

8 To lose one parent, Mr Worthing, may be regarded as a misfortune; to lose both looks like carelessness.
Oscar Wilde (1854–1900) Irish-born British dramatist.
The Importance of Being Earnest, I

LOVE

See also admiration, love and death, love and friendship, love and hate, love and marriage, lust, passion, sex

1 All is fair in love and war.
Proverb

2 All the world loves a lover.
Proverb

3 Love laughs at locksmiths.
Proverb

4 Love makes the world go round.
Proverb

5 Love me, love my dog.
Proverb

6 Love will find a way.
Proverb

7 Lucky at cards, unlucky in love.
Proverb

8 No love like the first love.
Proverb

9 Salt water and absence wash away love.
Proverb

10 The way to a man's heart is through his stomach.
Proverb

11 True love never grows old.
Proverb

12 When poverty comes in at the door, love flies out of the window.
Proverb

13 In Scarlet town, where I was born,
There was a fair maid dwellin',
Made every youth cry *Well-a-way!*
Her name was Barbara Allen.

All in the merry month of May,
When green buds they were swellin',
Young Jemmy Grove on his death-bed lay,
For love of Barbara Allen.

So slowly, slowly rase she up,
And slowly she came nigh him,
And when she drew the curtain by –
'Young man, I think you're dyin'!'.
Anonymous
Barbara Allen's Cruelty

14 Greensleeves was all my joy,
Greensleeves was my delight,
Greensleeves was my heart of gold,

And who but Lady Greensleeves.
Anonymous
Greensleeves

15 There were twa sisters sat in a bour;
Binnorie, O Binnorie!
There came a knight to be their wooer,
By the bonnie milldams o' Binnorie.
Anonymous
Binnorie

16 Oh, love is real enough, you will find it some
day, but it has one arch-enemy – and that is
life.
Jean Anouilh (1910–87) French dramatist.
Ardèle

17 Love is, above all, the gift of oneself.
Jean Anouilh
Ardèle

18 When it comes, will it come without warning
Just as I'm picking my nose?
Will it knock on my door in the morning,
Or tread in the bus on my toes?
Will it come like a change in the weather?
Will its greeting be courteous or rough?
Will it alter my life altogether?
O tell me the truth about love.
W. H. Auden (1907–73) British poet.
Twelve Songs, XII

19 Nuptial love maketh mankind; friendly love
perfecteth it; but wanton love corrupteth and
embaseth it.
Francis Bacon (1561–1626) English philosopher.
Essays, 'Of Love'

20 Women who love the same man have a kind
of bitter freemasonry.
Max Beerbohm (1872–1956) British writer.
Zuleika Dobson, Ch. 4

21 Love ceases to be a pleasure, when it ceases
to be a secret.
Aphra Behn (1640–89) English novelist and dramatist.
The Lover's Watch, 'Four o'clock'

22 Beloved, let us love one another: for love is
of God; and every one that loveth is born of
God, and knoweth God.
He that loveth not knoweth not God; for God
is love.
Bible: I John
4:7–8

23 If a man say, I love God, and hateth his
brother, he is a liar: for he that loveth not
his brother whom he hath seen, how can he
love God whom he hath not seen?
Bible: I John
4:20

24 There is no fear in love; but perfect love
casteth out fear: because fear hath torment.
He that feareth is not made perfect in love.
Bible: I John
4:18

25 Greater love hath no man than this, that a
man lay down his life for his friends.
Bible: John
15:13

26 Jesus said unto him, Thou shalt love the
Lord thy God with all thy heart, and with all
thy soul, and with all thy mind.
This is the first and great commandment.
And the second is like unto it, Thou shalt love
thy neighbour as thyself.
On these two commandments hang all the law
and the prophets.
Bible: Matthew
22:37–40

27 Love seeketh not itself to please,
Nor for itself hath any care,
But for another gives its ease,
And builds a Heaven in Hell's despair.
William Blake (1757–1827) British poet.
Songs of Experience, 'The Clod and the Pebble'

28 Love seeketh only Self to please,
To bind another to its delight,
Joys in another's loss of ease,
And builds a Hell in Heaven's despite.
William Blake
Songs of Experience, 'The Clod and the Pebble'

29 Although love dwells in gorgeous palaces, and
sumptuous apartments, more willingly than in
miserable and desolate cottages, it cannot be
denied but that he sometimes causes his
power to be felt in the gloomy recesses of
forests, among the most bleak and rugged
mountains, and in the dreary caves of a
desert . . .
Giovanni Boccaccio (1313–75) Italian writer and poet.
Decameron, 'Third Day'

30 I love thee with a love I seemed to lose
With my lost saints – I love thee with the
breath,
Smiles, tears, of all my life! – and, if God
choose,
I shall but love thee better after death.
Elizabeth Barrett Browning (1806–61) British poet.
Sonnets from the Portuguese, XLIII

31 Such ever was love's way; to rise, it stoops.
Robert Browning (1812–89) British poet.
A Death in the Desert

32 Green grow the rashes O,
Green grow the rashes O,
The sweetest hours that e'er I spend,
Are spent amang the lasses O!
Robert Burns (1759–96) Scottish poet.
Green Grow the Rashes

33 My love is like a red red rose
That's newly sprung in June:
My love is like the melodie
That's sweetly play'd in tune.
Robert Burns
A Red, Red Rose

34 Gin a body meet a body
Coming through the rye;
Gin a body kiss a body,
Need a body cry?
Robert Burns
Coming through the Rye

35 God is Love – I dare say. But what a
mischievous devil Love is!
Samuel Butler (1835–1902) British writer.
Notebooks

36 Of all the girls that are so smart
There's none like pretty Sally;
She is the darling of my heart
And she lives in our alley.
Henry Carey (c. 1690–1743) English poet and musician.
Sally in our Alley

37 There ain't a lady livin' in the land
As I'd swop for my dear old Dutch!
Albert Chevalier (1861–1923) British music-hall artist.
My Old Dutch

38 Many a man has fallen in love with a girl in a
light so dim he would not have chosen a suit
by it.
Maurice Chevalier (1888–1972) French singer and actor.
Attrib.

39 To the men and women who own men and
women
those of us meant to be lovers
we will not pardon you
for wasting our bodies and time
Leonard Cohen (1934–   ) Canadian poet.
The Energy of Slaves

40 Love and a cottage! Eh, Fanny! Ah, give me
indifference and a coach and six!
George Colman, the Elder (1732–94) British dramatist.
The Clandestine Marriage, I:2

41 See how love and murder will out.
William Congreve (1670–1729) British Restoration
dramatist.
The Double Dealer, IV:6

42 Lord, what is a lover that it can give? Why
one makes lovers as fast as one pleases, and
they live as long as one pleases, and they die
as soon as one pleases: and then if one
pleases one makes more.
William Congreve
The Way of the World, II:4

43 Say what you will, 'tis better to be left than
never to have been loved.
William Congreve
The Way of the World, II:1

44 Mad about the boy.
Noël Coward (1899–1973) British dramatist.
Title of song

45 Love is a sickness full of woes,
All remedies refusing;
A plant that with most cutting grows,

Most barren with best using.
Why so?
More we enjoy it, more it dies;
If not enjoyed, it sighing cries,
Hey ho.
Samuel Daniel (c. 1562–1619) English poet and dramatist.
Hymen's Triumph, I

46 It has been said that love robs those who
have it of their wit, and gives it to those who
have none.
Denis Diderot (1713–84) French writer.
Paradoxe sur le comédien

47 Come live with me, and be my love,
And we will some new pleasures prove
Of golden sands, and crystal brooks,
With silken lines, and silver hooks.
John Donne (1573–1631) English poet.
The Bait

48 I am two fools, I know,
For loving, and for saying so
In whining Poetry.
John Donne
The Triple Fool

49 O my America! my new-found-land,
My Kingdom, safeliest when with one man
man'd.
John Donne
Elegies, 19, 'Going To Bed'

50 It seems to me that he has never loved, that
he has only imagined that he has loved, that
there has been no real love on his part. I
even think that he is incapable of love; he is
too much occupied with other thoughts and
ideas to become strongly attached to anyone
earthly.
Anna Dostoevsky (1846–1918) Russian diarist and
writer.
Dostoevsky Portrayed by His Wife

51 And I was desolate and sick of an old
passion.
Ernest Dowson (1867–1900) British lyric poet.
Non Sum Qualis Eram Bonae Sub Regno Cynarae

52 You may not be an angel
'Cause angels are so few,
But until the day that one comes along
I'll string along with you.
Al Dubin (20th century) US songwriter.
Twenty Million Sweethearts

53 All mankind love a lover.
Ralph Waldo Emerson (1803–82) US poet and essayist.
Essays, 'Love'

54 Don't you think I was made for you? I feel
like you had me ordered – and I was
delivered to you – to be worn – I want you
to wear me, like a watch-charm or a button
hole bouquet – to the world.
Zelda Fitzgerald (1900–48) US writer.
Letter to F. Scott Fitzgerald, 1919

55 ... I don't want to live – I want to love
first, and live incidentally ...
Zelda Fitzgerald
Letter to F. Scott Fitzgerald, 1919

56 *Plaisir d'amour ne dure qu'un moment,*
Chagrin d'amour dure toute la vie.
Love's pleasure lasts but a moment; love's sor-
row lasts all through life.
Jean-Pierre Claris de Florian (1755–94) French writer
of fables.
Celestine

57 I'm leaning on a lamp-post at the corner of
the street,
In case a certain little lady walks by.
George Formby (1905–61) British comedian.
Leaning on a Lamp-post

58 Try thinking of love, or something.
Amor vincit insomnia.
Christopher Fry (1907–) British dramatist.
A Sleep of Prisoners

59 If with me you'd fondly stray,
Over the hills and far away.
John Gay (1685–1732) English poet and dramatist.
The Beggar's Opera

60 She who has never loved has never lived.
John Gay
Captives

61 Everyone has experienced that truth: that
love, like a running brook, is disregarded,
taken for granted; but when the brook
freezes over, then people begin to remember
how it was when it ran, and they want it to
run again.
Kahil Gibran (1833–1931) Lebanese mystic and poet.
Beloved Prophet (ed. Virginia Hilu)

62 It's a song of a merryman, moping mum,
Whose soul was sad, and whose glance was
glum,
Who sipped no sup, and who craved no crumb,
As he sighed for the love of a ladye.
W. S. Gilbert (1836–1911) British dramatist.
The Yeoman of the Guard, I

63 In love as in sport, the amateur status must
be strictly maintained.
Robert Graves (1895–1985) British poet and novelist.
Occupation: Writer

64 Love, love, love – all the wretched cant of
it, masking egotism, lust, masochism, fantasy
under a mythology of sentimental postures, a
welter of self-induced miseries and joys,
blinding and masking the essential
personalities in the frozen gestures of
courtship, in the kissing and the dating and
the desire, the compliments and the quarrels
which vivify its barrenness.
Germaine Greer (1939–) Australian-born British writer
and feminist.
The Female Eunuch

65 If you were the only girl in the world,

And I were the only boy.
George Grossmith the Younger (1874–1935) British
singer, actor, and songwriter.
The Bing Boys, 'If you were the Only Girl' (with Fred Thompson; 1884–1949)

66 Hello, Young Lovers, Wherever You Are.
Oscar Hammerstein (1895–1960) US lyricist.
From the musical *The King and I*
Song title

67 A lover without indiscretion is no lover at all.
Thomas Hardy (1840–1928) British novelist.
The Hand of Ethelberta, Ch. 20

68 'You must sit down,' says Love, 'and taste
My meat,'
So I did sit and eat.
George Herbert (1593–1633) English poet.
Love

69 My love she's but a lassie yet.
James Hogg (1770–1835) Scottish poet and writer.
Title of song

70 Pale hands I loved beside the Shalimar,
Where are you now? Who lies beneath your
spell?
Laurence Hope (Mrs M. H. Nicolson; 1804–1905)
British poet and songwriter.
The Garden of Kama and other Love Lyrics from India, 'Pale
Hands I Loved'

71 Look not in my eyes, for fear
They mirror true the sight I see,
And there you find your face too clear
And love it and be lost like me.
A. E. Housman (1859–1936) British scholar and poet.
A Shropshire Lad, 'March'

72 Love is like the measles; we all have to go
through with it.
Jerome K. Jerome (1859–1927) British humorist.
Idle Thoughts of an Idle Fellow

73 Love's like the measles – all the worse
when it comes late in life.
Douglas William Jerrold (1803–57) British dramatist.
Wit and Opinions of Douglas Jerrold, 'A Philanthropist'

74 Love is the wisdom of the fool and the folly
of the wise.
Samuel Johnson (1709–84) British lexicographer.
Johnsonian Miscellanies (ed. G. B. Hill), Vol. II

75 Drink to me only with thine eyes,
And I will pledge with mine;
Or leave a kiss but in the cup,
And I'll not look for wine.
The thirst that from the soul doth rise
Doth ask a drink divine;
But might I of Jove's nectar sup,
I would not change for thine.

I sent thee late a rosy wreath,
Not so much honouring thee,
As giving it a hope that there
It could not wither'd be.
Ben Jonson (1573–1637) English dramatist.
The Forest, IX, 'To Celia'

76 Come, my Celia, let us prove,
While we can, the sports of love,
Time will not be ours for ever,
He, at length, our good will sever.
Ben Jonson
Volpone, III:6

77 Love in a hut, with water and a crust,
Is – Love, forgive us! – cinders, ashes, dust;
Love in a palace is perhaps at last
More grievous torment than a hermit's fast.
John Keats (1795–1821) British poet.
Lamia, II

78 Soft adorings from their loves receive
Upon the honey'd middle of the night.
John Keats
The Eve of Saint Agnes, VI

79 I love a lassie.
Harry Lauder (Hugh MacLennon; 1870–1950) Scottish
music-hall artist.
Song title

80 You must always be a-waggle with LOVE.
D. H. Lawrence (1885–1930) British novelist.
Bibbles

81 I'm not sure if a mental relation with a
woman doesn't make it impossible to love
her. To know the *mind* of a woman is to end
in hating her. Love means the pre-cognitive
flow . . . it is the honest state before the
apple.
D. H. Lawrence
Letter to Dr Trigant Burrow, 3 Aug 1927

82 If there's anything that you want,
If there's anything I can do,
Just call on me,
And I'll send it along with love from me to you.
John Lennon (1940–80) British rock musician.
From Me to You (with Paul McCartney)

83 She loves you, yeh, yeh, yeh,
And with a love like that you know you should
be glad.
John Lennon
She Loves You (with Paul McCartney)

84 Two souls with but a single thought,
Two hearts that beat as one.
Maria Lovell (1803–77) British actress and dramatist.
Ingomar the Barbarian, II (transl. of Friedrich Halm)

85 Time was away and somewhere else,
There were two glasses and two chairs
And two people with one pulse.
Louis MacNeice (1907–63) Irish-born British poet.
Meeting Point

86 Come live with me, and be my love;
And we will all the pleasures prove
That hills and valleys, dales and fields,
Woods or steepy mountain yields.
Christopher Marlowe (1564–93) English dramatist.
The Passionate Shepherd to his Love

87 Let us roll all our strength and all

Our sweetness up into one ball,
And tear our pleasures with rough strife
Thorough the iron gates of life:
Thus, though we cannot make our sun
Stand still, yet we will make him run.
Andrew Marvell (1621–78) English poet.
To His Coy Mistress

88 Send two dozen roses to Room 424 and put
'Emily, I love you' on the back of the bill.
Groucho Marx (Julius Marx; 1895–1977) US comedian.
A Night in Casablanca

89 Because women can do nothing except love,
they've given it a ridiculous importance.
W. Somerset Maugham (1874–1965) British novelist.
The Moon and Sixpence, Ch. 41

90 Love is based on a view of women that is
impossible to those who have had any
experience with them.
H. L. Mencken (1880–1956) US journalist.

91 My heart shall be thy garden.
Alice Meynell (1847–1922) British poet.
The Garden

92 When a man is in love he endures more than
at other times; he submits to everything.
Friedrich Wilhelm Nietzsche (1844–1900) German
philosopher.
The Antichrist

93 I do not love thee! – no! I do not love thee!
And yet when thou art absent I am sad.
Caroline Elizabeth Sarah Norton (1808–77) British
poet.
I do Not Love Thee

94 K-K-Katy, beautiful Katy,
You're the only g-g-g-girl that I adore,
When the m-m-m-moon shines over the cow-
shed,
I'll be waiting at the k-k-k-kitchen door.
Geoffrey O'Hara (1882–1967) Canadian-born US
songwriter.
K-K-Katy (song)

95 By the time you swear you're his,
Shivering and sighing,
And he vows his passion is
Infinite, undying –
Lady, make a note of this:
One of you is lying.
Dorothy Parker (1893–1967) US writer.
Unfortunate Coincidence

96 Every love is the love before
In a duller dress.
Dorothy Parker
Death and Taxes

97 Love is like quicksilver in the hand. Leave
the fingers open and it stays. Clutch it, and it
darts away.
Dorothy Parker
Attrib.

98 Love's perfect blossom only blows

Where noble manners veil defect.
Angels may be familiar; those
Who err each other must respect.
Coventry Patmore (1823–96) British poet.
The Angel in the House, Bk. I, Prelude 2

99 Ye gods! annihilate but space and time.
And make two lovers happy.
Alexander Pope (1688–1744) British poet.
The Art of Sinking in Poetry, 11

100 I've Got You Under My Skin.
Cole Porter (1893–1964) US songwriter.
Born to Dance, song title

101 Night and day, you are the one,
Only you beneath the moon and under the
sun.
Cole Porter
The Gay Divorcee, 'Night and Day'

102 Let's Do It; Let's Fall in Love.
Cole Porter
Paris, song title

103 I have sometimes regretted living so close to
Marie . . . because I may be very fond of
her, but I am not quite so fond of her
company.
Marcel Proust (1871–1922) French novelist.
À la recherche du temps perdu: Sodome et Gomorrhe

104 There can be no peace of mind in love, since
the advantage one has secured is never
anything but a fresh starting-point for further
desires.
Marcel Proust
*À la recherche du temps perdu: À l'ombre des jeunes filles en
fleurs*

105 I loved you when you were inconstant. What
should I have done if you had been faithful?
Jean Racine (1639–99) French dramatist.
Andromaque, IV:5

106 If all the world and love were young,
And truth in every shepherd's tongue,
These pretty pleasures might me move
To live with thee, and be thy love.
Walter Raleigh (1554–1618) English explorer.
Answer to Marlow

107 There are very few people who are not
ashamed of having been in love when they no
longer love each other.
Duc de la Rochefoucauld (1613–80) French writer.
Maximes, 71

108 It takes a woman twenty years to make a
man of her son, and another woman twenty
minutes to make a fool of him.
Helen Rowland (1876–1950) US writer.
Reflections of a Bachelor Girl

109 To fear love is to fear life, and those who
fear life are already three parts dead.
Bertrand Russell (1872–1970) British philosopher.
Marriage and Morals

110 Of all forms of caution, caution in love is per-
haps the most fatal to true happiness.
Bertrand Russell
Marriage and Morals

111 Every little girl knows about love. It is only
her capacity to suffer because of it that
increases.
Françoise Sagan (1935–   ) French writer.
Daily Express

112 Liszt said to me today that God alone deserves to be loved. It may be true, but when
one has loved a man it is very different to
love God.
George Sand (Aurore Dupin, Baronne Dudevant; 1804–
76) French novelist.
Intimate Journal

113 True love's the gift which God has given
To man alone beneath the heaven.
Walter Scott (1771–1832) Scottish novelist.
The Lay of the Last Minstrel, V

114 Therefore love moderately: long love doth
so;
Too swift arrives as tardy as too slow.
William Shakespeare (1564–1616) English dramatist.
Romeo and Juliet, II:6

115 The triple pillar of the world transform'd
Into a strumpet's fool.
William Shakespeare
Antony and Cleopatra, I:1

116 There's beggary in the love that can be
reckon'd.
William Shakespeare
Antony and Cleopatra, I:1

117 If thou rememb'rest not the slightest folly
That ever love did make thee run into,
Thou hast not lov'd.
William Shakespeare
As You Like It, II:4

118 But love is blind, and lovers cannot see
The pretty follies that themselves commit.
William Shakespeare
The Merchant of Venice, II:6

119 For aught that I could ever read,
Could ever hear by tale or history,
The course of true love never did run
smooth.
William Shakespeare
A Midsummer Night's Dream, I:1

120 Love looks not with the eyes, but with the
mind;
And therefore is wing'd Cupid painted blind.
William Shakespeare
A Midsummer Night's Dream, I:1

121 The lunatic, the lover, and the poet,
Are of imagination all compact.
William Shakespeare
A Midsummer Night's Dream, V:1

122 A woman's face, with Nature's own hand painted,
Hast thou, the Master Mistress of my passion.
William Shakespeare
Sonnet 20

123 Let me not to the marriage of true minds
Admit impediments. Love is not love
Which alters when it alteration finds,
Or bends with the remover to remove.
O, no! it is an ever-fixed mark,
That looks on tempests and is never shaken.
William Shakespeare
Sonnet 116

124 Love alters not with his brief hours and weeks,
But bears it out even to the edge of doom.
If this be error, and upon me prov'd,
I never writ, nor no man ever lov'd.
William Shakespeare
Sonnet 116

125 To be wise and love
Exceeds man's might.
William Shakespeare
Troilus and Cressida, III:2

126 She never told her love,
But let concealment, like a worm i' th' bud,
Feed on her damask cheek. She pin'd in thought;
And with a green and yellow melancholy
She sat like Patience on a monument,
Smiling at grief.
William Shakespeare
Twelfth Night, II:4

127 Love sought is good, but given unsought is better.
William Shakespeare
Twelfth Night, III:1

128 Then must you speak
Of one that lov'd not wisely, but too well;
Of one not easily jealous, but, being wrought,
Perplexed in the extreme; of one whose hand,
Like the base Indian, threw a pearl away
Richer than all his tribe.
William Shakespeare
Othello, V:2

129 Nowadays we don't think much of a man's love for an animal; we laugh at people who are attached to cats. But if we stop loving animals, aren't we bound to stop loving humans too?
Alexander Solzhenitsyn (1918–) Soviet novelist.
Cancer Ward, Pt. I, Ch. 20

130 A woman despises a man for loving her, unless she returns his love.
Elizabeth Drew Stoddard (1823–1902) US novelist and poet.
Two Men, Ch. 32

131 I know she likes me,
'Cause she says so.
Eugene Stratton (1861–1918) British music-hall singer.
The Lily of Laguna

132 I hold it true, whate'er befall;
I feel it, when I sorrow most;
'Tis better to have loved and lost
Than never to have loved at all.
Alfred, Lord Tennyson (1809–92) British poet.
In Memoriam A.H.H., XXVII

133 Such a one do I remember, whom to look at was to love.
Alfred, Lord Tennyson
Locksley Hall

134 The rose was awake all night for your sake,
Knowing your promise to me;
The lilies and roses were all awake,
They sighed for the dawn and thee.
Alfred, Lord Tennyson
Maud, I

135 O tell her, brief is life but love is long.
Alfred, Lord Tennyson
The Princess, IV

136 God gives us love. Something to love
He lends us; but, when love is grown
To ripeness that on which it throve
Falls off, and love is left alone.
Alfred, Lord Tennyson
To J.S.

137 'Tis strange what a man may do, and a woman yet think him an angel.
William Makepeace Thackeray (1811–63) British novelist.
Henry Esmond, Ch. 7

138 All, everything that I understand, I understand only because I love.
Leo Tolstoy (1828–1910) Russian writer.
War and Peace, Bk. VII, Ch. 16

139 One can't live on love alone; and I am so stupid that I can do nothing but think of him.
Sophie Tolstoy (1844–1919) Russian writer.
A Diary of Tolstoy's Wife, 1860–1891

140 Those who have courage to love should have courage to suffer.
Anthony Trollope (1815–82) British novelist.
The Bertrams, Ch. 27

141 I doubt whether any girl would be satisfied with her lover's mind if she knew the whole of it.
Anthony Trollope
The Small House at Allington, Ch. 4

142 Walking My Baby Back Home.
Roy Turk (20th century) US songwriter.
Title of song

143 Love conquers all things: let us too give in to Love.
Virgil (Publius Vergilius Maro; 70–19 BC) Roman poet.
Eclogue, Bk. X

144 The boy I love is up in the gallery,
The boy I love is looking now at me.
George Ware (19th century) British songwriter.
The Boy in the Gallery

145 It is like a cigar. If it goes out, you can light
it again but it never tastes quite the same.
Lord Wavell (1883–1950) British field marshall.
Attrib.

146 Beware you be not swallowed up in books!
An ounce of love is worth a pound of
knowledge.
John Wesley (1703–91) British religious leader.
Life of Wesley (R. Southey), Ch. 16

147 I have found it impossible to carry the heavy
burden of responsibility and to discharge my
duties as King as I would wish to do without the help and support of the woman I
love.
Duke of Windsor (1894–1972) King of the United
Kingdom; abdicated 1936.
Radio broadcast, 11 Dec 1936

148 'Ah, love, love' he said. 'Is there anything
like it? Were you ever in love, Beach?'
'Yes, sir, on one occasion, when I was a
young under-footman. But it blew over.'
P. G. Wodehouse (1881–1975) British humorous
novelist.
Pigs Have Wings

149 There is a comfort in the strength of love;
'Twill make a thing endurable, which else
Would overset the brain, or break the heart.
William Wordsworth (1770–1850) British poet.
Michael, 448

150 Love fled
And paced upon the mountains overhead
And hid his face amid a crowd of stars.
W. B. Yeats (1865–1939) Irish poet.
When you are Old

151 But Love has pitched his mansion in
The place of excrement.
W. B. Yeats
Crazy Jane Talks with the Bishop

152 A pity beyond all telling
Is hid in the heart of love.
W. B. Yeats
The Pity of Love

LOVE AND DEATH

See also death, love

1 And for bonnie Annie Laurie
I'll lay me doun and dee.
William Douglas (1672–1748) Scottish poet.
Annie Laurie

2 For, Heaven be thanked, we live is such an
age,
When no man dies for love, but on the stage.
John Dryden (1631–1700) British poet and dramatist.
Mithridates, Epilogue

3 Love is my religion – I could die for that.
John Keats (1795–1821) British poet.
Letter to Fanny Brawne, 13 Oct 1819

4 How alike are the groans of love to those of
the dying.
Malcolm Lowry (1909–57) British novelist.
Under the Volcano, Ch. 12

5 It is very rarely that a man loves
And when he does it is nearly always fatal.
Hugh MacDiarmid (Christopher Murray Grieve; 1892–
1978) Scottish poet.
The International Brigade

6 Men have died from time to time, and worms
have eaten them, but not for love.
William Shakespeare (1564–1616) English dramatist.
As You Like It, IV:1

7 'Tis said that some have died for love.
William Wordsworth (1770–1850) British poet.
'Tis Said that some have Died

LOVE AND FRIENDSHIP

See also friendship, love

1 Love is blind; friendship closes its eyes.
Proverb

2 Friendship is a disinterested commerce
between equals; love, an abject intercourse
between tyrants and slaves.
Oliver Goldsmith (1728–74) Irish-born British writer.
The Good-Natured Man, I

3 Friendship is constant in all other things
Save in the office and affairs of love.
William Shakespeare (1564–1616) English dramatist.
Much Ado About Nothing, II:1

LOVE AND HATE

See also hate, love

1 Now hatred is by far the longest pleasure;
Men love in haste, but they detest at leisure.
Lord Byron (1788–1824) British poet.
Don Juan, XIII

2 *Odi et amo.*
I hate and love.
Catullus (c. 84–c. 54 BC) Roman poet.
Carmina, LXXXV

3 Heaven has no rage like love to hatred
turned,
Nor hell a fury like a woman scorned.
William Congreve (1670–1729) British Restoration
dramatist.
The Mourning Bride, III

4 Oh, I have loved him too much to feel no
hate for him.
Jean Racine (1639–99) French dramatist.
Andromaque, II:1

5 If one judges love by its visible effects, it looks more like hatred than like friendship.
Duc de la Rochefoucauld (1613–80) French writer.
Maximes, 72

LOVE AND MARRIAGE

See also love, marriage

1 Love and marriage, love and marriage,
Go together like a horse and carriage.
Sammy Cahn (Samuel Cohen; 1913–   ) US songwriter.
Our Town, 'Love and Marriage'

2 ALMA. I rather suspect her of being in love with him.
MARTIN. Her own husband? Monstrous! What a selfish woman!
Jennie Jerome Churchill (1854–1921) US-born British hostess and writer.
His Borrowed Plumes

3 Love is moral even without legal marriage, but marriage is immoral without love.
Ellen Key (Karolina Sofia Key; 1849–1926) Swedish writer.
The Morality of Woman and Other Essays, 'The Morality of Woman'

4 Any one must see at a glance that if men and women marry those whom they do not love, they must love those whom they do not marry.
Harriet Martineau (1802–76) British writer.
Society in America, Vol. III, 'Marriage'

5 Can't you read? The score demands *con amore*, and what are you doing? You are playing it like married men!
Arturo Toscanini (1867–1957) Italian conductor.
Criticizing the playing of an Austrian orchestra during rehearsal
Attrib.

6 The amount of women in London who flirt with their own husbands is perfectly scandalous. It looks so bad. It is simply washing one's clean linen in public.
Oscar Wilde (1854–1900) Irish-born British dramatist.
The Importance of Being Earnest, I

LOYALTY

See also betrayal, faithfulness, patriotism, support

1 Dog does not eat dog.
Proverb

2 There is honour among thieves.
Proverb

3 You cannot run with the hare and hunt with the hounds.
Proverb

4 Here's a health unto his Majesty . . .
Confusion to his enemies, . . .
And he that will not drink his health,
I wish him neither wit nor wealth,

Nor yet a rope to hang himself.
Anonymous
Here's a Health unto his Majesty

5 And Ruth said, Intreat me not to leave thee, or to return from following after thee: for whither thou goest, I will go; and where thou lodgest, I will lodge: thy people shall be my people, and thy God my God:
Where thou diest, will I die, and there will I be buried: the Lord do so to me, and more also, if ought but death part thee and me.
Bible: Ruth
1:16–17

6 The State, in choosing men to serve it, takes no notice of their opinions. If they be willing faithfully to serve it, that satisfies.
Oliver Cromwell (1599–1658) English soldier and statesman.
Said before the Battle of Marston Moor, 2 July 1644

7 We are all the President's men.
Henry Kissinger (1923–   ) German-born US politician and diplomat.
Said regarding the invasion of Cambodia, 1970
The Sunday Times Magazine, 4 May 1975

8 A man who will steal *for* me will steal *from* me.
Theodore Roosevelt (1858–1919) US Republican president.
Firing a cowboy who had applied Roosevelt's brand to a steer belonging to a neighbouring ranch
Roosevelt in the Bad Lands (Herman Hagedorn)

9 If this man is not faithful to his God, how can he be faithful to me, a mere man?
Theodoric (c. 445–526) King of the Ostrogoths.
Explaining why he had had a trusted minister, who had said he would adopt his master's religion, beheaded
Dictionnaire Encyclopédique (E. Guérard)

10 When I forget my sovereign, may God forget me!
Lord Thurlow (1731–1806) British lawyer.
Speech, House of Lords, 15 Dec 1778

11 Had I but served God as diligently as I have served the king, he would not have given me over in my gray hairs.
Cardinal Wolsey (1475–1530) English churchman.
Remark to Sir William Kingston
Negotiations of Thomas Wolsey (Cavendish)

LUCK

See also chance, superstition

1 A bad penny always turns up.
Proverb

2 A cat has nine lives.
Proverb

3 Finders keepers, losers weepers.
Proverb

4 It is better to be born lucky than rich.
Proverb

5 The devil looks after his own.
Proverb

6 There, but for the grace of God, goes John Bradford.
John Bradford (c. 1510–55) English Protestant martyr.
Said on seeing some criminals being led to execution
Attrib.

7 This is the temple of Providence where disciples still hourly mark its ways and note the system of its mysteries. Here is the one God whose worshippers prove their faith by their works and in their destruction still trust in Him.
F. H. Bradley (1846–1924) British philosopher.
Referring to Monte Carlo
Aphorisms

8 Fortune, that favours fools.
Ben Jonson (1573–1637) English dramatist.
The Alchemist, Prologue

9 I am a great believer in luck, and I find the harder I work the more I have of it.
Stephen Leacock (1869–1944) English-born Canadian economist and humorist.
Literary Lapses

10 The Eskimo had his own explanation. Said he: 'The devil is asleep or having trouble with his wife, or we should never have come back so easily.'
Robert Edwin Peary (1856–1920) US explorer.
The North Pole

11 We need greater virtues to sustain good fortune than bad.
Duc de la Rochefoucauld (1613–80) French writer.
Maximes, 25

12 'My aunt was suddenly prevented from going a voyage
in a ship what went down – would you call that a case
of Providential interference?'
'Can't tell: didn't know your aunt.'
Frederick Temple (1821–1902) British churchman.
Memoirs of Archbishop Temple (Sandford), Vol. II

LUST

See also animalism, desire, love, sex

1 Licence my roving hands, and let them go,
Before, behind, between, above, below.
John Donne (1573–1631) English poet.
Elegies, 18, 'Love's Progress'

2 What is commonly called love, namely the desire of satisfying a voracious appetite with a certain quantity of delicate white human flesh.
Henry Fielding (1707–54) British novelist.
Tom Jones, Bk. VI, Ch. 1

3 I'll come no more behind your scenes, David; for the silk stockings and white bosoms of your actresses excite my amorous propensities.
Samuel Johnson (1709–84) British lexicographer.
Said to the actor-manager David Garrick
Life of Johnson (J. Boswell), Vol. I

4 Oh, to be seventy again!
Oliver Wendell Holmes Jnr (1841–1935) US jurist.
Said in his eighty-seventh year, while watching a pretty girl
The American Treasury (C. Fadiman)

5 Stand close around, ye Stygian set,
With Dirce in one boat conveyed!
Or Charon, seeing, may forget
That he is old and she a shade.
Walter Savage Landor (1775–1864) British poet and writer.
In Greek mythology, Dirce, a follower of Dionysius, was killed by her great-nephews Amphion and Zethus because of her mistreatment of their mother Antiope; Charon was the ferryman who transported dead souls across the River Styx to the underworld
Dirce

6 Lolita, light of my life, fire of my loins. My sin, my Soul.
Vladimir Nabokov (1899–1977) Russian-born US novelist.
Lolita

7 Th' expense of spirit in a waste of shame
Is lust in action; and till action, lust
Is perjur'd, murd'rous, bloody, full of blame,
Savage, extreme, rude, cruel, not to trust;
Enjoy'd no sooner but despised straight.
William Shakespeare (1564–1616) English dramatist.
Sonnet 129

8 Nonconformity and lust stalking hand in hand through the country, wasting and ravaging.
Evelyn Waugh (1903–66) British novelist.
Decline and Fall, Pt. I, Ch. 5

LUXURY

See also extravagance, wealth

1 It's grand, and ye canna expect to be baith grand and comfortable.
J. M. Barrie (1860–1937) British novelist and dramatist.
The Little Minister, Ch. 10

2 The saddest thing I can imagine is to get used to luxury.
Charlie Chaplin (Sir Charles Spencer C.; 1889–1977) British film actor.
My Autobiography

3 In the affluent society no useful distinction can be made between luxuries and necessaries.
John Kenneth Galbraith (1908–) US economist.
The Affluent Society, Ch. 21

4 Give us the luxuries of life, and we will dispense with its necessities.
John Lothrop Motley (1814–77) US historian and diplomat.
Also quoted by Frank Lloyd Wright
The Autocrat of the Breakfast Table (O. W. Holmes), Ch. 6

5 How many things I can do without!

Socrates (469–399 BC) Athenian philosopher.
Examining the range of goods on sale at a market
Lives of the Eminent Philosophers (Diogenes Laertius), II

6 Beulah, peel me a grape.

Mae West (1892–1980) US actress.
I'm No Angel, film 1933

LYING

See also deception, honesty, truth

1 A liar is worse than a thief.

Proverb

2 The boy cried 'Wolf, wolf!' and the villagers came out to help him.

Aesop (6th century BC) Reputed Greek writer of fables.
Fables, 'The Shepherd's Boy'

3 It contains a misleading impression, not a lie. I was being economical with the truth.

Robert Armstrong (1913–) British civil servant.
Giving evidence on behalf of the British Government in an Australian court case, Nov 1986. Armstrong was, in fact, quoting Edmund Burke (1729–97).

4 Woe unto them that call evil good, and good evil; that put darkness for light, and light for darkness; that put bitter for sweet, and sweet for bitter!

Bible: Isaiah
5:20

5 Nobody speaks the truth when there's something they must have.

Elizabeth Bowen (1899–1973) Irish novelist.
The House in Paris, Ch. 5

6 A lie can be half-way round the world before the truth has got its boots on.

James Callaghan (1912–) British politician and prime minister.
Speech, 1 Nov 1976

7 It cannot in the opinion of His Majesty's Government be classified as slavery in the extreme acceptance of the word without some risk of terminological inexactitude.

Winston Churchill (1874–1965) British statesman.
Speech, House of Commons, 22 Feb 1906

8 The broad mass of a nation . . . will more easily fall victim to a big lie than to a small one.

Adolf Hitler (1889–1945) German dictator.
Mein Kampf, Ch. 10

9 She's too crafty a woman to invent a new lie when an old one will serve.

W. Somerset Maugham (1874–1965) British novelist.
The Constant Wife, II

10 It is hard to believe that a man is telling the truth when you know that you would lie if you were in his place.

H. L. Mencken (1880–1956) US journalist.
Prejudices

11 Unless a man feels he has a good enough memory, he should never venture to lie.

Michel de Montaigne (1533–92) French essayist.
Also quoted in *Le Menteur*, IV:5 by Pierre Corneille (1606–84)
Essais, I

12 He led a double life. Did that make him a liar? He did not feel a liar. He was a man of two truths.

Iris Murdoch (1919–) Irish-born British novelist.
The Sacred and Profane Love Machine

13 He who does not need to lie is proud of not being a liar.

Friedrich Wilhelm Nietzsche (1844–1900) German philosopher.
Nachgelassene Fragmente

14 It has made more liars out of the American people than Golf.

Will Rogers (1879–1935) US actor and humorist.
Referring to income tax
Saturday Review, 'A Rogers Thesaurus', 25 Aug 1962

15 In our country the lie has become not just a moral category but a pillar of the State.

Alexander Solzhenitsyn (1918–) Soviet novelist.
The Observer, 'Sayings of the Year', 29 Dec 1974

16 A lie is an abomination unto the Lord and a very present help in trouble.

Adlai Stevenson (1900–65) US statesman.
Speech, Jan 1951

17 That a lie which is all a lie may be met and fought with outright,
But a lie which is part a truth is a harder matter to fight.

Alfred, Lord Tennyson (1809–92) British poet.
The Grandmother

18 There was things which he stretched, but mainly he told the truth.

Mark Twain (Samuel Langhorne Clemens; 1835–1910) US writer.
The Adventures of Huckleberry Finn, Ch. 1

M

MADNESS

See also psychiatry, psychology

1 We all are born mad. Some remain so.

Samuel Beckett (1906–89) Irish novelist and dramatist.
Waiting for Godot, II

2 A knight errant who turns mad for a reason deserves neither merit nor thanks. The thing is to do it without cause.

Miguel de Cervantes (1547–1616) Spanish novelist.
Don Quixote, Pt. I, Ch. 25

3 The madman is not the man who has lost his

reason. The madman is the man who has lost everything except his reason.

G. K. Chesterton (1874–1936) British writer.
Orthodoxy, Ch. 1

4 Those whom God wishes to destroy, he first makes mad.

Euripides (c. 480–406 BC) Greek dramatist.
Fragment

5 With lack of sleep and too much understanding I grow a little crazy, I think, like all men at sea who live too close to each other and too close thereby to all that is monstrous under the sun and moon.

William Golding (1911–) British novelist.
Rites of Passage, '&'

6 Show me a sane man and I will cure him for you.

Carl Gustav Jung (1875–1961) Swiss psychoanalyst.
The Observer, 19 July 1975

7 Every one is more or less mad on one point.

Rudyard Kipling (1865–1936) Indian-born British writer.
Plain Tales from the Hills, 'On the Strength of a Likeness'

8 Madness need not be all breakdown. It may also be break-through. It is potential liberation and renewal as well as enslavement and existential death.

R. D. Laing (1927–89) British psychiatrist.
The Politics of Experience, Ch. 16

9 The world is becoming like a lunatic asylum run by lunatics.

David Lloyd George (1863–1945) British Liberal statesman.
The Observer, 'Sayings of Our Times', 31 May 1953

10 His father's sister had bats in the belfry and was put away.

Eden Phillpotts (1862–1960) British novelist and dramatist.
Peacock House, 'My First Murder'

11 A body seriously out of equilibrium, either with itself or with its environment, perishes outright. Not so a mind. Madness and suffering can set themselves no limit.

George Santayana (1863–1952) US philosopher.
The Life of Reason: Reason in Common Sense, 2

12 Though this be madness, yet there is method in't.

William Shakespeare (1564–1616) English dramatist.
Hamlet, II:2

13 Madness in great ones must not unwatch'd go.

William Shakespeare
Hamlet, III:1

14 O, let me not be mad, not mad, sweet heaven!
Keep me in temper; I would not be mad!

William Shakespeare
King Lear, I:5

15 If you talk to God, you are praying; if God talks to you, you have schizophrenia. If the dead talk to you, you are a spiritualist; if God talks to you, you are a schizophrenic.

Thomas Szasz (1920–) US psychiatrist.
The Second Sin

16 When we remember that we are all mad, the mysteries disappear and life stands explained.

Mark Twain (Samuel Longhorne Clemens; 1835–1910) US writer.

17 Men will always be mad and those who think they can cure them are the maddest of all.

Voltaire (François-Marie Arouet; 1694–1778) French writer.
Letter, 1762

18 I shudder and I sigh to think
That even Cicero
And many-minded Homer were
Mad as the mist and snow.

W. B. Yeats (1865–1939) Irish poet.
Mad as the Mist and Snow

MAJORITY

See also democracy, minority, public

1 'It's always best on these occasions to do what the mob do.'
'But suppose there are two mobs?' suggested Mr Snodgrass.
'Shout with the largest,' replied Mr Pickwick.

Charles Dickens (1812–70) British novelist.
Pickwick Papers, Ch. 13

2 A majority is always the best repartee.

Benjamin Disraeli (1804–81) British statesman.
Tancred, Bk. II, Ch. 14

3 The majority has the might – more's the pity – but it hasn't right . . . The minority is always right.

Henrik Ibsen (1828–1906) Norwegian dramatist.
An Enemy of the People, IV

4 The worst enemy of truth and freedom in our society is the compact majority. Yes, the damned, compact, liberal majority.

Henrik Ibsen
An Enemy of the People, IV

5 It is time for the great silent majority of Americans to stand up and be counted.

Richard Milhous Nixon (1913–) US president.
Election speech, Oct 1970

MALAPROPISMS

Remarks of a type associated with Mrs Malaprop in Sheridan's play *The Rivals*.

1 Our watch, sir, have indeed comprehended two aspicious persons.

William Shakespeare (1564–1616) English dramatist.
Much Ado About Nothing, III:5

2 Comparisons are odorous.
William Shakespeare
Much Ado About Nothing, III:5

3 A progeny of learning.
Richard Brinsley Sheridan (1751–1816) British dramatist.
The Rivals, I

4 Illiterate him, I say, quite from your memory.
Richard Brinsley Sheridan
The Rivals, II

5 It gives me the hydrostatics to such a degree.
Richard Brinsley Sheridan
The Rivals, III

6 As headstrong as an allegory on the banks of the Nile.
Richard Brinsley Sheridan
The Rivals, III

7 He is the very pine-apple of politeness!
Richard Brinsley Sheridan
The Rivals, III

8 If I reprehend any thing in this world, it is the use of my oracular tongue, and a nice derangement of epitaphs!
Richard Brinsley Sheridan
The Rivals, III

MANKIND

See also evolution, human condition, human nature, men, misanthropy, philanthropy, public, society, women

1 Pray consider what a figure a man would make in the republic of letters.
Joseph Addison (1672–1719) British essayist.
Ancient Medals

2 Either a beast or a god.
Aristotle (384–322 BC) Greek philosopher.
Politics, Bk. I

3 Whatever this is that I am, it is a little flesh and breath, and the ruling part.
Marcus Aurelius (121–180 AD) Roman emperor.
Meditations, Bk. II, Ch. 2

4 Drinking when we are not thirsty and making love all year round, madam; that is all there is to distinguish us from other animals.
Beaumarchais (1732–99) French dramatist.
Le Mariage de Figaro, II:21

5 And God said, Let us make man in our image, after our likeness: and let them have dominion over the fish of the sea, and over the fowl of the air, and over the cattle, and over all the earth, and over every creeping thing that creepeth upon the earth.
So God created man in his own image, in the image of God created he him; male and female created he them.
And God blessed them, and God said unto them, Be fruitful, and multiply, and replenish the earth, and subdue it: and have dominion over the fish of the sea, and over the fowl of the air, and over every living thing that moveth upon the earth.
Bible: Genesis
1:26–28

6 For Mercy has a human heart,
Pity a human face,
And Love, the human form divine,
And Peace, the human dress.
William Blake (1757–1827) British poet.
Songs of Innocence, 'The Divine Image'

7 What is man, when you come to think upon him, but a minutely set, ingenious machine for turning, with infinite artfulness, the red wine of Shiraz into urine?
Karen Blixen (Isak Dinesen; 1885–1962) Danish writer.
Seven Gothic Tales, 'The Dreamers'

8 Every animal leaves traces of what it was; man alone leaves traces of what he created.
Jacob Bronowski (1908–74) British scientist and writer.
The Ascent of Man, Ch. 1

9 Man is a noble animal, splendid in ashes, and pompous in the grave.
Thomas Browne (1605–82) English physician and writer.
Urn Burial, Ch. 5

10 A single sentence will suffice for modern man: he fornicated and read the papers.
Albert Camus (1913–60) French existentialist writer.
The Fall

11 Carlyle said that men were mostly fools. Christianity, with a surer and more reverend realism, says that they are all fools.
G. K. Chesterton (1874–1936) British writer.
Heretics, Ch. 12

12 Mankind is not a tribe of animals to which we owe compassion. Mankind is a club to which we owe our subscription.
G. K. Chesterton
Daily News, 10 Apr 1906

13 The evolution of the human race will not be accomplished in the ten thousand years of tame animals, but in the million years of wild animals, because man is and will always be a wild animal.
Charles Darwin (1887–1962) British life scientist.
The Next Ten Million Years, Ch. 4

14 On earth there is nothing great but man; in man there is nothing great but mind.
William Hamilton (1788–1856) Scottish philosopher.
Lectures on Metaphysics

15 The majority of men devote the greater part of their lives to making their remaining years unhappy.
Jean de La Bruyère (1645–96) French satirist.
Les Caractères

16 The anthropologist respects history, but he does not accord it a special value. He

conceives it as a study complementary to his own: one of them unfurls the range of human societies in time, the other in space.
Claude Lévi-Strauss (1908–) French anthropologist.
The Savage Mind

17 I'll give you my opinion of the human race ... Their heart's in the right place, but their head is a thoroughly inefficient organ.
W. Somerset Maugham (1874–1965) British novelist.
The Summing Up

18 Clearly, then, the city is not a concrete jungle, it is a human zoo.
Desmond Morris (1928–) British biologist and writer.
The Human Zoo, Introduction

19 There are one hundred and ninety-three living species of monkeys and apes. One hundred and ninety-two of them are covered with hair. The exception is a naked ape self-named *Homo sapiens*.
Desmond Morris
The Naked Ape, Introduction

20 Man, as he is, is not a genuine article. He is an imitation of something, and a very bad imitation.
P. D. Ouspensky (1878–1947) Russian-born occultist.
The Psychology of Man's Possible Evolution, Ch. 2

21 The human face is indeed, like the face of the God of some Oriental theogony, a whole cluster of faces, crowded together but on different surfaces so that one does not see them all at once.
Marcel Proust (1871–1922) French novelist.
À la recherche du temps perdu: À l'ombre des jeunes filles en fleurs

22 I wish I loved the Human Race;
I wish I loved its silly face;
I wish I liked the way it walks;
I wish I liked the way it talks;
And when I'm introduced to one
I wish I thought *What Jolly Fun!*
Walter Raleigh (1861–1922) British scholar.
Laughter from a Cloud, 'Wishes of an Elderly Man'

23 Everything is good when it leaves the Creator's hands; everything degenerates in the hands of man.
Jean Jacques Rousseau (1712–78) French philosopher.
Attrib.

24 I love mankind – it's people I can't stand.
Charles M. Schultz (1922–) US cartoonist.
Go Fly a Kite, Charlie Brown

25 After all, for mankind as a whole there are no exports. We did not start developing by obtaining foreign exchange from Mars or the moon. Mankind is a closed society.
E. F. Schumacher (1911–77) German-born economist.
Small is Beautiful, A Study of Economics as if People Mattered, Ch. 14

26 But man, proud man

Dress'd in a little brief authority,
Most ignorant of what he's most assur'd,
His glassy essence, like an angry ape,
Plays such fantastic tricks before high heaven
As makes the angels weep.
William Shakespeare (1564–1616) English dramatist.
Measure for Measure, II:2

27 What a piece of work is a man! How noble in reason! how infinite in faculties! in form and moving, how express and admirable! in action, how like an angel! in apprehension, how like a god! the beauty of the world! the paragon of animals! And yet, to me, what is this quintessence of dust? Man delights not me –no, nor woman neither.
William Shakespeare
Hamlet, II:2

28 How beauteous mankind is! O brave new world
That has such people in't!
William Shakespeare
The Tempest, V:1

29 Physically there is nothing to distinguish human society from the farm-yard except that children are more troublesome and costly than chickens and women are not so completely enslaved as farm stock.
George Bernard Shaw (1856–1950) Irish dramatist and critic.
Getting Married, Preface

30 Man, unlike any other thing organic or inorganic in the universe, grows beyond his work, walks up the stairs of his concepts, emerges ahead of his accomplishments.
John Steinbeck (1902–68) US novelist.
The Grapes of Wrath, Ch. 14

31 Glory to Man in the highest! for Man is the master of things.
Charles Swinburne (1837–1909) British poet.
Hymn of Man

32 I am a man, I count nothing human foreign to me.
Terence (Publius Terentius Afer; c. 190–159 BC) Roman poet.
Heauton Timorumenos

33 ... he willed that the hearts of Men should seek beyond the world and should find no rest therein; but they should have a virtue to shape their life, amid the powers and chances of the world.
J. R. R. Tolkien (1892–1973) British writer.
'He' is Ilúvatar, the Creator
The Silmarillion, Ch. 1

34 The highest wisdom has but one science – the science of the whole – the science explaining the whole creation and man's place in it.
Leo Tolstoy (1828–1910) Russian writer.
War and Peace, Bk.V, Ch. 2

35 One thousand years more. That's all *Homo sapiens* has before him.
H. G. Wells (1866–1946) British writer.
Diary (Harold Nicolson)

36 If anything is sacred the human body is sacred.
Walt Whitman (1819–92) US poet.
I Sing the Body Electric, 8

37 But there comes a moment in everybody's life when he must decide whether he'll live among human beings or not – a fool among fools or a fool alone.
Thornton Wilder (1897–1975) US novelist and dramatist.
The Matchmaker, IV

38 We're all of us guinea pigs in the laboratory of God. Humanity is just a work in progress.
Tennessee Williams (1911–83) US dramatist.
Camino Real, 12

39 If this belief from heaven be sent,
If such be Nature's holy plan,
Have I not reason to lament
What man has made of man?
William Wordsworth (1770–1850) British poet.
Lines written in Early Spring

MANNERS

See also courtesy, etiquette

1 Leave off first for manners' sake: and be not unsatiable, lest thou offend.
Bible: Ecclesiasticus
31:17

2 'Speak when you're spoken to!' the Red Queen sharply interrupted her.
Lewis Carroll (Charles Lutwidge Dodgson; 1832–98) British writer.
Through the Looking-Glass, Ch. 9

3 To Americans English manners are far more frightening than none at all.
Randall Jarrell (1914–65) US author.
Pictures from an Institution, Pt. I, Ch. 5

4 On the Continent people have good food; in England people have good table manners.
George Mikes (1912–87) Hungarian-born British writer.
How to be an Alien

5 Good breeding consists in concealing how much we think of ourselves and how little we think of other persons.
Mark Twain (Samuel Langhorne Clemens; 1835–1910) US writer.
Notebooks

6 Politeness is organised indifference.
Paul Valéry (1871–1945) French poet and writer.
Tel Quel

7 Manners are especially the need of the plain. The pretty can get away with anything.
Evelyn Waugh (1903–66) British novelist.
The Observer, 'Sayings of the Year,' 1962

8 Manners maketh man.
William of Wykeham (1324–1404) English churchman.
Motto of Winchester College and New College, Oxford

MARRIAGE

See also adultery, family, love and marriage, unfaithfulness

1 Better be an old man's darling than a young man's slave.
Proverb

2 Marriages are made in heaven.
Proverb

3 Marry in haste, and repent at leisure.
Proverb

4 Marry in Lent, and you'll live to repent.
Proverb

5 Marry in May, rue for aye.
Proverb

6 The first wife is matrimony, the second company, the third heresy.
Proverb

7 I had vaguely supposed that marriage in a registry office, while lacking both sanctity and style, was at least a swift, straightforward business. If not, then what was the use of it, even to the heathen? A few inquiries, however, showed it to be no such thing.
Richard Adams (1920–) British novelist.
The Girl in a Swing, Ch. 13

8 To marry a man out of pity is folly; and, if you think you are going to influence the kind of fellow who has 'never had a chance, poor devil,' you are profoundly mistaken. One can only influence the strong characters in life, not the weak; and it is the height of vanity to suppose that you can make an honest man of anyone.
Margot Asquith (1865–1945) The second wife of Herbert Asquith.
The Autobiography of Margot Asquith, Ch. 6

9 I married beneath me – all women do.
Nancy Astor (1879–1964) American-born British politician.
Dictionary of National Biography

10 It is a truth universally acknowledged, that a single man in possession of a good fortune must be in want of a wife.
Jane Austen (1775–1817) British novelist.
The opening words of the book
Pride and Prejudice, Ch. 1

11 Happiness in marriage is entirely a matter of chance.
Jane Austen
Pride and Prejudice, Ch. 6

12 Mrs Hall of Sherbourne was brought to bed yesterday of a dead child, some weeks before she expected, owing to a fright. I

suppose she happened unawares to look at her husband.
Jane Austen
Letter, 27 Oct 1798

13 Wives are young men's mistresses, companions for middle age, and old men's nurses.
Francis Bacon (1561–1626) English philosopher.
Essays, 'Of Marriage and Single Life'

14 He was reputed one of the wise men, that made answer to the question, when a man should marry? A young man not yet, an elder man not at all.
Francis Bacon
Essays, 'Of Marriage and Single Life'

15 I rather think of having a career of my own.
Arthur Balfour (1848–1930) British statesman.
When asked whether he was going to marry Margot Tennant
Autobiography (Margot Asquith), Ch. 9

16 It is easier to be a lover than a husband, for the same reason that it is more difficult to show a ready wit all day long than to produce an occasional *bon mot*.
Honoré de Balzac (1799–1850) French novelist.
Attrib.

17 The majority of husbands remind me of an orangutang trying to play the violin.
Honoré de Balzac
La Physiologie du mariage

18 No man should marry until he has studied anatomy and dissected at least one woman.
Honoré de Balzac
La Physiologie du mariage

19 My father argued sair – my mother didna speak,
But she looked in my face till my heart was like to break;
They gied him my hand but my heart was in the sea;
And so auld Robin Gray, he was gudeman to me.
Lady Ann Barnard (1750–1825) British poet.
Auld Robin Gray

20 I don't like your Christian name. I'd like to change it.
To his future wife. She replied, 'You can't, but you can change my surname.'
Thomas Beecham ((1879–1961) British conductor.
Attrib.

21 I think weddings is sadder than funerals, because they remind you of your own wedding. You can't be reminded of your own funeral because it hasn't happened. But weddings always make me cry.
Brendan Behan (1923–64) Irish playwright.
Richard's Cork Leg, I

22 Being a husband is a whole-time job. That is

why so many husbands fail. They cannot give their entire attention to it.
Arnold Bennett (1867–1931) British novelist.
The Title, I

23 Husbands, love your wives, and be not bitter against them.
Bible: Colossians
3:19

24 Let the husband render unto the wife due benevolence: and likewise also the wife unto the husband.
Bible: I Corinthians
7:3

25 But if they cannot contain, let them marry: for it is better to marry than to burn.
Bible: I Corinthians
7:9

26 But he that is married careth for the things that are of the world, how he may please his wife.
Bible: I Corinthians
7:33

27 Wherefore they are no more twain, but one flesh. What therefore God hath joined together, let not man put asunder.
Bible: Matthew
19:6

28 Even as Sara obeyed Abraham, calling him lord: whose daughters ye are, as long as ye do well, and are not afraid with any amazement.
Likewise, ye husbands, dwell with them according to knowledge, giving honour unto the wife, as unto the weaker vessel, and as being heirs together of the grace of life; that your prayers be not hindered.
Bible: I Peter
3:6–7

29 *Marriage*, n. The state or condition of a community consisting of a master, a mistress and two slaves, making in all two.
Ambrose Bierce (1842–?1914) US writer and journalist.
The Devil's Dictionary

30 To have and to hold from this day forward, for better for worse, for richer for poorer, in sickness and in health, to love and to cherish, till death us do part.
The Book of Common Prayer
Solemnization of Matrimony

31 'We stay together, but we distrust one another.'
'Ah, yes . . . but isn't that a definition of marriage?'
Malcolm Bradbury (1932–) British academic and novelist.
The History Man, Ch. 3

32 Ah, gentle dames! It gars me greet
To think how mony counsels sweet,
How mony lengthen'd sage advices,

The husband frae the wife despises!
Robert Burns (1759–96) Scottish poet.
Tam o' Shanter

33 Marriage is distinctly and repeatedly excluded from heaven. Is this because it is thought likely to mar the general felicity?
Samuel Butler (1835–1902) British writer.
Notebooks

34 Wedlock – the deep, deep peace of the double bed after the hurly-burly of the chaise-longue.
Mrs Patrick Campbell (Beatrice Stella Tanner; 1865–1940) British actress.
Jennie (Ralph G. Martin), Vol. II

35 She was a worthy womman al hir lyve,
Housbondes at chirche-dore she hadde fyve,
Withouten other companye in youthe.
Geoffrey Chaucer (c. 1342–1400) English poet.
Referring to the wife of Bath
The Canterbury Tales, Prologue

36 An archaeologist is the best husband any woman can have: the older she gets, the more interested he is in her.
Agatha Christie (1891–1976) British detective-story writer.
Attrib.

37 The most happy marriage I can picture or imagine to myself would be the union of a deaf man to a blind woman.
Samuel Taylor Coleridge (1772–1834) British poet.
Recollections (Allsop)

38 SHARPER: Thus grief still treads upon the heels of pleasure:
Marry'd in haste, we may repent at leisure.
SETTER: Some by experience find those words mis-plac'd:
At leisure marry'd, they repent in haste.
William Congreve (1670–1729) British Restoration dramatist.
The Old Bachelor, V:8

39 Courtship to marriage, as a very witty prologue to a very dull Play.
William Congreve
The Old Bachelor, V:10

40 I hope you do not think me prone to any iteration of nuptials.
William Congreve
The Way of the World, IV:12

41 Marriage is a wonderful invention; but then again so is a bicycle repair kit.
Billy Connolly (1942–) British comedian.
The Authorized Version

42 Says John, It is my wedding-day,
And all the world would stare,
If wife should dine at Edmonton,
And I should dine at Ware.
William Cowper (1731–1800) British poet.
John Gilpin

43 To-morrow is our wedding-day,

And we will then repair
Unto the Bell at Edmonton,
All in a chaise and pair.
William Cowper
John Gilpin

44 Daisy, Daisy, give me your answer, do!
I'm half crazy, all for the love of you!
It won't be a stylish marriage,
I can't afford a carriage,
But you'll look sweet upon the seat
Of a bicycle made for two!
Harry Dacre (19th century) British songwriter.
Daisy Bell

45 If a man stays away from his wife for seven years, the law presumes the separation to have killed him; yet according to our daily experience, it might well prolong his life.
Lord Darling (1849–1936) British judge.
Scintillae Juris

46 This man, she reasons, as she looks at her husband, is a poor fish. But he is the nearest I can get to the big one that got away.
Nigel Dennis (1912–) British writer.
Cards of Identity

47 'Old girl,' said Mr Bagnet, 'give him my opinion. You know it.'
Charles Dickens (1812–70) British novelist.
Bleak House, Ch. 27

48 Every woman should marry – and no man.
Benjamin Disraeli (1804–81) British statesman.
Lothair, Ch. 30

49 It destroys one's nerves to be amiable every day to the same human being.
Benjamin Disraeli
The Young Duke

50 Now one of the great reasons why so many husbands and wives make shipwreck of their lives together is because a man is always seeking for happiness, while a woman is on a perpetual still hunt for trouble.
Dorothy Dix (Elizabeth Meriwether Gilmer; 1861–1951) US journalist and writer.
Dorothy Dix, Her Book, Ch. 1

51 The husband was a teetotaller, there was no other woman, and the conduct complained of was that he had drifted into the habit of winding up every meal by taking out his false teeth and hurling them at his wife.
Arthur Conan Doyle (1856–1930) British writer.
A Case of Identity

52 Here lies my wife; here let her lie!
Now she's at rest, and so am I.
John Dryden (1631–1700) British poet and dramatist.
Epitaph Intended for Dryden's Wife

53 I am to be married within these three days; married past redemption.
John Dryden
Marriage à la Mode, I

54 So that ends my first experience with matrimony, which I always thought a highly overrated performance.
Isadora Duncan (1878–1927) US dancer.
The New York Times, 1923

55 Being an old maid is like death by drowning, a really delightful sensation after you cease to struggle.
Edna Ferber (1887–1968) US writer.
Wit's End (R. E. Drennan), 'Completing the Circle'

56 His designs were strictly honourable, as the phrase is; that is, to rob a lady of her fortune by way of marriage.
Henry Fielding (1707–54) British novelist.
Tom Jones, Bk. XI, Ch. 4

57 Composed that monstrous animal a husband and wife.
Henry Fielding
Tom Jones, Bk. XV, Ch. 9

58 When widows exclaim loudly against second marriages, I would always lay a wager, that the man, if not the wedding-day, is absolutely fixed on.
Henry Fielding
Amelia, Bk. VI, Ch. 8

59 One fool at least in every married couple.
Henry Fielding
Amelia, Bk. IX, Ch. 4

60 Most marriages don't add two people together. They subtract one from the other.
Ian Fleming (1908–64) British journalist and author.
Diamonds are Forever

61 Husbands are like fires. They go out when unattended.
Zsa Zsa Gabor (1919–) Hungarian-born US film star.
Newsweek, 28 Mar 1960

62 A man in love is incomplete until he has married. Then he's finished.
Zsa Zsa Gabor
Newsweek, 28 Mar 1960

63 Do you think your mother and I should have liv'd comfortably so long together, if ever we had been married?
John Gay (1685–1732) English poet and dramatist.
The Beggar's Opera

64 No, I shall have mistresses.
George II (1683–1760) King of Great Britain and Ireland.
Reply to Queen Caroline's suggestion, as she lay on her death-bed, that he should marry again after her death
Memoirs of George the Second (Hervey), Vol. II

65 I was ever of opinion, that the honest man who married and brought up a large family, did more service than he who continued single and only talked of population.
Oliver Goldsmith (1728–74) Irish-born British writer.
The Vicar of Wakefield, Ch. 1

66 I . . . chose my wife, as she did her wedding gown, not for a fine glossy surface, but such qualities as would wear well.
Oliver Goldsmith
The Vicar of Wakefield, Preface

67 The trouble with my wife is that she is a whore in the kitchen and a cook in bed.
Geoffrey Gorer (1905–85) British writer and anthropologist.
Exploring the English Character

68 When a woman gets married it is like jumping into a hole in the ice in the middle of winter; you do it once and you remember it the rest of your days.
Maxim Gorky (Aleksei Maksimovich Peshkov; 1868–1936) Russian writer.
The Lower Depths

69 The concept of two people living together for 25 years without having a cross word suggests a lack of spirit only to be admired in sheep.
A. P. Herbert (1890–1971) British writer and politician.
News Chronicle, 1940

70 The critical period in matrimony is breakfast-time.
A. P. Herbert
Uncommon Law

71 Then be not coy, but use your time;
And while ye may, go marry:
For having lost but once your prime,
You may for ever tarry.
Robert Herrick (1591–1674) English poet.
Hesperides, 'To the Virgins, to Make Much of Time'

72 Marriage has many pains, but celibacy has no pleasures.
Samuel Johnson (1709–84) British lexicographer.
Rasselas, Ch. 26

73 The triumph of hope over experience.
Samuel Johnson
Referring to the hasty remarriage of an acquaintance following the death of his first wife, with whom he had been most unhappy
Life of Johnson (J. Boswell), Vol. II

74 It has been discovered experimentally that you can draw laughter from an audience anywhere in the world, of any class or race, simply by walking on to a stage and uttering the words 'I am a married man'.
Ted Kavanagh (1892–1958) British radio scriptwriter.
News Review, 10 July 1947

75 Nothing is to me more distasteful than that entire complacency and satisfaction which beam in the countenances of a new-married couple.
Charles Lamb (1775–1834) British essayist.
Essays of Elia, 'A Bachelor's Complaint of Married People'

76 Same old slippers,
Same old rice,
Same old glimpse of

Paradise.

William James Lampton (1859–1917) British writer.
June Weddings

77 There was I, waiting at the church,
Waiting at the church, waiting at the church,
When I found he'd left me in the lurch,
Lor', how it did upset me! . . .
Can't get away to marry you today –
My wife won't let me.

Fred W. Leigh (19th century) British songwriter.
Waiting at the Church

78 I'm getting married in the morning!
Ding dong! the bells are gonna chime.
Pull out the stopper!
Let's have a whopper!
But get me to the church on time!

Alan Jay Lerner (1918–86) US songwriter.
My Fair Lady, II:3

79 I am in truth very thankful for not having
married at all.

Harriet Martineau (1802–76) British writer.
Harriet Martineau's Autobiography, Vol. I

80 . . . the early marriages of silly children . . .
where . . . every woman is married before
she well knows how serious a matter human
life is.

Harriet Martineau
Society in America, Vol. III, 'Marriage'

81 In no country, I believe, are the marriage
laws so iniquitous as in England, and the
conjugal relation, in consequence, so
impaired.

Harriet Martineau
Society in America, Vol. III, 'Marriage'

82 When married people don't get on they can
separate, but if they're not married it's
impossible. It's a tie that only death can
sever.

W. Somerset Maugham (1874–1965) British novelist.
The Circle, III

83 Marriage is like a cage; one sees the birds
outside desperate to get in, and those inside
equally desperate to get out.

Michel de Montaigne (1533–92) French essayist.
Essais, III

84 It has been said that a bride's attitude
towards her betrothed can be summed up in
three words: Aisle. Altar. Hymn.

Frank Muir (1920–) British writer and broadcaster.
Upon My Word! (Frank Muir and Dennis Norden), 'A Jug of
Wine'

85 One doesn't have to get anywhere in a
marriage. It's not a public conveyance.

Iris Murdoch (1919–) Irish-born British novelist.
A Severed Head

86 Writing is like getting married. One should

never commit oneself until one is amazed at
one's luck.

Iris Murdoch
The Black Prince, 'Bradley Pearson's Foreword'

87 Why have hamburger out when you've got
steak at home? That doesn't mean it's always
tender.

Paul Newman (1925–) US film actor.
Remark, Mar 1984

88 It is now known . . . that men enter local
politics solely as a result of being unhappily
married.

Cyril Northcote Parkinson (1919–) British historian
and writer.
Parkinson's Law, Ch. 10

89 Marriage may often be a stormy lake, but
celibacy is almost always a muddy horse-
pond.

Thomas Love Peacock (1785–1866) British novelist.
Melincourt

90 Sir, I have quarrelled with my wife; and a
man who has quarrelled with his wife is
absolved from all duty to his country.

Thomas Love Peacock
Nightmare Abbey, Ch. 11

91 Strange to say what delight we married
people have to see these poor fools decoyed
into our condition.

Samuel Pepys (1633–1703) English diarist.
Diary, 25 Dec 1665

92 When a man opens the car door for his wife,
it's either a new car or a new wife.

Prince Philip (1921–) The consort of Queen Elizabeth
II.
Remark, Mar 1988

93 He loved me, and 'twas right that he should,
for I had come to him as a girl-bride; we two
had made such wise provision in all our love
that our two hearts were moved in all things,
whether of joy or of sorrow, by a common
wish, more united in love than the hearts of
brother and sister.

Christine de Pisan (?1363–?1430) Italian poet.
Women of Medieval France (Pierce Butler)

94 A loving wife will do anything for her
husband except stop criticising and trying to
improve him.

J. B. Priestley (1894–1984) British novelist.
Rain on Godshill

95 It doesn't much signify whom one marries,
for one is sure to find next morning that it
was someone else.

Samuel Rogers (1763–1855) British poet.
Table Talk (ed. Alexander Dyce)

96 A married couple are well suited when both
partners usually feel the need for a quarrel at
the same time.

Jean Rostand (1894–1977) French biologist and writer.
Le Mariage

97 Never feel remorse for what you have thought about your wife; she has thought much worse things about you.
Jean Rostand
Le Mariage

98 When you see what some girls marry, you realize how they must hate to work for a living.
Helen Rowland (1876–1950) US writer.
Reflections of a Bachelor Girl

99 The Western custom of one wife and hardly any mistresses.
Saki (Hector Hugh Munro; 1870–1916) British writer.
Reginald in Russia

100 It takes two to make a marriage a success and only one a failure.
Herbert Samuel (1870–1963) British Liberal statesman.
A Book of Quotations

101 Marriage is nothing but a civil contract.
John Selden (1584–1654) English historian.
Table Talk

102 For a light wife doth make a heavy husband.
William Shakespeare (1564–1616) English dramatist.
The Merchant of Venice, V:1

103 Many a good hanging prevents a bad marriage.
William Shakespeare
Twelfth Night, I:5

104 Marriage is popular because it combines the maximum of temptation with the maximum of opportunity.
George Bernard Shaw (1856–1950) Irish dramatist and critic.
Man and Superman

105 It is a woman's business to get married as soon as possible, and a man's to keep unmarried as long as he can.
George Bernard Shaw
Man and Superman, II

106 Have you not heard
When a man marries, dies, or turns Hindoo,
His best friends hear no more of him?
Percy Bysshe Shelley (1792–1822) British poet.
Referring to Thomas Love Peacock, who worked for the East India Company and had recently married
Letter to Maria Gisborne, I

107 Married women are kept women, and they are beginning to find it out.
Logan Pearsall Smith (1865–1946) US writer.
Afterthoughts, 'Other people'

108 My definition of marriage: . . . .it resembles a pair of shears, so joined that they cannot be separated; often moving in opposite directions, yet always punishing anyone who comes between them.
Sydney Smith (1771–1845) British clergyman and essayist.
Memoir (Lady Holland)

109 A little in drink, but at all times yr faithful husband.
Richard Steele (1672–1729) Dublin-born British essayist.
Letter to his wife, 27 Sep 1708

110 Even if we take matrimony at its lowest, even if we regard it as no more than a sort of friendship recognized by the police.
Robert Louis Stevenson (1850–94) Scottish writer.
Virginibus Puerisque

111 Marriage is a step so grave and decisive that it attracts light-headed, variable men by its very awfulness.
Robert Louis Stevenson
Virginibus Puerisque

112 Marriage is like life in this – that it is a field of battle, and not a bed of roses.
Robert Louis Stevenson
Virginibus Puerisque

113 In marriage, a man becomes slack and selfish and undergoes a fatty degeneration of his moral being.
Robert Louis Stevenson
Virginibus Puerisque

114 Bachelor's fare; bread and cheese, and kisses.
Jonathan Swift (1667–1745) Irish-born Anglican priest and writer.
Polite Conversation, Dialogue 1

115 What they do in heaven we are ignorant of; what they do *not* we are told expressly, that they neither marry, nor are given in marriage.
Jonathan Swift
Thoughts on Various Subjects

116 He that loves not his wife and children, feeds a lioness at home and broods a nest of sorrows.
Jeremy Taylor (1613–67) English Anglican theologian.
Sermons, 'Married Love'

117 Or when the moon was overhead,
Came two young lovers lately wed;
'I am half sick of shadows,' said
The Lady of Shalott.
Alfred, Lord Tennyson (1809–92) British poet.
The Lady of Shalott, Pt. II

118 Remember, it is as easy to marry a rich woman as a poor woman.
William Makepeace Thackeray (1811–63) British novelist.
Pendennis, Ch. 28

119 This I set down as a positive truth. A woman with fair opportunities and without a positive hump, may marry whom she likes.
William Makepeace Thackeray
Vanity Fair, Ch. 4

120 Every night of her married life she has been late for school.
Dylan Thomas (1914–53) Welsh poet.
Under Milk Wood

121 It should be a very happy marriage – they are both so much in love with *him*.
Irene Thomas (1920–) British writer.
Attrib.

122 Divorce? Never. But murder often!
Sybil Thorndike (1882–1976) British actress.
Replying to a query as to whether she had ever considered divorce during her long marriage to Sir Lewis Casson
Attrib.

123 A man should not insult his wife publicly, at parties. He should insult her in the privacy of the home.
James Thurber (1894–1961) US humorist.
Thurber Country

124 Nearly all marriages, even happy ones, are mistakes: in the sense that almost certainly (in a more perfect world, or even with a little more care in this very imperfect one) both partners might have found more suitable mates. But the real soul-mate is the one you are actually married to.
J. R. R. Tolkien (1892–1973) British writer.
Letter to Michael Tolkien, 6–8 Mar 1941

125 Marriage is the only adventure open to the cowardly.
Voltaire (François-Marie Arouet; 1694–1778) French writer.
Thoughts of a Philosopher

126 Marriage is a great institition, but I'm not ready for an institution, yet.
Mae West (1892–1980) US actress.

127 I think women are basically quite lazy. Marriage is still a woman's best investment, because she can con some man into supporting her for the rest of his life.
Alan Whicker (1925–) British television broadcaster and writer.
The Observer, 'Sayings of the Week', 10 Sept 1972

128 And what would happen to my illusion that I am a force for order in the home if I wasn't married to the only man north of the Tiber who is even untidier than I am?
Katherine Whitehorn (1926–) British journalist.
Sunday Best, 'Husband-Swapping'

129 In married life three is company and two is none.
Oscar Wilde (1854–1900) Irish-born British dramatist.
The Importance of Being Earnest, I

130 Twenty years of romance makes a woman look like a ruin; but twenty years of marriage make her something like a public building.
Oscar Wilde
A Woman of No Importance, I

131 The best part of married life is the fights. The rest is merely so-so.
Thornton Wilder (1897–1975) US novelist and dramatist.
The Matchmaker, II

132 Of course, I do have a slight advantage over the rest of you. It helps in a pinch to be able to remind your bride that you gave up a throne for her.
Duke of Windsor (1894–1972) King of the United Kingdom; abdicated 1936.
Discussing the maintenance of happy marital relations
Attrib.

133 Judges, as a class, display, in the matter of arranging alimony, that reckless generosity that is found only in men who are giving away somebody else's cash.
P. G. Wodehouse (1881–1975) British humorous novelist.
Louder and Funnier

134 I can honestly say that I always look on Pauline as one of the nicest girls I was ever engaged to.
P. G. Wodehouse
Thank You Jeeves, Ch. 6

135 Wondering why one's friends chose to marry the people they did is unprofitable, but recurrent. One could so often have done so much better for them.
John Wyndham (1903–69) British science-fiction writer.
The Kraken Wakes

MARTYRDOM

See also execution

1 The king has been very good to me. He promoted me from a simple maid to be a marchioness. Then he raised me to be a queen. Now he will raise me to be a martyr.
Anne Boleyn (1507–36) Second wife of Henry VIII.
Notable Women in History (W. Abbot)

2 'Dying for an idea,' again, sounds well enough, but why not let the idea die instead of you?
Wyndham Lewis (1882–1957) British novelist.
The Art of Being Ruled, Pt. I, Ch. 1

3 I will burn, but this is a mere incident. We shall continue our discussion in eternity.
Michael Servetus (1511–53) Spanish physician and theologian.
Comment to the judges of the Inquisition after being condemned to be burned at the stake as a heretic
Borges: A Reader (E. Monegal)

4 And they blest him in their pain, that they were not left to Spain,
To the thumbscrew and the stake, for the glory of the Lord.
Alfred, Lord Tennyson (1809–92) British poet.
The Revenge, III

5 A thing is not necessarily true because a man dies for it.
Oscar Wilde (1854–1900) Irish-born British dramatist.
Oscariana

MARXISM

See also Communism, socialism

1 Karl Marx wasn't a Marxist all the time. He got drunk in the Tottenham Court Road.
Michael Foot (1913–) British Labour politician and journalist.
Behind The Image (Susan Barnes)

2 Marxian Socialism must always remain a portent to the historians of Opinion – how a doctrine so illogical and so dull can have exercised so powerful and enduring an influence over the minds of men, and, through them, the events of history.
John Maynard Keynes (1883–1946) British economist.
The End of Laissez-Faire, III

3 The workers have nothing to lose but their chains. They have a world to gain. Workers of the world, unite.
Karl Marx (1818–83) German philosopher and revolutionary.
The Communist Manifesto, 4

4 From each according to his abilities, to each according to his needs.
Karl Marx
Criticism of the Gotha Programme

5 The dictatorship of the proletariat.
Karl Marx
Attrib.

6 And what a prize we have to fight for: no less than the chance to banish from our land the dark divisive clouds of Marxist socialism.
Margaret Thatcher (1925–) British politician and prime minister.
Speech, Scottish Conservative Conference, 1983

MASCULINITY

See also men

1 It makes me feel masculine to tell you that I do not answer questions like this without being paid for answering them.
Lillian Hellman (1905–84) US dramatist.
When asked by *Harper's* magazine when she felt most masculine; this question had already been asked of several famous men
Reader's Digest, July 1977

2 You may have my husband, but not my horse. My husband won't need emasculating, and my horse I won't have you meddle with. I'll preserve one last male thing in the museum of this world, if I can.
D. H. Lawrence (1885–1930) British novelist.
St Mawr

MATERIALISM

See also greed, money, wealth

1 Benefits make a man a slave.
Arabic proverb
Proverb

2 Thinking to get at once all the gold that the goose could give, he killed it, and opened it only to find – nothing.
Aesop (6th century BC) Reputed Greek writer of fables.
Fables, 'The Goose with the Golden Eggs'

3 Jesus said unto him, If thou wilt be perfect, go and sell that thou hast, and give to the poor, and thou shalt have treasure in heaven: and come and follow me.
But when the young man heard that saying, he went away sorrowful: for he had great possessions.
Bible: Matthew
19:21–22

4 Maidens, like moths, are ever caught by glare,
And Mammon wins his way where Seraphs might despair.
Lord Byron (1788–1824) British poet.
Childe Harold's Pilgrimage, I

5 For gold in phisik is a cordial,
Therfore he lovede gold in special.
Geoffrey Chaucer (c. 1342–1400) English poet.
Referring to the doctor
The Canterbury Tales, Prologue

6 To be clever enough to get all that money, one must be stupid enough to want it.
G. K. Chesterton (1874–1936) British writer.
The Innocence of Father Brown

7 I never hated a man enough to give him diamonds back.
Zsa Zsa Gabor (1919–) Hungarian-born US film star.
The Observer, 'Sayings of the Week', 28 Aug 1957

8 What female heart can gold despise?
What cat's averse to fish?
Thomas Gray (1716–71) British poet.
Ode on the Death of a Favourite Cat

9 Man must choose whether to be rich in things or in the freedom to use them.
Ivan Illich (1926–) Austrian sociologist.
Deschooling Society, Ch. 4

10 In a consumer society there are inevitably two kinds of slaves: the prisoners of addiction and the prisoners of envy.
Ivan Illich
Tools for Conviviality

11 The almighty dollar, that great object of universal devotion throughout our land, seems to have no genuine devotees in these peculiar villages.
Washington Irving (1783–1859) US writer.
Wolfert's Roost, 'The Creole Village'

12 Good morning to the day: and, next, my
gold! –
Open the shrine, that I may see my saint.
Ben Jonson (1573–1637) English dramatist.
Volpone, I:1

13 Kissing your hand may make you feel very
very good but a diamond and safire bracelet
lasts forever.
Anita Loos (1891–1981) US novelist.
Gentlemen Prefer Blondes, Ch. 4

14 When an American heiress wants to buy a
man, she at once crosses the Atlantic. The
only really materialistic people I have ever
met have been Europeans.
Mary McCarthy (1912–89) US novelist.
On the Contrary 1962

15 Years ago a person, he was unhappy, didn't
know what to do with himself – he'd go to
church, start a revolution – *something*. Today
you're unhappy? Can't figure it out? What is
the salvation? Go shopping.
Arthur Miller (1915–   ) US dramatist.
The Price, I

16 Why is it no one ever sent me yet
One perfect limousine, do you suppose?
Ah no, it's always just my luck to get
One perfect rose.
Dorothy Parker (1893–1967) US writer.
One Perfect Rose

17 Diamonds Are A Girl's Best Friend.
Leo Robin (1899–1984) US songwriter.
Gentlemen Prefer Blondes, song title

18 Bell, book, and candle, shall not drive me
back,
When gold and silver becks me to come on.
William Shakespeare (1564–1616) English dramatist.
King John, III:3

19 The want of a thing is perplexing enough, but
the possession of it is intolerable.
John Vanbrugh (1664–1726) English architect and
dramatist.
The Confederacy, I:2

20 Conspicuous consumption of valuable goods is
a means of reputability to the gentleman of
leisure.
Thorstein Bunde Veblen (1857–1929) US social
scientist.
The Theory of the Leisure Class

21 What do you not drive human hearts into,
cursed
craving for gold!
Virgil (Publius Vergilius Maro; 70–19 BC) Roman poet.
Aeneid, Bk. III

22 There's something about a crowd like that
that brings a lump to my wallet.
Eli Wallach (1915–   ) US actor.
Remarking upon the long line of people at the box office before
one of his performances
Attrib.

23 A gold rush is what happens when a line of
chorus girls spot a man with a bank roll.
Mae West (1892–1980) US actress.
Klondike Annie, film 1936

MATHEMATICS

See also numbers

1 What is algebra exactly; is it those three-
cornered things?
J. M. Barrie (1860–1937) British novelist and dramatist.
Quality Street, II

2 I never could make out what those damned
dots meant.
Lord Randolph Churchill (1849–95) British Conservative
politician.
Referring to decimal points
Lord Randolph Churchill (W. S. Churchill)

3 As far as the laws of mathematics refer to
reality, they are not certain, and as far as
they are certain, they do not refer to reality.
Albert Einstein (1879–1955) German-born US physicist.
The Tao of Physics (F. Capra), Ch. 2

4 There is no 'royal road' to geometry.
Euclid (c. 300 BC) Greek mathematician.
Said to Ptolemy I when asked if there were an easier way to
solve theorems
Comment on Euclid (Proclus)

5 About binomial theorems I'm teeming with a
lot of news,
With many cheerful facts about the square on
the hypoteneuse.
W. S. Gilbert (1836–1911) British dramatist.
The Pirates of Penzance, I

6 MORIARTY. How are you at Mathematics?
HARRY SECOMBE. I speak it like a native.
Spike Milligan (1918–   ) British comic actor and author.
The Goon Show

7 The only way I can distinguish proper from
improper fractions
Is by their actions.
Ogden Nash (1902–71) US poet.
Ask Daddy, He Won't Know

8 One geometry cannot be more true than
another; it can only be more convenient.
Geometry is not true, it is advantageous.
Robert T. Pirsig (1928–   ) US writer.
Zen and the Art of Motorcycle Maintenance, Pt. III, Ch. 22

9 Let no one ignorant of mathematics enter
here.
Plato (429–347 BC) Greek philosopher.
Inscription written over the entrance to the Academy
Biographical Encyclopedia (I. Asimov)

10 The true spirit of delight, the exaltation, the
sense of being more than Man, which is the
touchstone of the highest excellence is to be
found in mathematics as surely as in poetry.
Bertrand Russell (1872–1970) British philosopher.
Mysticism and Logic

11 Mathematics, rightly viewed, possesses not only truth by supreme beauty – a beauty cold and austere like that of sculpture.
Bertrand Russell
Mysticism and Logic

12 Mathematics may be defined as the subject in which we never know what we are talking about, nor whether what we are saying is true.
Bertrand Russell
Mysticism and Logic, Ch. 4

13 Pure mathematics consists entirely of assertions to the effect that, if such and such a proposition is true of *anything*, then such and such another proposition is true of that thing. It is essential not to discuss whether the first proposition is really true, and not to mention what the anything is, of which it is supposed to be true.
Bertrand Russell
Mysticism and Logic, Ch. 5

14 Mathematics possesses not only truth, but supreme beauty –a beauty cold and austere, like that of sculpture.
Bertrand Russell
The Study of Mathematics

15 Numbers constitute the only universal language.
Nathaniel West (Nathan Weinstein; 1903–40) US novelist.
Miss Lonelyhearts

MEANING

See also purpose, words

1 'Then you should say what you mean,' the March Hare went on. 'I do,' Alice hastily replied; 'at least – at least I mean what I say – that's the same thing, you know.'
'Not the same thing a bit!' said the Hatter. 'Why, you might just as well say that 'I see what I eat' is the same thing as 'I eat what I see!"
Lewis Carroll (Charles Lutwidge Dodgson; 1832–98) British writer.
Alice's Adventures in Wonderland, Ch. 7

2 Take care of the sense, and the sounds will take care of themselves.
Lewis Carroll
Alice's Adventures in Wonderland, Ch. 9

3 'When *I* use a word,' Humpty Dumpty said in rather a scornful tone, 'it means just what I choose it to mean – neither more nor less.'
Lewis Carroll
Through the Looking-Glass, Ch. 6

4 Where in this small-talking world can I find
A longitude with no platitude?
Christopher Fry (1907–) British dramatist.
The Lady's Not for Burning, III

5 The least of things with a meaning is worth more in life than the greatest of things without it.
Carl Gustav Jung (1875–1961) Swiss psychoanalyst.
Modern Man in Search of a Soul

MEDICINE

See also disease, doctors, drugs, health and healthy living, illness, nurses, remedies

1 The prime goal is to alleviate suffering, and not to prolong life. And if your treatment does not alleviate suffering, but only prolongs life, that treatment should be stopped.
Christiaan Barnard (1922–) South African surgeon.

2 Medical men all over the world having merely entered into a tacit agreement to call all sorts of maladies people are liable to, in cold weather, by one name; so that one sort of treatment may serve for all, and their practice thereby be greatly simplified.
Jane Welsh Carlyle (1801–66) The wife of Thomas Carlyle.
Letter to John Welsh, 4 Mar 1837

3 A miracle drug is any drug that will do what the label says it will do.
Eric Hodgins (1899–1971) US writer and editor.
Episode

4 One of the most difficult things to contend with in a hospital is the assumption on the part of the staff that because you have lost your gall bladder you have also lost your mind.
Jean Kerr (1923–) US dramatist.
Please Don't Eat the Daisies

5 The ultimate indignity is to be given a bedpan by a stranger who calls you by your first name.
Maggie Kuhn (1905–) US writer and social activist.
The Observer, 20 Aug 1978

6 The art of medicine is generally a question of time.
Ovid (Publius Ovidius Naso; 43 BC–17 AD) Roman poet.
Remedia Amoris

7 Not even medicine can master incurable diseases.
Seneca (c. 4 BC–65 AD) Roman author.
Epistulae ad Lucilium, XCIV

8 Optimistic lies have such immense therapeutic value that a doctor who cannot tell them convincingly has mistaken his profession.
George Bernard Shaw (1856–1950) Irish dramatist and critic.
Misalliance, Preface

9 I've already had medical attention – a dog licked me when I was on the ground.
Neil Simon (1927–) US playwright.
Only When I Laugh (screenplay)

10 Formerly, when religion was strong and science weak, men mistook magic for

medicine, now, when science is strong and religion weak, men mistake medicine for magic.
Thomas Szasz (1920–) US psychiatrist.
The Second Sin

11 Human beings, yes, but not surgeons.
Rudolph Virchow (1821–1902) German pathologist.
Answering a query as to whether human beings could survive appendectomy, which had recently become a widespread practice
Anekdotenschatz (H. Hoffmeister)

12 The art of medicine consists of amusing the patient while Nature cures the disease.
Voltaire (François-Marie Arouet; 1694–1788) French writer.
Attrib.

MEDIOCRITY

See also inferiority

1 Only mediocrity can be trusted to be always at its best.
Max Beerbohm (1872–1956) British writer.
Conversations with Max (S.N. Behrman)

2 The world is made of people who never quite get into the first team and who just miss the prizes at the flower show.
Jacob Bronowski (1908–74) British scientist and writer.
The Face of Violence, Ch. 6

3 Mediocrity knows nothing higher than itself, but talent instantly recognizes genius.
Arthur Conan Doyle (1856–1930) British writer.
The Valley of Fear

4 Some men are born mediocre, some men achieve mediocrity, and some men have mediocrity thrust upon them. With Major Major it had been all three.
Joseph Heller (1923–) US novelist.
Catch-22, Ch. 9

5 Women want mediocre men, and men are working to be as mediocre as possible.
Margaret Mead (1901–78) US anthropologist.
Quote Magazine, 15 May 1958

6 With first-rate sherry flowing into second-rate whores,
And third-rate conversation without one single pause:
Just like a couple
Between the wars.
William Plomer (1903–73) South African poet and novelist.
Father and Son: 1939

7 It isn't evil that is ruining the earth, but mediocrity. The crime is not that Nero played while Rome burned, but that he played badly.
Ned Rorem (1923–) US composer and writer.
The Final Diary

8 Much of a muchness.
John Vanbrugh (1664–1726) English architect and dramatist.
The Provok'd Husband, I:1

MELANCHOLY

See also despair, sorrow

1 Nothing's so dainty sweet as lovely melancholy.
Francis Beaumont (1584–1616) English dramatist.
The Nice Valour, III:3

2 All my joys to this are folly,
Naught so sweet as Melancholy.
Robert Burton (1577–1640) English scholar and explorer.
Anatomy of Melancholy, Abstract

3 If there is a hell upon earth, it is to be found in a melancholy man's heart.
Robert Burton
Anatomy of Melancholy, Pt. I

4 Twentieth-Century Blues.
Noël Coward (1899–1973) British dramatist.
Title of song

5 I am aware of the damp souls of the housemaids
Sprouting despondently at area gates.
T. S. Eliot (1888–1965) US-born British poet and dramatist.
Morning at the Window

6 I am in that temper that if I were under water I would scarcely kick to come to the top.
John Keats (1795–1821) British poet.
Letter to Benjamin Bailey, 21 May 1818

7 My heart aches, and a drowsy numbness pains
My sense.
John Keats
Ode to a Nightingale

8 Ay, in the very temple of delight
Veil'd Melancholy has her sovran shrine.
Though seen of none save him whose strenuous tongue
Can burst Joy's grape against his palate fine.
John Keats
Ode on Melancholy

9 Where glowing embers through the room
Teach light to counterfeit a gloom,
Far from all resort of mirth,
Save the cricket on the hearth.
John Milton (1608–74) English poet.
Il Penseroso

10 Wrapt in a pleasing fit of melancholy.
John Milton
Comus

11 I was told I am a true cosmopolitan. I am
unhappy everywhere.
Stephen Vizinczey (1933–) Hungarian-born British
writer.
The Guardian, 7 Mar 1968

MEMORIALS

See also epitaphs, memory, obituaries, reputation

1 When I am dead, and laid in grave,
And all my bones are rotten,
By this may I remembered be
When I should be forgotten.
Anonymous
On a girl's sampler, 1736

2 All your better deeds
Shall be in water writ, but this in marble.
Francis Beaumont (1584–1616) English dramatist.
The Nice Valour, V:3

3 They shall grow not old, as we that are left
grow old:
Age shall not weary them, nor the years
condemn.
At the going down of the sun and in the
morning
We will remember them.
Laurence Binyon (1869–1943) British poet.
Poems For the Fallen

4 John Brown's body lies a-mouldering in the
grave,
His soul is marching on!
Charles Sprague Hall (19th century) US songwriter.
The song commemorates the American hero who died in the
cause of abolishing slavery
John Brown's Body

5 I have executed a memorial longer lasting
than bronze.
Horace (Quintus Horatius Flaccus; 65–8 BC) Roman poet.
Odes, III

6 In a larger sense we cannot dedicate, we
cannot consecrate, we cannot hallow this
ground. The brave men, living and dead, who
struggled here, have consecrated it far above
our power to add or detract. The world will
little note, nor long remember, what we say
here, but it can never forget what they did
here. It is for us, the living, rather to be
dedicated here to the unfinished work which
they who fought here have thus far so nobly
advanced. It is rather for us to be here
dedicated to the great task remaining before
us . . . that we here highly resolve that the
dead shall not have died in vain, that this
nation, under God, shall have a new birth of
freedom; and that government of the people,
by the people, and for the people, shall not
perish from the earth.
Abraham Lincoln (1809–65) US statesman.
Report of Lincoln's address at the dedication (19 Nov 1863) of
the national cemetery on the site of the Battle of Gettysburg

7 The monument sticks like a fishbone

in the city's throat.
Robert Lowell (1917–77) US poet.
For the Union Dead

8 In Flanders fields the poppies blow
Between the crosses, row on row,
That mark our place.
John McCrae (1872–1918) Canadian poet and doctor.
In Flanders Fields, 'Ypres Salient', 3 May 1915

9 I was told that the Chinese said they would
bury me by the Western Lake and build a
shrine to my memory. I have some slight
regret that this did not happen, as I might
have become a god, which would have been
very *chic* for an atheist.
Bertrand Russell (1872–1970) British philosopher.
The Autobiography of Bertrand Russell, Vol. II, Ch. 3

10 Men's evil manners live in brass: their
virtues
We write in water.
William Shakespeare (1564–1616) English dramatist.
Henry VIII, IV:2

11 I met a traveller from an antique land
Who said: Two vast and trunkless legs of
stone
Stand in the desert.
Percy Bysshe Shelley (1792–1822) British poet.
Referring to the legs of a broken statue of the Pharaoh Rame-
ses II (1301–1234 BC; Greek name, Ozymandias)
Ozymandias

12 Move Queen Anne? Most certainly not! Why
it might some day be suggested that *my*
statue should be moved, which I should much
dislike.
Victoria (1819–1901) Queen of the United Kingdom.
Said at the time of her Diamond Jubilee (1897), when it was
suggested that the statue of Queen Anne should be moved
from outside St. Paul's
Men, Women and Things (Duke of Portland), Ch. 5

MEMORY

See also memorials, nostalgia, past

1 Memories are hunting horns whose sound
dies on the wind.
Guillaume Apollinaire (Wilhelm de Kostrowitzky; 1880–
1918) Italian-born French poet.
Cors de Chasse

2 I have more memories than if I were a
thousand years old.
Charles Baudelaire (1821–67) French poet.
Spleen

3 Time whereof the memory of man runneth
not to the contrary.
William Blackstone (1723–80) British jurist.
Commentaries on the Laws of England, Bk. I, Ch. 18

4 Am in Birmingham. Where ought I to be?
G. K. Chesterton (1874–1936) British writer.
Telegram to his wife during a lecture tour
Portrait of Barrie (C. Asquith)

5 When I meet a man whose name I can't

remember, I give myself two minutes; then, if it is a hopeless case, I always say, And how is the old complaint?
Benjamin Disraeli (1804–81) British statesman.
Attrib.

6 I have forgot much, Cynara! gone with the wind,
Flung roses, roses riotously with the throng.
Ernest Dowson (1867–1900) British lyric poet.
Non Sum Qualis Eram Bonae Sub Regno Cynarae

7 Oh! don't you remember sweet Alice, Ben Bolt,
Sweet Alice, whose hair was so brown,
Who wept with delight when you gave her a smile,
And trembled with fear at your frown?
Thomas Dunn English (1819–1902) US lawyer and writer.
Ben Bolt

8 To endeavour to forget anyone is a certain way of thinking of nothing else.
Jean de La Bruyère (1645–96) French satirist.
Les Caractères

9 I never forget a face, but I'll make an exception in your case.
Groucho Marx (Julius Marx; 1895–1977) US comedian.
The Guardian, 18 June 1965

10 What a strange thing is memory, and hope; one looks backward, the other forward. The one is of today, the other is the Tomorrow. Memory is history recorded in our brain, memory is a painter, it paints pictures of the past and of the day.
Grandma Moses (Anna Mary Robertson Moses; 1860–1961) US primitive painter.
Grandma Moses, My Life's History (ed. Aotto Kallir), Ch. 1

11 The taste was that of the little crumb of madeleine which on Sunday mornings at Combray . . . , when I used to say good-day to her in her bedroom, my aunt Léonie used to give me, dipping it first in her own cup of real or of lime-flower tea.
Marcel Proust (1871–1922) French novelist.
A la recherche du temps perdu: Du côté de chez Swann

12 Thanks For the Memory.
Leo Robin (1899–1984) US songwriter.
Big Broadcast, song title

13 Remember me when I am gone away,
Gone far away into the silent land.
Christina Rossetti (1830–74) British poet.
Remember

14 Better by far you should forget and smile
Than that you should remember and be sad.
Christina Rossetti
Remember

15 To expect a man to retain everything that he has ever read is like expecting him to carry about in his body everything that he has ever eaten.
Arthur Schopenhauer (1788–1860) German philosopher.
Parerga and Paralipomena

16 Old men forget; yet all shall be forgot,
But he'll remember, with advantages,
What feats he did that day.
William Shakespeare (1564–1616) English dramatist.
Henry V, IV:3

17 Music, when soft voices die,
Rose leaves, when the rose is dead,
Are heaped for the beloved's bed;
And so thy thoughts, when thou art gone,
Love itself shall slumber on.
Percy Bysshe Shelley (1792–1822) British poet.
To –

18 As a perfume doth remain
In the folds where it hath lain,
So the thought of you, remaining
Deeply folded in my brain,
Will not leave me: all things leave me:
You remain.
Arthur Symons (1865–1945) British poet.
Memory

19 I suppose that the high-water mark of my youth in Columbus, Ohio, was the night the bed fell on my father.
James Thurber (1894–1961) US humorist.
My Life and Hard Times, Ch. 1

MEN

See also mankind, marriage, masculinity, sexes, women

1 One cannot be always laughing at a man without now and then stumbling on something witty.
Jane Austen (1775–1817) British novelist.
Pride and Prejudice, Ch. 40

2 A man's a man for a' that.
Robert Burns (1759–96) Scottish poet.
For a' that and a' that

3 It is men who face the biggest problems in the future, adjusting to their new and complicated role.
Anna Ford British newscaster.
Remark, Jan 1981

4 All men are rapists and that's all they are. They rape us with their eyes, their laws and their codes.
Marilyn French (1929–) US novelist.
The Women's Room

5 A man . . . is *so* in the way in the house!
Elizabeth Gaskell (1810–65) British novelist.
Cranford, Ch. 1

6 Probably the only place where a man can feel really secure is in a maximum security prison, except for the imminent threat of release.

Germaine Greer (1939–) Australian-born British writer and feminist.
The Female Eunuch

7 And let her learn through what kind of dust
He has earned his thirst and the right to quench it
And what sweat he has exchanged for his money
And the blood-weight of money. He'll humble her

Ted Hughes (1930–) British poet.
Selected Poems 1957–1981, 'Her Husband'

8 How beastly the bourgeois is
especially the male of the species.

D. H. Lawrence (1885–1930) British novelist.
How beastly the bourgeois is

9 One realizes with horror, that the race of men is almost extinct in Europe. Only Christ-like heroes and woman-worshipping Don Juans, and rabid equality-mongrels.

D. H. Lawrence
Sea and Sardinia, Ch. 3

10 Why can't a woman be more like a man?
Men are so honest, so thoroughly square;
Eternally noble, historically fair.

Alan Jay Lerner (1918–86) US songwriter.
My Fair Lady, II:4

11 He was formed for the ruin of our sex.

Tobias Smollett (1721–71) British novelist.
Roderick Random, Ch. 22

12 It is an ancient contention of my wife that I, in common with all other men, in any dispute between a female relative and a tradesman, side with the tradesman, partly from fear, partly from masculine clannishness, and most of all from a desire to stand well with the tradesman.

E. . Somerville (1858–1949) Irish writer.
Experiences of an Irish R.M., 'The Pug-nosed Fox'

13 Sometimes I think if there was a third sex men wouldn't get so much as a glance from me.

Amanda Vail (Warren Miller; 1921–66) US writer.
Love Me Little, Ch. 6

14 A man in the house is worth two in the street.

Mae West (1892–1980) US actress.
Belle of the Nineties, film 1934

MERCY

1 I seem forsaken and alone,
I hear the lion roar;
And every door is shut but one,
And that is Mercy's door.

William Cowper (1731–1800) British poet.
Olney Hymns, 33

2 The quality of mercy is not strain'd;
It droppeth as the gentle rain from heaven
Upon the place beneath. It is twice blest;
It blesseth him that gives and him that takes.

William Shakespeare (1564–1616) English dramatist.
The Merchant of Venice, IV:1

3 And her face so sweet and pleading, yet with sorrow pale and worn,
Touched his heart with sudden pity – lit his eye with misty light;
'Go, your lover lives!' said Cromwell; 'Curfew shall not ring tonight!'

Rose Hartwick Thorpe (1850–1939) US poet and novelist.
Curfew Shall Not Ring Tonight

MERIT

1 A good dog deserves a good bone.

Proverb

2 I don't deserve this, but I have arthritis, and I don't deserve that either.

Jack Benny (Benjamin Kubelsky; 1894–1974) US actor.
Said when accepting an award
Attrib.

3 But many that are first shall be last; and the last shall be first.

Bible: Matthew
19:30

4 GOLDSMITH: Here's such a stir about a fellow that has written one book, and I have written many.
JOHNSON: Ah, Doctor, there go two-and-forty sixpences you know to one guinea.

Samuel Johnson (1709–84) British lexicographer.
Referring to Beattie's *Essay on Truth*
Johnsonian Miscellanies (ed. G. B. Hill), Vol. I

5 I guess this is the week I earn my salary.

John Fitzgerald Kennedy (1917–63) US statesman.
Comment made during the Cuban missile crisis
Nobody Said It Better (M. Ringo)

6 Use every man after his desert, and who shall scape whipping?

William Shakespeare (1564–1616) English dramatist.
Hamlet, II:2

7 I wasn't lucky. I deserved it.

Margaret Thatcher (1925–) British politician and prime minister.
Said after receiving school prize, aged nine
Attrib.

8 The Rise of the Meritocracy.

Michael Young (1915–) British political writer.
Book title

MERRYMAKING

See also parties, pleasure

1 Come lasses and lads, get leave of your dads,
And away to the Maypole hie,

For every he has got him a she,
And the fiddler's standing by.
Anonymous
Come Lasses and Lads

2   There was a sound of revelry by night,
And Belgium's capital had gather'd then
Her Beauty and her Chivalry, and bright
The lamps shone o'er fair women and brave
men.
Lord Byron (1788–1824) British poet.
Childe Harold's Pilgrimage, III

3   Dost thou think, because thou art virtuous,
there shall be no more cakes and ale?
William Shakespeare (1564–1616) English dramatist.
Twelfth Night, II:3

4   We have heard the chimes at midnight.
William Shakespeare
Henry IV, Part Two, III:2

5   You must wake and call me early, call me
early, mother dear;
To-morrow 'ill be the happiest time of all the
glad New-year;
Of all the glad New-year, mother, the maddest
merriest day;
For I'm to be Queen o' the May, mother, I'm
to be Queen o' the May.
Alfred, Lord Tennyson (1809–92) British poet.
The May Queen

6   I love such mirth as does not make friends
ashamed to look upon one another next
morning.
Izaak Walton (1593–1683) English writer.
The Compleat Angler, Ch. 5

METAPHYSICS

See also philosophy

1   A blind man in a dark room – looking for a
black hat – which isn't there.
Lord Bowen (1835–94) British judge.
Characterization of a metaphysician
Attrib.

2   Metaphysics is the finding of bad reasons for
what we believe upon instinct; but to find
these reasons is no less an instinct.
F. H. Bradley (1846–1924) British philosopher.
Appearance and Reality, Preface

3   We used to think that if we knew one, we
knew two, because one and one are two. We
are finding that we must learn a great deal
more about 'and'.
Arthur Eddington (1882–1944) British astronomer.
The Harvest of a Quiet Eye (A. L. Mackay)

4   In other words, apart from the known and
the unknown, what else is there?
Harold Pinter (1930–) British dramatist.
The Homecoming, II

5   Whither is fled the visionary gleam?
Where is it now, the glory and the dream?

Our birth is but a sleep and a forgetting:
The Soul that rises with us, our life's Star,
Hath had elsewhere its setting,
And cometh from afar;
Not in entire forgetfulness,
And not in utter nakedness,
But trailing clouds of glory do we come
From God, who is our home:
Heaven lies about us in our infancy!
Shades of the prison-house begin to close
Upon the growing boy.
William Wordsworth (1770–1850) British poet.
Ode. Intimations of Immortality, IV

6   Hence in a season of calm weather
Though inland far we be,
Our souls have sight of that immortal sea
Which brought us hither . . .
William Wordsworth
Ode. Intimations of Immortality, IX

MILTON

1   Malt does more than Milton can,
To justify God's way to man.
A. E. Housman (1859–1936) British scholar and poet.
A Shropshire Lad

2   Milton, Madam, was a genius that could cut a
Colossus from a rock; but could not carve
heads upon cherry-stones.
Samuel Johnson (1709–84) British lexicographer.
Life of Johnson (James Boswell)

3   Milton's Devil as a moral being is far superior
to his God. . . . Milton has so far violated the
popular creed (if this shall be judged a
violation), as to have alleged no superiority of
moral virtue to his God over his Devil. And
this bold neglect of direct moral purpose is
the most decisive proof of Milton's genius.
Percy Bysshe Shelley (1792–1822) British poet.
Defence of Poetry

4   That mighty orb of song, The divine Milton.
William Wordsworth (1770–1850) British poet.
The Excursion

MIND

See also intellect, intelligence, thinking

1   *Brain,* n. An apparatus with which we think
that we think.
Ambrose Bierce (1842–?1914) US writer and journalist.
The Devil's Dictionary

2   We know the human brain is a device to
keep the ears from grating on one another.
Peter De Vries (1910–) US novelist.
Comfort me with Apples, Ch. 1

3   The pendulum of the mind oscillates between
sense and nonsense, not between right and
wrong.
Carl Gustav Jung (1875–1961) Swiss psychoanalyst.
Memories, Dreams, Reflections, Ch. 5

4 A mind not to be changed by place or time.
The mind is its own place, and in itself
Can make a Heaven of Hell, a Hell of Heaven.
John Milton (1608–74) English poet.
Paradise Lost, Bk. I

5 That's the classical mind at work, runs fine
inside but looks dingy on the surface.
Robert T. Pirsig (1928–) US writer.
Zen and the Art of Motorcycle Maintenance, Pt. III, Ch. 25

6 The dogma of the Ghost in the Machine.
Gilbert Ryle (1900–76) British philosopher.
The Concept of Mind, Ch. 1

7 If it is for mind that we are seaching the
brain, then we are supposing the brain to be
much more than a telephone-exchange. We
are supposing it a telephone-exchange along
with the subscribers as well.
Charles Scott Sherrington (1857–1952) British physiologist.
Man on his Nature

8 When people will not weed their own minds,
they are apt to be overrun with nettles.
Horace Walpole (1717–97) British writer.
Letter to Lady Ailesbury, 10 July 1779

9 The mind can also be an erogenous zone.
Raquel Welch (Raquel Tejada; 1940–) US film star.
Colombo's Hollywood (J. R. Colombo)

10 Strongest minds
Are often those of whom the noisy world
Hears least.
William Wordsworth (1770–1850) British poet.
The Excursion

MINORITY

See also majority

1 What's a cult? It just means not enough
people to make a minority.
Robert Altman (1922–) US film director.
The Observer, 1981

2 The majority has the might – more's the pity
– but it hasn't right . . . The minority is
always right.
Henrik Ibsen (1828–1906) Norwegian dramatist.
An Enemy of the People, IV

3 Minorities . . . are almost always in the right.
Sydney Smith (1771–1845) British clergyman and essayist.
The Smith of Smiths (H. Pearson), Ch. 9

MISANTHROPY

See also mankind

1 What though the spicy breezes
Blow soft o'er Ceylon's isle;
Though every prospect pleases,

And only man is vile . . .
Reginald Heber (1783–1826) British bishop and hymn writer.
From Greenland's Icy Mountains

2 I've always been interested in people, but
I've never liked them.
W. Somerset Maugham (1874–1965) British novelist.
The Observer, 'Sayings of the Week', 28 Aug 1949

3 I love mankind – it's people I can't stand.
Charles M. Schultz (1922–) US cartoonist.
Go Fly a Kite, Charlie Brown

4 Other people are quite dreadful. The only
possible society is oneself.
Oscar Wilde (1854–1900) Irish-born British dramatist.
An Ideal Husband, III

MISFORTUNE

See also accidents, curses, sorrow, suffering

1 It is easy to bear the misfortunes of others.
Proverb

2 It never rains but it pours.
Proverb

3 Prosperity doth best discover vice; but
adversity doth best discover virtue.
Francis Bacon (1561–1626) English philosopher.
Essays, 'Of Adversity'

4 Calamities are of two kinds. Misfortune to
ourselves and good fortune to others.
Ambrose Bierce (1842–?1914) US writer and journalist.
The Devil's Dictionary

5 There remaineth a rest for the people of
God:
And I have had troubles enough, for one.
Robert Browning (1812–89) British poet.
Old Pictures in Florence, XVII

6 Tragedie is to seyn a certeyn storie,
As olde bokes maken us memorie,
Of him that stood in greet prosperitee
And is y-fallen out of heigh degree
Into miserie, and endeth wrecchedly.
Geoffrey Chaucer (c. 1342–1400) English poet.
The Canterbury Tales, 'The Monk's Prologue'

7 For of fortunes sharp adversitee
The worst kinde of infortune is this,
A man to have ben in prosperitee,
And it remembren, what is passed is.
Geoffrey Chaucer
Troilus and Criseyde, 3

8 A chapter of accidents.
Earl of Chesterfield (1694–1773) English statesman.
Letter to his son, 16 Feb 1753

9 'I am a lone lorn creetur,' were Mrs
Gummidge's words . . . 'and everythink goes
contrairy with me.'
Charles Dickens (1812–70) British novelist.
David Copperfield, Ch. 3

10 Life is mostly froth and bubble;
Two things stand like stone,
Kindness in another's trouble,
Courage in your own.
Adam Lindsay Gordon (1833–70) Australian poet.
Ye Wearie Wayfarer, Fytte 8

11 Depend upon it that if a man talks of his misfortunes ·there is something in them that is not disagreeable to him; for where there is nothing but pure misery there never is any recourse to the mention of it.
Samuel Johnson (1709–84) British lexicographer.
Life of Johnson (J. Boswell), Vol. IV

12 There exist some evils so terrible and some misfortunes so horrible that we dare not think of them, whilst their very aspect makes us shudder; but if they happen to fall on us, we find ourselves stronger than we imagined, we grapple with our ill luck, and behave better than we expected we should.
Jean de La Bruyère (1645–96) French satirist.
Les Caractères

13 I never knew any man in my life who could not bear another's misfortunes perfectly like a Christian.
Alexander Pope (1688–1744) British poet.
Thoughts on Various Subjects

14 We are all strong enough to bear the misfortunes of others.
Duc de la Rochefoucauld (1613–80) French writer.
Maximes, 19

15 In the misfortune of our best friends, we always find something which is not displeasing to us.
Duc de la Rochefoucauld
Maximes, 99

16 Misery acquaints a man with strange bedfellows.
William Shakespeare (1564–1616) English dramatist.
The Tempest, II:2

17 When sorrows come, they come not single spies,
But in battalions!
William Shakespeare
Hamlet, IV:5

18 This is the excellent foppery of the world, that, when we are sick in fortune, often the surfeits of our own behaviour, we make guilty of our disasters the sun, the moon, and stars.
William Shakespeare
King Lear, I:2

MISOGYNY

See also women

1 I'd be equally as willing
For a dentist to be drilling
Than to ever let a woman in my life.
Alan Jay Lerner (1918–86) US songwriter.
My Fair Lady, I:2

2 How can I possibly dislike a sex to which Your Majesty belongs?
Cecil Rhodes (1853–1902) South African statesman.
Replying to Queen Victoria's suggestion that he disliked women
Rhodes (Lockhart)

3 Would you have me speak after my custom, as being a professed tyrant to their sex?
William Shakespeare (1564–1616) English dramatist.
Much Ado About Nothing, I:1

MISQUOTATIONS

1 Misquotations are the only quotations that are never misquoted.
Hesketh Pearson (1887–1964) British biographer.
Common Misquotations

2 A widely-read man never quotes accurately ... Misquotation is the pride and privilege of the learned.
Hesketh Pearson
Common Misquotations

Some examples

3 Had I been present at the Creation, I would have given some useful hints for the better ordering of the universe.
Alfonso the Wise (c. 1221–84) King of Castile and Léon.
Referring to the complicated Ptolemaic model of the universe. Often quoted as, 'Had I been consulted I would have recommended something simpler'
Attrib.

4 We have ways of making men talk.
Anonymous
Film catchphrase, often repeated as 'We have ways of making you talk'
Lives of a Bengal Lancer

5 That's one small step for man, one giant leap for mankind.
Neil Armstrong (1930–) US astronaut.
Said on stepping onto the moon. Often quoted as, 'small step for a man . . . ' (which is probably what he intended)
Remark, 21 July 1969

6 I have seldom spoken with greater regret, for my lips are not yet unsealed. Were these troubles over I would make a case, and I guarantee that not a man would go into the Lobby against us.
Stanley Baldwin (1867–1947) British statesman.
Referring to the Abyssinian crisis; usually misquoted as 'My lips are sealed'
Speech, House of Commons, 10 Dec 1935

7 And behold joy and gladness, slaying oxen, and killing sheep, eating flesh, and drinking wine: let us eat and drink; for tomorrow we shall die.
Bible: Isaiah 22:13
A similar sentiment is expressed in Corinthians 15:32–33. Often misquoted as 'let us eat, drink, and be merry'

8 So when they continued asking him, he lifted up himself, and said unto them, He that is without sin among you, let him first cast a stone at her.
Bible: John 8:7
Often misquoted as 'cast the first stone'

9 Then said Jesus unto him, Put up again thy sword into his place: for all they that take the sword shall perish with the sword.
Bible: Matthew 26:52
Often misquoted as 'They that live by the sword shall die by the sword'

10 Pride goeth before destruction, and an haughty spirit before a fall.
Bible: Proverbs 16:18
Often misquoted as 'Pride goeth before a fall'

11 Play it, Sam. Play 'As Time Goes By.'
Humphrey Bogart (1899–1957) US film star.
Often misquoted as 'Play it again, Sam'
Casablanca

12 You dirty double-crossing rat!
James Cagney (1899–1986) US actor.
Usually misquoted by impressionists as 'You dirty rat'
Blonde Crazy

13 I have nothing to offer but blood, toil, tears and sweat.
Winston Churchill (1874–1965) British statesman.
On becoming prime minister. Often misquoted as 'blood, sweat and tears'
Speech, House of Commons, 13 May 1940

14 War is the continuation of politics by other means.
Karl von Clausewitz (1780–1831) Prussian general.
The usual misquotation of 'War is nothing but a continuation of politics with the admixture of other means'
Vom Kriege

15 'Excellent!' I cried. 'Elementary,' said he.
Arthur Conan Doyle (1856–1930) British writer.
Watson talking to Sherlock Holmes; Holmes's reply is often misquoted as 'Elementary my dear Watson'
The Crooked Man

16 I got there fustest with the mostest.
Nathan Bedford Forrest (1821–77) Confederate general.
Popular misquotation of his explanation of his success in capturing Murfreesboro; his actual words were, 'I just took the short cut and got there first with the most men'
A Civil War Treasury (B. Botkin)

17 I never said, 'I want to be alone.' I only said, 'I want to be *left* alone.' There is all the difference.
Greta Garbo (1905–90) Swedish-born US film star.
Garbo (John Bainbridge)

18 Take your hare when it is cased . . .
Hannah Glasse (18th century) English writer.
Often misquoted as, 'First catch your hare' and wrongly attributed to Mrs Beaton
The Art of Cookery Made Plain and Easy, Ch. 1

19 Once I built a rail-road,

Now it's done.
Brother, can you spare a dime?
E. Y. Harburg (1898–1981) US lyricist.
Often quoted as 'Buddy can you spare a dime'
New Americana, 'Brother Can You Spare a Dime'.

20 I am happy now that Charles calls on my bedchamber less frequently than of old. As it is, I now endure but two calls a week and when I hear his steps outside my door I lie down on my bed, close my eyes, open my legs and think of England.
Lady Alice Hillingdon (1857–1940) Wife of 2nd Baron Hillingdon.
Often mistakenly attributed to Queen Victoria
Journal (1912)

21 Jerry Ford is so dumb that he can't fart and chew gum at the same time.
Lyndon B. Johnson (1908–73) US statesman.
Sometimes quoted as '. . . can't walk and chew gum'
A Ford, Not a Lincoln (R. Reeves), Ch. 1

22 Alas, poor Yorick! I knew him, Horatio: a fellow of infinite jest, of most excellent fancy.
William Shakespeare (1564–1616) English dramatist.
Often misquoted as 'I knew him well'
Hamlet, V:1

23 I always did like a man in uniform. And that one fits you grand. Why don't you come up sometime and see me?
Mae West (1892–1980) US actress.
Often misquoted as 'Come up and see me some time'
She Done Him Wrong, film 1933

MISTAKES

See also imperfection

1 Two wrongs do not make a right.
Proverb

2 It is worse than immoral, it's a mistake.
Dean Acheson (1893–1971) US lawyer and statesman.
Describing the Vietnam war. See also BOULAY DE LA MEURTHE.
Quoted by Alistair Cooke in his radio programme Letter from America

3 The weak have one weapon: the errors of those who think they are strong.
Georges Bidault (1899–1983) French statesman.
The Observer, 1962

4 It is worse than a crime, it is a blunder.
Antoine Boulay de la Meurthe (1761–1840) French politician.
See also ACHESON. Referring to the summary execution of the Duc d'Enghien by Napoleon, 1804
Attrib.

5 I guess that'll hold the little bastards.
Don Carney (1897–1954) US broadcaster.
Carney was ending a children's radio show and thought that he was off the air
Attrib.

6 I beseech you, in the bowels of Christ, think it possible you may be mistaken.
Oliver Cromwell (1599–1658) English soldier and statesman.
Letter to the General Assembly of the Church of Scotland, 3 Aug 1650

7 Better send them a Papal Bull.
Lord Curzon (1859–1925) British politician.
Written in the margin of a Foreign Office document. The phrase 'the monks of Mount Athos were violating their vows' had been misprinted as '. . . violating their cows'
Life of Lord Curzon (Ronaldshay), Vol. III, Ch. 15

8 Yes, once – many, many years ago. I thought I had made a wrong decision. Of course, it turned out that I had been right all along. But I was wrong to have *thought* that I was wrong.
John Foster Dulles (1888–1959) US politician.
On being asked whether he had ever been wrong
Facing the Music (H. Temianka)

9 Pardon me, madam, but *I* am my brother.
Karl Gustav Jacob Jacobi (1804–51) German mathematician.
On being mistaken by a lady for his brother
Men of Mathematics (M. H. Jacobi)

10 Erratum. In my article on the Price of Milk, 'Horses' should have read 'Cows' throughout.
J. B. Morton (1893–1979) British journalist.
The Best of Beachcomber

11 The man who makes no mistakes does not usually make anything.
Edward John Phelps (1822–1900) US lawyer and diplomat.
Speech, Mansion House, London, 24 Jan 1899

12 A man should never be ashamed to own he has been in the wrong, which is but saying, in other words, that he is wiser to-day than he was yesterday.
Alexander Pope (1688–1744) British poet.
Thoughts on Various Subjects

13 To err is human, to forgive, divine.
Alexander Pope
An Essay on Criticism

14 The follies which a man regrets the most in his life, are those which he didn't commit when he had the opportunity.
Helen Rowland (1876–1950) US writer.
Guide To Men

15 What time is the next swan?
Leo Slezak (1873–1946) Czechoslovakian-born tenor.
When the mechanical swan left the stage without him during a performance of Lohengrin
What Time Is the Next Swan? (Walter Slezak)

16 We often discover what *will* do, by finding out what will not do; and probably he who never made a mistake never made a discovery.
Samuel Smiles (1812–1904) British writer.
Self-Help, Ch. 11

17 Human blunders usually do more to shape history than human wickedness.
A. J. P. Taylor (1906–) British historian.
The Origins of the Second World War, Ch. 10

18 Well, if I called the wrong number, why did you answer the phone?
James Thurber (1894–1961) US humorist.
Cartoon caption

19 If we had more time for discussion we should probably have made a great many more mistakes.
Leon Trotsky (Lev Davidovich Bronstein; 1879–1940) Russian revolutionary.
My Life

20 The physician can bury his mistakes, but the architect can only advise his client to plant vines.
Frank Lloyd Wright (1869–1959) US architect.
New York Times Magazine, 4 Oct 1953

MISTRUST

See also suspicion, trust

1 After shaking hands with a Greek, count your fingers.
Proverb

2 While I see many hoof-marks going in, I see none coming out.
Aesop (6th century BC) Reputed Greek writer of fables.
Fables, 'The Lion, the Fox, and the Beasts'

3 The lion and the calf shall lie down together but the calf won't get much sleep.
Woody Allen (Allen Stewart Konigsberg; 1935–) US film actor.
Without Feathers, 'The Scrolls'

4 The louder he talked of his honour, the faster we counted our spoons.
Ralph Waldo Emerson (1803–82) US poet and essayist.
Conduct of Life, 'Worship'

5 Let me remind you what the wary fox said once upon a time to the sick lion: 'Because those footprints scare me, all directed your way, none coming back.'
Horace (Quintus Horatius Flaccus; 65–8 BC) Roman poet.
Epistles, I

6 But if he does really think that there is no distinction between virtue and vice, why, Sir, when he leaves our houses let us count our spoons.
Samuel Johnson (1709–84) British lexicographer.
Life of Johnson (J. Boswell), Vol. I

7 *Quis custodiet ipsos custodes?*
Who is to guard the guards themselves?
Juvenal (Decimus Junius Juvenalis; 60–130 AD) Roman satirist.
Satires, VI

8 Ye diners-out from whom we guard our spoons.

Lord Macaulay (1800–59) British historian.
Letter to Hannah Macaulay, 29 June 1831

9 Let me have men about me that are fat;
Sleek-headed men, and such as sleep o' nights.
Yon Cassius has a lean and hungry look;
He thinks too much. Such men are dangerous.

William Shakespeare (1564–1616) English dramatist.
Julius Caesar, I:2

10 An ally has to be watched just like an enemy.

Leon Trotsky (Lev Davidovich Bronstein; 1879–1940) Russian revolutionary.
Expansion and Coexistence (A. Ulam)

11 *Equo ne credite, Teucri.*
Quidquid id est timeo Danaos et dona ferentis.
Do not trust the horse, Trojans. Whatever it is, I fear the Greeks even when they bring gifts.

Virgil (Publius Vergilius Maro; 70–19 BC) Roman poet.
Aeneid, Bk. II

MIXED METAPHORS

See also Goldwynisms

1 If you open that Pandora's Box you never know what Trojan 'orses will jump out.

Ernest Bevin (1881–1951) British trade-union leader and politician.
Referring to the Council of Europe
Ernest Bevin and the Foreign Office (Sir Roderick Barclay)

2 Every director bites the hand that lays the golden egg.

Samuel Goldwyn (Samuel Goldfish; 1882–1974) Polish-born US film producer.
Attrib.

3 You ought to take the bull between the teeth.

Samuel Goldwyn
Attrib.

4 Mr Speaker, I smell a rat; I see him forming in the air and darkening the sky; but I'll nip him in the bud.

Boyle Roche (1743–1807) British politician.
Attrib.

MODERATION

See also excess

1 Moderation in all things.

Proverb

2 You can have too much of a good thing.

Proverb

3 By God, Mr Chairman, at this moment I stand astonished at my own moderation!

Clive of India (1725–74) British soldier and governor of Bengal.
Reply during Parliamentary Inquiry, 1773

4 Not too much zeal.

Talleyrand (Charles Maurice de Talleyrand-Périgord; 1754–1838) French politician.
Attrib.

5 Moderation is a fatal thing, Lady Hunstanton. Nothing succeeds like excess.

Oscar Wilde (1854–1900) Irish-born British dramatist.
A Woman of No Importance, III

MODESTY

1 Nurse, take away the candle and spare my blushes.

Henry James (1843–1916) US novelist.
On being informed, whilst confined to his bed, that he had been awarded the Order of Merit
The American Treasury (C. Fadiman)

2 It was involuntary. They sank my boat.

John Fitzgerald Kennedy (1917–63) US statesman.
Responding to praise of his courage whilst serving in the US navy against the Japanese in World War II
Nobody Said It Better (M. Ringo)

3 In some remote regions of Islam it is said, a woman caught unveiled by a stranger will raise her skirt to cover her face.

Raymond Mortimer (1895–1980) British literary critic and writer.
Colette

4 If you want people to think well of you, do not speak well of yourself.

Blaise Pascal (1623–62) French philosopher and mathematician.
Pensées, I

5 Be modest! It is the kind of pride least likely to offend.

Jules Renard (1894–1910) French writer.
Journal

6 . . . the nuns who never take a bath without wearing a bathrobe all the time. When asked why, since no man can see them, they reply 'Oh, but you forget the good God.'

Bertrand Russell (1872–1970) British philosopher.
The Basic Writings, Pt. II, Ch. 7

7 I have often wished I had time to cultivate modesty . . . But I am too busy thinking about myself.

Edith Sitwell (1887–1964) British poet and writer.
The Observer, 'Sayings of the Week', 30 Apr 1950

MONARCHY

See also royalty

1 The best reason why Monarchy is a strong government is that it is an intelligible government. The mass of mankind understand it, and they hardly anywhere in the world understand any other.

Walter Bagehot (1826–77) British economist and journalist.
The English Constitution, 'The Monarchy'

2 The Sovereign has, under a constitutional

monarchy such as ours, three rights – the right to be consulted, the right to encourage, the right to warn.
Walter Bagehot
The English Constitution, 'The Monarchy'

3 God grant him peace and happiness but never understanding of what he has lost.
Stanley Baldwin (1867–1947) British statesman.
Referring to Edward VIII's abdication

4 That the king can do no wrong, is a necessary and fundamental principle of the English constitution.
William Blackstone (1723–80) British jurist.
Commentaries on the Laws of England, Bk. III, Ch. 17

5 The king never dies.
William Blackstone
Commentaries on the Laws of England, Bk. I, Ch. 7

6 I would rather hew wood than be a king under the conditions of the King of England.
Charles X (1757–1836) King of France.
Encyclopaedia Britannica

7 There is no middle course between the throne and the scaffold.
Charles X
Said to Talleyrand, who is said to have replied 'You are forgetting the postchaise'
Attrib.

8 Magna Charta is such a fellow, that he will have no sovereign.
Edward Coke (1552–1634) English lawyer and politician.
Speaking on the Lords Amendment to the Petition of Right, 17 May 1628
Hist. Coll. (Rushworth), I

9 The influence of the Crown has increased, is increasing, and ought to be diminished.
John Dunning (1731–83) British lawyer and politician.
Motion passed by the House of Commons, 1780

10 There will soon be only five kings left – the Kings of England, Diamonds, Hearts, Spades and Clubs.
Farouk I (1920–65) The last king of Egypt.
Remark made to Lord Boyd-Orr

11 Kings govern by means of popular assemblies only when they cannot do without them.
Charles James Fox (1749–1806) British Whig politician.
Attrib.

12 I will govern according to the common weal, but not according to the common will.
James I (1566–1625) King of England.
History of the English People (J. R. Green)

13 A constitutional king must learn to stoop.
Leopold II (1835–1909) King of the Belgians.
Instructing Prince Albert, the heir apparent, to pick up some papers that had fallen onto the floor
The Mistress (Betty Kelen)

14 *L'État c'est moi.*
I am the State.
Louis XIV (1638–1715) French king.
Attrib.

15 There is something behind the throne greater than the King himself.
William Pitt the Elder (1708–78) British statesman.
Speech, House of Lords, 2 Mar 1770

16 The right divine of kings to govern wrong.
Alexander Pope (1688–1744) British poet.
The Dunciad, IV

17 A king is a thing men have made for their own sakes, for quietness' sake. Just as if in a family one man is appointed to buy the meat.
John Selden (1584–1654) English historian.
Table Talk

18 Every subject's duty is the King's; but every subject's soul is his own.
William Shakespeare (1564–1616) English dramatist.
Henry V, IV:1

19 There's such divinity doth hedge a king
That treason can but peep to what it would.
William Shakespeare
Hamlet, IV:5

20 Not all the water in the rough rude sea
Can wash the balm from an anointed king;
The breath of worldly men cannot depose
The deputy elected by the Lord.
William Shakespeare
Richard II, III:2

21 Uneasy lies the head that wears a crown.
William Shakespeare
Henry IV, Part Two, III:1

22 The king reigns, and the people govern themselves.
Louis Adolphe Thiers (1797–1877) French statesman and historian.
In an unsigned article attributed to Thiers
Le National, 20 Jan 1830

23 As guardian of His Majesty's conscience.
Lord Thurlow (1731–1806) British lawyer.
Speech, House of Lords, 1779

24 The monarchy is a labour-intensive industry.
Harold Wilson (1916–) British politician and prime minister.
The Observer, 13 Feb 1977

25 The king reigns, but does not govern.
Jan Zamoyski (1541–1605) Grand chancellor of Poland.
Speech, Polish Parliament, 1605

MONEY

See also bribery, economics, extravagance, greed, materialism, thrift, wealth

1 Easy come, easy go.
Proverb

2 Out of debt, out of danger.
Proverb

3 Take care of the pence, and the pounds will take care of themselves.
Proverb

4 I can't afford to waste my time making money.
Jean Louis Rodolphe Agassiz (1807–73) Swiss naturalist.
When asked to give a lecture for a fee
Attrib.

5 It does seem to be true that the more you get the more you spend. It is rather like being on a golden treadmill.
Charles Allsop (1940–) Commodities broker.
Remark, Dec 1988

6 Business, you know, may bring money, but friendship hardly ever does.
Jane Austen (1775–1817) British novelist.
Emma, Ch. 34

7 Money is like muck, not good except it be spread.
Francis Bacon (1561–1626) English philosopher.
See also MURCHISON
Essays, 'Of Seditions and Troubles'

8 Money, it turned out, was exactly like sex, you thought of nothing else if you didn't have it and thought of other things if you did.
James Baldwin (1924–87) US writer.
Nobody Knows My Name

9 I'm tired of Love: I'm still more tired of Rhyme.
But Money gives me pleasure all the Time.
Hilaire Belloc (1870–1953) French-born British poet.
Fatigue

10 A feast is made for laughter, and wine maketh merry: but money answereth all things.
Bible: Ecclesiastes
10:19

11 For the love of money is the root of all evil: which while some coveted after, they have erred from the faith, and pierced themselves through with many sorrows.
Bible: I Timothy
6:10

12 If it's a good script, I'll do it. And if it's a bad script, and they pay me enough, I'll do it.
George Burns (1896–) US comedian.
Remark, Nov 1988

13 Straighteners, managers and cashiers of the Musical Banks.
Samuel Butler (1835–1902) British writer.
Erewhon, Ch. 9

14 It has been said that the love of money is the root of all evil. The want of money is so quite as truly.
Samuel Butler
Erewhon, Ch. 20

15 What makes all doctrines plain and clear? About two hundred pounds a year.
Samuel Butler
Hudibras, Pt. III

16 It is a kind of spiritual snobbery that makes people think that they can be happy without money.
Albert Camus (1913–60) French existentialist writer.
Notebooks, 1935–1942

17 Where large sums of money are concerned, it is advisable to trust nobody.
Agatha Christie (1891–1976) British detective-story writer.
Endless Night, Bk. II, Ch. 15

18 How pleasant it is to have money.
Arthur Hugh Clough (1819–61) British poet.
Dipsychus, Bk. I

19 But then one is always excited by descriptions of money changing hands. It's much more fundamental than sex.
Nigel Dennis (1912–) British writer.
Cards of Identity

20 Buy an annuity cheap, and make your life interesting to yourself and everybody else that watches the speculation.
Charles Dickens (1812–70) British novelist.
Martin Chuzzlewit, Ch. 18

21 Ah, take the Cash in hand and waive the Rest;
Oh, the brave Music of a *distant* Drum!
Edward Fitzgerald (1809–83) British poet.
The Rubáiyát of Omar Khayyám (1st edn.), XII

22 It is only the poor who pay cash, and that not from virtue, but because they are refused credit.
Anatole France (Jacques Anatole François Thibault; 1844–1924) French writer.
A Cynic's Breviary (J. R. Solly)

23 Money differs from an automobile, a mistress or cancer in being equally important to those who have it and those who do not.
John Kenneth Galbraith (1908–) US economist.
Attrib.

24 If possible honestly, if not, somehow, make money.
Horace (Quintus Horatius Flaccus; 65–8 BC) Roman poet.
Epistles, I

25 We all know how the size of sums of money appears to vary in a remarkable way according as they are being paid in or paid out.
Julian Huxley (1887–1975) British biologist.
Essays of a Biologist, 5

26 Money is like manure. If you spread it around it does a lot of good. But if you pile it up in one place it stinks like hell.
Clint Murchison Jnr (1895–1969) US industrialist.
Following BACON
Time Magazine, 16 June 1961

27 There are few ways in which a man can be

more innocently employed than in getting money.

Samuel Johnson (1709–84) British lexicographer.
Life of Johnson (J. Boswell), Vol. II

28 You don't seem to realize that a poor person who is unhappy is in a better position than a rich person who is unhappy. Because the poor person has hope. He thinks money would help.

Jean Kerr (1923–) US dramatist.
Poor Richard

29 Clearly money has something to do with life
– In fact, they've a lot in common, if you enquire:
You can't put off being young until you retire.

Philip Larkin (1922–85) British poet.
Money

30 For I don't care too much for money,
For money can't buy me love.

John Lennon (1940–80) British rock musician.
Can't Buy Me Love (with Paul McCartney)

31 The working classes are never embarrassed by money – only the absence of it.

Ken Livingstone (1945–) British Labour politician.
Speech, Sept 1987

32 What's a thousand dollars? Mere chicken feed. A poultry matter.

Groucho Marx (Julius Marx; 1895–1977) US comedian.
The Cocoanuts

33 Do they allow tipping on the boat?
– Yes, sir.
Have you got two fives?
– Oh, yes, sir.
Then you won't need the ten cents I was going to give you.

Groucho Marx
A Night at the Opera

34 Money is like a sixth sense without which you cannot make a complete use of the other five.

W. Somerset Maugham (1874–1965) British novelist.
Of Human Bondage, Ch. 51

35 Money can't buy friends, but you can get a better class of enemy.

Spike Milligan (1918–) British comic actor and author.
Puckoon, Ch. 6

36 Some people's money is merited
And other people's is inherited.

Ogden Nash (1902–71) US poet.
The Terrible People

37 Check enclosed.

Dorothy Parker (1893–1967) US writer.
Giving her version of the two most beautiful words in the English language
Attrib.

38 Money is good for bribing yourself through the inconveniences of life.

Gottfried Reinhardt (1911–) Austrian film producer.
Picture, 'Looks Like We're Still in Business' (Lillian Ross)

39 My boy . . . always try to rub up against money, for if you rub up against money long enough, some of it may rub off on you.

Damon Runyon (1884–1946) US writer.
Furthermore, 'A Very Honourable Guy'

40 He that wants money, means, and content, is without three good friends.

William Shakespeare (1564–1616) English dramatist.
As You Like It, III:2

41 I can get no remedy against this consumption of the purse; borrowing only lingers and lingers it out, but the disease is incurable.

William Shakespeare
Henry IV, Part Two, I:2

42 Put money in thy purse.

William Shakespeare
Othello, I:3

43 Lack of money is the root of all evil.

George Bernard Shaw (1856–1950) Irish dramatist and critic.
Man and Superman, 'Maxims for Revolutionists.'

44 The trouble, Mr Goldwyn is that you are only interested in art and I am only interested in money.

George Bernard Shaw
Turning down Goldwyn's offer to buy the screen rights of his plays
The Movie Moguls (Philip French), Ch. 4

45 Nothing links man to man like the frequent passage from hand to hand of cash.

Walter Richard Sickert (1860–1942) British impressionist painter.
A Certain World (W. H. Auden)

46 Pieces of eight!

Robert Louis Stevenson (1850–94) Scottish writer.
Treasure Island, Ch. 10

47 I think I could be a good woman if I had five thousand a year.

William Makepeace Thackeray (1811–63) British novelist.
Vanity Fair, Ch. 36

48 No one would have remembered the Good Samaritan if he'd only had good intentions. He had money as well.

Margaret Thatcher (1925–) British politician and prime minister.
Television interview, 1980

49 The easiest way for your children to learn about money is for you not to have any.

Katherine Whitehorn (1926–) British journalist.
How to Survive Children

50 You can be young without money but you can't be old without it.

Tennessee Williams (1911–83) US dramatist.
Cat on a Hot Tin Roof, I

51 All these financiers, all the little gnomes of

Zürich and the other financial centres, about whom we keep on hearing.
Harold Wilson (1916–) British politician and prime minister.
Speech, House of Commons, 12 Nov 1956

MONTHS

See also seasons

1 March comes in like a lion and goes out like a lamb.
Proverb

2 Ne'er cast a clout till May be out.
Proverb

3 The cuckoo comes in April, and stays the month of May; sings a song at midsummer, and then goes away.
Proverb

4 Thirty days hath September,
April, June, and November;
All the rest have thirty-one,
Excepting February alone,
And that has twenty-eight days clear
And twenty-nine in each leap year.
Anonymous
See also GRAFTON
Stevins Manuscript, c. 1555

5 There are twelve months in all the year,
As I hear many men say,
But the merriest month in all the year
Is the merry month of May.
Anonymous
Robin Hood and the Widow's Three Sons

6 And after April, when May follows,
And the whitethroat builds, and all the swallows!
Robert Browning (1812–89) British poet.
Home Thoughts from Abroad

7 Whan that Aprille with his shoures sote
The droghte of Marche hath perced to the rote.
Geoffrey Chaucer (c. 1342–1400) English poet.
The Canterbury Tales, Prologue

8 April is the cruellest month, breeding
Lilacs out of the dead land, mixing
Memory and desire, stirring
Dull roots with spring rain.
T. S. Eliot (1888–1965) US-born British poet and dramatist.
The Waste Land, 'The Burial of the Dead'

9 Thirty days hath November,
April, June and September,
February hath twenty-eight alone,
And all the rest have thirty-one.
Richard Grafton (d. c. 1572) English chronicler and printer.
Abridgement of the Chronicles of England, Introduction

10 No warmth, no cheerfulness, no healthful ease,

No comfortable feel in any member –
No shade, no shine, no butterflies, no bees,
No fruits, no flowers, no leaves, no birds, –
November!
Thomas Hood (1799–1845) British poet.
No!

11 February, fill the dyke
With what thou dost like.
Thomas Tusser (1524–80) English farmer.
Five Hundred Points of Good Husbandry, 'February's Husbandry'

12 Sweet April showers
Do spring May flowers.
Thomas Tusser
Five Hundred Points of Good Husbandry, 'April's Husbandry'

MOON

See also astronomy, space, universe

1 I saw the new moon late yestreen
Wi' the auld moon in her arm;
And if we gang to sea master;
I fear we'll come to harm.
Anonymous
The 'new moon in the old moon's arms' is generally regarded as a sign of bad weather
Sir Patrick Spens

2 The moving Moon went up the sky,
And no where did abide:
Softly she was going up,
And a star or two beside.
Samuel Taylor Coleridge (1772–1834) British poet.
The Rime of the Ancient Mariner, IV

3 who knows if the moon's
a balloon, coming out of a keen city
in the sky – filled with pretty people?
e. e. cummings (1894–1962) US poet.
Used for the title and epigraph of David Niven's first volume of autobiography, *The Moon's a Balloon*, about his experiences in the film industry

4 So sicken waning moons too near the sun,
And blunt their crescents on the edge of day.
John Dryden (1631–1700) British poet and dramatist.
Annus Mirabilis

5 For years politicians have promised the moon, I'm the first one to be able to deliver it.
Richard Milhous Nixon (1913–) US president.
Radio message to astronauts on the moon, 20 Jul 1969

6 Oh! shine on, shine on, harvest moon
Up in the sky.
I ain't had no lovin'
Since April, January, June or July.
Jack Norworth (1879–1959) US vaudeville comedian and songwriter.
Shine On, Harvest Moon (song)

MORALITY

See also integrity, principles, righteousness

1 In his own way each man must struggle, lest the moral law become a far-off abstraction utterly separated from his active life.
Jane Addams (1860–1935) US social worker.
Twenty Years at Hull House

2 No morality can be founded on authority, even if the authority were divine.
A. J. Ayer (1910–89) British philosopher.
Essay on Humanism

3 Morality's not practical. Morality's a gesture. A complicated gesture learnt from books.
Robert Bolt (1924–) British playwright.
A Man for All Seasons

4 The propriety of some persons' seems to consist in having improper thoughts about their neighbours.
F. H. Bradley (1846–1924) British philosopher.
Aphorisms

5 And there isn't any way that one can get rid of the guilt of having a nice body by saying that one can serve society with it, because that would end up with oneself as what? There simply doesn't seem to be any moral place for flesh.
Margaret Drabble (1939–) British novelist.
A Summer Bird-Cage, Ch. 10

6 What is moral is what you feel good after, and what is immoral is what you feel bad after.
Ernest Hemingway (1899–1961) US novelist.
Death in the Afternoon

7 The quality of moral behaviour varies in inverse ratio to the number of human beings involved.
Aldous Huxley (1894–1964) British novelist.
Grey Eminence, Ch. 10

8 Finally, there is an imperative which commands a certain conduct immediately . . . This imperative is Categorical . . . This imperative may be called that of Morality.
Immanuel Kant (1724–1804) German philosopher.
Grundlegung zur Metaphysik der Sitten, II

9 Morality which is based on ideas, or on an ideal, is an unmitigated evil.
D. H. Lawrence (1885–1930) British novelist.
Fantasia of the Unconscious, Ch. 7

10 We know no spectacle so ridiculous as the British public in one of its periodical fits of morality.
Lord Macaulay (1800–59) British historian.
Literary Essays Contributed to the 'Edinburgh Review', 'Moore's 'Life of Lord Byron''

11 It is a public scandal that gives offence, and it is no sin to sin in secret.
Molière (Jean Baptiste Poquelin; 1622–73) French dramatist.
Tartuffe, IV:5

12 Morality in Europe today is herd-morality.
Friedrich Wilhelm Nietzsche (1844–1900) German philosopher.
Jenseits von Gut und Böse

13 We have, in fact, two kinds of morality side by side; one which we preach but do not practise, and another which we practise but seldom preach.
Bertrand Russell (1872–1970) British philosopher.
Sceptical Essays

14 All universal moral principles are idle fancies.
Marquis de Sade (1740–1814) French novelist.
The 120 Days of Sodom

15 Without doubt the greatest injury . . . was done by basing morals on myth, for sooner or later myth is recognized for what it is, and disappears. Then morality loses the foundation on which it has been built.
Herbert Samuel (1870–1963) British Liberal statesman.
Romanes Lecture, 1947

16 Morality consists in suspecting other people of not being legally married.
George Bernard Shaw (1856–1950) Irish dramatist and critic.
The Doctor's Dilemma

17 He never does a proper thing without giving an improper reason for it.
George Bernard Shaw
Major Barbara, III

18 The so-called new morality is too often the old immorality condoned.
Lord Shawcross (1902–) British Labour politician and lawyer.
The Observer, 17 Nov 1963

19 'Twas Peter's drift
To be a kind of moral eunuch.
Percy Bysshe Shelley (1792–1822) British poet.
Peter Bell the Third

20 Moral indignation is in most cases 2 percent moral, 48 percent indignation and 50 percent envy.
Vittorio De Sica (1901–74) Italian film director.
The Observer, 1961

21 If your morals make you dreary, depend upon it, they are wrong.
Robert Louis Stevenson (1850–94) Scottish writer.
Across the Plains

22 Victorian values . . . were the values when our country became great.
Margaret Thatcher (1925–) British politician and prime minister.
Television interview, 1982

23 Morals are an acquirement – like music, like a foreign language, like piety, poker, paralysis – no man is born with them.
Mark Twain (Samuel Langhorne Clemens; 1835–1910) US writer.
Seventieth Birthday

MORTALITY

See also death, equality in death, human condition, immortality, life, life and death, time, transience

1 All men are mortal.
Proverb

2 Mortality, behold and fear!
What a change of flesh is here!
Francis Beaumont (1584–1616) English dramatist.
On the Tombs in Westminster Abbey

3 That lyf so short, the craft so long to lerne,
Th' assay so hard, so sharp the conquerynge.
Geoffrey Chaucer (c. 1342–1400) English poet.
See also HIPPOCRATES
The Parliament of Fowls

4 What argufies pride and ambition?
Soon or late death will take us in tow:
Each bullet has got its commission,
And when our time's come we must go.
Charles Dibdin (1745–1814) British actor and dramatist.
Each Bullet has its Commission

5 All humane things are subject to decay,
And, when Fate summons, Monarchs must obey.
John Dryden (1631–1700) British poet and dramatist.
Mac Flecknoe

6 The Wine of Life keeps oozing drop by drop,
The Leaves of Life keep falling one by one.
Edward Fitzgerald (1809–83) British poet.
The Rubáiyát of Omar Khayyám (4th edn.), VIII

7 Is life a boon?
If so, it must befall
That Death, whene'er he call,
Must call too soon.
W. S. Gilbert (1836–1911) British dramatist.
The lines are written on Arthur Sullivan's memorial in the Embankment gardens
The Yeoman of the Guard, I

8 I was not unaware that I had begotten a mortal.
Goethe (1749–1832) German poet and dramatist.
On learning of his son's death
The Story of Civilization (W. Durant), Vol. X

9 Man wants but little here below,
Nor wants that little long.
Oliver Goldsmith (1728–74) Irish-born British writer.
Edwin and Angelina, or the Hermit

10 The boast of heraldry, the pomp of pow'r,
And all that beauty, all that wealth e'er gave,
Awaits alike th' inevitable hour,
The paths of glory lead but to the grave.
Thomas Gray (1716–71) British poet.
Elegy Written in a Country Churchyard

11 I expect to pass through this world but once; any good thing therefore that I can do, or any kindness that I can show to any fellow-creature, let me do it now; let me not defer or neglect it, for I shall not pass this way again.
Stephen Grellet (1773–1855) French-born US missionary.
Attrib
Treasure Trove (John o'London)

12 The life so short, the craft so long to learn.
Hippocrates (c. 460–c. 377 BC) Greek physician.
Describing medicine. It is often quoted in Latin as *Ars longa, vita brevis*, and interpreted as 'Art lasts, life is short'. *See also* CHAUCER
Aphorisms, I

13 Life's short span forbids us to enter on far-reaching hopes.
Horace (Quintus Horatius Flaccus; 65–8 BC) Roman poet.
Odes, I

14 Art is long, and Time is fleeting,
And our hearts, though stout and brave,
Still, like muffled drums, are beating
Funeral marches to the grave.
Henry Wadsworth Longfellow (1807–82) US poet.
See also HIPPOCRATES
A Psalm of Life

15 *Inque brevi spatio mutantur saecla animantum
Et quasi cursores vitai lampada tradunt.*
The generations of living things pass in a short time, and like runners hand on the torch of life.
Lucretius (Titus Lucretius Carus; c. 99–55 BC) Roman philosopher.
On the Nature of the Universe, II

16 Fear no more the heat o' th' sun
Nor the furious winter's rages;
Thou thy worldly task hast done,
Home art gone, and ta'en thy wages.
Golden lads and girls all must,
As chimney-sweepers, come to dust.
William Shakespeare (1564–1616) English dramatist.
Cymbeline, IV:2

17 Our revels now are ended. These our actors,
As I foretold you, were all spirits, and
Are melted into air, into thin air;
And, like the baseless fabric of this vision,
The cloud-capp'd towers, the gorgeous palaces,
The solemn temples, the great globe itself,
Yea, all which it inherit, shall dissolve,
And, like this insubstantial pageant faded,
Leave not a rack behind. We are such stuff
As dreams are made on; and our little life
Is rounded with a sleep.
William Shakespeare
The Tempest, IV:1

18 Old and young, we are all on our last cruise.
Robert Louis Stevenson (1850–94) Scottish writer.
Virginibus Puerisque

19 The woods decay, the woods decay and fall,
The vapours weep their burthen to the ground,
Man comes and tills the field and lies beneath,
And after many a summer dies the swan.
Alfred, Lord Tennyson (1809–92) British poet.
Tithonus

20 A power is passing from the earth
To breathless Nature's dark abyss;
But when the great and good depart,
What is it more than this –

That Man who is from God sent forth,
Doth yet again to God return? –
Such ebb and flow must ever be,
Then wherefore should we mourn?
William Wordsworth (1770–1850) British poet.
Referring to Charles James Fox, the hero of the liberal Whigs,
who died in 1806
Lines on the Expected Dissolution of Mr. Fox

21 The clouds that gather round the setting sun
Do take a sober colouring from an eye
That hath kept watch o'er man's mortality.
William Wordsworth
Ode. Intimations of Immortality, XI

22 I am moved to pity, when I think of the
brevity of human life, seeing that of all this
host of men not one will still be alive in a
hundred years' time.
Xerxes (d. 465 BC) King of Persia.
On surveying his army

23 That is no country for old men. The young
In one another's arms, birds in the trees
– Those dying generations – at their song,
The salmon-falls, the mackerel-crowded seas,
Fish, flesh, or fowl, commend all summer long
Whatever is begotten, born, and dies.
W. B. Yeats (1865–1939) Irish poet.
Sailing to Byzantium, I

24 Man wants but little, nor that little long.
Edward Young (1683–1765) British poet.
Night Thoughts

MOTIVE

See also purpose

1 Never ascribe to an opponent motives
meaner than your own.
J. M. Barrie (1860–1937) British novelist and dramatist.
Speech, St Andrews, 3 May 1922

2 The last temptation is the greatest treason:
To do the right deed for the wrong reason.
T. S. Eliot (1888–1965) US-born British poet and
dramatist.
Murder in the Cathedral, I

3 Because it is there.
George Mallory (1886–1924) British mountaineer.
Answer to the question 'Why do you want to climb Mt.
Everest?'
George Mallory (D. Robertson)

4 Nobody ever did anything very foolish except
from some strong principle.
Lord Melbourne (1779–1848) British statesman.
The Young Melbourne (Lord David Cecil)

5 The heart has its reasons which reason does
not know.
Blaise Pascal (1623–62) French philosopher and
mathematician.
Pensées, IV

6 Men are rewarded and punished not for what
they do, but rather for how their acts are
defined. This is why men are more
interested in better justifying themselves than
in better behaving themselves.
Thomas Szasz (1920–) US psychiatrist.
The Second Sin

MOUNTAINS

1 Mountains interposed
Make enemies of nations, who had else,
Like kindred drops, been mingled into one.
William Cowper (1731–1800) British poet.
The Task

2 Separate from the pleasure of your company,
I don't much care if I never see another
mountain in my life.
Charles Lamb (1775–1834) British essayist.
Letter to William Wordsworth, 30 Jan 1801

3 Mountains are the beginning and the end of
all natural scenery.
John Ruskin (1819–1900) British art critic and writer.
Modern Painters, Vol. IV

4 They say that if the Swiss had designed
these mountains they'd be rather flatter.
Paul Theroux (1941–) US-born writer.
Referring to the Alps
The Great Railway Bazaar, Ch. 28

MOURNING

See also death, loss, regret, sorrow

1 We met . . . Dr Hall in such very deep
mourning that either his mother, his wife, or
himself must be dead.
Jane Austen (1775–1817) British novelist.
Letter to Cassandra Austen, 17 May 1799

2 I am distressed for thee, my brother
Jonathan: very pleasant hast thou been unto
me: thy love to me was wonderful, passing
the love of women.
How are the mighty fallen, and the weapons of
war perished!
Bible: II Samuel
1:26–27

3 With proud thanksgiving, a mother for her
children,
England mourns for her dead across the sea.
Laurence Binyon (1869–1943) British poet.
In response to the slaughter of World War I
Poems For the Fallen

4 MEDVEDENKO. Why do you wear black all the
time?

MASHA. I'm in mourning for my life, I'm unhappy.
Anton Chekhov (1860–1904) Russian dramatist.
The Seagull, I

5 There's a one-eyed yellow idol to the north
of Khatmandu,
There's a little marble cross below the town;
There's a broken-hearted woman tends the
grave of Mad Carew
And the Yellow God forever gazes down.
J. Milton Hayes (1884–1940) British writer.
The Green Eye of the Yellow God

6 What we call mourning for our dead is
perhaps not so much grief at not being able
to call them back as it is grief at not being
able to want to do so.
Thomas Mann (1875–1955) German novelist.
The Magic Mountain

7 In a cavern, in a canyon,
Excavating for a mine
Dwelt a miner, Forty-niner,
And his daughter, Clementine.
Oh, my darling, Oh, my darling, Oh, my dar-
ling Clementine!
Thou art lost and gone for ever, dreadful sor-
ry, Clementine.
Percy Montrose (19th century) US songwriter.
Clementine

8 She is far from the land where her young
hero sleeps,
And lovers are round her, sighing:
But coldly she turns from their gaze, and
weeps,
For her heart in his grave is lying.
Thomas Moore (1779–1852) Irish poet.
Irish Melodies, 'She is Far'

9 And my poor fool is hang'd! No, no, no life!
Why should a dog, a horse, a rat have life,
And thou no breath at all? Thou'lt come no
more,
Never, never, never, never.
William Shakespeare (1564–1616) English dramatist.
King Lear, V:3

10 Alas, poor Yorick! I knew him, Horatio: a
fellow of infinite jest, of most excellent fancy.
William Shakespeare
Hamlet, V:1

11 O, wither'd is the garland of the war,
The soldier's pole is fall'n! Young boys and
girls
Are level now with men. The odds is gone,
And there is nothing left remarkable
Beneath the visiting moon.
William Shakespeare
Antony and Cleopatra, IV:13

12 But I have that within which passes show –
these but the trappings and the suits of woe.
William Shakespeare
Hamlet, I:2

13 If thou didst ever hold me in thy heart,

Absent thee from felicity awhile,
And in this harsh world draw thy breath in
pain,
To tell my story.
William Shakespeare
Hamlet, V:2

14 I weep for Adonais – he is dead!
O, weep for Adonais! though our tears
Thaw not the frost which binds so dear a head!
Percy Bysshe Shelley (1792–1822) British poet.
Prompted by the death of Keats
Adonais, I

15 A lady asked me why, on most occasions, I
wore black. 'Are you in mourning?'
'Yes.'
'For whom are you in mourning?'
'For the world.'
Edith Sitwell (1887–1964) British poet and writer.
Taken Care Of, Ch. 1

16 Home they brought her warrior dead.
She nor swoon'd, nor utter'd cry:
All her maidens, watching said,
'She must weep or she will die.'
Alfred, Lord Tennyson (1809–92) British poet.
The Princess, VI

MURDER

See also assassination, crime, killing

1 Lizzie Borden took an axe
And gave her mother forty whacks;
When she saw what she had done
She gave her father forty-one!
Anonymous
On 4 Aug 1892 in Fall River, Massachusetts, Lizzie Borden
was acquitted of the murder of her stepmother and her fa-
ther

2 And the Lord said unto Cain, Where is Abel
thy brother? And he said, I know not: Am I
my brother's keeper?
And he said, What hast thou done? the voice of
thy brother's blood crieth unto me from the
ground.
Bible: Genesis
4:9–10

3 I've been accused of every death except the
casualty list of the World War.
Al Capone (1899–1947) Italian-born US gangster.
The Bootleggers (Kenneth Allsop), Ch. 11

4 Mordre wol out, that see we day by day.
Geoffrey Chaucer (c. 1342–1400) English poet.
The Canterbury Tales, 'The Nun's Priest's Tale'

5 See how love and murder will out.
William Congreve (1670–1729) British Restoration
dramatist.
The Double Dealer, IV:6

6 Murder considered as one of the Fine Arts.
Thomas De Quincey (1785–1859) British writer.
Essay title

7 I made a remark a long time ago. I said I was very pleased that television was now showing murder stories, because it's bringing murder back into its rightful setting – in the home.

Alfred Hitchcock (1889–1980) British film director.
The Observer, 'Sayings of the Week', 17 Aug 1969

8 It takes two to make a murder. There are born victims, born to have their throats cut.

Aldous Huxley (1894–1964) British novelist.
Point Counter Point

9 Murder, like talent, seems occasionally to run in families.

G. H. Lewes (1817–78) British philosopher and writer.
The Physiology of Common Life, Ch. 12

10 Put out the light, and then put out the light.
If I quench thee, thou flaming minister,
I can again thy former light restore,
Should I repent me; but once put out thy light,
Thou cunning'st pattern of excelling nature,
I know not where is that Promethean heat
That can thy light relume.

William Shakespeare (1564–1616) English dramatist.
Othello, V:2

11 Murder most foul, as in the best it is;
But this most foul, strange, and unnatural.

William Shakespeare
Hamlet, I:5

12 I met Murder on the way –
He had a mask like Castlereagh.

Percy Bysshe Shelley (1792–1822) British poet.
Viscount Castlereagh (1769–1822) was British foreign secretary (1812–22); he was highly unpopular and became identified with such controversial events as the Peterloo massacre of 1819
The Mask of Anarchy, 5

13 Other sins only speak; murder shrieks out.

John Webster (1580–1625) English dramatist.
The Duchess of Malfi, IV:2

MUSEUMS

1 The Arab who builds himself a hut out of the marble fragments of a temple in Palmyra is more philosophical than all the curators of the museums in London, Munich or Paris.

Anatole France (Jacques Anatole François Thibault; 1844–1924) French writer.
The Crime of Sylvestre Bonnard

2 If there was a little room somewhere in the British Museum that contained only about twenty exhibits and good lighting, easy chairs, and a notice imploring you to smoke, I believe I should become a museum man.

J. B. Priestley (1894–1984) British novelist.
Self-Selected Essays, 'In the British Museum'

3 There is in the British Museum an enormous

mind. Consider that Plato is there cheek by jowl with Aristotle; and Shakespeare with Marlowe. This great mind is hoarded beyond the power of any single mind to possess it.

Virginia Woolf (1882–1941) British novelist.
Jacob's Room, Ch. 9

MUSIC

See also criticism, musicians, opera, singing

1 Music helps not the toothache.
Proverb

2 Nothing is capable of being well set to music that is not nonsense.

Joseph Addison (1672–1719) British essayist.
The Spectator, 18

3 The music teacher came twice each week to bridge the awful gap between Dorothy and Chopin.

George Ade (1866–1944) US dramatist and humorist.
Attrib.

4 Brass bands are all very well in their place – outdoors and several miles away.

Thomas Beecham (1879–1961) British conductor.
Attrib.

5 The English may not like music – but they absolutely love the noise it makes.

Thomas Beecham
The Wit of Music (L. Ayre)

6 The sound of the harpsichord resembles that of a bird-cage played with toasting-forks.

Thomas Beecham
Attrib.

7 There are two golden rules for an orchestra: start together and finish together. The public doesn't give a damn what goes on in between.

Thomas Beecham
Beecham Stories (H. Atkins and A. Newman)

8 A musicologist is a man who can read music but can't hear it.

Thomas Beecham
Beecham Remembered (H. Procter-Gregg)

9 When I composed that, I was conscious of being inspired by God Almighty. Do you think I can consider your puny little fiddle when He speaks to me?

Ludwig van Beethoven (1770–1827) German composer.
Said when a violinist complained that a passage was unplayable
Music All Around Me (A. Hopkins)

10 *Fiddle, n.* An instrument to tickle human ears by function of a horse's tail on the entrails of a cat.

Ambrose Bierce (1842–?1914) US writer and journalist.
The Devil's Dictionary

11 Down South where I come from you don't go around hitting too many white keys.
Eubie Blake (1883–1983) US pianist and ragtime composer.
When asked why his compositions contained so many sharps and flats
Attrib.

12 Piping down the valleys wild,
Piping songs of pleasant glee,
On a cloud I saw a child.
William Blake (1757–1827) British poet.
Songs of Innocence, Introduction

13 'Pipe a song about a Lamb!'
So I piped with merry cheer.
William Blake
Songs of Innocence, Introduction

14 No one really understood music unless he was a scientist, her father had declared, and not just a scientist, either, oh, no, only the real ones, the theoreticians, whose language was mathematics.
Pearl Buck (1892–1973) US novelist.
The Goddess Abides, Pt. I

15 Music has charms to soothe a savage breast.
William Congreve (1670–1729) British Restoration dramatist.
The Mourning Bride, I

16 Strange how potent cheap music is.
Noël Coward (1899–1973) British dramatist.
Private Lives

17 Music is the arithmetic of sounds as optics is the geometry of light.
Claude Debussy (1862–1918) French composer.
Attrib.

18 The century of aeroplanes deserves its own music. As there are no precedents I must create anew.
Claude Debussy
Attrib.

19 When I was 25, Bartok needed me, a young man who would get up on the podium, play his music and be whistled at for it.
Antal Dorati (1906–) American conductor and composer.
Remark, Apr 1986

20 Music was invented to confirm human loneliness.
Lawrence Durrell (1912–) British novelist.
Clea

21 Beethoven's Fifth Symphony is the most sublime noise that ever penetrated into the ear of man.
E. M. Forster (1879–1970) British novelist.
Howards End, Ch. 5

22 The hills are alive with the sound of music
With the songs they have sung
For a thousand years.
Oscar Hammerstein (1895–1960) US lyricist.
The Sound of Music, title song

23 I do not see any reason why the devil should have all the good tunes.
Rowland Hill (1744–1833) British clergyman.
Attrib.

24 Never compose anything unless the not composing of it becomes a positive nuisance to you.
Gustav Holst (1874–1934) British composer.
Letter to W. G. Whittaker

25 Since Mozart's day composers have learned the art of making music throatily and palpitatingly sexual.
Aldous Huxley (1894–1964) British novelist.
Along the Road, 'Popular music'

26 The only sensual pleasure without vice.
Samuel Johnson (1709–84) British lexicographer.
Referring to music
Johnsonian Miscellanies (ed. G. B. Hill), Vol. II

27 Heard melodies are sweet, but those unheard
Are sweeter; therefore, ye soft pipes, play on.
John Keats (1795–1821) British poet.
Ode on a Grecian Urn

28 But I can't listen to music too often. It affects your nerves, makes you want to say stupid, nice things, and stroke the heads of people who could create such beauty while living in this vile hell.
Lenin (Vladimir Ilich Ulyanov; 1870–1924) Russian revolutionary leader.
Lenin and the Russian Revolution (Christopher Hill)

29 There's sure no passion in the human soul,
But finds its food in music.
George Lillo (1693–1739) English dramatist.
Fatal Curiosity, I:2

30 Music, Maestro, Please.
Herb Magidson (20th century) US songwriter.
Song title

31 Music is not written in red, white and blue. It is written in the heart's blood of the composer.
Nellie Melba (Helen Porter Mitchell; 1861–1931) Australian soprano.
Melodies and Memories

32 Music creates order out of chaos; for rhythm imposes unanimity upon the divergent, melody imposes continuity upon the disjointed, and harmony imposes compatibility upon the incongruous.
Yehudi Menuhin (1916–) US-born British violinist.
The Sunday Times, 10 Oct 1976

33 The melting voice through mazes running;
Untwisting all the chains that tie
The hidden soul of harmony.
John Milton (1608–74) English poet.
L'Allegro

34 The song that we hear with our ears is only the song that is sung in our hearts.
Ouida (Marie Louise de la Ramée; 1839–1908) British novelist.
Wisdom, Wit and Pathos, 'Ariadne'

35 What a terrible revenge by the culture of the Negroes on that of the whites.
Ignacy Paderewski (1860–1941) Polish pianist, composer, and statesman.
Referring to jazz
Attrib.

36 Music is your own experience, your thoughts, your wisdom. If you don't live it, it won't come out of your horn.
Charlie Parker (1920–55) US black jazz musician.
Hear Me Talkin' to Ya (Nat Shapiro and Nat Hentoff)

37 Music and women I cannot but give way to, whatever my business is.
Samuel Pepys (1633–1703) English diarist.
Diary, 9 Mar 1666

38 The basic difference between classical music and jazz is that in the former the music is always greater than its performance – whereas the way jazz is performed is always more important than what is being played.
André Previn (1929–   ) German-born conductor.
An Encyclopedia of Quotations about Music (Nat Shapiro)

39 Seated one day at the organ,
I was weary and ill at ease,
And my fingers wandered idly
Over the noisy keys.
. . .
But I struck one chord of music,
Like the sound of a great Amen.
Adelaide Anne Procter (1825–64) British poet.
Better known in the setting by Sir Arthur Sullivan
Legends and Lyrics, 'A Lost Chord'

40 I have already heard it. I had better not go: I will start to get accustomed to it and finally like it.
Nikolai Rimsky-Korsakov (1844–1908) Russian composer.
Referring to music by Debussy
Conversations with Stravinsky (Robert Craft and Igor Stravinsky)

41 Give me a laundry-list and I'll set it to music.
Gioacchino Rossini (1792–1868) Italian operatic composer.
Attrib.

42 To be played with both hands in the pocket.
Erik Satie (1866–1925) French composer.
Direction on one of his piano pieces
The Unimportance of Being Oscar (O. Levant)

43 The sonatas of Mozart are unique; they are too easy for children, and too difficult for artists.
Artur Schnabel (1882–1951) Austrian concert pianist.
An Encyclopedia of Quotations about Music (Nat Shapiro)

44 I am never merry when I hear sweet music.
William Shakespeare (1564–1616) English dramatist.
The Merchant of Venice, V:1

45 The man that hath no music in himself,
Nor is not mov'd with concord of sweet sounds,
Is fit for treasons, stratagems, and spoils.
William Shakespeare
The Merchant of Venice, V:1

46 If music be the food of love, play on,
Give me excess of it, that, surfeiting,
The appetite may sicken and so die.
William Shakespeare
Twelfth Night, I:1

47 I wish the Government would put a tax on pianos for the incompetent.
Edith Sitwell (1887–1964) British poet and writer.
Letters, 1916–1964

48 Jazz will endure just as long as people hear it through their feet instead of their brains.
John Philip Sousa (1854–1932) US composer, conductor, and writer.
Attrib.

49 I don't write modern music. I only write good music.
Igor Stravinsky (1882–1971) Russian-born US composer.
To journalists on his first visit to America, 1925

50 My music is best understood by children and animals.
Igor Stravinsky
The Observer, 'Sayings of the Week', 8 Oct 1961

51 Music that gentlier on the spirit lies,
Than tir'd eyelids upon tir'd eyes.
Alfred, Lord Tennyson (1809–92) British poet.
The Lotos-Eaters, 'Choric Song'

52 Oh I'm a martyr to music.
Dylan Thomas (1914–53) Welsh poet.
Under Milk Wood

53 The cello is not one of my favourite instruments. It has such a lugubrious sound, like someone reading a will.
Irene Thomas (1920–   ) British writer.
Attrib.

54 God tells me how he wants this music played – and you get in his way.
Arturo Toscanini (1867–1957) Italian conductor.
Etude (Howard Tubman)

55 You know, sometimes I don't even like music.
Sir William Walton (1902–83) British composer.
Remark, Mar 1982

56 When I play on my fiddle in Dooney,
Folk dance like a wave of the sea.
W. B. Yeats (1865–1939) Irish poet.
The Fiddler of Dooney

MUSICIANS

See also critics, singers

General quotes

1 Musicians don't retire; they stop when there's no more music in them.
Louis Armstrong (1900–71) US jazz trumpeter.
The Observer, 'Sayings of the Week', 21 Apr 1968

2 Off with you! You're a happy fellow, for you'll give happiness and joy to many other people. There is nothing better or greater than that!
Ludwig van Beethoven (1770–1827) German composer.
Said to Franz Liszt when Liszt, aged 11, had visited Beethoven and played for him
Beethoven: Letters, Journals and Conversations (M. Hamburger)

3 The public doesn't want a new music: the main thing it demands of a composer is that he be dead.
Arthur Honegger (1892–1955) French composer.
Attrib.

4 Of all musicians, flautists are most obviously the ones who know something we don't know.
Paul Jennings (1918–) British humorous writer.
The Jenguin Pennings, 'Flautists Flaunt Afflatus'

5 The conductor has the advantage of not seeing the audience.
André Kostalenetz (1903–80) Russian-born conductor.
Attrib.

6 You see, our fingers are circumcised, which gives it a very good dexterity, you know, particularly in the pinky.
Itzhak Perlman (1945–) Israeli violinist.
Responding to an observation that many great violinists are Jewish
Close Encounters (M. Wallace)

7 Sometimes, I think, not so much am I a pianist, but a vampire. All my life I have lived off the blood of Chopin.
Arthur Rubinstein (1887–1982) Polish-born US pianist.
Attrib.

8 The notes I handle no better than many pianists. But the pauses between the notes – ah, that is where the art resides.
Artur Schnabel (1882–1951) Austrian concert pianist.
Chicago Daily News, 11 June 1958

9 A good composer does not imitate; he steals.
Igor Stravinsky (1882–1971) Russian-born composer.
Twentieth Century Music (Peter Yates)

Specific quotes

10 A master is dead. Today we sing no more.
Johannes Brahms (1833–97) German composer.
Stopping a choral rehearsal on hearing of the death of Wagner
Brahms (P. Latham)

11 Bach is like an astronomer who, with the aid of ciphers, finds the most wonderful stars.
Frédéric Chopin (1810–49) Polish composer and pianist.
Letter to Delphine Potocka

12 Wagner is the Puccini of music.
J. B. Morton (1893–1979) British journalist.
Attrib.

13 My dear hands. Farewell, my poor hands.
Sergei Rachmaninov (1873–1943) Russian composer.
On being informed that he was dying from cancer
The Great Pianists (H. Schonberg)

14 When a piece gets difficult make faces.
Artur Schnabel (1882–1951) Austrian concert pianist.
Advice given to the pianist Vladimir Horowitz
The Unimportance of Being Oscar (O. Levant)

15 Music owes as much to Bach as religion to its founder.
Robert Schumann (1810–56) German composer.
Attrib.

16 Brahms is just like Tennyson, an extraordinary musician with the brains of a third-rate village policeman.
George Bernard Shaw (1856–1950) Irish dramatist and critic.
Letter to Packenham Beatty, 4 Apr 1893

17 Unlike many contemporaries, he never writes paper music; everything has first been vividly heard by an inner ear of amazing acuteness. This faculty explains the speed at which he composes. The processes of trial and error take place mostly in the head.
Desmond Shaw-Taylor (1907–) British music critic.
Referring to Benjamin Britten
Sunday Times, 17 Nov 1963

18 Walton wrote *Belshazzar's Feast* in that barn out there. He made such a frightful din on the piano we had to banish him from the house.
Sacheverell Sitwell (1897–) British writer.
The Times, Profile, 16 Nov 1982

19 He was the only pianist I have ever seen who did not grimace. That is a great deal.
Igor Stravinsky (1882–1971) Russian-born US composer.
Referring to Rachmaninov
Conversations with Igor Stravinsky (Igor Stravinsky and Robert Craft)

20 Rachmaninov's immortalizing totality was his scowl. He was a six-and-a-half-foot-tall scowl.
Igor Stravinsky
Conversations with Igor Stravinsky (Igor Stravinsky and Robert Craft)

21 Ah, a German and a genius! a prodigy, admit him!
Jonathan Swift (1667–1745) Irish-born Anglican priest and writer.
Learning of the arrival of Handel: Swift's last words
Attrib.

MYTHS

1 Science must begin with myths, and with the criticism of myths.
Karl Popper (1902–) Austrian-born British philosopher.
British Philosophy in the Mid-Century (ed. C. A. Mace)

2 A myth is, of course, not a fairy story. It is the presentation of facts belonging to one category in the idioms appropriate to another. To explode a myth is accordingly not to deny the facts but to re-allocate them.
Gilbert Ryle (1900–76) British philosopher.
The Concept of Mind, Introduction

N

NAKEDNESS

1 Nakedness is uncomely as well in mind, as body.
Francis Bacon (1561–1626) English philosopher.
Essays, 'Of Simulation and Dissimulation'

2 Lives there the man that can figure a naked Duke of Windlestraw addressing a naked House of Lords?
Thomas Carlyle (1795–1881) Scottish historian and essayist.
Sartor Resartus, Bk. I, Ch. 9

3 a pretty girl who naked is
is worth a million statues.
e. e. cummings (1894–1962) US poet.
Collected Poems, 133

4 No woman so naked as one you can see to be naked underneath her clothes.
Michael Frayn (1933–) British journalist and writer.
Constructions

5 How idiotic civilization is! Why be given a body if you have to keep it shut up in a case like a rare, rare fiddle?
Katherine Mansfield (1888–1923) New-Zealand-born British writer.
Bliss and Other Stories, 'Bliss'

6 JOURNALIST. Didn't you have anything on?
M. M. I had the radio on.
Marilyn Monroe (Norma-Jean Baker; 1926–62) US film star.
Attrib.

NAMES

1 Ball . . . how very singular.
Thomas Beecham (1879–1961) British conductor.
To a man called Ball
Sir Thomas Beecham (N. Cardus)

2 Known by the *sobriquet* of 'The artful Dodger.'
Charles Dickens (1812–70) British novelist.
Oliver Twist, Ch. 8

3 I'm called Little Buttercup – dear Little Buttercup,
Though I could never tell why.
W. S. Gilbert (1836–1911) British dramatist.
HMS Pinafore, I

4 A nickname is the heaviest stone that the devil can throw at a man.
William Hazlitt (1778–1830) British essayist.
Nicknames

5 No, Groucho is not my real name. I'm breaking it in for a friend.
Groucho Marx (Julius Marx; 1895–1977) US comedian.
Attrib.

6 O Romeo, Romeo! wherefore art thou Romeo?
William Shakespeare (1564–1616) English dramatist.
Romeo and Juliet, II:2

7 What's in a name? That which we call a rose By any other name would smell as sweet.
William Shakespeare
Romeo and Juliet, II:2

8 'It's giving girls names like that', said Buggins, 'that nine times out of ten makes 'em go wrong. It unsettles 'em. If ever I was to have a girl, if ever I was to have a dozen girls, I'd call 'em all Jane.'
H. G. Wells (1866–1946) British writer.
Referring to the name Euphemia
Kipps, Bk. I, Ch. 4

NASTINESS

See also cruelty, hurt

1 But are they all horrid, are you sure they are all horrid?
Jane Austen (1775–1817) British novelist.
Northanger Abbey, Ch. 6

2 I do not want people to be very agreeable, as it saves me the trouble of liking them a great deal.
Jane Austen
Letter, 24 Dec 1798

3 There is an unseemly exposure of the mind, as well as of the body.
William Hazlitt (1778–1830) British essayist.
On Disagreeable People

4 Because I am a bastard.
Ernest Hemingway (1899–1961) US novelist.
When asked why he had deserted his wife for another woman
Americans in Paris (B. Morton)

5 He was one of those born neither to obey nor to command, but to be evil to the commander and the obeyer alike. Perhaps

there was nothing in life that he had much wanted to do, except to shoot rabbits and hit his father on the jaw, and both these things he had done.

John Masefield (1878–1967) British poet.
The Bird of Dawning

6 One of the worst things about life is not how nasty the nasty people are. You know that already. It is how nasty the nice people can be.

Anthony Powell (1905–) British novelist.
A Dance to the Music of Time: The Kindly Ones, Ch. 4

7 I can't see that she could have found anything nastier to say if she'd thought it out with both hands for a fortnight.

Dorothy L. Sayers (1893–1957) British writer.
Busman's Holiday, 'Prothalamion'

8 'I grant you that he's not two-faced,' I said. 'But what's the use of that when the one face he has got is so peculiarly unpleasant?'

C. P. Snow (1905–80) British novelist.
The Affair, Ch. 4

9 Malice is like a game of poker or tennis; you don't play it with anyone who is manifestly inferior to you.

Hilde Spiel (1911–) Austrian writer.
The Darkened Room

NATIONALITY

See also Americans, British

1 He was born an Englishman and remained one for years.

Brendan Behan (1923–64) Irish playwright.
The Hostage, I

2 PAT. He was an Anglo-Irishman.
MEG. In the blessed name of God, what's that?
PAT. A Protestant with a horse.

Brendan Behan
The Hostage, I

3 England is a paradise for women, and hell for horses: Italy a paradise for horses, hell for women.

Robert Burton (1577–1640) English scholar and explorer.
Anatomy of Melancholy, Pt. III

4 The Almighty in His infinite wisdom did not see fit to create Frenchmen in the image of Englishmen.

Winston Churchill (1874–1965) British statesman.
Speech, House of Commons, 10 Dec 1942

5 For he might have been a Roosian,
A French, or Turk, or Proosian,
Or perhaps Ital-ian!
But in spite of all temptations
To belong to other nations,
He remains an Englishman!

W. S. Gilbert (1836–1911) British dramatist.
HMS Pinafore, II

6 The Saxon is not like us Normans. His manners are not so polite.
But he never means anything serious till he talks about justice and right,
When he stands like an ox in the furrow with his sullen set eyes on your own,
And grumbles, 'This isn't fair dealing,' my son, leave the Saxon alone.

Rudyard Kipling (1865–1936) Indian-born British writer.
Norman and Saxon

7 Great artists have no country.

Alfred de Musset (1810–57) French dramatist and poet.
Lorenzaccio, I:5

8 I am not an Athenian or a Greek, but a citizen of the world.

Socrates (469–399 BC) Athenian philosopher.
Of Banishment (Plutarch)

9 Men of England! You wish to kill me because I am a Frenchman. Am I not punished enough in not being born an Englishman?

Voltaire (François-Marie Arouet; 1694–1778) French writer.
Addressing an angry London mob who desired to hang him because he was a Frenchman
Attrib.

10 We are all American at puberty; we die French.

Evelyn Waugh (1903–66) British novelist.
Diaries, 'Irregular Notes', 18 July 1961

NATIONS

See also places

1 The day of small nations has long passed away. The day of Empires has come.

Joseph Chamberlain (1836–1914) British politician.
Speech, Birmingham, 12 May 1904

2 The nations which have put mankind and posterity most in their debt have been small states – Israel, Athens, Florence, Elizabethan England.

Dean Inge (1860–1954) British churchman.
Wit and Wisdom of Dean Inge (ed. Marchant)

3 This agglomeration which was called and which still calls itself the Holy Roman Empire was neither holy, nor Roman, nor an empire.

Voltaire (François-Marie Arouet; 1694–1778) French writer.
Essai sur les moeurs et l'esprit des nations, LXX

NATURE

See also animals, birds, countryside, ecology, flowers, human nature, science

1 All things are artificial, for nature is the art of God.

Thomas Browne (1605–82) English physician and writer.
Religio Medici, Pt. I

2 Ye banks and braes o' bonnie Doon,
How can ye bloom sae fresh and fair?

How can ye chant, ye little birds,
And I sae weary fu' o' care?
Robert Burns (1759–96) Scottish poet.
Ye Banks and Braes

3   There is a pleasure in the pathless woods,
There is a rapture on the lonely shore,
There is society, where none intrudes,
By the deep Sea, and music in its roar:
I love not Man the less, but Nature more.
Lord Byron (1788–1824) British poet.
Childe Harold's Pilgrimage, IV

4   Nature admits no lie.
Thomas Carlyle (1795–1881) Scottish historian and
essayist.
Latter-Day Pamphlets, 5

5   Is ditchwater dull? Naturalists with
microscopes have told me that it teems with
quiet fun.
G. K. Chesterton (1874–1936) British writer.
The Spice of Life

6   Nature is but a name for an effect
Whose cause is God.
William Cowper (1731–1800) British poet.
The Task

7   All my life through, the new sights of Nature
made me rejoice like a child.
Marie Curie (1867–1934) Polish chemist.
Pierre Curie

8   By viewing Nature, Nature's handmaid, art,
Makes mighty things from small beginnings
grow.
John Dryden (1631–1700) British poet and dramatist.
Annus Mirabilis

9   All Nature wears one universal grin.
Henry Fielding (1707–54) British novelist.
Tom Thumb the Great, I:1

10   Natural science does not simply describe and
explain nature, it is part of the interplay
between nature and ourselves.
Werner Heisenberg (1901–76) German physicist.
Physics and Philosophy

11   In nature there are neither rewards nor
punishments – there are consequences.
Robert G. Ingersoll (1833–99) US lawyer and agnostic.
Lectures & Essays, 'Some Reasons Why'

12   Nature is very consonant and conformable
with herself.
Isaac Newton (1642–1727) British scientist.
Opticks, Bk. III

13   It is far from easy to determine whether she
has proved a kind parent to man or a
merciless step-mother.
Pliny the Elder (Gaius Plinius Secundus; 23–79 AD)
Roman scholar.
Natural History, VII

14   Nature abhors a vacuum.
François Rabelais (1483–1553) French satirist.
Attrib.

15   Are God and Nature then at strife
That Nature lends such evil dreams?
So careful of the type she seems,
So careless of the single life.
Alfred, Lord Tennyson (1809–92) British poet.
In Memoriam A.H.H.

16   Nature is usually wrong.
James Whistler (1834–1903) US painter.
The Gentle Art of Making Enemies

17   After you have exhausted what there is in
business, politics, conviviality, and so on –
have found that none of these finally satisfy,
or permanently wear – what remains?
Nature remains.
Walt Whitman (1819–92) US poet.
Specimen Days, 'New Themes Entered Upon'

18   Nature never did betray
The heart that loved her.
William Wordsworth (1770–1850) British poet.
Lines composed a few miles above Tintern Abbey

19   Earth fills her lap with pleasures of her own:
Yearnings she hath in her own natural kind.
William Wordsworth
Ode. Intimations of Immortality, VI

20   Come forth into the light of things,
Let Nature be your Teacher.
William Wordsworth
The Tables Turned

21   Another race hath been, and other palms are
won.
Thanks to the human heart by which we live,
Thanks to its tenderness, its joys and fears,
To me the meanest flower that blows can give
Thoughts that do often lie too deep for tears.
William Wordsworth
Ode. Intimations of Immortality, IX

22   O chestnut tree, great rooted blossomer,
Are you the leaf, the blossom or the bole?
O body swayed to music; O brightening glance,
How can we know the dancer from the dance?
W. B. Yeats (1865–1939) Irish poet.
Among School Children

NAVY

See also boats, officers, sea, war

1   Ye Mariners of England
That guard our native seas,
Whose flag has braved, a thousand years,
The battle and the breeze –
Your glorious standard launch again
To match another foe!
And sweep through the deep,
While the stormy winds do blow, –
While the battle rages loud and long,
And the stormy winds do blow.
Thomas Campbell (1777–1844) British poet.
Ye Mariners of England

2 Don't talk to me about naval tradition. It's nothing but rum, sodomy, and the lash.
Winston Churchill (1874–1965) British statesman.
Former Naval Person (Sir Peter Gretton), Ch. 1

3 There were gentlemen and there were seamen in the navy of Charles the Second. But the seamen were not gentlemen; and the gentlemen were not seamen.
Lord Macaulay (1800–59) British historian.
History of England, Vol. I, Ch. 3

4 The Fleet's lit up. It is like fairyland; the ships are covered with fairy lights.
Thomas Woodroofe (1899–1978) British radio broadcaster.
Said during commentary at the Coronation Review of the Royal Navy, May 1937

NAZISM

See also fascism, Germany, Hitler, Jews, World War II

1 I herewith commission you to carry out all preparations with regard to ... a *total solution* of the Jewish question, in those territories of Europe which are under German influence.
Hermann Goering (1893–1946) German leader.
The Rise and Fall of the Third Reich (William Shirer)

2 *Kraft durch Freude.*
Strength through joy.
Robert Ley (1890–1945) German Nazi.
German Labour Front slogan

3 The former allies had blundered in the past by offering Germany too little, and offering even that too late, until finally Nazi Germany had become a menace to all mankind.
Allan Nevins (1890–1971) US historian.
Current History, May 1935

4 In Germany, the Nazis came for the Communists and I didn't speak up because I was not a Communist. Then they came for the Jews and I didn't speak up because I was not a Jew. Then they came for the trade unionists and I didn't speak up because I was not a trade unionist. Then they came for the Catholics and I was a Protestant so I didn't speak up. Then they came for me ... By that time there was no one to speak up for anyone.
Martin Niemöller (1892–1984) German pastor.
Concise Dictionary of Religious Quotations (W. Neil)

NECESSITY

1 Beggars can't be choosers.
Proverb

2 Necessity is the mother of invention.
Proverb

3 Needs must when the devil drives.
Proverb

4 Necessity is the plea for every infringement of human freedom. It is the argument of tyrants; it is the creed of slaves.
William Pitt the Younger (1759–1806) British statesman.
Speech, House of Commons, 18 Nov 1783

5 O, reason not the need! Our basest beggars Are in the poorest thing superfluous. Allow not nature more than nature needs, Man's life is cheap as beast's.
William Shakespeare (1564–1616) English dramatist.
King Lear, II:4

6 Teach thy necessity to reason thus: There is no virtue like necessity.
William Shakespeare
Richard II, I:3

7 Necessity knows no law.
Publilius Syrus (1st century BC) Roman dramatist.
Attrib.

8 I find no hint throughout the universe Of good or ill, of blessing or of curse; I find alone Necessity Supreme.
James Thomson (1834–82) British poet.
The City of Dreadful Night, XIV

NEGLECT

1 A little neglect may breed mischief, ... for want of a nail, the shoe was lost; for want of a shoe the horse was lost; and for want of a horse the rider was lost.
Benjamin Franklin (1706–90) US scientist and statesman.
Poor Richard's Almanack

2 The general idea, of course, in any first-class laundry is to see that no shirt or collar ever comes back twice.
Stephen Leacock (1869–1944) English-born Canadian economist and humorist.
Winnowed Wisdom, Ch. 6

3 The dust and silence of the upper shelf.
Lord Macaulay (1800–59) British historian.
Literary Essays Contributed to the 'Edinburgh Review', 'Milton'

4 What time he can spare from the adornment of his person he devotes to the neglect of his duties.
William Hepworth Thompson (1810–86) British academic.
Referring to the Cambridge Professor of Greek, Sir Richard Jebb
With Dearest Love to All (M. R. Bobbit), Ch. 7

NEIGHBOURS

1 Love your neighbour, yet pull not down your hedge.
Proverb

2 Thou shalt love thy neighbour as thy self.
Bible: Matthew
22:39

3 My apple trees will never get across

And eat the cones under his pines, I tell him.
He only says, 'Good fences make good
neighbours.'
Robert Frost (1875–1963) US poet.
North of Boston, 'Mending Wall'

4 For it is your business, when the wall next
door catches fire.
Horace (Quintus Horatius Flaccus; 65–8 BC) Roman poet.
Epistles, I

NEPOTISM

1 I am against government by crony.
Harold L. Ickes (1874–1952) US Republican politician.
Comment on his resignation as Secretary of the Interior (1946)
after a dispute with President Truman

2 I can't see that it's wrong to give him a little
legal experience before he goes out to
practice law.
John Fitzgerald Kennedy (1917–63) US statesman.
On being criticized for making his brother Robert attorney
general
Nobody Said It Better (M. Ringo)

NEUROSIS

See also psychiatry, psychology

1 Neurosis has an absolute genius for
malingering. There is no illness which it
cannot counterfeit perfectly . . . If it is capable
of deceiving the doctor, how should it fail to
deceive the patient?
Marcel Proust (1871–1922) French novelist.
À la recherche du temps perdu: Le Côté de Guermantes

2 Everything great in the world is done by
neurotics; they alone founded our religions
and created our masterpieces.
Marcel Proust
The Perpetual Pessimist (Sagittarius and George)

3 Neurosis is the way of avoiding non-being by
avoiding being.
Paul Tillich (1886–1965) German-born US theologian.
The Courage to Be

NEWSPAPERS

See also editors, journalism

1 *The Times* has made many ministries.
Walter Bagehot (1826–77) British economist and
journalist.
The English Constitution, 'The Cabinet'

2 Deleted by French censor.
James Gordon Bennett (1841–1918) US newspaper
owner and editor.
Used to fill empty spaces in his papers during World War I
when news was lacking
Americans in Paris (B. Morton)

3 Price of Herald three cents daily. Five cents
Sunday. Bennett.
James Gordon Bennett
Telegram to William Randolph Hearst, when he heard that
Hearst was trying to buy his paper
The Life and Death of the Press Barons (P. Brandon)

4 Reading someone else's newspaper is like
sleeping with someone else's wife. Nothing
seems to be precisely in the right place, and
when you find what you are looking for, it is
not clear then how to respond to it.
Malcolm Bradbury (1932–) British academic and
novelist.
Stepping Westward, Bk. I, Ch. 1

5 *The Times* is speechless and takes three
columns to express its speechlessness.
Winston Churchill (1874–1965) British statesman.
Referring to Irish Home Rule
Speech, Dundee, 14 May 1908

6 I believe it has been said that one copy of
The Times contains more useful information
than the whole of the historical works of
Thucydides.
Richard Cobden (1804–65) British politician.
Speech, Manchester, 27 Dec 1850

7 Nothing is news until it has appeared in *The
Times*.
Ralph Deakin (1888–1952) Foreign News Editor of *The
Times*.
Attrib.

8 All the news that's fit to print.
Adolph Simon Ochs (1858–1935) US newspaper
publisher.
The motto of the *New York Times*

9 Well, there are only two posh papers on a
Sunday – the one you're reading and this
one.
John Osborne (1929–) British dramatist.
Look Back in Anger, I

10 Written by office boys for office boys.
Marquess of Salisbury (1830–1903) British statesman.
Reaction to the launch of the *Daily Mail*, 1896
Northcliffe, an Intimate Biography (Hamilton Fyfe), Ch. 4

11 The *Pall Mall Gazette* is written by
gentlemen for gentlemen.
William Makepeace Thackeray (1811–63) British
novelist.
Pendennis, Ch. 32

12 'The *Beast* stands for strong mutually
antagonistic governments everywhere', he
said. 'Self-sufficiency at home, self-assertion
abroad.'
Evelyn Waugh (1903–66) British novelist.
Scoop, Bk. I, Ch. 1

13 News is what a chap who doesn't care much
about anything wants to read. And it's only
news until he's read it. After that it's dead.
Evelyn Waugh
Scoop, Bk. I, Ch. 5

14 They were not so much published as carried screaming into the street.
H. G. Wells (1866–1946) British writer.
War In the Air

NOBILITY

See also aristocracy, honour

1 There is surely a piece of divinity in us, something that was before the elements, and owes no homage unto the sun.
Thomas Browne (1605–82) English physician and writer.
Religio Medici, Pt. II

2 *Noblesse oblige.*
Nobility has its own obligations.
Duc de Lévis (1764–1830) French writer and soldier.
Maximes et Réflexions

3 The high sentiments always win in the end, the leaders who offer blood, toil, tears and sweat always get more out of their followers than those who offer safety and a good time. When it comes to the pinch, human beings are heroic.
George Orwell (Eric Blair; 1903–50) British novelist.
The Art of Donald McGill

4 This was the noblest Roman of them all. All the conspirators save only he Did that they did in envy of great Caesar.
William Shakespeare (1564–1616) English dramatist.
Julius Caesar, V:5

5 His life was gentle, and the elements So mixed in him that Nature might stand up And say to all the world, 'This was a man!'
William Shakespeare
Julius Caesar, V:5

6 There is
One great society alone on earth: The noble living and the noble dead.
William Wordsworth (1770–1850) British poet.
The Prelude, XI

7 Thy soul was like a star, and dwelt apart.
William Wordsworth
Sonnets, 'Milton! thou shouldst'

NONCOMMITMENT

1 We know what happens to people who stay in the middle of the road. They get run over.
Aneurin Bevan (1897–1960) British Labour politician.
The Observer, 'Sayings of the Week', 9 Dec 1953

2 Let them eat the lie and swallow it with their bread. Whether the two were lovers or no, they'll have accounted to God for it by now. I have my own fish to fry.
Miguel de Cervantes (1547–1616) Spanish novelist.
Don Quixote, Pt. I, Ch. 25

3 The Right Hon. gentleman has sat so long on the fence that the iron has entered his soul.
David Lloyd George (1863–1945) British Liberal statesman.
Referring to Sir John Simon
Attrib.

NONSENSE

See also humour

1 If all the world were paper, And all the sea were ink, And all the trees were bread and cheese, What should we do for drink?
Anonymous
If All the World were Paper

2 If ever there was a case of clearer evidence than this of persons acting in concert together, this case is that case.
William Arabin (1773–1841) British judge.
Arabinesque at Law (Sir R. Megarry)

3 The fleas that tease in the high Pyrenees.
Hilaire Belloc (1870–1953) French-born British poet.
Tarantella

4 What happens to the hole when the cheese is gone?
Bertolt Brecht (1898–1956) German dramatist.
Mother Courage, VI

5 Twinkle, twinkle, little bat! How I wonder what you're at! Up above the world you fly! Like a teatray in the sky.
Lewis Carroll (Charles Lutwidge Dodgson; 1832–98) British writer.
Alice's Adventures in Wonderland, Ch. 7

6 For the Snark *was* a Boojum, you see.
Lewis Carroll
The Hunting of the Snark

7 'Twas brillig, and the slithy toves Did gyre and gimble in the wabe; All mimsy were the borogoves, And the mome raths outgrabe.
Lewis Carroll
Through the Looking-Glass, Ch. 1

8 Now, *here,* you see, it takes all the running *you* can do, to keep in the same place. If you want to get somewhere else, you must run at least twice as fast as that!
Lewis Carroll
Through the Looking-Glass, Ch. 2

9 'The time has come,' the Walrus said, 'To talk of many things: Of shoes – and ships – and sealing-wax – Of cabbages – and kings – And why the sea is boiling hot – And whether pigs have wings.'
Lewis Carroll
Through the Looking-Glass, Ch. 4

10 Colourless green ideas sleep furiously.
Noam Chomsky (1928–) US academic linguist.
Used by Chomsky to demonstrate that an utterance can be
grammatical without having meaning
Syntactic Structures

11 Go, and catch a falling star,
Get with child a mandrake root,
Tell me, where all past years are,
Or who cleft the Devil's foot.
John Donne (1573–1631) English poet.
Go and Catch a Falling Star

12 So she went into the garden to cut a
cabbage-leaf; to make an apple-pie; and at
the same time a great she-bear, coming up
the street, pops its head into the shop.
'What! no soap?' So he died, and she very
imprudently married the barber; and there
were present the Picninnies, and the
Joblillies, and the Garyalies, and the grand
Panjandrum himself, with the little round
button at top, and they all fell to playing the
game of catch as catch can, till the gun
powder ran out at the heels of their boots.
Samuel Foote (1720–77) British actor and dramatist.
Nonsense composed to test the actor Charles Macklin's claim
that he could memorize anything

13 If the man who turnips cries,
Cry not when his father dies,
'Tis a proof that he had rather
Have a turnip than his father.
Samuel Johnson (1709–84) British lexicographer.
Johnsonian Miscellanies (ed. G. B. Hill), Vol. I

14 Three quarks for Muster Mark!
James Joyce (1882–1941) Irish novelist.
The word quark has since been adopted by physicists for hypo-
thetical elementary particles
Finnegans Wake

15 Lord Ronald said nothing; he flung himself
from the room, flung himself upon his horse
and rode madly off in all directions.
Stephen Leacock (1869–1944) English-born Canadian
economist and humorist.
Nonsense Novels, 'Gertrude the Governess'

16 On the Coast of Coromandel
Where the early pumpkins blow,
In the middle of the woods
Lived the Yonghy-Bonghy-Bò.
Edward Lear (1812–88) British artist and writer.
The Courtship of the Yonghy-Bonghy-Bò

17 The Dong! – the Dong!
The wandering Dong through the forest goes!
The Dong! – the Dong!
The Dong with a luminous Nose!
Edward Lear
The Dong with a Luminous Nose

18 Far and few, far and few,
Are the lands where the Jumblies live;
Their heads are green, and their hands are
blue,

And they went to sea in a sieve.
Edward Lear
The Jumblies

19 He has many friends, laymen and clerical.
Old Foss is the name of his cat:
His body is perfectly spherical,
He weareth a runcible hat.
Edward Lear
Nonsense Songs, preface

20 The Owl and the Pussy-Cat went to sea
In a beautiful pea-green boat,
They took some honey, and plenty of money,
Wrapped up in a five-pound note.
Edward Lear
The Owl and the Pussy-Cat

21 Serve up in a clean dish, and throw the
whole out of the window as fast as possible.
Edward Lear
To make an Amblongus Pie

22 As I was going up the stair
I met a man who wasn't there.
He wasn't there again to-day.
I wish, I wish he'd stay away.
Hughes Mearns (1875–1965) US writer.
The Psychoed

23 I'm walking backwards till Christmas.
Spike Milligan (1918–) British comic actor and author.
The Goon Show

NORMALITY

1 She always says she dislikes the abnormal, it
is so obvious. She says the normal is so
much more simply complicated and
interesting.
Gertrude Stein (1874–1946) US writer.
The Autobiography of Alice B. Toklas

2 My suit is pale yellow. My nationality is
French, and my normality has been often
subject to question.
Tennessee Williams (1911–83) US dramatist.
Camino Real, Block 4

NOSTALGIA

See also homesickness, memory, past, regret

1 Were we closer to the ground as children, or
is the grass emptier now?
Alan Bennett (1934–) British playwright.
Forty Years On

2 Play it, Sam. Play 'As Time Goes By.'
Humphrey Bogart (1899–1957) US film star.
Often misquoted as 'Play it again, Sam'
Casablanca

3 Stands the Church clock at ten to three?
And is there honey still for tea?
Rupert Brooke (1887–1915) British poet.
The Old Vicarage, Grantchester

4 John Anderson my jo, John,

When we were first acquent,
Your locks were like the raven,
Your bonnie brow was brent.
Robert Burns (1759–96) Scottish poet.
John Anderson My Jo

5 The 'good old times' – all times when old
are good –
Are gone.
Lord Byron (1788–1824) British poet.
The Age of Bronze, I

6 Nothing recalls the past so potently as a
smell.
Winston Churchill (1874–1965) British statesman.
My Early Life

7 What peaceful hours I once enjoyed!
How sweet their memory still!
But they have left an aching void
The world can never fill.
William Cowper (1731–1800) British poet.
Olney Hymns, 1

8 I'm sitting on the stile, Mary,
Where we sat, side by side.
Countess of Dufferin (1807–67) British poet.
Lament of the Irish Emigrant

9 I remember, I remember,
The house where I was born,
The little window where the sun
Came peeping in at morn;
He never came a wink too soon,
Nor brought too long a day,
But now, I often wish the night
Had borne my breath away!
Thomas Hood (1799–1845) British poet.
I Remember

10 Into my heart an air that kills
From yon far country blows:
What are those blue remembered hills,
What spires, what farms are those?
A. E. Housman (1859–1936) British scholar and poet.
A Shropshire Lad, 'The Welsh Marches'

11 With rue my heart is laden
For golden friends I had,
For many a rose-lipt maiden
And many a lightfoot lad.
A. E. Housman
A Shropshire Lad, 'The Welsh Marches'

12 I have had playmates, I have had companions
In my days of childhood, in my joyful school-
days –
All, all are gone, the old familiar faces.
Charles Lamb (1775–1834) British essayist.
The Old Familiar Faces

13 For love that time was not as love is
nowadays.
Thomas Malory (1400–71) English writer.
Morte d'Arthur, Bk. XX, Ch. 3

14 Oft in the stilly night,
Ere Slumber's chain has bound me,

Fond Memory brings the light
Of other days around me;
The smiles, the tears,
Of boyhood's years,
The words of love then spoken;
The eyes that shone,
Now dimmed and gone,
The cheerful hearts now broken!
Thomas Moore (1779–1852) Irish poet.
National Airs, 'Oft in the Stilly Night'

15 Fings Ain't Wot They Used T'Be.
Frank Norman (1931–80) British dramatist and
broadcaster.
Title of musical

16 Before the war, and especially before the
Boer War, it was summer all the year round.
George Orwell (Eric Blair; 1903–50) British novelist.
Coming Up for Air, Pt. II, Ch. 1

17 They spend their time mostly looking forward
to the past.
John Osborne (1929–) British dramatist.
Look Back in Anger, II:1

18 Come to me in the silence of the night;
Come in the speaking silence of a dream;
Come with soft rounded cheeks and eyes as
bright
As sunlight on a stream;
Come back in tears,
O memory, hope, love of finished years.
Christina Rossetti (1830–74) British poet.
Echo

19 For now I see the true old times are dead,
When every morning brought a noble chance,
And every chance brought out a noble knight.
Alfred, Lord Tennyson (1809–92) British poet.
Idylls of the King, 'The Passing of Arthur'

20 Dear as remembered kisses after death,
And sweet as those by hopeless fancy feign'd
On lips that are for others: deep as love,
Deep as first love, and wild with all regret;
O Death in Life, the days that are no more.
Alfred, Lord Tennyson
The Princess, IV

21 And the stately ships go on
To their haven under the hill;
But O for the touch of a vanish'd hand,
And the sound of a voice that is still!
Alfred, Lord Tennyson
Break, Break, Break

22 *Mais où sont les neiges d'antan?*
But where are the snows of yesteryear?
François Villon (1431–85) French poet.
Ballade des dames du temps jadis

23 Where are the boys of the Old Brigade?
Frederic Edward Weatherly (1848–1929) British lawyer
and songwriter.
The Old Brigade

24 Sweet childish days, that were as long

As twenty days are now.
William Wordsworth (1770–1850) British poet.
To a Butterfly, I've Watched you now

NOTHING

1 Nothing can be created out of nothing.
Lucretius (Titus Lucretius Carus; c. 99–55 BC) Roman philosopher.
On the Nature of the Universe, I

2 Nothing will come of nothing. Speak again.
William Shakespeare (1564–1616) English dramatist.
King Lear, I:1

NOVELS

See also books, criticism, fiction, literature, writers, writing

1 My scrofulous French novel
On grey paper with blunt type!
Robert Browning (1812–89) British poet.
Soliloquy of the Spanish Cloister

2 A good novel tells us the truth about its hero; but a bad novel tells us the truth about its author.
G. K. Chesterton (1874–1936) British writer.
Heretics, Ch. 15

3 When I want to read a novel I write one.
Benjamin Disraeli (1804–81) British statesman.
Attrib.

4 Yes – oh dear, yes – the novel tells a story.
E. M. Forster (1879–1970) British novelist.
Aspects of the Novel, Ch. 2

5 The romance of *Tom Jones*, that exquisite picture of human manners, will outlive the palace of the Escurial and the imperial eagle of the house of Austria.
Edward Gibbon (1737–94) British historian.
Autobiography

6 Historians tell the story of the past, novelists the story of the present.
Edmond de Goncourt (1822–96) French novelist.
Journal

7 The only obligation to which in advance we may hold a novel, without incurring the accusation of being arbitrary, is that it be interesting.
Henry James (1843–1916) US novelist.
Partial Portraits, 'The Art of Fiction'

8 Far too many relied on the classic formula of a beginning, a muddle, and an end.
Philip Larkin (1922–85) British poet.
Referring to modern novels
New Fiction, 15 (January 1978)

9 I am a man, and alive . . . For this reason I am a novelist. And being a novelist, I consider myself superior to the saint, the scientist, the philosopher, and the poet, who are all great masters of different bits of man alive, but never get the whole hog.
D. H. Lawrence (1885–1930) British novelist.
Phoenix, 'Why the Novel Matters'

10 I would sooner read a time-table or a catalogue than nothing at all. They are much more entertaining than half the novels that are written.
W. Somerset Maugham (1874–1965) British novelist.
The Summing Up

11 An interviewer asked me what book I thought best represented the modern American woman. All I could think of to answer was: *Madame Bovary*.
Mary McCarthy (1912–89) US novelist.
On the Contrary

12 People think that because a novel's invented, it isn't true. Exactly the reverse is the case. Biography and memoirs can never be wholly true, since they cannot include every conceivable circumstance of what happened. The novel can do that.
Anthony Powell (1905–) British novelist.
A Dance to the Music of Time: Hearing Secret Harmonies, Ch. 3

13 The detective novel is the art-for-art's-sake of yawning Philistinism.
V. S. Pritchett (1900–) British short-story writer.
Books in General, 'The Roots of Detection'

14 It is the sexless novel that should be distinguished: the sex novel is now normal.
George Bernard Shaw (1856–1950) Irish dramatist and critic.
Table-Talk of G.B.S.

15 A novel is a mirror walking along a main road.
Stendhal (Henri Beyle; 1783–1842) French novelist.
Le Rouge et le noir, Ch. 49

16 A novel is a static thing that one moves through; a play is a dynamic thing that moves past one.
Kenneth Tynan (1927–80) British theatre critic.
Curtains

17 The novel being dead, there is no point to writing made-up stories. Look at the French who will not and the Americans who cannot.
Gore Vidal (1925–) US novelist.
Myra Breckinridge, Ch. 2

NOVELTY

See also conservatism, innovation, progress

1 All the rivers run into the sea; yet the sea is not full; unto the place from whence the rivers come, thither they return again.
All things are full of labour; man cannot utter it: the eye is not satisfied with seeing, nor the ear filled with hearing.
The thing that hath been, it is that which shall be; and that which is done is that which shall

be done: and there is no new thing under the sun.
Bible: Ecclesiastes
1:7–9

2 Most of the change we think we see in life
Is due to truths being in and out of favour.
Robert Frost (1875–1963) US poet.
The Black Cottage

3 There are three things which the public will always clamour for, sooner or later: namely, Novelty, novelty, novelty.
Thomas Hood (1799–1845) British poet.
Announcement of *Comic Annual*, 1836

4 It is the customary fate of new truths to begin as heresies and to end as superstitions.
T. H. Huxley (1825–95) British biologist.
The Coming of Age of the Origin of Species

5 New opinions are always suspected, and usually opposed, without any other reason but because they are not already common.
John Locke (1632–1704) English philosopher.
An Essay Concerning Human Understanding, dedicatory epistle

6 Rummidge . . . had lately suffered the mortifying fate of most English universities of its type (civic redbrick): having competed strenuously for fifty years with two universities chiefly valued for being old, it was, at the moment of drawing level, rudely overtaken in popularity and prestige by a batch of universities chiefly valued for being new.
David Lodge (1935–) British author.
Changing Places, Ch. 1

7 There are no new truths, but only truths that have not been recognized by those who have perceived them without noticing.
Mary McCarthy (1912–89) US novelist.
On the Contrary

8 There is always something new out of Africa.
Pliny the Elder (Gaius Plinius Secundus; 23–79 AD) Roman scholar.
Natural History, VIII

9 All great truths begin as blasphemies.
George Bernard Shaw (1856–1950) Irish dramatist and critic.
Annajanska

10 If we do not find anything pleasant, at least we shall find something new.
Voltaire (François-Marie Arouet; 1694–1778) French writer.
Candide, Ch. 17

NUCLEAR WEAPONS

See also weapons

1 Now we are all sons of bitches.
Kenneth Bainbridge (1904–) US physicist.
After the first atomic test
The Decision to Drop the Bomb

2 If you carry this resolution and follow out all its implications and do not run away from it you will send a Foreign Minister, whoever he may be, naked into the conference chamber.
Aneurin Bevan (1897–1960) British Labour politician.
Opposing a motion advocating unilateral nuclear disarmament
Speech, Labour Party Conference, 3 Oct 1957

3 The way to win an atomic war is to make certain it never starts.
Omar Nelson Bradley (1893–1981) US general.
The Observer, 'Sayings of the Week', 20 Apr 1952

4 The Bomb brought peace but man alone can keep that peace.
Winston Churchill (1874–1965) British statesman.
Speech, House of Commons, 16 Aug 1945

5 If only I had known, I should have become a watchmaker.
Albert Einstein (1879–1955) German-born US physicist.
Reflecting on his role in the development of the atom bomb
New Statesman, 16 Apr 1965

6 Surely the right course is to test the Russians, not the bombs.
Hugh Gaitskell (1906–63) British Labour politician.
Observer, 'Sayings of the Week', 23 June 1957

7 We thus denounce the false and dangerous programme of the arms race, of the secret rivalry between peoples for military superiority.
John Paul II (Karol Wojtyla; 1920–) Polish pope (1978–).
The Observer, 'Sayings of the Week', 19 Dec 1976

8 Preparing for suicide is not a very intelligent means of defence.
Bruce Kent (1929–) British campaigner for nuclear disarmament
The Observer, 'Sayings of the Week', 10 Aug 1986

9 Hitherto man had to live with the idea of death as an individual; from now onward mankind will have to live with the idea of its death as a species.
Arthur Koestler (1905–83) Hungarian-born British writer.
Referring to the development of the atomic bomb
Peter's Quotations (Laurence J. Peter)

10 The statesmen of the world who boast and threaten that they have Doomsday weapons are far more dangerous, and far more estranged from 'reality', than many of the people on whom the label 'psychotic' is affixed.
R. D. Laing (1927–89) British psychiatrist.
The Divided Self, Preface

11 At first it was a giant column that soon took the shape of a supramundane mushroom.
William L. Laurence (1888–1977) US journalist.
Referring to the explosion of the first atomic bomb, over Hiroshima, 6 Aug 1945
The New York Times, 26 Sept 1945

12 The atom bomb is a paper tiger which the

United States reactionaries use to scare
people.
Mao Tse-Tung (1893–1976) Chinese communist leader.
Interview, Aug 1946

13 As a military man who has given half a
century of active service, I say in all sincerity
that the nuclear arms race has no military
purpose. Wars cannot be fought with nuclear
weapons; their existence only adds to our
perils because of the illusions which they
have generated.
Louis Mountbatten of Burma (1900–79) British admiral
and colonial administrator.
Speech, Strasbourg, 11 May 1979

14 We knew the world would not be the same.
J. Robert Oppenheimer (1904–67) US physicist.
After the first atomic test
The Decision to Drop the Bomb

15 It was on this issue, the nuclear defence of
Britain, on which I left the Labour Party, and
on this issue I am prepared to stake my
entire political career.
David Owen (1938–) British politician.
The Observer, 'Sayings of the Week', 9 Nov 1986

16 To adopt nuclear disarmament would be akin
to behaving like a virgin in a brothel.
David Penhaligon (1944–86) British politician.
The Guardian, 1980

17 You may reasonably expect a man to walk a
tightrope safely for ten minutes; it would be
unreasonable to do so without accident for
two hundred years.
Bertrand Russell (1872–1970) British philosopher.
On the subject of nuclear war between the USA and the
Soviets
The Tightrope Men (D. Bagley)

18 There is no evil in the atom; only in men's
souls.
Adlai Stevenson (1900–65) US statesman.
Speech, Hartford, Connecticut, 18 Sept 1952

19 For Hon. Members opposite the deterrent is
a phallic symbol. It convinces them that they
are men.
George Wigg (1900–76) British politician.
The Observer, 'Sayings of the Week', 8 Mar 1964

NUMBERS

See also mathematics, statistics

1 Round numbers are always false.
Samuel Johnson (1709–84) British lexicographer.
Life of Johnson (J. Boswell), Vol. III

2 No, I don't know his telephone number. But
it was up in the high numbers.
John Maynard Keynes (1883–1946) British economist.
Attrib.

3 No, it is a very interesting number, it is the
smallest number expressible as a sum of two
cubes in two different ways.
Srinivasa Ramanujan (1887–1920) Indian mathematician.
The mathematician G. H. Hardy had referred to the number –
1729 as 'dull'
Collected Papers of Srinivasa Ramanujan

4 Oh, quite easy! The Septuagint minus the
Apostles.
Arthur Woollgar Verrall (1851–1912) British classicist.
Reply to a person who thought the number 58 difficult to
remember

NURSERY RHYMES

A selection is given here. The form used is that most commonly used today – not the one in the original publication.

1 A frog he would a-wooing go,
Heigh ho! says Rowley,
A frog he would a-wooing go,
Whether his mother would let him or no.
With a rowley, powley, gammon and spinach,
Heigh ho! says Anthony Rowley.
Melismata (Thomas Ravenscroft)

2 All the birds of the air
Fell a-sighing and a-sobbing,
When they heard the bell toll
For poor Cock Robin.
Tommy Thumb's Pretty Song Book

3 As I was going to St Ives,
I met a man with seven wives.
Each wife had seven sacks
Each sack had seven cats,
Each cat had seven kits,
How many were going to St Ives?
Mother Goose's Quarto

4 Baa, baa, black sheep,
Have you any wool?
Yes, sir, yes, sir,
Three bags full;
One for the master,
And one for the dame,
And one for the little boy
Who lives down the lane.
Tommy Thumb's Pretty Song Book

5 Bobby Shafto's gone to sea,
Silver buckles on his knee;
He'll come back and marry me,
Bonny Bobby Shafto!
Songs for the Nursery

6 Boys and girls come out to play,
The moon doth shine as bright as day.
Useful Transactions in Philosophy (William King)

7 Come, let's to bed
Says Sleepy-head;
Tarry a while, says Slow;
Put on the pan;
Says Greedy Nan,
Let's sup before we go.
Gammer Gurton's Garland (R. Christopher)

8 Curly locks, Curly locks,
Wilt thou be mine?
Thou shalt not wash dishes
Nor yet feed the swine,
But sit on a cushion
And sew a fine seam,
And feed upon strawberries,
Sugar and cream
Infant Institutes

9 Ding dong, bell,
Pussy's in the well.
Who put her in?
Little Johnny Green.
Who pulled her out?
Little Tommy Stout.
Mother Goose's Melody

10 Doctor Foster went to Gloucester
In a shower of rain:
He stepped in a puddle,
Right up to his middle,
And never went there again.
The Nursery Rhymes of England (J. O. Halliwell)

11 Eena, meena, mina, mo,
Catch a nigger by his toe;
If he hollers, let him go,
Eena, meena, mina, mo.
Games and Songs of American Children (Newell)

12 Georgie Porgie, pudding and pie,
Kissed the girls and made them cry;
When the boys came out to play,
Georgie Porgie ran away.
The Nursery Rhymes of England (J. O. Halliwell)

13 Goosey, goosey gander,
Whither shall I wander?
Upstairs and downstairs
And in my lady's chamber.
Gammer Gurton' Garland

14 Hey diddle diddle,
The cat and the fiddle,
The cow jumped over the moon;
The little dog laughed
To see such sport,
And the dish ran away with the spoon.
Mother Goose's Melody

15 Hickory, dickory, dock,
The mouse ran up the clock.
The clock struck one,
The mouse ran down,
Hickory, dickory, dock.
Tommy Thumb's Pretty Song Book

16 Hot cross buns!
Hot cross buns!
One a penny, two a penny,
Hot cross buns!
Christmas Box

17 How many miles to Babylon?
Three score miles and ten.
Can I get there by candle-light?

Yes, and back again.
If your heels are nimble and light,
You may get there by candle-light.
Songs for the Nursery

18 Humpty Dumpty sat on a wall,
Humpty Dumpty had a great fall.
All the king's horses,
And all the king's men,
Couldn't put Humpty together again.
Gammer Gurton's Garland

19 Hush-a-bye, baby, on the tree top,
When the wind blows the cradle will rock;
When the bough breaks the cradle will fall,
Down will come baby, cradle, and all.
Mother Goose's Melody

20 I had a little nut tree,
Nothing would it bear
But a silver nutmeg
And a golden pear;
The King of Spain's daughter
Came to visit me,
And all for the sake
Of my little nut tree.
Newest Christmas Box

21 I had a little pony,
His name was Dapple Grey;
I lent him to a lady
To ride a mile away.
She whipped him, she lashed him,
She rode him through the mire;
I would not lend my pony now,
For all the lady's hire.
Poetical Alphabet

22 I love sixpence, jolly little sixpence,
I love sixpence better than my life;
I spent a penny of it, I lent a penny of it,
And I took fourpence home to my wife.
Gammer Gurton's Garland

23 I'm the king of the castle,
Get down you dirty rascal.
Brand's Popular Antiquities

24 Jack and Jill went up the hill
To fetch a pail of water;
Jack fell down and broke his crown,
And Jill came tumbling after.
Mother Goose's Melody

25 Jack Sprat could eat no fat,
His wife could eat no lean,
And so between them both you see,
They licked the platter clean.
Paroemiologia Anglo-Latina (John Clark)

26 Ladybird, ladybird,
Fly away home,
Your house is on fire
And your children all gone.
Tommy Thumb's Pretty Song Book

27 Little Bo-peep has lost her sheep,
And can't tell where to find them;

Leave them alone, and they'll come home,
Bringing their tails behind them.
Gammer Gurton's Garland

28 Little Boy Blue,
Come blow your horn,
The sheep's in the meadow,
The cow's in the corn.
Famous Tommy Thumb's Little Story Book

29 Little Jack Horner
Sat in the corner,
Eating a Christmas pie;
He put in his thumb,
And pulled out a plum,
And said, What a good boy am I!
Namby Pamby (Henry Carey)

30 Little Miss Muffet
Sat on a tuffet,
Eating her curds and whey;
There came a big spider,
Who sat down beside her
And frightened Miss Muffet away.
Songs for the Nursery

31 Little Tommy Tucker,
Sings for his supper:
What shall we give him?
White bread and butter
How shall he cut it
Without a knife?
How will be be married
Without a wife?
Tommy Thumb's Pretty Song Book

32 London Bridge is falling down,
My fair lady.
Namby Pamby (Henry Carey)

33 Mary, Mary, quite contrary,
How does your garden grow?
With silver bells and cockle shells,
And pretty maids all in a row.
Tom Thumb's Pretty Song Book

34 Monday's child is fair of face,
Tuesday's child is full of grace,
Wednesday's child is full of woe,
Thursday's child has far to go,
Friday's child is loving and giving,
Saturday's child works hard for his living,
And the child that is born on the Sabbath day
Is bonny and blithe, and good and gay.
Traditions of Devonshire (A. E. Bray)

35 My mother said that I never should
Play with the gypsies in the wood;
If I did, she would say,
Naughty girl to disobey.
Come Hither (Walter de la Mare)

36 Old Mother Hubbard
Went to the cupboard,
To fetch her poor dog a bone;
But when she got there
The cupboard was bare

And so the poor dog had none.
The Comic Adventures of Old Mother Hubbard and Her Dog

37 One, two,
Buckle my shoe;
Three, four,
Knock at the door.
Songs for the Nursery

38 Pat-a-cake, pat-a-cake, baker's man,
Bake me a cake as fast as you can;
Pat it and prick it, and mark it with B,
Put it in the oven for baby and me.
The Campaigners (Tom D'Urfey)

39 Peter Piper picked a peck of pickled pepper;
A peck of pickled pepper Peter Piper picked;
If Peter Piper picked a peck of pickled pepper,
Where's the peck of pickled pepper Peter Piper picked?
Peter Piper's Practical Principles of Plain and Perfect Pronunciation

40 Polly put the kettle on,
Polly put the kettle on,
Polly put the kettle on,
We'll all have tea.
Sukey take it off again,
Sukey take it off again,
Sukey take it off again,
They've all gone away.
Traditional

41 Pussy cat, pussy cat, where have you been?
I've been to London to look at the queen.
Pussy cat, pussy cat, what did you there?
I frightened a little mouse under her chair.
Songs for the Nursery

42 Ride a cock-horse to Banbury Cross,
To see a fine lady upon a white horse;
Rings on her fingers and bells on her toes,
And she shall have music wherever she goes.
Gammer Gurton's Garland

43 Ring-a-ring o'roses,
A pocket full of posies,
A-tishoo! A-tishoo!
We all fall down.
Mother Goose (Kate Greenaway)

44 Round and round the garden
Like a teddy bear;
One step, two step,
Tickle you under there!
Traditional

45 Rub-a-dub-dub,
Three men in a tub,
And who do you think they be?
The butcher, the baker,
The candlestick-maker,
And they all sailed out to sea.
Christmas Box

46 See-saw, Margery Daw,
Jacky shall have a new master;
Jacky shall have but a penny a day,

Because he can't work any faster.
Mother Goose's Melody

47 Simple Simon met a pieman,
Going to the fair;
Says Simple Simon to the pieman,
Let me taste your ware.
Says the pieman to Simple Simon,
Show me first your penny;
Says Simple Simon to the pieman,
Indeed I have not any.
Simple Simon (Chapbook Advertisement)

48 Sing a song of sixpence,
A pocket full of rye;
Four and twenty blackbirds,
Baked in a pie.
When the pie was opened,
The birds began to sing;
Wasn't that a dainty dish,
To set before the king? The king was in his
counting-house,
Counting out his money;
The queen was in the parlour,
Eating bread and honey.
The maid was in the garden,
Hanging out the clothes,
When down came a blackbird,
And pecked off her nose.
Tommy Thumb's Pretty Song Book

49 Solomon Grundy,
Born on a Monday,
Christened on Tuesday,
Married on Wednesday,
Took ill on Thursday,
Worse on Friday,
Died on Saturday,
Buried on Sunday.
This is the end
Of Solomon Grundy.
The Nursery Rhymes of England (J. O. Halliwell)

50 The lion and the unicorn
Were fighting for the crown;
The lion beat the unicorn
All round about the town.
Useful Transactions in Philosophy (William King)

51 The Queen of Hearts
She made some tarts,
All on a summer's day;
The Knave of Hearts
He stole the tarts,
And took them clean away.
The European Magazine

52 There was a crooked man, and he walked a
crooked mile,
He found a crooked sixpence against a crooked
stile:
He bought a crooked cat, which caught a
crooked mouse,
And they all lived together in a little crooked
house.
The Nursery Rhymes of England (J. O. Halliwell)

53 There was an old woman
Lived under a hill,
And if she's not gone
She lives there still.
Academy of Complements

54 There was an old woman who lived in a
shoe,
She had so many children she didn't know what
to do;
She gave them some broth without any bread;
She whipped them all soundly and put them to
bed.
Gammer Gurton's Garland

55 The twelfth day of Christmas,
My true love sent to me
Twelve lords a-leaping,
Eleven ladies dancing,
Ten pipers piping,
Nine drummers drumming,
Eight maids a-milking,
Seven swans a-swimming,
Six geese a-laying,
Five gold rings,
Four colly birds,
Three French hens,
Two turtle doves, and
A partridge in a pear tree.
Mirth without Mischief

56 Thirty days hath September,
April, June, and November;
All the rest have thirty-one,
Excepting February alone
And that has twenty-eight days clear
And twenty-nine in each leap year.
Abridgement of the Chronicles of England (Richard Grafton)

57 This is the farmer sowing his corn,
That kept the cock that crowed in the morn,
That waked the priest all shaven and shorn,
That married the man all tattered and torn,
That kissed the maiden all forlorn,
That milked the cow with the crumpled horn,
That tossed the dog,
That worried the cat,
That killed the rat,
That ate the corn,
That lay in the house that Jack built.
Nurse Truelove's New-Year-Gift

58 This little piggy went to market,
This little piggy stayed at home,
This little piggy had roast beef,
This little piggy had none,
And this little piggy cried, Wee-wee-wee-wee-
wee,
I can't find my way home.
The Famous Tommy Thumb's Little Story Book

59 Three blind mice, see how they run!
They all run after the farmer's wife,
Who cut off their tails with a carving knife,
Did you ever see such a thing in your life,

As three blind mice?
Deuteromelia (Thomas Ravenscroft)

60 Tinker,
Tailor,
Soldier,
Sailor,
Rich man,
Poor man,
Beggarman,
Thief.
Popular Rhymes and Nursery Tales (J. O. Halliwell)

61 Tom, he was a piper's son,
He learnt to play when he was young,
And all the tune that he could play
Was 'Over the hills and far away'.
Tom, The Piper's Son

62 Tom, Tom, the piper's son,
Stole a pig and away he run;
The pig was eat
And Tom was beat,
And Tom went howling down the street.
Tom, The Piper's Son

63 Two little dicky birds,
Sitting on a wall;
One named Peter,
The other named Paul,
Fly away, Peter!
Fly away, Paul!
Come back, Peter!
Come back, Paul!
Mother Goose's Melody

64 Wee Willie Winkie runs through the town
upstairs and downstairs and in his nightgown,
Rapping at the window, crying through the
lock,

Are the children all in their beds? It's past
eight o'clock.
In *Whistle-Binkie* (W. Miller)

65 What are little boys made of?
Frogs and snails
And puppy-dogs' tails,
That's what little boys are made of.
What are little girls made of?
Sugar and spice
And all that's nice,
That's what little girls are made of.
Nursery Rhymes (J. O. Halliwell)

66 Where are you going to, my pretty maid?
I'm going a-milking, sir, she said.
Archaeologia Cornu-Britannica (William Pryce)

67 What is your fortune, my pretty maid?
My face is my fortune, sir, she said.
Then I can't marry you, my pretty maid.
Nobody asked you, sir, she said.
Archaeologia Cornu-Britannica (William Pryce)

68 Who killed Cock Robin?
I, said the Sparrow,
With my bow and arrow,
I killed Cock Robin.
Who saw him die?
I, said the Fly,
With my little eye,
I saw him die.
Tommy Thumb's Pretty Song Book

69 Yankee Doodle came to town,
Riding on a pony;
He stuck a feather in his cap
And called it macaroni.
Gammer Gurton's Garland

O

OBEDIENCE

1 Children, obey your parents in the Lord: for
this is right.
Bible: Ephesians
6:1

2 'She still seems to me in her own way a
person born to command,' said Luce . . .
'I wonder if anyone is born to obey,' said
Isabel.
'That may be why people command rather bad-
ly, that
they have no suitable material to work on.'
Ivy Compton-Burnett (1892–1969) British novelist.
Parents and Children, Ch. 3

3 It is much safer to obey than to rule.
Thomas à Kempis (Thomas Hemmerken; c. 1380–1471)
German monk.
The Imitation of Christ, I

4 'Forward the Light Brigade!'

Was there a man dismay'd?
Not tho' the soldier knew
Some one had blunder'd:
Their's not to make reply,
Their's not to reason why,
Their's but to do and die:
Into the valley of Death
Rode the six hundred.
Alfred, Lord Tennyson (1809–92) British poet.
The Charge of the Light Brigade

OBESITY

See also food, greed

1 Outside every fat man there is an even fatter
man trying to close in.
Kingsley Amis (1922–) British novelist.
See also CONNOLLY, ORWELL
One Fat Englishman, Ch. 3

2 Who's your fat friend?

'Beau' Brummel (George Bryan Brummell; 1778–1840) British dandy.
Referring to George, Prince of Wales
Reminiscences (Gronow)

3 Just the other day in the Underground I enjoyed the pleasure of offering my seat to three ladies.

G. K. Chesterton (1874–1936) British writer.
Suggesting that fatness had its consolations
Das Buch des Lachens (W. Scholz)

4 I want to reassure you I am not this size, really – dear me no, I'm being amplified by the mike.

G. K. Chesterton
At a lecture in Pittsburgh
The Outline of Sanity: A Life of G. K. Chesterton (S. D. Dale)

5 Imprisoned in every fat man a thin one is wildly signalling to be let out.

Cyril Connolly (1903–74) British journalist.
See also AMIS, ORWELL
The Unquiet Grave

6 O fat white woman whom nobody loves,
Why do you walk through the fields in gloves
. . .
Missing so much and so much?

F. M. Cornford (1886–1960) British poet.
To a Fat Lady Seen from a Train

7 I see no objection to stoutness, in moderation.

W. S. Gilbert (1836–1911) British dramatist.
Iolanthe, I

8 I'm fat, but I'm thin inside. Has it ever struck you that there's a thin man inside every fat man, just as they say there's a statue inside every block of stone?

George Orwell (Eric Blair; 1903–50) British novelist.
See also AMIS, CONNOLLY
Coming Up For Air, Pt. I, Ch. 3

9 My advice if you insist on slimming: Eat as much as you like – just don't swallow it.

Harry Secombe (1921–) Welsh singer, actor, and comedian.
Daily Herald, 5 Oct 1962

10 Falstaff sweats to death
And lards the lean earth as he walks along.

William Shakespeare (1564–1616) English dramatist.
Henry IV, Part One, II:2

11 I have more flesh than another man, and therefore more frailty.

William Shakespeare
Henry IV, Part One, III:3

12 She fitted into my biggest armchair as if it had been built round her by someone who knew they were wearing armchairs tight about the hips that season.

P. G. Wodehouse (1881–1975) British humorous novelist.
My Man Jeeves, 'Jeeves and the Unbidden Guest'

13 The Right Hon. was a tubby little chap who looked as if he had been poured into his clothes and had forgotten to say 'When!'

P. G. Wodehouse
Very Good Jeeves!, 'Jeeves and the Impending Doom'

OBITUARIES

See also death, epitaphs, memorials

1 With the newspaper strike on I wouldn't consider it.

Bette Davis (Ruth Elizabeth Davis; 1908–89) US film star.
When told that a rumour was spreading that she had died
Book of Lists (I. Wallace)

2 I've just read that I am dead. Don't forget to delete me from your list of subscribers.

Rudyard Kipling (1865–1936) Indian-born British writer.
Writing to a magazine that had mistakenly published an announcement of his death
Anekdotenschatz (H. Hoffmeister)

3 In these days a man is nobody unless his biography is kept so far posted up that it may be ready for the national breakfast-table on the morning after his demise.

Anthony Trollope (1815–82) British novelist.
Doctor Thorne, Ch. 25

4 Reports of my death are greatly exaggerated.

Mark Twain (Samuel Langhorne Clemens; 1835–1910) US writer.
On learning that his obituary had been published
Cable to the Associated Press

OBJECTIVITY

See also perspective, subjectivity

1 *Sir Roger* told them, with the air of a man who would not give his judgment rashly, that 'much might be said on both sides'.

Joseph Addison (1672–1719) British essayist.
Sir Roger de Coverley was a fictional archetype of the old-fashioned and eccentric country squire
The Spectator, 122

2 Thus I live in the world rather as a Spectator of mankind, than as one of the species, by which means I have made myself a speculative statesman, soldier, merchant, and artisan, without ever meddling with any practical part of life.

Joseph Addison
The Spectator, 1

3 Only reason can convince us of those three fundamental truths without a recognition of which there can be no effective liberty: that what we believe is not necessarily true; that what we like is not necessarily good; and that all questions are open.

Clive Bell (1881–1964) British art critic.
Civilization, Ch. 5

4 I am a camera with its shutter open, quite passive, recording, not thinking.
Christopher Isherwood (1904–86) British novelist.
Goodbye to Berlin

5 The man who sees both sides of a question is a man who sees absolutely nothing at all.
Oscar Wilde (1854–1900) Irish-born British dramatist.
The Critic as Artist, Pt. 2

OBLIGATION

See also duty

1 The debt which cancels all others.
Charles Caleb Colton (?1780–1832) British clergyman and writer.
Lacon, Vol. II

2 It is the nature of men to be bound by the benefits they confer as much as by those they receive.
Machiavelli (1469–1527) Italian statesman.
The Prince

OBLIVION

1 Many brave men lived before Agamemnon's time; but they are all, unmourned and unknown, covered by the long night, because they lack their sacred poet.
Horace (Quintus Horatius Flaccus; 65–8 BC) Roman poet.
Odes, IV

2 No, no, go not to Lethe, neither twist Wolf's-bane, tight-rooted, for its poisonous wine.
John Keats (1795–1821) British poet.
Ode on Melancholy

3 Annihilating all that's made
To a green thought in a green shade.
Andrew Marvell (1621–78) English poet.
The Garden

OBSESSIONS

1 I have three phobias which, could I mute them, would make my life as slick as a sonnet, but as dull as ditch water: I hate to go to bed, I hate to get up, and I hate to be alone.
Tallulah Bankhead (1903–68) US actress.
Tallulah, Ch. 1

2 *Papyromania* – compulsive accumulation of papers . . .
Papyrophobia – abnormal desire for 'a clean desk'.
Laurence J. Peter (1919–90) Canadian writer.
The Peter Principle, Glossary

OBSTRUCTION

1 I'll put a spoke among your wheels.
Francis Beaumont (1584–1616) English dramatist.
The Mad Lover, III:6

2 If any of you know cause, or just impediment.
The Book of Common Prayer
Solemnization of Matrimony

3 There was only one catch and that was Catch-22, which specified that a concern for one's own safety in the face of dangers that were real and immediate was the process of a rational mind.
Joseph Heller (1923–) US novelist.
Catch-22, Ch. 5

OCCUPATIONS

See also doctors, lawyers, police

1 A priest sees people at their best, a lawyer at their worst, but a doctor sees them as they really are.
Proverb

2 Every man to his trade.
Proverb

3 Jack of all trades, master of none.
Proverb

4 Old soldiers never die, they simply fade away.
Proverb

5 Once a parson always a parson.
Proverb

6 Sailors have a port in every storm.
Proverb

7 Doctors bury their mistakes. Lawyers hang them. But journalists put theirs on the front page.
Anonymous

8 The ugliest of trades have their moments of pleasure. Now, if I were a grave-digger, or even a hangman, there are some people I could work for with a great deal of enjoyment.
Douglas William Jerrold (1803–57) British dramatist.
Wit and Opinions of Douglas Jerrold, 'Ugly Trades'

9 He did not know that a keeper is only a poacher turned outside in, and a poacher a keeper turned inside out.
Charles Kingsley (1819–75) British writer.
The Water Babies, Ch. 1

10 Under the spreading chestnut tree
The village smithy stands;
The smith, a mighty man is he,
With large and sinewy hands;
And the muscles of his brawny arms
Are strong as iron bands.
Henry Wadsworth Longfellow (1807–82) US poet.
The Village Blacksmith

11 The trained nurse has given nursing the human, or shall we say, the divine touch, and made the hospital desirable for patients with

serious ailments regardless of their home advantages.

Charles H. Mayo (1865–1939) US physician.
Collected Papers of the Mayo Clinic and Mayo Foundation

12 I have nothing against undertakers personally. It's just that I wouldn't want one to bury my sister.

Jessica Mitford (1917–) British writer.
Attrib. in *Saturday Review*, 1 Feb 1964

13 If I didn't start painting, I would have raised chickens.

Grandma Moses (Anna Mary Robertson Moses; 1860–1961) US primitive painter.
Grandma Moses, My Life's History (ed. Aotto Kallir), Ch. 3

14 No *man*, not even a doctor, ever gives any other definition of what a nurse should be than this – 'devoted and obedient.' This definition would do just as well for a porter. It might even do for a horse. It would not do for a policeman.

Florence Nightingale (1820–1910) British nurse.
Notes on Nursing

15 The trained nurse has become one of the great blessings of humanity, taking a place beside the physician and the priest, and not inferior to either in her mission.

William Osler (1849–1919) Canadian physician.
Aequanimitas, with Other Addresses, 'Nurse and Patient'

16 A doctor who doesn't say too many foolish things is a patient half-cured, just as a critic is a poet who has stopped writing verse and a policeman a burglar who has retired from practice.

Marcel Proust (1871–1922) French novelist.
À la recherche du temps perdu: Le Côté de Guermantes

17 Everybody hates house-agents because they have everybody at a disadvantage. All other callings have a certain amount of give and take; the house-agent simply takes.

H. G. Wells (1866–1946) British writer.
Kipps, Bk. III, Ch. 1

18 The best careers advice to give to the young is 'Find out what you like doing best and get someone to pay you for doing it.'

Katherine Whitehorn (1926–) British journalist.
The Observer, 1975

OFFICERS

See also army, navy, soldiers, war

1 Any officer who shall behave in a scandalous manner, unbecoming the character of an officer and a gentleman shall . . . be cashiered.

Anonymous
The words 'conduct unbecoming the character of an officer' are a direct quotation from the Naval Discipline Act (10 Aug 1860), Article 24
Articles of War (1872), *Disgraceful Conduct*, 79

2 If Kitchener was not a great man, he was, at least, a great poster.

Margot Asquith (1865–1945) The second wife of Herbert Asquith.
Kitchener: Portrait of an Imperialist (Sir Philip Magnus), Ch. 14

3 In defeat unbeatable; in victory unbearable.

Winston Churchill (1874–1965) British statesman.
Referring to Viscount Montgomery
Ambrosia and Small Beer (E. Marsh), Ch. 5

4 Jellicoe was the only man on either side who could lose the war in an afternoon.

Winston Churchill
The Observer, 'Sayings of the Week', 13 Feb 1927

5 War is too important to be left to the generals.

Georges Clemenceau (1841–1929) French statesman.
A similar remark is attributed to Talleyrand
Attrib.

6 When I was a lad I served a term
As office boy to an Attorney's firm.
I cleaned the windows and I swept the floor,
And I polished up the handle of the big front door.
I polished up that handle so carefullee
That now I am the Ruler of the Queen's Navee!

W. S. Gilbert (1836–1911) British dramatist.
HMS Pinafore, I

7 Stick close to your desks and never go to sea,
And you all may be Rulers of the Queen's Navee!

W. S. Gilbert
HMS Pinafore, I

8 LUDENDORFF: The English soldiers fight like lions.
HOFFMANN: True. But don't we know that they are lions led by donkeys.

Max Hoffmann (1869–1927) German general.
Referring to the performance of the British army in World War I
The Donkeys (A. Clark)

9 I can't spare this man; he fights.

Abraham Lincoln (1809–65) US statesman.
Resisting demands for the dismissal of Ulysses Grant
Attrib.

10 The Nelson touch.

Lord Nelson (1758–1805) British admiral.
Diary, 9 Oct 1805

11 Nelson, born in a fortunate hour for himself and for his country, was always in his element and always on his element.

George Macaulay Trevelyan (1876–1962) British historian.
History of England, Bk. V, Ch. 5

12 I didn't fire him because he was a dumb son of a bitch, although he was, but that's not against the law for generals. If it was, half to three-quarters of them would be in gaol.

Harry S. Truman (1884–1972) US statesman.
Referring to General MacArthur
Plain Speaking (Merle Miller)

13 I don't know what effect these men will have on the enemy, but, by God, they frighten me.

Duke of Wellington (1769–1852) British general and statesman.
Referring to his generals
Attrib.

14 It is not the business of generals to shoot one another.

Duke of Wellington
Refusing an artillery officer permission to fire upon Napoleon himself during the Battle of Waterloo, 1815
Attrib.

15 Not upon a man from the colonel to the private in a regiment – both inclusive. We may pick up a marshal or two perhaps; but not worth a damn.

Duke of Wellington
Said during the Waterloo campaign, when asked whether he anticipated any desertions from Napoleon's army
Creevey Papers, Ch. X

16 I used to say of him that his presence on the field made the difference of forty thousand men.

Duke of Wellington
Referring to Napoleon
Notes of Conversations with the Duke of Wellington (Stanhope), 2 Nov 1831

OLD AGE

See also age, longevity

1 Grey hairs are death's blossoms.
Proverb

2 You can't teach an old dog new tricks.
Proverb

3 When you are forty, half of you belongs to the past . . . And when you are seventy, nearly all of you.
Jean Anouilh (1910–87) French dramatist.

4 I will never be an old man. To me, old age is always fifteen years older than I am.
Bernard Baruch (1870–1965) US financier and presidential adviser.
The Observer 'Sayings of the Week', 21 Aug 1955

5 Better is a poor and a wise child than an old and foolish king, who will no more be admonished.
Bible: Ecclesiastes
4:13

6 With the ancient is wisdom; and in length of days understanding.
Bible: Job
12:12

7 To be old is to be part of a huge and ordinary multitude . . . the reason why old age was venerated in the past was because it was extraordinary.
Ronald Blythe (1922–) British author.
The View in.Winter

8 Old age takes away from us what we have inherited and gives us what we have earned.
Gerald Brenan (Edward Fitzgerald Brenan; 1894–1987) British writer.
Thoughts in a Dry Season, 'Life'

9 As a white candle
In a holy place,
So is the beauty
Of an aged face.
Joseph Campbell (1879–1944) Irish poet.
The Old Woman

10 'You are old, Father William,' the young man said,
'And your hair has become very white;
And yet you incessantly stand on your head –
Do you think at your age, it is right?'
Lewis Carroll (Charles Lutwidge Dodgson; 1832–98) British writer.
See also Robert SOUTHEY
Alice's Adventures in Wonderland, Ch. 5

11 Old age is the out-patients' department of purgatory.
Lord Cecil (1869–1956) British politician.
The Cecils of Hatfield House (David Cecil)

12 I prefer old age to the alternative.
Maurice Chevalier (1888–1972) French singer and actor.
Attrib.

13 Old-age, a second child, by Nature curs'd
With more and greater evils than the first,
Weak, sickly, full of pains; in ev'ry breath
Railing at life, and yet afraid of death.
Charles Churchill (1731–64) British poet.
Gotham, I

14 Oh to be seventy again.
Georges Clemenceau (1841–1929) French statesman.
Remark on his eightieth birthday, noticing a pretty girl in the Champs Elysées
Ego 3 (James Agate)

15 So, perhaps, I may escape otherwise than by death the last humiliation of an aged scholar, when his juniors conspire to print a volume of essays and offer it to him as a sign that they now consider him senile.
Robin George Collingwood (1889–1943) British philosopher and archaeologist.
Autobiography

16 When a man fell into his anecdotage it was a sign for him to retire from the world.
Benjamin Disraeli (1804–81) British statesman.
Lothair, Ch. 28

17 I grow old . . . I grow old . . .

I shall wear the bottoms of my trousers rolled.
T. S. Eliot (1888–1965) US-born British poet and dramatist.
The Love Song of J. Alfred Prufrock

18 Shall I part my hair behind? Do I dare to eat a peach?
I shall wear white flannel trousers, and walk upon the beach.
I have heard the mermaids singing, each to each.
T. S. Eliot
The Love Song of J. Alfred Prufrock

19 Old age brings along with its uglinesses the comfort that you will soon be out of it, – which ought to be a substantial relief to such discontented pendulums as we are.
Ralph Waldo Emerson (1803–82) US poet and essayist.
Journal

20 He cannot bear old men's jokes. That is not new. But now he begins to think of them himself.
Max Frisch (1911–) Swiss dramatist and novelist.
Sketchbook 1966–71

21 Time goes by: reputation increases, ability declines.
Dag Hammarskjöld (1905–61) Swedish diplomat.
Diaries, 1964

22 And now in age I bud again,
After so many deaths I live and write;
I once more smell the dew and rain,
And relish versing; O, my only Light,
It cannot be
That I am he
On whom Thy tempests fell all night.
George Herbert (1593–1633) English poet.
The Flower

23 It is so comic to hear oneself called old, even at ninety I suppose!
Alice James (1848–92) US diarist.
Letter to William James, 14 June 1889
The Diary of Alice James (ed. Leon Edel)

24 There is a wicked inclination in most people to suppose an old man decayed in his intellects. If a young or middle-aged man, when leaving a company, does not recollect where he laid his hat, it is nothing; but if the same inattention is discovered in an old man, people will shrug up their shoulders, and say, 'His memory is going.'
Samuel Johnson (1709–84) British lexicographer.
Life of Johnson (J. Boswell), Vol. IV

25 Perhaps being old is having lighted rooms Inside your head, and people in them, acting. People you know, yet can't quite name.
Philip Larkin (1922–85) British poet.
The Old Fools

26 A 'Grand Old Man'. That means on our continent any one with snow white hair who has kept out of jail till eighty.
Stephen Leacock (1869–1944) English-born Canadian economist and humorist.
The Score and Ten

27 Old age is woman's hell.
Ninon de Lenclos (1620–1705) French courtesan.
Attrib.

28 From the earliest times the old have rubbed it into the young that they are wiser than they, and before the young had discovered what nonsense this was they were old too, and it profited them to carry on the imposture.
W. Somerset Maugham (1874–1965) British novelist.
Cakes and Ale, Ch. 9

29 Being seventy is not a sin.
Golda Meir (1898–1978) Russian-born Israeli stateswoman.
Reader's Digest (July 1971), 'The Indestructible Golda Meir'

30 A ready means of being cherished by the English is to adopt the simple expedient of living a long time. I have little doubt that if, say, Oscar Wilde had lived into his nineties, instead of dying in his forties, he would have been considered a benign, distinguished figure suitable to preside at a school prize-giving or to instruct and exhort scoutmasters at their jamborees. He might even have been knighted.
Malcolm Muggeridge (1903–) British writer.
Tread Softly for you Tread on my Jokes

31 I prefer to forget both pairs of glasses and pass my declining years saluting strange women and grandfather clocks.
Ogden Nash (1902–71) US poet.
Peekaboo, I Almost See You

32 Age only matters when one is ageing. Now that I have arrived at a great age, I might just as well be twenty.
Pablo Picasso (1881–1973) Spanish painter.
The Observer, Shouts and Murmurs, 'Picasso in Private' (John Richardson)

33 See how the world its veterans rewards!
A youth of frolics, an old age of cards.
Alexander Pope (1688–1744) British poet.
Moral Essays, II

34 Growing old is like being increasingly penalized for a crime you haven't committed.
Anthony Powell (1905–) British novelist.
A Dance to the Music of Time: Temporary Kings, Ch. 1

35 Darling, I am growing old,
Silver threads among the gold.
Eben Rexford (1848–1916) British songwriter.
Silver Threads Among the Gold

36 Age seldom arrives smoothly or quickly. It's more often a succession of jerks.
Jean Rhys (1894–1979) Dominican-born British novelist.
The Observer, 'Sayings of the Week', 25 May 1975

37 As I grow older and older,
And totter towards the tomb,
I find that I care less and less
Who goes to bed with whom.
Dorothy L. Sayers (1893–1957) British writer.
That's Why I Never Read Modern Novels

38 Last scene of all,
That ends this strange eventful history,
Is second childishness and mere oblivion;
Sans teeth, sans eyes, sans taste, sans every
thing.
William Shakespeare (1564–1616) English dramatist.
As You Like It, II:7

39 I have liv'd long enough.
My way of life
Is fall'n into the sear, the yellow leaf;
And that which should accompany old age,
As honour, love, obedience, troops of friends,
I must not look to have.
William Shakespeare
Macbeth, V:3

40 That time of year thou mayst in me behold
When yellow leaves, or none, or few, do hang
Upon those boughs which shake against the
cold,
Bare ruin'd choirs, where late the sweet birds
sang.
William Shakespeare
Sonnet 73

41 Old men are dangerous; it doesn't matter to
them what is going to happen to the world.
George Bernard Shaw (1856–1950) Irish dramatist and
critic.
Heartbreak House

42 You are old, Father William, the young man
cried,
The few locks which are left you are grey;
You are hale, Father William, a hearty old
man,
Now tell me the reason, I pray.
Robert Southey (1774–1843) British poet.
See also Lewis CARROLL
The Old Man's Comforts, and how he Gained them

43 Being over seventy is like being engaged in a
war. All our friends are going or gone and
we survive amongst the dead and the dying
as on a battlefield.
Muriel Spark (1918–) British novelist.
Memento Mori, Ch. 4

44 There are so few who can grow old with a
good grace.
Richard Steele (1672–1729) Dublin-born British essayist.
The Spectator, 263

45 The greatest problem about old age is the
fear that it may go on too long.
A. J. P. Taylor (1906–) British historian.
Observer 'Sayings of the Week', 1 Nov 1981

46 Sleeping as quiet as death, side by wrinkled

side, toothless, salt and brown, like two old
kippers in a box.
Dylan Thomas (1914–53) Welsh poet.
Under Milk Wood

47 Old age is the most unexpected of all the
things that happen to a man.
Leon Trotsky (Lev Davidovich Bronstein; 1879–1940)
Russian revolutionary.
Diary in Exile, 8 May 1935

48 There is nothing funny or commendable about
old age. It is a miserable affliction which
brings a sort of imbecility to those who suffer
from it and distresses everyone else.
Auberon Waugh (1939–) British novelist.
The Diaries of Auberon Waugh 1976–1985, 'July 21, 1982'

49 The gods bestowed on Max the gift of
perpetual old age.
Oscar Wilde (1854–1900) Irish-born British dramatist.
Referring to Max Beerbohm
Attrib.

50 It is a terrible thing for an old woman to
outlive her dogs.
Tennessee Williams (1911–83) US dramatist.
Camino Real

51 He was either a man of about a hundred and
fifty who was rather young for his years or a
man of about a hundred and ten who had
been aged by trouble.
P. G. Wodehouse (1881–1975) British humorous
novelist.
Wodehouse at Work to the End (Richard Usborne), Ch. 6

52 The wiser mind
Mourns less for what age takes away
Than what it leaves behind.
William Wordsworth (1770–1850) British poet.
The Fountain

53 Provoke
The years to bring the inevitable yoke.
William Wordsworth
Ode. Intimations of Immortality, VIII

54 When you are old and gray and full of sleep,
And nodding by the fire, take down this book,
And slowly read, and dream of the soft look
Your eyes had once, and of their shadows
deep. . .
W. B. Yeats (1865–1939) Irish poet.
When you are Old

ONE-UPMANSHIP

See also snobbery, superiority

1 Keeping up with the Joneses was a full-time
job with my mother and father. It was not
until many years later when I lived alone that
I realized how much cheaper it was to drag
the Joneses down to my level.
Quentin Crisp (?1910–) Model, publicist, and writer.
The Naked Civil Servant

2 There is no doubt that basic weekendmanship

should contain some reference to Important Person Play.

Stephen Potter (1900–69) British writer.
Lifemanship, Ch. 2

3 *How to be one up* – how to make the other man feel that something has gone wrong, however slightly.

Stephen Potter
Lifemanship, Introduction

OPERA

See also music, singing

1 I do not mind what language an opera is sung in so long as it is a language I don't understand.

Edward Appleton (1892–1965) British physicist.
The Observer, 'Sayings of the Week,' 28 Aug 1955

2 No good opera plot can be sensible, for people do not sing when they are feeling sensible.

W. H. Auden (1907–73) British poet.
Time, 29 Dec 1961

3 The opera isn't over till the fat lady sings.

Dan Cook US journalist.
Washington Post, 13 June 1978

4 People are wrong when they say the opera isn't what it used to be. It is what it used to be. That's what's wrong with it.

Noël Coward (1899–1973) British dramatist.
Design for Living

5 Opera in English, is, in the main, just about as sensible as baseball in Italian.

H. L. Mencken (1880–1956) US journalist.
The Frank Muir Book (Frank Muir)

6 I sometimes wonder which would be nicer – an opera without an interval, or an interval without an opera.

Ernest Newman (1868–1959) British music critic.
Berlioz, Romantic and Classic, (ed. Peter Heyworth)

7 His vocal cords were kissed by God.

Harold Schoenberg (1915–) US music critic.
Referring to Luciano Pavarotti
The Times, 30 June 1981

8 Tenors are noble, pure and heroic and get the soprano. But baritones are born villains in opera. Always the heavy and never the hero.

Leonard Warren (1911–60) US baritone singer.
The New York World Telegram, 13 Feb 1957

9 Like German opera, too long and too loud.

Evelyn Waugh (1903–66) British novelist.
Giving his opinions of warfare after the Battle of Crete, 1941
Attrib.

10 An unalterable and unquestioned law of the musical world required that the German text of French operas sung by Swedish artists should be translated into Italian for the clearer understanding of English speaking audiences.

Edith Wharton (1862–1937) US novelist.
The Age of Innocence, Bk. I, Ch. 1

OPINIONS

See also ideas

1 We must say that the same opinions have arisen among men in cycles, not once, twice, nor a few times, but infinitely often.

Aristotle (384–322 BC) Greek philosopher.
Meteorologica

2 They that approve a private opinion, call it opinion; but they that mislike it, heresy: and yet heresy signifies no more than private opinion.

Thomas Hobbes (1588–1679) English philosopher.
Leviathan, Pt. I, Ch. 11

3 The superiority of one man's opinion over another's is never so great as when the opinion is about a woman.

Henry James (1843–1916) US novelist.
The Tragic Muse, Ch. 9

4 'Tis with our judgments as our watches, none Go just alike, yet each believes his own.

Alexander Pope (1688–1744) British poet.
An Essay on Criticism

5 The fact that an opinion has been widely held is no evidence whatever that it is not utterly absurd.

Bertrand Russell (1872–1970) British philosopher.
Attrib.

6 It is folly of too many to mistake the echo of a London coffee-house for the voice of the kingdom.

Jonathan Swift (1667–1745) Irish-born Anglican priest and writer.
The Conduct of the Allies

7 So many men, so many opinions.

Terence (Publius Terentius Afer; c. 190–159 BC) Roman poet.
Phormio

8 I agree with no man's opinion. I have some of my own.

Ivan Turgenev (1818–83) Russian novelist.
Fathers and Sons, Ch. 13

OPPORTUNITY

See also chance, present

1 All's grist that comes to the mill.
Proverb

2 Every dog has his day.
Proverb

3 Hoist your sail when the wind is fair.
Proverb

4 Make hay while the sun shines.
Proverb

5 Nothing ventured, nothing gained.
Proverb

6 Opportunity seldom knocks twice.
Proverb

7 Strike while the iron is hot.
Proverb

8 Whenever you fall, pick up something.
Oswald Theodore Avery (1877–1955) Canadian bacteriologist.
Attrib.

9 A wise man will make more opportunities than he finds.
Francis Bacon (1561–1626) English philosopher.
Essays, 'Of Ceremonies and Respects'

10 Cast thy bread upon the waters: for thou shalt find it after many days.
Bible: Ecclesiastes
11:1

11 Let him now speak, or else hereafter for ever hold his peace.
The Book of Common Prayer
Solemnization of Matrimony

12 Opportunities are usually disguised as hard work, so most people don't recognise them.
Ann Landers (1918–) US journalist.
Attrib.

13 One can present people with opportunities. One cannot make them equal to them.
Rosamond Lehmann (1901–90) British novelist.
The Ballad and the Source

14 Equality of opportunity means equal opportunity to be unequal.
Iain Macleod (1913–70) British politician.
Way Of Life (John Boyd Carpenter)

15 Grab a chance and you won't be sorry for a might have been.
Arthur Ransome (1884–1967) British novelist.
We Didn't Mean to Go to Sea

16 There is a tide in the affairs of men
Which, taken at the flood, leads on to fortune;
Omitted, all the voyage of their life
Is bound in shallows and in miseries.
On such a full sea are we now afloat,
And we must take the current when it serves,
Or lose our ventures.
William Shakespeare (1564–1616) English dramatist.
Julius Caesar, IV:3

17 Why, then the world's mine oyster,
Which I with sword will open.
William Shakespeare
The Merry Wives of Windsor, II:2

18 I missed the chance of a lifetime, too. Fifty

lovelies in the rude and I'd left my Bunsen burner home.
Dylan Thomas (1914–53) Welsh poet.
Portrait of the Artist as a Young Dog, 'One Warm Saturday'

OPPOSITES

See also conflict, difference

1 It takes all sorts to make a world.
Proverb

2 Fish die belly-upward and rise to the surface; it is their way of falling.
André Gide (1869–1951) French novelist.
Journals

3 The poet and the dreamer are distinct,
Diverse, sheer opposite, antipodes.
The one pours out a balm upon the world,
The other vexes it.
John Keats (1795–1821) British poet.
The Fall of Hyperion, I

4 Oh, East is East, and West is West, and never the twain shall meet.
Rudyard Kipling (1865–1936) Indian-born British writer.
The Ballad of East and West

5 War is Peace, Freedom is Slavery, Ignorance is Strength.
George Orwell (Eric Blair; 1903–50) British novelist.
Nineteen Eighty-Four

6 Doublethink means the power of holding two contradictory beliefs in one's mind simultaneously, and accepting both of them.
George Orwell
Nineteen Eighty-Four

7 The sublime and the ridiculous are often so nearly related that it is difficult to class them separately. One step above the sublime makes the ridiculous; and one step above the ridiculous makes the sublime again.
Thomas Paine (1737–1809) British writer.
The Age of Reason, Pt. 2

OPPOSITION

See also government, politics

1 It has been said that England invented the phrase, 'Her Majesty's Opposition'.
Walter Bagehot (1826–77) British economist and journalist.
See HOBHOUSE
The English Constitution, 'The Monarchy'

2 The duty of an opposition is to oppose.
Lord Randolph Churchill (1849–95) British Conservative politician.
Lord Randolph Churchill (W. S. Churchill)

3 When I invented the phrase 'His Majesty's

Opposition' he paid me a compliment on the fortunate hit.

John Cam Hobhouse (1786–1869) British politician.
Speaking about Canning
Recollections of a Long Life, II, Ch. 12

4   One fifth of the people are against everything all the time.

Robert Kennedy (1925–68) US politician.
The Observer, 'Sayings of the Week', 10 May 1964

5   . . . I have spent many years of my life in opposition and I rather like the role.

Eleanor Roosevelt (1884–1962) US writer and lecturer.
Letter to Bernard Baruch, 18 Nov 1952

OPPRESSION

See also imprisonment, indoctrination, power politics, slavery, tyranny

1   When Israel was in Egypt land,
Let my people go,
Oppressed so hard they could not stand,
Let my people go.
Go down, Moses,
Way-down in Egypt land,
Tell old Pharaoh
To let my people go.

Anonymous
Negro spiritual

2   Christ in this country would quite likely have been arrested under the Suppression of Communism Act.

Joost de Blank (1908–68) Dutch-born British churchman.
Referring to South Africa
The Observer, 'Sayings of the Week', 27 Oct 1963

3   The enemies of Freedom do not argue; they shout and they shoot.

Dean Inge (1860–1954) British churchman.
The End of an Age, Ch. 4

4   If you want a picture of the future, imagine a boot stamping on a human face – for ever.

George Orwell (Eric Blair; 1903–50) British novelist.
Nineteen Eighty-Four

5   In the first days of the revolt you must kill: to shoot down a European is to kill two birds with one stone, to destroy an oppressor and the man he oppresses at the same time: there remain a dead man, and a free man.

Jean-Paul Sartre (1905–80) French writer.
The Wretched of the Earth (F. Fanon), Preface

OPTIMISM

See also hope

1   After a storm comes a calm.
Proverb

2   Every cloud has a silver lining.
Proverb

3   It's an ill wind that blows nobody any good.
Proverb

4   It will all come right in the wash.
Proverb

5   Look on the bright side.
Proverb

6   No news is good news.
Proverb

7   Nothing so bad but it might have been worse.
Proverb

8   The darkest hour is just before the dawn.
Proverb

9   Tomorrow is another day.
Proverb

10   When one door shuts, another opens.
Proverb

11   While there's life there's hope.
Proverb

12   Are we downhearted? No!

Anonymous
A favourite expression of the British soldiers during World War I
Attrib.

13   What's the use of worrying?
It never was worth while,
So, pack up your troubles in your old kit-bag,
And smile, smile, smile.

George Asaf (George H. Powell; 1880–1951) US songwriter.
Pack up Your Troubles in Your Old Kit-bag

14   Let other pens dwell on guilt and misery.

Jane Austen (1775–1817) British novelist.
Mansfield Park, Ch. 48

15   *Future*, n. That period of time in which our affairs prosper, our friends are true and our happiness is assured.

Ambrose Bierce (1842–?1914) US writer and journalist.
The Devil's Dictionary

16   My sun sets to rise again.

Robert Browning (1812–89) British poet.
At the 'Mermaid'

17   No, at noonday in the bustle of man's worktime
Greet the unseen with a cheer!

Robert Browning
Epilogue to Asolando

18   Don't you know each cloud contains Pennies from Heaven?

Johnny Burke (1908–64) US songwriter.
Pennies from Heaven

19   The optimist proclaims we live in the best of all possible worlds; and the pessimist fears this is true.

James Cabell (1879–1958) US novelist and journalist.
The Silver Stallion

20 The place where optimism most flourishes is the lunatic asylum.

Havelock Ellis (1859–1939) British sexologist.
The Dance of Life

21 Two men look out through the same bars:
One sees the mud, and one the stars.

Frederick Langbridge (1849–1923) British religious writer.
A Cluster of Quiet Thoughts

22 The worst is not
So long as we can say 'This is the worst'.

William Shakespeare (1564–1616) English dramatist.
King Lear, IV:1

23 Now is the winter of our discontent
Made glorious summer by this sun of York.

William Shakespeare
Richard III, I:1

24 Life may change, but it may fly not;
Hope may vanish, but can die not;
Truth be veiled, but still it burneth;
Love repulsed, – but it returneth!

Percy Bysshe Shelley (1792–1822) British poet.
Hellas, I

25 The latest definition of an optimist is one who fills up his crossword puzzle in ink.

Clement King Shorter (1857–1926) British journalist and critic.
The Observer, 'Sayings of the Week', 22 Feb 1925

26 I am an optimist, unrepentant and militant. After all, in order not to be a fool an optimist must know how sad a place the world can be. It is only the pessimist who finds this out anew every day.

Peter Ustinov (1921–) British actor.
Dear Me, Ch. 9

27 All is for the best in the best of possible worlds.

Voltaire (François-Marie Arouet; 1694–1778) French writer.
Candide, Ch. 30

28 We are all in the gutter, but some of us are looking at the stars.

Oscar Wilde (1854–1900) Irish-born British dramatist.
Lady Windermere's Fan, III

29 Nor greetings where no kindness is, nor all
The dreary intercourse of daily life,
Shall e'er prevail against us, or disturb
Our cheerful faith, that all which we behold
Is full of blessings.

William Wordsworth (1770–1850) British poet.
Lines composed a few miles above Tintern Abbey

ORDER

1 I am an orderly man. I say this with no sense of false modesty, or of conceit. . . . Being orderly, as a matter of fact, can be excessively tiresome and it often irritates me greatly, but I cannot pull away.

Dirk Bogarde (1921–) British actor and writer.
An Orderly Man, Ch. 1

2 'Where shall I begin, please your Majesty?' he asked.
'Begin at the beginning' the King said, gravely, 'and go on till you come to the end: then stop.'

Lewis Carroll (Charles Lutwidge Dodgson; 1832–98) British writer.
Alice's Adventures in Wonderland, Ch. 11

3 Order is heaven's first law.

Alexander Pope (1688–1744) British poet.
An Essay on Man, IV

4 O, when degree is shak'd,
Which is the ladder of all high designs,
The enterprise is sick!

William Shakespeare (1564–1616) English dramatist.
Troilus and Cressida, I:3

5 How sour sweet music is
When time is broke and no proportion kept!
So is it in the music of men's lives.

William Shakespeare
Richard II, V:5

6 A place for everything, and everything in its place.

Samuel Smiles (1812–1904) British writer.
Thrift, Ch. 5

ORIGINALITY

See also imitation, innovation

1 Anything that is worth doing has been done frequently. Things hitherto undone should be given, I suspect, a wide berth.

Max Beerbohm (1872–1956) British writer.
Mainly on the Air

2 An original writer is not one who imitates nobody, but one whom nobody can imitate.

Vicomte de Chateaubriand (1768–1848) French diplomat and writer.
Génie du Christianisme

3 A thought is often original, though you have uttered it a hundred times.

Oliver Wendell Holmes (1809–94) US writer.
The Autocrat of the Breakfast Table, Ch. 1

4 All good things which exist are the fruits of originality.

John Stuart Mill (1806–73) British philosopher.
On Liberty, Ch. 3

5 Nothing has yet been said that's not been said before.

Terence (Publius Terentius Afer; c. 190–159 BC) Roman poet.
Eunuchus, Prologue

6 Another unsettling element in modern art is that common symptom of immaturity, the dread of doing what has been done before.

Edith Wharton (1862–1937) US novelist.
The Writing of Fiction, Ch. 1

ORTHODOXY

See also conformity

1   The difference between Orthodoxy or My-doxy and Heterodoxy or Thy-doxy.
Thomas Carlyle (1795–1881) Scottish historian and essayist.
A similar remark is attributed to the British churchman William Warburton (1698–1779)
History of the French Revolution, Pt. II, Bk. IV, Ch. 2

2   The word 'orthodoxy' not only no longer means being right; it practically means being wrong.
G. K. Chesterton (1874–1936) British writer.
Heretics, Ch. 1

3   Worldly wisdom teaches that it is better for the reputation to fail conventionally than to succeed unconventionally.
John Maynard Keynes (1883–1946) British economist.
The General Theory of Employment, Interest and Money, Bk. IV, Ch. 12

OSTENTATION

See also affectation

1   That's it, baby, if you've got it, flaunt it.
Mel Brooks (Melvyn Kaminsky; 1926–) US film director.
The Producers

2   The possession of a book becomes a substitute for reading it.
Anthony Burgess (John Burgess Wilson; 1917–) British novelist.
New York Times Book Review

3   Wealth has never been a sufficient source of honour in itself. It must be advertised, and the normal medium is obtrusively expensive goods.
John Kenneth Galbraith (1908–) US economist.
The Affluent Society, Ch. 7

4   When I meet those remarkable people whose company is coveted, I often wish they would show off a little more.
Desmond MacCarthy (1877–1952) British writer and theatre critic.
Theatre, 'Good Talk'

5   She's like the old line about justice – not only must be done but must be seen to be done.
John Osborne (1929–) British dramatist.
Time Present, I

6   With the great part of rich people, the chief employment of riches consists in the parade of riches.
Adam Smith (1723–90) Scottish economist.
The Wealth of Nations

OXFORD

See also Cambridge, education, England

1   Home of lost causes, and forsaken beliefs, and unpopular names, and impossible loyalties!
Matthew Arnold (1822–88) British poet and critic.
Essays in Criticism, First Series, Preface

2   That sweet City with her dreaming spires
She needs not June for beauty's heightening.
Matthew Arnold
Thyrsis

3   Oxford is on the whole more attractive than Cambridge to the ordinary visitor; and the traveller is therefore recommended to visit Cambridge first, or to omit it altogether if he cannot visit both.
Karl Baedeker (1801–59) German publisher.
Baedeker's Great Britain, 'From London to Oxford'

4   The King to Oxford sent a troop of horse,
For Tories own no argument but force:
With equal skill to Cambridge books he sent,
For Whigs admit no force but argument.
William Browne (1692–1774) English physician.
A reply to TRAPP
Literary Anecdotes (Nichols), Vol. III

5   Very nice sort of place, Oxford, I should think, for people that like that sort of place.
George Bernard Shaw (1856–1950) Irish dramatist and critic.
Man and Superman, II

6   The King, observing with judicious eyes
The state of both his universities,
To Oxford sent a troop of horse, and why?
That learned body wanted loyalty;
To Cambridge books, as very well discerning
How much that loyal body wanted learning.
Joseph Trapp (1679–1747) English churchman and academic.
Written after George I donated the Bishop of Ely's library to Cambridge; for reply see BROWNE
Literary Anecdotes (Nichols), Vol. III

7   Oxford is, and always has been, full of cliques, full of factions, and full of a particular non-social snobbiness.
Mary Warnock (1924–) British philosopher and educationalist.
The Observer, 2 Nov 1980

P

PAINTING

See also art, artists

1   Buy old masters. They fetch a better price than old mistresses.
Lord Beaverbrook (1879–1964) British newspaper owner and politician.
Attrib.

2 *Painting, n.* The art of protecting flat surfaces from the weather and exposing them to the critic.
Ambrose Bierce (1842–?1914) US writer and journalist.
The Devil's Dictionary

3 Good painters imitate nature, bad ones spew it up.
Miguel de Cervantes (1547–1616) Spanish novelist.
El Licenciado Vidriera

4 It's either easy or impossible.
Salvador Dali (1904–89) Spanish painter.
Reply when asked if he found it hard to paint a picture
Attrib.

5 Never mind about my soul, just make sure you get my tie right.
James Joyce (1882–1941) Irish novelist.
Responding to the painter Patrick Tuohy's assertion that he wished to capture Joyce's soul in his portrait of him
James Joyce (R. Ellmann)

6 If people only knew as much about painting as I do, they would never buy my pictures.
Edwin Landseer (1802–73) British painter and sculptor.
Said to W. P. Frith
Landseer the Victorian Paragon (Campbell Lennie), Ch. 12

7 I mix them with my brains, sir.
John Opie (1761–1807) British painter.
When asked what he mixed his colours with
Self-Help (Samuel Smiles), Ch. 4

8 A picture has been said to be something between a thing and a thought.
Samuel Palmer (1805–81) British landscape painter.
Life of Blake (Arthur Symons)

9 If I like it, I say it's mine. If I don't I say it's a fake.
Pablo Picasso (1881–1973) Spanish painter.
When asked how he knew which paintings were his
The Sunday Times, 10 Oct 1965

10 I paint objects as I think them, not as I see them.
Pablo Picasso
Attrib.

11 Painting is a blind man's profession. He paints not what he sees, but what he feels, what he tells himself about what he has seen.
Pablo Picasso
Journals (Jean Cocteau), 'Childhood'

12 It's better like that, if you want to kill a picture all you have to do is to hang it beautifully on a nail and soon you will see nothing of it but the frame. When it's out of place you see it better.
Pablo Picasso
Explaining why a Renoir in his apartment was hung crooked
Picasso: His Life and Work (Ronald Penrose)

13 It is bad enough to be condemned to drag around this image in which nature has

imprisoned me. Why should I consent to the perpetuation of the image of this image?
Plotinus (205–270 AD) Egyptian-born Greek philosopher.
Refusing to have his portrait painted
Attrib.

14 I just keep painting till I feel like pinching. Then I know it's right.
Pierre Auguste Renoir (1841–1919) French impressionist painter.
Explaining how he achieved such lifelike flesh tones in his nudes
Attrib.

15 Every time I paint a portrait I lose a friend.
John Singer Sargent (1856–1925) US portrait painter.
Attrib.

16 Portraits of famous bards and preachers, all fur and wool from the squint to the kneecaps.
Dylan Thomas (1914–53) Welsh poet.
Under Milk Wood

17 My business is to paint not what I know, but what I see.
Joseph Turner (1775–1851) British painter.
Responding to a criticism of the fact that he had painted no portholes on the ships in a view of Plymouth
Proust: The Early Years (G. Painter)

PARASITES

1 Many a man who thinks to found a home discovers that he has merely opened a tavern for his friends.
Norman Douglas (1868–1952) British novelist.
South Wind, Ch. 24

2 A free-loader is a confirmed guest. He is the man who is always willing to come to dinner.
Damon Runyon (1884–1946) US writer.
Short Takes, 'Free-Loading Ethics'

3 So, naturalist observe, a flea
Hath smaller fleas that on him prey,
And these have smaller fleas to bite 'em.
And so proceed *ad infinitum*.
Jonathan Swift (1667–1745) Irish-born Anglican priest and writer.
On Poetry

4 But was there ever dog that praised his fleas?
W. B. Yeats (1865–1939) Irish poet.
To a Poet, who would have me Praise certain Bad Poets, Imitators of His and Mine

PARIS

See also France

1 If you are lucky enough to have lived in Paris as a young man, then wherever you go for the rest of your life, it stays with you, for Paris is a moveable feast.
Ernest Hemingway (1899–1961) US novelist.
A Moveable Feast, Epigraph

2 Paris is worth a mass.
Henri IV (1553–1610) King of France.
Said on entering Paris (March 1594), having secured its submission to his authority by becoming a Roman Catholic
Attrib.

3 Is Paris burning?
Adolf Hitler (1889–1945) German dictator.
Referring to the liberation of Paris, 1944

4 As an artist, a man has no home in Europe save in Paris.
Friedrich Wilhelm Nietzsche (1844–1900) German philosopher.
Ecce Homo

5 I love Paris in the springtime.
Cole Porter (1893–1964) US songwriter.
Can-Can, 'I Love Paris'

PAROCHIALISM

See also self-interest, selfishness

1 This fellow did not see further than his own nose.
Jean de La Fontaine (1621–95) French poet.
Fables, III, 'Le Renard et le Bouc'

2 A broken head in Cold Bath Fields produces a greater sensation among us than three pitched battles in India.
Lord Macaulay (1800–59) British historian.
Speech, 10 July 1833

3 'That is well said,' replied Candide, 'but we must cultivate our garden.'
Voltaire (François-Marie Arouet; 1694–1778) French writer.
Candide, Ch. 30

PARTIES

See also society

1 The sooner every party breaks up the better.
Jane Austen (1775–1817) British novelist.
Emma, Ch. 25

2 And bring hither the fatted calf, and kill it; and let us eat, and be merry:
For this my son was dead, and is alive again; he was lost, and is found. And they began to be merry.
Bible: Luke
15:23–24

3 I entertained on a cruising trip that was so much fun that I had to sink my yacht to make my guests go home.
F. Scott Fitzgerald (1896–1940) US novelist.
The Crack-Up, 'Notebooks, K'

4 I was one of the few guests who had actually been invited. People were not invited – they went there.
F. Scott Fitzgerald
The Great Gatsby, Ch. 3

5 HE. Have you heard it's in the stars
Next July we collide with Mars?
SHE. Well, did you evah! What a swell party this is.
Cole Porter (1893–1964) US songwriter.
High Society 'Well, Did You Evah!'

6 Certainly, there is nothing else here to enjoy.
George Bernard Shaw (1856–1950) Irish dramatist and critic.
Said at a party when his hostess asked him whether he was enjoying himself
Pass the Port (Oxfam)

7 'So like one's first parties' said Miss Runcible 'being sick with other people singing.'
Evelyn Waugh (1903–66) British novelist.
Vile Bodies

8 She had heard someone say something about an Independent Labour Party, and was furious that she had not been asked.
Evelyn Waugh
Vile Bodies

9 The Life and Soul, the man who will never go home while there is one man, woman or glass of anything not yet drunk.
Katherine Whitehorn (1926–) British journalist.
Sunday Best, 'Husband-Swapping'

PARTING

See also departure, greetings, separation

1 Adieu, adieu, kind friends, adieu, adieu, adieu,
I can no longer stay with you, stay with you.
I'll hang my harp on a weeping willow-tree.
And may the world go well with thee.
Anonymous
There is a Tavern in the Town

2 There is a tavern in the town,
And there my dear love sits him down,
And drinks his wine 'mid laughter free,
And never, never thinks of me.

Fare thee well, for I must leave thee,
Do not let this parting grieve thee,
And remember that the best of friends must part.
Anonymous
There is a Tavern in the Town

3 Farewell and adieu to you,
Fair Spanish Ladies
Farewell and adieu to you, Ladies of Spain.
Anonymous
Spanish Ladies

4 Forty years on, when afar and asunder
Parted are those who are singing to-day.
E. E. Bowen (1836–1901) British writer.
Forty Years On (the Harrow school song)

5 Parting is all we know of heaven,

And all we need of hell.
Emily Dickinson (1830–86) US poet.
My Life Closed Twice Before its Close

6 Since there's no help, come let us kiss and
part –
Nay, I have done, you get no more of me;
And I am glad, yea glad with all my heart
That thus so cleanly I myself can free.
Michael Drayton (1563–1631) English poet.
Sonnets, 61

7 But tha mun dress thysen, an' go back to thy
stately homes of England, how beautiful they
stand. Time's up! Time's up for Sir John, an'
for little Lady Jane! Put thy shimmy on, Lady
Chatterley!
D. H. Lawrence (1885–1930) British novelist.
Lady Chatterley's Lover, Ch. 15

8 It was not like your great and gracious ways!
Do you, that have nought other to lament,
Never, my Love, repent
Of how, that July afternoon,
You went,
With sudden, unintelligible phrase, – And
frightened eye,
Upon your journey of so many days,
Without a single kiss or a good-bye?
Coventry Patmore (1823–96) British poet.
The Unknown Eros, Bk. I, 'Departure'

9 It is seldom indeed that one parts on good
terms, because if one were on good terms
one would not part.
Marcel Proust (1871–1922) French novelist.
À la recherche du temps perdu: La Prisonnière

10 Good night, good night! Parting is such
sweet sorrow
That I shall say good night till it be morrow.
William Shakespeare (1564–1616) English dramatist.
Romeo and Juliet, II:2

11 Farewell! thou art too dear for my
possessing,
And like enough thou know'st thy estimate:
The charter of thy worth gives thee releasing;
My bonds in thee are all determinate.
William Shakespeare
Sonnet 87

12 Good-by-ee! – good-bye-ee!
Wipe the tear, baby dear, from your eye-ee.
Tho' it's hard to part, I know,
I'll be tickled to death to go.
Don't cry-ee! – don't sigh-ee!
There's a silver lining in the sky-ee! –
Bonsoir, old thing! cheerio! chin-chin!
Nahpoo! Toodle-oo! Good-bye-ee!
R. P. Weston (20th century) British songwriter.
Good-bye-ee! (with Bert Lee)

PASSION

See also emotion, love

1 The man who is master of his passions is
Reason's slave.
Cyril Connolly (1903–74) British journalist.
Turnstile One (ed. V. S. Pritchett)

2 A man who has not passed through the
inferno of his passions has never overcome
them.
Carl Gustav Jung (1875–1961) Swiss psychoanalyst.
Memories, Dreams, Reflections, Ch. 9

3 For ever warm and still to be enjoy'd,
For ever panting and for ever young;
All breathing human passion far above,
That leaves a heart high-sorrowful and cloy'd,
A burning forehead, and a parching tongue.
John Keats (1795–1821) British poet.
Ode on a Grecian Urn

4 It is with our passions as it is with fire and
water, they are good servants, but bad
masters.
Roger L'Estrange (1616–1704) English journalist and
writer.
Aesop's Fables, 38

5 And hence one master-passion in the breast,
Like Aaron's serpent,
swallows up the rest.
Alexander Pope (1688–1744) British poet.
An Essay on Man, II

6 The ruling passion, be it what it will
The ruling passion conquers reason still.
Alexander Pope
Moral Essays, III

7 Passion, you see, can be destroyed by a
doctor. It cannot be created.
Peter Shaffer (1926–) British dramatist.
Equus, II:35

8 So I triumphed ere my passion, sweeping
thro' me, left me dry,
Left me with the palsied heart, and left me
with the jaundiced eye.
Alfred, Lord Tennyson (1809–92) British poet.
Locksley Hall

9 Strange fits of passion have I known:
And I will dare to tell,
But in the lover's ear alone,
What once to me befell.
William Wordsworth (1770–1850) British poet.
Strange Fits of Passion

PAST

See also experience, future, history, memory, nostalgia, present, regret, time

1 Even God cannot change the past.
Agathon (c. 446–401 BC) Athenian poet and playwright.
Nicomachean Ethics (Aristotle), VI

2 There is always something rather absurd
about the past.
Max Beerbohm (1872–1956) British writer.
1880

3 A king lived long ago,
In the morning of the world,
When earth was nigher heaven than now.
Robert Browning (1812–89) British poet.
Pippa Passes, Pt. I

4 Study the past, if you would divine the future.
Confucius (K'ung Fu-tzu; 551–479 BC) Chinese philosopher.
Analects

5 The past is a foreign country: they do things differently there.
L. P. Hartley (1895–1972) British novelist.
The Go-Between

6 Look back, and smile at perils past.
Walter Scott (1771–1832) Scottish novelist.
The Bridal of Triermain, Introduction

7 The past is the only dead thing that smells sweet.
Edward Thomas (1878–1917) British poet.
Early One Morning

8 Keep off your thoughts from things that are past and done;
For thinking of the past wakes regret and pain.
Arthur Waley (1889–1966) British poet and translator.
Translation from the Chinese of Po-Chü-I
Resignation

9 The past, at least, is secure.
Daniel Webster (1782–1852) US statesman.
Speech, US Senate, 26 Jan 1830

PATIENCE

See also endurance, persistence

1 A watched pot never boils.
Proverb

2 Everything comes to him who waits.
Proverb

3 First things first.
Proverb

4 Patience is a virtue.
Proverb

5 Rome was not built in a day.
Proverb

6 We must learn to walk before we can run.
Proverb

7 Wait and see.
Herbert Henry Asquith (1852–1928) British statesman.
In various speeches, 1910

8 *Patience*, n. A minor form of despair, disguised as a virtue.
Ambrose Bierce (1842–?1914) US writer and journalist.
The Devil's Dictionary

9 The bud may have a bitter taste,

But sweet will be the flower.
William Cowper (1731–1800) British poet.
Olney Hymns, 35

10 Beware the Fury of a Patient Man.
John Dryden (1631–1700) British poet and dramatist.
Absalom and Achitophel, I

11 Patience and passage of time do more than strength and fury.
Jean de La Fontaine (1621–95) French poet.
Fables, II, 'Le Lion et le Rat'

12 Though patience be a tired mare, yet she will plod.
William Shakespeare (1564–1616) English dramatist.
Henry V, II:1

13 It is very strange . . . that the years teach us patience; that the shorter our time, the greater our capacity for waiting.
Elizabeth Taylor (1912–75) British writer.
A Wreath of Roses, Ch. 10

PATIENTS

1 Keep a watch also on the faults of the patients, which often make them lie about the taking of things prescribed.
Hippocrates (c. 460–c. 377 BC) Greek physician.
Decorum, 14

2 The sick man is a parasite of society. In certain cases it is indecent to go on living. To continue to vegetate in a state of cowardly dependence upon doctors and special treatments, once the meaning of life, the right to life has been lost, ought to be regarded with the greatest contempt by society.
Friedrich Wilhelm Nietzsche (1844–1900) German philosopher.
The Twilight of the Idols, 'Skirmishes in a War with the Age'

PATRIOTISM

See also homesickness, loyalty, war

1 What pity is it
That we can die but once to serve our country!
Joseph Addison (1672–1719) British essayist.
Cato, IV:4

2 Speak for England.
Leopold Amery (1873–1955) British statesman.
Shouted to Arthur Greenwood, Labour Party spokesman, before he began to speak in a House of Commons debate immediately preceding the declaration of war, 2 Sept 1939

3 That this house will in no circumstances fight for its King and country.
Anonymous
Motion passed at the Oxford Union, 9 Feb 1933

4 Patriotism is seen not only as the last refuge

of the scoundrel but as the first bolt-hole of the hypocrite.

Melvyn Bragg (1939–) British author and television presenter.
Speak for England, Introduction

5 'My country, right or wrong' is a thing that no patriot would think of saying, except in a desperate case. It is like saying 'My mother, drunk or sober.'

G. K. Chesterton (1874–1936) British writer.
The Defendant

6 Be England what she will,
With all her faults, she is my country still.

Charles Churchill (1731–64) British poet.
The Farewell

7 England, with all thy faults, I love thee still,
My country.

William Cowper (1731–1800) British poet.
The Task

8 Our country! In her intercourse with foreign nations, may she always be in the right; but our country, right or wrong.

Stephen Decatur (1779–1820) US naval officer.
Speech, Norfolk, Virginia, Apr 1816

9 Nationalism is an infantile disease. It is the measles of mankind.

Albert Einstein (1879–1955) German-born US physicist.
Einstein: A Study in Simplicity (Edwin Muller)

10 I have never understood why one's affections must be confined, as once with women, to a single country.

John Kenneth Galbraith (1908–) US economist.
A Life in our Times

11 Anyone who wants to carry on the war against the outsiders, come with me. I can't offer you either honours or wages; I offer you hunger, thirst, forced marches, battles and death. Anyone who loves his country, follow me.

Giuseppe Garibaldi (1807–82) Italian general and political leader.
Garibaldi (Guerzoni)

12 That kind of patriotism which consists in hating all other nations.

Elizabeth Gaskell (1810–65) British novelist.
Sylvia's Lovers, Ch. 1

13 I only regret that I have but one life to lose for my country.

Nathan Hale (1755–76) US revolutionary hero.
Speech before his execution, 22 Sept 1776

14 Unlike so many who find success, she remained a 'dinkum hard-swearing Aussie' to the end.

Arnold Haskell (1903–80) English writer on ballet.
Referring to Dame Nellie Melba
Waltzing Matilda

15 *Dulce et decorum est pro patria mori.*

It is a sweet and seemly thing to die for one's country.

Horace (Quintus Horatius Flaccus; 65–8 BC) Roman poet.
Odes, III

16 We don't want to fight, but, by jingo if we do,
We've got the ships, we've got the men, we've got the money too.
We've fought the Bear before, and while Britons shall be true,
The Russians shall not have Constantinople.

George William Hunt (c. 1829–1904) British writer.
We Don't Want to Fight

17 Patriotism is the last refuge of a scoundrel.

Samuel Johnson (1709–84) British lexicographer.
Life of Johnson (J. Boswell), Vol. II

18 And so, my fellow Americans: ask not what your country can do for you – ask what you can do for your country. My fellow citizens of the world: ask not what America will do for you, but what together we can do for the freedom of man.

John Fitzgerald Kennedy (1917–63) US statesman.
Inaugural address, 20 Jan 1961

19 Those who prate about Blimpish patriotism in the mode of Margaret Thatcher are also the ones who will take millions off the caring services of this country.

Neil Kinnock (1942–) British politician.
Speech, Labour Party Conference, Brighton, 1983

20 I would die for my country . . . but I would not let my country die for me.

Neil Kinnock
Speech on nuclear disarmament, 1987

21 'Take my drum to England, hang et by the shore,
Strike et when your powder's runnin' low;
If the Dons sight Devon, I'll quit the port o' Heaven,
An' drum them up the Channel as we drummed them long ago.'

Henry John Newbolt (1862–1938) British poet.
Drake's Drum

22 But cared greatly to serve God and the King,
And keep the Nelson touch.

Henry John Newbolt
Minora Sidera

23 The old Lie: *Dulce et decorum est Pro patria mori.*

Wilfred Owen (1893–1918) British poet.
Dulce et decorum est

24 If I were an American, as I am an Englishman, while a foreign troop was landed in my country, I never would lay down my arms, – never – never – never!

William Pitt the Elder (1708–78) British statesman.
Speech, House of Lords, 18 Nov 1777

25 There is no room in this country for hyphenated Americanism.
Theodore Roosevelt (1858–1919) US Republican president.
Speech, New York, 12 Oct 1915

26 There can be no fifty-fifty Americanism in this country. There is room here for only one hundred per cent Americanism.
Theodore Roosevelt
Speech, Saratoga, 19 July 1918

27 Patriots always talk of dying for their country and never of killing for their country.
Bertrand Russell (1872–1970) British philosopher.
The Autobiography of Bertrand Russell

28 Not that I lov'd Caesar less, but that I lov'd Rome more.
William Shakespeare (1564–1616) English dramatist.
Julius Caesar, III:2

29 True patriotism is of no party.
Tobias Smollett (1721–71) British novelist.
The Adventures of Sir Launcelote Greaves

30 Patriotism to the Soviet State is a revolutionary duty, whereas patriotism to a bourgeois State is treachery.
Leon Trotsky (Lev Davidovich Bronstein; 1879–1940) Russian revolutionary.
Disputed Barricade (Fitzroy Maclean)

31 I was born an American; I will live an American; I shall die an American.
Daniel Webster (1782–1852) US statesman.
Speech, US Senate, 17 July 1850

32 'Shoot, if you must, this old gray head, But spare your country's flag,' she said.

A shade of sadness, a blush of shame, Over the face of the leader came.
John Greenleaf Whittier (1807–92) US poet.
Barbara Frietchie

33 There is one certain means by which I can be sure never to see my country's ruin; I will die in the last ditch.
William III (1650–1702) King of England.
History of England (Hume)

PATRONAGE

See also promotion

1 *Patron.* Commonly a wretch who supports with insolence, and is paid with flattery.
Samuel Johnson (1709–84) British lexicographer.
Dictionary of the English Language

2 Is not a Patron, my Lord, one who looks with unconcern on a man struggling for life in the water, and, when he has reached ground, encumbers him with help? The notice which you have been pleased to take of my labours, had it been early, had it been kind; but it has been delayed till I am indifferent, and cannot enjoy it; till I am solitary, and cannot impart it; till I am known, and do not want it.
Samuel Johnson
Letter to Lord Chesterfield, 7 Feb 1755
Life of Johnson (J. Boswell), Vol. I

PEACE

See also war and peace

1 The wolf also shall dwell with the lamb, and the leopard shall lie down with the kid; and the calf and the young lion and the fatling together: and a little child shall lead them. And the cow and the bear shall feed; their young ones shall lie down together: and the lion shall eat straw like the ox. And the sucking child shall play on the hole of the asp, and the weaned child shall put his hand on the cockatrice' den. They shall not hurt nor destroy in all my holy mountain: for the earth shall be full of the knowledge of the Lord, as the waters cover the sea.
Bible: Isaiah
11:6–9

2 There is no peace, saith the Lord, unto the wicked.
Bible: Isaiah
48:22

3 Peace I leave with you, my peace I give unto you: not as the world giveth, give I unto you. Let not your heart be troubled, neither let it be afraid.
Bible: John
14:27

4 *Peace,* n. In international affairs, a period of cheating between two periods of fighting.
Ambrose Bierce (1842–?1914) US writer and journalist.
The Devil's Dictionary

5 Give peace in our time, O Lord.
The Book of Common Prayer
Morning Prayer, Versicles

6 Don't tell me peace has broken out.
Bertolt Brecht (1898–1956) German dramatist.
Mother Courage, VIII

7 I believe it is peace for our time . . . peace with honour.
Neville Chamberlain (1869–1940) British statesman.
Broadcast after Munich Agreement, 1 Oct 1938

8 Anythin' for a quiet life, as the man said wen he took the sitivation at the lighthouse.
Charles Dickens (1812–70) British novelist.
Pickwick Papers, Ch. 43

9 Lord Salisbury and myself have brought you back peace – but a peace I hope with honour.
Benjamin Disraeli (1804–81) British statesman.
Speech, House of Commons, 16 July 1878

10 Let us have peace.

Ulysses Simpson Grant (1822–85) US general.
On accepting nomination
Letter, 29 May 1868

11 Arms alone are not enough to keep the peace – it must be kept by men.

John Fitzgerald Kennedy (1917–63) US statesman.
The Observer, 'Sayings of the Decade', 1962

12 And who will bring white peace
That he may sleep upon his hill again?

Vachel Lindsay (1879–1931) US poet.
Abraham Lincoln Walks at Midnight

13 The issues are the same. We wanted peace on earth, love, and understanding between everyone around the world. We have learned that change comes slowly.

Paul McCartney (1943–   ) British rock musician.
The Observer, 'Sayings of the Week', 7 June 1987

14 Roll up that map: it will not be wanted these ten years.

William Pitt the Younger (1759–1806) British statesman.
On learning that Napoleon had won the Battle of Austerlitz
Attrib.

15 Nation shall speak peace unto nation.

Montague John Rendall (1862–1950) British schoolmaster.
Motto of BBC, 1927

16 Here, where the world is quiet;
Here, where all trouble seems
Dead winds' and spent waves' riot
In doubtful dreams of dreams.

Algernon Charles Swinburne (1837–1909) British poet.
The Garden of Proserpine

17 We are the true peace movement.

Margaret Thatcher (1925–   ) British politician and prime minister.
The Times, 1983

18 And I shall have some peace there, for peace comes dropping slow,
Dropping from the veils of the morning to where the cricket sings.

W. B. Yeats (1865–1939) Irish poet.
The Lake Isle of Innisfree

PERCEPTION

1 If the doors of perception were cleansed everything would appear to man as it is, infinite.

William Blake (1757–1827) British poet.
The Marriage of Heaven and Hell, 'A Memorable Fancy'

2 Man's Desires are limited by his Perceptions; none can desire what he has not perceived.

William Blake
There is no Natural Religion

3 'What,' it will be questioned, 'when the sun rises, do you not see a round disc of fire somewhat like a guinea?' 'O no, no, I see an innumerable company of the heavenly host crying, 'Holy, Holy, Holy is the Lord God Almighty!"

William Blake
Descriptive Catalogue, 'The Vision of Judgment'

4 I saw it, but I did not realize it.

Elizabeth Peabody (1804–94) US educationalist.
Giving a Transcendentalist explanation for her accidentally walking into a tree
The Peabody Sisters of Salem (L. Tharp)

PERFECTION

See also imperfection

1 The pursuit of perfection, then, is the pursuit of sweetness and light... He who works for sweetness and light united, works to make reason and the will of God prevail.

Matthew Arnold (1822–88) British poet and critic.
Culture and Anarchy, Ch. 1

2 The year's at the spring,
And day's at the morn;
Morning's at seven;
The hill-side's dew-pearled;
The lark's on the wing;
The snail's on the thorn;
God's in His heaven –
All's right with the world.

Robert Browning (1812–89) British poet.
Pippa Passes, Pt. I

3 What's come to perfection perishes.
Things learned on earth, we shall practise in heaven.
Works done least rapidly, Art most cherishes.

Robert Browning
Old Pictures in Florence, XVII

4 You would attain to the divine perfection,
And yet not turn your back upon the world.

Henry Wadsworth Longfellow (1807–82) US poet.
Michael Angelo

5 Perfection has one grave defect; it is apt to be dull.

W. Somerset Maugham (1874–1965) British novelist.
The Summing Up

6 Whoever thinks a faultless piece to see,
Thinks what ne'er was, nor is, nor e'er shall be.

Alexander Pope (1688–1744) British poet.
An Essay on Criticism

7 Oysters are more beautiful than any religion ... There's nothing in Christianity or Buddhism that quite matches the sympathetic unselfishness of an oyster.

Saki (Hector Hugh Munro; 1870–1916) British writer.
The Match-Maker

8 Everything's Coming Up Roses.

Stephen Sondheim (1930–   ) US composer and lyricist.
Song title

9 Finality is death. Perfection is finality. Nothing is perfect. There are lumps in it.
James Stephens (1882–1950) Irish novelist.
The Crock of Gold

PERSISTENCE

See also determination, endurance, patience

1 If the mountain will not come to Mahomet, Mahomet must go to the mountain.
Proverb

2 Never say die.
Proverb

3 Slow but sure wins the race.
Proverb

4 And ye shall be hated of all men for my name's sake: but he that endureth to the end shall be saved.
Bible: Matthew
10:22

5 If at first you don't succeed,
Try, try again.
William Edward Hickson (1803–70) British educationalist.
Try and Try Again

6 A man may write at any time, if he will set himself doggedly to it.
Samuel Johnson (1709–84) British lexicographer.
Life of Johnson (J. Boswell), Vol. I

7 The drop of rain maketh a hole in the stone, not by violence, but by oft falling.
Hugh Latimer (1485–1555) English churchman.
See also LUCRETIUS; OVID
Sermon preached before Edward VI

8 Keep right on to the end of the road.
Harry Lauder (Hugh MacLennon; 1870–1950) Scottish music-hall artist.
Song title

9 You persisted for a certain number of years like a stammer. You were a *stammer*, if you like, of Space-Time.
Wyndham Lewis (1882–1957) British novelist.
The Human Age, 'The Childermass'

10 Constant dripping hollows out a stone.
Lucretius (Titus Lucretius Carus; c. 99–55 BC) Roman philosopher.
On the Nature of the Universe, I. *See also* LATIMER; OVID

11 Dripping water hollows out a stone, a ring is worn away by use.
Ovid (Publius Ovidius Naso; 43 BC–17 AD) Roman poet.
See also LATIMER; LUCRETIUS
Epistulae Ex Ponto, Bk. IV

12 I am a kind of burr; I shall stick.
William Shakespeare (1564–1616) English dramatist.
Measure for Measure, IV:3

PERSPECTIVE

See also objectivity

1 'Tis distance lends enchantment to the view, And robes the mountain in its azure hue.
Thomas Campbell (1777–1844) British poet.
Pleasures of Hope, I

2 One sees great things from the valley; only small things from the peak.
G. K. Chesterton (1874–1936) British writer.
The Hammer of God

3 Fleas know not whether they are upon the body of a giant or upon one of ordinary size.
Walter Savage Landor (1775–1864) British poet and writer.
Imaginary Conversations, 'Southey and Porson'

4 Everything must be taken seriously, nothing tragically.
Louis Adolphe Thiers (1797–1877) French statesman and historian.
Speech, French National Assembly, 24 May 1873

PERSUASION

1 They will conquer, but they will not convince.
Miguel de Unamuno y Jugo (1864–1936) Spanish writer.
Referring to the Franco rebels
Attrib.

2 There is a holy, mistaken zeal in politics, as well as religion. By persuading others we convince ourselves.
Junius An unidentified writer of letters (1769–72) to the *London Public Advertiser*.
Letter, 19 Dec 1769

3 For a priest to turn a man when he lies a-dying, is just like one that has a long time solicited a woman, and cannot obtain his end; at length makes her drunk, and so lies with her.
John Selden (1584–1654) English historian.
Table Talk

4 The President spends most of his time kissing people on the cheek in order to get them to do what they ought to do without getting kissed.
Harry S. Truman (1884–1972) US statesman.
The Observer, 'Sayings of the Week', 6 Feb 1949

PERVERSITY

See also petulance, stubbornness

1 If it's heaven for climate, it's hell for company.
J. M. Barrie (1860–1937) British novelist and dramatist.
The Little Minister, Ch. 3

2 Never the time and the place

And the loved one all together!

Robert Browning (1812–89) British poet.
Never the Time and the Place

3   For 'tis a truth well known to most,
    That whatsoever thing is lost –
    We seek it, ere it come to light,
    In every cranny but the right.

    William Cowper (1731–1800) British poet.
    The Retired Cat

4   Let's find out what everyone is doing,
    And then stop everyone from doing it.

    A. P. Herbert (1890–1971) British writer and politician.
    Let's Stop Somebody

5   I had never had a piece of toast
    Particularly long and wide,
    But fell upon the sanded floor,
    And always on the buttered side.

    James Payn (1830–98) British writer and editor.
    Chambers's Journal, 2 Feb 1884

6   Adam was but human – this explains it all.
    He did not want the apple for the apple's
    sake, he wanted it only because it was
    forbidden.

    Mark Twain (Samuel Langhorne Clemens; 1835–1910)
    US writer.
    Pudd'nhead Wilson's Calendar, Ch. 2

PESSIMISM

1   Pessimism, when you get used to it, is just
    as agreeable as optimism.

    Arnold Bennett (1867–1931) British novelist.
    Things that have Interested Me, 'The Slump in Pessimism'

2   Scratch a pessimist, and you find often a
    defender of privilege.

    Lord Beveridge (1879–1963) British economist.
    The Observer, 'Sayings of the Week', 17 Dec 1943

3   The optimist proclaims we live in the best of
    all possible worlds; and the pessimist fears
    this is true.

    James Cabell (1879–1958) US novelist and journalist.
    The Silver Stallion

4   He who despairs over an event is a coward,
    but he who holds hopes for the human
    condition is a fool.

    Albert Camus (1913–60) French existentialist writer.
    The Rebel

5   A Hard Rain's A-Gonna Fall.

    Bob Dylan (Robert Allen Zimmerman; 1941–   ) US
    popular singer.
    Song title

6   Sleep is good, death is better; but of course,
    the best thing would be never to have been
    born at all.

    Heinrich Heine (1797–1856) German poet and writer.
    Morphine

7   Nothing to do but work,
    Nothing to eat but food,
    Nothing to wear but clothes,

To keep one from going nude.

Benjamin Franklin King (1857–94) American humorist.
The Pessimist

8   If we see light at the end of the tunnel it is
    the light of an oncoming train.

    Robert Lowell (1917–77) US poet.
    Day by Day

9   How many pessimists end up by desiring the
    things they fear, in order to prove that they
    are right.

    Robert Mallet (1915–   ) French writer.
    Apostilles

10 A pessimist is a man who looks both ways
    before crossing a one-way street.

    Laurence J. Peter (1919–90) Canadian writer.
    Peter's Quotations

11 It is not, nor it cannot come to good.

    William Shakespeare (1564–1616) English dramatist.
    Hamlet, I:2

PETULANCE

See also perversity, stubbornness

1   She refused to begin the 'Beguine'
    Tho' they besought her to
    And with language profane and obscene
    She curs'd the man who taught her to
    She curs'd Cole Porter too!

    Noël Coward (1899–1973) British dramatist.
    Sigh No More, 'Nina'

2   He has to learn that petulance is not
    sarcasm, and that insolence is not invective.

    Benjamin Disraeli (1804–81) British statesman.
    Said of Sir C. Wood
    Speech, House of Commons, 16 Dec 1852

3   I am the emperor, and I want dumplings.

    Ferdinand I (1793–1875) Emperor of Austria.
    The Fall of the House of Habsburg (E. Crankshaw)

4   I hate a fellow whom pride, or cowardice, or
    laziness drives into a corner, and who does
    nothing when he is there but sit and *growl*;
    let him come out as I do, and *bark*.

    Samuel Johnson (1709–84) British lexicographer.
    Life of Johnson (J. Boswell), Vol. IV

PHILISTINISM

See also arts, books, culture

1   For this class we have a designation which
    now has become pretty well known, and
    which we may as well still keep for them,
    the designation of Philistines.

    Matthew Arnold (1822–88) British poet and critic.
    Referring to the middle class
    Culture and Anarchy, Ch. 3

2   The great apostle of the Philistines, Lord
    Macaulay.

    Matthew Arnold
    Joubert

3 The finest collection of frames I ever saw.

Humphry Davy (1778–1829) British chemist.
When asked what he thought of the Paris art galleries
Attrib.

4 When I hear anyone talk of Culture, I reach for my revolver.

Hermann Goering (1893–1946) German leader.
Attrib. to Goering but probably said by Hanns Johst

5 I've never been in there . . . but there are only three things to see, and I've seen colour reproductions of all of them.

Harold W. Ross (1892–1951) US journalist.
Referring to the Louvre
A Farewell to Arms (Ernest Hemingway)

6 All my wife has ever taken from the Mediterranean – from that whole vast intuitive culture – are four bottles of Chianti to make into lamps, and two china condiment donkeys labelled Sally and Peppy.

Peter Shaffer (1926–) British dramatist.
Equus, I:18

7 Particularly against books the Home Secretary is. If we can't stamp out literature in the country, we can at least stop it being brought in from outside.

Evelyn Waugh (1903–66) British novelist.
Vile Bodies, Ch. 2

8 Listen! There never was an artistic period. There never was an Art-loving nation.

James Whistler (1834–1903) US painter.
Attrib.

PHILOSOPHERS

See also philosophy

1 All are lunatics, but he who can analyze his delusion is called a philosopher.

Ambrose Bierce (1842–?1914) US writer and journalist.
Epigrams

2 There is nothing so absurd but some philosopher has said it.

Cicero (106–43 BC) Roman orator and statesman.
De Divinatione, II

3 To a philosopher no circumstance, however trifling, is too minute.

Oliver Goldsmith (1728–74) Irish-born British writer.
The Citizen of the World

4 Philosophers never balance between profit and honesty, because their decisions are general, and neither their passions nor imaginations are interested in the objects.

David Hume (1711–76) Scottish philosopher.
A Treatise of Human Nature

5 I doubt if the philosopher lives, or ever has lived, who could know himself to be heartily despised by a street boy without some irritation.

T. H. Huxley (1825–95) British biologist.
Evolution and Ethics

6 In the philosopher there is nothing whatever impersonal; and, above all, his morality bears decided and decisive testimony to *who he is* – that is to say, to the order of rank in which the innermost drives of his nature stand in relation to one another.

Friedrich Wilhelm Nietzsche (1844–1900) German philosopher.
Jenseits von Gut und Böse

7 Not to care for philosophy is to be a true philosopher.

Blaise Pascal (1623–62) French philosopher and mathematician.
Pensées, I

8 Three passions, simple but overwhelmingly strong, have governed my life: the longing for love, the search for knowledge, and unbearable pity for the suffering of mankind.

Bertrand Russell (1872–1970) British philosopher.
The Autobiography of Bertrand Russell, Prologue

9 Philosophers are as jealous as women. Each wants a monopoly of praise.

George Santayana (1863–1952) US philosopher.
Dialogues In Limbo

10 There are now-a-days professors of philosophy but not philosophers.

Henry David Thoreau (1817–62) US writer.
Walden, 'Economy'

PHILOSOPHY

See also logic, metaphysics, philosophers, thinking

1 The principles of logic and metaphysics are true simply because we never allow them to be anything else.

A. J. Ayer (1910–89) British philosopher.
Language, Truth and Logic

2 The formula 'Two and two make five' is not without its attractions.

Fedor Mikhailovich Dostoevsky (1821–81) Russian novelist.
Notes from the Underground

3 If we take in our hand any volume; of divinity or school metaphysics, for instance; let us ask, *Does it contain any abstract reasoning concerning quantity or number?* No. *Does it contain any experimental reasoning, concerning matter of fact and existence?* No. Commit it then to the flames: for it can contain nothing but sophistry and illusion.

David Hume (1711–76) Scottish philosopher.
An Enquiry Concerning Human Understanding

4 We are perpetually moralists, but we are geometricians only by chance. Our intercourse with intellectual nature is necessary; our speculations upon matter are voluntary, and at leisure.

Samuel Johnson (1709–84) British lexicographer.
Lives of the English Poets, 'Milton'

5 I refute it *thus*.

Samuel Johnson
Replying to Boswell's contention that they were unable to refute Bishop Berkeley's theory of matter, by kicking a large stone with his foot
Life of Johnson (J. Boswell), Vol. I

6 There are innumerable questions to which the inquisitive mind can in this state receive no answer: Why do you and I exist? Why was this world created? Since it was to be created, why was it not created sooner?

Samuel Johnson
Life of Johnson (J. Boswell), Vol. III

7 Do not all charms fly
At the mere touch of cold philosophy?

John Keats (1795–1821) British poet.
Lamia, II

8 Axioms in philosophy are not axioms until they are proved upon our pulses; we read fine things but never feel them to the full until we have gone the same steps as the author.

John Keats
Letter to J. H. Reynolds, 3 May 1818

9 There will be no end to the troubles of states, or indeed, my dear Glaucon, of humanity itself, till philosophers become kings in this world, or till those we now call kings and rulers really and truly become philosophers.

Plato (429–347 BC) Greek philosopher.
Republic, Bk. 5

10 We thought philosophy ought to be patient and unravel people's mental blocks. Trouble with doing that is, once you've unravelled them, their heads fall off.

Frederic Raphael (1931–) British author.
The Glittering Prizes: A Double Life, III:2

11 Matter . . . a convenient formula for describing what happens where it isn't.

Bertrand Russell (1872–1970) British philosopher.
An Outline of Philosophy

12 Philosophy is the replacement of category-habits by category-disciplines.

Gilbert Ryle (1900–76) British philosopher.
The Concept of Mind, Introduction

13 It is a great advantage for a system of philosophy to be substantially true.

George Santayana (1863–1952) US philosopher.
The Unknowable

14 Philosophy is the product of wonder.

A. N. Whitehead (1861–1947) British philosopher.
Nature and Life, Ch. 1

15 The history of Western philosophy is, after all, no more than a series of footnotes to Plato's philosophy.

A. N. Whitehead
Attrib.

16 My advice to you is not to inquire why or

whither, but just enjoy your ice-cream while it's on your plate, – that's my philosophy.

Thornton Wilder (1897–1975) US novelist and dramatist.
The Skin of Our Teeth, I

17 Philosophy, as we use the word, is a fight against the fascination which forms of expression exert upon us.

Ludwig Wittgenstein (1889–1951) Austrian philosopher.
The Blue Book

18 Philosophy is not a theory but an activity.

Ludwig Wittgenstein
Tractatus Logico-Philosophicus, Ch. 4

PHOTOGRAPHY

1 Photography can never grow up if it imitates some other medium. It has to walk alone; it has to be itself.

Berenice Abbott (b. 1898) US photographer.
Infinity, 'It Has to Walk Alone'

2 Most things in life are moments of pleasure and a lifetime of embarrassment; photography is a moment of embarrassment and a lifetime of pleasure.

Tony Benn (1925–) British politician.
The Sunday Times, 31 Dec 1989

3 The camera cannot lie. But it can be an accessory to untruth.

Harold Evans (1928–) British journalist.
Pictures on a Page

4 As far as I knew, he had never taken a photograph before, and the summit of Everest was hardly the place to show him how.

Edmund Hillary (1919–) New Zealand mountaineer.
Referring to Tenzing Norgay, his companion on the conquest of Mt Everest (1953)
High Adventure

5 The modern pantheist not only sees the god in everything, he takes photographs of it.

D. H. Lawrence (1885–1930) British novelist.
St Mawr

6 I have for instance among my purchases . . . several original Mona Lisas and all painted (according to the Signature) by the great artist Kodak.

Spike Milligan (1918–) British comic actor and author.
A Dustbin of Milligan, 'Letters to Harry Secombe'

7 A photograph is not only an image (as a painting is an image), an interpretation of the real; it is also a trace, something directly stencilled off the real, like a footprint or a death mask.

Susan Sontag (1933–) US novelist and essayist.
On Photography

PLACES

See also Britain, Europe

1 The shortest way out of Manchester is notoriously a bottle of Gordon's gin.
William Bolitho (1890–1930) British writer.
Attrib.

2 Nothing and no one can destroy the Chinese people. They are relentless survivors. They are the oldest civilized people on earth. Their civilization passes through phases but its basic characteristics remain the same. They yield, they bend to the wind, but they never break.
Pearl Buck (1892–1973) US novelist.
China, Past and Present, Ch. 1

3 India is a geographical term. It is no more a united nation than the Equator.
Winston Churchill (1874–1965) British statesman.
Speech, Royal Albert Hall, 18 Mar 1931

4 There are few virtues which the Poles do not possess and there are few errors they have ever avoided.
Winston Churchill
Speech, House of Commons, 1945

5 Latins are tenderly enthusiastic. In Brazil they throw flowers at you. In Argentina they throw themselves.
Marlene Dietrich (Maria Magdalene von Losch; 1904–)
German-born film star.
Newsweek, 24 Aug 1959

6 I find it hard to say, because when I was there it seemed to be shut.
Clement Freud (1924–) British Liberal politician and broadcaster.
On being asked for his opinion of New Zealand. Similar remarks have been attributed to others
BBC radio, 12 Apr 1978

7 From Greenland's icy mountains,
From India's coral strand,
Where Afric's sunny fountains
Roll down their golden sand.
Reginald Heber (1783–1826) British bishop and hymn writer.
From Greenland's Icy Mountains

8 Dublin, though a place much worse than London, is not so bad as Iceland.
Samuel Johnson (1709–84) British lexicographer.
Letter to Mrs Christopher Smart
Life of Johnson (J. Boswell), Vol. IV

9 Asia is not going to be civilized after the methods of the West. There is too much Asia and she is too old.
Rudyard Kipling (1865–1936) Indian-born British writer.
Life's Handicap, 'The Man Who Was'

10 On the road to Mandalay
Where the flyin'-fishes play.
Rudyard Kipling
The Road to Mandalay

11 And all lying mysteriously within the Australian underdark, that peculiar, lost weary aloofness of Australia. There was the vast town of Sydney. And it didn't seem to be real, it seemed to be sprinkled on the surface of a darkness into which it never penetrated.
D. H. Lawrence (1885–1930) British novelist.
Kangaroo, Ch. 1

12 So you're going to Australia! Well, I made twenty thousand pounds on my tour there, but of course *that* will never be done again. Still, it's a wonderful country, and you'll have a good time. What are you going to sing? All I can say is – sing 'em muck! It's all they can understand!
Nellie Melba (Helen Porter Mitchell; 1861–1931)
Australian soprano.
Speaking to Clara Butt
Clara Butt: Her Life Story (W. H. Ponder)

13 I shook hands with a friendly Arab . . . I still have my right hand to prove it.
Spike Milligan (1918–) British comic actor and author.
A Dustbin of Milligan, 'Letters to Harry Secombe'

14 Jerusalem the golden,
With milk and honey blest,
Beneath thy contemplation
Sink heart and voice opprest.
John Mason Neale (1818–66) British churchman.
Jerusalem the Golden

15 Once a jolly swagman camped by a billy-bong,
Under the shade of a coolibah tree,
And he sang as he sat and waited for his billy-boil,
'You'll come a-waltzing, Matilda, with me.'
Andrew Barton Paterson (1864–1941) Australian journalist and poet.
Waltzing Matilda

16 Even the Hooligan was probably invented in China centuries before we thought of him.
Saki (Hector Hugh Munro; 1870–1916) British writer.
Reginald on House-Parties

17 Great God! this is an awful place.
Captain Robert Falcon Scott (1868–1912) British explorer.
Referring to the South Pole
Journal, 17 Jan 1912

18 The South African Police would leave no stone unturned to see that nothing disturbed the even terror of their lives.
Tom Sharpe (1928–) British novelist.
Indecent Exposure, Ch. 1

19 Cusins is a very nice fellow, certainly: nobody would ever guess that he was born in Australia.
George Bernard Shaw (1856–1950) Irish dramatist and critic.
Major Barbara, I

20 The Japanese have perfected good manners and made them indistinguishable from rudeness.
Paul Theroux (1941–) US-born writer.
The Great Railway Bazaar, Ch. 2

21 I'm Charley's aunt from Brazil, where the nuts come from.
Brandon Thomas (1856–1914) British actor and dramatist.
Charley's Aunt, I

PLAYS

See also acting, actors, criticism, literature, Shakespeare, theatre, writers, writing

1 Now a whole is that which has a beginning, a middle, and an end.
Aristotle (384–322 BC) Greek philosopher.
Referring specifically to the dramatic form of tragedy
Poetics, Ch. 7

2 One of Edward's Mistresses was Jane Shore, who has had a play written about her, but it is a tragedy and therefore not worth reading.
Jane Austen (1775–1817) British novelist.
The History of England

3 In the theatre the audience want to be surprised – but by things that they expect.
Tristan Bernard (1866–1947) French dramatist.
Contes, Repliques et Bon Mots

4 Prologues precede the piece – in mournful verse;
As undertakers – walk before the hearse.
David Garrick (1717–79) British actor and manager.
Apprentice, Prologue

5 He always hurries to the main event and whisks his audience into the middle of things as though they knew already.
Horace (Quintus Horatius Flaccus; 65–8 BC) Roman poet.
Ars Poetica

6 I think you would have been very glad if I had written it.
Alexis Piron (1689–1773) French poet and dramatist.
Discussing Voltaire's *Sémiramis* with him after its poor reception on the first night
Cyclopaedia of Anecdotes (K. Arvine)

7 Depending upon shock tactics is easy, whereas writing a good play is difficult. Pubic hair is no substitute for wit.
J. B. Priestley (1894–1984) British novelist.
Outcries and Asides

8 My soul; sit thou a patient looker-on;
Judge not the play before the play is done:
Her plot hath many changes, every day
Speaks a new scene; the last act crowns the play.
Francis Quarles (1592–1644) English poet.
Epigram, Respice Finem

9 Rehearsing a play is making the word flesh. Publishing a play is reversing the process.
Peter Shaffer (1926–) British dramatist.
Equus, Note

10 If it be true that good wine needs no bush, 'tis true that a good play needs no epilogue.
William Shakespeare (1564–1616) English dramatist.
As You Like It, Epilogue

11 The play's the thing
Wherein I'll catch the conscience of the King.
William Shakespeare
Hamlet, II:2

12 A good many inconveniences attend play-going in any large city, but the greatest of them is usually the play itself.
Kenneth Tynan (1927–80) British theatre critic.
New York Herald Tribune

13 A novel is a static thing that one moves through; a play is a dynamic thing that moves past one.
Kenneth Tynan
Curtains

14 The play was a great success, but the audience was a disaster.
Oscar Wilde (1854–1900) Irish-born British dramatist.
Referring to a play that had recently failed
Attrib.

PLEASURE

See also debauchery, happiness, leisure, merrymaking

1 No pleasure without pain.
Proverb

2 And if the following day, he chance to find
A new repast, or an untasted spring,
Blesses his stars, and thinks it luxury.
Joseph Addison (1672–1719) British essayist.
Cato, I:4

3 One half of the world cannot understand the pleasures of the other.
Jane Austen (1775–1817) British novelist.
Emma, Ch. 9

4 Then I commended mirth, because a man hath no better thing under the sun, than to eat, and to drink, and to be merry: for that shall abide with him of his labour the days of his life, which God giveth him under the sun.
Bible: Ecclesiastes
8:15

5 He who bends to himself a Joy
Doth the wingèd life destroy;
But he who kisses the Joy as it flies
Lives in Eternity's sunrise.
William Blake (1757–1827) British poet.
Gnomic Verses

6 Pleasure after all is a safer guide than either right or duty.
Samuel Butler (1835–1902) British writer.
The Way of All Flesh, Ch. 19

7 Though sages may pour out their wisdom's treasure,
There is no sterner moralist than Pleasure.
Lord Byron (1788–1824) British poet.
Don Juan, III

8 In Xanadu did Kubla Khan
A stately pleasure-dome decree:

Where Alph, the sacred river, ran
Through caverns measureless to man
Down to a sunless sea.
Samuel Taylor Coleridge (1772–1834) British poet.
Kubla Khan

9 It was a miracle of rare device,
A sunny pleasure-dome with caves of ice!
Samuel Taylor Coleridge
Kubla Khan

10 Nothing can permanently please, which does
not contain in itself the reason why it is so,
and not otherwise.
Samuel Taylor Coleridge
Biographia Literaria, Ch. 14

11 For present joys are more to flesh and blood
Than a dull prospect of a distant good.
John Dryden (1631–1700) British poet and dramatist.
The Hind and the Panther, III

12 The art of pleasing consists in being pleased.
William Hazlitt (1778–1830) British essayist.
On Manner

13 People must not do things for fun. We are
not here for fun. There is no reference to
fun in any Act of Parliament.
A. P. Herbert (1890–1971) British writer and politician.
Uncommon Law

14 Pleasure is very seldom found where it is
sought; our brightest blazes of gladness are
commonly kindled by unexpected sparks.
Samuel Johnson (1709–84) British lexicographer.
The Idler

15 No man is a hypocrite in his pleasures.
Samuel Johnson
Life of Johnson (J. Boswell), Vol. IV

16 If I had no duties, and no reference to
futurity, I would spend my life in driving
briskly in a post-chaise with a pretty woman.
Samuel Johnson
Life of Johnson (J. Boswell), Vol. III

17 Give me books, fruit, French wine and fine
weather and a little music out of doors,
played by somebody I do not know.
John Keats (1795–1821) British poet.
Letter to Fanny Keats, 29 Aug 1819

18 Life would be tolerable, were it not for its
amusements.
George Cornewall Lewis (1806–63) British statesman
and writer.
The Perpetual Pessimist (Sagittarius and George)

19 A little of what you fancy does you good.
Marie Lloyd (1870–1922) British music-hall singer.
Song title

20 Who loves not wine, woman and song,
Remains a fool his whole life long.
Martin Luther (1483–1546) German Protestant.
Attrib.

21 My candle burns at both ends;

It will not last the night;
But ah, my foes, and oh my friends –
It gives a lovely light!
Edna St Vincent Millay (1892–1950) US poet.
A Few Figs from Thistles, 'First Fig'

22 To sport with Amaryllis in the shade,
Or with the tangles of Neaera's hair.
John Milton (1608–74) English poet.
Lycidas

23 Hence, vain deluding Joys,
The brood of Folly without father bred!
John Milton
Il Penseroso

24 Great lords have their pleasures, but the
people have fun.
Baron de Montesquieu (1689–1755) French writer.
Pensées diverses

25 I wish thee as much pleasure in the reading,
as I had in the writing.
Francis Quarles (1592–1644) English poet.
Emblems, 'To the Reader'

26 Pleasures are all alike simply considered in
themselves . . . He that takes pleasure to
hear sermons enjoys himself as much as he
that hears plays.
John Selden (1584–1654) English historian.
Table Talk

27 Pleasure is nothing else but the intermission
of pain.
John Selden
Table Talk

28 A Good Time Was Had by All.
Stevie Smith (Florence Margaret Smith; 1902–71) British
poet.
Book title

29 This is the best moment of my life, since my
Granny caught her tit in the mangle.
Daley Thompson (Francis Morgan T.; 1958–   ) British
decathlete.
On winning the decathlon at the Olympics
The Guardian, 1984

30 Everyone is dragged on by their favourite
pleasure.
Virgil (Publius Vergilius Maro; 70–19 BC) Roman poet.
Eclogue, Bk. II

31 All the things I really like to do are either
immoral, illegal, or fattening.
Alexander Woollcott (1887–1943) US journalist.
Attrib.

32 Pleasures newly found are sweet
When they lie about our feet.
William Wordsworth (1770–1850) British poet.
To the Small Celandine

POETRY

See also criticism, inspiration, literature, poetry and prose,
poets

1 For this reason poetry is something more philosophical and more worthy of serious attention than history.
Aristotle (384–322 BC) Greek philosopher.
Poetics, Ch. 9

2 A criticism of life under the conditions fixed for such a criticism by the laws of poetic truth and poetic beauty.
Matthew Arnold (1822–88) British poet and critic.
Essays in Criticism, Second Series, 'The Study of Poetry'

3 I think it will be found that the grand style arises in poetry, when a noble nature, poetically gifted, treats with simplicity or with severity a serious subject.
Matthew Arnold
Closing words
On Translating Homer

4 The difference between genuine poetry and the poetry of Dryden, Pope, and all their school, is briefly this: their poetry is conceived and composed in their wits, genuine poetry is conceived and composed in the soul.
Matthew Arnold
Thomas Gray

5 Now Ireland has her madness and her weather still,
For poetry makes nothing happen.
W. H. Auden (1907–73) British poet.
In Memory of W. B. Yeats, II

6 Too many people in the modern world view poetry as a luxury, not a necessity like petrol. But to me it's the oil of life.
John Betjeman (1906–84) British poet.
The Observer, 'Sayings of the Year', 1974

7 Poetry is as much a part of the universe as mathematics and physics. It is not a cleverer device or recreation, unless the Eternal is clever.
Edmund Blunden (1896–1974) British poet.
Speech on his election as Professor of Poetry at Oxford University, 1966

8 Nothing so difficult as a beginning
In poesy, unless perhaps the end.
Lord Byron (1788–1824) British poet.
Don Juan, IV

9 I have nothing to say, I am saying it, and that is poetry.
John Cage (1912–) US composer.
In *The Sunday Times* (quoted by Cyril Connolly), 10 Sept 1972

10 For the godly poet must be chaste himself, but there is no need for his verses to be so.
Catullus (c. 84–c. 54 BC) Roman poet.
Carmina, XVI

11 That willing suspension of disbelief for the moment, which constitutes poetic faith.
Samuel Taylor Coleridge (1772–1834) British poet.
Biographia Literaria, Ch. 14

12 Poetry's unnat'ral; no man ever talked poetry 'cept a beadle on boxin' day.
Charles Dickens (1812–70) British novelist.
Pickwick Papers, Ch. 33

13 I am afeered that werges on the poetical, Sammy.
Charles Dickens
Said by Sam Weller
Pickwick Papers, Ch. 33

14 Poetry is not a turning loose of emotion, but an escape from emotion; it is not the expression of personality, but an escape from personality.
T. S. Eliot (1888–1965) US-born British poet and dramatist.
Tradition and the Individual Talent

15 All one's inventions are true, you can be sure of that. Poetry is as exact a science as geometry.
Gustave Flaubert (1821–80) French novelist.
Letter to Louise Colet, 14 Aug 1853

16 We all write poems; it is simply that poets are the ones who write in words.
John Fowles (1926–) British novelist.
The French Lieutenant's Woman, Ch. 19

17 Writing free verse is like playing tennis with the net down.
Robert Frost (1875–1963) US poet.
Speech, Milton Academy, 17 May 1935

18 Rightly thought of there is poetry in peaches . . . even when they are canned.
Harley Granville-Barker (1877–1946) British actor and dramatist.
The Madras House, I

19 If Galileo had said in verse that the world moved, the Inquisition might have let him alone.
Thomas Hardy (1840–1928) British novelist.
The Later Years of Thomas Hardy (F. E. Hardy)

20 Even when poetry has a meaning, as it usually has, it may be inadvisable to draw it out . . . Perfect understanding will sometimes almost extinguish pleasure.
A. E. Housman (1859–1936) British scholar and poet.
The Name and Nature of Poetry

21 'Why Sir, it is much easier to say what it is not. We all *know* what light is; but it is not easy to *tell* what it is.'
Samuel Johnson (1709–84) British lexicographer.
When asked, 'What is poetry'
Life of Johnson (J. Boswell), Vol. III

22 A drainless shower
Of light is poesy; 'tis the supreme of power;
'Tis might half slumb'ring on its own right arm.
John Keats (1795–1821) British poet.
Sleep and Poetry

23 A long poem is a test of invention which I

take to be the Polar star of poetry, as fancy is the sails, and imagination the rudder.
John Keats
Letter to Benjamin Bailey, 8 Oct 1817

24 We hate poetry that has a palpable design upon us – and if we do not agree, seems to put its hand in its breeches pocket. Poetry should be great and unobtrusive, a thing which enters into one's soul, and does not startle or amaze it with itself, but with its subject.
John Keats
Letter to J. H. Reynolds, 3 Feb 1818

25 If poetry comes not as naturally as leaves to a tree it had better not come at all.
John Keats
Letter to John Taylor, 27 Feb 1818

26 When power narrows the areas of man's concern, poetry reminds him of the richness and diversity of his existence.
John Fitzgerald Kennedy (1917–63) US statesman.
Address at Dedication of the Robert Frost Library, 26 Oct 1963

27 Perhaps no person can be a poet, or can even enjoy poetry, without a certain unsoundness of mind.
Lord Macaulay (1800–59) British historian.
Literary Essays Contributed to the 'Edinburgh Review', 'Milton'

28 Poem me no poems.
Rose Macaulay (1889–1958) British writer.
Poetry Review, Autumn 1963

29 Poetry is a comforting piece of fiction set to more or less lascivious music.
H. L. Mencken (1880–1956) US journalist.
Prejudices, 'The Poet and his Art'

30 Blest pair of Sirens, pledges of Heaven's joy, Sphere-born harmonious sisters, Voice and Verse.
John Milton (1608–74) English poet.
At a Solemn Music

31 Rhyme being no necessary adjunct or true ornament of poem or good verse, in longer works especially, but the invention of a barbarous age, to set off wretched matter and lame metre.
John Milton
Paradise Lost, The Verse. Preface to 1668 ed.

32 The troublesome and modern bondage of Rhyming.
John Milton
Paradise Lost, The Verse. Preface to 1668 ed.

33 . . . poetry, 'The Cinderella of the Arts.'
Harriet Monroe (1860–1936) US poet and editor.
Famous American Women (Hope Stoddard), 'Harriet Monroe'

34 Above all I am not concerned with Poetry.

My subject is War, and the pity of War. The Poetry is in the pity.
Wilfred Owen (1893–1918) British poet.
Poems, Preface

35 Curst be the verse, how well so'er it flow, That tends to make one worthy man my foe.
Alexander Pope (1688–1744) British poet.
Epistle to Dr. Arbuthnot

36 For three years, out of key with his time, He strove to resuscitate the dead art Of poetry to maintain 'the sublime' In the old sense. Wrong from the start.
Ezra Pound (1885–1972) US poet.
Pour l'élection de son sépulcre

37 It is a perfectly possible means of overcoming chaos.
I. A. Richards (1893–1979) British critic.
Science and Poetry

38 A sonnet is a moment's monument, – Memorial from the Soul's eternity To one dead deathless hour.
Dante Gabriel Rossetti (1828–82) British painter and poet.
The House of Life, Introduction

39 What is poetry? The suggestion, by the imagination, of noble grounds for the noble emotions.
John Ruskin (1819–1900) British art critic and writer.
Modern Painters, Vol. III

40 The truest poetry is the most feigning.
William Shakespeare (1564–1616) English dramatist.
As You Like It, III:3

41 The poet's eye, in a fine frenzy rolling, Doth glance from heaven to earth, from earth to heaven; And as imagination bodies forth The forms of things unknown, the poet's pen Turns them to shapes, and gives to airy nothing A local habitation and a name.
William Shakespeare
A Midsummer Night's Dream, V:1

42 Not marble, nor the gilded monuments Of princes, shall outlive this powerful rhyme.
William Shakespeare
Sonnet 55

43 The lunatic, the lover, and the poet, Are of imagination all compact.
William Shakespeare
A Midsummer Night's Dream, V:1

44 Poetry is the record of the best and happiest moments of the happiest and best minds.
Percy Bysshe Shelley (1792–1822) British poet.
A Defence of Poetry

45 One of the purposes of poetry is to show the dimensions of man that are, as Sir Arthur

Eddington said 'midway in scale between the atom and the star.'
Edith Sitwell (1887–1964) British poet and writer.
Rhyme and Reason

46 My poems are hymns of praise to the glory of life.
Edith Sitwell
Collected Poems, 'Some Notes on My Poetry'

47 A man does not write poems about what he knows, but about what he does not know.
Robin Skelton (1925–) British academic.
Teach Yourself Poetry

48 These poems, with all their crudities, doubts, and confusions, are written for the love of Man and in praise of God, and I'd be a damn' fool if they weren't.
Dylan Thomas (1914–53) Welsh poet.
Collected Poems, Note

49 What was it Chaucer
Said once about the long toil
That goes like blood to the poem's making?
Leave it to nature and the verse sprawls,
Limp as bindweed, if it break at all
Life's iron crust.
R. S. Thomas (1913–) Welsh poet.
Poetry for Supper

50 Having verse set to music is like looking at a painting through a stained glass window.
Paul Valéry (1871–1945) French poet and writer.
Attrib.

51 Hence no force however great can stretch a cord however fine into an horizontal line which is accurately straight: there will always be a bending downwards.
William Whewell (1794–1866) British philosopher and mathematician.
An example of unintentional versification
Elementary Treatise on Mechanics (1819 edition), Ch. 4

52 No one will ever get at my verses who insists upon viewing them as a literary performance.
Walt Whitman (1819–92) US poet.
A Backward Glance O'er Travel'd Roads

53 I would rather have written those lines than take Quebec.
James Wolfe (1727–59) British general.
Referring to Gray's Elegy, on the eve of the Battle of Quebec, 1759
Attrib.

54 Poetry is the spontaneous overflow of powerful feelings: it takes its origin from emotion recollected in tranquillity.
William Wordsworth (1770–1850) British poet.
Lyrics Ballads, Preface

55 Out of the quarrel with others we make rhetoric; out of the quarrel with ourselves we make poetry.
W. B. Yeats (1865–1939) Irish poet.
Essay

POETRY AND PROSE

See also poetry, prose

1 Poetry is not the proper antithesis to prose, but to science. Poetry is opposed to science, and prose to metre.
Samuel Taylor Coleridge (1772–1834) British poet.
Lectures and Notes of 1818, I

2 I wish our clever young poets would remember my homely definitions of prose and poetry; that is, prose = words in their best order; – poetry = the best words in the best order.
Samuel Taylor Coleridge
Table Talk

3 Prose on certain occasions can bear a great deal of poetry: on the other hand, poetry sinks and swoons under a moderate weight of prose.
Walter Savage Landor (1775–1864) British poet and writer.
Imaginary Conversations, 'Archdeacon Hare and Walter Landor'

4 For to write good prose is an affair of good manners. It is, unlike verse, a civil art . . . . Poetry is baroque.
W. Somerset Maugham (1874–1965) British novelist.
The Summing Up

5 Poetry is to prose as dancing is to walking.
John Wain (1925–) British novelist and poet.
Talk, BBC radio, 13 Jan 1976

6 The poet gives us his essence, but prose takes the mould of the body and mind entire.
Virginia Woolf (1882–1941) British novelist.
The Captain's Death Bed, 'Reading'

7 There neither is, nor can be, any *essential* difference between the language of prose and metrical composition.
William Wordsworth (1770–1850) British poet.
Lyrical Ballads, Preface

8 O'CONNOR. How are you?
W.B.Y. Not very well, I can only write prose today.
W. B. Yeats (1865–1939) Irish poet.
Attrib.

POETS

See also Chaucer, criticism, Milton, poetry, Shakespeare, writers

General quotes

1 Poets and painters are outside the class system, or rather they constitute a special class of their own, like the circus people and the gipsies.
Gerald Brenan (Edward Fitzgerald Brenan; 1894–1987) British writer.
Thoughts in a Dry Season, 'Writing'

2 The Fleshly School of Poetry.

Robert Williams Buchanan (1841–1901) British poet and writer.
Referring to Swinburne, William Morris, D. G. Rossetti, etc
Title of article in the *Contemporary Review*, Oct 1871

3 A poet without love were a physical and metaphysical impossibility.

Thomas Carlyle (1795–1881) Scottish historian and essayist.
Critical and Miscellaneous Essays, 'Burns'

4 A true poet does not bother to be poetical. Nor does a nursery gardener scent his roses.

Jean Cocteau (1889–1963) French poet and artist.
Professional Secrets

5 Immature poets imitate; mature poets steal.

T. S. Eliot (1888–1965) US-born British poet and dramatist.
Philip Massinger

6 To be a poet is a condition rather than a profession.

Robert Graves (1895–1985) British poet and novelist.
Horizon

7 Shelley and Keats were the last English poets who were at all up to date in their chemical knowledge.

J. B. S. Haldane (1892–1964) British geneticist.
Daedalus or Science and the Future

8 Not gods, nor men, nor even booksellers have put up with poets' being second-rate.

Horace (Quintus Horatius Flaccus; 65–8 BC) Roman poet.
Ars Poetica

9 Sir, there is no settling the point of precedency between a louse and a flea.

Samuel Johnson (1709–84) British lexicographer.
When Maurice Morgann asked him who he considered to be the better poet – Smart or Derrick
Life of Johnson (J. Boswell), Vol. IV

10 For ne'er
Was flattery lost on poet's ear:
A simple race! they waste their toil
For the vain tribute of a smile.

Walter Scott (1771–1832) Scottish novelist.
The Lay of the Last Minstrel, IV

11 There have been many most excellent poets that have never versified, and now swarm many versifiers that need never answer to the name of poets.

Philip Sidney (1554–86) English poet and courtier.
The Defence of Poesy

12 I hate the whole race . . . There is no believing a word they say – your professional poets, I mean – there never existed a more worthless set than Byron and his friends for example.

Duke of Wellington (1769–1852) British general and statesman.
Lady Salisbury's diary, 26 Oct 1833

Specific quotes

13 Reader! I am to let thee know,
Donne's Body only, lyes below:
For, could the grave his Soul comprize,
Earth would be richer than the skies.

Anonymous
Epitaph, written on the wall above Donne's grave the day after his burial

14 It always seems to me that the right sphere for Shelley's genius was the sphere of music, not of poetry.

Matthew Arnold (1822–88) British poet and critic.
Maurice de Guérin, Footnote

15 When Byron's eyes were shut in death,
We bow'd our head and held our breath.
He taught us little: but our soul
Had *felt* him like the thunder's roll.

Matthew Arnold
Memorial Verses

16 He spoke, and loos'd our heart in tears.
He laid us as we lay at birth
On the cool flowery lap of earth.

Matthew Arnold
Referring to Wordsworth
Memorial Verses

17 Time may restore us in his course
Goethe's sage mind and Byron's force:
But where will Europe's latter hour
Again find Wordsworth's healing power?

Matthew Arnold
Memorial Verses

18 Earth, receive an honoured guest:
William Yeats is laid to rest.
Let the Irish vessel lie
Emptied of its poetry.

W. H. Auden (1907–73) British poet.
In Memory of W. B. Yeats, III

19 So long as Byron tried to write Poetry with a capital P, to express deep emotions and profound thoughts, his work deserved that epithet he most dreaded, *una seccatura . . .* His attempts to write satirical heroic couplets were less unsuccessful, but aside from the impossibility of equaling Dryden and Pope in their medium, Byron was really a comedian, not a satirist.

W. H. Auden
The Dyer's Hand

20 He was the one English love poet who was not afraid to acknowledge that he was composed of body, soul, and mind; and who faithfully recorded all the pitched battles, alarms, treaties, sieges, and fanfares of that extraordinary triangular warfare.

Rupert Brooke (1887–1915) British poet.
Referring to John Donne
John Donne

21 The great Metaquizzical poet.

Lord Byron (1788–1824) British poet.
Said of Wordsworth
Letter to John Murray, 19 Jan 1821

22 Here is Johnny Keats piss-a-bed poetry. No
more Keats, I entreat.
Lord Byron
Letter to the publisher John Murray, 12 Oct 1821

23 If they had said the sun and the moon was
gone out of the heavens it could not have
struck me with the idea of a more awful and
dreary blank in the creation than the words:
Byron is dead.
Jane Welsh Carlyle (1801–66) The wife of Thomas
Carlyle.
Letter to Thomas Carlyle, 1824

24 A weak, diffusive, weltering, ineffectual man.
Thomas Carlyle (1795–1881) Scottish historian and
essayist.
Referring to Coleridge
Attrib.

25 How great a possibility; how small a realized
result.
Thomas Carlyle
Referring to Coleridge
Letter to Ralph Waldo Emerson, 12 Aug 1834

26 A gifted Byron rises in his wrath; and feeling
too surely that he for his part is not 'happy',
declares the same in very violent language,
as a piece of news that may be interesting. It
evidently has surprised him much. One
dislikes to see a man and poet reduced to
proclaim on the streets such tidings.
Thomas Carlyle
Past and Present

27 He could not think up to the height of his
own towering style.
G. K. Chesterton (1874–1936) British writer.
Speaking of Tennyson
The Victorian Age in Literature, Ch. 3

28 With Donne, whose muse on dromedary
trots,
Wreathe iron pokers into true-love knots.
Samuel Taylor Coleridge (1772–1834) British poet.
On Donne's Poetry

29 The misfortune is, that he has begun to write
verses without very well understanding what
metre is.
Samuel Taylor Coleridge
Referring to Tennyson
Table Talk

30 The world is rid of Lord Byron, but the
deadly slime of his touch still remains.
John Constable (1776–1837) British landscape painter.
Letter to John Fisher, three weeks after Byron's death.

31 Few writers have shown a more
extraordinary compass of powers than Donne;
for he combined what no other man has ever
done – the last sublimation of subtlety with
the most impassioned majesty.
Thomas De Quincey (1785–1859) British writer.
Referring to John Donne
Blackwood's Magazine, Dec 1828

32 This illustrious man, the largest and most
spacious intellect, the subtlest and the most
comprehensive, in my judgement, that has
yet existed amongst men.
Thomas De Quincey
Talking of Coleridge
Recollections of the Lake Poets

33 He seems to me the most *vulgar-minded*
genius that ever produced a great effect in
literature.
George Eliot (Mary Ann Evans; 1819–80) British
novelist.
Referring to Byron
Letter, 21 Sept 1869

34 Blake . . . knew what interested him, and he
therefore presents only the essential, only, in
fact, what can be presented, and need not be
explained . . . He approached everything with
a mind unclouded by current opinions. There
was nothing of the superior person about
him. This makes him terrifying.
T. S. Eliot (1888–1965) US-born British poet and
dramatist.
The Sacred Wood

35 Blake is damned good to steal from!
Henry Fuseli (1741–1825) Swiss artist.
Life of Blake (Alexander Gilchrist)

36 *Hugo – hélas!*
André Gide (1869–1951) French novelist.
Replying to an inquiry as to whom he considered the finest
poet of the 19th century
André Gide–Paul Valéry Correspondence 1890–1942

37 He has no sense of the ludicrous, and, as to
God, a worm crawling in a privy is as worthy
an object as any other, all being to him
indifferent. So to Blake the Chimney
Sweeper etc. He is ruined by vain struggles
to get rid of what presses on his brain – he
attempts impossibles.
William Hazlitt (1778–1830) British essayist.
Referring to Blake
Diary (Henry Crabb Robinson)

38 He talked on for ever; and you wished him
to talk on for ever.
William Hazlitt
Referring to Coleridge
Lectures on the English Poets, Lecture VIII, 'On the Living
Poets'

39 His thoughts did not seem to come with
labour and effort; but as if borne on the
gusts of genius, and as if the wings of his
imagination lifted him from off his feet.
William Hazlitt
Referring to Coleridge
Lectures on the English Poets, Lecture VIII, 'On the Living
Poets'

40 He had a fire in his eye, a fever in his blood,
a maggot in his brain, a hectic flutter in his
speech, which mark out the philosophic
fanatic.
William Hazlitt
Referring to Shelley
Table Talk

41 The most original poet now living, and the one whose writings could the least be spared; for they have no substitutes elsewhere.
William Hazlitt
Referring to Wordsworth
The Spirit of the Age

42 Dr Donne's verses are like the peace of God; they pass all understanding.
James I (1566–1625) King of England.
Attrib.

43 He was dull in a new way, and that made many people think him *great*.
Samuel Johnson (1709–84) British lexicographer.
Referring to the poet Thomas Gray
Life of Johnson (J. Boswell), Vol. II

44 Milton, Madam, was a genius that could cut a Colossus from a rock; but could not carve heads upon cherry-stones.
Samuel Johnson
When Miss Hannah More had wondered why Milton could write the epic *Paradise Lost* but only very poor sonnets
Life of Johnson (J. Boswell), Vol. IV

45 For Shelley's nature is utterly womanish. Not merely his weak points, but his strong ones, are those of a woman. Tender and pitiful as a woman; and yet, when angry, shrieking, railing, hysterical as a woman . . . The nature of a woman looks out of that wild, beautiful, girlish face – the nature: but not the spirit.
Charles Kingsley (1819–75) British writer.
Thoughts on Shelley and Byron

46 Mad, bad, and dangerous to know.
Lady Caroline Lamb (1785–1828) The wife of William Lamb.
Said of Byron in her journal
Journal

47 Separate from the pleasure of your company, I don't much care if I never see another mountain in my life.
Charles Lamb (1775–1834) British essayist.
Letter to Wordsworth, 30 Jan 1801

48 His face when he repeats his verses hath its ancient glory, an Archangel a little damaged.
Charles Lamb
Referring to Coleridge
Letter, 26 Apr 1816

49 Keats, at a time when the phrase had not yet been invented, practised the theory of art for art's sake. He is the type, not of the poet, but of the artist. He was not a great personality, his work comes to us as a greater thing than his personality. When we read his verse, we think of the verse, not of John Keats.
F. R. Leavis (1895–1978) British literary critic.
Revaluation

50 Walt Whitman who laid end to end words

never seen in each other's company before outside of a dictionary.
David Lodge (1935–) British author.
Changing Places, Ch. 5

51 Your works will be read after Shakespeare and Milton are fogotten – and not till then.
Richard Porson (1759–1808) British classicist.
Giving his opinion of the poems of Robert Southey
Quotable Anecdotes (L. Meissen)

52 Mr Wordsworth, a stupid man, with a decided gift for portraying nature in vignettes, never yet ruined anyone's morals, unless, perhaps, he has driven some susceptible persons to crime in a very fury of boredom.
Ezra Pound (1885–1972) US poet.
Future, Nov 1917

53 I weep for Adonais – he is dead!
O, weep for Adonais! though our tears
Thaw not the frost which binds so dear a head!
And thou, sad Hour, selected from all years
To mourn our loss, rouse thy obscure compeers,
And teach them thine own sorrow, say: 'With me
Died Adonais; till the Future dares
Forget the Past, his fate and fame shall be
An echo and a light unto eternity!'
Percy Bysshe Shelley (1792–1822) British poet.
Written on the death of Keats
Adonais

54 People sometimes divide others into those you laugh at and those you laugh with. The young Auden was someone you could laugh-at-with.
Stephen Spender (1909–) British poet.
Address, W. H. Auden's memorial service, Oxford 27 Oct 1973

55 Blake, in the hierarchy of the inspired, stands very high indeed. If one could strike an average among poets, it would probably be true to say that, as far as inspiration is concerned, Blake is to the average poet, as the average poet is to the man in the street. All poetry, to be poetry at all, must have the power of making one, now and then, involuntarily ejaculate: 'What made him think of that?' With Blake, one is asking the question all the time.
Lytton Strachey (1880–1932) British writer.
Books and Characters

56 Blake is the only poet who sees all temporal things under a form of eternity . . . Where other poets use reality as a spring-board into space, he uses it as a foothold on his return from flight.
Arthur Symons (1865–1945) British poet.
William Blake

57 Wordsworth was a tea-time bore, the great Frost of literature, the verbose, the humourless, the platitudinary reporter of

Nature in her dullest moods. Open him at any page: and there lies the English language not, as George Moore said of Pater, in a glass coffin, but in a large, sultry, and unhygienic box.
Dylan Thomas (1914–53) Welsh poet.
Letter to Pamela Hansford Johnson, 1933

58 The Poet of Immortal Youth.
Henry Van Dyke
Keats

59 He found in stones the sermons he had already hidden there.
Oscar Wilde (1854–1900) Irish-born British dramatist.
Referring to Wordsworth
The Decay of Lying

60 There is no doubt that this poor man was mad, but there is something in the madness of this man which interests me more than the sanity of Lord Byron and Walter Scott.
William Wordsworth (1770–1850) British poet.
Talking of Blake
Reminiscences (Henry Crabb Robinson)

61 I see a schoolboy when I think of him
With face and nose pressed to a sweetshop window.
W. B. Yeats (1865–1939) Irish poet.
Referring to Keats
Attrib.

62 That William Blake
Who beat upon the wall
Till Truth obeyed his call.
W. B. Yeats
An Acre of Grass

POLICE

1 When constabulary duty's to be done –
A policeman's lot is not a happy one.
W. S. Gilbert (1836–1911) British dramatist.
The Pirates of Penzance, II

2 The police are the only 24-hour social service in the country.
Commander Alex Marnoch
Remark, Feb 1983

3 Policemen are numbered in case they get lost.
Spike Milligan (1918–) British comic actor and author.
The Last Goon Show of All

4 A thing of duty is a boy for ever.
Flann O'Brien (Brian O'Nolan; 1911–66) Irish novelist and journalist.
About policemen always seeming to be young-looking
The Listener, 24 Feb 1977

5 Reading isn't an occupation we encourage among police officers. We try to keep the paper work down to a minimum.
Joe Orton (1933–67) British dramatist.
Loot, II

6 My father didn't create you to arrest me.
Lord Peel (1829–1912) British politician.
Protesting against his arrest by the police, recently established by his father
Attrib.

7 One always has the air of someone who is lying when one speaks to a policeman.
Charles-Louis Philippe (1874–1909) French novelist.
Les Chroniques du canard sauvage

POLITICIANS

See also Churchill, compliments, government, Hitler, Houses of Parliament, insults, politics

General quotes

1 No man has come so near our definition of a constitutional statesman – the powers of a first-rate man and the creed of a second-rate man.
Walter Bagehot (1826–77) British economist and journalist.
Historical Essays, 'The Character of Sir Robert Peel'

2 Politics and the fate of mankind are shaped by men without ideas and without greatness. Men who have greatness within them don't go in for politics.
Albert Camus (1913–60) French existentialist writer.
Notebooks, 1935–42

3 a politician is an arse upon which everyone has sat except a man.
e. e. cummings (1894–1962) US poet.
A Politician

4 When I was a boy I was told that anybody could become President of the United States. I am beginning to believe it.
Clarence Seward Darrow (1857–1938) US lawyer.
Attrib.

5 There are two problems in my life. The political ones are insoluble and the economic ones are incomprehensible.
Alec Douglas-Home (1903–) British statesman.
Speech, Jan 1964

6 For Politicians neither love nor hate.
John Dryden (1631–1700) British poet and dramatist.
Absalom and Achitophel, I

7 Since a politician never believes what he says, he is surprised when others believe him.
Charles De Gaulle (1890–1970) French general and statesman.
Attrib.

8 In order to become the master, the politician poses as the servant.
Charles De Gaulle
Attrib.

9 I have come to the conclusion that politics

are too serious a matter to be left to the politicians.
Charles De Gaulle
Attrib.

10 I always voted at my party's call,
And I never thought of thinking for myself at all.
W. S. Gilbert (1836–1911) British dramatist.
HMS Pinafore, I

11 The prospect of a lot
Of dull MPs in close proximity,
All thinking for themselves is what
No man can face with equanimity.
W. S. Gilbert
Iolanthe, I

12 'Do you pray for the senators, Dr Hale?' 'No, I look at the senators and I pray for the country.'
Edward Everett Hale (1822–1909) US author and clergyman.
New England Indian Summer (Van Wyck Brooks)

13 Politicians are the same everywhere. They promise to build bridges even where there are no rivers.
Nikita Khrushchev (1894–1971) Soviet statesman.
Attrib., Oct 1960

14 Political renegades always start their career of treachery as 'the best men of all parties' and end up in the Tory knackery.
Neil Kinnock (1942–) British politician.
Speech, Welsh Labour Party Conference, 1985

15 A politician is a person with whose politics you don't agree; if you agree with him he is a statesman.
David Lloyd George (1863–1945) British Liberal statesman.
Attrib.

16 When you're abroad you're a statesman: when you're at home you're just a politician.
Harold Macmillan (1894–1986) British politician and prime minister.
Speech, 1958

17 It is very unfair to expect a politician to live in private up to the statements he makes in public.
W. Somerset Maugham (1874–1965) British novelist.
The Circle

18 A statesman is a politician who places himself at the service of the nation. A politician is a statesman who places the nation at his service.
Georges Pompidou (1911–74) French statesman.
The Observer, 'Sayings of the Year', 30 Dec 1973

19 All political lives, unless they are cut off in mid-stream at a happy juncture, end in failure.
Enoch Powell (1912–) British politician.
Sunday Times, 6 Nov 1977

20 Above any other position of eminence, that of Prime Minister is filled by fluke.
Enoch Powell
The Observer, 'Sayings of the Week' 8 Mar 1987

21 A number of anxious dwarfs trying to grill a whale.
J. B. Priestley (1894–1984) British novelist.
Outcries and Asides

22 Get thee glass eyes,
And, like a scurvy politician, seem
To see the things thou dost not.
William Shakespeare (1564–1616) English dramatist.
King Lear, IV:6

23 He knows nothing; and he thinks he knows everything. That points clearly to a political career.
George Bernard Shaw (1856–1950) Irish dramatist and critic.
Major Barbara, III

24 All politicians have vanity. Some wear it more gently than others.
David Steel (1938–) British politician.
The Observer, 'Sayings of the Week', 14 July 1985

25 A politician is a statesman who approaches every question with an open mouth.
Adlai Stevenson
Also attrib. to Arthur Goldberg
The Fine Art of Political Wit (L. Harris)

26 Whoever could make two ears of corn or two blades of grass to grow upon a spot of ground where only one grew before would deserve better of mankind and do more essential service to his country than the whole race of politicians put together.
Jonathan Swift (1667–1745) Irish-born Anglican priest and writer.
Gulliver's Travels, 'Voyage to Brobdingnag', Ch. 7

27 In politics, if you want anything said, ask a man; if you want anything done, ask a woman.
Margaret Thatcher (1925–) British politician and prime minister.
The Changing Anatomy of Britain (Anthony Sampson)

28 A politician is a man who understands government, and it takes a politician to run a government. A statesman is a politician who's been dead ten or fifteen years.
Harry S. Truman (1884–1972) US statesman.
New York World Telegram and Sun, 12 Apr 1958

29 Politicians can forgive almost anything in the way of abuse; they can forgive subversion, revolution, being contradicted, exposed as liars, even ridiculed, but they can never forgive being ignored.
Auberon Waugh (1939–) British novelist and critic.
The Observer, 11 Oct 1981

30 It is a pity, as my husband says, that more

politicians are not bastards by birth instead of vocation.

Katherine Whitehorn (1926–) British journalist.
The Observer, 1964

Specific quotes

31 It is fitting that we should have buried the Unknown Prime Minister by the side of the Unknown Soldier.

Herbert Henry Asquith (1852–1928) British statesman.
Said at Bonar Law's funeral, 5 Nov 1923
Attrib.

32 He believes, with all his heart and soul and strength, that there *is* such a thing as truth; he has the soul of a martyr with the intellect of an advocate.

Walter Bagehot
Referring to Gladstone
Historical Essays, 'Mr Gladstone'

33 If I rescued a child from drowning, the Press would no doubt headline the story 'Benn grabs child'.

Tony Benn (1925–) British politician.
The Observer, 'Sayings of the Week', 2 Mar 1975

34 A dessicated calculating machine.

Aneurin Bevan (1897–1960) British Labour politician.
Referring to Hugh Gaitskell
Hugh Gaitskell (W. T. Rodgers)

35 There is no reason to attack the monkey when the organ-grinder is present.

Aneurin Bevan
The 'monkey' was Selwyn Lloyd; the 'organ-grinder' was Harold Macmillan
Speech, House of Commons

36 She is trying to wear the trousers of Winston Churchill.

Leonid Brezhnev (1906–82) Soviet statesman.
Referring to Margaret Thatcher
Speech, 1979

37 He was not merely a chip off the old block, but the old block itself.

Edmund Burke (1729–97) British politician.
Referring to William Pitt the Younger's first speech in the House of Commons, 26 Feb 1781
Attrib.

38 Mr Macmillan is the best prime minister we have.

R. A. Butler (1902–82) British Conservative politician.
Often quoted in the form above. In fact, Butler simply answered 'Yes' to the question 'Would you say that this is the best prime minister we have?'
Interview, London Airport, Dec 1955

39 Pitt is to Addington
As London is to Paddington.

George Canning (1770–1827) British statesman.
The Oracle

40 The seagreen Incorruptible.

Thomas Carlyle (1795–1881) Scottish historian and essayist.
Referring to Robespierre
History of the French Revolution, Pt. II, Bk. IV, Ch. 4

41 She is clearly the best man among them.

Barbara Castle (1910–) British politician.
Referring to Margaret Thatcher
The Castle Diaries

42 An old man in a hurry.

Lord Randolph Churchill (1849–95) British Conservative politician.
Referring to Gladstone
Speech, June 1886

43 I remember, when I was a child, being taken to the celebrated Barnum's circus, which contained an exhibition of freaks and monstrosities, but the exhibit . . . which I most desired to see was the one described as 'The Boneless Wonder'. My parents judged that that spectacle would be too revolting and demoralising for my youthful eyes, and I have waited 50 years to see the boneless wonder sitting on the Treasury Bench.

Winston Churchill (1874–1965) British statesman.
Referring to Ramsey MacDonald
Speech, House of Commons, 28 Jan 1931

44 I have never seen a human being who more perfectly represented the modern conception of a robot.

Winston Churchill
Referring to the Soviet statesman Molotov
The Second World War

45 In Franklin Roosevelt there died the greatest American friend we have ever known and the greatest champion of freedom who has ever brought help and comfort from the New World to the Old.

Winston Churchill
The Second World War

46 In private conversation he tries on speeches like a man trying on ties in his bedroom to see how he would look in them.

Lionel Curtis (1872–1955) British writer.
Referring to Winston Churchill
Letter to Nancy Astor, 1912

47 Not even a public figure. A man of no experience. And of the utmost insignificance.

Lord Curzon (1859–1925) British politician.
Referring to Stanley Baldwin on his appointment as Prime Minister
Curzon: The Last Phase (Harold Nicolson)

48 If a traveller were informed that such a man was leader of the House of Commons, he may well begin to comprehend how the Egyptians worshipped an insect.

Benjamin Disraeli (1804–81) British statesman.
Referring to Lord John Russell
Attrib.

49 He is used to dealing with estate workers. I

cannot see how anyone can say he is out of touch.

Lady Caroline Douglas-Home (1937–) Daughter of Alec Douglas-Home.
Referring to her father's suitability to his new role as prime minister
Daily Herald, 21 Oct 1963 (Jon Akass)

50 For the past few months she has been charging about like some bargain-basement Boadicea.

Denis Healey (1917–) British Labour politician.
Referring to Margaret Thatcher
The Observer, 'Sayings of the Week', 7 Nov 1982

51 I am the Gromyko of the Labour party.

Denis Healey
Alluding to Andrei Gromyko (1909–89), Soviet statesman who was foreign minister from 1957 to 1985
Attrib.

52 He would rather follow public opinion than lead it.

Harry Hopkins (1890–1946) US politician.
Referring to Roosevelt
Attrib.

53 If a man were to go by chance at the same time with Burke under a shed, to shun a shower, he would say – 'this is an extraordinary man.'

Samuel Johnson (1709–84) British lexicographer.
Referring to Edmund Burke
Life of Johnson (J. Boswell), Vol. IV

54 Do you realize the responsibility I carry? I'm the only person standing between Nixon and the White House.

John Fitzgerald Kennedy (1917–63) US statesman.
Said to Arthur Schlesinger, 13 Oct 1960; Richard Nixon was the Republican candidate in the 1960 US Presidential election
A Thousand Days (Arthur M. Schlesinger, Jnr)

55 This goat-footed bard, this half-human visitor to our age from the hag-ridden magic and enchanted woods of Celtic antiquity.

John Maynard Keynes (1883–1946) British economist.
Referring to Lloyd George
Essays and Sketches in Biography

56 We have heard of people being thrown to the wolves, but never before have we heard of a man being thrown to the wolves with a bargain on the part of the wolves that they would not eat him.

Bonar Law (1858–1923) British statesman.
Referring to the fact that the then war minister, Col Seely, had offered his resignation
Speech, House of Common, Mar 1914

57 Look at that man's eyes. You will hear more of him later.

Bonar Law
Referring to Mussolini
Attrib.

58 Poor Bonar can't bear being called a liar. Now I don't mind.

David Lloyd George (1863–1945) British Liberal statesman.
Referring to Bonar Law, prime minister 1922–23
Stanley Baldwin (G. M. Young)

59 He saw foreign policy through the wrong end of a municipal drainpipe.

David Lloyd George
Referring to Neville Chamberlain
The Fine Art of Political Wit (Harris), Ch. 6

60 So restless Cromwell could not cease
In the inglorious arts of peace.

Andrew Marvell (1621–78) English poet.
An Horatian Ode upon Cromwell's Return from Ireland

61 Sit down, man. You're a bloody tragedy.

James Maxton (1885–1946) Scottish Labour leader.
Said to Ramsay MacDonald when he made his last speech in Parliament
Attrib.

62 The rogue elephant among British prime ministers.

Dr Kenneth Morgan (1934–) British historian.
Referring to Lloyd George
Life of David Lloyd George

63 I am not and never have been, a man of the right. My position was on the left and is now in the centre of politics.

Oswald Mosley (1896–1980) British politician.
The Times, 26 Apr 1968

64 Argue as you please, you are nowhere, that grand old man, the Prime Minister, insists on the other thing.

Lord Northcote (1818–87) British statesman.
Referring to Gladstone; the phrase, and its acronym GOM, became his nickname – temporarily reversed to MOG ('Murderer of Gordon') in 1885, after the death of General Gordon at Khartoum
Speech, Liverpool, 12 Apr 1882

65 How could they tell?

Dorothy Parker (1893–1967) US writer.
Reaction to news of the death of Calvin Coolidge, US President 1923–29; also attributed to H. L. Mencken
You Might As Well Live (J. Keats)

66 Coolidge is a better example of evolution than either Bryan or Darrow, for he knows when not to talk, which is the biggest asset the monkey possesses over the human.

Will Rogers (1879–1935) US actor and humorist.
Saturday Review, 'A Rogers Thesaurus', 25 Aug 1962

67 Stalin hates the guts of all your top people. He thinks he likes me better, and I hope he will continue to do so.

Franklin D. Roosevelt (1882–1945) US Democratic president.
The Hinge of Fate (Winston S. Churchill), Ch. 11

68 I will not accept if nominated, and will not serve if elected.

General William Sherman (1820–91) US general.
Replying to a request that he accept the Republican presidential nomination
Attrib.

69 He was the Messiah of the new age, and his crucifixion was yet to come.

George Edward Slocombe (1894–1963) British journalist.
Referring to Woodrow Wilson and his visit to the Versailles conference
Mirror to Geneva

70 Nixon is the kind of politician who would cut down a redwood tree, then mount the stump for a conservation speech.

Adlai Stevenson (1900–65) US statesman.
Attrib.

71 I hope Mrs Thatcher will go until the turn of the century looking like Queen Victoria.

Norman Tebbitt (1931–) British Conservative politician.
The Observer, 'Sayings of the Week', 17 May 1987

72 If a woman like Eva Peron with no ideals can get that far, think how far I can go with all the ideals that I have.

Margaret Thatcher (1925–) British politician and prime minister.
The Sunday Times, 1980

73 Introducing Super-Mac.

Vicky (Victor Weisz; 1913–66) German-born British cartoonist.
Cartoon caption depicting Harold Macmillan as Superman
Evening Standard, 6 Nov 1958

74 The danger to the country, to Europe, to her vast Empire, which is involved in having all these great interests entrusted to the shaking hand of an old, wild, and incomprehensible man of 82½, is very great!

Victoria (1819–1901) Queen of the United Kingdom.
Reaction to Gladstone's fourth and last appointment as prime minister, 1892
Letter to Lord Lansdowne, 12 Aug 1892

75 He speaks to Me as if I was a public meeting.

Victoria
Referring to Gladstone
Collections and Recollections (G. W. E. Russell), Ch. 14

POLITICS

See also Communism, democracy, diplomacy, government, Houses of Parliament, monarchy, opposition, politicians, power politics, socialism

1 Politics, as a practice, whatever its professions, has always been the systematic organisation of hatreds.

Henry Brooks Adams (1838–1918) US historian.
The Education of Henry Adams

2 He warns the heads of parties against believing their own lies.

John Arbuthnot (1667–1735) Scottish writer and physician.
The Art of Political Lying

3 Man is by nature a political animal.

Aristotle (384–322 BC) Greek philosopher.
Politics, Bk. I

4 The accursed power which stands on Privilege
(And goes with Women, and Champagne, and Bridge)
Broke – and Democracy resumed her reign:
(Which goes with Bridge, and Women and Champagne).

Hilaire Belloc (1870–1953) French-born British poet.
Epigrams, 'On a Great Election'

5 Every Briton is at heart a Tory – especially every British Liberal.

Arnold Bennett (1867–1931) British novelist.
Journal

6 Politics is a blood sport.

Aneurin Bevan (1897–1960) British Labour politician.
My Life with Nye (Jennie Lee)

7 No attempt at ethical or social seduction can eradicate from my heart a deep burning hatred for the Tory Party . . . So far as I am concerned they are lower than vermin.

Aneurin Bevan
Speech, Manchester, 4 July 1949

8 Politics is not an exact science.

Bismarck (1815–98) German statesman.
Speech, Prussian Chamber, 18 Dec 1863

9 Politics is not a science . . . but an art.

Bismarck
Speech, Reichstag, 15 Mar 1884

10 South Africa will not allow the double standards and hypocrisy of the Western world, even in the application of legal principles, to stand in the way of our responsibility to protect our country.

P. W. Botha (1916–) South African politican and president.
Speech, May 1986

11 You won't force South Africans to commit national suicide.

P. W. Botha
Speech, Aug 1986

12 Politics are usually the executive expression of human immaturity.

Vera Brittain (1893–1970) British writer and feminist.
The Rebel Passion

13 Party loyalty lowers the greatest of men to the petty level of the masses.

Jean de La Bruyère (1645–96) French satirist.
Les Caractères

14 Politics is the art of the possible.
R. A. Butler (1902–82) British Conservative politician.
Often attrib. to Butler but used earlier by others, including Bismarck
The Art of the Possible, Epigraph

15 The healthy stomach is nothing if not conservative. Few radicals have good digestions.
Samuel Butler (1835–1902) British writer.
Notebooks

16 I am not made for politics because I am incapable of wishing for, or accepting the death of my adversary.
Albert Camus (1913–60) French existentialist writer.
The Rebel

17 Detente is like the race in 'Alice in Wonderland' where everyone had to have a prize.
Lord Carrington (1919–) British politician.
Speech, Mar 1980

18 What a genius the Labour Party has for cutting itself in half and letting the two parts writhe in public.
Cassandra (William Neil Cannon; 1910–67) Irish journalist.
The Daily Mirror

19 Labour is not fit to govern.
Winston Churchill (1874–1965) British statesman.
Election speech, 1920

20 The disastrous element in the Labour party is its intellectuals.
George Norman Clark (1890–1979) British historian.
A Man of the Thirties (A. L. Rowse)

21 We now are, as we always have been, decidedly and conscientiously attached to what is called the Tory, and which might with more propriety be called the Conservative, party.
John Wilson Croker (1780–1857) British Tory politician.
The first use of the term 'Conservative Party'
In *Quarterly Review*, Jan 1830

22 A Conservative government is an organized hypocrisy.
Benjamin Disraeli (1804–81) British statesman.
Speech, 17 Mar 1845

23 The right honourable gentleman caught the Whigs bathing, and walked away with their clothes.
Benjamin Disraeli
Referring to Sir Robert Peel
Speech, House of Commons, 28 Feb 1845

24 During the last few weeks I have felt that the Suez Canal was flowing through my drawing room.
Clarissa Eden (1920–85) Wife of Anthony Eden.
Said during the Suez crisis of 1956
Attrib.

25 All terrorists, at the invitation of the Government, end up with drinks at the Dorchester.
Hugh Gaitskell (1906–63) British Labour politician.
Letter to *The Guardian*, 23 Aug 1977 (Dora Gaitskell)

26 There are some of us . . . who will fight, fight, fight, and fight again to save the party we love.
Hugh Gaitskell
After his policy for a nuclear deterrent had been defeated
Speech, Labour Party conference, Scarborough, 3 Oct 1960

27 There are times in politics when you must be on the right side and lose.
John Kenneth Galbraith (1908–) US economist.
The Observer, 'Sayings of the Week', 11 Feb 1968

28 Few things are as immutable as the addiction of political groups to the ideas by which they have once won office.
John Kenneth Galbraith
The Affluent Society, Ch. 13

29 There is just one rule for politicians all over the world. Don't say in Power what you say in Opposition: if you do you only have to carry out what the other fellows have found impossible.
John Galsworthy (1867–1933) British novelist.
Maid in Waiting

30 It isn't worth a pitcher of warm spit.
John Nance Garner (1868–1937) US Democratic vice-president.
Referring to the Vice-Presidency; sometimes 'piss' is substituted for 'spit'
Attrib.

31 I myself have become a Gaullist only little by little.
Charles De Gaulle (1890–1970) French general and statesman.
The Observer, 'Sayings of the Year', 29 Dec 1963

32 I often think it's comical
How Nature always does contrive
That every boy and every gal
That's born into the world alive
Is either a little Liberal
Or else a little Conservative!
W. S. Gilbert (1836–1911) British dramatist.
Iolanthe, II

33 If the British public falls for this, I say it will be stark, staring bonkers.
Lord Hailsham (1907–) British Conservative politician.
Referring to Labour policy in the 1964 general-election campaign
Press conference, Conservative Central Office, 12 Oct 1964

34 A great party is not to be brought down because of a scandal by a woman of easy virtue and a proved liar.
Lord Hailsham
Referring to the Profumo affair, in BBC interview, 13 June 1963
The Pendulum Years, Ch. 3 (Bernard Levin)

35 Their Europeanism is nothing but imperialism with an inferiority complex.
Denis Healey (1917–) British Labour politician.
Referring to the policies of the Conservative party
The Observer, 'Sayings of the Week', 7 Oct 1962

36 I don't think that modesty is the oustanding characteristic of contemporary politics, do you?
Edward Heath (1916–) British politician and prime minister.
Remark, Dec 1988

37 The essential thing is the formation of the political will of the nation: that is the starting point for political action.
Adolf Hitler (1889–1945) German dictator.
Speech, Düsseldorf, 27 Jan 1932

38 A little rebellion, now and then, is a good thing, and as necessary in the political world as storms in the physical.
Thomas Jefferson (1743–1826) US statesman.

39 If you're in politics and you can't tell when you walk into a room who's for you and who's against you, then you're in the wrong line of work.
Lyndon B. Johnson (1908–73) US statesman.
The Lyndon Johnson Story (B. Mooney)

40 Sir, I perceive you are a vile Whig.
Samuel Johnson (1709–84) British lexicographer.
Speaking to Sir Adam Fergusson
Life of Johnson (J. Boswell), Vol. II

41 Why, Sir, most schemes of political improvement are very laughable things.
Samuel Johnson
Life of Johnson (J. Boswell), Vol. II

42 Politics are now nothing more than a means of rising in the world.
Samuel Johnson
Life of Johnson (J. Boswell), Vol. II

43 The idea that there is a model Labour voter, a blue-collar council house tenant who belongs to a union and has 2.4 children, a five-year-old car and a holiday in Blackpool, is patronizing and politically immature.
Neil Kinnock (1942–) British politician.
Speech, 1986

44 Proportional Representation, I think, is fundamentally counter-democratic.
Neil Kinnock
Marxism Today, 1983

45 States, like men, have their growth, their manhood, their decrepitude, their decay.
Walter Savage Landor (1775–1864) British poet and writer.
Imaginary Conversations, 'Pollio and Calvus'

46 If it were necessary to give the briefest possible definition of imperialism we should have to say that imperialism is the monopoly stage of capitalism.
Lenin (Vladimir Ilich Ulyanov; 1870–1924) Russian revolutionary leader.
Imperialism, the Highest Stage of Capitalism, Ch. 7

47 In every age the vilest specimens of human nature are to be found among demagogues.
Lord Macaulay (1800–59) British historian.
History of England, Vol. I, Ch. 5

48 I thought the best thing to do was to settle up these little local difficulties, and then turn to the wider vision of the Commonwealth.
Harold Macmillan (1894–1986) British politician and prime minister.
Referring to resignation of ministers
Attrib., London Airport, 7 Jan 1958

49 There are three groups that no prime minister should provoke: the Treasury, the Vatican, and the National Union of Mineworkers.
Harold Macmillan
First used by Stanley Baldwin
Attrib.

50 First of all the Georgian silver goes, and then that nice furniture that used to be in the saloon. Then the Canalettos go.
Harold Macmillan
Referring to privatization of profitable nationalized industries
Speech, House of Lords, 1985

51 In politics, as in grammar, one should be able to tell the substantives from the adjectives. Hitler was a substantive; Mussolini only an adjective. Hitler was a nuisance. Mussolini was bloody. Together a bloody nuisance.
Salvador de Madariaga y Rogo (1886–1978) Spanish diplomat and writer.
Attrib.

52 Every intellectual attitude is latently political.
Thomas Mann (1875–1955) German novelist.
The Observer, 11 Aug 1974

53 All reactionaries are paper tigers.
Mao Tse-Tung (1893–1976) Chinese communist leader.
Quotations from Chairman Mao Tse-Tung, Ch. 6

54 McCarthyism is Americanism with its sleeves rolled.
Joseph R. McCarthy (1908–57) US senator.
Speech, 1952

55 The expression 'positive neutrality' is a contradiction in terms. There can be no more positive neutrality than there can be a vegetarian tiger.
V. K. Krishna Menon (1896–1974) Indian barrister and writer.
The New York Times, 18 Oct 1960

56 We cannot change our policy now. After all, we are not political whores.
Benito Mussolini (1883–1945) Italian dictator.
Hitler (Alan Bullock), Ch. 8

57 I still love you, but in politics there is no heart, only head.

Napoleon I (Napoleon Bonaparte; 1769–1821) French emperor.
Referring to his divorce, for reasons of state, from the Empress Josephine (1809)
Bonaparte (C. Barnett)

58 In our time, political speech and writing are largely the defence of the indefensible.

George Orwell (Eric Blair; 1903–50) British novelist.
Politics and the English Language

59 I used to say that politics was the second lowest profession and I have come to know that it bears a great similarity to the first.

Ronald Reagan (1911–) US politician and president.
The Observer, 13 May 1979

60 Please assure me that you are all Republicans!

Ronald Reagan
Addressing the surgeons on being wheeled into the operating theatre for an emergency operation after an assassination attempt
Presidential Anecdotes (P. Boller)

61 Remember this, Griffin. The revolution eats its own. Capitalism re-creates itself.

Mordecai Richler (1931–) Canadian novelist.
Cocksure, Ch. 22

62 The more you read about politics, you got to admit that each party is worse than the other.

Will Rogers (1879–1935) US actor and humorist.
Saturday Review, 'A Rogers Thesaurus', 25 Aug 1962

63 England elects a Labour Government. When a man goes in for politics over here, he has no time to labour, and any man that labours has no time to fool with politics. Over there politics is an obligation; over here it's a business.

Will Rogers
Autobiography, Ch. 14

64 You have to clean your plate.

Lord Rosebery (1847–1929) British statesman.
Said to the Liberal Party
Speech, Chesterfield, 16 Dec 1901

65 The collection of prejudices which is called political philosophy is useful provided that it is not called philosophy.

Bertrand Russell (1872–1970) British philosopher.
The Observer, 'Sayings of the Year', 1962

66 History is past politics, and politics present history.

John Robert Seeley (1834–95) British historian.
Quoting the historian E. A. Freeman
The Growth of British Policy

67 If ever there's any emergence of a fourth party in this country, the task of the Liberal party is to strangle it at birth.

Cyril Smith (1928–) British Liberal politician.
The Guardian, 1981

68 If Her Majesty stood for Parliament – if the Tory Party had any sense and made Her its leader instead of that grammar school twit Heath – us Tories, mate, would win every election we went in for.

Johnny Speight (1920–) British television scriptwriter.
Till Death Do Us Part

69 The Republican form of Government is the highest form of government; but because of this it requires the highest type of human nature – a type nowhere at present existing.

Herbert Spencer (1820–1903) British philosopher.
Essays, 'The Americans'

70 The tasks of the party are . . . to be cautious and not allow our country to be drawn into conflicts by warmongers who are accustomed to have others pull the chestnuts out of the fire for them.

Joseph Stalin (J. Dzhugashvili; 1879–1953) Soviet statesman.
Speech, 8th Congress of the Communist Party, 6 Jan 1941

71 Disdain is the wrong word, but perhaps affection is too strong a word

David Steel (1938–) British politician.
Referring to his attitude to the Liberal party
The Observer, 'Sayings of the Week', 22 Sept 1985

72 Go back to your constituencies and prepare for government!

David Steel
Speech to party conference, 1985

73 I sense that the British electorate is now itching to break out once and for all from the discredited straight-jacket of the past.

David Steel
The Times, 2 June 1987

74 An independent is a guy who wants to take the politics out of politics.

Adlai Stevenson (1900–65) US statesman.
The Art Of Politics.

75 Politics is perhaps the only profession for which no preparation is thought necessary.

Robert Louis Stevenson (1850–94) Scottish writer.
Familiar Studies of Men and Books, 'Yoshida-Torajiro'

76 Socialists treat their servants with respect and then wonder why they vote Conservative.

Tom Stoppard (1937–) Czech-born British dramatist.
Lord Malquist and Mr Moon, Pt. V, Ch. 1

77 Revolts, republics, revolutions, most
No graver than a schoolboy's barring out.

Alfred, Lord Tennyson (1809–92) British poet.
The Princess, Conclusion

78 Any woman who understands the problems of running a home will be nearer to understanding the problems of running a country.

Margaret Thatcher (1925–) British politician and prime minister.
The Observer, 8 May 1979

79 I can trust my husband not to fall asleep on a public platform and he usually claps in the right places.
Margaret Thatcher
Observer, 20 Aug 1978

80 Britain is no longer in the politics of the pendulum, but of the ratchet.
Margaret Thatcher
Speech, Institute of Public Relations, 1977

81 Politics is the art of preventing people from taking part in affairs which properly concern them.
Paul Valéry (1871–1945) French poet and writer.
Tel quel

82 Any American who is prepared to run for President should automatically, by definition, be disqualified from ever doing so.
Gore Vidal (1925–) US novelist.
Attrib.

83 Politics come from man. Mercy, compassion and justice come from God.
Terry Waite (1939–) British churchman.
The Observer, 'Sayings of the Week', 13 Jan 1985

84 The hungry hare has no frontiers and doesn't follow ideologies. The hungry hare goes where it finds the food. And the other hares don't block its passage with the tanks.
Lech Wałesa (1943–) Polish trade unionist.
Interview, 1981

85 A writer of crook stories ought never to stop seeking new material.
Edgar Wallace (1875–1932) British thriller writer.
Said when a candidate for Parliament
The Long Weekend (Alan Hodge)

86 He stood twice for Parliament, but so diffidently that his candidature passed almost unnoticed.
Evelyn Waugh (1903–66) British novelist.
Decline and Fall, Pt. III, Ch. 1

87 Pappenhacker says that every time you are polite to a proletarian you are helping to bolster up the capitalist system.
Evelyn Waugh
Scoop, Bk. I, Ch. 5

88 The Labour Party is going about the country stirring up apathy.
William Whitelaw (1918–) British politician.
Attrib.

89 The Labour party is like a stage-coach. If you rattle along at great speed everybody inside is too exhilarated or too seasick to cause any trouble. But if you stop everybody gets out and argues about where to go next.
Harold Wilson (1916–) British politician and prime minister.
Harold Wilson, The Authentic Portrait (Leslie Smith)

90 Hence the practised performances of latter-day politicians in the game of musical daggers: never be left holding the dagger when the music stops.
Harold Wilson
The Governance of Britain, Ch. 2

91 A week is a long time in politics.
Harold Wilson
First said in 1965 or 1966, and repeated on several occasions
Attrib.

POLLUTION

See conservation, ecology, environment

POP MUSIC

1 Rock'n'roll is part of a pest to undermine the morals of the youth of our nation. It . . . brings people of both races together.
Anonymous
Statement by the North Alabama Citizens' Council in the 1950s

2 Give me that rock'n'roll music,
Any old way you choose it,
It's got to be rock'n'roll music,
If you want to dance with me.
The Beatles British pop group.
Rock'n'roll music

3 Listen kid, take my advice, never hate a song that has sold half a million copies.
Irving Berlin (Israel Baline; 1888–1989) Russian-born US composer.
Giving advice to Cole Porter
Attrib.

4 Roll Over Beethoven.
Chuck Berry (1931–) US rock-and-roll musician.
Song title.

5 Hail, hail rock'n'roll'.
Deliver me from the days of old.
Chuck Berry
Hail, hail, rock'n'roll

6 Do they merit vitriol, even a drop of it? Yes, because they corrupt the young, persuading them that the mature world, which produced Beethoven and Schweitzer, sets an even higher value on the transient anodynes of youth than does youth itself . . . They are the Hollow Men. They are electronic lice.
Anthony Burgess (1917–) British novelist.
Referring to disc jockeys
Punch, 20 Sept 1967

7 Canned music is like audible wallpaper.
Alistair Cooke (1908–) British broadcaster.
Attrib.

8 Strange how potent cheap music is.
Noël Coward (1899–1973) British dramatist.
Private Lives

9 I think popular music in this country is one of

the few things in the twentieth century that have made giant strides in reverse.

Bing Crosby (Harry Lillis Crosby; 1904–77) US singer.
Interview in *This Week*

10 Yea, some of them are about ten minutes long, others five or six.

Bob Dylan (Robert Allen Zimmerman; 1941–) US songwriter.
On being asked in an interview, to say something about his songs
Attrib.

11 Rock Around the Clock.

Bill Haley and The Comets US rock-and-roll band.
Song title

12 We're more popular than Jesus Christ now. I don't know which will go first, Rock and Roll or Christianity.

John Lennon (1940–80) British rock musician.
The Beatles Illustrated Lyrics

13 What a terrible revenge by the culture of the Negroes on that of the Whites.

Ignacy Paderewski (1860–1941) Polish pianist.
Referring to jazz
Attrib.

14 Every popular song has at least one line or sentence that is perfectly clear – the line that fits the music.

Ezra Pound (1885–1972) US poet and critic.
Attrib.

15 It's only rock and roll
But I like it.

The Rolling Stones British rock band.
It's Only Rock and Roll

16 Jazz will endure just as long as people hear it through their feet instead of their brains.

John Philip Sousa (1854–1932) US composer, conductor, and writer.
Attrib.

POPULARITY

See also fame

1 Do not let that trouble Your Excellency; perhaps the greetings are intended for me.

Ludwig van Beethoven (1770–1827) German composer.
Said when walking with Goethe, when Goethe complained about greetings from passers-by
Thayer's Life of Beethoven (E. Forbes)

2 Everybody hates me because I'm so universally liked.

Peter De Vries (1910–) US novelist.
The Vale of Laughter, Pt. I

3 Popularity is a crime from the moment it is sought; it is only a virtue where men have it whether they will or no.

Lord Halifax (1633–95) English statesman.
Political, Moral and Miscellaneous Thoughts and Reflections

4 Popularity? It's glory's small change.

Victor Hugo (1802–85) French writer.
Ruy Blas, III

5 The worse I do, the more popular I get.

John Fitzgerald Kennedy (1917–63) US statesman.
Referring to his popularity following the failure of the US invasion of Cuba
The People's Almanac (D. Wallechinsky)

6 We're more popular than Jesus Christ now. I don't know which will go first. Rock and roll or Christianity.

John Lennon (1940–80) British rock musician.
The Beatles Illustrated Lyrics

7 He's liked, but he's not well liked.

Arthur Miller (1915–) US dramatist.
Death of a Salesman, I

8 I don't resent his popularity or anything else. Good Lord, I co-starred with Errol Flynn once.

Ronald Reagan (1911–) US politician and president.
Remark, Dec 1987

9 He hasn't an enemy in the world, and none of his friends like him.

Oscar Wilde (1854–1900) Irish-born British dramatist.
Said of G. B. Shaw
Sixteen Self Sketches (Shaw), Ch. 17

PORNOGRAPHY

See also censorship, prudery, sex

1 This is the kind of show that gives pornography a bad name.

Clive Barnes (1927–) British-born theatre and ballet critic.
Reviewing *Oh, Calcutta!*
Attrib.

2 I don't think pornography is very harmful, but it is terribly, terribly boring.

Noël Coward (1899–1973) British dramatist.
The Observer, 'Sayings of the Week', 24 Sept 1972

3 Pornography is the attempt to insult sex, to do dirt on it.

D. H. Lawrence (1885–1930) British novelist.
Phoenix, 'Pornography and Obscenity'

4 Its avowed purpose is to excite sexual desire, which, I should have thought, is unnecessary in the case of the young, inconvenient in the case of the middle aged, and unseemly in the old.

Malcolm Muggeridge (1903–) British writer.
Tread Softly For You Tread On My Jokes, 1966

5 *Lady Chatterley's Lover* is a book that all Christians might read with profit.

John Robinson (1919–83) Bishop of Woolwich.
Said in the court case against Penguin Books
Attrib.

6 Don't be daft. You don't get any pornography on there, not on the telly. Get filth, that's

all. The only place you get pornography is in yer Sunday papers.
Johnny Speight (1920–) British television scriptwriter.
Till Death Do Us Part

POSSIBILITY

1 The grand Perhaps!
Robert Browning (1812–89) British poet.
Bishop Blougram's Apology

2 However, one cannot put a quart in a pint cup.
Charlotte Perkins Gilman (1860–1935) US writer.
The Living of Charlotte Perkins Gilman

3 Your If is the only peace-maker; much virtue in If.
William Shakespeare (1564–1616) English dramatist.
As You Like It, V:4

POSTERITY

See also death, fame, future, immortality, reputation

1 Think of your forefathers! Think of your posterity!
John Quincy Adams (1767–1848) Sixth president of the USA.
Speech, Plymouth, Massachusetts, 22 Dec 1802

2 We are always doing something for posterity, but I would fain see posterity do something for us.
Joseph Addison (1672–1719) British essayist.
The Spectator, 583

3 Let us honour if we can
The vertical man
Though we value none
But the horizontal one.
W. H. Auden (1907–73) British poet.
Epigraph for Poems

4 When a man is in doubt about this or that in his writing, it will often guide him if he asks himself how it will tell a hundred years hence.
Samuel Butler (1835–1902) British writer.
Notebooks

5 I think I shall be among the English Poets after my death.
John Keats (1795–1821) British poet.
Letter to George and Georgiana Keats, 14 Oct 1818

6 A writer's ambition should be to trade a hundred contemporary readers for ten readers in ten years' time and for one reader in a hundred years' time.
Arthur Koestler (1905–83) Hungarian-born British writer.
New York Times Book Review, 1 Apr 1951

7 Damn the age. I'll write for antiquity.
Charles Lamb (1775–1834) British essayist.
Referring to his lack of payment for the *Essays of Elia*
English Wits (L. Russell)

8 Now I'm dead in the grave with my lips moving
And every schoolboy repeating my words by heart.
Osip Mandelstam (1891–1938) Russian poet.
Poems, No. 306

9 My time has not yet come either; some are born posthumously.
Friedrich Wilhelm Nietzsche (1844–1900) German philosopher.
Ecce Homo

POVERTY

See also hunger, poverty and wealth

1 From clogs to clogs in three generations.
Proverb

2 Poverty is not a crime.
Proverb

3 To some extent, if you've seen one city slum you've seen them all.
Spiro Agnew (1918–) US politician.
Election speech, Detroit, 18 Oct 1968

4 To be poor and independent is very nearly an impossibility.
William Cobbett (1763–1835) British journalist and writer.
Advice to Young Men

5 He found it inconvenient to be poor.
William Cowper (1731–1800) British poet.
Charity

6 Poverty and oysters always seem to go together.
Charles Dickens (1812–70) British novelist.
Pickwick Papers, Ch. 22

7 Poverty, therefore, was comparative. One measured it by a sliding scale. One was always poor, in terms of those who were richer.
Margaret Drabble (1939–) British novelist.
The Radiant Way

8 There's no scandal like rags, nor any crime so shameful as poverty.
George Farquhar (1678–1707) Irish dramatist.
The Beaux' Strategem, I:1

9 The very poor are unthinkable and only to be approached by the statistician and the poet.
E. M. Forster (1879–1970) British novelist.
Howards End

10 It is only the poor who are forbidden to beg.
Anatole France (Jacques Anatole François Thibault; 1844–1924) French writer.
Crainquebille

11 No sir, tho' I was born and bred in England, I can dare to be poor, which is the only thing now-a-days men are asham'd of.
John Gay (1685–1732) English poet and dramatist.
Polly

12 Is it possible that my people live in such awful conditions? . . . I tell you, Mr Wheatley, that if I had to live in conditions like that I would be a revolutionary myself.
George V (1865–1936) King of the United Kingdom.
On being told Mr Wheatley's life story
The Tragedy of Ramsay MacDonald (L. MacNeill Weir), Ch. 16

13 Let not Ambition mock their useful toil,
Their homely joys, and destiny obscure;
Nor Grandeur hear with a disdainful smile,
The short and simple annals of the poor.
Thomas Gray (1716–71) British poet.
Elegy Written in a Country Churchyard

14 People who are much too sensitive to demand of cripples that they run races ask of the poor that they get up and act just like everyone else in society.
Michael Harrington (1928–) US socialist and writer.
The Other America

15 I want there to be no peasant in my kingdom so poor that he is unable to have a chicken in his pot every Sunday.
Henri IV (1553–1610) King of France.
Hist. de Henry le Grand (Hardouin de Péréfixe)

16 Seven cities warr'd for Homer, being dead,
Who, living, had no roof to shroud his head.
Thomas Heywood (c. 1574–1641) English dramatist.
The Hierarchy of the Blessed Angels

17 Oh! God! that bread should be so dear,
And flesh and blood so cheap!
Thomas Hood (1799–1845) British poet.
The Song of the Shirt

18 Hard to train to accept being poor.
Horace (Quintus Horatius Flaccus; 65–8 BC) Roman poet.
Odes, I

19 It is easy enough to say that poverty is no crime. No; if it were men wouldn't be ashamed of it. It is a blunder, though, and is punished as such. A poor man is despised the whole world over.
Jerome K. Jerome (1859–1927) British humorist.
Idle Thoughts of an Idle Fellow

20 Resolve not to be poor: whatever you have, spend less. Poverty is a great enemy to human happiness; it certainly destroys liberty, and it makes some virtues impracticable and others extremely difficult.
Samuel Johnson (1709–84) British lexicographer.
Life of Johnson (J. Boswell), Vol. IV

21 The misfortunes of poverty carry with them nothing harder to bear than that it exposes men to ridicule.
Juvenal (Decimus Junius Juvenalis; 60–130 AD) Roman satirist.
Satires, III

22 It's not easy for people to rise out of

obscurity when they have to face straitened circumstances at home.
Juvenal
Satires, III

23 We're really all of us bottomly broke. I haven't had time to work in weeks.
Jack Kerouac (1922–69) US novelist.
On the Road, Pt. I

24 Few, save the poor, feel for the poor.
Letitia Landon (1802–38) British poet and novelist.
The Poor

25 'The Workhouse' – always a word of shame, grey shadow falling on the close of life, most feared by the old (even when called The Infirmary); abhorred more than debt, or prison, or beggary, or even the stain of madness.
Laurie Lee (1914–) British novelist and poet.
Cider with Rosie

26 Look at me: I worked my way up from nothing to a state of extreme poverty.
Groucho Marx (Julius Marx; 1895–1977) US comedian.
Monkey Business

27 The forgotten man at the bottom of the economic pyramid.
Franklin D. Roosevelt (1882–1945) US Democratic president.
Speech on radio, 7 Apr 1932

28 The poor don't know that their function in life is to exercise our generosity.
Jean-Paul Sartre (1905–80) French writer.
Words

29 The heart of the matter, as I see it, is the stark fact that world poverty is primarily a problem of two million villages, and thus a problem of two thousand million villagers.
E. F. Schumacher (1911–77) German-born economist.
Small is Beautiful, A Study of Economics as if People Mattered, Ch. 13

30 CUSINS. Do you call poverty a crime?
UNDERSHAFT. The worst of all crimes. All the other crimes are virtues beside it.
George Bernard Shaw (1856–1950) Irish dramatist and critic.
Major Barbara, IV

31 . . . the poor are our brothers and sisters. . . . people in the world who need love, who need care, who have to be wanted.
Mother Teresa (Agnes Gonxha Bojaxhui; 1910–)
Yugoslavian missionary in Calcutta.
Time, 'Saints Among Us', 29 Dec 1975

32 There were times my pants were so thin I could sit on a dime and tell if it was heads or tails.
Spencer Tracy (1900–67) US film star.
Spencer Tracy (L. Swindell)

33 As for the virtuous poor, one can pity them,

of course, but one cannot possibly admire them.

Oscar Wilde (1854–1900) Irish-born British dramatist.
The Soul of Man under Socialism

34 But I, being poor, have only my dreams;
I have spread my dreams under your feet;
Tread softly because you tread on my dreams.

W. B. Yeats (1865–1939) Irish poet.
He Wishes for the Cloths of Heaven

POVERTY AND WEALTH

See also money, poverty, wealth

1 She was poor but she was honest
Victim of a rich man's game.
First he loved her, then he left her,
And she lost her maiden name.

See her on the bridge at midnight,
Saying 'Farewell, blighted love.'
Then a scream, a splash and goodness,
What is she a-doin' of?

It's the same the whole world over,
It's the poor wot gets the blame,
It's the rich wot gets the gravy.
Ain't it all a bleedin' shame?

Anonymous
She was Poor but she was Honest

2 There was a certain rich man, which was clothed in purple and fine linen, and fared sumptuously every day:
And there was a certain beggar named Lazarus, which was laid at his gate, full of sores,
And desiring to be fed with the crumbs which fell from the rich man's table: moreover the dogs came and licked his sores.
And it came to pass, that the beggar died, and was carried by the angels into Abraham's bosom: the rich man also died, and was buried;
And in hell he lift up his eyes, being in torments, and seeth Abraham afar off, and Lazarus in his bosom.

Bible: Luke
16:19–23

3 There are only two families in the world, my old grandmother used to say, The *Haves* and the *Have-Nots*.

Miguel de Cervantes (1547–1616) Spanish novelist.
Don Quixote, Pt. II, Ch. 20

4 'Two nations; between whom there is no intercourse and no sympathy; who are as ignorant of each other's habits, thoughts, and feelings, as if they were dwellers in different zones, or inhabitants of different planets; who are formed by a different breeding, are fed by a different food, are ordered by different manners, and are not governed by the same laws.'

'You speak of –' said Egremont, hesitatingly
'THE RICH AND THE POOR.'

Benjamin Disraeli (1804–81) British statesman.
Sybil, Bk. II, Ch. 5

5 Errors look so very ugly in persons of small means – one feels they are taking quite a liberty in going astray; whereas people of fortune may naturally indulge in a few delinquencies.

George Eliot (Mary Ann Evans; 1819–80) British novelist.
Janet's Repentance, Ch. 25

6 Whereas it has long been known and declared that the poor have no right to the property of the rich, I wish it also to be known and declared that the rich have no right to the property of the poor.

John Ruskin (1819–1900) British art critic and writer.
Unto this Last, Essay III

7 When the rich wage war it is the poor who die.

Jean-Paul Sartre (1905–80) French writer.
The Devil and the Good Lord

8 As long as men are men, a poor society cannot be too poor to find a right order of life, nor a rich society too rich to have need to seek it.

R. H. Tawney (1880–1962) British economist and historian.
The Acquisitive Society

POWER

See also influence, leadership, responsibility

1 Divide and rule.

Proverb

2 He who pays the piper calls the tune.

Proverb

3 Power tends to corrupt, and absolute power corrupts absolutely. Great men are almost always bad men . . . There is no worse heresy than that the office sanctifies the holder of it.

Lord Acton (1834–1902) British historian.
Often misquoted as 'Power corrupts . . .'
Letter to Bishop Mandell Creighton, 5 Apr 1887

4 A friend in power is a friend lost.

Henry Brooks Adams (1838–1918) US historian.
The Education of Henry Adams

5 Nothing destroyeth authority so much as the unequal and untimely interchange of power pressed too far, and relaxed too much.

Francis Bacon (1561–1626) English philosopher.
Essays, 'Of Empire'

6 He did not care in which direction the car

was travelling, so long as he remained in the driver's seat.
Lord Beaverbrook (1879–1964) British newspaper owner and politician.
Referring to Lloyd George
New Statesman, 14 June 1963

7 The strongest poison ever known
Came from Caesar's laurel crown.
William Blake (1757–1827) British poet.
Auguries of Innocence

8 The greater the power, the more dangerous the abuse.
Edmund Burke (1729–97) British politician.
Speech, House of Commons, 7 Feb 1771

9 If you think you have someone eating out of your hand, it's a good idea to count your fingers.
Martin Buxbaume
Attrib.

10 There is one thing about being President – nobody can tell you when to sit down.
Dwight D. Eisenhower (1890–1969) US general and statesman.
The Observer, 'Sayings of the Week', 9 Aug 1953

11 Men of power have not time to read; yet men who do not read are unfit for power.
Michael Foot (1913–) British Labour politician and journalist.
Debts Of Honour

12 Power is so apt to be insolent and Liberty to be saucy, that they are seldom upon good Terms.
Lord Halifax (1633–95) English statesman.
Political, Moral, and Miscellaneous Thoughts and Reflections

13 It was a symptom of Britain's post-war condition that anyone given power before his hair turned white was called a whizz-kid.
Clive James (1939–) Writer and broadcaster, born in Australia.
Falling Towards England, Ch. 18

14 Power is the ultimate aphrodisiac.
Henry Kissinger (1923–) German-born US politician and diplomat.
The Guardian, 28 Nov 1976

15 Power? It's like a dead sea fruit; when you achieve it, there's nothing there.
Harold Macmillan (1894–1986) British politician and prime minister.
Attrib.

16 It could never be a correct justification that, because the whites oppressed us yesterday when they had power, that the blacks must oppress them today because they have power.
Robert Mugabe (1925–) Zimbabwe politician and president.
Speech, Mar 1980

17 To reign is worth ambition, though in Hell:

Better to reign in Hell than serve in Heaven.
John Milton (1608–74) English poet.
Paradise Lost, Bk. I

18 Who controls the past controls the future. Who controls the present controls the past.
George Orwell (Eric Blair; 1903–50) British novelist.
Nineteen Eighty-Four

19 Unlimited power is apt to corrupt the minds of those who possess it.
William Pitt the Elder (1708–78) British statesman.
See also Lord ACTON
Speech, House of Lords, 9 Jan 1770

20 The megalomaniac differs from the narcissist by the fact that he wishes to be powerful rather than charming, and seeks to be feared rather than loved. To this type belong many lunatics and most of the great men of history.
Bertrand Russell (1872–1970) British philosopher.
The Conquest of Happiness

21 We are the masters at the moment – and not only for the moment, but for a very long time to come.
Lord Shawcross (1902–) British Labour politician and lawyer.
Sometimes quoted as, 'We are the masters now!'
House of Commons, 2 Apr 1946

22 The official world, the corridors of power, the dilemmas of conscience and egotism – she disliked them all.
C. P. Snow (1905–80) British novelist.
Homecomings, Ch. 22

23 You only have power over people so long as you don't take *everything* away from them. But when you've robbed a man of everything he's no longer in your power – he's free again.
Alexander Solzhenitsyn (1918–) Soviet novelist.
The First Circle, Ch. 17

24 Power corrupts, but lack of power corrupts absolutely.
Adlai Stevenson (1900–65) US statesman.
The Observer, Jan 1963

25 He aspired to power instead of influence, and as a result forfeited both.
A. J. P. Taylor (1906–) British historian.
Referring to Lord Northcliffe
English History, 1914–1945, Ch. 1

26 One Ring to rule them all, One Ring to find them,
One Ring to bring them all and in the darkness bind them.
J. R. R. Tolkien (1892–1973) British writer.
The Lord of the Rings, Pt. I: *The Fellowship of the Ring*, Ch. 2

27 The balance of power.
Robert Walpole (1676–1745) British statesman.
Speech, House of Commons

28 The good old rule
Sufficeth them, the simple plan,

That they should take, who have the power,
And they should keep who can.
William Wordsworth (1770–1850) British poet.
Rob Roy's Grave

29 The wrong sort of people are always in power because they would not be in power if they were not the wrong sort of people.
Jon Wynne-Tyson (1924–) British humorous writer.
Times Literary Supplement

POWER POLITICS

See also force, oppression, violence, weapons

1 Whatever happens, we have got
The Maxim Gun, and they have not.
Hilaire Belloc (1870–1953) French-born British poet.
Referring to African natives
The Modern Traveller

2 The great questions of our day cannot be solved by speeches and majority votes . . . but by iron and blood.
Bismarck (1815–98) German statesman.
Usually misquoted as 'blood and iron' – a form Bismarck himself used in 1886
Speech, Prussian Chamber, 30 Sept 1862

3 Guns will make us powerful; butter will only make us fat.
Hermann Goering (1893–1946) German leader.
Radio broadcast, 1936

4 A man may build himself a throne of bayonets, but he cannot sit on it.
Dean Inge (1860–1954) British churchman.
Wit and Wisdom of Dean Inge (ed. Marchant)

5 Every Communist must grasp the truth, 'Political power grows out of the barrel of a gun.'
Mao Tse-Tung (1893–1976) Chinese communist leader.
Selected Works, Vol II, 'Problems of War and Strategy', 6 Nov 1938

6 There is a homely adage which runs 'Speak softly and carry a big stick, you will go far'.
Theodore Roosevelt (1858–1919) US Republican president.
Speech, Minnesota State Fair, 2 Sept 1901

7 God is always on the side of the big battalions.
Vicomte de Turenne (1611–75) French marshal.
Attrib.

8 God is on the side not of the heavy battalions, but of the best shots.
Voltaire (François-Marie Arouet; 1694–1778) French writer.
Notebooks

PRACTICALITY

1 I have no dress except the one I wear every day. If you are going to be kind enough to give me one, please let it be practical and dark so that I can put it on afterwards to go to the laboratory.
Marie Curie (1867–1934) Polish chemist.
Referring to a wedding dress
Letter to a friend

2 What would you do with it? It is full of leprosy.
Father Damien (Joseph de Veuster; 1840–89) Belgian Roman Catholic missionary.
When asked on his deathbed whether he would leave another priest his mantle, like Elijah
Memoirs of an Aesthete (H. Acton)

3 The Arab who builds himself a hut out of the marble fragments of a temple in Palmyra is more philosophical than all the curators of the museums in London, Munich or Paris.
Anatole France (Jacques Anatole François Thibault; 1844–1924) French writer.
The Crime of Sylvestre Bonnard

4 Talk to him of Jacob's ladder, and he would ask the number of the steps.
Douglas William Jerrold (1803–57) British dramatist.
Wit and Opinions of Douglas Jerrold, 'A Matter-of-fact Man'

5 Don't carry away that arm till I have taken off my ring.
Lord Raglan (1788–1855) British field marshal.
Request immediately after his arm had been amputated following the battle of Waterloo
Dictionary of National Biography

6 Very well, then I shall not take off my boots.
Duke of Wellington (1769–1852) British general and statesman.
Responding to the news, as he was going to bed, that the ship in which he was travelling seemed about to sink
Attrib.

PRAISE

See also admiration, boasts, compliments, flattery

1 Self-praise is no recommendation.
Proverb

2 Just as it is always said of slander that something always sticks when people boldly slander, so it might be said of self-praise (if it is not entirely shameful and ridiculous) that if we praise ourselves fearlessly, something will always stick.
Francis Bacon (1561–1626) English philosopher.
The Advancement of Learning

3 Let us now praise famous men, and our fathers that begat us.
Bible: Ecclesiasticus
44:1

4 The advantage of doing one's praising for oneself is that one can lay it on so thick and exactly in the right places.
Samuel Butler (1835–1902) British writer.
The Way of All Flesh, Ch. 34

5 Fondly we think we honour merit then,

When we but praise ourselves in other men.
Alexander Pope (1688–1744) British poet.
An Essay on Criticism

6 To refuse praise reveals a desire to be praised twice over.
Duc de la Rochefoucauld (1613–80) French writer.
Maximes, 149

PRAYER

See also Christianity, faith, God, religion

1 Hail Mary, full of grace, the Lord is with thee: Blessed art thou among women, and blessed is the fruit of thy womb, Jesus.
Anonymous
Ave Maria, 11th century

2 From ghoulies and ghosties and long-leggety beasties
And things that go bump in the night,
Good Lord, deliver us!
Anonymous
Cornish

3 O Lord! thou knowest how busy I must be this day: if I forget thee, do not thou forget me.
Lord Astley (1579–1652) English Royalist general.
Prayer before taking part in the Battle of Edgehill
Memoires (Sir Philip Warwick)

4 But when ye pray, use not vain repetitions, as the heathen do: for they think that they shall be heard for their much speaking.
Be not ye therefore like unto them: for your Father knoweth what things ye have need of, before ye ask him.
After this manner therefore pray ye: Our Father which art in heaven, Hallowed be thy name.
Thy kingdom come. Thy will be done in earth, as it is in heaven.
Give us this day our daily bread.
And forgive us our debts, as we forgive our debtors.
And lead us not into temptation, but deliver us from evil: For thine is the kingdom, and the power, and the glory, for ever. Amen.
Bible: Matthew
6:7–13

5 To Mercy, Pity, Peace, and Love
All pray in their distress.
William Blake (1757–1827) British poet.
Songs of Innocence, 'The Divine Image'

6 When two or three are gathered together in thy Name thou wilt grant their requests.
The Book of Common Prayer
Morning Prayer, Prayer of St Chrysostom

7 A leap over the hedge is better than good men's prayers.
Miguel de Cervantes (1547–1616) Spanish novelist.
Don Quixote, Pt. I, Ch. 21

8 He prayeth well, who loveth well
Both man and bird and beast.
Samuel Taylor Coleridge (1772–1834) British poet.
The Rime of the Ancient Mariner, VII

9 He prayeth best, who loveth best
All things both great and small;
For the dear God who loveth us,
He made and loveth all.
Samuel Taylor Coleridge
The Rime of the Ancient Mariner, VII

10 Prayer makes the Christian's armour bright;
And Satan trembles when he sees
The weakest saint upon his knees.
William Cowper (1731–1800) British poet.
Olney Hymns, 29

11 The idea that He would take his attention away from the universe in order to give me a bicycle with three speeds is just so unlikely I can't go along with it.
Quentin Crisp (?1910–) Model, publicist, and writer.
The Sunday Times, 18 Dec 1977

12 Forgive, O Lord, my little jokes on Thee
And I'll forgive Thy great big one on me.
Robert Frost (1875–1963) US poet.
In the clearing, 'Cluster of Faith'

13 Religion's in the heart, not in the knees.
Douglas William Jerrold (1803–57) British dramatist.
The Devil's Ducat, I.2

14 The Beadsman, after thousand aves told,
For aye unsought-for slept among his ashes cold.
John Keats (1795–1821) British poet.
The Eve of Saint Agnes, I

15 Our dourest parsons, who followed the nonconformist fashion of long extemporary prayers, always seemed to me to be bent on bullying God. After a few 'beseech thees' as a mere politeness, they adopted a sterner tone and told Him what they expected from Him and more than hinted He must attend to His work.
J. B. Priestley (1894–1984) British novelist.
Outcries and Asides

16 I am just going to pray for you at St Paul's, but with no very lively hope of success.
Sydney Smith (1771–1845) British clergyman and essayist.
On meeting an acquaintance
The Smith of Smiths (H. Pearson), Ch. 13

17 If thou shouldst never see my face again,
Pray for my soul. More things are wrought by prayer
Than this world dreams of.
Alfred, Lord Tennyson (1809–92) British poet.
Idylls of the King, 'The Passing of Arthur'

18 Whatever a man prays for, he prays for a

miracle. Every prayer reduces itself to this:
'Great God grant that twice two be not four.'
Ivan Turgenev (1818–83) Russian novelist.
Prayer

PRECOCITY

See also children, youth

1 One of those men who reach such an acute
limited excellence at twenty-one that
everything afterward savours of anti-climax.
F. Scott Fitzgerald (1896–1940) US novelist.
The Great Gatsby, Ch. 1

2 Thank you, madam, the agony is abated.
Lord Macaulay (1800–59) British historian.
Replying, aged four, to a lady who asked if he had hurt himself
Life and Letters of Macaulay (Trevelyan), Ch. 1

PREJUDICE

See also equality, feminism, Jews, objectivity, racism, religion,
subjectivity

1 I am a Catholic. As far as possible I go to
Mass every day. As far as possible I kneel
down and tell these beads every day. If you
reject me on account of my religion, I shall
thank God that he has spared me the
indignity of being your representative.
Hilaire Belloc (1870–1953) French-born British poet.
Said in his first election campaign
Speech, Salford, 1906

2 Mother is far too clever to understand
anything she does not like.
Arnold Bennett (1867–1931) British novelist.
The Title

3 Common sense is the collection of prejudices
acquired by age eighteen.
Albert Einstein (1879–1955) German-born US physicist.
Scientific American, Feb 1976

4 Vegetarians have wicked, shifty eyes, and
laugh in a cold and calculating manner. They
pinch little children, steal stamps, drink
water, favour beards . . . wheeze, squeak,
drawl and maunder.
J. B. Morton (1893–1979) British journalist.
By the Way, '4 June'

5 . . . I *too well* know its truth, from
experience, that whenever any poor Gipsies
are encamped anywhere and crimes and
robberies &c. occur, it is invariably laid to
their account, which is shocking; and if they
are always looked upon as vagabonds, how
can they become good people?
Victoria (1819–1901) Queen of the United Kingdom.
Journal, 29 Dec 1836

6 I do not intend to prejudge the past.
William Whitelaw (1918–) British politician.
Said on arriving in Ulster as Minister for Northern Ireland
The Times, 3 Dec 1973

7 No Jewish blood runs among my blood,

but I am as bitterly and hardly hated
by every anti-semite
as if I were a Jew. By this
I am a Russian.
Yevgeny Yevtushenko (1933–) Soviet poet.
Babi Yar

PRESENT

See also future, opportunity, past, time

1 No time like the present.
Proverb

2 The past was nothing to her; offered no
lesson which she was willing to heed. The
future was a mystery which she never
attempted to penetrate. The present alone
was significant . . .
Kate Chopin (1851–1904) US writer.
The Awakening, Ch. 15

3 I have learned to live each day as it comes,
and not to borrow trouble by dreading
tomorrow. It is the dark menace of the
future that makes cowards of us.
Dorothy Dix (Elizabeth Meriwether Gilmer; 1861–1951)
US journalist and writer.
Dorothy Dix, Her Book, Introduction

4 Happy the Man, and happy he alone,
He who can call today his own:
He who, secure within, can say,
Tomorrow do thy worst, for I have liv'd today.
John Dryden (1631–1700) British poet and dramatist.
Translation of Horace, III

5 Ah, my Belovéd, fill the Cup that clears
TO-DAY of past Regrets and Future Fears:
To-morrow! – Why, To-morrow I may be
Myself with Yesterday's Sev'n thousand Years.
Edward Fitzgerald (1809–83) British poet.
The Rubáiyát of Omar Khayyám (1st edn.), XX

6 Gather ye rosebuds while ye may,
Old time is still a-flying:
And this same flower that smiles today
Tomorrow will be dying.
Robert Herrick (1591–1674) English poet.
Hesperides, 'To the Virgins, to Make Much of Time'

7 *Carpe diem.*
Seize the day.
Horace (Quintus Horatius Flaccus; 65–8 BC) Roman poet.
Odes, I

8 Drop the question what tomorrow may bring,
and count as profit every day that Fate
allows you.
Horace
Odes, I

9 While we're talking, time will have meanly
run on: pick today's fruits, not relying on the
future in the slightest.
Horace
Odes, I

10 Believe each day that has dawned is your

last. Some hour to which you have not been looking forward will prove lovely. As for me, if you want a good laugh, you will come and find me fat and sleek, in excellent condition, one of Epicurus' herd of pigs.
Horace
Epistles, I

11 We live in stirring times – tea-stirring times.
Christopher Isherwood (1904–86) British novelist.
Mr Norris Changes Trains

12 Redeem thy mis-spent time that's past;
Live this day, as if 'twere thy last.
Thomas Ken (1637–1711) English bishop.
A Morning Hymn

13 What is love? 'Tis not hereafter;
Present mirth hath present laughter;
What's to come is still unsure.
In delay there lies no plenty,
Then come kiss me, sweet and twenty;
Youth's a stuff will not endure.
William Shakespeare (1564–1616) English dramatist.
Twelfth Night, II:3

PRIDE

See also arrogance, conceit, egotism, self-respect

1 Pride goeth before destruction, and an haughty spirit before a fall.
Bible: Proverbs
16:18

2 He that is down needs fear no fall;
He that is low, no pride.
John Bunyan (1628–88) English writer.
The Pilgrim's Progress, 'Shepherd Boy's Song'

3 I know of no case where a man added to his dignity by standing on it.
Winston Churchill (1874–1965) British politician.
Attrib.

4 When the Lord sent me forth into the world, He forbade me to put off my hat to any high or low.
George Fox (1624–91) English religious leader.
Journal

5 And if you include me among the lyric poets, I'll hold my head so high it'll strike the stars.
Horace (Quintus Horatius Flaccus; 65–8 BC) Roman poet.
Odes, I

6 We are not ashamed of what we have done, because, when you have a great cause to fight for, the moment of greatest humiliation is the moment when the spirit is proudest.
Christabel Pankhurst (1880–1958) British suffragette.
Speech, Albert Hall, London, 19 Mar 1908

7 Yes; I am proud, I must be proud to see Men not afraid of God, afraid of me.
Alexander Pope (1688–1744) British poet.
Epilogue to the Satires, Dialogue II

8 Of all the causes which conspire to blind

Man's erring judgment, and misguide the mind,
What the weak head with strongest bias rules,
Is Pride, the never-failing vice of fools.
Alexander Pope
An Essay on Criticism

9 There is false modesty, but there is no false pride.
Jules Renard (1894–1910) French writer.
Journal

10 I am proud to have a son who died doing the job he loved for the country he loved.
Harry Taylor Father of soldier killed in Falklands war.
Remark, May 1982

11 The French want no-one to be their *superior*. The English want *inferiors*. The Frenchman constantly raises his eyes above him with anxiety. The Englishman lowers his beneath him with satisfaction. On either side it is pride, but understood in a different way.
Alexis de Tocqueville (1805–59) French writer, historian, and politician.
Voyage en Angleterre et en Irlande de 1835, 18 May

12 We cannot bring ourselves to believe it possible that a foreigner should in any respect be wiser than ourselves. If any such point out to us our follies, we at once claim those follies as the special evidences of our wisdom.
Anthony Trollope (1815–82) British novelist.
Orley Farm, Ch. 18

PRINCIPLES

See also integrity, morality

1 It is easier to fight for one's principles than to live up to them.
Alfred Adler (1870–1937) Austrian psychiatrist.
Alfred Adler (P. Bottome)

2 If one sticks too rigidly to one's principles one would hardly see anybody.
Agatha Christie (1891–1976) British detective-story writer.
Towards Zero, I

3 Whenever two good people argue over principles, they are both right.
Marie Ebner von Eschenbach (1830–1916) Austrian writer.
Aphorism

4 Well, sir, you never can tell. That's a principle in life with me, sir, if you'll excuse my having such a thing, sir.
George Bernard Shaw (1856–1950) Irish dramatist and critic.
You Never Can Tell, II

PRIVACY

1 The house of every one is to him as his castle and fortress.
Edward Coke (1552–1634) English lawyer and politician.
Semayne's Case

2 I never said, 'I want to be alone.' I only said, 'I want to be *left* alone.' There is all the difference.
Greta Garbo (1905–90) Swedish-born US film star.
Garbo (John Bainbridge)

3 The poorest man may in his cottage bid defiance to all the forces of the Crown. It may be frail – its roof may shake – the wind may blow through it – the storm may enter – the rain may enter – but the King of England cannot enter! – all his force dares not cross the threshold of the ruined tenement!
William Pitt the Elder (1708–78) British statesman.
Statesmen in the Time of George III (Lord Brougham), Vol. I

4 This is a free country, madam. We have a right to share your privacy in a public place.
Peter Ustinov (1921–) British actor.
Romanoff and Juliet, I

PROCRASTINATION

1 Never put off till tomorrow what you can do today.
Proverb

2 Put off the evil hour as long as you can.
Proverb

3 The road to hell is paved with good intentions.
Proverb

4 Give me chastity and continence, but not yet.
St Augustine of Hippo (354–430) Bishop of Hippo.
Confessions, Bk. VIII, Ch. 7

5 Procrastination is the thief of time.
Edward Young (1683–1765) British poet.
Night Thoughts

PROGRESS

See also change, conservatism, improvement, innovation, novelty, technology

1 The people who live in the past must yield to the people who live in the future. Otherwise the world would begin to turn the other way round.
Arnold Bennett (1867–1931) British novelist.
Milestones

2 All progress is based upon a universal innate desire on the part of every organism to live beyond its income.
Samuel Butler (1835–1902) British writer.
Notebooks

3 As enunciated today, 'progress' is simply a comparative of which we have not settled the superlative.
G. K. Chesterton (1874–1936) British writer.
Heretics, Ch. 2

4 New roads: new ruts.
G. K. Chesterton
Attrib.

5 What we call progress is the exchange of one nuisance for another nuisance.
Havelock Ellis (1859–1939) British sexologist.
Attrib.

6 All that is human must retrograde if it does not advance.
Edward Gibbon (1737–94) British historian.
Decline and Fall of the Roman Empire, Ch. 71

7 You cannot fight against the future. Time is on our side.
William Ewart Gladstone (1809–98) British statesman.
Advocating parliamentary reform
Speech, 1866

8 One step forward, two steps back . . . It happens in the lives of individuals, and it happens in the history of nations and in the development of parties.
Lenin (Vladimir Ilich Ulyanov; 1870–1924) Russian revolutionary leader.
One Step Forward, Two Steps Back

9 If I have seen further it is by standing on the shoulders of giants.
Isaac Newton (1642–1727) British scientist.
Letter to Robert Hooke, 5 Feb 1675

10 You can't say civilization don't advance, however, for in every war they kill you a new way.
Will Rogers (1879–1935) US actor and humorist.
Autobiography, Ch. 12

11 Organic life, we are told, has developed gradually from the protozoon to the philosopher, and this development, we are assured, is indubitably an advance. Unfortunately it is the philosopher, not the protozoon, who gives us this assurance.
Bertrand Russell (1872–1970) British philosopher.
Mysticism and Logic, Ch. 6

12 Man's 'progress' is but a gradual discovery that his questions have no meaning.
Antoine de Saint-Exupéry (1900–44) French novelist and aviator.
The Wisdom of the Sands

PROMISCUITY

See also sex

1 I see – she's the original good time that was had by all.
Bette Davis (Ruth Elizabeth Davis; 1908–89) US film star.
Referring to a starlet of the time
The Filmgoer's Book of Quotes (Leslie Halliwell)

2 Lady Capricorn, he understood, was still keeping open bed.
Aldous Huxley (1894–1964) British novelist.
Antic Hay, Ch. 21

3 The woman's a whore, and there's an end on't.

Samuel Johnson (1709–84) British lexicographer.
Referring to Lady Diana Beauclerk
Life of Johnson (J. Boswell), Vol. II

4 You were born with your legs apart. They'll send you to the grave in a Y-shaped coffin.

Joe Orton (1933–67) British dramatist.
What the Butler Saw, I

5 You know, she speaks eighteen languages. And she can't say 'No' in any of them.

Dorothy Parker (1893–1967) US writer.
Speaking of an acquaintance
Attrib.

6 I'm glad you like my Catherine. I like her too. She ruled thirty million people and had three thousand lovers. I do the best I can in two hours.

Mae West (1892–1980) US actress.
After her performance in *Catherine the Great*
Speech from the stage

PROMISES

1 Better is it that thou shouldest not vow, than that thou shouldest vow and not pay.

Bible: Ecclesiastes
5:5

2 I do set my bow in the cloud, and it shall be for a token of a covenant between me and the earth.

Bible: Genesis
9:13

3 The rule is, jam tomorrow and jam yesterday – but never jam today.

Lewis Carroll (Charles Lutwidge Dodgson; 1832–98) British writer.
Through the Looking-Glass, Ch. 5

4 If you feed people just with revolutionary slogans they will listen today, they will listen tomorrow, they will listen the day after tomorrow, but on the fourth day they will say 'To hell with you!'

Nikita Khrushchev (1894–1971) Soviet statesman.
Attrib.

5 A promise made is a debt unpaid.

Robert William Service (1874–1958) Canadian poet.
The Cremation of Sam McGee

6 Jam today, and men aren't at their most exciting: Jam tomorrow, and one often sees them at their noblest.

C. P. Snow (1905–80) British novelist.
The Two Cultures and the Scientific Revolution, 4

7 Promises and pie-crust are made to be broken.

Jonathan Swift (1667–1745) Irish-born Anglican priest and writer.
Polite Conversation, Dialogue 1

PROMOTION

See also patronage

1 Tired of knocking at Preferment's door.

Matthew Arnold (1822–88) British poet and critic.
The Scholar Gipsy

2 He had said he had known many kicked down stairs, but he never knew any kicked up stairs before.

Lord Halifax (1633–95) English statesman.
Original Memoirs (Burnet)

PROMPTNESS

1 Liberality lies less in giving liberally than in the timeliness of the gift.

Jean de La Bruyère (1645–96) French satirist.
Les Caractères

2 Punctuality is the politeness of kings.

Louis XVIII (1755–1824) French king.
Attrib.

3 Better never than late.

George Bernard Shaw (1856–1950) Irish dramatist and critic.
Responding to an offer by a producer to present one of Shaw's plays, having earlier rejected it
The Unimportance of Being Oscar (Oscar Levant)

4 He gives twice who gives promptly.

Publilius Syrus (1st century BC) Roman dramatist.
Attrib.

5 Punctuality is the virtue of the bored.

Evelyn Waugh (1903–66) British novelist.
Diaries, 'Irregular Notes', 26 Mar 1962

PRONUNCIATION

See also class, language, speech, spelling

1 Everybody has a right to pronounce foreign names as he chooses.

Winston Churchill (1874–1965) British statesman.
The Observer, 'Sayings of the Week', 5 Aug 1951

2 Oh my God! Remember you're in Egypt. The *skay* is only seen in Kensington.

Herbert Beerbohm Tree (1853–1917) British actor and theatre manager.
To a leading lady
Beerbohm Tree (Hesketh Pearson)

3 They spell it Vinci and pronounce it Vinchy; foreigners always spell better than they pronounce.

Mark Twain (Samuel Langhorne Clemens; 1835–1910) US writer.
The Innocents Abroad, Ch. 19

PROOF

1 One swallow does not make a summer.

Proverb

2 What is now proved was once only imagined.
William Blake (1757–1827) British poet.
The Marriage of Heaven and Hell, 'Proverbs of Hell'

3 If a man could pass through Paradise in a dream, and have a flower presented to him as a pledge that his soul had really been there, and if he found that flower in his hand when he awoke – Aye, and what then?
Samuel Taylor Coleridge (1772–1834) British poet.
Anima Poetae

4 Of course, before we *know* he is a saint, there will have to be miracles.
Graham Greene (1904–) British novelist.
The Power and the Glory, Pt. IV

5 If only I could get down to Sidcup! I've been waiting for the weather to break. He's got my papers, this man I left them with, it's got it all down there, I could prove everything.
Harold Pinter (1930–) British dramatist.
The Caretaker, I

6 Some circumstantial evidence is very strong, as when you find a trout in the milk.
Henry David Thoreau (1817–62) US writer.
Journal, 1850

PROPAGANDA

1 Propaganda is that branch of the art of lying which consists in nearly deceiving your friends without quite deceiving your enemies.
F. M. Cornford (1886–1960) British poet.
New Statesman, 15 Sept 1978

2 The greater the lie, the greater the chance that it will be believed.
Adolf Hitler (1889–1945) German dictator.
Mein Kampf

3 I wonder if we could contrive . . . some magnificent myth that would in itself carry conviction to our whole community.
Plato (429–347 BC) Greek philosopher.
Republic, Bk. 5

PROPHECY

See also beginning, future

1 'I saw the new moon late yestreen
Wi' the auld moon in her arm;
And if we gang to sea master,
I fear we'll come to harm.'
Anonymous
Sir Patrick Spens

2 And there arose not a prophet since in Israel like unto Moses, whom the Lord knew face to face.
Bible: Deuteronomy
34:10

3 I am signing my death warrant.
Michael Collins (1890–1922) Irish nationalist.
Said on signing the agreement with Great Britain, 1921, that

established the Irish Free State. He was assassinated in an ambush some months later
Peace by Ordeal (Longford), Pt. 6, Ch. 1

4 I will sit down now, but the time will come when you will hear me.
Benjamin Disraeli (1804–81) British statesman.
Maiden Speech, House of Commons, 7 Dec 1837

5 The lamps are going out over all Europe; we shall not see them lit again in our lifetime.
Lord Grey (1862–1933) British statesman.
Remark made on 3 Aug 1914, the eve of World War I

6 You ain't heard nothin' yet, folks.
Al Jolson (Asa Yoelson; 1886–1950) US actor and singer.
In the film *The Jazz Singer,* July 1927

7 For not wanting to consent to the divorce, which then afterwards will be recognized as unworthy, the King of the islands will be forced to flee, and one put in his place who has no sign of kingship.
Nostradamus (1503–66) French astrologer.
Thought to refer to the abdication of Edward VIII
The Prophecies of Nostradamus, Century X, 22

8 At night they will think they have seen the sun, when they see the half pig man: Noise, screams, battles seen fought in the skies. The brute beasts will be heard to speak.
Nostradamus
Thought to prophecy a 20th-century air-battle
The Prophecies of Nostradamus, Century I, 64

9 The blood of the just will be demanded of London burnt by fire in three times twenty plus six. The ancient lady will fall from her high position, and many of the same denomination will be killed.
Nostradamus
Believed to refer to the Great Fire of London, 1666. The 'ancient lady' is interpreted as the Cathedral of St. Paul's, which was destroyed in the fire
The Prophecies of Nostradamus, Century II, 51

10 *Après nous le déluge.*
After us the deluge.
Madame de Pompadour (1721–64) The mistress of Louis XV of France.
After the Battle of Rossbach, 1757

11 As I look ahead, I am filled with foreboding. Like the Roman, I seem to see 'the River Tiber foaming with much blood'.
Enoch Powell (1912–) British politician.
Talking about immigration
Speech in Birmingham, 20 Apr 1968

12 Beware the ides of March.
William Shakespeare (1564–1616) English dramatist.
Julius Caesar, I:2

13 Mr Turnbull had predicted evil consequences . . . and was now doing the best in his power to bring about the verification of his own prophecies.
Anthony Trollope (1815–82) British novelist.
Phineas Finn, Ch. 25

14 I see wars, horrible wars, and the Tiber
foaming with
much blood.
Virgil (Publius Vergilius Maro; 70–19 BC) Roman poet.
Part of the Sibyl's prophecy to Aeneas, foretelling his difficulties in winning a home in Italy
Aeneid, Bk. VI

15 When the Paris Exhibition closes, electric
light will close with it and no more will be
heard of it.
Erasmus Wilson

PROSE

See also books, criticism, fiction, literature, novels, poetry and prose, writing

1 Yet no one hears his own remarks as prose.
W. H. Auden (1907–73) British poet.
At a Party

2 Men will forgive a man anything except bad
prose.
Winston Churchill (1874–1965) British statesman.
Election speech, Manchester, 1906

3 Good heavens! I have been talking prose for
over forty years without realizing it.
Molière (Jean Baptiste Poquelin; 1622–73) French
dramatist.
Le Bourgeois Gentilhomme, II:4

PROTESTANTISM

See also Catholicism, Christianity, religion

1 The chief contribution of Protestantism to
human thought is its massive proof that God
is a bore.
H. L. Mencken (1880–1956) US journalist.
Notebooks, 'Minority Report'

2 'You're a Christian?' 'Church of England,' said
Mr Polly. 'Mm,' said the employer, a little
checked. 'For good all round business work,
I should have preferred a Baptist.'
H. G. Wells (1866–1946) British writer.
The History of Mr Polly, Pt. III, Ch. 1

3 Take heed of thinking. *The farther you go
from the church of Rome, the nearer you are
to God.*
Henry Wotton (1568–1639) English poet and diplomat.
Reliquiae Wottonianae (Izaak Walton)

PROVOCATION

1 My wife hath something in her gizzard, that
only waits an opportunity of being provoked
to bring up.
Samuel Pepys (1633–1703) English diarist.
Diary, 17 June 1668

2 Ask you what provocation I have had?
The strong antipathy of good to bad.
Alexander Pope (1688–1744) British poet.
Epilogue to the Satires, Dialogue II

PRUDENCE

See also caution, wisdom

1 A bird in the hand is worth two in the bush.
Proverb

2 Forewarned is forearmed.
Proverb

3 For want of a nail the shoe was lost; for
want of a shoe the horse was lost; for want
of a horse the rider was lost.
Proverb

4 Prevention is better than cure.
Proverb

5 It is always good
When a man has two irons in the fire.
Francis Beaumont (1584–1616) English dramatist.
The Faithful Friends, I:2

6 Put your trust in God, my boys, and keep
your powder dry.
Valentine Blacker (1778–1823) British soldier.
Oliver Cromwell's Advice

7 I'd much rather have that fellow inside my
tent pissing out, than outside my tent pissing
in.
Lyndon B. Johnson (1908–73) US statesman.
When asked why he retained J. Edgar Hoover at the FBI
Guardian Weekly, 18 Dec 1971

8 One should oblige everyone to the extent of
one's ability. One often needs someone
smaller than oneself.
Jean de La Fontaine (1621–95) French poet.
Fables, II, 'Le Lion et le Rat'

9 Any girl who was a lady would not even
think of having such a good time that she did
not remember to hang on to her jewelry.
Anita Loos (1891–1981) US novelist.
Gentlemen Prefer Blondes, Ch. 4

10 Be nice to people on your way up because
you'll meet 'em on your way down.
Wilson Mizner (1876–1933) US writer and wit.
Also attributed to Jimmy Durante
A Dictionary of Catch Phrases (Eric Partridge)

PRUDERY

See also censorship, pornography, puritanism

1 Would you allow your wife or your servant to
read this book?
Mervyn Griffith-Jones (1909–78) British lawyer.
As counsel for the prosecution in the *Lady Chatterley's Lover*
trial

2 Age will bring all things, and everyone
knows, Madame, that twenty is no age to be
a prude.
Molière (Jean Baptiste Poquelin; 1622–73) French
dramatist.
Le Misanthrope, III:4

3 An orgy looks particularly alluring seen through the mists of righteous indignation.
Malcolm Muggeridge (1903–) British writer.
The Most of Malcolm Muggeridge, 'Dolce Vita in a Cold Climate'

4 Obscenity is what happens to shock some elderly and ignorant magistrate.
Bertrand Russell (1872–1970) British philosopher.
Look magazine

PSYCHIATRY

See also madness, neurosis, psychology

1 To us he is no more a person
Now but a climate of opinion.
W. H. Auden (1907–73) British poet.
In Memory of Sigmund Freud

2 The trouble with Freud is that he never played the Glasgow Empire Saturday night.
Ken Dodd (1931–) British comedian.
TV interview, 1965

3 The psychic development of the individual is a short repetition of the course of development of the race.
Sigmund Freud (1856–1939) Austrian psychoanalyst.
Leonardo da Vinci

4 Anybody who goes to see a psychiatrist ought to have his head examined.
Samuel Goldwyn (Samuel Goldfish; 1882–1974) Polish-born US film producer.
Attrib.

5 Schizophrenic behaviour is a special strategy that a person invents in order to live in an unlivable situation.
R. D. Laing (1927–89) British psychiatrist.
The Politics of Experience

6 Schizophrenia cannot be understood without understanding despair.
R. D. Laing
The Divided Self, Ch. 2

7 The mystic sees the ineffable, and the psychopathologist the unspeakable.
W. Somerset Maugham (1874–1965) British novelist.
The Moon and Sixpence, Ch. 1

8 If the nineteenth century was the age of the editorial chair, ours is the century of the psychiatrist's couch.
Marshall McLuhan (1911–81) Canadian sociologist.
Understanding Media, Introduction

9 A psychiatrist is a man who goes to the Folies-Bergère and looks at the audience.
Mervyn Stockwood (1913–) British churchman.
The Observer, 'Sayings of the Week', 15 Oct 1961

10 Psychiatrists classify a person as neurotic if he suffers from his problems in living, and a psychotic if he makes others suffer.
Thomas Szasz (1920–) US psychiatrist.
The Second Sin

11 A neurotic is the man who builds a castle in the air. A psychotic is the man who lives in it. And a psychiatrist is the man who collects the rent.
Lord Robert Webb-Johnstone (b. 1879)
Collected Papers

12 He was meddling too much in my private life.
Tennessee Williams (1911–83) US dramatist.
Explaining why he had given up visiting his psychoanalyst
Attrib.

13 He is always called a nerve specialist because it sounds better, but everyone knows he's a sort of janitor in a looney bin.
P. G. Wodehouse (1881–1975) British humorous novelist.
The Inimitable Jeeves

PSYCHOLOGY

See also mind, psychiatry

1 What progress we are making. In the Middle Ages they would have burned me. Now they are content with burning my books.
Sigmund Freud (1856–1939) Austrian psychoanalyst.
Referring to the public burning of his books in Berlin
Letter to Ernest Jones, 1933

2 I don't think the profession of historian fits a man for psychological analysis. In our work we have to deal only with simple feelings to which we give generic names such as Ambition and Interest.
Jean-Paul Sartre (1905–80) French writer.
Nausea

PUBLIC

See also class, majority

1 *Vox populi, vox dei.*
The voice of the people is the voice of God.
Alcuin (c. 735–804) English theologian.
Letter to Charlemagne

2 But that vast portion, lastly, of the working-class which, raw and half-developed, has long lain half-hidden amidst its poverty and squalor, and is now issuing from its hiding-place to assert an Englishman's heaven-born privilege of doing as he likes, and is beginning to perplex us by marching where it likes, meeting where it likes, bawling what it likes, breaking what it likes – to this vast residuum we may with great propriety give the name of Populace.
Matthew Arnold (1822–88) British poet and critic.
Culture and Anarchy, Ch. 3

3 Our researchers into Public Opinion are content
That he held the proper opinions for the time of year;

When there was peace, he was for peace;
when there was war, he went.
W. H. Auden (1907–73) British poet.
The Unknown Citizen

4 You cannot make a man by standing a sheep
on its hind legs. But by standing a flock of
sheep in that position you can make a crowd
of men.
Max Beerbohm (1872–1956) British writer.
Zuleika Dobson, Ch. 9

5 The great Unwashed.
Henry Peter Brougham (1778–1868) Scottish lawyer
and politician.
Attrib.

6 The people are the masters.
Edmund Burke (1729–97) British politician.
Speech on the Economical Reform (House of Commons, 11 Feb
1780)

7 The public buys its opinions as it buys its
meat, or takes in its milk, on the principle
that it is cheaper to do this than to keep a
cow. So it is, but the milk is more likely to
be watered.
Samuel Butler (1835–1902) British writer.
Notebooks

8 The Public is an old woman. Let her
maunder and mumble.
Thomas Carlyle (1795–1881) Scottish historian and
essayist.
Journal, 1835

9 The people would be just as noisy if they
were going to see me hanged.
Oliver Cromwell (1599–1658) English soldier and
statesman.
Referring to a cheering crowd

10 If by the people you understand the
multitude, the *hoi polloi*, 'tis no matter what
they think; they are sometimes in the right,
sometimes in the wrong; their judgement is a
mere lottery.
John Dryden (1631–1700) British poet and dramatist.
Essay of Dramatic Poesy

11 Nor is the Peoples Judgment always true:
The Most may err as grosly as the Few.
John Dryden
Absalom and Achitophel, I

12 Ill fares the land, to hast'ning ills a prey,
Where wealth accumulates, and men decay;
Princes and lords may flourish, or may fade;
A breath can make them, as a breath has
made;
But a bold peasantry, their country's pride,
When once destroy'd, can never be supplied.
Oliver Goldsmith (1728–74) Irish-born British writer.
The Deserted Village

13 There is not a more mean, stupid, dastardly,
pitiful, selfish, spiteful, envious, ungrateful
animal than the public. It is the greatest of
cowards, for it is afraid of itself.
William Hazlitt (1778–1830) British essayist.
On Living to Oneself

14 Only constant repetition will finally succeed in
imprinting an idea on the memory of the
crowd.
Adolf Hitler (1889–1945) German dictator.
Mein Kampf, Ch. 6

15 The people long eagerly for just two things –
bread and circuses.
Juvenal (Decimus Junius Juvenalis; 60–130 AD) Roman
satirist.
Satires, X

16 They are only ten.
Lord Northcliffe (1865–1922) Irish-born British
newspaper proprietor.
Rumoured to have been a notice to remind his staff of his opin-
ion of the mental age of the general public
Attrib.

17 The multitude is always in the wrong.
Earl of Roscommon (1633–85) Irish-born English poet.
Essay on Translated Verse

18 Once the people begin to reason, all is lost.
Voltaire (François-Marie Arouet; 1694–1778) French
writer.
Letter to Damilaville, 1 Apr 1766

19 The century on which we are entering – the
century which will come out of this war –
can be and must be the century of the
common man.
Henry Wallace (1888–1965) US economist and politician.
Speech, 'The Price of Free World Victory', 8 May 1942

20 Our supreme governors, the mob.
Horace Walpole (1717–97) British writer.
Letter to Sir Horace Mann, 7 Sept 1743

21 I have no concern for the common man
except that he should not be so common.
Angus Wilson (1913–) British novelist.
No Laughing Matter

PUBLIC HOUSES

See also alcohol, drunkenness

1 A tavern chair is the throne of human felicity.
Samuel Johnson (1709–84) British lexicographer.
Johnsonian Miscellanies (ed. G. B. Hill), Vol. II

2 There is nothing which has yet been
contrived by man, by which so much
happiness is produced as by a good tavern or
inn.
Samuel Johnson
Life of Johnson (J. Boswell), Vol. II

3 Souls of poets dead and gone,
What Elysium have ye known,
Happy field or mossy cavern,
Choicer than the Mermaid Tavern?
Have ye tippled drink more fine

Than mine host's Canary wine?
John Keats (1795–1821) British poet.
Lines on the Mermaid Tavern

4 The hands of the clock have stayed still at half past eleven for fifty years. It is always opening time in the Sailors Arms.
Dylan Thomas (1914–53) Welsh poet.
Under Milk Wood

5 Come, Come, Come and have a drink with me
Down at the old 'Bull and Bush'.
Harry Tilzer (Albert von Tilzer; 1878–1956) British songwriter.
The Old Bull and Bush

PUBLISHING

See also books, editors

1 Publication is the male equivalent of childbirth.
Richard Acland (1906–   ) British politician and writer.
The Observer, 'Sayings of the Week', 19 May 1974

2 If I had been someone not very clever, I would have done an easier job like publishing. That's the easiest job I can think of.
A. J. Ayer (1910–89) British philosopher.
Remark, Sept 1984

3 I'll publish, right or wrong:
Fools are my theme, let satire be my song.
Lord Byron (1788–1824) British poet.
English Bards and Scotch Reviewers

4 Now Barabbas was a publisher.
Thomas Campbell (1777–1844) British poet.
Attrib.

5 Gentlemen, you must not mistake me. I admit that he is the sworn foe of our nation, and, if you will, of the whole human race. But, gentlemen, we must be just to our enemy. We must not forget that he once shot a bookseller.
Thomas Campbell
Excusing himself in proposing a toast to Napoleon at a literary dinner
The Life and Letters of Lord Macaulay (G. O. Trevelyan)

6 As repressed sadists are supposed to become policemen or butchers so those with irrational fear of life become publishers.
Cyril Connolly (1903–74) British journalist.
Enemies of Promise, Ch. 3

7 Let it be kept till the ninth year, the manuscript put away at home: you may destroy whatever you haven't published; once out, what you've said can't be stopped.
Horace (Quintus Horatius Flaccus; 65–8 BC) Roman poet.
Ars Poetica

8 My own motto is publish and be sued.
Richard Ingrams (1937–   ) British editor.
Referring to his editorship of *Private Eye*
BBC radio broadcast, 4 May 1977

9 The booksellers are generous liberal-minded men.
Samuel Johnson (1709–84) British lexicographer.
Life of Johnson (J. Boswell), Vol. I

10 Publish and be damned!
Duke of Wellington (1769–1852) British general and statesman.
On being offered the chance to avoid mention in the memoirs of Harriette Wilson by giving her money
Attrib.

PUNISHMENT

See also education, execution, imprisonment, retribution

1 Wherefore putting away lying, speak every man truth with his neighbour: for we are members one of another.
Be ye angry, and sin not: let not the sun go down upon your wrath:
Neither give place to the devil.
Let him that stole steal no more: but rather let him labour, working with his hands the thing which is good, that he may have to give to him that needeth.
Bible: Ephesians
4:25–28

2 When thou tillest the ground, it shall not henceforth yield unto thee her strength; a fugitive and a vagabond shalt thou be in the earth.
And Cain said unto the Lord, My punishment is greater than I can bear.
Bible: Genesis
4:12–13

3 Then the Lord rained upon Sodom and upon Gomorrah brimstone and fire from the Lord out of heaven.
Bible: Genesis
19:24

4 And surely your blood of your lives will I require; at the hand of every beast will I require it, and at the hand of man; at the hand of every man's brother will I require the life of man.
Whoso sheddeth man's blood, by man shall his blood be shed: for in the image of God made he man.
Bible: Genesis
9:5–6

5 There is no peace, saith the Lord, unto the wicked.
Bible: Isaiah
48:22

6 Love is a boy, by poets styl'd,
Then spare the rod, and spoil the child.
Samuel Butler (1612–80) English satirist.
Hudibras, Pt. II

7 Quoth he, 'The man hath penance done,

And penance more will do.'
Samuel Taylor Coleridge (1772–1834) British poet.
The Rime of the Ancient Mariner, V

8 Punishment is not for revenge, but to lessen crime and reform the criminal.
Elizabeth Fry (1780–1845) British prison reformer.
Biography of Distinguished Women (Sarah Josepha Hale)

9 As some day it may happen that a victim must be found
I've got a little list – I've got a little list
Of society offenders who might well be underground,
And who never would be missed – who never would be missed!
W. S. Gilbert (1836–1911) British dramatist.
The Mikado, I

10 My object all sublime
I shall achieve in time –
To let the punishment fit the crime –
The punishment fit the crime.
W. S. Gilbert
The Mikado, II

11 The billiard sharp whom any one catches,
His doom's extremely hard –
He's made to dwell –
In a dungeon cell
On a spot that's always barred.
And there he plays extravagant matches
In fitless finger-stalls
On a cloth untrue
With a twisted cue
And elliptical billiard balls.
W. S. Gilbert
The Mikado, II

12 The door flew open, in he ran,
The great, long, red-legged scissor-man.
Heinrich Hoffman (1809–74) German writer.
Struwwelpeter, 'The Little Suck-a-Thumb'

13 Corporal punishment is as humiliating for him who gives it as for him who receives it; it is ineffective besides. Neither shame nor physical pain have any other effect than a hardening one . . .
Ellen Key (Karolina Sofia Key; 1849–1926) Swedish writer.
The Century of the Child, Ch. 8

14 The refined punishments of the spiritual mode are usually much more indecent and dangerous than a good smack.
D. H. Lawrence (1885–1930) British novelist.
Fantasia of the Unconscious, Ch. 4

15 He must have known me had he seen me as he was wont to see me, for he was in the habit of flogging me constantly. Perhaps he did not recognize me by my face.
Anthony Trollope (1815–82) British novelist.
Autobiography, Ch. 1

16 I'm all for bringing back the birch, but only between consenting adults.
Gore Vidal (1925–) US novelist.
Said when asked by David Frost in a TV interview for his views about corporal punishment

PUNS

See also humour

1 When I am dead, I hope it may be said:
'His sins were scarlet, but his books were read.'
Hilaire Belloc (1870–1953) French-born British poet.
Epigrams, 'On His Books'

2 VISITOR. Ah, Bottomley, sewing?
BOTTOMLEY. No, reaping.
Horatio William Bottomley (1860–1933) British newspaper editor.
When found sewing mail bags
Horatio Bottomley (Julian Symons)

3 A man who could make so vile a pun would not scruple to pick a pocket.
John Dennis (1657–1734) British critic and dramatist.
The Gentleman's Magazine, 1781

4 Any stigma will do to beat a dogma.
Philip Guedalla (1889–1944) British writer.
Attrib.

5 His death, which happen'd in his berth,
At forty-odd befell:
They went and told the sexton, and
The sexton toll'd the bell.
Thomas Hood (1799–1845) British poet.
Faithless Sally Brown

6 For that old enemy the gout
Had taken him in toe!
Thomas Hood
Lieutenant Luff

7 The love that loves a scarlet coat
Should be more uniform.
Thomas Hood
Faithless Nelly Gray

8 Ben Battle was a soldier bold,
And used to war's alarms:
But a cannon-ball took off his legs,
So he laid down his arms!
Thomas Hood
Faithless Nelly Gray

9 For here I leave my second leg,
And the Forty-second Foot!
Thomas Hood
Faithless Nelly Gray

10 It is a pistol let off at the ear; not a feather to tickle the intellect.
Charles Lamb (1775–1834) British essayist.
Referring to the nature of a pun
Last Essays of Elia, 'Popular Fallacies'

11 Thou canst not serve both cod and salmon.

Ada Beddington Leverson (1862–1933) British writer.
Reply when offered a choice of fish at dinner
The Times, 7 Nov 1970

12 You know it's hard to hear what a bearded man is saying. He can't speak above a whisker.

Herman J. Mankiewicz (1897–1953) US journalist and screenwriter.
Wit's End (R. E. Drennan)

13 What's a thousand dollars? Mere chicken feed. A poultry matter.

Groucho Marx (Julius Marx; 1895–1977) US comedian.
The Cocoanuts

14 It has been said that a bride's attitude towards her betrothed can be summed up in three words: Aisle. Altar. Hymn.

Frank Muir (1920–) British writer and broadcaster.
Upon My Word! (Frank Muir and Dennis Norden), 'A Jug of Wine'

15 A thing of duty is a boy for ever.

Flann O'Brien (Brian O'Nolan; 1911–66) Irish novelist and journalist.
About policemen always seeming to be young-looking
The Listener, 24 Feb 1977

16 You can lead a whore to culture but you can't make her think.

Dorothy Parker (1893–1967) US writer.
Speech to American Horticultural Society

17 You can't teach an old dogma new tricks.

Dorothy Parker
Wit's End (R. E. Drennan)

18 I tried to resist his overtures, but he plied me with symphonies, quartettes, chamber music and cantatas.

S. J. Perelman (1904–79) US humorous writer.
Crazy Like a Fox, 'The Love Decoy'

19 Mother always told me my day was coming, but I never realized that I'd end up being the shortest knight of the year.

Gordon Richards (1904–86) British champion jockey.
Referring to his diminutive size, on learning of his knighthood
Attrib.

20 Private Means is dead,
God rest his soul,
Officers and fellow-rankers said.

Stevie Smith (Florence Margaret Smith; 1902–71) British poet.
Private Means is Dead

21 That's right. 'Taint yours, and 'taint mine.

Mark Twain (Samuel Langhorne Clemens; 1835–1910) US writer.
Agreeing with a friend's comment that the money of a particular rich industrialist was 'tainted'
Attrib.

22 To me Adler will always be Jung.

Max Wall (1908–) British comedian.
Telegram to Larry Adler on his 60th birthday

PURITANISM

See also prudery

1 A puritan's a person who pours righteous indignation into the wrong things.

G. K. Chesterton (1874–1936) British writer.
Attrib.

2 To the Puritan all things are impure, as somebody says.

D. H. Lawrence (1885–1930) British novelist.
Etruscan Places, 'Cerveteri'

3 The Puritan hated bear-baiting, not because it gave pain to the bear, but because it gave pleasure to the spectators.

Lord Macaulay (1800–59) British historian.
History of England, Vol. I, Ch. 2

4 Puritanism – The haunting fear that someone, somewhere, may be happy.

H. L. Mencken (1880–1956) US journalist.
A Book of Burlesques

PURITY

1 Caesar's wife must be above suspicion.

Proverb

2 I'm as pure as the driven slush.

Tallulah Bankhead (1903–68) US actress.
The Observer, 'Sayings of the Week', 24 Feb 1957

3 A simple maiden in her flower
Is worth a hundred coats-of-arms.

Alfred, Lord Tennyson (1809–92) British poet.
Lady Clara Vere de Vere, II

4 It is one of the superstitions of the human mind to have imagined that virginity could be a virtue.

Voltaire (François-Marie Arouet; 1694–1778) French writer.
Notebooks

5 Age cannot wither her, nor custom stale her infinite virginity.

Daniel Webster (1782–1852) US statesman.
Paraphrasing a line from Shakespeare's *Antony and Cleopatra* on hearing of Andrew Jackson's steadfast maintenance that his friend Peggy Eaton did not deserve her scandalous reputation
Presidential Anecdotes (P. Boller)

6 I used to be Snow White . . . but I drifted.

Mae West (1892–1980) US actress.
The Wit and Wisdom of Mae West (ed. J. Weintraub)

PURPOSE

See also futility, motive

1 Everything's got a moral, if only you can find it.

Lewis Carroll (Charles Lutwidge Dodgson; 1832–98) British writer.
Alice's Adventures in Wonderland, Ch. 9

2 What is the use of a new-born child?
Benjamin Franklin (1706–90) US scientist and statesman.
Response when asked the same question of a new invention
Life and Times of Benjamin Franklin (J. Parton), Pt. IV

3 A useless life is an early death.
Goethe (1749–1832) German poet and dramatist.
Iphegenie, I:2

4 Fortunately, in her kindness and patience, Nature has never put the fatal question as to the meaning of their lives into the mouths of most people. And where no one asks, no one needs to answer.
Carl Gustav Jung (1875–1961) Swiss psychoanalyst.
The Development of Personality

5 I go among the fields and catch a glimpse of a stoat or a fieldmouse peeping out of the withered grass – the creature hath a purpose and its eyes are bright with it. I go amongst the buildings of a city and I see a man

hurrying along – to what? the Creature has a purpose and his eyes are bright with it.
John Keats (1795–1821) British poet.
Letter, 1819

6 Riddle of destiny, who can show
What thy short visit meant, or know
What thy errand here below?
Charles Lamb (1775–1834) British essayist.
On an Infant Dying as soon as Born

7 Yes there is a meaning; at least for me, there is one thing that matters – to set a chime of words tinkling in the minds of a few fastidious people.
Logan Pearsall Smith (1865–1946) US writer.
Attrib.

8 It should not merely be useful and ornamental; it should preach a high moral lesson.
Lytton Strachey (1880–1932) British writer.
Referring to Prince Albert's plans for the Great Exhibition
Queen Victoria, Ch. 4

Q

QUOTATIONS

See also misquotation

1 It is a good thing for an uneducated man to read books of quotations.
Winston Churchill (1874–1965) British statesman.
My Early Life, Ch. 9

2 We prefer to believe that the absence of inverted commas guarantees the originality of a thought, whereas it may be merely that the utterer has forgotten its source.
Clifton Fadiman (1904–) US writer.
Any Number Can Play

3 When a thing has been said and said well, have no scruple. Take it and copy it.
Anatole France (Jacques Anatole François Thibault; 1844–1924) French writer.
In *The Routledge Dictionary of Quotations* (Robert Andrews)

4 Classical quotation is the *parole* of literary men all over the world.
Samuel Johnson (1709–84) British lexicographer.
Life of Johnson (J. Boswell), Vol. IV

5 Every quotation contributes something to the stability or enlargement of the language.
Samuel Johnson
Dictionary of the English Language

6 To be amused at what you read – that is the great spring of happy quotation.
C. E. Montague (1867–1928) British editor and writer.
A Writer's Notes on his Trade

7 If with the literate I am
Impelled to try an epigram
I never seek to take the credit

We all assume that Oscar said it.
Dorothy Parker (1893–1967) US writer.
Oscar Wilde

8 I might repeat to myself . . . a list of quotations from minds profound – if I can remember any of the damn things.
Dorothy Parker
The Little Hours

9 A book that furnishes no quotations is, *me judice*, no book – it is a plaything.
Thomas Love Peacock (1785–1866) British novelist.
Crotchet Castle, Ch. 9

10 It is gentlemanly to get one's quotations very slightly wrong. In that way one unprigs oneself and allows the company to correct one.
Lord Ribblesdale (1854–1925) British aristocrat.
The Light of Common Day (Lady D. Cooper)

11 To say that anything was a quotation was an excellent method, in Eleanor's eyes, for withdrawing it from discussion.
Saki (Hector Hugh Munro; 1870–1916) British writer.
The Jesting of Arlington Stringham

12 The devil can cite Scripture for his purpose.
William Shakespeare (1564–1616) English dramatist.
The Merchant of Venice, I:3

13 It's better to be quotable than to be honest.
Tom Stoppard (1937–) Czech-born British dramatist.
The Guardian

14 In the dying world I come from quotation is a national vice. It used to be the classics, now it's lyric verse.
Evelyn Waugh (1903–66) British novelist.
The Loved One

15 The nicest thing about quotes is that they give us a nodding acquaintance with the originator which is often socially impressive.
Kenneth Williams (1926–88) British comic actor.
Acid Drops

R

RABBITS

See also animals

1 The rabbit has a charming face;
Its private life is a disgrace.
Anonymous
The Rabbit

2 I shall tell you a tale of four little rabbits whose names were Flopsy, Mopsy, Cottontail and Peter.
Beatrix Potter (1866–1943) British children's writer.
The Tale of Peter Rabbit

RACISM

See also equality, freedom, human rights, Jews, oppression, prejudice, slavery

1 There was a young woman called Starkie,
Who had an affair with a darky.
The result of her sins
Was quadruplets, not twins –
One black, and one white, and two khaki.
Anonymous

2 It is a great shock at the age of five or six to find that in a world of Gary Coopers you are the Indian.
James Baldwin (1924–87) US writer.
Speech, Cambridge Union, 17 Feb 1965

3 The future is . . . black.
James Baldwin
The Observer, 'Sayings of the Week', 25 Aug 1963

4 Down South where I come from you don't go around hitting too many white keys.
Eubie Blake (1883–1983) US pianist and ragtime composer.
When asked why his compositions contained so many sharps and flats
Attrib.

5 My mother bore me in the southern wild,
And I am black, but O! my soul is white;
White as an angel is the English child,
But I am black, as if bereav'd of light.
William Blake (1757–1827) British poet.
Songs of Innocence, 'The Little Black Boy'

6 People think we do not understand our black and coloured countrymen. But there is a special relationship between us.
Elize Botha Wife of South African President, P. W. Botha.
Remark, May 1987

7 To like an individual because he's black is just as insulting as to dislike him because he isn't white.
e. e. cummings (1894–1962) US poet.
Attrib.

8 I suffer from an incurable disease – colour blindness.
Joost de Blank (1908–68) Dutch-born British churchman.
Attrib.

9 I'm a coloured, one-eyed Jew.
Sammy Davis Jnr (1925–) US singer.
When asked what his handicap was during a game of golf
Attrib.

10 The so-called white races are really pinko-gray.
E. M. Forster (1879–1970) British novelist.
A Passage to India, Ch. 7

11 When the white man came we had the land and they had the Bibles; now they have the land and we have the Bibles.
Dan George (1899–1982) Canadian Indian chief.
Attrib.

12 All those who are not racially pure are mere chaff.
Adolf Hitler (1889–1945) German dictator.
Mein Kampf, Ch. 2

13 I want to be the white man's brother, not his brother-in-law.
Martin Luther King (1929–68) US Black civil-rights leader.
New York Journal-American, 10 Sept 1962

14 Take up the White Man's burden –
And reap his old reward:
The blame of those ye better,
The hate of those ye guard.
Rudyard Kipling (1865–1936) Indian-born British writer.
The White Man's Burden

15 So 'ere's to you, Fuzzy-Wuzzy, at your 'ome in the Soudan;
You're a pore benighted 'eathen but a first-class fightin' man;
An' 'ere's to you, Fuzzy-Wuzzy, with your 'ayrick 'ead of 'air –
You big black boundin' beggar – for you broke a British square!
Rudyard Kipling
Fuzzy-Wuzzy

16 When old settlers say 'One has to understand the country', what they mean is, 'You have to get used to our ideas about the native.'

They are saying, in effect, 'Learn our ideas, or otherwise get out; we don't want you.'
Doris Lessing (1919–) British novelist.
Referring specifically to South Africa
The Grass is Singing, Ch. 1

17 When a white man in Africa by accident looks into the eyes of a native and sees the human being (which it is his chief preoccupation to avoid), his sense of guilt, which he denies, fumes up in resentment and he brings down the whip.
Doris Lessing
The Grass is Singing, Ch. 8

18 A coloured man can tell, in five seconds dead, whether a white man likes him or not. If the white man *says* he does, he is instantly – and usually quite rightly – mistrusted.
Colin MacInnes (1914–76) British novelist.
England, Half English, 'A Short Guide for Jumbles'

19 It's just like when you've got some coffee that's too black, which means it's too strong. What do you do? You integrate it with cream, you make it weak . . . It used to wake you up, now it puts you to sleep.
Malcolm X (1925–65) US Black leader.
Referring to Black Power and the Civil Rights movement
Malcolm X Speaks, Ch. 14

20 The soil of our country South Africa is destined to be the scene of the fiercest fight and the sharpest struggles to rid our continent of the last vestiges of white minority rule.
Nelson Mandela (1918–) South African lawyer and politician.
Said, June 1980

21 I have cherished the ideal of a democratic and free society in which all persons live together in harmony and with equal opportunites . . . if needs be, it is an ideal for which I am prepared to die.
Nelson Mandela
Speech, 11 Feb 1990, after his release from prison. Mandela was reiterating his words at his trial in 1964

22 One of the things that makes a Negro unpleasant to white folk is the fact that he suffers from their injustice. He is thus a standing rebuke to them.
H. L. Mencken (1880–1956) US journalist.
Notebooks, 'Minority Report'

23 He's really awfully fond of coloured people. Well, he says himself, he wouldn't have white servants.
Dorothy Parker (1893–1967) US writer.
Arrangements in Black and White

24 If you stay much longer you will go back with slitty eyes.
Prince Philip (1921–) The consort of Queen Elizabeth II.
Said to English students on a visit to China
Remark, Oct 1986

25 As I look ahead, I am filled with foreboding. Like the Roman, I seem to see 'the River Tiber foaming with much blood'.
Enoch Powell (1912–) British politician.
Talking about immigration
Speech in Birmingham, 20 Apr 1968

26 He liked to patronise coloured people and treated them as equals because he was quite sure they were not.
Bertrand Russell (1872–1970) British philosopher.
The Autobiography of Bertrand Russell

27 I don't believe in black majority rule ever in Rhodesia . . . not in a thousand years.
Ian Smith (1919–) Rhodesian (Zimbabwe) politician.
Speech, Mar 1976

28 We don't want apartheid liberalized. We want it dismantled. You can't improve something that is intrinsically evil.
Bishop Desmond Tutu (1931–) South African clergyman.
The Observer, 'Sayings of the Week', 10 Mar 1985

29 It seems that the British Government sees black people as expendable.
Bishop Desmond Tutu
Speech, June 1986

30 There are two kinds of blood, the blood that flows in the veins and the blood that flows out of them.
Julian Tuwim (1894–1954) Polish writer and poet.
We, the Polish Jews

READING

See also books, criticism, fiction, literacy, literature, novels, writing

1 Reading maketh a full man; conference a ready man; and writing an exact man.
Francis Bacon (1561–1626) English philosopher.
Essays, 'Of Studies'

2 He has only half learned the art of reading who has not added to it the even more refined accomplishments of skipping and skimming.
Arthur Balfour (1848–1930) British statesman.
Mr. Balfour (E. T. Raymond)

3 I read, much of the night, and go south in the winter.
T. S. Eliot (1888–1965) US-born British poet and dramatist.
The Waste Land, 'The Burial of the Dead'

4 A lonesome man on a rainy day who does not know how to read.
Benjamin Franklin (1706–90) US scientist and statesman.
On being asked what condition of man he considered the most pitiable
Wit, Wisdom, and Foibles of the Great (C. Shriner)

5 As writers become more numerous, it is natural for readers to become more indolent.
Oliver Goldsmith (1728–74) Irish-born British writer.
The Bee, 'Upon Unfortunate Merit'

6 Reading is sometimes an ingenious device for avoiding thought.

Arthur Helps (1813–75) British historian.
Friends in Council

7 ELPHINSTON. What, have you not read it through?
. . .
JOHNSON. No, Sir, do *you* read books *through*?

Samuel Johnson (1709–84) British lexicographer.
Life of Johnson (J. Boswell), Vol. II

8 A man ought to read just as inclination leads him; for what he reads as a task will do him little good.

Samuel Johnson
Life of Johnson (J. Boswell), Vol. I

9 I love to lose myself in other men's minds. When I am not walking, I am reading; I cannot sit and think. Books think for me.

Charles Lamb (1775–1834) British essayist.
Last Essays of Elia, 'Detached Thoughts on Books and Reading'

10 I'm re-reading it with a slow deliberate carelessness.

T. E. Lawrence (1888–1935) British soldier and writer.
Letter to Edward Marsh, 18 Apr 1929

11 To read too many books is harmful.

Mao Tse-Tung (1893–1976) Chinese communist leader.
The New Yorker, 7 Mar 1977

12 I have only read one book in my life and that is *White Fang*. It's so frightfully good I've never bothered to read another.

Nancy Mitford (1904–73) British writer.
The Pursuit Of Love

13 There are two motives for reading a book: one, that you enjoy it, the other that you can boast about it.

Bertrand Russell (1872–1970) British philosopher.
The Conquest of Happiness

14 People say that life is the thing, but I prefer reading.

Logan Pearsall Smith (1865–1946) US writer.
Afterthoughts, 'Myself'

15 Reading is to the mind what exercise is to the body.

Richard Steele (1672–1729) Dublin-born British essayist.
The Tatler, 147

16 Education . . . has produced a vast population able to read but unable to distinguish what is worth reading.

George Macaulay Trevelyan (1876–1962) British historian.
English Social History, Ch. 18

17 I have led a life of business so long that I have lost my taste for reading, and now – what shall I do?

Horace Walpole (1717–97) British writer.
Thraliana (K. Balderston)

18 Lady Peabury was in the morning room

reading a novel; early training gave a guilty spice to this recreation, for she had been brought up to believe that to read a novel before luncheon was one of the gravest sins it was possible for a gentlewoman to commit.

Evelyn Waugh (1903–66) British novelist.
Work Suspended, 'An Englishman's Home'

19 As in the sexual experience, there are never more than two persons present in the act of reading – the writer who is the impregnator, and the reader who is the respondent.

Elwyn Brooks White (1899–1985) US journalist and humorist.
The Second Tree from the Corner

REALISM

1 Mr Lely, I desire you would use all your skill to paint my picture truly like me, and not flatter me at all; but remark all these roughnesses, pimples, warts, and everything as you see me, otherwise I will never pay a farthing for it.

Oliver Cromwell (1599–1658) English soldier and statesman.
The origin of the expression 'warts and all'
Anecdotes of Painting (Horace Walpole), Ch. 12

2 If at first you don't succeed, try, try again. Then quit. No use being a damn fool about it.

W. C. Fields (1880–1946) US actor.

3 We must rediscover the distinction between hope and expectation.

Ivan Illich (1926–) Austrian sociologist.
Deschooling Society, Ch. 7

4 Better by far
For Johnny-the-bright-star,
To keep your head
And see his children fed.

John Sleigh Pudney (1909–77) British poet and writer.
For Johnny

REALITY

1 For I see now that I am asleep that I dream when I am awake.

Pedro Calderón de la Barca (1600–81) Spanish dramatist.
La Vida es Sueño, II

2 Human kind
Cannot bear very much reality.

T. S. Eliot (1888–1965) US-born British poet and dramatist.
Four Quartets, 'Burnt Norton'

3 Dear friend, theory is all grey,
And the golden tree of life is green.

Goethe (1749–1832) German poet and dramatist.
Faust, Pt. I

4 I fancy, for myself, that they are rather out of touch with reality; by reality I mean shops

like Selfridges, and motor buses, and the
Daily Express.

T. E. Lawrence (1888–1935) British soldier and writer.
Referring to expatriate authors living in Paris, such as James
Joyce
Letter to W. Hurley, 1 Apr 1929

5   If this were play'd upon a stage now, I could
condemn it as an improbable fiction.

William Shakespeare (1564–1616) English dramatist.
Twelfth Night, III:4

REASON

See also motive

1   Some who had received a liberal education at
the Colleges of Unreason, and taken the
highest degrees in hypothetics, which are
their principal study.

Samuel Butler (1835–1902) British writer.
Erewhon, Ch. 9

2   Reason is itself a matter of faith. It is an act
of faith to assert that our thoughts have any
relation to reality at all.

G. K. Chesterton (1874–1936) British writer.
Orthodoxy, Ch. 3

3   My dear friend, clear your *mind* of cant . . .
You may *talk* in this manner; it is a mode of
talking in Society: but don't *think* foolishly.

Samuel Johnson (1709–84) British lexicographer.
Life of Johnson (J. Boswell), Vol. IV

4   A man who does not lose his reason over
certain things has none to lose.

Gotthold Ephraim Lessing (1729–81) German
dramatist.
Emilia Galotti, IV:7

REBELLION

See also revolution

1   The defiance of established authority,
religious and secular, social and political, as a
world-wide phenomenon may well one day be
accounted the outstanding event of the last
decade.

Hannah Arendt (1906–75) German-born US philosopher
and historian.
Crises of the Republic, 'Civil Disobedience'

2   What is a rebel? A man who says no.

Albert Camus (1913–60) French existentialist writer.
The Rebel

3   No one can go on being a rebel too long
without turning into an autocrat.

Lawrence Durrell (1912–   ) British novelist.
Balthazar, II

4   When the People contend for their Liberty,
they seldom get anything by their Victory but
new masters.

Lord Halifax (1633–95) English statesman.
Political, Moral, and Miscellaneous Thoughts and Reflections

5   A little rebellion now and then is a good
thing.

Thomas Jefferson (1743–1826) US statesman.
Letter to James Madison, 30 Jan 1787

6   A riot is at bottom the language of the
unheard.

Martin Luther King (1929–68) US Black civil-rights
leader.
Chaos or Community, Ch. 4

7   Angry Young Man.

Leslie Paul (1905–85) British writer.
Book title

REGRET

See also apologies, memory, mourning, nostalgia, past, sorrow

1   It is no use crying over spilt milk.

Proverb

2   It's too late to shut the stable door after the
horse has bolted.

Proverb

3   What's done cannot be undone.

Proverb

4   One doesn't recognize in one's life the really
important moments – not until it's too late.

Agatha Christie (1891–1976) British detective-story
writer.
Endless Night, Bk. II, Ch. 14

5   This hand hath offended.

Thomas Cranmer (1489–1556) English churchman.
Memorials of Cranmer (Strype)

6   Were it not better to forget
Than but remember and regret?

Letitia Landon (1802–38) British poet and novelist.
Despondency

7   We might have been – These are but
common words,
And yet they make the sum of life's bewailing.

Letitia Landon
Three Extracts from the Diary of a Week

8   And so, I missed my chance with one of the
lords
Of life.
And I have something to expiate;
A pettiness.

D. H. Lawrence (1885–1930) British novelist.
Snake

9   Make it a rule of life never to regret and
never to look back. Regret is an appalling
waste of energy; you can't build on it; it's
only good for wallowing in.

Katherine Mansfield (1888–1923) New Zealand-born
British writer.
Attrib.

10 Maybe it would have been better if neither of us had been born.

Napoleon I (Napoleon Bonaparte; 1769–1821) French emperor.
Said while looking at the tomb of the philosopher Jean-Jacques Rousseau, whose theories had influenced the French Revolution
The Story of Civilization (W. Durant), Vol. II

11 Good-bye, I've barely said a word to you, it is always like that at parties, we never see the people, we never say the things we should like to say, but it is the same everywhere in this life. Let us hope that when we are dead things will be better arranged.

Marcel Proust (1871–1922) French novelist.
À la recherche du temps perdu: Sodome et Gomorrhe

12 The follies which a man regrets most in his life are those which he didn't commit when he had the opportunity.

Helen Rowland (1876–1950) US writer.
Reflections of a Bachelor Girl

13 But with the morning cool repentance came.

Walter Scott (1771–1832) Scottish novelist.
Rob Roy, Ch. 12

14 Things sweet to taste prove in digestion sour.

William Shakespeare (1564–1616) English dramatist.
Richard II, I:3

15 What's gone and what's past help
Should be past grief.

William Shakespeare
The Winter's Tale, III:2

16 O, pardon me, thou bleeding piece of earth,
That I am meek and gentle with these butchers!
Thou art the ruins of the noblest man
That ever lived in the tide of times.

William Shakespeare
Julius Caesar, III:1

17 To mourn a mischief that is past and gone
Is the next way to draw new mischief on.

William Shakespeare
Othello, I:3

18 When to the sessions of sweet silent thought
I summon up remembrance of things past,
I sigh the lack of many a thing I sought,
And with old woes new wail my dear time's waste.

William Shakespeare
Sonnet 30

19 Had I but serv'd my God with half the zeal
I serv'd my King, he would not in mine age
Have left me naked to mine enemies.

William Shakespeare
Henry VIII, III:2

20 The bitterest tears shed over graves are for words left unsaid and deeds left undone.

Harriet Beecher Stowe (1811–96) US novelist.
Little Foxes, Ch. 3

21 I never wonder to see men wicked, but I often wonder to see them not ashamed.

Jonathan Swift (1667–1745) Irish-born Anglican priest and writer.
Thoughts on Various Subjects

22 Though nothing can bring back the hour
Of splendour in the grass, of glory in the flower;
We will grieve not, rather find
Strength in what remains behind . . .

William Wordsworth (1770–1850) British poet.
Ode. Intimations of Immortality, IX

23 Men are we, and must grieve when even the shade
Of that which once was great is passed away.

William Wordsworth
Sonnets, 'Once did she hold'

RELIGION

See also atheism, belief, Bible, Catholicism, Christianity, Christmas, Church, damnation, devil, doomsday, faith, God, heaven, hell, Jews, martyrdom, prayer, Protestantism, Sunday

1 Karin needed nothing from God. He just had the power to kill her that's all; to destroy her flesh and blood, the tools without which she could not work.

Richard Adams (1920–) British novelist.
The Girl in a Swing, Ch. 28

2 Nearer, my God, to thee,
Nearer to thee!

Sarah F. Adams (1805–48) British poet and hymn writer.
Nearer My God to Thee

3 There is no salvation outside the church.

St Augustine of Hippo (354–430) Bishop of Hippo.
De Bapt., IV

4 The Jews and Arabs should sit down and settle their differences like good Christians.

Warren Austin (1877–1962) US politician and diplomat.
Attrib.

5 INDIGESTION, n. A disease which the patient and his friends frequently mistake for deep religious conviction and concern for the salvation of mankind. As the simple Red Man of the western wild put it, with, it must be confessed, a certain force: 'Plenty well, no pray; big bellyache, heap God.'

Ambrose Bierce (1842–?1914) US writer and journalist.
The Devil's Dictionary

6 If the concept of God has any validity or use, it can only be to make us larger, freer, and more loving. If God cannot do this, then it is time we got rid of Him.

James Baldwin (1924–87) US writer.
The Fire next Time

7 If I really believed that the Church of England came out of the loins of Henry VIII I could be as free as I liked about making changes, but I do not believe that.
Canon Peter Boulton British clergyman.
Remark, Mar 1987

8 Every day people are straying away from the church and going back to God. Really.
Lenny Bruce (1925–66) US comedian.
The Essential Lenny Bruce (ed. J. Cohen), 'Religions Inc.'

9 This Ariyan Eightfold Path, that is to say: Right view, right aim, right speech, right action, right living, right effort, right mindfulness, right contemplation.
Buddha (Gautama Siddhartha; c. 563–c. 483 BC) Indian religious teacher.
Some Sayings of the Buddha (F. L. Woodward)

10 Man is by his constitution a religious animal.
Edmund Burke (1729–97) British politician.
Reflections on the Revolution in France

11 One religion is as true as another.
Robert Burton (1577–1640) English scholar and explorer.
Anatomy of Melancholy, Pt. III

12 To be at all is to be religious more or less.
Samuel Butler (1835–1902) British writer.
Notebooks

13 Not a religion for gentlemen.
Charles II (1630–85) King of England.
Referring to Presbyterianism
History of My Own Time (Burnet), Vol. I, Bk. II, Ch. 2

14 Religion is by no means a proper subject of conversation in a mixed company.
Earl of Chesterfield (1694–1773) English statesman.
Letter to his godson

15 When your ladyship's faith has removed them, I will go thither with all my heart.
Earl of Chesterfield
Said to his sister, Lady Gertrude Hotham, when she suggested he go to a Methodist seminary in Wales to recuperate, recommending the views of the mountains
Attrib.

16 Talk about the pews and steeples
And the cash that goes therewith!
But the souls of Christian peoples . . .
Chuck it, Smith!
G. K. Chesterton (1874–1936) British writer.
Antichrist, or the Reunion of Christendom

17 Men will wrangle for religion; write for it; fight for it; anything but – live for it.
Charles Caleb Colton (?1780–1832) British clergyman and writer.
Lacon, Vol. I

18 Pray remember, Mr Dean, no dogma, no Dean.
Benjamin Disraeli (1804–81) British statesman.
Attrib.

19 'Sensible men are all of the same religion.'

'And pray what is that?' inquired the prince. 'Sensible men never tell.'
Benjamin Disraeli
Endymion, Bk. I, Ch. 81

20 In pious times, e'r Priest-craft did begin, Before Polygamy was made a Sin.
John Dryden (1631–1700) British poet and dramatist.
Absalom and Achitophel, I

21 Christian Science explains all cause and effect as mental, not physical.
Mary Baker Eddy (1821–1910) US religious leader.
Science and Health, with Key to the Scriptures

22 Sickness, sin and death, being inharmonious, do not originate in God, nor belong to His government.
Mary Baker Eddy
Science and Health, with Key to the Scriptures

23 Science without religion is lame, religion without science is blind.
Albert Einstein (1879–1955) German-born US physicist.
Out of My Later Years

24 The religions we call false were once true.
Ralph Waldo Emerson (1803–82) US poet and essayist.
Essays, 'Character'

25 Religion is an illusion and it derives its strength from the fact that it falls in with our instinctual desires.
Sigmund Freud (1856–1939) Austrian psychoanalyst.
New Introductory Lectures on Psychoanalysis, 'A Philosophy of Life'

26 Religion
Has made an honest woman of the supernatural,
And we won't have it kicking over the traces again.
Christopher Fry (1907–) British dramatist.
The Lady's Not for Burning, II

27 There exists no politician in India daring enough to attempt to explain to the masses that cows can be eaten.
Indira Gandhi (1917–84) Indian stateswoman.
New York Review of Books, 'Indira's Coup' (Oriana Fallaci)

28 The various modes of worship, which prevailed in the Roman world, were all considered by the people as equally true; by the philosopher, as equally false; and by the magistrate, as equally useful. And thus toleration produced not only mutual indulgence, but even religious concord.
Edward Gibbon (1737–94) British historian.
Decline and Fall of the Roman Empire, Ch. 2

29 As I take my shoes from the shoemaker, and my coat from the tailor, so I take my religion from the priest.
Oliver Goldsmith (1728–74) Irish-born British writer.
Life of Johnson (J. Boswell)

30 Those who marry God . . . can become

domesticated too – it's just as humdrum a marriage as all the others.

Graham Greene (1904–) British novelist.
A Burnt-Out Case, Ch. 1

31 Pray, good people, be civil. I am the Protestant whore.

Nell Gwyn (1650–87) English actress.
On being surrounded in her coach by an angry mob in Oxford at the time of the Popish Plot
Nell Gwyn (Bevan), Ch. 13

32 But as I rav'd and grew more fierce and wild
At every word,
Methought I heard one calling, 'Child';
And I replied, 'My Lord.'

George Herbert (1593–1633) English poet.
The Collar

33 The sedate, sober, silent, serious, sad-coloured sect.

Thomas Hood (1799–1845) British poet.
Referring to the Quakers
The Doves and the Crows

34 To become a popular religion, it is only necessary for a superstition to enslave a philosophy.

Dean Inge (1860–1954) British churchman.
Outspoken Essays

35 Many people believe that they are attracted by God, or by Nature, when they are only repelled by man.

Dean Inge
More Lay Thoughts of a Dean

36 Many people think they have religion when they are troubled with dyspepsia.

Robert G. Ingersoll (1833–99) US lawyer and agnostic.
Liberty of Man, Woman and Child, Section 3

37 Among all my patients in the second half of life . . . there has not been one whose problem in the last resort was not that of finding a religious outlook on life.

Carl Gustav Jung (1875–1961) Swiss psychoanalyst.
Modern Man in Search of a Soul

38 The author of the Satanic Verses book, which is against Islam, the Prophet and the Koran, and all those involved in its publication who were aware of its content, are sentenced to death. I ask all Moslems to execute them wherever they find them.

Ayatollah Ruholla Khomeini (1900-89) Iranian Shiite Muslim leader.
Speech, 14 Feb 1989

39 The month of Ramadan shall ye fast, in which the Koran was sent down from heaven, a direction unto men, and declarations of direction, and the distinction between good and evil.

Koran
Ch. II

40 But I suppose even God was born too late to trust the old religion –

all those setting out
that never left the ground,
beginning in wisdom, dying in doubt.

Robert Lowell (1917–77) US poet.
Tenth Muse

41 Here stand I. I can do no other. God help me. Amen.

Martin Luther (1483–1546) German Protestant.
Speech at the Diet of Worms, 18 Apr 1521

42 Abide with me; fast falls the eventide;
The darkness deepens; Lord, with me abide;
When other helpers fail, and comforts flee,
Help of the helpless, O, abide with me.

Henry Francis Lyte (1793–1847) British hymn writer.
Abide with Me

43 Religion . . . is the opium of the people.

Karl Marx (1818–83) German philosopher and revolutionary.
Criticism of the Hegelian Philosophy of Right, Introduction

44 Things have come to a pretty pass when religion is allowed to invade the sphere of private life.

Lord Melbourne (1779–1848) British statesman.
Attrib.

45 There are many who stay away from church these days because you hardly ever mention God any more.

Arthur Miller (1915–) US dramatist.
The Crucible, I

46 New Presbyter is but old Priest writ large.

John Milton (1608–74) English poet.
Sonnet: 'On the New Forcers of Conscience under the Long Parliament'

47 Man is quite insane. He wouldn't know how to create a maggot and he creates Gods by the dozen.

Michel de Montaigne (1533–92) French essayist.
Essais, II

48 There is a very good saying that if triangles invented a god, they would make him three-sided.

Baron de Montesquieu (1689–1755) French writer.
Lettres persanes

49 There's no reason to bring religion into it. I think we ought to have as great a regard for religion as we can, so as to keep it out of as many things as possible.

Sean O'Casey (1884–1964) Irish dramatist.
The Plough and the Stars, I

50 Organized religion is making Christianity political rather than making politics Christian.

Laurens Van der Post (1906–) South African novelist.
The Observer, 'Sayings of the Week', 9 Nov 1986

51 Unlike Christianity, which preached a peace that it never achieved, Islam unashamedly came with a sword.

Steven Runciman (1903–) British academic and diplomat.
A History of the Crusades, 'The First Crusade'

52 I call upon the intellectual community in this country and abroad to stand up for freedom of the imagination, an issue much larger than my book or indeed my life.
Salman Rushdie (1947–) Indian-born British novelist.
Press statement, 14 Feb 1989

53 I have been into many of the ancient cathedrals – grand, wonderful, mysterious. But I always leave them with a feeling of indignation because of the generations of human beings who have struggled in poverty to build these altars to the unknown god.
Elizabeth Stanton (1815–1902) US suffragette.
Diary

54 Whenever a man talks loudly against religion, – always suspect that it is not his reason, but his passions which have got the better of his creed.
Laurence Sterne (1713–68) Irish-born British writer.
Tristram Shandy

55 I believe in the Church, One Holy, Catholic and Apostolic, and I regret that it nowhere exists.
William Temple (1881–1944) British churchman.
Attrib.

56 Alas, O Lord, to what a state dost Thou bring those who love Thee!
St Teresa of Ávila (1515–82) Spanish mystic.
The Interior Castle, VI

57 It is spring, moonless night in the small town, starless and bible-black.
Dylan Thomas (1914–53) Welsh poet.
Under Milk Wood

58 I fled Him, down the nights and down the days;
I fled Him, down the arches of the years;
I fled Him, down the labyrinthine ways
Of my own mind; and in the mist of tears
I hid from Him, and under running laughter.
Francis Thompson (1859–1907) British poet.
The Hound of Heaven

59 Rock of ages, cleft for me,
Let me hide myself in Thee.
Augustus Montague Toplady (1740–78) British hymn writer.
Rock of Ages

60 Beware when you take on the Church of God. Others have tried and have bitten the dust.
Bishop Desmond Tutu (1931–) South African clergyman.
Speech, Apr 1987

61 In general the churches, visited by me too often on weekdays . . . bore for me the same relation to God that billboards did to Coca-Cola: they promoted thirst without quenching it.
John Updike (1932–) US novelist.
A Month of Sundays, Ch. 2

62 Jesus loves me – this I know,
For the Bible tells me so.
Susan Warner (1819–85) US novelist.
The Love of Jesus

63 Lord, I ascribe it to Thy grace,
And not to chance, as others do,
That I was born of Christian race,
And not a Heathen, or a Jew.
Isaac Watts (1674–1748) English theologian and hymn writer.
Divine Songs for Children, 'Praise for the Gospel'

64 Our God, our help in ages past,
Our hope for years to come,
Our shelter from the stormy blast,
And our eternal home.
Isaac Watts
Our God, Our Help in Ages Past

65 I have noticed again and again since I have been in the Church that lay interest in ecclesiastical matters is often a prelude to insanity.
Evelyn Waugh (1903–66) British novelist.
Decline and Fall, Pt. I, Ch. 8

66 There is a species of person called a 'Modern Churchman' who draws the full salary of a beneficed clergyman and need not commit himself to any religious belief.
Evelyn Waugh
Decline and Fall, Pt. II, Ch. 4

67 Religion is love; in no case is it logic.
Beatrice Webb (1858–1943) British economist and writer.
My Apprenticeship, Ch. 2

68 I look upon all the world as my parish.
John Wesley (1703–91) British religious leader.
Journal, 11 June 1739

69 Why do born-again people so often make you wish they'd never been born the first time?
Katherine Whitehorn (1926–) British journalist.
The Observer, 20 May 1979

70 So many gods, so many creeds,
So many paths that wind and wind,
While just the art of being kind
Is all the sad world needs.
Ella Wheeler Wilcox (1850–1919) US poet.
The World's Need

71 The itch of disputing will prove the scab of churches.
Henry Wotton (1568–1639) English poet and diplomat.
A Panegyric to King Charles

72 The Ethiopians say that their gods are snub-nosed and black, the Thracians that theirs have light blue eyes and red hair.
Xenophanes (c. 560–c. 478 BC) Greek poet and philosopher.
Fragment 15

73 No Jew was ever fool enough to turn Christian unless he was a clever man.
Israel Zangwill (1864–1926) British writer.
Children of the Ghetto, Ch. 1

REMEDIES

See also doctors, drugs, health and healthy living, illness, medicine

1 Cure the disease and kill the patient.
Francis Bacon (1561–1626) English philosopher.
Essays, 'Of Friendship'

2 The remedy is worse than the disease.
Francis Bacon
Essays, 'Of Seditions and Troubles'

3 Then Peter said, Silver and gold have I none; but such as I have give I thee: In the name of Jesus Christ of Nazareth rise up and walk.
Bible: Acts
3:6

4 And besought him that they might only touch the hem of his garment: and as many as touched were made perfectly whole.
Bible: Matthew
14:36

5 My father invented a cure for which there was no disease and unfortunately my mother caught it and died of it.
Victor Borge (1909–) Danish-born US composer, actor, and musical comedian.
In Concert

6 Well, now, there's a remedy for everything except death.
Miguel de Cervantes (1547–1616) Spanish novelist.
Don Quixote, Pt. II, Ch. 10

7 When a lot of remedies are suggested for a disease, that means it can't be cured.
Anton Chekhov (1860–1904) Russian dramatist.
The Cherry Orchard, II

8 Every day, in every way, I am getting better and better.
Émile Coué (1857–1920) French doctor.
Formula for a cure by autosuggestion

9 His Majestie began first to Touch for the Evil according to costome; Thus, his Majestie sitting under his State in the Banqueting house: The Chirurgeons cause the sick to be brought or led up to the throne, who kneeling, the King strokes their faces or cheekes with both his hands at once: at which instant a Chaplaine in his formalities, says, He put his hands upon them, & he healed them.
John Evelyn (1620–1706) English diarist.
Diary, 6 July 1660

10 Extreme remedies are most appropriate for extreme diseases.
Hippocrates (c. 460–c. 377 BC) Greek physician.
Aphorisms, I

11 As soon as he ceased to be mad he became merely stupid. There are maladies we must not seek to cure because they alone protect us from others that are more serious.
Marcel Proust (1871–1922) French novelist.
À la recherche du temps perdu: Le Côté de Guermantes

12 They all thought she was dead; but my father he kept ladling gin down her throat till she came to so sudden that she bit the bowl off the spoon.
George Bernard Shaw (1856–1950) Irish dramatist and critic.
Pygmalion, III

13 Our body is a machine for living. It is organized for that, it is its nature. Let life go on in it unhindered and let it defend itself, it will do more than if you paralyse it by encumbering it with remedies.
Leo Tolstoy (1828–1910) Russian writer.
War and Peace, Bk. X, Ch. 29

14 Sparrowhawks, Ma'am.
Duke of Wellington (1769–1852) British general and statesman.
Advice when asked by Queen Victoria how to remove sparrows from the Crystal Palace
Attrib.

15 There is only one cure for grey hair. It was invented by a Frenchman. It is called the guillotine.
P. G. Wodehouse (1881–1975) British humorous novelist.
The Old Reliable

RENUNCIATION

See also dismissal

1 Renounce the devil and all his works.
The Book of Common Prayer
Publick Baptism of Infants

2 I would rather be a brilliant memory than a curiosity.
Emma Eames (1865–1952) US opera singer.
Referring to her retirement at the age of 47
The Elephant that Swallowed a Nightingale (C. Galtey)

3 You won't have Nixon to kick around any more, gentlemen. This is my last Press Conference.
Richard Milhous Nixon (1913–) US president.
Press conference, after losing the election for the governorship of California, 2 Nov 1962

4 I'll break my staff,
Bury it certain fathoms in the earth,
And deeper than did ever plummet sound
I'll drown my book.
William Shakespeare (1564–1616) English dramatist.
The Tempest, V:1

5 It is very simple. The artists retired. The British remained.
James Whistler (1834–1903) US painter.
Explaining his resignation as president of the Royal Society of British Artists
Whistler Stories (D. Seitz)

REPARTEE

1 This is very true: for my words are my own, and my actions are my ministers'.
Charles II (1630–85) King of England.
Replying to Lord Rochester's suggested epitaph
King Charles II (A. Bryant)

2 Stand a little less between me and the sun.
Diogenes (412–322 BC) Greek philosopher.
When Alexander the Great asked if there was anything he wanted
Life of Alexander (Plutarch)

3 Oh! he is mad, is he? Then I wish he would bite some other of my generals.
George II (1683–1760) King of Great Britain and Ireland.
Replying to advisors who told him that General James Wolfe was mad
Attrib.

4 JUDGE WILLIS. What do you suppose I am on the Bench for, Mr Smith?
SMITH. It is not for me to attempt to fathom the inscrutable workings of Providence.
F. E. Smith (1872–1930) British lawyer and politician.
Frederick Elwin, Earl of Birkenhead (Lord Birkenhead), Vol. I, Ch. 9

5 LORD SANDWICH. You will die either on the gallows, or of the pox.
WILKES. That must depend on whether I embrace your lordship's principles or your mistress.
John Wilkes (1725–97) British politician.
Sometimes attrib. to Samuel Foote
Portrait of a Patriot (Charles Chenevix-Trench), Ch. 3

REPRESENTATION

1 Taxation without representation is tyranny.
James Otis (1725–83) US political activist.
As 'No taxation without representation' this became the principal slogan of the American Revolution
Attrib.

2 No annihilation without representation.
Arnold Toynbee (1889–1975) British historian.
Urging the need for a greater British influence in the UN 1947

REPUBLIC

See also democracy, State

1 Our object in the construction of the state is the greatest happiness of the whole, and not that of any one class.
Plato (429–347 BC) Greek philosopher.
Republic, Bk. 4

2 As there was no form of government common to the peoples thus segregated, nor tie of language, history, habit, or belief, they were called a Republic.
Evelyn Waugh (1903–66) British novelist.
Scoop, Bk. II, Ch. 1

REPUTATION

See also fame, posterity

1 For my name and memory, I leave it to men's charitable speeches, and to foreign nations, and the next ages.
Francis Bacon (1561–1626) English philosopher.
Will, 19 Dec 1625

2 I hold it as certain, that no man was ever written out of reputation but by himself.
Richard Bentley (1662–1742) English academic.
The Works of Alexander Pope (W. Warburton), Vol. IV

3 Reputation is a bubble which bursts when a man tries to blow it up for himself.
Emma Carleton
Attrib.

4 Die when I may, I want it said of me by those who know me best, that I have always plucked a thistle and planted a flower where I thought a flower would grow.
Abraham Lincoln (1809–65) US statesman.
Presidential Anecdotes (P. Boller)

5 Until you've lost your reputation, you never realize what a burden it was or what freedom really is.
Margaret Mitchell (1909–49) US novelist.
Gone with the Wind

6 Reputation, reputation, reputation! O, I have lost my reputation! I have lost the immortal part of myself, and what remains is bestial.
William Shakespeare (1564–1616) English dramatist.
Othello, II:3

7 Good name in man and woman, dear my lord,
Is the immediate jewel of their souls:
Who steals my purse steals trash; 'tis something, nothing;
'Twas mine, 'tis his, and has been slave to thousands;
But he that filches from me my good name
Robs me of that which not enriches him
And makes me poor indeed.
William Shakespeare
Othello, III:3

8 The purest treasure mortal times afford
Is spotless reputation; that away,
Men are but gilded loam or painted clay.
William Shakespeare
Richard II, I:1

9 I'm called away by particular business. But I leave my character behind me.
Richard Brinsley Sheridan (1751–1816) British dramatist.
The School for Scandal, II

10 Everything.
Mae West (1892–1980) US actress.
When asked what she wanted to be remembered for
Attrib.

RESEARCH

1 O speculator concerning this machine of ours let it not distress you that you impart

knowledge of it through another's death, but rejoice that our Creator has ordained the intellect to such excellence of perception.
Leonardo da Vinci (1452–1519) Italian artist.
Quaderni d'Anatomia, Vol. II

2 Research! A mere excuse for idleness; it has never achieved, and will never achieve any results of the slightest value.
Benjamin Jowett (1817–93) British theologian.
Unforgotten Years (Logan Pearsall Smith)

3 The aim of research is the discovery of the equations which subsist between the elements of phenomena.
Ernst Mach (1838–1916) Austrian physicist and philosopher.
Popular Scientific Lectures

4 Always verify your references.
Martin Joseph Routh (1755–1854) British scholar.
Attrib.

5 We haven't the money, so we've got to think.
Ernest Rutherford (1871–1937) British physicist.
Attrib.

6 The outcome of any serious research can only be to make two questions grow where only one grew before.
Thorstein Bunde Veblen (1857–1929) US social scientist.
The Place of Science in Modern Civilization

RESPECT

See also courtesy, self-respect

1 Let them hate, so long as they fear.
Lucius Accius (170–c. 85 BC) Roman tragic playwright.
Atreus, 'Seneca'

2 One does not arrest Voltaire.
Charles De Gaulle (1890–1970) French general and statesman.
Explaining why he had not arrested Jean-Paul Sartre for urging French soldiers in Algeria to desert
Attrib.

3 I hate victims who respect their executioners.
Jean-Paul Sartre (1905–80) French writer.
Altona

4 We owe respect to the living; to the dead we owe only truth.
Voltaire (François-Marie Arouet; 1694–1778) French writer.
Oeuvres, 'Première lettre sur Oedipe'

5 The old-fashioned respect for the young is fast dying out.
Oscar Wilde (1854–1900) Irish-born British dramatist.
The Importance of Being Earnest, I

RESPECTABILITY

1 Since when was genius found respectable?
Elizabeth Barrett Browning (1806–61) British poet.
Aurora Leigh, Bk. VI

2 Let them cant about decorum
Who have characters to lose.
Robert Burns (1759–96) Scottish poet.
The Jolly Beggars

3 Respectable means rich, and decent means poor. I should die if I heard my family called decent.
Thomas Love Peacock (1785–1866) British novelist.
Crotchet Castle, Ch. 3

4 So live that you wouldn't be ashamed to sell the family parrot to the town gossip.
Will Rogers (1879–1935) US actor and humorist.
Attrib.

RESPONSIBILITY

See also accusation

1 A bad workman always blames his tools.
Proverb

2 What the proprietorship of these papers is aiming at is power, and power without responsibility – the prerogative of the harlot through the ages.
Stanley Baldwin (1867–1947) British statesman.
Attacking the press barons Lords Rothermere and Beaverbrook. It was first used by KIPLING. *See also* DUKE OF DEVONSHIRE; STOPPARD
Speech, election rally, 18 Mar 1931

3 Each man the architect of his own fate.
Appius Caecus (4th–3rd century BC) Roman statesman.
De Civitate (Sallust), Bk. I

4 Everyone threw the blame on me. I have noticed that they nearly always do. I suppose it is because they think I shall be able to bear it best.
Winston Churchill (1874–1965) British statesman.
My Early Life, Ch. 17

5 Perhaps it is better to be irresponsible and right than to be responsible and wrong.
Winston Churchill
Party Political Broadcast, London, 26 Aug 1950

6 Good God, that's done it. He's lost us the tarts' vote.
Duke of Devonshire (1895–1950) Conservative politician.
Referring to Stanley BALDWIN's attack on newspaper proprietors; recalled by Harold Macmillan
Attrib.

7 What a man does defiles him, not what is done by others.
William Golding (1911–) British novelist.
Rites of Passage, 'Next Day'

8 It matters not how strait the gate,
How charged with punishments the scroll,
I am the master of my fate:

I am the captain of my soul.

William Ernest Henley (1849–1903) British writer.
Echoes, IV, 'Invictus. In Mem. R.T.H.B.'

9 Power without responsibility. – the
prerogative of the harlot throughout the ages.

Rudyard Kipling (1865–1936) Indian-born British writer.
Better known for its subsequent use by BALDWIN
Attrib.

10 Accuse not Nature, she hath done her part;
Do thou but thine.

John Milton (1608–74) English poet.
Paradise Lost, Bk. VIII

11 *We can believe what we choose.* We are
answerable for what we choose to believe.

Cardinal Newman (1801–90) British theologian.
Letter to Mrs Froude, 27 June 1848

12 You become responsible, forever, for what
you have tamed. You are responsible for
your rose.

Antoine de Saint-Exupéry (1900–44) French novelist
and aviator.
The Little Prince, Ch. 21

13 The salvation of mankind lies only in making
everything the concern of all.

Alexander Solzhenitsyn (1918–) Soviet novelist.
Nobel Lecture, 1970

14 The House of Lords, an illusion to which I
have never been able to subscribe –
responsibility without power, the prerogative
of the eunuch throughout the ages.

Tom Stoppard (1937–) Czech-born British dramatist.
See also BALDWIN
Lord Malquist and Mr Moon, Pt. VI, Ch. 1

15 For man is man and master of his fate.

Alfred, Lord Tennyson (1809–92) British poet.
Idylls of the King, 'The Marriage of Geraint'

16 The buck stops here.

Harry S. Truman (1884–1972) US statesman.
Sign kept on his desk during his term as president
Presidential Anecdotes (P. Boller)

17 In dreams begins responsibility.

W. B. Yeats (1865–1939) Irish poet.
Old Play, Epigraph, Responsibilities

REST

See also bed, idleness, leisure, sleep

1 Will there be beds for me and all who seek?
Yea, beds for all who come.

Christina Rossetti (1830–74) British poet.
Up-Hill

2 Unarm, Eros; the long day's task is done,
And we must sleep.

William Shakespeare (1564–1616) English dramatist.
Antony and Cleopatra, IV:12

3 It is well to lie fallow for a while.

Martin Farquhar Tupper (1810–89) British writer.
Proverbial Philosophy, 'Of Recreation'

RESULTS

1 Desperate cuts must have desperate cures.
Proverb

2 The little bit (two inches wide) of ivory on
which I work with so fine a brush as
produces little effect after much labour.

Jane Austen (1775–1817) British novelist.
Letter, 16 Dec 1816

3 Ye shall know them by their fruits. Do men
gather grapes of thorns, or figs of thistles?
Even so every good tree bringeth forth good
fruit; but a corrupt tree bringeth forth evil
fruit.
A good tree cannot bring forth evil fruit,
neither can a corrupt tree bring forth good
fruit.
Every tree that bringeth not forth good fruit is
hewn down, and cast into the fire.
Wherefore by their fruits ye shall know them.

Bible: Matthew
7:16–20

4 Our love of what is beautiful does not lead to
extravagance; our love of the things of the
mind does not make us soft.

Pericles (c. 495–429 BC) Greek statesman.
Part of the funeral oration, 430 BC, for the dead of the first
year of the Peloponnesian War
Attrib. in *Histories* Bk. II, Ch. 40 (Thucydides)

5 What dire offence from am'rous causes
springs,
What mighty contests rise from trivial things.

Alexander Pope (1688–1744) British poet.
The Rape of the Lock, I

RETRIBUTION

See also punishment, revenge

1 Give a thief enough rope and he'll hang
himself.
Proverb

2 *Nemo me impune lacessit.*
No one provokes me with impunity.

Anonymous
Motto of the Crown of Scotland

3 And if any mischief follow, then thou shalt
give life for life,
Eye for eye, tooth for tooth, hand for hand,
foot for foot,
Burning for burning, wound for wound, stripe
for stripe.

Bible: Exodus
21:23–25

4 Be not deceived: God is not mocked: for
whatsoever a man soweth, that shall he also
reap.
For he that soweth to his flesh shall of the
flesh reap corruption; but he that soweth to
the Spirit shall of the Spirit reap life
everlasting.

And let us not be weary in well doing: for in due season we shall reap, if we faint not.
Bible: Galatians
6:7–9

5 For they have sown the wind, and they shall reap the whirlwind: it hath no stalk: the bud shall yield no meal: if so be it yield, the strangers shall swallow it up.
Bible: Hosea
8:7

6 For I say unto you, That except your righteousness shall exceed the righteousness of the scribes and Pharisees, ye shall in no case enter into the kingdom of heaven.
Bible: Matthew
5:20

7 And if thy right eye offend thee, pluck it out, and cast it from thee: for it is profitable for thee that one of thy members should perish, and not that thy whole body should be cast into hell.
Bible: Matthew
5:29

8 For thou shalt heap coals of fire upon his head, and the Lord shall reward thee.
Bible: Proverbs
25:22

9 But men never violate the laws of God without suffering the consequences, sooner or later.
Lydia M. Child (1802–80) US abolitionist campaigner.
The Freedmen's Book, 'Toussaint L'Ouverture'

10 The Germans, if this Government is returned, are going to pay every penny; they are going to be squeezed, as a lemon is squeezed – until the pips squeak. My only doubt is not whether we can squeeze hard enough, but whether there is enough juice.
Eric Campbell Geddes (1875–1937) British politician.
Speech, Cambridge, 10 Dec 1918

RETURN

1 Poor wandering one!
Though thou hast surely strayed,
Take heart of grace,
Thy steps retrace,
Poor wandering one!
W. S. Gilbert (1836–1911) British dramatist.
The Pirates of Penzance, I

2 Ten o'clock . . . and back he'll come. I can just see him.
With vine leaves in his hair. Flushed and confident.
Henrik Ibsen (1828–1906) Norwegian dramatist.
Hedda Gabler, II

3 Better lo'ed ye canna be,

Will ye no come back again?
Carolina Nairne (1766–1845) Scottish songwriter.
Referring to Bonnie Prince Charlie
Bonnie Charlie's now awa!

REVENGE

See also retribution

1 Don't cut off your nose to spite your face.
Proverb

2 Revenge is a dish that tastes better cold.
Proverb

3 Revenge is sweet.
Proverb

4 Revenge is a kind of wild justice; which the more man's nature runs to, the more ought law to weed it out.
Francis Bacon (1561–1626) English philosopher.
Essays, 'Of Revenge'

5 A man that studieth revenge keeps his own wounds green.
Francis Bacon
Essays, 'Of Revenge'

6 Perish the Universe, provided I have my revenge.
Cyrano de Bergerac (1619–55) French writer.
La Mort d'Agrippine, IV

7 And the Lord said unto him, Therefore whosoever slayeth Cain, vengeance shall be taken on him sevenfold. And the Lord set a mark upon Cain, lest any finding him should kill him.
And Cain went out from the presence of the Lord, and dwelt in the land of Nod, on the east of Eden.
Bible: Genesis
4:15–16

8 I make war on the living, not on the dead.
Charles V (1500–58) Holy Roman Emperor.
After the death of Martin Luther, when it was suggested that he hang the corpse on a gallows
Attrib.

9 Rome shall perish – write that word
In the blood that she has spilt.
William Cowper (1731–1800) British poet.
Boadicea

10 Wisdom has taught us to be calm and meek,
To take one blow, and turn the other cheek;
It is not written what a man shall do
If the rude caitiff smite the other too!
Oliver Wendell Holmes (1809–94) US writer.
Non-Resistance

11 No one delights more in vengeance than a woman.
Juvenal (Decimus Junius Juvenalis; 60–130 AD) Roman satirist.
Satires, XIII

12 We had no use for the policy of the Gospels:

if someone slaps you, just turn the other cheek. We had shown that anyone who slapped us on our cheek would get his head kicked off.
Nikita Khrushchev (1894–1971) Soviet statesman.
Khrushchev Remembers, Vol. II

13 Revenge, at first though sweet,
Bitter ere long back on itself recoils.
John Milton (1608–74) English poet.
Paradise Lost, Bk. IX

14 Those who offend us are generally punished for the offence they give; but we so frequently miss the satisfaction of knowing that we are avenged!
Anthony Trollope (1815–82) British novelist.
The Small House at Allington, Ch. 50

REVOLUTION

See also French Revolution, rebellion, Russian Revolution

1 Inferiors revolt in order that they may be equal and equals that they may be superior. Such is the state of mind which creates revolutions.
Aristotle (384–322 BC) Greek philosopher.
Politics, Bk. V

2 All modern revolutions have ended in a reinforcement of the power of the State.
Albert Camus (1913–60) French existentialist writer.
The Rebel

3 The uprising of the masses implies a fabulous increase of vital possibilities; quite the contrary of what we hear so often about the decadence of Europe.
José Ortega y Gasset (1883–1955) Spanish philosopher.
The Revolt of the Masses, Ch. 2

4 Revolution is not the uprising against pre-existing order, but the setting-up of a new order contradictory to the traditional one.
José Ortega y Gasset
The Revolt of the Masses, Ch. 6

5 We are dancing on a volcano.
Comte de Salvandy (1795–1856) French nobleman.
A remark made before the July Revolution in 1830

6 Insurrection is an art, and like all arts it has its laws.
Leon Trotsky (Lev Davidovich Bronstein; 1879–1940) Russian revolutionary.
History of the Russian Revolution, Pt. III, Ch. 6

7 Revolutions are always verbose.
Leon Trotsky
History of the Russian Revolution, Pt. II, Ch. 12

8 The fundamental premise of a revolution is that the existing social structure has become incapable of solving the urgent problems of development of the nation.
Leon Trotsky
History of the Russian Revolution, Pt. III, Ch. 6

9 Revolution by its very nature is sometimes compelled to take in more territory than it is capable of holding. Retreats are possible – when there is territory to retreat from.
Leon Trotsky
Diary in Exile, 15 Feb 1935

10 The word 'revolution' is a word for which you kill, for which you die, for which you send the labouring masses to their death, but which does not possess any content.
Simone Weil (1909–43) French philosopher.
Oppression and Liberty, 'Reflections Concerning the Causes of Liberty and Social Oppression'

11 We invented the Revolution but we don't know how to run it.
Peter Weiss (1916–82) German novelist and dramatist.
Marat Sade, 15

12 Where the populace rise at once against the never-ending audacity of elected persons.
Walt Whitman (1819–92) US poet.
Song of the Broad Axe, 5

RIDICULE

See also contempt, satire

1 For what do we live, but to make sport for our neighbours, and laugh at them in our turn?
Jane Austen (1775–1817) British novelist.
Pride and Prejudice, Ch. 57

2 Few women care to be laughed at and men not at all, except for large sums of money.
Alan Ayckbourn (1939–   ) British dramatist.
The Norman Conquests, Preface

3 It often happens, that he who endeavours to ridicule other people, especially in things of a serious nature, becomes himself a jest, and frequently to his great cost.
Giovanni Boccaccio (1313–75) Italian writer and poet.
Decameron, 'Second Day'

4 Ridicule often checks what is absurd, and fully as often smothers that which is noble.
Walter Scott (1771–1832) Scottish novelist.
Quentin Durward

RIGHT

1 This the grave of Mike O'Day
Who died maintaining his right of way.
His right was clear, his will was strong.
But he's just as dead as if he'd been wrong.
Anonymous
Epitaph

2 A child becomes an adult when he realizes that he has a right not only to be right but also to be wrong.
Thomas Szasz (1920–   ) US psychiatrist.
The Second Sin

3 While I'd rather be right than president, at
any time I'm ready to be both.
Norman M. Thomas (1884–1968) US politician.
Referring to his lack of success in presidential campaigns. The
expression 'I'd rather be right than president' is also attributed to the US politician Henry Clay (1777–1852)
Come to Judgment (A. Whitman)

4 Right is more precious than peace.
Woodrow Wilson (1856–1925) US statesman.
Radio Times, 10 Sept 1964

RIGHTEOUSNESS

See also good, integrity, morality, virtue

1 The eternal *not ourselves* that makes for
righteousness.
Matthew Arnold (1822–88) British poet and critic.
Literature and Dogma, Ch. 8

2 Righteous people terrify me . . . Virtue is its
own punishment.
Aneurin Bevan (1897–1960) British Labour politician.
Aneurin Bevan 1897–1945 (Michael Foot)

3 Ye must leave righteous ways behind, not to
speak of unrighteous ways.
Buddha (Gautama Siddhartha; c. 563–c. 483 BC) Indian
religious teacher.
Some Sayings of the Buddha (F. L. Woodward)

4 The man of life upright,
Whose guiltless heart is free
From all dishonest deeds
Or thought of vanity.
Thomas Campion (1567–1620) English poet.
The Man of Life Upright

5 Good thoughts his only friends,
His wealth a well-spent age,
The earth his sober inn
And quiet pilgrimage.
Thomas Campion
The Man of Life Upright

6 Perhaps it is better to be irresponsible and
right than to be responsible and wrong.
Winston Churchill (1874–1965) British statesman.
Party Political Broadcast, London, 26 Aug 1950

7 Looks the whole world in the face,
For he owes not any man.
Henry Wadsworth Longfellow (1807–82) US poet.
The Village Blacksmith

8 Live among men as if God beheld you; speak
to God as if men were listening.
Seneca (c. 4 BC–65 AD) Roman author.
Epistles

RIVERS

1 I have seen the Mississippi. That is muddy
water. I have seen the St Lawrence. That is
crystal water. But the Thames is liquid
history.
John Burns (1858–1943) British Labour politician.
Attrib.

2 Ol' man river, dat ol' man river,
He must know sumpin', but don't say nothin',
He just keeps rollin', he keeps on rollin' along.
Oscar Hammerstein (1895–1960) US lyricist.
From the musical *Show Boat*
Ol' Man River

3 What is there to make so much of in the
Thames? I am quite tired of it. Flow, flow,
flow, always the same.
Duke of Queensberry (1724–1810) British peer.
Century of Anecdote (J. Timbs)

4 *Die Wacht am Rhein.*
The Watch on the Rhine.
Max Schneckenburger (1819–49) German poet.
Song title

5 Sweet Thames! run softly, till I end my
Song.
Edmund Spenser (1552–99) English poet.
Prothalamion, 18

6 I come from haunts of coot and hern,
I make a sudden sally
And sparkle out among the fern,
To bicker down a valley.
Alfred, Lord Tennyson (1809–92) British poet.
The Brook

ROYALTY

See also monarchy

1 The King over the Water.
Anonymous
Jacobite toast

2 'How different, how very different from the
home life of our own dear Queen!'
Anonymous
Remark about the character of Cleopatra as performed by Sarah Bernhardt

3 Here lies Fred,
Who was alive and is dead:
Had it been his father,
I had much rather;
Had it been his brother,
Still better than another;
Had it been his sister,
No one would have missed her;
Had it been the whole generation,
Still better for the nation:
But since 'tis only Fred,
Who was alive and is dead, –
There's no more to be said.
Anonymous
Referring to Frederick, Prince of Wales, eldest son of George
II and father of George III
Memoirs of George II (Horace Walpole)

4 The house is well, but it is you, Your
Majesty, who have made me too great for
my house.
Francis Bacon (1561–1626) English philosopher.
Reply when Elizabeth I remarked on the smallness of his house
After-dinner Stories and Anecdotes (L. Meissen)

5 Speed, bonny boat, like a bird on the wing;
'Onward', the sailors cry;
Carry the lad that's born to be king
Over the sea to Skye.
H. E. Boulton (1859–1935) Scottish songwriter.
Referring to Bonnie Prince Charlie
Skye Boat Song

6 Such grace had kings when the world begun!
Robert Browning (1812–89) British poet.
Pippa Passes, Pt. I

7 Kings are naturally lovers of low company.
Edmund Burke (1729–97) British politician.
Speech on the Economical Reform (House of Commons, 11 Feb 1780)

8 A better farmer ne'er brushed dew from lawn,
A worse king never left a realm undone!
Lord Byron (1788–1824) British poet.
Referring to George III
The Vision of Judgment, VIII

9 Conquering kings their titles take.
John Chandler (1806–76) British clergyman and writer.
Poem title

10 Brother, I am too old to go again to my travels.
Charles II (1630–85) King of England.
Referring to his exile, 1651–60
History of Great Britain (Hume), Vol. II, Ch. 7

11 The monarchy is the oldest profession in the world.
Charles, Prince of Wales (1948–) Eldest son of Elizabeth II.
Attrib.

12 Her Majesty is not a subject.
Benjamin Disraeli (1804–81) British statesman.
Responding to Gladstone's taunt that Disraeli could make a joke out of any subject, including Queen Victoria
Attrib.

13 I know I have the body of a weak and feeble woman, but I have the heart and stomach of a King, and of a King of England too.
Elizabeth I (1533–1603) Queen of England.
Speech at Tilbury on the approach of the Spanish Armada

14 Though God hath raised me high, yet this I count the glory of my crown: that I have reigned with your loves.
Elizabeth I
The Golden Speech, 1601

15 I will make you shorter by a head.
Elizabeth I
Sayings of Queen Elizabeth (Chamberlin)

16 I should like to be a horse.
Elizabeth II (1926–) Queen of the United Kingdom.
When asked about her ambitions when a child
Attrib.

17 I think that everyone will conceed that –

today of all days – I should begin by saying, 'My husband and I'.
Elizabeth II
On her silver-wedding
Speech, Guildhall, 1972

18 We're not a family; we're a firm.
George VI (1895–1952) King of the United Kingdom.
Our Future King (Peter Lane)

19 I'm prepared to take advice on leisure from Prince Philip. He's a world expert on leisure. He's been practising for most of his adult life.
Neil Kinnock (1942–) British politician.
Western Mail, 1981

20 I don't mind your being killed, but I object to your being taken prisoner.
Lord Kitchener (1850–1916) British field marshal.
Said to the Prince of Wales (later Edward VIII) when he asked to go to the Front
Journal (Viscount Esher), 18 Dec 1914

21 Ah, if I were not king, I should lose my temper.
Louis XIV (1638–1715) French king.
Attrib.

22 For God's sake, ma'am, let's have no more of that. If you get the English people into the way of making kings, you'll get them into the way of *un*making them.
Lord Melbourne (1779–1848) British statesman.
Advising Queen Victoria against granting Prince Albert the title of King Consort
Lord M. (Lord David Cecil)

23 You can divide my life into two. During the first part of my life I was an ordinary conventional naval officer, trying not to be different in the sense of being royal trying not to show myself off as being rich and ostentatious – like always using a small car to drive to the dockyard instead of my Rolls Royce.
Louis Mountbatten of Burma (1900–79) British admiral and colonial administrator.
Mountbatten, Hero of Our Time, Ch. 9 (Richard Hough)

24 He will go from resort to resort getting more tanned and more tired.
Westbrook Pegler (1894–1969) US journalist.
On the abdication of Edward VIII
Six Men (Alistair Cooke), Pt. II

25 I'm self-employed.
Prince Philip (1921–) The consort of Queen Elizabeth II.
Answering a query as to what nature of work he did
Attrib.

26 Not least among the qualities in a great King is a capacity to permit his ministers to serve him.
Cardinal Richelieu (1585–1642) French statesman.
Testament Politique, Maxims

27 Kings and such like are just as funny as politicians.
Theodore Roosevelt (1858–1919) US Republican president.
Mr Wilson's War (John Dos Passos), Ch. 1

28 The sun does not set in my dominions.
Friedrich von Schiller (1759–1805) German dramatist.
Said by Philip II
Don Carlos, I:6

29 Kings are earth's gods; in vice their law's their will.
William Shakespeare (1564–1616) English dramatist.
Pericles, I:1

30 For God's sake let us sit upon the ground
And tell sad stories of the death of kings:
How some have been depos'd, some slain in war,
Some haunted by the ghosts they have depos'd,
Some poison'd by their wives, some sleeping kill'd,
All murder'd – for within the hollow crown
That rounds the mortal temples of a king
Keeps Death his court.
William Shakespeare
Richard II, III:2

31 Ay, every inch a king.
William Shakespeare
King Lear, IV:6

32 I would not be a queen
For all the world.
William Shakespeare
Henry VIII, II:3

33 Albert was merely a young foreigner, who suffered from having no vices, and whose only claim to distinction was that he had happened to marry the Queen of England.
Lytton Strachey (1880–1932) British writer.
Queen Victoria, Ch. 5

34 Authority forgets a dying king.
Alfred, Lord Tennyson (1809–92) British poet.
Idylls of the King, 'The Passing of Arthur'

35 We are not amused!
Victoria (1819–1901) Queen of the United Kingdom.
Attrib.

36 I sat between the King and Queen. We left supper soon. My health was drunk. I then danced one more quadrille with Lord Paget. . . . I was *very* much amused.
Victoria
Journal, 16 June 1833

37 It has none, your Highness. Its history dates from today.
James Whistler (1834–1903) US painter.
Replying to a query from the Prince of Wales about the history of the Society of British Artists, which he was visiting for the first time
Whistler Stories (D. Seitz)

38 Now what do I do with *this*?
Duke of Windsor (1894–1972) King of the United Kingdom; abdicated 1936.
On being handed the bill after a lengthy stay in a luxury hotel
Attrib.

RUDENESS

See impertinence, insults

RULES

1 The exception proves the rule.
Proverb

2 Rules and models destroy genius and art.
William Hazlitt (1778–1830) British essayist.
On Taste

3 The golden rule is that there are no golden rules.
George Bernard Shaw (1856–1950) Irish dramatist and critic.
Man and Superman, 'Maxims for Revolutionists'

RUSSIA

See also Cold War, oppression, Russian Revolution

1 I cannot forecast to you the action of Russia. It is a riddle wrapped in a mystery inside an enigma.
Winston Churchill (1874–1965) British statesman.
Broadcast talk, 1 Oct 1939

2 Russia will certainly inherit the future. What we already call the greatness of Russia is only her pre-natal struggling.
D. H. Lawrence (1885–1930) British novelist.
Phoenix, Preface

3 Neither can you expect a revolution, because there is no new baby in the womb of our society. Russia is a collapse, not a revolution.
D. H. Lawrence
Phoenix, 'The Good Man'

4 Scratch the Russian and you will find the Tartar.
Joseph de Maistre (1753–1821) French monarchist.
Attributed also to Napoleon and Prince de Ligne

5 Absolutism tempered by assassination.
Ernst Friedrich Herbert Münster (1766–1839) Hanoverian statesman.
Referring to the Russian Constitution
Letter

6 It was the supreme expression of the mediocrity of the apparatus that Stalin himself rose to his position.
Leon Trotsky (Lev Davidovich Bronstein; 1879–1940) Russian revolutionary.
My Life, Ch. 40

7 From being a patriotic myth, the Russian people have become an awful reality.
Leon Trotsky
History of the Russian Revolution, Pt. III, Ch. 7

RUSSIAN REVOLUTION

See also revolution, Russia

1 Our hand will not tremble.

Joseph Stalin (J. Dzhugashvili; 1879–1953) Soviet statesman.
Reply to a telegraph from Lenin at the start of the Red Terror (1918) urging him to be merciless against the Bolsheviks' enemies

2 The 23rd of February was International Woman's Day . . . It had not occurred to anyone that it might become the first day of the revolution.

Leon Trotsky (Lev Davidovich Bronstein; 1879–1940) Russian revolutionary.
History of the Russian Revolution, Pt. I, Ch. 7

3 The revolution does not choose its paths: it made its first steps towards victory under the belly of a Cossack's horse.

Leon Trotsky
History of the Russian Revolution, Pt. I, Ch. 7

RUTHLESSNESS

1 Would that the Roman people had but one neck!

Caligula (Gaius Caesar; 12–41 AD) Roman Emperor.
Life of Caligula (Suetonius), Ch. 30

2 What millions died – that Caesar might be great!

Thomas Campbell (1777–1844) British poet.
Pleasures of Hope, II

3 Exterminate all brutes.

Joseph Conrad (Teodor Josef Konrad Korzeniowski; 1857–1924) Polish-born British novelist.
Heart of Darkness

4 I do not have to forgive my enemies, I have had them all shot.

Ramón Maria Narváez (1800–68) Spanish general and political leader.
Said on his deathbed, when asked by a priest if he forgave his enemies
Famous Last Words (B. Conrad)

5 3RD FISHERMAN. Master, I marvel how the fishes live in the sea.
1ST FISHERMAN. Why, as men do a-land – the great ones eat up the little ones.

William Shakespeare (1564–1616) English dramatist.
Pericles, II:1

6 The world continues to offer glittering prizes to those who have stout hearts and sharp swords.

F. E. Smith (1872–1930) British lawyer and politician.
Speech, Glasgow University, 7 Nov 1923

7 It is not enough to succeed. Others must fail.

Gore Vidal (1925–) US novelist.
Antipanegyric for Tom Driberg (G. Irvine)

S

SARCASM

1 Sarcasm I now see to be, in general, the language of the devil.

Thomas Carlyle (1795–1881) Scottish historian and essayist.
Sartor Resartus, Bk. II, Ch. 4

2 If you don't want to use the army, I should like to borrow it for a while. Yours respectfully, A. Lincoln.

Abraham Lincoln (1809–65) US statesman.
Letter to General George B. McClellan, whose lack of activity during the US Civil War irritated Lincoln

SATIRE

See also ridicule, sarcasm

1 It's hard not to write satire.

Juvenal (Decimus Junius Juvenalis; 60–130 AD) Roman satirist.
Satires, I

2 Satire should, like a polished razor keen, Wound with a touch that's scarcely felt or seen.

Lady Mary Wortley Montagu (1689–1762) English writer.
To the Imitator of the First Satire of Horace, Bk. II

3 Satire is a sort of glass, wherein beholders do generally discover everybody's face but their own.

Jonathan Swift (1667–1745) Irish-born Anglican priest and writer.
The Battle of the Books, 'Preface'

SATISFACTION

See also contentment

1 Youth will be served, every dog has his day, and mine has been a fine one.

George Henry Borrow (1803–81) British writer.
Lavengro, Ch. 92

2 I wasna fou, but just had plenty.

Robert Burns (1759–96) Scottish poet.
Death and Doctor Hornbrook

3 The reward of a thing well done is to have done it.

Ralph Waldo Emerson (1803–82) US poet and essayist.
Essays, 'New England Reformers'

SAYINGS

See also quotations

1 A platitude is simply a truth repeated till people get tired of hearing it.

Stanley Baldwin (1867–1947) British statesman.
Attrib.

2 The hunter for aphorisms on human nature has to fish in muddy water, and he is even condemned to find much of his own mind.
F. H. Bradley (1846–1924) British philosopher.
Aphorisms

3 The great writers of aphorisms read as if they had all known each other well.
Elias Canetti (1905–   ) Bulgarian-born novelist.
The Human Province

4 A proverb is much matter decorated into few words.
Thomas Fuller (1608–61) English historian.
The History of the Worthies of England, Ch. 2

5 A new maxim is often a brilliant error.
Chrétien Guillaume de Lamoignonde Malesherbes (1721–94) French statesman.
Pensées et maximes

6 A proverb is one man's wit and all men's wisdom.
Lord John Russell (1792–1878) British statesman.
Attrib.

7 A truism is on that account none the less true.
Herbert Samuel (1870–1963) British Liberal statesman.
A Book of Quotations

SCEPTICISM

See also doubt, proof

1 We don't believe in rheumatism and true love until after the first attack.
Marie Ebner von Eschenbach (1830–1916) Austrian writer.
Aphorism

2 I am too much of a sceptic to deny the possibility of anything.
T. H. Huxley (1825–95) British biologist.
Letter to Herbert Spencer, 22 Mar 1886

3 Truth, Sir, is a cow, which will yield such people no more milk, and so they are gone to milk the bull.
Samuel Johnson (1709–84) British lexicographer.
Life of Johnson (J. Boswell), Vol. I
Referring to sceptics

4 It is undesirable to believe a proposition when there is no ground whatever for supposing it true.
Bertrand Russell (1872–1970) British philosopher.
Sceptical Essays

5 She believed in nothing; only her scepticism kept her from being an atheist.
Jean-Paul Sartre (1905–80) French writer.
Words

6 The temerity to believe in nothing.
Ivan Turgenev (1818–83) Russian novelist.
Fathers and Sons, Ch. 14

SCIENCE

See also discovery, mathematics, Nature, progress, research, scientists, technology

1 That is the essence of science: ask an impertinent question, and you are on the way to the pertinent answer.
Jacob Bronowski (1908–74) British scientist and writer.
The Ascent of Man, Ch. 4

2 Physics becomes in those years the greatest collective work of science – no, more than that, the great collective work of art of the twentieth century.
Jacob Bronowski
The Ascent of Man, Ch. 10
Referring to the period around the turn of the century marked by the elucidation of atomic structure and the development of the quantum theory

3 There was a young lady named Bright,
Whose speed was far faster than light;
She set out one day
In a relative way,
And returned home the previous night.
Arthur Henry Reginald Buller (1874–1944) British botanist.
Limerick

4 That is how the atom is split. But what does it mean? To us who think in terms of practical use it means – Nothing!
Ritchie Calder (1898–   ) US engineer and sculptor.
The Daily Herald, 27 June 1932

5 It is, of course, a bit of a drawback that science was invented after I left school.
Lord Carrington (1919–   ) British statesman.
The Observer, 23 Jan 1983

6 When a distinguished but elderly scientist states that something is possible, he is almost certainly right. When he states that something is impossible, he is very probably wrong.
Arthur C. Clarke (1917–   ) British science-fiction writer.
Profiles of the Future

7 We have discovered the secret of life!
Francis Crick (1916–   ) British biophysicist.
Excitedly bursting into a Cambridge pub with James Watson to celebrate the fact that they had unravelled the structure of DNA
The Double Helix (J. D. Watson)

8 After all, science is essentially international, and it is only through lack of the historical sense that national qualities have been attributed to it.
Marie Curie (1867–1934) Polish chemist.
Memorandum, 'Intellectual Co-operation'

9 And new Philosophy calls all in doubt,
The Element of fire is quite put out;
The Sun is lost, and th' earth, and no man's wit
Can well direct him where to look for it.
John Donne (1573–1631) English poet.
An Anatomy of the World, 205

10 Electrical force is defined as something which causes motion of electrical charge; an electrical charge is something which exerts electric force.
Arthur Eddington (1882–1944) British astronomer.
The Nature of the Physical World

11 Man is slightly nearer to the atom than the stars. From his central position he can survey the grandest works of Nature with the astronomer, or the minutest works with the physicist.
Arthur Eddington
Stars and Atoms

12 When you are courting a nice girl an hour seems like a second. When you sit on a red-hot cinder a second seems like an hour. That's relativity.
Albert Einstein (1879–1955) German-born US physicist.
News Chronicle, 14 Mar 1949

13 The whole of science is nothing more than a refinement of everyday thinking.
Albert Einstein
Out of My Later Years

14 Science without religion is lame, religion without science is blind.
Albert Einstein
Out of My Later Years

15 God does not play dice.
Albert Einstein
Albert Einstein, Creator and Rebel (B. Hoffman), Ch. 10
Einstein's objection to the quantum theory, in which physical events can only be known in terms of probabilities. It is sometimes quoted as 'God does not play dice with the Universe'

16 A vacuum can only exist, I imagine, by the things which enclose it.
Zelda Fitzgerald (1900–48) US writer.
Journal, 1932

17 Shelley and Keats were the last English poets who were at all up to date in their chemical knowledge.
J. B. S. Haldane (1892–1964) British geneticist.
Daedalus or Science and the Future

18 MASTER: They split the atom by firing particles at it, at 5,500 miles a second.
BOY: Good heavens. And they only split it?
Will Hay (1888–1949) British comedian.
The Fourth Form at St Michael's

19 Science has 'explained' nothing; the more we know the more fantastic the world becomes and the profounder the surrounding darkness.
Aldous Huxley (1894–1964) British novelist.
Views Of Holland

20 Science is nothing but trained and organized common sense, differing from the latter only as a veteran may differ from a raw recruit: and its methods differ from those of common sense only as far as the guardsman's cut and thrust differ from the manner in which a savage wields his club.
T. H. Huxley (1825–95) British biologist.
Collected Essays, 'The Method of Zadig'

21 The great tragedy of Science – the slaying of a beautiful hypothesis by an ugly fact.
T. H. Huxley
Collected Essays, 'Biogenesis and Abiogenesis'

22 Reason, Observation, and Experience – the Holy Trinity of Science.
Robert G. Ingersoll (1833–99) US lawyer and agnostic.
The Gods

23 Life exists in the universe only because the carbon atom possesses certain exceptional properties.
James Jeans (1877–1946) British scientist.
The Mysterious Universe, Ch. 1

24 Science should leave off making pronouncements: the river of knowledge has too often turned back on itself.
James Jeans
The Mysterious Universe, Ch. 5

25 We have genuflected before the god of science only to find that it has given us the atomic bomb, producing fears and anxieties that science can never mitigate.
Martin Luther King (1929–68) US Black civil-rights leader.
Strength through Love, Ch. 13

26 In everything that relates to science, I am a whole Encyclopaedia behind the rest of the world.
Charles Lamb (1775–1834) British essayist.
Essays of Elia, 'The Old and the New Schoolmaster'

27 Water is H_2O, hydrogen two parts, oxygen one,
but there is also a third thing, that makes it water
and nobody knows what that is.
D. H. Lawrence (1885–1930) British novelist.
Pansies, 'The Third Thing'

28 Scientific discovery is a private event, and the delight that accompanies it, or the despair of finding it illusory does not travel.
Peter Medawar (1915–87) British immunologist.
Hypothesis and Imagination

29 *Laboratorium est oratorium.* The place where we do our scientific work is a place of prayer.
Joseph Needham (1900–) British biochemist.
The Harvest of a Quiet Eye (A. L. Mackay)

30 Do you really believe that the sciences would ever have originated and grown if the way had not been prepared by magicians, alchemists, astrologers and witches whose promises and pretensions first had to create a thirst, a hunger, a taste for *hidden* and *forbidden* powers? Indeed, infinitely more had to be *promised* than could ever be fulfilled in

order that anything at all might be fulfilled in the realms of knowledge.
Friedrich Wilhelm Nietzsche (1844–1900) German philosopher.
The Gay Science

31 There are no such things as applied sciences, only applications of science.
Louis Pasteur (1822–95) French scientist.
Address, 11 Sept 1872

32 Traditional scientific method has always been at the very *best*, 20-20 hindsight. It's good for seeing where you've been.
Robert T. Pirsig (1928–) US writer.
Zen and the Art of Motorcycle Maintenance, Pt. III, Ch. 24

33 Science must begin with myths, and with the criticism of myths.
Karl Popper (1902–) Austrian-born British philosopher.
British Philosophy in the Mid-Century (ed. C. A. Mace)

34 Should we force science down the throats of those that have no taste for it? Is it our duty to drag them kicking and screaming into the twenty-first century? I am afraid that it is.
George Porter (1920–) British chemist.
Speech, Sept 1986

35 Science without conscience is the death of the soul.
François Rabelais (1483–1553) French satirist.

36 The simplest schoolboy is now familiar with truths for which Archimedes would have sacrificed his life.
Ernest Renan (1823–92) French philosopher and theologian.
Souvenirs d'enfance et de jeunesse

37 If all the arts aspire to the condition of music, all the sciences aspire to the condition of mathematics.
George Santayana (1863–1952) US philosopher.
The Observer, 'Sayings of the Week', 4 Mar 1928

38 People must understand that science is inherently neither a potential for good nor for evil. It is a potential to be harnessed by man to do his bidding.
Glenn T. Seaborg (1912–) US physicist.
Associated Press interview with Alton Blakeslee, 29 Sept 1964

39 Science is the great antidote to the poison of enthusiasm and superstition.
Adam Smith (1723–90) Scottish economist.
The Wealth of Nations, Bk. V, Ch. 1

40 Her own mother lived the latter years of her life in the horrible suspicion that electricity was dripping invisibly all over the house.
James Thurber (1894–1961) US humorist.
My Life and Hard Times, Ch. 2

41 Modern Physics is an instrument of Jewry for the destruction of Nordic science . . . True physics is the creation of the German spirit.
Rudolphe Tomaschek (20th century) German scientist.
The Rise and Fall of the Third Reich (W. L. Shirer), Ch. 8

42 Science robs men of wisdom and usually converts them into phantom beings loaded up with facts.
Miguel de Unamuno y Jugo (1864–36) Spanish writer.
Essays and Soliloquies

43 The term Science should not be given to anything but the aggregate of the recipes that are always successful. All the rest is literature.
Paul Valéry (1871–1945) French poet and writer.
Moralités

44 Classical physics has been superseded by quantum theory: quantum theory is verified by experiments. Experiments must be described in terms of classical physics.
C. F. von Weizsäcker (1912–) German physicist and philosopher.
Attrib.

45 A science which hesitates to forget its founders is lost.
A. N. Whitehead (1861–1947) British philosopher.
Attrib.

46 The airplane stays up because it doesn't have the time to fall.
Orville Wright (1871–1948) US aviator.
Attrib.
Explaining the principles of powered flight

SCIENCE FICTION

1 Far out in the uncharted backwaters of the unfashionable end of the Western Spiral arm of the Galaxy lies a small unregarded yellow sun.
Orbiting this at a distance of roughly ninety-two million miles is an utterly insignificant little blue green planet whose ape-descended life forms are so amazingly primitive that they still think digital watches are a pretty neat idea.
Douglas Adams (1952–) British writer.
The Hitch Hiker's Guide to the Galaxy, Introduction

2 Science fiction is the search for a definition of mankind and his status in the universe which will stand in our advanced but confused state of knowledge (science), and is characteristically cast in the Gothic or post-Gothic mode.
Brian Aldiss (1925–) British science-fiction writer.
Trillion Year Spree, Ch. 1

3 *Star Maker* is really the one great grey holy book of science fiction . . .
Brian Aldiss
Referring to Olaf Stapledon's novel *Star Maker*
Trillion Year Spree, Ch. 8

SCIENTISTS

See also science

General quotes

1 When I find myself in the company of

scientists, I feel like a shabby curate who has strayed by mistake into a drawing-room full of dukes.

W. H. Auden (1907–73) British poet.
The Dyer's Hand

2 The true men of action in our time, those who transform the world, are not the politicians and statesmen, but the scientists. Unfortunately, poetry cannot celebrate them, because their deeds are concerned with things, not persons and are, therefore, speechless.

W. H. Auden
The Dyer's Hand

3 If you want to find out anything from the theoretical physicists about the methods they use, I advise you to stick closely to one principle: Don't listen to their words fix your attention on their deeds.

Albert Einstein (1879–1955) German-born US physicist.
The World As I See It

4 The physicists have known sin; and this is a knowledge which they cannot lose.

J. Robert Oppenheimer (1904–67) US physicist.
Lecture, Massachusetts Institute of Technology, 25 Nov 1947

5 He doubted the existence of the Deity but accepted Carnot's cycle, and he had read Shakespeare and found him weak in chemistry.

H. G. Wells (1866–1946) British writer.
Short Stories, 'The Lord of the Dynamos'

Specific quotes

6 Sir Humphry Davy
Abominated gravy.
He lived in the odium
Of having discovered Sodium.

Edmund Clerihew Bentley (1875–1956) British writer.
Biography for Beginners

7 Edison, whose inventions did as much as any to add to our material convenience, wasn't what we would call a scientist at all, but a supreme 'do-it-yourself' man – the successor to Benjamin Franklin.

Kenneth Clark (1903–83) British art historian.
Civilisation

8 I believe the souls of five hundred Sir Isaac Newtons would go to the making up of a Shakespeare or a Milton.

Samuel Taylor Coleridge (1772–1834) British poet.
Letter to Thomas Poole, 23 Mar 1801

9 I went to the Society where were divers experiments in Mr Boyle's Pneumatic Engine. We put in a snake but could not kill it by exhausting the air, only making it extremely sick, but a chick died of convulsions in a short space.

John Evelyn (1620–1706) English diarist.
Diary, 22 Apr 1661

10 Einstein – the greatest Jew since Jesus. I have no doubt that Einstein's name will still be remembered and revered when Lloyd George, Foch and William Hohenzollern share with Charlie Chaplin that uneluctable oblivion which awaits the uncreative mind.

J. B. S. Haldane (1892–1964) British geneticist.
Daedalus or Science and the Future

11 Bacon discovered the art of making reading-glasses . . . and various other mathematical and astronomical instruments. . . . That the ingredients of gunpowder and the art of making it were known to him is now undeniable; but the *humane philosopher* dreading the consequences of communicating the discovery to the world, transposed the letters of the Latin words which signify charcoal, which made the whole obscure.

Robert Henry
History of England

12 Had he not been an untidy man and apt to leave his cultures exposed on the laboratory table the spore of hyssop mould, the *penicillin notatum*, might never have floated in from Praed Street and settled on his dish of staphylococci.

André Maurois (Émile Herzog; 1885–1967) French writer.
Life of Alexander Fleming

13 Nature, and Nature's laws lay hid in night:
God said, Let *Newton be!* and all was light.

Alexander Pope (1688–1744) British poet.
For a reply, *see* John Collings SQUIRE
Epitaphs, 'Intended for Sir Isaac Newton'

14 It did not last: the Devil howling 'Ho!
Let Einstein be!' restored the status quo.

John Collings Squire (1884–1958) British journalist.
Answer to POPE's Epitaph for Newton
Epigrams, 'The Dilemma'

15 He snatched the lightning shaft from heaven, and the sceptre from tyrants.

Anne-Robert-Jacques Turgot (1727–81) French economist.
An inscription for a bust of Benjamin Franklin, alluding both to Franklin's invention of the lightning conductor and to his role in the American Revolution
Vie de Turgot (A. N. de Condorcet)

16 Already for thirty-five years he had not stopped talking and almost nothing of fundamental value had emerged.

James Dewey Watson (1928–) US geneticist.
Referring to Francis Crick
The Double Helix, Ch. 8

SCOTLAND

See also Britain, Scots

1 O ye'll tak' the high road, and I'll tak' the low road,
And I'll be in Scotland afore ye,
But me and my true love will never meet again,

On the bonnie, bonnie banks o' Loch Lomon'.
Anonymous
The Bonnie Banks o' Loch Lomon'

2 My heart's in the Highlands, my heart is not here;
My heart's in the Highlands a-chasing the deer;
Chasing the wild deer, and following the roe,
My heart's in the Highlands, wherever I go.
Robert Burns (1759–96) Scottish poet.
My Heart's in the Highlands

3 *Oats*. A grain, which in England is generally given to horses, but in Scotland supports the people.
Samuel Johnson (1709–84) British lexicographer.
Dictionary of the English Language

4 Norway, too, has noble wild prospects; and Lapland is remarkable for prodigious noble wild prospects. But, Sir, let me tell you, the noblest prospect which a Scotchman ever sees, is the high road that leads him to England!
Samuel Johnson
Life of Johnson (J. Boswell), Vol. I

5 Seeing Scotland, Madam, is only seeing a worse England.
Samuel Johnson
Life of Johnson (J. Boswell), Vol. III

6 Roamin' in the gloamin',
By the bonny banks of Clyde.
Harry Lauder (Hugh MacLennon; 1870–1950) Scottish music-hall artist.
Song

7 O Caledonia! stern and wild,
Meet nurse for a poetic child!
Land of brown heath and shaggy wood,
Land of the mountain and the flood,
Land of my sires! what mortal hand
Can e'er untie the filial band
That knits me to thy rugged strand!
Walter Scott (1771–1832) Scottish novelist.
The Lay of the Last Minstrel, VI

8 That knuckle-end of England – that land of Calvin, oat-cakes, and sulphur.
Sydney Smith (1771–1845) British clergyman and essayist.
Memoir (Lady Holland)

SCOTS

See also British, Scotland

1 You've forgotten the grandest moral attribute of a Scotsman, Maggie, that he'll do nothing which might damage his career.
J. M. Barrie (1860–1937) British novelist and dramatist.
What Every Woman Knows, II

2 There are few more impressive sights in the world than a Scotsman on the make.
J. M. Barrie
What Every Woman Knows, II

3 A Scotchman must be a very sturdy moralist who does not love Scotland better than truth.
Samuel Johnson (1709–84) British lexicographer.
Journey to the Western Islands of Scotland, 'Col'

4 BOSWELL. I do indeed come from Scotland, but I cannot help it . . .
JOHNSON. That, Sir, I find, is what a very great many of your countrymen cannot help.
Samuel Johnson
Life of Johnson (J. Boswell), Vol. I

5 Much may be made of a Scotchman, if he be *caught* young.
Samuel Johnson
Life of Johnson (J. Boswell), Vol. II
Referring to Lord Mansfield

6 Their learning is like bread in a besieged town: every man gets a little, but no man gets a full meal.
Samuel Johnson
Life of Johnson (J. Boswell), Vol. II
Referring to education in Scotland

7 I have been trying all my life to like Scotchmen, and am obliged to desist from the experiment in despair.
Charles Lamb (1775–1834) British essayist.
Essays of Elia, 'Imperfect Sympathies'

8 In all my travels I never met with any one Scotchman but what was a man of sense. I believe everybody of that country that has any, leaves it as fast as they can.
Francis Lockier (1667–1740) English writer.
Anecdotes (Joseph Spence)

9 Join a Highland regiment, me boy. The kilt is an unrivalled garment for fornication and diarrhoea.
John Masters (1914–83) British writer.
Bugles and a Tiger

10 It's ill taking the breeks aff a wild Highlandman.
Walter Scott (1771–1832) Scottish novelist.
The Fair Maid of Perth, Ch. 5

11 It is never difficult to distinguish between a Scotsman with a grievance and a ray of sunshine.
P. G. Wodehouse (1881–1975) British humorous novelist.
Wodehouse at Work to the End (Richard Usborne), Ch. 8

SCULPTURE

See art, artists

SEA

See also boats, Navy, seaside

1 The sea is calm to-night,
The tide is full, the moon lies fair
Upon the Straits.
Matthew Arnold (1822–88) British poet and critic.
Dover Beach

2 For all at last return to the sea – to
Oceanus, the ocean river, like the ever-
flowing stream of time, the beginning and the
end.
Rachel Carson (1907–64) US biologist.
The Sea Around Us
The closing words of the book

3 The voice of the sea speaks to the soul. The
touch of the sea is sensuous, enfolding the
body in its soft, close embrace.
Kate Chopin (1851–1904) US writer.
The Awakening, Ch. 6

4 The ice was here, the ice was there,
The ice was all around:
It cracked and growled, and roared and
howled,
Like noises in a swound!
Samuel Taylor Coleridge (1772–1834) British poet.
The Rime of the Ancient Mariner, I

5 We are as near to heaven by sea as by land.
Humphrey Gilbert (c. 1539–83) English navigator.
A Book of Anecdotes (D. George)
Remark made shortly before he went down with his ship *Squir-rel*

6 When men come to like a sea-life, they are
not fit to live on land.
Samuel Johnson (1709–84) British lexicographer.
Life of Johnson (J. Boswell), Vol. II

7 The snotgreen sea. The scrotumtightening
sea.
James Joyce (1882–1941) Irish novelist.
Ulysses

8 It keeps eternal whisperings around
Desolate shores, and with its mighty swell
Gluts twice ten thousand Caverns.
John Keats (1795–1821) British poet.
On the Sea

9 'Wouldst thou' – so the helmsman
answered–
'Learn the secret of the sea?
Only those who brave its dangers
Comprehend its mystery!'
Henry Wadsworth Longfellow (1807–82) US poet.
The Secret of the Sea

10 I must down to the seas again, to the lonely
sea and the sky,
And all I ask is a tall ship and a star to steer
her by,
And the wheel's kick and the wind's song and
the white sail's shaking,
And a grey mist on the sea's face and a grey
dawn breaking.
John Masefield (1878–1967) British poet.
Sea Fever
Often quoted using 'sea' rather than 'seas', and 'I must go
down' rather than 'I must down'

11 Rocked in the cradle of the deep.
Emma Millard (1787–1870) British songwriter.
Song

12 . . . the sea, trembling with a long line of

radiance, and showing in the clear distance
the sails of vessels stealing in every direction
along its surface.
Ann Radcliffe (1764–1823) British novelist.
The Italian

13 A life on the ocean wave,
A home on the rolling deep.
Epes Sargent (1813–80) US writer and dramatist.
A Life on the Ocean Wave

14 O hear us when we cry to Thee
For those in peril on the sea.
William Whiting (1825–78) British hymn writer.
Eternal Father Strong to Save

15 The sea! the sea!
Xenophon (430–354 BC) Greek historian.
Anabasis, IV:7

SEASIDE

See also sea

1 The Walrus and the Carpenter
Were walking close at hand;
They wept like anything to see
Such quantities of sand:
'If this were only cleared away,'
They said, 'it *would* be grand!'
Lewis Carroll (Charles Lutwidge Dodgson; 1832–98)
British writer.
Through the Looking-Glass, Ch. 4

2 It is the drawback of all sea-side places that
half the landscape is unavailable for purposes
of human locomotion, being covered by
useless water.
Norman Douglas (1868–1952) British novelist.
Alone, 'Mentone'

3 I do Like to be Beside the Seaside.
John A. Glover-Kind (19th century) US songwriter.
Song title

SEASONS

See also months

1 Sumer is icumen in,
Lhude sing cuccu!
Groweth sed, and bloweth med,
And springth the wude nu.
Anonymous
Cuckoo Song

2 Many human beings say that they enjoy the
winter, but what they really enjoy is feeling
proof against it.
Richard Adams (1920–) British novelist.
Watership Down, Ch. 50

3 All the live murmur of a summer's day.
Matthew Arnold (1882–88) British poet and critic.
The Scholar Gipsy

4 It is time for the destruction of error.
The chairs are being brought in from the
garden.

The summer talk stopped on that savage coast
Before the storms.
W. H. Auden (1907–73) British poet.
It is time

5   My beloved spake, and said unto me, Rise
up, my love, my fair one, and come away.
For, lo, the winter is past, the rain is over
and gone;
The flowers appear on the earth; the time of
the singing of birds is come, and the voice of
the turtle is heard in our land.
Bible: Song of Solomon
2:10–12

6   Now Spring, sweet laxative of Georgian
strains,
Quickens the ink in literary veins,
The Stately Homes of England ope their doors
To piping Nancy-boys and Crashing Bores.
Roy Campbell (1901–57) South African poet.
The Georgiad

7   Summer has set in with its usual severity.
Samuel Taylor Coleridge (1772–1834) British poet.
Quoted in Lamb's letter to V. Novello, 9 May 1826

8   Summer afternoon – summer afternoon; to
me those have always been the two most
beautiful words in the English language.
Henry James (1843–1916) US novelist.
A Backward Glance (Edith Wharton), Ch. 10

9   St Agnes Eve – Ah, bitter chill it was!
The owl, for all his feathers, was a-cold;
The hare limp'd trembling through the frozen
grass,
And silent was the flock in woolly fold.
John Keats (1795–1821) British poet.
The Eve of Saint Agnes, I

10 Four seasons fill the measure of the year;
There are four seasons in the mind of men.
John Keats
Four Seasons

11 Where are the songs of Spring? Ay, where
are they?
John Keats
To Autumn

12 Season of mists and mellow fruitfulness,
Close bosom-friend of the maturing sun;
Conspiring with him how to load and bless
With fruit the vines that round the thatch-
eaves run.
John Keats
To Autumn

13 No one thinks of winter when the grass is
green!
Rudyard Kipling (1865–1936) Indian-born British writer.
A St Helena Lullaby

14 In a somer season, when soft was the sonne.
William Langland (c. 1330–c. 1400) English poet.
The Vision of Piers Plowman, Prologue

15 Russia has two generals in whom she can
confide – Generals Janvier and Février.
Nicholas I (1796–1855) Tsar of Russia.
Referring to the Russian winter. Nicholas himself succumbed
to a February cold in 1855 – the subject of the famous
Punch Cartoon, 'General Février turned traitor', 10 Mar
1855
Attrib.

16 Winter is icummen in,
Lhude sing Goddamm,
Raineth drop and staineth slop
And how the wind doth ramm!
Sing: Goddamm.
Ezra Pound (1885–1972) US poet.
Ancient Music

17 Spring has returned. The earth is like a child
that knows poems.
Rainer Maria Rilke (1875–1926) Austrian poet.
Die Sonette an Orpheus, I, 21

18 In the bleak mid-winter
Frosty wind made moan,
Earth stood hard as iron,
Water like a stone;
Snow had fallen, snow on snow,
Snow on snow,
In the bleak mid-winter,
Long ago.
Christina Rossetti (1830–74) British poet.
Mid-Winter

19 The country habit has me by the heart,
For he's bewitched for ever who has seen,
Not with his eyes but with his vision, Spring
Flow down the woods and stipple leaves with
sun.
Vita Sackville-West (Victoria Sackville-West; 1892–1962)
British poet and novelist.
The Land, 'Winter'

20 When icicles hang by the wall,
And Dick the shepherd blows his nail,
And Tom bears logs into the hall,
And milk comes frozen home in pail,
When blood is nipp'd, and ways be foul,
Then nightly sings the staring owl:
'Tu-who;
Tu-whit, Tu-who' – A merry note.
While greasy Joan doth keel the pot.
William Shakespeare (1564–1616) English dramatist.
Love's Labour's Lost, V:2

21 If Winter comes, can Spring be far behind?
Percy Bysshe Shelley (1792–1822) British poet.
Ode to the West Wind

22 When the hounds of spring are on winter's
traces,
The mother of months in meadow or plain
Fills the shadows and windy places
With lisp of leaves and ripple of rain . . .
Algernon Charles Swinburne (1837–1909) British poet.
Atlanta in Calydon

23 The moans of doves in immemorial elms,

And murmuring of innumerable bees.
Alfred, Lord Tennyson (1809–92) British poet.
The Princess, VII

24 In the Spring a young man's fancy lightly
turns to thoughts of love.
Alfred, Lord Tennyson
Locksley Hall

25 It is a winter's tale
That the snow blind twilight ferries over the
lakes
And floating fields from the farm in the cup of
the vales.
Dylan Thomas (1914–53) Welsh poet.
A Winter's Tale

26 Spring is come home with her world-
wandering feet.
And all the things are made young with young
desires.
Francis Thompson (1859–1907) British poet.
The Night of Forebeing, 'Ode to Easter'

27 The comic almanacs give us dreadful pictures
of January and February; but, in truth, the
months which should be made to look gloomy
in England are March and April. Let no man
boast himself that he has got through the
perils of winter till at least the seventh of
May.
Anthony Trollope (1815–82) British novelist.
Doctor Thorne, Ch. 47

28 Like an army defeated
The snow hath retreated.
William Wordsworth (1770–1850) British poet.
Written in March

SECRECY

See also gossip

1 Only the nose knows
Where the nose goes
When the door close.
Muhammad Ali (Cassius Clay; 1942–) US boxer.
Remark, reported by Al Silverman
When asked whether a boxer should have sex before a big
fight

2 I have seldom spoken with greater regret,
for my lips are not yet unsealed. Were these
troubles over I would make a case, and I
guarantee that not a man would go into the
Lobby against us.
Stanley Baldwin (1867–1947) British statesman.
Speech, House of Commons, 10 Dec 1935
Referring to the Abyssinian crisis; usually misquoted as 'My
lips are sealed'

3 Curse not the king, no not in thy thought;
and curse not the rich in thy bedchamber: for
a bird of the air shall carry the voice, and
that which hath wings shall tell the matter.
Bible: Ecclesiastes
10:20

4 If thou hast heard a word, let it die with
thee; and be bold, it will not burst thee.
Bible: Ecclesiasticus
19:10

5 Stolen waters are sweet, and bread eaten in
secret is pleasant.
Bible: Proverbs
9:17

6 Mum's the word.
George Colman, the Younger (1762–1836) British
dramatist.
The Battle of Hexham, II:1

7 O fie miss, you must not kiss and tell.
William Congreve (1670–1729) British Restoration
dramatist.
Love for Love, II:10

8 I know that's a secret, for it's whispered
every where.
William Congreve
Love for Love, III:3

9 Three may keep a secret, if two of them are
dead.
Benjamin Franklin (1706–90) US scientist and statesman.
Poor Richard's Almanack

10 It is a secret in the Oxford sense: you may
tell it to only one person at a time.
Oliver Franks (1905–   ) British philosopher and
administrator.
Sunday Telegraph, 30 Jan 1977

SELF

See also self-confidence, etc.

1 Every man is his own worst enemy.
Proverb

2 God helps them that help themselves.
Proverb

3 He helps little that helps not himself.
Proverb

4 He travels fastest who travels alone.
Proverb

5 Lord, deliver me from myself.
Thomas Browne (1605–82) English physician and writer.
Religio Medici, Pt. II

6 I have always disliked myself at any given
moment; the total of such moments is my
life.
Cyril Connolly (1903–74) British journalist.
Enemies of Promise, Ch. 18

7 But I do nothing upon myself, and yet I am
mine own Executioner.
John Donne (1573–1631) English poet.
Devotions, 12

8 We never remark any passion or principle in

others, of which, in some degree or other, we may not find a parallel in ourselves.

David Hume (1711–76) Scottish philosopher.
A Treatise of Human Nature

9 Whenever I look inside myself I am afraid.

Cyril Joad (1891–1953) British writer and broadcaster.
The Observer, 'Sayings of the Week', 8 Nov 1942

10 All censure of a man's self is oblique praise. It is in order to shew how much he can spare.

Samuel Johnson (1709–84) British lexicographer.
Life of Johnson (J. Boswell), Vol. III

11 One should examine oneself for a very long time before thinking of condemning others.

Molière (Jean Baptiste Poquelin; 1622–73) French dramatist.
Le Misanthrope, III:4

12 Self-love seems so often unrequited.

Anthony Powell (1905–) British novelist.
The Acceptance World

13 Do not love your neighbour as yourself. If you are on good terms with yourself it is an impertinence; if on bad, an injury.

George Bernard Shaw (1856–1950) Irish dramatist and critic.
Man and Superman, 'Maxims for Revolutionists'

14 The unexamined life is not worth living.

Socrates (469–399 BC) Athenian philosopher.
Apology (Plato)

15 I am always with myself, and it is I who am my tormentor.

Leo Tolstoy (1828–1910) Russian writer.
Memoirs of a Madman

16 Meanwhile you will write an essay on 'self-indulgence'. There will be a prize of half a crown for the longest essay, irrespective of any possible merit.

Evelyn Waugh (1903–66) British novelist.
Decline and Fall, Pt. I, Ch. 5

17 I can't quite explain it, but I don't believe one can ever be unhappy for long provided one does just exactly what one wants to and when one wants to.

Evelyn Waugh
Decline and Fall, Pt. I, Ch. 5

18 I celebrate myself, and sing myself,
And what I assume you shall assume.

Walt Whitman (1819–92) US poet.
Song of Myself, 1

19 Behold, I do not give lectures or a little charity,
When I give I give myself.

Walt Whitman
Song of Myself, 40

20 I have said that the soul is not more than the body,
And I have said that the body is not more than the soul,

And nothing, but God, is greater to one than one's self is.

Walt Whitman
Song of Myself, 48

21 Do I contradict myself?
Very well then I contradict myself,
(I am large, I contain multitudes).

Walt Whitman
Song of Myself, 51

SELF-CONFIDENCE

See also shyness

1 Those who believe that they are exclusively in the right are generally those who achieve something.

Aldous Huxley (1894–1964) British novelist.
Proper Studies

2 I can honestly say that I was never affected by the question of the success of an undertaking. If I felt it was the right thing to do, I was for it regardless of the possible outcome.

Golda Meir (1898–1978) Russian-born Israeli stateswoman.
Golda Meir: Woman with a Cause (Marie Syrkin)

3 I wish I was as cocksure of anything as Tom Macaulay is of everything.

Lord Melbourne (1779–1848) British statesman.
Preface to Lord Melbourne's Papers (Earl Cowper)

4 'Tis an ill cook that cannot lick his own fingers.

William Shakespeare (1564–1616) English dramatist.
Romeo and Juliet, IV:2

5 'Are you not,' a Rugby master had asked him in discussing one of his essays, 'a little out of your depth here?' 'Perhaps, Sir,' was the confident reply, 'but I can swim.'

William Temple (1881–1944) British churchman.
William Temple (F. A. Iremonger)

6 I am certain that we will win the election with a good majority. Not that I am ever over-confident.

Margaret Thatcher (1925–) British politician and prime minister.
Evening Standard, 1987

7 If I ever felt inclined to be timid as I was going into a room full of people, I would say to myself, 'You're the cleverest member of one of the cleverest families in the cleverest class of the cleverest nation in the world, why should you be frightened?'

Beatrice Webb (1858–1943) British economist and writer.
Portraits from Memory (Bertrand Russell), 'Sidney and Beatrice Webb'

SELF-CONTROL

1 He that is slow to anger is better than the

mighty; and he that ruleth his spirit than he that taketh a city.

Bible: Proverbs
16:32

2 No one who cannot limit himself has ever been able to write.

Nicolas Boileau (1636–1711) French writer.
L'Art poétique, I

3 The highest possible stage in moral culture is when we recognize that we ought to control our thoughts.

Charles Darwin (1809–82) British life scientist.
Descent of Man, Ch. 4

4 When things are steep, remember to stay level-headed.

Horace (Quintus Horatius Flaccus; 65–8 BC) Roman poet.
Odes, II

5 If you can keep your head when all about you
Are losing theirs and blaming it on you.

Rudyard Kipling (1865–1936) Indian-born British writer.
If

6 He that would govern others, first should be The master of himself.

Philip Massinger (1583–1640) English dramatist.
The Bondman, I

7 Never lose your temper with the Press or the public is a major rule of political life.

Christabel Pankhurst (1880–1958) British suffragette.
Unshackled

SELF-DENIAL

See also abstinence, selflessness

1 Self-denial is not a virtue; it is only the effect of prudence on rascality.

George Bernard Shaw (1856–1950) Irish dramatist and critic.
Man and Superman, 'Maxims for Revolutionists'

2 Thy need is yet greater than mine.

Philip Sidney (1554–86) English poet and courtier.
Attrib.
Giving his own water bottle to a humble wounded soldier after he had himself been wounded

SELF-INTEREST

See also parochialism, selfishness

1 Every man for himself, and the devil take the hindmost.

Proverb

2 The land self-interest groans from shore to shore,
For fear that plenty should attain the poor.

Lord Byron (1788–1824) British poet.
The Age of Bronze, XIV

3 Anyone informed that the universe is expanding and contracting in pulsations of

eighty billion years has a right to ask, 'What's in it for me?'

Peter De Vries (1910–) US novelist.
The Glory of the Hummingbird, Ch. 1

4 The least pain in our little finger gives us more concern and uneasiness than the destruction of millions of our fellow-beings.

William Hazlitt (1778–1830) British essayist.
American Literature, 'Dr Channing'

5 It is difficult to love mankind unless one has a reasonable private income and when one has a reasonable private income one has better things to do than loving mankind.

Hugh Kingsmill (1889–1949) British writer.
God's Apology (R. Ingrams)

6 Self-interest speaks all sorts of tongues, and plays all sorts of roles, even that of disinterestedness.

Duc de la Rochefoucauld (1613–80) French writer.
Maximes, 39

SELFISHNESS

See also egotism, self-interest

1 I have been a selfish being all my life, in practice, though not in principle.

Jane Austen (1775–1817) British novelist.
Pride and Prejudice, Ch. 58

2 And this the burthen of his song,
For ever us'd to be,
I care for nobody, not I,
If no one cares for me.

Isaac Bickerstaffe (c. 1735–c. 1812) Irish dramatist.
Love in a Village, I

3 It's 'Damn you, Jack – I'm all right!' with you chaps.

David Bone (1874–1959) British sea captain and writer.
The Brassbounder, Ch. 3

4 The proud, the cold untroubled heart of stone,
That never mused on sorrow but its own.

Thomas Campbell (1777–1844) British poet.
Pleasures of Hope, I

SELF-KNOWLEDGE

1 Resolve to be thyself: and know, that he Who finds himself, loses his misery.

Matthew Arnold (1822–88) British poet and critic.
Self-Dependence

2 We confess our bad qualities to others out of fear of appearing naive or ridiculous by not being aware of them.

Gerald Brenan (Edward Fitzgerald Brenan; 1894–1987) British writer.
Thoughts in a Dry Season

3 'I know myself,' he cried, 'but that is all.'

F. Scott Fitzgerald (1896–1940) US novelist.
This Side of Paradise, Bk. II, Ch. 5

4 I do not know myself, and God forbid that I
should.
Goethe (1749–1832) German poet and dramatist.
Conversations with Eckermann, 10 Apr 1829

5 Know then thyself, presume not God to
scan,
The proper study of Mankind is Man.
Alexander Pope (1688–1744) British poet.
An Essay on Man, II

6 That true self-love and social are the same;
That virtue only makes our bliss below;
And all our knowledge is, ourselves to know.
Alexander Pope
An Essay on Man, IV

SELFLESSNESS

See also charity, self-denial

1 The way to get things done is not to mind
who gets the credit of doing them.
Benjamin Jowett (1817–93) British theologian.
Attrib.

2 To give and not to count the cost;
To fight and not to heed the wounds;
To toil and not to seek for rest;
To labour and not ask for any reward
Save that of knowing that we do Thy will.
St Ignatius Loyola (1491–1556) Spanish priest.
Prayer for Generosity

3 There is nothing in Christianity or Buddhism
that quite matches the sympathetic
unselfishness of an oyster.
Saki (Hector Hugh Munro; 1870–1916) British writer.
Chronicles of Clovis

SELF-MADE MEN

1 I know he is, and he adores his maker.
Benjamin Disraeli (1804–81) British statesman.
The Fine Art of Political Wit (L. Harris)
Replying to a remark made in defence of John Bright that he
was a self-made man

2 He was a self-made man who owed his lack
of success to nobody.
Joseph Heller (1923–) US novelist.
Catch-22, Ch. 3

3 A self-made man is one who believes in luck
and sends his son to Oxford.
Christina Stead (1902–83) Australian novelist.
House of All Nations, 'Credo'

SELF-PRESERVATION

See also survival

1 Look after number one.
Proverb

2 He that fights and runs away
May live to fight another day.
Anonymous
Musarum Deliciae

3 This animal is very bad; when attacked it
defends itself.
Anonymous
La Ménagerie (P. K. Théodore), 1828

4 In good King Charles's golden days,
When loyalty no harm meant,
A zealous High Churchman was I,
And so I got preferment.

And this is law, that I'll maintain,
Unto my dying day, Sir,
That whatsoever King shall reign,
I'll be the Vicar of Bray, Sir.
Anonymous
The Vicar of Bray

5 There was only one catch and that was
Catch-22, which specified that a concern for
one's own safety in the face of dangers that
were real and immediate was the process of
a rational mind.
Joseph Heller (1923–) US novelist.
Catch-22, Ch. 5

6 If a madman were to come into this room
with a stick in his hand, no doubt we should
pity the state of his mind; but our primary
consideration would be to take care of
ourselves. We should knock him down first,
and pity him afterwards.
Samuel Johnson (1709–84) British lexicographer.
Life of Johnson (J. Boswell), Vol. III

7 We intend to remain alive. Our neighbors
want to see us dead. This is not a question
that leaves much room for compromise.
Golda Meir (1898–1978) Russian-born Israeli
stateswoman.
Reader's Digest (July 1971), 'The Indestructible Golda Meir'

8 The better part of valour is discretion; in the
which better part I have saved my life.
William Shakespeare (1564–1616) English dramatist.
Henry IV, Part One, V:4

9 *J'ai vécu.*
I survived.
Abbé de Sieyès (1748–1836) French churchman.
Dictionnaire Encyclopédique (E. Guérard)
Replying to an enquiry concerning what he had done during the
Terror

10 Greater love hath no man than this, that he
lay down his friends for his life.
Jeremy Thorpe (1929–) British politician.
The Pendulum Years (Bernard Levin), Ch. 12
After Macmillan's 1962 Cabinet reshuffle

11 Scheherazade is the classical example of a
woman saving her head by using it.
Esme Wynne-Tyson (1898–) British writer.
Attrib.

SELF-RELIANCE

See also independence

1 If you want a thing well done, do it yourself.
Proverb

2 The gods help them that help themselves.
Aesop (6th century BC) Reputed Greek writer of fables.
Fables, 'Hercules and the Waggoner'

3 They do most by Books, who could do much
without them, and he that chiefly owes
himself unto himself, is the substantial Man.
Thomas Browne (1605–82) English physician and writer.
Christian Morals, Pt. II

4 Let the boy win his spurs.
Edward III (1312–77) King of England.
Attrib.
Replying to a suggestion that he should send reinforcements to
his son, the Black Prince, during the Battle of Crécy, 1346

5 The first rule in opera is the first rule in life:
see to everything yourself.
Nellie Melba (Helen Porter Mitchell; 1861–1931)
Australian soprano.
Melodies and Memories

6 The greatest thing in the world is to know
how to be self-sufficient.
Michel de Montaigne (1533–92) French essayist.
Essais, I

7 Our remedies oft in ourselves do lie,
Which we ascribe to heaven.
William Shakespeare (1564–1616) English dramatist.
All's Well that Ends Well, I:1

SELF-RESPECT

See also pride, respect

1 It is better to die on your feet than to live
on your knees.
Dolores Ibarruri (1895–1989) Spanish politician.
Speech, Paris, 1936

2 As for conceit, what man will do any good
who is not conceited? Nobody holds a good
opinion of a man who has a low opinion of
himself.
Anthony Trollope (1815–82) British novelist.
Orley Farm, Ch. 22

3 And, above all things, never think that you're
not good enough yourself. A man should
never think that. My belief is that in life
people will take you very much at your own
reckoning.
Anthony Trollope
The Small House at Allington, Ch. 32

4 When people do not respect us we are
sharply offended; yet deep down in his heart
no man much respects himself.
Mark Twain (Samuel Langhorne Clemens; 1835–1910)
US writer.
Notebooks

SENSATION

1 O for a life of sensations rather than of
thoughts!
John Keats (1795–1821) British poet.
Letter to Benjamin Bailey, 22 Nov 1817

2 'The story is like the wind', the Bushman
prisoner said. 'It comes from a far off place,
and we feel it.'
Laurens Van der Post (1906–) South African novelist.
A Story Like the Wind

SENTIMENTALITY

See also emotion

1 They had been corrupted by money, and he
had been corrupted by sentiment. Sentiment
was the more dangerous, because you
couldn't name its price. A man open to bribes
was to be relied upon below a certain figure,
but sentiment might uncoil in the heart at a
name, a photograph, even a smell
remembered.
Graham Greene (1904–) British novelist.
The Heart of the Matter

2 Sentimentality is a superstructure covering
brutality.
Carl Gustav Jung (1875–1961) Swiss psychoanalyst.
Reflections

3 One may not regard the world as a sort of
metaphysical brothel for emotions.
Arthur Koestler (1905–83) Hungarian-born British writer.
Darkness at Noon, 'The Second Hearing'

4 Sentimentality is only sentiment that rubs you
up the wrong way.
W. Somerset Maugham (1874–1965) British novelist.
A Writer's Notebook

5 She likes stories that make her cry – I think
we all do, it's so nice to feel sad when
you've nothing particular to be sad about.
Annie Sullivan (1866–1936) US teacher of the
handicapped.
Letter, 12 Dec 1887
Referring to Helen Keller

SEPARATION

See also absence, parting

1 My Bonnie lies over the ocean,
My Bonnie lies over the sea,
My Bonnie lies over the ocean,
Oh, bring back my Bonnie to me.
Anonymous
My Bonnie

2 If I should meet thee
After long years,
How should I greet thee? –
With silence and tears.
Lord Byron (1788–1824) British poet.
When we two parted

3 Absence from whom we love is worse than death.

William Cowper (1731–1800) British poet.
'Hope, like the Short-lived Ray'

4 As it will be the right of all, so it will be the duty of some, definitely to prepare for a separation, amicably if they can, violently if they must.

Josiah Quincy (1772–1864) US statesman.
Abridgement of Debates of Congress, Vol. IV, 14 Jan 1811

5 Every parting gives a foretaste of death; every coming together again a foretaste of the resurrection.

Arthur Schopenhauer (1788–1860) German philosopher.
Gedanken über vielerlei Gegenstände, XXVI

6 I do desire we may be better strangers.

William Shakespeare (1564–1616) English dramatist.
As You Like It, III:2

SERIOUSNESS

1 Angels can fly because they take themselves lightly.

G. K. Chesterton (1874–1936) British writer.
Orthodoxy, Ch. 7

2 Though this may be play to you, 'tis death to us.

Roger L'Estrange (1616–1704) English journalist and writer.
Aesop's Fables, 398

3 You must not think me necessarily foolish because I am facetious, nor will I consider you necessarily wise because you are grave.

Sydney Smith (1771–1845) British clergyman and essayist.
Letter to Bishop Blomfield

4 He rose by gravity; I sank by levity.

Sydney Smith
Attrib.
Comparing his career with that of his brother, Robert Percy Smith

SERMONS

See also brevity, speeches, verbosity

1 They are written as if sin were to be taken out of man like Eve out of Adam – by putting him to sleep.

Sydney Smith (1771–1845) British clergyman and essayist.
Anecdotes of the Clergy (J. Larwood)
Referring to boring sermons

2 I never quite forgave Mahaffy for getting himself suspended from preaching in the College Chapel. Ever since his sermons were discontinued, I suffer from insomnia in church.

George Tyrrell (1861–1909) Irish Catholic theologian.
As I Was Going Down Sackville Street (Oliver St John Gogarty), Ch. 25

3 Yes, about ten minutes.

Duke of Wellington (1769–1852) British general and statesman.
Attrib.
Responding to a vicar's query as to whether there was anything he would like his forthcoming sermon to be about

SERVICE

See also help

1 His lord said unto him, Well done, thou good and faithful servant: thou hast been faithful over a few things, I will make thee ruler over many things: enter thou into the joy of thy lord.

Bible: Matthew
25:21

2 Oh that I were an orange-tree,
That busy plant!
Then I should ever laden be,
And never want
Some fruit for Him that dressed me.

George Herbert (1593–1633) English poet.
Employment

3 All English shop assistants are Miltonists. All Miltonists firmly believe that 'they serve who only stand and wait.'

George Mikes (1912–87) Hungarian-born British writer.
How to be Inimitable

4 God doth not need
Either man's work or his own gifts. Who best
Bear his mild yoke, they serve him best: his state
Is kingly; thousands at his bidding speed,
And post o'er land and ocean without rest;
They also serve who only stand and wait.

John Milton (1608–74) English poet.
Sonnet: 'On his Blindness'

5 Small service is true service, while it lasts.

William Wordsworth (1770–1850) British poet.
To a Child, Written in her Album

SERVILITY

See also flattery, humility

1 Fine words and an insinuating appearance are seldom associated with true virtue.

Confucius (K'ung Fu-tzu; 551–479 BC) Chinese philosopher.
Analects

2 I am well aware that I am the 'umblest person going . . . .My mother is likewise a very 'umble person. We live in a numble abode.

Charles Dickens (1812–70) British novelist.
David Copperfield, Ch. 16
Said by Uriah Heep

3 Uriah, with his long hands slowly twining

over one another, made a ghastly writhe
from the waist upwards.
Charles Dickens
David Copperfield, Ch. 17

4 A pious man is one who would be an atheist
if the king were.
Jean de La Bruyère (1645–96) French satirist.
Les Caractères

5 Wit that can creep, and pride that licks the
dust.
Alexander Pope (1688–1744) British poet.
Epistle to Dr. Arbuthnot

6 You know that nobody is strongminded
around a President . . . it is always: 'yes sir',
'no sir' (the 'no sir' comes when he asks
whether you're dissatisfied).
George Edward Reedy (1917–) US government
official.
The White House (ed. R. Gordon Hoxie)

7 Whenever he met a great man he grovelled
before him, and my-lorded him as only a
free-born Briton can do.
William Makepeace Thackeray (1811–63) British
novelist.
Vanity Fair, Ch. 13

SEX

See also abstinence, adultery, animalism, contraception, debauchery, illegitimacy, lust, pornography, promiscuity, prudery, purity, sexes

1 Is sex dirty? Only if it's done right.
Woody Allen (Allen Stewart Konigsberg; 1935–) US
film actor.
All You've Ever Wanted to Know About Sex

2 It was the most fun I ever had without
laughing.
Woody Allen
Annie Hall

3 Don't knock it, it's sex with someone you
love.
Woody Allen
Annie Hall
Referring to masturbation

4 She sighed, she cried, she damned near died:
she said 'What shall I do?'
So I took her into bed and covered up her head
Just to save her from the foggy, foggy dew.
Anonymous
Weaver's Song

5 It is called in our schools 'beastliness', and
this is about the best name for it . . . should
it become a habit it quickly destroys both
health and spirits; he becomes feeble in body
and mind, and often ends in a lunatic asylum.
Robert Baden-Powell (1857–1941) British soldier and
founder of the Boy Scouts.
Referring to masturbation
Scouting for Boys

6 The great and terrible step was taken. What

else could you expect from a girl so
expectant? 'Sex,' said Frank Harris, 'is the
gateway to life.' So I went through the
gateway in an upper room in the Cafe Royal.
Enid Bagnold (1889–1981) British playwright.
Enid Bagnold's Autobiography

7 Money, it turned out, was exactly like sex,
you thought of nothing else if you didn't have
it and thought of other things if you did.
James Baldwin (1924–87) US writer.
Nobody Knows My Name

8 If God had meant us to have group sex, I
guess he'd have given us all more organs.
Malcolm Bradbury (1932–) British academic and
novelist.
Who Do You Think You Are?, 'A Very Hospitable Person'

9 It doesn't matter what you do in the
bedroom as long as you don't do it in the
street and frighten the horses.
Mrs Patrick Campbell (Beatrice Stella Tanner; 1865–
1940) British actress.
The Duchess of Jermyn Street (Daphne Fielding), Ch. 2

10 The Summer hath his joys,
And Winter his delights.
Though Love and all his pleasures are but
toys,
They shorten tedious nights.
Thomas Campion (1567–1620) English poet.
Now Winter Nights Enlarge

11 I'll wager you that in 10 years it will be
fashionable again to be a virgin.
Barbara Cartland (1902–) British romantic novelist.
The Observer, 'Sayings of the Week', 20 June 1976

12 I answer 20 000 letters a year and so many
couples are having problems because they
are not getting the right proteins and
vitamins.
Barbara Cartland
The Observer, 'Sayings of the Week', 31 Aug 1986

13 I said 10 years ago that in 10 years time it
would be smart to be a virgin. Now everyone
is back to virgins again.
Barbara Cartland
The Observer, 'Sayings of the Week', 12 July 1987

14 Have you not as yet observed that pleasure,
which is undeniably the sole motive force
behind the union of the sexes, is
nevertheless not enough to form a bond
between them? And that, if it is preceded by
desire which impels, it is succeeded by
disgust which repels? That is a law of nature
which love alone can alter.
Pierre Choderlos de Laclos (1741–1803) French
novelist.
Les Liaisons Dangereuses, Letter 131

15 She gave me a smile I could feel in my hip
pocket.
Raymond Chandler (1888–1959) US novelist.
Farewell, My Lovely, Ch. 18

16 When she raises her eyelids it's as if she were taking off all her clothes.
Colette (1873–1954) French novelist.
Claudine and Annie

17 No more about sex, it's too boring.
Lawrence Durrell (1912–) British novelist.
Tunc

18 He in a few minutes ravished this fair creature, or at least would have ravished her, if she had not, by a timely compliance, prevented him.
Henry Fielding (1707–54) British novelist.
Jonathan Wild, Bk. III, Ch. 7

19 Older women are best because they always think they may be doing it for the last time.
Ian Fleming (1908–64) British journalist and author.
Life of Ian Fleming (John Pearson)

20 Personally I know nothing about sex because I've always been married.
Zsa Zsa Gabor (1919–) Hungarian-born US film star.
The Observer, 'Sayings of the Week', 16 Aug 1987

21 Prostitution gives her an opportunity to meet people. It provides fresh air and wholesome exercise, and it keeps her out of trouble.
Joseph Heller (1923–) US novelist.
Catch-22, Ch. 33

22 But did thee feel the earth move?
Ernest Hemingway (1899–1961) US novelist.
For Whom the Bell Tolls, Ch. 13

23 My life with girls has ended, though till lately I was up to it and soldiered on not ingloriously; now on this wall will hang my weapons and my lyre, discharged from the war.
Horace (Quintus Horatius Flaccus; 65–8 BC) Roman poet.
Odes, III

24 People will insist . . . on treating the *mons Veneris* as though it were Mount Everest.
Aldous Huxley (1894–1964) British novelist.
Eyeless in Gaza, Ch. 30

25 A million million spermatozoa,
All of them alive:
Out of their cataclysm but one poor Noah
Dare hope to survive.
Aldous Huxley
Fifth Philosopher's Song

26 'Bed,' as the Italian proverb succinctly puts it, 'is the poor man's opera.'
Aldous Huxley
Heaven and Hell

27 Sexual intercourse began
In nineteen sixty-three
(Which was rather late for me) –
Between the end of the *Chatterley* ban
And the Beatles' first LP.
Philip Larkin (1922–85) British poet.
High Windows, 'Annus Mirabilis'

28 When Eve ate this particular apple, she became aware of her own womanhood, mentally. And mentally she began to experiment with it. She has been experimenting ever since. So has man. To the rage and horror of both of them.
D. H. Lawrence (1885–1930) British novelist.
Fantasia of the Unconscious, Ch. 7

29 Making love is the sovereign remedy for anguish.
Frédérick Leboyer (1918–) French obstetrician.
Birth without Violence

30 There was sex of course, but although both of them were extremely interested in sex, and enjoyed nothing better than discussing it, neither of them, if the truth be told, was quite so interested in actually having it, or at any rate in having it very frequently.
David Lodge (1935–) British author.
Nice Work, I

31 No sex without responsibility.
Lord Longford (1905–) British politician and social reformer.
The Observer, 'Sayings of the Week', 3 May 1954

32 The Duke returned from the wars today and did pleasure me in his top-boots.
Sarah, Duchess of Marlborough (1660–1744) Wife of John Churchill, 1st Duke of Marlborough.
Attributed to her in various forms; a more ambitious version goes ' . . . pleasure me three times in his top-boots'

33 FRIAR BARNARDINE. Thou hast committed –
BARABAS. Fornication: but that was in another country;
And beside the wench is dead.
Christopher Marlowe (1564–93) English dramatist.
The Jew of Malta, IV:1

34 Whoever named it necking was a poor judge of anatomy.
Groucho Marx (Julius Marx; 1895–1977) US comedian.
Attrib.

35 If sex is such a natural phenomenon, how come there are so many books on how to?
Bette Midler (1944–) US actress and comedienne.

36 Sex is one of the nine reasons for reincarnation . . . The other eight are unimportant.
Henry Miller (1891–1980) US novelist.
Big Sur and the Oranges of Hieronymus Bosch

37 There was a little girl
Who had a little curl
Right in the middle of her forehead,
When she was good she was very very good
And when she was bad she was very very popular.
Max Miller (Harold Sargent; 1895–1963) British music-hall comedian.
The Max Miller Blue Book

38 The daughter-in-law of Pythagoras said that a woman who goes to bed with a man ought to

lay aside her modesty with her skirt, and put it on again with her petticoat.
Michel de Montaigne (1533–92) French essayist.
Essais, I

39 Why do they put the Gideon Bibles only in the bedrooms where it's usually too late?
Christopher Darlington Morley (1890–1957) US writer.
Quotations for Speakers and Writers

40 The orgasm has replaced the Cross as the focus of longing and the image of fulfilment.
Malcolm Muggeridge (1903–) British writer.
The Most of Malcolm Muggeridge, 'Down with Sex'

41 It has to be admitted that we English have sex on the brain, which is a very unsatisfactory place to have it.
Malcolm Muggeridge
The Observer, 'Sayings of the Decade', 1964

42 It's all any reasonable child can expect if the dad is present at the conception.
Joe Orton (1933–67) British dramatist.
Entertaining Mr Sloane, III

43 If all the young ladies who attended the Yale promenade dance were laid end to end, no one would be the least surprised.
Dorothy Parker (1893–1967) US writer.
While Rome Burns (Alexander Woollcott)

44 I know it does make people happy but to me it is just like having a cup of tea.
Cynthia Payne (1934–) London housewife.
After her acquittal on a charge of controlling prostitutes in a famous 'sex-for-luncheon-vouchers' case, 8 Nov 1987

45 Love is not the dying moan of a distant violin – it's the triumphant twang of a bedspring.
S. J. Perelman (1904–79) US humorous writer.
Quotations for Speakers and Writers (A. Andrews)

46 On a sofa upholstered in panther skin Mona did researches in original sin.
William Plomer (1903–73) South African poet and novelist.
Mews Flat Mona

47 A PUSHING LADY. What are your views on love?
MME LEROI. Love? I make it constantly but I never talk about it.
Marcel Proust (1871–1922) French novelist.
À la recherche du temps perdu: Le Côté de Guermantes

48 The Christian view of sex is that it is, indeed, a form of holy communion.
John Robinson (1919–83) Bishop of Woolwich.
Giving evidence in the prosecution of Penguin Books for publishing *Lady Chatterley's Lover*

49 Sex is something I really don't understand too hot. You never know *where* the hell you are. I keep making up these sex rules for myself, and then I break them right away.
J. D. Salinger (1919–) US novelist.
The Catcher in the Rye, Ch. 9

50 Is it not strange that desire should so many years outlive performance?
William Shakespeare (1564–1616) English dramatist.
Henry IV, Part Two, II:4

51 Lechery, lechery! Still wars and lechery! Nothing else holds fashion.
William Shakespeare
Troilus and Cressida, V:2

52 Someone asked Sophocles, 'How do you feel now about sex? Are you still able to have a woman?' He replied, 'Hush, man; most gladly indeed am I rid of it all, as though I had escaped from a mad and savage master.'
Sophocles (c. 496–406 BC) Greek dramatist.
Republic (Plato), Bk. I

53 Masturbation: the primary sexual activity of mankind. In the nineteenth century it was a disease; in the twentieth, it's a cure.
Thomas Szasz (1920–) US psychiatrist.
The Second Sin

54 Traditionally, sex has been a very private, secretive activity. Herein perhaps lies its powerful force for uniting people in a strong bond. As we make sex less secretive, we may rob it of its power to hold men and women together.
Thomas Szasz
The Second Sin

55 Chasing the naughty couples down the grassgreen gooseberried double bed of the wood.
Dylan Thomas (1914–53) Welsh poet.
Under Milk Wood

56 Old Nat Burge sat . . . He was . . . watching the moon come up lazily out of the old cemetery in which nine of his daughters were lying, and only two of them were dead.
James Thurber (1894–1961) US humorist.
Let Your Mind Alone, 'Bateman Comes Home'

57 Surely you don't mean by unartificial insemination!
James Thurber
Attrib.
On being accosted at a party by a drunk woman who claimed she would like to have a baby by him

58 Familiarity breeds contempt – and children.
Mark Twain (Samuel Langhorne Clemens; 1835–1910) US writer.
Notebooks

59 Sex is the biggest nothing of all time.
Andy Warhol (Andrew Warhola; 1926–87) US pop artist.
Halliwell's Filmgoer's and Video Viewer's Companion

60 All this fuss about sleeping together. For physical pleasure I'd sooner go to my dentist any day.
Evelyn Waugh (1903–66) British novelist.
Vile Bodies, Ch. 6

61 When women go wrong, men go right after them.
Mae West (1892–1980) US actress.
The Wit and Wisdom of Mae West (ed. J. Weintraub)

62 It's not the men in my life that count; it's the life in my men.
Mae West
Attrib.

63 When I'm good I'm very good, but when I'm bad I'm better.
Mae West
Attrib.

64 I shall not say why and how I became, at the age of fifteen, the mistress of the Earl of Craven.
Harriette Wilson (1789–1846) British writer and courtesan.
Memoirs, Opening

65 A mistress should be like a little country retreat near the town, not to dwell in constantly, but only for a night and away.
William Wycherley (1640–1716) English dramatist.
The Country Wife, I:1

SEXES

See also feminism, marriage, men, sex, woman's role, women

1 As men
Do walk a mile, women should talk an hour,
After supper. 'Tis their exercise.
Francis Beaumont (1584–1616) English dramatist.
Philaster, II:4

2 And the man said, The woman whom thou gavest to be with me, she gave me of the tree, and I did eat.
And the Lord God said unto the woman, What is this that thou hast done? And the woman said, The serpent beguiled me, and I did eat.
And the Lord God said unto the serpent, Because thou hast done this, thou art cursed above all cattle, and above every beast of the field; upon thy belly shalt thou go, and dust shalt thou eat all the days of thy life:
And I will put enmity between thee and the woman, and between thy seed and her seed; it shall bruise thy head, and thou shalt bruise his heel.
Unto the woman he said, I will greatly multiply thy sorrow and thy conception; in sorrow thou shalt bring forth children; and thy desire shall be to thy husband, and he shall rule over thee.
And unto Adam he said, Because thou hast hearkened unto the voice of thy wife, and has eaten of the tree, of which I commanded thee, saying, Thou shalt not eat of it: cursed is the ground for thy sake; in sorrow shalt thou eat of it all the days of thy life.
Bible: Genesis
3:12–17

3 Mr. Darwin . . . has failed to hold definitely before his mind the principle that the difference of sex, whatever it may consist in, must itself be subject to natural selection and to evolution.
Antoinette Brown Blackwell (1825–1921) US feminist writer.
The Sexes Throughout Nature

4 Man's love is of man's life a thing apart,
'Tis woman's whole existence.
Lord Byron (1788–1824) British poet.
Don Juan, I

5 There is more difference within the sexes than between them.
Ivy Compton-Burnett (1892–1969) British novelist.
Mother and Son

6 In the sex-war thoughtlessness is the weapon of the male, vindictiveness of the female.
Cyril Connolly (1903–74) British journalist.
The Unquiet Grave

7 The average man is more interested in a woman who is interested in him than he is in a woman – any woman – with beautiful legs.
Marlene Dietrich (Maria Magdalene von Losch; 1904–)
German-born film star.
News item, 13 Dec 1954

8 The reason that husbands and wives do not understand each other is because they belong to different sexes.
Dorothy Dix (Elizabeth Meriwether Gilmer; 1861–1951)
US journalist and writer.
News item

9 I don't think men and women were meant to live together. They are totally different animals.
Diana Dors (1931–84) British actress.
Remark, May 1988

10 Where young boys plan for what they will achieve and attain, young girls plan for whom they will achieve and attain.
Charlotte Perkins Gilman (1860–1935) US writer.
Women and Economics, Ch. 5

11 Man has his will, – but woman has her way.
Oliver Wendell Holmes (1809–94) US writer.
The Autocrat of the Breakfast Table, Prologue

12 Boys will be boys – '
'And even that . . . wouldn't matter if we could only prevent girls from being girls.'
Anthony Hope (Anthony Hope Hawkins; 1863–1933)
British novelist.
The Dolly Dialogues

13 Christ called as his Apostles only men. He did this in a totally free and sovereign way.
John Paul II (Karol Wotjyla; 1920–) Polish pope.
Speech, Sept 1988

14 For men must work, and women must weep,
And there's little to earn, and many to keep,
Though the harbour bar be moaning.
Charles Kingsley (1819–75) British writer.
The Three Fishers

15 The silliest woman can manage a clever man; but it needs a very clever woman to manage a fool.
Rudyard Kipling (1865–1936) Indian-born British writer.
Plain Tales from the Hills, 'Three and – an Extra'

16 Perhaps at fourteen every boy should be in love with some ideal woman to put on a pedestal and worship. As he grows up, of course, he will put her on a pedestal the better to view her legs.
Barry Norman (1933–   ) British cinema critic and broadcaster.
The Listener

17 The seldom female in a world of males!
Ruth Pitter (1897–   ) British poet.
The Kitten's Eclogue, IV

18 Women have smaller brains than men.
Hojatolislam Rafsanjani Iranian politician.
Remark, July 1986

19 I often want to cry. That is the only advantage women have over men – at least they can cry.
Jean Rhys (1894–1979) Dominican-born British novelist.
Good Morning, Midnight, Pt. II

20 Woman's virtue is man's greatest invention.
Cornelia Otis Skinner (1901–79) US stage actress.
Attrib.

21 Man is a creature who lives not upon bread alone, but principally by catchwords; and the little rift between the sexes is astonishingly widened by simply teaching one set of catchwords to the girls and another to the boys.
Robert Louis Stevenson (1850–94) Scottish writer.
Virginibus Puerisque

22 Man is the hunter; woman is his game:
The sleek and shining creatures of the chase,
We hunt them for the beauty of their skins.
Alfred, Lord Tennyson (1809–92) British poet.
The Princess, V

23 Man for the field and woman for the hearth:
Man for the sword and for the needle she:
Man with the head and woman with the heart:
Man to command and woman to obey;
All else confusion.
Alfred, Lord Tennyson
The Princess, V

24 There are some meannesses which are too mean even for man – woman, lovely woman alone, can venture to commit them.
William Makepeace Thackeray (1811–63) British novelist.
A Shabby-Genteel Story, Ch. 3

25 The War between Men and Women.
James Thurber (1894–1961) US humorist.
Title of a series of cartoons

26 When a man confronts catastrophe on the road, he looks in his purse – but a woman looks in her mirror.
Margaret Turnbull (fl. 1920s–1942) US writer.
The Left Lady

27 Instead of this absurd division into sexes they ought to class people as static and dynamic.
Evelyn Waugh (1903–66) British novelist.
Decline and Fall, Pt. III, Ch. 7

28 All women become like their mothers. That is their tragedy. No man does. That's his.
Oscar Wilde (1854–1900) Irish-born British dramatist.
The Importance of Being Earnest, I

29 Women represent the triumph of matter over mind, just as men represent the triumph of mind over morals.
Oscar Wilde
The Picture of Dorian Gray, Ch. 4

30 Can the fact that Our Lord chose men as his Twelve Apostles be lightly dismissed?
Bishop of Winchester (1926–   ) British churchman.
Remark, July 1988

31 Why are women . . . so much more interesting to men than men are to women?
Virginia Woolf (1882–1941) British novelist.
A Room of One's Own

SHAKESPEARE

See also critcism, poets, writers

1 Others abide our question, Thou art free,
We ask and ask: Thou smilest and art still,
Out-topping knowledge.
Matthew Arnold (1822–88) British poet and critic.
Shakespeare

2 When he killed a calf he would do it in a high style, and make a speech.
John Aubrey (1626–1697) English antiquary.
Brief Lives, 'William Shakespeare'

3 Our myriad-minded Shakespeare.
Samuel Taylor Coleridge (1772–1834) British poet.
Biographia Literaria, Ch. 15

4 I have tried lately to read Shakespeare, and found it so intolerably dull that it nauseated me.
Charles Darwin (1809–82) British life scientist.
Autobiography

5 He was the man who of all modern, and perhaps ancient poets had the largest and most comprehensive soul.
John Dryden (1631–1700) British poet and dramatist.
Essay of Dramatic Poesy

6 He was naturally learned; he needed not the spectacles of books to read nature; he looked inwards, and found her there.
John Dryden
Essay of Dramatic Poesy

7 We can say of Shakespeare, that never has a

man turned so little knowledge to such great account.

T. S. Eliot (1888–1965) US-born British poet and dramatist.
The Classics and the Man of Letters (lecture)

8 The remarkable thing about Shakespeare is that he is really very good – in spite of all the people who say he is very good.

Robert Graves (1895–1985) British poet and novelist.
The Observer, 'Sayings of the Week', 6 Dec 1964

9 Shakespeare never had six lines together without a fault. Perhaps you may find seven, but this does not refute my general assertion.

Samuel Johnson (1709–84) British lexicographer.
Life of Johnson (J. Boswell), Vol. II

10 He was not of an age, but for all time!

Ben Jonson (1573–1637) English dramatist.
To the Memory of William Shakespeare

11 Sweet Swan of Avon!

Ben Jonson
To the Memory of William Shakespeare

12 When I read Shakespeare I am struck with wonder
That such trivial people should muse and thunder
In such lovely language.

D. H. Lawrence (1885–1930) British novelist.
When I Read Shakespeare

13 Or sweetest Shakespeare, Fancy's child,
Warble his native wood-notes wild.

John Milton (1608–74) English poet.
L'Allegro

14 Shakespeare – the nearest thing in incarnation to the eye of God.

Laurence Olivier (1907–89) British actor.
Kenneth Harris Talking To, 'Sir Laurence Olivier'

15 A man can be forgiven a lot if he can quote Shakespeare in an economic crisis.

Prince Philip (1921–) The consort of Queen Elizabeth II.
Attrib.

16 With the single exception of Homer, there is no eminent writer, not even Sir Walter Scott, whom I can despise so entirely as I despise Shakespeare when I measure my mind against his . . . It would positively be a relief to me to dig him up and throw stones at him.

George Bernard Shaw (1856–1950) Irish dramatist and critic.
Dramatic Opinions and Essays, Vol. 2

17 Wonderful women! Have you ever thought how much we all, and women especially, owe to Shakespeare for his vindication of women in these fearless, high-spirited, resolute and intelligent heroines?

Ellen Terry (1847–1928) British actress.
Four Lectures on Shakespeare, 'The Triumphant Women'

18 One of the greatest geniuses that ever existed, Shakespeare, undoubtedly wanted taste.

Horace Walpole (1717–97) British writer.
Letter to Wren, 9 Aug 1764

SHYNESS

See also self-confidence

1 I'm really a timid person – I was beaten up by Quakers.

Woody Allen (Allen Stewart Konigsberg; 1935–) US film actor.
Sleeper

2 A timid question will always receive a confident answer.

Lord Darling (1849–1936) British judge.
Scintillae Juris

3 Why so shy, my pretty Thomasina?
Thomasin, O Thomasin,
Once you were so promisin'.

Christopher Fry (1907–) British dramatist.
The Dark Is Light Enough, II

4 Shyness is just egotism out of its depth.

Penelope Keith British actress.
Remark, July 1988

5 Had we but world enough, and time,
This coyness, lady, were no crime.

Andrew Marvell (1621–78) English poet.
To His Coy Mistress

6 Shyness is *common* . . . . Self-consciousness it was always called when I was young, and that is what it is. To imagine that it shows a sense of modesty is absurd. *Modesty*. Why, I have never known a *truly* modest person to be the least bit shy.

Elizabeth Taylor (1912–75) British writer.
The Bush, 'You'll Enjoy It When You Get There'

SIGNATURES

1 Never sign a walentine with your own name.

Charles Dickens (1812–70) British novelist.
Pickwick Papers, Ch. 33
Said by Sam Weller

2 There, I guess King George will be able to read that.

John Hancock (1737–93) US revolutionary.
The American Treasury (C. Fadiman)
Referring to his signature, written in a bold hand, on the US Declaration of Independence

3 The hand that signed the treaty bred a fever,
And famine grew, and locusts came;
Great is the hand that holds dominion over
Man by a scribbled name.

Dylan Thomas (1914–53) Welsh poet.
The Hand that Signed the Paper

SILENCE

See also speech

1 A still tongue makes a wise head.
Proverb

2 Speech is silver, silence is golden.
Proverb

3 No voice; but oh! the silence sank
Like music on my heart.
Samuel Taylor Coleridge (1772–1834) British poet.
The Rime of the Ancient Mariner, VI

4 When you have nothing to say, say nothing.
Charles Caleb Colton (?1780–1832) British clergyman
and writer.
Lacon, Vol. I

5 For God's sake hold your tongue and let me love.
John Donne (1573–1631) English poet.
The Canonization

6 Silence is become his mother tongue.
Oliver Goldsmith (1728–74) Irish-born British writer.
The Good-Natured Man, II

7 That man's silence is wonderful to listen to.
Thomas Hardy (1840–1928) British novelist.
Under the Greenwood Tree, Ch. 14

8 Silence is as full of potential wisdom and wit
as the unhewn marble of great sculpture.
Aldous Huxley (1894–1964) British novelist.
Point Counter Point

9 Thou still unravish'd bride of quietness,
Thou foster-child of silence and slow time.
John Keats (1795–1821) British poet.
Ode on a Grecian Urn

10 Silence is the best tactic for him who
distrusts himself.
Duc de la Rochefoucauld (1613–80) French writer.
Maximes, 79

11 You get the impression that their normal
condition is silence and that speech is a slight
fever which attacks them now and then.
Jean-Paul Sartre (1905–80) French writer.
Nausea

12 Silence is the perfectest herald of joy: I were
but little happy if I could say how much.
William Shakespeare (1564–1616) English dramatist.
Much Ado About Nothing, II:1

13 Silence is the most perfect expression of
scorn.
George Bernard Shaw (1856–1950) Irish dramatist and
critic.
Back to Methuselah

14 The cruellest lies are often told in silence.
Robert Louis Stevenson (1850–94) Scottish writer.
Virginibus Puerisque

15 Whereof one cannot speak, thereon one must
remain silent.
Ludwig Wittgenstein (1889–1951) Austrian philosopher.
Tractatus Logico-Philosophicus, Ch. 7

SIMILARITY

See also analogy, difference

1 Birds of a feather flock together.
Proverbs

2 Great minds think alike.
Proverb

3 Like breeds like.
Proverb

4 Never mind, dear, we're all made the same,
though some more than others.
Noël Coward (1899–1973) British dramatist.
The Café de la Paix

5 I never knows the children. It's just six of
one and half-a-dozen of the other.
Captain Frederick Marryat (1792–1848) British
novelist.
The Pirate, Ch. 4

SIMPLICITY

1 'Excellent!' I cried. 'Elementary,' said he.
Arthur Conan Doyle (1856–1930) British writer.
The Crooked Man
Watson talking to Sherlock Holmes; Holmes's reply is often
misquoted as 'Elementary my dear Watson'

2 The ability to simplify means to eliminate the
unnecessary so that the necessary may
speak.
Hans Hofmann (1880–1966) German-born US painter.
Search for the Real

3 O holy simplicity!
John Huss (Jan Hus; c. 1369–1415) Bohemian religious
reformer.
Apophthegmata (Zincgreff-Weidner), Pt. III
On noticing a peasant adding a faggot to the pile at his execu-
tion

4 The trivial round, the common task,
Would furnish all we ought to ask;
Room to deny ourselves; a road
To bring us, daily, nearer God.
John Keble (1792–1866) British poet and clergyman.
The Christian Year, 'Morning'

5 A child of five would understand this.
Send somebody to fetch a child of five.
Groucho Marx (Julius Marx; 1895–1977) US comedian.
Duck Soup

6 Entities should not be multiplied
unnecessarily.
No more things should be presumed to exist
than are absolutely necessary.
William of Okham (c. 1280–1349) English philosopher.
'Okham's Razor'. Despite its attribution to William of Okham, it
was in fact a repetition of an ancient philosophical maxim

7 Anybody can shock a baby, or a television
audience. But it's too easy, and the effect is
disproportionate to the effort.
Richard G. Stern (1928–) US writer.
Golk, Ch. 4

8 Our life is frittered away by detail . . .
Simplify, simplify.
Henry David Thoreau (1817–62) US writer.
Walden, 'Where I lived, and What I Lived For'

SIN

See also evil, vice

1 Old sins cast long shadows.
Proverb

2 All sin tends to be addictive, and the terminal point of addiction is what is called damnation.
W. H. Auden (1907–73) British poet.
A Certain World

3 Wherefore putting away lying, speak every man truth with his neighbour: for we are members one of another.
Be ye angry, and sin not: let not the sun go down upon your wrath:
Neither give place to the devil.
Let him that stole steal no more: but rather let him labour, working with his hands the thing which is good, that he may have to give to him that needeth.
Bible: Ephesians
4:25–28

4 So when they continued asking him, he lifted up himself, and said unto them, He that is without sin among you, let him first cast a stone at her.
Bible: John
8:7

5 If we say that we have no sin, we deceive ourselves, and the truth is not in us.
If we confess our sins, he is faithful and just to forgive us our sins, and to cleanse us from all unrighteousness.
Bible: I John
1:8–9

6 Wherefore I say unto thee, Her sins, which are many, are forgiven; for she loved much: but to whom little is forgiven, the same loveth little.
Bible: Luke
7:47

7 But if ye will not do so, behold, ye have sinned against the Lord: and be sure your sin will find you out.
Bible: Numbers
32:23

8 We have erred, and strayed from thy ways like lost sheep.
The Book of Common Prayer
Morning Prayer, General Confession

9 We have left undone those things which we ought to have done; and we have done those things we ought not to have done.
The Book of Common Prayer
Morning Prayer, General Confession

10 A private sin is not so prejudicial in the world as a public indecency.
Miguel de Cervantes (1547–1616) Spanish novelist.
Don Quixote, Pt. II, Ch. 22

11 He said he was against it.
Calvin Coolidge (1872–1933) US president.
Attrib.
Reply when asked what a clergyman had said regarding sin in his sermon

12 It is my belief, Watson, founded upon my experience, that the lowest and vilest alleys of London do not present a more dreadful record of sin than does the smiling and beautiful countryside.
Arthur Conan Doyle (1856–1930) British writer.
Copper Beeches

13 Did wisely from Expensive Sins refrain,
And never broke the Sabbath, but for Gain.
John Dryden (1631–1700) British poet and dramatist.
Absalom and Achitophel, I

14 Sin brought death, and death will disappear with the disappearance of sin.
Mary Baker Eddy (1821–1910) US religious leader.
Science and Health, with Key to the Scriptures

15 There's nothing so artificial as sinning nowadays. I suppose it once was real.
D. H. Lawrence (1885–1930) British novelist.
St Mawr

16 Of Man's first disobedience, and the fruit
Of that forbidden tree, whose mortal taste
Brought death into the World, and all our woe. . .
John Milton (1608–74) English poet.
Paradise Lost, Bk. I

17 The only people who should really sin
Are the people who can sin with a grin.
Ogden Nash (1902–71) US poet.
I'm a Stranger Here Myself

18 She holds that it were better for sun and moon to drop from heaven, for the earth to fail, and for all the many millions who are upon it to die of starvation in extremest agony, as far as temporal affliction goes, than that one soul, I will not say, should be lost, but should commit one single venial sin, should tell one wilful untruth, . . . or steal one poor farthing without excuse.
Cardinal Newman (1801–90) British theologian.
Lectures on Anglican Difficulties, VIII
Referring to the Roman Catholic Church

19 At such an hour the sinners are still in bed resting up from their sinning of the night before, so they will be in good shape for more sinning a little later on.
Damon Runyon (1884–1946) US writer.
Runyon à la carte, 'The Idyll of Miss Sarah Brown'

20 Were't not for gold and women, there would be no damnation.
Cyril Tourneur (1575–1626) English dramatist.
The Revenger's Tragedy, II:1

SINCERITY

See also frankness, honesty, integrity

1 Best be yourself, imperial, plain and true!
Robert Browning (1812–89) British poet.
Bishop Blougram's Apology

2 What comes from the heart, goes to the heart.
Samuel Taylor Coleridge (1772–1834) British poet.
Table Talk

3 Some of the worst men in the world are sincere and the more sincere they are the worse they are.
Lord Hailsham (1907–) British Conservative politician.
The Observer, 'Sayings of the Week', 7 Jan 1968

4 I'm afraid of losing my obscurity. Genuineness only thrives in the dark. Like celery.
Aldous Huxley (1894–1964) British novelist.
Those Barren Leaves, Pt. I, Ch. 1

5 What's a man's first duty? The answer's brief: To be himself.
Henrik Ibsen (1828–1906) Norwegian dramatist.
Peer Gynt, IV:1

6 A little sincerity is a dangerous thing, and a great deal of it is absolutely fatal.
Oscar Wilde (1854–1900) Irish-born British dramatist.
The Critic as Artist, Pt. 2

SINGERS

See also musicians, singing

1 Swans sing before they die – 'twere no bad thing,
Did certain persons die before they sing.
Samuel Taylor Coleridge (1772–1834) British poet.
Epigram on a Volunteer Singer

2 A wandering minstrel I –
A thing of shreds and patches,
Of ballads, songs and snatches,
And dreamy lullaby!
W. S. Gilbert (1836–1911) British dramatist.
The Mikado, I

3 The Last of the Red-Hot Mamas.
Sophie Tucker (Sophia Abuza; 1884–1966) Russian-born US singer.
Dictionary of Biographical Quotation (J. Wintle and R. Kenin)
Description of herself

SINGING

See also music, opera, singers

1 You know whatta you do when you shit? Singing, it's the same thing, only up!
Enrico Caruso (1873–1921) Italian tenor.
Whose Little Boy Are You? (H. Brown)

2 I have a song to sing O!
Sing me your song, O!
W. S. Gilbert (1836–1911) British dramatist.
The Yeoman of the Guard, I

3 Just a little more reverence, please, and not so much astonishment.
Malcolm Sargent (1895–1967) British conductor.
2500 Anecdotes (E. Fuller)
Rehearsing the female chorus in 'For Unto Us a Child is Born' from Handel's *Messiah*

SLAVERY

See also imprisonment, oppression, racism

1 The future is the only kind of property that the masters willingly concede to slaves.
Albert Camus (1913–60) French existentialist writer.
The Rebel

2 There they are cutting each other's throats, because one half of them prefer hiring their servants for life, and the other by the hour.
Thomas Carlyle (1795–1881) Scottish historian and essayist.
Attrib.
Referring to the American Civil War

3 Slaves cannot breathe in England; if their lungs
Receive our air, that moment they are free;
They touch our country, and their shackles fall.
William Cowper (1731–1800) British poet.
The Task
A situation resulting from a judicial decision in 1772

4 The compact which exists between the North and the South is a covenant with death and an agreement with hell.
William Lloyd Garrison (1805–79) US abolitionist.
Resolution, Massachusetts Anti-Slavery Society, 27 Jan 1843

5 The whole commerce between master and slave is a perpetual exercise of the most boisterous passions, the most unremitting despotism on the one part, and degrading submissions on the other.
Thomas Jefferson (1743–1826) US statesman.
Notes on the State of Virginia

SLEEP

See also bed, dreams

1 One hour's sleep before midnight, is worth two after.
Proverb

2 Now I lay me down to sleep,
I pray the Lord my soul to keep.
If I should die before I wake,

I pray the Lord my soul to take.
Anonymous
New England Primer, 1781

3 Lay your sleeping head, my love,
Human on my faithless arm.
W. H. Auden (1907–73) British poet.
Lullaby

4 Rock-a-bye baby on the tree top,
When the wind blows the cradle will rock,
When the bough bends the cradle will fall,
Down comes the baby, cradle and all.
Charles Dupee Blake (1846–1903) British writer of
nursery rhymes.
Attrib.

5 Laugh and the world laughs with you; snore
and you sleep alone.
Anthony Burgess (John Burgess Wilson; 1917–)
British novelist.
Inside Mr. Enderby

6 Oh sleep! it is a gentle thing,
Beloved from pole to pole!
Samuel Taylor Coleridge (1772–1834) British poet.
The Rime of the Ancient Mariner, V

7 Golden slumbers kiss your eyes,
Smiles awake you when you rise.
Thomas Dekker (c. 1572–1632) English dramatist.
Patient Grissil, IV:2

8 It appears that every man's insomnia is as
different from his neighbor's as are their
daytime hopes and aspirations.
F. Scott Fitzgerald (1896–1940) US novelist.
The Crack-up, 'Sleeping and Waking'

9 Try thinking of love, or something.
Amor vincit insomnia.
Christopher Fry (1907–) British dramatist.
A Sleep of Prisoners

10 He's a wicked man that comes after children
when they won't go to bed and throws
handfuls of sand in their eyes.
Ernst Hoffmann (1776–1822) German composer.
The Sandman

11 The amount of sleep required by the average
person is about five minutes more.
Max Kauffmann
Attrib.

12 O soft embalmer of the still midnight.
John Keats (1795–1821) British poet.
To Sleep

13 Turn the key deftly in the oiled wards,
And seal the hushed casket of my soul.
John Keats
To Sleep

14 How do people go to sleep? I'm afraid I've
lost the knack. I might try busting myself
smartly over the temple with the nightlight. I
might repeat to myself, slowly and

soothingly, a list of quotations beautiful from
minds profound; if I can remember any of the
damn things.
Dorothy Parker (1893–1967) US writer.
The Little Hours

15 Sleep that knits up the ravell'd sleave of
care,
The death of each day's life, sore labour's
bath,
Balm of hurt minds, great nature's second
course,
Chief nourisher in life's feast.
William Shakespeare (1564–1616) English dramatist.
Macbeth, II:2

16 Sleep, Death's twin-brother, knows not
Death,
Nor can I dream of thee as dead.
Alfred, Lord Tennyson (1809–92) British poet.
In Memoriam A.H.H., LXVIII

17 There ain't no way to find out why a snorer
can't hear himself snore.
Mark Twain (Samuel Langhorne Clemens; 1835–1910)
US writer.
Tom Sawyer Abroad, Ch. 10

18 It was the time when first sleep begins for
weary
mortals and by the gift of the gods creeps over
them
most welcomely.
Virgil (Publius Vergilius Maro; 70–19 BC) Roman poet.
Aeneid, Bk. II

19 I haven't been to sleep for over a year.
That's why I go to bed early. One needs
more rest if one doesn't sleep.
Evelyn Waugh (1903–66) British novelist.
Decline and Fall, Pt. II, Ch. 3

20 I believe the greatest asset a head of state
can have is the ability to get a good night's
sleep.
Harold Wilson (1916–) British politician and prime
minister.
The World Tonight, BBC Radio, 16 Apr 1975

21 Dear God! the very houses seem asleep;
And all that mighty heart is lying still!
William Wordsworth (1770–1850) British poet.
Sonnets, 'Composed upon Westminster Bridge'

SMALLNESS

See also triviality

1 The best things come in small parcels.
Proverb

2 The Microbe is so very small
You cannot make him out at all.
Hilaire Belloc (1870–1953) French-born British poet.
More Beasts for Worse Children, 'The Microbe'

3 One cubic foot less of space and it would have constituted adultery.
Robert Benchley (1889–1945) US humorist.
Attrib.
Describing an office shared with Dorothy Parker

4 Small is beautiful.
E. F. Schumacher (1911–77) German-born economist.
Title of book

SMOKING

See also abstinence

1 Certainly not – if you don't object if I'm sick.
Thomas Beecham (1879–1961) British conductor.
When asked whether he minded if someone smoked in a non-smoking compartment
Attrib.

2 Tobacco, divine, rare, superexcellent tobacco, which goes far beyond all their panaceas, potable gold, and philosopher's stones, a sovereign remedy to all diseases.
Robert Burton (1577–1640) English scholar and explorer.
Anatomy of Melancholy

3 Jones – (who, I'm glad to say,
Asked leave of Mrs J. –)
Daily absorbs a clay
After his labours.
C. S. Calverley (1831–84) British poet.
Ode to Tobacco

4 I must point out that my rule of life prescribed as an absolutely sacred rite smoking cigars and also the drinking of alcohol before, after, and if need be during all meals and in the intervals between them.
Winston Churchill (1874–1965) British statesman.
The Second World War
Said during a lunch with the Arab leader Ibn Saud, when he heard that the king's religion forbade smoking and alcohol

5 It is quite a three-pipe problem.
Arthur Conan Doyle (1856–1930) British writer.
The Red-Headed League

6 What a blessing this smoking is! perhaps the greatest that we owe to the discovery of America.
Arthur Helps (1813–75) British historian.
Friends in Council

7 A custom loathsome to the eye, hateful to the nose, harmful to the brain, dangerous to the lungs, and in the black, stinking fume thereof, nearest resembling the horrible Stygian smoke of the pit that is bottomless.
James I (1566–1625) King of England.
A Counterblast to Tobacco

8 Neither do thou lust after that tawney weed tobacco.
Ben Jonson (1573–1637) English dramatist.
Bartholomew Fair, II:6

9 Ods me, I marvel what pleasure or felicity they have in taking their roguish tobacco. It is good for nothing but to choke a man, and fill him full of smoke and embers.
Ben Jonson
Every Man in His Humour, III:5

10 This very night I am going to leave off tobacco! Surely there must be some other world in which this unconquerable purpose shall be realized. The soul hath not her generous aspirings implanted in her in vain.
Charles Lamb (1775–1834) British essayist.
Letter to Thomas Manning, 26 Dec 1815

11 Dr Parr . . . asked him, how he had acquired his power of smoking at such a rate? Lamb replied, 'I toiled after it, sir, as some men toil after virtue.'
Charles Lamb
Memoirs of Charles Lamb (Talfourd)

12 He who lives without tobacco is not worthy to live.
Molière (Jean Baptiste Poquelin; 1622–73) French dramatist.
Don Juan, I:1

13 The very act of smoking a cigarette is, for many, a major source of Displacement Activities . . . They are stress-smokers, not drug-smokers, and in that capacity at least, smoking can play a valuable role in a society full of minute-by-minute tensions and pressures. It is so much more than a question of inhaling smoke.
Desmond Morris (1928–) British biologist.
Manwatching, 'Displacement Activities'

14 This vice brings in one hundred million francs in taxes every year. I will certainly forbid it at once – as soon as you can name a virtue that brings in as much revenue.
Napoleon III (1808–73) French emperor.
Anekdotenschatz (H. Hoffmeister)
Reply when asked to ban smoking

15 My doctor has always told me to smoke. He even explains himself: 'Smoke, my friend. Otherwise someone else will smoke in your place.'
Erik Satie (1866–1925) French composer.
Mémoires d'un amnésique

16 I have every sympathy with the American who was so horrified by what he had read of the effects of smoking that he gave up reading.
Henry G. Strauss
Quotations for Speakers and Writers (A. Andrews)

17 I asked a coughing friend of mine why he doesn't stop smoking. 'In this town it wouldn't do any good,' he explained. 'I happen to be a chain breather.'
Robert Sylvester (1907–75) US writer.
Bartlett's Unfamiliar Quotations (Leonard Louis Levinson)

18 We shall not refuse tobacco the credit of

being sometimes medical, when used temperately, though an acknowledged poison.

Jesse Torrey (1787–1834)
The Moral Instructor, Pt. IV

19 When I was young, I kissed my first woman, and smoked my first cigarette on the same day. Believe me, never since have I wasted any more time on tobacco.

Arturo Toscanini (1867–1957) Italian conductor.
Attrib.

20 There are people who strictly deprive themselves of each and every eatable, drinkable and smokable which has in any way acquired a shady reputation. They pay this price for health. And health is all they get for it.

Mark Twain (Samuel Langhorne Clemens; 1835–1910) US writer.

21 I've done it a hundred times!

Mark Twain
Attrib.
Referring to giving up smoking

22 Tobacco drieth the brain, dimmeth the sight, vitiateth the smell, hurteth the stomach, destroyeth the concoction, disturbeth the humors and spirits, corrupteth the breath, induceth a trembling of the limbs, exsiccateth the windpipe, lungs, and liver, annoyeth the milt, scorcheth the heart, and causeth the blood to be adjusted.

Tobias Venner (1577–1660)
Via Recta ad Vitam Longam

23 A cigarette is the perfect type of a perfect pleasure. It is exquisite, and it leaves one unsatisfied. What more can one want?

Oscar Wilde (1854–1900) Irish-born British dramatist.
The Picture of Dorian Gray, Ch. 6

SNOBBERY

See also aristocracy, class, one-upmanship

1 In our way we were both snobs, and no snob welcomes another who has risen with him.

Cecil Beaton (1904–80) British photographer.
Referring to Evelyn Waugh
Attrib.

2 And this is good old Boston,
The home of the bean and the cod,
Where the Lowells talk only to Cabots,
And the Cabots talk only to God.

John Collins Bossidy (1860–1928) US writer.
Toast at Holy Cross Alumni dinner, 1910

3 Of course they have, or I wouldn't be sitting here talking to someone like you.

Barbara Cartland (1902–) British romantic novelist.
Class (J. Cooper)
When asked in a radio interview whether she thought that British class barriers had broken down

4 I've danced with a man, who's danced with a girl, who's danced with the Prince of Wales.

Herbert Farjeon (1887–1945) British writer.
Picnic

5 His hatred of snobs was a derivative of his snobbishness, but made the simpletons (in other words, everyone) believe that he was immune from snobbishness.

Marcel Proust (1871–1922) French novelist.
À la recherche du temps perdu: Le Côté de Guermantes

6 I mustn't go on singling out names. One must not be a name-dropper, as Her Majesty remarked to me yesterday.

Norman St John Stevas (1929–) British politician.
Speech, Museum of the Year luncheon, 20 June 1979

7 He who meanly admires mean things is a Snob.

William Makepeace Thackeray (1811–63) British novelist.
The Book of Snobs, Ch. 2

8 It is impossible, in our condition of society, not to be sometimes a Snob.

William Makepeace Thackeray
The Book of Snobs, Ch. 3

9 She was – but I assure you that she was a very bad cook.

Louis Adolphe Thiers (1797–1877) French statesman and historian.
Attrib.
Defending his social status after someone had remarked that his mother had been a cook

10 My dear – the people we should have been seen dead with.

Rebecca West (Cicely Isabel Fairfield; 1892–1983) British novelist and journalist.
Times Literary Supplement, 1 Oct 1982
Cable sent to Noël Coward after learning they had both been on a Nazi death list

11 CECILY: When I see a spade I call it a spade.
GWENDOLEN: I am glad to say I have never seen a spade. It is obvious that our social spheres have been widely different.

Oscar Wilde (1854–1900) Irish-born British dramatist.
The Importance of Being Earnest, II

12 Never speak disrespectfully of Society, Algernon. Only people who can't get into it do that.

Oscar Wilde
The Importance of Being Earnest, III

SOCIALISM

See also Communism, Marxism

1 Why is it always the intelligent people who are socialists?

Alan Bennett (1934–) British playwright.
Forty Years On

2 The language of priorities is the religion of Socialism.

Aneurin Bevan (1897–1960) British Labour politician.
Aneurin Bevan (Vincent Brome), Ch. 1

3 The people's flag is deepest red;
It shrouded oft our martyred dead,
And ere their limbs grew stiff and cold,
Their heart's blood dyed its every fold.
Then raise the scarlet standard high!
Within its shade we'll live or die.
Tho' cowards flinch and traitors sneer,
We'll keep the red flag flying here.

James Connell (1852–1929) British socialist.
Traditionally sung at the close of annual conferences of the British Labour Party
The Red Flag, in *Songs that made History* (H. E. Piggot), Ch. 6

4 Socialism can only arrive by bicycle.

José Antonio Viera Gallo (1943–) Chilean politician.
Energy and Equity (Ivan Illich)

5 Only socialism would put up with it for so long. Capitalism would have gone bankrupt years ago.

Mikhail Gorbachov (1931–) Soviet statesman.
Talking of sub-standard workmanship in the Soviet Union
TV documentary, 23 March 1987

6 Well, what are you socialists going to do about me?

George V (1865–1936) King of the United Kingdom.
To Ramsay MacDonald at his first meeting as prime minister
Attrib.

7 We are all Socialists now.

William Harcourt (1827–1904) British statesman.
Attrib.

8 Compassion is not a sloppy, sentimental feeling for people who are underprivileged or sick . . . it is an absolutely practical belief that, regardless of a person's background, ability or ability to pay, he should be provided with the best that society has to offer.

Neil Kinnock (1942–) British politician.
Maiden speech, House of Commons, 1970

9 It is inconceivable that we could transform this society without a major extension of public ownership.

Neil Kinnock
Marxism Today, 1983

10 Under socialism *all* will govern in turn and will soon become accustomed to no one governing.

Lenin (Vladimir Ilich Ulyanov; 1870–1924) Russian revolutionary leader.
The State and Revolution, Ch. 6

11 As with the Christian religion, the worst advertisement for Socialism is its adherents.

George Orwell (Eric Blair; 1903–50) British novelist.
The Road to Wigan Pier, Ch. 11

12 To the ordinary working man, the sort you would meet in any pub on Saturday night,

Socialism does not mean much more than better wages and shorter hours and nobody bossing you about.

George Orwell
The Road to Wigan Pier, Ch. 11

13 The higher-water mark, so to speak, of Socialist literature is W. H. Auden, a sort of gutless Kipling.

George Orwell
The Road to Wigan Pier, Ch. 11

14 State socialism is totally alien to the British character.

Margaret Thatcher (1925–) British politician and prime minister.
The Times, 1983

15 We are redefining and we are restating our socialism in terms of the scientific revolution . . . the Britain that is going to be forged in the white heat of this revolution will be no place for restrictive practices or out-dated methods on either side of industry.

Harold Wilson (1916–) British politician and prime minister.
Speech, Labour Party Conference, 1 Oct 1963

SOCIETY

See also mankind

1 I am a sociable worker.

Brendan Behan (1923–64) Irish playwright.
The Hostage, II

2 Man was formed for society.

William Blackstone (1723–80) British jurist.
Commentaries on the Laws of England, Introduction

3 No man is an Island, entire of itself; every man is a piece of the Continent, a part of the main.

John Donne (1573–1631) English poet.
Devotions, 17

4 People who need people are the luckiest people in the world.

Bob Merrill (Robert Merrill; 1890–1977) US lyricist and composer.
People Who Need People

5 Our civilization . . . has not yet fully recovered from the shock of its birth – the transition from the tribal or 'closed society', with its submission to magical forces, to the 'open society' which sets free the critical powers of man.

Karl Popper (1902–) Austrian-born British philosopher.
The Open Society and Its Enemies

6 Man is not a solitary animal, and so long as social life survives, self-realization cannot be the supreme principle of ethics.

Bertrand Russell (1872–1970) British philosopher.
History of Western Philosophy, 'Romanticism'

7 Society is no comfort

To one not sociable.
William Shakespeare (1564–1616) English dramatist.
Cymbeline, IV:2

8 Man is a social animal.
Benedict Spinoza (Baruch de Spinoza; 1632–77) Dutch
philosopher.
Ethics

9 What men call social virtues, good fellowship,
is commonly but the virtue of pigs in a litter,
which lie close together to keep each other
warm. It brings men together in crowds and
mobs in bar-rooms and elsewhere, but it
does not deserve the name of virtue.
Henry David Thoreau (1817–62) US writer.
Journal, 1852

SOLDIERS

See also army, officers, war

1 It's Tommy this, an' Tommy that, an' 'Chuck
him out, the brute!'
But it's 'Saviour of 'is country' when the guns
begin to shoot.
Rudyard Kipling (1865–1936) Indian-born British writer.
Tommy

2 Oh, it's Tommy this, an' Tommy that, an'
'Tommy, go away';
But it's 'Thank you, Mister Atkins,' when the
band begins to play.
Rudyard Kipling
Tommy

3 They're changing guard at Buckingham Palace
Christopher Robin went down with Alice.
Alice is marrying one of the guard.
'A soldier's life is terrible hard,'
Says Alice.
A. A. Milne (1882–1956) British writer.
When We Were Very Young, 'Buckingham Palace'

4 Volunteers usually fall into two groups. There
are the genuinely courageous who are itching
to get at the throat of the enemy, and the
restless who will volunteer for anything in
order to escape from the boredom of what
they are presently doing.
David Niven (1909–83) British film actor.
The Moon's a Balloon, Ch. 12

5 Soldiers are citizens of death's grey land,
Drawing no dividend from time's tomorrows.
Siegfried Sassoon (1886–1967) British poet.
Dreamers

6 You are a very poor soldier: a chocolate
cream soldier!
George Bernard Shaw (1856–1950) Irish dramatist and
critic.
Arms and the Man, I

7 I never expect a soldier to think.
George Bernard Shaw
The Devil's Disciple, III

8 They're overpaid, overfed, oversexed and
over here.
Tommy Trinder (1909–89) British entertainer.
Attrib.
Referring to the G.I.s

9 He (the recruiting officer) asked me 'Why
tanks?' I replied that I preferred to go into
battle sitting down.
Peter Ustinov (1921–) British actor.
Dear Me

10 It all depends upon that article there.
Duke of Wellington (1769–1852) British general and
statesman.
The Age of Elegance (A. Bryant)
Indicating a passing infantryman when asked if he would be
able to defeat Napoleon

SOLITUDE

See also loneliness

1 Whosoever is delighted in solitude is either a
wild beast or a god.
Francis Bacon (1561–1626) English philosopher.
Essays, 'Of Friendship'

2 Alone, alone, all, all alone,
Alone on a wide wide sea!
And never a saint took pity on
My soul in agony.
Samuel Taylor Coleridge (1772–1834) British poet.
The Rime of the Ancient Mariner, IV

3 Oh for a lodge in some vast wilderness,
Some boundless contiguity of shade,
Where rumour of oppression and deceit,
Of unsuccessful or successful war,
Might never reach me more!
William Cowper (1731–1800) British poet.
The Task

4 Society, friendship, and love,
Divinely bestowed upon man,
Oh, had I the wings of a dove,
How soon would I taste you again!
William Cowper
Verses supposed to be written by Alexander Selkirk

5 I am monarch of all I survey,
My right there is none to dispute;
From the centre all round to the sea
I am lord of the fowl and the brute.
Oh, solitude! where are the charms
That sages have seen in thy face?
Better dwell in the midst of alarms,
Than reign in this horrible place.
William Cowper
Verses supposed to be written by Alexander Selkirk

6 I want to be alone.
Greta Garbo (1905–90) Swedish-born US film star.
Words spoken by Garbo in the film *Grand Hotel,* and associat-
ed with her for the rest of her career.

7 Far from the madding crowd's ignoble strife,
Their sober wishes never learn'd to stray;
Along the cool sequester'd vale of life

They kept the noiseless tenor of their way.
Thomas Gray (1716–71) British poet.
Elegy Written in a Country Churchyard

8 One of the pleasantest things in the world is
going on a journey; but I like to go by
myself.
William Hazlitt (1778–1830) British essayist.
On Going a Journey

9 It is a fine thing to be out on the hills alone.
A man can hardly be a beast or a fool alone
on a great mountain.
Francis Kilvert (1840–79) British diarist and clergyman.
Diary, 29 May 1871

10 In solitude
What happiness? who can enjoy alone,
Or, all enjoying, what contentment find?
John Milton (1608–74) English poet.
Paradise Lost, Bk. VIII

11 I want to be a movement
But there's no one on my side.
Adrian Mitchell (1932–) British writer and dramatist.
Loose Leaf Poem

12 A man must keep a little back shop where he
can be himself without reserve. In solitude
alone can he know true freedom.
Michel de Montaigne (1533–92) French essayist.
Essais, I

13 I never found the companion that was so
companionable as solitude.
Henry David Thoreau (1817–62) US writer.
Walden, 'Solitude'

14 Alas, Lord, I am powerful but alone. Let me
sleep the sleep of the earth.
Alfred de Vigny (1797–1863) French writer.
Moïse

15 For oft, when on my couch I lie
In vacant or in pensive mood,
They flash upon that inward eye
Which is the bliss of solitude.
William Wordsworth (1770–1850) British poet.
I Wandered Lonely as a Cloud

16 Behold her, single in the field,
Yon solitary Highland lass!
William Wordsworth
The Solitary Reaper

17 I will arise and go now, and go to Innisfree,
And a small cabin build there, of clay and wat-
tles made;
Nine bean rows will I have there, a hive for the
honey bee,
And live alone in the bee-loud glade.
W. B. Yeats (1865–1939) Irish poet.
The Lake Isle of Innisfree

SORROW

See also despair, melancholy, mourning, regret

1 Every tear from every eye

Becomes a babe in Eternity.
William Blake (1757–1827) British poet.
Auguries of Innocence

2 Do you hear the children weeping, O my
brothers,
Ere the sorrow comes with years?
Elizabeth Barrett Browning (1806–61) British poet.
The Cry of the Children

3 Follow thy fair sun, unhappy shadow.
Thomas Campion (1567–1620) English poet.
Follow Thy Fair Sun

4 One often calms one's grief by recounting it.
Pierre Corneille (1606–84) French dramatist.
Polyeucte, I:3

5 Tears were to me what glass beads are to
African traders.
Quentin Crisp (?1910–) Model, publicist, and writer.
The Naked Civil Servant

6 There is no greater sorrow than to recall a
time of happiness when in misery.
Dante (1265–1321) Italian poet.
Divine Comedy, Inferno, V

7 *Adieu tristesse*
Bonjour tristesse
Tu es inscrite dans les lignes du plafond.
Farewell sadness
Good day sadness
You are written in the lines of the ceiling.
Paul Éluard (Eugène Grindel; 1895–1952) French
surrealist poet.
La Vie immédiate

8 A moment of time may make us unhappy for
ever.
John Gay (1685–1732) English poet and dramatist.
The Beggar's Opera

9 Sadness is almost never anything but a form
of fatigue.
André Gide (1869–1951) French novelist.
Journals, 1922

10 They say my verse is sad: no wonder;
Its narrow measure spans
Tears of eternity, and sorrow,
Not mine, but man's.
A. E. Housman (1859–1936) British scholar and poet.
Last Poems, 'Fancy's Knell'

11 Then Sir Launcelot saw her visage, but he
wept not greatly, but sighed!
Thomas Malory (1400–71) English writer.
Morte d'Arthur, Bk. XXI, Ch. 11

12 Tears such as angels weep, burst forth.
John Milton (1608–74) English poet.
Paradise Lost, Bk. I

13 Art thou weary, art thou languid,
Art thou sore distressed?
John Mason Neale (1818–66) British churchman.
Art thou Weary?

14 Sorrow is tranquillity remembered in emotion.

Dorothy Parker (1893–1967) US writer.
Sentiment

15 Line after line my gushing eyes o'erflow,
Led through a sad variety of woe.

Alexander Pope (1688–1744) British poet.
Eloisa to Abelard

16 Not louder shrieks to pitying heav'n are cast,
When husbands, or when lap-dogs breathe their last.

Alexander Pope
The Rape of the Lock, III

17 As soon as one is unhappy one becomes moral.

Marcel Proust (1871–1922) French novelist.
À la recherche du temps perdu: À l'ombre des jeunes filles en fleurs

18 Happiness is beneficial for the body, but it is grief that develops the powers of the mind.

Marcel Proust
À la recherche du temps perdu: Le Temps retrouvé

19 It is such a secret place, the land of tears.

Antoine de Saint-Exupéry (1900–44) French novelist and aviator.
The Little Prince, Ch. 7

20 He's simply got the instinct for being unhappy highly developed.

Saki (Hector Hugh Munro; 1870–1916) British writer.
The Match-Maker

21 If you have tears, prepare to shed them now.

William Shakespeare (1564–1616) English dramatist.
Julius Caesar, III:2

22 Down, thou climbing sorrow,
Thy element's below.

William Shakespeare
King Lear, II:4

23 The secret of being miserable is to have leisure to bother about whether you are happy or not.

George Bernard Shaw (1856–1950) Irish dramatist and critic.
Misalliance, Preface

24 'Tis held that sorrow makes us wise.

Alfred, Lord Tennyson (1809–92) British poet.
In Memoriam A.H.H., CXIII

25 My regret
Becomes an April violet,
And buds and blossoms like the rest.

Alfred, Lord Tennyson
In Memoriam A.H.H., CXV

26 Tears, idle tears, I know not what they mean,
Tears from the depth of some divine despair.

Alfred, Lord Tennyson
The Princess, IV

27 A grief too much to be told, O queen, you bid me renew.

Virgil (Publius Vergilius Maro; 70–19 BC) Roman poet.
Aeneid, Bk. II
The opening words of Aeneas' account to Dido of the fall of Troy

---

SOUL

1 The eyes are the window of the soul.
Proverb

2 We cannot kindle when we will
The fire which in the heart resides,
The spirit bloweth and is still,
In mystery our soul abides.

Matthew Arnold (1822–88) British poet and critic.
Morality

3 And see all sights from pole to pole,
And glance, and nod, and bustle by;
And never once possess our soul
Before we die.

Matthew Arnold
A Southern Night

4 Man has no Body distinct from his Soul; for that called Body is a portion of Soul discerned by the five Senses, the chief inlets of Soul in this age.

William Blake (1757–1827) British poet.
The Marriage of Heaven and Hell, 'The Voice of the Devil'

5 Leave the flesh to the fate it was fit for! the spirit be thine!

Robert Browning (1812–89) British poet.
Saul, XIII

6 In the real dark night of the soul it is always three o'clock in the morning.

F. Scott Fitzgerald (1896–1940) US novelist.
The Crack-Up
See ST JOHN OF THE CROSS

7 That night, that year
Of now done darkness I wretch lay wrestling with (my God!) my God.

Gerard Manley Hopkins (1844–99) British Jesuit and poet.
Carrion Comfort

8 The dark night of the soul.

St John of the Cross (Juan de Yepes y Alvarez; 1542–91) Spanish churchman and poet.
English translation of *Noche obscura del alma*, the title of a poem; see also F. SCOTT FITZGERALD

9 Nor let the beetle, nor the death-moth be Your mournful Psyche.

John Keats (1795–1821) British poet.
Ode on Melancholy

10 And looks commercing with the skies,
Thy rapt soul sitting in thine eyes.

John Milton (1608–74) English poet.
Il Penseroso

11 I am positive I have a soul; nor can all the

books with which materialists have pestered the world ever convince me of the contrary.
Laurence Sterne (1713–68) Irish-born British writer.
A Sentimental Journey, 'Maria, Moulines'

12 Fair seed-time had my soul, and I grew up Fostered alike by beauty and by fear.
William Wordsworth (1770–1850) British poet.
The Prelude, I

SPACE

See also astronomy, discovery, exploration, moon, science, stars, sun, technology, universe

1 That's one small step for man, one giant leap for mankind.
Neil Armstrong (1930–) US astronaut.
Remark, 21 July 1969
Said on stepping onto the moon. Often quoted as, 'small step for a man . . . ' (which is probably what he intended)

2 Outer space is no place for a person of breeding.
Violet Bonham Carter (1887–1969) British politician.
The New Yorker

3 I am a passenger on the spaceship, Earth.
Richard Buckminster Fuller (1895–1983) US architect and inventor.
Operating Manual for Spaceship Earth

4 The Earth is just too small and fragile a basket for the human race to keep all its eggs in.
Robert Heinlein (1907–88) US science-fiction writer.
Speech

5 Space isn't remote at all. It's only an hour's drive away if your car could go straight upwards.
Fred Hoyle (1915–) British astronomer.
The Observer, 9 Sept 1979

6 This is the greatest week in the history of the world since the creation.
Richard Milhous Nixon (1913–) US president.
Attrib., 24 July 1969
Said when men first landed on the moon

7 Space is almost infinite. As a matter of fact we think it *is* infinite.
Dan Quayle (James Danforth Q.; 1946–) US statesman.
The Sunday Times, 31 Dec 1989

8 The astronauts! . . . Rotarians in outer space.
Gore Vidal (1925–) US novelist.
Two Sisters

SPECULATION

1 While to deny the existence of an unseen kingdom is bad, to pretend that we know more about it than its bare existence is no better.
Samuel Butler (1835–1902) British writer.
Erewhon, Ch. 15

2 If the world were good for nothing else, it is a fine subject for speculation.
William Hazlitt (1778–1830) British essayist.
Characteristics

3 I think the primary notion back of most gambling is the excitement of it. While gamblers naturally want to win, the majority of them derive pleasure even if they lose. The desire to win, rather than the excitement involved, seems to me the compelling force behind speculation.
Joseph Kennedy (1888–1969) US businessman.
The Kennedys, Ch. 2 (Peter Collier and David Horowitz)

SPEECH

See also silence, speeches, verbosity, words

1 Save your breath to cool your porridge.
Proverb

2 Speak when you are spoken to.
Proverb

3 Let your speech be alway with grace, seasoned with salt, that ye may know how ye ought to answer every man.
Bible: Colossians
4:6

4 Let thy speech be short, comprehending much in few words; be as one that knoweth and yet holdeth his tongue.
Bible: Ecclesiasticus
32:8

5 Even so the tongue is a little member, and boasteth great things. Behold, how great a matter a little fire kindleth!
Bible: James
3:5

6 But the tongue can no man tame; it is an unruly evil, full of deadly poison.
Bible: James
3:8

7 To know how to say what others only know how to think is what makes men poets or sages; and to dare to say what others only dare to think makes men martyrs or reformers – or both.
Elizabeth Charles (1828–96) British writer.
Chronicle of the Schönberg-Cotta Family

8 No, Sir, because I have time to think before I speak, and don't ask impertinent questions.
Erasmus Darwin (1731–1802) British physician, biologist, and poet.
Reminiscences of My Father's Everyday Life (Sir Francis Darwin)
Reply when asked whether he found his stammer inconvenient

9 The true use of speech is not so much to express our wants as to conceal them.
Oliver Goldsmith (1728–74) Irish-born British writer.
Essays, 'The Use of Language'

10 Most men make little use of their speech than to give evidence against their own understanding.
Lord Halifax (1633–95) English statesman.
Political, Moral, and Miscellaneous Thoughts and Reflections

11 Talking and eloquence are not the same: to speak, and to speak well, are two things.
Ben Jonson (1573–1637) English dramatist.
Timber, or Discoveries made upon Men and Matter

12 The thoughtless are rarely wordless.
Howard W. Newton
Attrib.

13 The most precious things in speech are pauses.
Ralph Richardson (1902–83) British actor.
Attrib.

14 But words once spoke can never be recall'd.
Earl of Roscommon (1633–85) Irish-born English poet.
Art of Poetry

15 Words may be false and full of art,
Sighs are the natural language of the heart.
Thomas Shadwell (1642–92) English dramatist.
Psyche, III

16 Speech was given to man to disguise his thoughts.
Talleyrand (Charles Maurice de Talleyrand-Périgord; 1754–1838) French politician.
Attrib.

SPEECHES

See also brevity, sermons, verbosity

1 I take the view, and always have done, that if you cannot say what you have to say in twenty minutes, you should go away and write a book about it.
Lord Brabazon of Tara (1910–74) British businessman and Conservative politician.
Attrib.

2 An after-dinner speech should be like a lady's dress – long enough to cover the subject and short enough to be interesting.
R. A. Butler (1902–82) British Conservative politician.
Remark made at an Anglo-Jewish dinner

3 He is one of those orators of whom it was well said, 'Before they get up they do not know what they are going to say; when they are speaking, they do not know what they are saying; and when they sit down, they do not know what they have said'.
Winston Churchill (1874–1965) British statesman.
Speech, House of Commons, 20 Dec 1912
Referring to Lord Charles Beresford

4 I dreamt that I was making a speech in the House. I woke up, and by Jove I was!
Duke of Devonshire (1833–1908) Conservative politician.
Thought and Adventures (W. S. Churchill)

5 For I have neither wit, nor words, nor worth,
Action, nor utterance, nor the power of speech,
To stir men's blood; I only speak right on.
William Shakespeare (1564–1616) English dramatist.
Julius Caesar, III:2

6 Don't quote Latin; say what you have to say, and then sit down.
Duke of Wellington (1769–1852) British general and statesman.
Attrib.
Advice to a new Member of Parliament

SPELLING

See also language, pronunciation, words, writing

1 Put it down a we, my lord, put it down a we!
Charles Dickens (1812–70) British novelist.
Pickwick Papers, Ch. 34

2 They spell it Vinci and pronounce it Vinchy; foreigners always spell better than they pronounce.
Mark Twain (Samuel Langhorne Clemens; 1835–1910) US writer.
The Innocents Abroad, Ch. 19

SPONTANEITY

See also impetuosity

1 Spontaneity is only a term for man's ignorance of the gods.
Samuel Butler (1835–1902) British writer.
Erewhon, Ch. 25

2 *L'acte gratuite.*
The unmotivated action.
André Gide (1869–1951) French novelist.
Les Caves du Vatican

3 Away with all ideals. Let each individual act spontaneously from the for ever incalculable prompting of the creative wellhead within him. There is no universal law.
D. H. Lawrence (1885–1930) British novelist.
Phoenix, Preface to 'All Things are Possible' by Leo Shostov

4 Nothing prevents us from being natural so much as the desire to appear so.
Duc de la Rochefoucauld (1613–80) French writer.
Maximes, 431

SPOONERISMS

Sayings associated with the Oxford clergyman and academic William Archibald Spooner (1844–1930).

1 You will find as you grow older that the weight of rages will press harder and harder on the employer.
Spooner (Sir W. Hayter), Ch. 6

2 I remember your name perfectly, but I just can't think of your face.

3 Kinquering Congs their titles take.

A scrambled announcement of the hymn in New College Chapel (probably apocryphal)

4 Let us drink to the queer old Dean.

5 Sir, you have tasted two whole worms; you have hissed all my mystery lectures and have been caught fighting a liar in the quad; you will leave Oxford by the town drain.

SPORT AND GAMES

See also cricket, fishing, football, golf, horses, hunting

1 Float like a butterfly
Sting like a bee.

Muhammad Ali (Cassius Clay; 1942–) US boxer.
Remark
Describing his boxing style

2 Follow up! Follow up! Follow up! Follow up! Follow up!
Till the field ring again and again,
With the tramp of the twenty-two men,
Follow up!

E. E. Bowen (1836–1901) British writer.
Forty Years On (the Harrow school song)

3 Life's too short for chess.

Henry James Byron (1834–84) British dramatist and actor.
Our Boys, I

4 There is plenty of time to win this game, and to thrash the Spaniards too.

Francis Drake (1540–96) British navigator and admiral.
Attrib.
Referring to the sighting of the Armada during a game of bowls, 20 July 1588

5 Exercise is bunk. If you are healthy, you don't need it: if you are sick, you shouldn't take it.

Henry Ford (1863–1947) US car manufacturer.
Attrib.

6 Bullfighting is the only art in which the artist is in danger of death and in which the degree of brilliance in the performance is left to the fighter's honour.

Ernest Hemingway (1899–1961) US novelist.
Death in the Afternoon, Ch. 9

7 When in doubt, win the trick.

Edmond Hoyle (1672–1769) English writer on card games.
Hoyle's Games, 'Whist, Twenty-four Short Rules for Learners'

8 The only athletic sport I ever mastered was backgammon.

Douglas William Jerrold (1803–57) British dramatist.
Douglas Jerrold (W. Jerrold), Vol. I, Ch. 1

9 It is unbecoming for a cardinal to ski badly.

John Paul II (Karol Wojtyla; 1920–) Polish pope (1978–).
John Paul II
Replying to the suggestion that it was inappropriate for him, a cardinal, to ski

10 I am sorry I have not learned to play at cards. It is very useful in life: it generates kindness and consolidates society.

Samuel Johnson (1709–84) British lexicographer.
Tour to the Hebrides (J. Boswell)

11 At what time does the dissipation of energy begin?

Lord Kelvin (1824–1907) British physicist.
Memories of a Scientific Life (A. Fleming)
On realizing that his wife was planning an afternoon excursion

12 Man is a gaming animal. He must always be trying to get the better in something or other.

Charles Lamb (1775–1834) British essayist.
Essays of Elia, 'Mrs Battle's Opinions on Whist'

13 O, he flies through the air with the greatest of ease,
This daring young man on the flying trapeze.

George Leybourne (?–1884) British songwriter.
The Man on the Flying Trapeze

14 I don't like this game.

Spike Milligan (1918–) British comic actor and author.
The Goon Show

15 Serious sport has nothing to do with fair play. It is bound up with hatred, jealousy, boastfulness, disregard of all rules and sadistic pleasure in witnessing violence; in other words it is war minus the shooting.

George Orwell (Eric Blair; 1903–50) British novelist.
The Sporting Spirit

16 Gamesmanship or The Art of Winning Games Without Actually Cheating.

Stephen Potter (1900–69) British writer.
Book title

17 For when the One Great Scorer comes
To write against your name,
He marks – not that you won or lost –
But how you played the game.

Grantland Rice (1880–1954) US sportswriter.
Alumnus Football

18 It was remarked to me by the late Mr Charles Roupell . . . that to play billiards well was a sign of an ill-spent youth.

Herbert Spencer (1820–1903) British philosopher.
Life and Letters of Spencer (Duncan), Ch. 20

19 I wanted a play that would paint the full face of sensuality, rebellion and revivalism. In South Wales these three phenomena have played second fiddle only to the Rugby Union which is a distillation of all three.

Gwyn Thomas (1913–81) British writer.
Jackie the Jumper (Introduction), 'Plays and Players' 19 Jan 1963

20 There's no secret. You just press the accelerator to the floor and steer left.
Bill Vukovich (1918–55) US motor-racing driver.
Attrib.
Explaining his success in the Indianapolis 500

SPRING

See months, seasons

STARING

1 It is better to be looked over than overlooked.
Mae West (1892–1980) US actress.
The Wit and Wisdom of Mae West (ed. J. Weintraub)

2 Don't go on looking at me like that, because you'll wear your eyes out.
Émile Zola (1840–1902) French novelist.
La Bête Humaine, Ch. 5

STARS

See also astronomy, moon, space, sun, universe

1 ... things called Stars appeared, which robbed men of their souls and left them unreasoning brutes, so that they destroyed the civilization they themselves had built up.
Isaac Asimov (1920–) US science-fiction writer.
On the fictional world of Lagash night comes once every 2049 years
Nightfall

2 And God made two great lights: the greater light to rule the day, and the lesser light to rule the night: he made the stars also.
Bible: Genesis
1:16

3 Look at the stars! look, look up at the skies!
O look at all the fire-folk sitting in the air!
The bright boroughs, the circle-citadels there!
Gerard Manley Hopkins (1844–99) British Jesuit and poet.
The Starlight Night

4 Bright star, would I were steadfast as thou art.
John Keats (1795–1821) British poet.
Bright Star

5 Twinkle, twinkle, little star,
How I wonder what you are!
Up above the world so high,
Like a diamond in the sky!
Jane Taylor (1783–1824) British writer.
Rhymes for the Nursery (with Ann Taylor), 'The Star'

6 For still I looked on that same star,
That fitful, fiery Lucifer,
Watching with mind as quiet as moss
Its light nailed to a burning cross.
Andrew John Young (1885–1971) Scottish poet.
The Evening Star

7 Stars lay like yellow pollen
That from a flower has fallen;
And single stars I saw
Crossing themselves in awe;
Some stars in sudden fear
Fell like a falling tear.
Andrew John Young
The Stars

STATE

See also democracy, government, republic

1 The only way to erect such a common power, as may be able to defend them from the invasion of foreigners, and the injuries of one another . . . is, to confer all their power and strength upon one man, or upon one assembly of men, that may reduce all their wills, by plurality of voices, unto one will . . . This is the generation of that great Leviathan, or rather (to speak more reverently) of that *Mortal God*, to which we owe under the *Immortal God*, our peace and defence.
Thomas Hobbes (1588–1679) English philosopher.
Leviathan, Pt. II, Ch. 17

2 So long as the state exists there is no freedom. When there is freedom there will be no state.
Lenin (Vladimir Ilich Ulyanov; 1870–1924) Russian revolutionary leader.
The State and Revolution, Ch. 5

3 In a free society the state does not administer the affairs of men. It administers justice among men who conduct their own affairs.
Walter Lippman (1889–1974) US editor and writer.
An Enquiry into the Principles of a Good Society

4 The worth of a State in the long run is the worth of the individuals composing it.
John Stuart Mill (1806–73) British philosopher.
On Liberty, Ch. 5

5 The state is an instrument in the hands of the ruling class for suppressing the resistance of its class enemies.
Joseph Stalin (J. Dzhugashvili; 1879–1953) Soviet statesman.
Stalin's Kampf (ed. M. R. Werner)

STATELY HOMES

See also architecture, aristocracy, houses

1 Now Spring, sweet laxative of Georgian strains,
Quickens the ink in literary veins,
The Stately Homes of England ope their doors
To piping Nancy-boys and Crashing Bores.
Roy Campbell (1901–57) South African poet.
The Georgiad

2 The Stately Homes of England
How beautiful they stand,
To prove the upper classes

Have still the upper hand.
Noël Coward (1899–1973) British dramatist.
Operette, 'The Stately Homes of England'

3 And though the Van Dycks have to go
And we pawn the Bechstein grand,
We'll stand by the Stately Homes of England.
Noël Coward
Operette, The Stately Homes of England

4 The stately homes of England,
How beautiful they stand!
Amidst their tall ancestral trees,
O'er all the pleasant land.
Felicia Dorothea Hemans (1793–1835) British poet.
The Homes of England

5 Those comfortably padded lunatic asylums
which are known, euphemistically, as the
stately homes of England.
Virginia Woolf (1882–1941) British novelist.
The Common Reader, 'Lady Dorothy Nevill'

STATISTICS

1 A witty statesman said, you might prove
anything by figures.
Thomas Carlyle (1795–1881) Scottish historian and
essayist.
Critical and Miscellaneous Essays, 'Chartism'

2 There are three kinds of lies: lies, damned
lies and statistics.
Benjamin Disraeli (1804–81) British statesman.
Autobiography (Mark Twain)

3 We are just statistics, born to consume
resources.
Horace (Quintus Horatius Flaccus; 65–8 BC) Roman poet.
Epistles, I

4 He uses statistics as a drunken man uses
lamp-posts – for support rather than
illumination.
Andrew Lang (1844–1912) Scottish writer and poet.
Treasury of Humorous Quotations

5 You cannot feed the hungry on statistics.
David Lloyd George (1863–1945) British Liberal
statesman.
Speech, 1904
Advocating Tariff Reform

6 Statistics will prove anything, even the truth.
Noël Moynihan (1916–) British doctor and writer.
Attrib.

7 To understand God's thoughts we must study
statistics, for these are the measure of his
purpose.
Florence Nightingale (1820–1910) British nurse.
Life . . . of Francis Galton (K. Pearson), Vol. II, Ch. 13

8 I am one of the unpraised, unrewarded
millions without whom Statistics would be a
bankrupt science. It is we who are born, who
marry, who die, in constant ratios.
Logan Pearsall Smith (1865–1946) US writer.
Trivia

9 A single death is a tragedy; a million is a
statistic.
Joseph Stalin (J. Dzhugashvili; 1879–1953) Soviet
statesman.
Attrib.

10 There are two kinds of statistics, the kind
you look up and the kind you make up.
Rex Todhunter Stout (1886–1975) US writer.
Death of a Doxy, Ch. 9

11 Facts speak louder than statistics.
Geoffrey Streatfield (1897–1978) British lawyer.
The Observer, 'Sayings of the Week', 19 Mar 1950

STRIKES

See also industrial relations

1 Not a penny off the pay; not a minute on the
day.
A. J. Cook (1885–1931) British trade-union leader.
Slogan used in the miners' strike, 1926

2 There is no right to strike against the public
safety by anybody, anywhere, any time.
Calvin Coolidge (1872–1933) US president.
Remark, 14 Sept 1919
Referring to the Boston police strike

3 The trouble with employers is that they only
like ballots so long as you lose them.
Jimmy Knapp (1940–) General Secretary of the
National Union of Railwaymen.
Referring to British Rail's decision to go to court following a
ballot solidly in favour of strike action
The Guardian, 1989

4 Another fact of life that will not have escaped
you is that, in this country, the twenty-four-
hour strike is like the twenty-four-hour flu.
You have to reckon on it lasting at least five
days.
Frank Muir (1920–) British writer and broadcaster.
You Can't Have Your Kayak and Heat It (Frank Muir and Dennis Norden), 'Great Expectations'

5 Have you noticed, the last four strikes we've
had, it's pissed down? It wouldn't be a bad
idea to check the weather reports before
they pull us out next time.
Johnny Speight (1920–) British television scriptwriter.
Till Death Do Us Part

STUBBORNNESS

See also determination, inflexibility, petulance

1 You can lead a horse to the water, but you
can't make him drink.
Proverb

2 Obstinate people can be divided into the
opinionated, the ignorant, and the boorish.
Aristotle (384–322 BC) Greek philosopher.
Nicomachean Ethics, Bk. VII

3 'Tis known by the name of perseverance in a good cause, – and of obstinacy in a bad one.
Laurence Sterne (1713–68) Irish-born British writer.
Tristram Shandy

STUPIDITY

See also foolishness, ignorance

1 His mind is open; yes, it is so open that nothing is retained; ideas simply pass through him.
F. H. Bradley (1846–1924) British philosopher.
Attrib.

2 He'd be sharper than a serpent's tooth, if he wasn't as dull as ditch water.
Charles Dickens (1812–70) British novelist.
Our Mutual Friend, Bk. III, Ch. 10

3 He is not only dull in himself, but the cause of dullness in others.
Samuel Foote (1720–77) British actor and dramatist.
Parody of a line from Shakespeare's *Henry IV, Part 2*
Life of Johnson (J. Boswell)

4 The trouble with Senator Long is that he is suffering from halitosis of the intellect. That's presuming Emperor Long has an intellect.
Harold L. Ickes (1874–1952) US Republican politician.
The Politics of Upheaval (A. M. Schlesinger Jnr), Pt. II, Ch. 14

5 Jerry Ford is so dumb that he can't fart and chew gum at the same time.
Lyndon B. Johnson (1908–73) US statesman.
A Ford, Not a Lincoln (R. Reeves), Ch. 1
Sometimes quoted as '. . . can't walk and chew gum'

6 That fellow seems to me to possess but one idea, and that is a wrong one.
Samuel Johnson (1709–84) British lexicographer.
Life of Johnson (J. Boswell), Vol. II

7 I've been married six months. She looks like a million dollars, but she only knows a hundred and twenty words and she's only got two ideas in her head. The other one's hats.
Eric Linklater (1889–1974) Scottish novelist.
Juan in America, Pt. II, Ch. 5

8 You've got the brain of a four-year-old boy, and I bet he was glad to get rid of it.
Groucho Marx (Julius Marx; 1895–1977) US comedian.
Horse Feathers

9 Music-hall songs provide the dull with wit, just as proverbs provide them with wisdom.
W. Somerset Maugham (1874–1965) British novelist.
A Writer's Notebook

10 Stupidity does not consist in being without ideas. Such stupidity would be the sweet, blissful stupidity of animals, molluscs and the gods. Human Stupidity consists in having lots of ideas, but stupid ones.
Henry de Montherlant (1896–1972) French novelist.
Notebooks

11 She has a Rolls body and a Balham mind.
J. B. Morton (1893–1979) British journalist.
The Best of Beachcomber, 'A Foul Innuendo'

12 I've examined your son's head, Mr Glum, and there's nothing there.
Frank Muir (1920–) British writer and broadcaster.
Take It from Here (Frank Muir and Dennis Norden), 1957

13 You beat your pate, and fancy wit will come; Knock as you please, there's nobody at home.
Alexander Pope (1688–1744) British poet.
Epigram

14 Against stupidity the gods themselves struggle in vain.
Friedrich von Schiller (1759–1805) German dramatist.
Die Jungfrau von Orleans, III:6

15 There is no sin except stupidity.
Oscar Wilde (1854–1900) Irish-born British dramatist.
The Critic as Artist, Pt. 2

STYLE

1 Style is the man himself.
Comte de Buffon (1707–88) French naturalist.
Discours sur le style

2 Style, like sheer silk, too often hides eczema.
Albert Camus (1913–60) French existentialist writer.
The Fall

3 An author arrives at a good style when his language performs what is required of it without shyness.
Cyril Connolly (1903–74) British journalist.
Enemies of Promise, Ch. 3

4 He has never been known to use a word that might send the reader to the dictionary.
William Faulkner (1897–1962) US novelist.
Attrib.
Referring to Ernest HEMINGWAY

5 Poor Faulkner. Does he really think big emotions come from big words? He thinks I don't know the ten-dollar words. I know them all right. But there are older and simpler and better words, and those are the ones I use.
Ernest Hemingway (1899–1961) US novelist.
Attrib.
In response to a jibe by William FAULKNER

6 All styles are good except the tiresome sort.
Voltaire (François-Marie Arouet; 1694–1778) French writer.
L'Enfant prodigue, Preface

7 In matters of grave importance, style, not sincerity, is the vital thing.
Oscar Wilde (1854–1900) Irish-born British dramatist.
The Importance of Being Earnest, III

SUBJECTIVITY

See also objectivity, prejudice

1 She was one of the people who say, 'I don't

know anything about music really, but I know what I like'.

Max Beerbohm (1872–1956) British writer.
Zuleika Dobson, Ch. 16

2 An apology for the Devil – it must be remembered that we have only heard one side of the case. God has written all the books.

Samuel Butler (1835–1902) British writer.
Notebooks

3 It is a general mistake to think the men we like are good for everything, and those we do not, good for nothing.

Lord Halifax (1633–95) English statesman.
Political, Moral and Miscellaneous Thoughts and Reflections

4 He who knows only his own side of the case knows little of that.

John Stuart Mill (1806–73) British philosopher.
On Liberty, Ch. 2

5 All the world is queer save thee and me, and even thou art a little queer.

Robert Owen (1771–1858) British social reformer.
Attrib., 1828
Referring to William Allen, his partner in business

6 To observations which ourselves we make We grow more partial for th' observer's sake.

Alexander Pope (1688–1744) British poet.
Moral Essays, I

7 Partisanship is our great curse. We too readily assume that everything has two sides and that it is our duty to be on one or the other.

James Harvey Robinson (1863–1936) US historian and educator.
The Mind in the Making

SUBURBIA

1 I come from suburbia, Dan, personally, I don't ever want to go back. It's the one place in the world that's further away than anywhere else.

Frederic Raphael (1931–) British author.
The Glittering Prizes: A Sex Life, I:3

2 She was more than ever proud of the position of the bungalow, so almost in the country.

Angus Wilson (1913–) British novelist.
A Bit Off the Map, 'A Flat Country Christmas'

SUCCESS

See also achievement, failure, victory

1 Nothing succeeds like success.
Proverb

2 Nothing is harder on your laurels than resting on them.
Anonymous

3 'Tis not in mortals to command success,

But we'll do more, Sempronius; we'll deserve it.

Joseph Addison (1672–1719) British essayist.
Cato, I:2

4 The penalty of success is to be bored by people who used to snub you.

Nancy Astor (1879–1964) American-born British politician.
Sunday Express, 12 Jan 1956

5 One's religion is whatever he is most interested in, and yours is Success.

J. M. Barrie (1860–1937) British novelist and dramatist.
The Twelve-Pound Look

6 All I think about is winning that bleedin' title.

Frank Bruno (1961–) British boxer.
Remark, Jan 1989

7 The only infallible criterion of wisdom to vulgar minds – success.

Edmund Burke (1729–97) British politician.
Letter to a Member of the National Assembly

8 Success is counted sweetest
By those who ne'er succeed.

Emily Dickinson (1830–86) US poet.
Success is Counted Sweetest

9 The moral flabbiness born of the bitch-goddess Success.

William James (1842–1910) US psychologist and philosopher.
Letter to H. G. Wells, 11 Sept 1906

10 Victory has a thousand fathers but defeat is an orphan.

John Fitzgerald Kennedy (1917–63) US statesman.
Attrib.

11 The shortest and best way to make your fortune is to let people see clearly that it is in their interests to promote yours.

Jean de La Bruyère (1645–96) French satirist.
Les Caractères

12 Sweet Smell of Success.

Ernest Lehman (1920–) US screenwriter.
Novel and film title

13 As is the case in all branches of art, success depends in a very large measure upon individual initiative and exertion, and cannot be achieved except by dint of hard work.

Anna Pavlova (1881–1931) Russian ballet dancer.
Pavlova: A Biography (ed. A. H. Franks), 'Pages of My Life'

14 To succeed in the world, we do everything we can to appear successful.

Duc de la Rochefoucauld (1613–80) French writer.
Maximes, 50

15 The only place where success comes before work is a dictionary.

Vidal Sassoon (1928–) British hair stylist.
Quoting one of his teachers in a BBC radio broadcast

16 There are no gains without pains.

Adlai Stevenson (1900–65) US statesman.
Speech, Chicago, 26 July 1952

SUFFERING

1 He that lives long suffers much.
Proverb

2 Who has never tasted what is bitter does not know what is sweet.
German proverb

3 There was a faith-healer of Deal,
Who said, 'Although pain isn't real,
If I sit on a pin
And it punctures my skin,
I dislike what I fancy I feel.'
Anonymous

4 One does not love a place the less for having suffered in it unless it has all been suffering, nothing but suffering.
Jane Austen (1775–1817) British novelist.
Persuasion, Ch. 20

5 Once drinking deep of that divinest anguish,
How could I seek the empty world again?
Emily Brontë (1818–48) British novelist.
Remembrance

6 I am convinced that we have a degree of delight, and that no small one, in the real misfortunes and pains of others.
Edmund Burke (1729–97) British politician.
On the Sublime and Beautiful, Pt. I

7 Pain – has an Element of Blank –
It cannot recollect
When it begun – or if there were
A time when it was not –.
Emily Dickinson (1830–86) US poet.
Poem

8 If suffer we must, let's suffer on the heights.
Victor Hugo (1802–85) French writer.
Contemplations, 'Les Malheureux'

9 The music, yearning like a God in pain.
John Keats (1795–1821) British poet.
The Eve of Saint Agnes, VII

10 Rather suffer than die is man's motto.
Jean de La Fontaine (1621–95) French poet.
Fables, I, 'La Mort et le Bûcheron'

11 A man who fears suffering is already suffering from what he fears.
Michel de Montaigne (1533–92) French essayist.
Essais, III

12 Every reformation must have its victims. You can't expect the fatted calf to share the enthusiasm of the angels over the prodigal's return.
Saki (Hector Hugh Munro; 1870–1916) British writer.
Reginald on the Academy

13 Remember that pain has this most excellent quality: if prolonged it cannot be severe, and if severe it cannot be prolonged.
Seneca (c. 4 BC–65 AD) Roman author.
Epistulae ad Lucilium, XCIV

14 Thou art a soul in bliss; but I am bound
Upon a wheel of fire, that mine own tears
Do scald like molten lead.
William Shakespeare (1564–1616) English dramatist.
King Lear, IV:7

15 I know, by sad experience, with what difficulty a mind, weakened by long and uninterrupted suffering, admits hope, much less assurance.
Sarah Siddons (1755–1831) English actress.
Letter to Mrs. FitzHugh, 14 July 1801

SUICIDE

See also death

1 If you must commit suicide . . . always contrive to do it as decorously as possible; the decencies, whether of life or of death, should never be lost sight of.
George Borrow (1803–81) British writer.
Lavengro, Ch. 23

2 The strangest whim has seized me . . . After all
I think I will not hang myself today.
G. K. Chesterton (1874–1936) British writer.
A Ballade of Suicide

3 Not only is suicide a sin, it is the sin. It is the ultimate and absolute evil, the refusal to take the oath of loyalty to life. The man who kills a man, kills a man. The man who kills himself kills all men; as far as he is concerned he wipes out the world.
G. K. Chesterton
Orthodoxy

4 Suicide is the worst form of murder, because it leaves no opportunity for repentance.
John Churton Collins (1848–1908)
Life and Memoirs of John Churton Collins (L. C. Collins), Appendix VII

5 There are many who dare not kill themselves for fear of what the neighbours might say.
Cyril Connolly (1903–74) British journalist.
The Unquiet Grave

6 The thought of suicide is a great source of comfort: with it a calm passage is to be made across many a bad night.
Friedrich Wilhelm Nietzsche (1844–1900) German philosopher.
Jenseits von Gut und Böse

7 Razors pain you
Rivers are damp;
Acids stain you;
And drugs cause cramp.
Guns aren't lawful;
Nooses give;
Gas smells awful;
You might as well live.
Dorothy Parker (1893–1967) US writer.
Enough Rope, 'Resumé'

8 When you're between any sort of devil and

the deep blue sea, the deep blue sea
sometimes looks very inviting.
Terence Rattigan (1911–77) British dramatist.
The Deep Blue Sea

9 Next week, or next month, or next year I'll
kill myself. But I might as well last out my
month's rent, which has been paid up, and
my credit for breakfast in the morning.
Jean Rhys (1894–1979) Dominican-born British novelist.
Good Morning, Midnight, Pt. II

10 It is against the law to commit suicide in this
man's town ... although what the law can
do to a guy who commits suicide I am never
able to figure out.
Damon Runyon (1884–1946) US writer.
Guys and Dolls

11 Dost thou not see my baby at my breast
That sucks the nurse asleep?
William Shakespeare (1564–1616) English dramatist.
Antony and Cleopatra, V:2
Holding the asp to her breast

12 To be, or not to be – that is the question;
Whether 'tis nobler in the mind to suffer
The slings and arrows of outrageous fortune,
Or to take arms against a sea of troubles,
And by opposing end them? To die, to sleep –
No more; and by a sleep to say we end
The heart-ache and the thousand natural
shocks
That flesh is heir to, 'tis a consummation
Devoutly to be wish'd. To die, to sleep;
To sleep, perchance to dream. Ay, there's the
rub;
For in that sleep of death what dreams may
come,
When we have shuffled off this mortal coil,
Must give us pause.
William Shakespeare
Hamlet, III:1

13 A still small voice spake unto me,
'Thou art so full of misery,
Were it not better not to be?'
Alfred, Lord Tennyson (1809–92) British poet.
The Two Voices

14 Never murder a man who is committing
suicide.
Woodrow Wilson (1856–1925) US statesman.
Mr Wilson's War (John Dos Passos), Pt. II, Ch. 10

SUITABILITY

1 In seed time learn, in harvest teach, in
winter enjoy.
William Blake (1757–1827) British poet.
The Marriage of Heaven and Hell, 'Proverbs of Hell'

2 A cow is a very good animal in the field; but
we turn her out of a garden.
Samuel Johnson (1709–84) British lexicographer.
The Personal History of Samuel Johnson (C. Hibbert)
Responding to Boswell's objections to the expulsion of six
Methodists from Oxford University

3 Today I dressed to meet my father's eyes;
yesterday it was for my husband's.
Julia (39 BC–14 AD) Daughter of Augustus.
Saturnalia (Macrobius)
On being complimented by her father, the emperor Augustus,
on her choice of a more modest dress than the one she had
worn the previous day

4 At Christmas I no more desire a rose
Than wish a snow in May's newfangled shows.
William Shakespeare (1564–1616) English dramatist.
Love's Labour's Lost, I:1

SUMMER

See months, seasons

SUMMONS

See also invitations

1 Go, for they call you, Shepherd, from the
hill.
Matthew Arnold (1822–88) British poet and critic.
The Scholar Gipsy

2 Whistle and she'll come to you.
Francis Beaumont (1584–1616) English dramatist.
Wit Without Money, IV:4

3 Mr Watson, come here; I want you.
Alexander Graham Bell (1847–1922) Scottish scientist.
Attrib.
The first telephone conversation, 10 Mar 1876, in Boston

4 Dauntless the slug-horn to my lips I set,
And blew. *Childe Roland to the Dark Tower
came.*
Robert Browning (1812–89) British poet.
Childe Roland to the Dark Tower Came, XXXIV

SUN

See also weather

1 The Sun came up upon the left,
Out of the sea came he!
And he shone bright, and on the right
Went down into the sea.
Samuel Taylor Coleridge (1772–1834) British poet.
The Rime of the Ancient Mariner, I

2 Busy old fool, unruly Sun,
Why dost thou thus,
Through windows and through curtains call on
us?
John Donne (1573–1631) English poet.
The Sun Rising

3 I have a horror of sunsets, they're so
romantic, so operatic.
Marcel Proust (1871–1922) French novelist.
À la recherche du temps perdu: Sodome et Gomorrhe

4 ... twentieth-century woman appears to
regard sunlight as a kind of cosmetic
effulgence with a light aphrodisiac content –
which makes it a funny thing that none of her
female ancestors are recorded as seeing it

the same way. Men, of course, just go on sweating in it from century to century.

John Wyndham (1903–69) British science-fiction writer.
The Kraken Wakes

SUNDAY

1 And on the seventh day God ended his work which he had made; and he rested on the seventh day from all his work which he had made.
Bible: Genesis
2:2

2 And he said unto them, The sabbath was made for man, and not man for the sabbath: Therefore the Son of man is Lord also of the sabbath.
Bible: Mark
2:27–28

3 Of all the days that's in the week
I dearly love but one day –
And that's the day that comes betwixt
A Saturday and Monday.
Henry Carey (c. 1690–1743) English poet and musician.
Sally in our Alley

4 The better day, the worse deed.
Matthew Henry (1662–1714) English nonconformist minister.
Exposition of the Old and New Testaments

5 The feeling of Sunday is the same everywhere, heavy, melancholy, standing still. Like when they say, 'As it was in the beginning, is now, and ever shall be, world without end.'
Jean Rhys (1894–1979) Dominican-born British novelist.
Voyage in the Dark, Ch. 4

SUPERIORITY

See also equality, excellence, one-upmanship, snobbery

1 My name is George Nathaniel Curzon,
I am a most superior person.
My face is pink, my hair is sleek,
I dine at Blenheim once a week.
Anonymous
The Masque of Balliol

2 The superior man is satisfied and composed; the mean man is always full of distress.
Confucius (K'ung Fu-tzu; 551–479 BC) Chinese philosopher.
Analects

3 The superior man is distressed by his want of ability.
Confucius
Analects

4 When you meet someone better than yourself, turn your thoughts to becoming his equal. When you meet someone not as good

as you are, look within and examine your own self.
Confucius
Analects

5 And lo! Ben Adhem's name led all the rest.
Leigh Hunt (1784–1859) British poet.
Abou Ben Adhem and the Angel

6 Though I've belted you an' flayed you,
By the livin' Gawd that made you,
You're a better man than I am, Gunga Din!
Rudyard Kipling (1865–1936) Indian-born British writer.
Gunga Din

7 Sir, you have the advantage of me.
– Not yet I haven't, but wait till I get you outside.
Groucho Marx (Julius Marx; 1895–1977) US comedian.
Monkey Business

8 Above the vulgar flight of common souls.
Arthur Murphy (1727–1805) Irish dramatist, writer, and actor.
Zenobia, V

9 I teach you the Superman. Man is something that is to be surpassed.
Friedrich Wilhelm Nietzsche (1844–1900) German philosopher.
Thus Spake Zarathustra

10 It is brought home to you . . . that it is only because miners sweat their guts out that superior persons can remain superior.
George Orwell (Eric Blair; 1903–50) British novelist.
The Road to Wigan Pier, Ch. 2

11 'I believe I take precedence,' he said coldly; 'you are merely the club Bore: I am the club Liar.'
Saki (Hector Hugh Munro; 1870–1916) British writer.
A Defensive Diamond

12 In the Country of the Blind the One-eyed Man is King.
H. G. Wells (1866–1946) British writer.
The Country of the Blind

SUPERNATURAL

See also fairies

1 From ghoulies and ghosties and long-leggety beasties
And things that go bump in the night,
Good Lord, deliver us!
Anonymous
Cornish prayer

2 Open Sesame!
The Arabian Nights (c. 1500) A collection of tales from the East.
The History of Ali Baba

3 Thou shalt not suffer a witch to live.
Bible: Exodus
22:18

4 For my part, I have ever believed, and do now know, that there are witches.
Thomas Browne (1605–82) English physician and writer.
Religio Medici, Pt. I

5 This time it vanished quite slowly, beginning with the end of the tail, and ending with the grin, which remained some time after the rest of it had gone.
Lewis Carroll (Charles Lutwidge Dodgson; 1832–98) British writer.
Alice's Adventures in Wonderland, Ch. 6
Describing the Cheshire Cat

6 A savage place! as holy and enchanted
As e'er beneath a waning moon was haunted
By woman wailing for her demon-lover!
Samuel Taylor Coleridge (1772–1834) British poet.
Kubla Khan

7 The girl is lost; she is burnt flesh.
Umberto Eco (1932–) Italian semiologist and writer.
Referring to a suspected witch
The Name of the Rose

8 Religion
Has made an honest woman of the supernatural,
And we won't have it kicking over the traces again.
Christopher Fry (1907–) British dramatist.
The Lady's Not for Burning, II

9 All argument is against it; but all belief is for it.
Samuel Johnson (1709–84) British lexicographer.
Life of Johnson (J. Boswell), Vol. III
Of the ghost of a dead person

10 'La belle Dame sans Merci
Hath thee in thrall!'
John Keats (1795–1821) British poet.
La Belle Dame Sans Merci

11 That old black magic has me in its spell.
Johnny Mercer (1909–76) US lyricist and composer.
That Old Black Magic

12 Once upon a midnight dreary, while I pondered, weak and weary,
Over many a quaint and curious volume of forgotten lore,
While I nodded, nearly napping, suddenly there came a tapping,
As of some one gently rapping, rapping at my chamber door.
Edgar Allan Poe (1809–49) US poet and writer.
The Raven

13 There are more things in heaven and earth, Horatio,
Than are dreamt of in your philosophy.
William Shakespeare (1564–1616) English dramatist.
Hamlet, I:5

14 This supernatural soliciting
Cannot be ill; cannot be good.
William Shakespeare
Macbeth, I:3

15 His face was a strong – a very strong – aquiline, with high bridge of the thin nose and peculiarly arched nostrils . . . The mouth . . . was fixed and rather cruel-looking, with peculiarly sharp white teeth; these protruded over the lips, whose remarkable ruddiness showed astonishing vitality in a man of his years.
Bram Stoker (1847–1912) Irish novelist.
Referring to Count Dracula
Dracula, Ch. 2

16 His eyes flamed red with devilish passion; the great nostrils of the white aquiline nose opened wide and quivered at the edges; and the white sharp teeth, behind the full lips of the blood-dripping mouth, champed together like those of a wild beast.
Bram Stoker
Dracula, Ch. 21

SUPERSTITION

See also luck

1 A dimple in the chin, a devil within.
Proverb

2 Meet on the stairs and you won't meet in heaven.
Proverb

3 One for sorrow, two for mirth; three for a wedding, four for a birth; five for silver, six for gold; seven for a secret, not to be told; eight for heaven, nine for hell; and ten for the devil's own sel.
Proverb
Referring to magpies or crows; there are numerous variants

4 See a pin and pick it up, all the day you'll have good luck; see a pin and let it lie, you'll want a pin before you die.
Proverb

5 Third time lucky.
Proverb

6 Of course I don't believe in it. But I understand that it brings you luck whether you believe in it or not.
Niels Bohr (1885–1962) Danish physicist.
Attrib.
When asked why he had a horseshoe on his wall

7 Superstition is the religion of feeble minds.
Edmund Burke (1729–97) British politician.
Reflections on the Revolution in France

8 Superstition is the poetry of life.
Goethe (1749–1832) German poet and dramatist.
Sprüche in Prosa, III

9 And some of the bigger bears try to pretend
That they came round the corner to look for a friend;
And they'll try to pretend that nobody cares

Whether you walk on the lines or the squares.
A. A. Milne (1882–1956) British writer.
When We Were Very Young, 'Lines and Squares'

10 They say there is divinity in odd numbers,
either in nativity, chance, or death.
William Shakespeare (1564–1616) English dramatist.
The Merry Wives of Windsor, V:1

11 Superstition sets the whole world in flames;
philosophy quenches them.
Voltaire (François-Marie Arouet; 1694–1778) French
writer.
Dictionnaire philosophique, 'Superstition'

SUPPORT

See also loyalty

1 He found him in a desert land, and in the
waste howling wilderness; he led him about,
he instructed him, he kept him as the apple
of his eye.
Bible: Deuteronomy
32:10

2 The finest plans have always been spoiled by
the littleness of those that should carry them
out. Even emperors can't do it all by
themselves.
Bertolt Brecht (1898–1956) German dramatist.
Mother Courage, VI

3 Either back us or sack us.
James Callaghan (1912–) British politician and prime
minister.
Speech, Labour Party Conference, Brighton, 5 Oct 1977

4 What I want is men who will support me
when I am in the wrong.
Lord Melbourne (1779–1848) British statesman.
Lord M. (Lord David Cecil)
Replying to someone who said he would support Melbourne as
long as he was in the right

5 While I cannot be regarded as a pillar, I must
be regarded as a buttress of the church,
because I support it from the outside.
Lord Melbourne
Attrib.

6 Ladies and gentleman, it takes more than one
to make a ballet.
Ninette de Valois (Edris Stannus; 1898–) British ballet
dancer and choreographer.
New Yorker

SURVIVAL

See also evolution, self-preservation

1 I haven't asked you to make me young again.
All I want is to go on getting older.
Konrad Adenauer (1876–1967) German statesman.
Attrib.
Replying to his doctor

2 The perpetual struggle for room and food.
Thomas Robert Malthus (1766–1834) British clergyman
and economist.
Essays on the Principle of Population

3 The thing-in-itself, the will-to-live, exists
whole and undivided in every being, even in
the tiniest; it is present as completely as in
all that ever were, are, and will be, taken
together.
Arthur Schopenhauer (1788–1860) German philosopher.
Parerga and Paralipomena

4 This is the Law of the Yukon, that only the
strong shall thrive;
That surely the weak shall perish, and only the
Fit survive.
Robert William Service (1874–1958) Canadian poet.
The Law of the Yukon

SUSPICION

See also mistrust

1 Suspicions amongst thoughts are like bats
amongst birds, they ever fly by twilight.
Francis Bacon (1561–1626) English philosopher.
Essays, 'Of Suspicion'

SWITZERLAND

See also Europe

1 Since both its national products, snow and
chocolate, melt, the cuckoo clock was
invented solely in order to give tourists
something solid to remember it by.
Alan Coren (1938–) British humorist and writer.
The Sanity Inspector, 'And Though They Do Their Best'

2 The Swiss who are not a people so much as
a neat clean quite solvent business.
William Faulkner (1897–1962) US novelist.
Intruder in the Dust, Ch. 7

3 I look upon Switzerland as an inferior sort of
Scotland.
Sydney Smith (1771–1845) British clergyman and
essayist.
Letter to Lord Holland, 1815

4 They say that if the Swiss had designed
these mountains they'd be rather flatter.
Paul Theroux (1941–) US-born writer.
The Great Railway Bazaar, Ch. 28
Referring to the Alps

5 In Italy for thirty years under the Borgias
they had warfare, terror, murder, bloodshed
– they produced Michelangelo, Leonardo da
Vinci and the Renaissance. In Switzerland
they had brotherly love, five hundred years
of democracy and peace, and what did they
produce . . . ? The cuckoo clock.
Orson Welles (1915–85) US film actor.
The Third Man

SYMPATHY

See also comfort

1 Sympathy – for all these people, for being foreigners – lay over the gathering like a woolly blanket; and no one was enjoying it at all.
Malcolm Bradbury (1932–) British academic and novelist.
Eating People is Wrong, Ch. 2

2 To be sympathetic without discrimination is so very debilitating.
Ronald Firbank (1886–1926) British novelist.
Vainglory

3 She was a machine-gun riddling her hostess with sympathy.
Aldous Huxley (1894–1964) British novelist.
Mortal Coils, 'The Gioconda Smile'

4 I can sympathize with people's pains, but not with their pleasures. There is something curiously boring about somebody else's happiness.
Aldous Huxley
Limbo, 'Cynthia'

5 To show pity is felt as a sign of contempt because one has clearly ceased to be an object of *fear* as soon as one is pitied.
Friedrich Wilhelm Nietzsche (1844–1900) German philosopher.
The Wanderer and His Shadow

6 I can sympathize with everything, except suffering.
Oscar Wilde (1854–1900) Irish-born British dramatist.
The Picture of Dorian Gray, Ch. 3

T

TACT

See also diplomacy

1 Leave well alone.
Proverb

2 Let sleeping dogs lie.
Proverb

3 Social tact is making your company feel at home, even though you wish they were.
Anonymous

4 One shouldn't talk of halters in the hanged man's house.
Miguel de Cervantes (1547–1616) Spanish novelist.
Don Quixote, Pt. I, Ch. 25

5 Tact consists in knowing how far we may go too far.
Jean Cocteau (1889–1963) French poet and artist.
In *Treasury of Humorous Quotations*

6 My advice was delicately poised between the cliché and the indiscretion.
Robert Runcie (1921–) British churchman (Archbishop of Canterbury).
Comment to the press concerning his advice to the Prince of Wales and Lady Diana Spencer on their approaching wedding, 13 July 1981

TALENT

See also genius, talent and genius

1 Whom the gods wish to destroy they first call promising.
Cyril Connolly (1903–74) British journalist.
Enemies of Promise, Ch. 3

2 Talent develops in quiet places, character in the full current of human life.
Goethe (1749–1832) German poet and dramatist.
Torquato Tasso, I

3 Middle age snuffs out more talent than even wars or sudden deaths do.
Richard Hughes (1900–) British writer.
The Fox in the Attic

4 There is no substitute for talent. Industry and all the virtues are of no avail.
Aldous Huxley (1894–1964) British novelist.
Point Counter Point

5 I think it's the most extraordinary collection of talent, of human knowledge, that has ever been gathered together at the White House – with the possible exception of when Thomas Jefferson dined alone.
John Fitzgerald Kennedy (1917–63) US statesman.
Said at a dinner for Nobel Prizewinners, 29 Apr 1962

6 It's not enough to be Hungarian, you must have talent too.
Alexander Korda (Sandor Kellner; 1893–1956) Hungarian-born British film director.
Alexander Korda (K. Kulik)

7 Let our children grow tall, and some taller than others if they have it in them to do so.
Margaret Thatcher (1925–) British politician and prime minister.
Speech, US tour, 1975

TALENT AND GENIUS

See also genius, talent

1 It takes people a long time to learn the difference between talent and genius, especially ambitious young men and women.
Louisa May Alcott (1832–88) US novelist.
Little Women, Pt. II

2 Mediocrity knows nothing higher than itself, but talent instantly recognizes genius.
Arthur Conan Doyle (1856–1930) British writer.
The Valley of Fear

3 Genius does what it must, and Talent does what it can.

Owen Meredith (Robert Bulwer-Lytton, 1st Earl of Lytton; 1831–91) British statesman and poet.
Last Words of a Sensitive Second-rate Poet

TASTE

See also difference, individuality

1 Good taste is better than bad taste, but bad taste is better than no taste.

Arnold Bennett (1867–1931) British novelist.
The Observer, 'Sayings of the Week', 24 Aug 1930

2 Taste is the feminine of genius.

Edward Fitzgerald (1809–83) British poet.
Letter to J. R. Lowell, Oct 1877

3 Our tastes greatly alter. The lad does not care for the child's rattle, and the old man does not care for the young man's whore.

Samuel Johnson (1709–84) British lexicographer.
Life of Johnson (J. Boswell), Vol. II

4 What is food to one man is bitter poison to others.

Lucretius (Titus Lucretius Carus; c. 99–55 BC) Roman philosopher.
On the Nature of the Universe, IV

5 The kind of people who always go on about whether a thing is in good taste invariably have very bad taste.

Joe Orton (1933–67) British dramatist.
Attrib.

6 The play, I remember, pleas'd not the million; 'twas caviare to the general.

William Shakespeare (1564–1616) English dramatist.
Hamlet, II:2

7 You had no taste when you married me.

Richard Brinsley Sheridan (1751–1816) British dramatist.
The School for Scandal, I

TAXATION

1 They can't collect legal taxes from illegal money.

Al Capone (1899–1947) Italian-born US gangster.
Objecting to the US Bureau of Internal Revenue claiming large sums in unpaid back tax
Capone (J. Kobler)

2 The hardest thing in the world to understand is income tax.

Albert Einstein (1879–1955) German-born US physicist.
Attrib.

3 The greatest harm that cometh of a king's poverty is, that he shall by necessity be forced to find exquisite means of getting goods, as to put in default some of his subjects that be innocent, and upon the rich men more than the poor, because they may the better pay.

John Fortescue (c. 1394–1476) English jurist.
The Governance of England

4 In this world nothing is certain but death and taxes.

Benjamin Franklin (1706–90) US scientist and statesman.
Letter to Jean-Baptiste Leroy, 13 Nov 1789

5 *Excise.* A hateful tax levied upon commodities.

Samuel Johnson (1709–84) British lexicographer.
Dictionary of the English Language

6 Sir, I now pay you this exorbitant charge, but I must ask you to explain to her Majesty that she must not in future look upon me as a source of income.

Charles Kemble (1775–1854) British actor.
On being obliged to hand over his income tax to the tax collector
Humour in the Theatre (J. Aye)

7 The avoidance of taxes is the only pursuit that still carries any reward.

John Maynard Keynes (1883–1946) British economist.
Attrib.

8 The Chancellor of the Exchequer is a man whose duties make him more or less of a taxing machine. He is intrusted with a certain amount of misery which it is his duty to distribute as fairly as he can.

Robert Lowe (1811–92) British lawyer and politician.
Speech, House of Commons, 11 Apr 1870

9 The taxpayer is someone who works for the federal government but doesn't have to take a civil service examination.

Ronald Reagan (1911–) US politician and president.
Attrib.

10 There is no art which one government sooner learns of another than that of draining money from the pockets of the people.

Adam Smith (1723–90) Scottish economist.
The Wealth of Nations

11 For God's sake, madam, don't say that in England for if you do, they will surely tax it.

Jonathan Swift (1667–1745) Irish-born Anglican priest and writer.
Responding to Lady Carteret's admiration for the quality of the air in Ireland
Lives of the Wits (H. Pearson)

TECHNOLOGY

See also progress, science

1 Give me a firm place to stand, and I will move the earth.

Archimedes (c. 287–212 BC) Greek mathematician.
On the Lever

2 Man is a tool-using animal.

Thomas Carlyle (1795–1881) Scottish historian and essayist.
Sartor Resartus, Bk. I, Ch. 5

3 Any sufficiently advanced technology is indistinguishable from magic.
Arthur C. Clarke (1917–) British science-fiction writer.
The Lost Worlds of 2001

4 Man is a tool-making animal.
Benjamin Franklin (1706–90) US scientist and statesman.
Life of Johnson (J. Boswell), 7 Apr 1778

5 One machine can do the work of fifty ordinary men. No machine can do the work of one extraordinary man.
Elbert Hubbard (1856–1915) US writer.
Roycroft Dictionary and Book of Epigrams

6 That plastic Buddha jars out a Karate screech

Before the soft words with their spores
The cosmetic breath of the gravestone

Death invented the phone it looks like the altar of death
Ted Hughes (1930–) British poet.
Selected Poems 1957–1981, 'Do not Pick up the Telephone'

7 Have strong suspicions that Crippen London cellar murderer and accomplice are amongst saloon passengers moustache taken off growing beard accomplice dressed as boy voice manner and build undoubtedly a girl both travelling as Mr and Master Robinson
Captain Kendall
This was the first time a wireless telegraphy message from a ship at sea led to the arrest of criminals
Telegram to Scotland Yard, 22 July 1910

8 It was difficult to decide whether the system that produced the kettle was a miracle of human ingenuity and co-operation or a colossal waste of resources, human and natural. Would we all be better off boiling our water in a pot hung over an open fire? Or was it the facility to do such things at the touch of a button that freed men, and more particularly women, from servile labour and made it possible for them to become literary critics?
David Lodge (1935–) British author.
Nice Work, V

9 The new electronic interdependence recreates the world in the image of a global village.
Marshall McLuhan (1911–81) Canadian sociologist.
The Gutenberg Galaxy

10 For tribal man space was the uncontrollable mystery. For technological man it is time that occupies the same role.
Marshall McLuhan
The Mechanical Bride, 'Magic that Changes Mood'

11 The machine threatens all achievement.
Rainer Maria Rilke (1875–1926) Austrian poet.
Die Sonette an Orpheus, II, 10

12 Pylons, those pillars

Bare like nude giant girls that have no secret.
Stephen Spender (1909–) British poet.
The Pylons

13 No man . . . who has wrestled with a self-adjusting card table can ever quite be the man he once was.
James Thurber (1894–1961) US humorist.
Let Your Mind Alone, 'Sex ex Machina'

14 I see no reason to suppose that these machines will ever force themselves into general use.
Duke of Wellington (1769–1852) British general and statesman.
Referring to steam locomotives
Geoffrey Madan's Notebooks (J. Gere)

TEETH

1 For years I have let dentists ride roughshod over my teeth: I have been sawed, hacked, chopped, whittled, bewitched, bewildered, tattooed, and signed on again; but this is cuspid's last stand.
S. J. Perelman (1904–79) US humorous writer.
Crazy Like a Fox, 'Nothing but the Tooth'

2 I'll dispose of my teeth as I see fit, and after they've gone, I'll get along. I started off living on gruel, and by God, I can always go back to it again.
S. J. Perelman
Crazy Like a Fox, 'Nothing but the Tooth'

3 Certain people are born with natural false teeth.
Robert Robinson (1927–) British writer and broadcaster.
BBC radio programme, *Stop the Week*, 1977

4 Adam and Eve had many advantages, but the principal one was that they escaped teething.
Mark Twain (Samuel Langhorne Clemens; 1835–1910) US writer.
The Tragedy of Pudd'nhead Wilson, Ch. 4

5 To lose a lover or even a husband or two during the course of one's life can be vexing. But to lose one's teeth is a catastrophe.
Hugh Wheeler (1912–87) British-born US writer.
A Little Night Music

TELEGRAMS

1 To hell with you. Offensive letter follows.
Anonymous
Telegram to Sir Alec Douglas-Home

2 Winston's back.
Anonymous
Signal to all ships of the Royal Navy from the Admiralty when Churchill was reappointed First Sea Lord, 3 Sept 1939

3 Streets full of water. Please advise.
Robert Benchley (1889–1945) US humorist.
Telegram sent to his editor on arriving in Venice
Attrib.

4 Price of Herald three cents daily.
James Gordon Bennett (1841–1918) US editor.
Telegram to William Randolph Hearst, when he heard that
Hearst was trying to buy his paper
The Life and Death of the Press Barons (P. Brandon)

5 Nothing to be fixed except your performance.
Noël Coward (1899–1973) British dramatist.
Replying to a telegram from the actress Gertrude Lawrence –
'Nothing wrong that can't be fixed' – referring to her part in
Coward's play *Private Lives*
Noël Coward and his Friends

6 Dear Mrs A., hooray hooray,
At last you are deflowered
On this as every other day
I love you. Noël Coward.
Noël Coward
Telegram to Gertrude Lawrence on her marriage to Richard
S. Aldrich

7 'Old Cary Grant fine. How you?'
Cary Grant (Archibald Leach; 1904–86) British-born US
film star.
Replying to a telegram sent to his agent inquiring: 'How old
Cary Grant?'
The Filmgoer's Book of Quotes (Leslie Halliwell)

8 ?
Victor Hugo (1802–85) French writer.
The entire contents of a telegram sent to his publishers asking
how *Les Misérables* was selling the reply was '!'
The Literary Life (R. Hendrickson)

9 Have strong suspicions that Crippen London
cellar murderer and accomplice are amongst
saloon passengers moustache taken off
growing beard accomplice dressed as boy
voice manner and build undoubtedly a girl
both travelling as Mr and Master Robinson.
Captain Kendall
This was the first time a wireless telegraphy message from a
ship at sea led to the arrest of criminals
Telegram to Scotland Yard, 22 July 1910

10 We have finished the job, what shall we do
with the tools?
Haile Selassie (1892–1975) Emperor of Ethiopia.
Telegram to Winston Churchill, mimicking his 'Give us the
tools, and we will finish the job'
Ambrosia and Small Beer, Ch. 4 (Edward Marsh)

11 Reports of my death are greatly exaggerated.
Mark Twain (Samuel Langhorne Clemens; 1835–1910)
US writer.
On learning that his obituary had been published
Cable to the Associated Press

12 Nurse unupblown.
Evelyn Waugh (1903–66) British novelist.
Cable sent after he had failed, while a journalist serving in
Ethiopia, to substantiate a rumour that an English nurse had
been blown up in an Italian air raid
Our Marvelous Native Tongue (R. Claiborne)

13 No, no, Oscar, you forget. When you and I
are together we never talk about anything
except me.
James Whistler (1834–1903) US painter.
Cable replying to Oscar Wilde's message: 'When you and I are
together we never talk about anything except ourselves'
The Gentle Art of Making Enemies

TELEVISION

1 Television is more interesting than people. If
it were not, we should have people standing
in the corners of our rooms.
Alan Coren (1938–) British humorist and writer.
In *The Times*

2 If any reader of this book is in the grip of
some habit of which he is deeply ashamed, I
advise him not to give way to it in secret but
to do it on television. No-one will pass him
with averted gaze on the other side of the
street. People will cross the road at the risk
of losing their own lives in order to say 'We
saw you on the telly'.
Quentin Crisp (?1910–) Model, publicist, and writer.
How to Become a Virgin

3 Television is an invention that permits you to
be entertained in your living room by people
you wouldn't have in your home.
David Frost (1939–) British television personality.
Attrib., CBS television, 1971

4 Television brought the brutality of war into
the comfort of the living room. Vietnam was
lost in the living rooms of America – not on
the battlefields of Vietnam.
Marshall McLuhan (1911–81) Canadian sociologist.
Montreal *Gazette*, 16 May 1975

5 Television? No good will come of this device.
The word is half Greek and half Latin.
C. P. Scott (1846–1932) British journalist.
Attrib.

TEMPTATION

1 Forbidden fruit is sweet.
Proverb

2 If you can't be good, be careful.
Proverb

3 I am not over-fond of resisting temptation.
William Beckford (1759–1844) British writer.
Vathek

4 Blessed is the man that endureth temptation:
for when he is tried, he shall receive the
crown of life, which the Lord hath promised
to them that love him.
Bible: James
1:12

5 All the deceits of the world, the flesh, and
the devil.
The Book of Common Prayer
Morning Prayer, Prayer of St Chrysostom

6 Not all that tempts your wand'ring eyes
And heedless hearts, is lawful prize;
Nor all, that glisters, gold.
Thomas Gray (1716–71) British poet.
Ode on the Death of a Favourite Cat

7 'You oughtn't to yield to temptation.'

'Well, somebody must, or the thing becomes absurd.'
Anthony Hope (Sir Anthony Hope Hawkins; 1863–1933) British novelist.
The Dolly Dialogues

8 ... with peaches and women, it's only the side next the sun that's tempting.
Ouida (Marie Louise de la Ramée; 1839–1908) British novelist.
Strathmore

9 I never resist temptation because I have found that things that are bad for me never tempt me.
George Bernard Shaw (1856–1950) Irish dramatist and critic.
The Apple Cart

10 I can resist everything except temptation.
Oscar Wilde (1854–1900) Irish-born British dramatist.
Lady Windermere's Fan, I

11 The only way to get rid of a temptation is to yield to it.
Oscar Wilde
Repeating a similar sentiment expressed by Clementina Stirling Graham (1782–1877)
The Picture of Dorian Gray, Ch. 2

THEATRE

See also acting, actors, audiences, criticism, literature, plays, Shakespeare

1 The reason why Absurdist plays take place in No Man's Land with only two characters is primarily financial.
Arthur Adamov (1908–70) Russian-born French dramatist.
Said at the Edinburgh International Drama Conference, 13 Sept 1963

2 It's one of the tragic ironies of the theatre that only one man in it can count on steady work – the night watchman.
Tallulah Bankhead (1903–68) US actress.
Tallulah, Ch. 1

3 Tragedy is if I cut my finger. Comedy is if I walk into an open sewer and die.
Mel Brooks (Melvyn Kaminsky; 1926–) US film director.
New Yorker, 30 Oct 1978

4 All tragedies are finish'd by a death,
All comedies are ended by a marriage.
Lord Byron (1788–1824) British poet.
Don Juan, III

5 You know, I go to the theatre to be entertained... I don't want to see plays about rape, sodomy and drug addiction... I can get all that at home.
Peter Cook (1937–) British writer and entertainer.
The Observer, caption to cartoon, 8 July 1962

6 Don't put your daughter on the stage, Mrs Worthington.
Noël Coward (1899–1973) British dramatist.
Title of song

7 Farce is the essential theatre. Farce refined becomes high comedy: farce brutalized becomes tragedy.
Gordon Craig (1872–1966) British actor.
The Story of my Days, Index

8 We participate in a tragedy; at a comedy we only look.
Aldous Huxley (1894–1964) British novelist.
The Devils of Loudon, Ch. 11

9 I never deliberately set out to shock, but when people don't walk out of my plays I think there is something wrong.
John Osborne (1929–) British dramatist.
The Observer, 'Sayings of the Week', 19 Jan 1975

10 I depict men as they ought to be, but Euripides portrays them as they are.
Sophocles (c. 496–406 BC) Greek dramatist.
Poetics (Aristotle)

11 The bad end unhappily, the good unluckily. That is what tragedy means.
Tom Stoppard (1937–) Czech-born British dramatist.
Rosencrantz and Guildenstern Are Dead, II

12 I would just like to mention Robert Houdin who in the eighteenth century invented the vanishing bird-cage trick and the theater matinée – may he rot and perish. Good afternoon.
Orson Welles (1915–85) US film actor.
Addressing the audience at the end of a matinée performance
Great Theatrical Disasters (G. Brandreth)

THEFT

See also crime

1 The fault is great in man or woman
Who steals a goose from off a common;
But what can plead that man's excuse
Who steals a common from a goose?
Anonymous
The Tickler Magazine, 1 Feb 1821

2 They will steal the very teeth out of your mouth as you walk through the streets. I know it from experience.
William Arabin (1773–1841) British judge.
Referring to the people of Uxbridge
Arabinesque at Law (Sir R. Megarry)

3 Prisoner, God has given you good abilities, instead of which you go about the country stealing ducks.
William Arabin
Arabinesque at Law (Sir R. Megarry)

4 I am laughing to think what risks you take to

try to find money in a desk by night where
the legal owner can never find any by day.

Honoré de Balzac (1799–1850) French novelist.
Said on waking to find a burglar in the room
Attrib.

5 Stolen sweets are best.

Colley Cibber (1671–1757) British actor and dramatist.
The Rival Fools, I

6 Travel light and you can sing in the robber's
face.

Juvenal (Decimus Junius Juvenalis; 60–130 AD) Roman
satirist.
Satires, X

7 Stolen sweets are always sweeter,
Stolen kisses much completer,
Stolen looks are nice in chapels,
Stolen, stolen, be your apples.

Hunt Leigh (1784–1859) British poet.
Song of Fairies Robbing an Orchard

THEORY

See also ideas

1 A thing may look specious in theory, and yet
be ruinous in practice; a thing may look evil
in theory, and yet be in practice excellent.

Edmund Burke (1729–97) British politician.
Impeachment of Warren Hastings, 19 Feb 1788

2 A theory can be proved by experiment; but
no path leads from experiment to the birth of
a theory.

Albert Einstein (1879–1955) German-born US physicist.
The Sunday Times, 18 July 1976

3 For hundreds of pages the closely-reasoned
arguments unroll, axioms and theorems
interlock. And what remains with us in the
end? A general sense that the world can be
expressed in closely-reasoned arguments, in
interlocking axioms and theorems.

Michael Frayn (1933–) British journalist and writer.
Constructions

4 Dear friend, theory is all grey,
And the golden tree of life is green.

Goethe (1749–1832) German poet and dramatist.
Faust, Pt. I

5 You know very well that unless you're a
scientist, it's much more important for a
theory to be shapely, than for it to be true.

Christopher Hampton (1946–) British writer and
dramatist.
The Philanthropist, Sc. 1

6 It is a good morning exercise for a research
scientist to discard a pet hypothesis every
day before breakfast. It keeps him young.

Konrad Lorenz (1903–89) Austrian zoologist.
On Aggression, Ch. 2

7 When the torrent sweeps a man against a
boulder, you must expect him to scream, and

you need not be surprised if the scream is
sometimes a theory.

Robert Louis Stevenson (1850–94) Scottish writer.
Virginibus Puerisque

THINKING

See also intellect, intelligence, mind, philosophy

1 I have always found that the man whose
second thoughts are good is worth watching.

J. M. Barrie (1860–1937) British novelist and dramatist.
What Every Woman Knows, III

2 Mirrors should think longer before they
reflect.

Jean Cocteau (1889–1963) French poet and artist.
The Sunday Times, 20 Oct 1963

3 *Cogito, ergo sum.*
I think, therefore I am.

René Descartes (1596–1650) French philosopher.
Le Discours de la méthode

4 The most fluent talkers or most plausible
reasoners are not always the justest thinkers.

William Hazlitt (1778–1830) British essayist.
On Prejudice

5 Most of one's life . . . is one prolonged effort
to prevent oneself thinking.

Aldous Huxley (1894–1964) British novelist.
Mortal Coils, 'Green Tunnels'

6 You can't think rationally on an empty
stomach, and a whole lot of people can't do it
on a full one either.

Lord Reith (1889–1971) British administrator.
Attrib.

7 People don't seem to realize that it takes
time and effort and preparation to think.
Statesmen are far too busy making speeches
to think.

Bertrand Russell (1872–1970) British philosopher.
Kenneth Harris Talking To: 'Bertrand Russell' (Kenneth Harris)

8 Many people would sooner die than think. In
fact they do.

Bertrand Russell
Thinking About Thinking (A. Flew)

9 My thought is *me*: that is why I can't stop. I
exist by what I think . . . and I can't prevent
myself from thinking.

Jean-Paul Sartre (1905–80) French writer.
Nausea

10 There is nothing either good or bad, but
thinking makes it so.

William Shakespeare (1564–1616) English dramatist.
Hamlet, II:2

11 Thinking is to me the greatest fatigue in the
world.

John Vanbrugh (1664–1726) English architect and
dramatist.
The Relapse, II:1

12 Great thoughts come from the heart.

Marquis de Vauvenargues (1715–47) French soldier and writer.
Réflexions et maximes

13 In order to draw a limit to thinking, we should have to be able to think both sides of this limit.

Ludwig Wittgenstein (1889–1951) Austrian philosopher.
Tractatus Logico-Philosophicus, Preface

THIRST

See also alcohol, desire, drinks, hunger

1 There are two reasons for drinking; one is, when you are thirsty, to cure it; the other, when you are not thirsty, to prevent it . . . Prevention is better than cure.

Thomas Love Peacock (1785–1866) British novelist.
Melincourt

2 I drink for the thirst to come.

François Rabelais (1483–1553) French satirist.
Gargantua, Bk. I, Ch. 5

3 As pants the hart for cooling streams
When heated in the chase.

Nahum Tate (1652–1715) Irish-born English poet.
New Version of the Psalms, 'As Pants the Hart'

THREATS

1 Violet Elizabeth dried her tears. She saw that they were useless and she did not believe in wasting her effects. 'All right,' she said calmly, 'I'll thcream then. I'll thcream, an' thcream, an' thcream till I'm thick.'

Richmal Crompton (Richmal Crompton Lamburn; 1890–1969) British writer.
Violet Elizabeth Bott, a character in the *William* books, had both a lisp and an exceptional ability to get her own way
Just William

2 If you start throwing hedgehogs under me, I shall throw two porcupines under you.

Nikita Khrushchev (1894–1971) Soviet statesman.
The Observer, 'Sayings of the Week', 10 Nov 1963

3 After I die, I shall return to earth as a gatekeeper of a bordello and I won't let any of you – not a one of you – enter!

Arturo Toscanini (1867–1957) Italian conductor.
Rebuking an incompetent orchestra
The Maestro: The Life of Arturo Toscanini (Howard Taubman)

THRIFT

See also extravagance, money

1 A penny saved is a penny earned.
Proverb

2 Keep something for a rainy day.
Proverb

3 Penny wise, pound foolish.
Proverb

4 I knew once a very covetous, sordid fellow, who used to say, 'Take care of the pence, for the pounds will take care of themselves.'

Earl of Chesterfield (1694–1773) English statesman.
Possibly referring to William Lowndes
Letter to his son, 6 Nov 1747

5 . . . we owe something to extravagance, for thrift and adventure seldom go hand in hand.

Jennie Jerome Churchill (1854–1921) US-born British hostess and writer.
Pearson's, 'Extravagance'

6 Thrift has nearly killed her on several occasions, through the agency of old sausages, slow-punctured tyres, rusty blades.

Margaret Drabble (1939–) British novelist.
The Radiant Way

7 Everybody is always in favour of general economy and particular expenditure.

Anthony Eden (1897–1977) British statesman.
The Observer, 'Sayings of the Week', 17 June 1956

8 Economy is going without something you do want in case you should, some day, want something you probably won't want.

Anthony Hope (Sir Anthony Hope Hawkins; 1863–1933) British novelist.
The Dolly Dialogues

9 What! Can't a fellow even enjoy a biscuit any more?

Duke of Portland (1857–1943) British peer.
On being informed that as one of several measures to reduce his own expenses he would have to dispense with one of his two Italian pastry cooks
Their Noble Lordships (S. Winchester)

10 A hole is the accident of a day, while a darn is premeditated poverty.

Edward Shuter (1728–76) British actor.
Explaining why he did not mend the holes in his stocking
Dictionary of National Biography

11 Beware of all enterprises that require new clothes.

Henry David Thoreau (1817–62) US writer.
Walden, 'Economy'

TIME

See also eternity, future, life, past, present, transience

1 An hour in the morning is worth two in the evening.
Proverb

2 There are only twenty-four hours in the day.
Proverb

3 There is a time and place for everything.
Proverb

4 Time and tide wait for no man.
Proverb

5 Time is a great healer.
Proverb

6 Time will tell.
Proverb

7 Except Time all other things are created.
Time is the creator; and Time has no limit,
neither top nor bottom.
The Persian Rivayat

8 To choose time is to save time.
Francis Bacon (1561–1626) English philosopher.
Essays, 'Of Dispatch'

9 VLADIMIR. That passed the time.
ESTRAGON. It would have passed in any case.
VLADIMIR. Yes, but not so rapidly.
Samuel Beckett (1906–89) Irish novelist and dramatist.
Waiting for Godot, I

10 I believe the twenty-four hour day has come
to stay.
Max Beerbohm (1872–1956) British writer.
A Christmas Garland, 'Perkins and Mankind'

11 Time is a great teacher, but unfortunately it
kills all its pupils.
Hector Berlioz (1803–69) French composer.
Almanach des lettres françaises

12 To every thing there is a season, and a time
to every purpose under the heaven:
A time to be born, and a time to die; a time to
plant, and a time to pluck up that which is
planted;
A time to kill, and a time to heal; a time to
break down, and a time to build up;
A time to weep, and a time to laugh; a time to
mourn, and a time to dance;
A time to cast away stones, and a time to gather stones together; a time to embrace, and a
time to refrain from embracing;
A time to get, and a time to lose; a time to
keep, and a time to cast away;
A time to rend, and a time to sew; a time to
keep silence, and a time to speak;
A time to love, and a time to hate; a time of
war, and a time of peace.
Bible: Ecclesiastes
3:1–8

13 Men talk of killing time, while time quietly
kills them.
Dion Boucicault (Dionysius Lardner Boursiquot; 1820–
90) Irish-born US actor and dramatist.
London Assurance, II:1

14 Time, like a loan from the bank, is something
you're only given when you possess so much
that you don't need it.
John Braine (1922–86) British novelist.
Room at the Top, Ch. 15

15 I recommend you to take care of the
minutes: for hours will take care of
themselves.
Earl of Chesterfield (1694–1773) English statesman.
Letter to his son, 6 Nov 1747

16 Time present and time past
Are both perhaps present in time future

And time future contained in time past.
T. S. Eliot (1888–1965) US-born British poet and
dramatist.
Four Quartets

17 Come, fill the Cup, and in the Fire of Spring
The Winter Garment of Repentance fling:
The Bird of Time has but a little way
To fly – and Lo! the Bird is on the Wing.
Edward Fitzgerald (1809–83) British poet.
The Rubáiyát of Omar Khayyám

18 Ah, fill the Cup: – what boots it to repeat
How Time is slipping underneath our Feet:
Unborn TOMORROW, and dead
YESTERDAY,
Why fret about them if TODAY be sweet!
Edward Fitzgerald
The Rubáiyát of Omar Khayyám

19 Dost thou love life? Then do not squander
time, for that's the stuff life is made of.
Benjamin Franklin (1706–90) US scientist and statesman.
Poor Richard's Almanack

20 You must remember this;
A kiss is just a kiss,
A sigh is just a sigh –
The fundamental things apply
As time goes by.
Herman Hupfeld (20th century) US songwriter.
From the film *Casablanca*
As Time Goes By

21 O aching time! O moments big as years!
John Keats (1795–1821) British poet.
Hyperion, I

22 We must use time as a tool, not as a couch.
John Fitzgerald Kennedy (1917–63) US statesman.
The Observer, 'Sayings of the Week', 10 Dec 1961

23 They shut the road through the woods
Seventy years ago.
Weather and rain have undone it again,
And now you would never know
There was once a road through the woods.
Rudyard Kipling (1865–1936) Indian-born British writer.
The Way Through the Woods

24 The Future is something which everyone
reaches at the rate of sixty minutes an hour,
whatever he does, whoever he is.
C. S. Lewis (1898–1963) British academic and writer.
The Screwtape Letters

25 I stood on the bridge at midnight,
As the clocks were striking the hour.
Henry Wadsworth Longfellow (1807–82) US poet.
The Bridge

26 The man is killing time – there's nothing
else.
Robert Lowell (1917–77) US poet.
The Drinker

27 Time wounds all heels.
Groucho Marx (Julius Marx; 1895–1977) US comedian.
Attrib.

28 A physician can sometimes parry the scythe

of death, but has no power over the sand in the hourglass.
Hester Lynch Piozzi (Mrs. Henry Thrale; 1741–1821) British writer.
Letter to Fanny Burney, 22 Nov 1781

29 It is only time that weighs upon our hands.
It is only time, and that is not material.
Sylvia Plath (1932–63) British poet.
Winter Trees, 'The Three Women'

30 They do that to pass the time, nothing more.
But Time is too large, it refuses to let itself be filled up.
Jean-Paul Sartre (1905–80) French writer.
Nausea

31 Ah! the clock is always slow;
It is later than you think.
Robert William Service (1874–1958) Canadian poet.
It is Later than You Think

32 Come what come may,
Time and the hour runs through the roughest day.
William Shakespeare (1564–1616) English dramatist.
Macbeth, I:3

33 Th' inaudible and noiseless foot of Time.
William Shakespeare
All's Well that Ends Well, V:3

34 Like as the waves make towards the pebbled shore,
So do our minutes hasten to their end.
William Shakespeare
Sonnet 60

35 Time hath, my lord, a wallet at his back,
Wherein he puts alms for oblivion,
A great-siz'd monster of ingratitudes.
William Shakespeare
Troilus and Cressida, III:3

36 In reality, *killing time*
Is only the name for another of the multifarious ways
By which Time kills us.
Osbert Sitwell (1892–1969) British writer.
Milordo Inglese

37 Time driveth onward fast,
And in a little while our lips are dumb.
Let us alone. What is it that will last?
All things are taken from us, and become
Portions and parcels of the dreadful Past.
Alfred, Lord Tennyson (1809–92) British poet.
The Lotos-Eaters, 'Choric Song'

38 Time is but the stream I go a-fishing in.
Henry David Thoreau (1817–62) US writer.
Walden, 'Where I Lived, and What I Lived For'

39 As if you could kill time without injuring eternity.
Henry David Thoreau
Walden, 'Economy'

40 But meanwhile it is flying, irretrievable time is flying.
Virgil (Publius Vergilius Maro; 70–19 BC) Roman poet.
Georgics, Bk. III

41 Time drops in decay,
Like a candle burnt out.
W. B. Yeats (1865–1939) Irish poet.
The Moods

42 The bell strikes one. We take no note of time
But from its loss.
Edward Young (1683–1765) British poet.
Night Thoughts

43 Time flies, death urges, knells call, heaven invites,
Hell threatens.
Edward Young
Night Thoughts

TITLES

See also aristocracy, courtesy, honour, nobility

1 As far as the 14th Earl is concerned, I suppose Mr Wilson, when you come to think of it, is the 14th Mr Wilson.
Alec Douglas-Home (1903–) British statesman.
On renouncing his peerage (as 14th Earl of Home) to become prime minister
TV interview, 21 Oct 1963

2 Madam I may not call you; mistress I am ashamed to call you; and so I know not what to call you; but howsoever, I thank you.
Elizabeth I (1533–1603) Queen of England.
Writing to the wife of the Archbishop of Canterbury, expressing her disapproval of married clergy
Brief View of the State of the Church (Harington)

3 Tyndall, I must remain plain Michael Faraday to the last; and let me now tell you, that if I accepted the honour which the Royal Society desires to confer upon me, I would not answer for the integrity of my intellect for a single year.
Michael Faraday (1791–1867) British scientist.
Said when Faraday was offered the Presidency of the Royal Society
Faraday as a Discoverer (J. Tyndall), 'Illustrations of Character'

4 Pooh-Bah (Lord High Everything Else)
W. S. Gilbert (1836–1911) British dramatist.
The Mikado, Dramatis Personae

5 I like the Garter; there is no damned merit in it.
Lord Melbourne (1779–1848) British statesman.
Lord Melbourne (H. Dunckley), 'On the Order of the Garter'

6 When I want a peerage, I shall buy one like an honest man.
Lord Northcliffe (1865–1922) Irish-born British newspaper proprietor.
Attrib.

7 Call me madame.

Francis Perkins (1882–1965) US social worker and politician.
Deciding the term of address she would prefer when made the first woman to hold a cabinet office in the USA
Familiar Quotations (J. Bartlett)

8 Mother always told me my day was coming, but I never realized that I'd end up being the shortest knight of the year.

Gordon Richards (1904–86) British champion jockey.
Referring to his diminutive size, on learning of his knighthood
Attrib.

9 Members rise from CMG (known sometimes in Whitehall as 'Call me God') to the KCMG ('Kindly Call me God') to . . . The GCMG ('God Calls me God').

Anthony Sampson (1926–) British writer and journalist.
Anatomy of Britain, Ch. 18

10 Titles distinguish the mediocre, embarrass the superior, and are disgraced by the inferior.

George Bernard Shaw (1856–1950) Irish dramatist and critic.
Man and Superman, 'Maxims for Revolutionists'

11 I've been offered titles, but I think they get one into disreputable company.

George Bernard Shaw
Gossip (A. Barrow)

12 After half a century of democratic advance, the whole process has ground to a halt with a 14th Earl.

Harold Wilson (1916–) British politician and prime minister.
Speech, Manchester, 19 Oct 1963

TOLERANCE

1 There is, however, a limit at which forbearance ceases to be a virtue.

Edmund Burke (1729–97) British politician.
Observations on a Publication, 'The Present State of the Nation'

2 No party has a monopoly over what is right.

Mikhail Gorbachov (1931–) Soviet statesman.
Speech, Mar 1986

3 It is flattering some men to endure them.

Lord Halifax (1633–95) English statesman.
Political, Moral and Miscellaneous Thoughts and Reflections

4 If you cannot mould yourself as you would wish, how can you expect other people to be entirely to your liking?

Thomas à Kempis (Thomas Hemmerken; c. 1380–1471) German monk.
The Imitation of Christ, I

5 We must respect the other fellow's religion, but only in the sense and to the extent that we respect his theory that his wife is beautiful and his children smart.

H. L. Mencken (1880–1956) US journalist.
Notebooks, 'Minority Report'

6 Steven's mind was so tolerant that he could have attended a lynching every day without becoming critical.

Thorne Smith (1892–1934) US humorist.
The Jovial Ghosts, Ch. 11

7 So long as a man rides his hobby-horse peaceably and quietly along the king's highway, and neither compels you or me to get up behind him, – pray, Sir, what have either you or I to do with it?

Laurence Sterne (1713–68) Irish-born British writer.
Tristram Shandy

8 It is because we put up with bad things that hotel-keepers continue to give them to us.

Anthony Trollope (1815–82) British novelist.
Orley Farm, Ch. 18

TRANSIENCE

See also life, mortality, time

1 Everything is only for a day, both that which remembers and that which is remembered.

Marcus Aurelius (121–180 AD) Roman emperor.
Meditations, Bk. IV, Ch. 35

2 Time is like a river made up of the events which happen, and its current is strong; no sooner does anything appear than it is swept away, and another comes in its place, and will be swept away too.

Marcus Aurelius
Meditations, Bk. IV, Ch. 43

3 Faith, Sir, we are here to-day, and gone tomorrow.

Aphra Behn (1640–89) English novelist and dramatist.
The Lucky Chance, IV

4 Vanity of vanities, saith the Preacher, vanity of vanities; all is vanity.
What profit hath a man of all his labour which he taketh under the sun?
One generation passeth away, and another generation cometh: but the earth abideth for ever.

Bible: Ecclesiastes
1:2–4

5 And I gave my heart to seek and search out by wisdom concerning all things that are done under heaven: this sore travail hath God given to the sons of man to be exercised therewith.
I have seen all the works that are done under the sun; and, behold, all is vanity and vexation of spirit.

Bible: Ecclesiastes
1:13–14

6 Whatsoever thy hand findeth to do, do it with thy might; for there is no work, nor device, nor knowledge, nor wisdom, in the grave, whither thou goest.

Bible: Ecclesiastes
9:10

7 And behold joy and gladness, slaying oxen, and killing sheep, eating flesh, and drinking wine: let us eat and drink; for tomorrow we shall die.
Bible: Isaiah
A similar sentiment is expressed in Corinthians 15:32–33
22:13

8 Heaven and earth shall pass away, but my words shall not pass away.
Bible: Matthew
24:35

9 Suddenly, as rare things will, it vanished.
Robert Browning (1812–89) British poet.
One Word More, IV

10 Now the peak of summer's past, the sky is overcast
And the love we swore would last for an age seems deceit.
C. Day Lewis (1904–72) British poet.
Hornpipe

11 They are not long, the days of wine and roses.
Ernest Dowson (1867–1900) British lyric poet.
Vitae Summa Brevis Spem Nos Vetat Incohare Longam

12 A little rule, a little sway,
A sunbeam in a winter's day,
Is all the proud and mighty have
Between the cradle and the grave.
John Dyer (1700–58) British poet.
Grongar Hill

13 The Worldly Hope men set their Hearts upon
Turns Ashes – or it prospers; and anon,
Like Snow upon the Desert's dusty face,
Lighting a little Hour or two – is gone.
Edward Fitzgerald (1809–83) British poet.
The Rubáiyát of Omar Khayyám, XIV

14 Fair daffodils, we weep to see
You haste away so soon:
As yet the early-rising sun
Has not attain'd his noon.
Stay, stay,
Until the hasting day
Has run
But to the even-song;
And, having pray'd together, we
Will go with you along.

We have short time to stay, as you,
We have as short a Spring;
As quick a growth to meet decay,
As you or any thing.
Robert Herrick (1591–1674) English poet.
Hesperides, 'To Daffodils'

15 Not to hope for things to last for ever, is what the year teaches and even the hour which snatches a nice day away.
Horace (Quintus Horatius Flaccus; 65–8 BC) Roman poet.
Odes, IV

16 Ships that pass in the night, and speak each other in passing;
Only a signal shown and a distant voice in the darkness;
So on the ocean of life we pass and speak one another,
Only a look and a voice; then darkness again and a silence.
Henry Wadsworth Longfellow (1807–82) US poet.
Tales of a Wayside Inn, 'The Theologian's Tale. Elizabeth'

17 But she was of the world where the fairest things have the worst fate. Like a rose, she has lived as long as roses live, the space of one morning.
François de Malherbe (1555–1628) French poet.
Consolation à M. du Périer

18 Our little systems have their day;
They have their day and cease to be.
Alfred, Lord Tennyson (1809–92) British poet.
In Memoriam A.H.H., Prologue

TRANSLATION

1 The original is unfaithful to the translation.
Jorge Luis Borges (1899–1986) Argentinian writer.
Referring to Henley's translation of Beckford's *Vathek*
Sobre el 'Vathek' de William Beckford

2 Translations (like wives) are seldom faithful if they are in the least attractive.
Roy Campbell (1901–57) South African poet.
Poetry Review

3 Poetry is what gets lost in translation.
Robert Frost (1875–1963) US poet.
Attrib

4 An idea does not pass from one language to another without change.
Miguel de Unamuno y Jugo (1864–1936) Spanish writer.
The Tragic Sense of Life

5 Humour is the first of the gifts to perish in a foreign tongue.
Virginia Woolf (1882–1941) British novelist.
The Common Reader

TRAVEL

See also boats, flying

1 Travel broadens the mind.
Proverb

2 Travel, in the younger sort, is a part of education; in the elder, a part of experience.
Francis Bacon (1561–1626) English philosopher.
Essays, 'Of Travel'

3 I have recently been all round the world and have formed a very poor opinion of it.
Thomas Beecham (1879–1961) British conductor.
Speech at the Savoy
The News Review, 22 Aug 1946

4 Rumbling under blackened girders, Midland,
bound for Cricklewood,
Puffed its sulphur to the sunset where the
Land of Laundries stood.
Rumble under, thunder over, train and tram al-
ternate go.
John Betjeman (1906–84) British poet.
Parliament Hill Fields

5 Before the Roman came to Rye or out to
Severn strode,
The rolling English drunkard made the rolling
English road.
G. K. Chesterton (1874–1936) British writer.
The Rolling English Road

6 The only way to be sure of catching a train
is to miss the one before it.
G. K. Chesterton
Vacances à tous prix, 'Le Supplice de l'heure' (P. Daninos)

7 Travelling is almost like talking with men of
other centuries.
René Descartes (1596–1650) French philosopher.
Le Discours de la méthode

8 How does it feel
To be without a home
Like a complete unknown
Like a rolling stone?
Bob Dylan (Robert Allen Zimmerman; 1941–) US
popular singer.
Like a Rolling Stone

9 I read, much of the night, and go south in
the winter.
T. S. Eliot (1888–1965) US-born British poet and
dramatist.
The Waste Land, 'The Burial of the Dead'

10 The woods are lovely, dark, and deep,
But I have promises to keep,
And miles to go before I sleep,
And miles to go before I sleep.
Robert Frost (1875–1963) US poet.
Stopping by Woods on a Snowy Evening

11 He gave the impression that very many cities
had rubbed him smooth.
Graham Greene (1904–) British novelist.
A Gun for Sale, Ch. 4

12 Motorists (as they used to be called) were
utterly irresponsible in their dealings with
each other and with the pedestrian public; for
their benefit homicide was legalised. The
basic principles of Equality were flouted,
while the opposing principle of Envy was
disastrously encouraged.
L. P. Hartley (1895–1972) British novelist.
Facial Justice, Ch. 5

13 One of the pleasantest things in the world is
going on a journey; but I like to go by
myself.
William Hazlitt (1778–1830) British essayist.
On Going a Journey

14 They change their clime, not their frame of
mind, who rush across the sea. We work
hard at doing nothing: we look for happiness
in boats and carriage rides. What you are
looking for is here, is at Ulubrae, if only
peace of mind doesn't desert you.
Horace (Quintus Horatius Flaccus; 65–8 BC) Roman poet.
Epistles, I

15 A man who has not been in Italy, is always
conscious of an inferiority, from his not
having seen what it is expected a man should
see. The grand object of travelling is to see
the shores of the Mediterranean.
Samuel Johnson (1709–84) British lexicographer.
Life of Johnson (J. Boswell), Vol. III

16 Much have I travell'd in the realms of gold,
And many goodly states and kingdoms seen.
John Keats (1795–1821) British poet.
On first looking into Chapman's Homer

17 Mr Stephenson having taken me on the
bench of the engine with him, we started at
about ten miles an hour. You cannot imagine
how strange it seemed to be journeying on
thus, without any visible cause of progressing
other than that magical machine, with its
flying white breath, and rhythmical
unwearying pace.
Fanny Kemble (1809–93) British actress and writer.
Record of a Girlhood

18 Like Brighton pier, all right as far as it goes,
but inadequate for getting to France.
Neil Kinnock (1942–) British politician.
Speech, House of Commons, 1981

19 Oh, mister porter, what shall I do?
I wanted to go to Birmingham, but they've car-
ried me on to Crewe.
Marie Lloyd (1870–1922) British music-hall singer.
Oh, Mister Porter

20 The great and recurrent question about
abroad is, is it worth getting there?
Rose Macaulay (1889–1958) British writer.
Attrib.

21 Whenever I prepare for a journey I prepare
as though for death. Should I never return,
all is in order. This is what life has taught
me.
Katherine Mansfield (1888–1923) New-Zealand-born
British writer.
The Journal of Katherine Mansfield, 1922

22 The car has become the carapace, the
protective and aggressive shell, of urban and
suburban man.
Marshall McLuhan (1911–81) Canadian sociologist.
Understanding Media, Ch. 22

23 *Rush hour:* that hour when traffic is almost
at a standstill.
J. B. Morton (1893–1979) British journalist.
Morton's Folly

24 It is the overtakers who keep the undertakers busy.

William Ewart Pitts (b. 1900) British chief constable.
The Observer, 'Sayings of the Week', 22 Dec 1963

25 Travel is the most private of pleasures. There is no greater bore than the travel bore. We do not in the least want to hear what he has seen in Hong-Kong.

Vita Sackville-West (Victoria Sackville-West; 1892–1962) British poet and novelist.
Passenger to Tehran, Ch. 1

26 A man should know something of his own country, too, before he goes abroad.

Laurence Sterne (1713–68) Irish-born British writer.
Tristram Shandy

27 Wealth I ask not; hope nor love,
Nor a friend to know me;
All I seek, the heaven above
And the road below me.

Robert Louis Stevenson (1850–94) Scottish writer.
Songs of Travel, 'The Vagabond'

28 For my part, I travel not to go anywhere, but to go. I travel for travel's sake. The great affair is to move.

Robert Louis Stevenson
Travels with a Donkey, 'Cheylard and Luc'

29 Travel is glamorous only in retrospect.

Paul Theroux (1941–) US-born writer.
The Observer, 'Sayings of the Week', 7 Oct 1979

30 Yes – around Concord.

Henry David Thoreau (1817–62) US writer.
On being asked whether he had travelled much
Attrib.

31 Commuter – one who spends his life
In riding to and from his wife;
A man who shaves and takes a train,
And then rides back to shave again.

Elwyn Brooks White (1899–1985) US journalist and humorist.
The Commuter

32 The Victorians had not been anxious to go away for the weekend. The Edwardians, on the contrary, were nomadic.

T. H. White (1906–64) British novelist.
Farewell Victoria, Ch. 4

TREASON

See also betrayal

1 Please to remember the Fifth of November,
Gunpowder Treason and Plot.
We know no reason why gunpowder treason
Should ever be forgot.

Anonymous
Traditional

2 During his Office, Treason was no Crime.
The Sons of Belial had a Glorious Time.

John Dryden (1631–1700) British poet and dramatist.
Absalom and Achitophel, I

3 Treason doth never prosper: what's the reason?
For if it prosper, none dare call it treason.

John Harington (1561–1612) English writer.
Epigrams, 'Of Treason'

4 Caesar had his Brutus – Charles the First, his Cromwell – and George the Third – ('Treason,' cried the Speaker) . . . *may profit by their example*. If *this* be treason, make the most of it.

Patrick Henry (1736–99) US statesman.
Speech, Virginia Convention, May 1765

TREES

See also countryside, Nature

1 And the Lord God took the man, and put him into the garden of Eden to dress it and to keep it. And the Lord God commanded the man, saying, Of every tree of the garden thou mayest freely eat:
But of the tree of the knowledge of good and evil, thou shalt not eat of it: for in the day that thou eatest thereof thou shalt surely die.

Bible: Genesis
2:15–17

2 O leave this barren spot to me!
Spare, woodman, spare the beechen tree.

Thomas Campbell (1777–1844) British poet.
The Beech-Tree's Petition

3 The poplars are felled, farewell to the shade,
And the whispering sound of the cool colonnade!

William Cowper (1731–1800) British poet.
The Poplar Field

4 On Wenlock Edge the wood's in trouble;
His forest fleece the Wrekin heaves;
The gale, it plies the saplings double,
And thick on Severn snow the leaves.

A. E. Housman (1859–1936) British scholar and poet.
A Shropshire Lad, 'The Welsh Marches'

5 Loveliest of trees, the cherry now
Is hung with bloom along the bough,
And stands about the woodland ride
Wearing white for Eastertide.

A. E. Housman
A Shropshire Lad, '1887'

6 I'm replacing some of the timber used up by my books. Books are just trees with squiggles on them.

Hammond Innes (1913–) British novelist.
Interview in *Radio Times*, 18 Aug 1984

7 As when, upon a trancèd summer-night,
Those green-rob'd senators of mighty woods,
Tall oaks, branch-charmèd by the earnest stars,
Dream, and so dream all night without a stir.

John Keats (1795–1821) British poet.
Hyperion, I

8 I think that I shall never see
A poem lovely as a tree.
Alfred Joyce Kilmer (1886–1918) US poet.
Trees

9 Poems are made by fools like me,
But only God can make a tree.
Alfred Joyce Kilmer
Trees

10 Yet once more, O ye laurels, and once more,
Ye myrtles brown, with ivy never sere,
I come to pluck your berries harsh and crude,
And with forced fingers rude
Shatter your leaves before the mellowing year.
John Milton (1608–74) English poet.
Lycidas

11 Woodman, spare that tree!
Touch not a single bough!
In youth it sheltered me,
And I'll protect it now.
George Pope Morris (1802–64) US journalist.
Woodman, Spare That Tree

12 I think that I shall never see
A billboard lovely as a tree.
Perhaps unless the billboards fall,
I'll never see a tree at all.
Ogden Nash (1902–71) US poet.
Song of the Open Road

13 The difference between a gun and a tree is a
difference of tempo. The tree explodes every
spring.
Ezra Pound (1885–1972) US poet.
Criterion, July 1937

TRIVIALITY

See also insignificance

1 Nothing matters very much, and very few
things matter at all.
Arthur Balfour (1848–1930) British statesman.
Attrib.

2 A Storm in a Teacup.
W. B. Bernard (1807–75) British dramatist.
Play title

3 As she frequently remarked when she made
any such mistake, it would be all the same a
hundred years hence.
Charles Dickens (1812–70) British novelist.
Said by Mrs Squeers
Martin Chuzzlewit, Ch. 9

4 Little things affect little minds.
Benjamin Disraeli (1804–81) British statesman.
Sybil, Bk. III, Ch. 2

5 You know my method. It is founded upon the
observance of trifles.
Arthur Conan Doyle (1856–1930) British writer.
The Boscombe Valley Mystery

6 It has long been an axiom of mine that the
little things are infinitely the most important.
Arthur Conan Doyle
A Case of Identity

7 Depend upon it, there is nothing so unnatural
as the commonplace.
Arthur Conan Doyle
A Case of Identity

8 'Is there any point to which you would wish
to draw my attention?'
'To the curious incident of the dog in the night-
time.'
'The dog did nothing in the night-time.'
'That was the curious incident,' remarked
Sherlock Holmes.
Arthur Conan Doyle
The Silver Blaze

9 To great evils we submit; we resent little
provocations.
William Hazlitt (1778–1830) British essayist.
On Great and Little Things

10 Little minds are interested in the
extraordinary; great minds in the
commonplace.
Elbert Hubbard (1856–1915) US writer.
Roycroft Dictionary and Book of Epigrams

11 What should I do? I think the best thing is to
order a new stamp to be made with my face
on it.
Charles (1887–1922) Emperor of Austria.
On hearing of his accession to emperor
Anekdotenschatz (H. Hoffmeister)

12 To suckle fools and chronicle small beer.
William Shakespeare (1564–1616) English dramatist.
Othello, II:1

13 It's deadly commonplace, but, after all, the
commonplaces are the great poetic truths.
Robert Louis Stevenson (1850–94) Scottish writer.
Weir of Hermiston, Ch. 6

14 Ah God! the petty fools of rhyme
That shriek and sweat in pigmy wars.
Alfred, Lord Tennyson (1809–92) British poet.
Literary Squabbles

TRUST

See also faith, mistrust

1 Trust ye not in a friend, put ye not
confidence in a guide: keep the doors of thy
mouth from her that lieth in thy bosom.
Bible: Micah
7:5

2 Never trust the man who hath reason to
suspect that you know he hath injured you.
Henry Fielding (1707–54) British novelist.
Jonathan Wild, Bk III, Ch. 4

3 We are inclined to believe those whom we do

not know because they have never deceived us.
Samuel Johnson (1709–84) British lexicographer.
The Idler

4 Never trust a husband too far, nor a bachelor too near.
Helen Rowland (1876–1950) US writer.
The Rubaiyat of a Bachelor

5 Would you buy a second-hand car from this man?
Mort Sahl (1926–) US political comedian.
Referring to President Nixon
Attrib.

TRUTH

See also facts, frankness, honesty, lying, sincerity

1 Better a lie that heals than a truth that wounds.
Proverb

2 Many a true word is spoken in jest.
Proverb

3 Tell the truth and shame the devil.
Proverb

4 Truth fears no trial.
Proverb

5 Truth is stranger than fiction.
Proverb

6 Truth will out.
Proverb

7 The truth that makes men free is for the most part the truth which men prefer not to hear.
Herbert Sebastian Agar (1897–1980) US writer.
A Time for Greatness

8 Plato is dear to me, but dearer still is truth.
Aristotle (384–322 BC) Greek philosopher.
Attrib.

9 Truth sits upon the lips of dying men.
Matthew Arnold (1822–88) British poet and critic.
Sohrab and Rustum

10 What is truth? said jesting Pilate, and would not stay for an answer.
Francis Bacon (1561–1626) English philosopher.
Essays, 'Of Truth'

11 And ye shall know the truth, and the truth shall make you free.
Bible: John
8:32

12 Pilate saith unto him, What is truth? And when he had said this, he went out again unto the Jews, and saith unto them, I find in him no fault at all.
Bible: John
18:38

13 A truth that's told with bad intent
Beats all the lies you can invent.
William Blake (1757–1827) British poet.
Auguries of Innocence

14 To treat your facts with imagination is one thing, to imagine your facts is another.
John Burroughs (1837–1921) US naturalist.
The Heart of Burroughs Journals

15 Some men love truth so much that they seem to be in continual fear lest she should catch a cold on overexposure.
Samuel Butler (1835–1902) British writer.
Notebooks

16 Agree to a short armistice with truth.
Lord Byron (1788–1824) British poet.
Don Juan, III

17 'Tis strange – but true; for truth is always strange;
Stranger than fiction: if it could be told,
How much would novels gain by the exchange!
Lord Byron
Don Juan, XIV

18 You can only find truth with logic if you have already found truth without it.
G. K. Chesterton (1874–1936) British writer.
The Man who was Orthodox

19 Much truth is spoken, that more may be concealed.
Lord Darling (1849–1936) British judge.
Scintillae Juris

20 Perjury is often bold and open. It is truth that is shamefaced – as, indeed, in many cases is no more than decent.
Lord Darling
Scintillae Juris

21 It is an old maxim of mine that when you have excluded the impossible, whatever remains, however improbable, must be the truth.
Arthur Conan Doyle (1856–1930) British writer.
The Beryl Coronet

22 Errors, like Straws, upon the surface flow;
He who would search for Pearls must dive below.
John Dryden (1631–1700) British poet and dramatist.
All for Love, Prologue

23 A man is to be cheated into passion, but to be reasoned into truth.
John Dryden
Religio Laici, Preface

24 Ethical axioms are found and tested not very differently from the axioms of science. Truth is what stands the test of experience.
Albert Einstein (1879–1955) German-born US physicist.
Out of My Later Years

25 Truth, like a torch, the more it's shook it shines.
William Hamilton (1788–1856) Scottish philosopher.
Discussions on Philosophy, title page

26 True and False are attributes of speech, not of things. And where speech is not, there is neither Truth nor Falsehood.
Thomas Hobbes (1588–1679) English philosopher.
Leviathan, Pt. I, Ch. 4

27 It's easy to make a man confess the lies he tells to himself; it's far harder to make him confess the truth.
Geoffrey Household (1900–88) British writer.
Rogue Male

28 I am certain of nothing but the holiness of the heart's affections and the truth of imagination – what the imagination seizes as beauty must be truth – whether it existed before or not.
John Keats (1795–1821) British poet.
Letter to Benjamin Bailey, 22 Nov 1817

29 I never can feel certain of any truth but from a clear perception of its beauty.
John Keats
Letter to George and Georgiana Keats, 16 Dec 1818–4 Jan 1819

30 'Beauty is truth, truth beauty,' – that is all Ye know on earth, and all ye need to know.
John Keats
Ode on a Grecian Urn

31 It is one thing to show a man that he is in an error, and another to put him in possession of truth.
John Locke (1632–1704) English philosopher.
An Essay Concerning Human Understanding, Bk. IV, Ch. 7

32 It is hard to believe that a man is telling the truth when you know that you would lie if you were in his place.
Henry Louis Mencken (1880–1956) US journalist.

33 Let her and Falsehood grapple; who ever knew Truth put to the worse, in a free and open encounter?
John Milton (1608–74) English poet.
Areopagitica

34 There can be no whitewash at the White House.
Richard Milhous Nixon (1913–) US president.
Referring to the Watergate scandal
The Observer, 'Sayings of the Week', 30 Dec 1973

35 Let us begin by committing ourselves to the truth, to see it like it is and to tell it like it is, to find the truth, to speak the truth and live with the truth. That's what we'll do.
Richard Milhous Nixon
Nomination acceptance speech, Miami, 8 Aug 1968

36 Truth has no special time of its own. Its hour is now – always.
Albert Schweitzer (1875–1965) French Protestant theologian, philosopher, physician, and musician.
Out of My Life and Thought

37 Truth telling is not compatible with the defence of the realm.
George Bernard Shaw (1856–1950) Irish dramatist and critic.
Heartbreak House

38 My way of joking is to tell the truth. It's the funniest joke in the world.
George Bernard Shaw
John Bull's Other Island, II

39 When truth is discovered by someone else, it loses something of its attractiveness.
Alexander Solzhenitsyn (1918–) Soviet novelist.
Candle in the Wind, 3

40 It takes two to speak the truth – one to speak, and another to hear.
Henry David Thoreau (1817–62) US writer.
A Week on the Concord and Merrimack Rivers

41 The only truths which are universal are those gross enough to be thought so.
Paul Valéry (1871–1945) French poet and writer.
Mauvaises Pensées et autres

42 But not even Marx is more precious to us than the truth.
Simone Weil (1909–43) French philosopher.
Oppression and Liberty, 'Revolution Proletarienne'

43 There are no whole truths; all truths are half-truths. It is trying to treat them as whole truths that plays the devil.
A. N. Whitehead (1861–1947) British philosopher.
Dialogues, 16

44 I believe that in the end the truth will conquer.
John Wycliffe (1329–84) English religious reformer.
Said to John of Gaunt, Duke of Lancaster, 1381
Short History of the English People (J. R. Green)

45 Truth is on the march; nothing can stop it now.
Émile Zola (1840–1902) French novelist.
Referring to the Dreyfus scandal
Attrib.

TYRANNY

See also authoritarianism, oppression

1 Nature has left this tincture in the blood,
That all men would be tyrants if they could.
Daniel Defoe (1660–1731) British journalist and writer.
The Kentish Petition, Addenda

2 'Twixt kings and tyrants there's this difference known;
Kings seek their subjects' good: tyrants their own.
Robert Herrick (1591–1674) English poet.
Hesperides, 'Kings and Tyrants'

3 A country governed by a despot is an inverted cone.
Samuel Johnson (1709–84) British lexicographer.
Life of Johnson (J. Boswell), Vol. III

4 It is better that a man should tyrannize over his bank balance than over his fellow citizens.
John Maynard Keynes (1883–1946) British economist.
The General Theory of Employment, Interest and Money, Bk. VI, Ch. 24

5 . . . whenever kingship approaches tyranny it is near its end, for by this it becomes ripe for division, change of dynasty, or total destruction, especially in a temperate climate . . . where men are habitually, morally and naturally free.
Nicholas of Oresme (c. 1320–82) Chaplain to Charles V of France.
De Moneta

6 Where laws end, tyranny begins.
William Pitt the Elder (1708–78) British statesman.
Speech, House of Lords, referring to the Wilkes case, 9 Jan 1770

U

UNCERTAINTY

See also doubt, indecision

1 If ifs and ans were pots and pans, there'd be no trade for tinkers.
Proverb

2 I have known uncertainty: a state unknown to the Greeks.
Jorge Luis Borges (1899–1986) Argentinian writer.
Ficciones, 'The Babylonian Lottery'

3 Of course not. After all, I may be wrong.
Bertrand Russell (1872–1970) British philosopher.
On being asked whether he would be prepared to die for his beliefs
Attrib.

UNDERSTANDING

See also intelligence, wisdom

1 And come hither, and I shall light a candle of understanding in thine heart, which shall not be put out, till the things be performed which thou shalt begin to write.
Bible: II Esdras
14:25

2 It is good to know what a man is, and also what the world takes him for. But you do not understand him until you have learnt how he understands himself.
F. H. Bradley (1846–1924) British philosopher.
Aphorisms

3 The people may be made to follow a course of action, but they may not be made to understand it.
Confucius (K'ung Fu-tzu; 551–479 BC) Chinese philosopher.
Analects

4 Only one man ever understood me. . . . And he didn't understand me.
Hegel (1770–1831) German philosopher.
Said on his deathbed
Famous Last Words (B. Conrad)

5 Even when poetry has a meaning, as it usually has, it may be inadvisable to draw it out . . . Perfect understanding will sometimes almost extinguish pleasure.
A. E. Housman (1859–1936) British scholar and poet.
The Name and Nature of Poetry

6 Thought must be divided against itself before it can come to any knowledge of itself.
Aldous Huxley (1894–1964) British novelist.
Do What You Will

7 She did her work with the thoroughness of a mind that reveres details and never quite understands them.
Sinclair Lewis (1885–1951) US novelist.
Babbitt, Ch. 18

8 I used to tell my husband that, if he could make *me* understand something, it would be clear to all the other people in the country.
Eleanor Roosevelt (1884–1962) US writer and lecturer.
Newspaper column, 'My Day', 12 Feb 1947

9 I have striven not to laugh at human actions, not to weep at them, nor to hate them, but to understand them.
Benedict Spinoza (Baruch de Spinoza; 1632–77) Dutch philosopher.
Tractatus Theologico-Politicus, Ch. 1

10 All, everything that I understand, I understand only because I love.
Leo Tolstoy (1828–1910) Russian writer.
War and Peace, Bk. VII, Ch. 16

UNEMPLOYMENT

See also idleness, work

1 My father did not wait around . . . he got on his bike and went out looking for work.
Norman Tebbitt (1931–) British Conservative politician.
Speech, Conservative Party conference, 1981

2 It's a recession when your neighbour loses his job; it's a depression when you lose your own.
Harry S. Truman (1884–1972) US statesman.
The Observer, 'Sayings of the Week', 6 Apr 1958

3 Something must be done.

Duke of Windsor (1894–1972) King of the United Kingdom; abdicated 1936.
Said while visiting areas of high unemployment in South Wales during the 1930s
Attrib.

UNFAITHFULNESS

See also adultery

1 Early one morning, just as the sun was rising,
I heard a maiden singing in the valley below:
'Oh, don't deceive me; Oh, never leave me!
How could you use a poor maiden so?'
Anonymous
Early One Morning

2 Swore to be true to each other, true as the stars above;
He was her man, but he done her wrong.
Anonymous
Frankie and Johnny

3 . . . today I was driving a little more slowly because of the rain, but that was the only difference between yesterday and today.
My wife had been unfaithful to me but there was still the same number of traffic lights to obey . . .
John Braine (1922–86) British novelist.
Life at the Top, Ch. 16

4 But I kissed her little sister,
And forgot my Clementine.
Percy Montrose (19th century) US songwriter.
Clementine

5 O, swear not by the moon, th' inconstant moon,
That monthly changes in her circled orb,
Lest that thy love prove likewise variable.
William Shakespeare (1564–1616) English dramatist.
Romeo and Juliet, II:2

6 His honour rooted in dishonour stood,
And faith unfaithful kept him falsely true.
Alfred, Lord Tennyson (1809–92) British poet.
Idylls of the King, 'Lancelot and Elaine'

7 No man worth having is true to his wife, or can be true to his wife, or ever was, or ever will be so.
John Vanbrugh (1664–1726) English architect and dramatist.
The Relapse, III:2

8 Why should marriage bring only tears?
All I wanted was a man
With a single heart,
And we would stay together
As our hair turned white,
Not somebody always after wriggling fish
With his big bamboo rod.
Chuo Wên-chün (?179–117 BC) Chinese poet.
Orchid Boat, Women Poets of China (Kenneth Rexroth and Ling Chung)

UNITY

1 A chain is no stronger than its weakest link.
Proverb

2 Union is strength.
Proverb

3 United we stand, divided we fall.
Proverb

4 That typically English characteristic for which there is no English name – *esprit de corps*.
Frank Ezra Adcock (1886–1968) British classicist.
Presidential address

5 And if one prevail against him, two shall withstand him; and a threefold cord is not quickly broken.
Bible: Ecclesiastes
4:12

6 And the whole earth was of one language, and of one speech.
Bible: Genesis
11:1

7 When bad men combine, the good must associate; else they will fall one by one, an unpitied sacrifice in a contemptible struggle.
Edmund Burke (1729–97) British politician.
Thoughts on the Cause of the Present Discontents

8 All for one, and one for all.
Alexandre Dumas, père (1802–70) French novelist and dramatist.
The Three Musketeers

9 We must indeed all hang together, or most assuredly, we shall all hang separately.
Benjamin Franklin (1706–90) US scientist and statesman.
Remark on signing the Declaration of Independence, 4 July 1776

10 No human relation gives one possession in another – every two souls are absolutely different. In friendship or in love, the two side by side raise hands together to find what one cannot reach alone.
Kahil Gibran (1833–1931) Lebanese mystic and poet.
Beloved Prophet (ed. Virginia Hilu)

11 Everyone has observed how much more dogs are animated when they hunt in a pack, than when they pursue their game apart. We might, perhaps, be at a loss to explain this phenomenon, if we had not experience of a similar in ourselves.
David Hume (1711–76) Scottish philosopher.
A Treatise of Human Nature

12 Now, is it to lower the price of corn, or isn't it? It is not much matter which we say, but mind, we must all say *the same*.
Lord Melbourne (1779–1848) British statesman.
Said at a cabinet meeting
The English Constitution (Bagehot), Ch. 1

UNIVERSE

See also astronomy, moon, space, stars, sun, world

1 Had I been present at the Creation, I would have given some useful hints for the better ordering of the universe.
Alfonso the Wise (c. 1221–84) King of Castile and León.
Referring to the complicated Ptolemaic model of the universe. Often quoted as, 'Had I been consulted I would have recommended something simpler'
Attrib.

2 The visible universe was an illusion or, more precisely, a sophism. Mirrors and fatherhood are abominable because they multiply it and extend it.
Jorge Luis Borges (1899–1986) Argentinian writer.
Ficciones, 'Tlön, Uqbar, Orbis Tertius'

3 I don't pretend to understand the Universe – it's a great deal bigger than I am . . . People ought to be modester.
Thomas Carlyle (1795–1881) Scottish historian and essayist.
Attrib.

4 MARGARET FULLER. I accept the universe.
CARLYLE. Gad! she'd better!
Thomas Carlyle
Attrib.

5 The cosmos is about the smallest hole that a man can hide his head in.
G. K. Chesterton (1874–1936) British writer.
Orthodoxy, Ch. 1

6 I am very interested in the Universe – I am specializing in the universe and all that surrounds it.
Peter Cook (1937–) British writer and entertainer.
Beyond the Fringe

7 My own suspicion is that the universe is not only queerer than we suppose, but queerer than we *can* suppose.
J. B. S. Haldane (1892–1964) British geneticist.
Possible Worlds, 'On Being the Right Size'

8 The universe is not hostile, nor yet is it friendly. It is simply indifferent.
John Haynes Holmes (1879–1964) US clergyman.
A Sensible Man's View of Religion

9 The universe begins to look more like a great thought than like a great machine.
James Jeans (1877–1946) British scientist.
The Mysterious Universe

10 The universe ought to be presumed too vast to have any character.
C. S. Peirce (1839–1914) US physicist.
Collected Papers, VI

V

VENICE

See also Europe

1 Streets full of water. Please advise.
Robert Benchley (1889–1945) US humorist.
Telegram sent to his editor on arriving in Venice
Attrib.

2 Venice is like eating an entire box of chocolate liqueurs at one go.
Truman Capote (1924–84) US novelist.
The Observer, 'Sayings of the Week', 26 Nov 1961

3 Venice, the eldest Child of Liberty.
She was a maiden City, bright and free.
William Wordsworth (1770–1850) British poet.
Venice, a republic since the Middle Ages, was conquered by Napoleon in 1797 and absorbed into his Kingdom of Italy in 1805
Sonnets, 'Once did she hold'

4 Once did she hold the gorgeous east in fee;
And was the safeguard of the west.
William Wordsworth
Sonnets, 'Once did she hold'

5 When she took unto herself a mate,
She must espouse the everlasting sea.
William Wordsworth
Sonnets, 'Once did she hold'

VERBOSITY

See also brevity, sermons, speech, speeches, writing

1 There was a young man of Japan
Whose limericks never would scan;
When they said it was so,
He replied, 'Yes, I know,
But I always try to get as many words into the last line as ever I possibly can.'
Anonymous

2 A sophistical rhetorician inebriated with the exuberance of his own verbosity.
Benjamin Disraeli (1804–81) British statesman.
Referring to Gladstone
Speech, 27 July 1878

3 But far more numerous was the Herd of such,
Who think too little, and who talk too much.
John Dryden (1631–1700) British poet and dramatist.
Absalom and Achitophel, I

4 Nothing is more despicable than a professional talker who uses his words as a quack uses his remedies.
François Fénelon (1651–1715) French writer and prelate.
Letter to M. Dacier

5 I have made this letter longer than usual,

only because I have not had the time to make it shorter.

Blaise Pascal (1623–62) French philosopher and mathematician.
Lettres provinciales, XVI

6 Words are like leaves; and where they most abound,
Much fruit of sense beneath is rarely found.

Alexander Pope (1688–1744) British poet.
An Essay on Criticism

VICE

See also crime, evil, sin, virtue and vice

1 When vice prevails, and impious men bear sway,
The post of honour is a private station.

Joseph Addison (1672–1719) British essayist.
Cato, IV:1

2 We make ourselves a ladder out of our vices if we trample the vices themselves underfoot.

St Augustine of Hippo (354–430) Bishop of Hippo.
Sermons, Bk. III, 'De Ascensione'

3 Often the fear of one evil leads us into a worse.

Nicolas Boileau (1636–1711) French writer.
L'Art poétique, I

4 The wickedness of the world is so great you have to run your legs off to avoid having them stolen from under you.

Bertolt Brecht (1898–1956) German dramatist.
The Threepenny Opera, I:3

5 Vice itself lost half its evil, by losing all its grossness.

Edmund Burke (1729–97) British politician.
Reflections on the Revolution in France

6 Vice is its own reward.

Quentin Crisp (?1910–) Model, publicist, and writer.
The Naked Civil Servant

7 In my time, the follies of the town crept slowly among us, but now they travel faster than a stagecoach.

Oliver Goldsmith (1728–74) Irish-born British writer.
She Stoops to Conquer, I

8 Wrongdoing can only be avoided if those who are not wronged feel the same indignation at it as those who are.

Solon (6th century BC) Athenian statesman.
Greek Wit (F. Paley)

9 Whenever I'm caught between two evils, I take the one I've never tried.

Mae West (1892–1980) US actress.
Attrib.

10 Never support two weaknesses at the same time. It's your combination sinners – your lecherous liars and your miserly drunkards –

who dishonour the vices and bring them into bad repute.

Thornton Wilder (1897–1975) US novelist and dramatist.
The Matchmaker, III

VICTORY

See also war

1 *Veni, vidi, vici.*
I came, I saw, I conquered.

Julius Caesar (100–44 BC) Roman general and statesman.
The Twelve Caesars (Suetonius)

2 Victory at all costs, victory in spite of all terror, victory however long and hard the road may be; for without victory there is no survival.

Winston Churchill (1874–1965) British statesman.
Speech, House of Commons, 13 May 1940

3 We triumph without glory when we conquer without danger.

Pierre Corneille (1606–84) French dramatist.
Le Cid, II:2

4 The most important thing in the Olympic Games is not winning but taking part . . . The essential thing in life is not conquering but fighting well.

Pierre de Coubertin (1863–1937) French educator and sportsman.
Speech, Banquet to Officials of Olympic Games, London, 24 July 1908

5 A game which a sharper once played with a dupe, entitled 'Heads I win, tails you lose.'

John Wilson Croker (1780–1857) British Tory politician.
Croker Papers

6 The happy state of getting the victor's palm without the dust of racing.

Horace (Quintus Horatius Flaccus; 65–8 BC) Roman poet.
Epistles, I

7 We've got no place in this outfit for good losers. We want tough hombres who will go in there and *win*!

Jonas Ingram US admiral.
Remark, 1926

8 They talk about who won and who lost. Human reason won. Mankind won.

Nikita Khrushchev (1894–1971) Soviet statesman.
Referring to the Cuban missiles crisis
The Observer, 'Sayings of the Week', 11 Nov 1962

9 Winning isn't everything, but wanting to win is.

Vince Lombardi (1913–70) US football coach.

10 How vainly men themselves amaze
To win the palm, the oak, or bays.

Andrew Marvell (1621–78) English poet.
The Garden

11 Who overcomes
By force, hath overcome but half his foe.

John Milton (1608–74) English poet.
Paradise Lost, Bk. I

12 See, the conquering hero comes!
Sound the trumpets, beat the drums!
Thomas Morell (1703–84) British classicist.
The libretto for Handel's oratorio
Joshua, Pt. III

13 We have met the enemy, and they are ours.
Oliver Hazard Perry (1785–1819) US naval officer.
Message sent reporting his victory in a naval battle on Lake Erie
Familiar Quotations (J. Bartlett)

14 Such another victory and we are ruined.
Pyrrhus (319–272 BC) King of Epirus.
Commenting upon the costliness of his victory at the Battle of Asculum, 279 BC
Life of Pyrrhus (Plutarch)

15 For when the One Great Scorer comes
To write against your name,
He marks – not that you won or lost –
But how you played the game.
Grantland Rice (1880–1954) US sportswriter.
Alumnus Football

16 I came; I saw; God conquered.
John III Sobieski (1624–96) King of Poland.
Announcing his victory over the Turks at Vienna to the pope (paraphrasing Caesar's 'veni, vidi, vici')
Attrib.

17 'And everybody praised the Duke,
Who this great fight did win.'
'But what good came of it at last?'
Quoth little Peterkin.
'Why that I cannot tell,' said he,
'But 'twas a famous victory.'
Robert Southey (1774–1843) British poet.
The Battle of Blenheim

18 The next greatest misfortune to losing a battle is to gain such a victory as this.
Duke of Wellington (1769–1852) British general and statesman.
Recollections (S. Rogers)

19 I always say that, next to a battle lost, the greatest misery is a battle gained.
Duke of Wellington
Diary (Frances, Lady Shelley)

20 By the splendour of God I have taken possession of my realm; the earth of England is in my two hands.
William the Conqueror (1027–87) King of England.
Said after falling over when coming ashore at Pevensey with his army of invasion
Attrib.

VIOLENCE

See also cruelty, force

1 A bit of shooting takes your mind off your troubles – it makes you forget the cost of living.
Brendan Behan (1923–64) Irish playwright.
The Hostage

2 So soon as the man overtook me, he was but a word and a blow.
John Bunyan (1628–88) English writer.
The Pilgrim's Progress, Pt. I

3 Two lovely black eyes,
Oh, what a surprise!
Only for telling a man he was wrong.
Two lovely black eyes!
Charles Coborn (1852–1945) US songwriter.
Two Lovely Black Eyes

4 It's possible to disagree with someone about the ethics of non-violence without wanting to kick his face in.
Christopher Hampton (1946–) British writer and dramatist.
Treats, Sc. 4

5 We are effectively destroying ourselves by violence masquerading as love.
R. D. Laing (1927–89) British psychiatrist.
The Politics of Experience, Ch. 13

6 If you strike a child, take care that you strike it in anger, even at the risk of maiming it for life. A blow in cold blood neither can nor should be forgiven.
George Bernard Shaw (1856–1950) Irish dramatist and critic.
Man and Superman, 'Maxims for Revolutionists'

VIRTUE

See also good, morality, purity, righteousness, virtue and vice

1 Virtue is like a rich stone, best plain set.
Francis Bacon (1561–1626) English philosopher.
Essays, 'Of Beauty'

2 As in nature things move violently to their place and calmly in their place, so virtue in ambition is violent, in authority settled and calm.
Francis Bacon
Essays, 'Of Great Place'

3 A good name is better than precious ointment; and the day of death than the day of one's birth.
It is better to go to the house of mourning, than to go to the house of feasting: for that is the end of all men; and the living will lay it to his heart.
Bible: Ecclesiastes
7:1–2

4 Finally, brethren, whatsoever things are true, whatsoever things are honest, whatsoever things are just, whatsoever things are pure, whatsoever things are lovely, whatsoever things are of good report; if there be any virtue; and if there be any praise, think on these things.
Bible: Philippians
4:8

5 Virtue consisted in avoiding scandal and venereal disease.
Robert Cecil (1913–) British writer.
Life in Edwardian England

6 My virtue's still far too small, I don't trot it out and about yet.
Colette (1873–1954) French novelist.
Claudine at School

7 To be able to practise five things everywhere under heaven constitutes perfect virtue . . . gravity, generosity of soul, sincerity, earnestness, and kindness.
Confucius (K'ung Fu-tzu; 551–479 BC) Chinese philosopher.
Analects

8 How next to impossible is the exercise of virtue! It requires a constant watchfulness, constant guard.
William Golding (1911–) British novelist.
Rites of Passage, 'Colley's Letter'

9 Good, but not religious-good.
Thomas Hardy (1840–1928) British novelist.
Under the Greenwood Tree, Ch. 2

10 The greatest offence against virtue is to speak ill of it.
William Hazlitt (1778–1830) British essayist.
On Cant and Hypocrisy

11 Only a sweet and virtuous soul,
Like season'd timber, never gives;
But though the whole world turn to coal,
Then chiefly lives.
George Herbert (1593–1633) English poet.
Virtue

12 Be good, sweet maid, and let who can be clever;
Do lovely things, not dream them, all day long;
And so make Life, and Death, and that For Ever,
One grand sweet song.
Charles Kingsley (1819–75) British writer.
A Farewell. To C. E. G.

13 To be discontented with the divine discontent, and to be ashamed with the noble shame, is the very germ and first upgrowth of all virtue.
Charles Kingsley
Health and Education

14 Most men admire
Virtue, who follow not her lore.
John Milton (1608–74) English poet.
Paradise Regained, Bk. I

15 When men grow virtuous in their old age,

they only make a sacrifice to God of the devil's leavings.
Alexander Pope (1688–1744) British poet.
Thoughts on Various Subjects

VIRTUE AND VICE

See also good and evil, vice, virtue

1 Our virtues and vices couple with one another, and get children that resemble both their parents.
Lord Halifax (1633–95) English statesman.
Political, Moral and Miscellaneous Thoughts and Reflections

2 Most usually our virtues are only vices in disguise.
Duc de la Rochefoucauld (1613–80) French writer.
Maximes, added to the 4th edition

3 Vice and virtues are products like sulphuric acid and sugar.
Hippolyte Adolphe Taine (1828–93) French writer and philosopher.
Histoire de la littérature anglaise, Introduction

VULGARITY

See also humour

1 You gotta have a swine to show you where the truffles are.
Edward Albee (1928–) US dramatist.
Who's Afraid of Virginia Woolf?, I

2 The aristocratic pleasure of displeasing is not the only delight that bad taste can yield. One can love a certain kind of vulgarity for its own sake.
Aldous Huxley (1894–1964) British novelist.
Vulgarity in Literature, Ch. 4

3 That fellow would vulgarize the day of judgment.
Douglas William Jerrold (1803–57) British dramatist.
Wit and Opinions of Douglas Jerrold, 'A Comic Author'

4 It is disgusting to pick your teeth. What is vulgar is to use a gold toothpick.
Louis Kronenberger (1904–80) US writer and literary critic.
The Cat and the Horse

5 With our James vulgarity begins at home, and should be allowed to stay there.
Oscar Wilde (1854–1900) Irish-born British dramatist.
Referring to the artist James Whistler
Letter to the *World*

6 I can't stand a naked light bulb, any more than I can a rude remark or a vulgar action.
Tennessee Williams (1911–83) US dramatist.
A Streetcar Named Desire, II:3

W

WALES

See also Britain, Welsh

1 The thing I value about Wales and Welsh background is that it has always been a genuinely more classless society than many people present England as being.
Geoffrey Howe (1926–) British politician.
The Observer, 'Sayings of the Week', 9 Nov 1986

2 The land of my fathers. My fathers can have it.
Dylan Thomas (1914–53) Welsh poet.
Referring to Wales
Dylan Thomas (John Ackerman)

3 Too many of the artists of Wales spend too much time about the position of the artist of Wales. There is only one position for an artist anywhere: and that is, upright.
Dylan Thomas
New Statesman, 18 Dec 1964

4 Make me content
With some sweetness
From Wales
Whose nightingales
Have no wings.
Edward Thomas (1878–1917) British poet.
Words

5 We can trace almost all the disasters of English history to the influence of Wales.
Evelyn Waugh (1903–66) British novelist.
Decline and Fall, Pt. I, Ch. 8

WAR

See also army, Cold War, defeat, navy, nuclear weapons, officers, patriotism, soldiers, victory, war and peace, weapons, World War II

1 Give them the cold steel, boys!
Lewis Addison Arminstead (1817–63) US general.
Exhortation given to his troops during the US Civil War
Attrib.

2 And we are here as on a darkling plain
Swept with confused alarms of struggle and flight,
Where ignorant armies clash by night.
Matthew Arnold (1822–88) British poet and critic.
Dover Beach

3 To save your world you asked this man to die:
Would this man, could he see you now, ask why?
W. H. Auden (1907–73) British poet.
Epitaph for an Unknown Soldier

4 Well, if you knows of a better 'ole, go to it.
Bruce Bairnsfather (1888–1959) British cartoonist.
Fragments from France

5 The only defence is in offence, which means that you have to kill more women and children more quickly than the enemy if you want to save yourselves.
Stanley Baldwin (1867–1947) British statesman.
Speech, Nov 1932

6 I think it is well also for the man in the street to realise that there is no power on earth that can protect him from being bombed. Whatever people may tell him, the bomber will always get through, and it is very easy to understand that, if you realise the area of space.
Stanley Baldwin
Speech, House of Commons, 10 Nov 1932

7 It takes twenty years or more of peace to make a man, it takes only twenty seconds of war to destroy him.
Baudouin I (1930–) King of Belgium.
Addressing US Congress, 12 May 1959

8 I have never understood this liking for war. It panders to instincts already catered for within the scope of any respectable domestic establishment.
Alan Bennett (1934–) British playwright.
Forty Years On, I

9 And ye shall hear of wars and rumours of wars: see that ye be not troubled: for all these things must come to pass, but the end is not yet.
For nation shall rise against nation, and kingdom against kingdom: and there shall be famines, and pestilences, and earthquakes, in divers places.
All these are the beginning of sorrows.
Bible: Matthew
24:6–8

10 Then said Jesus unto him, Put up again thy sword into his place: for all they that take the sword shall perish with the sword.
Bible: Matthew
26:52

11 If there is ever another war in Europe, it will come out of some damned silly thing in the Balkans.
Bismarck (1815–98) German statesman.
Remark to Ballen, shortly before Bismarck's death

12 C'est magnifique, mais ce n'est pas la guerre.
It is magnificent, but it is not war.
Pierre Bosquet (1810–61) French marshal.
Referring to the Charge of the Light Brigade at the Battle of Balaclava, 25 Oct 1854
Attrib.

13 The wrong war, at the wrong place, at the wrong time, and with the wrong enemy.
Omar Nelson Bradley (1893–1981) US general.
Said in evidence to a Senate inquiry, May 1951, over a propo-

sal by MacArthur that the Korean war should be extended into China

14 What they could do with round here is a good war.
Bertolt Brecht (1898–1956) German dramatist.
Mother Courage, I

15 A war of which we could say it left nothing to be desired will probably never exist.
Bertolt Brecht
Mother Courage, VI

16 War is like love, it always finds a way.
Bertolt Brecht
Mother Courage, VI

17 The Angel of Death has been abroad throughout the land: you may almost hear the beating of his wings.
John Bright (1811–89) British radical politician.
Referring to the Crimean War
Speech, House of Commons, 23 Feb 1855

18 If I should die, think only this of me:
That there's some corner of a foreign field
That is forever England.
Rupert Brooke (1887–1915) British poet.
The Soldier

19 War knows no power. Safe shall be my going,
Secretly armed against all death's endeavour;
Safe though all safety's lost; safe where men fall;
And if these poor limbs die, safest of all.
Rupert Brooke
Safety

20 Scots, wha hae wi' Wallace bled,
Scots, wham Bruce has aften led,
Welcome to your gory bed,
Or to victorie.
Robert Burns (1759–96) Scottish poet.
Scots, Wha Hae

21 When civil fury first grew high,
And men fell out they knew not why.
Samuel Butler (1612–80) English satirist.
Hudibras, Pt. I

22 War, war is still the cry, 'War even to the knife!'
Lord Byron (1788–1824) British poet.
Childe Harold's Pilgrimage, I

23 Tweedledum and Tweedledee
Agreed to have a battle;
For Tweedledum said Tweedledee
Had spoiled his nice new rattle.
Lewis Carroll (Charles Lutwidge Dodgson; 1832–98) British writer.
Through the Looking-Glass, Ch. 4

24 Carthage must be destroyed.
Cato the Elder (Marcius Porcius C.; 234–149 BC)
Roman statesman.
Life of Cato (Plutarch)

25 In war, whichever side may call itself the victor, there are no winners, but all are losers.
Neville Chamberlain (1869–1940) British statesman.
Speech, Kettering, 3 July 1938

26 Wars, conflict, it's all business. One murder makes a villain. Millions a hero. Numbers sanctify.
Charlie Chaplin (Sir Charles Spencer C.; 1889–1977)
British film actor.
Monsieur Verdoux

27 The redress of the grievances of the vanquished should precede the disarmament of the victors.
Winston Churchill (1874–1965) British statesman.
The Gathering Storm, Ch. 3

28 I said that the world must be made safe for at least fifty years. If it was only for fifteen to twenty years then we should have betrayed our soldiers.
Winston Churchill
Closing the Ring, Ch. 20

29 No one can guarantee success in war, but only deserve it.
Winston Churchill
Their Finest Hour

30 War is the continuation of politics by other means.
Karl von Clausewitz (1780–1831) Prussian general.
The usual misquotation of 'War is nothing but a continuation of politics with the admixture of other means'
Vom Kriege

31 Now, gentlemen, let us do something today which the world may talk of hereafter.
Lord Collingwood (1750–1810) British admiral.
Said before Trafalgar, 21 Oct 1805
Correspondence and Memoir of Lord Collingwood (G. L. Newnham; ed. Collingwood)

32 Come on, you sons of bitches! Do you want to live for ever?
Dan Daly (20th century) Sergeant in the US Marines.
Remark during Allied resistance at Belleau Wood, June 1918.
See also FREDERICK THE GREAT
Attrib.

33 If we lose this war, I'll start another in my wife's name.
Moshe Dayan (1915–81) Israeli general.
Attrib.

34 There is plenty of time to win this game, and to thrash the Spaniards too.
Francis Drake (1540–96) British navigator and admiral.
Referring to the sighting of the Armada during a game of bowls, 20 July 1588
Attrib.

35 I have singed the Spanish king's beard.
Francis Drake
Referring to the raid on Cadiz harbour, 1587
Attrib.

36 We are not at war with Egypt. We are in an armed conflict.

Anthony Eden (1897–1977) British statesman.
Speech, House of Commons, 4 Nov 1956

37 My centre is giving way, my right is in retreat; situation excellent. I shall attack.

Marshal Foch (1851–1929) French soldier.
Message sent during the second battle of the Marne, 1918
Biography of Foch (Aston), Ch. 13

38 Praise the Lord and pass the ammunition!

Howell Maurice Forgy (1908–83) US naval lieutenant.
Remark made during the Japanese attack on Pearl Harbor, 7 Dec 1941
Attrib. in *The Los Angeles Times*

39 I got there fustest with the mostest.

Nathan Bedford Forrest (1821–77) Confederate general.
Popular misquotation of his explanation of his success in capturing Murfreesboro; his actual words were, 'I just took the short cut and got there first with the most men'
A Civil War Treasury (B. Botkin)

40 Rascals, would you live for ever?

Frederick the Great (1712–86) King of Prussia.
Addressed to reluctant soldiers at the Battle of Kolin, 18 June 1757. *See also* DALY

41 Madam, I am the civilization they are fighting to defend.

Heathcote William Garrod (1878–1960) British classical scholar.
Replying to criticism that he was not fighting to defend civilization, during World War I
Oxford Now and Then (D. Balsdon)

42 I have many times asked myself whether there can be more potent advocates of peace upon earth through the years to come than this massed multitude of silent witnesses to the desolation of war.

George V (1865–1936) King of the United Kingdom.
Referring to the massed World War I graves in Flanders, 1922
Silent Cities (ed. Gavin Stamp)

43 You've got to forget about this civilian. Whenever you drop bombs, you're going to hit civilians.

Barry Goldwater (1909–) US politician.
Speech, New York, 23 Jan 1967

44 No terms except unconditional and immediate surrender can be accepted. I propose to move immediately upon your works.

Ulysses Simpson Grant (1822–85) US general.
Message to opposing commander, Simon Bolivar Buckner, during siege of Fort Donelson, 16 Feb 1862

45 Every position must be held to the last man: there must be no retirement. With our backs to the wall, and believing in the justice of our cause, each one of us must fight on to the end.

Douglas Haig (1861–1928) British general.
Order to the British Army, 12 Apr 1918

46 Gentlemen of the French Guard, fire first!

Lord Charles Hay (d. 1760) British soldier.
Said at the Battle of Fontenoy, 1745
Attrib.

47 I'd like to see the government get out of war altogether and leave the whole feud to private industry.

Joseph Heller (1923–) US novelist.
Catch 22

48 In starting and waging a war it is not right that matters, but victory.

Adolf Hitler (1889–1945) German dictator.
The Rise and Fall of the Third Reich (W. L. Shirer), Ch. 16

49 War? War is an organized bore.

Oliver Wendell Holmes Jnr (1841–1935) US jurist.
Yankee from Olympus (C. Bowen)

50 Older men declare war. But it is youth that must fight and die.

Herbert Clark Hoover (1874–1964) US statesman.
Speech, Republican National Convention, Chicago, 27 June 1944

51 East and west on fields forgotten
Bleach the bones of comrades slain,
Lovely lads and dead and rotten;
None that go return again.

A. E. Housman (1859–1936) British scholar and poet.
A Shropshire Lad, 'The Welsh Marches'

52 Elevate them guns a little lower.

Andrew Jackson (1767–1845) US statesman.
Order given whilst watching the effect of the US artillery upon the British lines at the Battle of New Orleans
Attrib.

53 I had always to remember that I could have lost the war in an afternoon.

Lord Jellicoe (1859–1935) British admiral.
Referring to the Battle of Jutland

54 The first casualty when war comes is truth.

Hiram Warren Johnson (1866–1945) US politician.
Speech, U.S. Senate, 1917

55 Formerly, a nation that broke the peace did not trouble to try and prove to the world that it was done solely from higher motives . . . *Now war has a bad conscience.* Now every nation assures us that it is bleeding for a human cause, the fate of which hangs in the balance of its victory. . . . No nation dares to admit the guilt of blood before the world.

Ellen Key (Karolina Sofia Key; 1849–1926) Swedish writer.
War, Peace, and the Future, Preface

56 Everything, everything in war is barbaric . . . But the worst barbarity of war is that it forces men collectively to commit acts against which individually they would revolt with their whole being.

Ellen Key
War, Peace, and the Future, Ch. 6

57 Our scientific power has outrun our spiritual power. We have guided missiles and misguided men.

Martin Luther King (1929–68) US Black civil-rights leader.
Strength to Love

58 The conventional army loses if it does not win. The guerrilla wins if he does not lose.

Henry Kissinger (1923–) German-born US politician and diplomat.
Foreign Affairs, XIII (Jan 1969), 'The Vietnam Negotiations'

59 The most persistent sound which reverberates through men's history is the beating of war drums.

Arthur Koestler (1905–83) Hungarian-born British writer.
Janus: A Summing Up, Prologue

60 If, therefore, war should ever come between these two countries, which Heaven forbid! it will not, I think, be due to irresistible natural laws, it will be due to the want of human wisdom.

Bonar Law (1858–1923) British statesman.
Referring to the UK and Germany
Speech, House of Commons, 27 Nov 1911

61 We have all lost the war. All Europe.

D. H. Lawrence (1885–1930) British novelist.
The Ladybird, 'The Ladybird'

62 It is well that war is so terrible; else we would grow too fond of it.

Robert E. Lee (1807–70) US general.
Speaking to another general during the battle of Fredericksburg
The American Treasury (C. Fadiman)

63 This war, like the next war, is a war to end war.

David Lloyd George (1863–1945) British Liberal statesman.
Referring to the popular opinion that World War I would be the last major war

64 'War is the continuation of politics'. In this sense war is politics and war itself is a political action.

Mao Tse-Tung (1893–1976) Chinese communist leader.
See also CLAUSEWITZ
Quotations from Chairman Mao Tse-Tung, Ch. 5

65 We are advocates of the abolition of war, we do not want war; but war can only be abolished through war, and in order to get rid of the gun it is necessary to take up the gun.

Mao Tse-Tung
Quotations from Chairman Mao Tse-Tung, Ch. 5

66 Television brought the brutality of war into the comfort of the living room. Vietnam was lost in the living rooms of America – not on the battlefields of Vietnam.

Marshall McLuhan (1911–81) Canadian sociologist.
Montreal *Gazette*, 16 May 1975

67 War will never cease until babies begin to come into the world with larger cerebrums and smaller adrenal glands.

H. L. Mencken (1880–1956) US journalist.
Notebooks, 'Minority Report'

68 War is the national industry of Prussia.

Comte de Mirabeau (1749–91) French statesman.
Attrib.

69 Fighting is like champagne. It goes to the heads of cowards as quickly as of heroes. Any fool can be brave on a battle field when it's be brave or else be killed.

Margaret Mitchell (1909–49) US novelist.
Gone with the Wind

70 War hath no fury like a non-combatant.

C. E. Montague (1867–1928) British editor and writer.
Disenchantment, Ch. 15

71 An empire founded by war has to maintain itself by war.

Baron de Montesquieu (1689–1755) French writer.
Considérations sur les causes de la grandeur et de la décadence des romains, Ch. 8

72 The U.S. has broken the second rule of war. That is, don't go fighting with your land army on the mainland of Asia. Rule One is don't march on Moscow. I developed these two rules myself.

Lord Montgomery (1887–1976) British field marshal.
Referring to the Vietnam war
Montgomery of Alamein (Chalfont)

73 The Minstrel Boy to the war has gone,
In the ranks of death you'll find him;
His father's sword he has girded on,
And his wild harp slung behind him.

Thomas Moore (1779–1852) Irish poet.
Irish Melodies, 'The Minstrel Boy'

74 It's the most beautiful battlefield I've ever seen.

Napoleon I (Napoleon Bonaparte; 1769–1821) French emperor.
Referring to carnage on the field of Borodino, near Moscow, after the battle (7 Sept 1812)
Attrib.

75 There rises the sun of Austerlitz.

Napoleon I
Said at the Battle of Borodino (7 Sept 1812), near Moscow; the Battle of Austerlitz (2 Dec 1805) was Napoleon's great victory over the Russians and Austrians

76 I don't care for war, there's far too much luck in it for my liking.

Napoleon III (1808–73) French emperor.
Said after the narrow but bloody French victory at Solferino (24 June 1859)
The Fall of the House of Habsburg (E. Crankshaw)

77 The sand of the desert is sodden red, –
Red with the wreck of a square that broke; –
The gatling's jammed and the colonel dead,
And the regiment blind with the dust and smoke.
The river of death has brimmed its banks
And England's far and honour a name.
But the voice of a schoolboy rallies the ranks:
'Play up! play up! and play the game!'

Henry John Newbolt (1862–1938) British poet.
Vitaî Lampada

78 Drake he's in his hammock till the great Armadas come.
(Capten, art tha sleepin' there below?)

Slung atween the round shot, listenin' for the
drum,
An dreamin' arl the time o' Plymouth Hoe.
Henry John Newbolt
Drake's Drum

79 War is war. The only good human being is a
dead one.
George Orwell (Eric Blair; 1903–50) British novelist.
Animal Farm, Ch. 4

80 Probably the Battle of Waterloo *was* won on
the playing-fields of Eton, but the opening
battles of all subsequent wars have been lost
there.
George Orwell
The Lion and the Unicorn, 'England, Your England'

81 The quickest way of ending a war is to lose
it.
George Orwell
Second Thoughts on James Burnham

82 The pallor of girls' brows shall be their pall;
Their flowers the tenderness of patient minds,
And each slow dusk a drawing-down of blinds.
Wilfred Owen (1893–1918) British poet.
Anthem for Doomed Youth

83 Red lips are not so red
As the stained stones kissed by the English
dead.
Wilfred Owen
Greater Love

84 I could not give my name to aid the slaughter
in this war, fought on both sides for grossly
material ends, which did not justify the
sacrifice of a single mother's son. Clearly I
must continue to oppose it, and expose it, to
all whom I could reach with voice or pen.
Sylvia Pankhurst (1882–1960) British suffragette.
The Home Front, Ch. 25

85 Stand your ground. Don't fire unless fired
upon, but if they mean to have a war, let it
begin here!
John Parker (1729–75) US general.
Command given at the start of the Battle of Lexington
Familiar Quotations (J. Bartlett)

86 War should belong to the tragic past, to
history: it should find no place on humanity's
agenda for the future.
John Paul II (Karol Wojtyla; 1920–) Polish pope
(1978–).
Speech, 1982

87 Don't cheer, boys; the poor devils are dying.
John Woodward Philip (1840–1900) US naval officer.
Restraining his victorious crew during the naval battle off San-
tiago in the Spanish-American War
Attrib.

88 Don't fire until you see the whites of their
eyes.
William Prescott (1726–95) US revolutionary soldier.
Command given at the Battle of Bunker Hill

89 War is, after all, the universal perversion.

We are all tainted: if we cannot experience
our perversion at first hand we spend our
time reading war stories, the pornography of
war; or seeing war films, the blue films of
war; or titillating our senses with the
imagination of great deeds, the masturbation
of war.
John Rae (1931–) British schoolmaster and writer.
The Custard Boys, Ch. 6

90 In a civil war, a general must know – and
I'm afraid it's a thing rather of instinct than of
practice – he must know exactly when to
move over to the other side.
Henry Reed (1914–86) British poet and dramatist.
Not a Drum was Heard: The War Memoirs of General Gland

91 And the various holds and rolls and throws
and breakfalls
Somehow or other I always seemed to put
In the wrong place. And as for war, my wars
Were global from the start.
Henry Reed
A Map of Verona, 'Lessons of the War', III

92 All Quiet on the Western Front.
Erich Maria Remarque (1898–1970) German novelist.
Title of novel

93 All wars are planned by old men
In council rooms apart.
Grantland Rice (1880–1954) US sportswriter.
Two Sides of War

94 (Fire – without hatred.)
Antonio Rivera (d. 1936) Spanish Nationalist hero.
Giving the order to open fire at the siege of the Alcázar
The Siege of the Alcázar (C. Eby)

95 More than an end to war, we want an end to
the beginnings of all wars.
Franklin D. Roosevelt (1882–1945) US Democratic
president.
Speech broadcast on the day after his death (13 Apr 1945)

96 They dashed on towards that *thin red line
tipped with steel.*
William Howard Russell (1820–1907) British journalist.
Description of the Russian charge against the British at the
Battle of Balaclava, 1854
The British Expedition to the Crimea

97 War is not an adventure. It is a disease. It is
like typhus.
Antoine de Saint-Exupéry (1900–44) French novelist
and aviator.
Flight to Arras

98 Sometime they'll give a war and nobody will
come.
Carl Sandburg (1878–1967) US author and poet.
The People, Yes

99 Man, it seemed, had been created to jab the
life out of Germans.
Siegfried Sassoon (1886–1967) British poet.
Memoirs of an Infantry Officer, Pt. I, Ch. 1

100 Safe with his wound, a citizen of life,
He hobbled blithely through the garden gate,

And thought: 'Thank God they had to amputate!'
Siegfried Sassoon
The One-Legged Man

101 If I were fierce and bald and short of breath,
I'd live with scarlet Majors at the Base,
And speed glum heroes up the line to death.
Siegfried Sassoon
Base Details

102 And when the war is done and youth stone dead
I'd toddle safely home and die – in bed.
Siegfried Sassoon
Base Details

103 'Good morning; good morning!' the general said
When we met him last week on our way to the line.
Now the soldiers he smiled at are most of 'em dead,
And we're cursing his staff for incompetent swine.
Siegfried Sassoon
The General

104 I am making this statement as a wilful defiance of military authority because I believe that the War is being deliberately prolonged by those who have the power to end it.
Siegfried Sassoon
Memoirs of an Infantry Officer, Pt. X, Ch. 3

105 All wars are popular for the first thirty days.
Arthur Schlesinger Jnr (1917–) US historian, educator, and author.
Attrib.

106 When you march into France, let the last man on the right brush the Channel with his sleeve.
Alfred Graf von Schlieffen (1833–1913) German general.
Referring to the Schlieffen plan
August 1914 (Barbara Tuchman), Ch. 2

107 When we, the Workers, all demand: 'What are we fighting for? . . .
Then, then we'll end that stupid crime, that devil's madness – War.
Robert William Service (1874–1958) Canadian poet.
Michael

108 Cry 'Havoc!' and let slip the dogs of war.
William Shakespeare (1564–1616) English dramatist.
Julius Caesar, III:1

109 Farewell the neighing steed and the shrill trump,
The spirit-stirring drum, th'ear piercing fife,
The royal banner, and all quality,
Pride, pomp, and circumstance, of glorious war!
William Shakespeare
Othello, III:3

110 The British soldier can stand up to anything except the British War Office.
George Bernard Shaw (1856–1950) Irish dramatist and critic.
The Devil's Disciple, II

111 I am tired and sick of war. Its glory is all moonshine . . . War is hell.
General William Sherman (1820–91) US general.
Attrib. in address, Michigan Military Academy, 19 June 1879

112 Who live under the shadow of a war,
What can I do that matters?
Stephen Spender (1909–) British poet.
Who live under the Shadow

113 To win in Vietnam, we will have to exterminate a nation.
Dr Benjamin Spock (1903–) US paediatrician and psychiatrist.
Dr Spock on Vietnam, Ch. 7

114 Yonder are the Hessians. They were bought for seven pounds and tenpence a man. Are you worth more? Prove it. Tonight the American flag floats from yonder hill or Molly Stark sleeps a widow!
John Stark (1728–1822) US general.
Urging on his troops at the Battle of Bennington in 1777
The American Treasury (C. Fadiman)

115 That's what you are. That's what you all are. All of you young people who served in the war. You are a lost generation.
Gertrude Stein (1874–1946) US writer.
A Moveable Feast (E. Hemingway)

116 War is capitalism with the gloves off.
Tom Stoppard (1937–) Czech-born British dramatist.
Travesties

117 Most sorts of diversion in men, children, and other animals, are an imitation of fighting.
Jonathan Swift (1667–1745) Irish-born Anglican priest and writer.
Thoughts on Various Subjects

118 The guerrilla fights the war of the flea, and his military enemy suffers the dog's disadvantages: too much to defend; too small, ubiquitous, and agile an enemy to come to grips with.
Robert Taber (20th century) US writer.
The War of the Flea, Ch. 2

119 They make a wilderness and call it peace.
Tacitus (c. 55–c. 120 AD) Roman historian.
Agricola, 30

120 Now all roads lead to France
And heavy is the tread
Of the living; but the dead
Returning lightly dance.
Edward Thomas (1878–1917) British poet.
Roads

121 Dead battles, like dead generals, hold the military mind in their dead grip.
Barbara W. Tuchman (1912–) US editor and writer.
August 1914, Ch. 2

122 They now *ring* the bells, but they will soon *wring* their hands.
Robert Walpole (1676–1745) British statesman.
Said when war was declared in 1739 with Spain, against Walpole's wishes
Memoirs of Sir Robert Walpole (W. Coxe)

123 I heard the bullets whistle, and believe me, there is something charming in the sound.
George Washington (1732–99) US statesman.
Referring to a recent skirmish in the French and Indian War
Presidential Anecdotes (P. Boller)

124 When the war broke out she took down the signed photograph of the Kaiser and, with some solemnity, hung it in the menservants' lavatory; it was her one combative action.
Evelyn Waugh (1903–66) British novelist.
Vile Bodies, Ch. 3

125 Like German opera, too long and too loud.
Evelyn Waugh
Giving his opinions of warfare after the Battle of Crete, 1941
Attrib.

126 It has been a damned serious business – Blücher and I have lost 30,000 men. It has been a damned nice thing – the nearest run thing you ever saw in your life . . . By God! I don't think it would have done if I had not been there.
Duke of Wellington (1769–1852) British general and statesman.
Referring to the Battle of Waterloo
Creevey Papers, Ch. X

127 Yes, and they went down very well too.
Duke of Wellington
Replying to the observation that the French cavalry had come up very well during the Battle of Waterloo
The Age of Elegance (A. Bryant)

128 A battle of giants.
Duke of Wellington
Referring to the Battle of Waterloo; said to Samuel Rogers
Attrib.

129 Up, Guards, and at 'em.
Duke of Wellington
Order given at the battle of Waterloo, 18 June 1815
Attrib.

130 The military don't start wars. The politicians start wars.
William Westmorland (1914–) US army officer.
Attrib.

131 As long as war is regarded as wicked, it will always have its fascination. When it is looked upon as vulgar, it will cease to be popular.
Oscar Wilde (1854–1900) Irish-born British dramatist.
The Critic as Artist, Pt. 2

132 You will be home before the leaves have fallen from the trees.
Wilhelm II (1859–1941) King of Prussia and Emperor of Germany.
Said to troops leaving for the Front, Aug 1914
August 1914 (Barbara Tuchman), Ch. 9

133 It is my Royal and Imperial Command that you . . . exterminate first the treacherous English, and . . . walk over General French's contemptible little Army.
Wilhelm II
Referring to the British Expeditionary Force; veterans of this force became known as 'Old Contemptibles'
The Times, 1 Oct 1914

134 There is such a thing as a man being too proud to fight.
Woodrow Wilson (1856–1925) US statesman.
Address to foreign-born citizens, 10 May 1915

135 The war we have just been through, though it was shot through with terror, is not to be compared with the war we would have to face next time.
Woodrow Wilson
Mr Wilson's War (John Dos Passos), Pt. V, Ch. 22

136 Once lead this people into war and they'll forget there ever was such a thing as tolerance.
Woodrow Wilson
Mr Wilson's War (John Dos Passos), Pt. III, Ch. 2

WAR AND PEACE

See also peace, war

1 Since wars begin in the minds of men, it is in the minds of men that the defences of peace must be constructed.
Anonymous
Constitution of UNESCO

2 And he shall judge among the nations, and shall rebuke many people: and they shall beat their swords into plowshares, and their spears into pruning-hooks: nation shall not lift up sword against nation, neither shall they learn war any more.
Bible: Isaiah
2:4

3 In war, resolution; in defeat, defiance; in victory, magnanimity; in peace, goodwill.
Winston Churchill (1874–1965) British statesman.
Epigram used by Sir Edward Marsh after World War II; used as 'a moral of the work' in Churchill's book
The Second World War

4 Those who can win a war well can rarely make a good peace and those who could make a good peace would never have won the war.
Winston Churchill
My Early Life, Ch. 26

5 My pacifism is not based on any intellectual theory but on a deep antipathy to every form of cruelty and hatred.
Albert Einstein (1879–1955) German-born US physicist.
Said on the outbreak of World War I
Attrib.

6 There never was a good war or a bad peace.
Benjamin Franklin (1706–90) US scientist and statesman.
Letter to Josiah Quincy, 11 Sept 1783

7 My argument is that War makes rattling good history; but Peace is poor reading.
Thomas Hardy (1840–1928) British novelist.
The Dynasts, II:5

8 He that makes a good war makes a good peace.
George Herbert (1593–1633) English poet.
Outlandish Proverbs, 420

9 The war ended, the explosions stopped.
The men surrendered their weapons
And hung around limply.
Peace took them all prisoner.
Ted Hughes (1930–) British poet.
Selected Poems 1957–1981, 'A Motorbike'

10 The statistics of suicide show that, for non-combatants at least, life is more interesting in war than in peace.
Dean Inge (1860–1954) British churchman.
The End of an Age

11 Peace hath her victories
No less renowned than war.
John Milton (1608–74) English poet.
Sonnet: 'To the Lord General Cromwell, May 1652'

12 Peace is not only better than war, but infinitely more arduous.
George Bernard Shaw (1856–1950) Irish dramatist and critic.
Heartbreak House (Preface)

13 Let him who desires peace, prepare for war.
Vegetius (Flavius Vegetius Renatus; 4th century AD) Roman writer.
Epitoma Rei Militaris, 3, 'Prologue'

14 When you're at war you think about a better life; when you're at peace you think about a more comfortable one.
Thornton Wilder (1897–1975) US novelist and dramatist.
The Skin of Our Teeth, III

WASTE

See also extravagance

1 Waste not, want not.
Proverb

2 Full many a gem of purest ray serene,
The dark unfathom'd caves of ocean bear:
Full many a flower is born to blush unseen,
And waste its sweetness on the desert air.
Thomas Gray (1716–71) British poet.
Elegy Written in a Country Churchyard

3 The world is too much with us; late and soon,
Getting and spending, we lay waste our powers:
Little we see in Nature that is ours.
William Wordsworth (1770–1850) British poet.
Sonnets, 'The world is too much with us'

WATER

See also drinks

1 Well, the principle seems the same. The water still keeps falling over.
Winston Churchill (1874–1965) British statesman.
When asked whether the Niagara Falls looked the same as when he first saw them
Closing the Ring, Ch. 5

2 Water, water, every where,
And all the boards did shrink;
Water, water, every where,
Nor any drop to drink.
Samuel Taylor Coleridge (1772–1834) British poet.
The Rime of the Ancient Mariner, II

3 Instead of drinking Coca Colas, turn on the tap and drink what the good Lord gave us.
Edwina Currie (1946–) British politician.
Speech, Nov 1988

4 Fish fuck in it.
W. C. Fields (1880–1946) US actor.
His reason for not drinking water
Attrib.

5 For any ceremonial purposes the otherwise excellent liquid, water, is unsuitable in colour and other respects.
A. P. Herbert (1890–1971) British writer and politician.
Uncommon Law

6 If you believe Cratinus from days of old,
Maecenas, (as you must know) no verse can give pleasure for long, nor last, that is written by drinkers of water.
Horace (Quintus Horatius Flaccus; 65–8 BC) Roman poet.
Epistles, I

7 The biggest waste of water in the country by far. You spend half a pint and flush two gallons.
Prince Philip (1921–) The consort of Queen Elizabeth II.
Speech, 1965

8 Human beings were invented by water as a device for transporting itself from one place to another.
Tom Robbins (1936–) US novelist.
Another Roadside Attraction

9 He who drinks a tumbler of London water has literally in his stomach more animated beings than there are men, women and children on the face of the globe.
Sydney Smith (1771–1845) British clergyman and essayist.
Letter

WEAKNESS

See also imperfection, yielding

1 The weakest goes to the wall.
Proverb

2 Oh, your precious 'lame ducks'!
John Galsworthy (1867–1933) British novelist.
The Man of Property, Pt. II, Ch. 12

3 A sheep in sheep's clothing.
Edmund Gosse (1849–1928) British writer and critic.
Referring to T. Sturge Moore. Sometimes attributed to Winston Churchill, referring to Clement Attlee
Under the Bridge (Ferris Greenslet), Ch. 12

4 Frailty, thy name is woman!
William Shakespeare (1564–1616) English dramatist.
Hamlet, I:2

WEALTH

See also capitalism, extravagance, materialism, money, ostentation, poverty and wealth

1 The best things in life are free.
Proverb

2 You can't take it with you when you go.
Proverb

3 Rich men's houses are seldom beautiful, rarely comfortable, and never original. It is a constant source of surprise to people of moderate means to observe how little a big fortune contributes to Beauty.
Margot Asquith (1865–1945) The second wife of Herbert Asquith.
The Autobiography of Margot Asquith, Ch. 17

4 A man who has a million dollars is as well off as if he were rich.
John Jacob Astor (1763–1848) US millionaire.
Attrib.

5 For the Lord thy God bringeth thee into a good land, a land of brooks of water, of fountains and depths that spring out of valleys and hills;
A land of wheat, and barley, and vines, and fig trees, and pomegranates; a land of oil olive, and honey;
A land wherein thou shalt eat bread without scarceness, thou shalt not lack any thing in it; a land whose stones are iron, and out of whose hills thou mayest dig brass.
When thou hast eaten and art full, then thou shalt bless the Lord thy God for the good land which he hath given thee.
Bible: Deuteronomy
8:7–10

6 For what shall it profit a man, if he shall gain the whole world, and lose his own soul? Or what shall a man give in exchange for his soul?
Bible: Mark
8:36–37

7 Lay not up for yourselves treasures upon earth, where moth and rust doth corrupt, and where thieves break through and steal:
But lay up for yourselves treasures in heaven, where neither moth nor rust doth corrupt, and where thieves do not break through nor steal:
For where your treasure is, there will your heart be also.
Bible: Matthew
6:19–21

8 Then said Jesus unto his disciples, Verily I say unto you, That a rich man shall hardly enter into the kingdom of heaven.
And again I say unto you, It is easier for a camel to go through the eye of a needle, than for a rich man to enter into the kingdom of God.
Bible: Matthew
19:23–24

9 The rich are the scum of the earth in every country.
G. K. Chesterton (1874–1936) British writer.
The Flying Inn

10 Poor Little Rich Girl.
Noël Coward (1899–1973) British dramatist.
Title of song

11 Riches have wings, and grandeur is a dream.
William Cowper (1731–1800) British poet.
The Task

12 FITZGERALD. The rich are different from us.
HEMINGWAY. Yes, they have more money.
F. Scott Fitzgerald (1896–1940) US novelist.
The Crack-Up, 'Notebooks, E'

13 Wealth is not without its advantages, and the case to the contrary, although it has often been made, has never proved widely persuasive.
John Kenneth Galbraith (1908–   ) US economist.
The Affluent Society, Ch. 1

14 The meek shall inherit the earth but not the mineral rights.
J. Paul Getty (1892–1976) US oil magnate.
Attrib.

15 If you can actually count your money you are not really a rich man.
J. Paul Getty
Gossip (A. Barrow)

16 As I walk along the Bois Bou-long,
With an independent air,
You can hear the girls declare,
'He must be a millionaire',
You can hear them sigh and wish to die,
You can see them wink the other eye
At the man who broke the Bank at Monte Carlo.
Fred Gilbert (1850–1903) British songwriter.
The Bois de Boulogne was a fashionable recreational area on the outskirts of Paris
The Man who Broke the Bank at Monte Carlo (song)

17 Sir, the insolence of wealth will creep out.
Samuel Johnson (1709–84) British lexicographer.
Life of Johnson (J. Boswell), Vol. III

18 Most of our people have never had it so good.
Harold Macmillan (1894–1986) British politician and prime minister.
Speech, Bedford Football Ground, 20 July 1957

19 And, as their wealth increaseth, so inclose Infinite riches in a little room.
Christopher Marlowe (1564–93) English dramatist.
The Jew of Malta, I:1

20 He must have killed a lot of men to have made so much money.
Molière (Jean Baptiste Poquelin; 1622–73) French dramatist.
Le Malade imaginaire, I:5

21 I am rich beyond the dreams of avarice.
Edward Moore (1712–57) British dramatist.
The Gamester, II

22 God shows his contempt for wealth by the kind of person he selects to receive it.
Austin O'Malley (1858–1932) US writer.

23 Who Wants to Be a Millionaire? I don't.
Cole Porter (1893–1964) US songwriter.
Who Wants to be a Millionaire?, title song

24 I am a millionaire. That is my religion.
George Bernard Shaw (1856–1950) Irish dramatist and critic.
Major Barbara

25 With the great part of rich people, the chief employment of riches consists in the parade of riches.
Adam Smith (1723–90) Scottish economist.
The Wealth of Nations

26 It is the wretchedness of being rich that you have to live with rich people.
Logan Pearsall Smith (1865–1946) US writer.
Afterthoughts, 'In the World'

27 If Heaven had looked upon riches to be a valuable thing, it would not have given them to such a scoundrel.
Jonathan Swift (1667–1745) Irish-born Anglican priest and writer.
Letter to Miss Vanhomrigh, 12–13 Aug 1720

28 I have had no real gratification or enjoyment of any sort more than my neighbor on the next block who is worth only half a million.
William Henry Vanderbilt (1821–85) US railway chief.
Famous Last Words (B. Conrad)

29 One can never be too thin or too rich.
Duchess of Windsor (Wallis Warfield Simpson; 1896–1986) The wife of the Duke of Windsor (formerly Edward VIII).
Attrib.

30 Just what God would have done if he had the money.
Alexander Woollcott (1887–1943) US journalist.
On being shown round Moss Hart's elegant country house and grounds
Attrib.

WEAPONS

See also nuclear weapons, power politics, war

1 If you carry this resolution and follow out all its implications and do not run away from it, you will send a Foreign Secretary, whoever he may be, naked into the conference chamber.
Aneurin Bevan (1897–1960) British Labour politician.
Referring to unilateral disarmament
Speech, Labour Party Conference, 2 Oct 1957

2 It was very successful, but it fell on the wrong planet.
Wernher von Braun (1912–77) German rocket engineer.
Referring to the first V2 rocket to hit London during World War II
Attrib.

3 We may find in the long run that tinned food is a deadlier weapon than the machine-gun.
George Orwell (Eric Blair; 1903–50) British novelist.
The Road to Wigan Pier, Ch. 6

4 Arms control so easily becomes an incantation rather than policy.
Richard Perle US politician.
Remark, Mar 1987

5 Today we have naming of parts. Yesterday,
We had daily cleaning. And tomorrow morning
We shall have what to do after firing. But today,
Today we have naming of parts.
Henry Reed (1914–86) British poet and dramatist.
Naming of Parts

6 They call it easing the Spring: it is perfectly easy
If you have any strength in your thumb: like the bolt,
And the breech, and the cocking-piece, and the point of balance,
Which in our case we have not got.
Henry Reed
Naming of Parts

7 Though loaded firearms were strictly forbidden at St Trinian's to all but Sixth-Formers . . . one or two of them carried automatics acquired in the holidays, generally the gift of some indulgent relative.
Ronald Searle (1920–) British cartoonist.
The Terror of St Trinian's, Ch. 3

8 But bombs *are* unbelievable until they actually fall.
Patrick White (1912–) British-born Australian novelist.
Riders in the Chariot, I:4

WEATHER

See also sun

1 Mackerel sky and mares' tails make lofty ships carry low sails.
Proverb

2 Rain before seven: fine before eleven.
Proverb

3 Rain, rain, go away, come again another day.
Proverb

4 Red sky at night, shepherd's delight; red sky in the morning, shepherd's warning.
Proverb

5 St. Swithin's Day, if thou dost rain, for forty days it will remain; St. Swithin's Day, if thou be fair, for forty days 'twill rain no more.
Proverb

6 The north wind does blow, and we shall have snow.
Proverb

7 What dreadful hot weather we have! It keeps me in a continual state of inelegance.
Jane Austen (1775–1817) British novelist.
Letter, 18 Sept 1796

8 I like the weather, when it is not rainy,
That is, I like two months of every year.
Lord Byron (1788–1824) British poet.
Beppo

9 This is a London particular . . . A fog, miss.
Charles Dickens (1812–70) British novelist.
Bleak House, Ch. 3

10 It ain't a fit night out for man or beast.
W. C. Fields (1880–1946) US actor.
The Fatal Glass of Beer

11 I'm singing in the rain, just singing in the rain;
What a wonderful feeling, I'm happy again.
Arthur Freed (1894–1973) US film producer and songwriter.
From the musical, *Hollywood Revue of 1929*
Singing in the Rain

12 This is the weather the cuckoo likes,
And so do I;
When showers betumble the chestnut spikes,
And nestlings fly:
And the little brown nightingale bills his best,
And they sit outside at 'The Travellers' Rest'.
Thomas Hardy (1840–1928) British novelist.
Weathers

13 This is the weather the shepherd shuns,
And so do I.
Thomas Hardy
Weathers

14 When two Englishmen meet, their first talk is of the weather.
Samuel Johnson (1709–84) British lexicographer.
The Idler

15 A snake came to my water-trough
On a hot, hot day, and I in pyjamas for the heat,
To drink there.
D. H. Lawrence (1885–1930) British novelist.
Snake

16 The British, he thought, must be gluttons for satire: even the weather forecast seemed to be some kind of spoof, predicting every possible combination of weather for the next twenty-four hours without actually committing itself to anything specific.
David Lodge (1935–) British author.
Changing Places, Ch. 2

17 Who has seen the wind?
Neither you nor I:
But when the trees bow down their heads,
The wind is passing by.
Christina Rossetti (1830–74) British poet.
Who Has Seen the Wind?

18 Blow, winds, and crack your cheeks; rage, blow.
You cataracts and hurricanoes, spout
Till you have drench'd our steeples, drown'd the cocks.
William Shakespeare (1564–1616) English dramatist.
King Lear, III:2

19 Rumble thy bellyful. Spit, fire; spout rain.
Nor rain, wind, thunder, fire, are my daughters
I tax not you, you elements, with unkindness.
William Shakespeare
King Lear, III:2

20 Poor naked wretches, wheresoe'er you are,
That bide the pelting of this pitiless storm,
How shall your houseless heads and unfed sides,
Your loop'd and window'd raggedness, defend you
From seasons such as these?
William Shakespeare
King Lear, III:4

21 So foul and fair a day I have not seen.
William Shakespeare
Macbeth, I:3

22 I am the daughter of Earth and Water,
And the nursling of the Sky;
I pass through the pores of the ocean and shores;
I change, but I cannot die,
For after the rain when with never a stain
The pavilion of Heaven is bare,
And the winds and sunbeams with their convex gleams
Build up the blue dome of air,
I silently laugh at my own cenotaph,
And out of the caverns of rain,
Like a child from the womb, like a ghost from the tomb,
I arise and unbuild it again.
Percy Bysshe Shelley (1792–1822) British poet.
The Cloud

23 I wield the flail of the lashing hail,
And whiten the green plains under,
And then again I dissolve it in rain,

And laugh as I pass in thunder.
Percy Bysshe Shelley
The Cloud

24 O Wild West Wind, thou breath of Autumn's being,
Thou, from whose unseen presence the leaves dead
Are driven, like ghosts from an enchanter fleeing,
Yellow, and black, and pale, and hectic red,
Pestilence-stricken multitudes.
Percy Bysshe Shelley
Ode to the West Wind

25 Heat, madam! It was so dreadful that I found there was nothing for it but to take off my flesh and sit in my bones.
Sydney Smith (1771–1845) British clergyman and essayist.
Discussing the hot weather with a lady acquaintance
Lives of the Wits (H. Pearson)

26 Willows whiten, aspens quiver,
Little breezes dusk and shiver.
Alfred, Lord Tennyson (1809–92) British poet.
The Lady of Shalott, Pt. I

WELSH

See also British, Wales

1 Eddy was a tremendously tolerant person, but he wouldn't put up with the Welsh. He always said, surely there's enough English to go round.
John Mortimer (1923–) British lawyer and dramatist.
Two Stars for Comfort, I:2

2 There are still parts of Wales where the only concession to gaiety is a striped shroud.
Gwyn Thomas (1913–81) British writer.
Punch, 18 June 1958

3 . . . an impotent people,
Sick with inbreeding,
Worrying the carcase of an old song.
R. S. Thomas (1913–) Welsh poet.
Welsh Landscape

4 'The Welsh,' said the Doctor, 'are the only nation in the world that has produced no graphic or plastic art, no architecture, no drama. They just sing,' he said with disgust, sing and blow down wind instruments of plated silver.'
Evelyn Waugh (1903–66) British novelist.
Decline and Fall, Pt. I, Ch. 8

WHISTLING

See also fear

1 The schoolboy, with his satchel in his hand,
Whistling aloud to bear his courage up.
Robert Blair (1699–1746) Scottish poet.
The Grave

2 I Whistle a Happy Tune.
Oscar Hammerstein (1895–1960) US lyricist.
From the musical *The King and I*
Song title

WINTER

See months, seasons

WISDOM

See also intelligence, knowledge, prudence, wisdom and foolishness

1 It is easy to be wise after the event.
Proverb

2 For in much wisdom is much grief: and he that increaseth knowledge increaseth sorrow.
Bible: Ecclesiastes
1:18

3 The words of wise men are heard in quiet more than the cry of him that ruleth among fools.
Bible: Ecclesiastes
9:17

4 The wisdom of a learned man cometh by opportunity of leisure: and he that hath little business shall become wise.
How can he get wisdom that holdeth the plough, and that glorieth in the goad, that driveth oxen, and is occupied in their labours, and whose talk is of bullocks?
Bible: Ecclesiasticus
38:24–25

5 With the ancient is wisdom; and in length of days understanding.
Bible: Job
12:12

6 No mention shall be made of coral, or of pearls: for the price of wisdom is above rubies.
Bible: Job
28:18

7 A wise man will hear, and will increase learning; and a man of understanding shall attain unto wise counsels:
To understand a proverb, and the interpretation; the words of the wise, and their dark sayings.
The fear of the Lord is the beginning of knowledge: but fools despise wisdom and instruction.
Bible: Proverbs
1:5–7

8 Wisdom is the principal thing; therefore get wisdom: and with all thy getting get understanding.
Bible: Proverbs
4:7

9 Wisdom reacheth from one end to another

mightily: and sweetly doth she order all things.
Bible: Wisdom
8:1

10 Does the Eagle know what is in the pit
Or wilt thou go ask the Mole?
Can Wisdom be put in a silver rod,
Or love in a golden bowl?
William Blake (1757–1827) British poet.
The Book of Thel, 'Thel's Motto'

11 I care not whether a man is Good or Evil; all that I care
Is whether he is a Wise Man or a Fool. Go! put off Holiness,
And put on Intellect.
William Blake
Jerusalem

12 Be wiser than other people if you can, but do not tell them so.
Earl of Chesterfield (1694–1773) English statesman.
Letter to his son, 19 Nov 1745

13 A sadder and a wiser man,
He rose the morrow morn.
Samuel Taylor Coleridge (1772–1834) British poet.
The Rime of the Ancient Mariner, VII

14 If one is too lazy to think, too vain to do a thing badly, too cowardly to admit it, one will never attain wisdom.
Cyril Connolly (1903–74) British journalist.
The Unquiet Grave

15 Knowledge dwells
In heads replete with thoughts of other men;
Wisdom in minds attentive to their own.
William Cowper (1731–1800) British poet.
The Task

16 Some are weather-wise, some are otherwise.
Benjamin Franklin (1706–90) US scientist and statesman.
Poor Richard's Almanack

17 Knowledge can be communicated but not wisdom.
Hermann Hesse (1877–1962) German novelist and poet.
Siddhartha

18 It is the province of knowledge to speak and it is the privilege of wisdom to listen.
Oliver Wendell Holmes (1809–94) US writer.
The Poet at the Breakfast Table, Ch. 10

19 Vain wisdom all, and false philosophy.
John Milton (1608–74) English poet.
Paradise Lost, Bk. II

20 The young man who has not wept is a savage, and the old man who will not laugh is a fool.
George Santayana (1863–1952) US philosopher.
Dialogues in Limbo, Ch. 3

21 Some folk are wise, and some are otherwise.
Tobias Smollett (1721–71) British novelist.
Roderick Random, Ch. 6

22 An ounce of a man's own wit is worth a ton of other people's.
Laurence Sterne (1713–68) Irish-born British writer.
Tristram Shandy

23 Oh, Vanity of vanities!
How wayward the decrees of Fate are;
How very weak the very wise,
How very small the very great are!
William Makepeace Thackeray (1811–63) British novelist.
Vanitas Vanitatum

24 It is never wise to try to appear to be more clever than you are. It is sometimes wise to appear slightly less so.
William Whitelaw (1918–) British politician.
The Observer, 'Sayings of the Year', 1975

WISDOM AND FOOLISHNESS

1 A wise man makes his own decisions, an ignorant man follows the public opinion.
Chinese Proverb

2 Then I saw that wisdom excelleth folly, as far as light excelleth darkness.
The wise man's eyes are in his head; but the fool walketh in darkness: and I myself perceived also that one event happeneth to them all.
Bible: Ecclesiastes
2:13–14

3 But God hath chosen the foolish things of the world to confound the wise; and God hath chosen the weak things of the world to confound the things which are mighty.
Bible: I Corinthians
1:27

4 For ye suffer fools gladly, seeing ye yourselves are wise.
Bible: II Corinthians
11:19

5 A fool sees not the same tree that a wise man sees.
William Blake (1757–1827) British poet.
The Marriage of Heaven and Hell, 'Proverbs of Hell'

6 Many have been the wise speeches of fools, though not so many as the foolish speeches of wise men.
Thomas Fuller (1608–61) English historian.
The Holy State and the Profane State

7 Give me the young man who has brains enough to make a fool of himself!
Robert Louis Stevenson (1850–94) Scottish writer.
Virginibus Puerisque

WOMAN'S ROLE

See also feminism, housework, marriage, women, sexes

1 Whoever rightly considers the order of things may plainly see the whole race of woman-

kind is by nature, custom, and the laws, made subject to man, to be governed according to his discretion: therefore it is the duty of every one of us that desires to have ease, comfort, and repose, with those men to whom we belong, to be humble, patient, and obedient, as well as chaste . . .

Giovanni Boccaccio (1313–75) Italian writer and poet.
Decameron, 'Ninth Day'

2 Mother is the dead heart of the family, spending father's earnings on consumer goods to enhance the environment in which he eats, sleeps and watches the television.

Germaine Greer (1939–) Australian-born British writer and feminist.
The Female Eunuch

3 These are rare attainments for a damsel, but pray tell me, can she spin?

James I (1566–1625) King of England.
On being introduced to a young girl proficient in Latin, Greek, and Hebrew
Attrib.

4 A man is in general better pleased when he has a good dinner upon his table, than when his wife talks Greek.

Samuel Johnson (1709–84) British lexicographer.
Johnsonian Miscellanies (ed. G. B. Hill), Vol. II

5 Women exist in the main solely for the propagation of the species.

Arthur Schopenhauer (1788–1860) German philosopher.

WOMEN

See also feminism, men, sexes, woman's role

1 A man of straw is worth a woman of gold.
Proverb

2 A woman's place is in the home.
Proverb

3 A woman's work is never done.
Proverb

4 The hand that rocks the cradle rules the world.
Proverb

5 Old-fashioned ways which no longer apply to changed conditions are a snare in which the feet of women have always become readily entangled.

Jane Addams (1860–1935) US social worker.
In *Newer Ideals of Peace*, 'Utilization of Women in City Government'

6 The woman that deliberates is lost.

Joseph Addison (1672–1719) British essayist.
Cato, IV:1

7 A woman seldom asks advice until she has bought her wedding clothes.

Joseph Addison
The Spectator, 475

8 . . . girls are so queer you never know what they mean. They say No when they mean Yes, and drive a man out of his wits for the fun of it . . .

Louisa May Alcott (1832–88) US novelist.
Little Women, Pt. II

9 Next to being married, a girl likes to be crossed in love a little now and then.

Jane Austen (1775–1817) British novelist.
Pride and Prejudice, Ch. 24

10 A woman, especially if she have the misfortune of knowing anything, should conceal it as well as she can.

Jane Austen
Northanger Abbey, Ch. 14

11 A lady's imagination is very rapid; it jumps from admiration to love, from love to matrimony in a moment.

Jane Austen
Pride and Prejudice, Ch. 6

12 Women – one half the human race at least – care fifty times more for a marriage than a ministry.

Walter Bagehot (1826–77) British economist and journalist.
The English Constitution, 'The Monarchy'

13 One is not born a woman, one becomes one.

Simone de Beauvoir (1908–86) French writer.
Le Deuxième Sexe (trans. The Second Sex)

14 You will find that the woman who is really kind to dogs is always one who has failed to inspire sympathy in men.

Max Beerbohm (1872–1956) British writer.
Zuleika Dobson, Ch. 6

15 And the Lord God caused a deep sleep to fall upon Adam, and he slept: and he took one of his ribs, and closed up the flesh instead thereof;
And the rib, which the Lord God had taken from man, made he a woman, and brought her unto the man.
And Adam said, This is now bone of my bones, and flesh of my flesh: she shall be called Woman, because she was taken out of Man. Therefore shall a man leave his father and his mother, and shall cleave unto his wife: and they shall be one flesh.
And they were both naked, the man and his wife, and were not ashamed.

Bible: Genesis
2:21–25

16 For the lips of a strange woman drop as an honeycomb, and her mouth is smoother than oil:
But her end is bitter as wormwood, sharp as a two-edged sword.

Bible: Proverbs
5:3–4

17 Who can find a virtuous woman? for her price is far above rubies

The heart of her husband doth safely trust in her, so that he shall have no need of spoil. She will do him good and not evil all the days of her life.
Bible: Proverbs
31:10–12

18 Why need the other women know so much?
Robert Browning (1812–89) British poet.
Any Wife to any Husband

19 The souls of women are so small,
That some believe they've none at all.
Samuel Butler (1612–80) English satirist.
Miscellaneous Thoughts

20 Brigands demand your money or your life; women require both.
Samuel Butler
Attrib.

21 I thought it would appear
That there had been a lady in the case.
Lord Byron (1788–1824) British poet.
Don Juan, V

22 Do you know why God withheld the sense of humour from women?
That we may love you instead of laughing at you.
Mrs Patrick Campbell (1865–1940) British actress.
To a man
The Life of Mrs Pat (M. Peters)

23 Women are much more like each other than men: they have, in truth, but two passions, vanity and love; these are their universal characteristics.
Earl of Chesterfield (1694–1773) English statesman.
Letter to his son, 19 Dec 1749

24 How lucky we are that women defend themselves so poorly! We should, otherwise, be no more to them than timid slaves.
Pierre Choderlos de Laclos (1741–1803) French novelist.
Les Liaisons Dangereuses, Letter 4

25 There is no fury like an ex-wife searching for a new lover.
Cyril Connolly (1903–74) British journalist.
The Unquiet Grave

26 Certain women should be struck regularly, like gongs.
Noël Coward (1899–1973) British dramatist.
Private Lives

27 Women never have young minds. They are born three thousand years old.
Shelagh Delaney (1939–) British dramatist.
A Taste of Honey, I:1

28 'She's the sort of woman now,' said Mould, . . . 'one would almost feel disposed to bury for nothing: and do it neatly, too!'
Charles Dickens (1812–70) British novelist.
Martin Chuzzlewit, Ch. 25

29 It is only the women whose eyes have been washed clear with tears who get the broad vision that makes them little sisters to all the world.
Dorothy Dix (Elizabeth Meriwether Gilmer; 1861–1951) US journalist and writer.
Dorothy Dix, Her Book, Introduction

30 She takes just like a woman, yes, she does
She makes love just like a woman, yes, she does
And she aches just like a woman
But she breaks just like a little girl.
Bob Dylan (Robert Allen Zimmerman; 1941–) US popular singer.
Just Like a Woman

31 I should like to know what is the proper function of women, if it is not to make reasons for husbands to stay at home, and still stronger reasons for bachelors to go out.
George Eliot (Mary Ann Evans; 1819–80) British novelist.
The Mill on the Floss, Ch. 6

32 In the room the women come and go
Talking of Michelangelo.
T. S. Eliot (1888–1965) US-born British poet and dramatist.
The Love Song of J. Alfred Prufrock

33 When a woman behaves like a man, why doesn't she behave like a nice man?
Edith Evans (1888–1976) British actress.
The Observer, 'Sayings of the Week', 30 Sept 1956

34 The great question . . . which I have not been able to answer, despite my thirty years of research into the feminine soul, is 'What does a woman want'?
Sigmund Freud (1856–1939) Austrian psychoanalyst.
Psychiatry in American Life (Charles Rolo)

35 How, like a moth, the simple maid
Still plays about the flame!
John Gay (1685–1732) English poet and dramatist.
The Beggar's Opera

36 You have to admit that most women who have done something with their lives have been disliked by almost everyone.
Françoise Gilot Artist and mistress of Picasso.
Remark, Oct 1987

37 Fighting is essentially a masculine idea; a woman's weapon is her tongue.
Hermione Gingold (1897–1987) British actress.
Attrib.

38 I know you do not make the laws but I also know that you are the wives and mothers, the sisters and daughters of those who do
. . .
Angelina Grimké (1805–79) US writer and reformer.
The Anti-Slavery Examiner (Sep 1836), 'Appeal to the Christian Women of the South'

39 My mother said it was simple to keep a man, you must be a maid in the living room, a cook in the kitchen and a whore in the bedroom. I said I'd hire the other two and take care of the bedroom bit.

Jerry Hall US model and actress.
Remark, Oct 1985

40 If men knew how women pass their time when they are alone, they'd never marry.

O. Henry (William Sidney Porter; 1862–1910) US short-story writer.
The Four Million Memoirs of a Yellow Dog

41 O! men with sisters dear,
O! men with mothers and wives!
It is not linen you're wearing out,
But human creatures' lives!

Thomas Hood (1799–1845) British poet.
The Song of the Shirt

42 A woman's preaching is like a dog's walking on his hinder legs. It is not done well; but you are surprised to find it done at all.

Samuel Johnson (1709–84) British lexicographer.
Life of Johnson (J. Boswell), Vol. I

43 No one delights more in vengeance than a woman.

Juvenal (Decimus Junius Juvenalis; 60–130 AD) Roman satirist.
Satires, XIII

44 When the Himalayan peasant meets the he-bear in his pride,
He shouts to scare the monster, who will often turn aside.
But the she-bear thus accosted rends the peasant tooth and nail
For the female of the species is more deadly than the male.

Rudyard Kipling (1865–1936) Indian-born British writer.
The Female of the Species

45 And a woman is only a woman, but a good cigar is a smoke.

Rudyard Kipling
The Betrothed

46 The First Blast of the Trumpet Against the Monstrous Regiment of Women.

John Knox (c. 1514–72) Scottish religious reformer.
Title of Pamphlet, 1558

47 Women run to extremes; they are either better or worse than men.

Jean de La Bruyère (1645–96) French satirist.
Les Caractères

48 So this gentleman said a girl with brains ought to do something else with them besides think.

Anita Loos (1891–1981) US novelist.
Gentlemen Prefer Blondes, Ch. 1

49 Women do not find it difficult nowadays to behave like men; but they often find it extremely difficult to behave like gentlemen.

Compton Mackenzie (1883–1972) British writer.
On Moral Courage

50 The Professor of Gynaecology began his course of lectures as follows: Gentlemen, woman is an animal that micturates once a day, defecates once a week, menstruates once a month, parturates once a year and copulates whenever she has the opportunity.

W. Somerset Maugham (1874–1965) British novelist.
A Writer's Notebook

51 A woman will always sacrifice herself if you give her the opportunity. It is her favourite form of self-indulgence.

W. Somerset Maugham
The Circle, III

52 Because women can do nothing except love, they've given it a ridiculous importance.

W. Somerset Maugham
The Moon and Sixpence, Ch. 41

53 I expect that Woman will be the last thing civilized by Man.

George Meredith (1828–1909) British novelist.
The Ordeal of Richard Feverel, Ch. 1

54 One tongue is sufficient for a woman.

John Milton (1608–74) English poet.
On being asked whether he would allow his daughters to learn foreign languages
Attrib.

55 Women would rather be right than reasonable.

Ogden Nash (1902–71) US poet.
Frailty, Thy Name Is a Misnomer

56 God created woman. And boredom did indeed cease from that moment – but many other things ceased as well! Woman was God's *second* mistake.

Friedrich Wilhelm Nietzsche (1844–1900) German philosopher.
The Antichrist

57 When a woman becomes a scholar there is usually something wrong with her sexual organs.

Friedrich Wilhelm Nietzsche
Bartlett's Unfamiliar Quotations (Leonard Louis Levinson)

58 There are already so many women in the world! Why then . . . was I born a woman, to be scorned by men in words and deeds?

Isotta Nogarola (1418–1466) Italian scholar and author.
Letter to Guarino Veronese

59 If women didn't exist, all the money in the world would have no meaning.

Aristotle Onassis (1906–75) Greek businessman.
Attrib.

60 Whether a pretty woman grants or withholds her favours, she always likes to be asked for them.

Ovid (Publius Ovidius Naso; 43 BC–17 AD) Roman poet.
Ars Amatoria

61 Most good women are hidden treasures who are only safe because nobody looks for them.

Dorothy Parker (1893–1967) US writer.
Obituary, *The New York Times*, 8 June 1967

62 My wife, who, poor wretch, is troubled with her lonely life.
Samuel Pepys (1633–1703) English diarist.
Diary, 19 Dec 1662

63 I don't think a prostitute is more moral than a wife, but they are doing the same thing.
Prince Philip (1921–) The consort of Queen Elizabeth II.
Remark, Dec 1988

64 There are two kinds of women – goddesses and doormats.
Pablo Picasso (1881–1973) Spanish painter.
Attrib.

65 Most women have no characters at all.
Alexander Pope (1688–1744) British poet.
Moral Essays, II

66 Men, some to business, some to pleasure take;
But every woman is at heart a rake.
Alexander Pope
Moral Essays, II

67 Woman's at best a contradiction still.
Alexander Pope
Moral Essays, II

68 Bah! I have sung women in three cities,
But it is all the same;
And I will sing of the sun.
Ezra Pound (1885–1972) US poet.
Cino

69 She really is a woman just like my mum.
Cliff Richard (1940–) British pop singer.
Remark, Aug 1988

70 The fundamental fault of the female character is that it has no sense of justice.
Arthur Schopenhauer (1788–1860) German philosopher.
Gedanken über vielerlei Gegenstände, XXVII

71 Do you not know I am a woman? When I think, I must speak.
William Shakespeare (1564–1616) English dramatist.
As You Like It, III:2

72 Frailty, thy name is woman!
William Shakespeare
Hamlet, I:2

73 I have no other but a woman's reason:
I think him so, because I think him so.
William Shakespeare
The Two Gentlemen of Verona, I:2

74 This Englishwoman is so refined
She has no bosom and no behind.
Stevie Smith (Florence Margaret Smith; 1902–71) British poet.
This Englishwoman

75 Womanhood is the great fact in her life; wifehood and motherhood are but incidental relations.
Elizabeth Stanton (1815–1902) US suffragette.
History of Woman Suffrage (with Susan B. Anthony and Mathilda Gage), Vol. I

76 The really original woman is the one who first imitates a man.
Italo Svevo (Ettore Schmitz; 1861–1928) Italian writer.
A Life, Ch. 8

77 God made the woman for the man,
And for the good and increase of the world.
Alfred, Lord Tennyson (1809–92) British poet.
Edwin Morris

78 How sweet are looks that ladies bend
On whom their favours fall!
Alfred, Lord Tennyson
Sir Galahad

79 I've got a woman's ability to stick to a job and get on with it when everyone else walks off and leaves it.
Margaret Thatcher (1925–) British politician and prime minister.
The Observer, 'Sayings of the Week', 16 Feb 1975

80 It is a great glory in a woman to show no more weakness than is natural to her sex, and not be talked of, either for good or evil by men.
Thucydides (c. 460–c. 400 BC) Greek historian and general.
History of the Peloponnesian War, Bk. II, Ch. 45

81 I was seized by the stern hand of Compulsion, that dark, unseasonable Urge that impels women to clean house in the middle of the night.
James Thurber (1894–1961) US humorist.
Alarms and Diversions, 'There's a Time for Flags'

82 I am a source of satisfaction to him, a nurse, a piece of furniture, a *woman* – nothing more.
Sophie Tolstoy (1844–1919) Russian writer.
A Diary of Tolstoy's Wife, 1860–1891

83 With many women I doubt whether there be any more effectual way of touching their hearts than ill-using them and then confessing it. If you wish to get the sweetest fragrance from the herb at your feet, tread on it and bruise it.
Anthony Trollope (1815–82) British novelist.
Miss Mackenzie, Ch. 10

84 Scarce, sir. Mighty scarce.
Mark Twain (Samuel Langhorne Clemens; 1835–1910) US writer.
Responding to the question 'In a world without women what would men become?'
Attrib.

85 Woman is unrivaled as a wet nurse.
Mark Twain
Attrib.

86 As if a woman of education bought things because she wanted 'em.
John Vanbrugh (1664–1726) English architect and dramatist.
The Confederacy, II:1

87 Once a woman has given you her heart you
can never get rid of the rest of her.
John Vanbrugh
The Relapse, II:1

88 Woman is always fickle and changing.
Virgil (Publius Vergilius Maro; 70–19 BC) Roman poet.
Aeneid, Bk. IV

89 I have often observed in women of her type
a tendency to regard all athletics as inferior
forms of fox-hunting.
Evelyn Waugh (1903–66) British novelist.
Decline and Fall, Pt. I, Ch. 10

90 'I will not stand for being called a woman in
my own house,' she said.
Evelyn Waugh
Scoop, Bk. I, Ch. 5

91 There is nothing in the whole world so
unbecoming to a woman as a Nonconformist
conscience.
Oscar Wilde (1854–1900) Irish-born British dramatist.
Lady Windermere's Fan, III

92 The question of the rights of women to hold
secular office is a quite separate matter and
should not in any way be connected to or
paralleled with the question of women's
ordination.
Cardinal Willebrands (1909–) Dutch ecclesiastic.
Remark, June 1986

93 I would venture to guess that Anon, who
wrote so many poems without signing them,
was often a woman.
Virginia Woolf (1882–1941) British novelist.
A Room of One's Own

94 Women have served all these centuries as
looking-glasses possessing the magic and
delicious power of reflecting the figure of
man at twice its natural size.
Virginia Woolf
A Room of One's Own

WONDER

See also admiration, curiosity

1 For all knowledge and wonder (which is the
seed of knowledge) is an impression of
pleasure in itself.
Francis Bacon (1561–1626) English philosopher.
The Advancement of Learning, Bk. I, Ch. 1

2 To see a World in a grain of sand,
And a Heaven in a wild flower,
Hold Infinity in the palm of your hand,
And Eternity in an hour.
William Blake (1757–1827) British poet.
Auguries of Innocence

3 Two things fill the mind with ever new and
increasing wonder and awe, the more often
and the more seriously reflection

concentrates upon them: the starry heaven
above me and the moral law within me.
Immanuel Kant (1724–1804) German philosopher.
Critique of Practical Reason, Conclusion

4 Philosophy is the product of wonder.
A. N. Whitehead (1861–1947) British philosopher.
Nature and Life, Ch. 1

WORDS

See also language, speech, verbosity

1 In the beginning was the Word, and the
Word was with God, and the Word was God.
Bible: – John
1:1

2 Actions speak louder than words.
Proverb

3 He said true things, but called them by
wrong names.
Robert Browning (1812–89) British poet.
Bishop Blougram's Apology

4 Oaths are but words, and words but wind.
Samuel Butler (1612–80) English satirist.
Hudibras, Pt. II

5 Be not the slave of Words.
Thomas Carlyle (1795–1881) Scottish historian and
essayist.
Sartor Resartus, Bk. I, Ch. 8

6 We must have a better word than
'prefabricated'. Why not 'ready-made'?
Winston Churchill (1874–1965) British statesman.
Closing the Ring, Appendix C

7 Words as is well known, are great foes of
reality.
Joseph Conrad (Teodor Josef Konrad Korzeniowski;
1857–1924) Polish-born British novelist.
Under Western Eyes

8 You can stroke people with words.
F. Scott Fitzgerald (1896–1940) US novelist.
The Crack-up

9 It was in the barbarous, gothic times when
words had a meaning; in those days, writers
expressed thoughts.
Anatole France (Jacques Anatole François Thibault;
1844–1924) French writer.
The Literary Life, 'M. Charles Morice'

10 Many terms which have now dropped out of
favour, will be revived, and those that are at
present respectable will drop out, if usage so
choose, with whom resides the decision and
the judgement and the code of speech.
Horace (Quintus Horatius Flaccus; 65–8 BC) Roman poet.
Ars Poetica

11 Thanks to words, we have been able to rise
above the brutes; and thanks to words, we
have often sunk to the level of the demons.
Aldous Huxley (1894–1964) British novelist.
Adonis and the Alphabet

12 *Net.* Anything reticulated or decussated at equal distances, with interstices between the intersections.

Samuel Johnson (1709–84) British lexicographer.
Dictionary of the English Language

13 Words are, of course, the most powerful drug used by mankind.

Rudyard Kipling (1865–1936) Indian-born British writer.
Speech, 14 Feb 1923

14 Words are men's daughters, but God's sons are things.

Samuel Madden (1686–1765) Irish writer.
Boulter's Monument

15 Until we learn the use of living words we shall continue to be waxworks inhabited by gramophones.

Walter De La Mare (1873–1956) British poet.
The Observer, 'Sayings of the Week', 12 May 1929

16 I am a Bear of Very Little Brain, and long words Bother me.

A. A. Milne (1882–1956) British writer.
Winnie-the-Pooh, Ch. 4

17 It is an important general rule always to refer to your friend's country establishment as a 'cottage'.

Stephen Potter (1900–69) British writer.
Lifemanship, Ch. 2

18 There is a Southern proverb, – fine words butter no parsnips.

Walter Scott (1771–1832) Scottish novelist.
The Legend of Montrose, Ch. 3

19 Man does not live by words alone, despite the fact that sometimes he has to eat them.

Adlai Stevenson (1900–65) US statesman.
Attrib.

20 She shrank from words, thinking of the scars they leave, which she would be left to tend when he had gone. If he spoke the truth, she could not bear it; if he tried to muffle it with tenderness, she would look upon it as pity.

Elizabeth Taylor (1912–75) British writer.
The Blush, 'The Letter Writers'

21 For words, like Nature, half reveal
And half conceal the Soul within.

Alfred, Lord Tennyson (1809–92) British poet.
In Memoriam A.H.H., V

22 No, my dear, it is *I* who am surprised; you are merely astonished.

Noah Webster (1758–1843) US lexicographer.
Responding to his wife's comment that she had been surprised to find him embracing their maid
Attrib.

WORK

See also effort, unemployment

1 All work and no play makes Jack a dull boy.
Proverb

2 No bees, no honey; no work, no money.
Proverb

3 Whatsoever thy hand findeth to do, do it with thy might; for there is no work, nor device, nor knowledge, nor wisdom, in the grave, whither thou goest.

Bible: Ecclesiastes
9:10

4 For even when we were with you, this we commanded you, that if any would not work, neither should he eat.

Bible: II Thessalonians
3:10

5 There is dignity in work only when it is work freely accepted.

Albert Camus (1913–60) French existentialist writer.
Notebooks, 1935–42

6 Work is the grand cure of all the maladies and miseries that ever beset mankind.

Thomas Carlyle (1795–1881) Scottish historian and essayist.
Speech, Edinburgh, 2 Apr 1886

7 Work is much more fun than fun.

Noël Coward (1899–1973) British dramatist.
The Observer, 'Sayings of the Week', 21 June 1963

8 By working faithfully eight hours a day you may eventually get to be a boss and work twelve hours a day.

Robert Frost (1875–1963) US poet.
Attrib.

9 When work is a pleasure, life is a joy! When work is a duty, life is slavery.

Maxim Gorky (Aleksei Maksimovich Peshkov; 1868–1936) Russian writer.
The Lower Depths

10 That one must do some work seriously and must be independent and not merely amuse oneself in life – this our mother has told us always, but never that science was the only career worth following.

Iréne Joliot-Curie (1897–1956) French scientist.
Recalling the advice of her mother, Marie Curie
A Long Way from Missouri (Mary Margaret McBride), Ch. 10

11 Horny-handed sons of toil.

Denis Kearney (1847–1907) US Labor leader.
Speech, San Francisco, c. 1878

12 It's been a hard day's night.

John Lennon (1940–80) British rock musician.
A Hard Day's Night (with Paul McCartney)

13 Life is too short to do anything for oneself that one can pay others to do for one.

W. Somerset Maugham (1874–1965) British novelist.
The Summing Up

14 The rise in the total of those employed is governed by Parkinson's Law and would be

much the same whether the volume of work were to increase, diminish or even disappear.
Cyril Northcote Parkinson (1919–) British historian and writer.
Parkinson's Law, Ch. 1

15 Work expands so as to fill the time available for its completion.
Cyril Northcote Parkinson
Parkinson's Law, Ch. 1

16 Work is necessary for man. Man invented the alarm clock.
Pablo Picasso (1881–1973) Spanish painter.
Attrib.

17 The harder you work, the luckier you get.
Gary Player (1935–) South African golfer.
Attrib.

18 They say hard work never hurt anybody, but I figure why take the chance.
Ronald Reagan (1911–) US politician and president.
Attrib.

19 If you have great talents, industry will improve them: if you have but moderate abilities, industry will supply their deficiency.
Joshua Reynolds (1723–92) British portrait painter.
Discourse to Students of the Royal Academy, 11 Dec 1769

20 I wish to preach, not the doctrine of ignoble ease, but the doctrine of the strenuous life.
Theodore Roosevelt (1858–1919) US Republican president.
Speech, Chicago, 10 Apr 1899

21 One of the symptoms of approaching nervous breakdown is the belief that one's work is terribly important. If I were a medical man, I should prescribe a holiday to any patient who considered his work important.
Bertrand Russell (1872–1970) British philosopher.
The Autobiography of Bertrand Russell, Vol. II, Ch. 5

22 The only place where success comes before work is a dictionary.
Vidal Sassoon (1928–) British hair stylist.
Quoting one of his teachers in a BBC radio broadcast

23 Pennies do not come from heaven. They have to be earned here on earth.
Margaret Thatcher (1925–) British politician and prime minister.
Sunday Telegraph, 1982

24 Work banishes those three great evils, boredom, vice, and poverty.
Voltaire (François-Marie Arouet; 1694–1778) French writer.
Candide, Ch. 30

25 How doth the little busy bee
Improve each shining hour,
And gather honey all the day
From every opening flower!
Isaac Watts (1674–1748) English theologian and hymn writer.
Divine Songs for Children, 'Against Idleness and Mischief'

26 Work is the curse of the drinking classes.
Oscar Wilde (1854–1900) Irish-born British dramatist.
Attrib.

27 I haven't got time to be tired.
Wilhelm I (1797–1888) King of Prussia and Emperor of Germany.
Said during his last illness

WORLD

See also confusion

1 For the world, I count it not an inn, but an hospital, and a place, not to live, but to die in.
Thomas Browne (1605–82) English physician and writer.
Religio Medici, Pt. II

2 As I walked through the wilderness of this world.
John Bunyan (1628–88) English writer.
The Pilgrim's Progress, Pt. I

3 The world degenerates and grows worse every day. . . . The calamities inflicted on Adam . . . were light in comparison with those inflicted on us.
Martin Luther (1483–1546) German Protestant.
Commentary on the Book of Genesis

WORLD WAR I

1 Belgium put the kibosh on the Kaiser,
Europe took a stick and made him sore;
And if Turkey makes a stand
She'll get ghurka'd and japanned,
And it won't be Hoch the Kaiser any more.
Anonymous
Song of World War I

2 Six million young men lie in premature graves, and four old men sit in Paris partitioning the earth.
Anonymous
New York Nation, 1919

3 Just for the word 'neutrality', a word which in wartime has so often been disregarded – just for a scrap of paper, Great Britain is going to make war on a kindred nation who desires nothing better than to be friends with her.
Theobald von Bethmann-Hollweg (1856–1921) German statesman.
Letter to Sir Edward Goschen, 4 Aug 1914

4 The battlefield is fearful. One is overcome by a peculiar sour, heavy and penetrating smell of corpses. . . . The legs of an Englishman, still encased in puttees, stick out of a trench, the corpse being built into the parapet; a soldier hangs his rifle on them.
Rudolph Binding
A Fatalist At War

5 The effects of the successful gas attack were horrible. I am not pleased with the idea of poisoning men. Of course the entire world

will rage about it first and then imitate us. All the dead lie on their backs with clenched fists; the whole field is yellow.
Rudolph Binding
A Fatalist At War

6 What did you do in the Great War, Daddy?
British Recruiting Poster

7 I shall fight before Paris, I shall fight in Paris, I shall fight behind Paris.
Georges Clemenceau (1841–1929) French statesman.
Speech, June 1918

8 We'll be over, we're coming over,
And we won't come back till it's over, over there.
George M. Cohan (1878–1942) US comedian.
American song of World War I

9 My centre is giving way, my right is in retreat; situation excellent. I shall attack.
Marshal Foch (1851–1929) French soldier.
Message sent during the second battle of the Marne, 1918
Biography of Foch (Aston), Ch. 13

10 This is not peace: it is an armistice for twenty years.
Marshal Foch
Attrib.

11 Please God – let there be victory, before the Americans arrive.
Douglas Haig
Diary, 1917

12 Every position must be held to the last man: there must be no retirement. With our backs to the wall, and believing in the justice of our cause, each one of us must fight on to the end.
Douglas Haig (1861–1928) British general.
Order to the British Army, 12 Apr 1918

13 If any question why we died,
Tell them because our fathers lied.
Rudyard Kipling (1865–1936) Indian-born British writer.
Epitaphs of War

14 I cannot get any sense of an enemy – only of a disaster.
D. H. Lawrence (1885–1930) British novelist.
Letter to Edward Marsh, Oct 1914

15 This war, like the next war, is a war to end war.
David Lloyd George (1863–1945) British Liberal statesman.

16 We travelled miles of trenches to reach the point we occupy. Some of the places we passed were liquid mud up to our knees. The town we passed through was an absolute ruin, not a house that is not blown to bits. I never saw the like of it, not a soul anywhere. I can't describe the look it has. It made me shiver – wooden crosses on the roadside and in places in the town marking the heroes' death – what devastation – a day of judgement more like. Man builds and then builds machines to destroy, well he seems to have made a better job of destroying this town.
Peter McGregor (1871–1916) Private soldier.
Letter to his wife, 21 June 1916

17 I feel my own life all the more precious and more dear in the presence of this deflowering of Europe. While it is true that the guns will effect a little useful weeding, I am furious with chagrin to think that the Minds, which were to have excelled the civilization of two thousand years, are being annihilated – and bodies, the product of aeons of Natural Selection, melted down to pay for political statues.
Wilfred Owen (1893–1918) British poet.
Letter, 28 Aug 1914

18 What passing-bells for these who die as cattle?
Only the monstrous anger of the guns,
Only the stuttering rifles' rapid rattle
Can patter out their hasty orisons.
Wilfred Owen
Anthem for Doomed Youth

19 Man, it seemed, had been created to jab the life out of Germans.
Siegfried Sassoon (1886–1967) British poet.
Memoirs of an Infantry Officer, Pt. I, Ch. 1

20 . . . The lecturer's voice still battered on my brain. 'The bullet and the bayonet are brother and sister.' 'If you don't kill him, he'll kill you.' 'Stick him between the eyes, in the throat, in the chest.' 'Don't waste good steel. Six inches are enough. What's the use of a foot of steel sticking out at the back of a man's neck? Three inches will do for him; when he coughs, go and look for another.'
Siegfried Sassoon
Memoirs of an Infantry Officer

21 On St Paul's steps I watched a recruiting meeting for some time. There was a tremendous crowd round and a soldier who looked like a Colonial was letting out for all he was worth. He had a number of men in uniform with him and every little while stopped and pointed his finger at some man in the crowd and shouted 'Why haven't you joined?' Of course everyone looked at the victim who felt called upon to make an excuse if he could, and one of the assistants pushed through the crowd to tackle the one singled out.
Robert Saunders Headmaster.
Letter to his son, 31 May 1915

22 When you march into France, let the last

man on the right brush the Channel with his sleeve.

Alfred Graf von Schlieffen (1833–1913) German general.
Referring to the Schlieffen plan
August 1914 (Barbara Tuchman), Ch. 2

23 We drove the Boche across the Rhine,
The Kaiser from his throne.
Oh, Lafayette, we've paid our debt,
For Christ's sake, send us home.

US Army song

24 You will be home before the leaves have fallen from the trees.

Wilhelm II (1859–1941) King of Prussia and Emperor of Germany.
Said to troops leaving for the Front, Aug 1914
August 1914 (Barbara Tuchman), Ch. 9

25 It is my Royal and Imperial Command that you . . . exterminate first the treacherous English, and . . . walk over General French's contemptible little Army.

Wilhelm II
Referring to the British Expeditionary Force; veterans of this force became known as 'Old Contemptibles'
The Times, 1 Oct 1914

26 There is such a thing as a man being too proud to fight.

Woodrow Wilson (1856–1925) US statesman.
Address to foreign-born citizens, 10 May 1915

27 My message today was a message of death for our young men. How strange it seems to applaud that.

Woodrow Wilson
Remark after his speech to Congress asking for a declaration of war, Apr 1917

28 There is a price which is too great to pay for peace, and that price can be put into one word. One cannot pay the price of self-respect.

Woodrow Wilson
Speech, Des Moines, Iowa, 1 Feb 1916

WORLD WAR II

See also Churchill, Germany, Hitler, Nazism, war

1 How horrible, fantastic, incredible, it is that we should be digging trenches and trying on gas-masks here because of a quarrel in a far-away country between people of whom we know nothing.

Neville Chamberlain (1869–1940) British statesman.
Referring to Germany's annexation of the Sudetenland
Radio broadcast, 27 Sept 1938

2 Hitler has missed the bus.

Neville Chamberlain
Speech, House of Commons, 4 Apr 1940

3 We have sustained a defeat without a war.

Winston Churchill (1874–1965)
Speech, House of Commons, 5 Oct 1938

4 We shall not flag or fail. We shall fight in France, we shall fight on the seas and oceans, we shall fight with growing confidence and growing strength in the air, we shall defend our island, whatever the cost may be, we shall fight on the beaches, we shall fight on the landing grounds, we shall fight in the fields and in the streets, we shall fight in the hills; we shall never surrender.

Winston Churchill
Speech, House of Commons, 4 June 1940

5 Let us therefore brace ourselves to our duties, and so bear ourselves that, if the British Empire and its Commonwealth last for a thousand years, men will still say: 'This was their finest hour'.

Winston Churchill
Referring to the forthcoming Battle of Britain
Speech, House of Commons, 18 June 1940

6 The battle of Britain is about to begin.

Winston Churchill
Speech, House of Commons, 18 June 1940

7 Never in the field of human conflict was so much owed by so many to so few.

Winston Churchill
Referring to the Battle of Britain pilots
Speech, House of Commons, 20 Aug 1940

8 We are waiting for the long-promised invasion. So are the fishes.

Winston Churchill
Radio broadcast to the French people, 21 Oct 1940

9 Give us the tools, and we will finish the job.

Winston Churchill
Referring to Lend-lease, which was being legislated in the USA
Radio broadcast, 9 Feb 1941

10 You do your worst, and we will do our best.

Winston Churchill
Addressed to Hitler
Speech, 14 July 1941

11 Do not let us speak of darker days; let us rather speak of sterner days. These are not dark days: these are great days – the greatest days our country has ever lived.

Winston Churchill
Address, Harrow School, 29 Oct 1941

12 When I warned them that Britain would fight on alone whatever they did, their Generals told their Prime Minister and his divided Cabinet: 'In three weeks England will have her neck wrung like a chicken.'
Some chicken! Some neck!

Winston Churchill
Referring to the French Government; see WEYGAND
Speech, Canadian Parliament, 30 Dec 1941

13 This is not the end. It is not even the beginning of the end. But it is, perhaps, the end of the beginning.

Winston Churchill
Referring to the Battle of Egypt
Speech, Mansion House, 10 Nov 1942

14 Wars are not won by evacuations.
Winston Churchill
Referring to Dunkirk
Their Finest Hour

15 Before Alamein we never had a victory.
After Alamein we never had a defeat.
Winston Churchill
The Hinge of Fate, Ch. 33

16 Peace with Germany and Japan on our terms
will not bring much rest . . . As I observed
last time, when the war of the giants is over
the wars of the pygmies will begin.
Winston Churchill
Triumph and Tragedy, Ch. 25

17 Now we can look the East End in the face.
Elizabeth the Queen Mother (1900–) The widow of
King George VI.
Surveying the damage caused to Buckingham Palace by a bomb
during the Blitz in World War II
Attrib.

18 This was the Angel of History! We felt its
wings flutter through the room. Was that not
the fortune we awaited so anxiously?
Joseph Goebbels (1897–1945) German politician.
Referring to Roosevelt's death
Diary

19 They entered the war to prevent us from
going into the East, not to have the East
come to the Atlantic.
Hermann Goering (1893–1946) German leader.
Referring to the war aims of the British in World War II
Nuremberg Diary (G. M. Gilbert)

20 The little ships, the unforgotten Homeric
catalogue of *Mary Jane* and *Peggy IV*, of
Folkestone Belle, *Boy Billy*, and *Ethel Maud*,
of *Lady Haig* and *Skylark* . . . the little ships
of England brought the Army home.
Philip Guedalla (1889–1944) British writer.
Referring to the evacuation of Dunkirk
Mr. Churchill

21 When Barbarossa commences, the world will
hold its breath and make no comment.
Adolf Hitler (1889–1945) German dictator.
Referring to the planned invasion of the USSR, Operation Bar-
barossa, which began on 22 June 1941
Attrib.

22 If we are going in without the help of Russia
we are walking into a trap.
David Lloyd George (1863–1945) British Liberal
statesman.
Speech, House of Commons, 3 Apr 1939

23 Dear Ike, Today I spat in the Seine.
General George Patton (1885–1945) US general.
Message sent to Eisenhower reporting his crossing of the
Seine in World War II
The American Treasury (C. Fadiman)

24 To make a union with Great Britain would be
fusion with a corpse.
Marshal Pétain (1856–1951) French marshal.
On hearing Churchill's suggestion for an Anglo-French union,
1940
Their Finest Hour (Winston S. Churchill), Ch. 10

25 Our great-grandchildren, when they learn
how we began this war by snatching glory
out of defeat . . . may also learn how the little
holiday steamers made an excursion to hell
and came back glorious.
J. B. Priestley (1894–1984) British novelist.
Referring to the British Expeditionary Force's evacuation from
Dunkirk
Broadcast, 5 June 1940

26 The best immediate defence of the United
States is the success of Great Britain
defending itself.
Franklin D. Roosevelt (1882–1945) US Democratic
president.
At press conference, 17 Dec 1940
Their Finest Hour (Winston S. Churchill), Ch. 28

27 Defeat of Germany means the defeat of
Japan, probably without firing a shot or losing
a life.
Franklin D. Roosevelt
The Hinge of Fate (Winston S. Churchill), Ch. 25

28 We have finished the job, what shall we do
with the tools?
Haile Selassie (1892–1975) Emperor of Ethiopia.
Telegram sent to Winston Churchill, mimicking his 'Give us the
tools, and we will finish the job'
Ambrosia and Small Beer, Ch. 4 (Edward Marsh)

29 If we see that Germany is winning the war
we ought to help Russia, and if Russia is
winning we ought to help Germany, and in
that way let them kill as many as possible.
Harry S. Truman (1884–1972) US statesman.
New York Times, 24 July 1941, when Russia was invaded by
Germany

30 In three weeks England will have her neck
wrung like a chicken.
Maxime Weygand (1867–1965) French general.
Said at the fall of France; see CHURCHILL
Their Finest Hour (Winston S. Churchill)

31 I fear we have only awakened a sleeping
giant, and his reaction will be terrible.
Isoroku Yamamoto (1884–1943) Japanese admiral.
Said after the Japanese attack on Pearl Harbor, 1941

WORLD-WEARINESS

1 Bankrupt of Life, yet Prodigal of Ease.
John Dryden (1631–1700) British poet and dramatist.
Absalom and Achitophel, I

2 Spare all I have, and take my life.
George Farquhar (1678–1707) Irish dramatist.
The Beaux' Stratagem, V:2

3 Death is a delightful hiding-place for weary
men.
Herodotus (c. 484 – c. 424 BC) Greek historian.
Histories, VII, 46

4 I am sick of this way of life. The weariness
and sadness of old age make it intolerable. I
have walked with death in hand, and death's
own hand is warmer than my own. I don't
wish to live any longer.
W. Somerset Maugham (1874 – 1965) British novelist.
Said on his ninetieth birthday
Familiar Medical Quotations (M. B. Strauss)

5 Stop the World, I Want to Get Off.
Anthony Newley (1931 –) British actor, composer,
singer, and comedian.
With Leslie Bricusse
Title of musical

6 How weary, stale, flat, and unprofitable,
Seem to me all the uses of this world!
William Shakespeare (1564 – 1616) English dramatist.
Hamlet, I:2

7 I have supp'd full with horrors.
William Shakespeare
Macbeth, V:5

8 I gin to be aweary of the sun,
And wish th' estate o' th' world were now
undone.
William Shakespeare
Macbeth, V:5

9 Death is not the greatest of ills; it is worse
to want to die, and not be able to.
Sophocles (c. 496 – 406 BC) Greek dramatist.
Electra, 1007

WORRY

See also misfortune

1 A trouble shared is a trouble halved.
Proverb

2 Don't meet troubles half-way.
Proverb

3 It will be all the same in a hundred years.
Proverb

4 Take things as they come.
Proverb

5 Begone, dull care! I prithee begone from me!
Begone, dull care, you and I shall never agree.
Anonymous
Begone Dull Care

6 Behold the fowls of the air: for they sow not,
neither do they reap, nor gather into barns;
yet your heavenly Father feedeth them. Are
ye not much better than they?
Which of you by taking thought can add one cu-
bit unto his stature?
And why take ye thought for raiment? Consider the lilies of the field, how they grow; they
toil not, neither do they spin:

And yet I say unto you, That even Solomon in
all his glory was not arrayed like one of these.
Wherefore, if God so clothe the grass of the
field, which today is, and tomorrow is cast into
the oven, shall he not much more clothe you,
O ye of little faith?
Therefore take no thought, saying, What shall
we eat? or, What shall we drink? or, Where-
withal shall we be clothed?
Bible: Matthew
6:26 – 31

7 But seek ye first the kingdom of God, and
his righteousness; and all these things shall
be added unto you.
Take therefore no thought for the morrow: for
the morrow shall take thought for the things
of itself. Sufficient unto the day is the evil
thereof.
Bible: Matthew
6:33 – 34

8 Just when we are safest, there's a sunset-
touch,
A fancy from a flower-bell, some one's death,
A chorus-ending from Euripides, –
And that's enough for fifty hopes and fears
As old and new at once as Nature's self,
To rap and knock and enter in our soul.
Robert Browning (1812 – 89) British poet.
Bishop Blougram's Apology

9 Before the cherry orchard was sold
everybody was worried and upset, but as
soon as it was all settled finally and once for
all, everybody calmed down, and felt quite
cheerful.
Anton Chekhov (1860 – 1904) Russian dramatist.
The Cherry Orchard, IV

10 When I look back on all these worries I
remember the story of the old man who said
on his deathbed that he had had a lot of
trouble in his life, most of which had never
happened.
Winston Churchill (1874 – 1965) British statesman.
Their Finest Hour

11 Care
Sat on his faded cheek.
John Milton (1608 – 74) English poet.
Paradise Lost, Bk. I

12 Worrying is the most natural and spontaneous
of all human functions. It is time to
acknowledge this, perhaps even to learn to
do it better.
Lewis Thomas (1913 –) US pathologist.
More Notes of a Biology Watcher, 'The Medusa and the Snail'

WRITERS

See also Chaucer, criticism, Dickens, Milton, poets, Shakespeare, writing

General quotes

1 A reader seldom peruses a book with

pleasure until he knows whether the writer of it be a black man or a fair man, of a mild or choleric disposition, married or a bachelor.
Joseph Addison (1672–1719) British essayist.
The Spectator, 1

2 Writers, like teeth, are divided into incisors and grinders.
Walter Bagehot (1826–77) British economist and journalist.
Estimates of some Englishmen and Scotchmen, 'The First Edinburgh Reviewers

3 The idea that it is necessary to go to a university in order to become a successful writer, or even a man or woman of letters (which is by no means the same thing), is one of those phantasies that surround authorship.
Vera Brittain (1893–1970) British writer and feminist.
On Being an Author, Ch. 2

4 Literary men are . . . a perpetual priesthood.
Thomas Carlyle (1795–1881) Scottish historian and essayist.
Critical and Miscellaneous Essays, 'The State of German Literature'

5 I believe the souls of five hundred Sir Isaac Newtons would go to the making up of a Shakespeare or a Milton.
Samuel Taylor Coleridge (1772–1834) British poet.
Letter to Thomas Poole, 23 Mar 1801

6 The faults of great authors are generally excellences carried to an excess.
Samuel Taylor Coleridge
Miscellanies, 149

7 A great writer creates a world of his own and his readers are proud to live in it. A lesser writer may entice them in for a moment, but soon he will watch them filing out.
Cyril Connolly (1903–74) British journalist.
Enemies of Promise, Ch. 1

8 The only way for writers to meet is to share a quick pee over a common lamp-post.
Cyril Connolly
The Unquiet Grave

9 Talent alone cannot make a writer. There must be a man behind the book.
Ralph Waldo Emerson (1803–82) US poet and essayist.
Goethe

10 Creative writers are always greater than the causes that they represent.
E. M. Forster (1879–1970) British novelist.
Gide and George

11 The reciprocal civility of authors is one of the most risible scenes in the farce of life.
Samuel Johnson (1709–84) British lexicographer.
Life of Sir Thomas Browne

12 Authors are easy to get on with – if you're fond of children.
Michael Joseph (1897–1958) British publisher.
The Observer, 1949

13 One man is as good as another until he has written a book.
Benjamin Jowett (1817–93) British theologian.
Letters of B. Jowett (Abbott and Campbell)

14 Our principal writers have nearly all been fortunate in escaping regular education.
Hugh MacDiarmid (Christopher Murray Grieve; 1892–1978) Scottish poet.
The Observer, 'Sayings of the Week', 29 Mar 1953

15 The trouble with our younger authors is that they are all in the sixties.
W. Somerset Maugham (1874–1965) British novelist.
The Observer, 'Sayings of the Week', 14 Oct 1951

16 A novelist is, like all mortals, more fully at home on the surface of the present than in the ooze of the past.
Vladimir Nabokov (1899–1977) Russian-born US novelist.
Strong Opinions, Ch. 20

17 I think that if a third of all the novelists and maybe two-thirds of all the poets now writing dropped dead suddenly, the loss to literature would not be great.
Charles Osborne (1927–) Author, critic, and Director of Arts Council.
Remark, Nov 1985

18 A list of authors who have made themselves most beloved and therefore, most comfortable financially, shows that it is our national joy to mistake for the first-rate, the fecund rate.
Dorothy Parker (1893–1967) US writer.
Wit's End (R. E. Drennan)

19 A novelist who writes nothing for 10 years finds his reputation rising. Because I keep on producing books they say there must be something wrong with this fellow.
J. B. Priestley (1894–1984) British novelist.
The Observer, 'Sayings of the Week', 21 Sept 1969

20 Everybody writes a book too many.
Mordecai Richler (1931–) Canadian novelist.
The Observer, 'Sayings of the Week', 9 Jan 1985

21 Among the many problems which beset the novelist, not the least weighty is the choice of the moment at which to begin his novel.
Vita Sackville-West (Victoria Sackville-West; 1892–1962) British poet and novelist.
The Edwardians, Ch. 1

22 When I was a little boy they called me a liar but now that I am a grown up they call me a writer.
Isaac Bashevis Singer (1904–) US novelist and short-story writer.
Remark, July 1983

23 No regime has ever loved great writers, only minor ones.
Alexander Solzhenitsyn (1918–) Soviet novelist.
The First Circle, Ch. 57

24 It is a sad feature of modern life that only women for the most part have time to write novels, and they seldom have much to write about.
Auberon Waugh (1939–) British novelist and critic.
Remark, June 1981

25 In my situation as Chancellor of the University of Oxford, I have been much exposed to authors.
Duke of Wellington (1769–1852) British general and statesman.
Collections and Recollections (G. W. E. Russell)

26 I think it's good for a writer to think he's dying; he works harder.
Tennessee Williams (1911–83) US dramatist.
The Observer, 'Sayings of the Week', 31 Oct 1976

27 Literature is strewn with the wreckage of men who have minded beyond reason the opinions of others.
Virginia Woolf (1882–1941) British novelist.
A Room of One's Own

28 It's not a writer's business to hold opinions.
W. B. Yeats (1865–1939) Irish poet.
Speaking to playwright, Denis Johnston
The Guardian, 5 May 1977

Specific quotes

29 More can be learnt from Miss Austen about the nature of the novel than from almost any other writer.
Walter Allen (1911–) British author and literary journalist.
The English Novel

30 From the beginning Wilde performed his life and continued to do so even after fate had taken the plot out of his hands.
W. H. Auden (1907–73) British poet.
Forewords and Afterwords

31 Shaw's judgements are often scatterbrained, but at least he has brains to scatter.
Max Beerbohm (1872–1956) British writer.
Conversation With Max (S. N. Behrens)

32 I have been told by hospital authorites that more copies of my works are left behind by departing patients than those of any other author.
Robert Benchley (1889–1945) US humorist.
Chips off the Old Benchley, 'Why Does Nobody Collect Me?'

33 He sipped at a weak hock and seltzer,
As he gazed at the London skies
Through the Nottingham lace of the curtains
Or was it his bees-winged eyes?
John Betjeman (1906–84) British poet.
The Arrest of Oscar Wilde at the Cadogan Hotel

34 That sovereign of insufferables.
Ambrose Bierce (1842–?1914) US writer and journalist.
Referring to Oscar Wilde
Wasp (San Francisco), 1882

35 Miller is not really a writer but a non-stop talker to whom someone has given a typewriter.
Gerald Brenan (Edward Fitzgerald Brenan; 1894–1987) British writer.
Referring to Henry Miller
Thoughts in a Dry Season, 'Literature'

36 I had not seen *Pride and Prejudice* till I read that sentence of yours, and then I got the book. And what did I find? An accurate daguerreotyped portrait of a commonplace face; a carefully fenced, highly cultivated garden, with neat borders and delicate flowers; but no glance of a bright, vivid physiognomy, no open country, no fresh air, no blue hill, no bonny beck. I should hardly like to live with her ladies and gentlemen, in their elegant but confined houses.
Charlotte Brontë (1816–55) British novelist.
Letter to G. H. Lewes, 12 Jan 1848

37 A budding young anthologist sought to include a Shaw piece in a new collection. 'I hope you understand', he wrote to Shaw, 'that I cannot afford to pay your usual fee as I am a very young man.' Shaw replied 'I'll wait for you to grow up.'
Bennett Cerf (1898–1971) US publisher, editor and writer.
Shake Well Before Using

38 G.B.S. looked aged and feeble and was dressed in very dark tweeds and a black overcoat. His white whiskers and pink face looked like an enamelled portrait, and had that pink lifeless quality of the very old.
Sir Henry Channon (1897–1958) Politician and writer.
Diary, 26 Feb 1944

39 Mr Shaw is (I suspect) the only man on earth who has never written any poetry.
G. K. Chesterton (1874–1936) British writer.
Referring to George Bernard Shaw
Orthodoxy, Ch. 3

40 His gaze was constantly fixed on himself; yet not on himself, but on his reflection in the looking-glass . . . Introspection of the genuine kind he never achieved . . . Wilde grew into a Pierrot who liked to play the prophet.
Harold Child
Writing of Oscar Wilde
Times Literary Supplement, 18 June 1908

41 . . . Old dread-death and dread-evil Johnson, that teacher of moping and melancholy . . . If the writings of this time-serving, mean, dastardly old pensioner had got a firm hold of the minds of the people at large, the people would have been bereft of their very souls.
William Cobbett (1763–1835) British journalist and writer.

42 Shaw relished every opportunity to have

himself painted, sketched, photographed or carved, because each likeness provided him with a new extension of himself.

Peter Conrad
The Observer, Multitude of Shaws, 7 Oct 1979

43 Wilde's voice was of the brown velvet order – mellifluous – rounded – in a sense giving it a plummy quality – rather on the adenotic side – but practically pure cello – and very pleasing.

Franklin Dyall
Life of Oscar Wilde (Hesketh Pearson)

44 A dangerous person to disagree with.

T. S. Eliot (1888–1965) US-born British poet and dramatist.
Referring to Samuel Johnson
The Metaphysical Poets

45 I am at a loss to understand why people hold Miss Austen's novels at so high a rate, which seem to me vulgar in tone, sterile in artistic invention, imprisoned in the wretched conventions of English society, without genius, wit, or knowledge of the world. Never was life so pinched and narrow. The one problem in the mind of the writer in both the stories I have read . . . is marriageableness.

Ralph Waldo Emerson (1803–82) US poet and essayist.
Journal, 1861

46 This pictorial account of the day-to-day life of an English gamekeeper is full of considerable interest to outdoor minded readers, as it contains many passages on pheasant-raising, the apprehending of poachers, ways to control vermin, and other chores and duties of the professional gamekeeper.
Unfortunately, one is obliged to wade through many pages of extraneous material in order to discover and savour those sidelights on the management of a midland shooting estate, and in this reviewer's opinion the book cannot take the place of J. R. Miller's *Practical Gamekeeping*.

Review of *Lady Chatterley's Lover*
Field and Stream

47 Lawrence himself is, as far as I know, the only prophetic novelist writing today – all the rest are fantasists or preachers: the only living novelist in whom the song predominates, who has the rapt bardic quality, and whom it is idle to criticize. . . . Nothing is more disconcerting than to sit down, so to speak, before your prophet, and then suddenly to receive his boot in the pit of your stomach.

E. M. Forster (1879–1970) British novelist.
Aspects of the Novel

48 Scott misunderstood it when he congratulated her for painting on a square of ivory. She is a miniaturist, but never two-dimensional. All her characters are round, or capable of rotundity.

E. M. Forster
Referring to Jane Austen
Aspects of the Novel

49 It's not good enough to spend time and ink in describing the penultimate sensations and physical movements of people getting into a state of rut . . . The body's never worthwhile, and the sooner Lawrence recognizes that, the better – the men we swear by – Tolstoy, Turgenev, Chekov, Maupassant, Flaubert, France – knew that great truth, they only use the body, and that sparingly, to reveal the soul.

John Galsworthy (1867–1933) British novelist.
Letter to Edward Garnett, 13 Apr 1914

50 Lunched with Pinker to meet D. H. Lawrence, that provincial genius. Interesting, but a type I could not get on with. Obsessed with self. Dead eyes, and a red beard, long pale narrow face. A strange bird.

John Galsworthy
Life and Letters of John Galsworthy (H. V. Marrot)

51 There is no arguing with Johnson; for when his pistol misses fire, he knocks you down with the butt end of it.

Oliver Goldsmith (1728–74) Irish-born British writer.
Life of Johnson (J. Boswell)

52 . . . But Mr Hardy's women are moulded of the same flesh as his men; they are liable to flutterings and tremblings; they are not always constant even when they are 'quite nice'; and some of them are actually 'of a coming-on disposition'.

Edmund Gosse (1849–1928) British writer and critic.
Speaker, 13 Sept 1890

53 Oscar Wilde did not dive very deeply below the surface of human nature, but found, to a certain extent rightly, that there is more on the surface of life than is seen by the eyes of most people.

J. T. Grein
Sunday Special, 9 Dec 1900

54 The work of Henry James has always seemed divisible by a simple dynastic arrangement into three reigns: James I, James II, and the Old Pretender.

Philip Guedalla (1889–1944) British writer.
Collected Essays, 'Men of Letters: Mr. Henry James'

55 His worst is better than any other person's best.

William Hazlitt (1778–1830) British essayist.
Referring to Walter Scott
English Literature, Ch. XIV, 'Sir Walter Scott'

56 He writes as fast as they can read, and he does not write himself down.

William Hazlitt
Referring to Walter Scott
English Literature, CH. XIV, 'Sir Walter Scott'

57 Dr Johnson's sayings would not appear so extraordinary, were it not for his *bow-wow way.*
Henry Herbert (1734–94) British general.
Life of Johnson (J. Boswell)

58 He identified genius with immunity from the cravings and turpitudes which make us human. Hence his regime of sexual continence which so confused and dismayed the women he persisted in loving, and hence too his abstinent diet of grated vegetables.
Michael Holroyd (1935–) British writer.
Referring to Shaw
The Genius of Shaw

59 To be with Lawrence was a kind of adventure, a voyage of discovery into newness and otherness . . . For Lawrence, existence was one continuous convalescence; it was as though he were newly re-born from a mortal illness every day of his life.
Aldous Huxley (1894–1964) British novelist.
The Letters of D. H. Lawrence, Introduction

60 He was unperfect, unfinished, inartistic; he was worse than provincial – he was parochial.
Henry James (1843–1916) US novelist.
Referring to Thoreau
Life of Nathaniel Hawthorne, Ch. 4

61 He is the richest author that ever grazed the common of literature.
Samuel Johnson (1709–84) British lexicographer.
Referring to Dr John Campbell
Life of Johnson (J. Boswell), Vol. I

62 What a commonplace genius he has, or a genius for the commonplace, I don't know which. He doesn't rank so terribly high, really. But better than Bernard Shaw, even then.
D. H. Lawrence (1885–1930) British novelist.
Referring to Hardy
Letter to Martin Secker, 24 July 1928

63 Charlotte Brontë, one cannot but feel after comparing her early work with modern bestsellers, was only unlike them in being fortunate in her circumstances, which gave her a cultured background, and in the age in which she lived, which did not get between her and her spontaneities.
Q. D. Leavis (1906–81) British writer.
Fiction and the Reading Public

64 A good man fallen among Fabians.
Lenin (Vladimir Ilich Ulyanov; 1870–1924) Russian revolutionary leader.
Referring to Bernard Shaw
Attrib.

65 The last gentleman in Europe.
Ada Beddington Leverson (1862–1933) British writer.
Said of Oscar Wilde
Letters to the Sphinx (Wilde), 'Reminiscences', 2

66 I ask you, is anything in life or literature, past or present, in earth, heaven or hell, anything more devastatingly tedious than D.H.L.'s interest in the human genitalia.
G. W. Lyttelton
Referring to D. H. Lawrence
The Lyttelton Hart-Davis Letters, 29 Mar 1956

67 In the foreground is that strange figure which is as familiar to us as the figures of those among whom we have been brought up, the gigantic body, the huge massy face, seamed with the scars of disease, the brown coat, the black worsted stockings, the grey wig with the scorched foretop, the dirty hands, the nails bitten and pared to the quick.
Lord Macaulay (1800–59) British historian.
Describing Samuel Johnson
Essays: 'Boswell's Life of Johnson'

68 Nothing very much happens in her books, and yet, when you come to the bottom of a page, you eagerly turn it to learn what will happen next. Nothing very much does and again you eagerly turn the page. The novelist who has the power to achieve this has the most precious gift a novelist can possess.
W. Somerset Maugham (1874–1965) British novelist.
Referring to Jane Austen
Ten Novels and Their Authors

69 I have discovered that our great favourite, Miss Austen, is my countrywoman . . . with whom mamma before her marriage was acquainted. Mamma says that she was then the prettiest, silliest, most affected, husband-hunting butterfly she ever remembers.
Mary Russell Mitford (1787–1855) British writer.
Referring to Jane Austen
Letter to Sir William Elford, 3 Apr 1815

70 English literature's performing flea.
Sean O'Casey (1884–1964) Irish dramatist.
Referring to P. G. Wodehouse
Attrib.

71 He is pretty certain to come back into favour. One of the surest signs of his genius is that women dislike his books.
George Orwell (Eric Blair; 1903–50) British novelist.
Referring to Conrad
New English Weekly, 23 July 1936

72 The foaming denouncers of the bourgeoisie, and the more-water-in-your-beer reformers of whom Shaw is the prototype.
George Orwell
The Road to Wigan Pier

73 If with the literate I am
Impelled to try an epigram
I never seek to take the credit
We all assume that Oscar said it.
Dorothy Parker (1893–1967) US writer.
Referring to Oscar Wilde
Attrib.

74 The poor son-of-a-bitch!
Dorothy Parker
Quoting from *The Great Gatsby* on paying her last respects to
F. Scott Fitzgerald
Thalberg: Life and Legend (B. Thomas)

75 Now that the old lion is dead, every ass
thinks he may kick at him.
Samuel Parr (1747–1825) British writer and scholar.
Referring to Dr Johnson
Life of Johnson (J. Boswell)

76 Even when conversing he could not keep
still: jumping up and down, crossing and
uncrossing his legs, shoving his hands in his
pockets and pulling them out, sitting straight
up or lying right back in his chair, bending
forward, stretching backward, never
remaining in one position for two minutes
together.
Hesketh Pearson (1887–1964) British biographer.
Bernard Shaw

77 Undeterred . . . ,Mr Lawrence has penned
another novel, *Women in Love*, which justly
merits the fate of its predecessor. I do not
claim to be a literary critic, but I know dirt
when I smell it and here it is in heaps –
festering, putrid heaps which smell to high
Heaven.
W. Charles Pilley Critic.
Review of *Women in Love*
John Bull, 17 Sept 1921

78 Detestable person but needs watching. I
think he learned the proper treatment of
modern subjects before I did.
Ezra Pound (1885–1972) US poet.
Referring to D. H. Lawrence
Letter to Harriet Monroe, Mar 1913

79 Waldo is one of those people who would be
enormously improved by death.
Saki (Hector Hugh Munro; 1870–1916) British writer.
Referring to Ralph Waldo Emerson
The Feast of Nemesis

80 Sherard Blaw, the dramatist who had
discovered himself, and who had given so
ungrudgingly of his discovery to the world.
Saki
The Unbearable Bassington, Ch. 13

81 The Big Bow-Wow strain I can do myself like
any now going; but the exquisite touch,
which renders ordinary commonplace things
and characters interesting, from the truth of
the description and the sentiment, is denied
to me.
Walter Scott (1771–1832) Scottish novelist.
In praise of Jane Austen
Journal, 14 Mar 1826

82 That young lady has a talent for describing
the involvements and feelings and characters

of ordinary life which is to me the most
wonderful thing I ever met with.
Walter Scott
Referring to Jane Austen
Journals, 14 Mar 1826

83 I enjoyed talking to her, but thought *nothing*
of her writing. I considered her 'a beautiful
little knitter'.
Edith Sitwell (1887–1964) British poet and writer.
Referring to Virginia Woolf
Letter to G. Singleton

84 That great Cham of literature, Samuel
Johnson.
Tobias Smollett (1721–71) British novelist.
Letter to John Wilkes, 16 Mar 1759

85 I wish you had not sent me Jane Eyre. It
interested me so much that I have lost (or
won if you like) a whole day in reading it at
the busiest period, with the printers I know
waiting for copy. Who the author can be I
can't guess – if a woman she knows her
language better than most ladies do, or has
had a 'classical' education. It is a fine book
though – the man & woman capital – the
style very generous and upright so to speak.
I thought it was Kinglake for some time.
W. M. Thackeray (1811–63) British novelist.
Referring to Charlotte Brontë
Letter to W. S. Williams, 23 Oct 1847

86 The poor little woman of genius! the fiery
little eager brave tremulous homely-faced
creature! . . . But you see she is a little bit of
a creature without a penny worth of good
looks, thirty years old I should think, buried
in the country, and eating up her own heart
there.
W. M. Thackeray
Referring to Charlotte Brontë
Letter to Lucy Baxter, 11 Mar 1853

87 George Too Shaw To Be Good.
Dylan Thomas (1914–53) Welsh poet.
Letter to Pamela Hansford Johnson, Oct 1933

88 William Congreve is the only sophisticated
playwright England has produced; and like
Shaw, Sheridan, and Wilde, his nearest
rivals, he was brought up in Ireland.
Kenneth Tynan (1927–80) British theatre critic.
Curtains, 'The Way of the World'

89 Jane Austen's books, too, are absent from
this library. Just that one omission alone
would make a fairly good library out of a
library that hadn't a book in it.
Mark Twain (Samuel Langhorne Clemens; 1835–1910)
US writer.
Following the Equator, Pt. II

90 I wouldn't give up writing about God at this
stage, if I was you. It would be like P. G.

Wodehouse dropping Jeeves half-way through the Wooster series.

Evelyn Waugh (1903–66) British novelist.
Said to Graham Greene, who proposed to write a political novel
Evelyn Waugh (Christopher Sykes)

91 He was over-dressed, pompous, snobbish, sentimental and vain. But he had an indeniable *flair* for the possibilities of commercial theatre.

Evelyn Waugh
Referring to Oscar Wilde
Harper's Bazaar, Nov 1930

92 Mr Bernard Shaw has no enemies but is intensely disliked by all his friends.

Oscar Wilde (1854–1900) Irish-born British dramatist.
Autobiographies (W. B. Yeats)

93 Of all the great Victorian writers, he was probably the most antagonistic to the Victorian age itself.

Edmund Wilson (1895–1972) US critic and writer.
Referring to Dickens
The Wound and the Bow, 'The Two Scrooges'

94 No one has written worse English than Mr Hardy in some of his novels – cumbrous, stilted, ugly, and inexpressive – yes, but at the same time so strangely expressive of something attractive to us in Mr Hardy himself that we would not change it for the perfection of Sterne at his best. It becomes coloured by its surroundings; it becomes literature.

Virginia Woolf (1882–1941) British novelist.
The Moment

95 I agree about Shaw – he is haunted by the mystery he flouts. He is an atheist who trembles in the haunted corridor.

W. B. Yeats (1865–1939) Irish poet.
Writing of Shaw
Letter to George Russell, 1 July 1921

WRITING

See also books, criticism, fiction, inspiration, letter-writing, literacy, literature, novels, plays, poetry, poetry and prose, prose, reading, style, writers

1 Every book must be chewed to get out its juice.

Chinese proverb
Proverb

2 The style is the man.

Proverb

3 Beneath the rule of men entirely great,
The pen is mightier than the sword.

Edward Bulwer-Lytton (1803–73) British novelist and politician.
Richelieu, II:2

4 From this it is clear how much more cruel the pen is than the sword.

Robert Burton (1577–1640) English scholar and explorer.
Anatomy of Melancholy, Pt. I

5 NINA. Your play's hard to act, there are no living people in it.

TREPLEV. Living people! We should show life neither as it is nor as it ought to be, but as we see it in our dreams.

Anton Chekhov (1860–1904) Russian dramatist.
The Seagull, I

6 Better to write for yourself and have no public, than write for the public and have no self.

Cyril Connolly (1903–74) British journalist.
Turnstile One (ed. V. S. Pritchett)

7 All good writing is *swimming under water* and holding your breath.

F. Scott Fitzgerald (1896–1940) US novelist.
Letter to Frances Scott Fitzgerald

8 No tears in the writer, no tears in the reader.

Robert Frost (1875–1963) US poet.
Collected Poems, Preface

9 Another damned, thick, square book! Always scribble, scribble, scribble! Eh! Mr Gibbon?

William, Duke of Gloucester (1743–1805) The brother of George III.
Addressing Edward Gibbon, author of *The History of the Decline and Fall of the Roman Empire*
Literary Memorials (Best)

10 You must write for children in the same way as you do for adults, only better.

Maxim Gorky (Aleksei Maksimovich Peshkov; 1868–1936) Russian writer.
Attrib.

11 You will have written exceptionally well if, by skilful arrangement of your words, you have made an ordinary one seem original.

Horace (Quintus Horatius Flaccus; 65–8 BC) Roman poet.
Ars Poetica

12 A bad book is as much a labour to write as a good one; it comes as sincerely from the author's soul.

Aldous Huxley (1894–1964) British novelist.
Point Counter Point

13 A man will turn over half a library to make one book.

Samuel Johnson (1709–84) British lexicographer.
Life of Johnson (J. Boswell), Vol. II

14 What is written without effort is in general read without pleasure.

Samuel Johnson
Johnsonian Miscellanies (ed. G. B. Hill), Vol. II

15 Read over your compositions, and wherever you meet with a passage which you think is particularly fine, strike it out.

Samuel Johnson
Recalling the advice of a college tutor
Life of Johnson (J. Boswell), Vol. II

16 No man but a blockhead ever wrote, except for money.
Samuel Johnson
Life of Johnson (J. Boswell), Vol. III

17 Many suffer from the incurable disease of writing, and it becomes chronic in their sick minds.
Juvenal (Decimus Junius Juvenalis; 60–130 AD) Roman satirist.
Satires, VII

18 Clear writers, like clear fountains, do not seem so deep as they are; the turbid look the most profound.
Walter Savage Landor (1775–1864) British poet and writer.
Imaginary Conversations, 'Southey and Porson'

19 I like to write when I feel spiteful: it's like having a good sneeze.
D. H. Lawrence (1885–1930) British novelist.
Letter to Lady Cynthia Asquith, Nov 1913

20 When once the itch of literature comes over a man, nothing can cure it but the scratching of a pen.
Samuel Lover (1797–1868) Irish novelist.
Handy Andy, Ch. 36

21 I shall not be satisfied unless I produce something that shall for a few days supersede the last fashionable novel on the tables of young ladies.
Lord Macaulay (1800–59) British historian.
Letter to Macvey Napier, 5 Nov 1841

22 There is an impression abroad that everyone has it in him to write one book; but if by this is implied a good book the impression is false.
W. Somerset Maugham (1874–1965) British novelist.
The Summing Up

23 I suffer from the disease of writing books and being ashamed of them when they are finished.
Baron de Montesquieu (1689–1755) French writer.
Pensées diverses

24 Writing is like getting married. One should never commit oneself until one is amazed at one's luck.
Iris Murdoch (1919–) Irish-born British novelist.
The Black Prince, 'Bradley Pearson's Foreword'

25 Poor Knight! he really had two periods, the first – a dull man writing broken English, the second – a broken man writing dull English.
Vladimir Nabokov (1899–1977) Russian-born US novelist.
The Real Life of Sebastian Knight, Ch. 1

26 True ease in writing comes from art, not chance,
As those move easiest who have learn'd to dance.

'Tis not enough no harshness gives offence,
The sound must seem an echo to the sense.
Alexander Pope (1688–1744) British poet.
An Essay on Criticism

27 Make 'em laugh; make 'em cry; make 'em wait.
Charles Reade (1814–84) British novelist and dramatist.
Advice to an aspiring writer
Attrib.

28 The profession of letters is, after all, the only one in which one can make no money without being ridiculous.
Jules Renard (1894–1910) French writer.
Journal

29 My scribbling pays me zero francs per line – not including the white spaces.
Marquis de Rochefort (1830–1913) French journalist.
Referring to his salary as a writer
Autant en apportent les mots (Pedrazzini)

30 No, this right hand shall work it all off.
Walter Scott (1771–1832) Scottish novelist.
Refusing offers of help following his bankruptcy in 1826
Century of Anecdote (J. Timbs)

31 Writing, when properly managed, (as you may be sure I think mine is) is but a different name for conversation.
Laurence Sterne (1713–68) Irish-born British writer.
Tristram Shandy

32 Whatever sentence will bear to be read twice, we may be sure was thought twice.
Henry David Thoreau (1817–62) US writer.
Journal, 1842

33 Not that the story need be long, but it will take a long while to make it short.
Henry David Thoreau
Letter, 16 Nov 1867

34 Three hours a day will produce as much as a man ought to write.
Anthony Trollope (1815–82) British novelist.
Autobiography, Ch. 15

35 I put the words down and push them a bit.
Evelyn Waugh (1903–66) British novelist.
Obituary, *New York Times*, 11 Apr 1966

36 All my novels are an accumulation of detail. I'm a bit of a bower-bird.
Patrick White (1912–) British-born Australian novelist.
Southerly, 139

37 Every great and original writer, in proportion as he is great and original, must himself create the taste by which he is to be relished.
William Wordsworth (1770–1850) British poet.
Lyrical Ballads, Preface

Y

YIELDING

See also determination, weakness

1 The concessions of the weak are the concessions of fear.
Edmund Burke (1729–97) British politician.
Speech on Conciliation with America (House of Commons, 22 Mar 1775)

2 He that complies against his will,
Is of his own opinion still.
Samuel Butler (1612–80) English satirist.
Hudibras, Pt. III

YOUTH

See also age, children

1 Better is a poor and a wise child than an old and foolish king, who will no more be admonished.
Bible: Ecclesiastes
4:13

2 It is good for a man that he bear the yoke in his youth.
Bible: Lamentations
3:27

3 Youth is something very new: twenty years ago no one mentioned it.
Coco Chanel (1883–1971) French dress designer.
Coco Chanel, Her Life, Her Secrets (Marcel Haedrich)

4 I remember my youth and the feeling that will never come back any more – the feeling that I could last for ever, outlast the sea, the earth, and all men; the deceitful feeling that lures us on to perils, to love, to vain effort – to death . . .
Joseph Conrad (Teodor Josef Konrad Korzeniowski; 1857–1924) Polish-born British novelist.
Youth

5 The young always have the same problem – how to rebel and conform at the same time. They have now solved this by defying their parents and copying one another.
Quentin Crisp (?1910–) Model, publicist, and writer.
The Naked Civil Servant

6 Almost everything that is great has been done by youth.
Benjamin Disraeli (1804–81) British statesman.
Coningsby, Bk. III, Ch. 1

7 I never dared be radical when young, for fear it would make me conservative when old.
Robert Frost (1875–1963) US poet.
Precaution

8 *Les enfants terribles.*
The embarrassing young.
Paul Gavarni (1801–66) French illustrator.
Title of a series of prints

9 It is the malady of our age that the young are so busy teaching us that they have no time left to learn.
Eric Hoffer (1902–) US writer.

10 Youth will come here and beat on my door, and force its way in.
Henrik Ibsen (1828–1906) Norwegian dramatist.
The Master Builder, I

11 Young men make great mistakes in life; for one thing, they idealize love too much.
Benjamin Jowett (1817–93) British theologian.
Letters of B. Jowett (Abbott and Campbell)

12 When all the world is young, lad,
And all the trees are green;
And every goose a swan, lad,
And every lass a queen;
Then hey for boot and horse, lad,
And round the world away:
Young blood must have its course, lad,
And every dog his day.
Charles Kingsley (1819–75) British writer.
Songs from The Water Babies, 'Young and Old'

13 Youth is a malady of which one becomes cured a little every day.
Benito Mussolini (1883–1945) Italian dictator.
Said on his 50th birthday

14 The atrocious crime of being a young man . . . I shall neither attempt to palliate nor deny.
William Pitt the Elder (1708–78) British statesman.
Speech, House of Commons, 27 Jan 1741

15 My salad days,
When I was green in judgment, cold in blood,
To say as I said then!
William Shakespeare (1564–1616) English dramatist.
Antony and Cleopatra, I:5

16 I would there were no age between ten and three and twenty, or that youth would sleep out the rest; for there is nothing in the between but getting wenches with child, wronging the ancientry, stealing, fighting.
William Shakespeare
The Winter's Tale, III:3

17 Far too good to waste on children.
George Bernard Shaw (1856–1950) Irish dramatist and critic.
10,000 Jokes, Toasts, and Stories (L. Copeland)

18 Live as long as you may, the first twenty years are the longest half of your life.
Robert Southey (1774–1843) British poet.
The Doctor, Ch. 130

KEYWORD INDEX

agitate to a. a bag of wind FOOTBALL, 9
Agnes St A. Eve – Ah, bitter chill it was SEASONS, 9
agnostic rather a compliment to be called an a. HUMILITY, 3
agongy a lonely spasm of helpless a. DEATH, 63
agree colours will a. in the dark DIFFERENCE, 7
don't say you a. with me AGREEMENT, 7
If two men on the same job a. AGREEMENT, 8
those who a. with us AGREEMENT, 4
Two of a trade can ne'er a. ARGUMENTS, 6
agreeable I do not want people to be very a. NASTINESS, 2
My idea of an a. person AGREEMENT, 2
agreement My people and I have come to an a. FREEDOM, 11
Whenever you accept our views we shall be in full a.
INFLEXIBILITY, 1
agrees a person who a. with me AGREEMENT, 3
agricultural the a. labourers . . . commute from London
COUNTRYSIDE, 7
agriculture when the nation depended on a. for its wealth
ECONOMICS, 17
Aids A. pandemic is a classic own-goal AIDS, 2
stop them catching A. . . . the wife AIDS, 4; ILLNESS, 3
ail what can a. thee, knight at arms ILLNESS, 10
ain't bet you a hundred bucks he a. in here ESCAPE, 1;
FUNERALS, 5
air cat is a diagram and pattern of subtle a. CATS, 5
Get your room full of good a. LONGEVITY, 2
my spirit found outlet in the a. FLYING, 1
the castles I have, are built with a. DREAMS, 9
to the Germans that of the a. EUROPE, 13
waste its sweetness on the desert a. WASTE, 2
airplane The a. stays up because it doesn't have the time to
fall SCIENCE, 46
airplanes a. . . . are wonderful things for other people to
FLYING, 2
I feel about a. the way I feel about diets FLYING, 2
airth Let them bestow on every a. a limb EXECUTION, 9
aisle A.. Altar. Hymn MARRIAGE, 84; PUNS, 14
aitches We have nothing to lose but our a. CLASS, 25
Alamein Before A. we never had a victory WORLD WAR II, 15
alarms confused a. of struggle and flight WAR, 2
albatross I shot the a. BIRDS, 2
Albert A. was merely a young foreigner ROYALTY, 33
that A. married beneath him CRITICISM, 10
alcohol A. . . . enables Parliament to do things at eleven
ALCOHOL, 55
A. is like love ALCOHOL, 19
discovered that a. was a food ALCOHOL, 66
alcoholic a. liquors have been used by the . . . best races
ALCOHOL, 50
ale a. from the Country of the Young KNOWLEDGE, 36
no more cakes and a. MERRYMAKING, 3
the spicy nut-brown a. ALCOHOL, 45
Alexander Some talk of A., and some of Hercules HEROISM, 1
algebra What is a. exactly MATHEMATICS, 1
Algerian And drink of my A. wine INSULTS, 7
Alice A. – Mutton; Mutton – A. INTRODUCTIONS, 1
Oh! don't you remember sweet A., Ben Bolt MEMORY, 7
alien amid the a. corn BIRDS, 5
State socialism is totally a. SOCIALISM, 14
alike so many million of faces . . . none a. INDIVIDUALITY, 3
alimony Judges . . . in the matter of arranging a. MARRIAGE, 133
alive Bliss was it in that dawn to be a. FRENCH REVOLUTION, 3
he is no longer a. DEATH, 26
if I am a. DEATH, 54
needst not strive . . . to keep a. KILLING, 2
not one will still be a. in a hundred years' time MORTALITY, 22
We intend to remain a. SELF-PRESERVATION, 7
all A. for one, and one for all UNITY, 8
A. good things ENDING, 1
a. our yesterdays LIFE, 43
A.'s well ENDING, 2
a man, take him for a. in a. ADMIRATION, 15; ADMIRATION, 15
are you sure they are a. horrid NASTINESS, 1
Christ is a., and in a. CHRISTIANITY, 2
Damn you, Jack – I'm a. right SELFISHNESS, 3
Ripeness is a. ENDURANCE, 17
'Tis a. thou art EQUALITY, 29
allegiance Not bound to swear a. to any master FREEDOM, 19
allegory headstrong as an a. MALAPROPISMS, 6
alley she lives in our a. LOVE, 36
allies former a. had blundered NAZISM, 5
all-round a wonderful a. man INSULTS, 6

ally An a. has to be watched MISTRUST, 10
Almighty If the A. himself played the violin EGOTISM, 6
almonds Don't eat too many a. FOOD, 15
alms a. for oblivion TIME, 35
alone A., alone, all, all alone SOLITUDE, 2
A. and palely loitering ILLNESS, 10
And we are left, or shall be left, a. DEFEAT, 9
better to be a. than in bad company FRIENDS, 15
I am here at the gate a. INVITATIONS, 2
I hate to be a. OBSESSIONS, 1
I want to be a. MISQUOTATIONS, 17; PRIVACY, 2; SOLITUDE, 1
No poet . . . has . . . meaning a. ARTS, 3
powerful but a. SOLITUDE, 14
She sleeps a. at last EPITAPHS, 1
To be a. is the fate of all great minds LONELINESS, 6;
GREATNESS, 11
We perish'd, each a. DEATH, 40
woe to him that is a. when he falleth FRIENDSHIP, 8
You come into the world a. HUMAN CONDITION, 13
Alph Where A., the sacred river, ran PLEASURE, 8
alphabet the remaining twenty-two letters of the a.
LEARNING, 7
altar Aisle. A.. Hymn MARRIAGE, 84; PUNS, 14
altars struggled in poverty to build these a. RELIGION, 53
alter I dare not a. these things INSPIRATION, 3
alternative a need to create an a. world FICTION, 3
I prefer old age to the a. OLD AGE, 12
always Minorities . . . are almost a. in the right MINORITY, 3
am in the infinite I A. IMAGINATION, 1
I think therefore I a. THINKING, 4
Amaryllis sport with A. in the shade PLEASURE, 22
amateur a. is an artist who supports himself with outside jobs
ARTISTS, 5
America . . . is the prize a. nation AMERICA, 38; GERMANY, 7
In love . . . the a. status LOVE, 63
the last time that I will take part as an a. FUNERALS, 7
amateurs a disease that afflicts a. ARTS, 2
nation of a. BRITISH, 9
amaze How vainly men themselves a. VICTORY, 10
ambiguity treat . . . her age with a. AGE, 48
ambition A., Distraction, Uglification, and Derision
EDUCATION, 9
A. should be made of sterner stuff AMBITION, 15
A writer's a. should be POSTERITY, 6
Every man has . . . an a. to be a wag HUMOUR, 16
Let not A. mock POVERTY, 13
Vaulting a., which o'er-leaps itself AMBITION, 16
What argufies pride and a. MORTALITY, 4
ambitious an a. man has as many masters AMBITION, 11
amblongus A. Pie NONSENSE, 9
ambulance Knocked down a doctor? With an a. ACCIDENTS, 6
Amen sound of a great A. MUSIC, 39
America A. . . . based on the dreams of spinsters AMERICA, 29
A. became top nation HISTORY, 31
A.! . . . God shed His grace on thee AMERICA, 4
A. . . . has gone directly from barbarism to degeneration
AMERICA, 8
A. is a country of young men AMERICA, 13
A. is a large, friendly dog AMERICA, 33
A. is just ourselves AMERICA, 1
A. is . . . the great Melting-Pot AMERICA, 40
A. is the only idealistic nation AMERICA, 37
A. . . . is the prize amateur nation AMERICA, 38; GERMANY, 7
ask not what A. will do for you PATRIOTISM, 18
A.'s really only a kind of Russia FUTURE, 5
behind the discovery of A. JEWS, 11
first come to pass in the heart of A. AMERICA, 12
His foreparents came to A. EQUALITY, 12
my A.! my new-found-land LOVE, 49
The business of A. is business AMERICA, 10
the greatest that we owe to the discovery of A. SMOKING, 6
the more absolute silence of A. ENGLAND, 24
The national dish of A. AMERICA, 27
Vietnam was lost in the living rooms of A. TELEVISION, 9;
WAR, 66
what makes A. what it is AMERICA, 30
when we think of thee, O A. AMERICA, 34
Why will A. not reach out . . . to Russia DIPLOMACY, 8
woman governs A. AMERICA, 24
American A. heiress wants to buy a man MATERIALISM, 14
A. system of rugged individualism AMERICA, 18
An A. is either a Jew, or an anti-Semite AMERICANS, 9

apartheid We don't want a. liberalized	RACISM, 28
apathy going about the country stirring up a.	POLITICS, 88
sheer a. and boredom	DISCOVERY, 4
ape having an a. for his grandfather	EVOLUTION, 10
Is man an a. or an angel	EVOLUTION, 8
It is not the a., nor the tiger	HUMAN NATURE, 23
the a. from which he is descended	EVOLUTION, 11
The exception is a naked a.	MANKIND, 19
ape-like The a. virtues without which	EDUCATION, 13
aphorisms The great writers of a.	SAYINGS, 3
The hunter for a. . . . has to fish in muddy water	SAYINGS, 3
aphrodisiac Fame is a powerful a.	FAME, 11
Power is the ultimate a.	POWER, 14
apologize a good rule in life never to a.	APOLOGIES, 5
It's too late to a.	INSULTS, 39
apology Never make a defence or a.	ACCUSATION, 2
apostates that peculiar malignity . . . characteristic of a.	BETRAYAL, 5
apostle great a. of the Philistines	PHILISTINISM, 2
Apostles The Septuagint minus the A.	NUMBERS, 4
apparatus *Brain*, n. An a. with which we think	MIND, 1
apparel a. oft proclaims the man	CLOTHES, 16
appeal The whole of art is an a. to a reality	ARTS, 6
appear Things are . . . what they a. to be	APPEARANCES, 19
appearance secret of a successful a.	APPEARANCE, 34
appearances A. are deceptive	APPEARANCES, 2
A. are not . . . a clue to the truth	APPEARANCES, 13
Keep up a.	APPEARANCES, 11
shallow people . . . do not judge by a.	APPEARANCES, 2
appeaser An a. is one who feeds a crocodile	DIPLOMACY, 6
appetite A. comes with eating	DESIRE, 13
a. may sicken and so die	MUSIC, 46
the desire of satisfying a voracious a.	LUST, 2
apple An a. a day	HEALTH AND HEALTHY LIVING, 1
as the a. of his eye	SUPPORT, 1
My a. trees will never get across	NEIGHBOURS, 3
want the a. for the a.'s sake	PERVERSITY, 6
When Eve ate this particular a.	SEX, 28
apple-pie An a. without some cheese	FOOD, 2
apples The silver a. of the moon	DESIRE, 18
applications only a. of science	SCIENCE, 31
applied no such things as a. sciences	SCIENCE, 31
appreciate I never 'a.'	BEAUTY, 29
appreciation total dependence on the a. of others	CHARM, 2
apprehend Intelligence is quickness to a.	INTELLIGENCE, 7
apprehensions elations and a. of growth	AGE, 36
approve They that a. . . . call it opinion	OPINIONS, 2
April And after A., when May follows	MONTHS, 6
A. is the cruellest month	MONTHS, 8
months . . . gloomy in England are March and A.	SEASONS, 27
My regret Becomes an A. violet	SORROW, 25
Now that A.'s there	ENGLAND, 8
Sweet A. showers	MONTHS, 12
Aprille Whan that A. with his shoures sote	MONTHS, 7
Arab I shook hands with a friendly A.	PLACES, 13
Arabia All the perfumes of A.	GUILT, 9
Arabs The Jews and A. should . . . settle their differences	RELIGION, 4
arch All experience is an a.	EXPERIENCE, 20
archaeologist An a. is the best husband	MARRIAGE, 36
Archangel an A. a little damaged	POETS, 48
archbishop the sign of an a. is a double-cross	CLERGY, 5
arch-enemy love . . . has one a. – and that is life	LOVE, 16
arches Underneath the a.	DREAMS, 7
Archimedes The . . . schoolboy is now familiar with truths for which A.	SCIENCE, 36
architect Each man the a. of his own fate	RESPONSIBILITY, 3
not a great sculptor or painter can be an a.	ARCHITECTURE, 4
the a. can only advise	MISTAKES, 20
architects a. were artists	ARTISTS, 12
architecture A. in general is frozen music	ARCHITECTURE, 10
Fashion is a.	FASHION, 1
What has happened to a. . . . that the only passers-by who can contemplate it	ARCHITECTURE, 6
ardua *Per a. ad astra*	AMBITION, 2
'arf An' rather less than 'a.	CLOTHES, 10
arguing I am not a. with you	ARGUMENTS, 18
In a. too, the parson own'd his skill	KNOWLEDGE, 17
argument All a. is against it	SUPERNATURAL, 9
I have found you an a.	ARGUMENTS, 10
I love a., I love debate	ARGUMENTS, 15
to get the best of an a.	ARGUMENTS, 4

work of art must start an a.	ART, 29
arguments beware of long a. and long beards	BREVITY, 6
the world can be expressed in . . . a.	THEORY, 3
Arian In three sips the A. frustrate	DRINKS, 2
aristocracy an absentee a.	IRELAND, 5
An a. in a republic is like a chicken	ARISTOCRACY, 10
a. . . . government by the badly educated	ARISTOCRACY, 5; DEMOCRACY, 3
a. to what is decent	CLASS, 16
displeased with a., call it *oligarchy*	GOVERNMENT, 12
If human beings could be propagated . . . a. would be . . . sound	ARISTOCRACY, 7
Unlike the male codfish . . . the British a. is	ARISTOCRACY, 16
aristocrat the gentleman from both the artist and the a.	CLASS, 35
aristocratic To be a. in Art	ART, 18
to distinguish . . . the a. class from the Philistines	CLASS, 3
arithmetic different branches of A.	EDUCATION, 9
Music is the a. of sounds	MUSIC, 17
arm An a. Rose up from . . . the lake	ARTHURIAN LEGEND, 3
Don't carry away that a. till I have . . . my ring	PRACTICALITY, 5
Human on my faithless a.	SLEEP, 3
armchair She fitted into my biggest a.	OBESITY, 12
arm'd a. with more than complete steel	JUSTICE, 16
Armenteers A mademoiselle from A.	FRANCE, 13
armies ignorant a. clash by night	WAR, 2
not a. . . . but flocks of sheep	DELUSION, 3
armistice an a. for twenty years	WORLD WAR I, 10
a short a. with truth	TRUTH, 16
armour Conceit is the finest a.	CONCEIT, 12
Prayer makes the Christian's a. bright	PRAYER, 10
arms Anger supplies the a.	ANGER, 7
A. control so easily becomes an incantation	WEAPONS, 4
For the theatre one needs long a.	ACTING, 4
I never would lay down my a.	PATRIOTISM, 24
I sing of a. and the man	ENDURANCE, 23
opening time in the Sailors A.	PUBLIC HOUSES, 4
So he laid down his a.	PUNS, 8
army An a. is a nation within a nation	ARMY, 4
An a. marches on its stomach	FOOD, 40
Chief of the A.	LAST WORDS, 45
contemptible little A.	WAR, 133
If you don't want to use the a., I should like to borrow it	SARCASM, 2
little ships of England brought the A. home	BOATS, 8; WORLD WAR II, 20
The a. ages men sooner than the law	ARMY, 6
The conventional a. loses if it does not win	WAR, 58
arrest My father didn't create you to a. me	POLICE, 6
One does not a. Voltaire	RESPECT, 2
arrested Christ . . . would quite likely have been a.	OPPRESSION, 2
arrive To travel hopefully is . . . better . . . than to a.	ANTICIPATION, 7
arrow Every a. . . . feels the attraction of earth	AMBITION, 13
I, said the Sparrow, With my bow and a.	NURSERY RHYMES, 68
I shot an a. into the air	CHANCE, 3
arse a politician is an a.	POLITICIANS, 3
Sit on your a. for fifty years	INDIFFERENCE, 4
arsenal a. of democracy	DEMOCRACY, 15
arson A., after all, is an artificial crime	FIRE, 5
art All a. deals with the absurd	ART, 19
All A. is quite useless	ART, 32
An a. can only be learned	LEARNING, 4
A. and religion first; then philosophy	IMPORTANCE, 3
A. . . . can go on mattering	ART, 5
a. constantly aspires towards . . . music	ART, 20
A. for art's sake	ART, 6, 8
A. has to move you	ART, 10
A. is a jealous mistress	ART, 7
A. is long, and Time is fleeting	MORTALITY, 14
A. is not a mirror . . . but a hammer	ART, 16
A. is not a special sauce	ART, 13
a. is not a weapon	ART, 11
A. is ruled . . . by the imagination	IMAGINATION, 3
A. is the imposing of a pattern	ART, 30
A. is the most intense mode	ART, 33
A. is . . . the transmission of feeling	ART, 27
a. is to give life a shape	ART, 2
A. never expresses anything	ART, 31
a. of pleasing consists	PLEASURE, 12
A. will make our streets as beautiful as the woods	DESIGN, 5

Miss A., . . . the prettiest, silliest, most affected, husband-
hunting butterfly — WRITERS, 69
Miss A.'s novels . . . sterile in artistic invention — WRITERS, 45
More can be learnt from Miss A. about . . . the novel
— WRITERS, 29
Austerlitz There rises the sun of A. — WAR, 75
Australia guess . . . he was born in A. — PLACES, 19
So you're going to A. — PLACES, 12
Australian I'm going to write the Great A. Novel — AMBITION, 19
Austria A. is Switzerland . . . with history added — EUROPE, 12
A. will astound the world — DIPLOMACY, 18
author An a. who speaks about his own books — EGOTISM, 5
bad novel tells us . . . about its a. — NOVELS, 2
He is the richest a. that ever grazed — WRITERS, 61
authority a. be a stubborn bear — BRIBERY, 4
A. forgets a dying king — ROYALTY, 34
man Dress'd in a little brief a. — MANKIND, 26
No morality can be founded on a. — MORALITY, 2
Nothing destroyeth a. so much — POWER, 5
place him in a. — CHARACTER, 2
The defiance of established a. — REBELLION, 1
the highest a. for believing that the meek shall inherit the Earth
— HUMILITY, 11
authors A. are easy to get on with — WRITERS, 12
much exposed to a. — WRITERS, 25
The faults of great a. — WRITERS, 6
their a. could not endure being wrong — CRIME, 2
The reciprocal civility of a. — WRITERS, 11
The trouble with our younger a. is — WRITERS, 15
automobile Money differs from an a. — MONEY, 23
avarice rich beyond the dreams of a. — WEALTH, 21
ave *a. atque vale* — GREETINGS, 4
avenged the satisfaction of knowing that we are a.
— REVENGE, 14
average Take the life-lie away from the a. man — DELUSION, 4
aves Beadsman, after thousand a. told — PRAYER, 14
Avilion To the island-valley of A. — AFTERLIFE, 10
avoidance The a. of taxes . . . still carries . . . reward
— TAXATION, 7
avoiding Reading . . . ingenious device for a. thought
— READING, 6
Avon Sweet Swan of A. — SHAKESPEARE, 11
a-waggle You must always be a. — LOVE, 80
awake At last a. — LIFE, 13
A.! for Morning in the Bowl of Night — DAY, 5
I dream when I am a. — REALITY, 1
The lilies and roses were all a. — LOVE, 134
We're very wide a., The moon and I — APPEARANCES, 15
away Over the hills and far a. — LOVE, 59
Take the soup a. — FOOD, 24
the big one that got a. — MARRIAGE, 46
aweary I gin to be a. of the sun — WORLD-WEARINESS, 8
awful And felt how a. goodness is — GOOD, 12
awfulness by its very a. — MARRIAGE, 111
awoke I a. one morning — FAME, 6
axe his keener eye The a.'s edge did try — EXECUTION, 16
Lizzie Borden took an a. — MURDER, 1
axioms A. in philosophy are not axioms — PHILOSOPHY, 8
the world can be expressed in . . . arguments, . . . a. and
theorems — THEORY, 3
aye A., and what then — PROOF, 3

B

baa B., b., black sheep — NURSERY RHYMES, 4
God ha' mercy on such as we, B.! Yah! Bah — DEBAUCHERY, 7
Babbitt one thing wrong with the B. house — HOME, 5
babbl'd b. of green fields — DEATH, 111
Babel B.; because the Lord did there confound the language
— LANGUAGE, 2
the tower of B. should have got language all mixed up
— LANGUAGE, 25
babies bit the b. in the cradles — ANIMALS, 5
If men had to have b. — BIRTH, 6
Other people's b. — BABIES, 4
putting milk into b. — CHILDREN, 18
War will never cease until b. — WAR, 67
wretched b. don't come until — BABIES, 3
You breed b. and you eat chips — FOOD, 49
baby Anybody can shock a b. — SIMPLICITY, 7
Don't throw the b. out — HASTE, 1
Every b. born into the world — BABIES, 2

hanging the b. on the clothes line to dry — INNOVATION, 2
Hush-a-bye, b., on the tree top — NURSERY RHYMES, 19
my b. at my breast — SUICIDE, 11
no new b. in the womb of our society — RUSSIA, 3
Rock-a-bye b. on the tree top — SLEEP, 4
Walking My B. Back Home — LOVE, 142
Babylon By the waters of B. we sit down and weep
— AMERICA, 34
How many miles to B. — NURSERY RHYMES, 17
Bach B. is like an astronomer — MUSICIANS, 11
J. S. B. — CRITICISM, 3
Music owes as much to B. — MUSICIANS, 15
bachelor B.'s fare — MARRIAGE, 114
Never trust . . . a b. too near — TRUST, 4
bachelors reasons for b. to go out — WOMEN, 31
back any of you at the b. who do not hear me — DISABILITY, 1
But at my b. I always hear — AGE, 37
Either b. us or sack us — SUPPORT, 3
I sit on a man's b. — HYPOCRISY, 17
turn your b. upon the world — PERFECTION, 4
Will ye no come b. again — RETURN, 3
backs With our b. to the wall . . . each . . . must fight on to the
end — WAR, 45; WORLD WAR I, 12
Bacon B. discovered the art of making reading-glasses
— SCIENTISTS, 11
When their lordships asked B. — BRIBERY, 1
bad a b. novel tells us the truth about its author — NOVELS, 2
A b. penny — LUCK, 1
A truth that's told with b. intent — TRUTH, 13
b. die late — GOOD AND EVIL, 3
B. girls don't have the time — DIARIES, 2
b. taste is better than no taste — TASTE, 1
Defend the b. against the worse — DECLINE, 3
It is as b. as b. can be — FOOD, 27
never was a b. peace — WAR AND PEACE, 6
nothing either good or b. — THINKING, 10
Nothing so b. but it might have been worse — OPTIMISM, 7
put up with b. things — TOLERANCE, 8
resolved to do something b. — DECISION, 3
she was a very b. cook — SNOBBERY, 9
so much b. in the best of us — GOOD AND EVIL, 1
strong antipathy of good to b. — PROVOCATION, 2
the name of . . . obstinacy in a b. one — STUBBORNNESS, 3
There's no such thing as a b. Picasso — INFERIORITY, 4
what I feel really b. about — LIBERALISM, 1
When b. men combine — UNITY, 7
when I'm b. I'm better — SEX, 63
badge Red B. of Courage — COURAGE, 7
badly If you want to do a thing b. — EFFORT, 6
Bailey When will you pay me? Say the bells of Old B.
— LONDON, 2
baker The butcher, the b., The candlestick-maker — NURSERY
RHYMES, 45
balance The b. of power — POWER, 27
balanced Food is an important part of a b. diet — FOOD, 32
balances thou art weighed in the b., and art found wanting
— JUDGMENT, 1
bald being b. – one can hear snowflakes — APPEARANCE, 11
Balfour Mr B.'s Poodle — HOUSES OF PARLIAMENT, 12
Balham She has a Rolls body and a B. mind — STUPIDITY, 11
Balkans some damned silly thing in the B. — WAR, 11
ball B. . . . how very singular — NAMES, 1
ballet it takes more than one to make a b. — SUPPORT, 6
To enter the . . . B. is to enter a convent — DANCING, 8
balloon the moon's a b. — MOON, 3
The Moon's a B. — BOOK, SONG, AND PLAY TITLES, 20
ballot The b. is stronger than the bullet — DEMOCRACY, 9
ballots employers . . . only like b. so long as you lose them
— STRIKES, 3
balm wash the b. from an anointed king — MONARCHY, 20
bananas hanging around like clumps of b. — INSULTS, 23
Banbury Ride a cock-horse to B. Cross — NURSERY RHYMES, 42
bandages to walk around . . . with only a few light b. on
— BEAUTY, 32
bands Brass b. are all very well in their place — MUSIC, 4
ladies who pursue Culture in b. — CULTURE, 4
bang Not with a b. but a whimper — ENDING, 4
banish to b. . . . the dark divisive clouds of Marxist socialism
— MARXISM, 6
bank a b. that would lend money to such a poor risk
— BORROWING, 2
b. and shoal of time — ENDING, 5

better that a man should tyrannize over his b. balance
    TYRANNY, 4
I cried all the way to the b.   CRITICISM, 29
the b. was mightier than the sword   LIBERALISM, 3
the man who broke the B. at Monte Carlo   WEALTH, 16
bankrupt B. of Life   WORLD-WEARINESS, 1
banks cashiers of the Musical B.   MONEY, 13
Ye b. and braes   NATURE, 2
banned any book should be b.   CENSORSHIP, 4
banner A b. with the strange device, Excelsior   AMBITION, 12
Baptist For good all round business work, I should have
    preferred a B.   PROTESTANTISM, 2
bar an olfactory b.   FAMILIARITY, 6
no moaning of the b.   DUTY, 5
though hell should b. the way   DETERMINATION, 13
When I went to the B. as a very young man   LAW, 10
Barabbas B. was a publisher   PUBLISHING, 4
Barbara Her name was B. Allen   LOVE, 3
barbarians society distributes itself into B., Philistines, and
    Populace   AMERICA, 1
barbarity the . . . b. of war . . . forces men . . . to commit acts
    WAR, 56
the English seem . . . to act with the b. of tyrants   IRELAND, 31
barbarous the invention of a b. age   POETRY, 31
bard This goat-footed b.   POLITICIANS, 55
bards Portraits of famous b. and preachers   PAINTING, 16
bare Our ingress . . . Was naked and b.   LIFE, 32
Pylons, those pillars B.   TECHNOLOGY, 12
bargains rule for b.   BUSINESS, 5
barge The b. she sat in, like a burnish'd throne
    ADMIRATION, 13
baritones b. are born villains in opera   OPERA, 8
bark to hear the watch-dog's honest b.   DOGS, 1
Barking B. dogs   ACTION, 1
Barnum the celebrated B.'s circus   POLITICIANS, 43
barrage chemical b. has been hurled against the fabric of life
    ECOLOGY, 2
barrel out of the b. of a gun   POWER POLITICS, 5
you won't intoxicate with one glass someone who has . . . drunk
    . . . a . . . b.   EXPERIENCE, 10
barrenness quarrels which vivify its b.   LOVE, 64
barricade At some disputed b.   DEATH, 102
barring a schoolboy's b. out   POLITICS, 77
bar-rooms It brings men together in crowds and mobs in b.
    SOCIETY, 9
bars Nor iron b. a cage   IMPRISONMENT, 4
barter All government . . . is founded on compromise and b.
    COMPROMISE, 4
base doing good to b. fellows   CHARITY, 11
It takes a certain courage . . . to be truly b.   EVIL, 2
baseball as sensible as b. in Italian   OPERA, 5
based All progress is b.   PROGRESS, 2; EXTRAVAGANCE, 2
basing b. morals on myth   MORALITY, 15
basket Have you ever taken anything out of the clothes b.
    CLEANNESS, 3
bastard Because I am a b.   NASTINESS, 4
I hope you will not publicly call me a b.   INSULTS, 43
putting all my eggs in one b.   ILLEGITIMACY, 2
bastards It is a pity . . . that more politicians are not b.
    POLITICIANS, 30
that'll hold the little b.   MISTAKES, 5
bat black b., night, has flown   INVITATIONS, 2
They came to see me b. not to see you bowl   CRICKET, 1
Twinkle, twinkle, little b.   NONSENSE, 5
bath B. . . . once a week to avoid being a public menace
    CLEANNESS, 1
Oh! who can ever be tired of B.   ENGLAND, 1
the nuns who never take a b.   MODESTY, 6
bathing caught the Whigs b.   POLITICS, 23
something between a large b. machine   BOATS, 6
bathroom fierce and revolutionary in a b.   AMERICANS, 7
he goes to church as he goes to the b.   CLERGY, 4
bats b. in the belfry   MADNESS, 10
battalions God is always on the side of the big b.
    POWER POLITICS, 7
God is on the side not of the heavy b.   POWER POLITICS, 8
battering B. the gates of heaven   EXCESS, 14
battle A b. of giants   WAR, 128
greatest misery is a b. gained   VICTORY, 19
next greatest misfortune to losing a b.   VICTORY, 19
preferred to go into b. sitting down   SOLDIERS, 9
The b. of Britain   WORLD WAR II, 6

battlefield b. is fearful   WORLD WAR I, 4
the most beautiful b.   WAR, 74
we survive amongst the dead and the dying as on a b.
    OLD AGE, 43
battlements Fate sits on these dark b.   DESTINY, 17
battles Dead b., like dead generals   WAR, 121
bauble that fool's b., the mace   DISMISSAL, 4
baying b. for broken glass   ARISTOCRACY, 15
bayonet bullet and the b. are brother and sister   WORLD WAR
    I, 20
bayonets A man may build . . . a throne of b.
    POWER POLITICS, 4
bays To win the palm, the oak, or b.   VICTORY, 10
be If you want to b. happy, b.   HAPPINESS, 29
To b., or not to b.   SUICIDE, 12; LANGUAGE, 6
What must b., must b.   DESTINY, 1
beaches we shall fight on the b.   WORLD WAR II, 4
beacons Logical consequences are the scarecrows of fools and
    the b. of wise men   LOGIC, 3
beadle a b. on boxin' day   POETRY, 12
beads what glass b. are to African traders   SORROW, 5
Beadsman The B., after thousand aves told   PRAYER, 14
beak Take thy b. from out my heart   EVIL, 13
beaker a b. full of the warm South   ALCOHOL, 37
Beale Miss Buss and Miss B. Cupid's darts do not feel
    INSENSITIVITY, 1
be-all b. and the end-all here   ENDING, 5
bean The home of the b. and the cod   SNOBBERY, 2
bear a B. of Very Little Brain   WORDS, 16
any man . . . who could not b. another's misfortunes . . . like a
    Christian   MISFORTUNE, 13
authority be a stubborn b.   BRIBERY, 4
Exit, pursued by a b.   ANIMALS, 18
Human kind cannot b.   REALITY, 2
never . . . sell the b.'s skin   ANTICIPATION, 6
Round and round the garden Like a teddy b.
    NURSERY RHYMES, 44
they think I shall be able to b. it best   RESPONSIBILITY, 4
bear-baiting Puritan hated b.   PURITANISM, 3
beard singed the Spanish king's b.   WAR, 35
There was an Old Man with a b.   APPEARANCE, 19
bearded hard to hear what a b. man is saying   PUNS, 12
He reaps the b. grain at a breath   DEATH, 78
beards beware of long arguments and long b.   BREVITY, 6
men wore their b., like they wear their neckties
    APPEARANCE, 18
bears And dancing dogs and b.   ANIMALS, 12
And some of the bigger b. try to pretend   SUPERSTITION, 9
b. and lions growl and fight   ANIMALS, 20
beast b. of the earth   ANIMALS, 3; CREATION, 5
Dialect words – those terrible marks of the b.   CLASS, 15
Either a b. or a god   MANKIND, 2
for man or b.   WEATHER, 10
hardly be a b. or a fool alone on a great mountain   SOLITUDE, 9
Man's life is cheap as b.'s   NECESSITY, 5
The B. stands for strong mutually antagonistic governments
    NEWSPAPERS, 12
the mark . . . of the b.   DEVIL, 5
beastie Wee, sleekit, cow'rin', tim'rous b.   ANIMALS, 1
beastliness It is called in our schools 'b.'   SEX, 5
beastly Don't let's be b. to the Germans   GERMANY, 2
beat make the b. keep time with short steps   FUNERALS, 1
Two hearts that b. as one   LOVE, 84
beaten I was b. up by Quakers   SHYNESS, 1
public school, where . . . learning was painfully b. into him
    EDUCATION, 43
beats It b. as it sweeps as it cleans   ADVERTISING, 14
beautiful Against the b. . . . one can wage a pitiless war
    BEAUTY, 19
b. . . . for someone who could not read   AMERICA, 7
Give me my golf clubs . . . and a b. partner   DESIRE, 1
light, shade, and perspective . . . make it b.   BEAUTY, 16
many men, so b.   GUILT, 4
most b. things . . . are the most useless   BEAUTY, 33
Our love of what is b. does not lead to extravagance
    RESULTS, 4
Rich men's houses are seldom b.   WEALTH, 3
summer afternoon . . . two most b. words   SEASONS, 8
The good is the b.   GOOD, 13
the most b. battlefield   WAR, 74
the most b. woman I've ever seen   BEAUTY, 27
the name of which was B.   ARCHITECTURE, 2

the work comes out more b.	ARTS, 4
when a woman isn't b.	BEAUTY, 15
beautifully B. done	LAST WORDS, 66
beauty A thing of b. is a joy for ever	BEAUTY, 23
B. and the lust for learning	BEAUTY, 8
b. being the best of all we know	BEAUTY, 10
B. in distress	BEAUTY, 13
B. in things exists in the mind which contemplates them	BEAUTY, 21
B. is altogether in the eye of the beholder	BEAUTY, 22
b. is only sin deep	BEAUTY, 34
b. is only skin-deep	BEAUTY, 2
B. is potent	BEAUTY, 3
B. is truth, truth beauty	BEAUTY, 24; TRUTH, 30
B. itself doth of itself persuade The eyes of men	BEAUTY, 35
B. sat with me all the summer day	BEAUTY, 11
B. stands In the admiration . . . of weak minds	BEAUTY, 28
better to be first with an ugly woman than the hundredth with a b.	BEAUTY, 12
But b.'s self she is, When all her robes are gone	BEAUTY, 5
Clad in the b. of a thousand stars	BEAUTY, 26
Exuberance is B.	BEAUTY, 9
Fostered alike by b. and by fear	SOUL, 12
her b. made The bright world dim	BEAUTY, 37
Love built on b.	BEAUTY, 17
love permanence more than . . . b.	BRITISH, 3
Mathematics possesses . . . b.	MATHEMATICS, 14
perceive real b. in a person . . . older	BEAUTY, 6
She walks in b.	BEAUTY, 14
Teaches such b. as a woman's eye	LEARNING, 8
the b. Of an aged face	OLD AGE, 9
the laws of poetic truth and poetic b.	POETRY, 2
The pain passes, but the b. remains	ENDURANCE, 14
There is no excellent b.	BEAUTY, 7
this generation . . . found England a land of b.	ECOLOGY, 4
What *is* b., anyway? There's no such thing	BEAUTY, 29
because B. it is there	MOTIVE, 3
Becket Thomas B.	ASSASSINATION, 4
become What's b. of Waring	ABSENCE, 5
becoming I believe I am b. a god	LAST WORDS, 72
Sunburn is very b.	APPEARANCE, 9
bed and die – in b.	WAR, 102
And so to b.	BED, 7
B. . . . is the poor man's opera	SEX, 26
Each within our narrow b.	DEATH, 37
Go to b. with the lamb	BED, 2
Here comes a candle to light you to b.	LONDON, 2
Lady Capricorn, . . . was . . . keeping open b.	PROMISCUITY, 2
Never go to b. mad	ANGER, 3
nicer to stay in b.	BED, 5
So I took her into b. and covered up her head	SEX, 4
The b. be blest	BLESSING, 1
the night the b. fell on my father	MEMORY, 19
Wedlock – the . . . deep peace of the double b. after the . . . chaise-longue	MARRIAGE, 34
Who goes to b. with whom	OLD AGE, 37
woman who goes to b. with a man	SEX, 38
bedfellows Misery acquaints . . . strange b.	MISFORTUNE, 16
bedroom meeting in a darkened b. in a Brussels hotel	EUROPE, 18
beds Minds like b. always made up	INFLEXIBILITY, 4
Will there be b. for me and all who seek	REST, 1
bedspring the triumphant twang of a b.	SEX, 45
bee How doth the little busy b.	WORK, 25
Sting like a b.	SPORT AND GAMES, 1
Beecham B.'s pills are just the thing	DRUGS, 2
beechen spare the b. tree	TREES, 2
beef The roast b. of England	FOOD, 20
beefsteak Dr Johnson's morality was as English . . . as a b.	ENGLAND, 20
beer chronicle small b.	TRIVIALITY, 12
Did you ever taste b.	ALCOHOL, 24
Life isn't all b. and skittles	LIFE, 28
that bitter b. that tastes sweet	IMMORTALITY, 5
Beerbohm Max B.	OLD AGE, 49
bees murmuring of innumerable b.	SEASONS, 23
No b., no honey	WORK, 2
No shade, no shine, no butterflies, no b.	MONTHS, 10
bees-winged Or was it his b. eyes	WRITERS, 33
Beethoven B.'s Fifth Symphony is the most sublime noise	MUSIC, 21
Roll Over B.	POP MUSIC, 4
before I have been here b.	FAMILIARITY, 4
beg only the poor . . . are forbidden to b.	POVERTY, 10
beggar'd b. all description	ADMIRATION, 13
beggars B. can't be choosers	NECESSITY, 1
beggary b. in the love that can be reckon'd	LOVE, 116
no vice but b.	HYPOCRISY, 15
begin Are you sitting comfortably? Then I'll b.	BEGINNING, 13
B. at the beginning	ORDER, 2
beginning a b., a muddle, and an end	NOVELS, 8
As it was in the b.	ETERNITY, 2
a whole is that which has a b., a middle, and an end	PLAYS, 1
Begin at the b.	ORDER, 2
b. of fairies	FAIRIES, 2
b. of time according to our Chronologie	CREATION, 14
end of the b.	WORLD WAR II, 13
every man at the b. doth set forth good wine	ALCOHOL, 14
I like a film to have a b., a middle and an end	CINEMA, 3
in the b. God	CREATION, 2
in the b. was the word	WORDS, 1
Nothing so difficult as a b.	POETRY, 8
the b. of the end	DEFEAT, 8
beginnings end to the b. of all wars	WAR, 95
mighty things from small b.	NATURE, 8
begins my family b. with me	ANCESTRY, 3
begot what they were about when they b. me	FAMILY, 40
begotten Whatever is b., born, and dies	MORTALITY, 23
beguine She refused to begin the 'B.'	PETULANCE, 1
When they begin the b.	HAPPINESS, 16
begun There is an old saying 'well b. is half done'	BEGINNING, 11
behaving men are more interested in . . . justifying themselves than in . . . b.	MOTIVE, 6
behaviour The quality of moral b. varies	MORALITY, 7
behind In the dusk, with a light b. her	AGE, 29
led his regiment from b.	COWARDICE, 4
part my hair b.	OLD AGE, 18
behold all which we b. Is full of blessings	OPTIMISM, 29
B. her, single in the field	SOLITUDE, 16
b. it was a dream	DREAMS, 3
beholder Beauty is . . . in the eye of the b.	BEAUTY, 22
beige It's b.! My color	ARCHITECTURE, 1
being in him we live, and move, and have our b.	GOD, 5
Knowledge is proportionate to b.	KNOWLEDGE, 20
To kill a human b.	KILLING, 4
Belfast British troops were patrolling the streets of B.	IRELAND, 4
belfry bats in the b.	MADNESS, 10
belief *Action will furnish b.*	BELIEF, 5
believe a verb meaning 'to b. falsely'	BELIEF, 8
b. in the life to come	AFTERLIFE, 2
B. it or not	BELIEF, 6
B. nothing of what you hear	BELIEF, 1
don't b. in . . . true love until after the first attack	SCEPTICISM, 1
I b. because it is impossible	BELIEF, 7
I b. I am becoming a god	LAST WORDS, 72
I b. in the Church	RELIGION, 55
I don't b. in fairies	FAIRIES, 1
inclined to b. those whom we do not know	TRUST, 3
Infidelity . . . consists in professing to b.	INTEGRITY, 5
it brings you luck whether you b. . . . or not	SUPERSTITION, 6
They didn't b. me	BEAUTY, 30
undesirable to b. a proposition	SCEPTICISM, 4
We can b. what we choose	RESPONSIBILITY, 11
what we b. is not necessarily true	OBJECTIVITY, 3
you must b. in God	FAITH, 12
believes He b. . . . that there *is* such a thing as truth	POLITICIANS, 32
politician never b. what he says	POLITICIANS, 7
bell B., book, and candle	MATERIALISM, 18
for whom the b. tolls	DEATH, 45
I'll b. the cat	COURAGE, 10
The b. strikes one	TIME, 42
The sexton toll'd the b.	PUNS, 5
Unto the B. at Edmonton	MARRIAGE, 43
Bellamy I could eat one of B.'s veal pies	LAST WORDS, 52; FOOD, 41
belle La b. Dame sans Merci	SUPERNATURAL, 10
bellies their b. were full	HUNGER, 3
bells Ring out, wild b., and let him die	ENDING, 7
Rings on her fingers and b. on her toes	NURSERY RHYMES, 42
The b. of hell go ting-a-ling-a-ling	DEATH, 16

'Twould ring the b. of Heaven — ANIMALS, 12
With silver b. and cockle shells — GARDENS, 1
belly Every man with a b. full of the classics — CLASSICS, 7
to banish hunger by rubbing the b. — HUNGER, 5
upon thy b. shalt thou go — SEXES, 2
victory under the b. of a Cossack's horse — RUSSIAN REVOLUTION, 3
bellyful Rumble thy b. — WEATHER, 19
below Capten, art thou sleepin' there b. — WAR, 78
Down and away b. — DEPARTURE, 1
What thy errand here b. — PURPOSE, 9
Ben Adhem And lo! B.'s name led all the rest — SUPERIORITY, 5
Ben Battle B. was a soldier bold — PUNS, 8
bench What do you suppose I am on the B. for — REPARTEE, 4
benefactors gratitude to most b. is the same as . . . for dentists — INGRATITUDE, 3
benefits B. make a man a slave — MATERIALISM, 1
It is the nature of men to be bound by the b. they confer — OBLIGATION, 2
benevolence husband render unto the wife due b. — MARRIAGE, 24
bereav'd I am black, as if b. of light — RACISM, 5
Berkeley A Nightingale Sang in B. Square — BIRDS, 7
Berliner Ich bin ein B. — GERMANY, 6
Bernhardt Sarah B.'s funeral — ACTORS, 12
berries I come to pluck your b. — TREES, 10
berth His death, which happen'd in his b. — PUNS, 5
Things hitherto undone should be given . . . a wide b. — ORIGINALITY, 1
Bertie I'm Burlington B. — BED, 3
best all that's b. of dark and bright — BEAUTY, 14
as in the b. it is — MURDER, 11
beauty being the b. of all we know — BEAUTY, 11
b. of life is but intoxication — DRUNKENNESS, 10
b. that is known and thought in the world — CRITICISM, 1
b. words in the b. order — POETRY AND PROSE, 2
Culture, the acquainting ourselves with the b. — CULTURE, 1
For home is b. — HOME, 9
His worst is better than any other person's b. — WRITERS, 55
It was the b. of times — FRENCH REVOLUTION, 1
look at the b. book . . . price of a turbot . . . — BOOKS, 37
Men of few words are the b. — BREVITY, 8
Stolen sweets are b. — THEFT, 5
The b. is the enemy of the good — EXCELLENCE, 4
The b. of friends — FRIENDSHIP, 6
the b. of possible worlds — OPTIMISM, 27
The b. things in life — WEALTH, 1
the shortest works are always the b. — BREVITY, 4
we live in the b. of all possible worlds — OPTIMISM, 19; PESSIMISM, 3
we will do our b. — WORLD WAR II, 10
bestial what remains is b. — REPUTATION, 6
bestow Let them b. on every airth a limb — EXECUTION, 9
best-seller A b. . . . because it was selling well — FAME, 5
A b. is the gilded tomb of a mediocre talent — BOOKS, 40
bet I b. my money on the bob-tail nag — HORSES, 6
Bethlehem O come ye to B. — CHRISTMAS, 16
O little town of B. — CHRISTMAS, 11
betimes to be up b. — BED, 8
betray Nature never did b. — NATURE, 18
betraying if I had to choose between b. my country and b. my friend — BETRAYAL, 3
betrothed a bride's attitude towards her b. — MARRIAGE, 84; PUNS, 14
better a far, far, b. thing — EXECUTION, 6
always . . . trying to get the b. — SPORT AND GAMES, 12
b. is he . . . who hath not seen the evil work . . . under the sun — EVIL, 3
b. strangers — SEPARATION, 6
B. than a play — HOUSES OF PARLIAMENT, 1
b. to have loved and lost — LOVE, 132
b. to have no opinion of God — GOD, 3
b. to marry than to burn — MARRIAGE, 25
for b. for worse — MARRIAGE, 30
He is no b. — ILLNESS, 1
I am getting b. and b. — REMEDIES, 8
if you knows of a b. 'ole — WAR, 4
I've got to admit it's getting b. — IMPROVEMENT, 2
something b. than our brains to depend upon — ARISTOCRACY, 4
the old is b. — AGE, 12; ALCOHOL, 15
when I'm bad I'm b. — SEX, 63

When you meet someone b. . . . turn your thoughts to becoming his equal — SUPERIORITY, 4
You're a b. man than I am, Gunga Din — SUPERIORITY, 6
Beulah B., peel me a grape — LUXURY, 6
bewailing the sum of life's b. — REGRET, 1
beware all should cry, B. — CAUTION, 9
B. of the dog — DOGS, 1
B. of the man who does not return your blow — FORGIVENESS, 14
bewildered Bewitched, Bothered and B. — CONFUSION, 5
I was b. once — CONFUSION, 2
bewitched B., Bothered and Bewildered — CONFUSION, 5
beyond All decent people live b. their incomes nowadays — EXTRAVAGANCE, 4
Bible have used the B. as if it was a constable's handbook — BIBLE, 6
searching through the B. for loopholes — BIBLE, 5
that book is the B. — BIBLE, 1
The B. is literature — BIBLE, 10
the B. tells me so — RELIGION, 62
The English B. — BIBLE, 7
There's a B. on that shelf there — BIBLE, 9
Bibles they have the land and we have the B. — RACISM, 11
bicycle a b. made for two — MARRIAGE, 44
Socialism can only arrive by b. — SOCIALISM, 4
big A b. man has no time — FAME, 9
A government . . . b. enough to give you all you want — GOVERNMENT, 11
B. Brother is watching you — AUTHORITARIANISM, 5
b. emotions come from b. words — STYLE, 5
he was too b. for them — CONCEIT, 5
the b. one that got away — MARRIAGE, 46
The b. print giveth and the fine print taketh away — BUSINESS, 20
bigger it's a great deal b. — UNIVERSE, 3
bike he got on his b. — UNEMPLOYMENT, 1
bill put 'Emily, I love you' on the back of the b. — LOVE, 88
billboard A b. lovely as a tree — TREES, 12
billboards the churches . . . bore for me the same relation to that b. did to Coca-Cola — RELIGION, 61
billiard The b. sharp whom any one catches — PUNISHMENT, 11
billiards to play b. well — SPORT AND GAMES, 18
Billy B. . . . Fell in the fire — FIRE, 2
billy-bong Once a jolly swagman camped by a b. — PLACES, 15
biographies History is the essence of . . . b. — BIOGRAPHY, 3; HISTORY, 1
biography a man is nobody unless his b. — OBITUARIES, 3
history . . . the b. of great men — GREATNESS, 6; HISTORY, 8
how difficult it is to write b. — BIOGRAPHY, 6
no history; only b. — BIOGRAPHY, 5; HISTORY, 12
birch I'm all for bringing back the b. — PUNISHMENT, 16
bird A b. in the hand — PRUDENCE, 1
a b. of the air shall carry the voice — SECRECY, 3
Lo! the B. is on the Wing — TIME, 17
She's only a b. in a gilded cage — IMPRISONMENT, 3
The B. of Time — TIME, 17
bird-cage a b. played with toasting-forks — MUSIC, 6
Robert Houdin who . . . invented the vanishing b. trick and the theater matinée – may he rot and perish. Good afternoon — THEATRE, 12
birds All the b. of the air — NURSERY RHYMES, 2
b. . . . caught in the snare — CHANCE, 2
B. of a feather — SIMILARITY, 1
no b. sing — ILLNESS, 10
No fruits, no flowers, no leaves, no b. — MONTHS, 1
spring now comes unheralded by the return of the b. — ECOLOGY, 1
that make fine b. — CLOTHES, 1
Two little dicky b., Sitting on a wall — NURSERY RHYMES, 63
where late the sweet b. sang — OLD AGE, 40
Birmingham Am in B. — MEMORY, 4
One has no great hopes from B. — ENGLAND, 2
birth B., and copulation, and death — LIFE AND DEATH, 4
B. may be a matter of a moment — BIRTH, 7
From b. to age eighteen, a girl needs good parents — AGE, 62
no credentials . . . not even . . . a certificate of b. — ARISTOCRACY, 8
no cure for b. and death — LIFE AND DEATH, 11
The history of man for the nine months preceding his b. — BIRTH, 5
what you were before your b. — AFTERLIFE, 2
birthday A diplomat . . . always remembers a woman's b. — AGE, 28
If one doesn't get b. presents — GIFTS, 5

boats messing about in b. BOATS, 7
we look for happiness in b. and carriage rides TRAVEL, 14
Bobby B. Shafto's gone to sea NURSERY RHYMES, 5
bob-tail I bet my money on the b. nag HORSES, 6
Boche drove the B. across the Rhine WORLD WAR I, 23
bodies many b. of the saints which slept arose LAST WORDS, 11
our dead b. must tell the tale ENDURANCE, 16
well-developed b., fairly developed minds EDUCATION, 18
body A b. seriously out of equilibrium MADNESS, 11
a sound mind in a sound b. HEALTH AND HEALTHY LIVING, 10
b. of a weak and feeble woman ROYALTY, 13
company, . . . have neither a soul to lose nor a b. to kick BUSINESS, 22
fear made manifest on the b. DISEASE, 16
Happiness is beneficial for the b. SORROW, 18
Man has no B. distinct from his Soul SOUL, 4
mind that makes the b. rich APPEARANCES, 22
more familiar with Africa than my own b. INNOCENCE, 8
Our b. is a machine for living REMEDIES, 13
the gigantic b., the huge massy face WRITERS, 67
the human b. is sacred MANKIND, 36
the soul is not more than the b. SELF, 20
Why be given a b. if you . . . keep it shut up NAKEDNESS, 5
Bognor Bugger B. LAST WORDS, 30
boil b. at different degrees INDIVIDUALITY, 4
boiler The United States is like a gigantic b. AMERICA, 16
boldness B., and again boldness COURAGE, 8
bomb god of science . . . has given us the atomic b. SCIENCE, 25
bombed no power on earth that can protect him from being b. WAR, 6
bombs b. *are* unbelievable until they . . . fall WEAPONS, 8
Come, friendly b., and fall on Slough ENGLAND, 4
drop b. . . . hit civilians WAR, 43
Ears like b. APPEARANCE, 7
test the Russians, not the b. NUCLEAR WEAPONS, 6
bon to produce an occasional *b. mot* MARRIAGE, 16
Bonaparte The three-o'-clock in the morning courage, which B. thought was the rarest COURAGE, 24
Bonar Poor B. can't bear being called a liar POLITICIANS, 58
bondage Of Human B. BOOK, SONG, AND PLAY TITLES, 16
bone The nearer the b. FOOD, 5
boneless the b. wonder POLITICIANS, 43
bones Bleach the b. of comrades slain WAR, 51
Heat, madam! . . . to take off my flesh and sit in my b. WEATHER, 25
Of his b. are coral made DEATH, 107
The healthy b. of a single Pomeranian grenadier DIPLOMACY, 4
bonhomie Overcame his natural b. ECONOMICS, 3
bonjour *B. tristesse* SORROW, 7
bonkers If the British public falls for this . . . it will be . . . b. POLITICS, 33
bonnie *By the b. milldams o' Binnorie* LOVE, 15
My B. lies over the ocean SEPARATION, 1
Oh, bring back my B. to me SEPARATION, 1
bonny the child that is born on the Sabbath day Is b. and blithe, and good and gay NURSERY RHYMES, 34
bonum *Summum b.* GOOD, 3
boojum Snark *was* a B. NONSENSE, 6
book A b. may be amusing BOOKS, 5
A b.'s a b., although there's nothing in't BOOKS, 10
A b. that furnishes no quotations is, . . . a plaything QUOTATIONS, 9
a b. that is a b. flowers once BOOKS, 23
a b. to kill time CRITICISM, 1
A good b. is the best of friends BOOKS, 44
A good b. is the precious life-blood BOOKS, 28
An angel writing in a b. of gold DREAMS, 11
Another damned, thick, square b. WRITING, 9
any b. should be banned CENSORSHIP, 4
Bell, b., and candle MATERIALISM, 18
b. is not harmless . . . consciously offended BOOKS, 17
dainties that are bred in a b. IGNORANCE, 13
do not throw this b. about BOOKS, 7
Everybody writes a b. too many WRITERS, 20
Every b. must be chewed WRITING, 1
go away and write a b. about it SPEECHES, 1
Go, litel b. BOOKS, 13
half a library to make one b. WRITING, 13
he who destroys a good b., kills reason BOOKS, 20
If a b. is worth reading BOOKS, 35
I have only read one b. READING, 12

I'll drown my b. RENUNCIATION, 4
moral or an immoral b. BOOKS, 46
never got around to reading the b. CRITICISM, 33
Never judge a cover by its b. BOOKS, 24
that everyone has it in him to write one b. WRITING, 22
The number one b. . . . was written by a committee BIBLE, 8
The possession of a b. OSTENTATION, 2
There are two motives for reading a b. READING, 3
There is not any b. Or face DEATH, 126
There must be a man behind the b. WRITERS, 9
unprintable b. that is readable BOOKS, 30
What is the use of a b. BOOKS, 12
What you don't know would make a great b. IGNORANCE, 15
When a b. is boring, they yawn openly BOOKS, 39
without mentioning a single b. BOOKS, 32
Would you allow your wife . . . to read this b. PRUDERY, 1
You can't tell a b. APPEARANCES, 8
books against b. the Home Secretary is PHILISTINISM, 7
All b. are divisible into two classes BOOKS, 36
An author who speaks about his own b. EGOTISM, 5
be not swallowed up in b. LOVE, 146; KNOWLEDGE, 34
between a man of sense and his b. BOOKS, 14
B. and friends BOOKS, 1; FRIENDS, 1
B. are a load of crap BOOKS, 22
B. are . . . a mighty bloodless substitute for life BOOKS, 42
B. are made . . . like pyramids BOOKS, 18
B. are well written, or badly written BOOKS, 46
b. by which the printers have lost BOOKS, 19
B. cannot always please BOOKS, 15
b. cannot be killed by fire BOOKS, 34
B., I don't know what you see in them BOOKS, 45
B. must follow sciences BOOKS, 4
B. . . . propose to *instruct* or to *amuse* BOOKS, 16
B. think for me READING, 9
b. . . . written by people who don't understand them BOOKS, 25
Borrowers of b. BORROWING, 6
but b. never die BOOKS, 34
come not, Lucifer! I'll burn my b. DAMNATION, 4
Few b. today are forgivable BOOKS, 21
Give me b., fruit, French wine and fine weather PLEASURE, 17
God has written all the b. SUBJECTIVITY, 2
His b. were read BOOKS, 6; PUNS, 5
If my b. had been any worse CINEMA, 1
I keep my b. at the British Museum BOOKS, 9
Morality's a gesture. . . . learnt from b. MORALITY, 3
No furniture so charming as b. BOOKS, 41
of making many b. there is no end BOOKS, 8
poring over miserable b. LEARNING, 9
Prolonged . . . reviewing of b. involves constantly *inventing* reactions CRITICISM, 36
proper study of mankind is b. LITERATURE, 5
replacing some of the timber used up by my b. TREES, 6
Some b. are to be tasted BOOKS, 3
Some b. are undeservedly forgotten BOOKS, 2
the b. of the hour BOOKS, 36
The b. one reads in childhood . . . create in one's mind a . . . false map BOOKS, 29
the disease of writing b. WRITING, 23
The reading of all good b. LITERATURE, 3
To read too many b. READING, 11
We all know that b. burn BOOKS, 34
Whenever b. are burned CENSORSHIP, 1
When I think of all the b. I have read LIFE, 53
women dislike his b. WRITERS, 71
bookseller he once shot a b. PUBLISHING, 5
booksellers b. are generous liberal-minded men PUBLISHING, 9
nor even b. have put up with poets' being second-rate POETS, 8
boon Is life a b. MORTALITY, 7
boorish the opinionated, the ignorant, and the b. STUBBORNNESS, 2
boot imagine a b. stamping on a human face OPPRESSION, 4
Booth B. died blind FAITH, 13
boots before the truth has got its b. on LYING, 6
If ever he went to school without any b. CONCEIT, 5
Very well, then I shall not take off my b. PRACTICALITY, 6
Bo-peep Little B. has lost her sheep NURSERY RHYMES, 27
bordello After I die, I shall return to earth as a gatekeeper of a b. THREATS, 3
border Through all the wide B. CHIVALRY, 9
bore A b. is a man who BORES, 5
A healthy male adult b. BORES, 8

B., n. A person who talks — BORES, 1
Every hero becomes a b. — HEROISM, 5
He is an old b. — BORES, 7
Is not life . . . too short . . . to b. ourselves — BOREDOM, 6
no greater b. than the travel b. — TRAVEL, 25
proof that God is a b. — PROTESTANTISM, 1
War is an organized b. — WAR, 49
you are . . . the club B.: I am the club Liar — SUPERIORITY, 11
bored aged diplomats to be b. — DIPLOMACY, 1
Bores and *B.* — BORES, 2
Dear World, I am leaving you because I am b. — LAST WORDS, 60
I wanted to be b. to death — BOREDOM, 2
Punctuality is the virtue of the b. — PROMPTNESS, 5
We were as nearly b. as enthusiasm would permit — CRITICISM, 17
When you're b. with yourself — BOREDOM, 7
boredom sheer apathy and b. — DISCOVERY, 4
The effect of b. on a large scale — BOREDOM, 5
three great evils, b., vice, and poverty — WORK, 24
bores he b. for England — BORES, 4
the *B.* and *Bored* — BORES, 2
boring curiously b. about . . . happiness — SYMPATHY, 4
Somebody's b. me, I think it's me — BORES, 6
you ought to be ashamed of . . . being b. — BOREDOM, 4
born a silly little mouse will be b. — DISAPPOINTMENT, 3
As soon as man is b. — DEATH, 3
a time to be b., and a time to die — TIME, 12
best . . . never to have been b. at all — PESSIMISM, 6
better if neither of us had been b. — REGRET, 10
b. again, not of corruptible seed — DEATH, 29
b. to obey — OBEDIENCE, 2
B. under one law — HUMAN CONDITION, 9
Every moment one is b. — LIFE AND DEATH, 13
he is not conscious of being b. — LIFE AND DEATH, 7
He was b. an Englishman — NATIONALITY, 1
I was b. at the age of twelve — CINEMA, 2
I was b. old — AGE, 60
joy that a man is b. into the world — BIRTH, 1
Man was b. free — FREEDOM, 45
natural to die as to be b. — DEATH, 23
No, thank you, I was b. intoxicated — DRUNKENNESS, 18
One is not b. a woman — WOMEN, 13
one of woman b. — BIRTH, 9
Some are b. great — GREATNESS, 12
Some men are b. mediocre — MEDIOCRITY, 4
sucker b. every minute — GULLIBILITY, 1
The house where I was b. — NOSTALGIA, 9
to have been b. — BIRTH, 4
to the manner b. — CUSTOM, 3
We are all b. mad — MADNESS, 1
Whatever is begotten, b., and dies — MORTALITY, 23
born-again b. people . . . make you wish — RELIGION, 69
boroughs The bright b., the circle-citadels there — STARS, 3
borrow If you don't want to use the army, I should like to b. it — SARCASM, 2
men who b. — BORROWING, 5
borrowed B. garments — BORROWING, 1
Britain has lived . . . on b. time — BRITAIN, 5
borrower Neither a b. nor a lender be — BORROWING, 8; INTEGRITY, 4
borrowers B. of books — BORROWING, 6
borrowing be not made a beggar by banqueting upon b. — BORROWING, 3
b. dulls the edge of husbandry — BORROWING, 8; INTEGRITY, 6
bosom Abraham's b. — POVERTY AND WEALTH, 2
a capital b. to hang jewels upon — APPEARANCE, 13
not a b. to repose upon — APPEARANCE, 13
boss working . . . eight hours a day . . . get to be a b. — WORK, 8
Boston A B. man — AMERICANS, 2
this is good old B. — SNOBBERY, 2
both Dreaming on b. — AGE, 52
said on b. sides — OBJECTIVITY, 1
bother long words B. me — WORDS, 16
bothered Bewitched, B. and Bewildered — CONFUSION, 5
Botticelli If B. were alive today — ARTISTS, 21
bottinney b. means a knowledge of plants — EDUCATION, 14
bottle Yo-ho-ho, and a b. of rum — ALCOHOL, 60
bottles It is with . . . people as with . . . b. — CHARACTER, 17
the English have hot-water b. — ENGLISH, 24
bottom b. of the economic pyramid — POVERTY, 27
the best reasons . . . for remaining at the b. — AMBITION, 6
bough Loaf of Bread beneath the B. — CONTENTMENT, 3

bought b. things because she wanted 'em — WOMEN, 86
bouillabaisse B. is only good because cooked by the French — FOOD, 17; FRANCE, 5
boulder When the torrent sweeps a man against a b. — THEORY, 7
Boulogne There was an old man of B. — INNUENDO, 1
bound Tomorrow my hands will be b. — EXECUTION, 1
bouquet the b. is better than the taste — ALCOHOL, 49
bourgeois *B.*, . . . is an epithet — CLASS, 16
How beastly the b. is — MEN, 8
bourgeoisie the British b. have spoken of themselves as gentlemen — CLASS, 35
bourn from whose b. No traveller returns — AFTERLIFE, 9
bovine The cow is of the b. ilk — ANIMALS, 16
bow B., bow, ye lower middle classes — CLASS, 13
I, said the Sparrow, With my b. and arrow — NURSERY RHYMES, 68
Says the great bell at B. — LONDON, 2
bowels in the b. of Christ — MISTAKES, 6
bower-bird I'm a bit of a b. — WRITING, 36
bowl inverted B. we call The Sky — DESTINY, 8
love in a golden b. — WISDOM, 10
They came to see me bat not to see you b. — CRICKET, 3
bow-wow Daddy wouldn't buy me a b. — DOGS, 14
box B. about: 'twill come to my father anon — FAMILY, 6
Take that black b. away — CINEMA, 10
boy And said, What a good b. am I — NURSERY RHYMES, 29
a secret way . . . of getting at a b. — EVIL, 8
A thing of duty is a b. for ever — POLICE, 4; PUNS, 15
every b. and every gal That's born into the world alive — POLITICS, 32
If . . . I were the only b. — LOVE, 65
I'm farther off from heav'n Than when . . . a b. — INNOCENCE, 6
Let the b. win his spurs — SELF-RELIANCE, 4
Love is a b. — PUNISHMENT, 6; INDULGENCE, 1
Mad about the b. — LOVE, 44
rarely . . . one can see in a little b. the promise of a man — CHILDREN, 20
Shades of the prison-house begin to close Upon the growing b. — METAPHYSICS, 5
The b. I love is up in the gallery — LOVE, 144
The b. stood on the burning deck — COURAGE, 14
the little b. Who lives down the lane — NURSERY RHYMES, 4
When I was a little b. they called me a liar — WRITERS, 22
boyhood The smiles, the tears, Of b.'s years — NOSTALGIA, 14
boys As flies to wanton b. — DESTINY, 19
B. and girls come out to play — NURSERY RHYMES, 4
B. are capital fellows in their own way — CHILDREN, 31
B. do not grow up gradually — CHILDREN, 19
B. will be boys — SEXES, 12
Claret is the liquor for b. — ALCOHOL, 32
Girls and b. grow up more normally together — EDUCATION, 45
Where are the b. of the Old Brigade — NOSTALGIA, 23
Where . . . b. plan for what . . . young girls plan for whom — SEXES, 10
Written by office b. for office b. — NEWSPAPERS, 10
bracelet diamond and safire b. lasts forever — MATERIALISM, 13
braces I had b. on my teeth and got high marks — APPEARANCE, 24
braes Ye banks and b. — NATURE, 2
Brahms B. . . . an extraordinary musician — MUSICIANS, 16
brain a Bear of Very Little B. — WORDS, 16
b. attic stocked with all the furniture that he is likely to use — KNOWLEDGE, 13
B., n. An apparatus with which we think — MIND, 1
If it is for mind that we are seaching the b. — MIND, 7
Let schoolmasters puzzle their b. — ALCOHOL, 29
the human b. is a device to keep the ears from grating — MIND, 2
Tobacco drieth the b. — SMOKING, 22
we are supposing the b. . . . more than a telephone-exchange — MIND, 7
with no deep researches vex the b. — CLARITY, 1
You've got the b. of a four-year-old boy — STUPIDITY, 8
brains a girl with b. ought to do something else — WOMEN, 48
b. enough to make a fool of himself — WISDOM AND FOOLISHNESS, 7
I mix them with my b. — PAINTING, 7
something better than our b. to depend upon — ARISTOCRACY, 4
What good are b. to a man — INTELLIGENCE, 8
braking British civil service . . . effective b. mechanism — BUREAUCRACY, 10
branch Cut is the b. that might have grown — DEATH, 80
brandy I am not well; pray get me . . . b. — FIRST IMPRESSIONS, 3
brass B. bands are all very well in their place — MUSIC, 4

C

cabbages c. and kings | NONSENSE, 9
The c. are coming now | ENGLAND, 4
cabin'd c., cribb'd, confin'd, bound in | FEAR, 11
cabs busy driving c. and cutting hair | GOVERNMENT, 7
Caesar *Ave C., morituri te salutant* | LAST WORDS, 4
C.! dost thou lie so low | DEATH, 105
C. had his Brutus – Charles the First, his Cromwell | TREASON, 4
C.'s wife | PURITY, 1
I always remember that I am C.'s daughter | EXTRAVAGANCE, 3
I come to bury C. | EVIL, 16
Not that I lov'd C. less | PATRIOTISM, 28
Regions C. never knew | ENGLAND, 13
Rose . . . where some buried C. bled | FLOWERS, 4
that C. might be great | RUTHLESSNESS, 2
Caesar's C. laurel crown | POWER, 7
C. wife must be above suspicion | INTEGRITY, 2
cage Marriage is like a c. | MARRIAGE, 83
Nor iron bars a c. | IMPRISONMENT, 4
robin redbreast in a c. | IMPRISONMENT, 1
She's only a bird in a gilded c. | IMPRISONMENT, 3
caged We think c. birds sing, when indeed they cry | IMPRISONMENT, 6
Cain the Lord set a mark upon C. | REVENGE, 9
caitiff If the rude c. smite the other too | REVENGE, 10
cake Bake me a c. as fast as you can | NURSERY RHYMES, 38
Let them eat c. | HUNGER, 10
cakes no more c. and ale | MERRYMAKING, 3
Calais 'C.' lying in my heart | DEFEAT, 5
Calamities C. are of two kinds | MISFORTUNE, 4
the c. of life | CLASS, 8
calamity Whatsoever . . . the private c., I hope it will not interfere with the public business of the country | FIRE, 3
calculating A dessicated c. machine | POLITICIANS, 34
Caledonia C.! stern and wild | SCOTLAND, 7
calf but the c. won't get much sleep | MISTRUST, 3
he killed a c. . . . in a high style | SHAKESPEARE, 2
the fatted c. | PARTIES, 2
call one clear c. for me | DUTY, 5
called c. a cold a cold | ILLNESS, 2
calm sea is c. to-night | SEA, 1
Wisdom has taught us to be c. and meek | REVENGE, 10
calories the only thing that matters is c. | HEALTH AND HEALTHY LIVING, 8
calumnies C. are answered best | INSULTS, 22
Calvary the place, which is called C. | EXECUTION, 3
Calvin land of C., oat-cakes, and sulphur | SCOTLAND, 8
Cambridge C. people rarely smile | CAMBRIDGE, 2
Oxford is on the whole more attractive than C. | CAMBRIDGE, 1; OXFORD, 2
Spring and summer did happen in C. | CAMBRIDGE, 4
The young C. group | CLASSIFICATION, 2
To C. books | CAMBRIDGE, 6; OXFORD, 6
With equal skill to C. books he sent | CAMBRIDGE, 3; OXFORD, 3
came I c.; I saw; God conquered | VICTORY, 16
I c., I saw, I conquered | VICTORY, 1
I c. like Water | LIFE AND DEATH, 5
camel easier for a c. to go through the eye of a needle | WEALTH, 8
Camelot many-tower'd C. | ARTHURIAN LEGEND, 2
To look down to C. | CURSES, 4
camels the c. and the sand | CINEMA, 9
camera I am a c. | OBJECTIVITY, 4
The c. cannot lie. But . . . | PHOTOGRAPHY, 3
Campland This is C., an invisible country | IMPRISONMENT, 5
campus three major administrative problems on a c. | EDUCATION, 28
can Talent does what it c. | TALENT AND GENIUS, 4
cancel to c. half a Line | DESTINY, 7
cancels debt which c. all others | OBLIGATION, 1
cancer C.'s a Funny Thing | DISEASE, 20
chronic diseases more destructive to life than c. | DISEASE, 26
candid save me, from the c. friend | FRANKNESS, 7
candidates C. should not attempt more than six | BIBLE, 2
candle a c. of understanding | UNDERSTANDING, 1
Bell, book, and c. | MATERIALISM, 18
blow out your c. . . . to find your way | GUIDANCE, 2
It is burning a farthing c. at Dover | CRITICISM, 19
light a c. to the sun | FUTILITY, 4
Like a c. burnt out | TIME, 41
little c. throws his beams | GOOD, 15

My c. burns at both ends | PLEASURE, 21
Out, out, brief c. | LIFE, 43
take away the c. and spare my blushes | MODESTY, 1
we shall this day light such a c., by God's grace, in England [as I trust shall never be put out. | EXECUTION, 15
candle-light Can I get there by c. | NURSERY RHYMES, 17
candles She would rather light c. than curse the darkness | COMPLIMENTS, 6
candlestick The butcher, the baker, The c.-maker | NURSERY RHYMES, 45
canem *Cave c.* | DOGS, 1
canker killing as the c. to the rose | CORRUPTION, 4
canned C. music is like audible wallpaper | POP MUSIC, 7
cannibal Better sleep with a sober c. than a drunken Christian | DRUNKENNESS, 16
cannon-ball c. took off his legs | PUNS, 8
canoe every man paddle his own c. | INDEPENDENCE, 3
Canossa We will not go to C. | DETERMINATION, 6
cant clear your *mind* of c. . . . | REASON, 3
love – all the wretched c. of it | LOVE, 64
where the Greeks had modesty, we have c. | HYPOCRISY, 13
can't 'C.' will be the epitaph of the British Empire | BRITISH EMPIRE, 5
capability Negative C. | DOUBT, 6
capable c. of being well set to music | MUSIC, 2
capital Boys are c. fellows in their own way | CHILDREN, 31
capitalism C. re-creates | POLITICS, 61
c. . . . : the process whereby American girls turn into American women | CAPITALISM, 3
I am going to fight c. | CAPITALISM, 11
imperialism is the monopoly stage of c. | POLITICS, 46
Lenin was the first to discover that c. 'inevitably' caused war | CAPITALISM, 14
militarism . . . is one of the chief bulwarks of c. | CAPITALISM, 5
unacceptable face of c. | CAPITALISM, 4
We cannot remove the evils of c. | CAPITALISM, 6
capitalist C. production begets . . . its own negation | CAPITALISM, 9
Not every problem someone has with his girlfriend is . . . due to . . . c. . . . production | CAPITALISM, 8
capitulate I will be conquered; I will not c. | DETERMINATION, 9
Capricorn Lady C., . . . was . . . keeping open bed | PROMISCUITY, 2
captain C. of the *Pinafore* | CONCEIT, 9
I am the c. of my soul | RESPONSIBILITY, 2
captains C. of industry | LEADERSHIP, 4
capten C., art tha sleepin' there below | WAR, 78
captive Beauty stands . . . Led c. | BEAUTY, 28
car always using a small c. to drive to the dockyard instead of my Rolls Royce | ROYALTY, 23
The c. has become the carapace | TRAVEL, 22
carapace The car has become the c. | TRAVEL, 22
carbon c. atom possesses certain exceptional properties | SCIENCE, 23
carbuncle Like a c. on the face of an old and valued friend | ARCHITECTURE, 4
card wrestled with a self-adjusting c. table | TECHNOLOGY, 13
cardinal unbecoming for a c. to ski badly | SPORT AND GAMES, 9
cards an old age of c. | OLD AGE, 33
I have not learned to play at c. | SPORT AND GAMES, 10
care age is full of c. | AGE, 54
Begone, dull c. | WORRY, 5
C. Sat on his faded cheek | WORRY, 1
I c. for nobody | SELFISHNESS, 2
I don't c. for war | WAR, 76
Our progress . . . Is trouble and c. | LIFE, 32
People who are always taking c. of their health are like misers | HYPOCHONDRIA, 2
pleasures are their only c. | EXPLOITATION, 2
Sleep that knits up the ravell'd sleave of c. | SLEEP, 15
so vain . . . c. for the opinion of those we don't c. for | CONCEIT, 8
take c. of the minutes | TIME, 15
Take c. of the pence | THRIFT, 4
what is past my help is past my c. | INDIFFERENCE, 1
career a lover with any other c. in view | COMMITMENT, 6
having a c. of my own | MARRIAGE, 15
Miss Madeleine Philips . . . was a c. | COMMITMENT, 6
nothing which might damage his c. | SCOTS, 1
science was the only c. worth following | WORK, 10
careers The best c. advice to give to the young | OCCUPATIONS, 18

careful be very c. o' vidders CAUTION, 11
careless first fine c. rapture BIRDS, 1
carelessness To lose one parent, ... a misfortune; to lose
 both looks like c. LOSS, 8
 with a slow deliberate c. READING, 10
cares Nobody c. much at heart about Titian ARTISTS, 20
 the earth where c. abound BIRDS, 11
careth he that is married c. ... how he may please his wife
  MARRIAGE, 26
cargo With a c. of ivory BOATS, 12
 With a c. of Tyne coal BOATS, 13
caring take millions off the c. services PATRIOTISM, 19
Carling I'll bet he drinks C. Black Label ADVERTISING, 13
carpe C. diem PRESENT, 7
carpenter Walrus and the C. SEASIDE, 1
carpet a Turkey c. bears to a picture CRITICISM, 31
 only men in rags ... Mistake themselves for c. bags
  ETIQUETTE, 5
carriage Go together like a horse and c. LOVE AND MARRIAGE, 1
 very small second-class c. BOATS, 3
 we look for happiness in boats and c. rides TRAVEL, 14
carriages when they think they are alone in railway c.
  HABIT, 6
Carthage C. must be destroyed WAR, 24
Cary Grant Old C. fine TELEGRAMS, 7
Casanova C. had lots of fun AIDS, 3
case If ever there was a c. of clearer evidence NONSENSE, 2
 in our c. we have not got WEAPONS, 6
 the c. is still before the courts ARGUMENTS, 7
 the reason of the c. LAW, 21
 there had been a lady in the c. ... WOMEN, 21
 The world is everything that is the c. LOGIC, 4
casements Charm'd magic c. BIRDS, 5
cash Nothing links man to man like ... c. MONEY, 45
 One cannot assess in terms of c. ... a church tower
  ENVIRONMENT, 1
 only the poor who pay c. MONEY, 22
 take the c. in hand MONEY, 21
cashiers c. of the Musical Banks MONEY, 13
casino I have come to regard ... courts ... as a c.
  JUSTICE, 11
cask A c. of wine ALCOHOL, 1
casket seal the hushed c. of my soul SLEEP, 13
Cassius C. has a lean and hungry look MISTRUST, 1
cassock C., band, and hymn-book too CLERGY, 15
cassowary If I were a c. CLERGY, 15
cast c. thy bread upon the waters OPPORTUNITY, 10
 he that is without sin ... let him first c. a stone SIN, 4
 pale c. of thought CONSCIENCE, 5
 The die is c. IRREVOCABILITY, 4
caste measure the social c. of a person CLASS, 2
casteth perfect love c. out fear LOVE, 24; FEAR, 3
casting It is no good c. out devils DEVIL, 9
castle A c. called Doubting Castle DESPAIR, 1
 A neurotic is the man who builds a c. in the air PSYCHIATRY, 11
 The house of every one is to him as his c. PRIVACY, 1
Castlereagh Murder ... had a mask like C. MURDER, 12
castles C. in the air DREAMS, 8
 Pale Death kicks his way ... into ... the c. of kings
  EQUALITY, 28
 the c. I have, are built with air DREAMS, 9
casualty except the c. list of the World War MURDER, 3
 The first c. when war comes WAR, 54
cat A c. has nine lives LUCK, 2
 A c. may look EQUALITY, 1
 a C. of such deceitfulness CATS, 2
 c. is a diagram and pattern of subtle air CATS, 5
 God ... a cosmic Cheshire c. GOD, 27
 Had Tiberius been a c. CATS, 1
 He bought a crooked c., which caught a crooked mouse
  NURSERY RHYMES, 52
 he is a very fine c. CATS, 4
 Hey diddle diddle, The c. and the fiddle NURSERY RHYMES, 14
 I'll bell the c. COURAGE, 10
 More ways of killing a c. CHOICE, 3
 That tossed the dog, That worried the c. NURSERY RHYMES, 57
 The C., the Rat, and Lovell our dog INSULTS, 12
 What c.'s averse to fish MATERIALISM, 8
 When I play with my c. CATS, 6
 When the c.'s away ABSENCE, 3
cataclysm Out of their c. but one poor Noah Dare hope to
 survive SEX, 25

catastrophe to lose one's teeth is a c. TEETH, 5
 When a man confronts c. ... a woman looks in her mirror
  SEXES, 26
catch Go, and c. a falling star NONSENSE, 11
 only one c. and that was Catch-22 OBSTRUCTION, 3;
  SELF-PRESERVATION, 5
Catch-22 only one catch and that was C. OBSTRUCTION, 3;
  SELF-PRESERVATION, 5
catchwords Man is a creature who lives ... by c. SEXES, 21
categorical This imperative is C. MORALITY, 8
cathedrals the ancient c. – grand, wonderful, mysterious
  RELIGION, 53
Catherine I'm glad you like my C. PROMISCUITY, 6
Catholic I am a C. ... I go to Mass every day PREJUDICE, 1
 I have a C. soul, but a Lutheran stomach CATHOLICISM, 4
 I'm still a C. CATHOLICISM, 12
 quite lawful for a C. woman to avoid pregnancy by ...
 mathematics CONTRACEPTION, 5
 who, like you, your Holiness, is a Roman C. CATHOLICISM, 3
Catholics C. and Communists have committed great crimes
  COMMITMENT, 4
 they may be C. but they are not Christians INSULTS, 31
 We know these new English C. CATHOLICISM, 7
cats All c. are grey EQUALITY, 2
 A lotta c. copy the Mona Lisa IMITATION, 1
 what c. most appreciate ... is ... entertainment value CATS, 3
cattle Actors should be treated like c. ACTORS, 5
 O Mary, go and call the c. home AGRICULTURE, 4
 these who die as c. WORLD WAR I, 18
cause for what high c. This darling of the Gods DESTINY, 13
 the name of perseverance in a good c. STUBBORNNESS, 3
causes Home of lost c. OXFORD, 1
 they should declare the c. which impel them to ... separation
  INDEPENDENCE, 2
cavaliero a perfect c. HEROISM, 4
cavaliers C. (Wrong but Wromantic) HISTORY, 27
cave C. canem DOGS, 1
 I should be like a lion in a c. of savage Daniels ENEMIES, 7
caverns Gluts twice ten thousand C. SEA, 8
 Through c. measureless to man PLEASURE, 8
caves be c. ... in which his shadow will be shown GOD, 39
 sunny pleasure-dome with c. of ice PLEASURE, 9
caviare c. to the general TASTE, 6
cease have their day and c. to be TRANSIENCE, 18
 I will not c. from mental fight ENGLAND, 5
 restless Cromwell could not c. POLITICIANS, 60
ceases forbearance c. to be a virtue TOLERANCE, 1
celebrate I c. myself SELF, 18
celebrity A c. ... works hard ... to become known FAME, 1
 The c. ... known for his well-knownness FAME, 4
celerity C. is never more admir'd IMPETUOSITY, 3
celery Genuineness ... Like c. SINCERITY, 4
 two thousand people crunching c. at the same time FOOD, 46
Celia Come, my C., let us prove LOVE, 76
celibacy c. is ... a muddy horse-pond MARRIAGE, 89
cello The c. is not one of my favourite instruments MUSIC, 53
cemetery old c. in which nine of his daughters were lying
  SEX, 56
censor Deleted by French c. NEWSPAPERS, 2
censorship Assassination ... the extreme form of c.
  ASSASSINATION, 5
 C. ... depraving and corrupting CENSORSHIP, 3
censure All c. of a man's self SELF, 10
centre I love being at the c. of things COMMITMENT, 5
 My c. is giving way WORLD WAR I, 9
century The c. on which we are entering ... must be the c. of
 the common man PUBLIC, 19
 The great man ... walks across his c. INFLUENCE, 9
 the twentieth c. will be ... the c. of Fascism FASCISM, 2
cereal Do you know what breakfast c. is made of FOOD, 16
cerebrums larger c. and smaller adrenal glands WAR, 67
certain I am c. that we will win the election with a good
 majority SELF-CONFIDENCE, 6
 nothing is c. but death and taxes TAXATION, 4
 Nothing is c. but death DEATH, 9
 One thing is c. LIFE, 24
certainties begin with c. CERTAINTY, 1; DOUBT, 1
 His doubts are better than ... c. DOUBT, 5
cesspit people swirling about in a human c. AIDS, 1
cesspool London, that great c. LONDON, 2
Ceylon spicy breezes Blow soft o'er C.'s isle MISANTHROPY, 1
chaff An editor ... separates the wheat from the c. EDITORS, 3

not racially pure are mere c. — RACISM, 12
chain A c. is no stronger — UNITY, 1
the flesh to feel the c. — IMPRISONMENT, 2
chains c. that tie The hidden soul of harmony — MUSIC, 33
It's often safer to be in c. — FREEDOM, 24
Man . . . everywhere he is in c. — FREEDOM, 45
nothing to lose but their c. — MARXISM, 3
chair Give Dayrolles a c. — LAST WORDS, 16
the nineteenth century was the age of the editorial c. — PSYCHIATRY, 8
chaise All in a c. and pair — MARRIAGE, 43
chaise-longue Wedlock – the . . . deep peace of the double bed after the . . . c. — MARRIAGE, 34
chalices In old time we had treen c. and golden priests — CLERGY, 8
cham That great C. of literature, Samuel Johnson — WRITERS, 84
chamber rapping at my c. door — SUPERNATURAL, 12
Upstairs and downstairs And in my lady's c. — NURSERY RHYMES, 13
chambermaid a man would be as happy in the arms of a c. — IMAGINATION, 5
chamois springing from blonde to blonde like the c. of the Alps — AMERICANS, 14
champagne Fighting is like c. — WAR, 69
like a glass of c. that has stood — HOUSES OF PARLIAMENT, 2
water flowed like c. — ABSTINENCE, 4
chance every c. brought out a noble knight — NOSTALGIA, 19
Grab a c. — OPPORTUNITY, 15
time and c. happeneth to them all — CHANCE, 2
chancellor C. of the Exchequer — TAXATION, 8
change C. is not made without inconvenience — CHANGE, 11
c. is the very essence of life — CHANGE, 8
I c., but I cannot die — WEATHER, 22
If you leave a thing alone you leave it to a torrent of c. — CONSERVATISM, 1
Most of the c. we think we see — NOVELTY, 2
Most women set out to try to c. a man — CHANGE, 5
Plus ça c. — CONSTANCY, 3
Popularity? . . . glory's small c. — POPULARITY, 4
The more things c. — CONSTANCY, 3
There is a certain relief in c. — CHANGE, 12
The wind of c. — CHANGE, 15
changed All c., c. utterly — BEAUTY, 41
changeth The old order c. — CHANGE, 19
changez C. vos amis — FRIENDS, 8
changing c. scenes of life — CHANGE, 18
Woman is always fickle and c. — WOMEN, 88
Channel dream you are crossing the C. — BOATS, 6
let the last man . . . brush the C. with his sleeve — WAR, 106; WORLD WAR I, 22
chaos a perfectly possible means of overcoming c. — POETRY, 37
The grotesque c. of a Labour council – a *Labour* council — INCOMPETENCE, 2
chapel Devil always builds a c. there — DEVIL, 7
chapels c. had been churches — ACTION, 11
chaplain twice a day the C. called — IMPRISONMENT, 8
Chaplin C. is no business man — ACTORS, 15
chaps Biography is about C. — BIOGRAPHY, 1
chapter c. of accidents — MISFORTUNE, 8; ACCIDENTS, 7
character I had become a woman of . . . c. — CHARACTER, 6
I leave my c. behind — REPUTATION, 9
What is c. but the determination of incident — CHARACTER, 13
characteristic typically English c. — ENGLISH, 3; UNITY, 4
characters c. in one of my novels — FICTION, 2
her c. are round, or capable of rotundity. — WRITERS, 48
involvements and feelings and c. of ordinary life — WRITERS, 82
Most women have no c. — WOMEN, 65
charge Electrical force . . . causes motion of electrical c. — SCIENCE, 10
charged it was c. against me — INDIFFERENCE, 7
Charing Cross between Heaven and C. — HEAVEN, 13
I went out to C., to see Major-general Harrison hanged — EXECUTION, 22
the full tide of human existence is at C. — LONDON, 9
chariot Swing low sweet c. — DEATH, 17
the dust beneath thy c. wheel — HUMILITY, 2
Time's winged c. — AGE, 37
charity C. begins at home — CHARITY, 1, 10
C. is the power of defending that which we know to be indefensible — CHARITY, 12; HOPE, 5
c. never faileth — CHARITY, 6

c. suffereth long, and is kind — CHARITY, 6
In c. there is no excess — CHARITY, 3
knowledge puffeth up, but c. edifieth — CHARITY, 7; KNOWLEDGE, 8
lectures or a little c. — SELF, 19
now abideth faith, hope, c. — CHARITY, 6
the greatest of these is c. — CHARITY, 6
The living need c. — CHARITY, 2
The man who leaves money to c. in his will — BEQUESTS, 3
without c. are nothing worth — CHARITY, 9
Charles Caesar had his Brutus – C. the First, his Cromwell — TREASON, 4
There were gentlemen and . . . seamen in the navy of C. the Second — NAVY, 3
Charley I'm C.'s aunt from Brazil — PLACES, 21
Charlie C. is my darling — ADMIRATION, 9
charm Conversation has a kind of c. — CONVERSATION, 8
Oozing c. . . . He oiled his way — CHARM, 3
The c. is purely romantic — IDEALISM, 7
charming c. people have something to conceal — CHARM, 2
I heard the bullets whistle, . . . c. in the sound — WAR, 123
It is c. to totter into vogue — AGE, 64
People are either c. or tedious — CHARM, 4
charms Whose c. all other maids surpass — ADMIRATION, 9
Charon C., seeing, may forget — LUST, 5
Chartreuse religious system that produced green C. — ALCOHOL, 51
chaste godly poet must be c. himself — POETRY, 10
chastity Give me c. and continence — PROCRASTINATION, 4
Chatterley Put thy shimmy on, Lady C. — PARTING, 7
Chaucer C., I confess, is a rough diamond — CHAUCER, 4
C. . . . I think obscene and contemptible — CHAUCER, 1
read C. still with as much pleasure — CHAUCER, 3
Chawcer pity that C. . . . was so unedicated — CHAUCER, 3
cheap flesh and blood so c. — POVERTY, 17
cheating *Peace . . . a period of c.* — PEACE, 4
check C. enclosed — MONEY, 37
dreadful is the c. — IMPRISONMENT, 2
cheek Care Sat on his faded c. — WORRY, 11
the c. that doth not fade — APPEARANCE, 17
turn the other c. — REVENGE, 1
whosoever shall smite thee on thy right c. — ENEMIES, 2
cheeks Blow, winds, and crack your c. — WEATHER, 18
cheer cups, That c. but not inebriate — DRINKS, 4
Don't c., boys; the poor devils are dying — WAR, 87
cheerful God loveth a c. giver — GENEROSITY, 2
cheerfulness No warmth, no c., no healthful ease — MONTHS, 10
cheese 265 kinds of c. — FRANCE, 6
bread and c., and kisses — MARRIAGE, 114
c. – toasted, mostly — DREAMS, 5
when the c. is gone — NONSENSE, 4
chemical c. barrage has been hurled against the fabric of life — ECOLOGY, 2
Shelley and Keats were . . . up to date in . . . c. knowledge — POETS, 7; SCIENCE, 17
cheque Any general statement is like a c. — GENERALIZATIONS, 3
Mrs Claypool's c. will come back to you — HUMOUR, 45
Chequer-board a C. of Nights and Days — DESTINY, 6
cherish to love and to c. — MARRIAGE, 30
cherry Before the c. orchard was sold — WORRY, 9
C. ripe, ripe, ripe — BUSINESS, 6
Loveliest of trees, the c. — TREES, 2
Till 'C. ripe' themselves do cry — ADMIRATION, 4
chess Life's too short for c. — SPORT AND GAMES, 3
the devil played at c. with me — EXPLOITATION, 1
chess-board c. is the world; the pieces . . . the phenomena of the universe — GOD, 28
chest Fifteen men on the dead man's c. — ALCOHOL, 60
chestnut O c. tree — NATURE, 4
Under the spreading c. tree — OCCUPATIONS, 7
chestnuts warmongers who . . . have others pull the c. out of the fire — POLITICS, 70
chew he can't fart and c. gum at the same time — STUPIDITY, 5
chewing c. little bits of String — FOOD, 8
chic very c. for an atheist — MEMORIALS, 9
chicken a c. in his pot every Sunday — POVERTY, 15
England will have her neck wrung like a c. — WORLD WAR II, 30
Some c. — WORLD WAR II, 12
chickens children are more troublesome and costly than c. — MANKIND, 29
count their c. ere they're hatched — ANTICIPATION, 5
Don't count your c. — ANTICIPATION, 4

If I didn't start painting, I would have raised c.
OCCUPATIONS, 13
You don't set a fox to watching the c. EXPERIENCE, 21
chief C. Defect of Henry King FOOD, 8
C. of the Army LAST WORDS, 45
child A c. becomes an adult when RIGHT, 2
A c. deserves the maximum respect CHILDREN, 28
A c.'s a plaything for an hour CHILDREN, 32
all any reasonable c. can expect SEX, 42
better . . . a poor and a wise c. than an old and foolish king
OLD AGE, 5; YOUTH, 1
C.! do not throw this book about BOOKS, 7
c. of five would understand this SIMPLICITY, 5
flourish in a c. of six CHILDREN, 9
getting wenches with c. YOUTH, 16
He who shall teach the c. to doubt DOUBT, 3
If you strike a c. VIOLENCE, 6
nobody's c. LONELINESS, 1
Now at last our c. is just like all children EQUALITY, 27
One stops being a c. when . . . telling one's trouble does not
make it better DISILLUSION, 5
receive one such little c. in my name CHILDREN, 14
spoil the c. PUNISHMENT, 6; INDULGENCE, 1
sweetest Shakespeare, Fancy's c. SHAKESPEARE, 13
The business of being a c. CHILDREN, 26
The C. is Father of the Man AGE, 68
The mother-c. relationship is paradoxical FAMILY, 16
There are only two things a c. will share willingly CHILDREN, 38
unless the play is stopped, the c. cannot . . . go on
AUDIENCES, 2
unto us a c. is born CHRISTMAS, 6
What is the use of a new-born c. PURPOSE, 2
when I was a c., I spake as a c. CHARITY, 6
wise father that knows his own c. FAMILY, 38
childbirth Death and taxes and c. EXPEDIENCY, 1
Mountains will heave in c. DISAPPOINTMENT, 3
the male equivalent of c. PUBLISHING, 1
Childe C. Roland to the Dark Tower SUMMONS, 4
childhood The books one reads in c. . . . create in one's mind a
. . . false map BOOKS, 29
childish I put away c. things CHARITY, 4
Sweet c. days NOSTALGIA, 24
childishness second c. OLD AGE, 38
children a Friend for little c. Above the bright blue sky
GOD, 36
Anybody who hates c. and dogs CHILDREN, 21; DOGS, 6
Are the c. all in their beds? It's past eight o'clock NURSERY
RHYMES, 64
as c. fear to go in the dark DEATH, 22
a wicked man that comes after c. SLEEP, 10
c. are more troublesome and costly than chickens MANKIND, 29
C. aren't happy with nothing to ignore FAMILY, 31
c. are true judges of character CHILDREN, 4; DISEASE, 7
C. have never been very good at listening CHILDREN, 6
C. . . . have no use for psychology. They detest sociology
BOOKS, 39
c., obey your parents OBEDIENCE, 1
C. should acquire . . . heroes and villains from fiction HISTORY, 3
C. sweeten labours CHILDREN, 5
C. with Hyacinth's temperament . . . merely know more
CHARACTER, 18
Come dear c. DEPARTURE, 1
desire not a multitude of unprofitable c. CHILDREN, 11
Do you hear the c. weeping SORROW, 2
English are growing demented about c. CHILDREN, 41
except ye . . . become as little c. CHILDREN, 13
Familiarity breeds . . . c. SEX, 58
Far too good to waste on c. YOUTH, 17
He that has no c. ADVICE, 3
He that loves not his wife and c. MARRIAGE, 116
his wife is beautiful and his c. smart TOLERANCE, 5
I love all my c. FAMILY, 11
in sorrow thou shalt bring forth c. SEXES, 2
I've lost one of my c. this week LOSS, 7
Let our c. grow tall TALENT, 7
like a c.'s party taken over by the elders AGE, 26
make your c. *capable of honesty* is the beginning of education
HONESTY, 6
Many c. are suffering from muesli-belt malnutrition FOOD, 35
Men are but c. of a larger growth AGE, 21
more careful of the breed of their horses and dogs than of their
c. FAMILY, 33

Most of the people . . . will be c. FUNERALS, 1
My music . . . understood by c. and animals MUSIC, 50
Never have c. CHILDREN, 40
Now at last our child is just like all c. EQUALITY, 27
Parents learn a lot from their c. CHILDREN, 37
provoke not your c. FAMILY, 9
She had so many c. she didn't know what to do NURSERY
RHYMES, 54
the c. I might have had CHILDREN, 34
the early marriages of silly c. MARRIAGE, 80
To bear many c. is considered . . . an investment CHILDREN, 22
We have no c., except me CHILDREN, 7
Were we closer to the ground as c. NOSTALGIA, 1
when they started life as c. CHILDREN, 3
write for c. . . . as you do for adults WRITING, 10
You can do anything with c. if you only play with them
CHILDREN, 16
chill St Agnes Eve – Ah, bitter c. it was SEASONS, 9
chime to set a c. of words tinkling in . . . a few fastidious
people PURPOSE, 7
chimes c. at midnight MERRYMAKING, 4
chimney sixty horses wedged in a c. JOURNALISM, 24
chimney-sweepers As c., come to dust MORTALITY, 16
China Even the Hooligan was probably invented in C.
PLACES, 16
On a slow boat to C. BOATS, 10
The infusion of a C. plant DRINKS, 1
Chinese Nothing . . . can destroy the C. people PLACES, 2
chip c. off the old block POLITICIANS, 37
chips You breed babies and you eat c. FOOD, 49
chirche-dore Housbondes at c. MARRIAGE, 35
chivalry age of c. is gone EUROPE, 2
The age of c. is never past CHIVALRY, 6
Chi Wen Tzu C. always CAUTION, 10
Chloë In the spring . . . your lovely C. APPEARANCE, 32
chocolate a c. cream soldier SOLDIERS, 4
both its national products, snow and c., melt SWITZERLAND, 1
Venice is like eating . . . c. liqueurs VENICE, 2
choice Hebrew word . . . *timshel* . . . gives a c. CHOICE, 1
choir Sweet singing in the c. CHRISTMAS, 5
choirs Bare ruin'd c. OLD AGE, 40
choose *We can believe what we c.* RESPONSIBILITY, 11
Chopin I have lived off the blood of C. MUSICIANS, 7
to bridge the awful gap between Dorothy and C. MUSIC, 3
chord c. of music MUSIC, 39
chorus a dozen are only a c. BEAUTY, 18
chose *plus c'est la même c.* CONSTANCY, 3
Christ C. is all, and in all CHRISTIANITY, 6
C. . . . would quite likely have been arrested OPPRESSION, 2
churches have kill'd their C. CLERGY, 14
I beseech you, in the bowels of C. MISTAKES, 6
The Jews have produced . . . C., Spinoza, and myself
CONCEIT, 16
We're more popular than Jesus C. POPULARITY, 6
Who dreamed that C. has died in vain CHRISTIANITY, 39
Christendom wisest fool in C. FOOLISHNESS, 13
Christian A C. . . . feels Repentance on a Sunday HYPOCRISY, 19
any man . . . who could not bear another's misfortunes . . . like a
C. MISFORTUNE, 13
Better sleep with a sober cannibal than a drunken C.
DRUNKENNESS, 16
C. Science explains all cause and effect as mental RELIGION, 21
How very hard . . . To be a C. CHRISTIANITY, 20
I die a C. EXECUTION, 4
in what peace a C. can die LAST WORDS, 3
I was born of C. race RELIGION, 63
No Jew was ever fool enough to turn C. RELIGION, 73
object . . . to form C. men EDUCATION, 3
Onward, C. soldiers CHRISTIANITY, 3
several young women . . . would render the C. life intensely
difficult CHRISTIANITY, 31
The C. religion not only was at first attended with miracles
CHRISTIANITY, 29
The C. religion . . . cannot be believed by any reasonable person
without one CHRISTIANITY, 29
Christianity C. accepted as given a metaphysical system
CHRISTIANITY, 30
C., . . . but why journalism CHRISTIANITY, 2; JOURNALISM, 3
C. has done a great deal for love CHRISTIANITY, 24
C. has made of death a terror CHRISTIANITY, 36
C. is part of the Common Law of England CHRISTIANITY, 26

C. is the most materialistic of all great religions
CHRISTIANITY, 42
C. . . . says that they are all fools
MANKIND, 11
C. the one great curse
CHRISTIANITY, 35
C. . . . the one immortal blemish of mankind
CHRISTIANITY, 35
decay of C.
ALCOHOL, 51
His C. was muscular
CHRISTIANITY, 23
local cult called C.
CHRISTIANITY, 28
loving C. better than Truth
CHRISTIANITY, 22
Rock and roll or C.
POPULARITY, 6
Christians C. awake, salute the happy morn
CHRISTMAS, 12
Onward, C., onward go
ENDURANCE, 24
settle their differences like good C.
RELIGION, 4
these C. love one another
CHRISTIANITY, 45
they may be Catholics but they are not C.
INSULTS, 31
Christ-like C. heroes and woman-worshipping Don Juans
MEN, 9
Christmas At C. I no more desire a rose
SUITABILITY, 4
C. should fall out in the Middle of Winter
CHRISTMAS, 1
Eating a C. pie
NURSERY RHYMES, 29
For C. comes but once a year
CHRISTMAS, 19
I'm walking backwards till C.
NONSENSE, 23
Let them know it's C.
CHARITY, 4
perceive C. through its wrapping
CHRISTMAS, 20
'Twas the night before C.
CHRISTMAS, 14
Christopher C. Robin went down with Alice
SOLDIERS, 4
chronicle c. small beer
TRIVIALITY, 12
the c. of wasted time
HISTORY, 32
Chronologie beginning of time according to our C.
CREATION, 14
church an alien C.
IRELAND, 5
Beware when you take on the C. of God
RELIGION, 60
But get me to the c. on time
MARRIAGE, 78
he'd go to c., start a revolution – *something*
MATERIALISM, 15
he goes to c. as he goes to the bathroom
CLERGY, 3
I believe in the C.
RELIGION, 55
If I really believed that the C. of England
RELIGION, 7
straying away from the c.
RELIGION, 8
The blood of the martyrs is the seed of the C.
CHRISTIANITY, 44
The C. exists
CHURCH, 5
The C.'s one foundation
CHRISTIANITY, 40
The farther you go from the c. of Rome
PROTESTANTISM, 3
There are many who stay away from c.
RELIGION, 45
There is no salvation outside the c.
RELIGION, 3
There was I, waiting at the c.
MARRIAGE, 77
where MCC ends and the C. of England begins
CHURCH, 4
churches chapels had been c.
ACTION, 11
c. have kill'd their Christ
CLERGY, 14
the c. . . . bore for me the same relation to God that billboards
did to Coca-Cola
RELIGION, 61
The itch of disputing . . . the scab of c.
RELIGION, 71
churchman a species of person called a 'Modern C.'
RELIGION, 66
churchyard A piece of c. fits everybody
DEATH, 2
Cicero C. And . . . Homer were *Mad as the mist and snow*
MADNESS, 18
cider c. and tinned salmon
FOOD, 47
cigar a good c. is a smoke
WOMEN, 45
It is like a c. . . . . it never tastes quite the same
LOVE, 145
cigarette A c. is . . . a perfect pleasure
SMOKING, 23
I kissed my first woman, and smoked my first c.
SMOKING, 19
Cinderella poetry, 'The C. of the Arts.'
POETRY, 33
cinema c. is truth twenty-four times a second
CINEMA, 4
circle All things from eternity . . . come round in a c.
HISTORY, 5
circumcised our fingers are c.
MUSICIANS, 6
When they c. Herbert Samuel
INSULTS, 27
circumcision atheism, breast-feeding, c.
INDULGENCE, 3
circumlocution C. Office
BUREAUCRACY, 5
circumstance Pride, pomp, and c.
WAR, 109
To a philosopher no c., . . . is too minute
PHILOSOPHERS, 3
circumstances to face straitened c. at home
POVERTY, 22
circumstantial Some c. evidence is very strong
PROOF, 6
circuses bread and c.
PUBLIC, 15
cities I have sung women in three c.
WOMEN, 68
many c. had rubbed him smooth
TRAVEL, 1
The government burns down whole c.
INJUSTICE, 10
citizen a c. of the world
NATIONALITY, 8; COURTESY, 2
citizens All free men, . . . are c. of Berlin
GERMANY, 4
city every man in the c. wants a farm
ENVY, 5
first c. Cain
GARDENS, 6

great c. . . . has the greatest men and women
GREATNESS, 15
hiring taxis to scuttle around a c.
INCOMPETENCE, 2
I go amongst the buildings of a c.
PURPOSE, 5
It is a c. where you can see a sparrow fall
IRELAND, 12
the c. is not a concrete jungle, it is a human zoo
MANKIND, 18
the c. of perspiring dreams
CAMBRIDGE, 5
civil In a c. war, a general must know
WAR, 90
civilian forget about this c.
WAR, 43
civilians drop bombs . . . hit c.
WAR, 43
civilisation Disinterested intellectual curiosity . . . life blood of
. . . c.
CURIOSITY, 9
civility C. costs nothing
COURTESY, 1
The reciprocal c. of authors
WRITERS, 11
civilization As c. advances, poetry . . . declines
CIVILIZATION, 8
C. is a method of living
CIVILIZATION, 1
C. is . . . equal respect for all men
CIVILIZATION, 1
How idiotic c. is
NAKEDNESS, 5
If people dug up the remains of this c.
ARTISTS, 16
It is so stupid of modern c.
DEVIL, 8
little in c. to appeal to a Yeti
CIVILIZATION, 7
Madam, I am the c. they are fighting to defend
WAR, 41
Our c. is founded on the shambles
DEATH, 63
The degree of a nation's c.
CIVILIZATION, 9
the Renaissance was . . . the green end of one of c.'s hardest
winters
CIVILIZATION, 5
without the usual interval of c.
AMERICA, 8
You can't say c. don't advance
PROGRESS, 1
civilized it proved that I was in a c. society
EXECUTION, 21
Woman will be the last thing c. by Man
WOMEN, 53
civil service British c. . . . effective braking mechanism
BUREAUCRACY, 10
clap Don't c. too hard
ENTHUSIASM, 6
clapped c. the glass to his sightless eye
BLINDNESS, 6
claret C. is the liquor for boys
ALCOHOL, 32
drink a dozen of C. on my Tomb
ALCOHOL, 35
look for the second cheapest c. . . . and say, 'Number 22'
ALCOHOL, 48
said of c.
ALCOHOL, 11
class an . . . young Englishman of our upper c.
ARISTOCRACY, 1
a special machine for the suppression of one c. by another
CAPITALISM, 7
Because there's no fourth c.
HUMILITY, 8
Discussion in c., which means
EDUCATION, 39
Every c. is unfit to govern
GOVERNMENT, 2
for one c. to appreciate the wrongs of another
CLASS, 32
For this c. we have . . . the designation of Philistines
PHILISTINISM, 1
Like many of the upper c.
ARISTOCRACY, 2
Poets and painters are outside the c. system
ARTISTS, 1
Poets and painters . . . constitute a special c.
POETS, 1
The constitution . . . first and second c. citizens
CLASS, 40
The history of all . . . society is the history of c. struggles
CLASS, 22
The one c. you do *not* belong to
CLASS, 23
the proletariat will . . . wage a c. struggle for Socialism
CLASS, 18
The state is an instrument . . . of the ruling c.
STATE, 5
Without c. differences, . . . living theatre
ENGLAND, 9
classes back the masses against the c.
CLASS, 14
Hats divide generally into three c.
CLOTHES, 19
I'm not interested in c.
CLASS, 20
responsible and the irresponsible c.
CLASS, 17
classical C. quotation is the *parole* of literary men
QUOTATIONS, 4
That's the c. mind at work
MIND, 5
The basic difference between c. music and jazz
MUSIC, 38
Classicism C., . . . the literature that gave . . . pleasure to their
great-grandfathers
LITERATURE, 16
classics Every man with a belly full of the c.
CLASSICS, 7
The c. are only primitive literature
CLASSICS, 6
clay absorbs a c. After his labours
SMOKING, 3
clean Bath . . . once a day to be passably c.
CLEANLINESS, 1
c. your plate
POLITICS, 64
hard to be funny when you have to be c.
HUMOUR, 28
clear His right was c., his will was strong
RIGHT, 1
if he could make *me* understand . . . it would be c. to all
UNDERSTANDING, 8
clearing-house the C. of the World
ECONOMICS, 5
cleft Rock of ages, c. for me
RELIGION, 59
Clementine Dwelt a miner, Forty-niner, And his daughter, C.
MOURNING, 7

clenched   You cannot shake hands with a c. fist
                                          INFLEXIBILITY, 2
Cleopatra   Had C.'s nose been shorter   APPEARANCE, 29
clergy   c. are men   CLERGY, 6
I never saw . . . the c. were beloved in any nation   CLERGY, 12
clergyman   c. whose mendicity is only equalled by their
mendacity   CLERGY, 13
good enough to be a c.   CLERGY, 9
clerk   diplomatic history is . . . what one c. said to another c.
                                          HISTORY, 37
the smartness of an attorney's c.   INSULTS, 15
clever   Be good, sweet maid, and let who can be c.   VIRTUE, 12
c. man . . . came of . . . stupid people INTELLIGENCE, 2
It's c., but is it art   ART, 12
never wise to try to appear . . . more c.   WISDOM, 24
no use trying to be c.   ACADEMICS, 3
To be c. enough to get . . . money, one must be stupid
                                          MATERIALISM, 6
cleverest   You're the c. member of . . . the c. nation in the
world   SELF-CONFIDENCE, 7
cleverness   height of c. is . . . to conceal it   INTELLIGENCE, 6
cliché   The c. is dead poetry   LANGUAGE, 3
climate   common where the c.'s sultry   ADULTERY, 1
If it's heaven for c.   PERVERSITY, 1
climb   Fain would I c., yet fear I to fall   AMBITION, 14
clime   change their c., not their frame of mind, who rush across
the sea   TRAVEL, 14
Clive   What I like about C.   DEATH, 26
clock   c. in the steeple strikes one   ALCOHOL, 68
grandfather's c.   CLOCKS, 2
Rock Around the C.   POP MUSIC, 11
Stands the Church c. at ten to three   NOSTALGIA, 3
The c. struck one, The mouse ran down   NURSERY RHYMES, 15
The mouse ran up the c.   NURSERY RHYMES, 15
clocks   hands of c. in railway stations   CHILDREN, 19
pass my declining years saluting . . . grandfather c.   OLD AGE, 31
the c. were striking the hour   TIME, 25
clogs   From c. to c.   POVERTY, 1
cloke   knyf under the c.   HYPOCRISY, 7
Clootie   Satan, Nick, or C.   DEVIL, 6
close   a breathless hush in the C. tonight   CRICKET, 1
regretted living so c. to Marie   LOVE, 103
closed   Mankind is a c. society   MANKIND, 25
the transition from the . . . 'c. society', . . . to the 'open society'
                                          SOCIETY, 5
closet   sleep in your c. rather than   ENGLISH, 8
close-up   Life is a tragedy . . . in c.   LIFE, 17
closing   c. time in the gardens of the West   CAPITALISM, 1
clothes   After that you just take the girl's c. off   ALCOHOL, 19
as if she were taking off all her c.   SEX, 16
bought her wedding c.   WOMEN, 7
enterprises that require new c.   THRIFT, 11
Fine c. are good   CLOTHES, 9
hanging the baby on the c. line to dry   INNOVATION, 2
Have you ever taken anything out of the c. basket
                                          CLEANNESS, 3
if it be our c. alone which fit us for society   CLOTHES, 4
most fun you can have with your c. on   ADVERTISING, 3
Nothing to wear but c.   PESSIMISM, 2
No woman so naked as . . . underneath her c.   NAKEDNESS, 4
walked away with their c.   POLITICS, 23
wrapped him in swaddling c.   CHRISTMAS, 7
cloud   Every c. has a silver lining   OPTIMISM, 2
fiend hid in a c.   BIRTH, 3
I wandered lonely as a c.   FLOWERS, 14
clouds   But trailing c. of glory   METAPHYSICS, 5
c. that gather round the setting sun   MORTALITY, 21
clout   Ne'er cast a c.   MONTHS, 2
clown   I remain just one thing . . . and that is a c.   HUMOUR, 6
club   I don't want to belong to any c.   HUMOUR, 46
Mankind is a c.   MANKIND, 12
takes you so far from the c. house   GOLF, 3
the best c. in London   HOUSES OF PARLIAMENT, 7
the most exclusive c. there is   ENGLISH, 9
cluster   The human face is . . . a whole c. of faces   MANKIND, 21
Clyde   the bonny banks of C.   SCOTLAND, 6
CMG   Members rise from C.   TITLES, 9
coach   c. and six horses through the Act of Settlement
                                          IRELAND, 13
indifference and a c. and six   LOVE, 40
coal   though the whole world turn to c.   VIRTUE, 11
coals   heap c. of fire upon his head   RETRIBUTION, 8

coaster   Dirty British c.   BOATS, 13
cobwebs   Laws are like c.   LAW, 27
laws were like c.   LAW, 6
Coca-Cola   the churches . . . bore for me the same relation to
God that billboards did to C.   RELIGION, 61
Coca Colas   Instead of drinking C.   WATER, 3
cocaine   C. isn't habit-forming   ADDICTION, 1
cock   He was like a c.   ARROGANCE, 3
That kept the c. that crowed in the morn   NURSERY RHYMES, 57
waiting for the c. to crow   BETRAYAL, 4
we owe a c. to Aesculapius   LAST WORDS, 65
cockles   Crying, C. and mussels! alive, alive, O   BUSINESS, 1
cockroach   to choose between him and a c. as a companion
                                          INSULTS, 46
cocksure   as c. of anything   SELF-CONFIDENCE, 3
cod   piece of c. passes all understanding   FOOD, 33
serve both c. and salmon   PUNS, 11
the c.'s wallop is always fresh made   COMMUNISM, 5
The home of the bean and the c.   SNOBBERY, 2
codfish   Unlike the male c. . . . the British aristocracy is
                                          ARISTOCRACY, 16
coffee   c. that's too black . . . You integrate it with cream
                                          RACISM, 19
C. which makes the politician wise   DRINKS, 6
measured out my life with c. spoons   LIFE, 23
coffee-house   c. is folly . . . to mistake the echo of a . . . c. for
the . . . kingdom   OPINIONS, 1
coffin   the silver plate on a c.   INSULTS, 32
cogito   C., ergo sum   THINKING, 4
coil   shuffled off this mortal c.   SUICIDE, 12
coke   Happiness is like c.   HAPPINESS, 11
cold   a period of c. peace   COLD WAR, 3
blow hot and c. with the same breath   INDECISION, 1
C. Pastoral   ETERNITY, 3
I beg c. comfort   COMFORT, 3
she should catch a c. on overexposure   TRUTH, 15
The Irish, . . . are needed in this c. age   IRISH, 4
we are . . . in the midst of a c. war   COLD WAR, 1
We called a c. a c.   ILLNESS, 2
coldly   c. she turns from their gaze, and weeps   MOURNING, 8
Coliseum   While stands the C., Rome shall stand   EUROPE, 5
collapse   Russia is a c., not a revolution   RUSSIA, 7
collapses   Force . . . c. through its own mass   JUDGMENT, 9
collar   no shirt or c. ever comes back twice   NEGLECT, 2
collections   those mutilators of c.   BORROWING, 6
collective   the greatest c. work of science   SCIENCE, 2
college   I am Master of this c.   ACADEMICS, 2
Like so many ageing c. people   ACADEMICS, 4
colleges   a liberal education at the C. of Unreason   REASON, 1
colonel   The gatling's jammed and the c. dead   WAR, 77
colonnade   whispering sound of the cool c.   TREES, 3
colour   an incurable disease – c. blindness   RACISM, 8
Any c., so long as it's black   CHOICE, 1
water, is unsuitable in c.   WATER, 5
coloured   I'm a c., one-eyed Jew   DISABILITY, 2; RACISM, 9
colourless   C. green ideas   NONSENSE, 10
colours   All c. will agree in the dark   DIFFERENCE, 7
clashed his c. together like cymbals   ARTISTS, 10
combine   When bad men c.   UNITY, 7
combustion   the Immaculate Conception was spontaneous c.
                                          CATHOLICISM, 9
come   C. what come may   TIME, 32
Mr Watson, c. here; I want you   SUMMONS, 3
O c. all ye faithful   CHRISTMAS, 16
Thou'lt c. no more   MOURNING, 9
Whistle and she'll c. to you   SUMMONS, 1
Why don't you c. up sometime   MISQUOTATIONS, 23;
                                          INVITATIONS, 3
Will ye no c. back again   RETURN, 3
comedian   A c. can only last   HUMOUR, 24
comedies   c. are ended by a marriage   THEATRE, 4
comedy   All I need to make a c.   HUMOUR, 5
at a c. we only look   THEATRE, 8
C. is if I walk into an open sewer and die   THEATRE, 3
C., like sodomy, is an unnatural act   HUMOUR, 12
C., we may say, is society   HUMOUR, 23
Farce refined becomes high c.   THEATRE, 7
Life is . . . a c. in long-shot   LIFE, 17
What a fine c. this world would be   LIFE, 20
world is a c. to those who think   LIFE, 51
comes   Everything c. to him who waits   PATIENCE, 2
comfort   carrion c., Despair, not feast on thee   DESPAIR, 4

From ignorance our c. flows — IGNORANCE, 12
I beg cold c. — COMFORT, 3
thought of suicide is a great . . . c. — SUICIDE, 6
Two loves I have, of c. and despair — CONFLICT, 7
until his friends came to c. him — ENDURANCE, 8
comfortable to be baith grand and c. — LUXURY, 1
comfortably Are you sitting c.? Then I'll begin — BEGINNING, 13
comic It is so c. to hear oneself called old — OLD AGE, 23
coming C. through the rye — LOVE, 34
he . . . c. after me is preferred before me — CHRISTIANITY, 11
command mortals to c. success — SUCCESS, 3
one of those born neither to obey nor to c. — NASTINESS, 5
people c. rather badly — OBEDIENCE, 2
commandments fear God, and keep his c. — GOD, 9
Where there aren't no Ten C. — DESIRE, 9
commas absence of inverted c. guarantees . . . originality — QUOTATIONS, 2
commend forced to c. her highly — INSINCERITY, 3
into thy hands I c. my spirit — LAST WORDS, 10
commended The man who gets angry . . . in the right way . . . is c. — ANGER, 1
commendeth obliquely c. himself — CRITICISM, 7
comment C. is free but facts are sacred — JOURNALISM, 27
commentators rather give me c. plain — CLARITY, 1
commerce Friendship is a disinterested c. between equals — LOVE AND FRIENDSHIP, 2
honour sinks where c. long prevails — BUSINESS, 12
commercing looks c. with the skies — SOUL, 10
commission A Royal C. is a broody hen — BUREAUCRACY, 6
Each bullet has got its c. — MORTALITY, 4
commit woman alone, can . . . c. them — SEXES, 24
committee A c. is a cul-de-sac — BUREAUCRACY, 4
A c. should consist of three men — DEMOCRACY, 18
The number one book . . . was written by a c. — BIBLE, 8
commodity C., *Firmness*, and *Delight* — ARCHITECTURE, 14
common C. Law of England — LAW, 15
C. sense is the collection of prejudices — PREJUDICE, 3
good thing, to make it too c. — ENGLAND, 37
He nothing c. did or mean — EXECUTION, 7
lose the c. touch — IDEALISM, 2
seldom attribute c. sense — AGREEMENT, 4
the happiness of the c. man — GOVERNMENT, 6
The trivial round, the c. task — SIMPLICITY, 4
'Tis education forms the c. mind — EDUCATION, 44
trained and organized c. sense — SCIENCE, 20
common-looking The Lord prefers c. people — APPEARANCE, 21
common man I have no concern for the c. — PUBLIC, 21
commonplace nothing so unnatural as the c. — TRIVIALITY, 7
renders . . . c. things and characters interesting — WRITERS, 81
unassuming c. Of Nature — FLOWERS, 13
commonplaces c. are the great poetic truths — TRIVIALITY, 13
Commons The C., faithful to their system — GOVERNMENT, 16
Commonwealth a C. of Nations — BRITISH EMPIRE, 7
turn to the wider vision of the C. — POLITICS, 48
Communism arrested under the Suppression of C. Act — OPPRESSION, 2
C. continued to haunt Europe as a spectre — COMMUNISM, 10
C. is like prohibition — COMMUNISM, 6
C. is Soviet power plus the electrification — COMMUNISM, 4
For us in Russia c. is a dead dog — COMMUNISM, 7
communist Every c. has a fascist frown — COMMUNISM, 8; FASCISM, 4
your grandson will . . . be a C. — COMMUNISM, 3
Communists Catholics and C. have committed great crimes — COMMITMENT, 4
In Germany, the Nazis came for the C. — NAZISM, 4
community journalism. . . . keeps us in touch with the ignorance of the c. — JOURNALISM, 32
Marriage . . . a c. . . . making in all two — MARRIAGE, 29
the c. of Europe — EUROPE, 15
commute the agricultural labourers . . . c. from London — COUNTRYSIDE, 7
commuter C. . . . riding to and from his wife — TRAVEL, 31
compact the damned, c., liberal majority — MAJORITY, 4
companion to choose between him and a cockroach as a c. — INSULTS, 46
companionable so c. as solitude — SOLITUDE, 13
companions Boys . . . are unwholesome c. for grown people — CHILDREN, 31
c. for middle age — MARRIAGE, 13
company better to be alone than in bad c. — FRIENDS, 15

c., . . . have neither a soul to lose nor a body to kick — BUSINESS, 22
Crowds without c. — LONDON, 7
find myself in the c. of scientists — SCIENTISTS, 1
I've been offered titles . . . get one into disreputable c. — TITLES, 11
pleasure of your c. — MOUNTAINS, 2
Take the tone of the c. — CONFORMITY, 3
Tell me what c. thou keepest — FRIENDS, 7
You never expected justice from a c. — BUSINESS, 22
comparative progress is simply a c. — PROGRESS, 3
compare any she belied with false c. — ANALOGY, 4
c. thee to a summer's day — COMPLIMENTS, 4
Learn, c., collect the facts — EDUCATION, 42
compared The war we have just been through, . . . is not to be c. — WAR, 135
comparisons c. are odious — ANALOGY, 2
C. are odorous — MALAPROPISMS, 2
compass my heart shall be The faithful c. — FAITHFULNESS, 4
compassion But a certain Samaritan . . . had c. on him — CHARITY, 8
competition happiest conversation where there is no c. — CONVERSATION, 5
complacency c. and satisfaction . . . in . . . a new-married couple — MARRIAGE, 75
complain one hardly knows to whom to c. — COMPLAINTS, 2
complaint Anno domini . . . the most fatal c. — DEATH, 61
how is the old c. — MEMORY, 5
I want to register a c. — COMPLAINTS, 5
complaints The imaginary c. of indestructible old ladies — HYPOCHONDRIA, 3
complete now I feel like a c. idiot — INFERIORITY, 1
complex Wherever an inferiority c. exists, there is . . . reason — INFERIORITY, 2
compliance by a timely c. — SEX, 18
compliment returned the c. — GOD, 50
compose Never c. . . . unless . . . not composing . . . becomes a positive nuisance — MUSIC, 24
composed When I c. that, I was . . . inspired by God — MUSIC, 9
composer A good c. does not imitate — MUSICIANS, 9
composition difference between . . . prose and metrical c. — POETRY AND PROSE, 7
comprehended c. two aspicious persons — MALAPROPISMS, 1
compromise All government . . . is founded on c. and barter — COMPROMISE, 4
C. used to mean that half a loaf — COMPROMISE, 5
not a question that leaves much room for c. — SELF-PRESERVATION, 7
compulsion seized by the stern hand of C. — WOMEN, 81
compulsory c. and irreproachable idleness — ARMY, 3
computers so many c. . . . use them in the search for love — CRITICISM, 53
comrade stepping where his c. stood — COURAGE, 18
comrades Bleach the bones of c. slain — WAR, 51
conceal Addresses . . . c. our whereabouts — ADDRESSES, 1
height of cleverness is . . . to c. it — INTELLIGENCE, 6
speech only to c. their thoughts — HUMAN NATURE, 24
concealed Much truth is spoken, . . . more . . . c. — TRUTH, 19
concealing Good breeding consists in c. how . . . we think of ourselves — MANNERS, 5
concealment c., like a worm i' th' bud — LOVE, 126
conceit C. is the finest armour — CONCEIT, 1
conceited I would grow intolerably c. — CONCEIT, 21
what man will do any good who is not c. — SELF-RESPECT, 2
concept If the c. of God has — RELIGION, 6
conception if the dad is present at the c. — SEX, 42
the Immaculate C. was spontaneous combustion — CATHOLICISM, 9
concepts walks up the stairs of his c. — MANKIND, 30
concessions The c. of the weak are the c. of fear — YIELDING, 1
conclusions Life is the art of drawing . . . c. — LIFE, 16
concord toleration produced . . . religious c. — RELIGION, 28
Yes – around C. — TRAVEL, 30
concurrence fortuitous c. of atoms — CHANCE, 4
condemn No man can justly censure or c. another — JUDGMENT, 5
condemned If God were suddenly c. to live the life — HUMAN CONDITION, 4
Man is c. to be free — FREEDOM, 47
condemning One should examine oneself . . . before . . . c. others — SELF, 11
condition fools decoyed into our c. — MARRIAGE, 91
hopes for the human c. — PESSIMISM, 4

The c. of man . . . is a c. of war HUMAN CONDITION, 10
the Jews have made a contribution to the human c. JEWS, 14
To be a poet is a c. POETS, 6
wearisome c. of humanity HUMAN CONDITION, 9
conditioned Americans have been c. to respect newness
AMERICANS, 11
conditions my people live in such awful c. POVERTY, 12
condoms hope people will learn to love c. AIDS, 3
conduct C. . . . to the prejudice of good order and military
discipline ARMY, 2
conductor c. has the advantage MUSICIANS, 3
conference naked into the c. chamber WEAPONS, 1
confess It's easy to make a man c. . . . lies TRUTH, 27
Men will c. HUMOUR, 8
only c. our little faults IMPERFECTION, 11
We c. our bad qualities . . . out of fear SELF-KNOWLEDGE, 2
confessing I am ashamed of c. INNOCENCE, 5
women . . . ill-using them and then c. it WOMEN, 83
confidence never dedicated to something you have complete c.
in FANATICISM, 4
Three addresses always inspire c. ADDRESSES, 2
confident There are two things which I am c. I can do very
well CRITICISM, 18
confin'd cabin'd, cribb'd, c., bound in FEAR, 11
confined I should hardly like to live . . . in their elegant but c.
houses · WRITERS, 36
conflict We are in an armed c. WAR, 36
conform how to rebel and c. at the same time YOUTH, 5
conformable Nature is very consonant and c. NATURE, 12
confound the weak things of the world to c. the . . . mighty
WISDOM AND FOOLISHNESS, 3
Congreve C. is the only sophisticated playwright WRITERS, 88
Congs Kinquering C. their titles take SPOONERISMS, 3
connect Only c. COMMUNICATION, 1
conquer in the end the truth will c. TRUTH, 44
They will c., but . . . not convince PERSUASION, 1
We'll fight and we'll c. COURAGE, 13
when we c. without danger VICTORY, 3
conquered I came; I saw; God c. VICTORY, 16
I came, I saw, I c. VICTORY, 1
I will be c.; I will not capitulate DETERMINATION, 9
the English seem . . . to have c. and peopled half the world
BRITISH EMPIRE, 8
conquering C. kings ROYALTY, 9
not c. but fighting well VICTORY, 4
See, the c. hero comes VICTORY, 12
conquest The Roman C. was, however, a *Good Thing*
HISTORY, 29
conscience a Nonconformist c. WOMEN, 91
As guardian of His Majesty's c. MONARCHY, 23
c. does make cowards of us all CONSCIENCE, 5
C. is a coward CONSCIENCE, 3
C. is the inner voice CONSCIENCE, 4
C. is the internal perception of the rejection of a particular wish
CONSCIENCE, 2
dilemmas of c. and egotism POWER, 22
freedom of speech, freedom of c., and the prudence never to
practise . . . them FREEDOM, 50
I cannot . . . cut my c. to fit this year's fashions INTEGRITY, 3
I'll catch the c. of the King PLAYS, 11
Now war has a bad c. WAR, 55
Science without c. SCIENCE, 35
why is my liberty judged of another man's c. CONSCIENCE, 1;
FREEDOM, 3
consent No one can make you feel inferior without your c.
INFERIORITY, 5
consequence physicians . . . mistake subsequence for c.
DOCTORS, 5
consequences men never violate the laws of God without
suffering the c. RETRIBUTION, 9
conservatism c. . . . adherence to the old and tried
CONSERVATISM, 5
c. is based upon the idea CONSERVATISM, 1
conservative C. government is an organized hypocrisy
POLITICS, 22
Or else a little C. POLITICS, 32
The radical invents the views. . . . the c. adopts them
CONSERVATISM, 7
to what is called the Tory . . . called the C., party POLITICS, 21
which makes a man more c. CONSERVATISM, 4
consider When I c. how my light is spent BLINDNESS, 5
considerable to appear c. in his native place FAME, 12

consistency C. is contrary to nature CONSTANCY, 2
consonant Nature is very c. and conformable NATURE, 12
conspiracy not a Party, it is a c. COMMUNISM, 1
People of the same trade . . . conversation ends in a c.
BUSINESS, 21
conspirators All the c. NOBILITY, 4
constabulary When c. duty's to be done POLICE, 1
constant A c. guest HOSPITALITY, 1
Friendship is c. in all other things LOVE AND FRIENDSHIP, 3
constitution The c. . . . first and second class citizens
CLASS, 40
The principles of a free c. GOVERNMENT, 10
constitutional A c. king must learn to stoop MONARCHY, 13
c. right DEMOCRACY, 10
definition of a c. statesman POLITICIANS, 1
construction Our object in the c. of the state REPUBLIC, 1
consultations dictator . . . always take some c.
AUTHORITARIANISM, 6
consulted the right to be c., . . . to encourage, . . . to warn
MONARCHY, 2
consume more history than they can c. EUROPE, 14
statistics, born to c. resources STATISTICS, 3
consumer In a c. society there are . . . two kinds of slaves
MATERIALISM, 10
consumes Man . . . c. without producing CAPITALISM, 10
consummation a c. Devoutly to be wish'd SUICIDE, 12
consumption Conspicuous c. . . . is a means of reputability
MATERIALISM, 20
this c. of the purse MONEY, 41
contemplates Beauty in things exists in the mind which c.
them BEAUTY, 21
contemplation right mindfulness, right c. RELIGION, 9
contemporary I am no one's c. – ever DENIAL, 2
to trade a hundred c. readers for POSTERITY, 6
contempt attention to the inside . . . c. for the outside
BOOKS, 14
she was only an Object of C. CONTEMPT, 1
To show pity is felt as a sign of c. SYMPATHY, 5
contemptible c. little Army WAR, 133; WORLD WAR I, 25
content desire is got without c. CONTENTMENT, 6
contented How is it . . . that no one lives c. with his lot
DISCONTENT, 4
If you are foolish enough to be c., don't show it COMPLAINTS, 3
With what I most enjoy c. least DISCONTENT, 8
contentment Where wealth and freedom reign, c. fails
BUSINESS, 12
contests mighty c. rise from trivial things RESULTS, 5
continence Give me chastity and c. PROCRASTINATION, 4
that melancholy sexual perversion known as c. ABSTINENCE, 6
continent On the C. people have good food MANNERS, 4
continental C. people have sex life ENGLISH, 24
continual c. state of inelegance WEATHER, 7
continuation All diplomacy is a c. of war DIPLOMACY, 14
War is the c. of politics WAR, 30
contraception a terrific story about oral c. CONTRACEPTION, 2
contraceptive It's like having a totally efficient c. FUTURE, 5
contraceptives C. should be used CONTRACEPTION, 6
Skullion had little use for c. CONTRACEPTION, 7
contract Every law is a c. LAW, 22
Marriage is . . . but a civil c. MARRIAGE, 101
contradict Do I c. myself SELF, 21
contradiction brook no c. DOCTORS, 9
Man is . . . an everlasting c. to himself INTELLECT, 3
Woman's at best a c. WOMEN, 67
contrairy everythink goes c. with me MISFORTUNE, 9
contraries Without C. is no progression CONFLICT, 4
contrariwise 'C.,' continued Tweedledee LOGIC, 1
contrary Mary, Mary, quite c. GARDENS, 1; NURSERY RHYMES, 33
On the c. LAST WORDS, 40
control we ought to c. our thoughts SELF-CONTROL, 3
controversies savage c. . . . no good evidence either way
ARGUMENTS, 14
controversy that c. is either superfluous or hopeless
ARGUMENTS, 12
convenient modern view of life is always to seek what is more
c. DISEASE, 37
Nobody is forgotten when it is c. to remember him
EXPEDIENCY, 3
convent To enter the . . . Ballet is to enter a c. DANCING, 8
convention a c. which says you must not make species extinct
CONSERVATION, 7
conventional The c. army loses if it does not win WAR, 58

conventionally to fail c.	ORTHODOXY, 3
conversation a c. with the finest men	LITERATURE, 3
And third-rate c.	MEDIOCRITY, 6
a proper subject of c.	RELIGION, 14
C. . . . elicits secrets from us	CONVERSATION, 8
C. has a kind of charm	CONVERSATION, 8
c. must be an exchange of thought	CONVERSATION, 7
happiest c. where there is no competition	CONVERSATION, 5
make his c. perfectly delightful	INSULTS, 35
Questioning is not the mode of c.	CONVERSATION, 4
There is no such thing as c.	CONVERSATION, 2
Writing . . . is but a different name for c.	WRITING, 31
Your ignorance cramps my c.	IGNORANCE, 8
conversationalist the c. who adds 'in other words'	
	CONVERSATION, 6
conversing Even when c. he could not keep still	WRITERS, 76
converted difficult for a Jew to be c.	JEWS, 6
convince They will conquer, but . . . not c.	PERSUASION, 1
cook a good c., as cooks go	HUMOUR, 52
Any c. should be able to	GOVERNMENT, 14
C. is a little unnerved	ETIQUETTE, 1
ill c. that cannot lick his own fingers	SELF-CONFIDENCE, 4
she was a very bad c.	SNOBBERY, 9
cookery c. do	FOOD, 37
cooking woman accepted c. . . . but man . . . made of it a	
recreation	FOOD, 43
cooks Too many c.	HELP, 5
Coolidge C. is a better example of evolution	POLITICIANS, 66
copier c. of nature can never produce anything great	
	IMITATION, 4
copies more c. of my works are left behind	WRITERS, 32
copulation Birth, and c., and death	LIFE AND DEATH, 4
copy A lotta cats c. the Mona Lisa	IMITATION, 1
copying by defying their parents and c. one another	YOUTH, 5
coral C. is far more red	ANALOGY, 3
Of his bones are c. made	DEATH, 107
cord a threefold c. is not quickly broken	UNITY, 5
cordial gold in phisik is a c.	MATERIALISM, 5
cordiale La c. entente	DIPLOMACY, 15
corn amid the alien c.	BIRDS, 7
make two ears of c. . . . grow . . . where only one grew before	
	POLITICIANS, 26
That ate the c.	NURSERY RHYMES, 57
the meadows rich with c.	AMERICA, 35
corner a c. in the thing I love	JEALOUSY, 6
some c. of a foreign field	WAR, 18
corners people standing in the c. of our rooms	TELEVISION, 1
Cornish twenty thousand C. men	EXECUTION, 10
Coromandel On the Coast of C.	NONSENSE, 16
coronets Kind hearts are more than c.	ARISTOCRACY, 12
corps English characteristic . . . esprit de c.	ENGLISH, 3
corpse He'd make a lovely c.	DEATH, 41
he makes a very handsome c.	DEATH, 56
corpses They are for prima donnas or c. . . .	FLOWERS, 11
corpuscles make the c. of the blood glow	JEWS, 8
correct Astronomy teaches the c. use	ASTRONOMY, 4
correction It is a stupidity . . . to busy oneself with the c. of	
the world	IMPROVEMENT, 3
correctly anxious to do the wrong thing c.	ETIQUETTE, 7
corridors c. of power	POWER, 22
corroboration c . . . . in the records of Somerset House	
	HUMILITY, 11
corrupt Among a people generally c.	CORRUPTION, 1
power is apt to c.	POWER, 19
Power tends to c.	POWER, 3
corrupted They had been c. by money	SENTIMENTALITY, 1
corruptible born again, not of c. seed	DEATH, 29
corruption C., the most infallible symptom of constitutional	
liberty	CORRUPTION, 2
corrupts lack of power c. absolutely	POWER, 24
corse As his c. to the rampart	FUNERALS, 10
cosmetic sunlight as a kind of c. effulgence	SUN, 4
cosmetics In the factory we make c.	COSMETICS, 3
cosmopolitan I was told I am a true c.	MELANCHOLY, 11
cosmos c. is about the smallest hole	UNIVERSE, 5
cost To give and not to count the c.	SELFLESSNESS, 2
cottage Love and a c.	LOVE, 40
poorest man may in his c. bid defiance to . . . the Crown	
	PRIVACY, 3
to refer to your friend's country establishment as a 'c.'	
	WORDS, 17

cottages Pale Death kicks his way equally into the c. of the	
poor	EQUALITY, 28
couch the century of the psychiatrist's c.	PSYCHIATRY, 8
time as a tool not as a c.	TIME, 22
when on my c. I lie	SOLITUDE, 15
cough Jeeves coughed one soft, low, gentle c.	ANALOGY, 5
coughing keeping people from c.	ACTING, 9
council The grotesque chaos of a Labour c.	INCOMPETENCE, 2
counsel C. of her country's gods	BRITAIN, 7
sometimes c. take – and sometimes Tea	DRINKS, 7
count Don't c. your chickens	ANTICIPATION, 4
If you can . . . c. your money you are not . . . rich man	
	WEALTH, 15
To give and not to c. the cost	SELFLESSNESS, 2
countenance the Lord lift up his c. upon thee	BLESSING, 4
counter-democratic Proportional Representation . . . is	
fundamentally c.	POLITICS, 44
counterpoint Too much c.; what is worse, Protestant c.	
	CRITICISM, 3
counties see the coloured c.	COUNTRYSIDE, 6
countries preferreth all c. before his own	DISCONTENT, 7
country absolved from all duty to his c.	MARRIAGE, 90
a c. diversion	COUNTRYSIDE, 1
A c. governed by a despot	TYRANNY, 7
a c. of young men	AMERICA, 13
affections must be confined . . . to a single c.	PATRIOTISM, 10
A man should know something of his own c.	TRAVEL, 26
an honest man sent to lie abroad for . . . his c.	DIPLOMACY, 21
Anybody can be good in the c.	COUNTRYSIDE, 10
Anyone who loves his c., follow me	PATRIOTISM, 11
Counsel of her c.'s gods	BRITAIN, 7
c. from whose bourn no traveller returns	AFTERLIFE, 9
God made the c.	COUNTRYSIDE, 9
go down into the c.	DECEPTION, 7
Great artists have no c.	NATIONALITY, 7
How I leave my c.	LAST WORDS, 51
I have but one life to lose for my c.	PATRIOTISM, 13
I love thee still, My c.	PATRIOTISM, 7
I would die for my c.	PATRIOTISM, 20
loathe the c.	COUNTRYSIDE, 1
My c., right or wrong	PATRIOTISM, 5
nothing good . . . in the c.	COUNTRYSIDE, 4
Our c. is the world	AMERICA, 14
our c., right or wrong	PATRIOTISM, 8
proud of the position of the bungalow, . . . in the c.	SUBURBIA, 2
she is my c. still	PATRIOTISM, 6
That is no c. for old men	MORTALITY, 23
The history of every c. begins in the heart	HISTORY, 9
The idiot who praises . . . every c. but his own	DISCONTENT, 2
The past is a foreign c.	PAST, 5
The soil of our c.	RACISM, 20
The undiscover'd c.	AFTERLIFE, 9
This c. . . . belongs to the people who inhabit it	DEMOCRACY, 10
to leave his c. as good as he had found it	DUTY, 1
understanding the problems of running a c.	POLITICS, 78
we can die but once to serve our c.	PATRIOTISM, 1
what was good for our c.	BUSINESS, 28
When I am in the c. I wish to vegetate	COUNTRYSIDE, 5
countryside a more dreadful record of sin than . . . c.	SIN, 12
c. is one of the most heavily man-made habitats	
	CONSERVATION, 8
county The sound of the English c. families	ARISTOCRACY, 15
couple A married c. are well suited	MARRIAGE, 15
couples so many c. . . . not getting the right proteins	SEX, 12
courage be strong and of a good c.	GOD, 8
C. is the price . . . for granting peace	COURAGE, 12
c. to love . . . courage to suffer	LOVE, 140
good deal of physical c. to ride a horse	ALCOHOL, 40; HORSES, 8
tale . . . of . . . c. of my companions	ENDURANCE, 16
The Red Badge of C.	COURAGE, 7
three o'clock in the morning c.	COURAGE, 24
Whistling aloud to bear his c. up	WHISTLING, 1
course c. of true love never did run smooth	LOVE, 119
courteous If a man be . . . c. to strangers	COURTESY, 3
courtesy C. is not dead	COURTESY, 4
courting When you are c. a nice girl	SCIENCE, 12
courts I have come to regard . . . c. . . . as a casino	JUSTICE, 11
the case is still before the c.	ARGUMENTS, 1
courtship C. to marriage	MARRIAGE, 39
covenant a c. between me and the earth	PROMISES, 2
a c. with death	SLAVERY, 2
cover Never judge a c. by its book	BOOKS, 24

covet thou shalt not c.   GOD, 10
cow A c. is a very good animal in the field   SUITABILITY, 2
That milked the c. with the crumpled horn   NURSERY RHYMES, 57
The c. is of the bovine ilk   ANIMALS, 16
The c. jumped over the moon   NURSERY RHYMES, 14
till the c. comes home   ETERNITY, 1
Truth, Sir, is a c.   SCEPTICISM, 3
Why buy a c.   FUTILITY, 1
coward better to be the widow of a hero than the wife of a c.   COURAGE, 15
Conscience is a c.   CONSCIENCE, 3
No c. soul is mine   COURAGE, 3
None but a c. . . . has never known fear   COWARDICE, 7
The c. does it with a kiss   KILLING, 8
cowardice guilty of Noël C.   COWARDICE, 1
cowardly Marriage is the only adventure open to the c.   MARRIAGE, 125
cowards C. die many times   COWARDICE, 9
the future . . . makes c. of us   PRESENT, 3
Thus conscience does make c. of us all   CONSCIENCE, 5
cowboy easier to get an actor to be a c.   ACTING, 6
cows daring . . . to explain . . . that c. can be eaten   RELIGION, 27
'Horses' should have read 'C.'   MISTAKES, 10
The c. in the corn   NURSERY RHYMES, 28
coxcomb to hear a c. ask two hundred guineas   CRITICISM, 18
coyness This c., lady, were no crime   SHYNESS, 5
compassion C. is not a sloppy, sentimental feeling   SOCIALISM, 8
cracked The c. looking glass of a servant   IRELAND, 9
cradle Between the c. and the grave   TRANSIENCE, 12
Rocked in the c. of the deep   SEA, 11
The hand that rocks the c.   INFLUENCE, 9
cradles bit the babies in the c.   ANIMALS, 5
craft the c. so long to lerne   MORTALITY, 3
The life so short, the c. so long to learn   MORTALITY, 12
craftsmanship Skill without imagination is c.   ART, 26
crafty too c. a woman to invent a new lie   LYING, 9
cranny We seek . . . In every c. but the right   PERVERSITY, 3
crap Books are a load of c.   BOOKS, 22
Craven why and how I became . . . mistress of the Earl of C.   SEX, 64
crazy going to go c., living this epidemic every minute   DISEASE, 24
grow a little c. . . . like all men at sea   MADNESS, 5
cream coffee that's too black . . . You integrate it with c.   RACISM, 19
create My father didn't c. you to arrest me   POLICE, 6
created God c. . . . the earth   CREATION, 2
man alone leaves traces of what he c.   MANKIND, 8
Man, . . . had been c. to jab the life out of Germans   WAR, 99
Thou hast c. us for Thyself   HUMAN CONDITION, 2
we cannot be c. for this sort of suffering   AFTERLIFE, 6
creates he c. Gods by the dozen   RELIGION, 47
creation greatest week . . . since the c.   SPACE, 6
Had I been present at the C.   UNIVERSE, 1
The art of c. is older   CREATION, 16
creator All right, my lord c., Don Miguel   DEATH, 69
c. had a purpose in equipping us with a neck   COURAGE, 45
Man . . . hasn't been a c., only a destroyer   ECOLOGY, 3
virtue in the c. is not the same as virtue in the creature   CREATION, 12
creature No c. smarts . . . as a fool   FOOLISHNESS, 17
the c. hath a purpose and its eyes are bright with it   PURPOSE, 5
Who kills a man kills a reasonable c.   BOOKS, 27
creatures call these delicate c. ours   JEALOUSY, 6
From fairest c. we desire increase   BEAUTY, 36
credentials no c. . . . not even . . . a certificate of birth   ARISTOCRACY, 8
credit The way to get things done is not to mind who gets the c.   SELFLESSNESS, 1
creditors my oldest c. would hardly know me   APPEARANCE, 14
not everyone who wishes makes c.   BORROWING, 7
credits c. would still read 'Rubinstein, God, and Piatigorsky'   EGOTISM, 6
credulity C. is . . . the child's strength   INNOCENCE, 7
creed got the better of his c.   RELIGION, 54
the c. of a second-rate man   POLITICIANS, 3
wrought . . . the c. of creeds   CHRISTIANITY, 43
creeds So many gods, so many c.   RELIGION, 70; KINDNESS, 6
Vain are the thousand c.   BELIEF, 3

creep I wants to make your flesh c.   FEAR, 8
Wit that can c.   SERVILITY, 5
creepers Jeepers C.   EYES, 2
creetur lone lorn c.   MISFORTUNE, 9
crème you would have been the c. de la c.   EXCELLENCE, 3
Crete The people of C. . . . make more history   EUROPE, 14
cricket c. as organised loafing   CRICKET, 7
c. is the greatest thing that God ever created   CRICKET, 6
I do love c. – it's so very English   CRICKET, 2; FOOTBALL, 2
If the French noblesse had been capable of playing c. with their peasants   ARISTOCRACY, 13; CRICKET, 8
It's not in support of c.   CRICKET, 1; GOLF, 1
the c. on the hearth   MELANCHOLY, 9
where the c. sings   PEACE, 18
Cricklewood Midland, bound for C.   TRAVEL, 4
cried I c. all the way to the bank   CRITICISM, 29
crieth thy brother's blood c. unto me   MURDER, 2
crime all c. is due to the repressed desire for aesthetic expression   CRIME, 6
Arson, after all, is an artificial c.   FIRE, 5
C., like virtue, has its degrees   CRIME, 5
Do you call poverty a c.   POVERTY, 30
If poverty is the mother of c., stupidity is its father   CRIME, 4
man's greatest c.   BIRTH, 4
no . . . c. so shameful as poverty   POVERTY, 8
The atrocious c. of being a young man   YOUTH, 14
the Napoleon of c.   CRIME, 3
The punishment fit the c.   PUNISHMENT, 10
This coyness, lady, were no c.   SHYNESS, 5
Treason was no C.   TREASON, 2
worse than a c., it is a blunder   MISTAKES, 4
crimes Catholics and Communists have committed great c.   COMMITMENT, 4
history . . . a tableau of c. and misfortunes   HISTORY, 35
how many c. committed   CRIME, 2
Oh liberty! . . . What c. are committed in thy name   EXECUTION, 27; FREEDOM, 44
Crippen strong suspicions that C. London cellar murderer   TECHNOLOGY, 7; TELEGRAMS, 9
crisp Deep and c. and even   CHRISTMAS, 15
critic A c. is a man who   CRITICS, 20
A good c. . . . narrates the adventures of his mind   CRITICS, 5
A good drama c. is   CRITICS, 21
c. spits on what is done   CRITICS, 8
Nor in the c. let the man be lost   CRITICS, 14
the function of the c.   CRITICS, 1
critical c. judgement is so exquisite   CRITICS, 6
nothing if not c.   CRITICISM, 46
criticism A great deal of contemporary c.   CRITICISM, 8
As far as c. is concerned   CRITICISM, 52
c. is a letter to the public   CRITICISM, 41
my own definition of c.   CRITICISM, 1
People ask you for c.   CRITICISM, 34
The Stealthy School of C.   CRITICISM, 43
criticize don't c. What you can't understand   CHANGE, 6
criticizing The pleasure of c.   CRITICISM, 26
critics Asking a working writer . . . about c.   CRITICS, 7
c. all are ready made   CRITICS, 2
C. are more malicious about poetry   CRITICS, 9
c. . . . desire our blood, not our pain   CRITICS, 13
music c. . . . . small and rodent-like with padlocked ears   CRITICS, 18
The greater part of c. are parasites   CRITICS, 16
crocodile An appeaser is one who feeds a c.   DIPLOMACY, 6
crocodiles wisdom of the c.   HYPOCRISY, 5
Cromwell Caesar had his Brutus – Charles the First, his C.   TREASON, 4
restless C. could not cease   POLITICIANS, 60
ruins that C. knocked about a bit   INNUENDO, 2
crony government by c.   NEPOTISM, 1
crook A writer of c. stories   POLITICS, 85
I am not a c.   DENIAL, 3
the symbol of a bishop is a c.   CLERGY, 5
crooked the c. timber of humanity   HUMAN NATURE, 15
There was a c. man, and he walked a c. mile   NURSERY RHYMES, 52
crop watering the last year's c.   FUTILITY, 6
crops Man . . . Laid the c. low   AGRICULTURE, 5
cross Don't c. the bridge   ANTICIPATION, 2
Hot c. buns! . . . One a penny, two a penny   NURSERY RHYMES, 16
no c., no crown   ENDURANCE, 12

The orgasm has replaced the C. — SEX, 40
When I survey the wondrous C. — HUMILITY, 13
cross-bow With my c. I shot — BIRDS, 1
crossed a girl likes to be c. in love a little now and then — WOMEN, 9
crosses wooden c. on the roadside — WORLD WAR I, 16
crossword an optimist . . . fills up his c. puzzle in ink — OPTIMISM, 25
crow sun had risen to hear him c. — ARROGANCE, 3
waiting for the cock to c. — BETRAYAL, 4
crowd a c. like that . . . brings a lump to my wallet — MATERIALISM, 22
And hid his face amid a c. of stars — LOVE, 150
Far from the madding c. — SOLITUDE, 7
crowds C. without company — LONDON, 7
If you can talk with c. and keep your virtue — IDEALISM, 2
It brings men together in c. and mobs in bar-rooms — SOCIETY, 9
crown no cross, no c. — ENDURANCE, 12
poorest man . . . bid defiance to . . . the C. — PRIVACY, 3
the c. of life — TEMPTATION, 4
The influence of the C. has increased — MONARCHY, 9
Uneasy lies the head that wears a c. — MONARCHY, 21
within the hollow c. — ROYALTY, 30
crucible America is God's C. — AMERICA, 40
crucified Where the dear Lord was c. — CHRISTIANITY, 1
you might try getting c. — CHRISTIANITY, 41
crucify Diseases c. the soul of man — DISEASE, 11
Do you want to c. the boy — CHRISTIANITY, 25
cruel A c. story runs on wheels — CRUELTY, 4
C., but composed and bland — CATS, 1
cruellest April is the c. month — MONTHS, 8
cruelty Man's inhumanity to man
we are all on our last c. — MORTALITY, 18
crumbs c. which fell from the rich man's table — POVERTY AND WEALTH, 2
cry I often want to c. — SEXES, 19
make 'em c. — WRITING, 27
mother, do not c. — LAST WORDS, 23
She likes stories that make her c. — SENTIMENTALITY, 5
the c. of him that ruleth among fools — WISDOM, 3
the only advantage women have over men – . . . they can c. — SEXES, 19
We think caged birds sing, when indeed they c. — IMPRISONMENT, 6
when we c. to Thee — SEA, 14
crying An infant c. in the night — HUMAN CONDITION, 20
It is no use c. — REGRET, 1
cubic One c. foot less — SMALLNESS, 3
cuckoo the c. clock was invented . . . to give tourists something solid — SWITZERLAND, 1
The c. comes in April — MONTHS, 3
This is the weather the c. likes — WEATHER, 12
cucumber A c. should be well sliced — FOOD, 28
cucumbers they are but c. after all — CRITICISM, 25
cul-de-sac A committee is a c. — BUREAUCRACY, 4
cult local c. called Christianity — CHRISTIANITY, 28
What's a c. — MINORITY, 1
cultivate c. our garden — PAROCHIALISM, 3
cultivated I do not want to die . . . until I have . . . c. the seed — ACHIEVEMENT, 6
culture C. is an instrument wielded by professors — CULTURE, 3
C. is the passion for sweetness and light — CULTURE, 2
C., the acquainting ourselves with the best — CULTURE, 1
ladies who pursue C. in bands — CULTURE, 4
terrible revenge by the c. of the Negroes — POP MUSIC, 13
two half-cultures do not make a c. — HALF MEASURES, 1
When I hear anyone talk of C. — PHILISTINISM, 4
You can lead a whore to c. — PUNS, 16
cultures apt to leave his c. exposed on the laboratory table — SCIENTISTS, 12
cup Ah, fill the C. — TIME, 18
Come, fill the C., and in the Fire of Spring — TIME, 17
tak a c. o' kindness yet — FRIENDSHIP, 13
cupboard But when she got there The c. was bare — NURSERY RHYMES, 36
Cupid wing'd C. painted blind — LOVE, 120
cups c., That cheer but not inebriate — DRINKS, 4
curators The Arab who builds . . . a hut out of . . . a temple . . . is more philosophical than . . . c. of the museums — MUSEUMS, 1; PRACTICALITY, 4
cur'd C. . . . of my disease — DOCTORS, 7
curds Eating her c. and whey — NURSERY RHYMES, 30

cure a c. for which there was no disease — REMEDIES, 5
C. the disease — DISEASE, 8; REMEDIES, 1
no c. for birth and death — LIFE AND DEATH, 11
Show me a sane man and I will c. him for you — MADNESS, 6
the c. for admiring the House of Lords — HOUSES OF PARLIAMENT, 3
There are maladies we must not seek to c. — REMEDIES, 11
Work is the grand c. — WORK, 6
cured the only disease you don't look forward to being c. of — DEATH, 79
What can't be c. — ENDURANCE, 3
curfew C. shall not ring tonight! — MERCY, 3
The C. tolls the knell of parting day — DAY, 6
curiosities How these c. would be quite forgot — GOSSIP, 7
curiosity C. killed the cat — CURIOSITY, 2
C. will conquer fear — CURIOSITY, 8
Disinterested intellectual c. . . . life blood of . . . civilisation — CURIOSITY, 9
I would rather be a brilliant memory than a c. — RENUNCIATION, 2
curious Be not c. in unnecessary matters — CURIOSITY, 3
I am c. to see what happens . . . to one who dies unshriven — LAST WORDS, 50
'That was the c. incident,' remarked . . . Holmes — TRIVIALITY, 4
curiouser C. and curiouser — CONFUSION, 3
curl There was a little girl Who had a little c. — SEX, 37
curly Curly locks, C. locks, Wilt thou be mine — NURSERY RHYMES, 8
currency I will not be a party to debasing the c. — ECONOMICS, 11
curse A c. is on her if she stay — CURSES, 4
Christianity the one great c. — CHRISTIANITY, 35
c. not the king, no not in thy thought — SECRECY, 3
Don't c. the darkness — FUTILITY, 4
She would rather light candles than c. the darkness — COMPLIMENTS, 6
The c. is come upon me — CURSES, 3
Work is the c. of the drinking classes — WORK, 26
cursed thou art c. above all cattle — SEXES, 2
curses C. . . . always come home to roost — CURSES, 2
curst C. be the verse — POETRY, 35
curtain An iron c. — COLD WAR, 2
I saw it at a disadvantage – the c. was up — CRITICISM, 55
Ring down the c. — LAST WORDS, 55
cushion Like a c., he always bore — IMPRESSIONABILITY, 2
custodiet Quis c. ipsos custodes — MISTRUST, 7
custom A c. loathsome to the eye, hateful to the nose — SMOKING, 7
Age . . . nor c. stale her infinite virginity — PURITY, 5
C. calls me to't — CUSTOM, 4
c. More honour'd in the breach than the observance — CUSTOM, 3
c. stale Her infinite variety — ADMIRATION, 14
C., then, is the great guide of human life — CUSTOM, 2
customer The c. is always right — BUSINESS, 18
customers When you are skinning your c. — BUSINESS, 14
cut c. to the heart — ANGER, 2
Don't c. off your nose — REVENGE, 1
the human pack is shuffled and c. — EDUCATION, 31
cuts he that c. off twenty years of life — DEATH, 104
cutting busy driving cabs and c. hair — GOVERNMENT, 7
cycles the same opinions have arisen among men in c. — OPINIONS, 1
cymbal a tinkling c. — CHARITY, 6
cymbals clashed his colours together like c. — ARTISTS, 10
Cynara faithful to thee, C. — FAITHFULNESS, 3
cynic c. is a man who — CYNICISM, 3
cynicism C. is an unpleasant way of saying the truth — CYNICISM, 2
C. is humour in ill-health — CYNICISM, 4
no literature can outdo the c. of real life — EXPERIENCE, 10

D

dad if the d. is present at the conception — SEX, 42
They fuck you up, your mum and d. — FAMILY, 24
Daddy D. wouldn't buy me a bow-wow — DOGS, 14
daffodils Fair d., we weep to see — TRANSIENCE, 14
host, of golden d. — FLOWERS, 14
I never saw d. so beautiful — FLOWERS, 14
dagger never be left holding the d. — POLITICS, 90
dainties d. that are bred in a book — IGNORANCE, 13
dainty Nothing's so d. sweet — MELANCHOLY, 1
Daisy D., give me your answer, do — MARRIAGE, 44
Dalhousie Alas! Lord and Lady D. are dead — DEATH, 85

what a man still plans . . . shows the . . . injustice in his d.
DEATH, 36
who fears dishonour more than d. HAPPINESS, 9
worse than d. SEPARATION, 3
you impart knowledge of it through another's d. RESEARCH, 1
deaths Any amusing d. DEATH, 34
it is chiefly our own d. that we mourn for FUNERALS, 3
debasing I will not be a party to d. the currency
ECONOMICS, 11
debate I love argument, I love d. ARGUMENTS, 15
debauchee *D.*, n. One who has . . . pursued pleasure
DEBAUCHERY, 3
debt A promise made is a d. unpaid PROMISES, 5
d. which cancels all others OBLIGATION, 1
Out of d. MONEY, 2
The nations which have put mankind . . . most in their d.
NATIONS, 2
debtor Not everyone is a d. BORROWING, 7
debts He that dies pays all d. DEATH, 108
decade fun to be in the same d. AGE, 47
decadence The difference between our d. and the Russians'
DECLINE, 12
decades D. have a delusive edge CLASSIFICATION, 3
decay as short a Spring; As quick a growth to meet d.
TRANSIENCE, 14
D. and disease are often beautiful DISEASE, 39
Macmillan seemed . . . to embody the national d. DECLINE, 5
Time drops in d. TIME, 41
woods d. and fall MORTALITY, 19
deceit love we swore . . . seems d. TRANSIENCE, 14
philosophy and vain d. CHRISTIANITY, 4
temper discretion with d. EDUCATION, 60
Where rumour of oppression and d. SOLITUDE, 3
deceitfulness a Cat of such d. CATS, 2
deceive if we say that we have no sin, we d. SIN, 5
To d. oneself DECEPTION, 1
deceived take heed . . . that your heart be not d.
CHRISTIANITY, 6
deceiving without quite d. your enemies PROPAGANDA, 1
decent aristocracy to what is d. CLASS, 16
d. means poor RESPECTABILITY, 8
the only d. thing . . . is to die at once BEQUESTS, 1
decision he is going to make 'a realistic d.' DECISION, 3
if usage so choose, with whom resides the d. WORDS, 10
decisive Marriage is a step so grave and d. MARRIAGE, 111
deck I am not going to spit on the d. DEPARTURE, 3
declaim Nay, Madam, when you are declaiming, d.
COMPLAINTS, 4
declare they should d. the causes which impel them to . . .
separation INDEPENDENCE, 1
declining pass my d. years saluting . . . grandfather clocks
OLD AGE, 31
decompose d. in a barrel of porter FUNERALS, 6
decomposing d. in the eternity of print CRITICISM, 56
decorated proverb . . . much matter d. SAYINGS, 4
decorum *Dulce et d. est* PATRIOTISM, 15
Let them cant about d. RESPECTABILITY, 2
decrepit you are not yet d. enough AGE, 22
decussated Anything reticulated or d. at equal distances
WORDS, 12
dedicated never d. to something you have complete confidence
in FANATICISM, 3
Dee Across the sands of D. AGRICULTURE, 4
deed a good d. to forget a poor joke HUMOUR, 4
good d. in a naughty world GOOD, 1
right d. for the wrong reason MOTIVE, 2
The better day, the worse d. SUNDAY, 4
deeds better d. shall be in water writ MEMORIALS, 2
The bitterest tears . . . are for words . . . unsaid and d. . . .
undone REGRET, 20
deep beauty is only sin d. BEAUTY, 34
D. and crisp and even CHRISTMAS, 15
Rocked in the cradle of the d. SEA, 11
what a very singularly d. young man ARROGANCE, 4
deeper d. than did ever plummet sound RENUNCIATION, 4
whelm'd in d. gulphs DEATH, 40
deeth D. is an end of every worldly sore LIFE AND DEATH, 3
defeat a d. without a war WORLD WAR II, 3
d. is an orphan SUCCESS, 10
D. of Germany means WORLD WAR II, 27
every victory turns into a d. DISILLUSION, 5
In d. unbeatable OFFICERS, 3

defeated man can be destroyed . . . not d. DEFEAT, 3
defect Chief D. of Henry King FOOD, 8
defence Never make a d. or apology ACCUSATION, 2
Preparing for suicide . . . means of d. NUCLEAR WEAPONS, 8
The best immediate d. of the United States WORLD WAR II, 26
The only d. is in offence WAR, 5
Truth telling is not compatible with the d. of the realm
TRUTH, 37
When you think about the d. of England ENGLAND, 3
defend I disapprove of what you say, but I will d. . . . your
right to say it FREEDOM, 51
defiance in defeat, d. WAR AND PEACE, 3
poorest man may in his cottage bid d. to . . . the Crown
PRIVACY, 3
The d. of established authority REBELLION, 1
defied Age will not be d. AGE, 7
defiles What a man does d. him RESPONSIBILITY, 7
defining Language is . . . a d. framework LANGUAGE, 27
definition Science fiction is the search for a d. of mankind
SCIENCE FICTION, 2
deflowering own life . . . more dear in the presence of this d.
of Europe WORLD WAR I, 17
defying by d. their parents and copying one another YOUTH, 5
degenerates everything d. in the hands of man MANKIND, 23
world d. and grows worse every day WORLD, 3
degeneration fatty d. of his moral being MARRIAGE, 113
degradation a . . . sense of intellectual d. after an interview
with a doctor DOCTORS, 4
degrading by labour d. to the makers DESIGN, 4
degree d. of delight SUFFERING, 6
when d. is shak'd ORDER, 4
degrees Crime, like virtue, has its d. CRIME, 5
We boil at different d. INDIVIDUALITY, 4
deid Gey few, and they're a' d. INDIVIDUALITY, 1
deities the d. so kindly DESTINY, 16
Deity doubted the existence of the D. SCIENTISTS, 5
to distinguish between the D. and the Drains GOD, 47
deleted D. by French censor NEWSPAPERS, 2
deliberate with a slow d. carelessness READING, 10
deliberates woman that d. is lost WOMEN, 6
deliberation D. is the work of many men ACTION, 9
delicacy the talent of flattering with d. FLATTERY, 4
delight a degree of d. SUFFERING, 6
Commodity, Firmness, and *D.* ARCHITECTURE, 14
Energy is Eternal D. EFFORT, 2
go to't with d. ENTHUSIASM, 8
Studies serve for d. EDUCATION, 5
Teach us d. in simple things GOOD, 7
The leaping light for your d. discovers DISCOVERY, 2
very temple of d. MELANCHOLY, 8
wept with d. when you gave her a smile MEMORY, 7
delighted Whosoever is d. in solitude SOLITUDE, 1
You have d. us long enough DISMISSAL, 2
delightful make his conversation perfectly d. INSULTS, 35
What a d. thing this perspective is ART, 28
delights Man d. not me MANKIND, 2
deliver d. me from myself SELF, 5
deluge After us the d. PROPHECY, 10
Après nous le d. PROPHECY, 10
delusion he who can analyze his d. is called a philosopher
PHILOSOPHERS, 1
delusions Many people have d. of grandeur DELUSION, 5
delusive Decades have a d. edge CLASSIFICATION, 3
delved When Adam d. CLASS, 4
demagogues the vilest specimens of human nature are . . .
found among d. POLITICS, 47
demand D. bare walls in your bedroom DESIGN, 1
demands the populace cannot exact their d. HOUSES OF
PARLIAMENT, 19
democracy arsenal of d. DEMOCRACY, 15
D. can't work DEMOCRACY, 5
D. . . . government by the uneducated ARISTOCRACY, 5;
DEMOCRACY, 3
D. is only an experiment in government DEMOCRACY, 6
D. means government by discussion DEMOCRACY, 1
D. passes into despotism DEMOCRACY, 13
D. resumed her reign POLITICS, 4
extreme d. or absolute oligarchy . . . will come GOVERNMENT, 4
grieved under a *d.*, call it *anarchy* GOVERNMENT, 12
In Switzerland they had . . . five hundred years of d. and peace
SWITZERLAND, 5
Man's capacity for evil makes d. necessary DEMOCRACY, 12

not the voting that's d.   DEMOCRACY, 17
world . . . made safe for d.   DEMOCRACY, 21
democratic the ideal of a d. and free society   RACISM, 21
thoroughly d. and patronise everybody   DEMOCRACY, 16
demon woman wailing for her d.-lover   SUPERNATURAL, 6
denial the highest praise of God consists in the d. of Him
     ATHEISM, 9
denies spirit that always d.   DENIAL, 1
Denmark rotten in the state of D.   CORRUPTION, 7
denounce We thus d. . . . the arms race   NUCLEAR WEAPONS, 7
dentist fuss about sleeping together . . . sooner go to my d.
     SEX, 60
dentists gratitude to most benefactors is the same as . . . for d.
     INGRATITUDE, 3
I have let d. ride roughshod over my teeth   TEETH, 1
The thought of d. gave him just the same sick horror   FEAR, 14
deny let him d. himself   CHRISTIANITY, 19
Those who d. freedom   FREEDOM, 28
depart D., . . . and let us have done with you   DISMISSAL, 1
lettest thou thy servant d. in peace   DEATH, 30
when the great and good d.   MORTALITY, 20
departure the time of my d. is at hand   FAITH, 6
depends It all d. upon that article there   SOLDIERS, 10
depraved No one . . . suddenly became d.   DEBAUCHERY, 6
depression Recession . . . a neighbour loses . . . d. . . . you lose
     ECONOMICS, 1
depth out of your d.   SELF-CONFIDENCE, 5
derangement a nice d. of epitaphs   MALAPROPISMS, 8
derision Ambition, Distraction, Uglification, and D.
     EDUCATION, 9
descend Never d. to the ways of those above you
     EQUALITY, 16
descended D. from the apes . . . hope it is not true
     EVOLUTION, 1
description beggar'd all d.   ADMIRATION, 13
descriptions d. of the fairest wights   HISTORY, 32
desert The sand of the d. is sodden red   WAR, 77
Use every man after his d.   MERIT, 6
deserts D. of vast eternity   AGE, 37
deserve I have arthritis, and I don't d. that either   MERIT, 2
deserved I wasn't lucky. I d. it   MERIT, 7
deserves At 50, everyone has the face he d.   AGE, 42
the government it d.   GOVERNMENT, 17
designing I am d. St Paul's   ARCHITECTURE, 1
desire antidote to d.   DESIRE, 6
a universal innate d.   PROGRESS, 2; EXTRAVAGANCE, 2
d. is got without content   CONTENTMENT, 6
D. is the very essence of man   DESIRE, 16
d. should so many years outlive performance   SEX, 50
d. to be praised twice over   PRAISE, 6
It provokes the d.   ALCOHOL, 53
nothing like d. for preventing the thing one says   DESIRE, 12
The D. of Man being Infinite   INFINITY, 1
Those who restrain D.   DESIRE, 2
to have few things to d.   FEAR, 1
to lose your heart's d.   DESIRE, 15
desired war which . . . left nothing to be d.   WAR, 15
desires He who d. but acts not   ACTION, 7
Man's D. are limited by his Perceptions   PERCEPTION, 2; DESIRE, 4
Strong enough to answer back to d.   CHARACTER, 11
than nurse unacted d.   DESIRE, 3
desiring pessimists end up by d. the things they fear
     PESSIMISM, 9
desist to d. from the experiment in despair   SCOTS, 7
desk what risks you take . . . to find money in a d.   THEFT, 4
desks Stick . . . to your d. and never go to sea   OFFICERS, 7
desolate d. and sick of an old passion   LOVE, 51
despair carrion comfort, D., not feast on thee   DESPAIR, 1
Don't d., not even over . . . despair   DESPAIR, 5
Patience, n. A minor form of d.   PATIENCE, 8
some divine d.   SORROW, 26
to desist from the experiment in d.   SCOTS, 7
without understanding d.   PSYCHIATRY, 6
despairs He who d. over an event is a coward   PESSIMISM, 4
desperate D. cuts   RESULTS, 1
desperation lives of quiet d.   DESPAIR, 6
despise I d. Shakespeare   SHAKESPEARE, 16
some other Englishman d. him   ENGLISH, 32
despised A poor man is d. the whole world over   POVERTY, 19
I doubt if the philosopher lives . . . who could know himself . . .
d. by a street boy   PHILOSOPHERS, 5

despises A woman d. a man for loving her   LOVE, 130
despond name of the slough was D.   DESPAIR, 2
despot A country governed by a d.   TYRANNY, 3
despotism Democracy passes into d.   DEMOCRACY, 13
extreme democracy or absolute oligarchy or d. will come
     GOVERNMENT, 4
France was a long d.   FRANCE, 2
dessicated A d. calculating machine   POLITICIANS, 34
destination I do not think this poem will reach its d.
     CRITICISM, 51
destiny I were walking with d.   DESTINY, 4
Riddle of d.   PURPOSE, 6
destroy Doth the wingèd life d.   PLEASURE, 5
He would like to d. his old diaries   CONCEIT, 20
Man . . . builds machines to d.   WORLD WAR I, 16
sought to d. institutions   INDIFFERENCE, 7
they shall not hurt nor d. in all my holy mountain   PEACE, 1
whom God wishes to d.   MADNESS, 4
Whom the gods wish to d.   TALENT, 1
destroy'd a bold peasantry . . . When once d.   PUBLIC, 12
destroyed man can be d. . . . not defeated   DEFEAT, 3
destroyer Man . . . hasn't been a creator, only a d.   ECOLOGY, 3
destroying simplifying something by d. nearly everything
     CIVILIZATION, 4
destroys he who d. a good book, kills reason   BOOKS, 27
destruction one purpose . . . d. of Hitler   HITLER, 1
Pride goeth before d.   MISQUOTATIONS, 1
detail life is frittered away by d.   SIMPLICITY, 8
details with the thoroughness of a mind that reveres d.
     UNDERSTANDING, 7
detective The d. novel is   NOVELS, 13
detente D. is like the race   POLITICS, 17
deterrent the d. is a phallic symbol   NUCLEAR WEAPONS, 19
detest they d. at leisure   LOVE AND HATE, 1
detestable D. person but needs watching   WRITERS, 78
detested D. sport   HUNTING, 2
Deutschland D., D. über alles   GERMANY, 3
device A banner with the strange d., Excelsior   AMBITION, 12
devil Abashed the d. . . . felt how awful goodness is   GOOD, 12
between any sort of d. and the deep blue sea   SUICIDE, 8
cleft the D.'s foot   NONSENSE, 11
D. always builds a chapel there   DEVIL, 7
d. can cite Scripture   QUOTATIONS, 12
given up believing in the d.   DEVIL, 8
I do not see . . . why the d. should have all the good tunes
     MUSIC, 23
Milton's D. as a moral being is far superior   MILTON, 3
nickname is the heaviest stone that the d. can throw   NAMES, 4
Renounce the d.   RENUNCIATION, 1
sacrifice . . . of the d.'s leavings   VIRTUE, 15
Sarcasm . . . the language of the d.   SARCASM, 1
The d. finds work   IDLENESS, 1
The D. is a gentleman   DEVIL, 1
The d. is not so black   DEVIL, 1
the D. knows Latin   LANGUAGE, 17
The D. looks after his own   LUCK, 6
the d. played at chess with me   EXPLOITATION, 1
the world, the flesh, and the d.   JOURNALISM, 25; TEMPTATION, 5
devilish eyes flamed red with d. passion   SUPERNATURAL, 16
devil's d. walking parody   ANIMALS, 9
It is no good casting out d.   DEVIL, 1
One more d.'-triumph and sorrow for angels   DAMNATION, 1
devotion The almighty dollar . . . object of universal d.
     MATERIALISM, 11
devour shed tears when they would d.   HYPOCRISY, 2
dew Just to save her from the foggy, foggy d.   SEX, 4
dexterity Your d. seems a happy compound   INSULTS, 15
diabetic Many a d. has stayed alive   DISEASE, 19
diagram cat is a d. and pattern of subtle air   CATS, 5
dialect a d. I understand very little   LANGUAGE, 19
D. words – those terrible marks of the beast   CLASS, 15
diamond
A d. is forever   ADVERTISING, 6
Chaucer, I confess, is a rough d.   CHAUCER, 2
D.! D.   ACCIDENTS, 5
more of rough than polished d.   BRITISH, 4
diamonds D. Are   MATERIALISM, 8
D. Are Forever   BOOK, SONG, AND PLAY TITLES, 6
My goodness those d. are lovely   GOOD, 17
to give him d. back   MATERIALISM, 9
diaries He would like to destroy his old d.   CONCEIT, 20
Let d., therefore   DIARIES, 1

direct can't d. a Laughton picture ACTORS, 16
direction 'God knows how you Protestants . . . have any sense
of d. CATHOLICISM, 12
directions rode madly off in all d. NONSENSE, 15
director Every d. bites the hand MIXED METAPHORS, 2
Theatre d.: a person ACTING, 1
dirt After the first four years the d. doesn't get any worse
HOUSEWORK, 3
I know d. when I smell it and here it is WRITERS, 77
Throw d. enough GOSSIP, 5
dirty Is sex d. SEX, 1
disadvantage d. of merely counting votes DEMOCRACY, 6
disagree Who shall decide when doctors d. DOCTORS, 6
disappointment Grief and d. give rise to anger EMOTION, 3
disapprove I d. of what you say, but I will defend . . . your
right to say it FREEDOM, 51
disarmament precede the d. of the victors WAR, 27
disaster the audience was a d. PLAYS, 14
disasters the middle station had the fewest d. CLASS, 8
trace . . . the d. of English history to . . . Wales WALES, 5
disbelief willing suspension of d. POETRY, 11
disciples d. . . . mark its ways and note . . . its mysteries
LUCK, 7
discomforts all the d. that will accompany my being blind
BLINDNESS, 7
discommendeth He who d. others CRITICISM, 7
discontent lent To youth and age . . . – d. DISCONTENT, 1
To be discontented with the divine d. VIRTUE, 13
winter of our d. OPTIMISM, 23
discontents the family . . . source of all our d. FAMILY, 25
discourse their d. was about hunting LANGUAGE, 19
discovered We have d. the secret of life SCIENCE, 7
discoverers They are ill d. that think there is no land
DISCOVERY, 3
discovery behind the d. of America JEWS, 11
D. consists of seeing what everybody has seen DISCOVERY, 8
he who never made a mistake never made a d. MISTAKES, 16
Scientific d. is a private event SCIENCE, 28
discretion better part of valour is d. SELF-PRESERVATION, 8
temper d. with deceit EDUCATION, 60
the years of d. AGE, 14
discrimination sympathetic without d. SYMPATHY, 2
discussion D. in class, which means EDUCATION, 39
more time for d. . . . more mistakes MISTAKES, 19
disdains He d. all things above his reach DISCONTENT, 4
disease a cure for which there was no d. REMEDIES, 5
amusing the patient while Nature cures the d. MEDICINE, 12
an incurable d. – colour blindness RACISM, 8
Cur'd . . . of my d. DOCTORS, 7
Cure the d. REMEDIES, 1
Decay and d. are often beautiful DISEASE, 39
D. is . . . of the place DISEASE, 34
d. known is half cured DISEASE, 1
dread d. which so prepares its victim . . . for death DISEASE, 14
Evil comes . . . like the d.; good . . . like the doctor GOOD AND
EVIL, 2
I am suffering from the particular d. HYPOCHONDRIA, 1
if the physician had the same d. upon him that I have
EXAMPLE, 7
I have Bright's d. HUMOUR, 50
Life is an incurable d. DISEASE, 13; LIFE, 19
only d. you don't look forward to being cured of DISEASE, 25
Only those in the last stage of d. CHILDREN, 4
remedies . . . suggested for a d. REMEDIES, 7
remedy is worse than the d. REMEDIES, 2
strange d. of modern life DISEASE, 6; LIFE, 5
the d. of writing books WRITING, 23
the incurable d. of writing WRITING, 17
the only d. you don't look forward to being cured of DEATH, 79
this long d., my life ENDURANCE, 13
diseases D. are the tax DISEASE, 31
d. . . . no less natural than the instincts which preserve him.
DISEASE, 32
Extreme remedies . . . for extreme d. REMEDIES, 10
Hungry Joe collected lists of fatal d. ILLNESS, 6
disgrace a d. to our family name of Wagstaff FAMILY, 28
disgracefully The world is d. managed COMPLAINTS, 2
disguise virtues are . . . vices in d. VIRTUE AND VICE, 2
dish And the d. ran away with the spoon NURSERY RHYMES, 14
a side d. he hadn't ordered CONTEMPT, 4
The national d. of America AMERICA, 27
dishes Thou shalt not wash d. NURSERY RHYMES, 8

dishonour honour rooted in d. UNFAITHFULNESS, 6
who fears d. more than death HAPPINESS, 9
disillusionments d. in the lives of the medieval saints
DECLINE, 9
disinclination d. to inflict pain upon oneself GOOD, 11
disinterested D. intellectual curiosity . . . life blood of . . .
civilisation CURIOSITY, 9
dislike I d. what I fancy I feel SUFFERING, 3
that *my* statue should be moved, which I should much d.
MEMORIALS, 12
The law of d. for the unlike JEWS, 15
disliked I have always d. myself SELF, 6
dismal the D. Science ECONOMICS, 4
Disney D. the most significant figure . . . since Leonardo
ART, 14
disobedience Of Man's first d. SIN, 16
disorder A sweet d. in the dress CLOTHES, 7
disposes God d. GOD, 30
dispute Many a long d. among divines ARGUMENTS, 5
disputing The itch of d. . . . the scab of churches RELIGION, 71
disreputable I've been offered titles . . . get one into d.
company TITLES, 11
disrespectfully Never speak d. of Society SNOBBERY, 3
dissipated still keep looking so d. DEBAUCHERY, 2
dissipation At what time does the d. of energy begin SPORT
AND GAMES, 11
d. without pleasure LONDON, 7
other things than d. . . . thicken the features APPEARANCE, 40
dissolve Fade far away, d. HUMAN CONDITION, 12
distance The d. doesn't matter BEGINNING, 8
disthressful She's the most d. country that iver yet was seen
IRELAND, 1
distinguish all there is to d. us from other animals MANKIND, 1
distinguished a sparrow alight upon my shoulder . . . I was
more d. by that HONOUR, 6
So it has come at last, the d. thing LAST WORDS, 41
When a d. but elderly scientist states SCIENCE, 4
distraction Ambition, D., Uglification, and Derision
EDUCATION, 9
distress All pray in their d. PRAYER, 5; PRAYER, 5
the mean man is always full of d. SUPERIORITY, 2
distrust shameful to d. one's friends FRIENDS, 12
stay together, but we d. one another MARRIAGE, 31
distrusts him who d. himself SILENCE, 10
disturb What isn't part of ourselves doesn't d. us HATE, 7
disturbances think of diseases as isolated d. in a healthy body
DISEASE, 3
ditch if he wasn't as dull as d. water STUPIDITY, 7
ditchwater Is d. dull NATURE, 5
diversion Most sorts of d. . . . are an imitation of fighting
WAR, 117
'tis a country d. COUNTRYSIDE, 1
diversity make the world safe for d. DIFFERENCE, 8
divide D. and rule POWER, 1
divided in their death they were not d. FRIENDSHIP, 9
Obstinate people can be d. into STUBBORNNESS, 2
Thought must be d. against itself UNDERSTANDING, 6
divine attain to the d. perfection PERFECTION, 4
The Hand that made us is d. CREATION, 1
The right d. of kings to govern wrong MONARCHY, 16
To be discontented with the d. discontent VIRTUE, 13
To err is human, to forgive, d. MISTAKES, 13; FORGIVENESS, 13
divines Many a long dispute among d. ARGUMENTS, 5
divinity a d. that shapes our ends DESTINY, 18
a piece of d. in us NOBILITY, 2
d. in odd numbers SUPERSTITION, 10
There's such d. doth hedge a king MONARCHY, 19
divisions How many d. has *he* got CATHOLICISM, 8
divorce D.? Never. But murder often MARRIAGE, 122
not wanting to consent to the d. PROPHECY, 7
do D. as I say, not as I do DISEASE, 33
D. as you would be done by EXAMPLE, 5
D. other men BUSINESS, 5
d. what the mob d. MAJORITY, 1
either d., or die ACTION, 6
for they know not what they d. FORGIVENESS, 4
I am to do what I please FREEDOM, 11
Let us d. or die ACTION, 6
Nature . . . hath done her part; D. thou but thine
RESPONSIBILITY, 10
Now what d. I d. with *this* ROYALTY, 38
Preachers say, D. as I say, not as I do EXAMPLE, 7

downhearted Are we d.? No — OPTIMISM, 12
dozen a d. are only a chorus — BEAUTY, 18
drain you will leave Oxford by the town d. — SPOONERISMS, 5
drainpipe wrong end of a municipal d. — POLITICIANS, 59
drains to distinguish between the Deity and the D. — GOD, 47
Drake D. he's in his hammock — WAR, 78
drama A good d. critic is — CRITICS, 21
dramatist Sherard Blaw, the d. who had discovered himself — WRITERS, 80
draught O, for a d. of vintage — ALCOHOL, 36
draw I d. what I feel in my body — ART, 9
drawbacks everything has its d. — FAMILY, 22
One of the d. of Fame — FAME, 13
drawing the Suez Canal was flowing through my d. room — POLITICS, 24
dread The d. of beatings — EDUCATION, 7
the d. of doing what has been done before — ORIGINALITY, 6
dreadful d. is the check — IMPRISONMENT, 2
Other people are quite d. — MISANTHROPY, 4
Portions and parcels of the d. Past — TIME, 37
some have called thee Mighty and d. — DEATH, 44
dreadnoughts A . . . Duke costs as much . . . as two D. — ARISTOCRACY, 9
dream All men d.: but not equally — DREAMS, 10
A sight to d. of — DESIRE, 5
awakened from the d. of life — LIFE AND DEATH, 12
Awoke one night from a deep d. of peace — DREAMS, 11
behold it was a d. — DREAMS, 3
d. of perfect bliss — DREAMS, 2
For life is but a d. — LIFE, 50
God will cease to d. you — DEATH, 69
Happiness is no vague d. — HAPPINESS, 21
hope is . . . the d. of those that wake — HOPE, 9
I d. when I am awake — REALITY, 1
I have a d. — EQUALITY, 15
The young men's vision, and the old men's d. — DREAMS, 5
To sleep, perchance to d. — SUICIDE, 12
warned of God in a d. — CHRISTMAS, 10
Where is it now, the glory and the d. — METAPHYSICS, 5
you d. you are crossing the Channel — BOATS, 6
dreamer The poet and the d. are distinct — OPPOSITES, 3
dreamers the d. of the day are dangerous men — DREAMS, 10
dreamin' d. . . . o' Plymouth Hoe — WAR, 78
dreaming after-dinner's sleep, d. on both — AGE, 52
a man d. I was a butterfly — DREAMS, 4
City with her d. spires — OXFORD, 2
dreams doubtful d. of d. — PEACE, 16
do we not live in d. — DREAMS, 13
dream our d. away — DREAMS, 7
D. and predictions — DREAMS, 1
Fanatics have their d. — FANATICISM, 2
For one person who d. of making fifty thousand pounds — LAZINESS, 3
I, being poor, have only my d. — POVERTY, 34
In d. begins responsibility — RESPONSIBILITY, 17
show life . . . as we see it in our d. — WRITING, 5
spread my d. under your feet — DREAMS, 14
Than this world d. of — PRAYER, 17
the city of perspiring d. — CAMBRIDGE, 5
We are such stuff As d. are made on — MORTALITY, 17
what d. may come — SUICIDE, 12
dreamt d. of in your philosophy — SUPERNATURAL, 13
I d. that I was making a speech — SPEECHES, 4
dreary d. intercourse of daily life — OPTIMISM, 29
Dying is a very dull, d. affair — DEATH, 84
If your morals make you d. — MORALITY, 21
Once upon a midnight d. — SUPERNATURAL, 12
dress I have no d. except the one I wear — PRACTICALITY, 1
put on a d. of guilt — GUILT, 6
sweet disorder in the d. — CLOTHES, 7
Those who make their d. . . . themselves — CLOTHES, 6
dress'd D. in a little brief authority — MANKIND, 26
dressed All d. up, with nowhere to go — FUTILITY, 11
Some fruit for Him that d. me — SERVICE, 2
Today I d. to meet my father's eyes — SUITABILITY, 3
dresses long d., . . . cover a multitude of shins — CLOTHES, 18
drink A good d. — ALCOHOL, 3
A little in d. — MARRIAGE, 109
Another little d. — ALCOHOL, 58
a rule never to d. by daylight — ALCOHOL, 43
A taste for d., combined with gout — ALCOHOL, 28
D. and the devil — ALCOHOL, 60

D. deep, or taste not the Pierian spring — KNOWLEDGE, 30
D.! for you know not whence you came — DESTINY, 9
d. may be said to be an equivocator with lechery — ALCOHOL, 53
D. to me only with thine eyes — LOVE, 75
First you take a d. . . . then the d. takes you — ALCOHOL, 25
I commended mirth . . . to eat . . . to d., and to be merry — PLEASURE, 4
let us eat and d. — MISQUOTATIONS, 7; TRANSIENCE, 7
never to refuse a d. after dark — ALCOHOL, 43
no one has yet found a way to d. for a living — ALCOHOL, 38
Nor any drop to d. — WATER, 2
One reason I don't d. — DRUNKENNESS, 6
she would never take a d. — ABSTINENCE, 11
soft d. at a party — ABSTINENCE, 2
that he has taken to d. — ALCOHOL, 61
There are five reasons we should d. — ALCOHOL, 8
we d. too much tea — DRINKS, 8
willing to taste any d. once — DRINKS, 3
woe unto them that . . . follow strong d. — ALCOHOL, 12
you shall d. twice while I d. once — DRUNKENNESS, 20
drinka D. a pinta milka day — ADVERTISING, 8
drinkers no verse can give pleasure . . . that is written by d. of water — WATER, 6
drinking D. . . . and making love — MANKIND, 4
d. deep of that divinest anguish — SUFFERING, 5
I have been d. it for sixty-five years and I am not dead — DRINKS, 9
let me die d. in an inn — ALCOHOL, 41
no d. after death — ALCOHOL, 26
resolve to give up smoking, d. and loving — ABSTINENCE, 5
smoking cigars and . . . d. of alcohol before, after, and . . . during — ALCOHOL, 21; SMOKING, 4
there's nothing like d. — ALCOHOL, 23
'Tis not the d. . . . but the excess — EXCESS, 7
two reasons for d. — THIRST, 1
Work is the curse of the d. classes — WORK, 26
drinks He who d. a little too much — ALCOHOL, 4
dripping Constant d. hollows out a stone — PERSISTENCE, 10
electricity was d. invisibly — SCIENCE, 40
driver in the d.'s seat — POWER, 6
driving busy d. cabs and cutting hair — GOVERNMENT, 7
I would spend my life in d. briskly in a post-chaise — PLEASURE, 16
drizzle the blasted English d. — DISCONTENT, 6
droghte d. of Marche — MONTHS, 7
dromedary Donne, whose muse on d. trots — POETS, 28
droop The day begins to d. — DAY, 2
drop Nor any d. to drink — WATER, 2
there are people whom one should like very well to d. — HURT, 2
dropping peace comes d. slow — PEACE, 18
dropsies there were people who died of d. — ALCOHOL, 33
dropt Mrs Montagu has d. me — HURT, 2
drown I'll d. my book — RENUNCIATION, 4
what pain it was to d. — DROWNING, 2
drowning A d. man — HOPE, 1
Being an old maid is like death by d. — MARRIAGE, 55
If I rescued a child from d. — POLITICIANS, 33; JOURNALISM, 7
not waving but d. — DROWNING, 3
drudge a harmless d. — LEXICOGRAPHY, 6
drudgery Learn to inure yourself to d. in science — EDUCATION, 42
drug A miracle d. is — MEDICINE, 7
d. is that substance which — DRUGS, 1
Words are . . . the most powerful d. — WORDS, 2
drugging Imperative d. . . . no longer . . . the chief function of the doctor — DRUGS, 11
drugs Half the modern d. could well be thrown out the window — DRUGS, 6
drum brave Music of a *distant* D. — MONEY, 21
Not a d. was heard — FUNERALS, 10
Take my d. to England — PATRIOTISM, 21
drums the beating of war d. — WAR, 59
drunk If, d. with sight of power, we loose — BOASTS, 4
man . . . must get d. — DRUNKENNESS, 10
My mother, d. or sober — PATRIOTISM, 14
not so think as you d. — DRUNKENNESS, 19
this meeting is d. — DRUNKENNESS, 11
you won't intoxicate with one glass someone who has . . . d. . . . a . . . barrel — EXPERIENCE, 10
drunkards There are more old d. — DRUNKENNESS, 1
drunken Better sleep with a sober cannibal than a d. Christian — DRUNKENNESS, 16

He uses statistics as a d. man uses lamp-posts STATISTICS, 4
What shall we do with the d. sailor DRUNKENNESS, 4
drunkenness A branch of the sin of d. DRUNKENNESS, 14
If . . . 'feeling good' could decide, d. would be . . . supremely
valid DRUNKENNESS, 13
dry old man in a d. month AGE, 23
out of these wet clothes and into a d. Martini ALCOHOL, 67
Dublin D., though . . . much worse than London PLACES, 8
In D.'s fair city, where the girls are so pretty BUSINESS, 1
duckling The Ugly D. BOOK, SONG, AND PLAY TITLES, 3
ducks you go about the country stealing d. THEFT, 4
your precious 'lame d.' WEAKNESS, 2
dug If people d. up the remains of this civilization ARTISTS, 16
duke A . . . D. costs as much . . . as two Dreadnoughts
ARISTOCRACY, 9
a naked D. of Windlestraw addressing a naked House of Lords
NAKEDNESS, 2
dulce D. et decorum est PATRIOTISM, 15
dull a doctrine so illogical and so d. MARXISM, 2
a very d. Play MARRIAGE, 39
Heaven . . . is a place so inane, so d. HEAVEN, 12
He was d. in a new way POETS, 43
if he wasn't as d. as ditch water STUPIDITY, 2
Music-hall songs provide the d. with wit STUPIDITY, 9
not only d. in himself STUPIDITY, 3
The prospect of a lot Of d. MPs POLITICIANS, 11
To make dictionaries is d. work LEXICOGRAPHY, 5
dullard The d.'s envy of brilliant men GREATNESS, 2
dumplings I am the emperor, and I want d. PETULANCE, 3
dunces the d. are all in confederacy against him GENIUS, 9
dupe The d. of friendship, and the fool of love BITTERNESS, 1
dusk In the d., with a light behind her AGE, 29
slow d. a drawing-down of blinds WAR, 82
dusky Midnight brought on the d. hour DAY, 12
dust A heap of d. alone remains EQUALITY, 29
As chimney-sweepers, come to d. MORTALITY, 16
d. shalt thou eat SEXES, 2
fear in a handful of d. FEAR, 9
fly . . . said, what a d. do I raise CONCEIT, 3
pride that licks the d. SERVILITY, 5
raised a d. COMPLAINTS, 1
The d. and silence of the upper shelf NEGLECT, 3
the d. beneath thy chariot wheel HUMILITY, 5
The d. of great persons' graves EQUALITY, 26
this quintessence of d. MANKIND, 27
Dutch my dear old D. LOVE, 37
duties he devotes to the neglect of his d. NEGLECT, 4
Property has its d. CAPITALISM, 2
duty absolved from all d. to his country MARRIAGE, 90
a stupid man . . . always declares that it is his d. DUTY, 4
A thing of d. is a boy for ever POLICE, 4; PUNS, 15
Do your d. and leave the rest to the Gods DUTY, 2
d. of an opposition OPPOSITION, 4
England expects every man will do his d. DUTY, 3
It is my d. to warn you that it will be used against you
JUSTICE, 6
more than a moral d. to speak one's mind FRANKNESS, 4
Nor law, nor d. bade me fight FLYING, 4
Patriotism . . . is a revolutionary d. PATRIOTISM, 30
right of all . . . d. of some SEPARATION, 4
the d. of being happy HAPPINESS, 27
this is the whole d. of man GOD, 9
What's a man's first d. SINCERITY, 5
when constabulary d.'s to be done POLICE, 1
dwarfs A number of anxious d. POLITICIANS, 21
dwell Let other pens d. on guilt and misery OPTIMISM, 14
dwelt She d. among the untrodden ways LONELINESS, 9
dyin' Young man, I think you're d.! LOVE, 13
dying alike are the groans of love to . . . d. LOVE AND DEATH, 4
All men are afraid of d. DEATH, 99
Don't cheer, boys; the poor devils are d. WAR, 87
D. for an idea MARTYRDOM, 2
D. is a very dull, dreary affair DEATH, 84
folly to shrink in fear, if this is d. DEATH, 91
For a priest to turn a man when he lies a-d. PERSUASION, 3
good for a writer to think he's d. WRITERS, 26
He had been, he said, a most unconscionable time d.
DEATH, 38
Here am I, d. DEATH, 94
I cannot forgive my friends for d. DEATH, 115
If this is d. LAST WORDS, 67
is it my birthday or am I d. LAST WORDS, 5

it is not death, but d., which is terrible DEATH, 49
'Tis not the d. for a faith FAITH, 18
Truth sits upon the lips of d. men TRUTH, 9
we survive amongst the dead and the d. as on a battlefield
OLD AGE, 43
dyke February, fill the d. MONTHS, 11
dykes our d., . . . are ten feet deep BOASTS, 6
dynamic class people as static and d. SEXES, 27
play is a d. thing NOVELS, 16; PLAYS, 13
dyspepsia when they are troubled with d. RELIGION, 36

E

ear a pistol let off at the e. PUNS, 10
jest's prosperity lies in the e. HUMOUR, 27
more is meant than meets the e. INNUENDO, 3
the e. begins to hear IMPRISONMENT, 9
Earl As far as the 14th E. is concerned TITLES, 1
the whole process has ground to a halt with a 14th E.
TITLES, 12
early A useless life is an e. death PURPOSE, 3
E. to bed BED, 1
E. to rise and early to bed BED, 9
good die e. GOOD AND EVIL, 3
nobody who does not rise e. BED, 4
The e. bird ANTICIPATION, 3
earn this is the week I e. my salary MERIT, 5
earned Old age . . . gives us what we have e. OLD AGE, 8
earning learning, e. and yearning LIFE, 36
ears A hungry stomach has no e. HUNGER, 8
can you waggle your e. BOOKS, 5
device to keep the e. from grating MIND, 2
Romans, countrymen, lend me your e. EVIL, 16
earth a covenant between me and the e. PROMISES, 2
But did thee feel the e. move SEX, 22
Cool'd . . . in the deep-delved e. ALCOHOL, 36
E. fills her lap with pleasures NATURE, 19
E. has not anything to show more fair LONDON, 14
E. is just too small and fragile a basket SPACE, 4
from whose face the e. and the heaven fled JUDGMENT, 4
God called the dry land E. CREATION, 3
God created . . . the e. CREATION, 2
heaven and e. shall pass away TRANSIENCE, 8
heav'n on e. HEAVEN, 6
hell upon e. . . . . in a melancholy man's heart MELANCHOLY, 3
I will move the e. TECHNOLOGY, 1
lards the lean e. as he walks OBESITY, 10
mine were princes of the e. JEWS, 2
more things in heaven and e. SUPERNATURAL, 13
passenger on the spaceship, E. SPACE, 3
so much of e. . . . . of heaven IMPETUOSITY, 4
the cool flowery lap of e. POETS, 16
The e. does not argue HUMAN NATURE, 25
the e. of England is in my two hands VICTORY, 20
the e. where cares abound BIRDS, 11
The meek do not inherit the e. HUMILITY, 6
This e. of majesty ENGLAND, 36
When e. was nigher heaven PAST, 3
ease done with so much e. CHARACTER, 7
Joys in another's loss of e. LOVE, 28
No warmth, no cheerfulness, no healthful e. MONTHS, 10
Prodigal of E. WORLD-WEARINESS, 1
True e. in writing comes from art WRITING, 26
easeful half in love with e. Death DEATH, 70
easier E. said than done ACTION, 3
it is much e. to say what it is not POETRY, 21
east E. is E., and West is West OPPOSITES, 4
E., west HOME, 1
hold the gorgeous e. in fee VENICE, 4
Now we can look the E. End in the face WORLD WAR II, 17
the e. wind made flesh AMERICANS, 2
to have the E. come to the Atlantic WORLD WAR II, 19
to prevent us from going into the E. WORLD WAR II, 19
wise men from the e. CHRISTMAS, 9
easy E. come MONEY, 1
It is e. to bear MISFORTUNE, 1
It is e. to be wise WISDOM, 1
It's either e. or impossible PAINTING, 4
eat Don't e. too many almonds FOOD, 15
E. as much as you like OBESITY, 2
e. moderately, having an ordinary mixed diet HEALTH AND
HEALTHY LIVING, 8

whether I e. your lordship's principles or your mistress
REPARTEE, 5
emotion Poetry is not a turning loose of e. POETRY, 14
Sorrow is tranquillity remembered in e. SORROW, 14
the degree of my aesthetic e. CRITICS, 1
emotional a well-bred sort of e. anarchy CLASSIFICATION, 2
emotions a sort of metaphysical brothel for e.
SENTIMENTALITY, 3
big e. come from big words STYLE, 5
noble grounds for the noble e. POETRY, 39
She ran . . . e. from A to B CRITICISM, 37
emperor An e. ought at least to die on his feet LAST WORDS, 72
I am the e., and I want dumplings PETULANCE, 3
the E. has nothing on INNOCENCE, 3
emperors e. can't do it all by themselves SUPPORT, 2
empire An e. founded by war WAR, 71
Great Britain has lost an E. BRITAIN, 1
How is the E. LAST WORDS, 31; BRITISH EMPIRE, 4
the downfall of the British E. BRITISH EMPIRE, 1
the Holy Roman Empire was neither holy, nor Roman, nor an
e. NATIONS, 3
to the French the e. of the land EUROPE, 13
empires The day of E. has come NATIONS, 1
employed innocently e. than in getting money MONEY, 27
The rise in the . . . e. is governed by Parkinson's Law
WORK, 14
employees Work . . . by those e. who have not yet reached . . .
incompetence INCOMPETENCE, 4
employer ideal of the e. . . . production without employees
INDUSTRIAL RELATIONS, 3
employers e. . . . only like ballots so long as you lose them
STRIKES, 4
employment I will undoubtedly have to seek . . . gainful e.
GOVERNMENT, 1
empty Bring on the e. horses LANGUAGE, 11
E. vessels FOOLISHNESS, 5
You can't think rationally on an e. stomach THINKING, 6
enchantment distance lends e. to the view PERSPECTIVE, 1
enclose A vacuum can only exist . . . by the things which e. it
SCIENCE, 16
enclosed Check e. MONEY, 37
encourage the right to be consulted, . . . to e., . . . to warn
MONARCHY, 1
to e. the others EXAMPLE, 9
encourager *pour e. les autres* EXAMPLE, 9
encyclopaedia a whole E. behind the rest of the world
SCIENCE, 26
end a beginning, a muddle, and an e. NOVELS, 8
an e. to the beginnings of all wars WAR, 95
a whole is that which has a beginning, a middle, and an e.
PLAYS, 1
beginning of the e. DEFEAT, 8
God be at my e., And at my departing GOD, 1
I like a film to have a beginning, a middle and an e. CINEMA, 3
I move softly towards the e. DEATH, 67
Keep right on to the e. of the road PERSISTENCE, 8
of making many books there is no e. BOOKS, 8
our minutes hasten to their e. TIME, 34
the e. is not yet WAR, 9
The *e.* is to build well ARCHITECTURE, 14
the e. of the beginning WORLD WAR I, 13
Walt Whitman who laid e. to e. POETS, 50
we're forbidden to know – what e. the gods have in store
DESTINY, 12
world without e. ETERNITY, 2
Yes, to the very e. ENDURANCE, 15
endeavour To e. to forget anyone MEMORY, 4
ended My life with girls has e. SEX, 23
The day Thou gavest, Lord, is e. DAY, 4
ending The quickest way of e. a war WAR, 81
endless History is an e. repetition HISTORY, 11
ends divinity that shapes our e. DESTINY, 18
my family begins . . . yours e. with you ANCESTRY, 3
endurance patient e. is godlike ENDURANCE, 9
endure For his mercies ay e. GOD, 37
It is flattering some men to e. them TOLERANCE, 3
Jazz will e. POP MUSIC, 16
Youth's a stuff will not e. PRESENT, 13
endured Job e. everything – until his friends came
ENDURANCE, 8
endures When a man is in love he e. more LOVE, 92
endureth blessed is the man that e. temptation TEMPTATION, 4

enemies Better a thousand e. ENEMIES, 1
designing mausoleums for his e. HATE, 6
do not have to forgive my e. LAST WORDS, 46; RUTHLESSNESS, 4
Even a paranoid can have e. ENEMIES, 4
love your e. ENEMIES, 3
Mountains interposed Make e. of nations MOUNTAINS, 1
The e. of Freedom OPPRESSION, 3
we have been mortal e. ever since ENEMIES, 5
enemy Every man is his own worst e. SELF, 1
hasn't an e. in the world POPULARITY, 9
I cannot get any sense of an e. WORLD WAR I, 14
It takes your e. and your friend . . . , to hurt you HURT, 3
no more sombre e. of good art BABIES, 1
Poverty is a great e. to human happiness POVERTY, 20
We have met the e., and they are ours VICTORY, 13
we must be just to our e. PUBLISHING, 5
energies quarrel . . . e. displayed in it are fine ARGUMENTS, 11
energy At what time does the dissipation of e. begin SPORT
AND GAMES, 11
E. is Eternal Delight EFFORT, 2
enfants *Allons, e., de la patrie* FRANCE, 10
Les e. terribles YOUTH, 8
engaged one of the nicest girls I was ever e. to
MARRIAGE, 134
engine indefatigable and unsavoury e. of pollution DOGS, 12
England A grain, which in E. is generally given to horses
SCOTLAND, 3
Be E. what she will PATRIOTISM, 6
but the King of E. cannot enter PRIVACY, 3
Christianity is part of the Common Law of E. CHRISTIANITY, 26
Common Law of E. LAW, 15
Damn you, E.. You're rotting ENGLAND, 32
E. elects a Labour Government POLITICS, 63
E. expects every man will do his duty DUTY, 3
E. is a nation of shopkeepers ENGLISH, 28
E. is a paradise for women NATIONALITY, 3
E. is the mother of parliaments ENGLAND, 6
E. is the paradise of women ENGLAND, 17
E. is the paradise of individuality ENGLAND, 35
E. mourns for her dead across the sea MOURNING, 3
E.'s green and pleasant land ENGLAND, 5
E.'s pleasant pastures ENGLAND, 5
E. . . . the envy of less happy lands ENGLAND, 14
E. . . . the workshop of the world ENGLAND, 16
E.! . . . What love I bore to thee HOMESICKNESS, 9
E. will have her neck wrung like a chicken WORLD WAR II, 30
E., with all thy faults PATRIOTISM, 7
For E.'s the one land ENGLAND, 7
For God's sake, madam, don't say that in E. for . . . they will
surely tax it TAXATION, 11
go back to thy stately homes of E. PARTING, 7
hardly be a town in the South of E. ENGLAND, 31
he bores for E. BORES, 4
in E. people have good table manners MANNERS, 4
In E., pop art and fine art ART, 15
In E. there is only silence or scandal ENGLAND, 27
It was twenty-one years ago that E. and I ENGLAND, 29
little ships of E. brought the Army home BOATS, 8;
WORLD WAR II, 20
Living in E., . . . must be like being married to a stupid . . . wife
ENGLAND, 18
no man in E. will take away my life ARROGANCE, 2
occurred nowhere but in E. ENGLAND, 11
Oh, to be in E. ENGLAND, 8
Old E. is lost BRITAIN, 10
rather hew wood than be . . . King of E. MONARCHY, 6
should they know of E. who only E. know ENGLAND, 2
Speak for E. PATRIOTISM, 2
Stately Homes of E. ARISTOCRACY, 6; STATELY HOMES, 2
that is forever E. WAR, 18
The best thing I know between France and E. FRANCE, 8
the earth of E. is in my two hands VICTORY, 20
the Kings of E., Diamonds, Hearts, Spades and Clubs
MONARCHY, 10
The Law of E. is a very strange one LAW, 8
The national sport of E. ENGLISH, 35
the old savage E., whose last blood flows still ENGLAND, 23
There'll always be an E. ENGLAND, 33
The roast beef of E. FOOD, 20
The stately homes of E. STATELY HOMES, 4
this generation . . . found E. a land of beauty ECOLOGY, 4
this realm, this E. ENGLAND, 36

excellences e. carried to an excess | WRITERS, 6
excellent everything that's e. | LAW, 11
Excelsior A banner with the strange device, E. | AMBITION, 12
exception I never forget a face, but I'll make an e. | MEMORY, 9
The e. proves the rule | RULES, 1
excess excellences carried to an e. | WRITERS, 6
e. is most exhilarating | EXCESS, 2
Give me e. of it | MUSIC, 46
In charity there is no e. | CHARITY, 3
Nothing succeeds like e. | MODERATION, 5; EXCESS, 15
The road of e. | EXCESS, 3
'Tis not the drinking . . . but the e. | EXCESS, 7
exchange conversation must be an e. of thought | CONVERSATION, 7
I stopped . . . to e. ideas | INFERIORITY, 1
Exchequer Chancellor of the E. | TAXATION, 8
exciting He found it less e. | COWARDICE, 2
Jam today, and men aren't at their most e. | PROMISES, 6
exclude we cannot e. the intellect from . . . any of our functions | INTELLECT, 4
excluded when you have e. the impossible | TRUTH, 21
exclusive the most e. club there is | ENGLISH, 29
excuse bet he's just using that as an e. | DEATH, 83
execution some are daily led to e. | EXECUTION, 23
executioner I am mine own E. | SELF, 7
executioners victims who respect their e. | RESPECT, 3
executive the e. expression of human immaturity | POLITICS, 12
exercise E. is bunk | HEALTH AND HEALTHY LIVING, 6; SPORT AND GAMES, 5
Prostitution . . . provides fresh air and wholesome e. | SEX, 21
exertion success depends . . . upon individual initiative and e. | EFFORT, 5; SUCCESS, 13
the e. is too much for me | LAUGHTER, 9
exhausted Our agenda is now e. | AGREEMENT, 6
exile New York . . . where every one is an e. | AMERICA, 15
exist Facts do not cease to e. | FACTS, 1
I e. by what I think | THINKING, 9
I feel . . . a certain difficulty in continuing to e. | LAST WORDS, 26
If God did not e. | GOD, 49
liberty cannot long e. | CORRUPTION, 1
No more things should be presumed to e. | SIMPLICITY, 6
existence A God who let us prove his e. | GOD, 15
disregard for the necessities of e. | CIVILIZATION, 9
Does it contain any experimental reasoning, concerning matter of fact and e. | PHILOSOPHY, 3
doubted the e. of the Deity | SCIENTISTS, 5
individual e. goes out in a lonely spasm of helpless agony | DEATH, 63
Let us contemplate e. | EXISTENCE, 2
mere e. is swollen to a horror | IDEALISM, 3
the sole purpose of human e. is to kindle a light | EXISTENCE, 3
the struggle for e. | EVOLUTION, 5
to deny the e. of an unseen kingdom is bad | SPECULATION, 1
to do something is to create e. | EXISTENCE, 5
exit E., pursued by a bear | ANIMALS, 18
exits They have their e. and their entrances | HUMAN CONDITION, 17
expect all any reasonable child can e. | SEX, 42
people e. me to neigh, grind my teeth | HORSES, 1
the audience want to be surprised . . . by things that they e. | PLAYS, 3
you e. other people to be . . . to your liking | TOLERANCE, 4
expectation the distinction between hope and e. | REALISM, 3
expectations the difference between our talents and our e. | DISAPPOINTMENT, 1
expects Blessed is the man who e. nothing | EXPECTATION, 3
England e. every man will do his duty | DUTY, 3
expediency the most useful thing about a principle . . . sacrificed to e. | EXPEDIENCY, 4
expendable British Government sees black people as e. | RACISM, 29
expenditure annual e. nineteen nineteen six | ECONOMICS, 7
in favour of . . . particular e. | THRIFT, 7
expense flatterers live at the e. of those who listen | FLATTERY, 6
who Would be at the e. of two | GOD, 17
experience All e. is an arch | EXPERIENCE, 20
An e. of women | EXPERIENCE, 12
E. is a good teacher | EXPERIENCE, 6
E. is never limited | EXPERIENCE, 16
E. isn't interesting | EXPERIENCE, 9
E. is the best teacher | EXPERIENCE, 2

E. is the mother | EXPERIENCE, 3
I can't see that it's wrong to give him a little legal e. | NEPOTISM, 2
Language is not simply a reporting device for e. | LANGUAGE, 27
moment's insight . . . worth a life's e. | EXPERIENCE, 15
my e. of life has been drawn from life itself | EXPERIENCE, 8
Notwithstanding the poverty of my . . . e. | CONTENTMENT, 4
Reason, Observation, and E. | SCIENCE, 22
the light which e. gives | EXPERIENCE, 11
The triumph of hope over e. | MARRIAGE, 73
experiences the child should be allowed to meet the real e. of life | CHILDREN, 30
experiment A theory can be proved by e. | THEORY, 2
existence remains a . . . lamentable e. | HAPPINESS, 22
no path leads from e. to . . . theory | THEORY, 2
to desist from the e. in despair | SCOTS, 7
experimental *Does it contain any e. reasoning, concerning matter of fact and existence* | PHILOSOPHY, 3
experiments divers e. in Mr Boyle's Pneumatic Engine | SCIENTISTS, 9
expert An e. . . . has made all the mistakes . . . in a very narrow field | EXPERTS, 2
An e. . . . knows some of the worst mistakes that can be made | EXPERTS, 3
Prince Philip. . . . a world e. on leisure | ROYALTY, 19
explanations less hideous than e. | EXPLANATIONS, 1
export I integrate the current e. drive | BUSINESS, 1
exposes A man who e. himself when he is intoxicated | DRUNKENNESS, 15
ex-president No candidate . . . elected e. by such a large majority | DEFEAT, 7
expression supreme e. of the mediocrity | RUSSIA, 5
the executive e. of human immaturity | POLITICS, 12
exquisite It is e., and it leaves one unsatisfied | SMOKING, 23
the e. touch . . . is denied to me | WRITERS, 8
ex-secretary attacking an e. of state | CHURCHILL, 1
exterminate E. all brutes | RUTHLESSNESS, 3
e. . . . the treacherous English | WAR, 133
extinct a convention which says you must not make species e. | CONSERVATION, 7
the Tasmanians . . . are now e. | ADULTERY, 5
extinguished glory of Europe is e. | EUROPE, 1
extraordinary Little minds are interested in the e. | TRIVIALITY, 10
the most e. collection of talent | TALENT, 5
this is an e. man | POLITICIANS, 53
extravagance e., . . . thrift and adventure | THRIFT, 5
Our love of what is beautiful does not lead to e. | RESULTS, 4
extreme E. remedies . . . for extreme diseases | REMEDIES, 10
extremism e. in the defence of liberty is no vice | EXCESS, 4
exuberance E. is Beauty | BEAUTY, 9
e. of his own verbosity | VERBOSITY, 2
ex-wife no fury like an e. searching for a new lover | WOMEN, 25
eye A custom loathsome to the e., hateful to the nose | SMOKING, 7
A person may be indebted for a nose or an e., . . . to a great-aunt | FAMILY, 20
a sober colouring from an e. | MORTALITY, 21
as the apple of his e. | SUPPORT, 1
clapped the glass to his sightless e. | BLINDNESS, 6
Every tear from every e. | SORROW, 1
e. for e. | RETRIBUTION, 1
He had but one e. | APPEARANCE, 12
his keener e. The axe's edge did try | EXECUTION, 16
less in this than meets the e. | CRITICISM, 2
man who looks you . . . in the e. . . . hiding something | INSINCERITY, 1
neither e. to see, nor tongue to speak | HOUSES OF PARLIAMENT, 11
such beauty as a woman's e. | LEARNING, 8
The e. is bigger | GREED, 2
There is a road from the e. to the heart | EMOTION, 1
the sort of e. that can open an oyster at sixty paces | APPEARANCE, 42
with an e. made quiet . . . We see into the life of things | DEATH, 133
with the jaundiced e. | PASSION, 8
eyeless E. in Gaza | BLINDNESS, 3
eye-lids the opening e. of the morn | DAY, 10
tir'd . . . upon tir'd eyes | MUSIC, 51
When she raises her e. | SEX, 16
eyes And on his grave, with shining e. | DEATH, 19

and throws . . . sand in their e.   SLEEP, 10
Drink to me only with thine e.   LOVE, 75
fortune and men's e.   DISCONTENT, 8
God be in my e., And in my looking   GOD, 1
I first set my e. on sweet Molly Malone   BUSINESS, 4
Look at that man's e.   POLITICIANS, 57
Look not in my e., for fear They mirror true the sight I see
                                                                       LOVE, 71
Love looks not with the e.   LOVE, 120
Mine e. have seen the glory of the coming of the Lord   GOD, 26
pearls that were his e.   DEATH, 107
the creature hath a purpose and its e. are bright with it
                                                                    PURPOSE, 5
the e. are the windows of the soul   EYES, 1
The e. are the window   SOUL, 1
The e. that shone, Now dimmed and gone   NOSTALGIA, 14
the whites of their e.   WAR, 88
Thy rapt soul sitting in thine e.   SOUL, 10
Two lovely black e.   VIOLENCE, 3
you'll wear your e. out   STARING, 2
Your e. shine like the pants   COMPLIMENTS, 3
eyesight with blinded e.   LEARNING, 9
Eyre I wish you had not sent me Jane E.   WRITERS, 85

F

Fabian Britain . . . F. Society writ large   BRITAIN, 8
Fabians A good man fallen among F.   WRITERS, 64
fabric chemical barrage has been hurled against the f. of life
                                                                 ECOLOGY, 2
the baseless f. of this vision   MORTALITY, 17
face Accustomed to her f.   FAMILIARITY, 3
a garden in her f.   ADMIRATION, 4
A good f. is a letter of recommendation   BEAUTY, 1
And hid his f. amid a crowd of stars   LOVE, 150
At 50, everyone has the f. he deserves   AGE, 42
everybody's f. but their own   SATIRE, 3
every man is responsible for his f.   APPEARANCE, 6
False f. must hide   DECEPTION, 5
from whose f. the earth and the heaven fled   JUDGMENT, 4
I have looked upon the f. of Agamemnon   HISTORY, 24
I never forget a f., but I'll make an exception   MEMORY, 3
Look in my f.; my name is Might-have-been   DISAPPOINTMENT, 6
Looks the whole world in the f.   RIGHTEOUSNESS, 7
My f. is my fortune, sir, she said   NURSERY RHYMES, 67
painting a f. and not washing   APPEARANCE, 15
Socialism with a human f.   COMMUNISM, 2
the f. that launch'd a thousand ships   BEAUTY, 25
The human f. is . . . a whole cluster of faces   MANKIND, 21
There is not any book Or f.   DEATH, 126
to order a new stamp . . . with my f. on it   TRIVIALITY, 11
your whole life shows in your f.   AGE, 6
faces All, all are gone, the old familiar f.   NOSTALGIA, 12
among so many million of f.   INDIVIDUALITY, 3
facetious You must not think me . . . foolish because I am f.
                                                          SERIOUSNESS, 3
fact the slaying of a beautiful hypothesis by an ugly f.
                                                              SCIENCE, 21
faction To die for f.   EXECUTION, 7
factory In the f. we make cosmetics   COSMETICS, 3
facts Comment is free but f. are sacred   JOURNALISM, 27
F. alone are wanted in life   FACTS, 1
F. do not cease to exist   FACTS, 2
F. speak louder than statistics   FACTS, 3; STATISTICS, 11
Learn, compare, collect the f.   EDUCATION, 42
Once a newspaper touches a story, the f. are lost
                                                          JOURNALISM, 22
phantom beings loaded up with f.   SCIENCE, 42
fade the cheek that doth not f.   APPEARANCE, 17
fail If they succeed, they f.   HOMOSEXUALITY, 3
Others must f.   RUTHLESSNESS, 4
to f. conventionally   ORTHODOXY, 3
failed Here lies Joseph, who f. in everything he undertook
                                                              FAILURE, 3
faileth charity never f.   CHARITY, 6
fails If thy heart f. thee   AMBITION, 7
failure All political lives . . . end in f.   POLITICIANS, 2
no success like f.   FAILURE, 2
we all contain f. and death within us   AGE, 36
faint Damn with f. praise   CRITICISM, 40
fair All is f.   LOVE, 1
all's f. in love and war   JUSTICE, 8

F. stood the wind for France   BOATS, 5
Grief has turned her f.   APPEARANCE, 41
Monday's child is f. of face   NURSERY RHYMES, 34
Serious sport has nothing to do with f. play   SPORT AND
                                                              GAMES, 15
So foul and f. a day   WEATHER, 21
the Brave deserves the F.   COURAGE, 11
There was a f. maid dwellin'   LOVE, 13
Whitehall . . . our attempts to be f. to everybody   BRITAIN, 3
faire Laissez f.   FREEDOM, 42
fairer thou art f. than the evening air   BEAUTY, 26
fairest the f. things have the worst fate   TRANSIENCE, 17
fairies I don't believe in f.   FAIRIES, 1
the beginning of f.   FAIRIES, 2
There are f. at the bottom of our garden   FAIRIES, 3
fairy A myth is, of course, not a f. story   MYTHS, 2
the f. tales of science   EXPERIENCE, 19
fairyland The Fleet's lit up. It is like f.   NAVY, 4
faith a life of doubt diversified by f.   DOUBT, 4
an absolute f. that all things are possible to God   FAITH, 10
And f. shines equal   COURAGE, 3
by f. the walls of Jericho fell down   FAITH, 2
F. . . . an illogical belief in . . . the improbable   FAITH, 14
F. consists in believing when it is beyond the power of reason
to believe   FAITH, 19
f., if it hath not works, is dead   FAITH, 7
f. is the substance of things hoped for   FAITH, 3
f. unfaithful kept him falsely true   UNFAITHFULNESS, 6
F. will move mountains   FAITH, 1
no need for any other f. than . . . faith in human beings
                                                             FAITH, 9
now abideth f., hope, charity   CHARITY, 6
O thou of little f., wherefore didst thou doubt   DOUBT, 2
Reason is itself a matter of f.   REASON, 2
the f. and morals hold Which Milton held   FREEDOM, 53
'Tis not the dying for a f.   FAITH, 18
we walk by f., not by sight   FAITH, 5
When your ladyship's f. has removed them   RELIGION, 15
whoever is moved by f. to assent to it   CHRISTIANITY, 29
faithful f. in love, . . . dauntless in war   CHIVALRY, 10
f. to thee, Cynara   FAITHFULNESS, 3
happiness of man that he be mentally f.   INTEGRITY, 5
If this man is not f. to his God   LOYALTY, 9
if you had been f.   LOVE, 105
my heart shall be The f. compass   FAITHFULNESS, 4
O come all ye f.   CHRISTMAS, 16
thou good and f. servant   SERVICE, 1
Translations (like wives) are seldom f.   TRANSLATION, 2
fake If I like it, . . . it's mine. If I don't . . . it's a f.   PAINTING, 9
fall and an haughty spirit before a f.   PRIDE, 1
Fain would I climb, yet fear I to f.   AMBITION, 14
The airplane stays up because it doesn't have the time to f.
                                                            SCIENCE, 46
Whenever you f., pick up something   OPPORTUNITY, 8
fallen A good man f. among Fabians   WRITERS, 64
y-f. out of heigh degree. Into miserie   MISFORTUNE, 6
falleth woe to him that is alone when he f.   FRIENDSHIP, 8
fallow lie f. for a while   REST, 3
false beware of f. prophets   DECEPTION, 2
F. face must hide what the false heart   DECEPTION, 5
f. to his friends . . . true to the public   HONESTY, 3
natural f. teeth   TEETH, 3
The religions we call f. were once true   RELIGION, 24
Thou canst not then be f.   BORROWING, 8; INTEGRITY, 6
thou shalt not bear f. witness   GOD, 10
True and F. are attributes of speech, not of things   TRUTH, 26
Vain wisdom all, and f. philosophy   WISDOM, 19
falsehood Let her and f. grapple   TRUTH, 33
falsely a verb meaning 'to believe f.'   BELIEF, 8
Falstaff F. sweats to death   OBESITY, 10
fame blush to find it f.   GOOD, 14
F. is a powerful aphrodisiac   FAME, 11
F. is like a river   FAME, 2
F. is sometimes like unto a . . . mushroom   FAME, 10
F. is the spur   FAME, 14
Here rests . . . A youth to fortune and to f. unknown   DEATH, 58
Love of f. is the last thing . . . to be parted from   FAME, 9
One of the drawbacks of F.   FAME, 13
The book written against f. . . . has the author's name on the
title-page   HYPOCRISY, 9
familiar old f. faces   NOSTALGIA, 12
familiarity F. breeds contempt   FAMILIARITY, 1

The only time . . . ever put up a f. INSULTS, 13
To f. and not to heed the wounds SELFLESSNESS, 2
too proud to f. WAR, 134
Ulster will f. IRELAND, 3
We don't want to f., but, by jingo if we do PATRIOTISM, 16
We'll f. and we'll conquer COURAGE, 13
we shall f. on the beaches WORLD WAR II, 4
when the f. begins within CONFLICT, 5
With our backs to the wall . . . each . . . must f. on to the end WAR, 45
You cannot f. against the future PROGRESS, 7

fighting F. is like champagne WAR, 69
Most sorts of diversion . . . are an imitation of f. WAR, 117
not conquering but f. well VICTORY, 4
What are we f. for WAR, 107

fights He that f. and runs away SELF-PRESERVATION, 2
I can't spare this man; he f. OFFICERS, 9

figure an oblong angular f. HUMOUR, 40

figures prove anything by f. STATISTICS, 1

film A wide screen . . . makes a bad f., twice as bad CINEMA, 2
I like a f. to have a beginning, a middle and an end CINEMA, 3

filmed written or thought, it can be f. CINEMA, 7

films Why . . . pay money to see bad f. CINEMA, 5

finality F. is death. Perfection is f. PERFECTION, 9

find terrible thing for a man to f. out HONESTY, 12
your sin will f. you out SIN, 7

finders F. keepers LUCK, 5

fine f. feathers that make f. birds CLOTHES, 1
In England, pop art and f. art ART, 15
The big print giveth and the f. print taketh away BUSINESS, 20

finer every baby . . . is a f. one BABIES, 2

finest their f. hour WORLD WAR II, 5

finger Moving F. writes DESTINY, 7
The least pain in our little f. SELF-INTEREST, 4

fingerlickin' It's f. good ADVERTISING, 15

fingernails if you don't stop biting your f. ARTISTS, 9

fingers F. were made before forks BEGINNING, 2
ill cook that cannot lick his own f. SELF-CONFIDENCE, 4
our f. are circumcised MUSICIANS, 6

finger-tips An accomplished man to his f. EXPERTS, 4

fings F. Ain't Wot They Used T'Be NOSTALGIA, 15

finished it is f. LAST WORDS, 9
We have f. the job TELEGRAMS, 10

finite Our knowledge can only be f. KNOWLEDGE, 8

fir The f. trees dark and high INNOCENCE, 6

fire All things, oh priests, are on f. FIRE, 1
Billy . . . Fell in the f. FIRE, 2
bound Upon a wheel of f. SUFFERING, 14
F. – without hatred WAR, 94
French Guard, f. first WAR, 46
heap coals of f. upon his head RETRIBUTION, 8
He had a f. in his eye, a fever in his blood POETS, 40
how great a matter a little f. kindleth SPEECH, 5
Ideas that enter the mind under f. INDOCTRINATION, 3
It is with our passions as it is with f. and water PASSION, 4
it is your business, when the wall next door catches f. NEIGHBOURS, 4
I warmed both hands before the f. of life LIFE AND DEATH, 8
London burnt by f. in three times twenty plus six PROPHECY, 9
The f. which in the heart resides SOUL, 3
two irons in the f. PRUDENCE, 5
what wind is to f. ABSENCE, 6

firearms Though loaded f. were strictly forbidden at St Trinian's WEAPONS, 7

fire-folk the f. sitting in the air STARS, 3

fireirons Saint Preux never kicked the f. IMPERFECTION, 5

fires Husbands are like f. MARRIAGE, 61

fireside A man may surely be allowed to take a glass of wine by his own f. FIRE, 4

firing he faced the f. squad; erect and motionless EXECUTION, 28

firm not a family; we're a f. ROYALTY, 18

firmness *Commodity, F.,* and *Delight* ARCHITECTURE, 14

first Because of my title, I was the f. COURAGE, 2
F. come HASTE, 2
F. impressions FIRST IMPRESSIONS, 1
F. things first PATIENCE, 5
If at f. you don't succeed PERSISTENCE, 5
many that are f. shall be last MERIT, 3
The constitution . . . f. and second class citizens CLASS, 40
The f. day a guest HOSPITALITY, 3
there is no last or f. EQUALITY, 6

which came f., the Greeks or the Romans IGNORANCE, 5
Who ever loved, that loved not at f. sight FIRST IMPRESSIONS, 6

first-aid His ideas of f. INCOMPETENCE, 6

first-rate the powers of a f. man and the creed of a second-rate man POLITICIANS, 1
to mistake for the f., the fecund rate WRITERS, 18

fish F. and guests HOSPITALITY, 2
F. die belly-upward OPPOSITES, 2
F. fuck in it WATER, 4
I have my own f. to fry NONCOMMITMENT, 2
No human being, . . . was ever so free as a f. FREEDOM, 46
Phone for the f. knives Norman ETIQUETTE, 4
This man . . . is a poor f. MARRIAGE, 46
What cat's averse to f. MATERIALISM, 8
white wine came up with the f. ETIQUETTE, 4

fishbone The monument sticks like a f. MEMORIALS, 7

fishermen a bite every time for f. HUMOUR, 47

fishes f. live in the sea RUTHLESSNESS, 5
So are the f. WORLD WAR II, 8

fishing Time is but the stream I go a-f. in TIME, 38

fishmonger She was a f., but sure 'twas no wonder BUSINESS, 1

fishy something f. about the French FRANCE, 4

fist You cannot shake hands with a clenched f. INFLEXIBILITY, 1

fit a pleasing f. of melancholy MELANCHOLY, 10
It is not f. that you should sit here DISMISSAL, 2
let the punishment f. the crime PUNISHMENT, 10
news that's f. to print NEWSPAPERS, 8
only the F. survive SURVIVAL, 4

fits periodical f. of morality MORALITY, 10
Strange f. of passion PASSION, 9

fittest Survival of the F. EVOLUTION, 7

five child of f. would understand this SIMPLICITY, 5
F. gold rings NURSERY RHYMES, 55
If you don't find a God by f. o'clock this afternoon ATHEISM, 7
practise f. things VIRTUE, 7
The formula 'Two and two make f.' PHILOSOPHY, 2

five-pound get a f. note as . . . a light for a cigarette GENEROSITY, 4

five-year-old real menace in dealing with a f. CHILDREN, 29

fixed Nothing to be f. except TELEGRAMS, 5

flabbiness The moral f. born of . . . Success SUCCESS, 9

flag But spare your country's f. PATRIOTISM, 32
keep the red f. flying here SOCIALISM, 3
Tonight the American f. floats from yonder hill WAR, 114

flame like a moth, the simple maid Still plays about the f. WOMEN, 35

flames Commit it then to the f. PHILOSOPHY, 3
Superstition sets the whole world in f. SUPERSTITION, 11

Flanders In F. fields MEMORIALS, 8
You have sent me a F. mare FIRST IMPRESSIONS, 8

flashing His f. eyes, his floating hair CAUTION, 9

flat Very f., Norfolk ENGLAND, 12
Vile snub-nose, f.-nosed ass APPEARANCE, 31

flatter not f. me REALISM, 1
We f. those we scarcely know HURT, 4

flatterer the brave beast is no f. HORSES, 7

flatterers f. live at the expense of those who listen FLATTERY, 6
Self-love . . . greatest of all f. CONCEIT, 14

flattering It is f. some men to endure them TOLERANCE, 3
the talent of f. with delicacy FLATTERY, 2

flattery consider whether . . . your f. is worth his having FLATTERY, 5
F. is all right FLATTERY, 8
f.'s the food of fools FLATTERY, 9
Imitation is the sincerest form of f. IMITATION, 2
ne'er Was f. lost POETS, 5
woman . . . to be gained by . . . f. FLATTERY, 4

flaunt if you've got it, f. it OSTENTATION, 1

flautists f. are most obviously the ones who know something we don't know MUSICIANS, 4

flea English literature's performing f. WRITERS, 70
man's whole frame is obvious to a f. CLARITY, 3
The guerrilla fights the war of the f. WAR, 118
the point of precedency between a louse and a f. POETS, 9

fleas dog that praised his f. PARASITES, 4
F. . . . upon the body of a giant PERSPECTIVE, 3
the f. in my bed were as good COMPLIMENTS, 1
The f. that tease in the high Pyrenees NONSENSE, 3
these have smaller f. to bite 'em PARASITES, 3

fled I f. Him, down the nights RELIGION, 58

those f. scare me, all directed your way, none coming back
MISTRUST, 5
you can have my f. HUMOUR, 44
footsteps home his f. he hath turn'd HOMESICKNESS, 6
foppery excellent f. of the world MISFORTUNE, 18
for neither f. nor against institutions INDIFFERENCE, 7
forbearance f. ceases to be a virtue TOLERANCE, 1
forbidden F. fruit TEMPTATION, 1
he wanted it only because it was f. PERVERSITY, 6
we're f. to know – what end the gods have in store
DESTINY, 12
force f. alone is but *temporary* FORCE, 2
F., if unassisted by judgement, collapses JUDGMENT, 9
F. is not a remedy FORCE, 1
Hence no f. however great POETRY, 51
Other nations use 'f.'; we Britons . . . use 'Might' BRITISH, 10
Who overcomes By f. VICTORY, 11
forced f. to commend her highly INSINCERITY, 3
force-feeding This universal, obligatory f. with lies
INDOCTRINATION, 2
forces one of the f. of nature GREATNESS, 10
Ford Jerry F. is so dumb STUPIDITY, 5
forefathers Think of your f. POSTERITY, 1
forehead A burning f., and a parching tongue PASSION, 3
foreign pronounce f. names as he chooses PRONUNCIATION, 1
wandering on a f. strand HOMESICKNESS, 2
foreigner f. should . . . be wiser than ourselves PRIDE, 12
foreigners f. speak English when our backs are turned
LANGUAGE, 10
f. . . . spell better than they pronounce PRONUNCIATION, 3;
SPELLING, 2
Sympathy . . . for being f. SYMPATHY, 1
foreparents His f. came to America EQUALITY, 12
forest His f. fleece the Wrekin heaves TREES, 4
Wandering in a vast f. at night GUIDANCE, 2
forests the f. of the night ANIMALS, 4
foretaste Every parting gives a f. of death SEPARATION, 5
forever That is f. England WAR, 18
forewarned F. is forearmed PRUDENCE, 2
forget Better by far you should f. and smile MEMORY, 14
Fade far away, dissolve, and . . . f. HUMAN CONDITION, 1
I f. what I was taught KNOWLEDGE, 35
I'll not f. old Ireland HOMESICKNESS, 1
I never f. a face, but I'll make an exception MEMORY, 1
Oh Lord! . . . if I f. thee, do not thou f. me PRAYER, 3
Old men f. MEMORY, 16
To endeavour to f. anyone MEMORY, 8
Were it not better to f. REGRET, 6
When I f. my sovereign LOYALTY, 10
forgivable Few books today are f. BOOKS, 21
forgive do not have to f. my enemies LAST WORDS, 46;
RUTHLESSNESS, 4
Father, f. them FORGIVENESS, 4
F. and forget FORGIVENESS, 1
how oft shall . . . I f. him FORGIVENESS, 6
Men will f. a man PROSE, 2
To err is human, to f., divine MISTAKES, 13; FORGIVENESS, 13
forgiven her sins, which are many, are f. FORGIVENESS, 5; SIN, 6
Once a woman has f. her man FORGIVENESS, 10
forgot auld acquaintance be f. FRIENDSHIP, 12
How these curiosities would be quite f. GOSSIP, 7
I have f. my part FAILURE, 5
forgotten I have f. more law than you ever knew INSULTS, 30
Nobody is f. when it is convenient to remember him
EXPEDIENCY, 3
The f. man POVERTY, 27
what has been learnt has been f. EDUCATION, 54
fork he had a f. INSULTS, 26
forks I had a knife and two f. left ETIQUETTE, 6
forlorn faery lands f. BIRDS, 5
The British postgraduate student is a lonely f. soul
EDUCATION, 31
form significant f. ART, 4
formed not f. by nature to bear ENDURANCE, 1
formidable Examinations are f. EXAMINATIONS, 1
forms from outward f. to win APPEARANCES, 12
formula Matter . . . a convenient f. PHILOSOPHY, 11
fornicated f. and read the papers MANKIND, 10
fornication F.: but that was in another country SEX, 33
forsaken my God, why hast thou f. me DESPAIR, 4
fortress f. built by Nature ENGLAND, 36
fortuitous f. concurrence of atoms CHANCE, 4

fortune f. and men's eyes DISCONTENT, 8
F. favours the brave COURAGE, 23
F., that favours fools LUCK, 8
greater virtues to sustain good f. LUCK, 11
Here rests . . . A youth to f. and to fame unknown DEATH, 58
hostages to f. FAMILY, 7
people of f. . . . a few delinquencies POVERTY AND WEALTH, 5
slings and arrows of outrageous f. SUICIDE, 12
to make your f. . . . let people see . . . it is in their interests to
promote yours SUCCESS, 11
What is your f., my pretty maid NURSERY RHYMES, 67
fortunes f. sharp adversitee MISFORTUNE, 1
share in the good f. of the mighty INJUSTICE, 2
forty F. years on PARTING, 4
I am just turning f. AGE, 35
I have been talking prose for over f. years PROSE, 3
Life begins at f. AGE, 61
look young till f. AGE, 20
made the difference of f. thousand men OFFICERS, 16
When you are f. OLD AGE, 3
forty-five That should assure us of . . . f. minutes of undisturbed
privacy INATTENTION, 2
forty-niner Dwelt a miner, F., And his daughter, Clementine
MOURNING, 1
forty-three She may very well pass for f. AGE, 29
forward looking f. to the past NOSTALGIA, 17
foster-child f. of silence and slow time SILENCE, 9
fou I wasna f. SATISFACTION, 2
fought better to have f. and lost DEFEAT, 1
I have f. a good fight FAITH, 6
foul Murder most f. MURDER, 11
So f. and fair a day WEATHER, 21
foul-mouthed English . . . are rather a f. nation ENGLISH, 18
found he f. it brick IMPROVEMENT, 1
I have f. it DISCOVERY, 1
Pleasure is . . . seldom f. where it is sought PLEASURE, 14
Suppose it had been someone else who f. you like this
ADULTERY, 6
foundation The Church's one f. CHRISTIANITY, 40
four at the age of f. . . . we're all Generals
AUTHORITARIANISM, 8
F. colly birds NURSERY RHYMES, 55
f. essential human freedoms HUMAN RIGHTS, 4
Great God grant that twice two be not f. PRAYER, 18
fourth a f. estate of the realm JOURNALISM, 21
Because there's no f. class HUMILITY, 8
on the f. day they will say 'To hell with you!' PROMISES, 4
four-year-old You've got the brain of a f. boy STUPIDITY, 8
fox a f. from his lair HUNTING, 4
Charles James F. MORTALITY, 20
The f. came home and he went to ground ANIMALS, 1
The f. knows many things ANIMALS, 2
the . . . f. said . . . to the sick lion: 'Because those footprints
scare me MISTRUST, 1
You don't set a f. to watching the chickens EXPERIENCE, 21
fox-hunting athletics as inferior forms of f. WOMEN, 89
fraction Only a residual f. is thought BUREAUCRACY, 7
fractions distinguish proper from improper f. MATHEMATICS, 7
fragrant a thousand f. posies FLOWERS, 7
frailty F., thy name is woman WEAKNESS, 4; WOMEN, 72
more flesh . . . more f. OBESITY, 11
frame all the Human F. requires FOOD, 2
change their clime, not their f. of mind, who rush across the
sea TRAVEL, 14
man's whole f. is obvious to a flea CLARITY, 3
frames The finest collection of f. PHILISTINISM, 1
framework Language is . . . a defining f. LANGUAGE, 27
France all roads lead to F. WAR, 120
Fair stood the wind for F. BOATS, 5
F. is a country where the money falls apart FRANCE, 16
F. was a long despotism FRANCE, 2
Had we gone the way of F. ECOLOGY, 8
Like Brighton pier, . . . inadequate for getting to F. TRAVEL, 18
The best thing I know between F. and England FRANCE, 8
Francis My cousin F. and I are in perfect accord
AGREEMENT, 1
frankincense gold, and f., and myrrh CHRISTMAS, 10
fraternité Liberté! Égalité! F. HUMAN RIGHTS, 3
frauds many of the great men of history are f. GREATNESS, 9
pious f. of friendship FRIENDSHIP, 18
free a f. society . . . where it is safe to be unpopular
FREEDOM, 49

All f. men, . . . are citizens of Berlin — GERMANY, 6
All human beings are born f. — HUMAN RIGHTS, 1
all men everywhere could be f. — FREEDOM, 27
f. as the road — FREEDOM, 17
F. Will and Predestination — DESTINY, 5
Greece might still be f. — EUROPE, 4
I'm with you on the f. press — JOURNALISM, 29
In a f. society the state . . . administers justice among men — STATE, 3
land of the f., and the home of the brave — AMERICA, 20
Man is condemned to be f. — FREEDOM, 47
Man was born f. — FREEDOM, 45
No human being, . . . was ever so f. as a fish — FREEDOM, 46
none the less f. than you were — ADAPTABILITY, 1
no such thing as a f. lunch — FRIENDSHIP, 7
safer to be in chains than to be f. — FREEDOM, 24
So f. we seem — FREEDOM, 4
the truth shall make you f. — TRUTH, 11
Thou art f. — SHAKESPEARE, 1
truth that makes men f. — TRUTH, 7
We have to believe in f. will — CHOICE, 4
We must be f. or die — FREEDOM, 53
Who would be f. — FREEDOM, 6
freedom enemies of F. — OPPRESSION, 3
fit to use their f. — FREEDOM, 29
flame of f. in their souls — KNOWLEDGE, 33
F.! Equality! Brotherhood — HUMAN RIGHTS, 4
F. is an indivisible word — HUMAN RIGHTS, 5
F. is the right to tell . . . do not want to hear — FREEDOM, 38
f. of speech, f. of conscience, and the prudence never to practise . . . them — FREEDOM, 50
F.'s just another word — FREEDOM, 25
f. to print . . . proprietor's prejudices — ADVERTISING, 5; JOURNALISM, 30
If f. were not so economically efficient — ECONOMICS, 8
In solitude alone can he know true f. — SOLITUDE, 12
Me this unchartered f. tires — FREEDOM, 52
Necessity is the plea for every infringement of human f. — NECESSITY, 4
None can love f. heartily, but good men — FREEDOM, 34
only f. can make security secure — FREEDOM, 40
So long as the state exists there is no f. — STATE, 2
stand up for f. of the imagination — RELIGION, 52
The worst enemy of truth and f. — MAJORITY, 4
Those who deny f. to others — FREEDOM, 28
Until you've lost your reputation, you never realize . . . what f. really is — REPUTATION, 5
what is F. — FREEDOM, 31
Your f. and mine cannot be separated — FREEDOM, 31
You took my f. away a long time ago — FREEDOM, 48
freedoms four essential human f. — HUMAN RIGHTS, 4
free-loader A f. is a confirmed guest — PARASITES, 2
freely nothing so f. as advice — ADVICE, 1
freemasonry a kind of bitter f. — LOVE, 20
free-will believe in f.. We've got no choice — HUMAN CONDITION, 19
French Bouillabaisse is only good because cooked by the F. — FOOD, 17; FRANCE, 5
dislike the F. from . . . vulgar antipathy — FRANCE, 15
everyone would always have spoken F. — LANGUAGE, 25
F. governments more selfish than most — GOVERNMENT, 8
F. Guard, fire first — WAR, 46
Give me books, fruit, F. wine and fine weather — PLEASURE, 17
I hate the F. — FRANCE, 7
Imagine the Lord talking F. — LANGUAGE, 12
I speak . . . Italian to women, F. to men — LANGUAGE, 7
My suit is pale yellow. My nationality is F. — NORMALITY, 2
something fishy about the F. — FRANCE, 4
The F. are wiser than they seem — APPEARANCES, 9
The F. want no-one to be their *superior* — PRIDE, 11
The F. will only be united under the threat of danger — FRANCE, 6
the German text of F. operas — OPERA, 10
There's something Vichy about the F. — FRANCE, 12
to the F. the empire of the land — EUROPE, 13
Frenchman F. must be always talking — FRANCE, 9
You must hate a F. — ENEMIES, 6
Frenchmen F. drink wine just like — ALCOHOL, 39
to create F. in the image of Englishmen — NATIONALITY, 4
frenzy poet's eye, in a fine f. rolling — POETRY, 4
fresh f. as is the month of May — CHARACTER, 4
the cod's wallop is always f. made — COMMUNISM, 5

freshen a mighty storm . . . to f. us up — CHANGE, 3
fret weariness, the fever, and the f. — HUMAN CONDITION, 12
Freud The trouble with F. — PSYCHIATRY, 2
Freudian the F., it is a very low, Central European sort of humour — HUMOUR, 13
Friday F.'s child is loving and giving — NURSERY RHYMES, 34
Worse on F. — NURSERY RHYMES, 49
friend A fav'rite has no f. — LONELINESS, 2
a F. for little children — GOD, 36
A f. in need — FRIENDSHIP, 1
A f. in power — POWER, 4
A f. should bear his f.'s infirmities — FRIENDS, 13
a good f., but bad acquaintance — FRIENDS, 3
A good f. is my nearest relation — FRIENDSHIP, 2
a new f. is as new wine — FRIENDS, 2
A woman can become a man's f. — FRIENDSHIP, 15
damned good-natured f. — FRIENDS, 14
Every time I paint a portrait I lose a f. — PAINTING, 15
forsake not an old f. — FRIENDS, 2
F. . . . masterpiece of Nature — FRIENDS, 7
f., wherefore art thou come — BETRAYAL, 1
He makes no f. — ENEMIES, 8
I might give my life for my f. — FRIENDSHIP, 27
In every f. we lose a part of ourselves — DEATH, 95
It takes your enemy and your f. . . . , to hurt you — HURT, 3
no f. like a sister — FAMILY, 36
save me, from the candid f. — FRANKNESS, 1
that a man lay down his wife for a f. — FRIENDSHIP, 21
trust ye not in a f. — TRUST, 1
When a f. dies out on us — FRIENDSHIP, 23
Whenever a f. succeeds — ENVY, 8
friendly Man is the only animal . . . on f. terms with the victims . . . he eats — HYPOCRISY, 6
so large, So f., and so rich — AMERICA, 2
friends Animals are such agreeable f. — ANIMALS, 10
better to drop thy f. — CLASS, 5
false to his f. . . . true to the public — HONESTY, 3
F., Romans, countrymen — EVIL, 16
Good thoughts his only f. — RIGHTEOUSNESS, 5
guessed you were f. — FRIENDSHIP, 10
Have no f. not equal — FRIENDS, 5
His best f. hear no more — MARRIAGE, 106
How few of his f.' houses — ILLNESS, 9
How to Win F. — INFLUENCE, 2
I cannot forgive my f. for dying — DEATH, 115
I don't trust him. We're f. — FRIENDSHIP, 11
I let down my f. — BETRAYAL, 6
In the misfortune of our best f. — MISFORTUNE, 15
Job endured everything – until his f. came — ENDURANCE, 8
lay down his f. for his life — SELF-PRESERVATION, 10
Money can't buy f. — MONEY, 35
none of his f. like him — POPULARITY, 9
not so much our f.' help that helps us — FRIENDSHIP, 17
Once more unto the breach, dear f. — COURAGE, 19
our f. are true and our happiness — OPTIMISM, 15
shameful to distrust one's f. — FRIENDS, 12
that a man lay down his life for his f. — LOVE, 25
the best of f. must part — PARTING, 2
troops of unrecording f. — LIFE, 48
with a little help from my f. — FRIENDS, 10
without three good f. — MONEY, 40
you choose your f. — FAMILY, 13; FRIENDS, 6
friendship A man, Sir, should keep his f. in constant repair — FRIENDS, 9
Business . . . may bring money, . . . f. hardly ever does — MONEY, 6
f. closes its eyes — LOVE AND FRIENDSHIP, 1; FRIENDSHIP, 5
F. is a disinterested commerce between equals — LOVE AND FRIENDSHIP, 2
F. is constant in all other things — LOVE AND FRIENDSHIP, 3
F. is unnecessary — FRIENDSHIP, 22
love . . . looks more like hatred than like f. — LOVE AND HATE, 5
Most f. is feigning — INSINCERITY, 4
Society, f., and love — SOLITUDE, 4
The dupe of f., and the fool of love — BITTERNESS, 1
To like . . . the same things, that is . . . true f. — FRIENDSHIP, 26
true bond of f. — FRIENDSHIP, 25
frighten by God, they f. me — OFFICERS, 13
f. the horses — SEX, 9
frightened My father was f. of his mother — FAMILY, 17
frittered life is f. away by detail — SIMPLICITY, 8
frivolity gay without f. — FUTURE, 1

G

No man is genuinely happy, married, who has to drink worse g. ALCOHOL, 44
she was dead; but my father he kept ladling g. REMEDIES, 12
The shortest way out of Manchester is . . . g. PLACES, 1
girded Pavilioned in splendour, and g. with praise GOD, 23
girl Every little g. knows about love LOVE, 111
From birth to age eighteen, a g. needs good parents AGE, 62
g. with brains WOMEN, 48
Give me a g. at an impressionable age IMPRESSIONABILITY, 3
If you were the only g. in the world LOVE, 65
one can . . . see in a little g. the threat of a woman CHILDREN, 20
One g. can be pretty BEAUTY, 18
park, a policeman and a pretty g. HUMOUR, 5
There was a little g. Who had a little curl SEX, 37
girlfriend Not every problem someone has with his g. is . . .
due to . . . capitalist . . . production CAPITALISM, 2
girls Boys and g. come out to play NURSERY RHYMES, 6
G. and boys grow up more normally together EDUCATION, 45
g. are so queer WOMEN, 8
g. from being g. SEXES, 12
g. . . . say No when they mean Yes WOMEN, 8
g. who wear glasses APPEARANCE, 27
if ever I was to have a dozen g., I'd call 'em all Jane NAMES, 8
little g. . . . slamming doors CHILDREN, 10
My life with g. has ended SEX, 23
one of the nicest g. I was ever engaged to MARRIAGE, 134
the . . . rift between the sexes is . . . widened by . . . teaching
. . . to the g. SEXES, 21
Treaties are like roses and young g. DIPLOMACY, 10
When you see what some g. marry MARRIAGE, 98
Where . . . boys plan for what . . . young g. plan for whom
SEXES, 10
give freely ye have received, freely g. GENEROSITY, 3; GIFTS, 1
g. me liberty or g. me death FREEDOM, 16
G. me your tired, . . . Your huddled masses AMERICA, 21
my peace I g. unto you PEACE, 3
such as I have g. I thee REMEDIES, 3
To g. and not to count the cost SELFLESSNESS, 4
When I g. I g. myself SELF, 19; SELF, 19
given I wish that God had not g. me what I prayed for
DISAPPOINTMENT, 7
I would have g. you another CHIVALRY, 5
gives He g. twice who g. promptly PROMPTNESS, 4
giving The manner of g. GIFTS, 4
gizzard My wife hath something in her g. PROVOCATION, 1
glad She had A heart . . . too soon made g.
IMPRESSIONABILITY, 1
with a love like that you know you should be g. LOVE, 83
you would have been very g. if I had written it PLAYS, 6
gladsome Let us with a g. mind Praise the Lord GOD, 37
Gladstone G. POLITICIANS, 32
Mr G. read Homer for fun CLASSICS, 2
glamorous g. only in retrospect TRAVEL, 10
Glasgow never played the G. Empire PSYCHIATRY, 2
glass baying for broken g. ARISTOCRACY, 15
He liked the sound of broken g. ARISTOCRACY, 2
on the other side of the g. LIFE, 11
Satire is a sort of g. SATIRE, 3
through a g., darkly CHARITY, 2
you won't intoxicate with one g. EXPERIENCE, 10
glasses girls who wear g. APPEARANCE, 27
glimpse I . . . catch a g. of a stoat PURPOSE, 5
Same old g. of Paradise MARRIAGE, 76
glisters Nor all that g. gold TEMPTATION, 6
glittering The world continues to offer g. prizes
RUTHLESSNESS, 6
glitters All that g. is not gold APPEARANCES, 2
gloamin Roamin' in the g.' SCOTLAND, 6
global my wars Were g. WAR, 91
the world in the image of a g. village TECHNOLOGY, 9
globe the great g. itself MORTALITY, 17
globule I can trace my ancestry back to a . . . g. ANCESTRY, 2
gloire Le jour de g. est arrivé FRANCE, 10
gloria Sic transit g. mundi GLORY, 3
glorious G. things of thee are spoken HEAVEN, 7
Happy and g. BRITAIN, 9
glory Another g. awaits us in heaven HEAVEN, 8
But trailing clouds of g. METAPHYSICS, 5
G. be to God for dappled things BEAUTY, 9
g., jest, and riddle of the world HUMAN CONDITION, 14
greatest g. is not in never falling ACHIEVEMENT, 3

I go on to g. LAST WORDS, 20
It is a great g. in a woman WOMEN, 80
Land of Hope and G. BRITAIN, 4
Mine eyes have seen the g. of the coming of the Lord GOD, 26
paths of g. lead but to the grave MORTALITY, 10
Popularity? . . . g.'s small change POPULARITY, 4
the g. of Europe is extinguished for ever EUROPE, 2
the Son of man coming . . . with power and great g.
DOOMSDAY, 2
To the greater g. of God CATHOLICISM, 2
we left him alone with his g. FUNERALS, 11
Where is it now, the g. and the dream METAPHYSICS, 5
Gloucester Doctor Foster went to G. NURSERY RHYMES, 10
glow make the corpuscles of the blood g. JEWS, 8
Glum I've examined your son's head, Mr G. STUPIDITY, 12
speed g. heroes . . . to death WAR, 101
gluttony G. is an emotional escape GREED, 5
gnomes the little g. of Zürich MONEY, 51
go a good cook, as cooks g. HUMOUR, 52
In the name of God, g.! DISMISSAL, 1
I shall be the last to g. out COURAGE, 2
Let us g. then, you and I DEPARTURE, 6
not to g. anywhere, but to g. TRAVEL, 28
stopped short – never to g. again CLOCKS, 3
whither thou goest, I will g. LOYALTY, 5
goal The g. stands up FOOTBALL, 3
goat-footed This g. bard POLITICIANS, 55
God Act of G. . . . *something which no reasonable man could*
have expected DISASTER, 3
A G. who let us prove his existence GOD, 15
a kind of Providence will . . . end . . . the acts of G. DISASTER, 2
A man with G. GOD, 31
America is G.'s Crucible AMERICA, 40
an absolute faith that all things are possible to G. FAITH, 10
an atheist half believes a G. FEAR, 15
An honest G. GOD, 29
Are G. and Nature then at strife NATURE, 15
better to have no opinion of G. GOD, 3
but for the grace of G. goes LUCK, 6
charged with the grandeur of G. GOD, 25
concept of G. has any validity RELIGION, 6
cricket is the greatest thing that G. ever created CRICKET, 6
effect Whose cause is G. NATURE, 6
Either a beast or a g. MANKIND, 2
either a wild beast or a g. SOLITUDE, 1
Even G. cannot change the past PAST, 7
even G. was born too late RELIGION, 40
Every man thinks G. is on his side GOD, 2
final proof of G.'s omnipotence GOD, 19
for which . . . the good G. prepare me BLINDNESS, 7
G. alone deserves to be loved LOVE, 112
G. as a working hypothesis GOD, 14
G. bless . . . G. damn LAST WORDS, 69
'G. bless us every one!' BLESSING, 6
G. can stand being told GOD, 43
G. could cause us considerable embarrassment DISCOVERY, 4
G. defend me from my friends FRIENDSHIP, 4
G. disposes GOD, 30
G. does not play dice SCIENCE, 15
G. erects a house of prayer DEVIL, 1
G. . . . first planted a garden GARDENS, 2
G. has written all the books SUBJECTIVITY, 2
G. helps them SELF, 7
G. is a gentleman GOD, 40
G. is always on the side of the big battalions POWER POLITICS, 7
G. is beginning to resemble . . . the last fading smile of a cosmic
Cheshire cat GOD, 27
G. is dead GOD, 39
G. is nothing more than an exalted father GOD, 22
G. is on the side . . . of the best shots POWER POLITICS, 8
G. is really only another artist GOD, 42
G. is subtle but he is not malicious GOD, 21
G. is the immemorial refuge of the incompetent GOD, 35
G. . . . just had the power to kill her RELIGION, 1
G. made everything out of nothing CREATION, 15
G. made the country COUNTRYSIDE, 2
G. save our gracious King BRITAIN, 9
G.'s gifts put man's best gifts GOD, 16
G. should go before such villains GOD, 44
G.'s in His heaven PERFECTION, 2
G. the first garden made GARDENS, 6
G. will cease to dream you DEATH, 69

how *can* they become g. people   PREJUDICE, 5
How g. is man's life, the mere living   LIFE, 14
If . . . 'feeling g.' could decide, drunkenness would be
    DRUNKENNESS, 13
If to do were as easy as to know what were g.   ACTION, 11
If you can't be g.   TEMPTATION, 2
I have fought a g. fight   FAITH, 6
it cannot come to g.   PESSIMISM, 11
It is g. to know what a man is   UNDERSTANDING, 2
It is seldom . . . one parts on g. terms   PARTING, 9
little of what you fancy does you g.   PLEASURE, 19
Men have never been g.   GOOD, 1
never was a g. war   WAR AND PEACE, 9
no hint throughout the universe Of g. or ill   NECESSITY, 8
Nothing can harm a g. man   GOOD, 16
nothing either g. or bad   THINKING, 10
nothing g. to be had in the country   COUNTRYSIDE, 7
One man is as g. as another   WRITERS, 13
Only g. girls keep diaries   DIARIES, 2
our people have never had it so g.   WEALTH, 18
Roman Conquest . . . a G. Thing   HISTORY, 29
science is . . . neither a potential for g. nor for evil   SCIENCE, 38
strong antipathy of g. to bad   PROVOCATION, 2
suppose the people g.   CORRUPTION, 6
The g. die early   GOOD AND EVIL, 3
The g. die first   GOOD AND EVIL, 5
The g. die young   DEATH, 10
The g. is oft interred with their bones   EVIL, 16
The g. is the beautiful   GOOD, 13
the g. must associate   UNITY, 7
The g. of the people   LAW, 7
The 'g. old times   NOSTALGIA, 5
The king has been very g. to me   MARTYRDOM, 1
the name of perseverance in a g. cause   STUBBORNNESS, 3
The only g. Indians I ever saw were dead   ENEMIES, 7
There is so much g. in the worst of us   GOOD AND EVIL, 1
the thing which is g.   PUNISHMENT, 1; SIN, 3
those who go about doing g.   CHARITY, 13
thou g. and faithful servant   SERVICE, 1
three ingredients in the g. life   LIFE, 36
to write g. prose is an affair of g. manners   POETRY AND
    PROSE, 4
what g. came of it at last   VICTORY, 17
What's the g. of a home   ABSENCE, 7
Whenever two g. people argue over principles   PRINCIPLES, 3
When I'm g. I'm very g.   SEX, 63
when the great and g. depart   MORTALITY, 20
Why care for grammar as long as we are g.   GRAMMAR, 8
You shouldn't say it is not g.   GOOD, 18
goodbye G. to All That   BOOK, SONG, AND PLAY TITLES, 10
Without a single kiss or a g.   PARTING, 8
good-bye-ee G.! – g.   PARTING, 13
goodness And felt how awful g. is   GOOD, 12
G. does not . . . make men happy   GOOD, 9
My g. those diamonds are lovely   GOOD, 17
Not to be wronged is to forgo . . . g.   INJUSTICE, 13
goods isn't a bad bit of g., the Queen   COMPLIMENTS, 1
good-temper'd a loyal, a gallant, a generous, an ingenious, and
g. people   FRANCE, 14
goodwill in peace, g.   WAR AND PEACE, 3
goose all the gold that the g. could give   MATERIALISM, 2
Goosey G., goosey gander   NURSERY RHYMES, 13
gored you tossed and g. several persons   CONVERSATION, 3
gorgeous hold the g. east in fee   VENICE, 4
Gospels We had no use for the policy of the G.   REVENGE, 12
gossips No one g. about . . . secret virtues   GOSSIP, 8
got Which in our case we have not g.   WEAPONS, 1
gout A taste for drink, combined with g.   ALCOHOL, 28
drink wine you have the g.   DISEASE, 38
G. . . . PHYSICIAN'S NAME FOR   DISEASE, 10
If gentlemen love the pleasant titillation of the g.   DISEASE, 21
that old enemy the g. Had taken him in toe   PUNS, 6; ILLNESS, 7
what is a cure for g.   DISEASE, 2
govern Every class is unfit to g.   GOVERNMENT, 2
Grammar, which can g. even kings   GRAMMAR, 6
He that would g. others   SELF-CONTROL, 6
I will g. according to the common weal   MONARCHY, 12
king reigns, but does not g.   MONARCHY, 25
Kings g. by . . . assemblies only when   MONARCHY, 11
Labour is not fit to g.   POLITICS, 19
No man is good enough to g. another man   DEMOCRACY, 8
Under socialism *all* will g.   SOCIALISM, 10

governed with how little wisdom the world is g.
    GOVERNMENT, 20
governing become accustomed to no one g.   SOCIALISM, 10
the right of g. was not property but a trust   GOVERNMENT, 9
government A g. . . . big enough to give you all you want
    GOVERNMENT, 11
a g. organization could do it that quickly   BUREAUCRACY, 3
All g. . . . is founded on compromise and barter   COMPROMISE, 4
As to religion, . . . duty of g. to protect all . . . professors
thereof   GOVERNMENT, 22
Democracy is only an experiment in g.   DEMOCRACY, 6
every g. . . . should have its old speeches burned
    GOVERNMENT, 27
g. by crony   NEPOTISM, 1
G., . . . is but a necessary evil   GOVERNMENT, 21
g. of the people, by the people, and for the people
    MEMORIALS, 6; DEMOCRACY, 11
I would not give half a guinea to live under one form of g.
    GOVERNMENT, 13
Monarchy is a strong g.   MONARCHY, 1
no man believes, that want of g., is any new kind of g.
    GOVERNMENT, 12
people's g.   GOVERNMENT, 31
prepare for g.   POLITICS, 72
The g. burns down whole cities   INJUSTICE, 10
the g. it deserves   GOVERNMENT, 17
the President is dead, but the G. lives   ASSASSINATION, 2
there was no form of g. common to the peoples   REPUBLIC, 2
the things which g. does . . . social progress   GOVERNMENT, 30
The worst g. is the most moral   GOVERNMENT, 18
We live under a g. of men and . . . newspapers
    GOVERNMENT, 23; JOURNALISM, 26
governments all G. are selfish   GOVERNMENT, 8
G. needs to have both shepherds and butchers
    GOVERNMENT, 29
The Beast stands for strong mutually antagonistic g.
    NEWSPAPERS, 12
governors Our supreme g., the mob   PUBLIC, 20
Gower moral G.   BOOKS, 13
grace but for the g. of God, goes   LUCK, 6
God in his mercy lend her g.   BEAUTY, 39
g. a summer queen   COUNTRYSIDE, 8
He had at least the g.   BRIBERY, 1
Lord, I ascribe it to Thy g.   RELIGION, 63
Such g. had kings   ROYALTY, 6
Tuesday's child is full of g.   NURSERY RHYMES, 34
graces the G. do not seem . . . natives of Great Britain
    BRITISH, 4
gracious A life that moves to g. ends   LIFE, 48
gradually Boys do not grow up g.   CHILDREN, 19
Grail What were they going to do with the G.   ARTHURIAN
    LEGEND, 1
grain A g., which in England is generally given to horses
    SCOTLAND, 3
He reaps the bearded g. at a breath   DEATH, 78
grammar down to posterity talking bad g.   GRAMMAR, 5
G., which can govern even kings   GRAMMAR, 6
I am . . . above g.   GRAMMAR, 7
Why care for g. as long as we are good   GRAMMAR, 8
grammatical I have laboured to refine our language to g. purity
    LANGUAGE, 14
gramophones waxworks inhabited by g.   WORDS, 15
grand A 'G. Old Man'   OLD AGE, 26
that g. old man   POLITICIANS, 64
The g. Perhaps   POSSIBILITY, 3
the g. style arises in poetry   POETRY, 3
to be baith g. and comfortable   LUXURY, 1
Grand Canyon coming across him at the G.   INSULTS, 33
grandeur g. is a dream   WEALTH, 11
g. of God   GOD, 25
Many people have delusions of g.   DELUSION, 2
grandfather g.'s clock   CLOCKS, 2
having an ape for his g.   EVOLUTION, 10
I don't know who my g. was   ANCESTRY, 5
pass my declining years saluting . . . g. clocks   OLD AGE, 31
grandmother I murdered my g. this morning   INATTENTION, 4
We have become a g.   AFFECTATION, 1
grandson I am much more concerned to know what his g. will
be   ANCESTRY, 5
your g. will . . . be a Communist   COMMUNISM, 1
granny G. caught her tit in the mangle   PLEASURE, 29
Grant Old Cary G. fine   AGE, 30

granted human beings have an . . . infinite capacity for taking
  things for g. HUMAN NATURE, 13
grape Beulah, peel me a g. LUXURY, 6
grapes I am sure the g. are sour ENVY, 4
  trampling out the vintage where the g. of wrath GOD, 26
grasp man's reach should exceed his g. AMBITION, 3
grass all flesh is as g. DEATH, 29
  There's a snake hidden in the g. DANGER, 7
grassgreen down the g. gooseberried double bed SEX, 55
gratification I have had no real g. . . . more than my neighbor
  . . . who is worth only half a million LAST WORDS, 71; WEALTH, 28
gratifying It is quite g. to feel guilty GUILT, 1
gratuite L'acte g. SPONTANEITY, 2
grave a-mouldering in the g. MEMORIALS, 4
  And digs my g. at each remove DEATH, 60
  And on his g., with shining eyes DEATH, 19
  Between the cradle and the g. TRANSIENCE, 12
  Dig the g. and let me lie DEATH, 119
  Funeral marches to the g. MORTALITY, 14
  her heart in his g. is lying MOURNING, 8
  I may dread The g. as little DEATH, 72
  I shall soon be laid in the quiet g. DEATH, 71
  Marriage is a step so g. and decisive MARRIAGE, 111
  no work, nor device, nor knowledge . . . in the g.
    TRANSIENCE, 6; WORK, 3
  O g., where is thy victory DEATH, 28, 93
  paths of glory lead but to the g. MORTALITY, 10
  The g.'s a fine and private place DEATH, 81
  the g. yawns for him BORES, 7
  To that dark inn, the g. DEATH, 100
grave-digger if I were a g., or . . . a hangman OCCUPATIONS, 8
graven any g. image GOD, 10
graves Six million young men lie in premature g. WORLD
    WAR I, 2
  The bitterest tears shed over g. REGRET, 20
  The dust of great persons' g. EQUALITY, 26
graveyards G. . . . people associate them with death DEATH, 25
gravity He rose by g.; I sank by levity SERIOUSNESS, 4
gray When you are old and g. OLD AGE, 54
Gray Robin G., he was gudeman to me MARRIAGE, 69
grazed He is the richest author that ever g. WRITERS, 61
great All my shows are g. CONCEIT, 11
  All things both g. and small PRAYER, 9
  Everything g. in the world is done by neurotics NEUROSIS, 2
  everything that is g. . . . done by youth YOUTH, 6
  fate of the g. wen LONDON, 5
  G. men are but life-sized GREATNESS, 8
  g. men have not commonly been g. scholars GREATNESS, 8
  G. oaks BEGINNING, 4
  History is full of ignominious getaways by the g. COWARDICE, 5
  how g. a matter a little fire kindleth SPEECH, 5
  How very small the very g. GREATNESS, 14; WISDOM, 23
  If I am a g. man GREATNESS, 9
  many of the g. men of history are frauds GREATNESS, 9
  No g. man lives in vain GREATNESS, 6; HISTORY, 8
  On earth there is nothing g. but man MANKIND, 14
  Some are born g. GREATNESS, 12
  the g. break through LAW, 25
  The g. man . . . walks across his century INFLUENCE, 6
  the g. ones eat up the little ones RUTHLESSNESS, 5
  the shade Of that which once was g. REGRET, 23
  To be g. is to be misunderstood GREATNESS, 7
  when the g. and good depart MORTALITY, 20
  you, . . . who have made me too g. for my house ROYALTY, 4
great-aunt A person may be indebted for a nose or an eye, . . .
  to a g. FAMILY, 20
Great Britain G. could say that she supported both sides
    DIPLOMACY, 17
  G. has lost an Empire BRITAIN, 1
  G. is going to make war on a kindred nation WORLD WAR I, 3
  To make a union with G. WORLD WAR II, 24
greater g. love hath no man LOVE, 25
  The g. the power POWER, 8
  Thy need is yet g. than mine SELF-DENIAL, 2
greatest great city . . . has the g. men and women
    GREATNESS, 15
  I'm the g. CONCEIT, 1
  the g. deeds require a certain insensitiveness INSENSITIVITY, 3
  The g. happiness of the g. number HAPPINESS, 3
  the g. of these is charity CHARITY, 6
great-grandfathers Classicism, . . . the literature that gave . . .
  pleasure to their g. LITERATURE, 16

greatness long farewell to all my g. HUMAN CONDITION, 16
  Men who have g. . . . don't go in for politics POLITICIANS, 2
  some have g. thrust upon 'em GREATNESS, 12
Greece Athens holds sway over all G. INFLUENCE, 8
  G. might still be free EUROPE, 4
  The isles of G. EUROPE, 3
Greek I . . . impress upon you the study of G. literature
    CLASSICS, 3
  it was G. to me CONFUSION, 8
  neither Jew nor G. CHRISTIANITY, 7
  Nobody can say a word against G. CLASSICS, 8
  small Latin and less G. CLASSICS, 5
  the intrigue of a G. of the lower empire INSULTS, 15
  The word is half G. and half Latin TELEVISION, 5
  We were taught . . . Latin and G. CLASSICS, 9
Greeks G. Had a Word LANGUAGE, 1
  I fear the G. even when they bring gifts MISTRUST, 11
  To the G. the Muse gave native wit CLASSICS, 4
  uncertainty: a state unknown to the G. UNCERTAINTY, 4
  which came first, the G. or the Romans IGNORANCE, 5
green a g. thought in a g. shade OBLIVION, 3; OBLIVION, 3
  for the wearin' o' the G. IRELAND, 1
  G. grow the rashes O LOVE, 32
  G. politics is not about being far left CONSERVATION, 5
  I was g. in judgment YOUTH, 15
  religious system that produced g. Chartreuse ALCOHOL, 51
  There is a g. hill far away CHRISTIANITY, 1
  tree of life is g. REALITY, 3; THEORY, 4
  When the g. woods laugh HAPPINESS, 5
green-ey'd jealousy . . . g. monster JEALOUSY, 5
Greenland From G.'s icy mountains PLACES, 7
green-rob'd g. senators of mighty woods TREES, 7
Greensleeves G. was all my joy LOVE, 14
greenwood Under the g. tree COUNTRYSIDE, 9
greetings g. where no kindness is OPTIMISM, 29
  perhaps the g. are intended for me POPULARITY, 1
grenadier The healthy bones of a single Pomeranian g.
    DIPLOMACY, 4
  With a tow, . . . row for the British G. HEROISM, 1
grew Three years and g. DEATH, 132
grey G. hairs are death's blossoms OLD AGE, 1
  theory is all g. REALITY, 3; THEORY, 4
  There is only one cure for g. hair. . . . the guillotine
    REMEDIES, 15
  well-belovèd's hair has threads of g. AGE, 69
grief A g. too much to be told SORROW, 27
  calms one's g. by recounting it SORROW, 4
  G. and disappointment give rise to anger EMOTION, 3
  G. has turned her fair APPEARANCE, 41
  in much wisdom is much g. KNOWLEDGE, 6; WISDOM, 2
  Should be past g. REGRET, 15
  The heart which g. hath cankered ALCOHOL, 18
grievances redress of the g. of the vanquished WAR, 27
grieve G. not that I die young DEATH, 59
  Men are we, and must g. REGRET, 23
grill be careful not to look like a mixed g. APPEARANCE, 9
grimace only pianist I have ever seen who did not g.
    MUSICIANS, 19
grin All Nature wears one universal g. NATURE, 9
  ending with the g., which remained some time
    SUPERNATURAL, 5
grind mills of God g. slowly GOD, 34
  yet they g. exceeding small GOD, 34
grinders Writers, like teeth, are divided into incisors and g.
    WRITERS, 2
grist All's g. that comes to the mill OPPORTUNITY, 1
groan men sit and hear each other g. HUMAN CONDITION, 12
groans How alike are the g. of love to those of the dying
    LOVE AND DEATH, 4
Gromyko the G. of the Labour party POLITICIANS, 51
grooves specialists . . . tend to think in g. EXPERTS, 6
Groucho had Marx been G. instead of Karl HUMOUR, 3
  No, G. is not my real name NAMES, 5
group A g. of closely related persons FAMILY, 27
grovelled Whenever he met a great man he g. SERVILITY, 7
groves And seek for truth in the g. of Academe EDUCATION, 3
grow Green g. the rashes O LOVE, 32
  make two ears of corn . . . g. . . . where only one grew before
    POLITICIANS, 26
  make two questions g. where only one RESEARCH, 6
  some of us never g. out AUTHORITARIANISM, 8
  They shall g. not old MEMORIALS, 3

grow'd   'I 'spect I g..'   CREATION, 13
growing   Be not afraid of g. slowly   ACHIEVEMENT, 2
G. old is like being increasingly penalized   OLD AGE, 34
growl   I hate a fellow . . . who does nothing . . . but sit and g.
   PETULANCE, 4
grown   Boys . . . are unwholesome companions for g. people
   CHILDREN, 31
one of the few English novels for g. up people   CRITICISM, 57
grown-ups   g. . . . have forgotten what it is like to be a child
   CHILDREN, 27
grows   Nothing g. well in the shade   GREATNESS, 5
growth   as short a Spring; As quick a g. to meet decay
   TRANSIENCE, 14
elations and apprehensions of g.   AGE, 36
G. is a greater mystery than death   AGE, 36
grub   it is poor g., poor pay, and easy work   AMERICA, 23;
   ENGLAND, 25
grumbling   the muttering grew to a g.   ANIMALS, 6
gruntled   far from feeling g.   DISCONTENT, 9
he was far from being g.   HUMOUR, 56
guarantee   No one can g. success in war   WAR, 29
guard   That g. our native seas   NAVY, 1
guardian   As g. of His Majesty's conscience   MONARCHY, 23
guards   Up, G., and at 'em   WAR, 129
Who is to guard the g. themselves   MISTRUST, 7
gudeman   Robin Gray, he was g. to me   MARRIAGE, 19
guerre   ce n'est pas la g.   WAR, 12
guerrilla   The g. fights the war of the flea   WAR, 118
The g. wins if he does not lose   WAR, 58
guest   A free-loader is a confirmed g.   PARASITES, 2
Earth, receive an honoured g.   POETS, 18
The g. who outstays   HOSPITALITY, 4
guests   the g. must be chosen as carefully as the wine
   ALCOHOL, 52
guide   Custom, then, is the great g. of human life   CUSTOM, 2
Everyman, I will go with thee, and be thy g.   GUIDANCE, 1
I have only a faint light to g. me   GUIDANCE, 2
guiding   little onward lend thy g. hand   GUIDANCE, 3
guillotine   There is only one cure for grey hair. . . . the g.
   REMEDIES, 15
guilt   Let other pens dwell on g. and misery   OPTIMISM, 14
Life without industry is g.   ART, 23
put on a dress of g.   GUILT, 6
guiltless   Whose g. heart is free   RIGHTEOUSNESS, 4
guilty   g. of Noël Cowardice   COWARDICE, 1
It is quite gratifying to feel g.   GUILT, 1
Let no g. man escape   JUSTICE, 9
ten g. persons escape than one innocent suffer   JUSTICE, 3
tremble like a g. thing surprised   DOUBT, 8
guinea   a round disc of fire somewhat like a g.   PERCEPTION, 3
I would not give half a g. to live under one form of government
   GOVERNMENT, 13
there go two-and-forty sixpences . . . to one g.   MERIT, 4
guineas   I have only five g. in my pocket   GENEROSITY, 5
Guinness   G. is good for you   ADVERTISING, 1
gulphs   whelm'd in deeper g. than he   DEATH, 40
gum   can't fart and chew g. at the same time
   MISQUOTATIONS, 21
gun   it is necessary to take up the g.   WAR, 65
The difference between a g. and a tree   TREES, 13
we have got The Maxim G.   POWER POLITICS, 1
gunfire   Thanks to the movies, g. has always sounded unreal
   CINEMA, 11
Gunga Din   You're a better man than I am, G.   SUPERIORITY, 6
gunpowder   G., Printing, and the Protestant Religion
   CIVILIZATION, 3
ingredients of g. . . . were known to him   SCIENTISTS, 3
guns   But it's 'Saviour of 'is country' when the g.   SOLDIERS, 1
Elevate them g. a little lower   WAR, 52
G. will make us powerful   POWER POLITICS, 4
gutless   W. H. Auden, a sort of g. Kipling   SOCIALISM, 13
gutter   We are all in the g.   OPTIMISM, 28
gypsies   My mother said that I never should Play with the g. in
   the wood   NURSERY RHYMES, 35

H

habit   a h. the pleasure of which increases with practise
   LETTER-WRITING, 1
H. is a great deadener   HABIT, 2
honour peereth in the meanest h.   APPEARANCES, 22
some h. of which he is deeply ashamed   TELEVISION, 2

habitation   to airy nothing A local h.   POETRY, 41
habits   Cultivate only the h.   HABIT, 5
Curious things, h.   HABIT, 3
h. that carry them far apart   HABIT, 4
Old h. die hard   HABIT, 1
hack   Do not h. me   EXECUTION, 17
had   you h. it in you   EXPECTATION, 2
hae   Scots, wha h.   WAR, 20
ha-ha   Funny peculiar, or funny h.   HUMOUR, 14
hail   All h., the power of Jesus' name   CHRISTIANITY, 37
h. and farewell   GREETINGS, 1
H., hail rock'n'roll'   POP MUSIC, 5
the flail of the lashing h.   WEATHER, 23
hair   busy driving cabs and cutting h.   GOVERNMENT, 7
if a woman have long h.   APPEARANCE, 5
part my h. behind   OLD AGE, 18
Take a h. of the dog   ALCOHOL, 8
To Crystal, h. was the most important   APPEARANCE, 26
you have lovely h.   BEAUTY, 15
half   And when they were only h. way up   ARMY, 1
h. a loaf is better than a whole   COMPROMISE, 5
I am only h. there when I am ill   ILLNESS, 12
I have not told h. of what I saw   LAST WORDS, 53
longest h. of your life   YOUTH, 1
One h. . . . cannot understand . . . the other   PLEASURE, 3
There is an old saying 'well begun is h. done'   BEGINNING, 11
half-a-dozen   six of one and h. of the other   SIMILARITY, 5
half-developed   the working-class which, raw and h.   PUBLIC, 2
half-wits   a wit out of two h.   FOOLISHNESS, 16
halitosis   h. of the intellect   STUPIDITY, 4
hall   one of the sparrows . . . flew . . . through the h.   LIFE, 9
We met . . . Dr H. in such very deep mourning   MOURNING, 1
hallowed   The place of justice is a h. place   JUSTICE, 7
halt   the whole process has ground to a h. with a 14th Earl
   TITLES, 12
halters   talk of h. in the hanged man's house   TACT, 4
halves   Never do things by h.   COMMITMENT, 2
hamburger   British h. thus symbolised . . . failure to provide its
   ordinary people with food   FOOD, 25
Why have h. out   MARRIAGE, 87
Hamelin   H. Town's in Brunswick   GERMANY, 1
hammer   Art is not a mirror . . . but a h.   ART, 16
hand   bite the h. that fed them   INGRATITUDE, 2
educate with the head instead of with the h.   EDUCATION, 29
h. that signed the treaty bred a fever   SIGNATURES, 3
little onward lend thy guiding h.   GUIDANCE, 3
No, this right h. shall work it all off   WRITING, 30
one of those parties which got out of h.   CHRISTIANITY, 21
Our h. will not tremble   RUSSIAN REVOLUTION, 1
put your h. into the h. of God   FAITH, 11
sweeten this little h.   GUILT, 9
The H. that made us is divine   CREATION, 1
The h. that rocks the cradle   WOMEN, 4
This h. hath offended   REGRET, 5
touch thy weaknesses with a delicate h.   IMPERFECTION, 8
handbook   have used the Bible as if it was a constable's h.
   BIBLE, 6
handful   for a h. of silver he left us   BETRAYAL, 2
handicraft   Art is not a h.   ART, 27
handkerchiefs   There is a ghost That eats h.   LOSS, 4
handle   I polished up the h. of the big front door   OFFICERS, 6
polished up the h. of the big front door   OFFICERS, 6
hands   don't raise your h. because I am also nearsighted
   DISABILITY, 1
Farewell, my poor h.   MUSICIANS, 13
He hath shook h. with time   DEATH, 51
he shakes h. with people's hearts   JOURNALISM, 5
into thy h. I commend my spirit   LAST WORDS, 5
Licence my roving h.   LUST, 1
Many h. make light work   HELP, 2
Pale h. I loved beside the Shalimar   LOVE, 70
Pilate . . . washed his h.   GUILT, 3
the earth of England is in my two h.   VICTORY, 20
To be played with both h. in the pocket   MUSIC, 42
Tomorrow my h. will be bound   EXECUTION, 1
You cannot shake h. with a clenched fist   INFLEXIBILITY, 1
handsome   H. is as handsome does   APPEARANCE, 2
hang   if you want to kill a picture all you have to do is to h. it
   beautifully   PAINTING, 12
I will find something . . . to h. him   EXECUTION, 26
I will not h. myself today   SUICIDE, 2
They h. us now in Shrewsbury jail   EXECUTION, 11

We must indeed all h. together — UNITY, 9
wretches h. that jury-men may dine — JUSTICE, 19
hanged if they were going to see me h. — PUBLIC, 9
I went out to Charing Cross, to see Major-general Harrison h. — EXECUTION, 22
Men are not h. for stealing — EXAMPLE, 5
talk of halters in the h. man's house — TACT, 4
to be h. for nonsense — EXECUTION, 7
when a man knows he is to be h. in a fortnight — EXECUTION, 12
hangin' they're h. Danny Deever in the mornin' — EXECUTION, 14
hanging H. and wiving goes by destiny — DESTINY, 20
h. prevents a bad marriage — MARRIAGE, 103
hangman if I were a grave-digger, or . . . a h. — OCCUPATIONS, 8
Hansard H. is history's ear — GOVERNMENT, 25
happen poetry makes nothing h. — POETRY, 5
happened most of which had never h. — WORRY, 10
happening h. to somebody else — HUMOUR, 25
happens Everything that h. h. as it should — DESTINY, 3
I just don't want to be there when it h. — DEATH, 13
life . . . seems to me preparation for something that never h. — LIFE, 53
Nothing h. — BOREDOM, 1
happiest h. time of all the glad New-year — MERRYMAKING, 5
Poetry is the record of the best and h. moments — POETRY, 44
happiness A lifetime of h. . . . hell on earth — HAPPINESS, 24
a man is always seeking for h. — MARRIAGE, 50
curiously boring about . . . h. — SYMPATHY, 4
greatest h. of the greatest number — HAPPINESS, 3
h. fails, existence remains . . . experiment — HAPPINESS, 22
H. in marriage — MARRIAGE, 11
H. is a mystery like religion — HAPPINESS, 7
H. is an imaginary condition — HAPPINESS, 28
H. is beneficial for the body — SORROW, 18
H. is like a butterfly — HAPPINESS, 15
H. is like coke — HAPPINESS, 11
H. is no laughing matter — HAPPINESS, 30
h. is not an ideal of reason — HAPPINESS, 13
H. is not best achieved — HAPPINESS, 18
H. is no vague dream — HAPPINESS, 21
H. is the only sanction of life — HAPPINESS, 22
h. makes them good — GOOD, 9
h. of man that he be mentally faithful — INTEGRITY, 5
H.? That's nothing more than health — HAPPINESS, 23
In Hollywood, if you don't have h. — CINEMA, 8
In solitude What h. — SOLITUDE, 10
I thought that success spelled h. — HAPPINESS, 15
It is of no moment to the h. of an individual — GOVERNMENT, 13
life, liberty, and the pursuit of h. — HUMAN RIGHTS, 3
nothing . . . by which so much h. is produced as by a good tavern — PUBLIC HOUSES, 2
one may fail to find h. in theatrical life — DANCING, 8
our friends are true and our h. — OPTIMISM, 15
Poverty is a great enemy to human h. — POVERTY, 20
recall a time of h. when in misery — SORROW, 6
result h. — ECONOMICS, 7
the greatest h. of the whole — REPUBLIC, 1
the greatest h. for the greatest numbers — HAPPINESS, 10
the h. of the common man — GOVERNMENT, 8
where . . . We find our h. — FRENCH REVOLUTION, 5
Who never knew the price of h. — HAPPINESS, 33
you'll give h. and joy — MUSICIANS, 4
you take away his h. — DELUSION, 4
happy Ask . . . whether you are h. — HAPPINESS, 14
be h. later on, but it's much harder — HAPPINESS, 2
Few people can be h. unless they hate — HATE, 7
Goodness does not . . . make men h. — GOOD, 9
H. Days — HAPPINESS, 31
h. families resemble each other — FAMILY, 43
H. the hare at morning — IGNORANCE, 4
H. the Man — PRESENT, 4
If you want to be h., be — HAPPINESS, 29
I have wanted only one thing to make me h. — DISCONTENT, 3
I've had a h. life — LAST WORDS, 34
I were but little h. — SILENCE, 12
laugh before one is h. — LAUGHTER, 8
Let us all be h., and live within our means — BORROWING, 12
man is h. so long as he choose to be h. — HAPPINESS, 26
Mankind are always h. for having been h. — HAPPINESS, 25; HAPPINESS, 25
Not the owner of many possessions will you be right to call h. — HAPPINESS, 9
One is h. as a result of one's own efforts — HAPPINESS, 21

People are never h. who want change — CONFORMITY, 5
policeman's lot is not a h. one — POLICE, 1
Puritanism – The haunting fear that someone . . . may be h. — PURITANISM, 4
That all who are h., are equally h. — HAPPINESS, 12
the duty of being h. — HAPPINESS, 27
. . . the one and only thing . . . that can make a man h. . . . — HAPPINESS, 8
There is a h. land — HEAVEN, 15
To make men h. — ADMIRATION, 10
We are never so h. nor so unhappy as we imagine — HAPPINESS, 17
what it is that makes a Scotchman h. — ALCOHOL, 34
hard Don't clap too h. — ENTHUSIASM, 6
H. and high to the stars — AMBITION, 2
I'm not h. – I'm frightfully soft — CHARACTER, 23
It's been a h. day's night — WORK, 12
Saturday's child works h. for his living — NURSERY RHYMES, 34
hard-faced A lot of h. men — HOUSES OF PARLIAMENT, 4
hardly the summit of Everest was h. the place — PHOTOGRAPHY, 4
hardness without h. will be sage — FUTURE, 1
hardships we shall be glad to remember even these h. — ENDURANCE, 22
Hardy But Mr H.'s women are moulded of . . . flesh — WRITERS, 52
Kiss me, H. — LAST WORDS, 47
No one has written worse English than Mr H. — WRITERS, 94
hare First catch your h. — MISQUOTATIONS, 18
Happy the h. at morning — IGNORANCE, 4
Take your h. when it is cased . . . — FOOD, 22
hares And little hunted h. — ANIMALS, 12
harlot society . . . pays a h. 25 times as much as it pays its Prime Minister — INJUSTICE, 14
the prerogative of the h. through the ages — RESPONSIBILITY, 2; JOURNALISM, 2
harm No people do so much h. — CHARITY, 13
harmony chains that tie The hidden soul of h. — MUSIC, 33
h. imposes compatibility upon the incongruous — MUSIC, 32
harp his wild h. slung behind him — WAR, 73
The h. that once — IRELAND, 11
harps To touch their h. of gold — CHRISTMAS, 17
harpsichon play on the h. — INSINCERITY, 3
harpsichord The sound of the h. — MUSIC, 6
harsh in this h. world — MOURNING, 13
hart As pants the h. for cooling streams — THIRST, 3
harvest His Royal Highness . . . prides himself upon . . . the excellent h. — ARROGANCE, 7
In seed time learn, in h. teach — SUITABILITY, 1
haste H. makes waste — HASTE, 3
Men love in h. — LOVE AND HATE, 1
More h., less speed — HASTE, 4
You h. away — TRANSIENCE, 14
Hastings ancestors on either side of the Battle of H. — ANCESTRY, 4
hat A gentleman . . . wouldn't hit a woman with his h. on — CHIVALRY, 1
call that thing under your h. a head — INSULTS, 19
He forbade me to put off my h. — PRIDE, 4
little man wears a shocking bad h. — CLOTHES, 20
looking for a black h. — METAPHYSICS, 1
Where did you get that h. — CLOTHES, 13
hatched chickens before they are h. — ANTICIPATION, 4
count their chickens before they're h. — ANTICIPATION, 5
hatchet I did it with my little h. — HONESTY, 10
hate feel no h. for him — LOVE AND HATE, 4
Few . . . can be happy unless they h. — HATE, 7
If you h. a person, you h. . . . yourself — HATE, 5
I h. a fellow . . . who does nothing . . . but sit and *growl* — PETULANCE, 4
I h. and love — LOVE AND HATE, 2
I h. everyone equally — HATE, 3
I h. the whole race . . . your professional poets — POETS, 12
I love or I h. — BEAUTY, 29
Let them h. — RESPECT, 1
never h. a song that has sold half a million copies — POP MUSIC, 3
not to weep at them, nor to h. them — UNDERSTANDING, 9
scarcely h. any one that we know — HATE, 4
to h. the man you have hurt — HUMAN NATURE, 22
You must h. a Frenchman — ENEMIES, 6
hated h. by every anti-semite as if I were a Jew — PREJUDICE, 7
h. of all men for my name's sake — PERSISTENCE, 4

A h. is a prophet in reverse — HISTORIANS, 6
Great abilities are not requisite for an H. — HISTORIANS, 3
h. fits a man for psychological analysis — PSYCHOLOGY, 2
The h. must have . . . some conception of how men . . . behave — HISTORIANS, 8
historians H. are like deaf people — HISTORIANS, 7
h. left blanks in their writings — HISTORIANS, 5
H. tell the story of the past — NOVELS, 6
history ancient h. . . . is no more than accepted fiction — HISTORY, 34
Austria is Switzerland . . . with h. added — EUROPE, 12
blunders usually do more to shape h. than . . . wickedness — MISTAKES, 17
deal of h. to produce . . . literature — LITERATURE, 7; HISTORY, 18
diplomatic h. is . . . what one clerk said to another clerk — HISTORY, 37
From today . . . there begins a new epoch in the h. of the world — BEGINNING, 9
He was . . . – a student of h. — EXPERIENCE, 18
h. . . . a tableau of crimes and misfortunes — HISTORY, 35
H. does not repeat itself — HISTORY, 6
H. gets thicker — HISTORY, 33
H. is more or less bunk — HISTORY, 13
H. is past politics — POLITICS, 66; HISTORY, 25
H. is philosophy teaching by examples — HISTORY, 10
H. is the essence of . . . biographies — BIOGRAPHY, 3; HISTORY, 7
H. is the sum total — HISTORY, 2
H. is . . . the wrong way of living — HISTORY, 11
H. is too serious — HISTORIANS, 4
h. must be false — HISTORY, 36
h. of the human spirit — CULTURE, 1
H. repeats itself — HISTORY, 1
'H.', Stephen said, 'is a nightmare' — HISTORY, 19
h. . . . the biography of great men — GREATNESS, 6; HISTORY, 8
h. . . . the register of the . . . misfortunes of mankind — HISTORY, 16
If men could learn from h. — EXPERIENCE, 11
It is impossible to write ancient h. — HISTORY, 21
Its h. dates from today — ROYALTY, 37
more h. than they can consume locally — EUROPE, 14
never looks like h. — HISTORY, 15
no h.; only biography — BIOGRAPHY, 5; HISTORY, 12
one of these is the h. of political power — HISTORY, 22
people . . . never have learned anything from h. — EXPERIENCE, 14
poetry is . . . more philosophical . . . than h. — POETRY, 1
Political h. is far too criminal . . . to be . . . fit . . . for the young — HISTORY, 3
Stratford, . . . suggests powdered h. — ENGLAND, 19
The attitude of the English . . . toward English h. — ENGLISH, 16
the greatest week in the h. of the world — SPACE, 6
The h. of all . . . society is the h. of class struggles — CLASS, 22
The h. of every country begins in the heart — HISTORY, 9
The most persistent sound . . . through men's h. — WAR, 59
the Thames is liquid h. — RIVERS, 1
This was the Angel of H. — WORLD WAR II, 18
trace . . . the disasters of English h. to . . . Wales — WALES, 5
War makes . . . good h. — WAR AND PEACE, 7
history-making Man is a h. creature — HISTORY, 4
hit a medley of your h. — INSULTS, 25
If you would h. the mark — AMBITION, 13
hither Come h. — COUNTRYSIDE, 9
Hitler every time H. occupies a country — HITLER, 4
Germany was the cause of H. — HITLER, 8
H. has carried out a revolution on our lines — FASCISM, 1
H. has missed the bus — WORLD WAR II, 2
H. showed surprising loyalty to Mussolini — HITLER, 5
H. was a nuisance. Mussolini was bloody — POLITICS, 51
I wouldn't believe H. was dead — HITLER, 6
one purpose, the destruction of H. — HITLER, 3
The people H. never understood — HITLER, 1
tipster who . . . reached H.'s level of accuracy — HITLER, 7
hobby-horse So long as a man rides his h. — TOLERANCE, 7
hobgoblin the h. of little minds — CONSTANCY, 1
hock He sipped at a weak h. and seltzer — WRITERS, 4
hog Rule all England under a h. — INSULTS, 14
hoi the multitude, the h. polloi — PUBLIC, 10
hoist H. your sail — OPPORTUNITY, 4
hold h. your tongue and let me love — SILENCE, 5
To have and to h. — MARRIAGE, 30
When every . . . thing you h. Is made of silver, or of gold — ECONOMICS, 9
holder office sanctifies the h. — POWER, 3

hole A h. is the accident — THRIFT, 10
if you knows of a better h. — WAR, 4
smallest h. . . . man can hide his head in — UNIVERSE, 5
What happens to the h. when the cheese is gone — NONSENSE, 4
holes the first law of h. . . . stop digging — ADVICE, 9
holiday the little h. steamers made an excursion to hell — WORLD WAR II, 25
holiness put off H. — WISDOM, 11
the h. of the heart's affections — IMAGINATION, 6; TRUTH, 28
who, like you, your H., is a Roman Catholic — CATHOLICISM, 3
Holland H. . . . lies so low they're only saved by being dammed — EUROPE, 8
hollers whatever you try to do, somebody jumps up and h. — HUMAN NATURE, 11
hollow within the h. crown — ROYALTY, 30
holly The h. and the ivy — CHRISTMAS, 5
The h. bears the crown — CHRISTMAS, 5
Hollywood In H., if you don't have happiness — CINEMA, 8
I should not have been invited to H. — CINEMA, 1
the attitude of a H. director toward love — ENGLISH, 16
holy dropped the word 'H.' to give it a more mass-market appeal — BIBLE, 4
everything that lives is h. — LIFE, 12
H., holy, holy, Lord God Almighty — GOD, 24
the Holy Roman Empire was neither h., nor Roman, nor an empire — NATIONS, 2
'Twas on a H. Thursday — CHILDREN, 17
home against books the H. Secretary is — PHILISTINISM, 7
Charity begins at h. — CHARITY, 10
Comin' for to carry me h. — DEATH, 17
eaten me out of house and h. — GREED, 11
English should give Ireland h. rule — IRELAND, 14
Father, . . . come h. with me now — ALCOHOL, 68
for de old folks at h. — HOMESICKNESS, 3
For h. is best — HOME, 9
For the old Kentucky H. far away — HOMESICKNESS, 4
give me a h. where the buffalo roam — HOMESICKNESS, 5
h. his footsteps he hath turn'd — HOMESICKNESS, 6
H. is heaven — DEBAUCHERY, 8
H. is h. — HOME, 3
H. is the sailor, h. from sea — DEATH, 119
H. is where — HOME, 3
H. of lost causes — OXFORD, 1
H. . . . where . . . they have to take you in — HOME, 4
I can get all that at h. — THEATRE, 5
Irish H. Rule is conceded — IRELAND, 15
Many a man who thinks to found a h. — PARASITES, 1
no h. . . . save in Paris — PARIS, 4
permits you to be entertained . . . by people you wouldn't have in your h. — TELEVISION, 3
Pleasure never is at h. — DISCONTENT, 5
She's leaving h. — DEPARTURE, 8
The Life and Soul, the man who will never go h. — PARTIES, 9
there's no place like h. — HOME, 7
till the cow comes h. — ETERNITY, 1
we come From God, who is our h. — METAPHYSICS, 5
What's the good of a h. — ABSENCE, 7
home-keeping h. youth — HOME, 8
homely A h. face . . . aided many women heavenward — APPEARANCE, 3
be never so h. — HOME, 3
h. wits — HOME, 8
Homer Cicero And . . . H. were *Mad as the mist and snow* — MADNESS, 18
even excellent H. nods — IMPERFECTION, 9
Mr Gladstone read H. for fun — CLASSICS, 2
Seven cities warr'd for H., being dead — POVERTY, 16
The author of that poem is either H. — ARGUMENTS, 8
homes go back to thy stately h. of England — PARTING, 7
the Stately H. of England — DECLINE, 1; STATELY HOMES, 1
home-sickness In h. you must keep moving — HOMESICKNESS, 7
homo The 'h.' is the legitimate child — HOMOSEXUALITY, 5
homos one of the stately h. of England — HOMOSEXUALITY, 2
homosexuals h. . . . set out to win the love of a 'real' man — HOMOSEXUALITY, 3
honest An h. broker — DIPLOMACY, 3
An h. God — GOD, 29
an h. man sent to lie abroad for . . . his country — DIPLOMACY, 21
An h. man's word — HONESTY, 1
give me six lines . . . by the most h. man — EXECUTION, 26
I am as h. as any man living — HONESTY, 3
It's better to be quotable than . . . h. — QUOTATIONS, 13

not an h. man HONESTY, 11
She was poor but she was h. POVERTY AND WEALTH, 1
then they get h. DOCTORS, 8
Though I am not naturally h. HONESTY, 9
Though I be poor, I'm h. HONESTY, 5
honestly If possible h., if not, somehow, make money
MONEY, 24
honesty H. is the best policy HONESTY, 2, 11
make your children *capable of h.* is the beginning of education
HONESTY, 6
Philosophers never balance between profit and h.
PHILOSOPHERS, 4
honey a land of oil olive, and h. WEALTH, 5
gather h. all the day WORK, 25
h. still for tea NOSTALGIA, 3
They took some h., and plenty of money NONSENSE, 20
honey'd the h. middle of the night LOVE, 78
honey-dew on h. hath fed CAUTION, 9
honi H. soit qui mal y pense EVIL, 1
honour All is lost save h. DEFEAT, 2
a prophet is not without h. HONOUR, 1
Brothers all In h. HONOUR, 7
His h. rooted in dishonour UNFAITHFULNESS, 6
h. is for the poor HUMILITY, 12
H. pricks me on HONOUR, 4
h. sinks where commerce long prevails BUSINESS, 12
h. thy father and thy mother GOD, 10
if I accepted the h. . . . I would not answer for the integrity of
my intellect TITLES, 3
Let us h. if we can POSTERITY, 3
only h. and life have been spared DEFEAT, 2
peace I hope with h. PEACE, 9
So h. peereth in the meanest habit APPEARANCES, 22
That chastity of h. HONOUR, 2
then they get h. DOCTORS, 8
There is h. among thieves LOYALTY, 2
To h. we call you COURAGE, 13
Wealth has never been a sufficient source of h. OSTENTATION, 3
we're fighting for this woman's h. HONOUR, 3
honourable His designs were strictly h. MARRIAGE, 56
hoof I see many h.-marks going in MISTRUST, 2
hooligan Even the H. was probably invented in China
PLACES, 16
hoorah He is without strict doubt a H. Henry ARISTOCRACY, 11
hooray Dear Mrs A., h. h. TELEGRAMS, 6
H. and up she rises DRUNKENNESS, 4
hope Abandon h., all ye who enter here HELL, 1
a faint h. that he will die HUMAN NATURE, 10
And what was dead was H. IMPRISONMENT, 9
H. for the best HOPE, 7
h. is . . . the dream of those that wake HOPE, 9
H. is the power of being cheerful CHARITY, 12; HOPE, 5
H. may vanish, but can die not OPTIMISM, 24
H. springs eternal in the human breast HOPE, 8
Land of H. and Glory BRITAIN, 4
no other medicine but only h. HOPE, 10
Not to h. for things to last for ever, is what the year teaches
TRANSIENCE, 15
now abideth faith, h., charity CHARITY, 6
Our h. for years to come RELIGION, 64
the distinction between h. and expectation REALISM, 3
The triumph of h. over experience MARRIAGE, 73
The Worldly H. men set their Hearts upon TRANSIENCE, 13
unconquerable h. HOPE, 4
What a strange thing is memory, and h. MEMORY, 10
what difficulty a mind . . . admits h. SUFFERING, 15
While there is life, there's h. HOPE, 6
Without all h. of day BLINDNESS, 4
hopeless that controversy is either superfluous or h.
ARGUMENTS, 12
hopes enough for fifty h. and fears WORRY, 8
Life's short span forbids us to enter on far-reaching h.
MORTALITY, 13
My h. no more must change their name FREEDOM, 52
Horatius brave H. COURAGE, 17
horde Society is now one polish'd h. BORES, 2
horizontal we value none But the h. one POSTERITY, 3
Horner Little Jack H. Sat in the corner NURSERY RHYMES, 29
Hornie Auld H., Satan, Nick DEVIL, 6
horns Memories are hunting h. MEMORY, 1
When you take the bull by the h. . . . CHANCE, 5
horny-handed H. sons of toil WORK, 11

horrible A strange, h. business, . . . good enough for
Shakespeare's day CRITICISM, 50
horrid are they all h. NASTINESS, 1
horror I have a h. of sunsets SUN, 3
mere existence is swollen to a h. IDEALISM, 3
The thought of dentists gave him just the same sick h.
FEAR, 14
horrors I have supp'd full with h. WORLD-WEARINESS, 7
horse A fly, Sir, may sting a stately h. CRITICS, 11
a pale h. DEATH, 31
A Protestant with a h. NATIONALITY, 2
Do not trust the h., Trojans MISTRUST, 11
good deal of physical courage to ride a h. ALCOHOL, 40;
HORSES, 8
Go together like a h. and carriage LOVE AND MARRIAGE, 1
I feel as a h. must feel INJUSTICE, 5
I know two things about the h. HORSES, 2
like to be a h. ROYALTY, 16
my kingdom for a h. HORSES, 10
nobody has any business to go around looking like a h.
APPEARANCE, 28
Ride a cock-h. to Banbury Cross NURSERY RHYMES, 42
the h., as a means of locomotion, is obsolete HORSES, 11
To confess that you are totally Ignorant about the H.
HORSES, 9
victory under the belly of a Cossack's h. RUSSIAN
REVOLUTION, 3
You can be in the H. Guards CLASS, 27
You can lead a h. to the water STUBBORNNESS, 1
You may have my husband, but not my h. MASCULINITY, 2
horsemanship princes learn no art truly, but . . . h. HORSES, 7
horse-pond celibacy is . . . a muddy h. MARRIAGE, 89
horses A grain, which in England is generally given to h.
SCOTLAND, 3
Bring on the empty h. LANGUAGE, 11
Dogs, like h., are quadrupeds ANIMALS, 15
England . . . hell for h. NATIONALITY, 3
England . . . hell of h. ENGLAND, 17
frighten the h. SEX, 9
'H.' should have read 'Cows' MISTAKES, 10
Men are . . . more careful of the breed of their h. and dogs
FAMILY, 33
sixty h. wedged in a chimney JOURNALISM, 24
swap h. in mid-stream CHANGE, 13
hospital h. is the assumption on the part of the staff
MEDICINE, 4
in a h. . . . the assumption . . . that because you have lost your
gall bladder HOSPITALITY, 7
the h. desirable for patients with serious ailments
OCCUPATIONS, 11
the world, I count it not an inn, but an h. WORLD, 1
host a happy h. makes a sad guest HOSPITALITY, 5
an innumerable company of the heavenly h. PERCEPTION, 3
of all this h. of men not one will still be alive in a hundred
years' time MORTALITY, 22
hostages h. given to fate FAMILY, 26
h. to fortune FAMILY, 7
hostile The universe is not h. UNIVERSE, 8
hostility your h. towards him FRIENDSHIP, 10
hot blow h. and cold with the same breath INDECISION, 1
H. cross buns! . . . One a penny, two a penny NURSERY
RHYMES, 16
hotel-keepers h. continue to give them TOLERANCE, 8
hotels I prefer temperance h. ALCOHOL, 64
hot-water the English have h. bottles ENGLISH, 24
Houdin Robert H. who . . . invented the vanishing bird-cage
trick THEATRE, 12
Houdini Harry H. ESCAPE, 1; FUNERALS, 5
hounded I will not be h. CHARACTER, 23
hounds And the cry of his h. HUNTING, 4
hour A child's a plaything for an h. CHILDREN, 32
An h. in the morning TIME, 1
at the rate of sixty minutes an h. TIME, 24
I also had my h. GLORY, 1
In the h. of death DEATH, 33
Milton! thou shouldst be living at this h. DECLINE, 15
nothing can bring back the h. REGRET, 22
one bare h. to live DAMNATION, 3
One h.'s sleep SLEEP, 1
Some h. to which you have not been looking forward will prove
lovely PRESENT, 10
the clocks were striking the h. TIME, 25

their finest h. — WORLD WAR II, 5
Time and the h. runs through — TIME, 32
To one dead deathless h. — POETRY, 38
hourglass the sand in the h. — TIME, 28
hours h. will take care of themselves — TIME, 15
Three h. a day — WRITING, 34
housbondes H. at chirche-dore — MARRIAGE, 35
house A h. is a machine for living in — HOUSES, 2
A man in the h. is worth two — MEN, 14
Cleaning your h. while your kids are still growing — HOUSEWORK, 4
get thee out . . . from thy father's h. — JEWS, 3
in my Father's h. are many mansions — HEAVEN, 3
The h. of every one is to him as his castle — PRIVACY, 1
The H. of Lords, an illusion — RESPONSIBILITY, 2
The H. of Lords . . . how to care for the elderly — HOUSES OF PARLIAMENT, 9
The h. where I was born — NOSTALGIA, 9
they all lived together in a little crooked h. — NURSERY RHYMES, 52
you, . . . who have made me too great for my h. — ROYALTY, 4
house-agents Everybody hates h. — OCCUPATIONS, 17
housekeeping H. ain't no joke — HOUSEWORK, 1
housemaids damp souls of the h. — MELANCHOLY, 5
House of Commons leader of the H. — POLITICIANS, 48
House of Lords Every man has a H. in his own head — HOUSES OF PARLIAMENT, 13
The H., an illusion — HOUSES OF PARLIAMENT, 18
The H. is a perfect eventide home — HOUSES OF PARLIAMENT, 17
The H. is the British Outer Mongolia — HOUSES OF PARLIAMENT, 5
The H. . . . kept efficient by . . . persistent absenteeism — HOUSES OF PARLIAMENT, 15
House of Peers The H., . . . Did nothing — HOUSES OF PARLIAMENT, 10
houses H. are built to live in — HOUSES, 1
plague o' both your h. — CURSES, 1
Rich men's h. are seldom beautiful — WEALTH, 3
the darkness inside h. — FEAR, 7
housewife don't pretend to be an ordinary h. — ACTORS, 19
h's drop thy 'H.' — CLASS, 5
Hubbard Old Mother H. Went to the cupboard — NURSERY RHYMES, 36
hue native h. of resolution — CONSCIENCE, 5
Hugo H. – hélas! — POETS, 36
human Adam was but h. — PERVERSITY, 6
All that is h. must retrograde — PROGRESS, 6
evolution of the h. race — MANKIND, 13
h. beings are heroic — NOBILITY, 3
h. beings have an . . . infinite capacity for taking things for granted — HUMAN NATURE, 13
H. beings were invented by water — WATER, 8
H. beings, yes, but not surgeons — MEDICINE, 11
H. kind cannot bear — REALITY, 2
h. nature . . . more of the fool — HUMAN NATURE, 3
H. on my faithless arm — SLEEP, 3
If h. beings could be propagated . . . aristocracy would be . . . sound — ARISTOCRACY, 7
I got disappointed in h. nature — HUMAN NATURE, 4
I have got lots of h. weaknesses — IMPERFECTION, 13
imagine a boot stamping on a h. face — OPPRESSION, 4
Ishmaelites . . . will not publicly eat h. flesh uncooked in Lent — CANNIBALISM, 2
I wish I loved the H. Race — MANKIND, 22
Mercy has a h. heart — MANKIND, 6
my opinion of the h. race — MANKIND, 17
No h. being, . . . was ever so free as a fish — FREEDOM, 46
no need for any other faith than . . . faith in h. beings — FAITH, 3
nothing h. foreign to me — MANKIND, 32
nothing to distinguish h. society from the farm-yard — MANKIND, 29
not linen you're wearing out, But h. creatures' lives — WOMEN, 41
the full tide of h. existence is at Charing-Cross — LONDON, 3
The h. face is . . . a whole cluster of faces — MANKIND, 21
The h. race, . . . many of my readers — HUMAN CONDITION, 5
the importance of the h. factor — INDUSTRIAL RELATIONS, 1
the vilest specimens of h. nature are . . . found among demagogues — POLITICS, 47
To err is h., to forgive, divine — MISTAKES, 13; FORGIVENESS, 13
To kill a h. being — KILLING, 4
When in the course of h. events, it becomes necessary — INDEPENDENCE, 2
you feel as if a h. being sitting inside were making fun of you — ANIMALS, 8

humanity Every year h. takes a step towards Communism — COMMUNISM, 3
H. is just a work in progress — MANKIND, 38
Oh wearisome condition of h. — HUMAN CONDITION, 9
That unremitting h. — DICKENS, 3
the crooked timber of h. — HUMAN NATURE, 15
The still, sad music of h. — EXPERIENCE, 22
human life being alone is a fundamental quality of h. — HUMAN CONDITION, 13
humble for the last time in my life, Your H. Servant — ARGUMENTS, 17
He'll h. her — MEN, 7
h. and meek are thirsting for blood — HUMILITY, 7
It is difficult to be h. — HUMILITY, 4
humiliating Corporal punishment is . . . h. for him who gives it — PUNISHMENT, 13
humiliation the last h. of an aged scholar — OLD AGE, 15
the moment of greatest h. is . . . when the spirit is proudest — PRIDE, 6
humility H. is only doubt — HUMILITY, 2
humour Cynicism is h. in ill-health — CYNICISM, 4
deficient in a sense of h. — HUMOUR, 9
Freudian . . . low . . . sort of h. — HUMOUR, 13
God withheld the sense of h. from women — WOMEN, 22
H. . . . the first of the gifts to perish — TRANSLATION, 5
own up to a lack of h. — HUMOUR, 8
Total absence of h. — HUMOUR, 10
hump A woman . . . without a positive h., may marry whom she likes — MARRIAGE, 119
Humpty H. Dumpty sat on a wall — NURSERY RHYMES, 18
hunchback The h. in the park — LONELINESS, 8
hundred a h. schools of thought contend — FREEDOM, 32
bet you a h. bucks he ain't in here — ESCAPE, 1; FUNERALS, 5
it would be all the same a h. years hence — TRIVIALITY, 3
I've done it a h. times — SMOKING, 21
Letting a h. flowers blossom — FREEDOM, 32
of all this host of men not one will still be alive in a h. years' time — MORTALITY, 22
to trade a h. contemporary readers for — POSTERITY, 6
Hungarian It's not enough to be H. — EUROPE, 9; TALENT, 6
hunger best sauce . . . is h. — HUNGER, 4
H. is the best sauce — HUNGER, 1
The war against h. — HUNGER, 7
to banish h. by rubbing the belly — HUNGER, 5
hungry A h. stomach has no ears — HUNGER, 8
h. as a hunter — HUNGER, 9
h. hare has no frontiers — POLITICS, 84
H. Joe collected lists of fatal diseases — ILLNESS, 3
h. sheep look up, and are not fed — CORRUPTION, 8
she makes h. Where most she satisfies — ADMIRATION, 14
You cannot feed the h. on statistics — STATISTICS, 5
hunt how much more dogs are animated when they h. in a pack — UNITY, 11
people who h. are the right people — HUNTING, 6
hunted tell the others by their h. expression — CHARITY, 15
hunter hungry as a h. — HUNGER, 9
Man is the h. — SEXES, 22
My heart is a lonely h. — LONELINESS, 5
The Heart Is a Lonely H. — BOOK, SONG, AND PLAY TITLES, 18
Hunter Dunn Miss J. H., Miss J. H. — ADMIRATION, 1
hunting Memories are h. horns — MEMORY, 1
their discourse was about h. — LANGUAGE, 19
when his half-civilized ancestors were h. the wild boar — JEWS, 2
hurrah h.! we bring the Jubilee — GLORY, 5
hurricanoes You cataracts and h. — WEATHER, 18
hurries h. to the main event — PLAYS, 5
hurry An old man in a h. — POLITICIANS, 42
H.! I never hurry. I have no time to hurry — HASTE, 12
So who's in a h. — ALCOHOL, 10
hurrying I see a man h. along – to what — PURPOSE, 5
hurt it h. too much to laugh — DISAPPOINTMENT, 8
It takes your enemy and your friend . . . , to h. you — HURT, 3
Those have most power to h. — HURT, 1
wish to h. — CRUELTY, 1
hurting Art . . . can go on mattering once it has stopped h. — ART, 5
husband An archaeologist is the best h. — MARRIAGE, 36
at all times yr faithful h. — MARRIAGE, 109
Being a h. is a whole-time job — MARRIAGE, 22
easier to be a lover than a h. — MARRIAGE, 16
happened unawares to look at her h. — MARRIAGE, 12
h. render unto the wife due benevolence — MARRIAGE, 24

visible universe was an i. UNIVERSE, 2
illusions It's life's i. I recall LIFE, 35
illustrious This i. man, the largest and most spacious intellect
POETS, 32
ill-will I bear no i. against those responsible for this
FORGIVENESS, 16
image any graven i. GOD, 10
A photograph is not only an i. PHOTOGRAPHY, 7
fall down and worship the golden i. DOOMSDAY, 1
If God made us in His i. GOD, 50
make man in our own i. MANKIND, 5; CREATION, 6
Why should I consent to the perpetuation of the i. of this i.
PAINTING, 13
imaginary Happiness is an i. condition HAPPINESS, 28
imagination A lady's i. is very rapid WOMEN, 11
Art is ruled . . . by the i. IMAGINATION, 3
I. and fiction . . . three quarters of our real life IMAGINATION, 9
I.! . . . I put it first years ago ACTING, 11
I. without skill gives us modern art ART, 26
no i. and . . . no compassion IMAGINATION, 4
not an ideal of reason but of i. HAPPINESS, 13
of i. all compact LOVE, 121; POETRY, 43
stand up for freedom of the i. RELIGION, 52
The primary i. IMAGINATION, 1
treat your facts with i. is one thing TRUTH, 14
truth of i. IMAGINATION, 6; TRUTH, 28
imagine never so happy . . . as we i. HAPPINESS, 17
imagined What is now proved was . . . i. PROOF, 2
imagining How reconcile this world . . . with . . . my i.
BLINDNESS, 2
imitate A good composer does not i. MUSICIANS, 9
An original writer is . . . one whom nobody can i.
ORIGINALITY, 2
never failed to i. CHILDREN, 6
obliged to i. himself, and to repeat IMITATION, 5
people . . . usually i. each other IMITATION, 3
imitates Photography can never grow up if it i.
PHOTOGRAPHY, 1
imitation I. is the sincerest form of flattery FLATTERY, 1;
IMITATION, 2
Man . . . is an i. MANKIND, 20
immaculate the I. Conception was spontaneous combustion
CATHOLICISM, 9
Immanuel call his name I. CHRISTIANITY, 9
immature the i. man . . . wants to die nobly for a cause
AGE, 58
immaturity common symptom of i. ORIGINALITY, 6
the executive expression of human i. POLITICS, 12
immoral moral or an i. book BOOKS, 46
the things I really like . . . are either i., illegal, or fattening
PLEASURE, 31
worse than i. MISTAKES, 2
immorality the most rigid code of i. ENGLISH, 6
immortal I have lost the i. part REPUTATION, 6
make me i. with a kiss BEAUTY, 25
Our souls have sight of that i. sea METAPHYSICS, 6
Why are you weeping? Did you imagine that I was i. LAST
WORDS, 44
immortality I . . . want to achieve i. . . . through not dying
IMMORTALITY, 1
just ourselves And I. DEATH, 42
immutable Few things are as i. POLITICS, 28
impediment cause, or just i. OBSTRUCTION, 2
imperative This i. is Categorical MORALITY, 8
imperfection i. itself may have its . . . perfect state
IMPERFECTION, 7
imperial be yourself, i., plain and true SINCERITY, 1
imperialism i. is the monopoly stage of capitalism POLITICS, 46
Their Europeanism is . . . i. with an inferiority complex
POLITICS, 35
impersonal In the philosopher there is nothing whatever i.
PHILOSOPHERS, 4
impertinent ask an i. question SCIENCE, 1
impetuous such i. blood IMPETUOSITY, 4
importance Official dignity . . . in inverse ratio to . . . i.
DIPLOMACY, 12
important One doesn't recognize . . . the really i. moments . . .
until it's too late REGRET, 4
that basic weekendmanship should contain . . . I. Person Play
ONE-UPMANSHIP, 2
the little things are infinitely the most i. TRIVIALITY, 6
imposed wish to be i. on, and then are EXPLOITATION, 2

impossibility a physical and metaphysical i. POETS, 3
impossible complete sorrow is as i. EMOTION, 6
I believe because it is i. BELIEF, 7
It's either easy or i. PAINTING, 4
something is i., he is . . . wrong SCIENCE, 6
when you have excluded the i. TRUTH, 21
impotent an i. people, Sick with inbreeding WELSH, 3
impregnator the writer . . . is the i. READING, 19
impression knowledge and wonder . . . is an i. of pleasure
KNOWLEDGE, 5; WONDER, 1
impressionable Give me a girl at an i. age
IMPRESSIONABILITY, 3
impressions i. . . . lasting as . . . an oar upon the water
INSIGNIFICANCE, 1
improbable an i. fiction REALITY, 5
Faith . . . an illogical belief in . . . the i. FAITH, 14
whatever remains, however i., must be the truth TRUTH, 21
improper I only hope it is not i. ETIQUETTE, 3
impropriety I. is the soul of wit HUMOUR, 19
improved enormously i. by death WRITERS, 79
improvement most schemes of political i. are very laughable
POLITICS, 41
impulse the i. of the moment FLATTERY, 2
the need to talk is a primary i. IMPETUOSITY, 1
impulses Mistrust first i. FIRST IMPRESSIONS, 7
impure To the Puritan all things are i. PURITANISM, 2
in you had it i. you EXPECTATION, 2
inactivity wise and masterly i. GOVERNMENT, 16
inadequate Like Brighton pier, . . . i. for getting to France
TRAVEL, 18
inarticulate speak for the i. and the submerged JOURNALISM, 4
inartistic He was unperfect, unfinished, i. WRITERS, 70
inbreeding an impotent people, Sick with i. WELSH, 3
incest except i. and folk-dancing EXPERIENCE, 7
inch every i. a king ROYALTY, 31
Give him an i. GREED, 1
inches They that die by famine die by i. HUNGER, 6
incident What is i. but the illustration of character
CHARACTER, 13
incisors Writers, like teeth, are divided into i. and grinders
WRITERS, 2
inclination A man ought to read just as i. leads him
READING, 8
incoherent I'm not i. CONFUSION, 7
income Annual i. twenty pounds ECONOMICS, 7
difficult to love mankind . . . private i. SELF-INTEREST, 5
hardest thing . . . to understand is i. tax TAXATION, 2
her Majesty . . . must not . . . look upon me as a source of i.
TAXATION, 6
live beyond its i. PROGRESS, 2; EXTRAVAGANCE, 2
incomes people live beyond their i. EXTRAVAGANCE, 2
incompetence Work . . . by those employees who have not yet
reached . . . i. INCOMPETENCE, 4
incompetent a tax on pianos for the i. MUSIC, 47
God is the immemorial refuge of the i. GOD, 35
i. swine WAR, 103
incomplete A man in love is i. until . . . married MARRIAGE, 62
incomprehensible an old, wild, and i. man POLITICIANS, 74
inconvenience Change is not made without i. CHANGE, 11
inconveniences A good many i. attend play-going PLAYS, 12
inconvenient i. to be poor POVERTY, 5
incorruptible seagreen I. POLITICIANS, 40
the dead shall be raised i. DEATH, 28
increase from fairest creatures we desire i. BEAUTY, 36
increased influence of the Crown has i. MONARCHY, 9
incurable Not even medicine can master i. diseases
MEDICINE, 7
the i. disease of writing WRITING, 17
Ind Outshone the wealth of Ormus and of I. DEVIL, 10
indecency prejudicial . . . as a public i. SIN, 10
The older one grows the more one likes i. AGE, 67
indecent It requires one to assume such i. postures
CRICKET, 9
much more i. . . . than a good smack PUNISHMENT, 14
sent down for i. behaviour EDUCATION, 58
indecision Nothing is so exhausting as i. INDECISION, 2
indefatigable i. and unsavoury engine of pollution DOGS, 12
indefensible political speech and writing are largely the defence
of the i. POLITICS, 58
independent an I. Labour Party PARTIES, 8
An i. . . . wants to take the politics out of politics POLITICS, 74
to become fully i. FAMILY, 16

insufferable   It is Oxford that has made me i.   EDUCATION, 6
insult   adding i. to injuries   AGGRAVATION, 1
A man should not i. his wife publicly   MARRIAGE, 123
sooner forgotten than an i.   INSULTS, 12
insulted   anyone here whom I have not i.   INSULTS, 10
insured   you cannot be i. for the accidents . . . most likely to happen   ACCIDENTS, 1
insurrection   I. is an art   REVOLUTION, 6
integrate   I i. the current export drive   BUSINESS, 4
integrity   if I accepted the honour . . . I would not answer for the i. of my intellect   TITLES, 3
I. without knowledge is weak   INTEGRITY, 4; KNOWLEDGE, 24
intellect   a feather to tickle the i.   PUNS, 10
a road . . . that does not go through the i.   EMOTION, 5
halitosis of the i.   STUPIDITY, 4
his i. is not replenished   IGNORANCE, 13
i. is . . . fooled by the heart   EMOTION, 4
I. is invisible   INTELLECT, 7
put on I.   WISDOM, 11
take care not to make the i. our god   INTELLECT, 1
the soul of a martyr with the i. of an advocate   POLITICIANS, 32
The voice of the i. is a soft one   INTELLECT, 2
we cannot exclude the i. from . . . any of our functions   INTELLECT, 4
intellects   highest i., like the tops of mountains   INTELLECT, 5
There is a wicked inclination . . . to suppose an old man decayed in his i.   OLD AGE, 24
intellectual   an i. . . . mind watches itself   INTELLECTUALS, 5
Beware of the artist who's an i.   ARTISTS, 3
Every i. attitude is latently political   POLITICS, 52
i., but I found it too difficult   HUMILITY, 9
i. . . . doesn't know how to park a bike   INTELLECTUALS, 1
I've been called many things, but never an i.   INTELLECTUALS, 3
Man is an i. animal   INTELLECT, 3
The word I. suggests   INTELLECTUALS, 2
thirdly, i. ability   EDUCATION, 3
intellectuals   vanishing race. . . . the i.   INTELLECTUALS, 7
intelligence   I. is quickness to apprehend   INTELLIGENCE, 7
i. is the great polluter   ENVIRONMENT, 4
The more i. . . . the more . . . one finds original   INTELLIGENCE, 5
intelligent   A really i. man feels what other men . . . know   INTELLIGENCE, 4
Each generation imagines itself . . . more i.   AGE, 43
i. people . . . are socialists   SOCIALISM, 1
stupid are cocksure . . . i. full of doubt   DOUBT, 7
The i. are to the intelligentsia   INTELLIGENCE, 1
intelligentsia   intelligent are to the i.   INTELLIGENCE, 1
intelligible   to aim at being i.   COMMUNICATION, 2
intended   i. to give you some advice   ADVICE, 8
intensity   excellence of every art is its i.   ARTS, 5
intent   A truth that's told with bad i.   TRUTH, 13
prick the sides of my i.   AMBITION, 16
intercourse   dreary i. of daily life   OPTIMISM, 29
Sexual i. began In nineteen sixty-three   SEX, 3
interest   How can I take an i. in my work   ENTHUSIASM, 1
It is not my i. to pay the principal, nor my principle to pay the i.   BORROWING, 5
interested   always been i. in people   MISANTHROPY, 2
The average man is . . . i. in a woman who is i. in him   SEXES, 7
interests   all these great i. entrusted to the shaking hand   POLITICIANS, 74
intérieur   'Vive l'i.   HISTORY, 30; HUMOUR, 53
intermission   Pleasure is . . . i. of pain   PLEASURE, 27
international   I. Woman's Day   RUSSIAN REVOLUTION, 2
science is essentially i.   SCIENCE, 8
interrupted   Mr Wordsworth is never i.   INTERRUPTIONS, 3
interval   an opera without an i., or an i. without an opera   OPERA, 6
intolerably   I would grow i. conceited   CONCEIT, 21
intoxicate   you won't i. with one glass someone who has . . . drunk . . . a . . . barrel   EXPERIENCE, 10
intoxicated   A man who exposes himself when he is i.   DRUNKENNESS, 15
No, thank you, I was born i.   DRUNKENNESS, 18
intoxication   best of life is . . . i.   DRUNKENNESS, 3
intrigue   the i. of a Greek of the lower empire   INSULTS, 15
introduce   let me i. you to that leg of mutton   INTRODUCTIONS, 1
introduction   I could buy back my i.   INTRODUCTIONS, 4
introspection   I. . . . he never achieved   WRITERS, 40

intrudes   society, where none i.   NATURE, 3
invade   when religion is allowed to i. . . . private life   RELIGION, 44
invalid   an invaluable permanent i. called Bunbury   DECEPTION, 7
invasion   no stand can be made against i. by an idea   IDEAS, 2
the long-promised i.   WORLD WAR II, 8
invective   insolence is not i.   PETULANCE, 2; IMPERTINENCE, 1
invent   it would be necessary to i. Him   GOD, 49
inventing   Prolonged . . . reviewing of books involves constantly i. reactions   CRITICISM, 36
invention   A long poem is a test of i.   POETRY, 23
Woman's virtue is man's greatest i.   SEXES, 20
inventions   All one's i. are true   POETRY, 15
investment   There is no finer i.   CHILDREN, 18
To bear many children is considered . . . an i.   CHILDREN, 22
inviolable   the i. shade   HOPE, 4
invisible   the only evil that walks I.   HYPOCRISY, 12
invisibly   electricity was dripping i.   SCIENCE, 40
invited   People were not i. – they went there   PARTIES, 4
involuntary   It was i. They sank my boat   MODESTY, 2
inward   They flash upon that i. eye   SOLITUDE, 5
inwards   he looked i., and found her   SHAKESPEARE, 6
Ireland   a picture of a relief map of I.   APPEARANCE, 4
English should give I. home rule   IRELAND, 14
How's poor ould I., and how does she stand   IRELAND, 11
I'll not forget old I.   HOMESICKNESS, 3
Ireland   I never met anyone in I. who understood the Irish question   IRELAND, 6
I. is the old sow   IRELAND, 8
I would have liked to go to I.   IRELAND, 17
Now I. has her madness   POETRY, 3
The moment . . . I. is mentioned   IRELAND, 16
The problem with I.   IRELAND, 10
Irish   All races have . . . economists, with the exception of the I.   IRISH, 5
as I. as Black Americans   IRISH, 6
I. . . . devotion to higher arts   IRISH, 5
That is the I. Question   IRELAND, 5
The English and Americans dislike only *some* I.   IRISH, 3
The I. and the Jews have a psychosis   IRISH, 2; JEWS, 1
The I. are a fair people   IRISH, 7
The I., . . . are needed in this cold age   IRISH, 4
The I. don't know what they want   IRISH, 8
Irishman   Put an I. on the spit   IRISH, 1
iron   An i. curtain   COLD WAR, 2
blood and i.   POWER POLITICS, 2
I do, and I also wash and i. them   HOUSEWIVES, 5
muscles . . . Are strong as i. bands   OCCUPATIONS, 10
rule them with a rod of i.   LEADERSHIP, 2
the i. enter into his soul   BITTERNESS, 1
the i. has entered his soul   NONCOMMITMENT, 3
will wink and hold out mine i.   COWARDICE, 8
ironies   Life's Little I.   LIFE, 26
irons   two i. in the fire   PRUDENCE, 5
irrelevant   the most i. thing in nature   FAMILY, 23
irreproachable   compulsory and i. idleness   ARMY, 3
irresponsible   better to be i. and right   RESPONSIBILITY, 5; RIGHTEOUSNESS, 6
Irving   I. reminded me of a pig   ACTORS, 20
Ishmaelites   I. . . . will not publicly eat human flesh uncooked in Lent   CANNIBALISM, 1
Islam   In some remote regions of I.   MODESTY, 3
I. unashamedly came with a sword   RELIGION, 51
island   No man is an I.   SOCIETY, 3
islands   less known by the British than these selfsame British I.   BRITISH, 3
isle   Kelly from the I. of Man   ABSENCE, 8
this sceptred i.   ENGLAND, 36
isles   The i. of Greece   EUROPE, 5
Israel   When I. was in Egypt land   OPPRESSION, 1
Italian   as sensible as baseball in I.   OPERA, 5
I speak . . . I. to women, French to men   LANGUAGE, 1
Italians   The I. will laugh at me   HITLER, 4
Italy   A man who has not been in I.   TRAVEL, 15
I. a paradise for horses   NATIONALITY, 3
itch   The i. of disputing . . . the scab of churches   RELIGION, 71
the i. of literature   WRITING, 20
iteration   i. of nuptials   MARRIAGE, 40
itself   Love seeketh not i. to please   LOVE, 27
ivy   The holly and the i.   CHRISTMAS, 5

J

jab Man, . . . had been created to j. the life out of Germans
WAR, 99
J'accuse J. ACCUSATION, 3
Jack Damn you, J. – I'm all right SELFISHNESS, 3
J. and Jill went up the hill To fetch a pail of water NURSERY
RHYMES, 24
J. of all trades OCCUPATIONS, 3
J. Sprat could eat no fat NURSERY RHYMES, 25
Little J. Horner Sat in the corner NURSERY RHYMES, 29
the house that J. built NURSERY RHYMES, 57
jackals J. piss at their foot BOOKS, 18
Jackson J. standing like a stone wall DETERMINATION, 5
Jacob Talk to him of J.'s ladder PRACTICALITY, 4
the traffic of J.'s ladder HEAVEN, 13
jail being in a ship is being in a j. BOATS, 9
jam J. today, and men aren't at their most exciting
PROMISES, 6
The rule is, j. tomorrow and j. yesterday PROMISES, 3
James The work of Henry J. has always seemed divisible
WRITERS, 54
Jane if ever I was to have a dozen girls, I'd call 'em all J.
NAMES, 8
Time's up for Sir John, an' for little Lady J. PARTING, 7
Janvier Generals J. and Février SEASONS, 1
Japan There was a young man of J. VERBOSITY, 1
Japanese The J. have perfected good manners PLACES, 20
jaundiced with the j. eye PASSION, 8
jaw-jaw To j. is better than to war-war DIPLOMACY, 5
jazz J. . . . people hear it through their feet MUSIC, 48
J. will endure POP MUSIC, 16
The basic difference between classical music and j. MUSIC, 38
the J. Age . . . became less and less an affair of youth AGE, 26
jealous a j. God GOD, 10
Art is a j. mistress ART, 7
jealousy J. . . . feeling alone among smiling enemies
JEALOUSY, 2
of j.; It is the green-ey'd monster JEALOUSY, 5
the ear of j. heareth all things JEALOUSY, 1
Jeepers J. Creepers EYES, 2
jeering laughing and j. at everything . . . strange ENGLISH, 30
jeers j. at Fate ENVY, 2
Jeeves J. coughed one soft, low, gentle cough ANALOGY, 5
like P. G. Wodehouse dropping J. WRITERS, 90
Jefferson when Thomas J. dined alone TALENT, 5
jelly Out vile j. EYES, 3
Jemmy Young J. Grove on his death-bed lay LOVE, 13
Jenny J. kissed me when we met KISSING, 5
Jericho by faith the walls of J. fell down FAITH, 2
Jerusalem J. ENGLAND, 5
J. the golden PLACES, 14
Till we have built J. ENGLAND, 5
jest a fellow of infinite j. MOURNING, 10
A j.'s prosperity lies in the ear HUMOUR, 27
glory, j., and riddle of the world HUMAN CONDITION, 14
Life is a j. LIFE, 25
jesting j. Pilate TRUTH, 10
Jesus All hail, the power of J.' name CHRISTIANITY, 37
Gentle J. HUMILITY, 4
If J. Christ were to come to-day BELIEF, 4
J. loves me – this I know RELIGION, 62
J. was . . . a first-rate political economist CHRISTIANITY, 8
We're more popular than J. Christ now POP MUSIC, 12
when J. was born in Bethlehem of Judaea CHRISTMAS, 9
jeunesse Si j. savait AGE, 24
Jew An American is either a J., or an anti-Semite
AMERICANS, 9
difficult for a J. to be converted JEWS, 6
hated by every anti-semite as if I were a J. PREJUDICE, 7
Hath not a J. eyes EQUALITY, 22
I'm a coloured, one-eyed J. DISABILITY, 2; RACISM, 9
I'm not really a J.; just J.-ish HALF MEASURES, 2
I was born of Christian race, And not a Heathen, or a J.
RELIGION, 63
neither J. nor Greek CHRISTIANITY, 7
no intellectual society can flourish where a J. feels . . . uneasy
JEWS, 7
No J. was ever fool enough to turn Christian RELIGION, 73
Pessimism is a luxury that a J. never can allow himself JEWS, 9
jewelry she did not remember . . . her j. PRUDENCE, 11
jewels a capital bosom to hang j. upon APPEARANCE, 13
Jewish A J. man with parents alive JEWS, 13

a *total solution* of the J. question NAZISM, 1
best that is in the J. blood JEWS, 8
I'm not really a Jew; just J. HALF MEASURES, 2
Jewry Modern Physics is an instrument of J. SCIENCE, 1
Jews But spurn the J. JEWS, 5
King of the J. CHRISTMAS, 9
not enough prisons . . . in Palestine to hold all the J. JEWS, 10
The Irish and the J. have a psychosis IRISH, 2; JEWS, 1
The J. and Arabs should . . . settle their differences RELIGION, 4
the J. bring the unlike into the heart of *every milieu* JEWS, 15
the J. have made a contribution to the human condition
JEWS, 14
The J. have produced . . . Christ, Spinoza, and myself
CONCEIT, 16
To choose The J. JEWS, 4
Jill Jack and J. went up the hill To fetch a pail of water
NURSERY RHYMES, 24
Jingo We don't want to fight, but, by j. if we do
PATRIOTISM, 16
jo John Anderson my j. NOSTALGIA, 4
job Being a husband is a whole-time j. MARRIAGE, 22
If two men on the same j. agree AGREEMENT, 8
We have finished the j. TELEGRAMS, 10; WORLD WAR II, 28
we will finish the j. WORLD WAR II, 9
woman's ability to stick to a j. WOMEN, 79
Job J. endured everything – until his friends came
ENDURANCE, 8
jockey the . . . cup is given to the j. INJUSTICE, 5
Joe Hungry J. collected lists of fatal diseases ILLNESS, 6
John D'ye ken J. Peel HUNTING, 4
J. Anderson my jo NOSTALGIA, 4
J. Brown's body MEMORIALS, 4
Matthew, Mark, Luke and J. BLESSING, 1
Time's up for Sir J., an' for little Lady Jane PARTING, 7
Johnny J. head-in-air IDEALISM, 5
J.-the-bright-star REALISM, 4
J. underground IDEALISM, 5
Little J. Head-in-Air CHILDREN, 24
Johnson Dr J.'s morality was as English . . . as a beefsteak
ENGLAND, 20
Dr J.'s sayings WRITERS, 57
Old dread-death and dread-evil J. WRITERS, 41
That great Cham of literature, Samuel J. WRITERS, 84
There is no arguing with J. WRITERS, 51
John Wayne J. is dead ACTORS, 9
join He's gone to j. the majority DEATH, 18
will you j. the dance DANCING, 2
joined what . . . God hath j. together MARRIAGE, 27
Why haven't you j. WORLD WAR I, 21
joke A j.'s a very serious thing HUMOUR, 7
a j. with a double meaning HUMOUR, 2
A rich man's j. is always funny FLATTERY, 3
good deed to forget a poor j. HUMOUR, 4
Housekeeping ain't no j. HOUSEWORK, 1
The coarse j. proclaims HUMOUR, 18
different taste in j. is a . . . strain on the affections HUMOUR, 11
Forgive . . . my little j. on Thee PRAYER, 12
He cannot bear old men's j. OLD AGE, 20
I don't make j. GOVERNMENT, 24
joking My way of j. is to tell the truth TRUTH, 38
jolly There was a j. miller HAPPINESS, 4
Joneses drag the J. down to my level ONE-UPMANSHIP, 1
Joseph Here lies J., who failed in everything he undertook
FAILURE, 3
journalism Christianity, . . . but why j. CHRISTIANITY, 2;
JOURNALISM, 3
J. is the only job that requires no degrees JOURNALISM, 12
j. . . . keeps us in touch with the ignorance of the community
JOURNALISM, 32
J. largely consists of saying 'Lord Jones is dead' JOURNALISM, 13
J. . . . the challenge of filling . . . space JOURNALISM, 31
j. what will be grasped at once LITERATURE, 1; JOURNALISM, 14
journalist the functions of the modern j. JOURNALISM, 15
to bribe or twist . . . the British j. JOURNALISM, 33
journalists j. put theirs on the front page OCCUPATIONS, 7
J. say a thing that they know isn't true JOURNALISM, 8
journey I prepare for a j. . . . as though for death TRAVEL, 21
long j. . . . must bid the company farewell LAST WORDS, 57
One of the pleasantest things in the world is going on a j.
SOLITUDE, 8; TRAVEL, 13
Our j. had advanced DEATH, 43
journeying You cannot imagine how strange it seemed to be j.
TRAVEL, 17

K

time quietly k. them | TIME, 13
Who k. a man k. a reasonable creature | BOOKS, 27; BOOKS, 27
Yet each man k. the thing he loves | KILLING, 8
kilt The k. is an unrivalled garment for fornication | SCOTS, 9
kind a k. parent . . . or a merciless step-mother | NATURE, 14
being k. Is all the sad world needs | RELIGION, 70; KINDNESS, 6
charity suffereth long, and is k. | CHARITY, 6
He was a vicious man, but very k. | CHARACTER, 14
I love thee for a heart that's k. | KINDNESS, 2
One k. word | KINDNESS, 3
try to be k. | ACADEMICS, 3
kindle the sole purpose of human existence is to k. a light | EXISTENCE, 3
kindly a young person, who . . . marries or dies, is sure to be k. spoken of | HUMAN NATURE, 1
the deities so k. | DESTINY, 16
kindness a cup o' k. yet | FRIENDSHIP, 13
A Woman Killed with K. | BOOK, SONG, AND PLAY TITLES, 11
full o' th' milk of human k. | KINDNESS, 4
greetings where no k. is | OPTIMISM, 29
kill a wife with k. | KINDNESS, 5
recompense k. with k. | KINDNESS, 1
set a high value on spontaneous k. | FRIENDSHIP, 23
the k. of strangers | CHARITY, 23
unremembered acts Of k. and of love | KINDNESS, 7
kindred Like k. drops, been mingled | MOUNTAINS, 1
king A constitutional k. must learn to stoop | MONARCHY, 13
A k. is a thing | MONARCHY, 17
a k. may make a nobleman | CHIVALRY, 3
A k. of shreds and patches | INFERIORITY, 6
All the k.'s horses, And all the k.'s men | NURSERY RHYMES, 18
an atheist if the k. were | SERVILITY, 4
Authority forgets a dying k. | ROYALTY, 34
A worse k. never left a realm undone | ROYALTY, 8
better . . . a poor and a wise child than an old and foolish k. | OLD AGE, 5; YOUTH, 1
but the K. of England cannot enter | PRIVACY, 3
curse not the k., no not in thy thought | SECRECY, 3
every inch a k. | ROYALTY, 31
Every subject's duty is the K.'s | MONARCHY, 18
God save our Gracious K. | BRITAIN, 6
half the zeal I serv'd my K. | REGRET, 19
harm that cometh of a k.'s poverty | TAXATION, 3
heart and stomach of a K. | ROYALTY, 13
He played the K. as though | CRITICISM, 13
if I were not k., I should lose my temper | ROYALTY, 21
I'm the k. of the castle | NURSERY RHYMES, 23
I think the K. is but a man | EQUALITY, 21
k. reigns, but does not govern | MONARCHY, 25
rather hew wood than be . . . K. of England | MONARCHY, 19
such divinity doth hedge a k. | MONARCHY, 19
That whatsoever K. shall reign, I'll be the Vicar of Bray, Sir | SELF-PRESERVATION, 4
the k. can do no wrong | MONARCHY, 4
The k. has been very good to me | MARTYRDOM, 1
The k. never dies | MONARCHY, 5
The K. of Spain's daughter Came to visit me | NURSERY RHYMES, 20
The K. over the Water | ROYALTY, 1
The k. reigns, and the people govern themselves | MONARCHY, 22
The k. was in his counting-house, Counting out his money | NURSERY RHYMES, 48
The present life of men on earth, O k. | LIFE, 9
this house will in no circumstances fight for its K. and country | PATRIOTISM, 3
wash the balm from an anointed k. | MONARCHY, 20
kingdom It is folly . . . to mistake the echo of a . . . coffee-house for the . . . k. | OPINIONS, 1
my k. for a horse | HORSES, 10
No k. has . . . had as many . . . wars as the k. of Christ | CHRISTIANITY, 34
the k. of God is not in word, but in power | GOD, 12
kings Conquering k. their titles take | ROYALTY, 9
Grammar, which can govern even k. | GRAMMAR, 6
If you get the English people into the way of making k. | ROYALTY, 22
K. are earth's gods | ROYALTY, 29
K. . . . are just 'as funny | ROYALTY, 27
K. are naturally lovers of low company | ROYALTY, 7
K. govern by . . . assemblies only when | MONARCHY, 11
Or walk with K. | IDEALISM, 2

Pale Death kicks his way . . . into . . . the castles of k. | EQUALITY, 28
sad stories of the death of k. | ROYALTY, 30
Such grace had k. | ROYALTY, 6
teeming womb of royal k. | ENGLAND, 36
the K. of England, Diamonds, Hearts, Spades and Clubs | MONARCHY, 10
This royal throne of k. | ENGLAND, 36
till philosophers become k. | PHILOSOPHY, 9
'Twixt k. and tyrants there's this difference | TYRANNY, 2
kingship k. approaches tyranny it is near its end | TYRANNY, 5
kinquering K. Congs their titles take | SPOONERISMS, 3
Kipling W. H. Auden, a sort of gutless K. | SOCIALISM, 13
kippers like two old k. in a box | OLD AGE, 46
kiss A k. without a moustache | KISSING, 4
come let us k. and part | PARTING, 6
K. me, Hardy | LAST WORDS, 47
make me immortal with a k. | BEAUTY, 25
The coward does it with a k. | KILLING, 8
The k. of sun for pardon | GARDENS, 7
Then come k. me, sweet and twenty | PRESENT, 13
Without a single k. or a good-bye | PARTING, 8
you must not k. and tell | SECRECY, 7
You must remember this; A k. is just a k. | TIME, 20
kissed Being k. by a man who didn't wax his moustache | KISSING, 3
hail, master; and k. him | BETRAYAL, 1
I k. her little sister | UNFAITHFULNESS, 4
Jenny k. me when we met | KISSING, 2
k. her once by the pig-sty | EXPECTATION, 5
K. the girls and made them cry | NURSERY RHYMES, 12
Wherever one wants to be k. | COSMETICS, 2
kisses bread and cheese, and k. | MARRIAGE, 114
remembered k. after death | NOSTALGIA, 20
Stolen sweets are always sweeter, Stolen k. much completer | THEFT, 7
kissing K. don't last | FOOD, 37
K. Had to Stop | BOOK, SONG, AND PLAY TITLES, 7
The President spends most of his time k. | PERSUASION, 4
when the k. had to stop | KISSING, 1
kit-bag pack up your troubles in your old k. | OPTIMISM, 13
kitchen can't stand the heat, get out of the k. | ENDURANCE, 20
the way of all flesh . . . towards the k. | FOOD, 48
Kitchener If K. was not a great man, he was . . . a great poster | OFFICERS, 2
K-K-Katy K., beautiful Katy | LOVE, 94
knave The K. of Hearts He stole the tarts | NURSERY RHYMES, 51
knaves world is made up . . . of fools and k. | FOOLISHNESS, 11
knee-cap The soul started at the k. | ANIMALISM, 5
knew I k. him, Horatio | MOURNING, 10
much righter than one k. at say 17 or 23 | AGE, 45
knife I had a k. and two forks left | ETIQUETTE, 3
it keeps them on the k. | FOOD, 6
last twist of the k. | LIFE, 22
War even to the k. | WAR, 22
knight a verray parfit gentil k. | CHIVALRY, 4
every chance brought out a noble k. | NOSTALGIA, 19
I never realized that I'd end up being the shortest k. of the year | PUNS, 19; TITLES, 8
Poor K.! he really had two periods | WRITING, 25
There came a K. to be their wooer | LOVE, 15
what can ail thee, k. at arms | ILLNESS, 10
knights sorrier for my good k.' loss than for . . . my fair queen | LOSS, 3
knitter a beautiful little k. | WRITERS, 83
knives Phone for the fish k. Norman | ETIQUETTE, 1
knock Don't k. it | SEX, 3
K. as you please | STUPIDITY, 13
k. him down first, and pity him afterwards | SELF-PRESERVATION, 6
Three, four, K. at the door | NURSERY RHYMES, 37
know all Ye k. on earth | BEAUTY, 24; TRUTH, 30
A really intelligent man feels what other men . . . k. | INTELLIGENCE, 4
Children with Hyacinth's temperament . . . merely k. more | CHARACTER, 18
flautists are most obviously the ones who k. something we don't k. | MUSICIANS, 4
for they k. not what they do | FORGIVENESS, 1
I do not k. myself | SELF-KNOWLEDGE, 4
I k. myself | SELF-KNOWLEDGE, 3

I k. what I like SUBJECTIVITY, 1
K. then thyself, presume not God to scan SELF-KNOWLEDGE, 5
scarcely hate any one that we k. HATE, 4
the only person . . . I should like to k. EGOTISM, 11
To k. how to say what others only . . . think SPEECH, 7
What we k. of the past HISTORY, 17
What you don't k. IGNORANCE, 3
What you don't k. would make a great book IGNORANCE, 15
You k. . . . what you are KNOWLEDGE, 20
knowed The clever men at Oxford Know all that there is to be k. KNOWLEDGE, 18
knowing A woman, especially if she have the misfortune of k. anything WOMEN, 10
knowledge a k. of nothing KNOWLEDGE, 12
All k. is of itself of some value KNOWLEDGE, 23
all k. to be my province KNOWLEDGE, 4
all our k. is, ourselves to know SELF-KNOWLEDGE, 6
an age in which useless k. KNOWLEDGE, 22
an intimate k. of its ugly side DISILLUSION, 1
ask it for the k. of a lifetime ARTISTS, 22
civilizations . . . abandon the quest for k. KNOWLEDGE, 27
he giveth . . . k. to them that know understanding GOD, 7
If a little k. is dangerous, where is the man . . . out of danger KNOWLEDGE, 21
if a little k. was a dangerous thing KNOWLEDGE, 32
if education is . . . a mere transmission of k. EDUCATION, 37
Integrity without k. is weak INTEGRITY, 4; KNOWLEDGE, 24
K. advances by steps KNOWLEDGE, 28
k. and wonder . . . is an impression of pleasure KNOWLEDGE, 5; WONDER, 1
K. can be communicated but not wisdom WISDOM, 17
K. dwells In heads replete KNOWLEDGE, 11; WISDOM, 15
K. is Life with wings KNOWLEDGE, 15
K. is of two kinds KNOWLEDGE, 26
K. is proportioned to being KNOWLEDGE, 20
K. is the mother KNOWLEDGE, 1
K. itself is power KNOWLEDGE, 3
k. puffeth up CHARITY, 7; KNOWLEDGE, 8
lawyers . . . have taken away the key of k. LAWYERS, 5
let him receive the new k. HEAVEN, 4
light of k. in their eyes KNOWLEDGE, 33
never has a man turned so little k. to such great account SHAKESPEARE, 7
Our k. can only be finite KNOWLEDGE, 31
Out-topping k. SHAKESPEARE, 1
province of k. to speak KNOWLEDGE, 19; WISDOM, 18
the river of k. has too often turned back on itself SCIENCE, 24
the search for k. PHILOSOPHERS, 8
the tree of the k. of good and evil GARDENS, 3
What I don't know isn't k. ACADEMICS, 2
worth a pound of k. LOVE, 146; KNOWLEDGE, 34
you impart k. of it through another's death RESEARCH, 1
known apart from the k. and the unknown METAPHYSICS, 4
knows a woman who k. all . . . that can be taught KNOWLEDGE, 9
He that k. little IGNORANCE, 1
He that k. nothing IGNORANCE, 2
he thinks he k. everything POLITICIANS, 23
He who k. only his own side . . . knows little SUBJECTIVITY, 4
Only the nose k. . . . SECRECY, 1
knuckle-end k. of England SCOTLAND, 8
knyf The smyler with the k. HYPOCRISY, 7
Kodak painted . . . by the great artist K. PHOTOGRAPHY, 6
Kubla In Xanadu did K. Khan PLEASURE, 8

L

laboratorium *L. est oratorium* SCIENCE, 29
laboratory apt to leave his cultures exposed on the l. table SCIENTISTS, 12
We're all of us guinea pigs in the l. of God MANKIND, 38
labour all ye that l. and are heavy laden CHRISTIANITY, 18
A mountain in l. shouted so loud DISAPPOINTMENT, 4
an Independent L. Party PARTIES, 8
disastrous element in the L. party POLITICS, 20
England elects a L. Government POLITICS, 63
genius the L. Party has for cutting itself in half POLITICS, 18
L. is not fit to govern POLITICS, 19
little effect after much l. RESULTS, 2
Man . . . can only find relaxation from one . . . l. by taking up another CHANGE, 7
model L. voter POLITICS, 43

the Gromyko of the L. party POLITICIANS, 51
The grotesque chaos of a L. council – a L. council INCOMPETENCE, 2
The L. party is like a stage-coach POLITICS, 89
To l. and not ask for any reward SELFLESSNESS, 2
labours absorbs a clay After his l. SMOKING, 3
Children sweeten l. CHILDREN, 5
labyrinthine I fled Him, down the l. ways RELIGION, 58
lack l. of power corrupts absolutely POWER, 24
own up to a l. of humour HUMOUR, 8
lad many a lightfoot l. NOSTALGIA, 11
ladder behold a l. set up on earth HEAVEN, 1
Talk to him of Jacob's l. PRACTICALITY, 4
the traffic of Jacob's l. HEAVEN, 13
We make ourselves a l. out of our vices VICE, 2
ladies How sweet are looks that l. bend WOMEN, 78
lion among l. FEAR, 12
lady Dance, dance, dance little l. DANCING, 3
l. doth protest too much EXCESS, 8
l. of a certain age AGE, 17
My fair l. NURSERY RHYMES, 32
the L. Is a Tramp DECLINE, 2
The l.'s not for turning INFLEXIBILITY, 3
there had been a l. in the case WOMEN, 21
There is a l. sweet and kind FIRST IMPRESSIONS, 2
young l. named Bright SCIENCE, 3
ladybird L., l., Fly away home NURSERY RHYMES, 26
Lady Chatterley L.'s Lover . . . all Christians might read with profit PORNOGRAPHY, 5
Put thy shimmy on, L. Chatterley PARTING, 7
ladyship When your l.'s faith has removed them RELIGION, 15
Lafayette L., we are here GREETINGS, 4
laid all the young ladies who attended the Yale promenade dance were l. end to end SEX, 43
l. on with a trowel EXCESS, 9
laissez L. *faire* FREEDOM, 42
L. *faire*, l. *passer* FREEDOM, 13
lake An arm Rose up from . . . the l. ARTHURIAN LEGEND, 3
Marriage may often be a stormy l. MARRIAGE, 89
sedge is wither'd from the l. ILLNESS, 10
lamb Did he who made the L. make thee CREATION, 7
Little L., who made thee CREATION, 8
Mary had a little l. ANIMALS, 11
Pipe a song about a L. MUSIC, 13
the L. of God CHRISTIANITY, 12
to make the lion lie down with the l. HUMAN NATURE, 18
Lambeth doin' the L. walk DANCING, 5
lambs We're poor little l. DEBAUCHERY, 7
lame your precious 'l. ducks' WEAKNESS, 2
lament reason to l. What man has made of man MANKIND, 39
lamp my l. burns low and dim ENVY, 3
To keep a l. burning CHARITY, 21
lampada *vitai l.* MORTALITY, 15
lamp-post I'm leaning on a l. LOVE, 57
like asking a l. . . . about dogs CRITICS, 7
share a quick pee over a common l. WRITERS, 8
lamp-posts He uses statistics as a drunken man uses l. STATISTICS, 4
lamps l. are going out all over Europe PROPHECY, 5
new l. for old ones BUSINESS, 9
the people are forbidden to light l. INJUSTICE, 10
Ye living l. BIRDS, 6
Lancelot bold Sir L. CHIVALRY, 11
land England's green and pleasant l. ENGLAND, 5
For England's the one l. ENGLAND, 7
L. of Hope and Glory BRITAIN, 4
My native L. DEPARTURE, 4
the l. grows poorer and uglier every day ECOLOGY, 3
The l. of my fathers WALES, 2
There is a happy l. HEAVEN, 15
They are ill discoverers that think there is no l. DISCOVERY, 3
they have the l. and we have the Bibles RACISM, 11
to the French the empire of the l. EUROPE, 13
Unhappy the l. that has no heroes HEROISM, 3
We are as near to heaven by sea as by l. LAST WORDS, 32; SEA, 5
why Absurdist plays take place in No Man's L. THEATRE, 1
landlady The l. . . . is a parallelogram HUMOUR, 40
landlord Come l., fill the flowing bowl DRUNKENNESS, 3
the l. does not intend to repair LAST WORDS, 2
lands in faery l. forlorn BIRDS, 5
l. where the Jumblies live NONSENSE, 18

landscape   half the l. is . . . covered by useless water
    SEASIDE, 2
When will the l. tire the view   COUNTRYSIDE, 3
lane   the little boy Who lives down the l.   NURSERY RHYMES, 4
language   Babel; because the Lord did there confound the l.
    LANGUAGE, 2
I have laboured to refine our l. to grammatical purity
    LANGUAGE, 14
L. grows out of life   LANGUAGE, 22
L. is not simply a reporting device for experience
    LANGUAGE, 27
L. is only the instrument of science   LANGUAGE, 16
L., man! . . . it's LITERATURE   LITERATURE, 18
Literature is simply l. charged with meaning   LITERATURE, 15
she knows her l. better than most ladies do   WRITERS, 85
The English have no respect for their l.   ENGLISH, 32
the tower of Babel should have got l. all mixed up
    LANGUAGE, 25
the whole earth was of one l.   UNITY, 6
what l. an opera is sung in   OPERA, 1
when his l. performs what is required of it without shyness
    STYLE, 3
with l. profane and obscene   PETULANCE, 1
with no l. but a cry   HUMAN CONDITION, 20
languages   l. are the pedigree of nations   LANGUAGE, 15
she speaks eighteen l.. And she can't say 'No' in any of them
    PROMISCUITY, 5
the man who can be silent in several l.   DIPLOMACY, 11
who quoted dead l.   CRITICS, 1
lap   the cool flowery l. of earth   POETS, 16
lap-dogs   when l. breathe their last   SORROW, 16
lards   And l. the lean earth as he walks   OBESITY, 10
lark   No l. more blithe than he   HAPPINESS, 4
To hear the l. begin his flight   BIRDS, 8
larks   Four L. and a Wren   APPEARANCE, 8
lascivious   Poetry . . . set to more or less l. music   POETRY, 29
lash   rum, sodomy, and the l.   NAVY, 2
lass   On Richmond Hill there lives a l.   ADMIRATION, 7
lasses   Come l. and lads, get leave of your dads
    MERRYMAKING, 1
lassie   I love a l.   LOVE, 79
last   as if it were the l.   LIFE, 33
Die . . . the l. thing I shall do   LAST WORDS, 49
Don't wait for the L. Judgement   DOOMSDAY, 4
each day that has dawned is your l.   PRESENT, 10
'Fan vaulting' . . . belongs to the 'L.-supper-carved-on-a-peach-
stone'   ARCHITECTURE, 5
for the l. time in my life, Your Humble Servant   ARGUMENTS, 17
hoping that it will eat him l.   DIPLOMACY, 6
I shall be the l. to go out   COURAGE, 2
l. act crowns the play   PLAYS, 8
l. day but one   EDUCATION, 30
Nice guys finish l.   GOOD, 4
the feeling that I could l. for ever   YOUTH, 4
the l. shall be first   MERIT, 3
The l. straw   ENDURANCE, 2
the l. time that I will take part as an amateur   FUNERALS, 2
there is no l. or first   EQUALITY, 6
'Tis the L. Judgment's fire   DOOMSDAY, 1
we are all on our l. cruise   MORTALITY, 18
What is it that will l.   TIME, 37
late   Better never than l.   PROMPTNESS, 3
Never too l. to learn   AGE, 1
One doesn't recognize . . . the really important moments . . .
until it's too l.   REGRET, 4
So l. into the night   DEBAUCHERY, 4
We have met too l.   INFLUENCE, 4
later   It is l. than you think   TIME, 31
Latin   A gentleman need not know L.   EDUCATION, 34
A silly remark can be made in L.   LANGUAGE, 5
Don't quote L.   SPEECHES, 6
small L., and less Greek   CLASSICS, 5
the Devil knows L.   LANGUAGE, 17
The word is half Greek and half L.   TELEVISION, 5
We were taught . . . L. and Greek   CLASSICS, 9
Latins   L. are tenderly enthusiastic   PLACES, 1
latrine   used as a l. by some small animal   DRUNKENNESS, 2
laudanum   Whipping and abuse are like l.   CRUELTY, 5
laugh   I make myself l. at everything   LAUGHTER, 4
L. and grow fat   LAUGHTER, 1
L., and the world laughs with you   LAUGHTER, 10
L. before breakfast   LAUGHTER, 2

l. before one is happy   LAUGHTER, 8
Make 'em l.   WRITING, 27
not to l. at human actions   UNDERSTANDING, 9
old man who will not l.   AGE, 50; WISDOM, 20
The Italians will l. at me   HITLER, 4
laughable   most schemes of political improvement are very l.
    POLITICS, 41
laugh-at-with   Auden was someone you could l.   POETS, 54
laughed   Few women care to be l. at   RIDICULE, 2
on which one has not l.   LAUGHTER, 6
When the first baby l.   FAIRIES, 2
laughing   Happiness is no l. matter   HAPPINESS, 30
l. and jeering at everything . . . strange   ENGLISH, 30
One cannot be always l. at a man   MEN, 1
one may die without ever l.   LAUGHTER, 8
read the death of Little Nell without l.   DICKENS, 4;
    INSENSITIVITY, 4
the most fun I ever had without l.   SEX, 2
laughter   I said of l., it is mad   LAUGHTER, 5
I was convulsed with l.   INSULTS, 29
L. is pleasant   LAUGHTER, 9
L. is the best medicine   LAUGHTER, 3
l. is weakness   LAUGHTER, 7
present l.   PRESENT, 13
you can draw l. from an audience   MARRIAGE, 74
Laughton   can't direct a L. picture   ACTORS, 16
Launcelot   Sir L. saw her visage, but he wept not greatly
    SORROW, 11
laundries   Land of L.   TRAVEL, 4
laundry   Give me a l.-list   MUSIC, 41
The general idea . . . in any first-class l.   NEGLECT, 2
laurel   Caesar's l. crown   POWER, 7
laurel-bough   burned as Apollo's l.   DEATH, 80
laurels   Nothing is harder on your l.   SUCCESS, 2
once more, O ye l.   TREES, 10
The l. all are cut   ENDING, 4
Laurie   for bonnie Annie L.   LOVE AND DEATH, 1
law   Born under one l.   HUMAN CONDITION, 9
Common L. of England   LAW, 15
each man must struggle, lest the moral l. become . . . separated
    MORALITY, 1
Every l. is a contract   LAW, 22
Ignorance of the l.   LAW, 23
I have forgotten more l. than you ever knew   INSULTS, 30
No brilliance is needed in the l.   LAW, 19
Nor l., nor duty bade me fight   FLYING, 4
nothing is l. that is not reason   LAW, 21
Order is heaven's first l.   ORDER, 3
Or lesser breeds without the L.   BOASTS, 4
Prisons are built with stones of L.   HYPOCRISY, 4
rich men rule the l.   LAW, 13
The army ages men sooner than the l.   ARMY, 6
the first l. of holes . . . stop digging   ADVICE, 9
the greater part of the l. is learning to tolerate fools   LAW, 18
The l. does not concern itself   LAW, 5
the l. is a ass —   LAW, 9
The L. is the true embodiment   LAW, 11
The L. of dislike for the unlike   JEWS, 15
The L. of England is a very strange one   LAW, 8
the L. of the Yukon   SURVIVAL, 4
the magnificent fair play of the British criminal l.   JUSTICE, 6
The majestic egalitarianism of the l.   EQUALITY, 8
the moral l.   WONDER, 3
There is no universal l.   SPONTANEITY, 3
There's one l. for the rich   CLASS, 1
The rise in the . . . employed is governed by Parkinson's L.
    WORK, 14
th' windy side of the l.   LAW, 24
Lawrence   For L., existence was one continuous convalescence
    WRITERS, 59
L., that provincial genius   WRITERS, 50
L. . . . the only prophetic novelist writing today   WRITERS, 47
Mr L. has penned another novel   WRITERS, 77
laws   I know not whether L. be right   IMPRISONMENT, 10
L. are generally found to be nets   LAW, 25
L. are like cobwebs   LAW, 27
L. are like spider's webs   LAW, 26
L. grind the poor   LAW, 13
l. were like cobwebs   LAW, 6
L. were made to be broken   LAW, 20
rules of the game are what we call the l. of Nature   GOD, 28

the individual subject . . . 'has nothing to do with the l. but to obey them.'   LAW, 16
the l. of poetic truth and poetic beauty   POETRY, 2
the repeal of bad or obnoxious l.   LAW, 14
Where l. end, tyranny begins   TYRANNY, 6
who are formed by a different breeding, are fed by a different food, are ordered by different manners, and are not governed by the same l.   POVERTY AND WEALTH, 4
you do not make the l. but . . . are the wives . . . of those who do   WOMEN, 38
lawyer A client is fain to hire a l. to keep from . . . other lawyers   LAWYERS, 6
A l. has no business with . . . justice or injustice   JUSTICE, 13
A l. never goes   LAWYERS, 2
A l.'s opinion   LAWYERS, 3
He that is his own l.   LAWYERS, 1
No poet ever interpreted nature . . . as a l. interprets truth   LAW, 12
lawyers L. are the only persons in whom ignorance . . . is not punished   LAWYERS, 4
woe unto you, l.   LAWYERS, 5
laxative Now Spring, sweet l. of Georgian strains   SEASONS, 6; STATELY HOMES, 1
lay I never would l. down my arms   PATRIOTISM, 24
L. your sleeping head   SLEEP, 3
Lazarus L. . . . laid at his gate, full of sores   POVERTY AND WEALTH, 2
L. was not Questioned about after-lives   DEATH, 64
lazy be efficient if you're going to be l.   LAZINESS, 1
There are no ugly women, only l. ones   BEAUTY, 31
lead L., kindly Light   FAITH, 16
leader A l. who doesn't hesitate . . . is not fit to be a l.   LEADERSHIP, 7
I have to follow them, I am their l.   LEADERSHIP, 6
leadership men do not approach to l.   LEADERSHIP, 1
leap a great l. in the dark   LAST WORDS, 38
A l. over the hedge   PRAYER, 7
And twenty-nine in each l. year   NURSERY RHYMES, 56
one giant l. for mankind   SPACE, 1
leapt Into the dangerous world I l.   BIRTH, 3
learn L., compare, collect the facts   EDUCATION, 42
The life so short, the craft so long to l.   MORTALITY, 12
we could never l. to be brave . . . if there were only joy   ENDURANCE, 7
What we have to l. to do   LEARNING, 1
learned A l. man is an idler   EDUCATION, 50
He was naturally l.   SHAKESPEARE, 6
I am . . . of the opinion with the l.   AGREEMENT, 1
Misquotation is the pride and privilege of the l.   MISQUOTATIONS, 2
people . . . never have l. anything from history   EXPERIENCE, 14
the l. roast an egg   FOOD, 42
learning A little l. is a dangerous thing   KNOWLEDGE, 30
A progeny of l.   MALAPROPISMS, 3
beauty and the lust for l.   BEAUTY, 8
I have been l. how to die   DEATH, 128
I thought that I was l. how to live   DEATH, 128
l., earning and yearning   LIFE, 36
L. hath gained most   BOOKS, 19
L. is a treasure   KNOWLEDGE, 2
L. is but an adjunct   LEARNING, 8
L. without thought is labour lost   KNOWLEDGE, 10
public school, where . . . l. was painfully beaten into him   EDUCATION, 43
Their l. is like bread in a besieged town   SCOTS, 6
learnt I only remember what I've l.   KNOWLEDGE, 35
Soon l.   EDUCATION, 1
what has been l. has been forgotten   EDUCATION, 54
least death . . . the l. of all evils   DEATH, 20
L. said soonest mended   ARGUMENTS, 2
Strongest minds . . . the noisy world Hears l.   MIND, 10
leave Fare thee well, for I must l. thee   PARTING, 2
How I l. my country   LAST WORDS, 51
If you l. a thing alone you l. it to a torrent of change   CONSERVATISM, 1
L. well alone   TACT, 1
to l. his country as good as he had found it   DUTY, 1
leaves before the l. have fallen   WAR, 132
before the l. have fallen from the trees   WORLD WAR I, 24
If poetry comes not . . . as l. to a tree   POETRY, 25
No fruits, no flowers, no l., no birds   MONTHS, 10
Though l. are many, the root is one   AGE, 71

With vine l. in his hair   RETURN, 2
Words are like l.   VERBOSITY, 6
leaving became him like the l. it   DEATH, 109
She's l. home   DEPARTURE, 8
leavings sacrifice . . . of the devil's l.   VIRTUE, 15
lecher small gilded fly does l.   ANIMALISM, 7
lechery drink . . . an equivocator with l.   ALCOHOL, 53
Still wars and l.   SEX, 51
lectures l. or a little charity   SELF, 19
led l. by the nose with gold   BRIBERY, 4
leeches l. have red blood   LAST WORDS, 17
left a handful of silver he l. us   BETRAYAL, 2
And we are l., or shall be l., alone   DEFEAT, 9
better to be l. than never to have been loved   LOVE, 43
not l. to Spain   MARTYRDOM, 4
You just press the accelerator to the floor and steer l.   SPORT AND GAMES, 20
leg here I leave my second l.   PUNS, 9
legal collect l. taxes from illegal money   TAXATION, 1
legality do not let so great an achievement suffer from . . . l.   LAW, 17
legs apart from having two good l.   INTELLIGENCE, 3
cannon-ball took off his l.   PUNS, 9
there you sit with that magnificent instrument between your l.   INCOMPETENCE, 5
You were born with your l. apart   PROMISCUITY, 4
Leicester Square Good-bye Piccadilly, Farewell l.   HOMESICKNESS, 8
leisure Evil comes at l.   DISEASE, 12
gentleman of l.   MATERIALISM, 20
Men . . . detest at l.   LOVE AND HATE, 1
Prince Philip. . . . a world expert on l.   ROYALTY, 19
The secret of being miserable is to have l.   SORROW, 23
wisdom . . . cometh by opportunity of l.   LEISURE, 1; WISDOM, 4
lemon The Germans, . . . are going to be squeezed, as a l.   RETRIBUTION, 10
lend I would not l. my pony now, For all the lady's hire   NURSERY RHYMES, 21
lender Neither a borrower nor a l. be   BORROWING, 8; INTEGRITY, 6
lene As l. was his hors as is a rake   HORSES, 1
Lenin L.'s method leads to this   COMMUNISM, 11
L. was the first to discover that capitalism 'inevitably' caused war   CAPITALISM, 14
Lent Ishmaelites . . . will not publicly eat human flesh uncooked in L.   CANNIBALISM, 2
Leonardo Disney the most significant figure . . . since L.   ART, 14
leopard or the l. his spots   CHANGE, 1
leprosy It is full of l.   PRACTICALITY, 2
lerne gladly wolde he l.   CHARACTER, 5
less found it l. exciting   COWARDICE, 3
I love not Man the l.   NATURE, 3
l. in this than meets the eye   CRITICISM, 2
Specialist – A man who knows more and more about l. and l.   EXPERTS, 5
the l. they have . . . the more noise they make   CHARACTER, 17
let I l. down my friends   BETRAYAL, 6
kick you out, but . . . never l. you down   EDUCATION, 61
L. it be, l. it pass   FREEDOM, 42
Lethe go not to L.   OBLIVION, 2
letter I have made this l. longer   VERBOSITY, 6
thou unnecessary l.   INSULTS, 34
writing a l. and forgetting to sign his name   INSULTS, 5
letters His sayings are generally like women's l.   LETTER-WRITING, 3
The profession of l. . . . in which one can make no money without being ridiculous   WRITING, 28
the republic of l.   MANKIND, 1
When I pass my name in such large l.   FAME, 22
level-headed When things are steep, remember to stay l.   SELF-CONTROL, 4
levellers Your l. wish to level *down* as far as themselves   EQUALITY, 13
Leviathan that great L., or rather . . . that *Mortal God*   STATE, 1
levity He rose by gravity; I sank by l.   SERIOUSNESS, 4
lexicographer L. . . . harmless drudge   LEXICOGRAPHY, 6
to wake a l.   LEXICOGRAPHY, 4
liaison partly a l. man and partly P.R.O   BUSINESS, 4
liar A l. is worse   LYING, 1
He did not feel a l.   LYING, 12

Mr. Speaker, I said the honorable member was a l.
APOLOGIES, 4

Poor Bonar can't bear being called a l.
POLITICIANS, 58

When I was a little boy they called me a l.
WRITERS, 22

you are . . . the club Bore: I am the club L.
SUPERIORITY, 11

liars It has made more l.
LYING, 14

liberal a l. education at the Colleges of Unreason
REASON, 1

either a little L.
POLITICS, 32

ineffectual l.'s problem
LIBERALISM, 1

Just like an old l. Between the wars
LIBERALISM, 3

the damned, compact, l. majority
MAJORITY, 4

When a l. is abused, he says
LIBERALISM, 2

liberality L. lies less in giving liberally
PROMPTNESS, 1

liberal-minded booksellers are generous l. men
PUBLISHING, 9

Liberal party task of the L. is to strangle it at birth
POLITICS, 67

liberation truly mankind's war of l.
HUNGER, 7

liberté L.! Égalité! Fraternité
HUMAN RIGHTS, 2

liberties government will protect all l. but one
FREEDOM, 37

liberty condition upon which God hath given l.
FREEDOM, 9

Corruption . . . symptom of constitutional l.
CORRUPTION, 2

extremism in the defence of l. is no vice
EXCESS, 4

give me l. or give me death
FREEDOM, 16

If men are to wait for l.
FREEDOM, 29

It is true that l. is precious
FREEDOM, 26

l. cannot long exist
CORRUPTION, 1

l. for one person is constrained only
EQUALITY, 11

L. is the right to do everything
FREEDOM, 35

L. means responsibility
LIBERTY, 2

L. of action
FREEDOM, 13

L., too, must be limited
FREEDOM, 5

life, l., and the pursuit of happiness
HUMAN RIGHTS, 3

love of l. is the love of others
FREEDOM, 15

Oh l.! . . . What crimes are committed in thy name
EXECUTION, 27; FREEDOM, 44

Power . . . and L. . . . are seldom upon good Terms
POWER, 12; FREEDOM, 14

The l. of the individual must be thus far limited
FREEDOM, 33

The L. of the press
FREEDOM, 23

the price of l.
FREEDOM, 39

The tree of l. must be refreshed
FREEDOM, 21

thy chosen music, L.
FREEDOM, 54

Venice, the eldest Child of L.
VENICE, 3

When the People contend for their L.
REBELLION, 4

why is my l. judged of another man's conscience
CONSCIENCE, 1; FREEDOM, 3

Liberty-Hall This is L.
FREEDOM, 12

library A l. is thought in cold storage
BOOKS, 38

half a l. to make one book
WRITING, 13

put away in the lumber room of his l.
KNOWLEDGE, 13

lice They are electronic l.
POP MUSIC, 6

licence a l. to print your own money
BUSINESS, 24

A universal l. to be good
FREEDOM, 8

L. my roving hands
LUST, 1

Painters and poets . . . l. to dare anything
FREEDOM, 18

the rest love . . . l.
FREEDOM, 34

licks pride that l. the dust
SERVILITY, 5

lie A l. can be half-way round the world
LYING, 6

A l. is . . . help in trouble
LYING, 16

a l. which is part a truth
LYING, 17

A lot of people, . . . tell a l. with their last gasp
LAST WORDS, 1

a man . . . should never venture to l.
LYING, 11

an honest man sent to l. abroad for . . . his country
DIPLOMACY, 21

Better a l. that heals
TRUTH, 1

Father, I cannot tell a l.
HONESTY, 10

He who does not need to l. is proud
LYING, 13

L. follows by post
APOLOGIES, 1

more easily fall victim to a big l.
LYING, 8

My love and I would l.
COUNTRYSIDE, 6

Nature admits no l.
NATURE, 4

The camera cannot l.. But . . .
PHOTOGRAPHY, 3

The greater the l.
PROPAGANDA, 2

the l. has become . . . a pillar of the State
LYING, 15

The old L.
PATRIOTISM, 23

Those who live by . . . a l., and those who live by . . . the truth
HONESTY, 4

too crafty a woman to invent a new l.
LYING, 9

you would l. if you were in his place
TRUTH, 32

lied because our fathers l.
WORLD WAR I, 13

lies believing their own l.
POLITICS, 2

It's easy to make a man confess . . . l.
TRUTH, 27

l., damned l. and statistics
STATISTICS, 2

Only l. and evil come from letting people off
FORGIVENESS, 12

Optimistic l.
MEDICINE, 8

polite by telling l.
COURTESY, 3

The cruellest l. are . . . told in silence
SILENCE, 14

This universal, obligatory force-feeding with l.
INDOCTRINATION, 2

which way the head l.
EXECUTION, 24

life a keen observer of l.
INTELLECTUALS, 2

A l. that moves to gracious ends
LIFE, 48

Anythin' for a quiet l.
PEACE, 8

As our l. is very short
LIFE, 47

A well-written L.
BIOGRAPHY, 2

Bankrupt of L.
WORLD-WEARINESS, 1

because I love this l.
DEATH, 120

believe in the l. to come
AFTERLIFE, 1

Books are . . . a mighty bloodless substitute for l.
BOOKS, 42

brief is l. but love is long
LOVE, 135

chemical barrage has been hurled against the fabric of l.
ECOLOGY, 2

death after l. does greatly please
DEATH, 118

doctrine of the strenuous l.
WORK, 20

dreary intercourse of daily l.
OPTIMISM, 29

Football isn't a matter of l. and death
FOOTBALL, 7

For l. is but a dream
LIFE, 50

good shepherd giveth his l. for the sheep
CHRISTIANITY, 15

half of them prefer hiring their servants for l.
SLAVERY, 2

help me through this long disease, my l.
DISEASE, 29

hymns of praise to the glory of l.
POETRY, 46

I am the bread of l.
FAITH, 8

I am the resurrection, and the l.
CHRISTIANITY, 16

I am the way, the truth, and the l.
CHRISTIANITY, 17

I have but one l. to lose for my country
PATRIOTISM, 13

I have measured out my l.
LIFE, 23

Illness is the night-side of l.
ILLNESS, 15

I might give my l. for my friend
FRIENDSHIP, 27

Is l. a boon
MORTALITY, 7

Is not l. . . . too short . . . to bore ourselves
BOREDOM, 6

isn't l. a terrible thing
LIFE, 49

Is there another l.
AFTERLIFE, 6

It doesn't . . . matter what you do . . . , so long as you have your l.
LIFE, 29

It is only in the microscope that our l. looks so big
LIFE, 41

Its private l. is a disgrace
RABBITS, 1

I've had a happy l.
LAST WORDS, 34

I've looked at l. from both sides now
LIFE, 35

I warmed both hands before the fire of l.
LIFE AND DEATH, 8

lay down his friends for his l.
SELF-PRESERVATION, 10

L. begins at forty
LIFE, 1; AGE, 61

l. . . . effort to prevent . . . thinking
THINKING, 5

L. exists in the universe
SCIENCE, 23

L. flies
LIFE, 24

l., . . . happens almost exclusively in newspapers
JOURNALISM, 1

L. . . . happens . . . while you're busy making other plans
LIFE, 31

L. is a gamble
LIFE, 46

L. is a great surprise
LIFE AND DEATH, 10

L. is a jest
LIFE, 25

L. is a maze in which we take the wrong turning
LIFE, 18

L. is an incurable disease
DISEASE, 13; LIFE, 19

L. . . . is a predicament
LIFE, 40

L. is as tedious as a twice-told tale
LIFE, 42

L. is a tragedy . . . in close-up
LIFE, 17

L. is just a bowl
LIFE, 2

L. is just one damned thing after another
LIFE, 27

L. is like a sewer
LIFE, 30

L. is mostly froth and bubble
MISFORTUNE, 10

L. is not a spectacle or a feast
LIFE, 40

L. isn't all beer and skittles
LIFE, 28

L. is one long process
LIFE, 15

L. is sweet
LIFE, 3

L. is the art of drawing sufficient conclusions
LIFE, 16

l. is the thing
READING, 14

L. is too short to do anything for oneself
WORK, 13

L. is too short to learn German
LANGUAGE, 21

l., liberty, and the pursuit of happiness
HUMAN RIGHTS, 3

L.'s but a walking shadow
LIFE, 43

l. . . . seems to me preparation for something that never happens
LIFE, 53

L.'s Little Ironies
LIFE, 26

L.'s short span forbids us to enter on far-reaching hopes
MORTALITY, 13

lion   A l. among ladies   FEAR, 12
I hear the l. roar   MERCY, 1
I should be like a l. in a cave of savage Daniels   ENEMIES, 9
Now that the old l. is dead   WRITERS, 75
the . . . fox said . . . to the sick l.: 'Because those footprints
   scare me'   MISTRUST, 5
The l. and the unicorn   NURSERY RHYMES, 50
The nation had the l.'s heart   CHURCHILL, 5
the wary fox said . . . to the sick l.   MISTRUST, 5
to make the l. lie down with the lamb   HUMAN NATURE, 18
lioness   feeds a l. at home   MARRIAGE, 116
lionized   wasn't spoilt by being l.   FAME, 21
lions   bears and l. growl and fight   ANIMALS, 20
English soldiers fight like l.   OFFICERS, 8
l. led by donkeys   OFFICERS, 8
lip   He bit his l. in a manner   HUMOUR, 49
stiff upper l.   COURAGE, 5
lips   l. that touch liquor must never touch mine   ABSTINENCE, 12
My l. are sealed   SECRECY, 2
Red l. are not so red   WAR, 83
liquefaction   That l. of her clothes   CLOTHES, 8
liquidation   the l. of the British Empire   BRITISH EMPIRE, 2
liquor   If . . . Orientals . . . drank a l.   ALCOHOL, 17
lips that touch l. must never touch mine   ABSTINENCE, 12
liquors   alcoholic l. have been used by the . . . best races
   ALCOHOL, 50
Lisa   A lotta cats copy the Mona L.   IMITATION, 1
list   victim must be found I've got a little l.   PUNISHMENT, 9
listen   privilege of wisdom to l.   KNOWLEDGE, 19; WISDOM, 18
they will l. today, they will l. tomorrow   PROMISES, 4
listener   A good l. is a good talker with a sore throat
   CONVERSATION, 11
literacy   The ratio of l. to illiteracy   LITERACY, 1
literary   Classical quotation is the *parole* of l. men
   QUOTATIONS, 4
'Joe,' . . . the first great nonstop l. drinker   ALCOHOL, 63
L. men are . . . a perpetual priesthood   WRITERS, 4
literature   All that is l. seeks to communicate power   BOOKS, 16
All the rest is l.   SCIENCE, 43
American professors like their l. . . . dead   LITERATURE, 10
great deal of history to produce a little l.   LITERATURE, 7;
   HISTORY, 18
He knew everything about l. except how to enjoy it
   LITERATURE, 4
If we can't stamp out l.   PHILISTINISM, 7
I . . . impress upon you the study of Greek l.   CLASSICS, 3
itch of l.   WRITING, 20
Language, man! . . . it's L.   LITERATURE, 18
L. and butterflies are the two sweetest passions
   LITERATURE, 13
L. flourishes best   LITERATURE, 6
L. is mostly about having sex   LITERATURE, 11
L. is news   LITERATURE, 14
L. is simply language charged with meaning   LITERATURE, 15
L. is strewn with the wreckage of men   WRITERS, 27
L. is the orchestration of platitudes   LITERATURE, 19
l. . . . poisoned by its own secretions   LANGUAGE, 3
L. . . . something that will be read twice   LITERATURE, 1;
   JOURNALISM, 14
no l. can outdo the cynicism of real life   EXPERIENCE, 10
That great Cham of l., Samuel Johnson   WRITERS, 84
The Bible is l.   BIBLE, 10
litter   What men call social virtues, . . . is . . . but the virtue of
   pigs in a l.   SOCIETY, 9
little   Every l. helps   HELP, 1
He who knows only his own side . . . knows l.   SUBJECTIVITY, 4
it was a very l. one   ILLEGITIMACY, 1
L. things affect little minds   TRIVIALITY, 4
Man wants but l.   MORTALITY, 9; MORTALITY, 24
read the death of L. Nell without laughing   DICKENS, 4;
   INSENSITIVITY, 4
So l. done, so much to do   LAST WORDS, 58
the l. things are infinitely the most important   TRIVIALITY, 6
littleness   the l. of those that should carry them out
   SUPPORT, 2
live   anything but l. for it   RELIGION, 17
better to die on your feet than to l. on your knees
   SELF-RESPECT, 1
Come l. with me, and be my love   LOVE, 47, 86
Do you want to l. for ever   WAR, 32
eat to l., not l. to eat   FOOD, 38
he forgets to l.   LIFE AND DEATH, 7

Houses are built to l. in   HOUSES, 1
If God were suddenly condemned to l. the life   HUMAN
   CONDITION, 6
If you l. long enough, the venerability factor creeps in
   LONGEVITY, 3
I have learned to l. each day as it comes   PRESENT, 3
in him we l., and move, and have our being   GOD, 5
in Rome, l. as the Romans   CONFORMITY, 2
I thought that I was learning how to l.   DEATH, 128
I want to love first, and l. incidentally   LOVE, 55
Like a rose, she has lived as long as roses l.   TRANSIENCE, 17
L. all you can; it's a mistake not to   LIFE, 29
L. among men as if God beheld you   RIGHTEOUSNESS, 8
L. and learn   EXPERIENCE, 4
l. beyond its income   PROGRESS, 2; EXTRAVAGANCE, 2
l. dangerously   DANGER, 6
l. for ever or die in the attempt   IMMORTALITY, 3
L. that thou mayest desire to live again   AFTERLIFE, 7
Live that thou mayest desire to l. again   AFTERLIFE, 7
L. this day, as . . . thy last   PRESENT, 3
l. to fight another day   SELF-PRESERVATION, 2
l. with the gods   CONTENTMENT, 1
One can't l. on love alone   LOVE, 139
People do not l. nowadays   LIFE, 21
people l. beyond their incomes   EXTRAVAGANCE, 4
Rascals, would you l. for ever   WAR, 40
self-willed determination to l.   LIFE AND DEATH, 6
Teach me to l.   DEATH, 72
than to l. up to them   PRINCIPLES, 1
there shall no man see me, and l.   GOD, 11
those who l. . . . believe . . . to be the truth   HONESTY, 4
Those who l. by . . . a lie, and those who l. by . . . the truth
   HONESTY, 4
To l. with thee, and be thy love   LOVE, 106
we l. but to make sport   RIDICULE, 1
We l. in stirring times   PRESENT, 11
we must l. as though . . . never going to die   ACHIEVEMENT, 9
You might as well l.   SUICIDE, 7
lived   Never to have l. is best   LIFE, 54
no man . . . hath l. better than I   ACHIEVEMENT, 7
She . . . has never l.   LOVE, 60
slimy things l. on   GUILT, 4
livelihood   slave for l.   ENVY, 3
lives   He that l. long   SUFFERING, 1
He who l. by the sword   CONFLICT, 3
he who l. more l. than one   DEATH, 130
l. of quiet desperation   DESPAIR, 6
men devote the greater part of their l.   MANKIND, 15
no man loses any other life than . . . he now l.   LIFE, 7
living   A house is a machine for l. in   HOUSES, 2
Civilization is a method of l.   CIVILIZATION, 1
History is . . . the wrong way of l.   HISTORY, 11
How good is man's life, the mere l.   LIFE, 14
I make war on the l.   REVENGE, 8
It does not then concern either the l. or the dead   DEATH, 47
let the earth bring forth the l. creature   ANIMALS, 3; CREATION, 5
life had prepared Podduyev for l.   DEATH, 117
L. frugally . . . he died early   ABSTINENCE, 1
l. need charity   CHARITY, 2
no one has yet found a way to drink for a l.   ALCOHOL, 38
search the land of l. men   ADMIRATION, 12
Television . . . permits you to be entertained in your l. room
   TELEVISION, 3
The noble l. and the noble dead   NOBILITY, 6
two people l. together for 25 years without having a cross word
   MARRIAGE, 69
Vietnam was lost in the l. rooms of America   TELEVISION, 4;
   WAR, 66
We owe respect to the l.   RESPECT, 4
Livingstone   Dr L., I presume   GREETINGS, 3
Lloyd George   L.   POWER, 6
L. could not see a belt . . . hitting below it   INSULTS, 3
loaf   half a l. is better than a whole l.   COMPROMISE, 5
loafed   It is better to have l. and lost   LAZINESS, 4
loathe   I l. the country   COUNTRYSIDE, 1
lobby   not a man would go into the L. against us   SECRECY, 2
local   settle up these little l. difficulties   POLITICS, 48
Lochinvar   young L.   CHIVALRY, 9
lodge   a l. in some vast wilderness   SOLITUDE, 3
log-cabin   L. to White House   ACHIEVEMENT, 6
logic   L. must take care of itself   LOGIC, 5
people . . . not dealing with creatures of l.   HUMAN NATURE, 7

Some hour to which you have not been looking forward will
prove l.   PRESENT, 10
lover All mankind love a l.   LOVE, 53
a l. with any other career in view   COMMITMENT, 6
A l. without indiscretion is no l.   LOVE, 67
an ex-wife searching for a new l.   WOMEN, 25
easier to be a l. than a husband   MARRIAGE, 16
lunatic, the l., and the poet   LOVE, 121; POETRY, 43
satisfied with her l.'s mind   LOVE, 141
loverly Oh, wouldn't it be l.   DESIRE, 10
lovers Hello, Young L., Wherever You Are   LOVE, 66
l. cannot see The pretty follies   LOVE, 118
l. fled away into the storm   DEPARTURE, 7
make two l. happy   LOVE, 99
one makes l. as fast as one pleases   LOVE, 42
those of us meant to be l.   LOVE, 39
two young l. lately wed   MARRIAGE, 117
loves Anyone who l. his country, follow me   PATRIOTISM, 11
Every man l. what he is good at   ENTHUSIASM, 7
He that l. not his wife and children   MARRIAGE, 116
I have reigned with your l.   ROYALTY, 14
Two l. I have, of comfort and despair   CONFLICT, 7
lovesome garden is a l. thing   GARDENS, 4
loveth God l. a cheerful giver   GENEROSITY, 2
He prayeth best who l. best   PRAYER, 9
loving A woman despises a man for l. her   LOVE, 130
But if we stop l. animals   LOVE, 129
Friday's child is l. and giving   NURSERY RHYMES, 34
l. himself better than all   CHRISTIANITY, 22
most l. mere folly   INSINCERITY, 4
low Caesar! dost thou lie so l.   DEATH, 105
He that is l.   PRIDE, 2
Holland . . . lies so l. they're only saved by being dammed
                                                                 EUROPE, 8
I'll tak' the l. road   SCOTLAND, 1
Kings are naturally lovers of l. company   ROYALTY, 7
my lamp burns l. and dim   ENVY, 3
to put off my hat to . . . high or l.   PRIDE, 4
when your powder's runnin' l.   PATRIOTISM, 21
lower if the l. orders don't set us a good example   CLASS, 39
The l. one's vitality   ART, 3
lower-middle No one ever describes himself as belonging to
the l. class   CLASS, 23
lowly In l. pomp ride on to die   CHRISTIANITY, 32
meek and l. in heart   CHRISTIANITY, 18
Lowry Malcolm L. Late of the Bowery   EPITAPHS, 19
loyal a l. . . . and good-temper'd people   FRANCE, 14
loyalty Hitler showed surprising l. to Mussolini   HITLER, 2
Party l. lowers the greatest of men   POLITICS, 13
When l. no harm meant   SELF-PRESERVATION, 4
Lucifer come not, L.! I'll burn my books   DAMNATION, 4
that same star, That fitful, fiery L.   STARS, 6
luck A self-made man . . . believes in l.   SELF-MADE MEN, 3
it brings you l. whether you believe . . . or not   SUPERSTITION, 4
l., . . . the harder I work the more I have   LUCK, 9
l. to give the roar   CHURCHILL, 5
luckiest People who need people are the l.   SOCIETY, 4
lucky It is better to be born l.   LUCK, 4
I wasn't l. I deserved it   MERIT, 7
L. at cards   LOVE, 7
L. Jim   BOOK, SONG, AND PLAY TITLES, 2
ludicrous He has no sense of the l.   POETS, 37
lumber put away in the l. room of his library   KNOWLEDGE, 13
luminous Dong with a l. Nose   NONSENSE, 17
lump a crowd like that . . . brings a l. to my wallet
                                                                 MATERIALISM, 22
lunatic l. asylums . . . the stately homes   STATELY HOMES, 5
l., the lover, and the poet   LOVE, 121; POETRY, 43
lunatics All are l.   PHILOSOPHERS, 1
luncheon to read a novel before l. was one of the gravest sins
                                                                 READING, 18
lungs don't keep using your l.   LONGEVITY, 2
lured down which ideas are l. and . . . strangled
                                                                 BUREAUCRACY, 4
lust l. in action   LUST, 7
Nonconformity and l. stalking hand in hand   LUST, 5
lusteth the flesh l. against the Spirit   COMPROMISE, 3
Lutheran I have a Catholic soul, but a L. stomach
                                                                 CATHOLICISM, 4
luxuries Give us the l. of life   LUXURY, 4
luxury Blesses his stars, and thinks it l.   PLEASURE, 2

Every l. . . . – atheism, breast-feeding, circumcision
                                                                 INDULGENCE, 2
The saddest thing . . . to get used to l.   LUXURY, 2
lyf That l. so short   MORTALITY, 3
lying One of you is l.   LOVE, 95
the air of someone who is l. . . . to a policeman   POLICE, 7
lynching he could have attended a l. every day   TOLERANCE, 6
lyre on this wall hang my weapons and my l.   SEX, 23
lyric if you include me among the l. poets, I'll hold my head . . .
high . . .   PRIDE, 5

M

macaroni He stuck a feather in his cap And called it m.
                                               AMERICA, 3; NURSERY RHYMES, 69
Macaulay apostle of the Philistines, Lord M.   PHILISTINISM, 2
Lord M.   INSULTS, 35
Macavity there's no one like M.   CATS, 7
McCarthyism M. is Americanism   POLITICS, 54
MacDonald Ramsay M.   POLITICIANS, 61
mace that fool's bauble, the m.   DISMISSAL, 4
McGregor Don't go into Mr M.'s garden   CAUTION, 12
machine A m. for living in   DESIGN, 3
a taxing m.   TAXATION, 8
One m. can do the work of fifty ordinary men   TECHNOLOGY, 5
Our body is a m. for living   REMEDIES, 13
that magical m., with its flying white breath   TRAVEL, 7
the Ghost in the M.   MIND, 6
the great intangible m. of commercial tyranny   DESIGN, 3
The m. threatens   TECHNOLOGY, 11
The tall modern office building is the m.   DESIGN, 8
machine-gun a m. riddling her hostess   SYMPATHY, 3
machines no reason . . . these m. will ever force themselves
into general use   TECHNOLOGY, 14
machine tools I would like to suggest we . . . make him sit on
a crate of m.   ECONOMICS, 17
mackerel M. sky and mares' tails   WEATHER, 1
Macmillan M. is the best prime minister   POLITICIANS, 38
M. seemed . . . to embody the national decay   DECLINE, 5
mad escaped from a m. and savage master   SEX, 52
Every one is more or less m. on one point   MADNESS, 7
half of the nation is m.   ENGLISH, 33
he ceased to be m. he became merely stupid   REMEDIES, 11
he first makes m.   MADNESS, 4
I said of laughter, it is m.   LAUGHTER, 5
let me not be m.   MADNESS, 14
M. about the boy   LOVE, 44
M. as the Mist and Snow   MADNESS, 18
M., bad, and dangerous to know   POETS, 46
Men will always be m.   MADNESS, 17
Never go to bed m.   ANGER, 1
The dog . . . Went m. and bit the man   DOGS, 7
There is no doubt that this poor man was m.   POETS, 60
We all are born m.   MADNESS, 1
When we remember that we are all m.   MADNESS, 16
who turns m. for a reason   MADNESS, 2
madam M. I may not call you   TITLES, 2
madame Call me m.   TITLES, 7
Madame Bovary All I could think of . . . was: M.   NOVELS, 11
maddest those who think they can cure them are the m.
                                                                 MADNESS, 17
made Annihilating all that's m.   OBLIVION, 3
Don't you think I was m. for you   LOVE, 54
Do you know who m. you   CREATION, 13
Little Lamb, who m. thee   CREATION, 8
we're all m. the same   SIMILARITY, 4
Madeira We're from M.   EUROPE, 16
madeleine The taste was that of the little crumb of m.
                                                                 MEMORY, 11
mademoiselle A m. from Armenteers   FRANCE, 13
Madison How were the receipts today in M. Square Garden
                                                                 LAST WORDS, 1
madman If a m. were to come into this room
                                               SELF-PRESERVATION, 6
The m. . . . has lost everything except his reason   MADNESS, 3
The m. is not the man who has lost his reason   MADNESS, 3
Thou call'st me m.   INSULTS, 9
madness devil's m. – War   WAR, 107
Great Wits . . . to M. near alli'd   GENIUS, 4
M. and suffering can set themselves no limit   MADNESS, 13
M. in great ones   MADNESS, 11
M. need not be all breakdown   MADNESS, 8

M. . . . Laid the crops low — AGRICULTURE, 5
m. made the town — COUNTRYSIDE, 2
M. proposes — GOD, 30
m. right fair — CONFLICT, 7
m.'s greatest crime — BIRTH, 4
M.'s inhumanity to m. — CRUELTY, 2
M.'s life is cheap as beast's — NECESSITY, 5
M.'s love is of man's life a thing apart — SEXES, 4
m. so various — HUMAN NATURE, 9
m.'s worth something — CONFLICT, 5
m. that hath no music in himself — MUSIC, 45
m. that is born of a woman — HUMAN CONDITION, 1
m. that is young in years — AGE, 8
M. to command and woman to obey — SEXES, 23
M. wants but little — MORTALITY, 9
M. was born free — FREEDOM, 45
m. who . . . had the largest . . . soul — SHAKESPEARE, 5
m. who's untrue to his wife — INTELLECTUALS, 2
m. with all his noble qualities — EVOLUTION, 4
M. with the head and woman with the heart — SEXES, 23
mean m. is always full of distress — SUPERIORITY, 2
My mother said it was simple to keep a m. — WOMEN, 39
no m. . . . hath lived better than I — ACHIEVEMENT, 7
No m. is an Island — SOCIETY, 3
No m. is good enough to govern another — DEMOCRACY, 8
Nor in the critic let the m. be lost — CRITICS, 14
Nothing happens to any m. — ENDURANCE, 2
Nothing links m. to m. like . . . cash — MONEY, 45
No young m. believes he shall ever die — IMMORTALITY, 2
Of M.'s first disobedience — SIN, 16
On earth there is nothing great but m. — MANKIND, 14
One cannot be always laughing at a m. — MEN, 1
one m. pick'd out of ten thousand — HONESTY, 7
One m. shall have one vote — DEMOCRACY, 2
one small step for m. — SPACE, 1
only m. is vile — MISANTHROPY, 1
only place where a m. can feel . . . secure — MEN, 6
rarely . . . one can see in a little boy the promise of a m. — CHILDREN, 20
reason to lament What m. has made of m. — MANKIND, 39
She is clearly the best m. among them — POLITICIANS, 41
single sentence . . . for modern m. — MANKIND, 10
some meannesses . . . too mean even for m. — SEXES, 4
Style is the m. himself — STYLE, 1
superior m. is distressed by his want of ability — SUPERIORITY, 3
superior m. is satisfied — SUPERIORITY, 2
Tears of eternity, and sorrow, Not mine, but m.'s — SORROW, 10
that grand old m. — POLITICIANS, 64
That married the m. all tattered and torn — NURSERY RHYMES, 57
That's one small step for m. — MISQUOTATIONS, 5
The atrocious crime of being a young m. — YOUTH, 14
the century of the common m. — PUBLIC, 19
The Child is Father of the M. — AGE, 68
The history of m. for the nine months preceding his birth — BIRTH, 5
the honest m. who married — MARRIAGE, 65
The m. who makes no mistakes — MISTAKES, 11
the m. whose second thoughts are good — THINKING, 1
the only real danger that exists is m. himself — HUMAN NATURE, 14
The proper study of Mankind is M. — SELF-KNOWLEDGE, 5
The really original woman . . . imitates a m. — WOMEN, 76
There must be a m. behind the book — WRITERS, 9
There once was a m. who said — EXISTENCE, 4
the state . . . M. is in — GOD, 39
This is the state of m. — HUMAN CONDITION, 16
this is the whole duty of m. — GOD, 9
This was a m.! — NOBILITY, 5
'Tis strange what a m. may do — LOVE, 137
To the m.-in-the-street, who — INTELLECTUALS, 2
True love's the gift which God has given To m. alone — LOVE, 113
uneducated m. to read books of quotations — QUOTATIONS, 1
We have on our hands a sick m. — DECLINE, 7
We know nothing of m., far too little — HUMAN NATURE, 14
Well, he looks like a m. — HOMOSEXUALITY, 6
what a m. is to a ghost — INTELLIGENCE, 1
What a piece of work is a m. — MANKIND, 27
what a very singularly deep young m. — ARROGANCE, 4
What is m. . . . . a . . . machine for turning . . . the red wine of Shiraz into urine — MANKIND, 7
What's a m.'s first duty — SINCERITY, 5

When a m. is in love he endures more — LOVE, 92
When a woman behaves like a m. — WOMEN, 33
whether he is a Wise M. or a Fool — WISDOM, 11
Whoso would be a m. — CONFORMITY, 4
Why can't a woman be more like a m. — MEN, 10
Women who love the same m. — LOVE, 20
you asked this m. to die — WAR, 3
You cannot make a m. by standing a sheep — PUBLIC, 4
you'll be a M. my son — IDEALISM, 2
young m. not yet — MARRIAGE, 14
Manchester The shortest way out of M. is . . . gin — PLACES, 1
Mandalay On the road to M. — PLACES, 10
Manderley I dreamt I went to M. again — DREAMS, 6
mandrake Get with child a m. root — NONSENSE, 11
manger In a m. for His bed — CHRISTMAS, 2
laid him in a m. — CHRISTMAS, 7
mangle Granny caught her tit in the m. — PLEASURE, 29
Manhattan I like to walk around M. — AMERICA, 31
manhood m. a struggle — AGE, 19
mankind about the dreadful wood . . . runs a lost m. — GUILT, 2
a decent respect to the opinions of m. — INDEPENDENCE, 1
all M.'s epitome — HUMAN NATURE, 9
As I know more of m. — EXPECTATION, 1
difficult to love m. . . . . private income — SELF-INTEREST, 5
giant leap for m. — SPACE, 1
Human reason won. M. won — VICTORY, 8
I am willing to love all m., *except an American* — AMERICANS, 5
Ideal m. would abolish death — IDEALISM, 3
I love m. — MANKIND, 24; MISANTHROPY, 3
M. is a closed society — MANKIND, 25
M. is a club — MANKIND, 12
M. is not a tribe of animals — MANKIND, 12
Nazi Germany had become a menace to all m. — NAZISM, 3
proper study of m. is books — LITERATURE, 5
Spectator of m. — OBJECTIVITY, 2
The nations which have put m. . . . . most in their debt — NATIONS, 2
The proper study of M. is Man — SELF-KNOWLEDGE, 5
truly m.'s war of liberation — HUNGER, 1
man-made countryside is one of the most heavily m. habitats — CONSERVATION, 8
manners in England people have good table m. — MANNERS, 4
leave off first for m.' sake — MANNERS, 1
M. are . . . the need of the plain — MANNERS, 7
M. maketh man — MANNERS, 8
The Japanese have perfected good m. — PLACES, 2
the m. of a dancing master — CRITICISM, 22
the m. of a Marquis — CLASS, 12
To Americans English m. are . . . frightening — MANNERS, 3
Tom Jones . . . picture of human m. — NOVELS, 5
to write good prose is an affair of good m. — POETRY AND PROSE, 4
who are . . . ordered by different m. — POVERTY AND WEALTH, 4
mansion Back to its m. call the fleeting breath — DEATH, 57
mansions in my Father's house are many m. — HEAVEN, 3
manure The tree of liberty must be refreshed . . . It is its natural m. — FREEDOM, 21
many m. men, m. women, and m. children — CRITICISM, 23
so much owed by so m. — WORLD WAR II, 7
what can two do against so m. — AUDIENCES, 6
map a picture of a relief m. of Ireland — APPEARANCE, 1
Roll up that m. — PEACE, 14
The books one reads in childhood . . . create in one's mind a . . . false m. — BOOKS, 29
maps Geography is about M. — BIOGRAPHY, 1
mar likely to m. the general felicity — MARRIAGE, 33
Marathon mountains look on M. — EUROPE, 4
marble he . . . left it m. — IMPROVEMENT, 1
Not m., nor the gilded monuments — POETRY, 42
March Beware the ides of M. — PROPHECY, 12
M. comes in like a lion — MONTHS, 1
M., whan God first maked man — CREATION, 9
months . . . gloomy in England are M. and April — SEASONS, 27
Napoleon's armies used to m. on their stomachs — HISTORY, 30; HUMOUR, 53
Truth is on the m. — TRUTH, 45
Marche The droghte of M. — MONTHS, 7
marched He m. them up to the top of the hill — ARMY, 1
March Hare 'you should say what you mean', the M. went on — MEANING, 1
marching m. through Georgia — GLORY, 5
mare Though patience be a tired m. — PATIENCE, 12

memory   Everyone complains of his m.   JUDGMENT, 12
Fond M. brings the light Of other days   NOSTALGIA, 14
For my name and m., I leave it to . . . the next ages
REPUTATION, 1
His m. is going   OLD AGE, 24
How sweet their m. still   NOSTALGIA, 8
Illiterate him . . . from your m.   MALAPROPISMS, 4
I would rather be a brilliant m. than a curiosity
RENUNCIATION, 2
m. is a painter   MEMORY, 10
O m., hope, love of finished years   NOSTALGIA, 18
Time whereof the m. of man   MEMORY, 3
Unless a man feels he has a good enough m.   LYING, 11
What a strange thing is m., and hope   MEMORY, 10
men   all m. are created equal   HUMAN RIGHTS, 3
all m. have one entrance into life   BIRTH, 2
all m. would be tyrants   TYRANNY, 1
Christ called as his Apostles only m.   SEXES, 13
depict m. as they ought to be   THEATRE, 10
don't sleep with married m.   ADULTERY, 4
England . . . purgatory of m.   ENGLAND, 7
give place to better m.   DISMISSAL, 3
great city . . . has the greatest m. and women   GREATNESS, 15
Great m. are almost always bad m.   POWER, 3
great m. have not commonly been great scholars   GREATNESS, 8
happy breed of m.   ENGLAND, 36
I don't think m. and women were meant to live together
SEXES, 9
It brings m. together in crowds and mobs in bar-rooms
SOCIETY, 9
It is m. who face the biggest problems   MEN, 3
It's not the m. in my life that count   SEX, 62
Many m. would take the death-sentence   LIFE AND DEATH, 9
m. about me that are fat   MISTRUST, 9
m. and sea interpenetrate   ENGLAND, 11
M. are but children of a larger growth   AGE, 21
M. are . . . more careful of the breed of their horses and dogs
FAMILY, 33
M. are not hanged for stealing horses   EXAMPLE, 5
M. are we, and must grieve   REGRET, 23
m. . . . capable of every wickedness   EVIL, 7
M. come of age at sixty   AGE, 59
m. devote the greater part of their lives   MANKIND, 15
m. everywhere could be free   FREEDOM, 27
M. fear death   DEATH, 22
M. have never been good   GOOD, 1
M. of few words are the best m.   BREVITY, 8
m. represent . . . mind over morals   SEXES, 29
M.'s natures are alike   HABIT, 4
m. think all m. mortal   ARROGANCE, 11
M. will always be mad   MADNESS, 17
M. will confess   HUMOUR, 8
Most m. admire Virtue   VIRTUE, 14
O! m. with sisters dear   WOMEN, 41
Our Lord chose m.   SEXES, 30
rich m. rule the law   LAW, 13
schemes o' mice an' m.   DISAPPOINTMENT, 2
So many m., so many opinions   OPINIONS, 1
Such m. are dangerous   MISTRUST, 9
That all m. are equal   EQUALITY, 10
The many m., so beautiful   GUILT, 4
The mass of m. lead lives   DESPAIR, 6
the m. who borrow, and the m. who lend   BORROWING, 5
the only advantage women have over m. – . . . they can cry
SEXES, 19
the race of m. is almost extinct in Europe   MEN, 9
the tongues of m. and of angels   CHARITY, 6
The War between M. and Women   SEXES, 25
those m. have their price   CORRUPTION, 10
tide in the affairs of m.   OPPORTUNITY, 16
To famous m. all the earth is a sepulchre   FAME, 20
to form Christian m.   EDUCATION, 3
We live under a government of m. and . . . newspapers
GOVERNMENT, 23; JOURNALISM, 26
when m. and mountains meet   GREATNESS, 4
Why are women . . . so much more interesting to m.   SEXES, 31
Women . . . are either better or worse than m.   WOMEN, 47
Women have smaller brains than m.   SEXES, 18
menace   Nazi Germany had become a m. to all mankind
NAZISM, 3
mend   God won't, and we can't m. it   CONFUSION, 4

mendacity   clergyman whose mendicity is only equalled by their
m.   CLERGY, 13
mental   Christian Science explains all cause and effect as m.
RELIGION, 21
philosophy ought to . . . unravel people's m. blocks
PHILOSOPHY, 10
mentally   happiness of man that he be m. faithful   INTEGRITY, 5
merci   La belle Dame sans M.   SUPERNATURAL, 10
mercies   For his m. ay endure   GOD, 37
merciless   a kind parent . . . or a m. step-mother   NATURE, 13
mercury   'Twas a chilly day for Willie When the m. went down
HUMOUR, 30
mercy   And that is M.'s door   MERCY, 1
For M. has a human heart   MANKIND, 6
quality of m. is not strain'd   MERCY, 2
To M., Pity, Peace, and Love   PRAYER, 5
merit   no damned m. in it   TITLES, 5
Satan exalted sat, by m. raised   DEVIL, 10
meritocracy   The Rise of the M.   MERIT, 8
Mermaid   Choicer than the M. Tavern   PUBLIC HOUSES, 3
mermaids   I have heard the m. singing   OLD AGE, 18
merry   For the good are always the m.   HAPPINESS, 32
For tonight we'll m. be   DRUNKENNESS, 3
I am never m. when I hear sweet music   MUSIC, 44
I commended mirth . . . to eat . . . to drink, and to be m.
PLEASURE, 4
merryman   It's a song of a m.   LOVE, 62
message   the electric m. came   ILLNESS, 1
The medium is the m.   COMMUNICATION, 3
Messiah   He was the M. of the new age   POLITICIANS, 69
messing   m. about in boats   BOATS, 7
met   I m. a man who wasn't there   NONSENSE, 22
We have m. too late   INFLUENCE, 1
metaphor   all m. is poetry   LANGUAGE, 9
metaphysical   a physical and m. impossibility   POETS, 3
a sort of m. brothel for emotions   SENTIMENTALITY, 3
metaphysics   M. is the finding of bad reasons   METAPHYSICS, 2
metaquizzical   The great M. poet   POETS, 21
method   madness, yet there is m. in't   MADNESS, 3
Traditional scientific m. has always been   SCIENCE, 32
You know my m.   TRIVIALITY, 5
metre   Poetry is opposed to science, . . . prose to m.   POETRY
AND PROSE, 1
without . . . understanding what m.   POETS, 29
metrical   difference between . . . prose and m. composition
POETRY AND PROSE, 7
Mexico   Poor M.   AMERICA, 11
mice   schemes o' m. an' men   DISAPPOINTMENT, 2
Three blind m., see how they run   NURSERY RHYMES, 59
Michelangelo   If M. had been straight   HOMOSEXUALITY, 8
Talking of M.   WOMEN, 32
microbe   The M. is so very small   SMALLNESS, 2
microscope   It is only in the m. that our life looks so big
LIFE, 41
middle   a whole is that which has a beginning, a m., and an end
PLAYS, 1
Bow, bow, ye lower m. classes   CLASS, 13
I like a film to have a beginning, a m. and an end   CINEMA, 3
no m. course between the throne and the scaffold   MONARCHY, 7
One of the pleasures of m. age is to *find out* that one WAS
right   AGE, 45
people who stay in the m. of the road   COMPROMISE, 2;
NONCOMMITMENT, 1
the ease . . . move into the m. class   CLASS, 33
middle-class   part of English m. education is devoted to the
training of servants   EDUCATION, 65
respectable, m., . . . lady   AUDIENCES, 4
the healthy type that was essentially m.   CLASS, 10
Midland   M., bound for Cricklewood   TRAVEL, 4
midnight   chimes at m.   MERRYMAKING, 4
I stood on the bridge at m.   TIME, 25
It came upon the m. clear   CHRISTMAS, 17
M. brought on the dusky hour   DAY, 12
m. never come   DAMNATION, 3
Not to be abed after m.   BED, 8
Once upon a m. dreary   SUPERNATURAL, 12
See her on the bridge at m.   POVERTY AND WEALTH, 1
soft embalmer of the still m.   SLEEP, 12
To cease upon the m. with no pain   DEATH, 70
mid-stream   best to swap horses in m.   CHANGE, 13
mid-winter   In the bleak m.   SEASONS, 18
might   Fight the good fight with all thy m.   CHRISTIANITY, 33

The majority has the m.   MAJORITY, 3; MINORITY, 2
We m. have been   REGRET, 7
Might-have-been   Look in my face; my name is M.
     DISAPPOINTMENT, 6
mightier   pen is m. than the sword   WRITING, 3
mighty   Another m. empire overthrown   DEFEAT, 9
How are the m. fallen   MOURNING, 2
share in the good fortunes of the m.   INJUSTICE, 2
the weak things of the world to confound the . . . m.   WISDOM
     AND FOOLISHNESS, 3
mike   I'm being amplified by the m.   OBESITY, 4
Milan   he wants M., and so do I   AGREEMENT, 1
miles   m. to go before I sleep   TRAVEL, 10
militant   I am an optimist, unrepentant and m.   OPTIMISM, 26
militarism   m. . . . is one of the chief bulwarks of capitalism
     CAPITALISM, 5
military   The chief attraction of m. service   ARMY, 3
milk   as when you find a trout in the m.   PROOF, 6
drunk the m. of Paradise   CAUTION, 9
Gin was mother's m.   ALCOHOL, 56
putting m. into babies   CHILDREN, 18
too full o' th' m. of human kindness   KINDNESS, 4
Mill   John Stuart M. By a mighty effort of will   ECONOMICS, 3
miller   There was a jolly m.   HAPPINESS, 4
million   I have had no real gratification . . . more than my
   neighbor . . . who is worth only half a m.   LAST WORDS, 71;
     WEALTH, 28
man who has a m. dollars   WEALTH, 4
m. m. spermatozoa, All of them alive   SEX, 25
Son, here's a m. dollars   ADVICE, 10
millionaire   He must be a m.   WEALTH, 16
I am a m.. That is my religion   WEALTH, 24
Who Wants to Be a M.   WEALTH, 23
millions   take m. off the caring services   PATRIOTISM, 19
unrewarded m. without whom Statistics would be a bankrupt
   science   STATISTICS, 8
mills   m. of God grind slowly   GOD, 34
millstone   a m. . . . hanged about his neck   CHILDREN, 14
Milton   Malt does more than M. can   ALCOHOL, 31; MILTON, 1
M., Madam, was a genius   MILTON, 2; POETS, 44
M.'s Devil as a moral being is far superior   MILTON, 3
M.! thou shouldst be living at this hour   DECLINE, 15
The divine M.   MILTON, 4
the faith and morals hold Which M. held   FREEDOM, 53
the making up of a Shakespeare or a M.   WRITERS, 5
mimsy   All m. were the borogoves   NONSENSE, 7
min'   never brought to m.   FRIENDSHIP, 12
mince   dined on m., and slices of quince   FOOD, 31
mind   A good critic . . . narrates the adventures of his m.
     CRITICS, 1
an exaggerated stress on not changing one's m.   DECISION, 2
an unseemly exposure of the m.   NASTINESS, 3
A short neck denotes a good m.   APPEARANCE, 35
a sound m. in a sound body   HEALTH AND HEALTHY LIVING, 10
Beauty in things exists in the m. which contemplates them
     BEAUTY, 21
change their clime, not their frame of m., who rush across the
   sea   TRAVEL, 14
clear your m. of cant . . .   REASON, 3
Do you think my m. is maturing late   AGE, 41
If it is for m. that we are seaching the brain   MIND, 7
it's all in the m.   ILLNESS, 16
making things plain to uninstructed people was . . . best means
   of clearing . . . one's own m.   EDUCATION, 24
Many ideas grow better when transplanted into another m.
     IDEAS, 3
men represent . . . m. over morals   SEXES, 29
m. that makes the body rich   APPEARANCES, 22
never to ransack any m. but his own   IMITATION, 5
No m. is thoroughly well organized   HUMOUR, 9
our love . . . of the m. does not make us soft   RESULTS, 4
prodigious quantity of m.   INDECISION, 3
Reading is to the m.   READING, 15
someone whose m. watches itself   INTELLECTUALS, 5
spirit . . . of a sound m.   FEAR, 2
That's the classical m. at work   MIND, 5
the inquisitive m. can . . . receive no answer   PHILOSOPHY, 6
The m. can also be an erogenous zone   MIND, 9
The m. . . . Can make a Heaven of Hell   MIND, 4
The m. is its own place   MIND, 4
The pendulum of the m. oscillates between sense and nonsense
     MIND, 3

There is in the British Museum an enormous m.   MUSEUMS, 3
'Tis education forms the common m.   EDUCATION, 44
to change your m.   ADAPTABILITY, 1
To know the m. of a woman   LOVE, 81
true genius is a m. of large general powers   GENIUS, 7
what difficulty a m. . . . admits hope   SUFFERING, 15
Women represent . . . matter over m.   SEXES, 29
minded   If everybody m. their own business   CURIOSITY, 4
minds   All things can corrupt perverted m.   CORRUPTION, 5
Great m. think alike   SIMILARITY, 2
Little m. are interested in the extraordinary   TRIVIALITY, 10
marriage of true m.   LOVE, 123
M. are not ever craving   BOOKS, 15
M. like beds always made up   INFLEXIBILITY, 4
m. so impatient of inferiority   GRATITUDE, 1
Strongest m. . . . the noisy world Hears least   MIND, 10
Superstition is the religion of feeble m.   SUPERSTITION, 7
the hobgoblin of little m.   CONSTANCY, 1
To be alone is the fate of all great m.   LONELINESS, 6;
     GREATNESS, 11
well-developed bodies, fairly developed m.   EDUCATION, 18
When people will not weed their own m.   MIND, 8
miner   Dwelt a m., Forty-niner, And his daughter, Clementine
     MOURNING, 7
miners   it is only because m. sweat their guts out
     SUPERIORITY, 10
the Vatican, the Treasury and the m.   DIPLOMACY, 2
mingled   Like kindred drops, been m.   MOUNTAINS, 1
ministers   I don't mind how much my m. talk
     AUTHORITARIANISM, 7
my actions are my m.'   REPARTEE, 1
ministries   *The Times* has made many m.   NEWSPAPERS, 1
ministry   Women . . . care fifty times more for a marriage than a
   m.   WOMEN, 12
minorities   M. . . . are almost always in the right   MINORITY, 3
minority   not enough people to make a m.   MINORITY, 1
The m. is always right   MAJORITY, 3; MINORITY, 2
minstrel   A wandering m. I   SINGERS, 2
Ethereal m.   BIRDS, 11
The M. Boy   WAR, 73
minute   M. Particulars   GOOD, 2
not a m. on the day   STRIKES, 1
sucker born every m.   GULLIBILITY, 1
To a philosopher no circumstance, . . . is too m.
     PHILOSOPHERS, 3
minutes   at the rate of sixty m. an hour   TIME, 24
take care of the m.   TIME, 15
Yes, about ten m.   SERMONS, 3
miracle   a m. of rare device   PLEASURE, 9
man prays . . . for a m.   PRAYER, 18
miracles   before we *know* he is a saint, there will have to be
   m.   PROOF, 4
The Christian religion not only was at first attended with m.
     CHRISTIANITY, 29
mirror   A novel is a m.   NOVELS, 15
Art is not a m. . . . but a hammer   ART, 16
Look not in my eyes, for fear They m. true the sight I see
     LOVE, 71
When a man confronts catastrophe . . . a woman looks in her m.
     SEXES, 26
mirrors   M. and fatherhood are abominable   UNIVERSE, 2
M. should think longer   THINKING, 2
mirth   I commended m. . . . to eat . . . to drink, and to be merry
     PLEASURE, 4
I love such m. as does not make friends ashamed
     MERRYMAKING, 6
miscarriage   success and m. are empty sounds   DISILLUSION, 4
miscast   George Bernard Shaw is sadly m.   CRITICISM, 48
mischief   If you want to make m. . . . papers   JOURNALISM, 6
Satan finds . . . m. . . . For idle hands   IDLENESS, 10
thou little knowest the m. done   ACCIDENTS, 1
To mourn a m. that is past   REGRET, 17
mischievous   what a m. devil Love is   LOVE, 35
miserable   m. have no other medicine   HOPE, 10
poring over m. books   LEARNING, 6
The secret of being m. is to have leisure   SORROW, 23
miserie   y-fallen out of heigh degree. Into m.   MISFORTUNE, 1
miseries   all the maladies and m.   WORK, 6
misery   certain amount of m. . . . to distribute as fairly as he can
     TAXATION, 8
greatest m. is a battle gained   VICTORY, 19
he Who finds himself, loses his m.   SELF-KNOWLEDGE, 1

Land of the m. and the flood — SCOTLAND, 7
mountains all faith, so that I could remove m. — CHARITY, 6
England's m. green — ENGLAND, 5
highest intellects, like the tops of m. — INTELLECT, 5
if the Swiss had designed these m. — MOUNTAINS, 4; SWITZERLAND, 4
M. interposed Make enemies of nations — MOUNTAINS, 1
m. look on Marathon — EUROPE, 4
M. . . . the beginning and the end of all natural scenery — MOUNTAINS, 3
M. will heave in childbirth — DISAPPOINTMENT, 3
Two voices . . . one is of the sea, One of the m. — FREEDOM, 54
when men and m. meet — GREATNESS, 4
mourn countless thousands m. — CRUELTY, 2
it is chiefly our own deaths that we m. for — FUNERALS, 3
To m. a mischief that is past — REGRET, 17
mourning I'm in m. for my life — MOURNING, 4
in m. . . . for the world — MOURNING, 15
tedium is the very basis of m. — BOREDOM, 4
We met . . . Dr Hall in such very deep m. — MOURNING, 1
What we call m. for our dead — MOURNING, 6
with my m. . . . and new periwig — APPEARANCE, 30
mouse a silly little m. will be born — DISAPPOINTMENT, 3
He bought a crooked cat, which caught a crooked m. — NURSERY RHYMES, 52
leave room for the m. — EXCESS, 6
she brought forth a m. — DISAPPOINTMENT, 4
The m. ran up the clock — NURSERY RHYMES, 15
mouse-trap If a man make a better m. — FAME, 8
moustache A kiss without a m. — KISSING, 4
a man outside with a big black m. — APPEARANCE, 25
Being kissed by a man who didn't wax his m. — KISSING, 3
his nicotine eggyellow weeping walrus Victorian m. — APPEARANCE, 37
mouth A politician is a statesman . . . with an open m. — POLITICIANS, 25
butter wouldn't melt in her m. — ACTORS, 17
God be in my m., And in my speaking — GOD, 1
Keep your m. shut and your eyes open — CAUTION, 6
mouth-brothels Great restaurants are . . . nothing but m. — FOOD, 45
move But did thee feel the earth m. — SEX, 22
in him we live, and m., and have our being — GOD, 5
I will m. the earth — TECHNOLOGY, 1
The great affair is to m. — TRAVEL, 28
movement I want to be a m. — SOLITUDE, 11
We are the true peace m. — PEACE, 17
moves m., and mates, and slays — DESTINY, 6
Yet it m. — ASTRONOMY, 3
movie This is a m., not a lifeboat — EQUALITY, 23
movies Thanks to the m., gunfire has always sounded unreal — CINEMA, 11
moving In home-sickness you must keep m. — HOMESICKNESS, 7
m. Moon went up the sky — MOON, 2
people under suspicion are better m. — JUDGMENT, 10
The M. Finger writes — DESTINY, 7
Mozart The sonatas of M. are unique — MUSIC, 43
when M. was my age — AGE, 34
MPs The prospect of a lot Of dull M. — POLITICIANS, 11
much m. . . . said on both sides — OBJECTIVITY, 1
So little done, so m. to do — LAST WORDS, 58
so m. owed by so many to so few — WORLD WAR II, 7
muchness Much of a m. — MEDIOCRITY, 8
muck Money is like m. — MONEY, 7
sing 'em m. — PLACES, 12
mud One sees the m., and one the stars — OPTIMISM, 21
muddle a beginning, a m., and an end — NOVELS, 8
muddle-headed He's a m. fool — FOOLISHNESS, 12
muddy The hunter for aphorisms . . . has to fish in m. water — SAYINGS, 2
muesli Many children are suffering from m.-belt malnutrition — FOOD, 35
Muffet Little Miss M. Sat on a tuffet — NURSERY RHYMES, 30
multiplied Entities should not be m. — SIMPLICITY, 6
multiply be fruitful and m. — MANKIND, 5; CREATION, 6
multitude long dresses, . . . cover a m. of shins — CLOTHES, 18
The m. is always in the wrong — PUBLIC, 17
this massed m. of silent witnesses to . . . war — WAR, 42
multitudes I contain m. — SELF, 21
mum M.'s the word — SECRECY, 6
They fuck you up, your m. and dad — FAMILY, 24
mumble maunder and m. — PUBLIC, 8

mundi *Sic transit gloria m.* — GLORY, 3
murder Divorce? Never. But m. often — MARRIAGE, 122
love and m. will out — LOVE, 41; MURDER, 5
m. back into its rightful setting – in the home — MURDER, 7
M. considered as one of the Fine Arts — MURDER, 6
M. . . . had a mask like Castlereagh — MURDER, 12
M., like talent, seems . . . to run in families — MURDER, 9
M. most foul — MURDER, 11
m. shrieks out — MURDER, 13
Never m. a man who is committing suicide — SUICIDE, 14
Olivier had m. in his heart — ACTORS, 14
put m. on a mass-production basis — DESIGN, 6
So it was m. — DEATH, 83
Sooner m. an infant in its cradle — DESIRE, 3
murdered I m. my grandmother this morning — INATTENTION, 4
murderer Kill a man, and you are a m. — KILLING, 7
strong suspicions that Crippen London cellar m. — TECHNOLOGY, 7
murderous at Yuletide men are the more m. — CHRISTMAS, 13
murmuring m. of innumerable bees — SEASONS, 23
muscular His Christianity was m. — CHRISTIANITY, 23
Muse To the Greeks the M. gave native wit — CLASSICS, 4
mused Lancelot m. a little space — BEAUTY, 39
museum the m. of this world — MASCULINITY, 2
museums more philosophical than . . . curators of the m. — PRACTICALITY, 3
The Arab who builds . . . a hut out of . . . a temple . . . is more philosophical than . . . curators of the m. — MUSEUMS, 1
mushroom a supramundane m. — NUCLEAR WEAPONS, 11
Fame is sometimes like unto a . . . m. — FAME, 10
to stuff a m. — HOUSEWORK, 2
music a martyr to m. — MUSIC, 52
Architecture . . . is frozen m. — ARCHITECTURE, 10
art constantly aspires towards . . . m. — ART, 20
a young man who would . . . play his m. and be whistled at for it — MUSIC, 19
Canned m. is like audible wallpaper — POP MUSIC, 7
capable of being well set to m. — MUSIC, 2
century of aeroplanes deserves its own m. — MUSIC, 18
chord of m. — MUSIC, 39
food in m. — MUSIC, 29
God tells me how he wants this m. played — MUSIC, 54
Having verse set to m. — POETRY, 50
how potent cheap m. is — MUSIC, 16
How sour sweet m. is — ORDER, 5
I don't write modern m. — MUSIC, 49
If all the arts aspire to the condition of m. — SCIENCE, 37
If m. be the food of love — MUSIC, 46
I'll set it to m. — MUSIC, 41
In m., the punctuation is absolutely strict — ACTING, 10
line that fits the m. — POP MUSIC, 14
making m. throatily and palpitatingly sexual — MUSIC, 25
man that hath no m. in himself — MUSIC, 45
m. . . . affects your nerves — MUSIC, 28
M. and women I cannot but give way to — MUSIC, 37
M. begins to atrophy — ARTS, 7
M. . . . confirm human loneliness — MUSIC, 20
M. creates order out of chaos — MUSIC, 32
m. critics. . . . small and rodent-like with padlocked ears — CRITICS, 18
M. has charms to soothe — MUSIC, 15
M. helps not — MUSIC, 1
M. is not written in red, white and blue — MUSIC, 31
M. is the arithmetic of sounds — MUSIC, 17
M. is your own experience — MUSIC, 36
M., Maestro, Please — MUSIC, 30
M. owes as much to Bach — MUSICIANS, 15
M. that gentlier on the spirit lies — MUSIC, 51
M., when soft voices die — MEMORY, 17
never merry when I hear sweet m. — MUSIC, 44
Poetry . . . set to more or less lascivious m. — POETRY, 29
popular m. . . . made giant strides in reverse — POP MUSIC, 9
potent cheap m. is — POP MUSIC, 8
public doesn't want a new m. — MUSICIANS, 1
silence sank like m. — SILENCE, 3
sometimes I don't even like m. — MUSIC, 55
The English may not like m. — MUSIC, 5
The hills are alive with the sound of m. — MUSIC, 22
The m. teacher came twice each week — MUSIC, 3
thy chosen m., Liberty — FREEDOM, 54
Van Gogh's ear for m. — INSULTS, 44
Wagner is the Puccini of m. — MUSICIANS, 12
musical cashiers of the M. Banks — MONEY, 13

N

o'erstep not the modesty of n. — ACTION, 10
one of N.'s Gentlemen — CHIVALRY, 7
one of the forces of n. — GREATNESS, 10
rules of the game are what we call the laws of N. — GOD, 28
science . . . is . . . the interplay between n. and ourselves — NATURE, 10
secret of the arts is to correct n. — ARTS, 8
the most irrelevant thing in n. — FAMILY, 23
the spectacles of books to read n. — SHAKESPEARE, 6
to see the absurd n. of Englishmen — ENGLISH, 30
True wit is n. to advantage dress'd — HUMOUR, 22
unassuming common-place Of N. — FLOWERS, 13
We need more understanding of human n. — HUMAN NATURE, 14
wonderful case of n. imitating art — ACTORS, 2
you can't call yourself a great work of n. — INSULTS, 42
natures Men's n. are alike — HABIT, 4
N. ancient power was lost — DECLINE, 11
naught N. so sweet as Melancholy — MELANCHOLY, 2
nauseate I n. walking — COUNTRYSIDE, 1
Navee Ruler of the Queen's N. — OFFICERS, 6
Rulers of the Queen's N. — OFFICERS, 7
navy There were gentlemen and . . . seamen in the n. of Charles the Second — NAVY, 3
Nazi N. Germany had become a menace to all mankind — NAZISM, 3
Nazis In Germany, the N. came for the Communists — NAZISM, 4
near I wished to be n. my mother — BIRTH, 10
nearer N., my God, to thee — RELIGION, 2
the n. you are to God — PROTESTANTISM, 3
nearest the n. run thing you ever saw — WAR, 126
nearsighted don't raise your hands because I am also n. — DISABILITY, 1
neat round, n., not gaudy — GARDENS, 9
necessary Government, . . . is but a n. evil — GOVERNMENT, 21
necessities disregard for the n. of existence — CIVILIZATION, 9
we will dispense with its n. — LUXURY, 4
necessity I find alone N. Supreme — NECESSITY, 8
N. is the mother — NECESSITY, 2
N. is the plea for every infringement of human freedom — NECESSITY, 4
N. knows no law — NECESSITY, 7
no virtue like n. — NECESSITY, 6
neck A short n. denotes a good mind — APPEARANCE, 35
creator had a purpose in equipping us with a n. — COURAGE, 16
England will have her n. wrung like a chicken — WORLD WAR II, 30
go to the bottom with my principles round my n. — EXPEDIENCY, 2
my n. is very short — EXECUTION, 19
Some n. — WORLD WAR II, 12
the Roman people had but one n. — RUTHLESSNESS, 1
necking Whoever named it n. — SEX, 34
neckties men wore their beards, like they wear their n. — APPEARANCE, 18
Ned no more work for poor old N. — DEATH, 53
need artist is someone who produces things that people don't n. — ARTISTS, 8
reason not the n. — NECESSITY, 5
Thy n. is yet greater than mine — SELF-DENIAL, 2
needle easier for a camel to go through the eye of a n. — WEALTH, 8
needs N. must — NECESSITY, 3
to each according to his n. — MARXISM, 4
You artists produce something that nobody n. — ARTISTS, 9
negation Capitalist production begets . . . its own n. — CAPITALISM, 9
negative Europe is the unfinished n. — AMERICA, 26
N. Capability — DOUBT, 6
neglect A little n. may breed mischief — NEGLECT, 1
he devotes to the n. of his duties — NEGLECT, 4
negligent Celerity . . . admired . . . by the n. — IMPETUOSITY, 3
Negro makes a N. unpleasant to white folk — RACISM, 22
Negroes revenge by the culture of the N. — MUSIC, 35
neiges les n. d'antan — NOSTALGIA, 22
neighbor I have had no real gratification . . . more than my n. — LAST WORDS, 71; WEALTH, 28
neighbour better mouse-trap than his n. — FAME, 8
death . . . had been his next-door n. — DEATH, 101
Death is my n. now — DEATH, 48
Do not love your n. as yourself — SELF, 13
It's a recession when your n. — UNEMPLOYMENT, 2
love thy n. as thyself — LOVE, 26
told men to love their n. — HUNGER, 3

neighbours fear of what the n. might say — SUICIDE, 5
improper thoughts about n. — MORALITY, 4
make sport for our n. — RIDICULE, 1
neither better if n. of us had been born — REGRET, 10
Nell read the death of Little N. without laughing — DICKENS, 4; INSENSITIVITY, 4
Nelly let not poor N. starve — LAST WORDS, 15
Nelson keep the N. touch — OFFICERS, 10; PATRIOTISM, 22
N., born in a fortunate hour — OFFICERS, 11
nerve called a n. specialist because it sounds better — PSYCHIATRY, 13
nerves It destroys one's n. to be amiable every day — MARRIAGE, 49
nervous One of the symptoms of approaching n. breakdown — WORK, 21
nest broods a n. of sorrows — MARRIAGE, 116
nets Laws are generally found to be n. — LAW, 25
nettle stroke a n., And it stings you for your pains — DECISION, 1
nettles apt to be overrun with n. — MIND, 8
neurosis N. has an absolute genius for malingering — NEUROSIS, 1
N. is the way of avoiding non-being — NEUROSIS, 3
neurotic Acting is the expression of a n. impulse — ACTING, 3
A n. is the man who builds a castle in the air — PSYCHIATRY, 11
Psychiatrists classify a person as n. — PSYCHIATRY, 10
neurotics Everything great in the world is done by n. — NEUROSIS, 2
neutrality 'positive n.' is a contradiction in terms — POLITICS, 55
never Better n. than late — PROMPTNESS, 3
I n. would lay down my arms — PATRIOTISM, 24
Love? I make it constantly but I n. talk about it — SEX, 47
N., n., n., n. — MOURNING, 9
our people have n. had it so good — WEALTH, 18
Than n. to have loved at all — LOVE, 132
nevermore Quoth the Raven, 'N.' — EVIL, 13
Nevershit like you was Lady N. — AFFECTATION, 2
new He that will not apply n. remedies — INNOVATION, 1
He was dull in a n. way — POETS, 43
He was the Messiah of the n. age — POLITICIANS, 69
n. book is published, read an old one — BOOKS, 33
n. deal for the American people — AMERICA, 28
N. roads: new ruts — PROGRESS, 4
Revolution is . . . the setting-up of a n. order — REVOLUTION, 4
something n. out of Africa — NOVELTY, 8
There are no n. truths — NOVELTY, 7
there is no n. thing under the sun — NOVELTY, 1
we shall find something n. — NOVELTY, 10
We stand today on the edge of a n. frontier — BEGINNING, 12
You suddenly understand something . . . in a n. way — LEARNING, 6
Youth is something very n. — YOUTH, 3
new-found-land my n. — LOVE, 49
newness Americans have been conditioned to respect n. — AMERICANS, 11
news Bad n. travels fast — DISASTER, 1
Literature is n. — LITERATURE, 14
n. that's fit to print — NEWSPAPERS, 8
No n. is good n. — OPTIMISM, 6; JOURNALISM, 9; JOURNALISM, 9
Nothing is n. until it has appeared in *The Times*. — NEWSPAPERS, 7
only n. until he's read it. After that it's dead — NEWSPAPERS, 13
when a man bites a dog that is n. — JOURNALISM, 11
newspaper good n., . . . is a nation talking to itself — JOURNALISM, 23
I read the n. avidly — JOURNALISM, 10
Once a n. touches a story, the facts are lost — JOURNALISM, 22
Reading someone else's n. — NEWSPAPERS, 4
With the n. strike on — OBITUARIES, 1
newspapers I'm with you on the free press. It's the n. — JOURNALISM, 29
life, . . . happens almost exclusively in n. — JOURNALISM, 1
N. always excite curiosity — JOURNALISM, 19
We live under a government of men and . . . n. — GOVERNMENT, 23; JOURNALISM, 26
Newton Let N. be! — SCIENTISTS, 13
Newtons souls of five hundred Sir Isaac N. — SCIENTISTS, 8; WRITERS, 5
New York N. is a small place — AMERICA, 39
N. . . . that unnatural city — AMERICA, 15
Niagara one wouldn't *live* under N. — INSULTS, 3
nice Be n. to people on your way up — PRUDENCE, 10
how nasty the n. people can be — NASTINESS, 6
N. guys finish last — GOOD, 4

Sugar and spice And all that's n. NURSERY RHYMES, 65
Nicely-Nicely what N. dies of will be over-feeding GREED, 8
nicest English people . . . are surely the *n.* people in the world
ENGLISH, 21
Nicholas St N. soon would be there CHRISTMAS, 14
Nick Satan, N., or Clootie DEVIL, 6
nickname n. is the heaviest stone that the devil can throw
NAMES, 4
nicotine his n. eggyellow weeping walrus Victorian moustache
APPEARANCE, 37
nigger Catch a n. by his toe NURSERY RHYMES, 11
niggers He's gone whar de good n. go DEATH, 53
night An infant crying in the n. HUMAN CONDITION, 20
calm passage . . . across many a bad n. SUICIDE, 1
Come to me in the silence of the n. NOSTALGIA, 18
Do not go gentle into that good n. DEATH, 125
From morn to n., my friend ENDURANCE, 15
Gwine to run all n. HORSES, 6
ignorant armies clash by n. WAR, 2
It ain't a fit n. out WEATHER, 4
money in a desk by n. THEFT, 4
moonless n. in the small town RELIGION, 57
Morning in the Bowl of N. DAY, 5
N. and day LOVE, 101
Oft in the stilly n., Ere Slumber's chain NOSTALGIA, 14
only one man . . . can count on steady work – the n. watchman
THEATRE, 2
perils . . . of this n. DANGER, 3
real dark n. of the soul SOUL, 6
returned home the previous n. SCIENCE, 3
Ships that pass in the n. TRANSIENCE, 16
So late into the n. DEBAUCHERY, 4
sound of revelry by n. MERRYMAKING, 2
the black bat, n., has flown INVITATIONS, 2
the darkness he called N. CREATION, 2
The dark n. of the soul SOUL, 8
the honey'd middle of the n. LOVE, 78
The n. is dark, and I am far from home FAITH, 16
wish the n. Had borne my breath away NOSTALGIA, 9
nightingale A N. Sang in Berkeley Square BIRDS, 7
N., . . . A creature of a 'fiery heart' BIRDS, 2
The n. does sit so late BIRDS, 6
nightingales From Wales Whose n. WALES, 4
nightmare 'History', Stephen said, 'is a n.' HISTORY, 19
nights a Chequer-board of N. and Days DESTINY, 6
The weariest n. . . . must . . . end ENDURANCE, 11
They shorten tedious n. SEX, 10
nihilist a part-time n. COMMITMENT, 3
Nile dam . . . the N. with bulrushes FREEDOM, 7
nine N. drummers drumming NURSERY RHYMES, 55
ninepence I have but n. in ready money CONVERSATION, 2
ninety stood n. years on the floor CLOCKS, 2
Nineveh Quinquireme of N. BOATS, 12
nip I'll n. him in the bud MIXED METAPHORS, 4
Nixon N. . . . would cut down a redwood tree POLITICIANS, 70
standing between N. and the White House POLITICIANS, 54
You won't have N. to kick around RENUNCIATION, 3
no become accustomed to n. one governing SOCIALISM, 10
girls . . . say N. when they mean Yes WOMEN, 8
It's n. go the picture palace INDIFFERENCE, 4
rebel . . . man who says n. REBELLION, 3
she speaks eighteen languages. And she can't say 'N.' in any of
them PROMISCUITY, 5
why Absurdist plays take place in N. Man's Land THEATRE, 1
Noah Out of their cataclysm but one poor N. SEX, 25
nobility N. has its own obligations NOBILITY, 2
The n. . . . snored through the Sermon ARISTOCRACY, 4
noble a n. nature, . . . treats . . . a serious subject POETRY, 3
Englishman never enjoys himself except for a n. purpose
ENGLISH, 19
n. grounds for the n. emotions POETRY, 39
Ridicule . . . smothers that which is n. RIDICULE, 4
The n. living and the n. dead NOBILITY, 6
nobleman a king may make a n. CHIVALRY, 3
nobleness perfect plainness of speech . . . perfect n. BIBLE, 1
noblesse If the French n. had been capable of playing cricket
with their peasants ARISTOCRACY, 13; CRICKET, 5
noblest n. man That ever lived in the tide of times REGRET, 16
n. Roman of them all NOBILITY, 4
nobly the immature man . . . wants to die n. for a cause
AGE, 58
nobody a man is n. unless his biography OBITUARIES, 3

I care for n. SELFISHNESS, 2
N. asked you, sir, she said NURSERY RHYMES, 67
whom n. loves OBESITY, 6
nod A n. is as good as a wink BLINDNESS, 1
the land of N. REVENGE, 7
nods even excellent Homer n. IMPERFECTION, 9
noise A loud n. at one end BABIES, 5
dreadful of waters in my ears DROWNING, 4
the less they have . . . the more n. they make CHARACTER, 17
they . . . love the n. it makes MUSIC, 5
Those people . . . are making such a n. AUDIENCES, 3
noises Like n. in a swound SEA, 4
noisy Strongest minds . . . the n. world Hears least MIND, 10
The people would be just as n. PUBLIC, 9
nominated I will not accept if n. POLITICIANS, 68
No-more I am also called N. DISAPPOINTMENT, 6
non-being Neurosis is the way of avoiding n. NEUROSIS, 3
non-combatant War hath no fury like a n. WAR, 70
nonconformist a N. conscience WOMEN, 91
man must be a n. CONFORMITY, 5
Why do you have to be a n. CONFORMITY, 6
nonconformity N. and lust stalking hand in hand LUST, 8
none N. but the Brave COURAGE, 11
nonsense you intend to talk n. AMERICANS, 4
non-U U and N. CLASS, 28
non-violence to disagree . . . about . . . n. without wanting to
kick VIOLENCE, 4
noon From morn To n. he fell DECLINE, 4
from n. to dewy eve DECLINE, 4
O dark, dark, dark, amid the blaze of n. BLINDNESS, 4
Norfolk bear him up the N. sky HUNTING, 1
Very flat, N. ENGLAND, 12
Norgay Tenzing N. PHOTOGRAPHY, 4
Norma Jean Goodbye N. ACTORS, 18
normal the n. is so . . . interesting NORMALITY, 1
Normans The Saxon is not like us N. NATIONALITY, 6
north The n. wind does blow WEATHER, 6
nose A custom loathsome to the eye, hateful to the n.
SMOKING, 7
A person may be indebted for a n. . . . to a great-aunt
FAMILY, 20
Dong with a luminous N. NONSENSE, 17
Had Cleopatra's n. been shorter APPEARANCE, 29
led by the n. with gold BRIBERY, 1
My n. is huge APPEARANCE, 31
Only the n. knows SECRECY, 1
This fellow did not see further than his . . . n. PAROCHIALISM, 1
will it come without warning Just as I'm picking my n. LOVE, 18
nostrils God . . . breathed into his n. GARDENS, 3
not Believe it or n. BELIEF, 2
HOW N. TO DO IT BUREAUCRACY, 5
note The world will little n., nor long remember MEMORIALS, 6
notes the pauses between the n. MUSICIANS, 8
nothin You ain't heard n.' yet PROPHECY, 6
nothing Blessed is the man who expects n. EXPECTATION, 3
Certainly, there is n. else here to enjoy PARTIES, 6
Children aren't happy with n. to ignore FAMILY, 31
Death is n. AFTERLIFE, 5
doing n. for each other FRIENDSHIP, 16
from n. to a state of extreme poverty POVERTY, 26
God made everything out of n. CREATION, 15
have n. whatever to do with it DEATH, 84
N. can be created out of nothing NOTHING, 1
n. can bring back the hour REGRET, 22
n. either good or bad THINKING, 4
N., except my genius CONCEIT, 25
N. happens BOREDOM, 1
n. if not critical CRITICISM, 46
n. is certain but death and taxes TAXATION, 4
n., . . . is greater . . . than one's self SELF, 20
n. is had for n. EFFORT, 4
n. is law that is not reason LAW, 21
N. long HUMAN NATURE, 9
N. matters very much TRIVIALITY, 2
N. to do but work PESSIMISM, 7
n. to do with the case APPEARANCE, 16
N. will come of n. NOTHING, 2
opened it only to find – n. MATERIALISM, 2
Signifying n. LIFE, 43
sooner read a time-table . . . than n. NOVELS, 13
take *more* than n. LANGUAGE, 4
The House of Peers, . . . Did n. HOUSES OF PARLIAMENT, 10

the sort of woman now, . . . said Mould, ... one would
almost feel disposed to bury for n.　　　　WOMEN, 28
The temerity to believe in n.　　　　SCEPTICISM, 6
those who were up to n.　　　　INTRIGUE, 2
To marvel at n. is just about the one and only thing
　　　　HAPPINESS, 8
When you have n. to say, say n.　　　　SILENCE, 4
Where some people are very wealthy and others have n.
　　　　GOVERNMENT, 4
nothingness the n. shows through　　　　CREATION, 15
notice The State, in choosing men . . . takes no n. of their
opinions　　　　LOYALTY, 6
notices One never n. what has been done　　　ACHIEVEMENT, 4
nought N.'s had, all's spent　　　　CONTENTMENT, 6
nourisher Chief n. in life's feast　　　　SLEEP, 15
novel Among the many problems . . . the choice of the moment
. . . to begin his n.　　　　WRITERS, 21
A n. is a mirror　　　　NOVELS, 15
A n. is a static thing　　　　NOVELS, 16; PLAYS, 13
because a n.'s invented, it isn't true　　　　NOVELS, 12
good n. tells us the truth　　　　NOVELS, 2
I'm going to write the Great Australian N.　　AMBITION, 19
not a n. to be tossed aside lightly　　　　CRITICISM, 38
scrofulous French n.　　　　NOVELS, 1
The detective n. is　　　　NOVELS, 13
the last fashionable n. on the tables of young ladies　WRITING, 21
The n. being dead　　　　NOVELS, 17
the n. tells a story　　　　NOVELS, 4
The only obligation to which . . . we may hold a n.　NOVELS, 7
the sex n. is now normal　　　　NOVELS, 14
to read a n. before luncheon was one of the gravest sins
　　　　READING, 18
When I want to read a n.　　　　NOVELS, 3
novelist A n. is, like all mortals　　　　WRITERS, 16
n. who writes nothing for 10 years　　　　WRITERS, 19
the most precious gift a n. can possess　　　　WRITERS, 68
novelists if a third of all the n. . . . dropped dead　WRITERS, 17
n. the story of the present　　　　NOVELS, 4
There are many reasons why n. write　　　　FICTION, 3
novels characters in one of my n.　　　　FICTION, 2
It is a sad feature . . . that only women . . . have time to write
n.　　　　WRITERS, 24
one of the few English n. for grown up people　　CRITICISM, 57
novelty N., n., n.　　　　NOVELTY, 3
November N.　　　　MONTHS, 10
Please to remember the Fifth of N.　　　　TREASON, 1
Thirty days hath N.　　　　MONTHS, 9
now We are all Socialists n.　　　　SOCIALISM, 7
nowhere All dressed up, with n. to go　　　　FUTILITY, 11
He's a real N. Man　　　　FUTILITY, 8
noxious the most n. is a tourist　　　　BRITISH, 7
nuclear adopt n. disarmament　　　　NUCLEAR WEAPONS, 16
Wars cannot be fought with n. weapons　　NUCLEAR WEAPONS, 13
nude To keep one from going n.　　　　PESSIMISM, 7
nudity you don't need the n.　　　　CINEMA, 1
nuisance exchange of one n. for another n.　　　PROGRESS, 5
Inflation in the Sixties was a n.　　　　ECONOMICS, 13
Never compose . . . unless . . . not composing . . . becomes a
positive n.　　　　MUSIC, 24
nuisances a change of n. is as good as a vacation　CHANGE, 14
number *abstract reasoning concerning quantity or n.*
　　　　PHILOSOPHY, 3
a very interesting n.　　　　NUMBERS, 3
Look after n. one　　　　SELF-PRESERVATION, 1
numbers divinity in odd n.　　　　SUPERSTITION, 10
N. . . . only universal language　　　　MATHEMATICS, 15
Round n.　　　　NUMBERS, 1
the greatest happiness for the greatest n.　　　HAPPINESS, 10
up in the high n.　　　　NUMBERS, 2
numble We live in a n. abode　　　　SERVILITY, 2
numbness drowsy n. pains My sense　　　　MELANCHOLY, 7
nun the upbringing a n. would envy　　　　INNOCENCE, 8
nuns the n. who never take a bath　　　　MODESTY, 1
nuptials prone to any iteration of n.　　　　MARRIAGE, 40
nurse any other definition of what a n. should be
　　　　OCCUPATIONS, 14
N. unupblown　　　　BREVITY, 9; TELEGRAMS, 12
The trained n. has become one of the great blessings of
humanity　　　　OCCUPATIONS, 15
The trained n. has given nursing the human . . . touch
　　　　OCCUPATIONS, 11
nurseries n. of all vice　　　　EDUCATION, 16

nurses old men's n.　　　　MARRIAGE, 13
nut I had a little n. tree, Nothing would it bear　　NURSERY
RHYMES, 20
nut-brown the spicy n. ale　　　　ALCOHOL, 45
nutmeg But a silver n.　　　　NURSERY RHYMES, 20

O

oak Heart of o. are our ships　　　　COURAGE, 13
To win the palm, the o., or bays　　　　VICTORY, 10
oar impressions . . . lasting as . . . an o. upon the water
　　　　INSIGNIFICANCE, 1
oat This bread I break was once the o.　　　AGRICULTURE, 5
oat-cakes land of Calvin, o., and sulphur　　　SCOTLAND, 8
oaths O. are but words　　　　WORDS, 4
obedience The reluctant o. of distant provinces　DIPLOMACY, 5
obey born to o.　　　　OBEDIENCE, 2
children, o. your parents　　　　OBEDIENCE, 1
one of those born neither to o. nor to command　NASTINESS, 5
safer to o. than to rule　　　　OBEDIENCE, 3
obeyed Nature, . . . must be o.　　　　HUMAN NATURE, 5
object o. will be, if possible to form Christian men
　　　　EDUCATION, 3
objectionable its own animality either o. or funny　HUMOUR, 18
obligation The only o. to which . . . we may hold a novel
　　　　NOVELS, 7
To the University of Oxford I acknowledge no o.
　　　　EDUCATION, 20
oblige One should o. everyone to . . . one's ability　PRUDENCE, 8
oblivion alms for o.　　　　TIME, 35
o. which awaits the uncreative mind　　　　SCIENTISTS, 10
oblong an o. angular figure　　　　HUMOUR, 40
obscene Chaucer . . . I think o. and contemptible　CHAUCER, 1
would not say that our Press is o.　　　　JOURNALISM, 20
obscenity O. . . . happens to shock some elderly . . . magistrate
　　　　PRUDERY, 4
obscure I strive to be brief, and I become o.　　BREVITY, 2
observance More honour'd in the breach than the o.
　　　　CUSTOM, 3
the o. of trifles　　　　TRIVIALITY, 5
observation Reason, O., and Experience　　　SCIENCE, 22
observations To o. which ourselves we make　SUBJECTIVITY, 6
observe Whenever you o. an animal closely　　ANIMALS, 8
obsolete the horse, as a means of locomotion, is o.
　　　　HORSES, 11
obstinacy the name of . . . o. in a bad one　STUBBORNNESS, 3
obstinate O. people can be divided into　STUBBORNNESS, 2
occupation for ever apologizing for his o.　　BUSINESS, 15
occur Accidents will o.　　　　ACCIDENTS, 4
ocean A life on the o. wave　　　　SEA, 13
on the o. of life we pass　　　　TRANSIENCE, 16
We mortals cross the o.　　　　HUMAN CONDITION, 4
whilst the great o. of truth lay all undiscovered before me
　　　　DISCOVERY, 6
o'clock Three o. is always too late or too early　　DAY, 13
octopus dear o. from whose tentacles we never quite escape
　　　　FAMILY, 39
odd How o. Of God　　　　JEWS, 4
This world is very o. we see　　　　CONFUSION, 4
odds The o. is gone　　　　MOURNING, 11
odi O. et amo　　　　LOVE AND HATE, 2
odious comparisons are o.　　　　ANALOGY, 2
little o. vermin　　　　ENGLISH, 34
One is not superior . . . because one sees the world in an o.
light　　　　CYNICISM, 1
odorous Comparisons are o.　　　　MALAPROPISMS, 2
Oedipuses a tense and peculiar family, the O.　CLASSICS, 1
o'er Returning were as tedious as go o.　　　　GUILT, 7
o'er-leaps Vaulting ambition, which o. itself　AMBITION, 16
off Days o.　　　　LEISURE, 4
offence dire o. from am'rous causes springs　　RESULTS, 5
greatest o. against virtue　　　　VIRTUE, 10
It is a public scandal that gives o.　　　　MORALITY, 11
The only defence is in o.　　　　WAR, 5
offend the kind of pride least likely to o.　　　MODESTY, 5
Those who o. us are generally punished　　　REVENGE, 14
offended This hand hath o.　　　　REGRET, 5
This hath not o. the king　　　　EXECUTION, 20
When people do not respect us we are sharply o.
　　　　SELF-RESPECT, 4
offensive You are extremely o.　　　　IMPERTINENCE, 4
office not describe holding public o.　　　GOVERNMENT, 1

o. sanctifies the holder	POWER, 3
Written by o. boys for o. boys	NEWSPAPERS, 10
officer unbecoming the character of an o.	OFFICERS, 1
official O. dignity . . . in inverse ratio to . . . importance	
	DIPLOMACY, 12
offspring Heaven has granted me no o.	CONCEIT, 24
often 'Do you come here o.	ANIMALISM, 6
oiled Oozing charm . . . He o. his way	CHARM, 3
ointment a good name is better than precious o.	VIRTUE, 3
Okie O. use' to mean you was from Oklahoma	INSULTS, 37
Oklahoma Okie use' to mean you was from O.	INSULTS, 37
old All evil comes from the o.	AGE, 3
an o., wild, and incomprehensible man	POLITICIANS, 74
a sight to make an o. man young	BEAUTY, 38
Before we grow o. and die	AGE, 72
being o. is having lighted rooms	OLD AGE, 25
Better be an o. man's darling	MARRIAGE, 1
first sign of o. age	AGE, 31
for de o. folks at home	HOMESICKNESS, 3
gift of perpetual o. age	OLD AGE, 49
Growing o. is like being increasingly penalized	OLD AGE, 34
He cannot bear o. men's jokes	OLD AGE, 20
I am o. enough to be – in fact am – your mother	AGE, 39
I grow o. . . . I grow o.	OLD AGE, 17
I love everything that's o.	CONSERVATISM, 2
inclination . . . to suppose an o. man decayed in his intellects	
	OLD AGE, 24
I prefer o. age to the alternative	OLD AGE, 12
It is so comic to hear oneself called o.	OLD AGE, 23
I was born o.	AGE, 60
I will never be an o. man	OLD AGE, 4
man . . . as o. as the woman he feels	AGE, 38
new book is published, read an o. one	BOOKS, 33
no more work for poor o. Ned	DEATH, 53
o. age a regret	AGE, 49
O. age brings . . . the comfort that you will soon be out of it	
	OLD AGE, 19
O. age is . . . crossed off names in an address book	AGE, 13
o. age is . . . older than I am	OLD AGE, 4
O. age is the out-patients' department	OLD AGE, 11
o. age . . . the fear that it may go on too long	OLD AGE, 45
O. men are dangerous	OLD AGE, 41
O. men forget	MEMORY, 16
O. sins	SIN, 1
one has to be very o. before one learns how to be amused	
	AGE, 16
redress the balance of the O.	AMERICA, 5
Say I'm growing o., but add, Jenny kissed me	KISSING, 2
so few who can grow o. with a good grace	OLD AGE, 44
Tell me the o., o. story	CHRISTIANITY, 27
terrible thing for an o. woman to outlive her dogs	OLD AGE, 50
that grand o. man	POLITICIANS, 64
That is no country for o. men	MORTALITY, 23
that o. serpent	DEVIL, 4
the o. have reminiscences	AGE, 49
the o. have rubbed it into the young that they are wiser	OLD
	AGE, 28
the o. is better	AGE, 12; ALCOHOL, 15
The o. man has his death	DEATH, 11
There are no o. men any more	AGE, 63
They shall grow not o.	MEMORIALS, 3
they think he is growing o.	AGE, 33
To be o. is to be part of a . . . multitude	OLD AGE, 7
too much Asia and she is too o.	PLACES, 9
too o. to go again to my travels	ROYALTY, 10
When you are o. and gray	OLD AGE, 54
Where are the boys of the O. Brigade	NOSTALGIA, 23
'You are o.,' Father William	OLD AGE, 10
old age nothing funny or commendable about o.	OLD AGE, 48
older make way for an o. man	DISMISSAL, 6
O. men declare war	WAR, 50
perceive real beauty in a person . . . o.	BEAUTY, 6
The o. one grows the more one likes indecency	AGE, 67
to go on getting o.	SURVIVAL, 1
old-fashioned o. respect for the young	RESPECT, 5
O. ways which no longer apply	WOMEN, 5
olfactory an o. bar	FAMILIARITY, 6
oligarchy displeased with *aristocracy*, call it o.	GOVERNMENT, 12
extreme democracy or absolute o. . . . will come	
	GOVERNMENT, 4
olive a land of oil o., and honey	WEALTH, 5
Olivier O. had murder in his heart	ACTORS, 14

Olympic The most important thing in the O. Games	VICTORY, 4
ominous an idea . . . to be fashionable is o.	FASHION, 6
omnipotence final proof of God's o.	GOD, 19
on O. with the dance	DANCING, 1
they get o., then they get *honour*	DOCTORS, 8
once For Christmas comes but o. a year	CHRISTMAS, 19
O. more unto the breach, dear friends	COURAGE, 19
One dies only o.	DEATH, 87
you have dined in every house in London – o.	BORES, 9
you shall drink twice while I drink o.	DRUNKENNESS, 20
one All for o., and o. for all	UNITY, 8
How to be o. up	ONE-UPMANSHIP, 3
if we knew o., we knew two	METAPHYSICS, 3
o. and o. are two	METAPHYSICS, 3
The number o. book . . . was written by a committee	BIBLE, 8
one-eyed o. yellow idol to the north of Khatmandu	
	MOURNING, 5
the O. Man is King	SUPERIORITY, 12
one-handed Give me a o. economist	ECONOMICS, 20
oneself It is a stupidity . . . to busy o. with the correction of	
the world	IMPROVEMENT, 3
One should examine o. . . . before . . . condemning others	
	SELF, 11
only possible society is o.	MISANTHROPY, 4
onions carry their own o. when cycling abroad	FRANCE, 3
onward little to lend thy guiding hand	GUIDANCE, 3
O., Christian soldiers	CHRISTIANITY, 3
O., Christians, onward go	ENDURANCE, 24
open I declare this thing o. – whatever it is	ARCHITECTURE, 7
O. Sesame	SUPERNATURAL, 2
opening o. time in the Sailors Arms	PUBLIC HOUSES, 4
opera an o. without an interval, or an interval without an o.	
	OPERA, 6
baritones are born villains in o.	OPERA, 8
Bed . . . is the poor man's o.	SEX, 125
Like German o., too long and too loud	OPERA, 9; WAR, 126
No good o. plot can be sensible	OPERA, 2
O. in English	OPERA, 5
o. isn't what it used to be	OPERA, 4
The first rule in o. is the first rule in life	SELF-RELIANCE, 5
The o. isn't over till the fat lady sings	OPERA, 3
what language an o. is sung in	OPERA, 1
operas the German text of French o.	OPERA, 10
opinion A man . . . must have a very good o. of himself	
	CONCEIT, 2
better to have no o. of God	GOD, 3
fact that an o. has been widely held	OPINIONS, 5
give him my o.	MARRIAGE, 47
he is . . . Now but a climate of o.	PSYCHIATRY, 1
heresy signifies no more than private o.	OPINIONS, 2
He would rather follow public o.	POLITICIANS, 52
I agree with no man's o.	OPINIONS, 8
I am . . . of the o. with the learned	AGREEMENT, 1
Nobody holds a good o. of a man who has a low o. of himself	
	SELF-RESPECT, 2
nothing to admire except his o.	CRITICS, 6
of his own o. still	YIELDING, 2
so vain . . . care for the o. of those we don't care for	
	CONCEIT, 8
the English think of an o. as something . . . to hide	ENGLISH, 17
The superiority of one man's o. over another's	OPINIONS, 3
They that approve . . . call it o.	OPINIONS, 2
opinionated the o., the ignorant, and the boorish	
	STUBBORNNESS, 2
opinions a decent respect to the o. of mankind	
	INDEPENDENCE, 2
New o. are always suspected	NOVELTY, 5
not a writer's business to hold o.	WRITERS, 28
So many men, so many o.	OPINIONS, 5
the proper o. for the time of year	PUBLIC, 3
The public buys its o. as it buys its meat	PUBLIC, 7
the same o. have arisen among men in cycles	OPINIONS, 1
The State, in choosing men . . . takes no notice of their o.	
	LOYALTY, 5
The wish to spread those o. that we hold	ENGLISH, 7
opium Religion . . . is the o. of the people	RELIGION, 43
opium-dose an o. for keeping beasts of burden	BIBLE, 8
opponent Never ascribe to an o. motives meaner than your	
own	MOTIVE, 1
opportunist rather be an o. and float	EXPEDIENCY, 1
opportunities A wise man will make more o.	OPPORTUNITY, 9
One can present people with o.	OPPORTUNITY, 13

oyster bold man that first eat an o. COURAGE, 20;
FOOLISHNESS, 19
nothing . . . quite matches the sympathetic unselfishness of an o. PERFECTION, 7
the sort of eye that can open an o. at sixty paces APPEARANCE, 42
world's mine o. OPPORTUNITY, 17
oysters Poverty and o. POVERTY, 6

P

pace this petty p. from day to day LIFE, 43
Pacific salutes the Admiral of the P. ARROGANCE, 10
pacifism My p. is not based on . . . intellectual theory WAR
AND PEACE, 5
pack how much more dogs are animated when they hunt in a
p. UNITY, 11
the human p. is shuffled and cut EDUCATION, 31
paddle every man p. his own canoe INDEPENDENCE, 3
padlocked music critics. . . . small and rodent-like with p. ears CRITICS, 18
pagan A P. suckled in a creed outworn DISCONTENT, 10
pageant insubstantial p. faded MORTALITY, 17
paid I do not answer questions like this without being a. MASCULINITY, 1
pain a gentleman . . . never inflicts p. CHIVALRY, 8
Although p. isn't real SUFFERING, 3
critics . . . desire our blood, not our p. CRITICS, 13
disinclination to inflict p. upon oneself GOOD, 11
I feel no p., dear mother, now ALCOHOL, 9
momentary intoxication with p. CRUELTY, 1
Neither shame nor physical p. have any . . . effect PUNISHMENT, 13
owes its pleasures to another's p. HUNTING, 2
P. – has an Element of Blank SUFFERING, 7
Pleasure is . . . intermission of p. PLEASURE, 27
Remember that p. has this most excellent quality SUFFERING, 13
The least p. in our little finger SELF-INTEREST, 4
The p. passes, but the beauty remains ENDURANCE, 14
they blest him in their p. MARTYRDOM, 4
what p. it was to drown DROWNING, 2
yearning like a God in p. SUFFERING, 9
pains no gains without p. ENDURANCE, 19
paint flinging a pot of p. in the public's face CRITICISM, 45
I p. objects as I think them ARTISTS, 17; PAINTING, 10
My business is to p. . . . what I see PAINTING, 17
not a portrait to look like the subject ARTISTS, 13
to p. the lily EXCESS, 10
painted As idle as a p. ship BOATS, 3
I am p. as the greatest little dictator AUTHORITARIANISM, 6
Most women are not so young as they are p. COSMETICS, 1
p. . . . by the great artist Kodak PHOTOGRAPHY, 6
painter A p. should not paint what he sees ARTISTS, 7
I am married to Beatrice Salkeld, a p. CHILDREN, 7
I could have become a real p. LAST WORDS, 39
memory is a p. MEMORY, 10
not a great sculptor or p. can be an architect ARCHITECTURE, 4
painters Good p. imitate nature PAINTING, 3
P. and poets . . . licence to dare anything FREEDOM, 18
Poets and p. are outside the class system ARTISTS, 1; POETS, 1
painting a great difference between p. a face APPEARANCE, 15
If I didn't start p., I would have raised chickens OCCUPATIONS, 13
If people only knew . . . about p. PAINTING, 6
I just keep p. till I feel like pinching. Then I know it's right PAINTING, 14
P. is a blind man's profession PAINTING, 11
p. on a square of ivory WRITERS, 48
P., . . . protecting flat surfaces from the weather PAINTING, 2
pajamas I shot an elephant in my p. HUMOUR, 41
palace Love in a p. LOVE, 77
palaces Mid pleasures and p. though we may roam HOME, 7
pale a p. horse DEATH, 31
Palestine not enough prisons . . . in P. to hold all the Jews JEWS, 13
pall The pallor of girls' brows shall be their p. WAR, 82
Palladium Liberty of the press is the P. of . . . rights FREEDOM, 23
pallor The p. of girls' brows shall be their pall WAR, 82
palm happy state of getting the victor's p. without the dust of
racing VICTORY, 6
To win the p., the oak, or bays VICTORY, 10

palms p. before my feet GLORY, 1
palsied with the p. heart PASSION, 8
pan Put on the p.; Says Greedy Nan NURSERY RHYMES, 7
Pandora open that P.'s Box . . . Trojan 'orses will jump out MIXED METAPHORS, 1
Panjandrum the grand P. NONSENSE, 12
pantheist The modern p. not only PHOTOGRAPHY, 5
pants There were times my p. were so thin POVERTY, 32
Your eyes shine like the p. COMPLIMENTS, 3
papacy Since God has given us the p. . . . enjoy it CATHOLICISM, 8
The P. is not other than the Ghost of the deceased Roman
Empire CATHOLICISM, 5
paper reactionaries are p. tigers POLITICS, 53
The atom bomb is a p. tiger NUCLEAR WEAPONS, 12
This p. will no doubt be found interesting CRITICISM, 11
Where were you fellows when the p. was blank EDITORS, 1
papers fornicated and read the p. MANKIND, 10
only two posh p. on a Sunday NEWSPAPERS, 9
papyromania P. – compulsive accumulation OBSESSIONS, 2
papyrophobia P. – abnormal desire OBSESSIONS, 2
parables great p., . . . but false art CRITICISM, 27
parade the chief employment of riches consists in the p. of
riches OSTENTATION, 6; WEALTH, 25
paradise A p. for a sect FANATICISM, 2
drunk the milk of P. CAUTION, 9
England is a p. for women NATIONALITY, 3
England is the p. of individuality ENGLAND, 35
Grant me p. in this world HEAVEN, 14
If a man could pass through P. PROOF, 3
Same old glimpse of P. MARRIAGE, 76
to hope for P. is to live in P. HEAVEN, 9
Wilderness is P. enow CONTENTMENT, 3
paragon the p. of animals MANKIND, 27
parallel We never remark any passion . . . in others, of which,
. . . we may not find a p. SELF, 8
parallelogram The landlady . . . is a p. HUMOUR, 40
paralyse p. it by encumbering it with remedies REMEDIES, 13
paranoid Even a p. can have enemies ENEMIES, 4
parasite The sick man is a p. of society PATIENTS, 1
parcels Portions and p. of the dreadful Past TIME, 37
pardon God may p. you, but I never can FORGIVENESS, 11
God will p. me. It is His trade LAST WORDS, 36
the government that should ask me for a p. FORGIVENESS, 9
pardoned The women p. all FORGIVENESS, 8
parent a kind p. . . . or a merciless step-mother NATURE, 13
To lose one p., . . . a misfortune; to lose both looks like
carelessness LOSS, 8
parents A Jewish man with p. alive JEWS, 13
by defying their p. and copying one another YOUTH, 5
children, obey your p. OBEDIENCE, 1
Don't hold your p. up to contempt FAMILY, 46
From birth to age eighteen, a girl needs good p. AGE, 62
joys of p. are secret FAMILY, 8
necessary precautions to avoid having p. FAMILY, 12
P. . . . a disappointment to their children FAMILY, 34
P. . . . bones on which children sharpen their teeth FAMILY, 45
P. learn a lot from their children CHILDREN, 37
the way p. obey their children FAMILY, 47
what p. were created for FAMILY, 31
Paris delivered of a city bigger than P. DISAPPOINTMENT, 1
Good Americans, when they die, go to P. AMERICANS, 1
I love P. PARIS, 5
Is P. burning PARIS, 4
no home . . . save in P. PARIS, 4
P. is worth a mass PARIS, 2
when good Americans die they go to P. AMERICANS, 13
parish all the world as my p. RELIGION, 68
park The hunchback in the p. LONELINESS, 6
Parkinson The rise in the . . . employed is governed by P.'s
Law WORK, 14
par-lee-voo Hinky, dinky, p. FRANCE, 13
Parliament build your House of P. upon the river HOUSES OF
PARLIAMENT, 19
He stood twice for P. POLITICS, 86
If Her Majesty stood for P. POLITICS, 68
no reference to fun in any Act of P. PLEASURE, 13
P. is the longest running farce GOVERNMENT, 2
parliaments England . . . mother of p. ENGLAND, 6
parlour Will you walk into my p. INVITATIONS, 1
parochial worse than provincial – he was p. WRITERS, 70
parody devil's walking p. ANIMALS, 9

parole   Classical quotation is the *p.* of literary men
QUOTATIONS, 4
parrot   to sell the family p.   RESPECTABILITY, 4
parsnips   fine words butter no p.   WORDS, 18
parson   If P. lost his senses   ANIMALS, 12
In arguing too, the p. own'd his skill   KNOWLEDGE, 17
Once a p.   OCCUPATIONS, 5
parsons   Our dourest p.   PRAYER, 15
part   I have forgot my p.   FAILURE, 5
In every friend we lose a p. of ourselves   DEATH, 95
it is a little flesh and breath, and the ruling p.   MANKIND, 3
let us kiss and p.   PARTING, 6
till death us do p.   MARRIAGE, 30
We only p. to meet again   FAITHFULNESS, 4
particular   a London p. . . . A fog   WEATHER, 9
did nothing in p.   HOUSES OF PARLIAMENT, 10
particulars   Minute P.   GOOD, 2
parties   it is always like that at p.   REGRET, 11
one of those p. which got out of hand   CHRISTIANITY, 21
parting   Every p. gives a foretaste of death   ⟨SEPARATION, 5
P. is all we know of heaven   PARTING, 5
P. is such sweet sorrow   PARTING, 10
partisanship   P. is our great curse   SUBJECTIVITY, 7
partly   Man p. is   AMBITION, 4
partridge   well-shot woodcock, p., snipe   HUNTING, 1
parts   It is seldom . . . one p. on good terms   PARTING, 9
one man in his time plays many p.   HUMAN CONDITION, 17
Today we have naming of p.   WEAPONS, 5
part-time   p. nihilist   COMMITMENT, 3
party   A great p. is not to be brought down   POLITICS, 34
best number for a dinner p. is two   FOOD, 23
Heard there was a p.   ACCIDENTS, 2
I always voted at my p.'s call   POLITICIANS, 10
No p. has a monopoly over what is right   TOLERANCE, 2
soft drink at a p.   ABSTINENCE, 2
The p. is the rallying-point for the . . . working class
COMMUNISM, 9
The sooner every p. breaks up the better   PARTIES, 1
Well, did you evah! What a swell p.   PARTIES, 5
pass   ideas simply p. through him   STUPIDITY, 1
I shall not p. this way again   MORTALITY, 11
p. for forty-three   AGE, 29
Praise the Lord and p. the ammunition   WAR, 38
They shall not p.   DETERMINATION, 14
To p. away ere life hath lost its brightness   DEATH, 59
passage   calm p. . . . across many a bad night   SUICIDE, 6
Patience and p. of time   PATIENCE, 14
passageways   smell of steaks in p.   FOOD, 18
passed   That p. the time   TIME, 9
passengers   fools and p. drink at sea   BOATS, 15
passeront   *Ils ne p. pas*   DETERMINATION, 14
passes   Men seldom make p.   APPEARANCE, 27
passeth   the peace of God, which p. all understanding
BLESSING, 5
passion   All breathing human p. far above   PASSION, 3
cheated into p., but . . . reasoned into truth   TRUTH, 23
Culture is the p. for sweetness and light   CULTURE, 2
desolate and sick of an old p.   LOVE, 51
Master Mistress of my p.   LOVE, 122
one master-p. . . . swallows up the rest   PASSION, 5
p. and party blind our eyes   EXPERIENCE, 11
P. . . . can be destroyed by a doctor   PASSION, 7
p. in the human soul   MUSIC, 29
So I triumphed ere my p.   PASSION, 8
Strange fits of p.   PASSION, 9
The p. and the life, whose fountains are within
APPEARANCES, 12
The ruling p. conquers reason still   PASSION, 6
We never remark any p. . . . in others, of which, . . . we may
not find a parallel   SELF, 8
passions   A man who has not passed through the inferno of his
p.   PASSION, 2
It is with our p. as it is with fire and water   PASSION, 4
Literature and butterflies are the two sweetest p.
LITERATURE, 13
not his reason, but his p.   RELIGION, 54
The man who is master of his p.   PASSION, 1
Three p., simple but overwhelmingly strong, have governed my
life   PHILOSOPHERS, 8
past   Even God cannot change the p.   PAST, 1
half of you belongs to the p.   OLD AGE, 3
Historians tell the story of the p.   NOVELS, 6

I do not . . . prejudge the p.   PREJUDICE, 6
Keep off your thoughts from things that are p.   PAST, 8
looking forward to the p.   NOSTALGIA, 17
Nothing recalls the p. so potently as a smell   NOSTALGIA, 6
people who live in the p.   PROGRESS, 1
Portions and parcels of the dreadful P.   TIME, 37
remembrance of things p.   REGRET, 18
something . . . absurd about the p.   PAST, 2
Study the p.   PAST, 4
The only thing I regret about my p. life   AGE, 9
The p., at least, is secure   PAST, 9
The p. is a foreign country   PAST, 5
The p. is the only dead thing   PAST, 7
The p. was a sleep   BEGINNING, 7
The p. was nothing . . . The future was a mystery   PRESENT, 2
Those who cannot remember the p.   HISTORY, 23
to know nothing but the present, or nothing but the p.
CONSERVATISM, 4
what is p. my help is p. my care   INDIFFERENCE, 1
what's p. help Should be p. grief   REGRET, 15
What we know of the p. is   HISTORY, 17
Who controls the p. controls the future   POWER, 18
pastoral   Cold P.   ETERNITY, 3
pastures   fresh woods, and p. new   CHANGE, 16
pat   P.-a-cake, pat-a-cake, baker's man   NURSERY RHYMES, 38
P. it and prick it, and mark it with B   NURSERY RHYMES, 38
patches   king of shreds and p.   INFERIORITY, 6
thing of shreds and p.   SINGERS, 2
pate   You beat your p.   STUPIDITY, 13
patent   The people – could you p. the sun   DISCOVERY, 7
path   the primrose p. of dalliance   EXAMPLE, 8
world will make a . . . p. to his door   FAME, 8
patience   like P. on a monument   LOVE, 126
P. and passage of time   PATIENCE, 11
P. is a virtue   PATIENCE, 4
P., n. A minor form of despair   PATIENCE, 8
the years teach us p.   PATIENCE, 13
Though p. be a tired mare   PATIENCE, 12
patient   A disease which the p. and his friends frequently
mistake for deep religious conviction   RELIGION, 5
A doctor . . . is a p. half-cured   OCCUPATIONS, 16
amusing the p. while Nature cures the disease   MEDICINE, 12
Fury of a P. Man   PATIENCE, 10
kill the p.   REMEDIES, 1
Like a p. etherized upon a table   DEPARTURE, 6
p. endurance is godlike   ENDURANCE, 9
patients   the faults of the p.   PATIENTS, 1
patrie   *Allons, enfants, de la p.*   FRANCE, 10
patriot   A good historian . . . is a p.   HISTORIANS, 1
He was a great p. . . . provided . . . that he really is dead
ADMIRATION, 17
The summer soldier and the sunshine p.   COWARDICE, 6
patriotism   Blimpish p. in the mode of Margaret Thatcher
PATRIOTISM, 19
P. . . . is a revolutionary duty   PATRIOTISM, 30
p. is not enough   LAST WORDS, 14
P. . . . looking out for yourself while   AMERICA, 9
P. . . . the last refuge   PATRIOTISM, 4, 17
p. which consists in hating all other nations   PATRIOTISM, 12
True p. is of no party   PATRIOTISM, 29
patriots   P. always talk of dying for their country
PATRIOTISM, 27
patron   Is not a P., my Lord, one who looks with unconcern
PATRONAGE, 2
patronise   He liked to p. coloured people   RACISM, 26
patronizing   A p. disposition . . . has its meaner side
CHARACTER, 8
The idea that there is a model Labour voter, . . . is p.
POLITICS, 43
pattern   p. of excelling nature   MURDER, 10
paucity   the p. of human pleasures   HUNTING, 5
Paul   One named Peter, The other named P.   NURSERY
RHYMES, 63
Paul's   I am designing St P.   ARCHITECTURE, 1
pause   Now I'll have *eine kleine P.*   LAST WORDS, 24
pauses   the p. between the notes   MUSICIANS, 8
pavilion   The p. of Heaven is bare   WEATHER, 22
pavilioned   P. in splendour, and girded with praise   GOD, 23
pay   better . . . not vow, than . . . vow and not p.   PROMISES, 1
get someone to p. you for doing it   OCCUPATIONS, 18
it is poor grub, poor p., and easy work   AMERICA, 23;
ENGLAND, 25

Life is too short to do anything . . . one can p. others to do
WORK, 13
Not a penny off the p. STRIKES, 1
we cannot p. too dearly for it JUSTICE, 15
pays He who p. the piper POWER, 2
peace And who will bring white p. PEACE, 12
a period of cold p. COLD WAR, 3
Arms alone are not enough to keep the p. PEACE, 11
Courage is the price . . . for granting p. COURAGE, 1
depart in p. DEATH, 30
hereafter for ever hold his p. OPPORTUNITY, 11
In Switzerland they had brotherly love . . . and p.
SWITZERLAND, 5
in what p. a Christian can die LAST WORDS, 3
it is in the minds of men that the defences of p. must be
constructed WAR AND PEACE, 1
I will die in p. LAST WORDS, 75
Let him who desires p., prepare for war WAR AND PEACE, 13
Let us have p. PEACE, 10
life is more interesting in war than in p. WAR AND PEACE, 10
make a wilderness and call it p. WAR, 119
makes a good war makes a good p. WAR AND PEACE, 8
May God deny you p. GLORY, 2
my p. I give unto you PEACE, 3
Nation shall speak p. PEACE, 15
never was a good war or a bad p. WAR AND PEACE, 6
no p. . . . unto the wicked PEACE, 2; PUNISHMENT, 5
P. . . . a period of cheating PEACE, 4
p. comes dropping slow PEACE, 18
p. for our time PEACE, 7
p. has broken out PEACE, 6
P. hath her victories WAR AND PEACE, 11
p. I hope with honour PEACE, 9
p. in our time PEACE, 5
P. is not only better than war WAR AND PEACE, 12
P. is poor reading WAR AND PEACE, 7
P., the human dress MANKIND, 5
P. took them all prisoner WAR AND PEACE, 9
p. with honour PEACE, 7
price which is too great to pay for p. WORLD WAR I, 28
The Bomb brought p. but man alone NUCLEAR WEAPONS, 1
the inglorious arts of p. POLITICIANS, 60
the p. of God, which passeth all understanding BLESSING, 5
the Prince of P. CHRISTMAS, 6
There can be no p. of mind in love LOVE, 104
They made p. between us ENEMIES, 5
those who could make a good p. WAR AND PEACE, 4
War is P. OPPOSITES, 1
We are the true p. movement PEACE, 17
We wanted p. on earth PEACE, 13
When there was p., he was for p. PUBLIC, 18
peach dare to eat a p. OLD AGE, 18
'Fan vaulting' . . . belongs to the 'Last-supper-carved-on-a-p.-
stone' ARCHITECTURE, 5
peaches poetry in p. POETRY, 18
with p. and women, it's . . . the side next the sun that's
tempting TEMPTATION, 8
peak One sees . . . only small things from the p.
PERSPECTIVE, 2
Silent, upon a p. in Darien DISCOVERY, 5
pear And a golden p. NURSERY RHYMES, 20
pearl base Indian, threw a p. away LOVE, 128
pearls He who would search for P. TRUTH, 22
p. before swine FOOLISHNESS, 9
p. that were his eyes DEATH, 107
peas I always eat p. with honey FOOD, 6
peasantry a bold p. . . . When once destroy'd PUBLIC, 12
peasants If the French noblesse had been capable of playing
cricket with their p. ARISTOCRACY, 13; CRICKET, 8
peck Peter Piper picked a p. of pickled pepper NURSERY
RHYMES, 39
peculiar a tense and p. family, the Oedipuses CLASSICS, 1
Funny p., or funny ha-ha HUMOUR, 14
pedestal at fourteen every boy should be in love with some
ideal woman . . . on a p. SEXES, 16
pedigree languages are the p. of nations LANGUAGE, 15
pee share a quick p. over a common lamp-post WRITERS, 1
Peel D'ye ken John P. HUNTING, 4
P.'s smile INSULTS, 32
Sir Robert P. POLITICIANS, 1
peer A life p. is like a mule HOUSES OF PARLIAMENT, 16
peerage When I want a p., I shall buy one TITLES, 6

peers Fears, prejudices, misconceptions – those are the p.
HOUSES OF PARLIAMENT, 13
pen how much more cruel the p. WRITING, 4
less brilliant p. than mine CONCEIT, 4
nothing can cure it but the scratching of a p. WRITING, 20
p. is mightier than the sword WRITING, 3
penance The man hath p. done PUNISHMENT, 7
pence Take care of the p. MONEY, 1
Take care of the p. THRIFT, 4
pendulum politics of the p., but of the ratchet POLITICS, 80
The p. of the mind oscillates between sense and nonsense
MIND, 3
penetrable most things are p. BRIBERY, 2
pennies P. do not come from heaven WORK, 23
P. from Heaven OPTIMISM, 18
penny A p. saved THRIFT, 1
One a p., two a p. NURSERY RHYMES, 16
I don't owe a p. to a single soul BORROWING, 13
In for a p. COMMITMENT, 1
Not a p. off the pay STRIKES, 1
P. wise THRIFT, 3
pens Let other p. dwell on guilt and misery OPTIMISM, 14
people a loyal, a gallant, a generous, an ingenious, and good-
temper'd p. FRANCE, 14
always been interested in p. MISANTHROPY, 2
Be nice to p. on your way up PRUDENCE, 10
Boys . . . are unwholesome companions for grown p.
CHILDREN, 31
good of the p. LAW, 7
government of the p., by the p., and for the p.
DEMOCRACY, 11; MEMORIALS, 6
Hell is other p. HELL, 6
How do p. go to sleep SLEEP, 14
If p. behaved in the way nations do GOVERNMENT, 32
if the p. . . . can be reached with the truth DEMOCRACY, 14
indictment against an whole p. ACCUSATION, 1
It is with . . . p. as with . . . bottles CHARACTER, 17
Most of the p. . . . will be children FUNERALS, 1
my p. live in such awful conditions POVERTY, 12
Once the p. begin to reason PUBLIC, 18
p. . . . are attracted by God RELIGION, 35
P. are either charming or tedious CHARM, 4
P. are not fallen angels CRITICISM, 27
p. are the masters PUBLIC, 6
p. may be made to follow a course of action UNDERSTANDING, 3
P. must help one another HELP, 7
p. . . . not dealing with creatures of logic HUMAN NATURE, 7
p.'s government GOVERNMENT, 31
p. standing in the corners of our rooms TELEVISION, 9
p. under suspicion are better moving JUDGMENT, 10
p. . . . usually imitate each other IMITATION, 3
P. who like this sort of thing CRITICISM, 30
P. who need people are the luckiest SOCIETY, 4
p. whose company is coveted OSTENTATION, 4
p. who stay in the middle of the road NONCOMMITMENT, 1
P. will cross the road . . . to say 'We saw you on the telly'
TELEVISION, 2
Pleasant p. are just as real as horrible p. HUMAN NATURE, 6
Religion . . . is the opium of the p. RELIGION, 43
show my head to the p. EXECUTION, 2
the bludgeoning of the p. DEMOCRACY, 5
The Lord prefers common-looking p. APPEARANCE, 21
the p. are forbidden to light lamps INJUSTICE, 1
The p. – could you patent the sun DISCOVERY, 7
the p. we should have been seen dead with SNOBBERY, 10
The p. would be just as noisy PUBLIC, 9
The Swiss . . . are not a p. so much as a . . . business
SWITZERLAND, 2
This country . . . belongs to the p. who inhabit it
DEMOCRACY, 10
thy p. shall be my p. LOYALTY, 5
two p. with one pulse LOVE, 85
we are not a small p. BRITAIN, 9
When . . . it becomes necessary for one p. to dissolve . . .
political bonds INDEPENDENCE, 2
When the P. contend for their Liberty REBELLION, 4
You can fool too many of the p. DECEPTION, 6
people's The p. flag is deepest red SOCIALISM, 1
pepper Peter Piper picked a peck of pickled p. NURSERY
RHYMES, 39
Sergeant P.'s BOOK, SONG, AND PLAY TITLES, 14
perception any truth but from a clear p. TRUTH, 29

poorer for richer for p.   MARRIAGE, 30
poorest p. man may in his cottage bid defiance to . . . the
  Crown   PRIVACY, 3
pop In England, p. art and fine art   ART, 15
poplars The p. are felled   TREES, 3
poppies the p. blow   MEMORIALS, 8
populace society distributes itself into
  Barbarians, Philistines, and P.   AMERICA, 1
  the p. cannot exact their demands   HOUSES OF PARLIAMENT, 19
  this vast residuum we may . . . give the name of P.   PUBLIC, 2
popular Nothing can render them p.   CLERGY, 12
  The worse I do, the more p. I get   POPULARITY, 5
  We're more p. than Jesus Christ   POP MUSIC, 12; POPULARITY, 6
popularity I don't resent his p.   POPULARITY, 8
  P.? . . . glory's small change   POPULARITY, 4
  P. is a crime   POPULARITY, 3
population a starving p.   IRELAND, 5
  P. growth . . . environmental damage   CONSERVATION, 3
  P., . . . increases in a geometrical ratio   ECONOMICS, 15
populi vox p., vox dei   PUBLIC, 1
porcupines I shall throw two p. under you   THREATS, 2
Porlock by a person on business from P.   INTERRUPTIONS, 1
pornography P. is the attempt to insult sex   PORNOGRAPHY, 3
  p. . . . it is terribly, terribly boring   PORNOGRAPHY, 2
  p. of war   WAR, 89
  show that gives p. a bad name   PORNOGRAPHY, 1
  You don't get any p. . . . on the telly   PORNOGRAPHY, 6
port Any p. in a storm   DANGER, 1
  'it would be p. if it could'   ALCOHOL, 11
porter Oh, mister p., what shall I do   TRAVEL, 19
portion best p. of a good man's life   KINDNESS, 7
portions P. and parcels of the dreadful Past   TIME, 37
portrait Every man's work . . . is always a p. of himself
                                                                 ARTS, 1
  Every time I paint a p. I lose a friend   PAINTING, 15
  not paint a p. to look like the subject   ARTISTS, 13
portraits P. of famous bards and preachers   PAINTING, 16
portraying What sort of God are we p.   GOD, 20
posh only two p. papers on a Sunday   NEWSPAPERS, 9
posies beds of roses . . . fragrant p.   FLOWERS, 7
position only one p. for an artist   WALES, 3
possessing too dear for my p.   PARTING, 11
possession No human relation gives one p. in another
                                                                 UNITY, 10
  P. is nine points   LAW, 4
  The p. of a book   OSTENTATION, 2
  the p. of it is intolerable   MATERIALISM, 19
possessions Not the owner of many p. will you be right to call
  happy   HAPPINESS, 9
  p. for a moment of time   LAST WORDS, 22
possibility How great a p.   POETS, 25
  too much of a sceptic to deny the p. of anything   SCEPTICISM, 2
possible something is p., he is . . . right   SCIENCE, 6
  the art of the p.   POLITICS, 14
post of honour is a private station   VICE, 1
post-chaise I would spend my life in driving briskly in a p.
                                                                 PLEASURE, 16
posterity doing something for p.   POSTERITY, 2
  The nations which have put mankind and p. most in their debt
                                                                 NATIONS, 2
  Think of your p.   POSTERITY, 1
  Thy p. shall sway   ENGLAND, 13
postgraduate The British p. student is a lonely forlorn soul
                                                                 EDUCATION, 31
postscript all the pith is in the p.   LETTER-WRITING, 3
  that which was most material in the p.   LETTER-WRITING, 2
postures It requires one to assume such indecent p.
                                                                 CRICKET, 9
potent how p. cheap music is   MUSIC, 16; POP MUSIC, 8
potter Who is the P.   CREATION, 10
poultry A p. matter   MONEY, 32; PUNS, 3
pound the p. . . . in your pocket   ECONOMICS, 21
pounds My dear fellow, . . . I only ask you for twenty-five p.
                                                                 BORROWING, 11
  the p. will take care of themselves   THRIFT, 4
  two hundred p. a year   MONEY, 15
pouvait si vieillesse p.   AGE, 24
poverty a darn is . . . p.   THRIFT, 10
  crime so shameful as p.   POVERTY, 8
  Do you call p. a crime   POVERTY, 30
  from nothing to a state of extreme p.   POVERTY, 26

generations . . . have struggled in p. to build these altars
                                                                 RELIGION, 53
If p. is the mother of crime, stupidity is its father   CRIME, 4
It is easy enough to say that p. is no crime   POVERTY, 19
Loneliness . . . is the most terrible p.   LONELINESS, 7
Notwithstanding the p. of my . . . experience   CONTENTMENT, 4
P. and oysters   POVERTY, 6
p. . . . is a blunder   POVERTY, 19
P. is a great enemy to human happiness   POVERTY, 20
P. is an anomaly to rich people   HUNGER, 2
P. is not a crime   POVERTY, 2
P., therefore, was comparative   POVERTY, 7
The misfortunes of p.   POVERTY, 21
three great evils, boredom, vice, and p.   WORK, 24
world p. is primarily a problem of two million villages
                                                                 POVERTY, 29
powder keep your p. dry   PRUDENCE, 6
  when your p.'s runnin' low   PATRIOTISM, 21
powdered Stratford, . . . suggests p. history   ENGLAND, 19
power All that is literature seeks to communicate p.   BOOKS, 16
  As we make sex less secretive, we may rob it of its p.
                                                                 SEX, 54
  corridors of p.   POWER, 22
  Germany will be . . . a world p.   GERMANY, 4
  greater the p.   POWER, 8
  He aspired to p.   POWER, 25
  If, drunk with sight of p., we loose   BOASTS, 4
  its source of p.: ownership   CAPITALISM, 6
  Knowledge itself is p.   KNOWLEDGE, 3
  love of p. is the love of ourselves   FREEDOM, 15
  Men of p. have not time to read   POWER, 11
  one of these is the history of political p.   HISTORY, 22
  P. . . . and Liberty . . . are seldom upon good Terms   POWER, 12;
                                                                 FREEDOM, 14
  p. before his hair turned white was called a whizz-kid
                                                                 POWER, 13
  P. corrupts   POWER, 24
  p. is apt to corrupt   POWER, 19
  P. is the ultimate aphrodisiac   POWER, 14
  P.? . . . like a dead sea fruit   POWER, 15
  P. tends to corrupt   POWER, 3
  p. without responsibility   RESPONSIBILITY, 2, 9; JOURNALISM, 2
  The accursed p. which stands on Privilege   POLITICS, 4
  The balance of p.   POWER, 27
  the blacks must oppress them today because they have p.
                                                                 POWER, 16
  the kingdom of God is not in word, but in p.   GOD, 12
  they . . . take, who have the p.   POWER, 28
  War knows no p.   WAR, 19
  When p. narrows the areas of man's concern   POETRY, 26
  wrong sort of people are always in p.   POWER, 29
  You only have p. over people   POWER, 23
powerful Guns will make us p.   POWER POLITICS, 3
  The rich and p. know   GOD, 2
powerless Brief and p.   HUMAN CONDITION, 15
powers a taste for *hidden* and *forbidden* p.   SCIENCE, 30
  Headmasters have p.   EDUCATION, 12
  the p. of a first-rate man and the creed of a second-rate man
                                                                 POLITICIANS, 1
pox You will die either on the gallows, or of the p.
                                                                 REPARTEE, 5
practical Compassion is . . . an absolutely p. belief   SOCIALISM, 8
  meddling with any p. part of life   OBJECTIVITY, 2
  P. men, . . . are usually the slaves of some defunct economist
                                                                 INFLUENCE, 5
practice a thing may look evil in theory, . . . in p. excellent
                                                                 THEORY, 1
  P. makes perfect   EXPERIENCE, 5
practiced A genius! For thirty-seven years I've . . . and now
  they call me a genius   GENIUS, 8
practise P. what you preach   EXAMPLE, 1
  two kinds of morality . . . one which we preach but do not p.
                                                                 MORALITY, 13
praise bury Caesar, not to p. him   EVIL, 16
  Damn with faint p.   CRITICISM, 40
  envy is a kind of p.   ENVY, 6
  if we p. ourselves fearlessly, something will always stick
                                                                 PRAISE, 2
  I will p. any man that will p. me   FLATTERY, 7
  Let us with a gladsome mind P. the Lord   GOD, 37
  My poems are hymns of p.   POETRY, 46
  Pavilioned in splendour, and girded with p.   GOD, 23

The p. of logic and metaphysics are true   PHILOSOPHY, 1
Whenever two good people argue over p.   PRINCIPLES, 3
whether I embrace your lordship's p. or your mistress
   REPARTEE, 5
whoever is moved . . . is conscious of a continued miracle . . .
which subverts all the p. of his understanding   CHRISTIANITY, 29
print decomposing in the eternity of p.   CRITICISM, 56
news that's fit to p.   NEWSPAPERS, 8
pleasant, sure, to see one's name in p.   BOOKS, 10
The big p. giveth and the fine p. taketh away   BUSINESS, 20
printers those books by which the p. have lost   BOOKS, 19
printing Gunpowder, P., and the Protestant Religion
   CIVILIZATION, 3
priorities The language of p. is   SOCIALISM, 2
prison an extraordinarily pleasant p.   LEXICOGRAPHY, 1
Anyone who has been to . . . public school will . . . feel . . . at
home in p.   EDUCATION, 62
Stone walls do not a p. make   IMPRISONMENT, 4
the true place for a just man is also a p.   JUSTICE, 24
The world . . . is but a large p.   EXECUTION, 23
prisoner I object to your being taken p.   ROYALTY, 20
Peace took them all p.   WAR AND PEACE, 9
P., God has given you good abilities   THEFT, 3
prisoners If this is the way Queen Victoria treats her p.
   IMPRISONMENT, 11
p. of addiction and . . . prisoners of envy   MATERIALISM, 10
prisons not enough p. . . . in Palestine to hold all the Jews
   JEWS, 10
P. are built with stones of Law   HYPOCRISY, 4
privacy a right to share your p. in a public place   PRIVACY, 1
That should assure us of . . . forty-five minutes of undisturbed
p.   INATTENTION, 2
private He was meddling too much in my p. life   PSYCHIATRY, 12
P. Means is dead   PUNS, 20
Scientific discovery is a p. event   SCIENCE, 28
sex has been a very p., secretive activity   SEX, 54
The grave's a fine and p. place   DEATH, 81
Travel is the most p. of pleasures   TRAVEL, 25
Whatsoever . . . the p. calamity, I hope it will not interfere with
the public business of the country   FIRE, 3
when religion is allowed to invade . . . p. life   RELIGION, 44
privilege a defender of p.   PESSIMISM, 2
an Englishman's heaven-born p. of doing as he likes   PUBLIC, 2
The accursed power which stands on P.   POLITICS, 4
prize Men p. the thing ungain'd   DESIRE, 14
Not all that tempts your wand'ring eyes . . . is lawful p.
   TEMPTATION, 6
prizes just miss the p. at the flower show   MEDIOCRITY, 2
The world continues to offer glittering p.   RUTHLESSNESS, 6
P.R.O partly a liaison man and partly P.   BUSINESS, 4
problem ineffectual liberal's p.   LIBERALISM, 1
Not every p. someone has with his girlfriend is . . . due to . . .
capitalist . . . production   CAPITALISM, 8
the p. as I see it   LANGUAGE, 6
problems Among the many p. . . . the choice of the moment
. . . to begin his novel   WRITERS, 21
There are two p. in my life   POLITICIANS, 5
procession A torchlight p.   ALCOHOL, 46
prodigal P. of Ease   WORLD-WEARINESS, 1
producing Man . . . consumes without p.   CAPITALISM, 10
production Capitalist p. begets . . . its own negation
   CAPITALISM, 9
profession Politics is . . . the only p.   POLITICS, 75
The price . . . for pursuing any p.   DISILLUSION, 1
professor A p. is one who talks in someone else's sleep
   ACADEMICS, 1
professors American p. like their literature clear and cold and
pure and very dead   LITERATURE, 1
As to religion, . . . duty of government to protect all . . . p.
thereof   GOVERNMENT, 22
Culture is an instrument wielded by p.   CULTURE, 3
now-a-days p. of philosophy but not philosophers
   PHILOSOPHERS, 10
profit Drop . . . what tomorrow may bring . . . count as p. every
day that Fate allows you   PRESENT, 8
No p. grows where is no pleasure   EDUCATION, 49
Philosophers never balance between p. and honesty
   PHILOSOPHERS, 4
trouble with the p. system   BUSINESS, 27
profound turbid look the most p.   WRITING, 18
progeny A p. of learning   MALAPROPISMS, 3
progress All p. is based   PROGRESS, 2; EXTRAVAGANCE, 2

Man's 'p.' is but a gradual discovery   PROGRESS, 12
Our p. . . . Is trouble and care   LIFE, 32
P. . . . depends on retentiveness   HISTORY, 23
'p.' is simply a comparative   PROGRESS, 3
the things which government does . . . social p.
   GOVERNMENT, 30
What p. . . . In the Middle Ages   PSYCHOLOGY, 1
What we call p. is   PROGRESS, 5
progression Without Contraries is no p.   CONFLICT, 4
prohibition Communism is like p.   COMMUNISM, 6
proletarian you are polite to a p. you . . . bolster up the
capitalist system   POLITICS, 87
proletariat The dictatorship of the p.   MARXISM, 5
the p. will . . . wage a class struggle for Socialism   CLASS, 11
prologues P. precede the piece   PLAYS, 4
prolonged the War is being deliberately p.   WAR, 104
promise A p. made is a debt unpaid   PROMISES, 5
rarely . . . one can see in a little boy the p. of a man
   CHILDREN, 20
promised Only do always in health what you have often p. to
do when you are sick   ILLNESS, 14
promises P. and pie-crust are made to be broken   PROMISES, 7
young man of p.   CHURCHILL, 3
promisin' Once you were so p.   SHYNESS, 3
promptly He gives twice who gives p.   PROMPTNESS, 4
pronounce foreigners . . . spell better than they p.
   PRONUNCIATION, 3; SPELLING, 2
last words which I should p. in this Academy   ARTISTS, 18
p. foreign names as he chooses   PRONUNCIATION, 1
spell it Vinci and p. it Vinchy   PRONUNCIATION, 3; SPELLING, 2
pronouncements Science should leave off making p.
   SCIENCE, 24
propaganda P. . . . consists in nearly deceiving your friends
   PROPAGANDA, 1
propagated If human beings could be p. . . . aristocracy would
be . . . sound   ARISTOCRACY, 7
propagation Women exist . . . solely for the p. of the species
   WOMAN'S ROLE, 5
propensities the silk stockings and white bosoms . . . excite my
amorous p.   LUST, 3
proper He never does a p. thing without . . . an improper
reason   MORALITY, 17
The p. study of Mankind is Man   SELF-KNOWLEDGE, 5
property poor have no right to the p. of the rich   POVERTY AND
   WEALTH, 6
P. has its duties   CAPITALISM, 2
P. is organised robbery   CAPITALISM, 13
P. is theft   CAPITALISM, 12
The future is the only kind of p.   SLAVERY, 1
the right of governing was not p. but a trust   GOVERNMENT, 9
prophecies bring about the verification of his own p.
   PROPHECY, 13
prophet A historian is a p. in reverse   HISTORIANS, 6
a p. is not without honour   HONOUR, 1
there arose not a p. . . . like unto Moses   PROPHECY, 2
The sons of the p. were brave men and bold   COURAGE, 1
proportion strangeness in the p.   BEAUTY, 7
Proportional Representation P. . . . fundamentally counter-
democratic   POLITICS, 44
proposes Man p.   GOD, 30
proposition undesirable to believe a p.   SCEPTICISM, 4
propriety The p. of . . . having improper thoughts about . . .
neighbours   MORALITY, 4
prose anything except bad p.   PROSE, 2
difference between . . . p. and metrical composition   POETRY AND
   PROSE, 7
I can only write p. today   POETRY AND PROSE, 8
I have been talking p. for over forty years   PROSE, 3
no one hears his own remarks as p.   PROSE, 1
Poetry is opposed to science, . . . p. to metre   POETRY AND
   PROSE, 1
Poetry is to p.   POETRY AND PROSE, 5
poetry sinks and swoons under . . . p.   POETRY AND PROSE, 3
P. . . . can bear a great deal of poetry   POETRY AND PROSE, 3
p. = words in their best order   POETRY AND PROSE, 2
the p. for God   LANGUAGE, 13
to write good p. is an affair of good manners   POETRY AND
   PROSE, 4
prosper Treason doth never p.   TREASON, 3
prosperitee A man to have ben in p.   MISFORTUNE, 7
him that stood in greet p.   MISFORTUNE, 6
prosperity P. doth best discover vice   MISFORTUNE, 3

put   I p. away childish things   CHARITY, 6
p. up with bad things   TOLERANCE, 8
pygmies   wars of the p. will begin   WORLD WAR II, 16
pyjamas   I in p. for the heat   WEATHER, 15
pylons   P., those pillars Bare   TECHNOLOGY, 12
pyramid   bottom of the economic p.   POVERTY, 27
pyramids   Books are made . . . like p.   BOOKS, 18
Pyrenees   The fleas that tease in the high P.   NONSENSE, 3

Q

quack   uses his words as a q. uses his remedies   VERBOSITY, 4
quad   I am always about in the Q.   EXISTENCE, 1
no one about in the Q.   EXISTENCE, 4
quadrupeds   Dogs, like horses, are q.   ANIMALS, 15
Quakers   I was beaten up by Q.   SHYNESS, 1
qualifications   actor. . . . q., including no money   ACTORS, 6
qualities   Almost every man . . . attempts to display q. which he
does not possess   DECEPTION, 3
q. . . . . necessary for success upon the stage   ACTING, 11
quantity   abstract reasoning concerning q. or number
   PHILOSOPHY, 3
a prodigious q. of mind   INDECISION, 2
quarks   Three q. for Muster Mark   NONSENSE, 14
quarrel   a q. in a far-away country   WORLD WAR II, 1
a q. in the streets is . . . to be hated   ARGUMENTS, 11
It takes . . . one to make a q.   ARGUMENTS, 9
Out of the q. . . . . we make rhetoric   POETRY, 55
q. at the same time   MARRIAGE, 96
q. . . . . energies displayed in it are fine   ARGUMENTS, 11
The justice of my q.   JUSTICE, 16
quarrelled   I did not know that we had ever q.   ARGUMENTS, 16
I have q. with my wife   MARRIAGE, 90
quarrels   q. which vivify its barrenness   LOVE, 64
Q. would not last   ARGUMENTS, 13
quart   cannot put a q. in a pint cup   POSSIBILITY, 2
Quebec   I would rather have written those lines than take Q.
   POETRY, 53
queen   Fella belong Mrs Q.   LANGUAGE, 20
he . . . happened to marry the Q.   ROYALTY, 33
how very different from the home life of our own dear Q.!
   ROYALTY, 2
isn't a bad bit of goods, the Q.   COMPLIMENTS, 1
I've been to London to look at the q.   NURSERY RHYMES, 51
I would not be a q. For all the world   ROYALTY, 32
Move Q. Anne? Most certainly not   MEMORIALS, 12
sorrier for my good knights' loss than for . . . my fair q.
   LOSS, 3
the British warrior q.   BRITAIN, 7
The Q. of Hearts She made some tarts   NURSERY RHYMES, 48
The q. was in the parlour, Eating bread and honey   NURSERY
   RHYMES, 48
queenly   She keeps on being Q.   AFFECTATION, 3
queens   for q. I might have enough   LOSS, 3
queer   All the world is q.   SUBJECTIVITY, 5
girls are so q.   WOMEN, 3
the q. old Dean   SPOONERISMS, 4
There's nowt so q.   DIFFERENCE, 6
thou art a little q.   SUBJECTIVITY, 5
queerer   the universe is . . . q. than we can suppose
   UNIVERSE, 7
questing   plashy fen passes the q. vole   ANIMALS, 21
question   a good q. for you to ask   DIPLOMACY, 9
A timid q. will . . . receive a confident answer   SHYNESS, 2
man who sees both sides of a q.   OBJECTIVITY, 5
Nature has never put the fatal q. as to the meaning of their
lives   PURPOSE, 4
No q. is ever settled Until   ARGUMENTS, 19
not a wise q. for me to answer   DIPLOMACY, 9
q. . . . . which I have not been able to answer   WOMEN, 34
That is the Irish Q.   IRELAND, 5
that is the q.   SUICIDE, 12
the q. that we do not know   KNOWLEDGE, 29
To be, or not to be: that is the q.   LANGUAGE, 6
questioning   Q. is not the mode of conversation
   CONVERSATION, 4
questionings   Those obstinate q.   DOUBT, 8
questions   all q. are open   OBJECTIVITY, 3
I do not answer q. like this without being paid   MASCULINITY, 1
make two q. grow where only one   RESEARCH, 6
queue   An Englishman . . . forms an orderly q. of one
   ENGLISH, 23

quiet   Anythin' for a q. life   PEACE, 8
Here, where the world is q.   PEACE, 16
quietness   unravish'd bride of q.   SILENCE, 9
quince   dined on mince, and slices of q.   FOOD, 31
quintessence   this q. of dust   MANKIND, 27
quotable   It's better to be q. than . . . honest   QUOTATIONS, 13
quotation   Classical q. is the parole of literary men
   QUOTATIONS, 4
Every q. contributes something   QUOTATIONS, 5
q. is a national vice   QUOTATIONS, 14
the great spring of happy q.   QUOTATIONS, 6
To say that anything was a q.   QUOTATIONS, 11
quotations   A book that furnishes no q. is, . . . a plaything
   QUOTATIONS, 9
a list of q.   QUOTATIONS, 8
good thing . . . to read books of q.   QUOTATIONS, 1
It needs no dictionary of q.   EYES, 1
q. very slightly wrong   QUOTATIONS, 10
quote   can q. Shakespeare in an economic crisis
   SHAKESPEARE, 15
quotes   q. . . . . give us a nodding acquaintance with the originator
   QUOTATIONS, 15

R

rabbit   The r. has a charming face   RABBITS, 1
rabbits   a tale of four little r.   RABBITS, 2
except to shoot r. and hit his father on the jaw   NASTINESS, 5
race   A loftier r.   KNOWLEDGE, 33
I wish I loved the Human R.   MANKIND, 22
my opinion of the human r.   MANKIND, 17
Slow and steady wins the r.   HASTE, 7
races   human species . . . composed of two distinct r.
   BORROWING, 5
the r. of Europe are melting   AMERICA, 40
Rachmaninov   R.'s immortalizing totality was his scowl
   MUSICIANS, 20
racially   not r. pure are mere chaff   RACISM, 12
racing   happy state of getting the victor's palm without the dust
of r.   VICTORY, 6
rack   Leave not a r. behind   MORTALITY, 17
radical   A r. is a man   IDEALISM, 6
I never dared be r. when young   YOUTH, 7
The r. invents the views. . . . the conservative adopts them
   CONSERVATISM, 7
radicals   Few r. have good digestions   POLITICS, 15
radio   I had the r. on   NAKEDNESS, 6
Simply a r. personality   CHURCHILL, 8
radioactive   The Irish Sea is naturally r.   ECOLOGY, 6
rage   all Heaven in a r.   IMPRISONMENT, 8
R., rage, against the dying of the light   DEATH, 125
rages   the weight of r.   SPOONERISMS, 1
rags   no scandal like r.   POVERTY, 8
only men in r. . . . . Mistake themselves for carpet bags
   ETIQUETTE, 5
railing   R. at life, and yet afraid of death   OLD AGE, 13
railway   when they think they are alone in r. carriages   HABIT, 6
raiment   they parted his r., and cast lots   FORGIVENESS, 4
rain   A Hard R.'s A-Gonna Fall   PESSIMISM, 3
drop of r. maketh a hole in the stone   PERSISTENCE, 7
droppeth as the gentle r.   MERCY, 2
falls not hail, r., or any snow   AFTERLIFE, 10
He comes in the terrible R.   CHRISTIANITY, 39
R. before seven   WEATHER, 2
R., rain, go away   WEATHER, 3
singing in the r.   WEATHER, 11
rainbow   Somewhere over the r.   DESIRE, 8
the R. gave thee birth   BIRDS, 3
raineth   it r. on the just   JUSTICE, 4
rains   It never r. but it pours   MISFORTUNE, 2
rainy   Keep something for a r. day   THRIFT, 2
when it is not r.   WEATHER, 8
raise   My God shall r. me up   FAITH, 17
Now he will r. me to be a martyr   MARTYRDOM, 1
rake   every woman is at heart a r.   WOMEN, 66
lene . . . as is a r.   HORSES, 4
rallying-point   The party is the r. for the . . . working class
   COMMUNISM, 9
Ralph   R. wept for the end of innocence   INNOCENCE, 5
Ramadan   month of R. shall ye fast   RELIGION, 39
Randolph   the only part of R. that was not malignant
   INSULTS, 41

rapidly but not so r.   TIME, 9
rapists All men are r.   MEN, 4
rapping r. at my chamber door   SUPERNATURAL, 12
rapture a r. on the lonely shore   NATURE, 3
  The first fine careless r.   BIRDS, 1
rare as r. things will, it vanished   TRANSIENCE, 9
  keep it shut up . . . like a r., r. fiddle   NAKEDNESS, 5
rascal Get down you dirty r.   NURSERY RHYMES, 23
rascals R., would you live for ever   WAR, 40
rat Mr Speaker, I smell a r.   MIXED METAPHORS, 4
  That killed the r.   NURSERY RHYMES, 57
ratchet politics of the pendulum, but of the r.   POLITICS, 80
rather It's all been r. lovely   LAST WORDS, 43
rationalized Happiness . . . should never be r.   HAPPINESS, 7
rats R.! They fought the dogs   ANIMALS, 5
ravages What do the r. of time not injure   AGE, 32
raven Quoth the R., 'Nevermore'   EVIL, 13
ravished He . . . r. this fair creature   SEX, 18
raw the working-class which, r. and half-developed   PUBLIC, 2
razor Satire should, like a polished r. keen   SATIRE, 2
razors R. pain you   SUICIDE, 7
reach a man's r. should exceed his grasp   AMBITION, 3
reactionaries r. are paper tigers   POLITICS, 53
read A lonesome man . . . who does not know how to r.   READING, 4
  A man ought to r. just as inclination leads him   READING, 8
  beautiful . . . for someone who could not r.   AMERICA, 7
  books. . . . criticized and r. by people who don't understand them   BOOKS, 25
  do *you* r. books *through*   READING, 7
  Education . . . has produced a vast population able to r.   READING, 16
  everybody wants to have r.   LITERATURE, 17
  he had r. of the effects of smoking   SMOKING, 16
  He writes as fast as they can r.   WRITERS, 56
  His books were r.   BOOKS, 6; PUNS, 1
  In my early years I r. very hard   KNOWLEDGE, 25
  I've just r. that I am dead   OBITUARIES, 2
  King George will be able to r. that   SIGNATURES, 2
  Men of power have not time to r.   POWER, 11
  R., mark, learn and inwardly digest   LEARNING, 3
  sooner r. a time-table . . . than nothing   NOVELS, 10
  When I want to r. a novel   NOVELS, 3
  will bear to be r. twice, . . . was thought twice   WRITING, 32
reader A r. seldom peruses a book with pleasure   WRITERS, 1
  not to inform the r.   BUREAUCRACY, 1
  send the r. to the dictionary   STYLE, 4
  the writer . . . is the impregnator, . . . the r. . . . is the respondent   READING, 19
readers his r. are proud to live in it   WRITERS, 7
  The human race, . . . many of my r.   HUMAN CONDITION, 1
  to trade a hundred contemporary r. for   POSTERITY, 6
  Was there ever yet anything written . . . that was wished longer by its r.   LITERATURE, 4
reading as much pleasure in the r.   PLEASURE, 25
  a substitute for r. it   OSTENTATION, 2
  a tragedy and therefore not worth r.   PLAYS, 2
  but I prefer r.   READING, 14
  half learned the art of r.   READING, 2
  If a book is worth r.   BOOKS, 35
  I have led a life of business so long that I have lost my taste for r.   READING, 17
  I loitered my life away, r. books   DISCONTENT, 3
  I shall lose no time in r. it   INATTENTION, 1
  Peace is poor r.   WAR AND PEACE, 7
  R. . . . ingenious device for avoiding thought   READING, 6
  R. isn't an occupation we encourage among police officers   POLICE, 5
  R. is to the mind   READING, 15
  R. maketh a full man   READING, 1
  The r. of all good books   LITERATURE, 3
  There are two motives for r. a book   READING, 3
  When I am not walking, I am r.   READING, 9
ready critics all are r. made   CRITICS, 2
  I have but ninepence in r. money   CONVERSATION, 2
ready-made Why not . . . r.   WORDS, 6
Reagan disastrous fire in President R.'s library both books were destroyed   INSULTS, 20
real I could have become a r. painter   LAST WORDS, 39
  It's the r. thing   ADVERTISING, 16
  Nothing ever becomes r. till it is experienced   EXPERIENCE, 17
  whether Zelda and I are r.   FICTION, 2

realistic he is going to make 'a r. decision'   DECISION, 3
reality art . . . r. which is . . . in our minds   ARTS, 6
  As far as the laws of mathematics refer to r.   MATHEMATICS, 3
  by r. I mean shops like Selfridges   REALITY, 4
  Cannot bear very much r.   REALITY, 2
  statesmen of the world . . . are far more dangerous, and far more estranged from . . . r.   NUCLEAR WEAPONS, 10
  The whole of art is an appeal to a r.   ARTS, 4
realize I saw it, but I did not r. it   PERCEPTION, 4
realm A worse king never left a r. undone   ROYALTY, 8
realms travell'd in the r. of gold   TRAVEL, 16
reap sown the wind . . . r. the whirlwind   RETRIBUTION, 5
  whatsoever a man soweth, that shall he also r.   RETRIBUTION, 4
reaper a R. whose name is Death   DEATH, 78
reaping No, r.   PUNS, 2
reappear all great events and personalities in . . . history r.   HISTORY, 20
reason A man who does not lose his r.   REASON, 4
  Faith consists in believing when it is beyond the power of r. to believe   FAITH, 19
  happiness is not an ideal of r.   HAPPINESS, 13
  He never does a proper thing without . . . an improper r.   MORALITY, 17
  he who destroys a good book, kills r.   BOOKS, 27
  Human r. won. Mankind won   VICTORY, 8
  it was neither rhyme nor r.   CRITICISM, 35
  man . . . is R.'s slave   PASSION, 1
  nothing is law that is not r.   LAW, 21
  not to r. why   OBEDIENCE, 4
  Once the people begin to r.   PUBLIC, 18
  Only r. can convince us   OBJECTIVITY, 3
  R. is itself a matter of faith   REASON, 2
  r. not the need   NECESSITY, 5
  R., Observation, and Experience   SCIENCE, 22
  right deed for the wrong r.   MOTIVE, 2
  The madman . . . has lost everything except his r.   MADNESS, 3
  the r. of the case   LAW, 21
  The ruling passion conquers r. still   PASSION, 6
  who turns mad for a r.   MADNESS, 4
  woman's r.   WOMEN, 73
reasonable Act of God . . . *something which no r. man could have expected*   DISASTER, 3
  figure of 'The R. Man'   LAW, 15
  Who kills a man kills a r. creature   BOOKS, 27
reasoners most plausible r.   THINKING, 4
reasoning *abstract r. concerning quantity or number*   PHILOSOPHY, 3
  Does it contain any experimental r., concerning matter of fact and existence   PHILOSOPHY, 3
reasons Metaphysics is the finding of bad r.   METAPHYSICS, 2
  never give your r.   JUDGMENT, 11
  r. for not printing any list of subscribers   FRANKNESS, 2
  The heart has its r.   MOTIVE, 5
  two r. for drinking   THIRST, 1
rebel how to r. and conform at the same time   YOUTH, 5
  What is a r.   REBELLION, 2
rebellion A little r. now and then   REBELLION, 5
  little r. . . . is a good thing   POLITICS, 38
recall The Gods themselves cannot r. their gifts   IRREVOCABILITY, 2
receipts How were the r. today in Madison Square Garden   LAST WORDS, 6
receive whoso shall r. one such little child   CHILDREN, 14
received freely ye have r., freely give   GENEROSITY, 3; GIFTS, 2
receiver your wife . . . is a r. of stolen goods   INSULTS, 21
reception men that . . . hinder the r. of every work   CRITICS, 10
recession R. when . . . neighbour loses his job   ECONOMICS, 18; UNEMPLOYMENT, 2
reckon'd beggary in the love that can be r.   LOVE, 116
reckoning take you . . . at your own r.   SELF-RESPECT, 3
recognize did not r. me by my face   PUNISHMENT, 15
recoils Revenge . . . back on itself r.   REVENGE, 13
recompense R. injury with justice   KINDNESS, 1
reconcile How r. this world . . . with . . . my imagining   BLINDNESS, 2
  It takes a long while for a . . . trustful person to r. himself to . . . God   FAITH, 15
recounting calms one's grief by r. it   SORROW, 4
recreation woman accepted cooking . . . but man . . . made of it a r.   FOOD, 43
red Coral is far more r.   ANALOGY, 3
  it's not even r. brick, but white tile   CLASS, 26

. . . leeches have r. blood — LAST WORDS, 17
R. Badge of Courage — COURAGE, 7
Red lips are not so r. — WAR, 83
R. sky at night — WEATHER, 4
The people's flag is deepest r. — SOCIALISM, 3
The sand of the desert is sodden r. — WAR, 77
thin r. line tipped with steel — WAR, 96
redemption married past r. — MARRIAGE, 53
red-hot The Last of the R. Mamas — SINGERS, 3
redundancy hiring taxis . . . handing out r. notices to its own workers — INCOMPETENCE, 2
redwood Nixon . . . would cut down a r. tree — POLITICIANS, 70
reeling R. and Writhing — EDUCATION, 9
references Always verify your r. — RESEARCH, 4
refined One of those r. people — CLASS, 6
reflection a r. of the British Museum Reading Room — INTELLECTUALS, 8
reform All r. . . . will prove unavailing — CHANGE, 1
Any attempt to r. the university — EDUCATION, 25
reformation Every r. must have its victims — SUFFERING, 12
refreshed The tree of liberty must be r. — FREEDOM, 21
refuge God is the immemorial r. of the incompetent — GOD, 35
Idleness . . . the r. of weak minds — IDLENESS, 3
Patriotism is the last r. — PATRIOTISM, 17
refuse To r. praise — PRAISE, 6
refused She r. to begin the 'Beguine' — PETULANCE, 1
refute I r. it *thus* — PHILOSOPHY, 5
regardless r. of their doom — IGNORANCE, 7
regime No r. has ever loved great writers — WRITERS, 23
regiment led his r. from behind — COWARDICE, 3
register history . . . the r. of the . . . misfortunes of mankind — HISTORY, 16
I want to r. a complaint — COMPLAINTS, 5
registry marriage in a r. office — MARRIAGE, 7
regret I have seldom spoken with greater r. — MISQUOTATIONS, 6
My r. Becomes an April violet — SORROW, 2
R. is an appalling waste of energy — REGRET, 9
remember and r. — REGRET, 6
wild with all r. — NOSTALGIA, 20
regrets the Cup that clears TO-DAY of past R. — PRESENT, 5
The follies which a man r. — REGRET, 12
rehearsing R. a play is making the word flesh — PLAYS, 9
reign Better to r. in Hell — POWER, 17
reigned I have r. with your loves — ROYALTY, 14
reigns king r., but does not govern — MONARCHY, 25
reject If you r. me on account of my religion — PREJUDICE, 1
rejoice new sights of Nature made me r. — NATURE, 7
related A group of closely r. persons — FAMILY, 27
relation If a man's character is to be abused . . . there's nobody like a r. to do the business — FAMILY, 42
No human r. gives one possession in another — UNITY, 10
relations Fate chooses your r. — FAMILY, 13; FRIENDS, 1
great men have their poor r. — FAMILY, 14
relaxation Man . . . can only find r. from one . . . labour by taking up another — CHANGE, 7
relief For this r. much thanks — COMFORT, 2
There is a certain r. in change — CHANGE, 12
thou wilt give thyself r. — LIFE, 33
religion a feeling of inward tranquillity which r. is powerless to bestow — CLOTHES, 5
Art and r. first; then philosophy — IMPORTANCE, 3
As to r., . . . duty of government to protect all . . . professors thereof — GOVERNMENT, 22
brothels with bricks of R. — HYPOCRISY, 4
Fascism is a r. — FASCISM, 2
If you reject me on account of my r. — PREJUDICE, 1
Love is my r. — LOVE AND DEATH, 3
Many people think they have r. — RELIGION, 36
Men will wrangle for r. — RELIGION, 17
no reason to bring r. into it — RELIGION, 49
Not a r. for gentlemen — RELIGION, 13
Nothing is so fatal to r. as indifference — INDIFFERENCE, 1
One r. is as true as another — RELIGION, 11
One's r. . . . yours is Success — SUCCESS, 5
R. Has made an honest woman of the supernatural — RELIGION, 26; SUPERNATURAL, 8
R. is an illusion — RELIGION, 25
R. is by no means a proper subject — RELIGION, 14
R. is love — RELIGION, 67
R. . . . is the opium of the people — RELIGION, 43
r. of feeble minds — SUPERSTITION, 7
r. of Socialism — SOCIALISM, 2

R.'s in the heart — PRAYER, 13
Science without r. is lame — RELIGION, 23; SCIENCE, 14
Sensible men are all of the same r. — RELIGION, 19
talks loudly against r. — RELIGION, 54
that God is interested only . . . in r. — GOD, 48
To become a popular r. — RELIGION, 34
when r. is allowed to invade . . . private life — RELIGION, 44
when r. was strong . . . men mistook magic for medicine — MEDICINE, 10
religions a country with thirty-two r. and only one sauce — AMERICA, 32
sixty different r., and only one sauce — ENGLAND, 10
The r. we call false were once true — RELIGION, 24
religious frequently mistake for deep r. conviction — RELIGION, 5
a r. animal — RELIGION, 1
first, r. and moral principles — EDUCATION, 2
not r.-good — VIRTUE, 9
r. outlook on life — RELIGION, 37
skilled appeals to r. prejudice — EVOLUTION, 10
To be at all is to be r. — RELIGION, 2
relished the taste by which he is . . . r. — WRITING, 37
reluctant The r. obedience of distant provinces — DIPLOMACY, 16
remarkable nothing left r. Beneath the visiting moon — MOURNING, 11
remedies Extreme r. . . . for extreme diseases — REMEDIES, 10
He that will not apply new r. — INNOVATION, 1
Not even r. can master — DISEASE, 35
Our r. oft in ourselves do lie — SELF-RELIANCE, 7
paralyse it by encumbering it with r. — REMEDIES, 13
r. . . . suggested for a disease — REMEDIES, 7
remedy a r. for everything except death — REMEDIES, 6
a sovereign r. to all diseases — SMOKING, 2
Force is not a r. — FORCE, 1
r. is worse than the disease — DISEASE, 9; REMEDIES, 2
Tis a sharp r., but a sure one — EXECUTION, 25
remember I only r. what I've learnt — KNOWLEDGE, 35
I r., I r. — NOSTALGIA, 9; INNOCENCE, 6
Oh! don't you r. sweet Alice, Ben Bolt — MEMORY, 7
one man to r. me — LAST WORDS, 59
r. and regret — REGRET, 6
R. me when I am gone away — MEMORY, 13
she did not r. . . . her jewelry — PRUDENCE, 9
The world will little note, nor long r. — MEMORIALS, 6
we shall be glad to r. even these hardships — ENDURANCE, 22
We will r. them — MEMORIALS, 4
When I meet a man whose name I can't r. — MEMORY, 5
remembered By this may I r. be When I should be forgotten — MEMORIALS, 1
I r. my God — GOD, 46
remembrance r. of things past — REGRET, 18
reminiscences the old have r. — AGE, 49
remorse r. for what you have thought about your wife — MARRIAGE, 97
remove all faith, so that I could r. mountains — CHARITY, 6
Renaissance the R. was . . . the green end of one of civilization's hardest winters — CIVILIZATION, 5
render husband r. unto the wife due benevolence — MARRIAGE, 24
rendezvous a r. with Death — DEATH, 102
renegades Political r. always start their career of treachery — POLITICIANS, 14
renewal urban r. in New York City — EDUCATION, 25
rent they r. out my room — EXPEDIENCY, 1
repair the landlord does not intend to r. — LAST WORDS, 2
repartee A majority is always the best r. — MAJORITY, 2
repast A new r., or an untasted spring — PLEASURE, 2
repay whatsoever thou spendest more . . . I will r. — CHARITY, 8
repeal the r. of bad or obnoxious laws — LAW, 14
repeat History does not r. itself — HISTORY, 6
obliged to imitate himself, and to r. — IMITATION, 5
repeated A platitude is simply a truth r. — SAYINGS, 1
repent Do you . . . , my Love, r. — PARTING, 8
r. at leisure — MARRIAGE, 38
repentance A Christian . . . feels R. on a Sunday — HYPOCRISY, 19
There's no r. in the grave — DEATH, 129
with the morning cool r. — REGRET, 13
repetition constant r. will finally succeed in imprinting an idea — PUBLIC, 14
History is an endless r. — HISTORY, 11
replenished His intellect is not r. — IGNORANCE, 13
replied And I r., 'My Lord.' — RELIGION, 32
reporter A r. is a man who has renounced everything — JOURNALISM, 25

R. Gray, he was gudeman to me — MARRIAGE, 19
Who killed Cock R. — NURSERY RHYMES, 68
robot the modern conception of a r. — POLITICIANS, 44
rock R. and roll or Christianity — POPULARITY, 6
R. Around the Clock — POP MUSIC, 11
R. of ages, cleft for me — RELIGION, 59
upon this r. I will build my church — CHURCH, 1
With my little stick of Blackpool r. — FOOD, 21
rocked R. in the cradle of the deep — SEA, 11
rock'n'roll Give me that r. music — POP MUSIC, 2
R. is part of a pest — POP MUSIC, 1
rocks The hand that r. the cradle — INFLUENCE, 9
rod he that spareth his r. hateth his son — CHILDREN, 15
rule them with a r. of iron — LEADERSHIP, 2
spare the r. — PUNISHMENT, 6; INDULGENCE, 1
rode and r. madly off in all directions — NONSENSE, 15
rodent-like music critics.... small and r. with padlocked ears — CRITICS, 18
Roland *Childe R. to the Dark Tower came* — SUMMONS, 4
role he saw his r. as being that of Moses — LEADERSHIP, 9
roll R. up that map — PEACE, 14
rolled bottoms of my trousers r. — OLD AGE, 17
rolling Like a r. stone — TRAVEL, 8
The r. English drunkard — TRAVEL, 5
Rolls She has a R. body and a Balham mind — STUPIDITY, 11
Rolls Royce always using a small car to drive to the dockyard instead of my R. — ROYALTY, 23
Roma *R. locuta est* — AUTHORITARIANISM, 1
Roman noblest R. of them all — NOBILITY, 4
the Holy R. Empire was neither holy, nor R., nor an empire — NATIONS, 3
The Papacy is not other than the Ghost of the deceased R. Empire — CATHOLICISM, 5
the R. people had but one neck — RUTHLESSNESS, 1
romance The r. of *Tom Jones* — NOVELS, 5
Twenty years of r. makes a woman look like a ruin — MARRIAGE, 130
Romans Friends, R., countrymen, lend me your ears — EVIL, 16
which came first, the Greeks or the R. — IGNORANCE, 5
romantic The charm is purely r. — IDEALISM, 7
Romanticism R. is ... presenting people with the literary works ... affording ... the greatest ... pleasure — LITERATURE, 16
Rome I lov'd R. more — PATRIOTISM, 28
R. has spoken; the case is concluded — AUTHORITARIANISM, 1
R.'s gross yoke Drops off — INFLUENCE, 1
R. shall perish — REVENGE, 8
R.'s just a city like anywhere else — EUROPE, 1
R. was not built — PATIENCE, 5
The farther you go from the church of R. — PROTESTANTISM, 3
When in R. — CONFORMITY, 2
when R. falls – the World — EUROPE, 5
Romeo Romeo! wherefore art thou R. — NAMES, 4
room All I want is a r. somewhere — DESIRE, 10
before my little r. — FLOWERS, 2
I have only slipped away into the next r. — AFTERLIFE, 5
Infinite riches in a little r. — WEALTH, 19
no r. for them in the inn — CHRISTMAS, 7
The perpetual struggle for r. and food — SURVIVAL, 2
There is always r. at the top — AMBITION, 18
who sneaked into my r. at three o'clock this morning — COMPLAINTS, 5
rooms being old is having lighted r. — OLD AGE, 25
Roosevelt the kind of nation that President R. hoped for — AMBITION, 10
roost Curses ... always come home to r. — CURSES, 5
root love of money is the r. of all evil — MONEY, 11
the r. of all sins — DRUNKENNESS, 5
Though leaves are many, the r. is one — AGE, 71
rope Give a thief enough r. — RETRIBUTION, 1
rose a r. By any other name — NAMES, 4
A r. without a thorn — ADMIRATION, 7
At Christmas I no more desire a r. — SUITABILITY, 4
killing as the canker to the r. — CORRUPTION, 4
Like a r., she has lived as long as roses live — TRANSIENCE, 17
mighty lak' a r. — BABIES, 6
One perfect r. — MATERIALISM, 16
R. ... where some buried Caesar bled — FLOWERS, 4
That which sets ... The budding r. above the r. full blown — FRENCH REVOLUTION, 4
the last r. of summer — FLOWERS, 9
You are responsible for your r. — RESPONSIBILITY, 12

rosebuds Gather ye r. while ye may — PRESENT, 6
roses a wreath of r. — FLOWERS, 1
days of wine and r. — TRANSIENCE, 11
Everything's Coming Up R. — PERFECTION, 8
Flung r., r. riotously — MEMORY, 1
hand that gives you r. — GENEROSITY, 1
I will make thee beds of r. — FLOWERS, 7
I would like my r. to see you — COMPLIMENTS, 1
Nor does a ... gardener scent his r. — POETS, 4
not a bed of r. — MARRIAGE, 112
Plant thou no r. — DEATH, 98
Ring-a-ring o'r. — NURSERY RHYMES, 43
R. are flowering in Picardy — COMPLIMENTS, 9
Send two dozen r. to Room 424 — LOVE, 88
so with r. overgrown — GARDENS, 10
The lilies and r. were all awake — LOVE, 134
Treaties are like r. and young girls — DIPLOMACY, 10
rot lie in cold obstruction, and to r. — DEATH, 106
we r. and r. — LIFE, 44
Rotarians The astronauts! ... R. in outer space — SPACE, 8
rotten r. in the state of Denmark — CORRUPTION, 7
rotting Damn you, England. You're r. — ENGLAND, 32
rough-hew R. them how we will — DESTINY, 18
round R. and round the garden Like a teddy bear — NURSERY RHYMES, 44
r., neat, not gaudy — GARDENS, 9
The trivial r., the common task — SIMPLICITY, 4
roundabouts What's lost upon the r. — LOSS, 2
Roundheads R. (Right but Repulsive) — HISTORY, 27
roving we'll go no more a r. — DEBAUCHERY, 4
row Row upon r. with strict impunity — DEATH, 121
rowed All r. fast — BOATS, 1
Rowley Heigh ho! says R. — NURSERY RHYMES, 1
royal A R. Commission is a broody hen — BUREAUCRACY, 6
Once in r. David's city — CHRISTMAS, 2
trying not to be different in the sense of being r. — ROYALTY, 23
rub R.-a-dub-dub, Three men in a tub — NURSERY RHYMES, 45
there's the r. — SUICIDE, 12
try to r. up against money — MONEY, 39
rubies her price is far above r. — WOMEN, 17
the price of wisdom is above r. — WISDOM, 6
Rubinstein Arthur R. — EGOTISM, 6
rubs sentimentality ... r. you up the wrong way — SENTIMENTALITY, 4
rude Fifty lovelies in the r. — OPPORTUNITY, 18
The right people are r. — IMPERTINENCE, 3
rue With r. my heart is laden — NOSTALGIA, 1
rug Stop ... those dogs ... peeing on my cheapest r. — DOGS, 9
rugby R. Union which is a distillation — SPORT AND GAMES, 19
ruin for the r. of our sex — MEN, 11
I am inclined to notice the r. in things — EUROPE, 11
Twenty years of romance makes a woman look like a r. — MARRIAGE, 130
ruined Such another victory and we are r. — VICTORY, 14
ruining they will end by r. our idea — FASCISM, 1
ruins r. that Cromwell knocked about a bit — INNUENDO, 2
rule A little r., a little sway — TRANSIENCE, 12
English should give Ireland home r. — IRELAND, 14
I don't believe in black majority r. — RACISM, 27
Irish Home R. is conceded — IRELAND, 15
One Ring to r. them all — POWER, 26
R. all England under a hog — INSULTS, 14
r. them with a rod of iron — LEADERSHIP, 2
safer to obey than to r. — OBEDIENCE, 3
The first r. in opera is the first r. in life — SELF-RELIANCE, 5
ruler I am the R. of the Queen's Navee — OFFICERS, 6
rulers R. of the Queen's Navee — OFFICERS, 7
rules R. and models destroy genius and art — RULES, 2
r. of the game are what we call the laws of Nature — GOD, 28
the hand that r. the world — INFLUENCE, 9
there are no golden r. — RULES, 3
two golden r. for an orchestra — MUSIC, 7
ruleth the cry of him that r. among fools — WISDOM, 3
ruling The state is an instrument ... of the r. class — STATE, 5
rum r., sodomy, and the lash — NAVY, 2
Yo-ho-ho, and a bottle of r. — ALCOHOL, 60
rumble R. thy bellyful — WEATHER, 19
rumour Where r. of oppression and deceit — SOLITUDE, 1
run Gwine to r. all night — HORSES, 6
He can r., but he can't hide — ESCAPE, 1
You cannot r. with the hare — LOYALTY, 3
runcible ate with a r. spoon — FOOD, 31

He weareth a r. hat — NONSENSE, 19
runners like r. hand on the torch of life — MORTALITY, 15
running drive out nature with a pitchfork . . . she'll be
constantly r. back — HUMAN NATURE, 12
it takes all the r. *you* can do, to keep in the same place
— NONSENSE, 8
rush *R. hour:* that hour when — TRAVEL, 23
rushes Green grow the r. O — LOVE, 32
Ruskin I doubt that art needed R. — CRITICS, 17
Russia For us in R. communism is a dead dog — COMMUNISM, 7
going in without the help of R. , — WORLD WAR II, 22
R. is a collapse, not a revolution — RUSSIA, 3
the greatness of R. is only her pre-natal struggling — RUSSIA, 2
Why will America not reach out . . . to R. — DIPLOMACY, 8
Russian Scratch the R. and . . . find the Tartar — RUSSIA, 4
the R. people have become — RUSSIA, 7
Russians our decadence and the R.' — DECLINE, 12
test the R., not the bombs — NUCLEAR WEAPONS, 6
rustling r. in unpaid-for silk — CONTENTMENT, 7
rut It's not good enough . . . getting into a state of r.
— WRITERS, 49
people getting into a state of r. — CRITICISM, 14
ruts New roads: new r. — PROGRESS, 4
rye Coming through the r. — LOVE, 34

S

Sabbath never broke the S., but for Gain — SIN, 13
the child that is born on the S. day Is bonny and blithe, and
good and gay — NURSERY RHYMES, 34
sabotage All business sagacity reduces itself . . . to . . . s.
— BUSINESS, 25
sack Either back us or s. us — SUPPORT, 3
sacred the human body is s. — MANKIND, 36
sacrifice A woman will always s. herself — WOMEN, 51
s. . . . of the devil's leavings — VIRTUE, 15
this war . . . which did not justify the s. of a single mother's son
— WAR, 84
sacrificed the most useful thing about a principle . . . s. to
expediency — EXPEDIENCY, 4
sad Becoming an Anglo-Catholic must . . . be a s. business
— CATHOLICISM, 11
being kind Is all the s. world needs — RELIGION, 70; KINDNESS, 6
when thou art absent I am s. — LOVE, 93
sadder A s. and a wiser man — WISDOM, 13
sadists repressed s. . . . become policemen or butchers
— PUBLISHING, 4
sadness Good day s. — SORROW, 7
S. . . . a form of fatigue — SORROW, 9
safe Better be s. than sorry — CAUTION, 1
make the world s. for diversity — DIFFERENCE, 8
The only way to be absolutely s. — CAUTION, 13
safeguard the s. of the west — VENICE, 4
safer s. to obey than to rule — OBEDIENCE, 3
safest Just when we are s. — WORRY, 8
safety Safe though all s.'s lost — WAR, 19
s. is in our speed — HASTE, 6
sage without hardness will be s. — FUTURE, 1
said a great deal to be s. For being dead — DEATH, 26
Nothing has yet been s. that's not been s. before
— ORIGINALITY, 5
they do not know what they have s. — SPEECHES, 3
'Tis s. that some have died for love — LOVE AND DEATH, 7
When a thing has been s. and s. well — QUOTATIONS, 3
sailor No man will be a s. — BOATS, 9
Tinker, Tailor, Soldier, S. — NURSERY RHYMES, 60
sailors opening time in the S. Arms — PUBLIC HOUSES, 4
S. have a port — OCCUPATIONS, 6
saint before we *know* he is a s., there will have to be miracles
— PROOF, 4
I consider myself superior to the s., the scientist — NOVELS, 9
never a s. took pity on My soul — SOLITUDE, 2
S. Preux never kicked the fireirons — IMPERFECTION, 5
St Ives As I was going to S. — NURSERY RHYMES, 3
saints All are not s. — HYPOCRISY, 1
many bodies of the s. which slept arose — LAST WORDS, 11
sake Art for art's s. — ART, 6
sakes king . . . men have made for their own s. — MONARCHY, 17
salad My s. days — YOUTH, 15
salary The s. of the chief executive — BUSINESS, 10
this is the week I earn my s. — MERIT, 5
sales Today's s. should be better than yesterday's — BUSINESS, 2

Salkeld I am married to Beatrice S., a painter — CHILDREN, 7
sally a sudden s. — RIVERS, 6
There's none like pretty S. — LOVE, 36
salmon cider and tinned s. — FOOD, 47
serve both cod and s. — PUNS, 11
the choice between smoked s. and tinned s. — FOOD, 50
salt nobody likes having s. rubbed into their wounds
— AGGRAVATION, 2
S. water and absence — LOVE, 9
speech . . . seasoned with s. — SPEECH, 3
salvation There is no s. outside the church — RELIGION, 3
The s. of mankind — RESPONSIBILITY, 13
Sam Play it, S. — MISQUOTATIONS, 11; NOSTALGIA, 2
Samaritan But a certain S. . . . had compassion on him
— CHARITY, 8
No one would have remembered the Good S. — MONEY, 48
ready enough to do the S. — CHARITY, 20
Samarkand the Golden Road to S. — KNOWLEDGE, 14
same he is much the s. — ILLNESS, 1
It will be all the s. — WORRY, 3
it would be all the s. a hundred years hence — TRIVIALITY, 3
principle seems the s. — WATER, 1
we must all say *the s.* — UNITY, 12
we're all made the s. — SIMILARITY, 4
samite Clothed in white s. — ARTHURIAN LEGEND, 3
Samuel When they circumcised Herbert S. — INSULTS, 27
sanction Happiness is the only s. of life — HAPPINESS, 22
sand and throws . . . s. in their eyes — SLEEP, 10
The s. of the desert is sodden red — WAR, 77
They wept . . . to see Such quantities of s. — SEASIDE, 1
throw the s. against the wind — FUTILITY, 5
World in a grain of s. — WONDER, 2
sane Show me a s. man and I will cure him for you
— MADNESS, 6
sans S. teeth, sans eyes, sans taste, sans every thing — OLD
AGE, 38
Sappho Where burning S. loved — EUROPE, 3
sarcasm petulance is not s. — PETULANCE, 2; IMPERTINENCE, 1
S. . . . the language of the devil — SARCASM, 1
sardines Life is . . . like a tin of s. — LIFE, 10
sat The . . . gentleman has s. so long on the fence
— NONCOMMITMENT, 3
Satan And S. trembles — PRAYER, 10
beheld S. as lightning fall from heaven — DEVIL, 2
S. exalted sat, by merit raised — DEVIL, 10
S. finds . . . mischief . . . For idle hands — IDLENESS, 10
S., Nick, or Clootie — DEVIL, 5
satanic author of the S. Verses book . . . sentenced to death
— RELIGION, 38
satire hard not to write s. — SATIRE, 1
S. is a sort of glass — SATIRE, 3
S. should, like a polished razor keen — SATIRE, 2
satirists S. should be heard and not seen — CRITICISM, 48
satisfaction complacency and s. . . . in . . . a new-married
couple — MARRIAGE, 75
the s. of knowing that we are avenged — REVENGE, 14
satisfied his soul is s. with what is assigned to him
— CONTENTMENT, 1
The superior man is s. — SUPERIORITY, 2
Saturday betwixt A S. and Monday — SUNDAY, 3
Died on S. — NURSERY RHYMES, 49
S.'s child works hard for his living — NURSERY RHYMES, 34
what he did on S. — HYPOCRISY, 19
satyr man is . . . either a stoic or a s. — AGE, 44
sauce a country with thirty-two religions and only one s.
— AMERICA, 32
Art is not a special s. — ART, 13
sixty different religions, and only one s. — ENGLAND, 10
The best s. in the world — HUNGER, 4
savage a time when Britain had a s. culture — CIVILIZATION, 2
s. place! as holy and enchanted — SUPERNATURAL, 6
soothe a s. breast — MUSIC, 15
The young man who has not wept is a s. — AGE, 50; WISDOM, 20
savaged s. by a dead sheep — INSULTS, 18
savait *Si jeunesse s.* — AGE, 24
save S. your breath — SPEECH, 1
To s. a man's life against his will is . . . killing him — KILLING, 1
saved he that endureth to the end shall be s. — PERSISTENCE, 4
they only s. the world — HEROISM, 2
saviour But it's 'S. of 'is country' when the guns — SOLDIERS, 1
saw I came; I s.; God conquered — VICTORY, 16
I came, I s., I conquered — VICTORY, 1

scribbling My s. pays me zero francs per line – not including the white spaces WRITING, 29
script If it's a good s. MONEY, 12
Scripture devil can cite S. QUOTATIONS, 12
scrofulous s. French novel NOVELS, 1
sculptor not a great s. or painter can be an architect ARCHITECTURE, 8
scum of the s. of the earth ARMY, 5
The rich are the s. of the earth WEALTH, 9
scutcheon I bear no other s. JOURNALISM, 17
sea all the s. were ink NONSENSE, 1
Alone on a wide wide s. SOLITUDE, 2
change their clime . . . who rush across the s. TRAVEL, 14
Down to a sunless s. PLEASURE, 8
espouse the everlasting s. VENICE, 5
fishes live in the s. RUTHLESSNESS, 5
For all at last return to the s. SEA, 2
For those in peril on the S. SEA, 14
grow a little crazy . . . like all men at s. MADNESS, 5
kings of the s. DEPARTURE, 2
Learn the secret of the s. SEA, 9
like throwing water into the s. CHARITY, 11
men and s. interpenetrate ENGLAND, 11
Out of the s. came he SUN, 1
Over the s. to Skye ROYALTY, 5
Owl and the Pussy-Cat went to s. NONSENSE, 20
precious stone set in the silver s. ENGLAND, 36
s., trembling with a long line of radiance SEA, 12
Stick . . . to your desks and never go to s. OFFICERS, 7
The s. is calm to-night SEA, 1
The s.! the s. SEA, 15
The voice of the s. speaks to the soul SEA, 3
to the English that of the s. EUROPE, 13
We are as near to heaven by s. as by land LAST WORDS, 32; SEA, 5
when they can see nothing but s. DISCOVERY, 3
why the s. is boiling hot NONSENSE, 9
sea-change doth suffer a s. DEATH, 107
seagreen The s. Incorruptible POLITICIANS, 40
sealed My lips are s. SECRECY, 2
sea-life When men come to like a s. SEA, 6
seam And sew a fine s. NURSERY RHYMES, 8
seamen There were gentlemen and . . . s. in the navy of Charles the Second NAVY, 3
the s. were not gentlemen NAVY, 3
search in s. of a great perhaps LAST WORDS, 56
s. for knowledge PHILOSOPHERS, 8
s. the land of living men ADMIRATION, 12
seas I must down to the s. again SEA, 10
That guard our native s. NAVY, 1
the waters called he S. CREATION, 3
seaside Beside the S. SEASIDE, 1
the drawback of all s. places SEASIDE, 2
season a perfectly ghastly s. . . . for you Spanish dancers CHARITY, 5
Only in the mating s. ANIMALISM, 6
S. of mists and mellow fruitfulness SEASONS, 12
to every thing there is a s. TIME, 12
seasoned speech . . . s. with salt SPEECH, 3
seasons a man for all s. ADAPTABILITY, 4
Four s. fill the measure SEASONS, 10
seat the pleasure of offering my s. to three ladies OBESITY, 3
seated S. . . . at the organ MUSIC, 39
sea-water Wealth is like s. GREED, 9
second The constitution . . . first and s. class citizens CLASS, 40
second-hand Would you buy a s. car TRUST, 5
second-rate an infallible sign of the s. INFERIORITY, 5
nor even booksellers have put up with poets' being s. POETS, 8
the creed of a s. man POLITICIANS, 1
secret a s. in the Oxford sense SECRECY, 10
a s. way . . . of getting at a boy EVIL, 8
bread eaten in s. is pleasant SECRECY, 5
I know that's a s. SECRECY, 8
it is no sin to sin in s. MORALITY, 11
joys of parents are s. FAMILY, 8
Learn the s. of the sea SEA, 9
not to give way to it in s. TELEVISION, 3
s. of reaping the greatest fruitfulness . . . from life DANGER, 6
Three may keep a s. SECRECY, 9
We have discovered the s. of life SCIENCE, 7
when it ceases to be a s. LOVE, 21

secreted Not in Utopia, . . . Or some s. island FRENCH REVOLUTION, 5
secretive As we make sex less s., we may rob it of its power SEX, 54
secrets Conversation . . . elicits s. from us CONVERSATION, 8
sect paradise for a s. FANATICISM, 2
sedate, sober, silent, serious, sad-coloured s. RELIGION, 33
secure only place where a man can feel . . . s. MEN, 6
The past, at least, is s. PAST, 9
security only freedom can make s. secure FREEDOM, 40
Sedan in a flood of tears and a S. chair HUMOUR, 35
sedge s. has wither'd from the lake ILLNESS, 10
seducers evil men and s. EVIL, 4
see change we think we s. NOVELTY, 2
Come up and s. me some time' MISQUOTATIONS, 23
complain we cannot s. COMPLAINTS, 1
I s. none coming out MISTRUST, 2
It is . . . at my age I now begin to s. things as they really are LAST WORDS, 25
My business is to paint . . . what I s. PAINTING, 17
s. . . . into a hypocrite HYPOCRISY, 8
seem to s. things thou dost not POLITICIANS, 22
there shall no man s. me, and live GOD, 11
Why don't you come up sometime and s. me INVITATIONS, 3
seed Fair s.-time had my soul SOUL, 12
I do not want to die . . . until I have . . . cultivated the s. ACHIEVEMENT, 6
In s. time learn, in harvest teach SUITABILITY, 1
seeing S. is believing BELIEF, 2
seek I will undoubtedly have to s. . . . gainful employment GOVERNMENT, 1
To toil and not to s. for rest SELFLESSNESS, 2
We s. him here, we s. him there ABSENCE, 9
We s. it, ere it comes to light PERVERSITY, 3
seem Things are not always what they s. APPEARANCES, 5
seen Who has s. the wind WEATHER, 17
sees fool s. not the same tree WISDOM AND FOOLISHNESS, 5
What, when drunk, one s. in other women COMPLIMENTS, 7
Seine Today I spat in the S. WORLD WAR II, 23
seize S. the day PRESENT, 7
seldom s. attribute common sense AGREEMENT, 4
selection Natural S. EVOLUTION, 6
self All censure of a man's s. SELF, 10
nothing, . . . is greater . . . than one's s. SELF, 20
sickness enlarges the dimensions of a man's s. ILLNESS, 11
to thine own s. be true BORROWING, 8; INTEGRITY, 6
self-adjusting No man . . . who has wrestled with a s. card table TECHNOLOGY, 13
self-assertion Self-sufficiency at home, s. abroad NEWSPAPERS, 12
self-denial S. is not a virtue SELF-DENIAL, 1
self-employed I'm s. ROYALTY, 25
self-indulgence her favourite form of s. WOMEN, 51
write an essay on 's.' SELF, 16
self-interest S. speaks all sorts of tongues SELF-INTEREST, 6
selfish all Governments are s. GOVERNMENT, 8
a man becomes slack and s. MARRIAGE, 113
French governments more s. than most GOVERNMENT, 8
I have been a s. being all my life SELFISHNESS, 1
self-love S. is the greatest of all flatterers CONCEIT, 14
S. seems so often unrequited CONCEIT, 13
S. . . . unrequited SELF, 12
true s. and social are the same SELF-KNOWLEDGE, 6
self-made A s. man . . . believes in luck SELF-MADE MEN, 3
a s. man who owed his lack of success to nobody SELF-MADE MEN, 2
self-praise S. is no recommendation PRAISE, 1
Selfridges by reality I mean shops like S. REALITY, 4
self-sufficiency S. at home, self-assertion abroad NEWSPAPERS, 12
self-sufficient know how to be s. SELF-RELIANCE, 6
selling A best-seller . . . because it was s. well FAME, 5
semed he s. bisier than he was APPEARANCES, 10
senators Do you pray for the s., Dr Hale POLITICIANS, 12
green-rob'd s. of mighty woods TREES, 7
senile a sign that they now consider him s. OLD AGE, 15
seniors earnest advice from my s. ADVICE, 15
sensations life of s. rather than of thoughts SENSATION, 1
sense because Americans won't listen to s. AMERICANS, 6
between a man of s. and his books BOOKS, 14
Common s. is the collection of prejudices PREJUDICE, 3
drowsy numbness pains my s. MELANCHOLY, 7

Let's talk s. to the American people — ENDURANCE, 19
Money is like a sixth s. — MONEY, 34
seldom attribute common s. — AGREEMENT, 4
Take care of the s. — MEANING, 2
The sound must seem an echo to the s. — WRITING, 26
trained and organized common s. — SCIENCE, 20
senses If Parson lost his s. — ANIMALS, 12
sensible S. men are all of the same religion — RELIGION, 19
sensitive more s. one is to great art — ART, 3
sensual The only s. pleasure without vice — MUSIC, 26
sent If this belief from heaven be s. — MANKIND, 39
sentence S. first – verdict afterwards — INJUSTICE, 4
structure of the . . . British s. — GRAMMAR, 3
sentences The most attractive s. are not perhaps the wisest — LANGUAGE, 24
sentiment Sentimentality is only s. — SENTIMENTALITY, 4
sentimentality S. is a superstructure covering brutality — SENTIMENTALITY, 4
S. is only sentiment — SENTIMENTALITY, 4
s. . . . rubs you up the wrong way — SENTIMENTALITY, 4
sentiments high s. always win in the end — NOBILITY, 3
sentinels men . . . who stand as s. in the avenues of fame — CRITICS, 10
separation prepare for a s. — SEPARATION, 4
they should declare the causes which impel them to . . . s. — INDEPENDENCE, 2
September Clear in the cool S. morn — AMERICA, 35
Thirty days hath S., April, June, and November — NURSERY RHYMES, 56
Septuagint The S. minus the Apostles — NUMBERS, 4
sepulchre To famous men all the earth is a s. — FAME, 20
sepulchres whited s. — HYPOCRISY, 3
seraphs Mammon wins his way where S. might despair — MATERIALISM, 4
serious a damned s. business — WAR, 126
A joke's a very s. thing — HUMOUR, 7
a noble nature, . . . treats . . . a s. subject — POETRY, 3
Mix a little foolishness with your s. plans — FOOLISHNESS, 14
they are too s. — FRANCE, 14
seriously Everything must be taken s., nothing tragically — PERSPECTIVE, 4
sermons Ever since his s. were discontinued — SERMONS, 2
He found in stones the s. . . . hidden there — POETS, 59
He that takes pleasure to hear s. — PLEASURE, 26
serpent that old s. — DEVIL, 4
the s. beguiled me — SEXES, 2
servant for the last time in my life, Your Humble S. — ARGUMENTS, 17
The cracked looking glass of a s. — IRELAND, 9
the politician poses as the s. — POLITICIANS, 8
thou good and faithful s. — SERVICE, 1
servants Few men have been admired by their s. — ADMIRATION, 8
good s., but bad masters — PASSION, 4
half of them prefer hiring their s. for life — SLAVERY, 2
he wouldn't have white s. — RACISM, 23
part of English middle-class education is devoted to the training of s. — EDUCATION, 65
S. should not be ill — CLASS, 7
Socialists treat their s. with respect — POLITICS, 76
We teachers can only help . . . as s. — EDUCATION, 38
serve capacity to permit his ministers to s. him — ROYALTY, 26
They also s. who only stand and wait — SERVICE, 4
served I must have things daintily s. — ETIQUETTE, 1
Youth will be s. — SATISFACTION, 1
service I will see you in the vestry after s. — CLERGY, 11
Small s. is true s. — SERVICE, 5
serviettes kiddies have crumpled the s. — ETIQUETTE, 1
Sesame Open S. — SUPERNATURAL, 2
sessions s. of sweet silent thought — REGRET, 18
set all, except their sun, is s. — EUROPE, 3
best plain s. — VIRTUE, 1
sets on which the sun never s. — BRITISH EMPIRE, 6
setting clouds that gather round the s. sun — MORTALITY, 21
settled No question is ever s. Until — ARGUMENTS, 19
Thank God, that's s. — BORROWING, 9
settlement coach and six horses through the Act of S. — IRELAND, 13
seven his acts being s. ages — HUMAN CONDITION, 17
S. swans a-swimming — NURSERY RHYMES, 55
seventh God . . . rested on the s. day — SUNDAY, 1

seventy Being over s. is like being engaged in a war — OLD AGE, 43
Being s. is not a sin — OLD AGE, 29
Oh, to be s. again — LUST, 4; OLD AGE, 14
sever a tie that only death can s. — MARRIAGE, 82
severe if prolonged it cannot be s. — SUFFERING, 13
sewage piped growing volumes of s. into the sea — ENVIRONMENT, 2
sewer s. in a glass-bottomed boat — CORRUPTION, 9
sex As we make s. less secretive, we may rob it of its power — SEX, 54
both of them were extremely interested in s. — SEX, 30
Christian view of s. — SEX, 48
Continental people have s. life — ENGLISH, 24
farmyard world of s. — ANIMALISM, 2
How can I . . . dislike a s. to which Your Majesty belongs — MISOGYNY, 2
If s. is such a natural phenomenon — SEX, 35
if there was a third s. — MEN, 13
In the s.-war thoughtlessness is the weapon of the male — SEXES, 6
Is s. dirty — SEX, 1
it's s. with someone you love — SEX, 3
Literature is mostly about having s. — LITERATURE, 8
meant us to have group s. — SEX, 11
Money, it turned out, was exactly like s. — MONEY, 8; SEX, 7
much more fundamental than s. — MONEY, 19
no more weakness than is natural to her s. — WOMEN, 80
No s. without responsibility — SEX, 31
Personally I know nothing about s. — SEX, 20
Pornography is the attempt to insult s. — PORNOGRAPHY, 3
professed tyrant to their s. — MISOGYNY, 3
s. has been a very private, secretive activity — SEX, 54
S. is one of the nine reasons for reincarnation — SEX, 36
S. is something I really don't understand — SEX, 49
S. is the biggest nothing — SEX, 59
'S.,' . . . 'is the gateway to life.' — SEX, 6
s. . . . must itself be subject . . . to evolution — SEXES, 3
the s. novel is now normal — NOVELS, 14
we English have s. on the brain — ENGLISH, 27; SEX, 41
sexes husbands and wives . . . belong to different s. — SEXES, 8
more difference within the s. than between them — SEXES, 5
that pleasure, which is undeniably the sole motive force behind the union of the s. — SEX, 14
the . . . rift between the s. is . . . widened — SEXES, 2
sexton went and told the s. — PUNS, 4
sexual avowed purpose is to excite s. desire — PORNOGRAPHY, 4
Industrial relations are like s. relations — INDUSTRIAL RELATIONS, 2
music throatily . . . s. — MUSIC, 25
shabby For tamed and s. tigers — ANIMALS, 12
shade a green thought in a green s. — OBLIVION, 3
inviolable s. — HOPE, 4
No s., no shine, no butterflies, no bees — MONTHS, 10
Nothing grows well in the s. — GREATNESS, 1
the s. Of that which once was great — REGRET, 23
shadow be caves . . . in which his s. will be shown — GOD, 39
lose the substance by grasping at the s. — GREED, 4
unhappy s. — SORROW, 3
Who live under the s. of a war — WAR, 112
Your s. at morning — FEAR, 9
shadows brooding tragedy and its dark s. can be lightened — HISTORY, 14
half sick of s. — MARRIAGE, 117
shak'd when degree is s. — ORDER, 1
Shakespeare after S. and Milton are fogotten — POETS, 51
A strange, horrible business, . . . good enough for S.'s day — CRITICISM, 50
Besides S. and me, who do you think there is — CONCEIT, 15
I despise S. — SHAKESPEARE, 16
myriad-minded S. — SHAKESPEARE, 2
reading S. by flashes of lightning — CRITICISM, 9
S., I come — LAST WORDS, 19
S. is . . . really very good — SHAKESPEARE, 8
S. never had six lines together without a fault — SHAKESPEARE, 9
S. – the nearest thing — SHAKESPEARE, 14
S., undoubtedly wanted taste — SHAKESPEARE, 18
sweetest S., Fancy's child — SHAKESPEARE, 13
the making up of a S. or a Milton — WRITERS, 3
the right to criticize S. — CRITICISM, 47
tried lately to read S. — SHAKESPEARE, 4
We can say of S. — SHAKESPEARE, 7
When I read S. I am struck — SHAKESPEARE, 12

being s. with other people singing | PARTIES, 7
Dante makes me s. | LAST WORDS, 13
I am s. at heart | COMFORT, 2
if you don't object if I'm s. | SMOKING, 1
make any man s. to hear her | INSINCERITY, 3
The prayer that . . . heals the s. | FAITH, 10
The s. man is a parasite of society | PATIENTS, 2
the wary fox said . . . to the s. lion | MISTRUST, 5
We have on our hands a s. man | DECLINE, 7
sickness in s. and in health | MARRIAGE, 30
Love is a s. | LOVE, 45
s. enlarges the dimensions of a man's self | ILLNESS, 11
S., sin and death . . . do not originate in God | RELIGION, 22
Sidcup If only I could get down to S. | PROOF, 5
side A door is what a dog is . . . on the wrong s. of | DOGS, 17
a s. dish he hadn't ordered | CONTEMPT, 3
He who knows only his own s. . . . knows little | SUBJECTIVITY, 4
Time is on our s. | PROGRESS, 7
sides Do not . . . write on both s. of the paper | EXAMINATIONS, 2
said on both s. | OBJECTIVITY, 1
We . . . assume that everything has two s. | SUBJECTIVITY, 7
sighed They s. for the dawn and thee | LOVE, 134
sighs over the Bridge of S. into eternity | DEATH, 74
S. are the natural language of the heart | SPEECH, 15
sight a s. to make an old man young | BEAUTY, 38
Out of s. | ABSENCE, 2
we walk by faith, not by s. | FAITH, 5
Who ever loved, that loved not at first s. | FIRST IMPRESSIONS, 6
sightless clapped the glass to his s. eye | BLINDNESS, 6
sights And see all s. from pole to pole | SOUL, 3
few more impressive s. in the world | SCOTS, 3
sign Never s. a walentine | SIGNATURES, 1
s. of an ill-spent youth | SPORT AND GAMES, 18
writing a letter and forgetting to s. his name | INSULTS, 7
significant s. form | ART, 4
signifying S. nothing | LIFE, 43
signing I am s. my death warrant | PROPHECY, 3
silence Come to me in the s. of the night | NOSTALGIA, 6
foster-child of s. and slow time | SILENCE, 9
In England there is only s. or scandal | ENGLAND, 27
Make him a bishop, and you will s. him | CLERGY, 4
occasional flashes of s. | INSULTS, 35
S. is as full of potential wisdom | SILENCE, 8
S. is become his mother tongue | SILENCE, 6
S. is the best tactic | SILENCE, 10
S. is the perfectest herald of joy | SILENCE, 12
S. is the . . . perfect expression of scorn | SILENCE, 13
s. sank Like music | SILENCE, 1
Sorrow and s. are strong | ENDURANCE, 9
That man's s. is wonderful to listen to | SILENCE, 7
The cruellest lies are . . . told in s. | SILENCE, 14
The dust and s. of the upper shelf | NEGLECT, 3
the impression that their normal condition is s. | SILENCE, 11
the more absolute s. of America | ENGLAND, 24
The rest is s. | DEATH, 103
With s. and tears | SEPARATION, 2
silent burst Into that s. sea | EXPLORATION, 1
the great s. majority | MAJORITY, 6
the man who can be s. in several languages | DIPLOMACY, 11
thereon one must remain s. | SILENCE, 15
silicon If s. had been a gas | EXAMINATIONS, 3
silk rustling in unpaid-for s. | CONTENTMENT, 7
s., too often hides eczema | STYLE, 2
the s. stockings and white bosoms . . . excite my amorous propensities | LUST, 3
silks Whenas in s. my Julia goes | CLOTHES, 8
silly A s. remark can be made in Latin | LANGUAGE, 5
it's lovely to be s. at the right moment | FOOLISHNESS, 4
some damned s. thing in the Balkans | WAR, 11
silver First of . . . Georgian s. goes | POLITICS, 50
for a handful of s. | BETRAYAL, 2
s. and gold have I none | REMEDIES, 3
S. buckles on his knee | NURSERY RHYMES, 5
S. threads among the gold | OLD AGE, 35
The s. apples of the moon | DESIRE, 18
When every . . . thing you hold Is made of s., or of gold | ECONOMICS, 9
silvery the s. adamant walls of life's exclusive city | DEATH, 75
Silvia Who is S.? What is she | ADMIRATION, 16
Simon Simple S. met a pieman | NURSERY RHYMES, 47
simple A s. race | POETS, 10

short and s. annals of the poor | POVERTY, 13
Teach us delight in s. things | GOOD, 7
simplicity O holy s. | SIMPLICITY, 3
simplify ability to s. means | SIMPLICITY, 2
S., simplify | SIMPLICITY, 8
simplifying s. something by destroying nearly everything | CIVILIZATION, 4
sin A branch of the s. of drunkenness | DRUNKENNESS, 14
All s. tends to be addictive | SIN, 2
a more dreadful record of s. than . . . countryside | SIN, 12
A private s. is not so prejudicial | SIN, 10
beauty is only s. deep | BEAUTY, 34
Being seventy is not a s. | OLD AGE, 29
He that is without s. | MISQUOTATIONS, 8; SIN, 4
if we say that we have no s., we deceive | SIN, 5
it is no s. to s. in secret | MORALITY, 11
nicest boy who ever committed the s. of whisky | ALCOHOL, 59
no s. but to be rich | HYPOCRISY, 15
no s. except stupidity | STUPIDITY, 15
people who can s. with a grin | SIN, 17
Sickness, s. and death . . . do not originate in God | RELIGION, 22
S. brought death | DEATH, 46; SIN, 14
than that one soul . . . should commit one single venial s. | SIN, 18
They are written as if s. were to be taken out . . . by . . . sleep | SERMONS, 1
which taketh away the s. of the world | CHRISTIANITY, 12
your s. will find you out | SIN, 7
sincere Some of the worst men in the world are s. | SINCERITY, 3
sincerest Imitation . . . s. of flattery | IMITATION, 2
sincerity A little s. is a dangerous thing | SINCERITY, 6
style, not s., is the vital thing | STYLE, 7
sinecure a widow . . . is a kind of s. | EXPEDIENCY, 7
sinews Anger is one of the s. of the soul | ANGER, 4
sing Can't act. Can't s. | ACTORS, 8
Did certain persons die before they s. | SINGERS, 1
I'd like to teach the world to s. | ADVERTISING, 12
I will s. of the sun | WOMEN, 68
S. a song of sixpence | NURSERY RHYMES, 48
The Welsh . . . just s. | WELSH, 4
singed s. the Spanish king's beard | WAR, 35
singing s. in the rain | WEATHER, 11
To hear the lark . . . s. . . . From his watch-tower in the skies | BIRDS, 8
when you shit? S., it's the same thing | SINGING, 1
single a s. man in possession of a good fortune must be in want of a wife | MARRIAGE, 10
begins with a s. step | BEGINNING, 1
Behold her, s. in the field | SOLITUDE, 16
singular Ball . . . how very s. | NAMES, 1
sink The s. is the great symbol of the bloodiness of family life | FAMILY, 29
sinn'd More s. against than sinning | INJUSTICE, 12
sinners At such an hour the s. are still in bed | SIN, 19
It's your combination s. . . . who dishonour the vices | VICE, 2
sinning nothing so artificial as s. nowadays | SIN, 15
sins atone for the s. of your fathers | INJUSTICE, 7
from Expensive S. refrain | SIN, 13
gravest s. it was possible for a gentlewoman to commit | READING, 18
her s., which are many, are forgiven | FORGIVENESS, 5; SIN, 6
His s. were scarlet | BOOKS, 6; PUNS, 15
One of the unpardonable s., . . . , is . . . to go about unlabelled | CLASSIFICATION, 1
she must not reheat his s. for breakfast | FORGIVENESS, 10
though your s. be as scarlet | FORGIVENESS, 3
Sir I am S. Oracle | EGOTISM, 8
Sirens Blest pair of S. | POETRY, 30
sister I kissed her little s. | UNFAITHFULNESS, 4
no friend like a s. | FAMILY, 36
sisters And so do his s. | FAMILY, 2
little s. to all the world | WOMEN, 29
O! men with s. dear | WOMEN, 1
sit I will s. down now | PROPHECY, 4
men s. and hear each other groan | HUMAN CONDITION, 12
nobody can tell you when to s. down | POWER, 10
say what you have to say, and then s. down | SPEECHES, 6
So I did s. and eat | LOVE, 68
sitting Are you s. comfortably? Then I'll begin | BEGINNING, 13
by s. down round you | HOUSES OF PARLIAMENT, 19
I do most of my work s. down | HUMOUR, 32

so companionable as s. — SOLITUDE, 13
s.! where are the charms — SOLITUDE, 5
the bliss of s. — SOLITUDE, 15
Whosoever is delighted in s. — SOLITUDE, 1
Solomon S. Grundy, Born on a Monday — NURSERY RHYMES, 49
solution A difficulty for every s. — BUREAUCRACY, 7
total s. of the Jewish question — NAZISM, 2
some I . . . may be s. time — LAST WORDS, 48
s. more than others — SIMILARITY, 4
You can fool s. of the people all the time — DECEPTION, 4
somebody s. may be looking — CONSCIENCE, 4
someone I wouldn't be . . . talking to s. like you — SNOBBERY, 3
like sleeping with s. else's wife — NEWSPAPERS, 4
Somerset corroboration . . . in the records of S. House — HUMILITY, 11
something Everybody was up to s. — INTRIGUE, 2
S. must be done — UNEMPLOYMENT, 3
S. nasty in the woodshed — EVIL, 9
sometime Why don't you come up s. and see me — INVITATIONS, 3
somewhere 'Tis always morning s. — BEGINNING, 10
son An only s., sir, might expect more indulgence — FAMILY, 19
I've examined your s.'s head, Mr Glum — STUPIDITY, 12
the S. of man coming . . . with power — DOOMSDAY, 2
sonatas The s. of Mozart are unique — MUSIC, 43
song I have a s. to sing O — SINGING, 2
the s. that is sung in our hearts — MUSIC, 34
Who loves not wine, woman and s. — PLEASURE, 20
songs Sing no sad s. — DEATH, 98
Where are the s. of Spring — SEASONS, 11
sonne soft was the s. — SEASONS, 14
sonnet I have three phobias which . . . would make my life as slick as a s. — OBSESSIONS, 1
s. is a moment's monument — POETRY, 38
son-of-a-bitch The poor s. — WRITERS, 74
sons I have a wife, I have s. — FAMILY, 26
Now we are all s. of bitches — NUCLEAR WEAPONS, 1
S. of Belial had a Glorious Time — TREASON, 2
sophistry it can contain nothing but s. and illusion — PHILOSOPHY, 3
Universities incline wits to s. and affectation — EDUCATION, 4
sores Lazarus . . . laid at his gate, full of s. — POVERTY AND WEALTH, 2
sorrow Down, thou climbing s. — SORROW, 22
in s. thou shalt bring forth children — SEXES, 2
Much in s., oft in woe — ENDURANCE, 24
One for s. — SUPERSTITION, 3
Parting is such sweet s. — PARTING, 10
Pure and complete s. is as impossible — EMOTION, 6
S. and silence are strong — ENDURANCE, 3
S. is tranquillity remembered in emotion — SORROW, 14
s. makes us wise — SORROW, 24
Tears of eternity and s. — SORROW, 10
There is no greater s. — SORROW, 6
Through the night of doubt and s. — ENDURANCE, 5
sorrows When s. come, they come not single spies — MISFORTUNE, 17
sort that like that s. of place — OXFORD, 5
Soudan to you, Fuzzy-Wuzzy, at your 'ome in the S. — RACISM, 15
sought Love s. is good — LOVE, 127
Pleasure is . . . seldom found where it is s. — PLEASURE, 14
soul And never once possess our s. — SOUL, 3
Anger is one of the sinews of the s. — ANGER, 4
Artists are not engineers of the s. — ART, 11
a . . . s. like season'd timber — VIRTUE, 11
become a living s. — DEATH, 133
company, . . . have neither a s. to lose nor a body to kick — BUSINESS, 22
education is a leading out of what is . . . in the pupil's s. — EDUCATION, 55
Education is . . . the s. of a society — EDUCATION, 11
Fair seed-time had my s. — SOUL, 12
His s. is marching on — MEMORIALS, 4
his s. is satisfied with what is assigned to him — CONTENTMENT, 1
I am positive I have a s. — SOUL, 11
I am the captain of my s. — RESPONSIBILITY, 8
Impropriety is the s. of wit — HUMOUR, 19
In mystery our s. abides — SOUL, 2
I pray the Lord my s. to keep — SLEEP, 1
Man has no Body distinct from his S. — SOUL, 4
My s. in agony — SOLITUDE, 2

my s. is white — RACISM, 5
Never mind about my s. . . . get my tie right — PAINTING, 5
No coward s. is mine — COURAGE, 3
passion in the human s. — MUSIC, 29
Raises from Hell a human s. — HELL, 1
real dark night of the s. — SOUL, 6
seal the hushed casket of my s. — SLEEP, 13
than that one s. . . . should commit one single venial sin — SIN, 18
The British postgraduate student is a lonely forlorn s. — EDUCATION, 31
The dark night of the s. — SOUL, 8
the . . . essence of a human s. — BOOKS, 11
the eyes are the windows of the s. — EYES, 1
the iron enter into his s. — BITTERNESS, 3
the iron has entered his s. — NONCOMMITMENT, 3
the largest and most comprehensive s. — SHAKESPEARE, 5
The Life and S., the man who will never go home — PARTIES, 9
The s. hath not her generous aspirings — SMOKING, 10
the s. is not more than the body — SELF, 20
the s. of a martyr with the intellect of an advocate — POLITICIANS, 32
The s. started at the knee-cap — ANIMALISM, 5
The S. that rises with us, our life's Star — METAPHYSICS, 5
The voice of the sea speaks to the s. — SEA, 3
Thy rapt s. sitting in thine eyes — SOUL, 10
Thy s. was like a star, and dwelt apart — NOBILITY, 7
souls Above the vulgar flight of common s. — SUPERIORITY, 8
damp s. of the housemaids — MELANCHOLY, 5
Our s. have sight of that immortal sea — METAPHYSICS, 5
s. of five hundred Sir Isaac Newtons — SCIENTISTS, 8; WRITERS, 5
S. of poets dead and gone — PUBLIC HOUSES, 3
Stars . . . robbed men of their s. — STARS, 1
The s. of women are so small — WOMEN, 19
Two s. dwell, alas! in my breast — CONFLICT, 6
Two s. with but a single thought — LOVE, 84
sound full of s. and fury — LIFE, 43
s. of a great Amen — MUSIC, 39
The hills are alive with the s. of music — MUSIC, 22
The most persistent s. . . . through men's history — WAR, 59
The s. must seem an echo to the sense — WRITING, 26
The s. of the English county families — ARISTOCRACY, 15
the trumpet shall s. — DEATH, 28
whispering s. of the cool colonnade — TREES, 3
sounding s. brass — CHARITY, 6
sounds Music is the arithmetic of s. — MUSIC, 17
the s. will take care of themselves — MEANING, 2
soup concludes that it will . . . make better s. — IDEALISM, 4
S. of the evening, beautiful S. — FOOD, 13
Take the s. away — FOOD, 24
sour How s. sweet music is — ORDER, 5
I am sure the grapes are s. — ENVY, 4
source her Majesty . . . must not . . . look upon me as a s. of income — TAXATION, 6
sourest sweetest things turn s. — CORRUPTION, 8
south beaker full of the warm S. — ALCOHOL, 37
go s. in the winter — READING, 8; TRAVEL, 9
hardly be a town in the S. of England — ENGLAND, 31
South Africa S. will not allow the double standards — POLITICS, 10
South African The S. Police would leave no stone unturned — PLACES, 18
South Africans You won't force S. — POLITICS, 11
southern mother bore me in the s. wild — RACISM, 5
sovereign he will have no s. — MONARCHY, 8
That s. of insufferables — WRITERS, 34
The S. has, under a constitutional monarchy . . . three rights — MONARCHY, 2
When I forget my s. — LOYALTY, 10
Soviet Communism is S. power plus the electrification — COMMUNISM, 4
The ship follows S. custom — CLASS, 34
sow Ireland is the old s. — IRELAND, 8
like a s. that hath overwhelm'd all her litter — HUMOUR, 26
soweth whatsoever a man s., that shall he also reap — RETRIBUTION, 4
sown A lovelier flower . . . was never s. — DEATH, 132
soya workers' flats in fields of s. beans — FUTURE, 2
space annihilate but s. and time — LOVE, 99
In the United States there is more s. — AMERICA, 30
Outer s. is no place — SPACE, 2
range of human societies in time, the other in s. — MANKIND, 16
S. is almost infinite — SPACE, 7

S. isn't remote at all — SPACE, 5
spaceship passenger on the s., Earth — SPACE, 3
spade When I see a s. I call it a s. — SNOBBERY, 11
Spain Farewell and adieu to you, Ladies of S. — PARTING, 3
not left to S. — MARTYRDOM, 4
spam he wanted steak and they offered s. — DISAPPOINTMENT, 5
span Life's short s. forbids us . . . far-reaching hopes — MORTALITY, 13
Spaniards the S. seem wiser than they are — APPEARANCES, 9
time to win this game, and to thrash the S. — SPORT AND GAMES, 4; WAR, 34
Spanish I speak S. to God — LANGUAGE, 7
singed the S. king's beard — WAR, 35
spare I can't s. this man; he fights — OFFICERS, 9
S. all I have — WORLD-WEARINESS, 2
S. the rod — CHILDREN, 1; INDULGENCE, 1; PUNISHMENT, 6
Woodman, s. that tree — TREES, 11
spareth he that s. his rod hateth his son — CHILDREN, 15
sparrow a s. alight upon my shoulder . . . I was more distinguished by that — HONOUR, 6
I, said the S., With my bow and arrow — NURSERY RHYMES, 68
It is a city where you can see a s. fall — IRELAND, 12
Sparrowhawks S., Ma'am — REMEDIES, 14
sparrows one of the s. . . . flew . . . through the hall — LIFE, 9
spasm a lonely s. of helpless agony — DEATH, 63
spat So he stood up and s. on the ceiling — HUMOUR, 31
Today I s. in the Seine — WORLD WAR II, 23
speak I didn't s. up — NAZISM, 4
I only s. right on — SPEECHES, 9
Let him now s. — OPPORTUNITY, 11
more than a moral duty to s. one's mind — FRANKNESS, 4
Never s. ill of the dead — DEATH, 8
province of knowledge to s. — KNOWLEDGE, 19; WISDOM, 18
some . . . s. . . . before they think — IMPETUOSITY, 2
S. softly and carry a big stick — POWER POLITICS, 6
s. to God as if men were listening — RIGHTEOUSNESS, 8
S. when you are spoken to — SPEECH, 2; MANNERS, 2
time to think before I s. — SPEECH, 8
When I think, I must s. — WOMEN, 71
Whereof one cannot s. — SILENCE, 15
speaking An Englishman's way of s. — CLASS, 19
People talking without s. — FUTILITY, 10
when . . . s., they do not know what they are saying — SPEECHES, 3
specialist called a nerve s. because it sounds better — PSYCHIATRY, 13
S. – A man who knows more and more about less and less — EXPERTS, 5
specialists s. . . . tend to think in grooves — EXPERTS, 6
species the idea of its death as a s. — NUCLEAR WEAPONS, 9
the one s. I wouldn't mind seeing vanish — DOGS, 3
Women exist . . . solely for the propagation of the s. — WOMAN'S ROLE, 5
spectacle Life is not a s. — LIFE, 40
spectator a S. of mankind — OBJECTIVITY, 2
spectre Communism continued to haunt Europe as a s. — COMMUNISM, 10
speculation If the world were good for . . . s. — SPECULATION, 2
speech An after-dinner s. should be like a lady's dress — SPEECHES, 2
freedom of s. and expression — HUMAN RIGHTS, 4
freedom of s., freedom of conscience, and the prudence never to practise . . . them — FREEDOM, 50
I dreamt that I was making a s. — SPEECHES, 4
let thy s. be short — SPEECH, 4
perfect plainness of s. . . . perfect nobleness — BIBLE, 1
S. is silver — SILENCE, 2
s. only to conceal their thoughts — HUMAN NATURE, 24
s. . . . seasoned with salt — SPEECH, 3
S. was given to man to disguise his thoughts — SPEECH, 16
The most precious things in s. — SPEECH, 13
The true use of s. — SPEECH, 9
the whole earth was . . . of one s. — UNITY, 6
True and False are attributes of s., not of things — TRUTH, 26
speeches every government . . . should have its old s. burned — GOVERNMENT, 27
he tries on s. like a man trying on ties — POLITICIANS, 46
Many have been the wise s. of fools — WISDOM AND FOOLISHNESS, 6
solved by s. and majority votes — POWER POLITICS, 2
Statesmen are far too busy making s. — THINKING, 7
speechless *The Times* is s. — NEWSPAPERS, 5

speed safety is in our s. — HASTE, 6
s. was faster than light — SCIENCE, 3
spell s. it Vinci and pronounce it Vinchy — PRONUNCIATION, 3; SPELLING, 2
spend s. a single day really well — GOOD, 6
spendest whatsoever thou s. more . . . I will repay — CHARITY, 8
spending Getting and s. — WASTE, 3
Riches are for s. — EXTRAVAGANCE, 1
spent Nought's had, all's s. — CONTENTMENT, 6
When I consider how my light is s. — BLINDNESS, 5
spermatozoa million million s., All of them alive — SEX, 25
spheres our social s. have been widely different — SNOBBERY, 11
spice Sugar and s. And all that's nice — NURSERY RHYMES, 65
Variety's the very s. of life — CHANGE, 4
spider said a s. to a fly — INVITATIONS, 1
spies sorrows . . . come not single s. — MISFORTUNE, 17
spilt the blood that she has s. — REVENGE, 9
spin rare attainments . . . but . . . can she s. — WOMAN'S ROLE, 3
spinning from eternity s. the thread of your being — DESTINY, 2
Spinoza The Jews have produced . . . Christ, S., and myself — CONCEIT, 16
spires City with her dreaming s. — OXFORD, 2
spirit and an haughty s. before a fall — PRIDE, 1
Give me the s. — APPEARANCES, 20
Hail to thee, blithe S. — BIRDS, 10
history of the human s. — CULTURE, 1
into thy hands I commend my s. — LAST WORDS, 10
Music that gentlier on the s. lies — MUSIC, 51
my s. found outlet in the air — FLYING, 1
s. . . . of a sound mind — FEAR, 2
the flesh lusteth against the S. — COMPROMISE, 3
the fruit of the S. is love, joy, peace — CHRISTIANITY, 8
the meanest . . . deeds require s. and talent — INSENSITIVITY, 3
The s. burning but unbent — DETERMINATION, 7
the s. . . . is willing — IMPERFECTION, 4
the S. of God moved upon . . . the waters — CREATION, 2
the s. that always denies — DENIAL, 1
Th' expense of s. in a waste of shame — LUST, 7
spiritualist If the dead talk to you, you are a s. — MADNESS, 15
spit a pitcher of warm s. — POLITICS, 30
I am not going to s. on the deck — DEPARTURE, 3
spiteful I like to write when I feel s. — WRITING, 19
spits Who s. against the wind — CONFORMITY, 1
spleen S. can subsist on any kind of food — ANGER, 5
splendour Pavilioned in s., and girded with praise — GOD, 23
splinters teeth like s. — APPEARANCE, 7
split They s. the atom by firing particles at — SCIENCE, 18
when I s. an infinitive . . . it stays s. — GRAMMAR, 2
spoil Don't s. the ship — ECONOMICS, 1
s. the child — PUNISHMENT, 6; INDULGENCE, 1
spoke s. among your wheels — OBSTRUCTION, 1
spoken Speak when you're s. to — MANNERS, 2
spontaneous set a high value on s. kindness — FRIENDSHIP, 19
the Immaculate Conception was s. combustion — CATHOLICISM, 9
Worrying is the most natural and s. of . . . functions — WORRY, 12
spoof even the weather forecast seemed to be some kind of s. — WEATHER, 16
spoon And the dish ran away with the s. — NURSERY RHYMES, 14
S. feeding . . . teaches us nothing but the shape of the spoon — EDUCATION, 19
spoons diners-out from whom we guard our s. — MISTRUST, 8
let us count our s. — MISTRUST, 6
the faster we counted our s. — MISTRUST, 4
sport Blood s. is brought to its ultimate refinement — JOURNALISM, 18
In love as in s., the amateur status — LOVE, 63
kill us for their s. — DESTINY, 19
Serious s. has nothing to do with fair play — SPORT AND GAMES, 15
s. would be as tedious as to work — LEISURE, 3
The national s. of England — ENGLISH, 35
The only athletic s. I ever mastered — SPORT AND GAMES, 8
to make s. for our neighbours — RIDICULE, 1
sportsman But He was never . . . A S. — HUNTING, 7
spot Out, damned s. — GUILT, 8
spotless s. reputation — REPUTATION, 8
spots or the leopard his s. — CHANGE, 1
sprang I s. to the stirrup — HORSES, 3
sprat Throw out a s. — CHANCE, 1
spreading Under the s. chestnut tree — OCCUPATIONS, 10
spring A new repast, or an untasted s. — PLEASURE, 2
as short a S.; As quick a growth to meet decay — TRANSIENCE, 14
By chilly finger'd s. — FLOWERS, 5

can S. be far behind SEASONS, 21
Drink deep, or taste not the Pierian s. KNOWLEDGE, 30
flowers that bloom in the s. APPEARANCE, 16
hounds of s. are on winter's traces SEASONS, 22
In the S. a young man's fancy SEASONS, 24
In the s. . . . your lovely Chloë APPEARANCE, 32
lived light in the s. LIFE, 4
Now S., sweet laxative of Georgian strains SEASONS, 6
S. and summer did happen in Cambridge CAMBRIDGE, 4
S. has returned SEASONS, 17
S. is come home SEASONS, 26
s. now comes unheralded by the return of the birds
ECOLOGY, 1
S. . . . stipple leaves with sun SEASONS, 19
there would be S. no more DECLINE, 11
They call it easing the S. WEAPONS, 6
The year's at the s. PERFECTION, 2
Thrice welcome, darling of the s. BIRDS, 14
Where are the songs of S. SEASONS, 11
spring-board poets use reality as a s. into space POETS, 56
spur A s. in the head INSPIRATION, 1
Fame is the s. FAME, 14
spurs Let the boy win his s. SELF-RELIANCE, 4
spurts They move forward in s. CHILDREN, 19
square Shed his blood . . . given a s. deal JUSTICE, 21
squares walk on the lines of the s. SUPERSTITION, 9
squeezed The Germans, . . . are going to be s., as a lemon
RETRIBUTION, 10
squire Bless the s. and his relations CLASS, 9
stable It's too late to shut the s. door REGRET, 2
staff I'll break my s. RENUNCIATION, 4
stage All the world's a s. HUMAN CONDITION, 17
Don't put your daughter on the s. THEATRE, 6
If this were play'd upon a s. REALITY, 5
no man dies for love, but on the s. LOVE AND DEATH, 2
qualities . . . necessary for success upon the s. ACTING, 11
the Attic s. LIFE, 6
this great s. of fools HUMAN CONDITION, 18
we go quite off this s. DEATH, 95
stagecoach You will hear more good things on . . . a s. from
London to Oxford INTELLECTUALS, 6
stair As I was going up the s. NONSENSE, 22
stairs he had known many kicked down s. PROMOTION, 2
walks up the s. of his concepts MANKIND, 30
stake To the thumbscrew and the s. MARTYRDOM, 4
Stalin If Mr S. dies DIPLOMACY, 9
S. hates the guts of POLITICIANS, 67
stammer You persisted . . . like a s. PERSISTENCE, 9
stamp If we can't s. out literature PHILISTINISM, 7
the indelible s. of his lowly origin EVOLUTION, 4
to order a new s. . . . with my face on it TRIVIALITY, 11
stand a firm place to s. TECHNOLOGY, 1
no time to s. and stare IDLENESS, 4
s. not upon the order of . . . going DISMISSAL, 8
S. your ground . . . if they mean to have a war, let it begin
here WAR, 85
They also serve who only s. and wait SERVICE, 4
We s. today on the edge of a new frontier BEGINNING, 12
standards South Africa will not allow the double s.
POLITICS, 10
stands S. the Church clock NOSTALGIA, 3
star a s. or two beside MOON, 2
Being a s. has made it possible FAME, 7
Bright s., would I were steadfast STARS, 4
Go, and catch a falling s. NONSENSE, 11
Hitch your wagon to a s. AMBITION, 8
one s. differeth from another . . . in glory ASTRONOMY, 1
Remember you are a s. ACTORS, 4
Someday I'll wish upon a s. DESIRE, 7
Sunset and evening s. DUTY, 5
that same s., That fitful, fiery Lucifer STARS, 4
The desire of the moth for the s. HUMOUR, 38
The Soul that rises with us, our life's S. METAPHYSICS, 5
Thy soul was like a s., and dwelt apart NOBILITY, 7
Twinkle, twinkle, little s. STARS, 4
we have seen his s. in the east CHRISTMAS, 9
stare no time to stand and s. IDLENESS, 4
Stark Tonight the American flag floats from yonder hill or Molly
S. sleeps a widow WAR, 114
Starkie There was a young woman called S. RACISM, 1
starry the s. heaven above me WONDER, 3
Under the wide and s. sky DEATH, 119

stars Clad in the beauty of a thousand s. BEAUTY, 26
Hard and high to the s. AMBITION, 2
he made the s. also CREATION, 4; STARS, 2
I'll hold my head so high it'll strike the s. PRIDE, 5
Look at the s. STARS, 3
One sees the mud, and one the s. OPTIMISM, 21
some of us are looking at the s. OPTIMISM, 28
Some s. . . . Fell like a falling tear STARS, 7
S. . . . robbed men of their souls STARS, 1
strives to touch the s. AMBITION, 17
Tempt not the s. DESTINY, 10
The s. grew bright in the winter sky ANIMALS, 13
the Stone that puts the S. to Flight DAY, 5
The Syrian s. look down DEATH, 19
We are merely the s.' tennis-balls DESTINY, 23
what is the s. CURIOSITY, 7
star-spangled 'Tis the s. banner AMERICA, 20
start Wrong from the s. POETRY, 36
starts make certain it never s. NUCLEAR WEAPONS, 3
starve Let not poor Nelly s. LAST WORDS, 8
starving all around you people are s. CAPITALISM, 11
state a s. in the proper sense of the word CAPITALISM, 7
attacking an ex-secretary of s. CHURCHILL, 1
I am the S. MONARCHY, 14
In a free society the s. . . . administers justice among men
STATE, 3
O Lord, to what a s. . . . those who love Thee RELIGION, 56
Our object in the construction of the s. REPUBLIC, 1
reinforcement of the power of the S. REVOLUTION, 2
So long as the s. exists there is no freedom STATE, 2
S. socialism is totally alien SOCIALISM, 14
the lie has become . . . a pillar of the S. LYING, 15
The S., in choosing men . . . takes no notice of their opinions
LOYALTY, 6
The s. is an instrument . . . of the ruling class STATE, 5
the s. . . . Man is in GOD, 39
The worth of a S. STATE, 4
stately go back to thy s. homes of England PARTING, 7
lunatic asylums . . . the s. homes STATELY HOMES, 5
S. Homes of England ope their doors STATELY HOMES, 1
The S. Homes of England ARISTOCRACY, 6; STATELY
HOMES, 2, 3, 4
statement Any general s. is like a cheque GENERALIZATIONS, 3
states S., like men, have their growth, . . . , their decay
POLITICS, 45
statesman abroad you're a s. POLITICIANS, 16
A politician is a s. . . . with an open mouth POLITICIANS, 25
A s. is a politician who's been dead POLITICIANS, 18, 28
definition of a constitutional s. POLITICIANS, 1
if you agree with him he is a s. POLITICIANS, 15
statesmen S. are far too busy making speeches THINKING, 7
s. . . . estranged from reality NUCLEAR WEAPONS, 10
static class people as s. and dynamic SEXES, 7
novel is a s. thing NOVELS, 16; PLAYS, 13
station honour is a private s. VICE, 1
stationmaster The s.'s whiskers are of a Victorian bushiness
APPEARANCE, 43
stations always know our proper s. CLASS, 9
statistics Facts speak louder than s. FACTS, 3; STATISTICS, 11
He uses s. as a drunken man uses lamp-posts STATISTICS, 4
lies, damned lies and s. STATISTICS, 2
s., born to consume resources STATISTICS, 3
S. will prove anything STATISTICS, 6
There are two kinds of s. STATISTICS, 10
unrewarded millions without whom S. would be a bankrupt
science STATISTICS, 8
we must study s. STATISTICS, 7
You cannot feed the hungry on s. STATISTICS, 5
statue that *my* s. should be moved, which I should much dislike
MEMORIALS, 12
there's a s. inside every block of stone OBESITY, 8
statues worth a million s. NAKEDNESS, 3
stay S., stay, Until the hasting day Has run TRANSIENCE, 14
stay-at-home Sweet S. CONTENTMENT, 2
steak he wanted s. and they offered spam DISAPPOINTMENT, 5
when you've got s. at home MARRIAGE, 87
steaks smell of s. in passageways FOOD, 18
steal A man who will s. *for* me will s. *from* me LOYALTY, 8
thou shalt not s. GOD, 10
stealing hanged for s. horses EXAMPLE, 5
steals what can plead that man's excuse Who s. a common
from a goose THEFT, 1

strife God and Nature then at s. NATURE, 15
With phantoms an unprofitable s. LIFE AND DEATH, 12
strike If you s. a child VIOLENCE, 6
no right to s. against the public safety STRIKES, 2
S. while the iron is hot OPPORTUNITY, 7
themselves must s. the blow FREEDOM, 6
the twenty-four-hour s. STRIKES, 4
where ever you meet with a passage . . . s. it out WRITING, 15
strikes the last four s. we've had, it's pissed down STRIKES, 5
Strindberg S. when you have a temperature LITERATURE, 12
string chewing little bits of S. FOOD, 8
strings 'There are s.', said Mr Tappertit, 'in the human heart . . .' EMOTION, 2
stripling yon pale s. EXPECTATION, 4
strive I s. to be brief, and I become obscure BREVITY, 2
men should s. to learn HUMAN CONDITION, 21
needst not s. . . . to keep alive KILLING, 15
To s., to seek, to find, and not to yield DETERMINATION, 15
strives s. to touch the stars AMBITION, 17
stroke man fears . . . only the s. of death DEATH, 21
none so fast as s. BOATS, 2
strong be s. and of a good courage GOD, 8
disarm the s. and arm the weak INJUSTICE, 6
how sublime . . . To suffer and be s. ENDURANCE, 10
Sorrow and silence are s. ENDURANCE, 9
S. enough to answer back to desires CHARACTER, 11
s. enough to bear the misfortunes of others MISFORTUNE, 14
the errors of those who think they are s. MISTAKES, 3
the s. shall thrive SURVIVAL, 4
the wall is s. IMPRISONMENT, 10
woe unto them that . . . follow s. drink ALCOHOL, 12
strongest S. minds . . . the noisy world Hears least MIND, 10
strongminded nobody is s. around a President SERVILITY, 6
strove I s. with none LIFE AND DEATH, 8
struck Certain women should be s. regularly WOMEN, 26
structure s. of the . . . British sentence GRAMMAR, 3
struggle each man must s., lest the moral law become . . .
separated MORALITY, 1
manhood a s. AGE, 19
The perpetual s. for room and food SURVIVAL, 2
the s. for existence EVOLUTION, 5
struggles The history of all . . . society is the history of class s. CLASS, 22
struggling the greatness of Russia is only her pre-natal s. RUSSIA, 2
strumpet a s.'s fool LOVE, 115
struts player that s. and frets LIFE, 43
stubborn s. spear-men COURAGE, 18
student an over-ambitious essay by a second-year s. CRITICS, 15
a s. to the end of my days LEARNING, 5
He was . . . – a s. of history EXPERIENCE, 18
studies S. serve for delight EDUCATION, 5
study much s. is a weariness of the flesh BOOKS, 8
s. what you most affect EDUCATION, 49
The proper s. of Mankind is Man SELF-KNOWLEDGE, 5
the result of previous s. FLATTERY, 2
studying By s. the masters EXPERTS, 1
stuff Ambition should be made of sterner s. AMBITION, 15
such s. as dreams are made on MORTALITY, 17
The future is made of the same s. FUTURE, 8
to s. a mushroom HOUSEWORK, 2
stumble they s. that run fast HASTE, 11
stumbling the . . . world was s. . . . in social blindness BLINDNESS, 2
stupid anger makes us all s. ANGER, 6
clever man . . . came of . . . s. people INTELLIGENCE, 2
he ceased to be mad he became merely s. REMEDIES, 11
Living in England, . . . must be like being married to a s. . . . wife ENGLAND, 18
s. are cocksure . . . intelligent full of doubt DOUBT, 7
The s. neither forgive FORGIVENESS, 15
To be clever enough to get . . . money, one must be s. MATERIALISM, 6
stupidity Against s. the gods . . . struggle in vain STUPIDITY, 14
Human S. consists in having lots of ideas STUPIDITY, 10
If poverty is the mother of crime, s. is its father CRIME, 4
It is a s. . . . to busy oneself with the correction of the world IMPROVEMENT, 3
no sin except s. STUPIDITY, 15
Stygian resembling the horrible S. smoke of the pit SMOKING, 7

ye S. set LUST, 5
style s. is the man himself STYLE, 1
s., not sincerity, is the vital thing STYLE, 7
s. . . . often hides eczema STYLE, 2
the grand s. arises in poetry POETRY, 3
The s. is the man WRITING, 2
styles All s. are good except the tiresome sort STYLE, 6
subject a noble nature, . . . treats . . . a serious s. POETRY, 3
Every s.'s duty is the King's MONARCHY, 18
Her Majesty is not a s. ROYALTY, 12
the individual s. . . . 'has nothing to do with the laws but to obey them.' LAW, 16
subjects Although there exist many thousand s. CONVERSATION, 1
subjunctive S. to the last, he preferred GRAMMAR, 9
sublime a step from the s. to the ridiculous DECLINE, 6
Beethoven's Fifth Symphony is the most s. noise MUSIC, 21
how s. . . . To suffer and be strong ENDURANCE, 10
The s. and the ridiculous OPPOSITES, 7
submerged speak for the inarticulate and the s. JOURNALISM, 4
submit To great evils we s.; we resent little provocations TRIVIALITY, 9
subscribers reasons for not printing any list of s. FRANKNESS, 2
subsequence physicians . . . mistake s. for consequence DOCTORS, 5
substance faith is the s. of things hoped for FAITH, 3
lose the s. by grasping at the shadow GREED, 4
substantial he that chiefly owes himself . . . is the s. Man SELF-RELIANCE, 3
substantives tell the s. from the adjectives POLITICS, 51
substitute a s. for reading it OSTENTATION, 2
no s. for talent TALENT, 4
substitutes and finally a single dictator s. himself COMMUNISM, 11
subtle Time, the s. thief of youth AGE, 40
suburbia I come from s. SUBURBIA, 1
subverts a continued miracle in his own person, which s. all the principles of his understanding CHRISTIANITY, 29
succeed don't s., try, try again. Then quit REALISM, 2
If at first you don't s. PERSISTENCE, 5
If they s., they fail HOMOSEXUALITY, 3
I'm . . . ugly enough to s. on my own INDEPENDENCE, 1
It is not enough to s. RUTHLESSNESS, 7
Never having been able to s. in the world ENVY, 9
those who ne'er s. SUCCESS, 8
to s. unconventionally ORTHODOXY, 3
succeeds Nothing s. SUCCESS, 1
Whenever a friend s. ENVY, 8
success a self-made man who owed his lack of s. to nobody SELF-MADE MEN, 2
I thought that s. spelled happiness HAPPINESS, 15
I was never affected by the question of the s. SELF-CONFIDENCE, 2
no s. like failure FAILURE, 2
not in mortals to command s. SUCCESS, 3
no very lively hope of s. PRAYER, 16
only place where s. comes before work SUCCESS, 15; WORK, 22
religion . . . yours is S. SUCCESS, 5
secret of my s. JEALOUSY, 4
s. and miscarriage are empty sounds DISILLUSION, 4
s. . . . by dint of hard work EFFORT, 5; SUCCESS, 13
s. depends . . . upon individual initiative and exertion EFFORT, 5; SUCCESS, 13
S. is counted sweetest SUCCESS, 8
Sweet Smell of S. SUCCESS, 12
The moral flabbiness born of . . . S. SUCCESS, 9
The penalty of s. SUCCESS, 4
two to make a marriage a s. MARRIAGE, 100
successful It was very s. WEAPONS, 2
we do everything we can to appear s. SUCCESS, 14
sucker a s. born every minute GULLIBILITY, 1
suckle To s. fools TRIVIALITY, 12
sucks s. the nurse asleep SUICIDE, 11
suddenly No one . . . s. became depraved DEBAUCHERY, 6
sued publish and be s. PUBLISHING, 8
Suez Ship me somewhere east of S. DESIRE, 9
the S. Canal was flowing through my drawing room POLITICS, 24
suffer courage to love . . . courage to s. LOVE, 140
how sublime . . . To s. and be strong ENDURANCE, 10
If s. we must, let's s. on the heights SUFFERING, 8

T

talking for thirty-five years he had not stopped t.
SCIENTISTS, 16

Frenchman must be always t.
FRANCE, 9

good newspaper, . . . is a nation t. to itself
JOURNALISM, 23

I wouldn't be . . . t. to someone like you
SNOBBERY, 2

People t. without speaking
FUTILITY, 10

T. and eloquence are not the same
SPEECH, 11

T. of Michelangelo
WOMEN, 32

While we're t., time will have meanly run on
PRESENT, 9

tall Let our children grow t.
TALENT, 7

tally-ho Maybe it's that t. lads attitude
INSULTS, 38

tambourine Hey! Mr T. Man
LEISURE, 2

tame the tongue can no man t.
SPEECH, 6

tamper Who am I to t. with a masterpiece
CONCEIT, 27

tangerine t. trees and marmalade skies
IMAGINATION, 7

tankard heart which grief hath cankered . . . remedy – the T.
ALCOHOL, 18

tanned getting more t. and more tired
ROYALTY, 24

tapeworm as fitted to survive . . . as as a t.
EVOLUTION, 9

Tara's through T. halls
IRELAND, 11

tarmac t. over the whole of England
CONSERVATION, 2

tarnished neither t. nor afraid
COURAGE, 6

tarry having lost . . . your prime, You may for ever t.
MARRIAGE, 71

Tartar Scratch the Russian and . . . find the T.
RUSSIA, 4

tarts He's lost us the t.' vote
RESPONSIBILITY, 6; JOURNALISM, 16

she made some t.
FOOD, 12

The Queen of Hearts She made some t.
NURSERY RHYMES, 51

Tarzan Me? T.
CINEMA, 13

task No t. is a long one but the t. on which one dare not start
BEGINNING, 6

The trivial round, the common t.
SIMPLICITY, 4

Tasmanians the T. . . . are now extinct
ADULTERY, 5

taste bad t. is better than no t.
TASTE, 1

different t. in jokes is a . . . strain on the affections
HUMOUR, 11

Drink deep, or t. not the Pierian spring
KNOWLEDGE, 30

Every one to his t.
DIFFERENCE, 2

great common sense and good t.
CHARACTER, 22

I suspect his t. in higher matters
FOOD, 29

no t. when you married me
TASTE, 7

people who always go on about . . . good t.
TASTE, 5

Shakespeare, undoubtedly wanted t.
SHAKESPEARE, 18

T. is the feminine of genius
TASTE, 2

the bouquet is better than the t.
ALCOHOL, 49

the t. by which he is . . . relished
WRITING, 37

The t. was that of the little crumb of madeleine
MEMORY, 11

Things sweet to t. prove . . . sour
REGRET, 14

willing to t. any drink once
DRINKS, 3

tasted Sir, you have t. two whole worms
SPOONERISMS, 5

Some books are to be t.
BOOKS, 3

tastes It is like a cigar. . . . it never t. quite the same
LOVE, 145

Our t. greatly alter
TASTE, 3

There is no accounting for t.
DIFFERENCE, 5

taught a woman who knows all . . . that can be t.
KNOWLEDGE, 9

I forget what I was t.
KNOWLEDGE, 35

tavern A t. chair is the throne
PUBLIC HOUSES, 1

he has . . . opened a t. for his friends
PARASITES, 1

nothing . . . by which so much happiness is produced as by a good t.
PUBLIC HOUSES, 2

There is a t. in the town
PARTING, 2

tawney that t. weed tobacco
SMOKING, 8

tax A hateful t.
TAXATION, 5

For God's sake, madam, don't say that in England for . . . they will surely t. it
TAXATION, 11

hardest thing . . . to understand is income t.
TAXATION, 2

taxation T. without representation
REPRESENTATION, 1

taxes collect legal t. from illegal money
TAXATION, 1

Death and t. and childbirth
EXPEDIENCY, 5

The avoidance of t. . . . still carries . . . reward
TAXATION, 7

taxi done almost every human activity inside a t.
BOASTS, 1

taxis hiring t. . . . handing out redundancy notices to its own workers
INCOMPETENCE, 2

taxpayer The t. is someone who works for the federal government
TAXATION, 9

Tay Beautiful Railway Bridge of the Silv'ry T.
DISASTER, 1

tea Dinner, Lunch and T.
FOOD, 7

honey still for t.
NOSTALGIA, 3

it is just like having a cup of t.
SEX, 44

sometimes counsel take – and sometimes T.
DRINKS, 7

Take some more t.
LANGUAGE, 4

T. for Two, and Two for T.
DRINKS, 5

we drink too much t.
DRINKS, 8

When I makes t. I makes t.
HUMOUR, 39; HUMOUR, 39

teach Don't t. your grandmother
ADVICE, 2

For every person wishing to t.
EDUCATION, 48

He who shall t. the child to doubt
DOUBT, 3

It is no matter what you t. them first
EDUCATION, 26

You can't t. an old dog
OLD AGE, 2

teacher Experience is a good t.
EXPERIENCE, 6

Time is a great t., but . . . kills all its pupils
TIME, 11

teachers We t. can only help . . . as servants
EDUCATION, 38

teaches He who cannot, t.
EDUCATION, 52

teacup Storm in a T.
TRIVIALITY, 7

team Is my t. ploughing
AGRICULTURE, 3

team games The British, being brought up on t.
HOUSES OF PARLIAMENT, 14

tear Every t. from every eye
SORROW, 1

Some stars . . . Fell like a falling t.
STARS, 7

tears blood, toil, t. and sweat
EFFORT, 3

foolish t. upon my grave
HYPOCRISY, 16

He spoke, and loos'd our heart in t.
POETS, 16

If you have t., prepare to shed them
SORROW, 21

in a flood of t. and a Sedan chair
HUMOUR, 35

mine own t. Do scald
SUFFERING, 14

No t. in the writer
WRITING, 7

our t. Thaw not the frost
MOURNING, 14

shed t. when they would devour
HYPOCRISY, 2

T., idle tears
SORROW, 26

T. such as angels weep
SORROW, 12

T. were to me
SORROW, 5

The bitterest t. . . . are for words . . . unsaid and deeds . . . undone
REGRET, 20

the land of t.
SORROW, 19

The smiles, the t., Of boyhood's years
NOSTALGIA, 14

the women whose eyes have been washed . . . with t.
WOMEN, 29

Violet Elizabeth dried her t.
THREATS, 1

With silence and t.
SEPARATION, 2

teas T., Where small talk dies
CONVERSATION, 9

tease The fleas that t. in the high Pyrenees
NONSENSE, 3

tea-stirring t. times
PRESENT, 11

teatray Like a t. in the sky
NONSENSE, 5

teche gladly wolde he lerne, and gladly t.
CHARACTER, 5

technological For t. man it is time
TECHNOLOGY, 10

technology t. . . . indistinguishable from magic
TECHNOLOGY, 3

tedious People are either charming or t.
CHARM, 4

They shorten t. nights
SEX, 10

tedium t. is the very basis of mourning
BOREDOM, 4

teeth I had braces on my t. and got high marks
APPEARANCE, 24

I have let dentists ride roughshod over my t.
TEETH, 1

I'll dispose of my t. as I see fit
TEETH, 2

It is necessary to clean the t. frequently
ETIQUETTE, 4

natural false t.
TEETH, 3

take the bull between the t.
MIXED METAPHORS, 3

taking out his false t. and hurling them at his wife
MARRIAGE, 51

They will steal the very t. out of your mouth
THEFT, 2

to lose one's t. is a catastrophe
TEETH, 5

white sharp t.
SUPERNATURAL, 16

teething they escaped t.
TEETH, 4

teetotaller a beer t., not a champagne t.
ALCOHOL, 54

no woman should marry a t.
ABSTINENCE, 10

teetotallers T. lack the sympathy
ABSTINENCE, 3

telephone I don't know his t. number
NUMBERS, 2

telephone-exchange we are supposing the brain . . . more than a t.
MIND, 7

television but to do it on t.
TELEVISION, 2

eats, sleeps and watches the t.
WOMAN'S ROLE, 2

stay at home and see bad t. for nothing
CINEMA, 5

T. brought the brutality of war
TELEVISION, 4; WAR, 66

T. is more interesting than people
TELEVISION, 1

T.? No good will come
TELEVISION, 5

T. . . . permits you to be entertained in your living room
TELEVISION, 3

tell do not t. them so
WISDOM, 12

How could they t.
POLITICIANS, 65

people who love to t. us what to do
ENGLISH, 22

T. the truth
TRUTH, 3

you must not kiss and t.
SECRECY, 7

you never can t.. That's a principle
PRINCIPLES, 4

thorn A rose without a t. ADMIRATION, 7
thorough How . . . t. these Germans always managed to be GERMANY, 5
thoroughness with the t. of a mind that reveres details UNDERSTANDING, 7
thou Book of Verse – and T. CONTENTMENT, 3
thought a green t. in a green shade OBLIVION, 3
A library is t. in cold storage BOOKS, 38
A society . . . of individuals . . . capable of original t. would probably be unendurable IDEAS, 6
A t. is often original ORIGINALITY, 3
conversation must be an exchange of t. CONVERSATION, 7
evil is wrought by want of t. EVIL, 10
Learning without t. is labour lost KNOWLEDGE, 10
My t. is me THINKING, 9
Only a residual fraction is t. BUREAUCRACY, 8
pale cast of t. CONSCIENCE, 5
Reading . . . ingenious device for avoiding t. READING, 6
sessions of sweet silent t. REGRET, 18
silent form, dost tease us out of t. ETERNITY, 3
something between a thing and a t. PAINTING, 8
T. must be divided against itself UNDERSTANDING, 6
t. only to justify their injustices HUMAN NATURE, 24
t. without learning is perilous KNOWLEDGE, 10
Two souls' with but a single t. LOVE, 84
What was once t. IDEAS, 1
will bear to be read twice, . . . was t. twice WRITING, 32
thoughtless t. are rarely wordless SPEECH, 6
thoughtlessness In the sex-war t. is the weapon of the male SEXES, 6
thoughts Great t. come from the heart THINKING, 12
Keep off your t. from things that are past PAST, 8
man whose second t. are good THINKING, 1
our life is what our t. make it LIFE, 8
sensations rather than of t. SENSATION, 1
speech only to conceal their t. HUMAN NATURE, 24
Speech . . . to disguise . . . t. SPEECH, 16
Suspicions amongst t. SUSPICION, 1
the meanest flower . . . can give T. NATURE, 21
To understand God's t. STATISTICS, 7
we ought to control our t. SELF-CONTROL, 3
thousand I can draw for a t. pounds CONVERSATION, 5
I could be a good woman if I had five t. MONEY, 47
if I were a t. years old MEMORY, 2
One t. years more. That's all *Homo sapiens* has MANKIND, 35
the face that launch'd a t. ships BEAUTY, 25
The thought of two t. people crunching celery FOOD, 46
Victory has a t. fathers SUCCESS, 6
What's a t. dollars MONEY, 32; PUNS, 13
thread from eternity spinning the t. of your being DESTINY, 2
threads well-belovèd's hair has t. of grey AGE, 69
threat one can . . . see in a little girl the t. of a woman CHILDREN, 20
three A committee should consist of t. men DEMOCRACY, 18
There are only t. events in a man's life LIFE AND DEATH, 7
there are only t. things to see PHILISTINISM, 5
thought t. times before taking action CAUTION, 10
T. French hens NURSERY RHYMES, 55
t. fundamental truths OBJECTIVITY, 3
T. little maids from school CHILDREN, 23
t. o'clock in the morning courage COURAGE, 24
T. o'clock is always too late or too early DAY, 13
t. things . . . the public will always clamour for NOVELTY, 3
T. years she grew DEATH, 132
we galloped all t. HORSES, 3
who sneaked into my room at t. o'clock this morning COMPLAINTS, 5
£300 let loose upon the world with £300 BRITISH, 1
threefold a t. cord is not quickly broken UNITY, 5
three-pipe a t. problem SMOKING, 5
three-sided if triangles invented a god, they would make him t. RELIGION, 48
thrift extravagance, . . . t. and adventure THRIFT, 5
T. has nearly killed her THRIFT, 6
thrive strong shall t. SURVIVAL, 4
throat A good listener is a good talker with a sore t. CONVERSATION, 11
throats cutting each other's t. SLAVERY, 2
throne A man may build . . . a t. of bayonets POWER POLITICS, 4
A tavern chair is the t. PUBLIC HOUSES, 1
barge . . . like a burnished t. ADMIRATION, 13
High on a t. of royal state DEVIL, 10

It helps . . . to remind your bride that you gave up a t. for her MARRIAGE, 132
no middle course between the t. and the scaffold MONARCHY, 7
royal t. of kings ENGLAND, 36
something behind the t. MONARCHY, 15
throve that on which it t. Falls off LOVE, 136
throw t. an egg into an electric fan AMBITION, 9
t. away the dearest thing he ow'd DEATH, 109
thrush That's the wise t. BIRDS, 1
Thucydides the historical works of T. NEWSPAPERS, 6
thumbscrew To the t. and the stake MARTYRDOM, 4
thunder laugh as I pass in t. WEATHER, 23
Thurlow No man . . . so wise as T. looked APPEARANCES, 14
Thursday T.'s child has far to go NURSERY RHYMES, 34
Took ill on T. NURSERY RHYMES, 49
'Twas on a Holy T. CHILDREN, 17
thyself Be so true to t. INTEGRITY, 1
Know then t., presume not God to scan SELF-KNOWLEDGE, 1
Resolve to be t. SELF-KNOWLEDGE, 1
Tiber married to the only man north of the T. . . . untidier than I am MARRIAGE, 128
the River T. foaming with much blood PROPHECY, 11, 14; RACISM, 25
Tiberius Had T. been a cat CATS, 1
tickle a feather to t. the intellect PUNS, 10
ticky-tacky They're all made out of t. HOUSES, 4
tide a t. in the affairs of men OPPORTUNITY, 16
ever lived in the t. of times REGRET, 16
the full t. of human existence is at Charing-Cross LONDON, 9
The t. is full SEA, 1
The western t. crept up DROWNING, 1
tides the waters of the heart Push in their t. EMOTION, 5
tidings good t. of great joy CHRISTMAS, 8
tie Never mind about my soul . . . get my t. right PAINTING, 5
tiger It is not the ape, nor the t. HUMAN NATURE, 23
The atom bomb is a paper t. NUCLEAR WEAPONS, 12
T.! T.! burning bright ANIMALS, 4
tigers Dictators ride to and fro upon t. AUTHORITARIANISM, 3
For tamed and shabby t. ANIMALS, 12
reactionaries are paper t. POLITICS, 53
tightrope You may reasonably expect a man to walk a t. safely NUCLEAR WEAPONS, 17
tile it's not even red brick, but white t. CLASS, 26
timber a . . . soul like season'd t. VIRTUE, 11
replacing some of the t. used up by my books TREES, 6
Timbuctoo On the plains of T. CLERGY, 15
time a book to kill t. CRITICISM, 32
Aging . . . the only . . . way to live a long t. LONGEVITY, 1
A Good T. Was Had by All PLEASURE, 28
And t., that takes survey of all the world, Must have a stop DEATH, 110
annihilate but space and t. LOVE, 99
Art is long, and T. is fleeting MORTALITY, 14
As if you could kill t. TIME, 39
As t. goes by TIME, 20
As T. Goes By NOSTALGIA, 2
a t. to be born, and a t. to die TIME, 12
big man has no t. FAME, 9
But get me to the church on t. MARRIAGE, 78
chronicle of wasted t. HISTORY, 2
do not squander t. TIME, 19
Even such is T. FAITH, 17
For technological man it is t. TECHNOLOGY, 10
Had we but world enough, and t. SHYNESS, 1
He hath shook hands with t. DEATH, 51
Hurry! I never hurry. I have no t. to hurry HASTE, 12
I haven't got t. to be tired WORK, 27
I . . . may be some t. LAST WORDS, 48
inaudible and noiseless foot of T. TIME, 33
time irretrievable t. is flying TIME, 40
I shall lose no t. in reading it INATTENTION, 1
It is only t. that weighs TIME, 29
it's for such a long t. DEATH, 87
killing t. Is only . . . another of the multifarious ways By which Time kills us TIME, 36
make the beat keep t. with short steps FUNERALS, 1
Men talk of killing t. TIME, 13
moment of t. LAST WORDS, 22
My t. has not yet come POSTERITY, 1
Never before have we had so little t. HASTE, 9
Never the t. and the place PERVERSITY, 2
not had the t. to make it shorter VERBOSITY, 5

the fruit Of that forbidden t. — SIN, 16
The t. of liberty must be refreshed — FREEDOM, 21
the t. of life — GARDENS, 3
the t. of the knowledge of good and evil — GARDENS, 3
t. of life is green — REALITY, 3; THEORY, 4
treen In old time we had t. chalices and golden priests — CLERGY, 8
trees Loveliest of t., the cherry — TREES, 5
T. are poems — CONSERVATION, 4
Trelawny shall T. die — EXECUTION, 10
tremble Our hand will not t. — RUSSIAN REVOLUTION, 1
t. like a guilty thing surprised — DOUBT, 8
trembled And t. with fear at your frown — MEMORY, 7
trembles And Satan t. — PRAYER, 10
trenches digging t. and trying on gas-masks — WORLD WAR II, 1
trial T. by jury . . . a delusion — JUSTICE, 5
triangles if t. invented a god, they would make him three-sided — RELIGION, 48
tribe Abou Ben Adhem (may his t. increase!) — DREAMS, 11
Mankind is not a t. — MANKIND, 12
Richer than all his t. — LOVE, 128
tribute the vain t. of a smile — POETS, 10
trick When in doubt, win the t. — SPORT AND GAMES, 7
trifle Is t. sufficient for sweet — FOOD, 9
trifles observance of t. — TRIVIALITY, 5
snapper-up of unconsidered t. — BUSINESS, 19
trigger Whose Finger do you want on the T. — GOVERNMENT, 3
Trinian's Though loaded firearms were strictly forbidden at St T. — WEAPONS, 7
Trinity I the T. illustrate — DRINKS, 2
the Holy T. of Science — SCIENCE, 22
Triton Old T. blow his wreathed horn — DISCONTENT, 10
triumph One more devils'-t. and sorrow for angels — DAMNATION, 1
We t. without glory — VICTORY, 3
triumphed So I t. ere my passion — PASSION, 8
trivial mighty contests rise from t. things — RESULTS, 5
The t. round, the common task — SIMPLICITY, 4
triviality we are deluded by t. — DELUSION, 5
Trojan open that Pandora's Box . . . T. 'orses will jump out — MIXED METAPHORS, 1
Trojans Do not trust the horse, T. — MISTRUST, 11
troops t. of unrecording friends — LIFE, 48
trot I don't t. it out and about — VIRTUE, 6
trouble a lot of t. in his life — WORRY, 3
A t. shared — WORRY, 1
a woman is on a . . . hunt for t. — MARRIAGE, 50
it saves me the t. of liking them — NASTINESS, 2
man . . . is . . . full of t. — HUMAN CONDITION, 3
telling one's t. does not make it better — DISILLUSION, 5
Our progress . . . Is t. and care — LIFE, 32
Prostitution . . . keeps her out of t. — SEX, 21
troubled let not your heart be t. — PEACE, 3
troubles Don't meet t. half-way — WORRY, 2
I have had t. enough — MISFORTUNE, 5
pack up your t. in your old kit-bag — OPTIMISM, 13
take arms against a sea of t. — SUICIDE, 12
troublesome t. . . . bondage of Rhyming — POETRY, 32
trousers bottoms of my t. rolled — OLD AGE, 17
I shall wear white flannel t. — OLD AGE, 18
man should never put on his best t. — FREEDOM, 20
She is trying to wear the t. of Winston Churchill — POLITICIANS, 36
trout as when you find a t. in the milk — PROOF, 6
trowel laid on with a t. — EXCESS, 9
Troy from the shores of T. came destined an exile — ENDURANCE, 23
Now there are fields where T. once was — DECLINE, 8
true a great advantage for . . . philosophy to be . . . t. — PHILOSOPHY, 13
All one's inventions are t. — POETRY, 15
A thing is not necessarily t. — MARTYRDOM, 5
because a novel's invented, it isn't t. — NOVELS, 12
Be so t. to thyself — INTEGRITY, 1
be yourself, imperial, plain and t. — SINCERITY, 1
false to his friends . . . t. to the public — HONESTY, 3
Geometry is not t. — MATHEMATICS, 8
He said t. things — WORDS, 3
if they keep on saying it . . . it will be t. — JOURNALISM, 8
it's . . . more important for a theory to be shapely, than . . . t. — THEORY, 5
Journalists say a thing that they know isn't t. — JOURNALISM, 8

Many a t. word — TRUTH, 2
Mr. Speaker, I said the honorable member was a liar it is t. and I am sorry for it — APOLOGIES, 4
No man worth having is t. to his wife — UNFAITHFULNESS, 7
One religion is as t. as another — RELIGION, 11
Small service is t. service — SERVICE, 5
The religions we call false were once t. — RELIGION, 24
to thine own self be t. — BORROWING, 8; INTEGRITY, 6
T. and False are attributes of speech, not of things — TRUTH, 26
T. love never grows old — LOVE, 11
t. to you, darlin', in my fashion — FAITHFULNESS, 6
truism is . . . none the less t. — SAYINGS, 7
whatsoever things are t. — VIRTUE, 4
truffles a swine to show you where the t. are — VULGARITY, 1
truism A t. is on that account none the less true — SAYINGS, 7
truly A t. great man — GREATNESS, 1
trumpet the t. shall sound — DEATH, 28
trunkless Two vast and t. legs of stone — MEMORIALS, 11
trust I don't t. him. We're friends — FRIENDSHIP, 11
Never t. a husband too far — TRUST, 4
never t. a woman — AGE, 66
Never t. the man who . . . hath injured you — TRUST, 2
the one God whose worshippers . . . still t. in Him — LUCK, 7
the right of governing was not property but a t. — GOVERNMENT, 9
t. ye not in a friend — TRUST, 1
Where large sums of money are concerned, . . . t. nobody — MONEY, 17
trustful It takes a long while for a . . . t. person to reconcile himself to . . . God — FAITH, 15
trusting it never extended to t. him — HITLER, 2
truth And seek for t. in the groves of Academe — EDUCATION, 22
any t. but from a clear perception — TRUTH, 7
A platitude is simply a t. repeated — SAYINGS, 1
a short armistice with t. — TRUTH, 16
A t. that's told with bad intent — TRUTH, 13
a t. universally acknowledged — MARRIAGE, 10
Beauty is t., t. beauty — BEAUTY, 24; TRUTH, 30
before the t. has got its boots on — LYING, 6
cheated into passion, but . . . reasoned into t. — TRUTH, 23
cinema is t. twenty-four times a second — CINEMA, 11
Cynicism is an unpleasant way of saying the t. — CYNICISM, 2
dearer still is t. — TRUTH, 8
economical with the t. — LYING, 3
Every man has a right to utter what he thinks t. — FREEDOM, 22
few enthusiasts . . . speak the t. — ENTHUSIASM, 2
hard to believe . . . a man is telling the t. — LYING, 4
He believes . . . that there is such a thing as t. — POLITICIANS, 32
I am the way, the t., and the life — CHRISTIANITY, 17
if the people . . . can be reached with the t. — DEMOCRACY, 14
If you do not tell the t. about yourself — HONESTY, 13
in the end the t. will conquer — TRUTH, 44
it cannot compel anyone to tell the t. — LAW, 8
It takes two to speak the t. — TRUTH, 40
Let us begin by committing ourselves to the t. — TRUTH, 35
loving Christianity better than T. — CHRISTIANITY, 22
mainly he told the t. — LYING, 18
Much t. is spoken, . . . more . . . concealed — TRUTH, 19
My way of joking is to tell the t. — TRUTH, 38
Nobody speaks the t. when — LYING, 5
No poet ever interpreted nature . . . as a lawyer interprets t. — LAW, 12
not even Marx is more precious . . . than the t. — TRUTH, 42
Now I may wither into the t. — AGE, 71
Perjury . . . is t. that is shamefaced — TRUTH, 20
Photography is t. — CINEMA, 4
polite by telling the t. — COURTESY, 3
Pride and T. . . . That long to give themselves for wage — AGE, 70
put him in possession of t. — TRUTH, 31
Some men love t. so much — TRUTH, 15
speaking nothing but the t. — HONESTY, 12
the laws of poetic t. and poetic beauty — POETRY, 2
the t. is not in us — SIN, 5
the t. of imagination — IMAGINATION, 6; TRUTH, 28
the t. shall make you free — TRUTH, 11
the unclouded face of t. suffer wrong — JOURNALISM, 27
The worst enemy of t. and freedom — MAJORITY, 4
those who live . . . believe . . . to be the t. — HONESTY, 4
to the dead we owe only t. — RESPECT, 4
T. be veiled — OPTIMISM, 24

U

unremitting That u. humanity — DICKENS, 1
unrequited Self-love seems so often u. — CONCEIT, 13
unsaid The bitterest tears . . . are for words . . . u. and deeds . . . undone — REGRET, 20
unsatisfied It is exquisite, and it leaves one u. — SMOKING, 23
unsavoury indefatigable and u. engine of pollution — DOGS, 12
unsealed my lips are not yet u. — SECRECY, 2
unseemly an u. exposure of the mind — NASTINESS, 3
unseen to deny the existence of an u. kingdom is bad — SPECULATION, 1
unselfishness nothing . . . quite matches the sympathetic u. of an oyster — PERFECTION, 7; SELFLESSNESS, 3
unshriven I am curious to see what happens . . . to one who dies u. — LAST WORDS, 50
unsoundness no person can be a poet . . . without . . . u. of mind — POETRY, 27
unspeakable the psychopathologist the u. — PSYCHIATRY, 7
the u. in full pursuit of the uneatable — HUNTING, 8
unstoned I wouldn't have left a turn u. — CRITICISM, 54
untidier married to the only man north of the Tiber . . . u. than I am — MARRIAGE, 128
untravelled Gleams that u. world — EXPERIENCE, 20
untruth The camera . . . an accessory to u. — PHOTOGRAPHY, 3
unupblown Nurse u. — BREVITY, 9
unused left over from last year u. — ADVICE, 8
unwashed The great U. — PUBLIC, 5
unwholesome Boys . . . are u. companions for grown people — CHILDREN, 31

up *How to be one u.* — ONE-UPMANSHIP, 3
I saw it at a disadvantage – the curtain was u. — CRITICISM, 55
u. with which I will not put — GRAMMAR, 4
upbringing the u. a nun would envy — INNOCENCE, 8
upper Like many of the u. class — ARISTOCRACY, 2
the person that . . . has the u. hand will inevitably give place to another — CHARACTER, 16
the u. classes Have still the u. hand — ARISTOCRACY, 6; STATELY HOMES, 2
upper-middle Shirley Williams . . . a member of the u. class — CLASS, 38
upright man of life u. — RIGHTEOUSNESS, 4
upstairs U. and downstairs And in my lady's chamber — NURSERY RHYMES, 13
Uriah U., . . . made a ghastly writhe — SERVILITY, 3
urine What is man . . . a . . . machine for turning . . . the red wine of Shiraz into u. — MANKIND, 7
urn Can storied u. . . . Back to its mansion call the fleeting breath — DEATH, 57
usage if u. so choose, with whom resides the decision — WORDS, 10
use let u. be preferred before uniformity — HOUSES, 1
no reason . . . these machines will ever force themselves into general u. — TECHNOLOGY, 14
what is the u. of a book — BOOKS, 12
What is the u. of a new-born child — PURPOSE, 2
useful not merely . . . u. and ornamental — PURPOSE, 8
the most u. thing about a principle . . . sacrificed to expediency — EXPEDIENCY, 4
useless All Art is quite u. — ART, 32
A u. life is an early death — PURPOSE, 3
most beautiful things . . . are the most u. — BEAUTY, 33
uses all the u. of this world — WORLD-WEARINESS, 6
usual Business as u. — BRITISH, 7
Utopia Not in U., . . . Or some secreted island — FRENCH REVOLUTION, 5
U-turn U. if you want to — INFLEXIBILITY, 3

V

vacant In v. or in pensive mood — SOLITUDE, 15
vacation a change of nuisances is as good as a v. — CHANGE, 14
vacuum A v. can only exist . . . by the things which enclose it — SCIENCE, 16
vagabond a fugitive and a v. — PUNISHMENT, 2
vaguery For V. in the Field — INCOMPETENCE, 1
vain generous aspirings implanted in her in v. — SMOKING, 10
thou shalt not take the name of . . . God in v. — GOD, 10
V. are the thousand creeds — BELIEF, 3
V. wisdom all, and false philosophy — WISDOM, 19
vale *ave atque v.* — GREETINGS, 1
valet No man is a hero to his v. — FAMILIARITY, 2
valiant v. never taste of death but once — COWARDICE, 9

valid If . . . 'feeling good' could decide, drunkenness would be . . . supremely v. — DRUNKENNESS, 13
valley One sees great things from the v. — PERSPECTIVE, 2
valleys Piping down the v. wild — MUSIC, 12
valour The better part of v. is discretion — SELF-PRESERVATION, 8
valuable riches to be a v. thing — WEALTH, 27
value All knowledge is of itself of some v. — KNOWLEDGE, 23
Friendship . . . has no survival v. — FRIENDSHIP, 22
the price of everything and the v. of nothing — CYNICISM, 5
values ideas are of more importance than v. — INTELLECTUALS, 4
Victorian v. . . . . were the v. when our country — MORALITY, 22
Van Gogh V.'s ear for music — INSULTS, 44
vanished as rare things will, it v. — TRANSIENCE, 9
vanity all is v. and vexation of spirit — TRANSIENCE, 5
The v. of human life is like a river — LIFE, 39
v. and love . . . universal characteristics — WOMEN, 23
V. dies hard — CONCEIT, 17
V. of vanities — GREATNESS, 14; WISDOM, 25
V. plays lurid tricks — CONCEIT, 6
vanquished redress of the grievances of the v. — WAR, 27
variable light-headed, v. men — MARRIAGE, 111
varies quality of moral behaviour v. — MORALITY, 7
variety a sad v. of woe — SORROW, 15
custom stale her infinite v. — ADMIRATION, 14
V.'s the very spice of life — CHANGE, 4
various man so v., that he seem'd to be — HUMAN NATURE, 9
vary money appears to v. — MONEY, 25
vasectomy V. means not ever having to say you're sorry — CONTRACEPTION, 1
vast The universe ought to be presumed too v. — UNIVERSE, 10
Vatican One of the best warehouses I ever see was the V. — EUROPE, 19
the V., the Treasury and the miners — DIPLOMACY, 2
vaulting 'Fan v.' . . . belongs to the 'Last-supper-carved-on-a-peach-stone' — ARCHITECTURE, 5
veal I could eat one of Bellamy's v. pies — LAST WORDS, 52; FOOD, 41
vegetables you must talk to your v. — GARDENS, 5
vegetarianism useless for the sheep to pass resolutions in favour of v. — ARGUMENTS, 9
v. is the only road to salvation of some — HEALTH AND HEALTHY LIVING, 8
vegetarians V. have wicked, shifty eyes — PREJUDICE, 4
vegetate When I am in the country I wish to v. — COUNTRYSIDE, 5
veil the v. of the temple was rent in twain — LAST WORDS, 11
the v. which those who live call life — DEATH, 113
v. which those who live Call life — LIFE, 45
veils v. of the morning — PEACE, 18
Velasquez Why drag in V. — CONCEIT, 22
venerability If you live long enough, the v. factor creeps in — LONGEVITY, 3
vengeance No one delights more in v. than a woman — REVENGE, 11; WOMEN, 43
venial than that one soul . . . should commit one single v. sin — SIN, 18
Venice She only went to V. — INSULTS, 24
V. is like eating . . . chocolate liqueurs — VENICE, 2
V., the eldest Child of Liberty — VENICE, 3
ventured Nothing v. — OPPORTUNITY, 5
Venus She is V. when she smiles — COMPLIMENTS, 4
verb a v. meaning 'to believe falsely' — BELIEF, 8
verbose Revolutions are always v. — REVOLUTION, 7
verbosity inebriated with . . . his own v. — VERBOSITY, 1
Verdi strains of V. will come back to you tonight — HUMOUR, 45
verdict Sentence first – v. afterwards — INJUSTICE, 4
verification bring about the v. of his own prophecies — PROPHECY, 13
verify Always v. your references — RESEARCH, 4
veritas *In vino v.* — ALCOHOL, 17
vermin lower than v. — POLITICS, 7
vernal One impulse from a v. wood — LEARNING, 10
Versailles a lady at the court of V. — LANGUAGE, 1
verse Curst be the v. — POETRY, 35
Having v. set to music — POETRY, 50
If Galileo had said in v. that the world moved — POETRY, 17
no v. can give pleasure . . . that is written by drinkers of water — WATER, 1
Writing free v. — POETRY, 17
verses v. . . . as a literary performance — POETRY, 52
versified excellent poets that have never v. — POETS, 11
versifiers now swarm many v. — POETS, 11

W

No one can guarantee success in w.   WAR, 29
Now w. has a bad conscience   WAR, 55
Older men declare w.   WAR, 50
only twenty seconds of w. to destroy him   WAR, 7
on this wall will hang my weapons and my lyre, discharged from
the w.   SEX, 23
Stand your ground . . . if they mean to have a w., let it begin
here   WAR, 85
Television brought the brutality of w.   TELEVISION, 4; WAR, 66
that devil's madness – W.   WAR, 107
the . . . barbarity of w. . . . forces men . . . to commit acts
    WAR, 56
The first casualty when w. comes   WAR, 54
The quickest way of ending a w.   WAR, 81
there was w. in heaven   DEVIL, 4
the second rule of w.   WAR, 72
The W. between Men and Women   SEXES, 25
the W. is being deliberately prolonged   WAR, 104
the w. of the giants is over   WORLD WAR II, 16
The w. we have just been through, . . . is not to be compared
    WAR, 135
The wrong w., at the wrong place   WAR, 13
they'll give a w. and nobody will come   WAR, 98
this liking for w.   WAR, 8
this massed multitude of silent witnesses to . . . w.   WAR, 42
This w. . . . is a w. to end w.   WAR, 63
this w. . . . which did not justify the sacrifice of a single
mother's son   WAR, 84
Those who can win a w. well   WAR AND PEACE, 4
w. can only be abolished through w.   WAR, 65
w. ended, the explosions stopped   WAR AND PEACE, 9
W. even to the knife   WAR, 22
W. hath no fury like a non-combatant   WAR, 70
W. is, after all, the universal perversion   WAR, 89
W. is an organized bore   WAR, 49
W. is capitalism   WAR, 116
W. is hell   WAR, 111
W. is like love   WAR, 16
W. is not an adventure   WAR, 97
W. is Peace   OPPOSITES, 5
W. is the continuation of politics   MISQUOTATIONS, 14; WAR, 30, 64
W. is too important   OFFICERS, 5
W. is war   WAR, 79
W. knows no power   WAR, 19
W. makes rattling good history   WAR AND PEACE, 7
w. minus the shooting   SPORT AND GAMES, 15
W. should belong to the tragic past   WAR, 86
W. which . . . left nothing to be desired   WAR, 15
W. will never cease until babies   WAR, 67
we are . . . in the midst of a cold w.   COLD WAR, 1
We are not at w. with Egypt   WAR, 36
We have all lost the w.   WAR, 61
What they could do with round here is a good w.   WAR, 14
when there was w., he went   PUBLIC, 3
When the rich wage w.   POVERTY AND WEALTH, 7
when they learn how we began this w.   WORLD WAR II, 25
When you're at w. you think about a better life   WAR AND
PEACE, 14
Who live under the shadow of a w.   WAR, 112
wards key deftly in the oiled w.   SLEEP, 13
Ware And I should dine at W.   MARRIAGE, 42
warehouses One of the best w. I ever see was the Vatican
    EUROPE, 19
Waring What's become of W.   ABSENCE, 5
warmongers w. who . . . have others pull the chestnuts out of
the fire   POLITICS, 70
warmth No w., no cheerfulness, no healthful ease   MONTHS, 10
warn the right to be consulted, . . . to encourage, . . . to w.
    MONARCHY, 2
warned my Friends, be w. by me   FOOD, 7
warning will it come without w. Just as I'm picking my nose
    LOVE, 18
warrior the British w. queen   BRITAIN, 7
wars All w. are planned by old men   WAR, 93
All w. are popular for the first thirty days   WAR, 105
end to the beginnings of all w.   WAR, 95
Just like an old liberal Between the w.   LIBERALISM, 3
military don't start w.   WAR, 130
my w. Were global   WAR, 91
No kingdom has . . . had as many . . . w. as the kingdom of
Christ   CHRISTIANITY, 34
Still w. and lechery   SEX, 51

W. are not won by evacuations   WORLD WAR II, 14
W. cannot be fought with nuclear weapons   NUCLEAR
WEAPONS, 13
W., conflict, it's all business   WAR, 26
w., horrible w.   PROPHECY, 1
warts pimples, w., and everything as you see me   REALISM, 1
war-war To jaw-jaw is better than to w.   DIPLOMACY, 5
wary the w. fox said . . . to the sick lion   MISTRUST, 5
wash Don't w. your dirty linen   GOSSIP, 2
I do, and I also w. and iron them   HOUSEWORK, 5
washed Pilate . . . w. his hands   GUILT, 3
washing painting a face and not w.   APPEARANCE, 15
wasps w. and hornets break through   LAW, 27
waste biggest waste of water in the country   CONSERVATION, 6
Far too good to w. on children   YOUTH, 17
The years to come seemed w. of breath   FLYING, 4
W. not, want not   WASTE, 1
wasted most w. of all days   LAUGHTER, 6
wasting she did not believe in w. her effects   THREATS, 1
watch Either he's dead or my w. has stopped   DEATH, 82
keeping w. over their flock by night   CHRISTMAS, 8
The W. on the Rhine   RIVERS, 4
w. and pray   IMPERFECTION, 4
why not carry a w.   CLOCKS, 1
watch-dog to hear the w.'s honest bark   DOGS, 5
watched A w. pot   PATIENCE, 1
watches 'Tis with our judgments as our w.   OPINIONS, 4
watchmaker I should have become a w.   NUCLEAR WEAPONS, 5
watchman only one man . . . can count on steady work – the
night w.   THEATRE, 2
watch-tower To hear the lark . . . From his w. in the skies
    BIRDS, 8
water better deeds Shall be in w. writ   MEMORIALS, 2
biggest waste of w. in the country   WATER, 7
Dripping w. hollows out a stone   PERSISTENCE, 1
half the landscape is . . . covered by useless w.   SEASIDE, 4
He who drinks a tumbler of London w.   WATER, 9
Human beings were invented by w.   WATER, 8
I came like W.   LIFE AND DEATH, 5
if I were under w. I would scarcely kick   MELANCHOLY, 6
impressions . . . lasting as . . . an oar upon the w.
    INSIGNIFICANCE, 1
It is with our passions as it is with fire and w.   PASSION, 4
Like a bridge over troubled w.   COMFORT, 4
like throwing w. into the sea   CHARITY, 11
no verse can give pleasure . . . that is written by drinkers of w.
    WATER, 6
Streets full of w.   TELEGRAMS, 3; VENICE, 1
the w. that was made wine   ALCOHOL, 14
virtues we write in w.   MEMORIALS, 10
w. flowed like champagne   ABSTINENCE, 4
W. is H$_2$O, hydrogen two parts, oxygen one   SCIENCE, 27
w., is unsuitable in colour   WATER, 5
w. still keeps falling over   WATER, 1
W., water, every where   WATER, 2
Water, w., every where   WATER, 2
when I makes w. I makes w.   HUMOUR, 39
watering a-w. the last year's crop   FUTILITY, 6
Waterloo Battle of W.   WAR, 80, 128
Every man meets his W.   DEFEAT, 6
waters dreadful noise of w. in my ears   DROWNING, 2
stolen w. are sweet   SECRECY, 5
the earth shall be full . . . as the w. cover the sea   PEACE, 1
the Spirit of God moved upon . . . the w.   CREATION, 2
the w. of the heart Push in their tides   EMOTION, 5
water-trough A snake came to my w.   WEATHER, 15
Watson Mr W., come here; I want you   SUMMONS, 3
waves w. make towards the pebbled shore   TIME, 34
waxworks w. inhabited by gramophones   WORDS, 15
way A man . . . is *so* in the w.   MEN, 5
blow out your candle . . . to find your w.   GUIDANCE, 2
catch the nearest w.   KINDNESS, 4
I am the w., the truth, and the life   CHRISTIANITY, 17
in every war they kill you a new w.   PROGRESS, 10
plowman homeward plods his weary w.   DAY, 6
The w. to a man's heart   LOVE, 10
The w. to dusty death   LIFE, 43
though hell should bar the w.   DETERMINATION, 13
w. of all flesh   DEATH, 39; HUMAN NATURE, 21
woman has her w.   SEXES, 11
ways She dwelt among the untrodden w.   LONELINESS, 9
We have w. of making men talk   MISQUOTATIONS, 4

whipping   W. and abuse are like laudanum   CRUELTY, 5
who shall scape w.   MERIT, 6
whirlwind   sown the wind . . . reap the w.   RETRIBUTION, 5
whisker   can't speak above a w.   PUNS, 12
whisky   nicest boy who ever committed the sin of w.
   ALCOHOL, 59
That w. priest   CLERGY, 7
with education and w. the price it is   CHARACTER, 25
whispered   it's w. every where   SECRECY, 8
whispering   w. sound of the cool colonnade   TREES, 3
whisperings   It keeps eternal w. around   SEA, 8
whistle   I heard the bullets w., . . . charming in the sound
   WAR, 123
So was hir joly w. wel y-wet   ALCOHOL, 20
W. a Happy Tune   WHISTLING, 2
W. and she'll come to you   SUMMONS, 2
whistled   a young man who would . . . play his music and be w.
at for it   MUSIC, 19
whistles   They hang us now in Shrewsbury jail: The w. blow
forlorn   EXECUTION, 11
whistling   W. aloud to bear his courage up   WHISTLING, 1
white   architecture . . . only passers-by who can contemplate it
. . . are those . . . with a w. stick and a dog   ARCHITECTURE, 6
Britain . . . is going to be forged in the w. heat of this
revolution   SOCIALISM, 15
'E was w., clear w., inside   APPEARANCES, 16
If the w. man says he does   RACISM, 18
it's not even red brick, but w. tile   CLASS, 26
I used to be Snow W.   PURITY, 6
I want to be the w. man's brother   RACISM, 13
makes a Negro unpleasant to w. folk   RACISM, 22
my soul is w.   RACISM, 5
One black, and one w., and two khaki   RACISM, 1
so-called w. races   RACISM, 10
Take up the W. Man's burden –   RACISM, 14
the silk stockings and w. bosoms . . . excite my amorous
propensities   LUST, 3
The w. man knows how to make everything   CHARITY, 19
When a w. man in Africa   RACISM, 17
When the w. man came we had the land   RACISM, 11
Whitehall   W. . . . our attempts to be fair to everybody
   BRITAIN, 3
White House   gathered together at the W.   TALENT, 5
Log-cabin to W.   ACHIEVEMENT, 8
no whitewash at the W.   TRUTH, 34
standing between Nixon and the W.   POLITICIANS, 54
whites   because the w. oppressed us yesterday   POWER, 16
the w. of their eyes   WAR, 88
whitewash   no w. at the White House   TRUTH, 34
whither   w. thou goest, I will go   LOYALTY, 5
Whitman   Walt W. who laid end to end   POETS, 50
whizz-kid   power before his hair turned white was called a w.
   POWER, 13
who   W. is Silvia   ADMIRATION, 16
w. you are, you aren't anybody   FAME, 17
whole   a w. is that which has a beginning, a middle, and an end
   PLAYS, 1
if she knew the w. of it   LOVE, 141
the greatest happiness of the w.   REPUBLIC, 1
whom   for w. the bell tolls   DEATH, 45
'W. are you?' said he   GRAMMAR, 1
whore   a w. in the kitchen and a cook in bed   MARRIAGE, 67
I am the Protestant w.   RELIGION, 1
the morals of a w., and the manners of a dancing master
   CRITICISM, 22
the old man does not care for the young man's w.   TASTE, 3
The woman's a w.   PROMISCUITY, 3
'Tis Pity She's a w.   BOOK, SONG, AND PLAY TITLES, 9
You can lead a w. to culture   PUNS, 16
whorehouses   virgin territory for w.   AMERICA, 6
whores   After all, we are not political w.   POLITICS, 56
With first-rate sherry flowing into second-rate w.
   MEDIOCRITY, 6
whoreson   w. zed   INSULTS, 34
whoso   W. would be a man   CONFORMITY, 4
why   For every w.   ARGUMENTS, 3
occasions and causes w. and wherefore   EXPLANATIONS, 2
they knew not w.   WAR, 21
W. should I go   FUNERALS, 7
wicked   As long as war is regarded as w.   WAR, 131
no peace . . . unto the w.   PEACE, 2; PUNISHMENT, 5
the men of Sodom were w.   HOMOSEXUALITY, 1

There is a w. inclination . . . to suppose an old man decayed in
his intellects   OLD AGE, 24
to see men w.   REGRET, 21
wickedness   blunders usually do more to shape history than . . .
w.   MISTAKES, 17
men alone are quite capable of every w.   EVIL, 7
The w. of the world   VICE, 4
wide   Things hitherto undone should be given . . . a w. berth
   ORIGINALITY, 1
Widnes   attached even to W.   ENGLAND, 39
widow   a w. . . . is a kind of sinecure   EXPEDIENCY, 7
better to be the w. of a hero than the wife of a coward
   COURAGE, 15
Tonight the American flag floats . . . or Molly Stark sleeps a w.
   WAR, 114
you, my dear, will be my w.   JEALOUSY, 3
widows   When w. exclaim loudly against second marriages
   MARRIAGE, 58
wife   A loving w. will do anything   MARRIAGE, 94
A man should not insult his w. publicly   MARRIAGE, 123
A man who's untrue to his w.   INTELLECTUALS, 2
better to be the widow of a hero than the w. of a coward
   COURAGE, 15
Caesar's w. must be above suspicion   INTEGRITY, 2
chose my w. . . . for . . . qualities as would wear well
   MARRIAGE, 66
Commuter . . . riding to and from his w.   TRAVEL, 31
Here lies my w.   MARRIAGE, 52
He that has no w.   ADVICE, 4
he that is married careth . . . how he may please his w.
   MARRIAGE, 26
He that loves not his w. and children   MARRIAGE, 116
His w. could eat no lean   NURSERY RHYMES, 25
his w. is beautiful and his children smart   TOLERANCE, 5
If a man stays away from his w.   MARRIAGE, 45
I have a w., I have sons   FAMILY, 26
I have quarrelled with my w.   MARRIAGE, 90
light w. doth make a heavy husband   MARRIAGE, 102
man . . . shall cleave unto his w.   WOMEN, 15
Mother to dozens, And nobody's w.   BABIES, 4
My w. hath something in her gizzard   PROVOCATION, 1
My w. . . . is troubled with her lonely life   WOMEN, 62
My w. won't let me   MARRIAGE, 77
No man worth having is true to his w.   UNFAITHFULNESS, 7
one w. and hardly any mistresses   MARRIAGE, 99
remorse for what you have thought about your w.
   MARRIAGE, 97
single man . . . must be in want of a w.   MARRIAGE, 10
stop them catching AIDS . . . the w.   AIDS, 4
taking out his false teeth and hurling them at his w.
   MARRIAGE, 51
that a man lay down his w. for a friend   FRIENDSHIP, 21
that monstrous animal a husband and w.   MARRIAGE, 57
The first w. is matrimony   MARRIAGE, 6
The husband frae the w. despises   MARRIAGE, 32
the w. . . . the weaker vessel   MARRIAGE, 28
the w. who made Britain great again, . . . has to get her
husband to sign her tax form   FEMINISM, 13
When a man opens the car door for his w.   MARRIAGE, 92
Whose w. shall it be   ADULTERY, 7
w. had been unfaithful to me   UNFAITHFULNESS, 3
with a w. to tell him what to do   LAZINESS, 2
Would you allow your w. . . . to read this book   PRUDERY, 1
your w. . . . is a receiver of stolen goods   INSULTS, 21
wifehood   w. and motherhood are but incidental relations
   WOMEN, 75
wig   man with a w. to keep order   APPEARANCE, 38
wild   an old, w., and incomprehensible man   POLITICIANS, 74
mother bore me in the southern w.   RACISM, 5
Wilde   Oscar W. did not dive very deeply   WRITERS, 53
W. grew into a Pierrot   WRITERS, 40
W. performed his life   WRITERS, 30
W.'s voice was of the brown velvet order   WRITERS, 43
wilderness   a little w.   GARDENS, 10
a lodge in some vast w.   SOLITUDE, 3
plants left over from the Edwardian W.   CHANGE, 17
the w. of this world   WORLD, 2
W. is Paradise enow   CONTENTMENT, 3
wild-fowl   more fearful w. than your lion   FEAR, 12
will   complies against his w.   YIELDING, 5
Do what you w.   FREEDOM, 43
formation of the political w. of the nation   POLITICS, 37

His right was clear, his w. was strong   RIGHT, 1
John Stuart Mill By a mighty effort of w.   ECONOMICS, 3
let my w. replace reasoned judgement   AUTHORITARIANISM, 4
Man has his w.   SEXES, 11
The man who leaves money to charity in his w.   BEQUESTS, 3
We have to believe in free w.   CHOICE, 4
Where there's a w.   DETERMINATION, 2
W. ye no come back again   RETURN, 3
You w., Oscar, you w.   IMITATION, 7
William You are old, Father W.   OLD AGE, 10; OLD AGE, 42
Willie Wee W. Winkie runs through the town   NURSERY RHYMES, 64
willow a little tom-tit Sang . . . W., titwillow, titwillow   BIRDS, 4
willows W. whiten, aspens quiver   WEATHER, 26
will-power There is no such thing as a great talent without great w.   DETERMINATION, 4
will-to-live The thing-in-itself, the w., exists . . . in every being   SURVIVAL, 1
Wilson Mr W. . . . is the 14th Mr W.   TITLES, 1
win Heads I w.   VICTORY, 5
high sentiments always w. in the end   NOBILITY, 3
I am certain that we will w. the election with a good majority   SELF-CONFIDENCE, 6
The conventional army loses if it does not w.   WAR, 58
Those who can w. a war well   WAR AND PEACE, 4
wind Blow, blow, thou winter w.   INGRATITUDE, 4
gone with the w.   MEMORY, 6
Gone With the W.   BOOK, SONG, AND PLAY TITLES, 19
It's an ill w.   OPTIMISM, 3
like W. I go   LIFE AND DEATH, 5
of w. and limb   FAITHFULNESS, 2
O Wild West W.   WEATHER, 24
so famous, that it would permit me . . . to break w. in society   FAME, 3
The answer . . . is blowin' in the w.   FREEDOM, 10
The story is like the w.   SENSATION, 2
throw the sand against the w.   FUTILITY, 5
to agitate a bag of w.   FOOTBALL, 9
what w. is to fire   ABSENCE, 6
wherever the w. takes me I travel as a visitor   FREEDOM, 19
Who has seen the w.   WEATHER, 17
words but w.   WORDS, 4
windmills not giants but w.   DELUSION, 2
window Serve up . . . and throw . . . out of the w.   NONSENSE, 21
wine A Flask of W.   CONTENTMENT, 3
A man may surely be allowed to take a glass of w. by his own fireside   FIRE, 4
And drink of my Algerian w.   INSULTS, 7
days of w. and roses   TRANSIENCE, 11
drinks his w. 'mid laughter free   PARTING, 2
drink w. you have the gout   DISEASE, 38
for its poisonous w.   OBLIVION, 2
Frenchmen drink w. just like   ALCOHOL, 39
full of new w.   DRUNKENNESS, 8
Give me books, fruit, French w. and fine weather   PLEASURE, 17
good w. needs no bush   PLAYS, 10
look not thou upon the w. when it is red   ALCOHOL, 16
no man . . . having drunk old w. straightway desireth new   AGE, 12; ALCOHOL, 15
the guests must be chosen as carefully as the w.   ALCOHOL, 52
the water that was made w.   ALCOHOL, 14
the w. is in, the wit is out   DRUNKENNESS, 9
the w. was a farce and the food a tragedy   FOOD, 44
This w. upon a foreign tree   AGRICULTURE, 5
Truth comes out in w.   ALCOHOL, 47
use a little w. for thy stomach's sake   ALCOHOL, 13
What is man . . . a . . . machine for turning . . . the red w. of Shiraz into urine   MANKIND, 7
When the w. is in   ALCOHOL, 7
white w. came up with the fish   ETIQUETTE, 4
Who loves not w., woman and song   PLEASURE, 20
W. comes in at the mouth   AGE, 72
w. is a mocker   DRUNKENNESS, 9
wingèd Doth the w. life destroy   PLEASURE, 5
Time's w. chariot   AGE, 37
wings Fear lent w. to his feet   FEAR, 14
the w. of a dove   SOLITUDE, 4
whether pigs have w.   NONSENSE, 9
wink I will w. and hold out mine iron   COWARDICE, 8
never came a w. too soon   NOSTALGIA, 9
winners In war . . . there are no w.   WAR, 25

winning All I think about is w. that bleedin' title   SUCCESS, 6
not w. but taking part   VICTORY, 7
W. isn't everything, but wanting to win is   VICTORY, 9
Winston It hasn't taken W. long to get used to American ways   CHURCHILL, 1
The first time you meet W.   CHURCHILL, 6
W. has devoted the best years of his life   CHURCHILL, 7
W.'s back   TELEGRAMS, 2
W. with his hundred-horse-power mind   CHURCHILL, 2
winter human beings say that they enjoy the w.   SEASONS, 2
It is a w.'s tale   SEASONS, 25
No one thinks of w.   SEASONS, 13
the furious w.'s rages   MORTALITY, 16
The stars grew bright in the w. sky   ANIMALS, 13
the w. is past   SEASONS, 5
W. is icummen in   SEASONS, 16
w. of our discontent   OPTIMISM, 23
wintry sailed the w. sea   BOATS, 11
wisdom follies as the special evidences of our w.   PRIDE, 12
If one is too lazy to think . . . never attain w.   WISDOM, 14
in much w. is much grief   KNOWLEDGE, 6; WISDOM, 4
Knowledge can be communicated but not w.   WISDOM, 17
Love is the w. of the fool   LOVE, 74
privilege of w. to listen   KNOWLEDGE, 19; WISDOM, 18
proverb is one man's wit and all men's w.   SAYINGS, 3
proverbs provide them with w.   STUPIDITY, 9
Silence is . . . full of potential w.   SILENCE, 3
The highest w. has but one science   MANKIND, 34
The only infallible criterion of w.   SUCCESS, 7
the palace of w.   EXCESS, 3
the price of w. is above rubies   WISDOM, 6
therefore get w.   WISDOM, 8
Vain w. all, and false philosophy   WISDOM, 19
want of human w.   WAR, 60
W. be put in a silver rod   WISDOM, 10
w. . . . cometh by opportunity of leisure   LEISURE, 1; WISDOM, 4
w. excelleth folly, as . . . light excelleth darkness   WISDOM AND FOOLISHNESS, 2
W. has taught us to be calm and meek   REVENGE, 10
W. in minds attentive   KNOWLEDGE, 11; WISDOM, 15
W. is not additive   DEMOCRACY, 5
w. of the crocodiles   HYPOCRISY, 2
w. . . . sweetly doth . . . order all things   WISDOM, 9
with how little w. the world is governed   GOVERNMENT, 20
with the ancient is w.   OLD AGE, 6; WISDOM, 5
wise A w. man will make more opportunities   OPPORTUNITY, 5
Coffee which makes the politician w.   DRINKS, 6
How very weak the very w.   GREATNESS, 14; WISDOM, 23
Many have been the w. speeches of fools   WISDOM AND FOOLISHNESS, 6
more of the fool than of the w.   HUMAN NATURE, 3
No man . . . so w. as Thurlow looked   APPEARANCES, 14
sorrow makes us w.   SORROW, 24
The only wretched are the w.   IGNORANCE, 12
the w. forgive   FORGIVENESS, 15
To be w. and love   LOVE, 125
where ignorance is bliss, 'Tis folly to be w.   IGNORANCE, 4
w. man makes his own decisions   WISDOM AND FOOLISHNESS, 1
wisely deserves the name of happy who knows how to use the gods' gifts w.   HAPPINESS, 9
lov'd not w., but too well   LOVE, 128
wiser Be w. than other people   WISDOM, 12
foreigner should . . . be w. than ourselves   PRIDE, 12
sadder and a w. man   WISDOM, 13
The French are w. than they seem   APPEARANCES, 9
the old have rubbed it into the young that they are w.   OLD AGE, 28
w. to-day than . . . yesterday   MISTAKES, 12
wisest The most attractive sentences are not perhaps the w.   LANGUAGE, 24
wish Conscience is . . . rejection of a . . . w.   CONSCIENCE, 2
Justice is the . . . perpetual w.   JUSTICE, 14
most . . . w. they were the only one alive   EGOTISM, 5
Someday I'll w. upon a star   DESIRE, 7
The w. to hurt   CRUELTY, 1
The w. to spread those opinions that we hold   ENGLISH, 7
wished consummation devoutly to be w.   SUICIDE, 12
wishful There is w. thinking in Hell as well as on earth   DESIRE, 11
wit An ounce of a man's own w.   WISDOM, 22
Attic w.   HUMOUR, 21
a w. out of two half-wits   FOOLISHNESS, 16

X

Y

Z

NAME INDEX

Sterne, Laurence BITTERNESS, 3; FAMILY, 40; FRANCE, 14; HYPOCHONDRIA, 2; RELIGION, 54; SOUL, 11; STUBBORNNESS, 3; TOLERANCE, 7; TRAVEL, 26; WISDOM, 22; WRITING, 31

Stevas, Norman St John SNOBBERY, 6

Stevenson, Adlai COMPLIMENTS, 6; DISAPPOINTMENT, 8; EDITORS, 3; ENDURANCE, 19; FLATTERY, 8; FREEDOM, 49; LYING, 16; NUCLEAR WEAPONS, 18; POLITICIANS, 25, 70; POLITICS, 74; POWER, 24; SUCCESS, 16; WORDS, 19

Stevenson, Robert Louis ABSTINENCE, 10; ALCOHOL, 60; ANTICIPATION, 7; BOOKS, 42; CONCEIT, 17; DEATH, 119; DREAMS, 12; EXCESS, 13; HAPPINESS, 27; IMITATION, 6; MARRIAGE, 110, 111, 112, 113; MONEY, 46; MORALITY, 21; MORTALITY, 18; POLITICS, 75; SEXES, 21; SILENCE, 14; THEORY, 7; TRAVEL, 27, 28; TRIVIALITY, 13; WISDOM AND FOOLISHNESS, 7

Stocks, Mary HOUSES OF PARLIAMENT, 17

Stockwood, Mervyn PSYCHIATRY, 9

Stoddard, Elizabeth Drew LOVE, 130

Stoker, Bram SUPERNATURAL, 15, 16

Stone, I. F. LONGEVITY, 3

Stone, Samuel. J. CHRISTIANITY, 40

Stoppard, Tom ART, 26; ARTISTS, 6; CRITICS, 17; DEMOCRACY, 7; ETERNITY, 4; HOUSES OF PARLIAMENT, 18; JOURNALISM, 29; JUSTICE, 23; LIFE, 46; POLITICS, 76; QUOTATIONS, 13; RESPONSIBILITY, 14; THEATRE, 11; WAR, 116

Stout, Rex Todhunter AMERICA, 31; STATISTICS, 10

Stowe, Harriet Beecher CREATION, 13; CRUELTY, 5; INSPIRATION, 6; REGRET, 20

Strachey, John St Loe CATHOLICISM, 11; FASCISM, 5

Strachey, Lytton GOD, 47; LAST WORDS, 67; POETS, 55; PURPOSE, 8; ROYALTY, 33

Stratton, Eugene LOVE, 131

Strauss, Henry G. SMOKING, 16

Stravinsky, Igor CRITICS, 18; HASTE, 12; MUSIC, 49, 50; MUSICIANS, 9, 19, 20

Streatfield, Geoffrey FACTS, 8; STATISTICS, 11

Strindberg, August DOGS, 13

Stubbes, Philip FOOTBALL, 8

Sullivan, Annie ADVICE, 14; LANGUAGE, 22; SENTIMENTALITY, 5

Sully, Duc de ENGLAND, 38

Svevo, Italo WOMEN, 76

Swaffer, Hannen ADVERTISING, 5; JOURNALISM, 30

Swift, Jonathan BUSINESS, 23; CLERGY, 12; COURAGE, 20; DECLINE, 10; ENGLISH, 19; FLATTERY, 9; FOOLISHNESS, 19; GENIUS, 9; LAST WORDS, 68; LAW, 27; MARRIAGE, 114, 115; MUSICIANS, 21; OPINIONS, 6; PARASITES, 3; POLITICIANS, 26; PROMISES, 7; REGRET, 21; SATIRE, 3; TAXATION, 11; WAR, 117; WEALTH, 27

Swinburne, Algernon Charles MANKIND, 31; PEACE, 16; SEASONS, 22

Sydenham, Thomas DISEASE, 38

Sylvester, Robert BOOKS, 43; SMOKING, 17

Symonds, John Addington KNOWLEDGE, 33

Symons, Arthur MEMORY, 18; POETS, 56

Synge, John Millington LOSS, 6

Szasz, Thomas FORGIVENESS, 15; HAPPINESS, 28; MADNESS, 11; MEDICINE, 10; MOTIVE, 6; PSYCHIATRY, 10; RIGHT, 2; SEX, 53, 54

Szent-Györgyi, Albert DISCOVERY, 8

Taber, Robert WAR, 118

Tabrar, Joseph DOGS, 14

Tacitus FAME, 19; HUMAN NATURE, 22; WAR, 119

Taft, William Howard DEFEAT, 7

Tagore, Rabindranath DEATH, 120

Taine, Hippolyte Adolphe VIRTUE AND VICE, 3

Talleyrand AMERICA, 32; CHRISTIANITY, 41; DEFEAT, 8; FIRST IMPRESSIONS, 7; GOVERNMENT, 28; MODERATION, 4; SPEECH, 16

Tarkington, Booth ALCOHOL, 61

Tate, Allen DEATH, 121

Tate, Nahum CHANGE, 18; CHRISTMAS, 18; THIRST, 3

Taupin, Bernie ACTORS, 18

Tawney, R. H. POVERTY AND WEALTH, 8

Taylor, A. J. P. CAPITALISM, 14; COMMUNISM, 10; ENGLAND, 39; EXPERIENCE, 18; HISTORY, 33; HITLER, 7; MISTAKES, 17; OLD AGE, 45; POWER, 25

Taylor, Bert Leston BORES, 5

Taylor, Elizabeth ABSTINENCE, 11; ACTORS, 19; PATIENCE, 13; SHYNESS, 6; WORDS, 20

Taylor, Harry PRIDE, 10

Taylor, Jane STARS, 5

Taylor, Jeremy LIFE, 47; MARRIAGE, 116

Taylor, John CLOTHES, 17

Tebbitt, Norman POLITICIANS, 71; UNEMPLOYMENT, 1

Temple, Frederick CLERGY, 13; LUCK, 12

Temple, William CHRISTIANITY, 42; CHURCH, 5; CRICKET, 7; GOD, 48; HUMAN NATURE, 23; RELIGION, 55; SELF-CONFIDENCE, 5

Templeman, Mr Justice LAWYERS, 8

Tenniel, John DISMISSAL, 9

Tennyson, Alfred, Lord ACTION, 12; AFTERLIFE, 10; ARISTOCRACY, 12; ARTHURIAN LEGEND, 2, 3; BEAUTY, 38, 39; CHANGE, 19; CHIVALRY, 11; CHRISTIANITY, 43; CLERGY, 14; CONSTANCY, 4; COURAGE, 21; CURSES, 3, 4; DEATH, 122; DECLINE, 11; DESTINY, 21, 22; DETERMINATION, 15; DREAMS, 13; DUTY, 5; ENDING, 7; ENEMIES, 8; EXCESS, 14; EXPERIENCE, 19, 20; HUMAN CONDITION, 20; HYPOCRISY, 16; INTEGRITY, 7; INVITATIONS, 2; IRREVOCABILITY, 2; LEARNING, 9; LIFE, 48; LIFE AND DEATH, 13; LOVE, 132, 133, 134, 135, 136; LYING, 17; MARRIAGE, 117; MARTYRDOM, 4; MERRYMAKING, 5; MORTALITY, 19; MOURNING, 16; MUSIC, 51; NATURE, 15; NOSTALGIA, 19, 20, 21; OBEDIENCE, 4; PASSION, 8; POLITICS, 77; PRAYER, 17; PURITY, 3; RESPONSIBILITY, 15; RIVERS, 4; ROYALTY, 34; SEASONS, 23, 24; SEXES, 22, 23; SLEEP, 16; SORROW, 24, 25, 26; SUICIDE, 13; TIME, 37; TRANSIENCE, 18; TRIVIALITY, 14; UNFAITHFULNESS, 6; WEATHER, 26; WOMEN, 77, 78; WORDS, 21

Terence COURAGE, 23; MANKIND, 32; OPINIONS, 7; ORIGINALITY, 5

Teresa, Mother CHARITY, 21; FAMILY, 41; HUMILITY, 12; LONELINESS, 7; POVERTY, 31

Teresa of Avila, St RELIGION, 56

Terry, Ellen ACTING, 11; ACTORS, 20; DIARIES, 5; FUNERALS, 6; SHAKESPEARE, 17

Tertullian BELIEF, 7; CHRISTIANITY, 44, 45

Thackeray, William Makepeace FAITH, 18; FAMILY, 42; GREATNESS, 14; LOVE, 137; MARRIAGE, 118, 119; MONEY, 47; NEWSPAPERS, 11; SERVILITY, 7; SEXES, 24; SNOBBERY, 7, 8; WISDOM, 23; WRITERS, 85, 86

Thales LIFE AND DEATH, 14

Thatcher, Denis FEMINISM, 42; HOUSEWORK, 5

Thatcher, Margaret AFFECTATION, 1; ARGUMENTS, 15; AUTHORITARIANISM, 6, 7; CHARACTER, 23; CLASS, 33; COMMITMENT, 5; CONCEIT, 18, 19; ECOLOGY, 8; FEMINISM, 41; IDEALISM, 8; IDLENESS, 8; IMPERFECTION, 13; INFLEXIBILITY, 3; MARXISM, 6; MERIT, 7; MONEY, 48; MORALITY, 22; PEACE, 17; POLITICIANS, 27, 72; POLITICS, 78, 79, 80; SELF-CONFIDENCE, 6; SOCIALISM, 14; TALENT, 7; WOMEN, 79; WORK, 23

Thayer, W. M. ACHIEVEMENT, 8

Themistocles INFLUENCE, 8

Theodoric LOYALTY, 9

Theroux, Paul CLASS, 34; LANGUAGE, 23; MOUNTAINS, 4; PLACES, 20; SWITZERLAND, 4; TRAVEL, 29

Thiers, Louis Adolphe MONARCHY, 22; PERSPECTIVE, 4; SNOBBERY, 9

Thomas, Brandon PLACES, 21

Thomas, Dylan AGRICULTURE, 5; APPEARANCE, 37; BORES, 6; CLEANNESS, 2; DEATH, 123, 124, 125; EMOTION, 5; EXPECTATION, 5; INNOCENCE, 9; LIFE, 49; LONELINESS, 8; MARRIAGE, 120; MUSIC, 52; OLD AGE, 46; OPPORTUNITY, 18; PAINTING, 16; POETRY, 48; POETS, 57; PUBLIC HOUSES, 4; RELIGION, 57; SEASONS, 25; SEX, 55; SIGNATURES, 3; WALES, 2, 3; WRITERS, 87

Thomas, Edward DEATH, 126; ENGLAND, 40; PAST, 7; WALES, 4; WAR, 120

Thomas, Gwyn BUREAUCRACY, 9; GOSSIP, 9; SPORT AND GAMES, 19; WELSH, 2

Thomas, Irene CONTRACEPTION, 8; MARRIAGE, 121; MUSIC, 53

Thomas, Lewis WORRY, 12

Thomas, Lowell CINEMA, 9

Thomas, Norman M. RIGHT, 3

Thomas, R. S. INNOCENCE, 10; POETRY, 49; WELSH, 3

Thompson, Daley PLEASURE, 29

Thompson, E. P. EUROPE, 18

Thompson, Francis HEAVEN, 13; RELIGION, 58; SEASONS, 26

Thompson, William Hepworth IMPERFECTION, 14; NEGLECT, 4

Thomson, James BRITAIN, 13; LIFE, 50; NECESSITY, 8

Thomson, Jeff INSULTS, 38

Thomson, Joseph LONDON, 13

Thomson of Fleet, Lord BUSINESS, 24

Thoreau, Henry David ADVICE, 15; AFTERLIFE, 11; ARGUMENTS, 16; CHARITY, 22; COURAGE, 24; DESPAIR, 6; DISEASE, 39; HONOUR, 6; JUSTICE, 24; LANGUAGE, 24; PHILOSOPHERS, 10; PROOF, 6; SIMPLICITY, 8; SOCIETY, 9; SOLITUDE, 13; THRIFT, 11; TIME, 38, 39; TRAVEL, 30; TRUTH, 40; WRITING, 32, 33

Thorndike, Sybil MARRIAGE, 122

Thorpe, Jeremy SELF-PRESERVATION, 10

Thorpe, Rose Hartwick MERCY, 3

Thucydides FAME, 20; WOMEN, 80

Thurber, James ALCOHOL, 62, 63; BED, 5; CONFORMITY, 6; CRITICISM, 49; DECEPTION, 6; DECLINE, 12; EXECUTION, 28; HUMAN CONDITION, 21; HUMOUR, 54; LAST WORDS, 69; LAZINESS, 4; MARRIAGE, 123; MEMORY, 19; MISTAKES, 18; SCIENCE, 40; SEX, 56, 57; SEXES, 25; TECHNOLOGY, 13; WOMEN, 81

Thurlow, Lord LOYALTY, 10; MONARCHY, 23

Tilberis, Liz FASHION, 8

Tillich, Paul NEUROSIS, 3

Tilzer, Harry PUBLIC HOUSES, 5

Tintoretto HEAVEN, 14

Tocqueville, Alexis de PRIDE, 11

Tolkien, J. R. R. MANKIND, 33; MARRIAGE, 124; POWER, 26

Tolstoy, Leo ARMY, 3; ART, 27; EMOTION, 6; FAMILY, 43; HAPPINESS, 29; HISTORIANS, 7; HYPOCRISY, 17; LAST WORDS, 70; LOVE, 138; MANKIND, 34; REMEDIES, 13; SELF, 15; UNDERSTANDING, 10

Tolstoy, Sophie CONCEIT, 20; LOVE, 139; WOMEN, 82

Tomaschek, Rudolphe SCIENCE, 41

Tooke, John Horne ADULTERY, 7

Toplady, Augustus Montague RELIGION, 59

Torrey, Jesse SMOKING, 18

Toscanini, Arturo FLOWERS, 11; INCOMPETENCE, 5; INSULTS, 39; LOVE AND MARRIAGE, 5; MUSIC, 54; SMOKING, 19; THREATS, 3

Tourneur, Cyril SIN, 20

Toynbee, Arnold AMERICA, 33; REPRESENTATION, 2

Tracy, Spencer EQUALITY, 23; LEISURE, 4; POVERTY, 32

Trapp, Joseph CAMBRIDGE, 6; OXFORD, 6